August 9-13, 2015
Santiago, Chile

Association for
Computing Machinery

Advancing Computing as a Science & Profession

SIGIR 2015

Proceedings of the 38th International ACM SIGIR Conference on
Research and Development in Information Retrieval

Sponsored by:

ACM SIGIR

Supported by:

Baidu, Google, Microsoft Research, Yahoo Labs, eBay, Facebook, IBM, Yandex, Universidad de Chile, Universidad de Santiago de Chile, Universidad Técnica Federico Santa María, Pontificia Universidad Católica de Chile, Yahoo Labs-Latin America, Morgan & Claypool, NOW, and Springer

Association for
Computing Machinery

Advancing Computing as a Science & Profession

The Association for Computing Machinery
2 Penn Plaza, Suite 701
New York, New York 10121-0701

ISBN: 978-1-4503-3621-5 (Digital)

ISBN: 978-1-4503-3889-9 (Print)

Additional copies may be ordered prepaid from:

ACM Order Department
PO Box 30777
New York, NY 10087-0777, USA

Phone: 1-800-342-6626 (USA and Canada)
+1-212-626-0500 (Global)
Fax: +1-212-944-1318
E-mail: acmhelp@acm.org
Hours of Operation: 8:30 am – 4:30 pm ET

Printed in the USA

SIGIR 2015 General Chair's Welcome

It is my great pleasure to welcome you to Santiago de Chile, my hometown, and to the *38th International SIGIR Conference on Research and Development in Information Retrieval*, the premier annual forum for presentations of research in information retrieval (IR) and related topics. This five-day event has a broad technical program that we hope you find interesting, useful, and insightful.

Amazingly, *SIGIR 2015* is not only held in my hometown, but also where I did my high school studies. Could I ever imagine that? No way! So in this venue where I have plenty of mixed memories, we start the conference on Sunday with nine great tutorials, thanks to Yoelle Maarek; the Doctoral Consortium, organized by J. Shane Culpepper and Brian Davidson; and we finish the day with the opening reception in the central patio.

The next three days we have the core of the conference, highlighted with the keynotes by Nick Belkin (*Salton Award)* on how we interact with information, and ChengXiang Zhai on game theory applied to IR. We also have 70 technical papers selected by the program committee chaired by Mounia Lalmas, Alistair Moffat and Berthier Ribeiro-Neto. Thanks for your great and hard work! We also have 79 short papers and 12 demos presented in a special session before the banquet on Tuesday that will be held at a nearby palace on Cerro Santa Lucía. Thanks to Maarten de Rijke, Ee-Peng Lim and Ryen White for handling the short papers and Djoerd Hiemstra and Mirella Moro for arranging the demonstrations.

On Wednesday we also have the industry track, SIRIP, organized by Hang Li and Jaime Teevan. This track combines eight invited talks and four refereed papers. This day we have been able to keep the number of parallel tracks to just three, and also have the final panel on industry impact from academia, as a single track event. Finally, on Thursday we have seven interesting workshops, thanks to the committee chaired by Fernando Diaz and Diane Kelly.

None of this would be possible without the support of the local organizers from four universities and Yahoo Labs Latin America, all in Santiago. They are Universidad Católica de Chile, Universidad de Chile, Universidad de Santiago de Chile and Universidad Técnica Federico Santa María. They are represented by the local arrangements chair, Diego Arroyuelo, the finance chair, Mauricio Marín, and the website chair, Marcelo Mendoza. Thanks to all of them!

Without financial support, this conference would have been more austere. Thanks to our supporters, Baidu (platinum); Google, Microsoft Research and Yahoo Labs (gold); eBay (silver); Facebook, IBM and Yandex (bronze); and Morgan & Claypool, Now and Springer (associated publishers); we were able to provide many student scholarships, include lunches, and upgrade the social program. Thanks to Vanessa Murdock and Sergei Vassilvitskii for their great help on this.

Finally, we hope that you share your ideas with other researchers and practitioners, enjoy the social program, and have time to visit Santiago and other interesting places in this long and amazing country that is Chile, from the Atacama Desert to the Lake District and the Patagonia glaciers, always between the Andes Mountains and the Pacific Ocean, without forgetting the navel of the world, Rapa Nui or Easter Island. Thanks for coming, without you there would be no SIGIR!

Ricardo Baeza-Yates
SIGIR 2015 General Chair
Yahoo Labs, USA

Program Chairs' Preface

Welcome to SIGIR 2015, the 38th Annual International ACM-SIGIR Conference on Research and Development in Information Retrieval, the premier conference in the area. We acknowledge all those who submitted papers to the conference and gave the Program Committee an opportunity to evaluate their work for potential inclusion in the program. Huge thanks are owed to the 66 Senior Program Committee Members, 235 Program Committee Members, and the 41 additional referees, for their dedicated work in evaluating the submissions. That pool of people spans 32 countries and of the order of 200 institutions.

The conference received 361 submissions in to the full-paper track, a 7% decrease compared to 2014. Of these, 10 papers were subsequently withdrawn by the authors after having been noted in an initial vetting process as being unready for review. A number of other submissions were revised during the same filtering pass to ensure that they were sufficiently anonymized for the review process. A total of 351 papers then went to review.

As has been customary for many years, SIGIR 2015 employed a two-tier double-blind review process. Two Senior Program Committee Members (SPCMs) and three Program Committee Members (reviewers) were assigned to each paper. Once the three reviewers had completed their evaluations, the Primary SPCM for the paper led a discussion, based on which they wrote a meta-review that synthesized the range of opinions, and gave an overall evaluation, including (if required) further commentary based on their own evaluation of the work. The Secondary SPCM assigned to each paper double-checked the reviews and discussion, and in some cases provided an additional review. The PC Chairs ranked the submitted papers by the meta-review scores assigned by the Primary SPCM and Secondary SPCM, and then by the average score of the three reviewer scores. A Program Meeting was held in San Francisco on 9–10 April, with all of the Senior Program Committee invited to attend; fourteen of them were able to participate, plus the three Program Committee Chairs. All papers that could not be categorized as "clear accepts" or "clear rejects" based on the three first-tier reviews and the Primary SPCM's meta-review were discussed at the meeting, and in some cases re-read; and for many of them, further reviews or commentaries were added to the package of information that was eventually returned to authors. Reviews and acceptance notifications were emailed to all authors on April 16, four days ahead of schedule.

This process led to the selection of 70 papers for oral presentation at the conference, a 20% acceptance ratio, and consistent with the last several years.

A few statistics about the authorship of the 351 papers that were refereed: there were 1,188 author-paper combinations (an average of 3.4 authors per submitted paper) and a total of 944 distinct authors that submitted to the conference (an average of 1.3 submitted papers per author). One paper had nine coauthors, and two others had eight; only 29 of the submitted papers had a single author. There were 14 people who were each authors of five or more submissions, and between them those 14 people accounted for 85 (7%) of the author-paper combinations. Across the accepted papers, there were 257 author-paper combinations, and 222 distinct authors who have had papers accepted for presentation at SIGIR 2015.

In terms of country of origin, over the 351 refereed papers there were 261 author-paper combinations from the USA, 239 from China, 62 from Great Britain, 45 from Australia, and 42 from Singapore. Germany, the Netherlands, Spain, Brazil, and Canada completed the top ten countries, with a total of 37 different countries represented in the author pool. Amongst the 70 accepted papers, 21 different countries are represented, with the top 10 countries (by author-paper combinations) being the USA (77), China (38), Great Britain (17), the Netherlands (15), Spain and Italy (13), Australia, Brazil, Canada and Russia (9). Of the counties listed, Italy, the Netherlands, Russia, and Spain (in that order) had the highest ratios of successful authors to submitting authors. Denmark also scored well in this metric, off a smaller number of submitted author-paper combinations.

Breaking the 351 papers in to seven bands by paper number, which corresponds to forming groups of 50 papers defined by when the submission process was initiated for each paper, the numbers of accepted papers in the bands are 9, 9, 7, 6, 12, 11, and 16. Submitting the abstract close to the deadline seems to help the odds of being accepted; whether this is a significant outcome we leave for future work.

To summarize the themes of the oral presentations, we made a tag cloud from the 70 full paper titles using the tool provided at `https://www.jasondavies.com/wordcloud/`.

We hope that you enjoy the result, and the papers that it represents.

Alistair Moffat, Mounia Lalmas, Berthier Ribeiro-Neto
June 2015.

Short Papers

The Short Papers Track received 252 submissions, of which 79 were accepted (31% acceptance). Each submitted paper received three reviews in a double-blind process, together with an overall meta-review from one of the three Chairs. Short papers are four pages in length, and will be presented at the conference during what can be expected to be a highly engaging Poster Session. We thank the many referees who contributed to the reviewing process, and are particularly grateful to John Tait, who managed a separate Short Paper conflict of interest track for submissions co-authored by any of the three Chairs. We look forward to the lively discussions that always accompany the SIGIR Poster Session

Maarten de Rijke, Ee-Peng Lim, Ryen White
June 2015.

Demonstrations

The Demonstrations Track received 24 submissions of which 12 were accepted. We thank the pool of expert referees who assisted with the task of selecting the final set of demos. The results of their work will provide a stimulating complement to the conference's Poster Session; and we are confident that, as always, the successful presentations will generate extensive discussion and lead to further new ideas.

Djoerd Hiemstra, Mirella Moro
June 2015.

Doctoral Consortium

The Doctoral Consortium received 14 submissions this year, of which 10 were recommended for acceptance, with almost equal representation across Asia, Europe, and America. Having facilitated the review process, we are now looking forward to chairing the Consortium on the first day of the conference, and welcoming and working with these new members of our community. We are especially grateful to the 17 referees that assisted with our candidate selections, many of whom will also be mentors on the day.

Shane Culpepper, Brian Davison
June 2015.

Table of Contents

Session 3C: Entities

Session Chair: Krisztian Balog *(University of Stavanger)*

Session 4A: User Models

Session Chair: Diane Kelly *(University of North Carolina)*

Session 4B: Recommending

Session Chair: Paul Benett *(Microsoft Research)*

Session 4C: Classifying & Ranking

Session Chair: Yi Chang *(Yahoo Labs)*

Session 5A: Deep Learning

Session Chair: Berthier Ribeiro-Neto *(Google Brazil)*

Session 5B: Products

Session Chair: Grace Hui Yang *(Georgetown University)*

Session 5C: Locations

Session Chair: Craig Macdonald *(University of Glasgow)*

Session 6A: Experiment Design

Session Chair: Alistair Moffat *(University of Melbourne)*

Session 6B: Predicting

Session Chair: Djoerd Hiemstra *(University of Twente)*

Session 8A: Variability in Test Collections

Session Chair: Mark Smucker *(University of Waterloo)*

Session 8B: Citations

Session Chair: Mark Sanderson *(RMIT)*

Session 9A: Streams

Session Chair: Fernando Diaz *(Microsoft Research)*

Session 9B: Cards

Session Chair: Eugene Agichtein *(Emory University)*

Short Papers

Demonstrations

Doctoral Consortium

Industry Track Preface

Industry Track Invited Talks

Industry Track Refereed Papers

Tutorials

Workshops

SIGIR 2015 Conference Organization

Conference Chair:	Ricardo Baeza-Yates, Yahoo Labs, USA
Program Committee Chairs:	Mounia Lalmas, Yahoo Labs, UK Alistair Moffat, University of Melbourne, Australia Berthier Ribeiro-Neto, Google, Brazil, and UFMG, Brazil
Short Papers Chairs:	Maarten de Rijke, University of Amsterdam, The Netherlands Ee-Peng Lim, Singapore Management University, Singapore Ryen White, Microsoft Research, USA
Demonstrations Chairs:	Djoerd Hiemstra, University of Twente, The Netherlands Mirella Moro, Universidade Federal de Minas Gerais, Brazil
Tutorial Chair:	Yoelle Maarek, Yahoo Labs, Israel
Workshop Chairs:	Fernando Diaz, Microsoft Research, USA Diane Kelly, University of North Carolina at Chapel Hill, USA
Doctoral Consortium Chairs:	Shane Culpepper, RMIT University, Australia Brian Davison, Lehigh University, USA
Industry Day Chairs:	Hang Li, Huawei, China Jaime Teevan, Microsoft Research, USA
Best Paper Chair:	Susan Dumais, Microsoft Research, USA
Sponsorship Chairs:	Vanessa Murdock, Microsoft Research, USA Sergei Vassilvitskii, Google, USA
Local Arrangements Chair:	Diego Arroyuelo, UTFSM & Yahoo Labs, Chile
Finance Chair:	Mauricio Marín, Universidad de Santiago de Chile & Yahoo Labs, Chile
Publications Chairs:	Roberto González-Ibáñez, Universidad de Santiago de Chile, Chile Nicolás Hidalgo, Universidad de Santiago de Chile, Chile
Website Chair:	Marcelo Mendoza, UTFSM, Chile
Social Events Chairs:	Erika Rosas, Universidad de Santiago de Chile, Chile Carolina Bonacic, Universidad de Santiago de Chile & Yahoo Labs, Chile

Publicity Chair: Bárbara Poblete, Universidad de Chile, Chile

Venue Chair: Valeria Herskovic, Pontificia Universidad Católica de Chile, Chile

Local Organization Committee:
Sara Quiñones, Yahoo Labs, Chile
Rodrigo Scheihing, Yahoo Labs, Chile
Roberto Solar, Universidad de Santiago de Chile, Chile
Javier Velasco, Universidad de Santiago de Chile, Chile

Senior Program Committee:
Eugene Agichtein, Emory University, USA
James Allan, University of Massachusetts Amherst, USA
Javed A. Aslam, Northeastern University, USA
Leif Azzopardi, University of Glasgow, UK
Krisztian Balog, University of Stavanger, Norway
Nicholas J. Belkin, Rutgers University, USA
Paul Bennett, Microsoft Research, USA
Jamie Callan, Carnegie Mellon University, USA
David Carmel, Yahoo Labs, Israel
Ben Carterette, University of Delaware, USA
Carlos Castillo, Qatar Computing Research Institute, Qatar
Yi Chang, Yahoo Labs, USA
Charles L. A. Clarke, University of Waterloo, Canada
Kevyn Collins-Thompson, University of Michigan, USA
Nick Craswell, Microsoft, USA
Fabio Crestani, University of Lugano (USI) , Switzerland
Bruce Croft, University of Massachusetts Amherst, USA
Ronan Cummins, University of Cambridge, UK
Arjen P. de Vries, Centrum Wiskunde & Informatica, The Netherlands
Fernando Diaz, Microsoft Research, USA
David Elsweiler, University of Regensburg, Germany
Hui Fang, University of Delaware, USA
Jianfeng Gao, Microsoft Research, USA
Shlomo Geva, Queensland University of Technology, Australia
Marcos Goncalves, Universidade Federal de Minas Gerais, Brazil
Julio Gonzalo, UNED, Spain
Claudia Hauff, TU Delft, The Netherlands
Djoerd Hiemstra, University of Twente, The Netherlands
Xian-Sheng Hua, Microsoft Research, USA
Jimmy Huang, York University, Canada
Gareth Jones, Dublin City University, Ireland
Jaap Kamps, University of Amsterdam, The Netherlands
Gabriella Kazai, Lumi.do, UK
Diane Kelly, University of North Carolina at Chapel Hill, USA
Wessel Kraaij, Radboud University Nijmegen, The Netherlands
Oren Kurland, Technion, Israel

Program Committee (continued):

Marcus C. Fontoura, Microsoft, USA
Dayne Freitag, SRI International, USA
Ingo Frommholz, University of Bedfordshire, UK
Atsushi Fujii, Tokyo Institute of Technology, Japan
Patrick Gallinari, Université Pierre et Marie Curie, France
Debasis Ganguly, Dublin City University, Ireland
Bin Gao, Microsoft Research Asia, China
Eric Gaussier, Université Joseph Fourier, France
Fredric Gey, University of California at Berkeley, USA
Nazli Goharian, Georgetown University, USA
Peter B. Golbus, Wayfair LLC, USA
Siddharth Gopal, Carnegie Mellon University, USA
Brigitte Grau, LIMSI-CNRS, France
Qi Guo, Microsoft, USA
Maxim Gurevich, Bento Labs, USA
Cathal Gurrin, Dublin City University, Ireland
Ido Guy, Yahoo Labs, Israel
Jacek Gwizdka, University of Texas at Austin, USA
Martin Halvey, University of Strathclyde, UK
Sanda M. Harabagiu, University of Texas, Dallas
Donna Harman, NIST, USA
Morgan Harvey, Northumbria University, UK
Ahmed Hassan, Microsoft Research, USA
David Hawking, Microsoft, Australia
Ben He, Chinese Academy of Sciences, China
Daqing He, University of Pittsburgh, USA
Jiyin He, CWI, The Netherlands
Qi He, LinkedIn, USA
Katja Hofmann, Microsoft Research, UK
Liangjie Hong, Yahoo Labs, USA
Winston H. Hsu, National Taiwan University, Taiwan
Xuanjing Huang, Fudan University, China
Samuel Huston, Google, USA
Hervé Jégou, INRIA, France
Jing Jiang, Singapore Management University, Singapore
Hideo Joho, University of Tsukuba, Japan
Joemon M. Jose, University of Glasgow, UK
Min-Yen Kan, National University of Singapore, Singapore
Noriko Kando, National Institute of Informatics, Japan
Evangelos Kanoulas, University of Amsterdam, The Netherlands
David Karger, MIT, USA
Jussi Karlgren, Gavagai & KTH, Sweden
Makoto Kato, Kyoto University, Japan
Enver Kayaaslan, INRIA, France
Jaana Kekalainen, University of Tampere, Finland

Program Committee (continued):

Gonzalo Navarro, University of Chile, Chile
Michael L. Nelson, Old Dominion University, USA
Chong-Wah Ngo, City University of Hong Kong, China
Dong Nguyen, University of Twente, The Netherlands
Alexandros Ntoulas, Zynga, USA
Heather O'Brien, University of British Columbia, Canada
Iadh Ounis, University of Glasgow, UK
Paul Over, NIST, USA
Jiaul Paik, University of Maryland, USA
Laurence Park, University of Western Sydney, Australia
Gabriella Pasi, University of Milano-Bicocca, Italy
Virgil Pavlu, Northeastern University, USA
Jan Pedersen, Microsoft, USA
Jian Pei, Simon Fraser University, Canada
Raffaele Perego, Consiglio Nazionale delle Ricerche (CNR), Italy
Vassilis Plachouras, Thomson Reuters, UK
Barbara Poblete, Universidad de Chile, Chile
Martin Potthast, University of Weimar, Germany
Kunal Punera, Bento Labs, USA
Filip Radlinski, Microsoft, UK
Fiana Raiber, Technion, Israel
Karthik Raman, Cornell University, USA
Edie Rasmussen, University of British Columbia, Canada
Yongli Ren, RMIT University, Australia
Soo Young Rieh, University of Michigan, USA
Haggai Roitman, IBM Research, Israel
Dmitri Roussinov, University of Strathclyde, UK
Rodrygo Santos, Universidade Federal de Minas Gerais, Brazil
Shin'ichi Satoh, National Institute of Informatics, Japan
Jacques Savoy, University of Neuchatel, Switzerland
Ralf Schenkel, University of Passau, Germany
Pavel Serdyukov, Yandex, Russia
Chirag Shah, Rutgers University, USA
Jialie Shen, Singapore Management University, Singapore
Anna Shtok, Technion, Israel
Laurianne Sitbon, Queensland University of Technology, Australia
Catherine L. Smith, Kent State University, USA
Ian Soboroff, NIST, USA
Aya Soffer, IBM Research, Israel
Oren Somekh, Yahoo Labs, Israel
Alessandro Sordoni, Université de Montréal, Canada
Alessandro Sperduti, University of Padova, Italy
Torsten Suel, New York University, USA
Jian-Tao Sun, Microsoft, USA
Le Sun, Chinese Academy of Sciences, China

Program Committee (continued):

Mingxuan Sun, Louisiana State University, USA
Idan Szpektor, Yahoo Labs, Israel
S. M. M. Tahaghoghi, Microsoft, USA
Jiliang Tang, Arizona State University, USA
Paul Thomas, CSIRO, Australia
Anastasios Tombros, Queen Mary University of London, UK
Manos Tsagkias, 904Labs, The Netherlands
Theodora Tsikrika, Centre for Research and Technology Hellas, Greece
David Vallet, Google, Australia
Emre Velipasaoglu, OpsClarity, USA
Adriano Veloso, Universidade Federal de Minas Gerais, Brazil
Rossano Venturini, University of Pisa, Italy
Robert Villa, University of Sheffield, UK
Bin Wang, Chinese Academy of Sciences, China
Jian Wang, LinkedIn, USA
Lidan Wang, IBM Research, USA
Lidan Wang, University of Illinois, USA
Meng Wang, Hefei University of Technology, China
Quan Wang, Chinese Academy of Sciences, China
Xin-Jing Wang, Microsoft Research Asia, China
William Webber, University of Melbourne, Australia
Ingmar Weber, Qatar Computing Research Institute, Qatar
Wouter Weerkamp, 904Labs, The Netherlands
Gerhard Weikum, Max Planck Institute for Informatics, Germany
Ji-Rong Wen, Renmin University of China, China
Max L. Wilson, University of Nottingham, UK
Wei Wu, Microsoft Research Asia, China
Xiaobing Xue, Twitter, USA
Zheng Ye, York University, Canada
Xing Yi, Yahoo Labs, USA
Dawei Yin, Yahoo Labs, USA
Minoru Yoshida, University of Tokushima, Japan
Xiaojun Yuan, State University of New York at Albany, USA
Dell Zhang, University of London Birkbeck, UK
Lanbo Zhang, Twitter, USA
Min Zhang, Tsinghua University, China
Yi Zhang, Unversity of California at Santa Cruz, USA
Le Zhao, Google, USA
Ke Zhou, Yahoo Labs, UK
Mianwei Zhou, Yahoo Labs, USA
Nivio Ziviani, Universidade Federal de Minas Gerais, Brazil
Guido Zuccon, Queensland University of Technology, Australia

Short Papers Committee:

Mikhail Ageev, Moscow State University, Russia
Eugene Agichtein, Emory University, USA
M-Dyaa Albakour, University of Glasgow, UK
Omar Alonso, Microsoft, USA
Javed A. Aslam, Northeastern University, USA
Krisztian Balog, University of Stavanger, Norway
Klaus Berberich, Max Planck Institute for Informatics, Germany
Bodo Billerbeck, Microsoft, Australia
Roi Blanco, Yahoo Labs, UK
Paolo Boldi, University of Milan, Italy
Gloria Bordogna, Consiglio Nazionale delle Ricerche (CNR), Italy
Mohand Boughanem, IRIT-University of Tolouse, France
Andrei Broder, Google, USA
Hendra Bunyamin, University of Amsterdam, The Netherlands
Rui Cai, Microsoft, USA
B. Barla Cambazoglu, Yahoo Labs, Spain
Mark Carman, Monash University, Australia
Ben Carterette, University of Delaware, USA
Marc-Allen Cartright, Google, USA
Francine Chen, FX Palo Alto Laboratory, USA
Hsin-His Chen, National Taiwan University, Taiwan
Kevyn Collins-Thompson, University of Michigan, USA
Bin Cui, Peking University, China
Shane Culpepper, RMIT University, Australia
Saly Jo Cunningham, University of Waikato, New Zealand
Kareem Darwish, Qatar Computing Research Institute, Qatar
Emanuele Di Buccio, University of Padova, Italy
Giorgio Maria Di Nunzio, University of Padua, Italy
Debora Donato, StumbleUpon, USA
Miles Efron, University of Illinois at Urbana-Champaign, USA
Carsten Eickhoff, ETH Zurich, Switzerland
Yi Fang, Santa Clara University, USA
Nicola Ferro, University of Padova, Italy
Luanne Freund, University of British Columbia, Canada
Ingo Frommholz, University of Bedfordshire, UK
Patrick Gallinari, Université Pierre-et-Marie-Curie, France
Bin Gao, Microsoft, China
Wei Gao, Qatar Computing Research Institute, Qatar
Susan Gauch, University of Arkansas, USA
Ayse Goker, Robert Gordon University, UK
Brigitte Grau, Université Paris-Sud, France
David Graus, University of Amsterdam, The Netherlands
Artem Grotov, University of Amsterdam, The Netherlands
Jacek Gwizdka, University of Texas at Austin, USA
Claudia Hauff, TU Delft, The Netherlands

Short Papers Committee (continued):

Ben He, University of Chinese Academy of Sciences, China
Daqing He, University of Pittsburgh, USA
Jiyin He, CWI, The Netherlands
Katja Hofmann, Microsoft, UK
Frank Hopfgartner, University of Glasgow, UK
Jimmy Huang, York University, Canada
Adam Jatowt, Kyoto University, Japan
Jiepu Jiang, University of Massachusetts Amherst, USA
Hideo Joho, University of Tsukuba, Japan
Joemon Jose, University of Glasgow, UK
Jaap Kamps, University of Amsterdam, The Netherlands
Noriko Kando, National Institute of Informatics, Japan
Nattiya Kanhabua, L3S Research Center, Germany
Evangelos Kanoulas, University of Amsterdam, The Netherlands
Diane Kelly, University of North Carolina at Chapel Hill, USA
Liadh Kelly, Trinity College Dublin, Ireland
Irwin King, Chinese University of Hong Kong, China
Julia Kiseleva, Technical University of Eindhoven, The Netherlands
Alexander Kotov, Wayne State University, USA
Udo Kruschwitz, University of Essex, UK
Giridhar Kumaran, eBay, USA
Sanna Kumpulainen, University of Amsterdam, The Netherlands
Wai Lam, Chinese University of Hong Kong, China
Martha Larson, Delft University of Technology
Victor Lavrenko, University of Edinburgh, UK
Jochen Leidner, Thomson Reuters, UK
Chenglian Li, Wuhan University, China
Hui Li, University of Hong Kong, China
Shangsong Liang, University of Amsterdam, The Netherlands
Christina Lioma, University of Copenhagen, Denmark
Suzanne Little, Dublin City University, Ireland
Carla Teixeira Lopes, University of Porto, Portugal
Hao Ma, Microsoft, USA
Andrew MacFarlane, City University London, UK
Takuya Maekawa, Osaka University, Japan
Walid Magdy, Qatar Computing Research Institute, Qatar
Prasenjit Majumder, Dhirubhai Ambani Institute of ICT, India
Stephane Marchand-Maillet, University of Geneva, Switzerland
Ilya Markov, University of Amsterdam, The Netherlands
Paul McNamee, Johns Hopkins University, USA
Edgar Meij, Yahoo Labs, UK
Marie-Francine Moens, Katholieke Universiteit Leuven, Belgium
Michael L. Nelson, Microsoft, UK
Dong Nguyen, Twente University, The Netherlands

Doctoral Consortium Committee:

Eugene Agichtein, Emory University, USA
Leif Azzopardi, University of Glasgow, UK
Krisztian Balog, University of Stavanger, Norway
Charles L. A. Clarke, University of Waterloo, Canada
Kevyn Collins-Thompson, University of Michigan, USA
Claudia Hauff, TU Delft, The Netherlands
Gareth Jones, Dublin City University, Ireland
Diane Kelly, University of North Carolina at Chapel Hill, USA
Oren Kurland, Technion, Israel
Dave Lewis, Independent consultant, USA
Doug Oard, University of Maryland, USA
Iadh Ounis, University of Glasgow, UK
Denis Parra, Pontificia Universidad Católica de Chile, Chile
Mark Sanderson, RMIT University, Australia
Falk Scholer, RMIT University, Australia
Jaime Teevan, Microsoft Research, USA
Emine Yilmaz, University College London, UK

Doctoral Consortium Mentors:

Eugene Agichtein, Emory University, USA
Krisztian Balog, University of Stavanger, Norway
Charles L. A. Clarke, University of Waterloo, Canada
Kevyn Collins-Thompson, University of Michigan, USA
Claudia Hauff, TU Delft, The Netherlands
Gareth Jones, Dublin City University, Ireland
Diane Kelly, University of North Carolina at Chapel Hill, USA
Dave Lewis, Independent consultant, USA
Doug Oard, University of Maryland, USA
Iadh Ounis, University of Glasgow, UK
Denis Parra, Pontificia Universidad Católica de Chile, Chile
Mark Sanderson, RMIT University, Australia
Jaime Teevan, Microsoft Research, USA

SIGIR 2015 Sponsors & Supporters

SPONSORS

SIGIR
Special Interest Group on Information Retrieval

acm
Association for Computing Machinery

PLATINUM SUPPORTER

Baidu 百度

GOLD SUPPORTERS

Google

Microsoft Research

YAHOO! LABS

SILVER SUPPORTERS

ebay

BRONZE SUPPORTERS

facebook

IBM

Yandex

LOCAL SUPPORTERS

Pontificia Universidad Católica de Chile

Universidad de Chile

UdeSantiago de Chile

Universidad Tecnica Federico Santa Maria

YAHOO! LABS LATIN AMERICA

Affiliated Publishers

Morgan & Claypool Publishers

now the essence of knowledge

Springer

Using Sensor Metadata Streams to Identify Topics of Local Events in the City

M-Dyaa Albakour
University of Glasgow, UK
dyaa.albakour@glasgow.ac.uk

Craig Macdonald
University of Glasgow, UK
craig.macdonald@glasgow.ac.uk

Iadh Ounis
University of Glasgow, UK
iadh.ounis@glasgow.ac.uk

ABSTRACT

In this paper, we study the emerging Information Retrieval (IR) task of local event retrieval using sensor metadata streams. Sensor metadata streams include information such as the crowd density from video processing, audio classifications, and social media activity. We propose to use these metadata streams to identify the topics of local events within a city, where each event topic corresponds to a set of terms representing a type of events such as a concert or a protest. We develop a supervised approach that is capable of mapping sensor metadata observations to an event topic. In addition to using a variety of sensor metadata observations about the current status of the environment as learning features, our approach incorporates additional background features to model cyclic event patterns. Through experimentation with data collected from two locations in a major Spanish city, we show that our approach markedly outperforms an alternative baseline. We also show that modelling background information improves event topic identification.

1. INTRODUCTION

Local search is increasingly attracting more demand, whereby the users are interested to find out about places or events in their local vicinity [11]. Local event retrieval is an example of local search where users can retrieve a ranked list of local events of interest, such as music concerts, entertainment events or even protests. Recent work has addressed local event retrieval by using social media activity as a sensor to detect and rank events [1, 13]. However, social media may only cover very popular events as users may not necessarily comment on all events taking place in the city. Therefore, physical sensors that record observations about the status of the environment can provide additional evidence about the events taking place in the city. These sensors can take the form of visual sensors such as CCTV cameras, acoustic sensors such as microphones or possibly environmental sensors.

There is a wealth of research on identifying low-level human activities from acoustic and visual sensors. Often, this involves sensor signal processing to extract sensor features for modelling human activities. For example, Atrey *et al.* [2] developed a Gaussian Mixture Model using a variety of features derived from audio signal processing to classify human activities into vocal classes, such as talking and shouting, and non-vocal classes, such as walking and running. Similar approaches also used audio signal features to identify low-level human activities that are related to security incidents, such as breaking glass or explosions [7]. In addition to using acoustic sensors, several studies have been conducted to identify low-level human activities from videos. Since its introduction in 2002, the TRECVID evaluation campaign [9] has tackled a variety of content-based retrieval tasks from video recordings to support video search and navigation. This includes the semantic indexing of video segments, whereby videos are mapped to concepts, which can be certain objects or human activities [9]. Another related task is multimedia event detection, where the aim is to identify predefined classes of events in the videos. In this task, the existing effective approaches employ classifiers trained with motion features from the videos [10]. Moreover, classifying human interactions identified in video recordings has been studied to detect surveillance-related incidents [5].

Although the aforementioned approaches derive useful semantics about the multimedia content, they only consider low-level human activities. In other words, they provide sensor metadata describing low-level human activities in the physical environment. However, to the best of our knowledge, no previous work has investigated combining these sensor metadata to detect and retrieve higher level complex events taking place in the city, such as music concerts or entertainment shows, which may involve several lower level human actions. In this paper, we propose an approach for combining sensor metadata streams to support local event retrieval. Our major contribution in this paper is devising a supervised machine learning approach that combines sensor metadata to identify the topic of a potential event happening at a particular time in a certain location of the city. The topic corresponds to a set of terms representing a type of events, such as a concert or a protest. Our approach uses features from acoustic, visual and social sensor metadata. We also incorporate background features from past observations to model events that exhibit cyclic patterns such as traffic jams at peak times. To develop our supervised approach, we perform two necessary steps. First, we obtain event annotations on a pool of candidate video and audio recordings of two vibrant locations in the centre of a major Spanish city over a period of two weeks. Second, we use the obtained annotations to map typical events taking place in those locations into coherent topics using a topic mod-

SIGIR '15, August 09 - 13, 2015, Santiago, Chile
© 2015 ACM. ISBN 978-1-4503-3621-5/15/08...$15.00.
DOI: http://dx.doi.org/10.1145/2766462.2767837 .

elling technique. Through experimentation with the data collected, we evaluate the accuracy of our event topic identification approach and shows that it markedly outperforms an alternative baseline. The results also show the effectiveness of the background features in improving the accuracy of event topic identification.

2. PROBLEM STATEMENT

In this paper, we tackle the problem of event topic identification. The aim is to combine the sensor metadata observations captured at different locations in a city to identify topics of potential high-level events taking place within certain locations. Formally, for a location l_i in a city, we denote the sensor metadata observations captured at time t_j in that location l_i by the vector $\overrightarrow{N}_{\langle l_i, t_j \rangle}$. The sensor metadata observations may include the crowd density identified from captured videos in the location, low-level audio events identified from the acoustic sensors installed in the location or social media activities, such as tweets posted by people at the location. The problem of event topic identification is to use the vector $\overrightarrow{N}_{\langle l_i, t_j \rangle}$ to map the tuple of time and location $\langle l_i, t_j \rangle$ to a certain topic $p_x \in \mathcal{P}$ described by a set of terms T_x; where $\mathcal{P}$ is a set of predefined topics.

In a previous work [1], the textual content of public tweets has been used as the only source of sensor metadata observation to identify topics of local events. Although this has worked well on popular events that attract social media activities, it did not work as well on more localised events that may not attract coverage on the social media. To alleviate this shortcoming, we introduce *physical* sensor metadata streams that can provide an additional evidence for the topic of an event, namely video and audio metadata observations. However, this requires understanding the semantics of visual scenes or audio recordings, which remains an open challenge. Indeed, there is no known taxonomy that maps sensor metadata to topics of high level events. To address this challenge, we propose to learn the topic associated with a tuple $\langle l_i, t_j \rangle$ from *labelled* training data using features extracted from the sensor observations $\overrightarrow{N}_{\langle l_i, t_j \rangle}$.

For this purpose, and to collect labelled training data, we obtain event annotations on a pool of videos that are identified as potential candidates to contain events. Furthermore, to extract a predefined set of coherent event topics, we apply topic modelling on the descriptions of the annotated events. We detail the event annotation and the topic extraction in Section 4. Next, we describe the sensor data collection.

3. SENSOR DATA COLLECTION

Our study considers two locations in the city centre of Santander in Spain. The first location is the geographical and business heart of the city; it is a major square opposite to the municipality building. The second location is a popular open market in the city, where hundreds of people go every day for shopping, located behind the municipality building. Both locations represent vibrant and busy areas, where we expect to observe high-level events of interest such as music concerts, entertainment shows or even protests. The data collection started since the 11th October 2013 in both locations.

Table 1 provides a summary of the sensor data collection and the metadata produced by processing the output from the microphones and the camera in each location. For producing the audio metadata, a supervised classifier using feed forward multilayer perceptron network and low-level audio features, such as those described in [6], was developed for each of the following 6 audio classes described in Table 1: "crowd", "traffic, "music", "applause", "speaker", and "siren". For video metadata, the video was processed for crowd analysis where we calculate the crowd density, in desired areas, by estimating the foreground components of the video. In addition to the acoustic and visual sensors, we collected parallel social media activity in the city. In particular, using the Twitter Public Streaming API[1], we obtained tweets related to each location (as identified by their geo-locations).

Table 1: Summary of sensor data collection

Locations	2 (square & market)
Physical sensors	A camera and microphones (in each location)
Raw output	1600x1200 video @ 20fps 16Khz audio @ 64kbits/s (audio is multiplexed with the video)
Audio metadata	classification scores for 6 audio classes (i) "crowd": noise from a crowd of people (ii) "traffic": car and road noises (iii) "music": music played outdoors (iv) "applause": applause, yelling or cheering (v) "speaker": speech over loud speakers (vi) "siren": noise of police cars & ambulances
Video metadata	crowd density in the scene
Twitter	geo-tagged tweets within each location

4. EVENT POOLING AND ANNOTATION

In this section, we describe our approach for obtaining event annotations on the recordings collected from the two locations. Recall from Section 2, that our ranking units (the documents) are tuples of time and location. Each tuple represents a segment of recordings at a location. The length of the segment, the sampling rate to obtain the tuples, can be predefined and we follow [1] in setting the sampling rate to 15 minutes. Coarser- or finer-grained sampling rate can be investigated in future work for different types of events e.g. emergency events may require a finer-grained sampling.

For annotation, we consider a period of 2 weeks starting from 19 October 2013, around a week after the start of the data collection (11 October 2013) to allow the estimation of background features. Since it is expensive to examine all recordings and annotate them with events, we employ a pooling approach [4], as commonly used in IR campaigns, such as TREC.

For pooling, we identify candidate segments of videos where high-level events may have occurred by applying the change component of the event retrieval framework in [1]. In particular, the change component of this framework identifies segments where sensor metadata observations change unusually in a location, e.g. unusual change in crowd density. We use 4 different types of sensor metadata observations to generate the pool (a subset of those listed in Table 1): (i) the median values of the video crowd density, (ii) the median values of the crowd audio classification score, (iii) the median values of the music audio classification score, and (iv) the total number of tweets posted. As a result, we obtain a total of 155 candidate segments. The video recording software produced videos with lengths of either 30 minutes or 1 hour, and the total number of video recordings that correspond to the 155 segments are 69 videos.

The generated candidate segments of videos were then annotated by two groups of human annotators, English and Spanish annotators, who were asked to examine the videos,

[1] `https://dev.twitter.com/streaming/public`

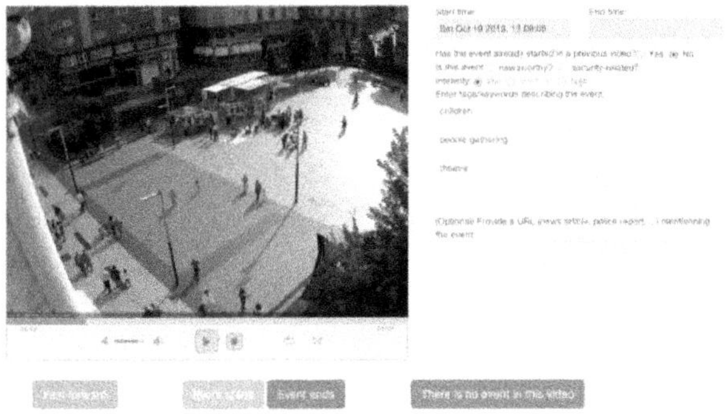

Figure 1: A snapshot from the annotation interface.

Table 2: Statistics of annotated videos

Annotators	unique videos	annot. ratio	mutliple annotations	Agreement
4 English	29	29/69= 42%	1 video	100%
5 Spanish	47	47/69= 68%	13 videos	77%
Both	55	55/69= 79%	21 videos	71%

describe events that they observe by typing in terms, and rate their intensity on a 3-point scale (Low, Medium, and High) according to how likely they are to generate public interest. The intensity is akin to graded relevance used in traditional IR evaluation approaches [12]. We provided the annotators with a web-based interface, of which we show a snapshot in Figure 1.

Statistics for the obtained annotations are summarised in Table 2. From the last row we observe that we obtain a total of 55 annotated videos, of which 21 were annotated by more than one annotator. The agreement between annotators is estimated by converting the intensity levels to binary decisions, using "Medium" as a threshold. We observe that a reasonable agreement is achieved in all cases (lowest is 71%), which gives us confidence in the annotations obtained.

For the set of annotated pooled segments, we obtain terms describing events that were identified in these segments. For each annotated segment, we construct a virtual document that consists of all of the terms provided by the annotators. Since the pooled videos were annotated by both spanish and english annotators, these virtual documents are bilingual and contain English and/or Spanish terms. To cluster events into various topics, we propose to use topic modelling on the document collection of all constructed virtual documents of terms. We use the Latent Dirichlet Allocation (LDA) topic modelling implemented in the Mallet toolkit [8]. In Table 3, we list the top terms of 7 identified topics from the English annotations only. From the table, we can observe that the identified topics are reasonable where we see some interesting associations of terms that describe typical high-level events taking place in the square and the market, e.g. 'demonstration' and 'show' in topic 4, and 'children' and 'entertainment' in topic 6.

5. LEARNING EVENT TOPICS

In this section, we discuss our supervised approach for event topic identification, where the aim is to identify the topic of a segment $\langle l_i, t_j \rangle$ using the sensor metadata observations $\overrightarrow{N}_{\langle l_i, t_j \rangle}$. To train our supervised approach, we construct a *labelled* dataset of event topics from the annotated video pool collected in Section 4. The labelled data consists of segments (tuples of time and location) labelled with either an event topic or with the label 'no event' indicating that no event of interest has occurred in the corresponding

Table 3: Topics identified with topic modelling using the English annotations

Topic	Top terms of the topic
Topic 1	loudspeaker people fanfare police drums procession
Topic 2	microphone rings speech public claps
Topic 3	gathering plaza people booth theatre music
Topic 4	demonstration sitting event sound speak show
Topic 5	market protest cars ongoing children fair
Topic 6	children people shopping middle entertainment
Topic 7	music singing playing guy bells whistles

Table 4: Distribution of labels

Lab.	#	**Lab.**	#	**Lab.**	#	**Lab.**	#
top.1	12	top.3	2	top.5	0	top.7	11
top.2	8	top.4	32	top.6	24	no event	66

time and location. We labelled each annotated segment in the pool to the most probable topic according to the LDA topic modelling configured by setting the number of topics to 7.[2] Unlabelled segments or where the annotators did not identify any event are associated to the 'no event' label. To illustrate the volume of the data and the distribution of labels, we detail in Table 4 the number of segments for each label when using topic modelling on all Spanish and English annotations and setting the number of topics to 7.

We consider the problem of identifying the topic of a pooled segment as a classification task. Using the constructed labelled data, we train a binary classifier for each of the labels with features derived from various sensor metadata streams. Our intuition is that such labelled data would allow us to learn the semantics of a combination of sensor metadata. In other words we aim to match sensor metadata to topics defined using the annotations. For training the classifier, we investigate two main sets of features for the segment, *observation features* and *background features*. Table 5 summarises those features. The *observation features* are extracted from the sensor metadata observed in the location and time corresponding to the segment. The *background features* aim to model past observations and cyclic patterns of activities that take place over time in the same location. The intuition is that some events are periodic and exhibit a long-term pattern, e.g. traffic jams at peak times resulting in a high traffic audio classification score, or entertainment shows taking place in the square at the same time on the weekends. Modelling cyclic patterns, i.e. daily and weekly cycles, from the sensor metadata observations would enable the supervised classifier to identify recurring background events or noise which are not of interest such as traffic jams. Similarly, it would help to identify recurring events of interest such as entertainment shows.

Using the labelled dataset of segments along with the features described in Table 5, we apply supervised machine learning to learn a binary classifier for each label. In particular, we experiment with Random Forests [3] as a learning algorithm.[3] Next we conduct a number of experiments to evaluate the accuracy of our classifier and the effectiveness of the various devised features.

6. EXPERIMENTS

To evaluate our approach for identifying the topic of a candidate segment, we use the dataset of labelled segments

[2]We use 7 topics since we have observed that with this setting we obtain the most coherent topics after experimenting with other alternatives (varying the number of topics between 5 and 10)

[3]We also experimented with other supervised machine learning algorithms, such as naive Bayes and SVM, but due to the space limit, we only report results with Random Forests since they achieve the best performances and the conclusions with other algorithms are similar.

Table 5: Features devised for topic identification

8 Observation features		
Audio features	6	median of the classification score for each audio class (crowd, traffic, music, applause, speaker, siren)
Video features	1	median of the crowd density score
Twitter features	1	number of tweets geotagged within the location in the past one hour
16 Background features		
Daily aggregates	8	for each of our 8 observation features its daily median from all available past observations at the same time from previous days
Weekly aggregates	8	for each of our 8 observation features its median from all available past observations at the same time on the same day of previous weeks
Total	24	

Table 6: Performance of topic identification

Approach	F_1 Accuracy	Precision	Recall
Majority baseline	0.254	0.181	0.426
Obs. Feat.	0.686	0.705	0.697
Obs. & Daily	0.740	0.759	0.761
Obs. & Weekly	0.715	0.715	0.729
Obs. & All background	**0.766**	**0.781**	**0.762**

described in Section 5. We perform a 10-fold cross validation and report the average accuracy across all labels (a label for each topic and the label 'no event'). In addition to using different instantiations of our classifier, we also compare our classifier to an alternative baseline. The "majority" baseline assigns the most common label in the training data to the segments in the testing data. Table 6 summarises the results.

We observe from the table that all instantiations of our approach are markedly better than the majority baseline. In particular, when using only the observation features our approach achieves an F_1 accuracy of 0.686. We also observe that this performance further increases when using the background features. Indeed the best performance is achieved when using all background features along with the observation features ($F_1 = 0.766$). This illustrates that modelling cyclic patterns by aggregating sensor metadata from previous observations helps in better identifying whether a candidate segment represents an event and in identifying the topic of an event.

Furthermore, we conduct an ablation study to identify which features are more effective for topic identification. We remove one of our 8 observation features when learning the classifier. We report the results in Table 7. For example, the row headed "- (Audio crowd)" means that we use all the observation features apart from the audio crowd score. We observe that removing any of the features results in a degrading of performance for accuracy and precision. This is an interesting observation and highlights the importance of having rich metadata describing the environment for identifying the topics high-level events. However, we also observe that the performance degrades most when removing the audio crowd score and the crowd density features. This suggests that the crowd level, as detected by the acoustic or visual sensors, is important to identify events and to distinguish their topic.

7. CONCLUSIONS

In this paper, we proposed an approach for combining sensor metadata streams to identify the topics of events happening within a city. Our approach trains a classifier to identify topics of candidate segments of recordings. Our results are promising and show that combining features from a variety of sensors (acoustic, visual and social) and modelling cyclic

Table 7: Results of the ablation study

Model	F_1 Accuracy	Precision	Recall
All observation features	**0.686**	**0.705**	**0.697**
- (Audio crowd)	0.635	0.624	0.635
- (Audio traffic)	0.681	0.678	0.691
- (Audio applause)	0.680	0.678	**0.697**
- (Audio music)	0.685	0.682	**0.697**
- (Audio speaker)	0.657	0.656	0.665
- (Audio siren)	0.656	0.655	0.665
- (Video crowd)	0.652	0.651	0.665
- Twitter	0.682	0.677	0.697

patterns from past observations provides the best accuracy for event topic identification. These results pave the way towards more robust implementations of local event retrieval that harness both physical and social sensor streams.

Acknowledgments

This work has been carried out in the scope of the EC co-funded project SMART (FP7-287583) and also in the integrated Multimedia City Data project funded by the Economic and Social Research Council.

8. REFERENCES

[1] M.-D. Albakour, C. Macdonald, and I. Ounis. Identifying local events by using microblogs as social sensors. In *Proc. of OAIR'13*.

[2] P. K. Atrey, M. Maddage, and M. S. Kankanhalli. Audio based event detection for multimedia surveillance. In *Proc. of ICASSP'06*.

[3] L. Breiman. Random forests. *Machine learning*, 45(1):5–32, 2001.

[4] C. Buckley and E. M. Voorhees. Retrieval evaluation with incomplete information. In *Proc. of SIGIR'04*.

[5] F. Chen and W. Wang. Activity recognition through multi-scale dynamic bayesian network. In *Proc. of VSMM'10*.

[6] J. Dennis, Q. Yu, H. Tang, H. D. Tran, and H. Li. Temporal coding of local spectrogram features for robust sound recognition. In *Proc. of ICASSP'13*.

[7] A. Dufaux, L. Besacier, M. Ansorge, and F. Pellandini. Automatic sound detection and recognition for noisy environment. In *Proc. of EUSIPCO'00*.

[8] A. K. McCallum. Mallet: A machine learning for language toolkit. http://mallet.cs.umass.edu, 2002.

[9] P. Over, G. Awad, M. Michel, J. Fiscus, G. Sanders, W. Kraaij, A. F. Smeaton, and G. Quénot. TRECVID 2014 – An overview of the goals, tasks, data, evaluation mechanisms and metrics. In *Proc. of TRECVID'14*.

[10] S. Phan, T. D. Ngo, V. Lam, S. Tran, D.-D. Le, D. A. Duong, and S. Satoh. Multimedia event detection using segment-based approach for motion feature. *Journal of Signal Processing Systems*, 74(1):19–31, 2014.

[11] G. Sterling. Study: 43 percent of total google search queries are local. http://searchengineland.com/study-43-percent-of-total-google-search-queries-have-local-intent-135428. Accessed: 5 October 2012.

[12] E. M. Voorhees. Evaluation by highly relevant documents. In *Proc. of SIGIR'01*, pages 74–82, 2001.

[13] M. Walther and M. Kaisser. Geo-spatial event detection in the twitter stream. In *Advances in Information Retrieval*, pages 356–367. Springer, 2013.

StarSum: A Simple Star Graph for Multi-document Summarization

Mohammed Al-Dhelaan
Department of Computer Science
King Saud University
Riyadh, Saudi Arabia
mdhelaan@ksu.edu.sa

ABSTRACT

Graph-based approaches for multi-document summarization have been widely used to extract top sentences for a summary. Traditionally, the documents' cluster is modeled as a graph of the cluster's sentences only which might limit the ability of recognizing topically discriminative sentences in regard to other clusters. In this paper, we propose StarSum a star bipartite graph which models sentences and their topic signature phrases. The approach ensures sentence similarity and content importance from the graph structure. We extract sentences in an approach that guarantees diversity and coverage which are crucial for multi-document summarization. Regardless of the simplicity of the approach in ranking, a DUC experiment shows the effectiveness of StarSum compared to different baselines.

Categories and Subject Descriptors

I.2.7 [**ARTIFICIAL INTELLIGENCE**]: Natural Language Processing—*Text analysis*

Keywords

Text summarization; Text graphs; Multi-document summarization; Topic signatures

1. INTRODUCTION

Multi-document text summarization is the process of automatically producing a concise summary version representing a group of related documents. Graph-based text summarization algorithms have been widely used for multi-document summarization where sentences are modeled as vertices and their similarities or content overlap are modeled as edges. After constructing the graph, an eigenvector centrality measure, as in PageRank[2], is used to rank the vertices. Notable algorithms as in TextRank[12] and LexRank[5] have shown tremendous success in text summarization. However, it is not clear if they capture important characteristics for multi-document summarization as in coverage and diversity.

SIGIR'15, August 09 - 13, 2015, Santiago, Chile.
© 2015 ACM. ISBN 978-1-4503-3621-5/15/08 ...$15.00.
DOI: http://dx.doi.org/10.1145/2766462.2767790 .

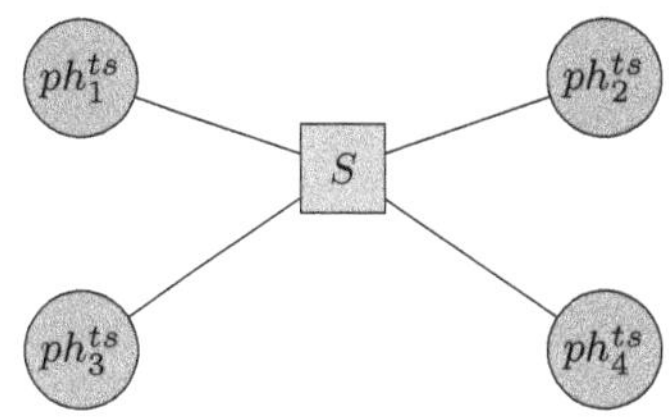

Figure 1: StarSum example: S represents a sentence and ph^{ts} represents topic signature phrase(bigram)

Moreover, when constructing the graph edges, all words are used to determine the sentences similarity which might overestimate the importance of longer sentences. Therefore, we propose an approach that addresses such limitations while maintaining simplicity.

In this paper, we propose a new graph-based summarizer that combines topic signature phrases with sentences in a star bipartite graph, called StarSum. Sentences are modeled as central nodes while their topic signature phrases are modeled around the sentences. This way we can rank sentences not only based on their relations to other sentences but also to how many topic signature phrases do they cover. For example, assume a sentence S_i has a relation to three other sentences. It is not clear if the traditional homogeneous graphs differentiate between whether S_i shares a small or large set of words with all three sentences regardless of the edge weight. Imagine for instance that S_i shares $\{w_1, ..., w_4\}$ with all three sentences, which means an edge weight of 4 between all sentences with S_i. Now, if S_i shares different sets of words with all three sentences each of which is of 4 words, it would mean that the sentence cover more information and would probably be more suitable for a summary regardless of the edge weights. It is clear that if the sentence shares more words, then it should be ranked higher than a sentence with fewer important words.

By explicitly representing words in the graph, we overcome the aforementioned problem. Moreover, by only considering topic signatures we have a less condensed graph which makes clustering the graph to components easier and ensures diversity. We show that by using a simple degree centrality of sentences with their topic signature phrases and neighboring sentences we can easily ensure coverages. The experimental work shows the effectiveness of our approach regardless of its simplicity compared to eigenvector centrality measures.

2. PROPOSED APPROACH

The proposed approach StarSum combines topic signatures bigrams with sentences in a star graph for multi-document summarization. By using topical bigrams, we ensure the selection of sentences that are topical in respect to different clusters of documents. We start by describing the extraction of topic signatures; then we explain the proposed StarSum graph-based approach.

2.1 Topic Signatures

Topic signatures[9] are unigrams, or bigrams in our case, that describe the topics of a giving document compared to a background corpus. These descriptive bigrams are found by using the log-likelihood ratios $\log \lambda$ of two different hypotheses. We have the input document cluster as D_I, and the background corpus as D_B which is all the other clusters. To calculate the log-likelihood ratio of a given bigram $\log \lambda(ph) \ni ph = w_{i-1}w_i$, we form two different hypotheses. The first one is H_1 which assumes to have the same probability of occurrence of ph in both D_I and D_B giving us $P(ph|D_I) = P(ph|D_B)$, and is considered the null hypothesis. The second hypothesis, H_2, which assumes that ph has higher probability of occurrence in the input D_I compared to D_B giving us $P(ph|D_I) > P(ph|D_B)$ which indicates that ph is descriptive. The log-likelihood ratio is calculated as $\log \lambda = \log \frac{L(H_1)}{L(H_2)}$ where L is calculated by using the binomial distribution from the Bernoulli trials of sequences of bigrams.

To find topic signature bigrams, we use $-2 \log \lambda$ to test the statistical significance of their occurrences, which is asymptotically approximated to the χ^2 distribution. We classify bigrams to be descriptive if their $R(ph) = 1$ iff$(-2\log \lambda(ph) > 10.83), 0$ which is equal to confidence level of 0.001. All the significant bigrams are stored for each input cluster separately as $D_I = \{ph_1^{ts}, ..., ph_n^{ts} | R(ph^{ts}) = 1\}$.

2.2 StarSum: Combining Topic Signatures with Sentences

After explaining the topic signature extraction, we move on to describe our proposed approach StarSum, which models sentences with their topic signature bigrams in a bipartite graph. By modeling the relations between sentences and their topical phrases in a graph, we ensure that saliency scores of sentences depend on the topicality of their phrases as well as their connectivity to other sentences. Our approach is designed to cover two main properties of summaries in a multi-document settings: diversity and coverage. First, we describe our approach to ensure diversity of main topics. Second, we describe our ranking approach that ensures coverage.

Before we describe our approach to ensure diversity in summaries, let us define the StarSum graph. Let $G(V_1 \cup V_2, E)$ be a bipartite star graph where $V_1 \cup V_2$ is a set of finite vertices, and E is a set of finite edges connecting V_1 and V_2. The set of sentences is denoted as $V_1 = \{S_1, ..., S_n\}$, and the set of topic signature bigrams as $V_2 = \{ph_1^{ts}, ..., ph_n^{ts}\}$. We are interested on ranking V_1 only. To have a diversified ranking of sentences, traditional approaches use clustering algorithms which might be computationally intensive for well connected graphs. However, since we only model sentences with their topic signatures as opposed to all words or phrases, the graph G is loosely connected. We can simply decompose the graph G to different graph components $G = \{G_1, ..., G_n\}$ that loosely represent different topics of the document cluster. We greedily choose the top ranked sentence from each graph component G_i starting with the largest component in number of vertices to the smallest. Therefore, we have a diversified list of sentences that cover the main topics of the document cluster. Next, we explain the ranking approach for sentences and how we measure the saliency scores for them.

Our saliency scores of sentences are measured in a way to ensure coverage of the topic within a given graph component G_i. The rank of sentences in a graph component is measured by the degree centrality of the sentence vertices, which chooses the sentence that covers the topic well. However, instead of only using the degree centrality, which is the number of topic signature bigrams in the sentence, we use both the first-order degree which is the number of phrases, and the second-order which are the number of other sentences that share topic signature phrases. Let us define $N(v, d)$ to be the neighborhood set of vertices for vertex v of order d. For example, $N(v, 1)$ is only the set of adjacent vertices to v. Therefore, the rank of the sentences is measured as:

$$R(v) = \frac{|N(v,2)| - 1}{length(v)} \tag{1}$$

Where $|N(v, 2)|$ is the total number of vertices in the neighborhood set which contains topic signature phrases and sentences that share these phrases with sentence v, we subtract one since we do not want to count v, and $length(v)$ is the total number of bigrams in sentence v for penalizing long sentences. The final summary is then constructed as:

$$Summary = \bigcup_{G_i} \arg\max_{v \in G_i} R(v) \tag{2}$$

We keep picking top sentences from each graph component, starting from the largest, until we reach the summary length. If we cover all the graph components but have not reached the summary length, we start over in a round robin fashion.

The intuition behind the StarSum approach is that assessing sentences' appropriateness for summaries should not only be about sentence similarity, as in number of common words or cosine similarity. Instead, it should be about both containing topical phrases and sharing them with other sentences. Therefore, modeling the topic signature phrases in the graph is important to ensure rewarding sentences that are more topically informative. Additionally, despite its simplicity, StarSum is an effective approach for guaranteeing diversity and coverage compared to other eigenvector approaches that uses a random walk.

3. EXPERIMENT

To evaluate how our proposed approach compares to other baselines, we use Task 2 of the Document Understanding Conference dataset (DUC 2001) which is designated for multi-document summarization. The DUC is an English news benchmark for text summarization. The dataset is clustered to 30 news topics where each cluster contains roughly 10 documents[1]. Each cluster has 3 different human written summaries that are considered as the golden summaries

[1]we used the 30 topics in the test set only

Table 1: Multi-document Summarization Results over DUC 2001

	ROUGE-1	ROUGE-2	ROUGE-3	ROUGE-L
Log Likelihood	0.47433	0.31205	0.26083	0.45782
TextRank + MMR	0.47545	0.31768	0.26979	0.45569
LexRank + MMR	0.51071	0.35801	0.31120	0.49046
Hypergraph + MMR	0.51612	0.37431	0.32444	0.50291
StarSum	0.52337	0.39148	0.34649	0.51193

to compare against all multi-document summarization algorithms[2]. All the baseline algorithms are set to produce a 100 word summary, which will be compared against the 100 word summary of the gold set. The topic signatures are calculated by assigning D_I to the current cluster, and the D_B to the other 29 clusters. For the preprocessing, we remove punctuations, lowercase all characters, and stem the text with Porter stemmer.

We use the well-known recall metric ROUGE [10] for evaluating the automated summaries. The metric measures the overlap between the generated summaries and the human summaries. We use 5 different options for ROUGE which depends on the size of the textual unit. ROUGE-1 is the unigram measure which shows the most agreement with human judges[10]. Additionally, we use the bigram measure ROUGE-2, the trigram measure ROUGE-3, ROUGE-4, and ROUGE-L for the longest common subsequence of words.

We use a number of different baselines to test our StarSum approach validity through ROUGE[10]. The baselines are common graph-based approaches that generally use an eigenvector centrality algorithms for ranking vertices and extracting the top sentences. The baselines are chosen to directly examine whether our simple approach for ensuring coverage and diversity is effective. The baselines used for comparison are described as follows:

- **Log Likelihood** Similar to[4], topic signatures of words are calculated to rank the sentences. Each sentence is ranked by the density of topic signature unigrams over the length of the sentence.

- **TextRank+MMR** This is well-known approach that builds a graph of sentences based on the overlap of words [12]. Specifically, edge weights are defined as the number of common words between the two sentences divided by the sentences' length. Sentences are then ranked by using a weighted PageRank[2] approach. To compare such approach to StarSum which uses diversity, we combine TextRank with a Maximal Marginal Relevance (MMR)[3]in a similar approach to[17]. The MMR is a simple reranker for ensuring diversity of top sentences.

- **LexRank+MMR** LexRank[5] builds a graph of sentences where the edge weight is the cosine similarity of the two sentences being greater than 0.1. Then we compute the rank of vertices by using a weighted PageRank approach. After ranking the vertices, we use an MMR approach to ensure diversity in the summary.

- **Hypergraph+MMR** This is a state-of-the-art algorithm that models sentences as hyperedges in a hypergraph and words as vertices[1]. It also uses unigram topic signatures in the hyperedge weights so the surfer in the random walk will prefer sentences that contain more topic signatures.

- **StarSum (unigram)** This baseline is built as a star graph between sentences and unigram topic signatures to validate the use of bigram in the proposed approach.

[2]The total is actually 29 clusters. Given that the organizers made a mistake in cluster d31's summaries, it was excluded from our experiment

The experimental results in Table 1 shows that regardless of StarSum's simplicity, it still outperforms computationally intensive approaches. Additionally, it slightly outperforms a state-of-the-art approach that uses random walks with topic signatures on a hypergraph. The improvement over baselines is noticed in all different options of ROUGE which shows the validity of the approach. Moreover, the usage of topic signature bigrams has outperformed using unigrams topic signatures in the StarSum approach in Table 2. This shows that informative bigrams are more important in highlighting salient sentences compared to unigrams in the StarSum algorithm.

To understand why StarSum works well despite its simple algorithmic design, we show how the intuition behind it is slightly different than eigenvector centrality approaches. StarSum is tailored toward two goals: coverage and diversity, where the random walk approaches focus on the prestige of vertices. It is not clear if prestige ensures either diversity or coverage. Additionally, modeling the relation between topic signature bigrams and sentences ensures that we prefer sentences that both contain many topical bigrams and share many connections with other sentences.

The efficiency of the StarSum ranking comes from the fact that it is simply a degree centrality approach. To get the rank of sentence v, the algorithm only needs to traverse the local neighborhood of that sentence. This means that for a single node v, the running time will be $\mathcal{O}(|V_n|+|E_n|)$ which is linear in v's local neighborhood n. In algorithms that use PageRank, the ranking of a node is dependent on the entire graph structure and number of iterations until convergence. Additionally, our approach avoids doing any sentence pair similarity calculation as in most of the baseline approaches which is of quadratic time.

4. RELATED WORK

Summarizing a cluster of documents through graphs has been extensively researched. The most notable work is TextRank[12] and LexRank[5]. In TextRank[12], the edge weights are defined using the words overlap normalized by the length of the two sentences. A weighted PageRank is then used to rank the sentences. Similarly in LexRank[5], a PageRank approach is used to rank vertices but the edge weights are based on cosine similarity between the two sentences. To ensure diversity, some enhanced approaches cluster the graph first as in C-LexRank[13], or enhance the random walk process as in DivRank[11].

Table 2: Comparision between bigram StarSum and unigram StarSum

	ROUGE-1	ROUGE-2	ROUGE-3	ROUGE-L
StarSum (unigram)	0.46915	0.37690	0.33750	0.45944
StarSum (bigram)	0.52337	0.39148	0.34649	0.51193

Other approaches model both sentences and words in a bipartite graph fashion and approach the task as mutual reinforcement between keywords and sentences[14, 16]. However, they are different approaches than StarSum since we are using the log likelihood to identify important phrases a priori to enhance sentence selection. Some new approaches have relied on the log likelihood of word association in sentences[7] which shows their importance in summarization. Additionally, Yih et al. [15] proposed an approach to find sentences that maximize the coverage of informative words. They recognized informative words by frequency and position of words. Similarly, Gillick and Favre[6] proposed to use Integer Linear Programming to find sentences that cover important bigrams based on their document frequency. Both approach do not use discriminative weighting approach as in topic signature. A recent survey on text summarization comparing baselines with state-of-the-art approaches can be found in[8].

5. CONCLUSION & FUTURE WORK

In this work, we proposed a simple, yet effective, star graph that combines topic signature bigrams and sentences. We ensure diversity by decomposing the StarSum graph into different components and picking top sentences from each different component, and we ensure coverage by ranking sentences through their degree connection to other topic phrases and sentences. The experiment showed the effectiveness of our approach by outperforming all other baselines. The results highlighted the shortcoming of using an eigenvector approach on graphs which ranks sentences based on their prestige as opposed to diversity and coverage. Moreover, the simplicity of the StarSum should be appealing to systems that needs to scale to large collection of documents as in the modern Information Retrieval systems.

In the future, we plan to experiment with more datasets and different summary length. Additionally, we will test our approach in related summarization tasks as query-focused summarization. Also, we will experiment with different setup for calculating the topic signature statistics and examine whether it changes the accuracy of summarization. For example, studying the effect of changing the statistical significance level for finding topic signatures. Moreover, we plan to test using a larger background dataset for finding topic signature phrases. Additionally, testing the use of trigrams, in addition to bigrams, and whether they improve the quality of the summaries is in our future plans.

6. REFERENCES

[1] A. Bellaachia and M. Al-Dhelaan. Multi-document hyperedge-based ranking for text summarization. In *CIKM*, pages 1919–1922, 2014.

[2] S. Brin and L. Page. The anatomy of a large-scale hypertextual web search engine. In *WWW*, pages 107–117, 1998.

[3] J. Carbonell and J. Goldstein. The use of mmr, diversity-based reranking for reordering documents and producing summaries. In *SIGIR*, pages 335–336, 1998.

[4] J. M. Conroy, J. D. Schlesinger, and D. P. O'Leary. Topic-focused multi-document summarization using an approximate oracle score. In *COLING-ACL*, pages 152–159, 2006.

[5] G. Erkan and D. R. Radev. Lexrank: graph-based lexical centrality as salience in summarization. *Journal of Artificial Intelligence Research*, 22(1):457–479, Dec. 2004.

[6] D. Gillick and B. Favre. A scalable global model for summarization. In *ILP*, pages 10–18, 2009.

[7] O. Gross, A. Doucet, and H. Toivonen. Document summarization based on word associations. In *SIGIR*, pages 1023–1026, 2014.

[8] K. Hong, J. Conroy, B. Favre, A. Kulesza, H. Lin, and A. Nenkova. A repository of state of the art and competitive baseline summaries for generic news summarization. In *LREC*, pages 1608–1616, Reykjavik, Iceland, May 2014.

[9] C.-Y. Lin and E. Hovy. The automated acquisition of topic signatures for text summarization. In *COLING*, pages 495–501, 2000.

[10] C.-Y. Lin and E. Hovy. Automatic evaluation of summaries using n-gram co-occurrence statistics. In *NAACL*, pages 71–78, 2003.

[11] Q. Mei, J. Guo, and D. Radev. Divrank: The interplay of prestige and diversity in information networks. In *KDD*, pages 1009–1018. ACM, 2010.

[12] R. Mihalcea and P. Tarau. Textrank: Bringing order into texts. In D. Lin and D. Wu, editors, *EMNLP*, pages 404–411, Barcelona, Spain, July 2004.

[13] V. Qazvinian and D. R. Radev. Scientific paper summarization using citation summary networks. In *Coling 2008*, pages 689–696, Manchester, UK, August 2008.

[14] X. Wan, J. Yang, and J. Xiao. Towards an iterative reinforcement approach for simultaneous document summarization and keyword extraction. In *ACL*, pages 552–559, Prague, Czech Republic, 2007.

[15] W.-t. Yih, J. Goodman, L. Vanderwende, and H. Suzuki. Multi-document summarization by maximizing informative content-words. In *IJCAI*, pages 1776–1782, 2007.

[16] H. Zha. Generic summarization and keyphrase extraction using mutual reinforcement principle and sentence clustering. In *SIGIR*, pages 113–120, 2002.

[17] B. Zhang, H. Li, Y. Liu, L. Ji, W. Xi, W. Fan, Z. Chen, and W.-Y. Ma. Improving web search results using affinity graph. In *SIGIR*, pages 504–511, 2005.

When Relevance Judgement is Happening? An EEG-based Study

Marco Allegretti
Mitech Srl
Mantova, IT
marco.allegretti@mitechsrl.it

Yashar Moshfeghi
School of Computing Science
University of Glasgow
Glasgow, UK
Yashar.Moshfeghi@glasgow.ac.uk

Maria Hadjigeorgieva
School of Psychology
University of Glasgow
Glasgow, UK
maria.hadjigeorgieva@glasgow.ac.uk

Frank E. Pollick
School of Psychology
University of Glasgow
Glasgow, UK
Frank.Pollick@glasgow.ac.uk

Joemon M. Jose
School of Computing Science
University of Glasgow
Glasgow, UK
Joemon.Jose@glasgow.ac.uk

Gabriella Pasi
DISCo
University of Milano-Bicocca
Milan, IT
pasi@disco.unimib.it

ABSTRACT

Relevance is a central notion in Information Retrieval, but it is considered to be a difficult concept to define. We analyse brain signals for the first 800 milliseconds (ms) of a relevance assessment process to answer the question "when relevance is happening in the brain?" with the belief that it will lead to better operational definitions of relevance. For this purpose, we devised a user study in which we captured the brain response of 20 participants. Using a 64-channel EEG device, we measured the electrophysiological activity of the brain while the subjects were in the phase of giving an explicit judgement about the relevance of presented images according to a given topic. Analyses were then performed over different time windows of the recorded EEG signals using repeated measures ANOVA. Data reveal significant variation between relevance and non-relevance within the EEG signals from the presentation of the image to 800 milliseconds afterwards. At an early stage these differences were located at frontal and posterior electrode sites. However, at later stages these differences were located in central, centro-parietal and centro-frontal areas. Our findings are an important step towards (i) a better understanding of the concept of relevance and (ii) a more effective implicit feedback systems.

Categories and Subject Descriptors: H.3.3 Information Storage and Retrieval - *Information Search and Retrieval - Search Process*

General Terms: Performance, Experimentation

Keywords: Relevance, EEG

SIGIR'15, August 09 - 13, 2015, Santiago, Chile.
 ISBN 978-1-4503-3621-5/15/08 ...$15.00.
DOI: http://dx.doi.org/10.1145/2766462.2767811.

1. INTRODUCTION

In this paper we focus on the process of relevance assessment performed by humans in an image retrieval task. The main aim of this study is to identify the time frame in which the brain has the highest activities with regard to the process of relevance assessment from the moment of observing a stimulus. Identification of the period of time in which there is a clear association of the activation of brain regions with the task of relevance assessment can be the basis to detect implicit signals of the relevance of images. This may lead to robust definitions and implementation of the concept of relevance.

Relevance is a core notion in Information Retrieval. It has been advocated that the relevance of an information object to the information need of a specific user is a subjective and multidimensional concept, which encompasses various properties and characteristics of the sought information objects [3]. In Information Retrieval systems searchers express their information needs via a set of query words, a process considered to be uncertain and noisy [13]. A progressive disambiguation of the user information need can be achieved through an interactive and iterative process known as the relevance feedback cycle. This process may rely either on explicit or implicit user's indications of relevant objects that the system processes to construct a better representation of the user's needs. To account for the highly interactive nature of the IR task, a number of relevance feedback techniques have been introduced in the literature, which vary from explicit to implicit.

Techniques that rely on explicit feedback are cognitively difficult to use, and hence implicit feedback based systems have been proposed, which, though noisy, allow us to collect several distinct signals of the user's interests through the analysis of both the user's actions and user generated contents [14]. Over the last few years affective and physiological features have been considered as valid ground to define implicit feedback techniques [1, 10, 8]. For example, Arapakis et al., studied the role of emotions in information retrieval, and introduced a number of models [1, 2]. In their subsequent work, they showed that emotional features can be effectively included in building implicit feedback systems [2], and they can also be used to personalise searching [1]. Another example is the work by Moshfeghi et al. in which they demonstrated that, in addition to emotional features, physiological features can also be used to model relevance [8], and they can also be used to predict task types [9].

More recently, a new wave of research was initiated to better understand relevance by analysing brain activity. Moshfeghi et al. [10] show that it is possible to identify brain regions activated during the process of relevance judgement. Another example is the study conducted by Eugster et al. [4] using EEG to show that the frequency content of the EEG signal over extended time windows, along with Event Related Potentials (ERPs) can be used as an effective feature set for decoding relevance of text. Likewise, Kauppi et al. [6] using magnetoencephalography (MEG) show that the frequency content of the MEG signal along with eye movement data can be used for decoding relevance of images. Finally, Zhang et al, [15] show that brain signals monitored via EEG may be used to predict term relevance. Despite the great progress made over this period in terms of better understanding relevance and how to use it more unobtrusively, these studies fail to answer an important and complementary question which is *when* the relevance assessment is happening in the brain. In this paper we aim towards answering this research question.

We conjecture that EEG signals can be exploited to detect significant brain activities in the process of assessing relevance of images. In particular, we aim to identify the time frame in which that significative activity appears in a user's brain while they are assessing pictures. In this spirit, this paper reports the results of an EEG-based user study on image search. We therefore devised an experiment consisting of collecting data via a 64-node EEG in a lab-based user study, and analyzed the collected data off-line. In contrast to the approaches [4, 6], we examined the time variation of the amplitude of the EEG response to relevant and non-relevant items so as to better understand how the difference in relevance evolves over time. In fact, our hypothesis is that there is a time frame in which the EEG signals would be different for relevant documents from non-relevant documents. The rest of the paper is organised as follows: the experiment methodology is described in Section 2, results and discussion are presented in Section 3, and finally the paper is concluded in Section 4.

2. EXPERIMENTAL METHODOLOGY

In this section, we report detailed settings of our experimental methodology.

Experiment Design: This study used a within-subject design. The independent variable was the relevance (with two levels: relevant, and non-relevant), The dependent variables were the EEG signal of the brain.

Tasks: During the experiment, subjects were asked to judge the relevance of images according to a topic. The images used were selected from the ImageCLEF 2009 - Photo Retrieval Task[1]. To this end, 100 images (stimuli), 50 relevant and 50 non-relevant, were shown to each subject. In order not to tire them, stimuli were presented in two separate tasks of 50 images each. For both tasks users could choose between two different topics from a total of four topics, one for each ImageCLEF used in the experiment (11, 49, 02 and 46).

Apparatus: The experiment was run in a purpose-designed room, with a soft light in order to avoid distractions. Stimuli were presented with E-Prime 2.0[2] installed on a PC with a video resolution of 1024 x 768 pixels. Subjects were able to interact with the computer via a keyboard.

EEG signals were recorded with a 64 Ag/AgCl electrodes BrainProducts cap (BrainCapMR)[3]. Eye movements and the electrical activity of the heart were monitored by 2 electrodes (EOG, which was the combination of VEOG and HEOG, and ECG), while the other 62 channels were placed on the scalp at the locations based on the International 10-20 system[5]. All the 64 channels were referred to the reference electrode placed in the middle of the scalp. Data was digitally sampled for analysis at 1024 Hz sampling rate with a 0.016 to 250 Hz analogue bandpass filter and a resolution of 0.5 μV per bit.

Participants: Data were collected from 20 participants (11 females and 9 males) with European origins (10 from UK and 10 from other EU countries). They were recruited from the University of Glasgow population (12 BSc, 5 MSc and 3 PhD) and the average age was 22.35 ($\pm$ 1.66) years (from 20 to 25). All of them had a normal or corrected-to-normal vision, no history of neurological or psychiatric disorders and declared not to be on any drug or medication which could affect their EEG.

Procedure: The user study was carried out in the following manner. The formal meeting with the participants took place in the laboratory setting. At the beginning of the session the participants were given an information sheet which explained the conditions of the experiment. They were then asked to sign a Consent Form and were notified about their right to withdraw at any point during the study, without affecting their legal rights or benefits. Then, they were given an Entry Questionnaire to fill in. The session proceeded with a brief tutorial on the use of the interface with a short training task.

Figure 1 shows how a stimulus was presented to participants. At the beginning, a fixation cross was shown for 1000 ms and it was used to capture the attention of the participant in the middle of the screen. Then, an image, which was randomly chosen among the 50, was presented for 1000 ms. During this period of time, from the appearance of the fixation cross on the screen to the disappearance of the image, the participant was asked to stay as relaxed as possible, and to try not to blink or move[4]. After the presentation of the stimulus, participants were asked to provide a feedback about relevance by pressing a key of the numeric keypad on the right-hand side of the keyboard. The subjects were instructed to press key 1 with the first finger of their right hand for positive feedback (which means the image was relevant), or press key 2 with the second finger for negative feedback. In order not to put any pressure on the participants, and reduce the probability of errors in pressing buttons, there were no time limits to answer the question. In the end, a blank screen was shown for 1500 ms to let them rest before the next picture.

[1]More information about the ImageCLEF 2009 - Photo Retrieval Task at: http://www.imageclef.org/2009/Photo. Relevant images were randomly taken from ImageCLEF 2009 tasks 11, 49, 03 and 46.

[2]E-Prime, Psychology Software Tools©. https://www.pstnet.com/

[3]Brain Products©. http://www.brainproducts.com

[4]These requirements are important in order to ensure good quality of the collected EEG signals.

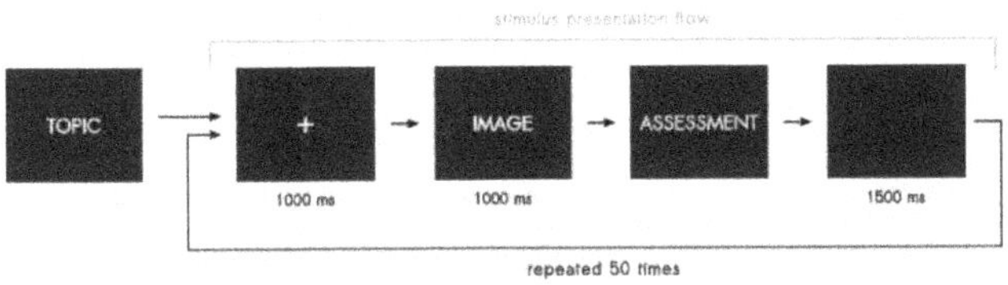

Figure 1: The figure shows the structure of a task. From the left, the first screen was dedicated to show the topic. Once ready, a participant could press any key on the keyboard to start. Firstly, a fixation cross was presented for 1000 ms. Then, a random image from the collection was shown for 1000 ms. This was followed by the question about relevance, which had no time limit. At the end, a black screen was shown for 1500 ms.

Finally, an Exit Questionnaire was administered at the end of the session. Participants were then asked to sign a payment form, prior to receiving the payment. Each study took approximately 100 minutes to complete. Users could only participate once. Prior to running the actual user study, a pilot study was performed using 5 participants to confirm that the process worked correctly and smoothly. A number of changes were made to the system based on feedback from the pilot study.

Preprocessing Steps: The acquired EEG signals were pre-processed using the tools provided by EEGLAB[5]. The pre-processing steps started by referencing the data to the common average (CAR). Then, a band-pass filter, from 0.3 to 40 Hz, was applied to remove power line noise. Epochs were then extracted from 500 ms before stimulus presentation to 1000 ms afterwards. Bad epochs containing only noise were manually removed. Finally, a spatial filter was run using Independent Component Analysis (ICA) in order to remove interference caused by eye blinking and other artifacts (e.g., muscle movement).

Time Frame Based Analysis: We decided to examine the behavior of the EEG signals across all the first 800 ms from the time when the stimuli was presented to the participants. In order do so, we defined four consecutive windows of time as follows: from 0 to 180 ms, from 180 to 300 ms, from 300 to 500 ms, and from 500 to 800 ms. A similar analysis strategy was adopted by Koelstra et al. [7] and included a time window of 300-500 ms. A decision for the other values used in these time boundaries was based on preliminary examination of the data, consideration of the task and consideration of the literature on the timing of EEG events in relation to perceptual and cognitive processing. For example, since approximately 150 milliseconds is the shortest duration of Event Related Potential (ERP) related to visual object categorization [12] we chose 0-180ms as our first epoch to include any such ultra-rapid potentials. Following Koelstra et al. we also chose 300-500 ms, a range that would include activity such as the P300, which has been related to attentional and memory processing [11].

Statistical Analysis of Button Responses: The collected responses were compared to the relevance assessment set (Qrel) provided with the ImageCLEF 2009 tasks. In general, the overall accuracy was 0.89 (± 0.10). In particular, the accuracy over relevant stimuli was 0.90 (± 0.12), while over non-relevant stimuli it was 0.87 (± 0.14). Regarding the response time, the overall mean response time was 676 (± 506) ms, where an average of 669 (± 480) ms was taken by subjects to judge relevant images, while 683 (± 530) ms was taken to judge non-relevant ones.

[5]EEGLAB is an open source Matlab toolbox for electrophysiological signal processing. http://sccn.ucsd.edu/eeglab/

3. RESULTS & DISCUSSIONS

This section presents the analysis of our EEG results. We firstly calculated the mean value for each channel obtained by averaging over the 20 participants' recorded signals and over the target window of time for two conditions: relevance and non-relevance. The Mean Significant Difference (MSD) was then calculated between the two conditions in each time range. This was calculated by subtracting the mean signal for the non-relevant condition from the mean signal for the relevant one. We finally obtained an F-value for each of the 62 electrodes by performing an ANOVA test.

Figure 2 shows topographical plots of the significance in difference (F-value) between the two conditions in the different time ranges. In these plots, the blue color indicates that there is no difference between relevance and non-relevance. Conversely, colors from yellow to red indicate a significant difference between two conditions, and the more the color is red the higher the difference. Moreover, the electrodes that carry significant differences ($p \leq 0.001$) are highlighted with a white dot.

0 - 180 ms This is the first window of time which goes from the initial presentation of the image to 180 ms afterwards. Looking at the first topographical plots on the left in Figure 2, it is clear that there are no apparent differences between the two conditions. This was also confirmed by an ANOVA test that did not reveal any significant effects. One possible reason for this lack of a difference between conditions is that this early time window is dominated by encoding of the stimulus features. Since both the relevant and non-relevant images are rich in detail it is possible that the coding of these stimulus features might mask any potential differences in processing relevance.

180 - 300 ms The window of time 180 - 300 ms shows an early process of implicit judgements of relevance. This process takes place in different areas of the scalp, as shown in the second topographical plot in Figure 2. The most relevant ones are located in the frontal area and in particular in F1 ($F(1,19) = 22.063$, $MSD = 1.123\mu V$) and AF4 ($F(1,19) =$, $MSD = 1.126\mu V$) locations. Since in both electrodes the MSD value is positive, the potential associated with relevance is greater than non-relevance.

300 - 500 ms This time-window shows (third topographical plot in Figure 2) that the positive value of MSD has moved to central areas. In particular, the most significant difference between the two conditions can be found in the electrodes located at C2 ($F(1,19) = 29.031$, $MSD = 1.074\mu V$) and CP2 ($F(1,19) = 27.655$, $MSD = 1.273\mu V$) positions on the scalp.

This window of time is also the same analysed by Koelstra et al. in their study. Looking at both our and their results, it is possible to state that they tally. In fact, the electrodes which carry the most significant differences between the two studies are very similar. In both experiments the area surrounding electrode CP2 is the one which carries the greatest difference between the two conditions[6].

500 - 800 ms The last window of time taken into account is the one which shows the most significant difference

[6]In our experiment the electrode which shows the greatest significant difference is C2. Since Koelstra et al. used a 32-channels EEG cap instead of a 64-channel one, they did not have this channel.

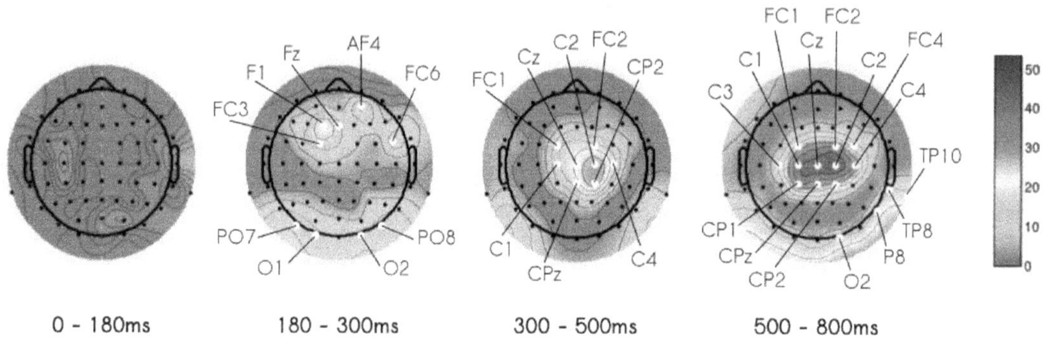

Figure 2: Topographical plots wihch show the significance of difference (F-value) between the two conditions in each window of time.

between relevance and non-relevance condition. As shown in the topographical plots in Figure 2, in the fourth plot the difference between the two conditions is more accentuated than in the third one. Nonetheless, it is possible to notice that the region of interest is still located in the centre of the scalp. In this last time range, the electrodes which carry the greatest difference between the two conditions are C2 ($F(1,19) = 53.369$, $MSD = 1.781\mu V$), Cz ($F(1,19) = 48.154$, $MSD = 1.800\mu V$) and C1 ($F(1,19) = 43.257$, $MSD = 1.848\mu V$).

Discussion Timing and topography of our results suggest a timecourse of processing relevance that involves an early stage in the time window of 180 - 300 ms and a later stage that begins around 300 ms and builds through 800 ms. This first stage was evident in the larger potentials for relevant images found at frontal and posterior electrode sites. The timing of this difference suggests a role for late perceptual encoding of relevance and might explain the fMRI activity reported by Moshfeghi et al [10] in the inferior temporal cortex. Moreover, this early difference in amplitude might be related to establishing differences in the EEG frequency content used as features in recent research [6, 4]. From 300 to 800 ms after the stimulus was presented, the mean difference between EEG signals elicited by relevant and non-relevant images became greater in the electrodes centered around Cz at the central area of the scalp. Similar results have been obtained by Eugster et al. [4]. They found a peak difference at 757 ms between relevant and non-relevant stimuli at the CZ and C4 electrode sites, arguing that this potential was due to processing of memory. Despite the different nature of the two studies (Eugster et al. focused on textual terms, while we focused on images), it is possible to assert that this later stage might be common across the visual modalities of text and image, and related to cognitive encoding of visual information. Hence, regardless of context, our brain needs around 800 ms to judge the relevance of a visually presented stimulus.

4. CONCLUSION

In this paper we aimed to answer a fundamental question which is *when* the relevance assessment is happening in the brain. Focusing on the process of assessing relevance of images, we tried to identify the time frame in which users' brain EEG signals are the strongest and most distinguishable from the time that the images are shown to them. Our hypothesis was that there is a time frame in which the difference between EEG signals elicited by relevant and non-relevant images would be significant. To investigate that, we analysed how relevance assessment evolves over different windows of time within the first 800 millisecond of relevance judgment. Our findings revealed time frames as well as regions which carry the most significant difference between relevance and non-relevance conditions within this period of time. Despite the fact that the process of relevance assessment is very complex, this novel study provides an important step towards unravelling the nature of relevance and operationalising it for IR processes.

5. REFERENCES

[1] I. Arapakis, K. Athanasakos, and J. M. Jose. A comparison of general vs personalised affective models for the prediction of topical relevance. In *SIGIR*, pages 371–378, 2010.

[2] I. Arapakis, Y. Moshfeghi, H. Joho, R. Ren, D. Hannah, and J. M. Jose. Enriching user profiling with affective features for the improvement of a multimodal recommender system. In *CIVR*, 2009.

[3] P. Borlund. The concept of relevance in ir. *Journal of the American Society for information Science and Technology*, 54:913–925, 2003.

[4] M. J. Eugster, T. Ruotsalo, M. M. Spapé, I. Kosunen, O. Barral, N. Ravaja, G. Jacucci, and S. Kaski. Predicting term-relevance from brain signals. In *SIGIR'14*, pages 425–434. ACM, 2014.

[5] H. Jasper. The ten-twenty electrode system of the international federation. In *Electroencephalogr Clin Neurophysiol*, volume 10, pages 371–375, 1958.

[6] J. P. Kauppi, M. Kandemir, V. M. Saarinen, L. Hirvenkari, L. Parkkonen, A. Klami, R. Hari, and S. Kaski. Towards brain-activity-controlled information retrieval: Decoding image relevance from MEG signals. *NeuroImage, in press*, 2015.

[7] S. Koelstra, C. Mühl, and I. Patras. Eeg analysis for implicit tagging of video data. In *ACII*, pages 1–6, 2009.

[8] Y. Moshfeghi and J. M. Jose. An effective implicit relevance feedback technique using affective, physiological and behavioural features. In *SIGIR*, pages 133–142, 2013.

[9] Y. Moshfeghi and J. M. Jose. On cognition, emotion, and interaction aspects of search tasks with different search intentions. In *WWW*, pages 931–942, 2013.

[10] Y. Moshfeghi, L. R. Pinto, F. E. Pollick, and J. M. Jose. Understanding relevance: An fmri study. In *ECIR*, pages 14–25, 2013.

[11] J. Polich. Updating p300: An integrative theory of p3a and p3b. volume 118, 2007.

[12] C. M. S. Thorpe, D. Fize. Speed of processing in the human visual system. volume 381, pages 520–522, 1996.

[13] P. Ingwersen, and Kalervo Järvelin. *The Turn: Integration of Information Seeking and Retrieval in Context.* Springer, 2005. xiv, 448 S. ISBN 1-4020-3850-X, 2006.

[14] R. W. White. Implicit feedback for interactive information retrieval, 2005.

[15] Y. Zhang, J. Zhang, M. Lease, and J. Gwizdka. Multidimensional relevance modeling via psychometrics and crowdsourcing. In *SIGIR'14*, pages 435–444. ACM, 2014.

Search Engine Evaluation based on Search Engine Switching Prediction

Olga Arkhipova Lidia Grauer Igor Kuralenok Pavel Serdyukov
Yandex LLC
{olycha, lidia, solar, pavser}@yandex-team.ru

ABSTRACT

In this paper we present a novel application of the search engine switching prediction model for online evaluation. We propose a new metric pSwitch for A/B-testing, which allows us to evaluate the quality of search engines in different aspects such as the quality of the user interface and the quality of the ranking function. pSwitch is a search session-level metric, which relies on the predicted probability that the session contains a switch to another search engine and reflects the degree of the failure of the session. We demonstrate the effectiveness and validity of pSwitch using A/B-testing experiments with real users of search engine Yandex. We compare our metric with recently proposed SpU (sessions per user) metric and other widely used query-level A/B metrics, such as Abandonment Rate and Time to First Click, which we used as our baseline metrics. We observed that pSwitch metric is more sensitive in comparison with those baseline metrics and also that pSwitch and SpU are more consistent with ground truth, than Abandonment Rate and Time to First Click.

Categories and Subject Descriptors: H.3.3 [Information Storage & Retrieval]: Information Search & Retrieval

Keywords: online evaluation; search engine switching

1. INTRODUCTION

Due to the intense competitiveness between commercial search engines, the correct evaluation of a search engine's quality is critical for its ability to constantly improve its quality and hence maintain its search market share. Since the impact of the tested improvements becomes relatively smaller with the time, sensitivity of evaluation measures becomes increasingly important. Two major approaches are used to evaluate search engine quality: Cranfield-style offline evaluation based on experts judgements [2] and online evaluation such as A/B-testing [6].

Despite the convenience of offline evaluation with document or search session labels provided by a group of experts, this approach has several considerable disadvantages, namely: expert judgements may not reflect the actual relevance, which is often user-specific; the process requires substantial costs and is also time consuming; some standard metrics do not necessarily correlate with user-centric performance measures. In contrast, the online evaluation approach, such as A/B testing, alleviates these disadvantages as it uses the implicit feedback of real users directly. In this case, the major challenge of online evaluation methods is establishing the relationship between the observed search behaviour and the relative quality of the search engines observing that behaviour. The idea of A/B-testing is the following: users are randomly assigned to two groups. During some period of time, the first (control) bucket of users is presented with the original version of the search engine (A), while the second (treatment) bucket of users is presented with the experimental version of the search engine (B). Successful search engine development requires making effective decisions towards improving all of its components, such as the ranking algorithm, the snippet generation algorithm, the ads ranking algorithm or the user interface. A/B testing, by design, allows to measure the effect of innovations in any of these components, but requires highly sensitive and easily interpretable metrics that would detect even subtle differences in the behavior of the users exposed to both versions of the system.

Many studies focused on the problem of predicting frustration or satisfaction of a searcher during her search session [3], but, to the best of our knowledge, there were no attempts to study the utility of such predictive models for the purposes of A/B testing. In this paper, we present a new metric for evaluating the quality of a search engine that can be used in A/B-testing and which is based on the prediction of the proportion of unsuccessful user sessions among all user sessions. We argue that this is possible by predicting if the user had a reason to switch to another search engine for each search session in each bucket. Indeed, in 57% of switches from one search engine to another the cause of the switch is a poor quality of search results [5]. However, low quality search results are not the only reason of switching, there are other reasons, including the need to verify the acquired knowledge or to find additional information (26%) [5]. Actually, any search engine aims to maximize its sufficiency and hence prevent switches to its competitors in all and, especially, in these 83% of cases, what means to improve relevance, authority and trustworthiness of its search results, as well as to increase the size of its document index. Although, search engine switches are good indicators of user dissatisfaction, search engines are able to observe them only for a small

SIGIR '15 August 09 - 13, 2015, Santiago, Chile

ACM 978-1-4503-3621-5/15/08 ...$15.00.
DOI: http://dx.doi.org/10.1145/2766462.2767786.

Table 1: **Characters assigned to actions. Characters with * were not presented in the final metric classifier**

H	short click on an organic result (< 10 sec)
C	normal click on an organic result (< 60 sec)
L	long click on an organic result ($\geq$ 60 sec)
S	skip of an organic result
O	query with a next action after a short time
V	query with a next action after a normal time
R	query with a next action after a long time
W *	click on a vertical search result
D *	click on an advertisement

share of users that are used to switch and whose web surfing activities can be tracked. To expand this to the entire audience, one needs to predict the potential switches: the switches that indeed occurred but were not detected or the switches that could occur if the users in the corresponding search sessions had the habit to use more than one search engine (there is always a considerable share of users that never uses more than one search engine [10])(see Section 2).

An online metric has to be applicable for comparing relative quality of modifications of search engines when they differ in different aspects such as ranking or user interface. We propose to use the probability that a session contains a switch to another search engine as such a metric (see Section 4.1).

In order to demonstrate that the proposed online metric is considerably more sensitive than the state-of-the-art online metrics [7, 9], we performed a series of A/B-testing experiments with the users of one of the most popular search engines (see Section 4).

2. SWITCHING PREDICTION MODEL

In this section we consider the problem of search engine switching prediction in a search session. We define a switch as an event of changing one search engine to another in order to continue the current search session. Actually, the fact of switching can be unambiguously detected only in a small part of the search sessions performed by users who installed the browser or the special browser toolbar plug-in developed by a search engine [10]. We used the Yandex browser/toolbar interaction logs collected in October 2014. For each session recorded in these logs, we could exactly detect the fact of switching from the search engine to other search engines. After that, we detected users, who had at least one switch from the search engine to other search engines in a given period. Then, we extracted a random sample of the search sessions of those "switching-tolerant" users from the period under study. Our final data set consisted of 224k search sessions, corresponding to 88k users. Further, we splited users into learn and test sets (1:1). In order to build a prediction model, we used a variation of stochastic gradient boosted decision trees [4]. The quality of the different versions of predictors that we describe in the paper was measured using Area Under Curve (AUC) measure.

Table 2: **The performance of feature groups**

feature group	**description**	**AUC with**	**AUC without**
Baseline	sequence based features	0.59	-
Baseline + "actions dwell time"	all features about time intervals between actions	0.617	0.728
Baseline + "query text"	query text features	**0.681**	0.673
Baseline + "user session number"	total number of user sessions during the day, current user session №	**0.66**	0.715
Baseline + "vertical results and ads appearance"	features about number of vertical results and ads appearance	0.601	0.727
Baseline + "session-level time"	session dwell time, session duration	0.623	0.727
Baseline + query text + session number	features from two groups	**0.7223**	**0.6547**

3. FEATURES SELECTION

We started from encoding each search session into an ordered set of characters representing a sequence of search actions. The alphabet for encoding is presented in Table 1. For example, using interaction logs, we encode the user session as follows: the user typed the query "toyota" and did not click anywhere. Seven seconds later, she reformulated her query "toyota celica" and, five seconds later, she clicked on the first result: image vertical search result. The next activity of that user happened after 2 minutes and it was a long click on the organic search result the third position. Using the full alphabet from Table 1, such a session would be encoded as (OOWSSL) and using the reduced version (without differentiation of clicked result types) as (OOLSSL). Our algorithm automatically extracts frequent subsequences of the characters that the sessions are represented by. Further, it uses these subsequences as binary features of the sessions. The classifier trained only with such sequence features (AUC = 0.59) was our baseline that we tried to improve with adding more features. Thus, we considered a number of session-level features, such as the duration of the session, the average duration of clicks, the level of advertising shown, etc (56 features). Every feature was included in the dataset with two normalizations, as in [8]. AUC of the classifier trained with the baseline features and all these additional features was 0.73. Feature selection is worth doing not only for evaluating feature performance, but also for selecting the optimal feature set and reducing the amount of the data to be stored during the production process. To select an optimal feature set, we grouped all features into the following groups: "actions dwell time" features, "query text"

Table 3: Top-10 features AUC

Minimum query length (characters) in the session	0.6607
Total number of user sessions during the given period (day)	0.6605
Maximum query length (characters) in the session	0.6481
Average query length (characters) in the session	0.6475
Current user session number during the given period (day)	0.6257
Average query length (words) in the session	0.6235
Minimum query length (words) in the session	0.6229
Maximum query length (words) in the session	0.6216
Time passed from the end of the previous user session before start of the current user session (user's absence time)	0.62
Share of unique clicked URLs among all clicked URLs per session	0.6173

features, "user session number" features, "vertical results and ads appearance" features and "session-level time" features. The descriptions of each feature group are presented in Table 2. We evaluated the utility of each of the feature groups in two ways: we trained a classifier only with the considered additional feature group and without this additional feature group (with baseline features always present). The results are presented in Table 2. Table 3 contains the top-10 most useful features across all the groups in terms of AUC. The most important features for switch prediction are the features from "query text" and "user session number" groups: combining them into one group gives us AUC = 0.722, so we select features only from these two groups to include into the final set of features (26 additional features).

4. SWITCH BASED EVALUATION METRIC

4.1 Metric description

Since search engine switching can be interpreted as an indication of the failure of the user's session, it can serve as a foundation for a search quality measure. We propose a new online metric for measuring and comparing the quality of the search engines via A/B-testing. Our metric is based on the prediction of the proportion of unsuccessful user sessions among all user sessions. Using the classsifier built in Section 3 we can predict the event of a switch for any user session and estimate the proportion of unsuccessful user sessions by the probability of switching averaged over all sessions in the experiment. We call our metric *pSwitch*:

$$pSwitch = \frac{1}{N}\sum_{i=1}^{N}\tilde{p}_{switch}(i)$$

Consider an A/B-testing experiment and suppose that the mean predicted switch probability in the experimental group is statistically significantly higher than the mean predicted switch probability in the control group: that indicates that the users in the experimental group are less satisfied. In order to measure the significance of the mean difference we used the bootstrap test [1] with sampling by users. We considered results to be significant in the case of p-value < 0.05.

4.2 Experimental setup

To analyze pSwitch, we conducted 8 online experiments testing different new features of search engine Yandex. All the experiments were manually inspected and labeled by a group of experts as degrading or improving (it means that we expected each feature to either degrade or improve the user experience). We regarded these labels as the ground truth that we expected our metrics to agree with. We also ran our experiments on 3 A/A-testing experiments [6] to control the validity of pSwitch: reliable online evaluation metrics must not signal about any differences in such experiments, as otherwise these metrics are not valid. All the A/A and A/B experiments were also evaluated by SpU (Sessions per User) [9], Abandonment Rate and Time to First Click, which we used as our baseline metrics. The users from the treatment buckets of the A/B-testing experiments were exposed to the following configurations of the search engine.

Experiments with vertical results (2 experiments) group of experiments consisted of one improvement and one degradation of vertical results.

Swap (1 experiment) In this case, we made the following changes of the original ranking: two random documents from positions 2-9 were swaped. We believe that the search engine generates rankings which are better than a random ordering on average, so we could assume that such swapping will lead to a degradation of the search quality.

Old ranking algorithm(1 experiment) In this case, we used a 1-year-old ranking algorithm instead of the current production algorithm. We treat it as a degradation of the ranking algorithm.

Ranking improvements (4 experiments) This group of experiments consisted of 4 improvements of the ranking algorithm.

In each experiment, the changes were substantial and had to be detected by an online evaluation metric that is supposed to be sensitive to the changes in the target aspects of search engine quality.

4.3 Experimental results

We evaluate the performance of the two pSwitch metrics: one based on the classifier with the full aplhabet and another based on the classifier with the reduced alphabet (without click type differentiation). The performances of the two types of pSwitch metric, SpU, Abandonment Rate and Time to First Click on the A/B dataset and A/A control dataset are presented in Table 4. P-values for SpU metric and pSwitch metrics were measured using the bootstrap test [1]. P-values for Time to First Click and Abandonment Rate are measured by Wilcoxon signed rank test. None of the metrics detected a significant difference in A/A experiments, so all metrics proved their validity for online evaluation. As we can see from Table 4, pSwitch metric with the reduced alphabet is much more sensitive than SpU metric and is more consistent with the ground truth then Time to First Click and Abandonment Rate. However, the outcome of the pSwitch metric based on the classifier with the full alphabet produced the result opposite to the ground truth for vertical results improvement experiment. The differences for other experimental groups are consistent with the ground truth. The reason for this contradiction is the inclusion into

Table 4: Experiment Results. Bootstrap by users. For each metric improvements are marked in green, degradations - in red, according to the metric diff. Expected color (the ground truth) is in the first column. "!" means that the metric diff is opposite to the ground truth. * - significance at 0.05, ** - at 0.01, *** - at 0,001

Experiment name	SpU pvalue	pSwitch pvalue (classifier with reduced alphabet)	pSwitch pvalue (classifier with full alphabet)	Abandonment Rate pvalue	Time to First Click pvalue
improvement 1	0.2662	0.0302 *	0,0228 *	0.04 (!*)	0.43
improvement 2	0.0834	0.25	0,313	0.02 *	0.82
improvement 3	0.16	0.33	0,0604	0.35	0.01 (!*)
improvement 4	0.0388 *	0.006 **	0,0016 **	0.12	0.78
vertical result improvement	0.0298 *	0.048 *	0,0144 (!*)	0 ***	0 ***
vertical result degradation	0.6918	0.65	0 ***	0.73	0 (!***)
swap	0.2788	0.0016 **	0.0002 ***	0.001 **	0.18
old formula	0.4498	0.007 **	0.0168 *	0.001 **	0.91
A/A control 1	0.67	0.22	0.236	0.54	0.23
A/A control 2	0.48	0.63	0.62	0.14	0.23
A/A control 3	0.89	0.68	0.67	0.85	0.58
correct decisions ratio	0.25	**0.625**	0.625	0.5	0.125
incorrect decisions ratio	0	**0**	0.125	0.125	0.25

the alphabet those actions whose appearance in the sequence depends not only on the users preferences, but is also directly affected by the experiment's design. Clicks on vertical results (W) and ads (D) are good examples of such actions. For example, if there are no vertical results on the SERP by design, a user cannot click on them and therefore there will be no (W) action in the user action sequence, that could lead to wrong results. Our baseline metrics Time to First Click and Abandonment Rate also had experiments with results, which are opposite to the ground truth (two experiments for Time to First Click and one - Abandonment Rate). SpU and pSwitch (classifier with reduced alphabet) metrics did not contradict the ground truth in any of the experiments.

5. CONCLUSIONS

In this paper, we proposed a new metric called pSwitch for evaluating the quality of search engines based on search engine switching prediction. To predict the probability of switching in a particular session, we presented the classification model that used a rich set of aggregated session features and sequences of search actions as features as well. We selected an optimal feature set and evaluated the performance of groups of features. We also presented a new direction of using models predicting of user frustration and a success during search sessions in A/B-testing. To analyze our metric, we conducted A/B-testing experiments with real users of search engine Yandex. We draw the attention to the importance of the action coding selection and illustrated this on real experiments. Our findings demonstrated that the new metric can be applied to evaluation of different aspects of a search engine. pSwitch is more sensitive in comparison with the recently proposed SpU metric and is also more consistent with the ground truth than query-level metrics, such as Abandonment Rate and Time to First Click. Since our work is the first to study an online evaluation metric based on search engine switching prediction, a variety of its extensions can be considered in the future. For instance, since our proposed metric can be used for evaluating different types of search engine's changes, not only the ones used in our experiments, we plan to demonstrate such applicability in the future experiments. Another direction of future work is the improvement of the classification model, which serves as the basis of our metric and might benefit from using a broader set of features and alternative classification methods.

6. AKNOWLEDGMENTS

We would like to thank Irina Orlova for her great contribution to this work.

7. REFERENCES

[1] M. R. Chernick and R. A. LaBudde. *An Introduction to Bootstrap Methods with Applications to R.* Wiley Publishing, 1st edition, 2011.

[2] C. Cleverdon. Readings in information retrieval. chapter The Cranfield Tests on Index Language Devices, pages 47–59. Morgan Kaufmann Publishers Inc., 1997.

[3] H. A. Feild, J. Allan, and R. Jones. Predicting searcher frustration. In *Proc. SIGIR 2010*, pages 34–41. ACM.

[4] J. H. Friedman. Stochastic gradient boosting. *Comput. Stat. Data Anal.*, 38(4):367–378, Feb. 2002.

[5] Q. Guo, R. W. White, Y. Zhang, B. Anderson, and S. T. Dumais. Why searchers switch: Understanding and predicting engine switching rationales. In *Proceedings SIGIR 2011*, pages 335–344. ACM.

[6] R. Kohavi, R. Longbotham, D. Sommerfield, and R. M. Henne. Controlled experiments on the web: Survey and practical guide. *Data Min. Knowl. Discov.*, 18(1):140–181, Feb. 2009.

[7] F. Radlinski and N. Craswell. Comparing the sensitivity of information retrieval metrics. In *Pr. SIGIR 2010*, pages 667–674. ACM.

[8] D. Savenkov, D. Lagun, and Q. Liu. Search engine switching detection based on user personal preferences and behavior patterns. In *Pr. SIGIR 2013*, pages 33–42. ACM.

[9] Y. Song, X. Shi, and X. Fu. Evaluating and predicting user engagement change with degraded search relevance. In *Pr. WWW 2013*, pages 1213–1224. International World Wide Web Conferences Steering Committee.

[10] R. W. White, A. Kapoor, and S. T. Dumais. Modeling long-term search engine usage. In *Pr. UMAP 2010.*

Time-Aware Authorship Attribution for Short Text Streams

Hosein Azarbonyad
Informatics Institute, University of Amsterdam
h.azarbonyad@uva.nl

Mostafa Dehghani
Institute for Logic, Language and Computation, University of Amsterdam
dehghani@uva.nl

Maarten Marx
Informatics Institute, University of Amsterdam
maartenmarx@uva.nl

Jaap Kamps
Institute for Logic, Language and Computation, University of Amsterdam
kamps@uva.nl

ABSTRACT

Identifying authors of short texts on Internet or social media based communication systems is an important tool against fraud and cybercrimes. Besides the challenges raised by the limited length of these short messages, evolving language and writing styles of authors of these texts makes authorship attribution difficult. Most current short text authorship attribution approaches only address the challenge of limited text length. However, neglecting the second challenge may lead to poor performance of authorship attribution for authors who change their writing styles.

In this paper, we analyse the temporal changes of word usage by authors of tweets and emails and based on this analysis we propose an approach to estimate the dynamicity of authors' word usage. The proposed approach is inspired by time-aware language models and can be employed in any time-unaware authorship attribution method. Our experiments on Tweets and the Enron email dataset show that the proposed time-aware authorship attribution approach significantly outperforms baselines that neglect the dynamicity of authors.

Categories and Subject Descriptors

H.3.3 [**Information Storage and Retrieval**]: Information Search and Retrieval

Keywords

Authorship Attribution; Time-Aware Language Models; Short Text Analysis

1. INTRODUCTION

Automatic authorship attribution is a growing research direction due to its legal and financial importance [12]. In the recent decade with the growth of Internet based communication facilities, much content on the web is in the form of short messages. Finding the author of a short message is important since much fraud and cybercrimes occur with exchanging emails and short messages. Usually cybercriminals tend to use an anonymous identity in the Internet based communication systems. Therefore, finding the authors of short texts could be useful for law enforcement agencies. As length of texts decreases, finding the author of the texts becomes more challenging [8, 10, 11].

SIGIR'15, August 09 - 13, 2015, Santiago, Chile.

ACM 978-1-4503-3621-5/15/08 ...$15.00.
DOI: http://dx.doi.org/10.1145/2766462.2767799 .

Current authorship attribution approaches neglect an important factor in human development: as a person matures or a significant event occurs in his life (such as changing job, getting married, moving in a new circle of friends, etc) over time the model of his writing style and the words used may change as well. As an example, Lancashire et al [7] analyses the temporal changes on the vocabulary usage by Agatha Christie and conclude that her vocabulary-size decreases over time. Cf. also [13]. As another example, Figure 1 shows the temporal changes of vocabulary usages of 133 Twitter users over a period of 40 months. The figure shows that the similarity of content to a fixed static corpus decreases over time. In fact, we can conclude that content generated at the current time is more similar to recent content than to older content. Current authorship attribution approaches neglect this fact and use all material generated by authors with the same influence.

This paper tries to answer two crucial questions in authorship attribution for short texts. The first research question is: Does the writing style of authors of short text change over time? And if so, do they change their writing styles by the same rate? The second research question is: How does the temporal change of writing styles of authors affect authorship attribution? And how we can capture the changes in the writing styles of authors and take the changes into account to overcome the effects of drift in authorship attribution?

We answer these questions using two datasets: one is collected from Twitter and the Enron email corpus [3]. We introduce a new time-aware authorship attribution approach which is inspired by time-based language models [9] and can be employed in any time-unaware authorship attribution method to consider the temporal drifts in authorship attribution process. Our evaluations on tweets and Enron datasets show that the proposed time-aware approach is able to incorporate the temporal changes in authors writing styles and outperforms two competitive baselines.

The paper is organized as follows. We review related work in Section 2. Section 3 contains our time-aware authorship attribution framework. The datasets and experiments are described in Section 4. We conclude in Section 5.

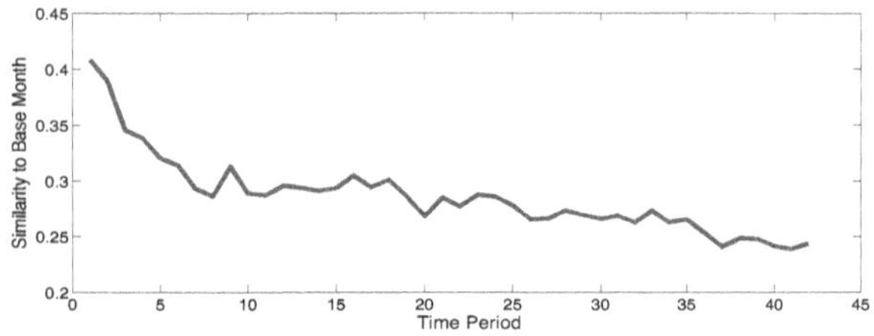

Figure 1: Vocabulary usage changes of Twitter users over time. A dataset containing 133 Twitter users and their written tweets is collected. The first two months of the users' activity in Twitter are considered as start period. Also, each following month is considered as a time period. The $x-axis$ shows the time periods and $y-axis$ shows the averaged similarity of the contents generated by the users at each time period with the content generated by them in the base time period. Cosine similarity over frequency of character 4-grams in users' contents is employed as similarity measure.

2. RELATED WORK

Authorship attribution approaches can be categorized into two main categories: similarity based approaches and machine learning based approaches [12]. Several studies showed that similarity based approaches outperform machine learning based methods when the number of candidate authors is high [5, 8]. In this paper, we only use similarity based approaches. Previous work showed that character n-grams are the most effective units for calculating the similarity of a given text with authors' profiles [1, 4, 12]. The SCAP method[1], which simply calculates the Jacard similarity of a given text and the profile texts of authors and assigns the given text to the most similar author, is the simplest similarity based approach. Among different similarity based methods, the *feature sampling method* proposed in [4] is the best performing method for authorship attribution. This method samples from all features (i.e., character n-grams) and calculates the similarity of the given text with all authors' profiles on the sampled features using cosine similarity. This process is repeated k times and the text is assigned to the author whose profile is most similar to the given text for a certain fixed number of the k times. (If no author achieves this threshold, no one is assigned). A variation of this method outperformed other approaches in the Authorship Verification task in which the goal is to determine if two documents are written by the same author [6]. Recent research focuses on authorship attribution for short texts [11, 8, 10]. Incorporating temporal changes of writing styles of authors has not been applied before in authorship attribution.

3. TIME-AWARE AUTHORSHIP ATTRIBUTION

Time-based language models have been shown to be effective in temporal information retrieval [9]. We use a similar approach in authorship attribution when we consider the temporal changes in authors' writings. We first divide the whole timeline of an author in time periods of a fixed length and then construct a language model for each period. In this work, we use character n-grams for our language models. In fact, the language model of each period is a probability distribution over n-grams of the texts generated in that period. For a new generated short text, we calculate its similarity with the language model constructed for each period weighted by a decay factor which is a function of the temporal difference of the date of the short text with the period. More specifically, the time-aware probability that a given short text s is written by an author a is calculated as follows:

$$P(s|a) = \sum_{t \in T \wedge t < t_s} decay(t_s - t) * P(s|\theta_{a_t}), \qquad (1)$$

where T is set of all periods. We discretize the whole timeline to T periods. $P(s|\theta_{a_t})$ is the probability that s is generated by the language model of author a in time period t. The function $decay()$ is a monotonically decreasing function, giving less weight to older periods. In section 3.1, we introduce different decay functions and study their effectiveness. We use character 4-grams as token units (features) and employ unigram language models [14] for estimating $P(s|\theta_{a_t})$. We construct a language model for t and first estimeate the likelihood of generating text s from language model of author a in time t as follows:

$$P(s|\theta_{a_t}) = \prod_{ng \in ngrams_s} p(ng|\theta_{a_t})^{c(ng, ngrams_s)}, \qquad (2)$$

where θ_{a_t} is the language model of a in time period t, $ngrams_s$ is all character n-grams extracted from s, and $c(ng, ngrams_s)$ is the frequency of n-gram ng in $ngrams_s$. $p(ng|\theta_{a_t})$ is calculated as follows using Jelinek-Mercer smoothing:

$$p(ng|\theta_{a_t}) = (1-\lambda) * p_{ml}(ng|d_{a_t}) + \lambda * p(ng|\mathcal{C}), \qquad (3)$$

where, d_{a_t} is a document containing all character n-grams of texts generated by a in time period t, $p_{ml}(ng|d_{a_t})$ is estimated using maximum likelihood, $\mathcal{C}$ is all character n-grams of whole corpus and $p(ng|\mathcal{C})$ is also estimated using maximum likelihood.

It is supposed that every author is equally likely before any piece of text is given and finally, the author of s is determined as follows:

$$\hat{a} = \operatorname*{argmax}_a P(s|a) \qquad (4)$$

We assign s to $\hat{a}$ if $P(s|a)$ is more than a predefined threshold.

We use this approach to extend the SCAP method[1] and the feature sampling method [4]. We use (1) to calculate similarity. When $decay()$ is the constant function assigning 1, we have a time-unaware approach. Otherwise the appraoch is time aware.

3.1 Decay Factor

Several decay functions have been proposed [2, 9]. In this paper, we compare a general decay function which is same for all users to a function which is specific for each user. The exponential decaying function is the most used method in temporal IR. However, Figure 1 shows that the writing styles of authors do not change that dramatically. Therefore, we use a linear decreasing function. We employ the slope of the curve plotted in Figure 1 as the slope of the general decay function. We use linear regression to estimate the slope and intercept parameters. Finally, the decay factor for a time period t is then calculated as follows:

$$decay(t) = \frac{1}{Z}(at + b), \qquad (5)$$

where Z is the normalizing factor (the sum of decay values for all periods should be 1), a and b are the parameters of the linear degrading function.

Changes in writing styles need not be the same for all authors. For estimating the parameters of specific degrading function for an author a, we first calculate the similarity of contents generated by a in each time period with the contents generated by him/her in start period and then plot a vocabulary usage change curve for a (similar to Figure 1). Then we use linear regression to estimate the slope and intercept parametrs of the plotted curve and employ the estimated parameters as the parameters of the specific decay function. Finally, the decay function for an author a at a time period t is calculated as follows:

$$decay_a(t) = \frac{1}{Z_a}(a_a t + b_a), \quad (6)$$

where a_a and b_a are the parameters of decay function for the author a.

4. DATASETS AND EXPERIMENTAL RESULTS

We describe the used datasets, explain the experiments and report our results.

4.1 Datasets

We use two different datasets: tweets and the Enron email corpus [3]. Both datasets contain short messages generated over a long period, and thus they are suitable for time-aware authorship attribution of short texts.

We collected tweets from users of Twitter who have tweeted for a long time. This dataset contains 133 users. The average number of tweets per user is 1820 and the average number of tweets of each user per month is 31. Tweets are written between 2010-01 and 2014-10. We divided this period into 46 months. Since character 4-grams have been shown to be the most effective units in authorship attribution [6, 8], we model texts and authors using unigram language models consisting of character 4-grams. The average and median number of 4-grams per month in this dataset are 61,677 and 101,867 respectively. The average length of tweets in this dataset is 101 characters with a the standard deviation of 42.

From the Enron dataset we selected mails from 15 prolific authors written between 1998-01 and 2002-09. We divided the corpus into 45 months. The average number of emails per person in this dataset is 3200 and the average and median number of emails written by a user per month in the selected dataset are 68 and 74 respectively. The average and median number of 4-grams per month in this dataset are 436,940 and 478,678 respectively. The average length of emails in this dataset is 648 characters with a standard deviation of 1253 and the median of 606.

4.2 Experimental results

We now discuss our results, following the two main research questions.

4.2.1 *Drift in word usage over time*

Starting with our first research question: Does the writing style of authors of short text change over time? And if so, do they change their writing styles by the same rate? Figure 1 shows that on average there is a change in vocabulary usages of authors. However, we expect that different users have different vocabulary usage change rates. Table 1 shows the statistics of the slopes of specific decay functions. We use the method described in Section 3.1 for estimating the slope of vocabulary usage change plot for each user. For calculating the similarity we use frequency of 4-grams. As can be seen from this table, the average of slopes of change plots of all users is almost zero. However there is a relatively large difference between maximum and minimum values of slopes in both datasets. This indicates that different authors change their vocabulary usage in different rates over the time.

Dataset	max	min	$average$	$median$	std
Enron(N=15)	0.09	-0.1	-0.007	-0.006	0.161
Tweets(N=133)	0.06	-0.07	-0.001	-0.002	0.07

Table 1: The statistics of slope a_a in the decay function 6 for different authors on Enron and Tweet dataset.

Dataset	Time-unaware	Time-aware(general)	Time-aware(specific)
Enron	0.87	0.88	0.94 (8%)$^{\blacktriangle}$
Tweets	0.69	0.71	0.80 (15%)$^{\blacktriangle}$

Table 2: Precision of feature sampling method on tweets and Enron dataset at Recall point of 0.3. ($^{\blacktriangle}$ indicates the significance using t-test, one-tailed, $p{-}value < 0.05$)

4.2.2 *Results of time-aware authorship attribution methods*

To see the effect of drift in authorship attribution, we first do time-unaware authorship attribution. We use 90% oldest messages generated by each author for constructing the author-model and use the remaining 10% newest messages to test different authorship attribution approaches. In time-aware approaches, we tested different lengths for time periods. Based on our experiments the best performance on both tweets and Enron datasets is achieved when we set the length of time periods to one month.

Figure 2 shows the precision-recall curves of time-aware SCAP, time-unaware SCAP, time-aware feature sampling, and time-unaware feature sampling methods on tweets and Enron datasets. We assign the given text to the found author if the similarity of the text with the author's model is more than a predefined threshold otherwise no authorship is made for the text. By changing the value of the threshold we achieved different values of precision and recall and plotted them in Figure 2. Precision is the proportion of correct attributions among all attributions made by the method and recall is the proportion of test samples for which and attribution made by the method and is correcet. As decay function we use specific decay function (Equation 6). We tested different values for the parameter of Jelinek-Mercer smoothing method λ and the number of iterations of feature sampling method k. The best results are achieved with $\lambda = 0.3$ and $k = 100$. In the results, these parameter values are used. Figure 2 shows that the precision of the time-aware approach is higher than the precision of time-unaware approach at different recall points both when we apply time-aware approach on simple SCAP method and when we apply it on feature sampling method. Also, from the results it can be concluded that the time-aware feature sampling method is the best performing method on both datasets.

The precision of feature sampling method using general and specific decay functions and without using decay function at recall of 0.3 is shown in Table 2. The results show that using the specific decay function gives significantly better performance compared to using the general decay function. Also, the precision of the time-aware method which uses general decay function is almost same as the precision of the time-unaware approach. In fact using a general decay function does not help to track the changes of writing styles of auhtors and can not distinguish between dynamic and static authors. The high value of precison on Enron dataset is mainly due to the low number of authors in this dataset which makes attribution easier.

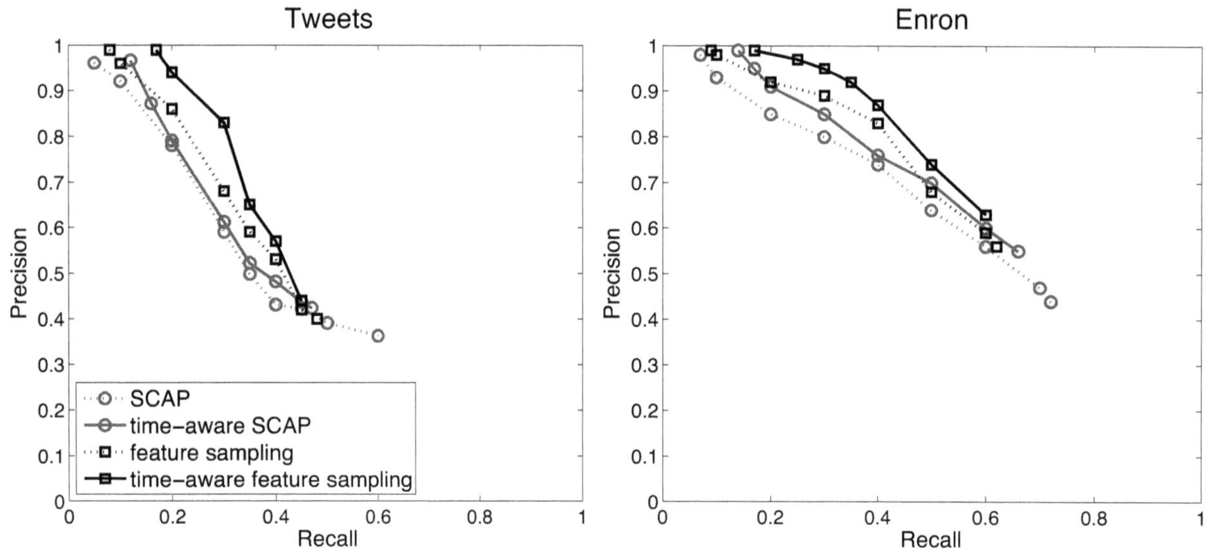

Figure 2: Precison-Recall curves of time-aware and time-unaware authorship attribution methods on tweets and Enron datasets.

5. CONCLUSIONS

We considered the effect of temporal change in the writing style and vocabulary usage of authors on the task of authorship attribution for short text streams. Our findings were based on two datasets, the Enron email corpus and an own-generated set of tweets from 133 authors who tweeted over a period of almost 4 years. We first investigated whether temporal change is a problem at all, and found that authors do change and that different authors change differently. We used a linearly decreasing temporal decay function to incorporate the temporal changes of authors' vocabulary usage in authorship attribution. We divided the whole timeline of authors into fixed size periods and constructed a language model for each period. In the evaluation we created time aware versions of two commonly used authorship attribution methods. In both methods the time-aware version performed significantly better than the "static" version, over both datasets.

Feature engineering is an interesting future research direction. Some (types of) features may change more than others, and we could incorporate that in our models.

Acknowledgements This research was supported by the Netherlands Organization for Scientific Research (ExPoSe project, NWO CI # 314.99.108; DiLiPaD project, NWO Digging into Data # 600.006.014) and by the European Community's Seventh Framework Program (FP7/2007-2013) under grant agreement ENVRI, number 283465.

6. REFERENCES

[1] G. Frantzeskou, E. Stamatatos, S. Gritzalis, C. E. Chaski, and B. S. Howald. Identifying authorship by byte-level n-grams: The source code author profile (SCAP) method. *IJDE*, 6(1), 2007.

[2] N. Kanhabua and K. Nørvåg. A comparison of time-aware ranking methods. SIGIR '11, pages 1257–1258, 2011.

[3] B. Klimt and Y. Yang. The enron corpus: A new dataset for email classification research. In *ECML'04*, pages 217–226, 2004.

[4] M. Koppel, J. Schler, and S. Argamon. Authorship attribution in the wild. *LREC*, 45(1):83–94, 2011.

[5] M. Koppel, J. Schler, S. Argamon, and E. Messeri. Authorship attribution with thousands of candidate authors. SIGIR '06, pages 659–660, 2006.

[6] M. Koppel and Y. Winter. Determining if two documents are written by the same author. *JASIST*, 65(1):178–187, 2014.

[7] I. Lancashire and G. Hirst. Vocabulary changes in agatha christie's mysteries as an indication of dementia: A case study. In *19th Annual Rotman Research Institute Conference Cognitive Aging: Research and Practice*, pages 1–5, 2009.

[8] R. Layton, P. Watters, and R. Dazeley. Authorship attribution for twitter in 140 characters or less. In *Cybercrime and Trustworthy Computing Workshop (CTC)*, pages 1–8, 2010.

[9] X. Li and W. B. Croft. Time-based language models. CIKM '03, pages 469–475, 2003.

[10] R. Schwartz, O. Tsur, A. Rappoport, and M. Koppel. Authorship attribution of micro-messages. In *EMNLP'13*, pages 1880–1891, 2013.

[11] R. S. Silva, G. Laboreiro, L. Sarmento, T. Grant, E. Oliveira, and B. Maia. Twazn me: Automatic authorship analysis of micro-blogging messages. NLDB'11, pages 161–168, 2011.

[12] E. Stamatatos. A survey of modern authorship attribution methods. *JASIST*, 60(3):538–556, 2009.

[13] M. van Dam and C. Hauff. Large-scale author verification: Temporal and topical influences. SIGIR '14, pages 1039–1042, 2014.

[14] C. Zhai and J. Lafferty. A study of smoothing methods for language models applied to information retrieval. *TOIS*, 22(2):179–214, 2004.

A Priori Relevance Based On Quality and Diversity Of Social Signals

Ismail Badache
IRIT Laboratory
University of Toulouse
Toulouse, France
Ismail.Badache@irit.fr

Mohand Boughanem
IRIT Laboratory
University of Toulouse
Toulouse, France
Mohand.Boughanem@irit.fr

ABSTRACT

Social signals (users' actions) associated with web resources (documents) can be considered as an additional information that can play a role to estimate a priori importance of the resource. In this paper, we are particularly interested in: first, showing the impact of signals diversity associated to a resource on information retrieval performance; second, studying the influence of their social networks origin on their quality. We propose to model these social features as prior that we integrate into language model. We evaluated the effectiveness of our approach on IMDb dataset containing 167438 resources and their social signals collected from several social networks. Our experimental results are statistically significant and show the interest of integrating signals diversity in the retrieval process.

Categories and Subject Descriptors

H.3.3 [**Information Storage and Retrieval**]: Information Search and Retrieval

General Terms

Retrieval model, Experimentation

Keywords

Social signals; Signals diversity; Priors; Language models

1. INTRODUCTION

Majority of information retrieval systems (SIR) exploit two classes of sources of evidence to rank documents in response to the user query. The first class, the most exploited, is dependent on the query, it concerns the term statistics such as term frequency, distribution of term in documents. The second class concerns query-independent factors, which measures a kind of quality or importance of the document. Among these factors, the number of incoming links to a document [12], PageRank [5], topical locality [7], the presence of URL [17], document authors [13] and social signals [11].

SIGIR '15, August 09 - 13, 2015, Santiago, Chile
Copyright 2015 ACM ISBN 978-1-4503-3621-5/15/08 ...$15.00.
http://dx.doi.org/10.1145/2766462.2767807.

In this paper we are interested in social signals associated to web resources. Nowadays, web pages include different social network buttons where users can express if they support or recommend content [1]. In this paper, we assume that, in addition to estimating a priori significance based on simply counting signals related to the resource [3], signals diversity associated to a resource can be also an index that indicates a resource interest beyond a social network or a community. The research questions addressed in this paper are the following:

1. How to estimate the signals diversity of a resource?
2. What is the impact of signals diversity on IR system?
3. Is there an influence of the social networks origin on the quality of their signals?

The remainder of this paper is organized as follows. Section 2 reviews some related work. Section 3 describes our social approach. In section 4, we evaluate the effectiveness of our proposed approach and discuss the results. Finally, we conclude the paper and announce some future work.

2. RELATED WORK

While considerable work has been done in the context of social IR there is still a lack of user studies that would analyze the impact of users' actions diversity in a resource from diverse viewpoints. Major existing works [3, 6, 10, 11] focus on how to improve IR effectiveness by exploiting the users' actions and their underlying social network. For instance, Chelaru et al. [6] study the impact of social signals (like, dislike, comment) on the effectiveness of search on YouTube. In [3, 4], the authors show the impact of different time-sensitive signals taken into account individually and grouped as social properties without considering their diversity in the resource.

Our work is distinguished from the state of art. Our approach is based on signals diversity in the resource to improve relevance ranking of conventional text search. We exploit various signals extracted from different social networks. We note that in previous works, diversity has been applied only to the textual content of the document [2] [16].

Our goal is to estimate the significance of the resource by taking into account signals diversity into the resource. These sources of evidence are incorporated into language model that provides a theoretical founded way to take into account the notion of a priori probability of a document.

3. SOCIAL SIGNALS DIVERSITY

Our approach consists in exploiting social signals and their diversity as a priori knowledge to take them into account in retrieval model. We rely on language model to model signals diversity as a prior probability.

3.1 Notation

Social information that we exploit within the framework of our model can be represented by 4-tuple <U, R, A, SN> where *U, R, A, SN* are finite sets of instances: *Users*, *Resources*, *Actions* and *Social Networks*.

Resources. We consider a collection $C=\{D_1, D_2, ...D_n\}$ of n documents. Each document (resource) D can be a Web page, video or other type of Web resources. We assume that resource D can be represented both by a set of textual keywords $D_w=\{D_{w_1}, D_{w_2}, ...D_{w_z}\}$ and a set of social actions A performed on this resource, $D_a=\{D_{a_1}, D_{a_2}, ...D_{a_m}\}$.

Actions. We assume a set $A=\{a_1, a_2, ...a_m\}$ of m actions that users can perform on the resources. These actions represent the relation between users $U=\{u_1, u_2, ...u_h\}$ and resources C. For instance, on Facebook, users can perform the following actions on resources: *like, share, comment.*

Social Properties. We consider a set $X=\{Popularity, Reputation\}$ of 2 social properties that characterize a document D. Each property is quantified by a specific actions group. These properties are modeled as a priori probability.

3.2 Query Likelihood and Document Priors

We exploit language models [15] to estimate the relevance of document to a query. The language modelling approach computes the probability $P(D|Q)$ of a document D being generated by query Q as follows:

$$P(D|Q) \overset{\text{rank}}{=} P(D) \cdot P(Q|D) = P(D) \cdot \prod_{w_i \in Q} P(w_i|D) \quad (1)$$

$P(D)$ is a document prior, i.e. query-independent feature representing the probability of seeing the document. The document prior is useful for representing and incorporating other sources of evidence in the retrieval process. w_i represents words of query Q. Estimating of $P(w_i|D)$ can be performed using different models (Jelineck Mercer, Dirichlet). The main contribution in this paper is how to estimate $P(D)$ by exploiting social signals.

3.3 Estimating Priors

According to our previous approach [3], the priors are estimated by a simply counting of actions performed on the resource. We assume that signals are independent, the general formula is the following:

$$P_x(D) = \prod_{a_i^x \in A} P_x(a_i^x) \quad (2)$$

$P_x(a_i)$ is estimated using maximum-likelihood:

$$P_x(a_i^x) = \frac{Count(a_i^x, D)}{Count(a_\bullet^x, D)} \quad (3)$$

To avoid Zero probability, we smooth $P_x(a_i)$ by collection C using Dirichlet. The formula becomes as follows:

$$P_x(D) = \prod_{a_i^x \in A} \left(\frac{Count(a_i^x, D) + \mu \cdot P(a_i^x|C)}{Count(a_\bullet^x, D) + \mu} \right) \quad (4)$$

$P_x(a_i|C)$ is estimated using maximum-likelihood:

$$P(a_i^x|C) = \frac{Count(a_i^x, C)}{Count(a_\bullet^x, C)} \quad (5)$$

Where:

- $x \in \{P, R\}$ refers to the social property (*popularity* or *reputation*) estimated from a set of specific actions.
- $a_\bullet^x$ the total number of all social signals associated with x property, in document D or in collection C.
- $P_x(D)$ represents the a priori probability of D.
- $Count(a_i^x, D)$ represents number of occurrence of specific action a_i^x performed on a resource. a_i^x designs action a_i related (or used) to measure x property.

We believe that the diversity of signals in a resource is an index that may indicate an interest beyond a social network or a community. Diversity and quantitative distribution of social signals in a resource may be considered as factors of relevance, i.e., a resource dominated by a single signal should be disadvantaged versus a resource with an equitable distribution of the signals. By applying diversity index of Shannon-Wiener [14], the corresponding formula is as follows:

$$Diversity_s(D) = -\sum_{i=1}^{m} P_x(a_i) \cdot log(P_x(a_i)) \quad (6)$$

Where $P(a_i)$ is defined above, and m represents the total number of signals.

The Shannon index is often accompanied by Pielou evenness index [14] :

$$Diversity_s^{Equit}(D) = \frac{Diversity_s(D)}{MAX(Diversity_s(D))} \quad (7)$$

Where:

$$MAX(Diversity_s(D)) = log(m) \quad (8)$$

The a priori probability $P_x(D)$ is estimated using the formula 4 multiplied by the diversity factor. The corresponding formula is as follows:

$$P_x(D) = \left(\prod_{a_i \in A} P_x(a_i) \right) \cdot Diversity_s^{Equit}(D) \quad (9)$$

4. EXPERIMENTAL EVALUATION

To validate our approach, we conducted a series of experiments on IMDb dataset. We evaluated the impact of signals diversity by combining it with language model.

4.1 Description of Test Dataset

We used a collection IMDb documents provided by INEX[1]. Each document describes a movie, and is represented by a set of metadata, and has been indexed according to keywords extracted from fields [3]. For each document, we collected

[1] https://inex.mmci.uni-saarland.de/tracks/dc/2011/

specific social signals via their corresponding API of 5 social networks listed in table 2. We chose 30 topics with their relevance judgments provided by INEX IMDb 2011[2]. In our study, we focused on the effectiveness of the top 1000 results. Table 1 shows an example of the documents containing social signals. The document URL is given by the following syntax: *http://www.imdb.com/title/{id}/*

Table 1: Instances of 2 documents with social signals

Id	Like	Share	Comment	+1
tt1730728	30	11	2	0
tt1922777	12363	11481	20614	238
Id	**Bookmark**		**Tweet**	**Share(LIn)**
tt1730728	0		2	0
tt1922777	12		2522	14

Table 2 presents the social signals that we take into account in order to estimate each social property.

Table 2: Exploited social signals in quantification

Property	Social signal	Network
Popularity	Number of *Comment*	Facebook
	Number of *Tweet*	Twitter
	Number of *Share(LIn)*	LinkedIn
	Number of *Share*	Facebook
Reputation	Number of *Like*	Facebook
	Number of *Mention* +1	Google+
	Number of *Bookmark*	Delicious

4.2 Results and Discussions

We conducted experiments with models based only on content of documents (Lucene Solr model[3] and Hiemstra language model without prior [9]), as well as approaches combining content and social properties as a priori probabilities of document. We note that the best value of $\mu \in [90, 100]$ The results are listed in table 3.

Table 3 summarizes the results of precisions@k for $k \in \{10, 20\}$, nDCG (Normalized Discounted Cumulative Gain) and MAP (Mean Average Precision). In [3, 4], authors have already shown that taking into account the social characteristics without considering diversity improves IR compared to models based only on the topical relevance. In order to check the significance of the results, we performed the Student test [8] and attached * (strong significance against Baseline (A) and (B)) and ** (very strong significance against Baseline (A) and (B)) to the performance number of each row in the table 3 when the p-value < 0.05 and p-value < 0.01 confidence level, respectively.

Before discussing the results we highlight that first we performed a correlation analysis by using the Spearman's correlation coefficient between signals diversity scores in the documents and their relevance. We found that the diversity represents a positive correlation with the relevance (Spearman's rho = 0.19), this result has aroused our interest and encourage us to exploit the diversity in our IR model. Table 3 (D) lists the results obtained by the integration of the signals diversity in the document. We notice that the NDCG and Precisions are generally better than the baseline listed in Table 3 (C) part when diversity is ignored.

We also notice that the both results are much more better than those obtained by topical models (Baseline (A) Without Priors) and Baseline (B) where signals are taken individually. This leads to our first conclusion, if multiple users of different social networks have found that a resource is useful, then it is more likely that other users will find these resources useful too.

Table 3: Results of P@{10, 20}, nDCG and MAP

IR Models	P@10	P@20	nDCG	MAP
(A) Baseline: Without Priors				
Lucene Solr	0.3411	0.3122	0.3919	0.1782
ML.Hiemstra	0.3700	0.3403	0.4325	0.2402
(B) Baseline: Single Priors				
Like	0.3938	0.3620	0.5130	0.2832
Share	0.4061	0.3649	0.5262	0.2905
Comment	0.3857	0.3551	0.5121	0.2813
Tweet	0.3879	0.3512	0.4769	0.2735
+1	0.3826	0.3468	0.5017	0.2704
Bookmark	0.3730	0.3414	0.4621	0.2600
Share (LIn)	0.3739	0.3432	0.4566	0.2515
(C) Baseline: Combination Priors				
TotalFacebook	0.4209	0.4102	0.5681	0.3125
Popularity	0.4316	0.4264	0.5801	0.3221
Reputation	0.4405	0.4272	0.5900	0.3260
All Criteria	0.4408	0.4262	0.5974	0.3300
All Properties	0.4629	0.4509	0.6203	0.3557
(D) With Considering Signals Diversity				
TotalFacebook^{Div}	0.4227*	0.4187*	0.5713*	0.3167*
Popularity^{Div}	0.4403**	0.4288**	0.5983**	0.3320**
Reputation^{Div}	0.4480**	0.4306**	0.6110**	0.3319**
All Criteria^{Div}	0.4463**	0.4318**	0.6174**	0.3325**
All Properties^{Div}	0.4689**	0.4563**	0.6245**	0.3571**

4.3 Quantitative and Qualitative Analysis

To better understand the effect of these social signals on the selection of relevant documents, we analyze their distribution in the all documents returned by 30 topics.

According to Table 4 we notice that the average frequency of the signals in the relevant documents is higher compared to irrelevant documents (ex. the average of *like* is 362 actions in the relevant documents while in irrelevant documents is 61 actions). We also note that the signals coming from Facebook capture the highest number of relevant documents (see Figure 2), knowing that they are many in irrelevant documents but with a much smaller average. This is due to the engagement rate on Facebook and its dynamic growth [1]. Therefore, the distinction between relevant documents and irrelevant documents is much more sensitive to signal frequency, i.e., relevant documents are characterized by a very high number of Facebook signals compared to the irrelevant documents (see Figure 1). The signals *tweet* and +1 come in second position with an average frequency, respectively, 97 and 29 actions in the relevant documents (see Figure 1). The signal of Delicious (Bookmark) is the weakest criterion among these signals, it appears in 429 relevant documents with an average frequency of 13 actions per document only. Concerning the signal of LinkedIn, we note that 95% of its actions of *share* are condensed in 601 relevant documents with an average frequency of 67 actions per document. However, the number of relevant documents captured by Linkedin *share* signal is very low compared to that captured by Facebook signals, this is due to LinkedIn engagement rate which is very low compared to Facebook, but LinkedIn *share* signal represents the most reliable source in terms of trust compared to other social signals. Therefore, we can say that the presence of this signal, whatever its frequency in a document represents a relevance index.

[2]https://inex.mmci.uni-saarland.de/tracks/dc/2011/
[3]http://lucene.apache.org/solr/

Table 4: **Statistics on the distribution of the signals in the documents (relevant and irrelevant)**

	Relevant documents containing signals			Relevant documents without signals	Irrelevant documents	
	Number of documents	Number of actions	Average	Number of documents	Number of actions	Average
Like	2210	800458	362.1981	555	1678040	61.6133
Share	2357	856009	363.1774	408	1862909	68.4012
Comment	1988	944023	474.8607	777	1901146	69.8052
Tweet	1735	168448	97.0884	1030	330784	12.1455
+1	790	23665	29.9556	1975	49727	1.8258
Bookmark	429	5654	13.1794	2336	20489	0.7523
Share (LIn)	601	**40446**	67.2985	2164	**2341**	0.0859
	Total relevant documents : 2765				Total irrelevant documents : 27235	

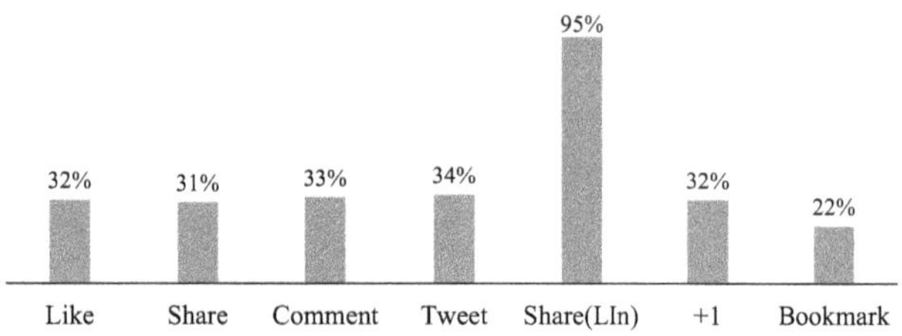

Figure 1: Signals % in the relevant documents

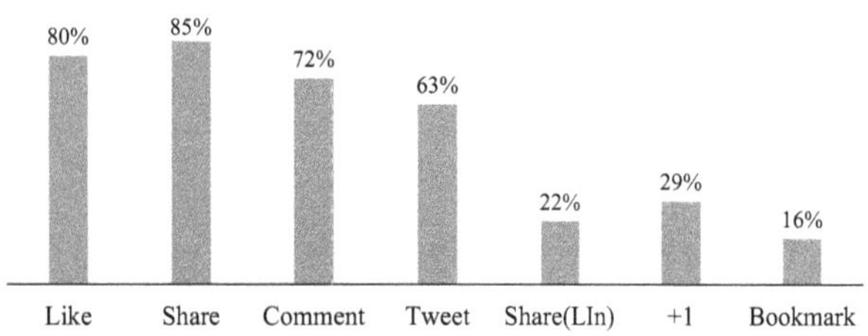

Figure 2: Relevant documents % containing signals

Finally, according to this preliminary statistical study, we observe that each social network has its own specific influence on the quality of its social signals. The quality of signals, provided by Facebook, Twitter, Google+ and Delicious, in a document depend on their frequencies, the more the signals are frequent on the resource, the more its a priori importance increases. However, the LinkedIn signal does not only depend on its frequency in the document because it has in itself a power of mature trust compared to the other signals. This amounts to the maturity of LinkedIn users who are well reputed compared to other social networks users.

5. CONCLUSION

We proposed in this paper a search model based on users' actions associated with a document. We proposed to estimate a social priors of a document by considering signals diversity. The proposed model is based on language model that incorporates this a priori knowledge. Experimental evaluation conducted on IMDb dataset shows that taking into account these social features in a textual model improves the quality of returned search results. Finally, to investigate the influence of social networks on the quality of signals, we developed a statistical study on the distribution of social signals for each social network in both relevant and irrelevant documents.

For future work, we plan to address some limitations of the current study. We plan to integrate other social data into proposed approach. Further experiments on another dataset are also needed. This is even with these simple elements, the first results encourage us to invest more this track.

6. REFERENCES

[1] O. Alonso and V. Kandylas. A study on placement of social buttons in web pages. *arXiv*, 2014.

[2] A. Angel and N. Koudas. Efficient diversity-aware search. In *SIGMOD*, pages 781–792, 2011.

[3] I. Badache and M. Boughanem. Social priors to estimate relevance of a resource. In *IIiX*, 2014.

[4] I. Badache and M. Boughanem. Document priors based on time-sensitive social signals. In *ECIR*, pages 617–622, 2015.

[5] S. Brin and L. Page. The anatomy of a large-scale hypertextual web search engine. In *WWW*, pages 107–117, 1998.

[6] S. Chelaru, C. Orellana-Rodriguez, and I. S. Altingovde. How useful is social feedback for learning to rank youtube videos? *WWW*, pages 1–29, 2013.

[7] Brian D Davison. Topical locality in the web. In *SIGIR*, pages 272–279, 2000.

[8] William Sealy Gosset. The probable error of a mean. *Biometrika*, 6(1):1–25, 1908. Originally published under the pseudonym "Student".

[9] D. Hiemstra. A linguistically motivated probabilistic model of information retrieval. In *ECDL*, pages 569–584, 1998.

[10] G. Kazai and N. Milic-Frayling. Effects of social approval votes on search performance. In *ITNG*, pages 1554–1559, 2009.

[11] A. Khodaei and C. Shahabi. Social-textual search and ranking. In *CrowdSearch*, pages 3–8, 2012.

[12] W. Kraaij, T. Westerveld, and D. Hiemstra. The importance of prior probabilities for entry page search. In *SIGIR*, pages 27–34, 2002.

[13] C. Macdonald and I. Ounis. Voting for candidates: adapting data fusion techniques for an expert search task. In *CIKM*, pages 387–396, 2006.

[14] EC. Pielou. Shannon's formula as a measure of specific diversity: its use and misuse. *American Naturalist*, pages 463–465, 1966.

[15] Jay M. Ponte and W. Bruce Croft. A language modeling approach to information retrieval. In *SIGIR*, pages 275–281, 1998.

[16] L. Qin, J. X Yu, and L. Chang. Diversifying top-k results. *VLDB Endowment*, 5(11):1124–1135, 2012.

[17] T. Westerveld, W. Kraaij, and D. Hiemstra. Retrieving web pages using content, links, urls and anchors. 2002.

Document Comprehensiveness and User Preferences in Novelty Search Tasks

Ashraf Bah
University of Delaware
Newark, Delaware, USA
ashraf@udel.edu

Praveen Chandar
University of Delaware
Newark, Delaware, USA
pcr@del.edu

Ben Carterette
University of Delaware
Newark, Delaware, USA
carteret@udel.edu

ABSTRACT

Different users may be attempting to satisfy different information needs while providing the same query to a search engine. Addressing that issue is addressing Novelty and Diversity in information retrieval. Novelty and Diversity search models the retrieval task wherein users are interested in seeing documents that are not only relevant, but also cover more aspects (or subtopics) related to the topic of interest. This is in contrast with the traditional IR task in which topical relevance is the only factor in evaluating search results. In this paper, we conduct a user study where users are asked to give a preference between one of two documents B and C given a query and also given that they have already seen a document A. We then test a total of ten hypotheses pertaining to the relationship between the "comprehensiveness" of documents (i.e. the number of subtopics a document is relevant to) and real users' preference judgments. Our results show that users are inclined to prefer documents with higher comprehensiveness, even when the prior document A already covers more aspects than the two documents being compared, and even when the less preferred document has a higher relevance grade. In fact, users are inclined to prefer documents with higher overall aspect-coverage even in cases where B and C are relevant to the same number of novel subtopics.

Categories and Subject Descriptors

H.3.3 [**Information Storage and Retrieval**]

Keywords: diversity; preference judgment; user study

1. INTRODUCTION

In the recent past, more and more researchers in information retrieval (IR) evaluation have directed their attention to evaluation measures that account for both redundancy and ambiguity in search. Novelty aims at dealing with redundancy in search results, while diversity aims at handling ambiguity in queries. Research in that direction has seen such an interest that two different IR evaluation conferences have organized diversity retrieval tasks. The Text Retrieval Conference (TREC) included a diversity retrieval task as part of the Web track between 2009 and 2012 [8]. Unlike its ad-hoc counterpart in the same track, the diversity task judged documents based on subtopics as well as to the topic as a whole. In the same manner, the NTCIR11-IMine task incorporates a subtask focused on diversified document retrieval for which different user intents must be taken into account [11].

SIGIR '15, August 09 - 13, 2015, Santiago, Chile

ACM 978-1-4503-3621-5/15/08...$15.00
DOI: http://dx.doi.org/10.1145/2766462.2767820

Popular evaluation metrics such as precision and recall do not account for intents and subtopics. Both assume binary relevance.

Newer metrics go beyond simple binary relevance, and use graded relevance instead. The shortcoming of binary relevance addressed by graded relevance is that some documents are simply more useful to users than others. Two of the most widely used metrics that make use of graded judgments are nDCG [10] and ERR [7]. What these two metrics do not account for, however, are different user intents and subtopics.

The simplest metric that accounts for different subtopics is subtopic recall [12]. Perhaps the more widely used measures in that category are α-nDCG [9] and ERR-IA [6]. These measures produce specific hypotheses about user preferences, and their recapitulative idea is that a user is always interested in seeing more novel subtopics, with decreasing interest in seeing redundant subtopics. Although this idea is sound, we argue that there are other factors that impact users' preferences. Specifically, we adopt an experimental design described by Chandar and Carterette [4] to show that users are interested in seeing more subtopics, but also that users are biased towards more "comprehensive" documents— that is, they prefer documents that cover the most subtopics regardless of how novel the subtopics are.

2. PREFERENCE JUDGMENTS

Absolute judgments in IR such as Boolean relevance and graded relevance have been used widely in the literature. An alternative is pairwise preference judgments, in which an assessor is presented with two documents and gives a preference to one document over the other. Early work on preference judgments in IR involved inferring preferences from those absolute judgments [2]. However more recently, pairwise (i.e. binary) preference judgments have been adopted as an alternative that may offer advantages in terms of alleviating the burden on assessors by reducing the complexity of the assessment, rendering the assessment task easier than assigning grades and reducing assessor disagreement [3].

The preference judgment scheme we adopt here, however, is a bit different and was first proposed by Chandar et al. [4]. This scheme is based on the so-called triplet framework, wherein given a query and a document A that the assessor is to pretend contains everything they know about the topics, the assessor chooses the *next* document they would like to see between two documents.

2.1 Data

For our experiments, we use 10 queries from the TREC 2012 Web track dataset [8]. The 10 queries selected are a sample of *broad* queries (i.e. queries good for *intrinsic diversity* tasks). Documents were selected for preference assessment from those judged for

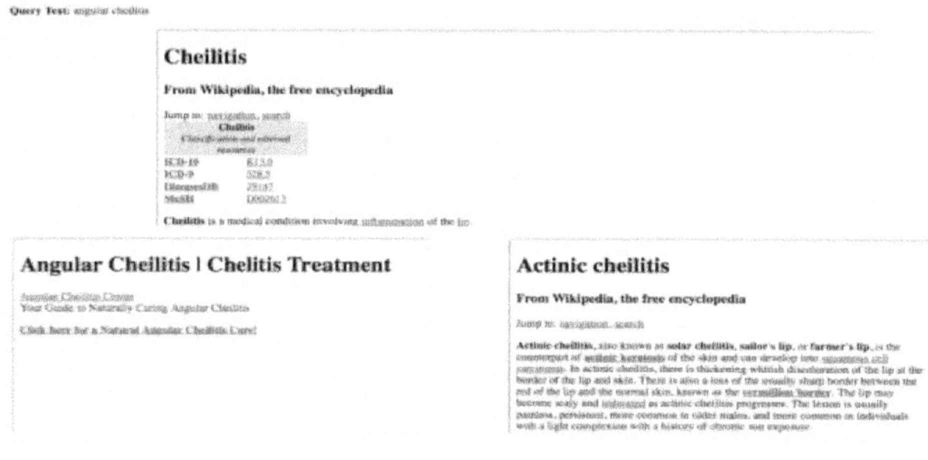

Figure 1. Screenshot of the HIT Layout

the Web track. All documents are therefore from the ClueWeb09 collection of millions of web pages. We use the publicly available subtopic relevance judgments produced by experienced NIST assessors and based on graded relevance. We use the publicly available subtopic relevance judgments produced by experienced NIST assessors and based on graded relevance. Since documents were not judged for subtopic relevance, we consider the maximum subtopic relevance grade of a document to be its topical relevance. For each one of the 10 queries, we obtained triplets from several users. In the next section, we describe the experimental design that yielded the triplets.

2.2 Experimental Design

The framework we adopt in our study for preference judgment is based on the work of Chandar and Carterette [4]. In the framework, an assessor (i.e. user) is shown three documents, one appearing at the top of the page, one appearing at the bottom left, and the third appearing at the bottom right. We will refer to the top document as D_T, and the bottom ones as D_1 and D_2, in concordance with naming conventions of Chandar and Carterette. Given D_T and a query, the assessor is asked to choose between D_1 and D_2. Essentially the assessor would need to indicate their preference for the *second* document they would like to see in a ranking by selecting either D_1 or D_2.

Since we have graded topical and subtopic relevance judgments for the documents, we can use that information to determine what subtopics each document is relevant to, as well as the corresponding relevance grades. A document can thus be represented as the set of subtopics it has been judged relevant to. For instance, $D_i = \{S_j, S_k\}$ means document i is relevant to subtopics j and k.

We used Amazon Mechanical Turk (AMT) [1]; an online labor marketplace to collect user judgments. AMT works as follow: a requestor creates a group of Human Intelligence Task (HITs) with various constraints and workers from the marketplace work to complete the tasks. Workers were instructed to assume that everything they know about the topic is in the top document, and they are now trying to find a document that would be most useful for learning more about the topic. No mentions of subtopics, novelty, or redundancy were given to them except as examples of properties assessors might take into account in their preferences (along with recency, ease of reading, and relevance). Each preference triplet consists of three documents, all of which were relevant to the topic; the documents were picked randomly from the data described in Section 2.1. One document appeared at the top followed by two documents below it. The HITs layout design, the quality control decisions and the HIT properties were the same as described by Carterette and Chandar [5]. Figure 1 shows an example of a triplet as it appeared in a HIT.

3. HYPOTHESES AND RESULTS

In this section we enumerate some specific hypotheses about relationships between document "comprehensiveness", ad-hoc relevance, and user preferences. Our goal is to test the degree to which comprehensiveness (in the sense of covering more aspects in relevance judgments) is more important to users than relevance; in general, we hypothesize that it is the more important of the two factors in their preferences.

3.1 Comprehensiveness Hypotheses

In the following, $D_1 > D_2$ means document D_1 is preferred to document D_2. $R_1 > R_2$ means document D_1 was judged by NIST assessors to have a higher ad-hoc relevance grade than document D_2. $S_1 > S_2$ means document D_1 contains more subtopics than document D_2. $S_1^{new} > S_2^{new}$ means document D_1 contains more novel subtopics (with respect to the subtopics already seen in D_T) than document D_2. Regardless of whether a document was placed on the left or right of a triplet, we will refer to the more comprehensive one as D_1.

3.1.1 Hypotheses Set 1 (H_1 through H_3).

This first set of hypotheses posits that a document D_1 with higher aspect coverage, in general, tends to be preferred by users – regardless of whether D_1 covers more novel aspects than the document it is being compared to. The three hypotheses are:

H_1: If $S_1 > S_2$ and $R_1 > R_2$ then $D_1 > D_2$. This means users prefer a document with higher aspect coverage and higher ad-hoc relevance grade than a document with lower aspect coverage and lower ad-hoc relevance grade.

H_2: If $S_1 > S_2$ and $R_1 < R_2$ then $D_1 > D_2$. This means users prefer a document with higher aspect coverage but lower ad-hoc relevance grade than a document with lower aspect coverage but higher ad-hoc relevance grade.

H_3: If $S_1 > S_2$ and $R_1 = R_2$ then $D_1 > D_2$. This means that for documents with equal ad-hoc relevance grade, users prefer a document with higher aspect coverage than a document with lower aspect coverage.

We expected H_1 to be largely true, and H_2 and H_3 to be more mitigated (or possibly inconclusive for H_2) due to the fact that relevance grades are an important factor as well. The results in

Table 1. Results for all the hypotheses, all results in the last column are significant (++) at p<0.01, except for H5 and H9

	Q 152	Q 157	Q 158	Q 167	Q171	Q 173	Q178	Q 184	Q 196	Q199	All Q
H1 true/false	196/ 22	87/ 13	148/19	97/ 28	181/31	155/30	119/51	157/19	108/53	136/22	1384/288 (82.78% true)++
H2 true/false	0/0	0/0	4/1	10/2	5/0	0/0	1/1	4/4	0/0	6/1	30/9 (76.92% true)++
H3 true/false	10/15	0/0	33/13	18/6	12/1	6/11	14/11	21/14	18/15	12/14	144/90 (61.54% true)++
H4 true/false	40/3	20/2	49/14	31/6	42/15	82/21	37/17	56/8	59/32	41/10	457/128 (78.12% true)++
H5 true/false	0/0	0/0	0/0	0/0	0/0	0/0	1/1	2/2	0/0	6/1	9/4 (69.23% true)
H6 true/false	4/1	0/0	21/4	0/0	0/0	2/7	6/1	1/6	5/2	8/6	47/27 (63.51% true)++
H7 true/false	181/21	67/11	97/5	79/24	149/18	73/9	105/50	115/11	49/21	91/11	1006/181 (84.75% true)++
H8 true/false	0/0	0/0	4/2	10/10	5/0	0/0	1/1	2/2	0/0	0/0	22/7 (75.86% true)++
H9 true/false	10/5	0/0	9/24	18/6	12/1	4/4	13/17	16/8	13/13	4/8	99/86 (53.51% true)
H10 true/false	15/1	20/2	63/18	20/5	32/13	84/28	18/5	49/16	64/34	59/18	424/140 (75.18% true)++
All H's T/F	293/68	194/28	400/100	283/87	306/79	406/110	315/155	423/90	316/170	363/91	3622/960++

Table 1 support our hypotheses that, a document D_1 with higher aspect coverage, in general, tend to be preferred by users – regardless of whether D_1 covers more novel aspects than the document D_2 it is being compared to. In fact, even H_2 and H_3 are true far more often than we expected them to be. According to the results, when D_1 covers more aspects than D_2 and D_1 also has a higher ad-hoc relevance grade than D_2, D_1 was by far preferred by users. In our experiment this happened 1384 times (82.78%), and failed to happen 288 times (17.22%).

The results also confirm H3 which posits that, for documents with equal ad-hoc relevance grade, users prefer the document with higher aspect coverage. And this happened 144 times (61.54%), and failed to happen 90 times (38.46%). H2 is also true more often than not, i.e. 30 times (76.92%) against 9 times (23.08%). The results, while proving H2 and H3 to be true, also suggest that when the least-comprehensive document has a higher relevance grade than the most-comprehensive document, the bias against the least-comprehensive document is reduced.

3.1.2 Hypotheses Set 2 (H_4 through H_6).

The second set of hypotheses zooms into special cases where the prior document D_1 (i.e. document shown at the top) has higher aspect coverage than each of D_1 and D_2 and posits that, even then, the document with higher aspect coverage is preferred by users. The three hypotheses are:

H_4: If $S_1 > S_2 \mid (S_T > S_1$ and $S_T > S_2)$ and $R_1 > R_2$ then $D_1 > D_2$. This means, given the prior document has higher aspect coverage than each of D_1 and D_2, users still prefer a document with higher aspect coverage and higher ad-hoc relevance grade than a document with lower aspect coverage and lower ad-hoc relevance grade.

H_5: If $S_1 > S_2 \mid (S_T > S_1$ and $S_T > S_2)$ and $R_1 < R_2$ then $D_1 > D_2$. This means, given the prior document has higher aspect coverage than each of D_1 and D_2, users prefer a document with higher aspect coverage but lower ad-hoc relevance grade than a document with lower aspect coverage but higher ad-hoc relevance grade.

H_6: If $S_1 > S_2 \mid (S_T > S_1$ and $S_T > S_2)$ and $R_1 = R_2$ then $D_1 > D_2$. This means given the prior document has higher aspect coverage than each of D_1 and D_2, for documents with equal ad-hoc relevance grade, users prefer a document with higher aspect coverage than a document with lower aspect coverage.

The results in Table 1 support the claims made by Hypotheses H_4 through H_6. That is, even when the prior document D_T has higher aspect coverage than each of D_1 and D_2, the document D_1 with higher aspect coverage is preferred by users. And here again, whether documents D_1 and D_2 have the same relevance grade or not, it is the one with the highest aspect coverage that gets selected by users as most preferred. Although, as we expected, H_5 and H_6 are more mitigated than H_4. H_4 is very often true (in 78.12% of qualifying user preferences): given D_T with higher aspect coverage than D_1 and D_2, the document D_1 with higher aspect coverage and higher ad-hoc relevance grade is preferred. Also, H_5 is often true (69.23% of qualifying user preferences, but this is not significant): given D_T with higher aspect coverage than D_1 and D_2, the document D_1 with higher aspect coverage but lower ad-hoc relevance grade is preferred. And finally, H_6 is also often true (63.51% true and 36.49% false): given D_T with higher aspect coverage than D_1 and D_2, the document D_1 with higher aspect coverage but same ad-hoc relevance grade as the other document, is preferred. However the proportions in which H_5 and H_6 are true are not as strong as that of H_4, which suggests that the bias against the least-comprehensive document is reduced in the cases of H_5 and H_6.

3.1.3 Hypotheses Set 3 (H_7 through H_9).

This second set of hypotheses focuses on "novel-comprehensiveness". Given a prior document D_T, a document D_1 is more "novel-comprehensive" than D_2 if D_1 covers more novel subtopics (with respect to the subtopics already seen in D_T). We posit that a document D_1 with higher novel aspect coverage, in general, tends to be preferred by users. The three hypotheses are:

H_7: If $S_1^{new} > S_2^{new}$ and $R_1 > R_2$ then $D_1 > D_2$. This means users prefer a document with higher novel-aspect coverage and higher ad-hoc relevance grade than a document with lower novel-aspect coverage and lower ad-hoc relevance grade.

H_8: If $S_1^{new} > S_2^{new}$ and $R_1 < R_2$ then $D_1 > D_2$. This means users prefer a document with higher novel-aspect coverage but lower ad-hoc relevance grade than a document with lower novel-aspect coverage but higher ad-hoc relevance grade.

H_9: If $S_1^{new} > S_2^{new}$ and $R_1 = R_2$ then $D_1 > D_2$. This means that for documents with equal ad-hoc relevance grade, users prefer a document with higher novel-aspect coverage than a document with lower novel-aspect coverage.

The results shown in Table 1 support hypotheses H_7 through H_9. In fact, H_7 is true in 1006 cases (84.75%), and fails 181 times (15.25%). This means when D_1 covers more novel aspects than D_2 and D_1 also has a higher ad-hoc relevance grade than D_2, D_1 was by far preferred by users. H_9 is true in 99 cases (53.51%), and fails 86 times (46.49%). This means when D_1 covers more novel aspects than D_2 but has same ad-hoc relevance grade as D_2, D_1 was still preferred by users, but not significantly. Also, H_8 is true only slightly more often than it is false. It is true 22 times (75.86%), and false 7 times (24.14%). These results suggest that when the least novel-comprehensive document has less than or equal ad-hoc relevance grade as the most novel-comprehensive document, the bias towards the most novel-comprehensive document is reduced.

3.1.4 Hypothesis H10.

This final hypothesis puts an emphasis on cases where the two documents being compared are equally "novel-comprehensive" – i.e. cover the same number of new subtopics – and posits that even in that case, users are more likely to prefer the one that covers the most number of subtopics.

H_{10}: If $S_1 > S_2 \mid (S_1^{new} = S_2^{new})$ then $D_1 > D_2$. This means users are more likely to prefer a document that covers the most number of subtopics, even when both documents contain the same number of novel-aspects. In other words, users are biased towards more comprehensive documents, even in cases where both documents have the same number of novel-aspects.

The result for this hypothesis is perhaps the most interesting one. It shows that, even when the two documents being compared are relevant to an equal number of novel aspects, users are more inclined to choose the one with the highest overall subtopic coverage. And this happens in 75.18% of cases.

It should be noted that there are very few cases (17 cases) where the preferred document covers more aspects but fewer novel-aspects; and even fewer cases (2 cases) where it contains more novel-aspects but fewer aspects.

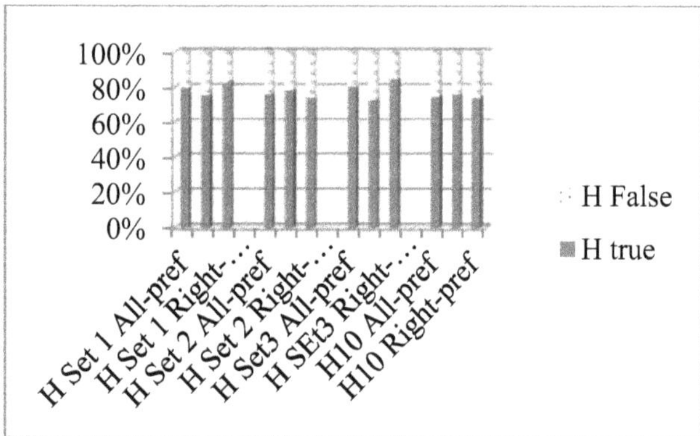

Figure 2. Comparison of proportions in which hypotheses are true/false for three cases (considering all-pref, left-pref only and right-pref only).

It is important to note that, in most cases, the document with higher aspect coverage (i.e. more comprehensive) is either more relevant or equally relevant to the other document. There were not many cases where one of the document being compared is more comprehensive but with lower ad-hoc relevance. So those cases are underrepresented, possibly due to the fact that documents with high coverage tend to be very relevant.

But is it the case that users prefer left docs to right docs (or vice versa) even when the preferred document has lower aspect coverage? That is, does the position of the document have an effect on it being preferred by a user? The results in Figure 2 suggest that is not the case. In fact, the proportions in which the hypotheses are true/false in both situations are relatively close. The triplets were indeed placed randomly in either left or right, that is, they are not placed according to any factor.

4. CONCLUSION AND FUTURE WORK

In this paper, we have used the triplet framework to empirically show that users tend to prefer in large proportions documents with high aspect coverage, regardless of the topical relevance grade. We asked users to choose, given a prior document D_T, between two documents D_1 and D_2 the one that is most useful for learning more about the topic. According to the results, users overwhelmingly prefer documents that are relevant to the largest number of aspects (i.e. highest aspect coverage), even when the prior document D_T already covers more subtopics than each of D_1 and D_2. In fact, even in cases where D_1 and D_2 are relevant to the same number of novel subtopics, the one that is relevant to the largest overall subtopics tends to be preferred.

ACKNOWLEDGMENTS

This material is based upon work supported by the National Science Foundation under Grant No. IIS-1350799. Any opinions, findings, and conclusions or recommendations expressed in this material are those of the authors and do not necessarily reflect the views of the National Science Foundation.

REFERENCES

[1] Amazon mechanical turk. http://www.mturk.com.

[2] Burges, C., Shaked, T., Renshaw, E., Lazier, A., Deeds, M., Hamilton, N., Hullen-der, G.: Learning to rank using gradient descent. In ICML. (2005)

[3] Carterette, B., Bennett, P. N., Chickering, D. M., & Dumais, S. T.: Here or there. In ECIR. (2008).

[4] Chandar, P. & Carterette, B.: What Qualities Do Users Prefer in Diversity Rankings? In Proc. WSDM Workshop on Diversity in Document Retrieval (2012)

[5] Chandar, P., & Carterette, B.: Using preference judgments for novel document retrieval. In SIGIR. (2012)

[6] Chapelle, O., Ji, S., Liao, C., Velipasaoglu, E., Lai, L., Wu, S. L.: Intent-based diversification of web search results: metrics and algorithms. IR14(6) (2011) 572-592

[7] Chapelle, O., Metlzer, D., Zhang, Y., ...: Expected reciprocal rank for graded relevance. In CIKM. (2009)

[8] Clarke, C. L., Craswell, N., & Soboroff, I.: Overview of the trec 2012 web track. In TREC (2012).

[9] Clarke, C. L., Kolla, M., Cormack, G. V., Vechtomova, O., Ashkan, A., Büttcher, S., ...: Novelty and diversity in information retrieval evaluation. In SIGIR. (2008)

[10] Järvelin, K., & Kekäläinen, J.: Cumulated gain-based evaluation of IR techniques. TOIS 20(4) (2002) 422-446

[11] Liu, Y., Song, R., Zhang, M., Dou, Z., Yamamoto, T., ...: Overview of the ntcir-11 imine task. In NTCIR. (2014).

[12] Zhai, C. X., Cohen, W. W., & Lafferty, J. (2003, July). Beyond independent relevance: methods and evaluation metrics for subtopic retrieval. In SIGIR (2003)

Cost-Aware Result Caching for Meta-Search Engines

Emre Bakkal
Middle East Technical University
Ankara, Turkey
emre.bakkal@metu.edu.tr

Ismail Sengor Altingovde
Middle East Technical University
Ankara, Turkey
altingovde@ceng.metu.edu.tr

Ismail Hakki Toroslu
Middle East Technical University
Ankara, Turkey
toroslu@ceng.metu.edu.tr

ABSTRACT

Our goal in this paper is to design cost-aware result caching approaches for meta-search engines. We introduce different levels of eviction, namely, query-, resource- and entry-level, based on the granularity of the entries to be evicted from the cache when it is full. We also propose a novel entry-level caching approach that is tailored for the meta-search scenario and superior to alternative approaches.

1. INTRODUCTION

The problem of combining search results that are obtained from several different and/or heterogeneous data sources are well studied in the IR and DB literature under various names, such as meta-search, federated-search and data fusion/aggregation (e.g., see [13]). In the context of Web search, a meta-search engine is a tool that forwards a submitted query to component search systems (so-called *resources* hereafter), collects the local top-k results from each of these systems and merges them to obtain a global top-k result. Although we have witnessed the domination of market by general purpose search engines in the last decade, the idea of a meta-search engine can be still useful in the context of specialized domains, such as shopping, healthcare or education. In such specialized domains, the result of a query submitted to a meta-search tool can be either directly presented to end-users, or can be post-processed to be consumed by other applications (e.g., extracting the product information for a price comparison engine in the context of shopping). In either case, the re-use of the results for previously seen queries, typically by constructing a *result cache*, is important not only for the efficiency and scalability of a meta-search system, but also for the availability (i.e., when the resources are temporarily unavailable [4]) and financial effectiveness (i.e., when a resource charges a processing fee per query).

Our goal in this work is to design cost-aware and dynamic result caching approaches to be employed in a meta-search scenario. To this end, as our first contribution, we introduce three different levels of eviction, namely, query-level, resource-level and entry-level, that arise naturally in the meta-search setup and indicate the granularity of the entries to be evicted from the cache when it is full. For each such eviction level, we utilize the well-known traditional and cost-aware eviction policies [11] to identify the actual entries that will be evicted, and hence, end up with several combinations representing alternative caching approaches. To the best of our knowledge, none of the earlier works consider the eviction at different granularities within a cost-aware framework, as we do here. Next, we propose a novel entry-level caching approach that is again cost-aware and exploits the special requirements of the meta-search scenario, i.e., the embarrassingly-parallel nature of processing a given query at each resource. These alternative caching approaches are evaluated using the cache miss-cost metric [11] in a large-scale simulation setup where the impact of various parameters (such as the number of resources, cache size and query cost distribution) is also investigated. Our simulation results show that the highest performance is obtained by using the entry-level caching approaches; and furthermore, our newly proposed approach outperforms both the traditional baselines and other cost-aware competitors.

SIGIR'15, August 9–13, 2015, Santiago, Chile.

ACM 978-1-4503-3621-5/15/08 ...$15.00
DOI: http://dx.doi.org/10.1145/2766462.2767813.

2. RELATED WORK

For general purpose search engines, result cache is a key component that improves the system efficiency and reduces the load at the backend. In earlier works, query results are cached in terms of the document identifiers [5, 8, 10] or full result pages including the title, URL and snippet of top-k results [9, 5, 2]. For the typical meta-search scenario with non-cooperative resources, the internal documents ids are neither available nor useful, and hence, we assume that the cache stores the results in the latter format.

The caching strategies can be broadly categorized as either static or dynamic [9]. A static cache determines items to be cached based on previous usage statistics and keeps the cache content intact until the next periodic update. In contrast, the dynamic caching strategies employ an eviction strategy to decide on the item to be removed when the cache is full; and they typically rely on the frequency and recency of the cached items, as in the well-known Least Frequently Used (LFU) and Least Recently Used (LRU) policies, respectively. More recently, the cost of generating and/or fetching the cached item is incorporated into the cache eviction policies; and furthermore, employed as a more realistic metric for evaluating the cache performance [11, 6]. Following this line of research, in this study, we tailor cost-aware caching approaches for meta-search engines.

In contrast to the case of general purpose search engines, caching for meta-search engines is an area that is left unexplored with the exception of a few works. In one of the earliest studies, Chidlovskii et al. propose a semantic cache at the client-side for a meta-search system [4]. Their work also mention the possibility of designing eviction strategies that take into account the cost of the cached entries; however the experimental evaluation only considers typical LRU policy and hit-rate as the efficiency metric. Lee et al. describe a popularity-driven caching strategy for meta-search engines; but again do not consider the notion of cost during caching and evaluation [7], as we do in this paper.

3. CACHING FOR META-SEARCH

We consider a meta-search framework where a broker search system forwards the query to component search systems that may include general purpose search engines as well as the APIs of Web 2.0 platforms, like YouTube or Twitter. The top-k result lists, R_i, from each such resource r_i, are returned to the broker; and merged there to obtain the global query result. We assume that for a given query q, there is an associated cost C_i to obtain the result R_i, which is the elapsed time for query processing at the target resource plus the network transfer time. Remarkably, the same resource can yield different costs for different queries, and the same query can incur different costs from different resources.

For a given query q and assuming there are N different resources r_1 to r_N, we store the vector $R_q : \langle (R_1, C_1), \ldots, (R_N, C_N) \rangle$ in the result cache. We believe it is preferable to store the local results from each resource rather than storing the merged (global) result (as in the earlier works like [4, 7]), as it allows more flexibility to switch to a different result merging algorithm and to apply separate mechanisms to invalidate cached results (e.g., results from more dynamic resources can be assigned a smaller time-to-live value). We consider a dynamic caching setup, as earlier works show that for reasonably large caches, dynamic caching approaches outperform the static counterparts [9].

3.1 Cost-aware eviction strategies

In the following discussion, a cache entry e can denote either the query result vector R_q, or a pair (R_i, C_i) in this vector; $C(e)$ denotes the cost of generating this entry, $F(e)$ denotes the frequency of this entry (i.e., submission frequency of the corresponding query in the past) and $S(e)$ denotes the entry size (in bytes). Using this notation, we summarize the cost-aware strategies that are described in [11] for evicting the entries from a dynamic result cache, as follows:

Least Costly Used (LCU). Evicts the cache entry e with the minimum cost $C(e)$.

Least Frequently and Costly Used (LFCU). Evicts the cache entry that has the minimum $H(e)$ value that is computed as $H(e) = C(e) \times F(e)^K$, where $K(> 1)$ is a parameter that aims to emphasize the impact of larger frequencies [11].

Greedy Dual Size (GDS). Evicts the cache entry that has the minimum $H(e)$ value that is computed as $H(e) = \frac{C(e)}{S(e)} + L$, where L value serves as an aging factor [3]. The L value is initialized to 0, and every time an entry gets evicted, it is set to the $H(e)$ value of the evicted entry.

Greedy Dual Size Frequency (GDSF). Evicts the cache entry that has the minimum $H(e)$ value that is computed as $H(e) = \frac{C(e)}{S(e)} \times F(e)^K + L$, where $K$and L values are computed as in the LFCU and GDS eviction strategies, respectively [1]. This strategy combines all four dimensions; namely, size, frequency, recency, and cost of the cached entries, while deciding the entry to be evicted. While the latter three dimensions are more likely to vary, we expect the size of the cached entries to be almost the same in practice; and hence, without loss of generality, all our discussions hereafter assume that the results from each resource take the same amount of space.

3.2 Eviction levels for meta-search

Our choice of storing the entire result vector $R_q : \langle (R_1, C_1), \ldots, (R_N, C_N) \rangle$ in the cache naturally and uniquely allows us to consider different granularities of eviction, as it is possible to evict the entire result vector of a query; or one or more entries from one or more result vectors. In this paper, we define three different caching approaches based on the eviction granularity (level), as follows:

Query-level (QL) eviction: When the cache is full, QL eviction determines a victim query using one of the cost-aware eviction strategies described in Section 3.1, and then evicts the *entire* result vector of the victim query. While doing so, the cost-aware strategies consider the cost of the evicted query, $C(e)$, as $\max(C_1, \ldots, C_n)$ where $(R_i, C_i) \in R_q$, since in meta-search the query is processed at all resources in *parallel*; so the overall latency is the maximum of these individual costs.

Resource-level (RL) eviction: In this approach, instead of evicting a query result as a whole, we first uniformly partition the cache space for each resource. Then, when the cache is full, the cost-aware eviction strategy determines a victim (R, C) pair to be removed from *each* resource partition.

Example. To illustrate the difference between query-level and resource-level approaches, we represent the cache content with the matrix M (for brevity) as shown in Figure 1. In the matrix, each row (column) is a query (resource), respectively; and the entries denote the cost of retrieving a query result from a particular resource. For simplicity, assume that we apply LCU as the cost-aware eviction strategy. In this case, when the cache is full, the QL approach evicts the entire result for q_2, i.e., the second row of the matrix, as $C(q_1)$, $C(q_2)$ and $C(q_3)$ are 45, 24 and 51, respectively. In contrast, the RL eviction approach determines the least-costly entry per resource; and in this case, the entries $M[1, 1]$ (i.e.; the result of q_1 from r_1), $M[2, 3]$ and $M[3, 2]$ are removed. In this case, the cache miss-cost is $1 + 4 + 8 = 13$, assuming q_1, q_2 and q_3 are re-submitted in the near future.

Entry-level (EL) eviction: As a third alternative, we consider each (R_i, C_i) pair as an independent cache entry; and when the cache is full, the eviction policy determines N victim pairs to be removed, so that a new query result vector R can be stored. Note that, in this case, several pairs from a particular query or resource can be removed. For instance, considering the cache contents in Figure 1 and assuming LCU, the entries $M[1, 1]$, $M[3, 1]$ and $M[2, 3]$ should be removed, as their costs lead to minimum total cost; i.e., 7.

Optimal solution for EL eviction. As the astute reader will realize, while the caching approach with entry-level eviction has much lower miss-cost than its competitors, it is not optimal. Indeed, a better solution should take into account the observation that if two pairs (R_i, C_i) and (R_j, C_j) are evicted for a query q; the miss-cost will not be $C_i + C_j$;

$$
M = \begin{array}{c} \\ q_1 \\ q_2 \\ q_3 \end{array} \begin{array}{c} \begin{array}{ccc} r_1 & r_2 & r_3 \end{array} \\ \begin{bmatrix} 1 & 12 & 45 \\ 5 & 24 & 4 \\ 3 & 8 & 51 \end{bmatrix} \end{array} \quad \begin{array}{l} \textbf{QL+LCU}: M[2,1], M[2,2], M[2,3] \\ \textbf{RL+LCU}: M[1,1], M[3,2], M[2,3] \\ \textbf{EL+LCU}: M[1,1], M[3,1], M[2,3] \end{array}
$$

Figure 1: Cache contents shown as a matrix (left) and evicted entries for each eviction level with LCU (right).

but $max(C_i, C_j)$, as R_i and R_j will be retrieved from the resources r_i and r_j in parallel. For example, in Figure 1, the optimal solution (i.e., with the least possible miss-cost) is evicting $M[1,1]$, $M[2,1]$ and $M[2,3]$, as the incurred miss-cost would be $1 + max(5,4) = 6$.

The optimal solution for the entry-level eviction can be computed using dynamic programming, in a similar fashion to that of the well-known 0-1 Knapsack problem. Let's define the matrix A to store the cost of query q using r resources in ascending order of the costs. Then, in each step, we attempt to add a new query to the solution, and while doing so, we compute (and store in a table) the costs when we evict entries for r resources from this new query, where $0 \leq r \leq N$, and entries for $N - r$ resources from the earlier queries. Hence, the recursive formula for the dynamic programming solution is:

$$
d(q,n) = \begin{cases} 0 & \text{if } n = 0, \\ \min\limits_{0 \leq r \leq N} (d(q-1, r) + A(q, n-r)) & \text{if } n > 0. \end{cases} \tag{1}
$$

Obviously, even computing the optimal cost has the computational complexity $O(MN^2)$, where M and N denote the number of queries in the cache and number of resources, respectively. Moreover, there is an additional overhead of updating the costs (using Equation 1) after each cache-miss and subsequent eviction of entries. Based on these run time requirements, it is not affordable to use the optimal solution as a cache management approach in practical systems.

Greedy solution for EL eviction. As a remedy, we propose a novel greedy algorithm that also takes into account the aforementioned parallel processing effect in meta-search scenario. In a nutshell, the algorithm works as follows: While storing the vector R_q for a query, the entries (R_i, C_i) in the vector are sorted wrt. C_i values. Next, for a pair that is at position p in the sorted list, its C' value is defined as $\frac{C_i}{p}$. Intuitively, this indicates that if we remove the entries up to and including position p; we will have size-p free space and the miss-cost for this query will be C_i; so the cost per space is $\frac{C_i}{p}$. Once these C' values are computed, any of the eviction strategies described in Section 3.1 can be employed; but taking into account the C' values while computing $H(e)$ values. Finally, when an entry (R_p, C_p) at position p is removed (along with all the entries at positions $p' < p$); we reduce the cost of all entries at higher positions by C_p; since the C_p (the current miss-cost for the query q) will be anyway incurred from this point on. For these entries, the C' values are also recomputed with respect to modified cost values. The new algorithm is called Greedy Parallel-Aware Caching Strategy (GPACS).

Example. To illustrate how GPACS operate, consider Figure 2 where each result vector R_q (of Figure 1) is sorted with respect to C_i values and corresponding C' values are shown per entry in the matrix M'. Note that, in practice, these values can be stored along with the actual entries; the matrix view is just for the illustration purposes. We again use LCU to evict entries; and in this case, we evict the entries $M[1,3]$ and $M[2,2]$ that have the lowest total costs (i.e., 1

$$
\begin{array}{l} R_{q1}: <(R_3,45),(R_2,12),(R_1,1)> \\ R_{q2}: <(R_2,24),(R_1,5),(R_3,4)> \\ R_{q3}: <(R_3,51),(R_2,8),(R_1,3)> \end{array} \quad M' = \begin{array}{c} \\ q_1 \\ q_2 \\ q_3 \end{array} \begin{array}{c} \begin{array}{ccc} p_1 & p_2 & p_3 \end{array} \\ \begin{bmatrix} 15 & 6 & 1 \\ 8 & 2.5 & 4 \\ 17 & 4 & 3 \end{bmatrix} \end{array}
$$

Figure 2: Re-sorted result vectors (left) and corresponding C' values shown as a matrix (right).

and 2.5, respectively) and yield a total of 3 empty spaces, as required to store a new query result. Note that, C' for $(R_1, 5)$ is 2.5; as 5 is divided by its position index, which 2.

Recall that selecting $M[2,2]$ means that we evict $(R_1, 5)$ pair at position 2 and all pairs in lower positions (i.e., $(R_3, 4)$ at position 1), so that we obtain 2 empty places in the cache. Finally, once $(R_1, 5)$ and $(R_3, 4)$ entries are evicted for q_2, the cost of the remaining $(R_2, 24)$ entry is updated as 19, since evicting this entry will bring an additional cost of 19 from this point on.

4. EVALUATION AND DISCUSSIONS

Setup. While there are public datasets (e.g., from TREC FedWeb Track) to evaluate the effectiveness of meta-search, the number of queries in these datasets are too small (i.e., up to 1,000 queries) to evaluate the performance of a result cache. Therefore, we construct a simulation setup as follows. We use an excerpt from the AOL query log [12] to simulate the repetition patterns of queries. For each query, we assume results from N different resources are retrieved and cached. For each such resource, we define an interval that represents the cost of retrieving results from this resource. Then, for each query q and resource r, we sample a cost value uniformly at random from the interval associated with this resource. We store these (R_i, C_i) values generated per query so that all caching strategies are evaluated under the same conditions.

Parameters. In our simulations, we used 500,000 queries from AOL log [12] in timestamp order. First 300,000 queries are used to warm-up the cache, and the rest are used for evaluation. We assume $N \in \{10, 50\}$, and all cost values are in [0, 1] range. We set the cost intervals for these resources in an ad hoc manner to model the fast, medium-speed and slow resources that exist in a real-life setting (e.g., fast and slow resources have the cost ranges [0, 0.3] and [0.8, 1], respectively). Note that, in practice, a meta-search engine can simply record the retrieval time for each query and resource, to apply the proposed caching approaches. We report simulation results for three different cache sizes, namely, caches that can store 10K, 50K and 100K query results for $N = 10$. We assume the same cache capacity when N is set to 50 (for the sake of fair comparison), hence the number of queries that can be cached drops accordingly, as 2K, 10K and 20K.

Evaluation metric. Since our goal by employing a cache is to reduce the total time cost for the meta-search system, we evaluate the proposed strategies in terms of the cost reduction percentage they achieve with respect to the no-caching case; i.e., when all results have to be retrieved for all 200,000 test queries from the scratch. As discussed before, for a given query q, if only some entries of R_q are located in the cache (i.e., cache hit), the miss-cost incurred for this query is maximum cost among the R_i's that caused a cache-miss.

Results. In Figure 3, we report the performance of query-level (QL), resource-level (RL) and entry-level (EL) caching approaches coupled with six different eviction strategies (i.e., traditional LRU and LFU strategies as well as the cost-

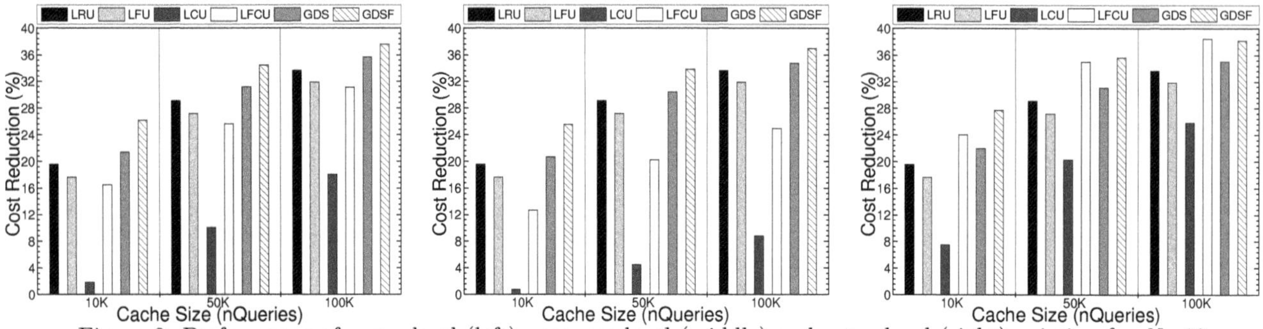

Figure 3: Performance of query-level (left), resource-level (middle) and entry-level (right) eviction for N=10.

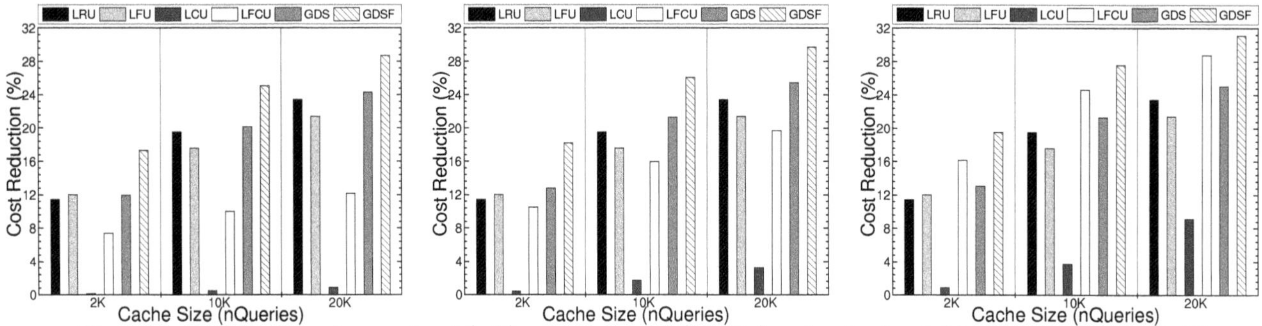

Figure 4: Performance of query-level (left), resource-level (middle) and entry-level (right) eviction for N=50.

Table 1: GPACS vs. best EL competitor (both with GDSF)

N=10			N=50		
Size	EL+GDSF	GPACS+GDSF	Size	EL+GDSF	GPACS+GDSF
100K	38.4%	39.1%	20K	31.1%	31.9%
50K	35.6%	36.2%	10K	26.1%	28.3%
10K	27.7%	28.4%	2K	18.2%	19.9%

aware strategies LCU, LFCU, GDS, and GDSF) for N=10 resources. Our findings are as follows: First, traditional strategies LRU and LFU are inferior to cost-aware strategies, especially, GDS and GDSF, in all cases. In particular, using only cost dimension is ineffective (as LCU is the worst performer in Figure 3) as an eviction strategy, while the GDSF strategy that takes into account all available clues (i.e., the cost, frequency and recency of queries) almost always yields the highest reduction in miss-costs. These findings are in line with those for web search engines [11]. Second, we compare the performances among the caching approaches with different eviction levels. Figure 3 shows that, in general, query-level eviction is better than resource-level eviction; and entry-level eviction outperforms both of the latter. For instance, the reduction in miss-costs is 37.6%, 37.0%, 38.2% for QL, RL and EL eviction approaches with GDSF strategy (for the cache of size 100K), respectively. This indicates that EL eviction is the most effective approach in the meta-search scenario. Figure 4 presents the results for N=50. We see that absolute gains slightly drop as the same cache capacity can now store a smaller number of queries. However, all the trends observed before also hold in Figure 4, implying the robustness of our findings under different settings.

Finally, Table 1 compares the performance of our novel GPACS algorithm to the best-performing case using EL eviction. It turns out that GPACS can yield up to 2% absolute improvements in terms of the cost reduction percentage.

Conclusion and future work. We introduced alternative eviction levels for result caches in a meta-search scenario, and showed that caching approaches with entry-level eviction outperforms those with query- and resource-level eviction. We also proposed a novel entry-level caching algorithm that is specifically tailored for meta-search and can further improve the performance. Our future work involves exploring cache refreshment issues in this setup.

Acknowledgements. This work is partially funded by the Ministry of Science, Industry and Technology of Turkey and by Huawei Inc. under the grant no 0441.STZ.2013-2.

5. REFERENCES

[1] M. Arlitt, L. Cherkasova, J. Dilley, R. Friedrich, and T. Jin. Evaluating content management techniques for web proxy caches. *SIGMETRICS Performance Evaluation Review*, 27(4):3–11, Mar. 2000.

[2] R. Baeza-Yates, A. Gionis, F. Junqueira, V. Murdock, V. Plachouras, and F. Silvestri. The impact of caching on search engines. In *SIGIR 2007*, pages 183–190, 2007.

[3] P. Cao and S. Irani. Cost-aware www proxy caching algorithms. In *USITS 1997*, pages 18–18, 1997.

[4] B. Chidlovskii, C. Roncancio, and M. Schneider. Semantic cache mechanism for heterogeneous web querying. *Computer Networks*, 31(11-16):1347–1360, 1999.

[5] T. Fagni, R. Perego, F. Silvestri, and S. Orlando. Boosting the performance of web search engines: Caching and prefetching query results by exploiting historical usage data. *ACM TOIS*, 24(1):51–78, Jan. 2006.

[6] Q. Gan and T. Suel. Improved techniques for result caching in web search engines. In *WWW 2009*, pages 431–440, 2009.

[7] S. H. Lee, J. S. Hong, and L. Kerschberg. A popularity-driven caching scheme for meta-search engines: An empirical study. In *DEXA 2001*, pages 877–886, 2001.

[8] M. Marin, V. Gil-Costa, and C. Gomez-Pantoja. New caching techniques for web search engines. In *HPDC 2010*, pages 215–226, 2010.

[9] E. P. Markatos. On caching search engine query results. *Computer Communications*, 24(2), 2001.

[10] R. Ozcan, I. S. Altingovde, B. B. Cambazoglu, F. P. Junqueira, and Özgür Ulusoy. A five-level static cache architecture for web search engines. *IPM*, 48(5):828–840, 2012.

[11] R. Ozcan, I. S. Altingovde, and O. Ulusoy. Cost-aware strategies for query result caching in web search engines. *ACM Transactions on the Web*, 5(2):9:1–9:25, May 2011.

[12] G. Pass, A. Chowdhury, and C. Torgeson. A picture of search. In *INFOSCALE 2006*, 2006.

[13] M. Shokouhi and L. Si. Federated search. *Foundations and Trends in Information Retrieval*, 5(1):1–102, 2011.

From Unlabelled Tweets to Twitter-specific Opinion Words

Felipe Bravo-Marquez, Eibe Frank, and Bernhard Pfahringer
Department of Computer Science, University of Waikato
Hamilton, New Zealand
fjb11@students.waikato.ac.nz, eibe@waikato.ac.nz, bernhard@waikato.ac.nz

ABSTRACT

In this article, we propose a word-level classification model for automatically generating a Twitter-specific opinion lexicon from a corpus of unlabelled tweets. The tweets from the corpus are represented by two vectors: a bag-of-words vector and a semantic vector based on word-clusters. We propose a distributional representation for words by treating them as the centroids of the tweet vectors in which they appear. The lexicon generation is conducted by training a word-level classifier using these centroids to form the instance space and a seed lexicon to label the training instances. Experimental results show that the two types of tweet vectors complement each other in a statistically significant manner and that our generated lexicon produces significant improvements for tweet-level polarity classification.

Categories and Subject Descriptors

I.2.7.7 [**Artificial Intelligence**]: Natural Language Processing—*Text Analysis*

General Terms

Experimentation, Measurement

Keywords

Lexicon Generation; Sentiment Analysis; Twitter

1. INTRODUCTION

Twitter[1] is a massive microblogging service in which users post short messages limited to 140 characters referred to as tweets. The large amount of personal opinions that is constantly generated on this platform has drawn increasing attention among the sentiment analysis research community.

The main challenge in analysing Twitter opinions is how to deal with the informal dialect used on this plattform, because it contains expressions such as acronyms, abbreviations, slang words, and misspelled words, that are not observed in traditional media [5].

[1] `http://www.twitter.com`

SIGIR'15, August 09 - 13, 2015, Santiago, Chile.

ACM 978-1-4503-3621-5/15/08 ...$15.00.
DOI: http://dx.doi.org/10.1145/2766462.2767770 .

Opinion lexicons, which are resources that associate words with sentiment polarities, play a central role in sentiment analysis applications [11]. However, most existing opinion lexicons focus on formal English expressions, and are unsuitable for Twitter sentiment analysis.

In this article, we propose a method for automatically generating a Twitter-oriented opinion lexicon from a collection of unlabelled tweets. We classify each word from a corpus into one of three different polarity classes: positive, negative, or neutral. The words are represented by vectors of attributes that are based on the context in which the words occur. We use a seed lexicon to label a sample of the words and train a linear classifier on the labelled instances. The fitted model is then used to classify the remaining unlabelled words.

Our approach based on word-level vectors takes the Distributional Hypothesis [7] as inspiration, which states that words occurring in the same contexts tend to have similar meanings. We exploit the short nature of Twitter messages to treat a whole tweet as a word's context, and we model tweets as vectors calculated from the textual content. We calculate word-level vectors based on the centroids of the tweet vectors in which a word occurs. In essence, we are assuming that words exhibiting a certain polarity are more likely to be used in contexts expressing the same polarity than in contexts exhibiting a different one.

We study and compare two different vector space models for tweet-level representation. The first is a high-dimensional bag-of-words model using word frequencies as dimension values. The second, is a semantic representation based on word-clusters. We rely on the Brown clustering algorithm [2] to tag a tweet according to a sequence of word clusters and create cluster frequency vectors.

Previous approaches for Twitter-specific lexicon generation rely on collections of tweets that were previously labelled to sentiment classes using distant supervision [13, 20] or pre-trained classifiers [1]. In contrast, our approach takes a raw collection of tweets and a seed lexicon to perform the generation. To the best of our knowledge, this is the first lexicon generation model for tweets in which a word-level classifier is trained using features calculated from unlabelled corpora.

The remainder of this article is organised as follows. In Section 2, we review some previous work on opinion lexicon generation. In Section 3, we formalise our word-level vector space models. Our main experiments and results are presented in Section 4. The conclusions are discussed in Section 5.

2. RELATED WORK

Lexicon generation techniques normally rely on a small seed lexicon which is expanded by exploiting word relations from two type of resources: a lexical database such as WordNet, or a corpus of documents. Methods based on WordNet consider semantic relations such as synonyms, antonyms, [9, 10] or dictionary definitions [3, 4] to perform the expansion. As semantic databases cover a fixed vocabulary, they are not suitable for the Twitter dialect. On the other hand, corpus approaches exploit statistical patterns observed in document corpora. Thus, they can potentially be applied to any domain. Statistical patterns can be computed using different types of methods, such as conjunction relations between adjectives [8], latent semantic analysis [16], and pointwise mutual information (PMI) [16, 17]. Previous work on Twitter lexicon generation computes the PMI between words and tweet-level sentiment labels. The tweets are automatically labelled to polarity classes using either distant supervision [13, 20] or self-training [1]. Distant supervision methods rely on strong sentiment clues found in a message such as emoticons [13, 20] or hashtags [13] to label the messages. Tweets where these clues are not observed are discarded. In the self-training approach [1], a message-level polarity classifier is trained from a corpus of manually labelled tweets and used to tag a large corpus of unlabelled tweets.

3. TWEET-CENTROID WORD VECTORS

In this section, we describe the word vectors for lexicon generation. These vectors are distributional representations [18] in which words are described according to their context. We assume that a word's context is the entire tweet in which it occurs. The first model we discuss is the bag-of-words (BOW) tweet-centroid model, which represents words according to the other words that co-occur with it.

Suppose we have a corpus $\mathcal{C}$ formed by n tweets $t_1, \ldots, t_n$, where each tweet t is a sequence of words. Let $\mathcal{V}$ be the vocabulary formed by the m different words $w_1, \ldots, w_m$ found in $\mathcal{C}$. The tweet-level bag-of-words model represents each tweet t as a m-dimensional vector $\overrightarrow{tb}$ where each dimension j has a numerical value $f_j(t)$ that corresponds to the frequency of the word w_j within the sequence of words of t.

For each word w, we define the word-tweet set $\mathcal{W}(w)$ as the set of tweets in which w is observed:

$$\mathcal{W}(w) = \{t : w \in t\} \tag{1}$$

We define the bag-of-words vector $\overrightarrow{wb}$ as as the centroid of all tweet vectors in which w is used. In other words, $\overrightarrow{wb}$ is an m-dimensional vector in which each dimension wb_j is calculated as follows:

$$wb_j = \sum_{t \in \mathcal{W}(w)} \frac{f_j(t)}{|\mathcal{W}(w)|} \tag{2}$$

However, because bag-of-word models tend to produce high-dimensional sparse vectors, we also study another word vector representation with lower dimensionality based on the interaction of word clusters.

Let c be a clustering function that maps the m words from $\mathcal{V}$ to a partition $\mathcal{S}$ containing k classes, with $k \ll m$. In our experiments, this function is trained in an unsupervised fashion from a corpus of tweets using the Brown clustering algorithm [2], which produces hierarchical clusters by maximising the mutual information of bigrams. These clusters have shown to be useful for tagging tweets according to part-of-speech classes [5].

We tag the word sequences of the tweets from $\mathcal{C}$ with the clustering function c. Afterwards, we create a new tweet-level vector $\overrightarrow{tc}$ of k dimensions based on the frequency of occurrence of a cluster s in the tweet. The cluster-based word vectors $\overrightarrow{wc}$ are calculated analogously to the bag-of-words vectors in the first approach. We take the centroids of the cluster-based vectors $\overrightarrow{tc}$ from the tweets of $\mathcal{W}(w)$, producing k-dimensional vectors for each word.

4. EXPERIMENTS

We evaluate the proposed vectors for lexicon generation using two different collections of tweets: the Edinburgh corpus (ED) [15], and the Stanford Twitter Sentiment corpus (STS)[2] [6].

The ED corpus is a collection of 97 million tweets acquired from the Twitter Streaming API covering multiple topics and languages. We take a random sample of 2.5 million English tweets from this collection. The STS corpus is a collection of 1.6 million English tweets collected by submitting queries with positive and negative emoticons to the Twitter search API. The emoticons are removed from the content. The ED corpus represents a realistic sample from a stream of tweets, whereas STS was intentionally manipulated to over-represent subjective tweets. We study these datasets to observe the effects of manipulating the collection of tweets for lexicon generation.

We tokenise the tweets from both collections and create the vectors $\overrightarrow{wb}$ and $\overrightarrow{wc}$ described in Section 3. The clustering function c was taken from the **TweetNLP** project[3]. This function was trained to produce 1000 different word clusters from a collection of around 56 million tweets using the Brown-clustering algorithm.

The two vectors $\overrightarrow{wb}, \overrightarrow{wc}$ are used as attributes to train a word-level classifier for lexicon generation. To avoid learning spurious relationships from infrequent words, vectors of words that occur in less than 10 tweets are discarded ($|\mathcal{W}(w)| < 10$). We also discard the dimensions from $\overrightarrow{wb}$ corresponding to those unfrequent words. Analogously, we remove all dimensions from $\overrightarrow{wc}$ associated with clusters appearing in less than 10 tweets.

We label the words that match a seed lexicon formed by words categorised into three sentiment categories: positive, negative, and neutral. The seed lexicon is built from the union of four existing hand-made lexicons, and a list of 87 positive and negative emoticons: *MPQA* [19], *Bing Liu* [11], *Afinn* [14], and *NRC-emotion lexicon* [12]. We discard all words labelled with conflicting polarities by different lexicons. The resulting seed lexicon has 3769 positive, 6414 negative, and 7088 neutral words. The main properties of the ED and STS datasets are summarised in Table 1.

Dataset	STS	ED
#tweets	1,600,000	2,500,000
#positive words	2,015	2,639
#negative words	2,621	3,642
#neutral words	3,935	5,085
#unlabelled words	36,451	67,692
#bag-of-words attributes	45,022	79,058
#cluster-vector attributes	993	999

Table 1: Dataset properties.

We first study the problem of classifying words into positive and negative classes. We train an L2-regularised logistic regression model with the regularisation C parameter set to 1.0 using LibLINEAR[4]. For performance estimation, we apply 10 times 10-folds cross-validation on the positive and negative labelled words from the two datasets. We compare three different instance spaces: bag-of-words vectors $\overrightarrow{wb}$, cluster vectors $\overrightarrow{wc}$, and the concatenation of both: $[wb_1, \ldots, wb_m, wc_1, \ldots, wc_k]$. We compare classification

[2] http://help.sentiment140.com/

[3] http://www.ark.cs.cmu.edu/TweetNLP/

[4] http://www.csie.ntu.edu.tw/~cjlin/liblinear/

accuracy and the weighted area under the ROC curve (AUC) obtained by the different instance spaces using a corrected resampled paired t-student test with an α level of 0.05. Results are displayed in Table 2. Statistically significant improvements over the bag-of-words approach are denoted with the symbol ∘.

Accuracy			
Dataset	BOW	CLUSTER	CONCAT
STS	75.52 ± 1.81	77.2 ± 1.9 ∘	**77.85** ± 1.94 ∘
ED	77.75 ± 1.54	77.62 ± 1.37	**79.15** ± 1.39 ∘
AUC			
Dataset	BOW	CLUSTER	CONCAT
STS	0.83 ± 0.02	0.84 ± 0.02 ∘	**0.85** ± 0.02 ∘
ED	0.85 ± 0.01	0.85 ± 0.01	**0.86** ± 0.01 ∘

Table 2: Word-level 2-class polarity classification performance.

We can observe that the classification results are slightly better for ED than STS. The cluster-based representation is better than the bag-of-words representation in STS. However, this pattern is not observed in ED. The concatenation of both vector models produces significant improvements in accuracy and AUC over the baseline in both datasets.

Accuracy			
Dataset	BOW	CLUSTER	CONCAT
STS	61.84 ± 1.46	64.42 ± 1.54 ∘	**64.57** ± 1.44 ∘
ED	62.93 ± 1.31	64.5 ± 1.16 ∘	**65.5** ± 1.19 ∘
AUC			
Dataset	BOW	CLUSTER	CONCAT
STS	0.77 ± 0.01	**0.79** ± 0.01 ∘	**0.79** ± 0.01 ∘
ED	0.78 ± 0.01	0.79 ± 0.01 ∘	**0.8** ± 0.01 ∘

Table 3: Word-level three-class polarity classification performance.

The detection of neutral words is an important task in sentiment analysis because it enables removal of non-opinion words from a passage of text. In the next experiment, we include neutral words to train a three-class polarity classifier. The classification results are given in Table 3. We can see that the classification performance is lower than in the previous experiment. The cluster-based vectors are significantly better than the bag-of-words vectors in both datasets. This suggests that word clusters are especially helpful in distinguishing neutral and non-neutral words. The concatenation of the two vectors achieves the best performance among all the experiments.

word	label	negative	neutral	positive
#recession	negative	0.603	0.355	0.042
#silicon_valley	neutral	0.043	0.609	0.348
bestfriends	positive	0.225	0.298	0.477
christamas	positive	0.003	0.245	0.751
comercials	negative	0.678	0.317	0.005
hhahaha	positive	0.112	0.409	0.479
powerpoint	neutral	0.068	0.802	0.13
psychotic	negative	0.838	0.138	0.024
widows	negative	0.464	0.261	0.275
yassss	positive	0.396	0.08	0.524

Table 4: Generated words example.

We use the three-class classifiers trained using both vectors to label the unlabelled words from the two collection of tweets. A sample of the generated words from the ED corpus with the estimated probabilities for negative, neutral, and positive classes is shown in Table 4.

As an additional validation for the generated words, we study their usefulness for classifying the overall polarity of Twitter messages. To do this, we compare the classification performance obtained by a simple classifier that uses attributes calculated from the seed lexicon, with the performance obtained by a classifier with attributes derived from both the seed lexicon and the generated words. The evaluation is done on three collections of tweets that were manually annotated to positive and negative classes: *6HumanCoded*[5], *Sanders*[6], and *SemEval*[7]. The number of positive and negative tweets of these datasets is given in Table 5.

	Positive	Negative	Total
6Coded	1340	949	2289
Sanders	570	654	1224
SemEval	5232	2067	7299

Table 5: Message-level polarity classification datasets.

The baseline of this experiment is a logistic regression model trained using the number of positive and negative words from the seed lexicon that are found within the tweet's content as attributes. For each expanded lexicon, we train a logistic regression model using the baseline attributes together with a positive and a negative score calculated as the weighted sum of the corresponding probabilities of words classified as positive or negative, respectively.

Accuracy			
Dataset	Baseline	STS	ED
Sanders	73.25 ± 3.51	74.76 ± 4.21	**76.58** ± 3.8 ∘
6-human	72.84 ± 2.57	75.08 ± 2.31 ∘	**76.42** ± 2.34 ∘
SemEval	77.72 ± 1.24	78.97 ± 1.31 ∘	**79.18** ± 1.22 ∘
AUC			
Dataset	Baseline	STS	ED
Sanders	0.78 ± 0.04	0.8 ± 0.04 ∘	**0.83** ± 0.04 ∘
6-human	0.79 ± 0.03	0.82 ± 0.03 ∘	**0.83** ± 0.02 ∘
SemEval	0.78 ± 0.02	0.82 ± 0.02 ∘	**0.84** ± 0.02 ∘

Table 6: Message-level classification performance.

The classification results obtained for message-level classification in the three datasets are shown in Table 6. We observe from the table that with the exception of the accuracy obtained by the STS-based lexicon on the Sanders dataset, the generated lexicons produce significant improvements over the baseline. Furthermore, the lexicon generated from the ED corpus outperforms the performance of the STS lexicon in accuracy and AUC score respectively. These results indicate that collections of tweets manipulated to over-represent subjective tweets such as STS, are not necessarily better for lexicon generation than random collections of tweets such as ED.

5. CONCLUSIONS

In this paper, we studied two distributional representations for classifying Twitter opinion words in a supervised fashion. Our experimental results show the usefulness of the generated words for message-level polarity classification. The main advantage of the

[5]`http://sentistrength.wlv.ac.uk/documentation/6humanCodedDataSets.zip`

[6]`http://www.sananalytics.com/lab/twitter-sentiment/`

[7]`http://www.cs.york.ac.uk/semeval-2013/task2/`

proposed technique is that it depends on resources that are relatively cheap to obtain: a seed lexicon, and a collection of unlabelled tweets. The former can be obtained from publicly available resources such as the ones used in this work, and the latter can be freely collected from the Twitter API. The source code and generated lexicons are released to the research community[8].

The proposed method does not depend on labelled tweets or tweets with emoticons, in contrast to previous approaches [1, 13, 20]. Thus, our model can be used to identify domain-specific opinion words by collecting tweets from the target domain. This could be useful in domains such as politics, in which emoticons are not frequently used to express negative and positive opinions.

Considering that our model represents words by the centroid of tweet-level vectors, we could extend it to include any kind of feature used for message-level sentiment classification. These features could include textual properties such as bigrams, part-of-speech tags, negations, among others. In future work, we will also study how to include attributes provided by low-dimensional distributed representations or word embeddings such as the neural language models implemented in the *Word2vec* library[9].

Finally, it would be possible to extend the model to produce a more fine-grained word-level categorisation based on emotion categories, e.g., anger, fear, surprise, and joy. This could be achieved by relying on the labels provided by an emotion-associated lexicon [12] and multi-label classification techniques.

6. REFERENCES

[1] L. Becker, G. Erhart, D. Skiba, and V. Matula. Avaya: Sentiment analysis on twitter with self-training and polarity lexicon expansion. In *Proceedings of the seventh international workshop on Semantic Evaluation Exercises*, SemEval'13, pages 333–340, 2013.

[2] P. F. Brown, P. V. Desouza, R. L. Mercer, V. J. D. Pietra, and J. C. Lai. Class-based n-gram models of natural language. *Computational linguistics*, 18(4):467–479, 1992.

[3] A. Esuli and F. Sebastiani. Determining the semantic orientation of terms through gloss classification. In *Proceedings of the 14th ACM International Conference on Information and Knowledge Management*, CIKM '05, pages 617–624, New York, NY, USA, 2005. ACM.

[4] A. Esuli and F. Sebastiani. Sentiwordnet: A publicly available lexical resource for opinion mining. In *In Proceedings of the 5th Conference on Language Resources and Evaluation*, LREC'06, pages 417–422, 2006.

[5] K. Gimpel, N. Schneider, B. O'Connor, D. Das, D. Mills, J. Eisenstein, M. Heilman, D. Yogatama, J. Flanigan, and N. A. Smith. Part-of-speech tagging for twitter: Annotation, features, and experiments. In *Proceedings of the 49th Annual Meeting of the Association for Computational Linguistics: Human Language Technologies: short papers-Volume 2*, pages 42–47. Association for Computational Linguistics, 2011.

[6] A. Go, R. Bhayani, and L. Huang. Twitter sentiment classification using distant supervision. *CS224N Project Report, Stanford*, 2009.

[7] Z. Harris. Distributional structure. *Word*, 10(23):146–162, 1954.

[8] V. Hatzivassiloglou and K. R. McKeown. Predicting the semantic orientation of adjectives. In *Proceedings of the 35th Annual Meeting of the Association for Computational Linguistics and Eighth Conference of the European Chapter of the Association for Computational Linguistics*, ACL '98, pages 174–181, Stroudsburg, PA, USA, 1997. Association for Computational Linguistics.

[9] M. Hu and B. Liu. Mining and summarizing customer reviews. In *Proceedings of the tenth ACM SIGKDD international conference on Knowledge discovery and data mining*, KDD '04, pages 168–177, New York, NY, USA, 2004. ACM.

[10] S.-M. Kim and E. Hovy. Determining the sentiment of opinions. In *Proceedings of the 20th International Conference on Computational Linguistics*, COLING '04, pages 1367–1373, Stroudsburg, PA, USA, 2004. Association for Computational Linguistics.

[11] B. Liu. *Sentiment Analysis and Opinion Mining*. Synthesis Lectures on Human Language Technologies. Morgan & Claypool Publishers, 2012.

[12] S. Mohammad and P. D. Turney. Crowdsourcing a word-emotion association lexicon. *Computational Intelligence*, 29(3):436–465, 2013.

[13] S. M. Mohammad, S. Kiritchenko, and X. Zhu. Nrc-canada: Building the state-of-the-art in sentiment analysis of tweets. In *Proceedings of the seventh international workshop on Semantic Evaluation Exercises*, SemEval'13, pages 321–327, 2013.

[14] F. Nielsen. A new ANEW: Evaluation of a word list for sentiment analysis in microblogs. In *Proceedings of the ESWC2011 Workshop on 'Making Sense of Microposts': Big things come in small packages*, #MSM2011, pages 93–98, 2011.

[15] S. Petrović, M. Osborne, and V. Lavrenko. The edinburgh twitter corpus. In *Proceedings of the NAACL HLT 2010 Workshop on Computational Linguistics in a World of Social Media*, WSA '10, pages 25–26, Stroudsburg, PA, USA, 2010. Association for Computational Linguistics.

[16] P. D. Turney. Thumbs up or thumbs down?: semantic orientation applied to unsupervised classification of reviews. In *Proceedings of the 40th Annual Meeting on Association for Computational Linguistics*, ACL '02, pages 417–424, Stroudsburg, PA, USA, 2002. Association for Computational Linguistics.

[17] P. D. Turney and M. L. Littman. Measuring praise and criticism: Inference of semantic orientation from association. *ACM Transactions on Information Systems (TOIS)*, 21(4):315–346, 2003.

[18] P. D. Turney and P. Pantel. From frequency to meaning: Vector space models of semantics. *J. Artif. Int. Res.*, 37(1):141–188, Jan. 2010.

[19] T. Wilson, J. Wiebe, and P. Hoffmann. Recognizing contextual polarity in phrase-level sentiment analysis. In *Proceedings of the Conference on Human Language Technology and Empirical Methods in Natural Language Processing*, HLT '05, pages 347–354, Stroudsburg, PA, USA, 2005. Association for Computational Linguistics.

[20] Z. Zhou, X. Zhang, and M. Sanderson. Sentiment analysis on twitter through topic-based lexicon expansion. In H. Wang and M. Sharaf, editors, *Databases Theory and Applications*, volume 8506 of *Lecture Notes in Computer Science*, pages 98–109. Springer International Publishing, 2014.

[8] `http://www.cs.waikato.ac.nz/ml/sa/lex.html#sigir15`

[9] `https://code.google.com/p/word2vec/`

The Best Published Result is Random: Sequential Testing and its Effect on Reported Effectiveness

Ben Carterette
Department of Computer and Information Sciences
University of Delaware
Newark, DE, USA 19716
carteret@udel.edu

ABSTRACT

Reusable test collections allow researchers to rapidly test different algorithms to find the one that works "best". But because of randomness in the topic sample, or in relevance judgments, or in interactions among system components, extreme results can be seen entirely due to chance, particularly when a collection becomes very popular. We argue that the best known published effectiveness on any given collection could be measured as much as 20% higher than its "true" intrinsic effectiveness, and that there are many other systems with lower measured effectiveness that could have substantially higher intrinsic effectiveness.

Categories and Subject Descriptors: H.3.4 [Information Storage and Retrieval] Performance Evaluation

General Terms: Experimentation, Measurement

Keywords: information retrieval; test collections; evaluation; statistical analysis

1. INTRODUCTION

Statistical significance testing is an important aspect of experimentation in IR. Without it, differences in effectiveness on the order of 5% would be difficult to interpret: they could represent a "real" improvement in effectiveness, or they could be the product of random noise. Significance testing helps us differentiate between the two [4, 5, 3].

That we use significance testing implies that we accept there is randomness in measuring effectiveness. There is randomness due to a topic sample, due to documents in a collection, due to relevance judgments, and other factors of a test collection. Significance testing asks whether the variance in effectiveness that can be ascribed directly to differences in the systems being tested outweighs those other sources of variance [1].

A full accounting of variance (such as that done for an ANOVA) could compute the total variance due to collection factors, suggesting that there is a "baseline" level of effectiveness for a given collection close to which we should expect to find most reasonable IR systems. It is the systems that are well above that baseline that we are most interested in, and in particular, the one with the maximum measured effectiveness is widely considered the best possible system to compare against.

SIGIR'15, August 09 - 13, 2015, Santiago, Chile.

ACM 978-1-4503-3621-5/15/08 ...$15.00.
DOI: http://dx.doi.org/10.1145/2766462.2767812.

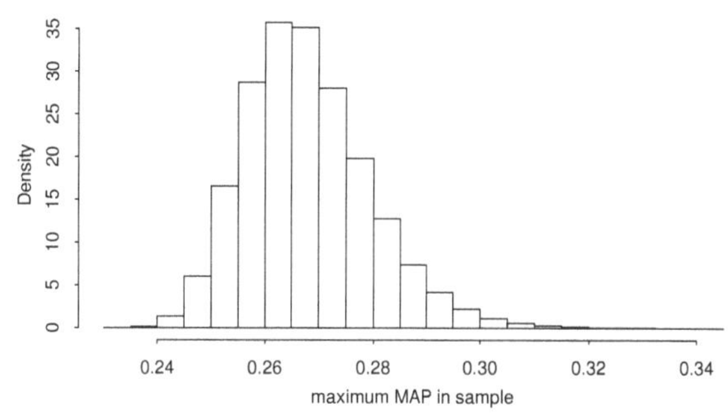

Figure 1: The distribution of the maximum of 100 samples from a normal distribution with mean 0.20 and standard deviation 0.027.

But just as two systems can have different measured effectiveness due to chance, a system can have effectiveness higher than the expected collection baseline due to chance. This randomness in turn means that there must be randomness in our determination of which system has produced the maximum value. It is actually *likely* that whatever method produces the largest measured effectiveness on a given collection has lower intrinsic effectiveness than reported. This is because of *sequential testing*: the more tests are done with a given collection, the more likely it becomes that an extreme effectiveness value will be observed.

Rather than take the maximum value at face value, we argue that we should analyze it in the context of other known results and the likelihood that such a value could be produced by a system whose intrinsic effectiveness is much lower simply due to random factors. Of course, the opposite is true as well: any given result could be produced by a system whose intrinsic effectiveness is much *higher*. We investigate both sides to argue that the intrinsic effectiveness of the best known system could be as much as 20% lower than reported, and systems as much as 20% less effective than the best could have intrinsic effectiveness much higher.

In Section 2 we introduce extreme value theory, and in Sections 3 and 4 we show how we can use it for deeper analysis of IR experiments. We conclude in Section 5 with some discussion about the implications of this work.

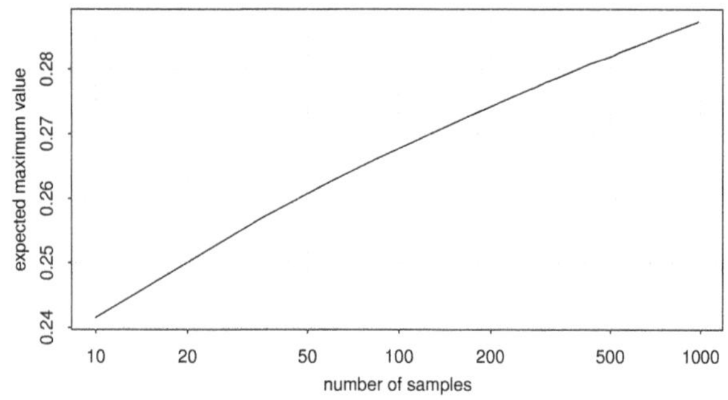

Figure 2: Increase in the expected maximum as the number of samples increases.

2. EXTREME VALUE DISTRIBUTIONS

Suppose we have 100 normal distributions, each of which has an identical population mean μ and population standard deviation σ. From each of these we sample 50 values and average them so that we have 100 sample means $\widehat{\mu}_1 \cdots \widehat{\mu}_{100}$. We can think of these as 100 measures of mean effectiveness over 50 topics from systems with the same intrinsic effectiveness. Each of them will be "close to" the population mean. But some will be further away than others, and in particular, one of them must be the maximum of the 100. Given that we've sampled 100 values, it is likely that whatever the maximum is, it will be more than two standard deviations above the population mean; that is, it will "look like" a significant improvement over the population mean even though it was sampled from exactly the same distribution.

Figure 1 shows the distribution of *maximum* MAP when 100 values are sampled from normal distributions with mean 0.20 and standard deviation 0.027. The mean of the distribution of maximums is 0.267, which, if taken at face value, would look like a 34% improvement over the mean of 0.2! Furthermore, 0.267 is outside of the 95% confidence interval around 0.2; in fact only 0.6% of the distribution is greater than 0.267. A full *99%* of the distribution of maximums is greater than the upper bound of the 95% confidence interval, meaning it is a near-certainty that out of 100 systems with identical intrinsic effectiveness, at least one will be measured above the 95% confidence interval around the mean.

Figure 2 shows the increase in expected maximum MAP as the number of samples increases. From this we argue that as the number of experiments performed on a particular collection increases, the expected maximum effectiveness reported on that collection will increase logarithmically, even if the "real" effectiveness of the systems being experimented on is not significantly different from the overall mean.

2.1 Extreme value theory

Extreme value theory is the area of statistics devoted to distributions of maximum and minimum sampled values [2]. The Gumbel distribution is an example of an extreme value distribution (EVD) that is useful for normally-distributed random variables. Its cumulative density function is:

$$P(X \leq x|\alpha, \beta) = e^{-e^{-(x-\alpha)/\beta}}$$

This could be the distribution of random variable X representing the maximum value of N samples from a normal distribution with mean μ and variance σ^2. In that case, the parameter α is equivalent to μ, and the parameter β is an increasing function of both σ^2 and N. The expected value of the maximum is then given as $\alpha + \gamma\beta$, where γ is Euler's constant, which has a value of about 0.5772. Since $\alpha = \mu$, γ is constant, and β is an increasing function of N, this means that the expected maximum increases with the number of identically-distributed samples.

2.2 Estimating an extreme value distribution

The exact relationship between β, σ^2, N has no closed form[1]. It is easy enough to estimate a Gumbel distribution using sampling, however. Given a population mean μ and population standard deviation σ, we sample n values from a normal distribution with those parameters N times (n represents the number of topics; N the number of systems), average those n values for each of the N samples, and take the maximum average. Over many trials, this produces an approximation of the Gumbel distribution.

We can simplify this further by just taking N samples from a normal distribution with mean μ and standard deviation $\sigma/\sqrt{n}$—the latter is known as the *standard error* or the *sampling distribution* of the mean. Figure 1 was generated this way, as was Figure 2.

3. ANALYSIS USING EVD

We typically answer statistical questions such as "is one algorithm better than another?" using *statistical hypothesis testing*. Procedures for hypothesis testing start by forming a reference distribution for the statistic in question (say, difference in mean effectiveness), then checking whether the measured value is in the tail of that distribution. If so, we say the systems are significantly different.

The extreme value question is "is this algorithm's effectiveness better than the *maximum* expected among N algorithms with the same intrinsic effectiveness on the same collection?" [2] Note that the question includes the number of samples N; this is a key difference between a one-off test of significance versus a test that accounts for the history of experiments done.

We would answer that question by forming a reference distribution for *maximum* effectiveness rather than mean effectiveness. That distribution must be based on variation across a sample of systems as well as topics, and must also be based on the number of systems N. It must be specific to a collection and an effectiveness measure, since different collections and measures exhibit different variability —average precision typically has low variance compared to other measures, while P@10 has high variance; more recent collections (which tend to be larger and more heterogeneous) like ClueWeb12 tend to exhibit higher variance than older (smaller and less heterogeneous) collections like WSJ or AP.

To form a reference distribution for a given collection and measure, we will first need to obtain a set of mean effectiveness values. Once obtained, we will assume that all of those values came from the same distribution: a normal distribution centered at their means, with variance equal to the variance of those means divided by the number of topics in

[1]Closed forms exist only for $N \leq 5$ [7].

[2]We use the phrase "intrinsic effectiveness" as a shorthand for "population effectiveness", which refers to the system's effectiveness measured over the full population of queries. In practice there may not be a finite population of queries that could be measured even in principle.

the collection (this is the variance of the sampling distribution). Then the *maximum* mean effectiveness has a Gumbel distribution, parameterized by α (the mean of the original normal distribution) and β (which is a function of the original variance as well as the number of means in the set); we estimate that distribution as described above.

Though we have described how to estimate a reference distribution that could be used in a significance test, we are not actually going to propose a significance test. Instead, we will use a reference distribution to analyze results reported using different collections.

3.1 TREC-7 run analysis

There were 103 submissions to TREC-7, so we have $N = 103$ mean average precisions (MAPs). The mean of means, which we will use for μ, is about 0.2; we consider this the "baseline" effectiveness by MAP for the collection. The standard deviation among means, which we will use for σ, is 0.08. We assume that each mean is drawn from a normal distribution with mean 0.2 and standard deviation $0.08/\sqrt{50}$, which is the standard deviation of the sampling distribution of the mean, also known as the standard error. To generate the reference maximum value distribution (MxVD), we repeatedly sample 103 values from a normal distribution with those parameters and take the maximum of those values.

One possible analysis similar to a significance test is as follows: identify the MAP in the MxVD such that 5% of the distribution is greater than or equal to that value. That represents the *minimum* MAP a system would need for us to conclude with high confidence that it is not just a random extreme value from a distribution with mean 0.2. In TREC-7, that value is about 0.2375. 35 of the 103 submitted runs have a MAP greater than 0.2375; we would say that it is likely 33 (95% of 35, since we expect 5% to be false positives) of those have intrinsic effectiveness above the overall mean. We could do the same for minimum MAP. We find that 5% of the minimum value distribution (MnVD) is less than 0.1625, and 34 TREC-7 submissions have MAPs lower than that. This leaves 34 systems with MAPs within the bounds of what would be expected given that we've sampled 103 total MAPs, the highest and lowest of which are nearly 20% different from the mean.

For the systems outside those bounds, we might also ask what distribution they could have reasonably come from. What is the *minimum* mean that could generate the maximum observed MAP with high enough probability that we do not consider it significant? Let us take the maximum MAP of any automatic TREC-7 run, since we expect *a priori* that manual runs will have higher MAPs. That is 0.303 for the `ok7ax` run [6]. Then the question is how *low* a population mean could produce an extreme value of 0.303 or higher (with the same variance and N) with probability 0.2. Applying a linear search, we find that value to be 0.2705, which is 11% lower than 0.303.

We might also ask how low a MAP we could measure when 103 are sampled from a distribution centered at 0.2705 rather than 0.2, or, what is the minimum MAP that we could observe with probability greater than 0.2 sampled from that distribution? It turns out that it could be as low as 0.2378. Therefore any MAP between 0.2378 and 0.303 could have come from a distribution centered at 0.27 if 103 values are sampled, and the probability of observing a MAP between those values is 60%.

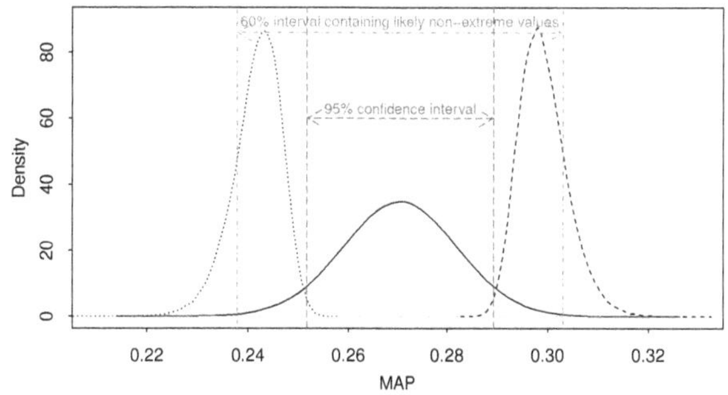

Figure 3: A normal distribution with mean 0.2705 and standard deviation 0.0114 (solid line), along with its maximum value distribution and minimum value distribution for $N = 103$. Blue lines show the 95% confidence interval of the normal distribution; red lines show the 60% interval in which non-extreme values are likely to fall.

venue	years	papers	stats
SIGIR	1995–2014	2,413	1,159 short, 1,254 long
ECIR	2005–2014	759	346 short, 413 long
CIKM	2005–2014	2,620	1,015 short, 1,605 long;

Table 1: IR research paper corpora.

To summarize, if we sample 103 mean average precisions from a distribution centered at 0.2705, there is a 20% chance the maximum sampled MAP would be greater than 0.303, and a 20% chance the minimum sampled MAP would be less than 0.2378. These bounds are outside of the 95% confidence interval around 0.2705, so would likely be considered statistically significantly different than 0.2705, even if the systems turned out to be equivalent over a much larger sample of topics. Figure 3 illustrates this, comparing the normal distribution and its 95% confidence interval to its extreme value distributions and the corresponding 60% interval in which non-extreme values are likely to fall.

The conclusion of this example is that there is a wide range of possible MAPs that are likely to be observed when sampling 100 from this distribution, significantly wider than is implied from its 95% confidence interval. The fact that the largest of them is 0.303 is random; under slightly different conditions that same system could have produced a MAP closer to 0.2378, and a system with a MAP of 0.24 could have produced a MAP of 0.3. Yet the change from 0.2378 to 0.303 represents a 27% improvement in effectiveness.

4. ANALYSIS OF IR EXPERIMENTS

In this section we analyze the IR literature to find distributions of effectiveness for different standard collections. We have a corpus of IR conference papers from 1995–2014, some statistics of which are shown in Table 1.We searched this corpus for papers using some standard collections: the Wall Street Journal (WSJ) and Associate Press (AP) collections on TREC disks, the GOV2 collection, the WT10g collection, and the TREC Robust 2004 track collection. We transcribed results from these papers, specifically mean effectiveness results. Then for a collection and a measure, we have a set of mean effectiveness values that we can analyze.

collection	N	μ	σ	max
Robust '04	55	0.2660	0.0024	0.3591
WSJ	31	0.2577	0.0108	0.4033
AP	31	0.2091	0.0096	0.2982
GOV2	17	0.2523	0.0144	0.3806
WT10g	17	0.1721	0.0059	0.2352

Table 2: Summary statistics on mean average precisions reported in published IR papers for different standard reusable collections.

collection	μ'	$\pm 20\%$ c.i.	# above l.b.
Robust '04	0.3448	(0.3384, 0.3591)	3
WSJ	0.3768	(0.3502, 0.4033)	5
AP	0.2747	(0.2513, 0.2982)	12
GOV2	0.3489	(0.3170, 0.3806)	6
WT10g	0.2227	(0.2096, 0.2352)	1

Table 3: Means of distributions that could produce the maximum values in Table 2 along with the 60% confidence interval for non-extreme values. The final column is the number of MAPs greater than the lower bound.

Table 2 shows summary statistics about data sets. Each row gives the number of results we transcribed (N), the mean of those results (μ), their standard deviation (σ), and the maximum MAP in our sample. Our Ns are fairly low, and necessarily a lower bound on the actual value of N. (In fact N cannot be known, since it includes experiments done but never published.)

Table 3 shows results of the analysis we described in Section 3.1. For each collection we report the mean μ' of the normal distribution for which the maximum value reported in Table 2 has 80% cumulative probability in the MxVD—so the upper 20th percentile value in this table is the same as the maximum in Table 2. The lower 20th percentile is the value of MAP at the 20th percentile in the MnVD for the distibution centered at μ'. These numbers are essentially a mean and 60% confidence bound (like the one in Figure 3) for a distribution that reasonably could have produced the maximum observed value for each collection.

The lower limit of the confidence interval is the value we are most interested in, as it gives an idea of how low measured effectiveness could be while intrinsic effectiveness is still competitive with the best observed effectiveness. Note that the ranges are wide, with the upper bound up to 20% higher than the lower (for GOV2) and over 15% for three of the collections (WSJ, AP, GOV2). The range is lowest for Robust '04, because that collection has a much larger number of topics (249) and therefore lower standard error.

The last column in Table 3 gives the number of systems in our sample with effectiveness greater than or equal to the minimum value. In all but WT10g there is more than one system that could reasonably be a candidate for "best performing" on the collection. If one performs slightly worse than another, it is most likely due to randomness.

5. CONCLUSION

We have argued that the best known result on any given test collection has a component of randomness due to the number of times the collection has been experimented with—something that is out of the control of and unknown to most researchers. Moreover, we have shown that the best known result could come from a system whose intrinsic effectiveness is as much as 20% lower than its observed mean, while a system with much lower observed effectiveness could have intrinsic effectiveness up to 20% greater. This means that there is a wide range of possible overlap in effectiveness, more than what is implied by the standard deviation normally computed for significance testing, due solely to the effect of reusing the collection, and enough that results that are statistically significantly different may actually not be once the extreme value distributions are taken into account.

This means there are extra considerations when reusing test collections and when comparing to best known results. The danger of reusable test collections is that the longer they are used, the more likely it is that an extreme value will be observed by chance alone. This implies that we must mentally adjust reported results downward some, particularly for older or very popular collections, and especially for methods that have not been shown to consistently work across collections. A relatively simple retrieval approach like BM25 that we know to work well in many different settings, is likely to be a better point of comparison than a much more complex model that happens to have the highest effectiveness on a single collection.

It also suggests that it is not always beneficial to rely on reusable test collections to advance the field. Proprietary collections can be beneficial in that they will not be used by as many different researchers, and thus their N may remain relatively small. Strictly non-reusable collections can never have $N > 1$, and therefore will never have an issue with extreme values being observed due to large N. Therefore it is probably best for the field to publish a portfolio of results across reusable test collections (which will always be good for unit testing, for prototyping, for training, and for failure analysis), proprietary collections (which can include data unavailable outside of the group that owns it, and therefore suggest new avenues of discovery), and non-reusable collections (which should be considered the true "test set").

Acknowledgments This material is based upon work supported by the National Science Foundation under Grant No. IIS-1350799. Any opinions, findings, and conclusions or recommendations expressed in this material are those of the authors and do not necessarily reflect the views of the National Science Foundation.

6. REFERENCES

[1] B. Carterette. Multiple testing in statistical analysis of systems-based information retrieval experiments. *ACM TOIS*, 30(1), 2012.

[2] S. Coles. *An Introduction to Statistical Modeling of Extreme Values.* Springer, 2001.

[3] M. Smucker, J. Allan, and B. Carterette. A comparison of statistical significance tests for information retrieval evaluation. In *Proceedings of CIKM*, pages 623–632, 2007.

[4] J. Tague. The pragmatics of information retrieval evaluation. pages 59–102. Buttersworth, 1981.

[5] C. J. van Rijsbergen. *Information Retrieval.* Butterworths, London, UK, 1979.

[6] E. M. Voorhees and D. Harman. Overview of the Seventh Text REtrieval Conference (TREC-7). In *Proceedings of the Seventh Text REtrieval Conference (TREC-7)*, pages 1–24, 1999.

[7] E. W. Weisstein. Gumbel distribution. From MathWorld–A Wolfram Web Resource. `http://mathworld.wolfram.com/GumbelDistribution.html`.

Load-sensitive CPU Power Management for Web Search Engines

Matteo Catena[1,3], Craig Macdonald[2], Nicola Tonellotto[3]
[1] Gran Sasso Science Institute, 67100 L'Aquila, Italy
[2] University of Glasgow, Glasgow, G12 8QQ, UK
[3] National Research Council of Italy, 56124 Pisa, Italy
{matteo.catena, nicola.tonellotto}@isti.cnr.it, craig.macdonald@glasgow.ac.uk

ABSTRACT

Web search engine companies require power-hungry data centers with thousands of servers to efficiently perform searches on a large scale. This permits the search engines to serve high arrival rates of user queries with low latency, but poses economical and environmental concerns due to the power consumption of the servers. Existing power saving techniques sacrifice the raw performance of a server for reduced power absorption, by scaling the frequency of the server's CPU according to its utilization. For instance, current Linux kernels include frequency governors i.e., mechanisms designed to dynamically throttle the CPU operational frequency. However, such general-domain techniques work at the operating system level and have no knowledge about the querying operations of the server. In this work, we propose to delegate CPU power management to search engine-specific governors. These can leverage knowledge coming from the querying operations, such as the query server utilization and load. By exploiting such additional knowledge, we can appropriately throttle the CPU frequency thereby reducing the query server power consumption. Experiments are conducted upon the TREC ClueWeb09 corpus and the query stream from the MSN 2006 query log. Results show that we can reduce up to ~24% a server power consumption, with only limited drawbacks in effectiveness w.r.t. a system running at maximum CPU frequency to promote query processing quality.

Categories and Subject Descriptors: H.3.3 [Information Storage & Retrieval]: Information Search & Retrieval
Keywords: Power Consumption, CPU Frequency Scaling, Search Engines

1. INTRODUCTION

Nowadays search engines are a fundamental part of the Web, due to its enormous size. In fact, most users turn to a search engine to look for the information they need, producing billions of searches every day. And yet, users want to quickly receive answers to their questions, and are not willing to wait long for queries to be served [15]. To achieve low latencies, user queries are processed in a distributed fashion by thousands of query servers, which are organized in clusters and hosted by a data center [1]. This distributed architecture promotes raw performance but also raises environmental and economical issues. In fact, data centers have high electricity consumption due to servers and telecommunications. Moreover, as servers generate heat, data centers need additional energy for thermal cooling.

Research in Information Retrieval on energy-efficiency for search engines has only started comparatively recently. Chowdhury was the first to explicitly write about Green Information Retrieval and to propose a research agenda to reduce power consumption in IR systems [5]. Recently, the research community has proposed some approaches for improving the energy efficiency of search engines data centers. These can involve workload consolidation among multiple query servers [6], caching mechanisms [8, 12, 14] or query routing between different data centers [10, 18]. These works focus on the behavior of either the whole distributed infrastructure or the single data-centre of a Web search engine. Conversely, our work focuses on the energy efficiency optimization of a query server within the data-centre's cluster.

The power consumption of a typical server is dominated by its CPU. This is particularly true at low utilization levels, where CPUs consume a fixed amount of power without performing any demanding computations. For this reason, Hoelzle and Barroso [9] report the data centers' need for *energy-proportional computing*, i.e., for hardware components with power consumption proportional to utilization.

Dynamic Frequency Scaling (DFS) technologies sacrifices CPU performance for lower power consumptions, by throttling processor's frequency [17]. By doing so, CPUs operating at low frequencies absorb less power but have lower performance than CPUs working at higher frequencies. Operating system (OS) kernels can exploit DFS to achieve energy savings, for instance by throttling the server CPU frequency accordingly to the processor utilization [3]. When the processor is under-utilized, a low CPU frequency is selected. Conversely, a high CPU frequency is picked when the processor is heavily utilized by the system. However, the OS misses domain-specific information on the search engine software and its interactions with the incoming user queries. We advocate that this information can help improving the energy proportionality of a search engine, as identified in [9].

We propose search engine-specific frequency governors that can better adapt to varying query workloads by leveraging domain-specific information. While DFS states are typically

SIGIR'15, August 09 - 13, 2015, Santiago, Chile.
© 2015 ACM. ISBN 978-1-4503-3621-5/15/08 ...$15.00.
DOI: http://dx.doi.org/10.1145/2766462.2767809.

managed by the OS, their functionality can be (partially) controlled by application-level code [3]. We build upon this functionality to develop our proposed solution i.e., search engine-specific frequency governors which control the CPU frequency from within the query server. Indeed, knowledge of query server utilization and load facilitate a more refined control of the processor to achieve power savings.

Recently, Lo et al. propose a centralized feedback-based DFS controller for search clusters [11]. Their approach achieves considerable power savings by trading off performance, so that latency constraints are barely met for any workload. However, the authors report several challenges in deploying their centralized solution on large clusters. On the other hand, our approach is decentralized as it works at the single query server level.

The contribution of this paper are as follows: (1) we propose to exploit query servers' knowledge (e.g., utilization, load) to throttle the CPU frequency via search engine-specific frequency governors (2) we experimentally demonstrate that our solutions can achieve significant power savings without markedly damaging the query processing quality w.r.t. standard frequency governors.

2. PROBLEM STATEMENT

We model a query server as a first-come first-served queue, where incoming queries wait to be processed upon arrival to the search engine. As soon as a processing thread is available, it picks the next query from the queue and starts processing it, in disjunctive mode. Queries arrive to the system with an arrival rate λ and are processed at a processing rate μ (both expressed in qps, i.e., queries per second). The query arrival rate can vary over time, due to fluctuations in the query load [16]. The query processing rate may change as well, because of the DFS mechanism: for lower CPU frequencies we expect lower power consumption but also lower μ values, as the CPU speed is reduced and query processing takes longer.

Search engines users are impatient [15], so we assume that query servers must process queries within a short time threshold τ since their arrival, e.g., 1 second. However, since a query can spend some time waiting in the queue, processing threads may actually have less than τ seconds to solve certain queries. Additionally, execution times are variable and some queries may require more time than others to be processed [4]. If our system cannot complete a query processing within the time budget, the retrieval phase is terminated early and results computed so far are returned [10]. This partial processing will likely have a negative impact on the effectiveness of the returned results; however, they can benefit from subsequent effectiveness-improving processing stages, e.g., machine-learned ranking [19]. Conversely, when a query exceeds τ seconds waiting in the queue, the server just drops it. In this case, the system returns no results.

The power consumed by a query server (measured in Watts) can be divided into two components: a static part which is continuously consumed to operate the hosting machine, and a dynamic (or operational) part which depends on the CPU usage to perform query processing activities. In this work, we propose to exploit DFS technology to dynamically change the query server CPU frequency to reduce the operational power consumption. Indeed, as shown in Figure 1, the average operational power consumed by the query server is directly correlated to the CPU frequency. Of course, the operational power consumed by the server varies for different incoming workloads, since the machine load varies with the number of queries requiring processing. Clearly, lower CPU frequencies consume less power but also increases the number of unanswered and partially processed queries, as lower frequencies decrease the query processing rate μ.

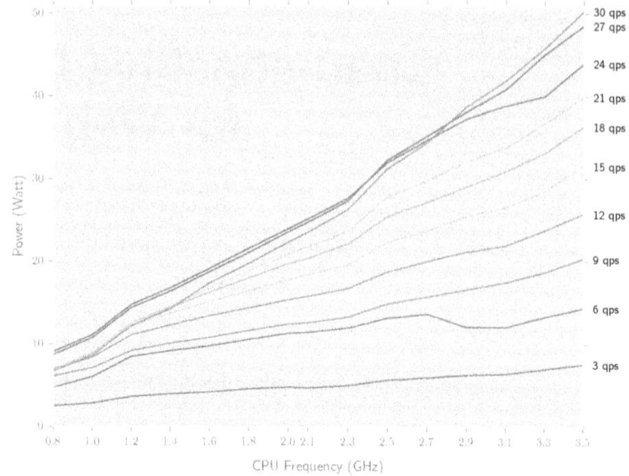

Figure 1: Average operational power (measured in Watts) consumed by a query server at different CPU frequencies and different workloads.

Hence, our goal is to reduce the power consumed by a query server to process queries, while providing an acceptable query processing quality.

3. PROPOSED SOLUTION

To achieve our goal, we propose to move CPU power management from the OS directly to the query server application code. The Linux OS leverages DFS to reduce power consumption. A CPU exposes a finite set of available operational frequencies to the OS kernel, which exploits software modules called *frequency governors* [3] to dynamically select the current operational frequency. OS governors vary the processor frequency according to metrics like the CPU utilization, i.e., the fraction of time a processor is busy performing computations. For instance, the `os-conservative` governor steps up the processor frequency when the CPU utilization is above a tunable threshold α (e.g., 0.8). Conversely, the CPU frequency is scaled down if utilization is below a tunable threshold β (e.g., 0.2). In any case, the OS governors select the CPU frequency using kernel-level information. They do not use application-specific information from the search engine, which we argue can help to improve the system energy efficiency. For this reason, we propose to delegate frequency scaling decisions to application-level modules, by implementing governors inside the search engine.

We develop two search engine-specific frequency governors, based on query server knowledge: `se-conservative` and `se-load`. The `se-conservative` governor is inspired by the `os-conservative` module, but it exploits the query server utilization instead of the raw CPU utilization. By using the query arrival and processing rates, the query server utilization ρ is computed as

$$\rho = \frac{\lambda}{k \cdot \mu} \tag{1}$$

where k is the number of threads processing queries [7]. The idea behind this governor is to maintain an acceptable query server utilization (e.g., 0.7 [7]) so that incoming queries can be easily processed without consuming too much power. Periodically, `se-conservative` computes the query server utilization and adjusts the CPU frequency. Frequency throttling is performed if ρ is above (resp. below) the tunable threshold α (resp. β). If an adjustment is required, `se-conservative` changes the processor frequency to obtain the desired utilization. The governor assumes that it will receive in the immediate future the same number of queries received during the last period. Using Equation (1), it computes the query processing rate necessary to obtain the target utilization. Finally, this governor selects the lowest frequency capable of producing such query processing rate, assuming processing rate directly proportional to CPU speed.

Our second governor, `se-load`, bases its frequency scaling decisions upon the number of queries N populating the query server, i.e., the queries currently queued or being processed. Given N, we define the query server load ℓ as:

$$\ell = \frac{N}{k} \tag{2}$$

Here, the principle is to reduce the query population in the server as fast as possible, when the query server load is too high (e.g. $\ell > 0.7$). Periodically, `se-load` observes the query server load and accordingly adjust the CPU frequency. If ℓ is greater than α, the processor is set to its maximum frequency. When ℓ is below β, the CPU frequency is stepped down from its current frequency to the next smaller one.

In the following section, we experiment in order to evaluate (a) how much power can be saved by using the search engine-specific frequency governors and (b) the corresponding impact on query processing quality.

4. EXPERIMENTAL SETUP

Experiments are conducted using the Terrier IR platform [13]. The platform is hosted on a dedicated Ubuntu 14.04 server; Linux kernel version is 3.13.0-45-generic. The machine is equipped with 32GB RAM and an 8-core Intel i7-4770K processor, which exposes 16 operational frequencies ranging from 800 MHz to 3.5 GHz. The ClueWeb09 (Cat. B) document collection is indexed to represent the first tier of a Web search engine. Stopwords are removed and the Porter stemmer is applied to all terms. The index stores document identifiers and term frequencies. The index is compressed with Elias-Fano encoding [20], and is kept in memory, shared among 8 query processing threads.

Queries are taken from the MSN 2006 query log and are submitted in real time to our system, while halving their original interarrival time. Since we use the first day of the dataset, every experiment take 12 hours to run; the average query load in 11.28 qps instead of the original 5.14, with a peak of 44 qps instead of 28.

For each query, we use BM25 to retrieve the top 1000 documents using WAND [2]. Upon arrival, queries are queued and have 1 second to be processed[1]. When this time expires before processing completion, query processing is early terminated and partial results are returned. If a query spends all its time in the queue, the system drops the query. The query is unanswered and an empty result list is returned.

[1]Approximatively 7% of the queries take at least one second to be solved.

For each experiment, we measure (a) the % of unanswered queries (%UQ), (b) the mean recall, relatively to an ideal system which has infinite time to process every query (RR) and (c) the power consumed by the query server (P). In particular, power consumption is measured at the server power socket by using an Alciom PowerSpy2 wattmeter. Measurements consider only the dynamic power consumption, i.e., we remove the power consumed by the server when idle (~41.8 Watt). Power is measured every 30 milliseconds and the mean value is reported for each experiment.

Our baselines are given by standard Linux frequency governors. In particular, we compare our approach to two baselines: `os-performance` which processes every query at the maximum CPU frequency; and `os-conservative` which adjusts the CPU frequency based on the processor utilization.

For `os-conservative`, frequency throttling decisions are taken every 0.08 milliseconds (the default value). Instead, our governors take decisions at every second, since we observe from the query log that the query arrival rate fluctuates every ~1.2 seconds in average.

While `os-performance` is parameterless, other governors are tested under two different configurations. One has relaxed thresholds ($\alpha = 0.8$, $\beta = 0.2$ – as in the `os-conservative` default setting), so that the query server is likely to maintain a certain CPU frequency for longer periods. The other configuration has tighter thresholds (selected as $\alpha = 0.8$, $\beta = 0.6$), so that the query server will promptly react to changes in utilization or load.

We consider our search engine-specific governors successful if they show reduced power consumption (P) than the baselines, without marked degradation to query processing quality, as measured by relative recall (RR) and % of unanswered queries (%UQ).

5. EXPERIMENTAL ANALYSIS

Governor	α	β	%UQ	RR	P
os-performance	-	-	0.342	**0.931**	41.765
os-conservative	0.8	0.2	**0.283**	0.929	38.569
	0.8	0.6	0.295	0.927	35.381
se-conservative	0.8	0.2	0.352	0.911	36.016
	0.8	0.6	0.315	0.900	**31.727**
se-load	0.8	0.2	0.312	0.913	35.455
	0.8	0.6	0.292	0.912	32.888

Table 1: Percentage of unanswered queries (%UQ), mean relative recall (RR) and mean consumed power (P, in Watt) for different frequency governors under various settings of α, β.

Experiments results are reported in Table 1. We observe that the `os-performance` baseline consumes the highest operational power (~ 42 Watt) and causes the query server to drop more than 0.3% of the incoming queries. However, under this configuration the system shows the best relative recall (0.931). Relative recall values are statistically significant according to paired t-tests ($p < 0.01$).

The query server using the `os-conservative` governor shows reduced power consumption w.r.t. a server equipped with the `os-performance` governor. Indeed, `os-conservative` can consume from ~8% to ~15% less power than a governor which always maintains the CPU at the maximum frequency.

Also, `os-conservative` drops less queries but provides a slightly worse relative recall.

Our first search engine-specific governor, `se-conservative`, leads to reduced power consumption if compared to `os-conservative` runs. In fact, our governor saves more than 6% in power consumption when relaxed thresholds are set ($\alpha = 0.8$, $\beta = 0.2$); and more than 10% using tight thresholds ($\alpha = 0.8$, $\beta = 0.6$). These power savings come at the price of small degradation in query processing quality: the percentage of unanswered queries increases by ~6% while the relative recall decreases by almost 2%, if we compare `se-conservative` to `os-conservative` with tight thresholds. Under the relaxed threshold, `se-conservative` drops ~24% more queries than `os-conservative`, while its relative recall diminishes of ~3% in comparison. When compared to `os-performance`, `se-conservative` can help saving from ~14% to ~24% in power consumption. Relative recall decreases by slightly more than 2% when using relaxed thresholds, and by almost 3% with tight ones. The percentage of unanswered queries increases of ~3% w.r.t. `os-performance` when `se-conservative` uses relaxed thresholds. However, dropped queries decrease by ~8% when tight thresholds are set.

Our second governor, namely `se-load`, obtains power savings similar to the `se-conservative` governor, but with a better query processing quality. Indeed, `se-load` saves more than 8% in power consumption when compared to `os-conservative` with relaxed thresholds. However, the relative recall detriment is less than 2% and the unanswered queries increment by just ~10%. When the governors are configured with tight thresholds, `se-load` saves 7% in power consumption w.r.t. `os-conservative`. At the same time, relative recall is damaged for less than 2% and no additional queries are dropped. When compared to `os-performance`, `se-load` saves from ~15% to ~21% in power consumption. Relative recall is damaged by ~2% under both threshold configurations. Instead, the percentage of unanswered queries benefits from our governor. Under relaxed thresholds, `se-load` drops ~9% less queries than `os-performance` and ~15% less queries remain unanswered by using tight thresholds.

Overall, experiments confirm that our approach is successful, as the search engine-specific governors show reduced power consumption than the two baselines. In particular, `se-conservative` provides the highest power saving. Relative recall (RR) and percentage of unanswered queries (%UQ) are not markedly damaged, especially when `se-load` is used.

6. CONCLUSIONS

In this work, we advocate that search engines infrastructures can save power at query server level, by leveraging knowledge on the server querying operations. We develop two search engine-specific frequency governors, `se-conservative` and `se-load`, which perform processor frequency throttling according to the query server utilization and load. By extensive experimentation, we evaluate the benefits and drawbacks of our approaches, compared to standard OS-level frequency governors. We find that `se-conservative` can help saving up to ~24% power w.r.t. a system which operates at maximum CPU frequency to promote query processing quality. Indeed, `se-conservative` damages by just ~3% both relative recall and percentage of unanswered queries. When compared to systems that use more energy efficient configurations, we find that our governors can still save at least 7% in power consumption. This gain costs only a limited detriment in relative recall (less than 2%) when `se-load` is used. Moreover, such power savings are important at data center-level too. Indeed, reduced CPU frequencies reduces heat output, and thus reduces thermal cooling expenditure. Greater power savings can be achieved by accepting more substantial degradation in query processing quality.

7. REFERENCES

[1] L. A. Barroso, J. Dean, and U. Hölzle. Web Search for a Planet: The Google Cluster Architecture. *IEEE Micro*, 23(2):22–28, 2003.

[2] A. Z. Broder, D. Carmel, M. Herscovici, A. Soffer, and J. Zien. Efficient query evaluation using a two-level retrieval process. In *CIKM*, 2003, pages 426–434.

[3] D. Brodowski. CPU frequency and voltage scaling code in the Linux kernel: Linux CPUFreq. `https://www.kernel.org/doc/Documentation/cpu-freq/index.txt`, Visited: 2015-02-16.

[4] S. Büttcher, C. L. A. Clarke and G. V. Cormack. *Information retrieval: Implementing and evaluating search engines*, 2010, MIT Press.

[5] G. Chowdhury. An agenda for green information retrieval research. *Information Processing & Management*, 48(6):1067–1077, 2012.

[6] A. Freire, C. Macdonald, N. Tonellotto, I. Ounis, and F. Cacheda. A Self-adapting Latency/Power Tradeoff Model for Replicated Search Engines. In *WSDM*, 2014, pages 13–22.

[7] M. Harchol-Balter. *Performance Modeling and Design of Computer Systems: Queueing Theory in Action.* Cambridge University Press, 2013.

[8] N. Hidalgo, E. Rosas, V. Gil-Costa, and M. Marin. Assessing Energy Efficiency in ISP and Web Search Engine Collaboration. In *WAINA*, 2014, pages 299–304.

[9] U. Hoelzle and L. A. Barroso. *The Datacenter As a Computer: An Introduction to the Design of Warehouse-Scale Machines.* Morgan and Claypool Publishers, 1st edition, 2009.

[10] E. Kayaaslan, B. B. Cambazoglu, R. Blanco, F. P. Junqueira, and C. Aykanat. Energy-price-driven Query Processing in Multi-center Web Search Engines. In *SIGIR*, 2011, pages 983–992.

[11] D. Lo, L. Cheng, R. Govindaraju, L. A. Barroso and C. Kozyrakis. Towards energy proportionality for large-scale latency-critical workloads. In *ISCA*, 2014, pages 301–312.

[12] M. Marin, V. Gil-Costa, and C. Gomez-Pantoja. New Caching Techniques for Web Search Engines. In *HPDC*, 2010, pages 215–226.

[13] C. Macdonald, R. McCreadie, R. Santos, and I. Ounis. From Puppy to Maturity: Experiences in Developing Terrier. In *OSIR Workshop*, 2012.

[14] F. B. Sazoglu, B. B. Cambazoglu, R. Ozcan, I. S. Altingovde, and O. Ulusoy. A Financial Cost Metric for Result Caching. In *SIGIR*, 2013, pages 873–876.

[15] E. Schurman and J. Brutlag. Performance related changes and their user impact. In *Proc. Velocity*, 2009, page 1.

[16] F. Silvestri. *Mining Query Logs: Turning Search Usage Data into Knowledge.* Foundations and Trends in IR, Now Publishers Inc., 2010.

[17] D. C. Snowdon, S. Ruocco, and G. Heiser. Power Management and Dynamic Voltage Scaling: Myths and Facts. In *PARC Workshop*, 2005.

[18] A. Teymorian, O. Frieder, and M. A. Maloof. Rank-energy Selective Query Forwarding for Distributed Search Systems. In *CIKM*, 2013, pages 389–398.

[19] N. Tonellotto, C. Macdonald, and I. Ounis. Efficient and effective retrieval using selective pruning. In *WSDM*, 2013, pages 63–72.

[20] S. Vigna. Quasi-succinct indices. In *WSDM*, 2013, pages 83–92.

Retrieval from Noisy E-Discovery Corpus in the Absence of Training Data

Anirban Chakraborty, Kripabandhu Ghosh and Swapan Kumar Parui
Computer Vision and Pattern Recognition Unit
Indian Statistical Institute, Kolkata, West Bengal, India
{chakraborty.abhi89, kripa.ghosh, swapan.parui}@gmail.com

ABSTRACT

OCR errors hurt retrieval performance to a great extent. Research has been done on modelling and correction of OCR errors. However, most of the existing systems use language dependent resources or training texts for studying the nature of errors. Not much research has been reported on improving retrieval performance from erroneous text when no training data is available. We propose a novel algorithm for detecting OCR errors and improving retrieval performance on an E-Discovery corpus. Our contribution is two-fold : (1) identifying erroneous variants of query terms for improvement in retrieval performance, and (2) presenting a scope for a possible error-modelling in the erroneous corpus where clean ground truth text is not available for comparison. Our algorithm does not use any training data or any language specific resources like thesaurus. It also does not use any knowledge about the language except that the word delimiter is blank space. The proposed approach obtained statistically significant improvements in recall over state-of-the-art baselines.

Categories and Subject Descriptors

H.3.3 [**Information Search and Retrieval**]: Clustering; Query formulation

General Terms

Algorithms, Legal Aspects

Keywords

Noisy Data, Co-occurrence, E-Discovery

1. INTRODUCTION

Erroneous text collections have posed challenges to the researchers. Many such collections have been created and researchers have tried several error modelling and correcting techniques on them. The techniques involve training models on sample pairs of correct and erroneous variants. But such exercise is possible only if the training samples are available. There are several text collections which are created directly by scanning hard copies and then OCRing them. The Illinois Institute of Technology Complex Document Information Processing Test Collection, version 1.0, referred to here as "IIT CDIP" [4] and informally in the TREC community as the "tobacco collection" is one such collection. It was created for the TREC Legal track. The text version was created by Optical Character Recognition (OCR) from the original document images. However, it contains a widespread of OCR errors which made it very difficult for the participants to achieve meaningful improvements on it. The size and the presence of OCR errors discouraged participation in the Legal task to an extent that the organizers decided not to use it further.

The unavailability of training data presents a different problem premise. Parapar et al. [7] combined the results of 5, 4, 3 and 2-grams with the actual terms. The parameters were trained on the TREC Confusion Track collection and tested on the TREC legal IIT CDIP 1.0 dataset. The method failed to produce significant improvement over a weak baseline in MAP. Moreover, they did not consider any recall specific evaluation measure which is vital for a legal IR retrieval. Also, a major drawback with the n-gram based methods is the increase in the size of the inverted index, which poses serious resource crisis and also slows down the retrieval process considerably. Ghosh et al. [2] proposed an algorithm based on word similarity and context information and an improved version was proposed by Chakraborty et al. [1]. We consider the later version as a baseline in our paper. A string matching technique (e.g., edit distance, n-gram overlaps, etc.) alone is not reliable in finding the erroneous variants of an error-free word due to homonymy. For example, word pairs like *industrial* and *industrious*, *kashmir* (place) and *kashmira* (name), etc. have very high string similarity and yet they are unrelated. Such mistakes are even so likely when we do not have a parallel error-free text collection to match the erroneous variants with the correct ones using the common context. However, context information can be used to get more reliable groups of erroneous variants. Context information can be harnessed effectively by word co-occurrence. We say that two words co-occur if they occur in a window of certain words between each other. Word co-occurrence has been successfully used in identifying better stems ([5], [6]) than methods that use string similarity alone [3].

SIGIR'15, August 09 - 13, 2015, Santiago, Chile.

DOI: http://dx.doi.org/10.1145/2766462.2767828.

The rest of the paper is organized as follows: we describe the proposed approach in Section 2, provide the results in Section 3, and conclude in Section 4.

2. PROPOSED APPROACH

We first describe two key terms used in our algorithm. Then we describe our algorithm.

2.1 Key Terms

2.1.1 Word Co-occurrence

We say that two words w_1 and w_2 co-occur if they appear in a window of size s ($s > 0$) words in the same document d. In our experiment we take the whole document as the window. Word co-occurrence gives a reliable measure of association between words as it reflects the degree of context match between the words. This association measure gets more strength when it is used in conjunction with a string matching measure. For example, two words with high string similarity are likely to be variants of each other if they share the same context as indicated by a high co-occurrence value between them. The word *industrious* is highly similar to *industrial*. But, they are not variants of each other. They can be easily segregated by examining their context match as they are unlikely to have a high co-occurrence frequency.

2.1.2 Longest Common Subsequence (LCS) similarity

Given a sequence $X = \langle x_1, x_2, ..., x_m \rangle$, another sequence $Z = \langle z_1, z_2, ..., z_k \rangle$ is a *subsequence* of X if there exists a strictly increasing sequence $\langle i_1, i_2, ..., i_k \rangle$ of indices of X such that for all j = 1,2,...,k, we have $x_{i_j} = z_j$. Now, given two sequences X and Y, we say that Z is a *common subsequence* of X and Y if Z is a subsequence of both X and Y. A *common subsequence* of X and Y that has the longest possible length is called a *longest common subsequence* or LCS of X and Y. For example, let $X = \langle A, B, C, B, D, A, B \rangle$ and $Y = \langle B, D, C, A, B, A \rangle$. Then, the sequence $\langle B, D, A, B \rangle$ is an LCS of X and Y. Note that LCS of X and Y is not in general unique.

In our problem, we consider sequences of characters or strings. For strings *industry* and *industrial*, an LCS is *industr*. Now, we define a similarity measure as follows :

$$LCS\_similarity(w_1, w_2) = \frac{StringLength(LCS(w_1,w_2))}{Maximum(StringLength(w_1), StringLength(w_2))}$$

So, $LCS\_similarity(industry, industrial)$

$$= \frac{StringLength(LCS(industry,industrial))}{Maximum(StringLength(industry), StringLength(industrial))} = \frac{StringLength(industr)}{Maximum(8,10)} = \frac{7}{10} = 0.7$$

Note that the value of LCS_similarity lies in the interval [0,1].

2.2 The Proposed Algorithm

Our algorithm has two major parts :

1. Grouping, and
2. Binding

2.2.1 Grouping

This part of our algorithm can be divided into the following sub-parts:

- **Filtering** :

  Let L be the lexicon or the set of all unique words in the documents in $\mathbb{C}$. Let $q \in \mathbb{Q}$ be a query such that $q = \{w_1, w_2, ..., w_n\}$, where w_i, $i \in \{1,2,...,n\}$, is a query word. We construct a set $L^{\alpha}_{w_i} = \{w \in L$: $LCS\_similarity(w, w_i) > \alpha\}$. In other words, $L^{\alpha}_{w_i}$ contains all the words in L that has $LCS\_similarity$ of more than a selection threshold α with the query word w_i. Since, α is a value of $LCS\_similarity$, α belongs to the interval $(0, 1)$.

- **Graph formation** :

  We now define a graph $G = (V,E)$ where V is the set $L^{\alpha}_{w_i}$ of words. For two words w_1, w_2 in $L^{\alpha}_{w_i}$, let $cf(w_1, w_2)$ denote the co-occurrence frequency over all the documents. If $cf(w_1, w_2) > 0$ then (w_1, w_2) defines an edge in E and the weight of the edge is defined as $cf(w_1, w_2)$.

- **Trimming** : Let the maximum edge weight of graph G be $max_e w$. Then, we eliminate those edges in G whose weight is less than β ($\beta \in (0, 100)$) per cent of $max_e w$. Let this new graph be called G_r. Then $G_r = (V, E_r)$ where $E_r = \{e \in E$: weight of $e \geq \beta$ % of $max_e w\}$. This step is done to eliminate the chance co-occurrences of words which are otherwise unrelated but happen to occur together in the same document by chance. The frequencies of such co-occurrence are very low. An example of such a situation can be - a lady named $Kashmira$ visited the place $Kashmir$ to spend her summer vacation. Note that the words $Kashmira$ and $Kashmir$ are not semantic variants of each other.

- **Clustering** : We now cluster the vertices of graph G_r based on the edge weights. The clustering algorithm is as follows :

  Two vertices v_1 and v_2 will belong to the same cluster if

  - either v_1 is the *strongest neighbour* of v_2
  - or v_2 is the *strongest neighbour* of v_1

  v_1 is the *strongest neighbour* of v_2 if out of all the neighbouring (adjacent) vertices of v_2, the edge weight of edge joining v_1 and v_2 is the maximum. This clustering algorithm was used by Paik et al. [6]. It is more convenient to use this algorithm over popular clustering algorithms like single-linkage, complete-linkage, k means and k nearest neighbour since it is parameter-free.

- **Weight assignment** : Given a cluster, the weight of each node is the degree of the node (i.e., the number of edges connected to the node). In Figure 1, we see a cluster containing the words *Tobacc*, *obacc* and *Tobac0*. The degrees of these three vertices are 2, 1 and 1 respectively. So, the weights of *Tobacc*, *obacc* and *Tobac0* are 2, 1 and 1 normalized into 0.5, 0.25 and 0.25 respectively.

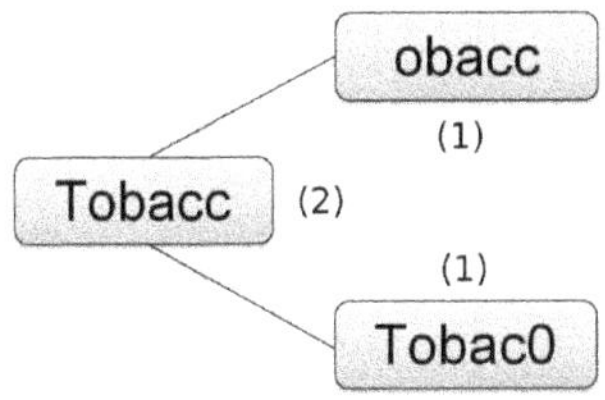

Figure 1: Weight assignment

2.2.2 *Binding*

Now, given a query word w_i, we need to find the erroneous variants from the OCRed corpus. Let $\mathbb{C} = \{Cl_1, Cl_2, ..., Cl_k\}$ be the set of all clusters formed from $L^{\alpha}_{w_i}$ (lexicon of the erroneous corpus) by the clustering algorithm discussed in the last subsection. So, each cluster Cl_j is of the form $\{(w_{j1}, wt_{j1}), (w_{j2}, wt_{j2}), .., (w_{jm}, wt_{j1})\}$, where (w_{jt}, wt_{jt}) is a word-weight pair in cluster Cl_j. In the clusters of $\mathbb{C}$, we look for the word that has the maximum $LCS\_similarity$ with w_i. Let $w_{closest} \in L^{\alpha}_{w_i}$ be the word such that $LCS\_similarity(w_{closest}, w_i) > LCS\_similarity(w_t, w_i)$, for all $w_t \in L^{\alpha}_{w_i} - \{w_{closest}\}$. Let $Cl_{closest} \in \mathbb{C}$ be the cluster containing $w_{closest}$. Then, we choose all the words in $Cl_{closest}$ as the erroneous variants of w_i. If there are more than one such $w_{closest}$ having maximum similarity with w_i, we do not choose any cluster.

A pictorial view of the algorithm is provided in Figure 2. For a *Query Word*, we get a *Subset of Lexicon* after filtering out from *Lexicon* based on an α threshold. *Co-occurrence Pairs' Block* represents the repository of all the co-occurrence information between all the word pairs in the document collection. For the *Subset of Lexicon*, the *Co-occurrence Pairs' Block* is used to read the co-occurrence values for this subset of words and form the *Graph*. Next, the *Graph* is trimmed using the β threshold and we get *Trimmed Graph*. Then, *Trimmed Graph* is clustered to get *Clusters*. After *weight assignment*, we get *Clusters (weighted nodes)*. Now, for the *Query Word*, we choose the appropriate cluster from *Clusters (weighted nodes)*. We call this process *Binding*. The chosen cluster (if any cluster is chosen), along with the *Query Word*, forms the *Expanded Query*. The *Expanded Query* is then used for retrieval.

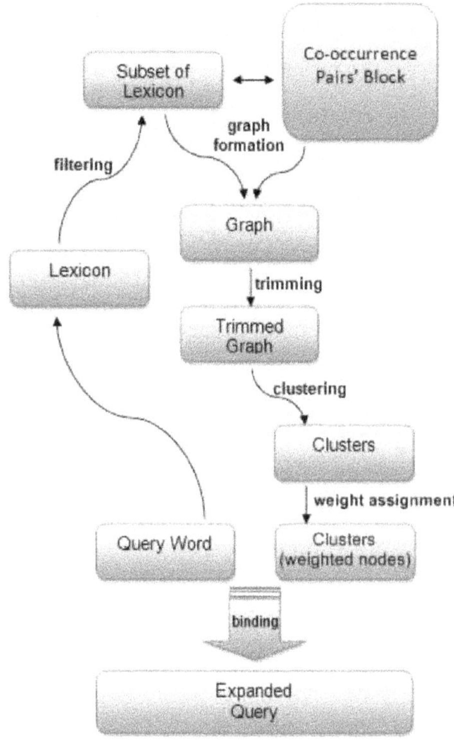

Figure 2: Algorithm : a pictorial view

3. RESULTS

We run our experiments on the IIT CDIP 1.0 dataset created for TREC Legal track. The collection statistics are shown in Table 1. We use the 43 topics of TREC Legal Ad Hoc 2007. We use only the **FinalQuery** field for our experiments. This query was prepared for Boolean retrieval and hence it contains Boolean operators like *OR* and *AND*. But, since we use it for ranked retrieval, we ignore the Boolean operators. We also convert the words in wildcard format like fertiliz!, phosphat!, agricultur! etc. to the shortest correct words like fertilize, phosphate, agriculture etc. respectively. The proximity operators like "w/15" are also dropped.

3.1 Performance

We have compared our approach with two baselines:

- The unexpanded query (*No Expansion*): Here retrieval is done solely on the basis of the original query terms. In other words, no query expansion is done here.
- Method proposed by Chakraborty et al. [1] (*KDIR*): Both co-occurrence and string similarity are used here. But the condition on co-occurrence of two words is quite relaxed resulting in more error variants.

Table 2 shows the results of the proposed approach. We see that the proposed approach produces superior performance in comparison to *No Expansion* and *KDIR*. The improvements in terms of MAP are only numerical. However, in Recall@100, the numerical improvements are also found to be *statistically significant* at 95% confidence level (p-value < 0.05) based on Wilcoxon signed-rank test [8]. The values of the parameters α and β are chosen by simple grid search in the intervals $(0, 1)$ and $(0, 100)$ respectively and the best result obtained is reported.

3.2 Error variants

Table 3 shows the error variants of some correct words in the corpus. We see that the proposed method is able to identify genuine error variants. For example, for the correct word *legal* the variants *egal*, *iegal*, *lega* and *legai* are identified. Several variants of *health* are also identified. All these variants are genuine error variants of *health*. Note here that LCS similarity between *health* and *iiealth* is 0.7143 and that between *health* and *wealth* (present in the corpus) is 0.8333. However, *iiealth* is identified as a variant while *wealth* is not. This is because the first pair has high co-occurrence frequency while the second pair has low co-occurrence frequency. So, both LCS similarity and co-occurrence have a role to play in identifying the error variants of a word. The proposed method is thus useful in the cleaning and error-modelling of the corpus where the clean text samples are not available for comparison and error-modelling.

	MAP	Recall@100
No Expansion	0.0899	0.1574
KDIR	0.0898	0.1658
Proposed	**0.0947** (+5.34%, +5.45%)	**0.1741**^{nk}(+10.6%, +5%)

Table 2: The table shows comparison of the proposed method with No Expansion and KDIR. Bold font shows the best value. Percentage improvements are shown in bracket. The super-scripts show significant improvements. The first letter of the less effective method appears in the super-script.

Term	Error variants
tobacco	lobacco, obacco, tabacco, tobacc, tobacca, tobaceo, tobacoo, tobaeco, tobaoco, tobecco, tohacco
smoking	smcking, smeking, smnking, smokiag, smokin, smokina, smokinc, smokine, smokinp, smokinq, smokins, smoktng, smolcing, smuking, snoking
mice	micee, miice, milce
oncology	0ncology, oncoiogy, oncolog, oncologv, oneology, onoology
polonium	olonium, poionium, polonlum
sewage	ewage, sewaqe
legal	egal, iegal, lega, legai
health	iiealth, heaith, hcalth, healt, healthy, bealth, healtb
securities	curities, secunties, securitles, seeurities
insurance	insuranee, lnsurance, nsurance
natural	atural, natura, naturai, naturall

Table 3: Error variants : IIT CDIP 1.0

Feature	Value
number of documents	6,910,192
number of tokens	6,524,494,574
number of unique terms	135,985,661
average document length	944.184

Table 1: Collection statistics for IIT CDIP 1.0

4. CONCLUSIONS

In this paper we have proposed a new paradigm which has not been well explored - improving IR performance from erroneous text without the availability of training data or language-specific resources. We have also proposed a novel algorithm to solve the problem on a large and extremely noisy E-Discovery corpus. The results show that we have achieved statistically significant improvements over the baselines in recall. Also, we have shown that the use of context information is extremely beneficial and reliable in agglomerating semantically related erroneous variants. In addition, the automatic identification of error variants lays a sound platform for the modelling of error patterns for the text corpora where the clean text sample is not available for comparison. We have seen that it is feasible to obtain useful error variants of the terms in the noisy corpus. This may be extremely useful in automatic cleaning of the IIT CDIP 1.0 corpus which, in its cleaned version, will be very important to the E-Discovery community.

5. REFERENCES

[1] A. Chakraborty, K. Ghosh, and U. Roy. A word association based approach for improving retrieval performance from noisy ocred text. KDIR '14, pages 450–456, Rome, Italy, Oct. 2014. SCITEPRESS.

[2] K. Ghosh and A. Chakraborty. Improving ir performance from ocred text using cooccurrence. *FIRE RISOT track 2012 working notes*, Dec. 2012.

[3] P. Majumder, M. Mitra, S. K. Parui, G. Kole, P. Mitra, and K. Datta. Yass: Yet another suffix stripper. *ACM Trans. on Information Systems*, 25(4):18:1–18:20, Oct. 2007.

[4] D. W. Oard, J. R. Baron, B. Hedin, D. D. Lewis, and S. Tomlinson. Evaluation of information retrieval for e-discovery. *Artificial Intelligence and Law*, 18(4):347–386, 2010.

[5] J. H. Paik, M. Mitra, S. K. Parui, and K. Järvelin. Gras: An effective and efficient stemming algorithm for information retrieval. *ACM Trans. on Information Systems*, 29(4):19:1–19:24, Dec. 2011.

[6] J. H. Paik, D. Pal, and S. K. Parui. A novel corpus-based stemming algorithm using co-occurrence statistics. In *ACM SIGIR*, SIGIR '11, pages 863–872, 2011.

[7] J. Parapar, A. Freire, and A. Barreiro. Revisiting n-gram based models for retrieval in degraded large collections. In *Proceedings of the 31th European Conference on IR Research on Advances in Information Retrieval*, ECIR '09, pages 680–684, Berlin, Heidelberg, 2009. Springer-Verlag.

[8] S. Siegel. *Nonparametric statistics for the behavioral sciences*. McGraw-Hill series in psychology. McGraw-Hill, 1956.

Opinion Spammer Detection in Web Forum

Yu-Ren Chen and Hsin-Hsi Chen
Department of Computer Science and Information Engineering, National Taiwan University
No. 1, Sec. 4, Roosevelt Rd., Taipei 10617, Taiwan
+886-2-33664888x311
chenaren@gmail.com; hhchen@ntu.edu.tw

ABSTRACT

In this paper, a real case study on opinion spammer detection in web forum is presented. We explore user profiles, maximum spamicity of first posts of users, burstiness of registration of user accounts, and frequent poster set to build a model with SVM with RBF kernel and frequent itemset mining. The proposed model achieves 0.6753 precision, 0.6190 recall, and 0.6460 F1 score. The result is promising because the ratio of opinion spammers in the test set is only 0.98%.

Categories and Subject Descriptors

H.3.3 [**INFORMATION STORAGE AND RETRIEVAL**]: Information Search and Retrieval –*Information filtering.*

General Terms

Algorithms, Design, Experimentation, Human Factors.

Keywords

Fake Web Review, Opinion Spammer Detection, Web Forum.

1. INTRODUCTION

Experience sharing is a common activity on the web. Users are often willing to contribute their experiences through various platforms. Genuine personal opinions will help users make right decisions. In contrast, fake opinions commonly used to promote specific targets will mislead users. Opinion spam and spammer detection aim at identifying fake review and reviewers.

Jindal and Liu [4] addressed the importance of opinion spam detection and proposed models to deal with this problem. Subsequently, the researches were extended to identify individual opinion spammers [2][5][9] and group opinion spammers [6][7]. Reviewers' behaviors, text similarity, linguistic features, rating patterns, relationships among reviewers, reviews and stores, and burstiness in reviews have been explored.

Evaluation is indispensable for this task, but no "true" ground truth data spam and non-spam are available. Jindal and Liu [4] collected reviews for four categories of products from amazon.com for model development and performance evaluation.

SIGIR '15, August 09 - 13, 2015, Santiago, Chile

ACM 978-1-4503-3621-5/15/08…$15.00
DOI: http://dx.doi.org/10.1145/2766462.2767766

Duplicate and near-duplicate reviews were regarded as fake reviews. The researches [2][5][7] were based on the this dataset for opinion spammer detection. Wang et al. [9] collected a large amount of store reviews from resellerratings.com for their experiments.

The evaluation methodologies are always based on human. Lim et al. [5] proposed a rigorous human evaluation procedure to examine a pool of ranked reviewers from different spammer detection methods. Mukherjee et al. [6] conducted a user study, and Mukherjee et al. [7] employed 8 expert judges for their work. Wang et al. [9] claimed suspicious reviewers who should have significant number of reviews satisfying three proposed conditions. Fei et al [2] argued that human evaluation was subjective, and proposed a complementary evaluation. They assumed that if a reviewer was labelled as a spammer, then all his/her reviews were considered as spam reviews. The above work showed some degrees of annotator agreement in human evaluation.

Different from the previous studies, this paper is based on a set of internal records of opinion spams leaked from a shady marketing campaign (see Section 2). To the best of our knowledge, it is the first research to study the behaviors of opinion spammers in web forum. The subtle nature of forum posts, low spam post of spammers, different types of spammer accounts, and interaction between forum posters are key issues.

This paper is organized as follows. Section 2 describes a real case in web forum. Section 3 shows some observations in the datasets. Section 4 proposes an opinion spammer detection model and discusses the experimental results under the real case study. Section 5 concludes the remarks.

2. A REAL CASE STUDY

2.1 Case Description

This paper studies a real case, *Samsung probed in Taiwan over 'fake web reviews'*, reported by BBC on 16 April 2013. A covert marketing campaign was carried out by a consulting firm that was a subsidiary company of one of the biggest IT companies in the world. In this campaign, hired posters were asked to promote a certain brand and denounce its rivals on web forums. The Fair Trade Commission (FTC) in Taiwan, investigated into the event and announced a decision on October 31, 2013 based on the leaked information and other documents, "the Samsung Taiwan, OpenTide Taiwan, and Sales & Profit International Co. concealed their identity and pretended to be regular private citizens to market their products on the Internet by making comparisons with and comments on the products of other enterprises." The three companies were imposed administrative fines of NT$10 million, NT$3 million and NT$50,000, respectively.

2.2 Disclosed Spreadsheets

The relevant articles describing the campaign were disclosed on *Taiwansamsungleaks*[1]. The leaked spreadsheets, which provide spam posts and spammers, are considered as ground truth for this study. Tables 1-3 show the attributes of user profiles, posts, and threads, respectively. A thread in a web forum is composed of a first post or replies by users. First post and reply are called posts.

Table 1. Attributes of User Profiles

Attribute	Description
uid	id of the user
reg_time	time of registration on the site
login_time	last time the user logged in
n_threads	number of threads initialized by the user
n_eff_posts	number of effective posts
n_posts	number of all posts
n_replies	number of replies, i.e., n_posts - n_threads
karma score	karma given by other users to the threads
p_phone	proportion of posts made on the smart phone

Table 2. Attributes of Posts

Attribute	Description
thid	id of the thread to which the post belong
time	submission time of the post
uid	id of the poster who made the post
uname	username of the poster
nfloor	position relative to other posts in the thread
pnum	page number on which the post is
content	structured content in *HTML*

Table 3. Attributes of Threads

Attribute	Description
thid	id of the thread
fid	id of the forum (board) in which the thread is
title	title of the thread
pages	number of pages in the thread
clicks	number of clicks (views) on this thread
time	submission time of the thread (=first post time)

2.3 Data Partition

We partition the leaked data into the following two post sets for training and testing, respectively, based on the submission time of the posts:

(1) 2011-post-set: Jan 2011-Dec 2011, and

(2) 2012-post-set: Jan 2012-May 2012.

The posts in the 2012-post-set may be posted by the same user in the 2011-post-set. To avoid the effects of writing styles of users on the performance of opinion spam/spammer detection, we remove all the posts by users who have posts in the 2011-post-set from the 2012-post-set. Table 4 lists the statistics of the remaining posts after removal.

We also assign user accounts to the 2011-user-set and 2012-user-set according to the submission time of their posts. Users who have submitted posts during the first period, but not the second one are put into 2011-user-set. Similarly, users who have submitted posts in the second period, but not the first are assigned to 2012-user-set. Now the question is in which set the users who have submitted posts in both periods should be put. Since we will use the opinion spam detection for first posts to assist opinion spammer detection, this set of users should not be in the test set. In other words, these users are assigned to 2011-user-set. Table 5 shows the statistics of the datasets for spammer detection. The dataset is available at http://nlg.csie.ntu.edu.tw/m01-corpus/.

Table 4. Statistics of posts in 2011-post- and 2012-post-sets

	#spam posts	#all posts	spam ratio
2011-post-set	1,883	159,432	1.12%
2012-post-set	414	32,932	1.26%

[1] http://taiwansamsungleaks.org/.

Table 5. Statistics of users in 2011-user- and 2012-user-sets

	#spammers	#all users	spammer ratio
2011-user-set	215	17,216	1.25%
2012-user-set	84	8,603	0.98%

3. SOME OBSERVATIONS

Spammers are the posters who had submitted any spam posts in web forum. We inspect the posts in the 2011-post-set and find that only about 33% of the posts by spammers in the 2011-user-set are spams. The low spam post ratio of spammers specifies that some "spammers" actually rarely spammed.

Spammers usually deliver their opinions in such a subtle way that the portion of the spam posts do not carry any opinions about the brands. Their purpose is to keep the discussion alive and bumping to attract more attention to the specific topics of the thread.

There are two types of spammer accounts in the dataset: (1) accounts of reputable posts who paid one or a few times to write quality long post to promote the brand, and (2) throwaway accounts shared internally among the spammers to synthesize public opinions. Throwaway accounts are often created in mass within a short period of time, as it takes much more effort to spread out the daunting task of registering throwaway accounts.

Because making spam posts is a job rather than a leisure activity for spammers, we observe that a higher percentage of spam posts are submitted during work time, compared to non-spam posts.

The threads initiated by spam first post are more active since they are written to draw attention and exposure. We measure the activeness of a thread with total number of posts in the thread, and find that spam threads tend to attract more replies, which can be either spam replies or non-spam replies.

We further examine 2011-post-set, and note that some threads contain multiple spam posts submitted by different accounts. It indicates collusion goes on between multiple spammers. These spammers usually express similar opinions in the same thread to reinforce the credibility, or to bump the thread to attract more attention to it.

4. OPINION SPAMMER DETECTION

We adopt *SVM with RBF kernel* from *Scikit-Learn* [8] after exploring various learning algorithms. In this section, we present the features used in opinion spammer detection. We scale each feature to zero mean and unit variance. In the latter experiments, we downsample the non-spammers in 2011-user-set by randomly removing 60% of them. The remaining forms a training set. The 2012-user-set is considered as a test set.

We first run 5-fold cross-validation multiple times on the training set to facilitate a grid search on C and γ with F1 score as the metric to optimize. The grid to search is represented below.

$(C, \gamma) \in \{10^x | -3 \leq x \leq 3, x \in \mathbb{Z}\} \times \{10^y | -5 \leq y \leq 2, y \in \mathbb{Z}\}$

Table 6 summarizes the experimental results of five models, M0-M4. Precision (**P**), Recall (**R**), and F-measuere (**F1**) are listed. M0 is an absolute baseline with random guessing. Intuitively, its performance is very bad due to very low spammer ratio, 0.98%. The detail of M1-M4 will be discussed in the following sections.

Table 6. Spam detection for first post using test set

Model	P	R	F1
M0: random baseline	0.0091	0.4588	0.0178
M1: user profile	0.0275	0.2262	0.0491
M2: M1+maximum spamicity	0.6102	0.4286	0.5035
M3: M2+burstiness of reg.	0.6731	0.4167	0.5147
M4: M3+frequent poster set	**0.6753**	**0.6190**	**0.6460**

4.1 User Profile

The last six attributes in user profile defined in Table 1 are used. We measure their usefulness in distinguishing the spammers from non-spammers by computing symmetric KL divergence as follows.

$$D_{KL}(P_{spammer} \| Q_{hammer}) + D_{KL}(Q_{hammer} \| P_{spammer})$$

where $P_{spammer}$ and Q_{hammer} are the distributions of an attribute under all spammers and non-spammers, respectively. Figure 1 shows the usefulness of these features. Spammers are more productive and reputable posters according to the number of the threads they make (n_threads), and the "karma scores" they have.

Figure 2 illustrates that (1) spammers tend to initiate more threads than non-spammers, and (2) on web forums, there are a lot of lurkers who regularly login and read posts, but barely participate in discussions. Figure 3 further depicts that some spammers tend to have higher "karma scores" than non-spammers.

Table 6 shows employing features from user profile, i.e., M1, increases F1 score compared with M0, but profile only is not sufficient to distinguish spammers from non-spammers effectively.

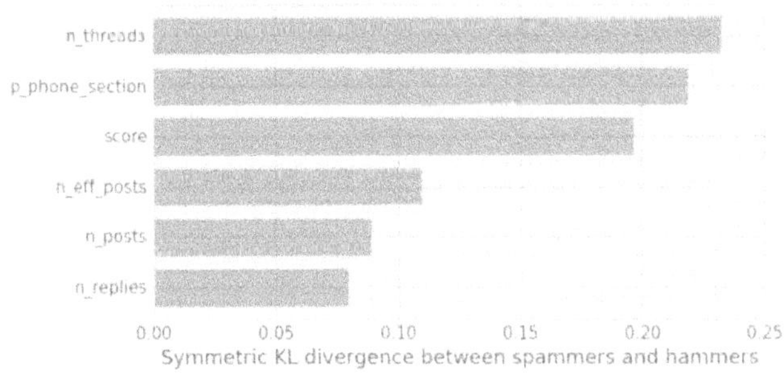

Figure 1. Usefulness of the features from user profies

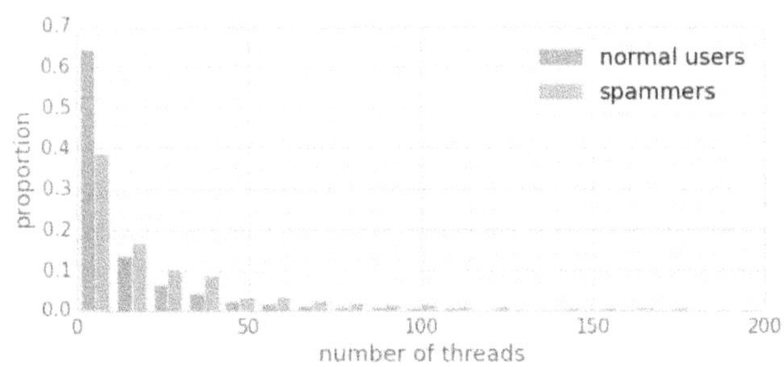

Figure 2. Number of threads initialized by spammers and non-spammers

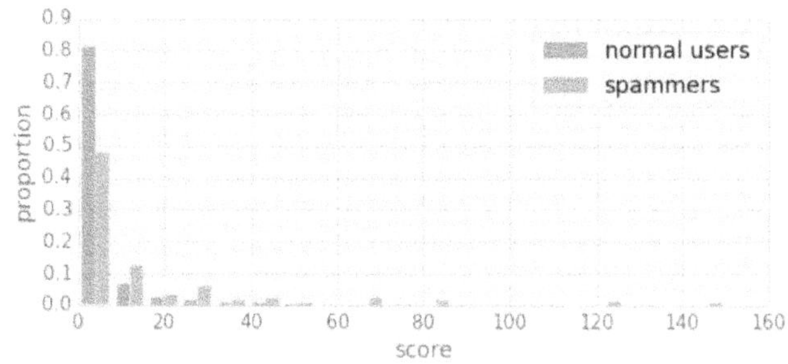

Figure 3. "Karma score" of spammers and non-spammers

4.2 Maximum Spamicity of First Posts

This section proposes a model to detect opinion spams from first posts, and consider the results as an additional feature.

4.2.1 Opinion Spam Detection for First Posts

We propose the following features, and employ 2011-post-set and 2012-post-set in Table 4 as training and test sets, respectively, to detect opinion spams from first posts. This model achieves 0.6667 precision, 0.5714 recall, and 0.6154 F1 score.

(1) Bag of Words

We first count the occurrence of each word in training set. Next, rare words with less than 5 occurrences are removed to avoid overfitting. Besides, words appearing in over 30% of the posts are regarded as stop words and also filtered. After the vocabulary is set up, we represent each post as a weighted word vector, where the weight of a word is its frequency in the post normalized by the length of the post.

We apply randomized PCA [3] on the post by word matrix to reduce the dimension. The desired number of dimension is tuned by the average F1 score with 5-fold cross-validation on training set. The average F1 score is the best when the bag-of-words is reduced to 150 components. Besides the contents of posts, the titles of threads are also informative. Thus we create another 50 bags-of-word features based on the titles, and combine these with the content parts to yield 200 features.

(2) Content Characteristics

A set of features derived from basic characteristics of the contents of the post is introduced in Table 7. We compute symmetric KL divergence to find which features exhibit the most different distributions between spams and hams, and add these 17 numerical features that characterize the contents of first posts.

(3) Submission Time

Spam posts tend to be submitted often during work time. To make use of this observation, we add a binary feature for each hour in a day and each day in a week, in total 24+7=31 features. If a first post is submitted during the hour or the day a feature corresponds to, then its value is 1; otherwise it is 0.

(4) Thread Activeness

We consider number of posts in a thread started by a first post as a feature, which measures the activeness of the thread.

4.2.2 Maximum Spamicity

A feature, **max_spamicity_fps**, is computed by taking the maximum of the spamicity estimates of all first posts submitted by a specific user. Because the definition of spammer is "whoever makes one or more spam posts", taking the maximum is a more sensible choice, compared to taking the mean or the median.

Table 7. Description of content characteristics

Attribute	Description
n_all	number of characters used in the post
n_words	number of words in the post
n_lines	number of lines in the post
n_hyperlinks	number of hyperlinks in the post
n_img	number of images added to the post
n_emoticon	number of emoticons used in the post
n_quote	number of quotations from previous posts
p_digit	proportion of digits
p_english	proportion of English characters
p_punct	proportion of punctuation characters
p_special	proportion of non-alphanumeric characters
p_wspace	proportion of white space characters
p_immediacy	proportion of first person pronouns
p_ntusd_pos	proportion of positive words in *NTUSD*
p_ntusd_neg	proportion of negative words in *NTUSD*
p_emoticon_pos	proportion of positive emoticons
p_emoticon_neg	proportion of negative emoticons

The model for first post spam detection in Section 4.2.1, which achieves higher precision than recall, is a plus here. If the model misses a spam first post of a specific spammer due to recall, it is still possible to detect other spam first posts by the spammer. On the contrary, if the model misidentifies a non-spam first post by a normal user as spam, i.e., low precision and high recall, and gives it a high spamicity estimate, then the value of **max_spamicity_fps** will be high for that user, who is thus likely to be misclassified as a spammer. Note the training set of posts does not contain any posts by any users in test set. The data splitting method guarantees a fair evaluation.

Table 6 shows the performance is significantly improved by almost 50% in F1 score when the **max_spamicity_fps** feature is introduced in M2. Further analysis finds that 54 out of the 84 spammers in test set, i.e., 64.3%, have submitted a spam post which is a first post in a thread. In principle, it is the maximum number of spammers that could be identified with this feature.

4.3 Burstiness of Registration of Accounts

In Section 3, we observe most of the throwaway spammer accounts are registered in bursts. Here, we propose a feature, **burstiness_reg**, which counts the number of accounts registered 20 days within the registration of the user account in discussion. A high **burstiness_reg** indicates the user account to be discussed is in a burst, so it is likely to be a throwaway spammer account. Table 6 shows adding this feature (i.e., M3) increases 0.0629 precision with the penalty of 0.0119 recall.

4.4 Frequent Poster Set

This section models the behavior of the collusion between spammers discussed in Section 3 with frequent itemset mining in data mining. Applying the shopping analogy to our scenario, user id of each post is an "item", and every 30 posts in a thread form a "basket". Each frequent poster set denotes a group of users that frequently appear together in threads. In our experiments, frequent itemset mining is conducted with the Orange library [1].

Rather than being incorporated the cue as a feature in our model, the mined frequent poster sets are used to examine the prediction outputs of the model M3 further. For each 3-element frequent poster set, we add up the spamicity prediction output by M3. If the sum is larger than a threshold, then we predict all users in this 3-element poster set to be spammers.

The model integrating the mined frequent poster sets, M4 shown in Table 6, increases recall from 0.4167 to 0.6190 without sacrificing precision, and achieves 0.6460 F1 score. The result is promising because the ratio of spammers in the test set is only 0.98%.

5. Conclusion

This paper investigates opinion spammer detection with a real case study. On the basis of a decent detection model for first posts, a quality model for spammer detection is proposed. In addition, leveraging the collusion between spammers significantly boosts the performance.

6. ACKNOWLEDGMENTS

This research was partially supported by National Taiwan University under grant NTU-ERP-104R890858, and Ministry of Science and Technology, under grant 102-2221-E-002-103-MY3.

7. REFERENCES

[1] Janez Demšar, Tomaž Curk, Aleš Erjavec, Črt Gorup, et al. Orange: Data mining toolbox in python. *Journal of Machine Learning Research*, 14:2349–2353, 2013.

[2] Geli Fei, Arjun Mukherjee, Bing Liu, Meichun Hsu, Malu Castellanos, and Riddhiman Ghosh. Exploiting burstiness in reviews for review spammer detection. In *Proceedings of the Seventh International AAAI Conference on Weblogs and Social Media* (ICWSM), pages 175-184, AAAI, 2013.

[3] Nathan Halko, Per-Gunnar Martinsson, and Joel A Tropp. Finding structure with randomness: Probabilistic algorithms for constructing approximate matrix decompositions. *SIAM review*, 53(2):217–288, 2011.

[4] Nitin Jindal and Bing Liu. Opinion spam and analysis. In *Proceedings of the 2008 International Conference on Web Search and Data Mining*, pages 219–230. ACM, 2008.

[5] Ee-Peng Lim, Viet-An Nguyen, Nitin Jindal, Bing Liu, and Hady Wirawan Lauw. Detecting product review spammers using rating behaviors. In *Proceedings of the 19th ACM International Conference on Information and Knowledge Management*, pages 939–948. ACM, 2010.

[6] Arjun Mukherjee, Bing Liu, Junhui Wang, Natalie Glance, and Nitin Jindal. Detecting group review spam. In *Proceedings of the 20th International Conference on World Wide Web*, pages 93–94. ACM, 2011.

[7] Arjun Mukherjee, Bing Liu, and Natalie Glance. Spotting fake reviewer groups in consumer reviews. In *Proceedings of 21st International World Wide Web Conference* (WWW 2012), pages 191-200, ACM, 2012.

[8] F. Pedregosa, G. Varoquaux, A. Gramfort, V. Michel, B. Thirion, O. Grisel, M. Blondel, P. Prettenhofer, R. Weiss, V. Dubourg, J. Vanderplas, A. Passos, D. Cournapeau, M. Brucher, M. Perrot, and E. Duchesnay. Scikitlearn: Machine learning in Python. *Journal of Machine Learning Research*, 12:2825–2830, 2011.

[9] Guan Wang, Sihong Xie, Bing Liu, and Philip S Yu. Review graph based online store review spammer detection. In *Proceedings of 2011 IEEE 11th International Conference on Data Mining (ICDM)*, pages 1242–1247. IEEE, 2011.

Multi-Faceted Recall of Continuous Active Learning for Technology-Assisted Review

Gordon V. Cormack
University of Waterloo
gvcormac@uwaterloo.ca

Maura R. Grossman*
Wachtell, Lipton, Rosen & Katz
mrgrossman@wlrk.com

ABSTRACT

Continuous active learning achieves high recall for technology-assisted review, not only for an overall information need, but also for various facets of that information need, whether explicit or implicit. Through simulations using Cormack and Grossman's TAR Evaluation Toolkit (SIGIR 2014), we show that continuous active learning, applied to a multi-faceted topic, efficiently achieves high recall for each facet of the topic. Our results assuage the concern that continuous active learning may achieve high overall recall at the expense of excluding identifiable categories of relevant information.

Categories and Subject Descriptors: H.3.3 Information Search and Retrieval: Search process, relevance feedback.

Keywords: Technology-assisted review; TAR; predictive coding; electronic discovery; e-discovery; test collections; relevance feedback; continuous active learning; CAL.

1. INTRODUCTION

The objective of technology-assisted review ("TAR"), first described in the context of electronic discovery ("eDiscovery") in legal matters [6], is to bring to the attention of a document reviewer substantially all relevant documents, and relatively few non-relevant ones, thereby maximizing recall and minimizing reviewer effort. The best reported results for TAR employ continuous active learning ("CAL"), in which a learning method presents the most-likely relevant documents to the reviewer in batches, the reviewer labels each document in each successive batch as relevant or not, and the labels are fed back to the learning method [6]. While CAL has been shown to achieve high recall with less effort than competing methods (including exhaustive manual review [7] and non-interactive supervised learning [6]), it has been suggested that CAL's emphasis on the most-likely relevant documents may bias it to prefer documents like the ones it finds first, causing it to fail to discover one or more important, but dissimilar, classes of relevant documents [11, 8].

In legal matters, an eDiscovery request typically comprises between several and several dozen requests for production ("RFPs"), each specifying a category of information sought. A review effort that fails to find documents relevant to each of the RFPs (assuming such documents exist) would likely be deemed deficient. In other domains, such as news services, topics are grouped into hierarchies, either explicit or implicit. A news-retrieval effort for "sports" that omits articles about "cricket" or "soccer" would likely be deemed inadequate, even if the vast majority of articles – about baseball, football, basketball, and hockey – were found. Similarly, a review effort that overlooked relevant short documents, spreadsheets, or presentations would likely also be seen as unsatisfactory.

We define a "facet" to be any identifiable subpopulation of the relevant documents, whether that subpopulation is defined by relevance to a particular RFP or subtopic, by file type, or by any other characteristic. Our objective is to determine whether CAL is able to achieve high recall over all facets, regardless of how they are identified. To this end, we used Cormack and Grossman's TAR Evaluation Toolkit ("Toolkit"),[1] grouping together the four RFPs supplied with the Toolkit as one overall topic, and treating each of the four RFPs as facets. We then computed recall as a function of review effort for the overall topic, as well as for each of the facets. We also computed recall separately for facets consisting of short documents, word-processing files, spreadsheets, and presentations.

We repeated our experiments, importing the Reuters RCV1-v2 dataset [10] into an adapted version of the Toolkit, using each of the RCV1-v2 top-level subject categories as an overall information need, and treating each of the 82 bottom-level subject categories as a facet.

2. TREC LEGAL TRACK EXPERIMENTS

In the Toolkit, we created a new overall topic, "all," by combining the topics supplied with the Toolkit (topics 201, 202, 203, and 207 from the TREC 2009 Legal Track [9]) as follows: As a seed set, we used 1,000 documents selected at random from the "seed query" hits in the Toolkit for the four topics [6, Table 3, p. 155]; as training and gold standards, we used the union of the respective standards supplied for the four topics, with the effect that, for both training and

*The views expressed herein are solely those of the author and should not be attributed to her firm or its clients.

[1] `http://cormack.uwaterloo.ca/cormack/tar-toolkit/`.

SIGIR'15, August 09-13, 2015, Santiago, Chile.
ACM 978-1-4503-3621-5/15/08.
DOI: http://dx.doi.org/10.1145/2766462.2767771 .

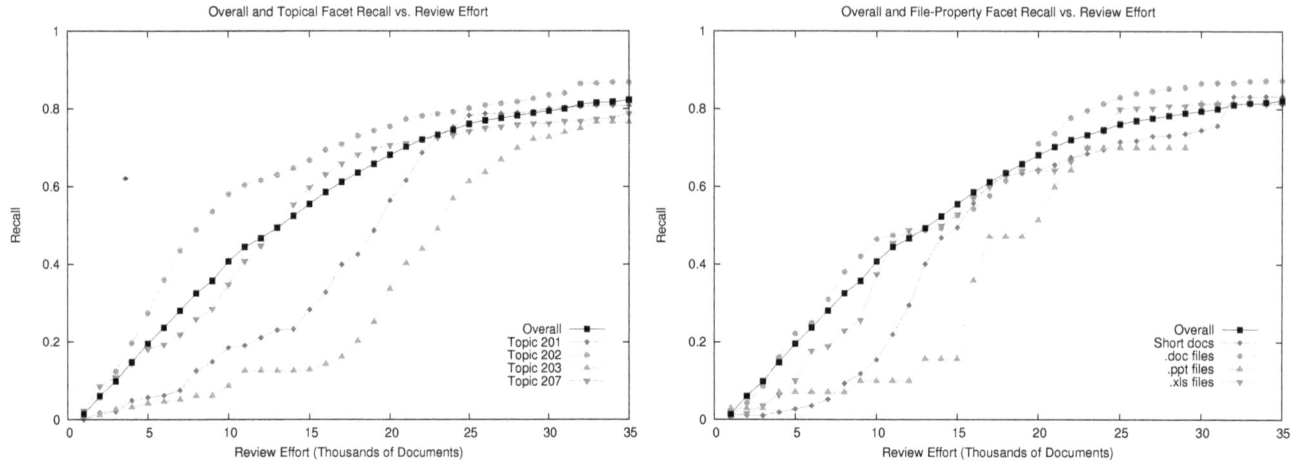

Figure 1: Overall and facet recall as a function of effort for the four TREC 2009 Legal Track topics. The left panel shows recall for an overall review effort, as well as recall with respect to each of four facets represented by the TREC topics. The right panel shows overall recall, as well as recall for facets represented by short documents, word-processing files, presentations, and spreadsheets.

evaluation, a document was considered relevant to the overall topic, "all," if it was relevant to any of the four facets represented by the Toolkit-supplied topics. We ran the "actkeysvm" CAL implementation, without modification, and captured the ordered list of documents presented for review. We computed recall for the "all" topic, and for each facet, at each position in the list.

We further evaluated recall with respect to four other facets: "short," ".doc," ".xls," and ".ppt," representing short documents ($< 1K$ bytes), word-processing files, spreadsheets, and presentations, respectively. Our results are shown in Figure 1. While it is apparent that, at the outset, topics 201 and 203, as well as short documents and presentations, lag behind; at high recall levels, there is little variance among the recall levels of the facets.

3. RCV1-V2 EXPERIMENTS

We next adapted the Toolkit to work with the RCV1-v2 dataset [10]. We used tf-idf Porter-stemmed word features, and SVM^{light}, following accepted practice [10]. We used as information needs the four top-level categories in the RCV1-v2 subject hierarchy, titled "corporate, industrial," "economics," "government and social," and "markets," with the corresponding subject codes, "CCAT," "ECAT," "GCAT," and "MCAT," respectively. As facets, we used the bottom-level categories in the RCV1-v2 subject hierarchy. We ignored the intermediate levels, as they are simple unions of the bottom-level categories. For seed queries, we used the titles of the top-level categories. We used the RCV1-v2 labels as both the training and gold standards.

Figure 2 shows overall and facet recall, as a function of review effort, for each of the four RCV1-v2 overall information needs. The results mirror those for the TREC 2009 dataset; however, a much higher level of recall is achieved, and convergence occurs as that higher level is approached. It appears that convergence coincides with a decline in marginal precision which, for these experiments, takes place in the neighborhood of 90% recall.

Among the results in Figure 2, one facet – "GMIL" – is an obvious outlier. Its recall reaches 80% only with double the review effort required for all other facets. In the RCV1-v2 collection, only five documents are labeled relevant to GMIL (bottom-level topic title: "Millennium Issues"). We examined these documents and found that four of them contain the phrase "millennium bug"; see, for example, the left panel of Table 1. We then searched the dataset and found 141 documents containing this same phrase, of which four were labeled relevant to GMIL, 48 were labeled relevant to some other facet of GCAT, and 93 were not labeled relevant to any facet. The right panel of Table 1 shows one such document. On reviewing these and other examples, we were unable to glean the criteria used to distinguish relevant from non-relevant documents, and thus attribute this outlier result to apparent mislabeling in the RCV1-v2 dataset.

4. WHEN TO STOP REVIEW

The objective of finding substantially all relevant documents suggests that CAL – or any other review effort – should continue until high recall has been achieved, and achieving higher recall would require disproportionate effort. Measuring recall is problematic, due to imprecision in the definition and assessment of relevance [3, 12, 8], and the effort, bias, and imprecision associated with sampling [2, 1, 8]. Accordingly, it is difficult to specify an absolute threshold value that constitutes "high recall," or to determine reliably that that such a threshold had been reached. Arguably, 75% to 80% recall would be sufficient for the TREC review detailed in Figure 1, because at that level, the recall for the facets is uniformly high, and a higher level can be achieved only with disproportionate effort. On the other hand, 90% or higher recall would be necessary to establish the adequacy of the RCV1-v2 reviews detailed in Figure 2. Only above 90% overall recall is the recall for facets uniformly high, and 90% recall is achievable with proportionate effort.

We suggest that, as an alternative to a fixed recall target, marginal precision might be a better indication of the completeness of a CAL review. In all of our experiments,

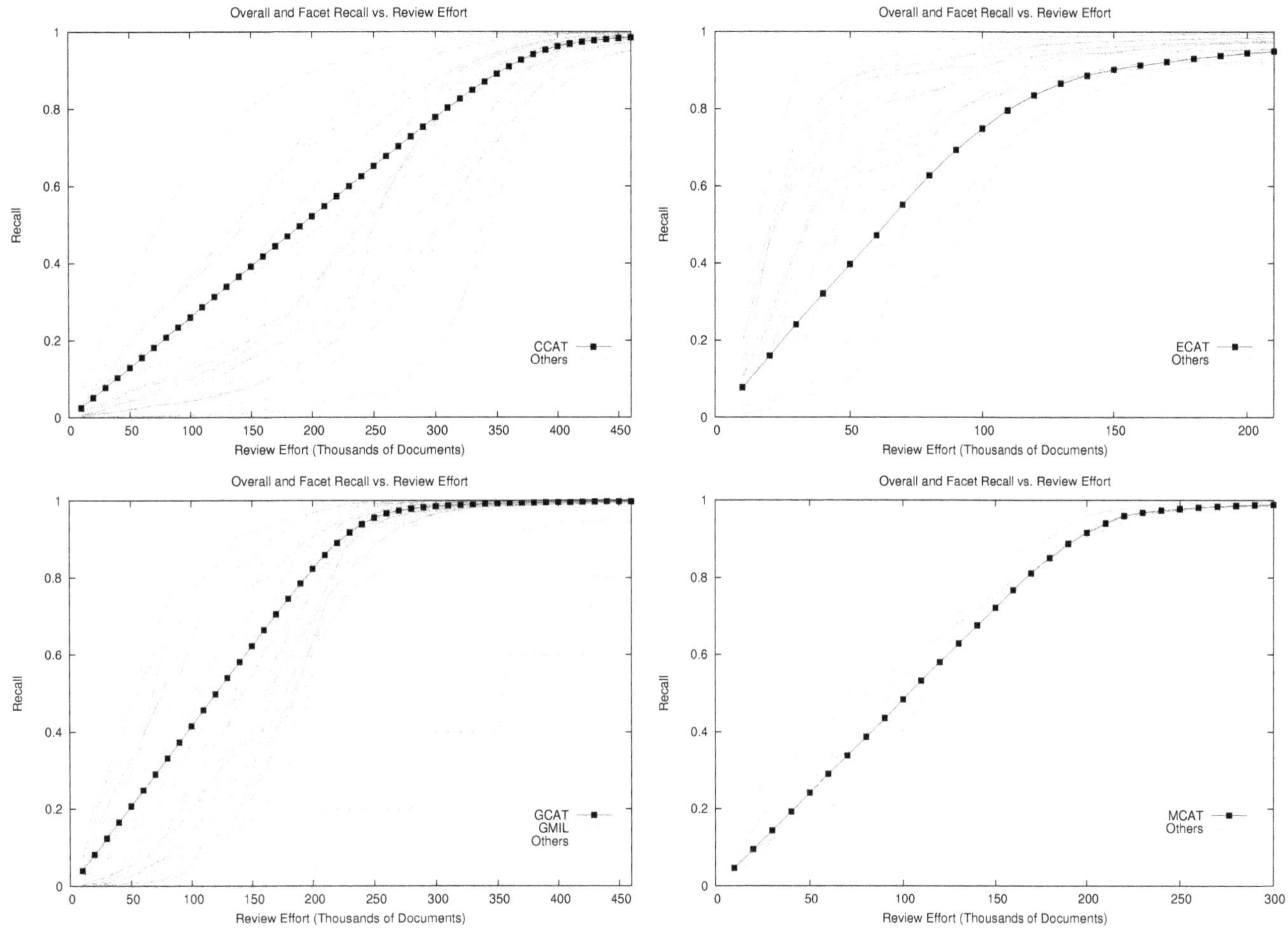

Figure 2: Overall and facet recall as a function of effort for the RCV1-v2 dataset.

we observed that the precision of each successive batch of 1,000 documents rose rapidly to nearly 100%, was sustained at nearly 100%, and then fell off. Table 2 illustrates that, in these experiments, stopping the review when marginal precision falls below one-tenth of its previously sustained value is a good predictor of high recall for the overall information need, as well as the facets, with proportionate effort.

5. DISCUSSION

A sign test shows our result to be significant ($p < 0.03$), by virtue of being observed for six of six separate experiments.

CAL is a greedy method that always chooses the most-likely relevant documents for review. It is to be expected that, at the outset, it chooses documents representing the easiest-to-identify facets, due to their subject matter, file properties, or abundance. As those documents are exhausted, others representing new facets become the most-likely relevant documents, until no more likely relevant documents remain. Only when the most-likely relevant documents from all facets have been exhausted, does marginal precision drop to a *de minimus* level.

While our findings suggest that it may be unnecessary, neither our theory of CAL's operation nor our results suggest that it would be harmful to train the learning method using additional seed documents – found by ad hoc means – to represent important facets that are are known to the reviewer at the outset, or become known during the course of the review process [5].

Our experiments suggest that when a review achieves sustained high precision, and then drops off substantially, one may have confidence that substantially all facets of relevance have been explored. In addition to offering a potentially better prediction of completeness, precision can be readily calculated throughout the review, while recall cannot. Further research is necessary to determine the extent to which marginal precision may afford a reliable quantitative estimate of review completeness, including coverage of different facets of relevance.

While sharing general motivation with efforts to achieve novelty and diversity in ad hoc retrieval [4], CAL seeks to achieve high recall rather than to reduce redundancy, and does so using a depth-first rather than breadth-first approach. We conducted an auxiliary experiment to investigate whether a strategy of using separate reviews for each facet would improve on the combined review strategy reported here. We found that the overall effort required to achieve 75% recall for every facet was higher for the separate review strategy. It remains to be seen whether other diversity-focused methods might improve on the purely depth-first results presented here.

Labeled "Relevant" in RCV1-v2	Labeled "Not relevant" in RCV1-v2
Okura up on millennium bug software demand. TOKYO 1997-08-15 Shares of Okura & Co Ltd surged on Friday afternoon due to the expectation that its software business would benefit from the so-called millennium bug problem. The stock was the top percentage gainer on the Tokyo Stock Exchange's first section in the afternoon session. Okura's shares were up 55 yen at 455 yen as of 0435 GMT. (c) Reuters Limited 1997-06-16	**Complete Business Solutions gets contract.** FARMINGTON HILLS, Mich. 1997-06-16 Complete Business Solutions Inc said early Monday that South Carolina Electric & Gas Co has awarded it a contract to manage and implement its Year 2000 code conversion project and deal with issues related to the "millennium bug". The project is expected to require changes to over three million lines of code at the utility and to be in the multi-million dollar range, Complete Business said. The company received the contract as part of a bidding process that included six other vendors. SCE&G is the principal subsidiary of SCANA Corp. ((- New York Newsdesk 212-859-1610)) (c) Reuters Limited 1997

Table 1: Conflicting relevance labels for category GMIL (bottom-level topic title: "Millennium Issues"). Of 141 documents in the RCV1-v2 collection containing the phrase "millennium bug," four were labeled "relevant," while 137 were labeled "not relevant."

	TREC	CCAT	ECAT	GCAT	GCAT (excl. GMIL)	MCAT
Review Effort (K-docs)	34	436	166	281	281	237
Overall Precision	0.587	0.856	0.664	0.848	0.848	0.840
Overall Recall	0.818	0.979	0.919	0.996	0.996	0.972
Overall F_1	0.684	0.913	0.771	0.916	0.916	0.901
Lowest Facet Recall	0.766	0.924	0.890	0.200	0.863	0.958

Table 2: Review effort and effectiveness when marginal precision (measured on the last batch of 1,000 documents) falls below 10%. Effort is measured in terms of thousands of documents reviewed; effectiveness is measured in terms of overall precision, recall, and F_1, as well as the lowest recall obtained for any facet.

6. CONCLUSION

For all experiments, our results are the same: CAL achieves high overall recall, while at the same time achieving high recall for the various facets of relevance, whether topics or file properties. While early recall is achieved for some facets at the expense of others, by the time high overall recall is achieved – as evidenced by a substantial drop in overall marginal precision – all facets (except for a single outlier case that we attribute to mislabeling) also exhibit high recall. Our findings provide reassurance that CAL can achieve high recall without excluding identifiable categories of relevant information.

7. REFERENCES

[1] M. Bagdouri, D. D. Lewis, and D. W. Oard. Sequential testing in classifier evaluation yields biased estimates of effectiveness. In *Proceedings of the 36th International ACM SIGIR Conference on Research and Development in Information Retrieval*, pages 933–936, 2013.

[2] M. Bagdouri, W. Webber, D. D. Lewis, and D. W. Oard. Towards minimizing the annotation cost of certified text classification. In *Proceedings of the 22nd ACM International Conference Information and Knowledge Management*, pages 989–998, 2013.

[3] D. C. Blair. STAIRS redux: Thoughts on the STAIRS evaluation, ten years after. *Journal of the American Society for Information Science*, 47(1):4–22, Jan. 1996.

[4] C. L. A. Clarke, M. Kolla, G. V. Cormack, O. Vechtomova, A. Ashkann, S. Büttcher, and I. MacKinnon. Novelty and diversity in information retrieval evaluation. In *Proceedings of the 31st Annual International ACM SIGIR Conference on Research and Development in Information Retrieval*, pages 659–666, 2008.

[5] G. Cormack and M. Mojdeh. Machine learning for information retrieval: TREC 2009 Web, Relevance Feedback and Legal Tracks. In *Eighteenth Text REtrieval Conference*, 2009.

[6] G. V. Cormack and M. R. Grossman. Evaluation of machine-learning protocols for technology-assisted review in electronic discovery. In *Proceedings of the 37th International ACM SIGIR Conference on Research and Development in Information Retrieval*, pages 153–162, 2014.

[7] M. R. Grossman and G. V. Cormack. Technology-assisted review in e-discovery can be more effective and more efficient than exhaustive manual review. *Richmond Journal of Law and Technology*, 17(3):1–48, 2011.

[8] M. R. Grossman and G. V. Cormack. Comments on "The implications of rule 26(g) on the use of technology-assisted review". *Federal Courts Law Review*, 7:285–313, 2014.

[9] B. Hedin, S. Tomlinson, J. R. Baron, and D. W. Oard. Overview of the TREC 2009 Legal Track. In *The Eighteenth Text REtrieval Conference*, 2009.

[10] D. D. Lewis, Y. Yang, T. G. Rose, and F. Li. RCV1: A new benchmark collection for text categorization research. *Journal of Machine Learning Research*, 5:361–397, 2004.

[11] K. Schieneman and T. Gricks. The implications of Rule 26(g) on the use of technology-assisted review. *Federal Courts Law Review*, 7(1):239–274, 2013.

[12] E. M. Voorhees. Variations in relevance judgments and the measurement of retrieval effectiveness. *Information Processing & Management*, 36(5):697–716, 2000.

Time Pressure and System Delays in Information Search

Anita Crescenzi
School of Information and Library Science, University of North Carolina
Chapel Hill, NC, USA
amcc@email.unc.edu

Diane Kelly
School of Information and Library Science, University of North Carolina
Chapel Hill, NC, USA
dianek@email.unc.edu

Leif Azzopardi
School of Computing Science, University of Glasgow
Glasgow, United Kingdom
leif@dcs.gla.ac.uk

ABSTRACT

We report preliminary results of the impact of time pressure and system delays on search behavior from a laboratory study with forty-three participants. To induce time pressure, we randomly assigned half of our study participants to a treatment condition where they were only allowed five minutes to search for each of four ad-hoc search topics. The other half of the participants were given no task time limits. For half of participants' search tasks (n=2), five second delays were introduced after queries were submitted and SERP results were clicked. Results showed that participants in the time pressure condition queried at a significantly higher rate, viewed significantly fewer documents per query, had significantly shallower hover and view depths, and spent significantly less time examining documents and SERPs. We found few significant differences in search behavior for system delay or interaction effects between time pressure and system delay. These initial results show time pressure has a significant impact on search behavior and suggest the design of search interfaces and features that support people who are searching under time pressure.

Categories and Subject Descriptors

H.3.3 [**Information Storage and Retrieval**]: Information Search and Retrieval—*Search Process*

Keywords

Search Behavior; Time Pressure; System Delays

1. INTRODUCTION

Recently, increased attention has been paid to how system delays impact search behavior and the user experience in the context of interactive information retrieval (IIR) [1, 8, 15, 16]. Users of search systems with slower query response times have been found to have lower perceptions of system usability and helpfulness [1]. Studies examining system delays have found users are tolerant of search delays up to a "tipping point" beyond which behaviors and perceptions change [15]. User sensitivity to delay varies across individuals, the average speed of the system used [1], and how the information is presented [15]. It has also been found that searchers who experience both query and document response delays view fewer documents, but mark a higher percentage as relevant, although the delay had no impact on the number of queries issued, the number of documents marked relevant, the depth of results inspected or search accuracy [8].

Although there has been a resurgence of interest in the impact of search system delay on user experience, a long line of research precedes this interest. In 1968, Miller [9] described system response times exceeding two seconds as changing the character of "man-computer conversational transactions" and provided a taxonomy of acceptable response times depending on the type and complexity of system interactions and the extent to which the response delay would disrupt the user's task. Since this early work, researchers have found that perceived wait time and the impact of delays can be reduced by informing users of the system response status [11], incrementally loading pages [2], or displaying filler text or images [6] while the system is processing its response.

While system delays have been investigated in IIR, one variable that has not been investigated much is time pressure. Research on time pressured decision-making has found that people adapt under time pressure: they may spend less time in each decision stage, spend less time processing individual pieces of information, accelerate the pace of the task or information processing, or even satisfice in their decisions [12]. Time has been shown to be an important contextual factor in search [13]; however, the impact of time pressure on search behaviors and perceptions is less well understood. Recent studies have have shown when searchers have less time to complete tasks, they have lower perceptions of their search performance [7] and task completion [17], less satisfaction with results [7, 17] and less knowledge gained [7]. Searchers also report lower pre-task search confidence [7] and more negative affect [7] and stress [17]. Time pressure has also been found to impact search satisfaction even when the same amount of time was given to complete tasks [4]. Finally, Mishra et al. [10] found dissatisfaction among people who searched for time-critical information.

In this paper, we report preliminary results of a study investigating the impact of time pressure, system delays and interaction effects on search behaviors and user experience. We present the results of our analyses of interaction measures as well as time pressure and delay manipulation checks.

SIGIR'15, August 09 - 13, 2015, Santiago, Chile

ACM 978-1-4503-3621-5/15/08 ...$15.00
DOI: http://dx.doi.org/10.1145/2766462.2767817.

2. METHOD

We conducted a laboratory experiment where we manipulated task time limit and system response time. To manipulate task time limit, half of the participants were given an unexpected task time limit just before they started the experimental search tasks. This time limit was presented via pop-up message after they completed the practice task and informed them they had only 5 minutes to complete each experimental search task (Figure 1). These instructions were intended to simulate a situation in which an urgent notification changes one's expectations about the time available to complete a task. The 5 minute time limit represented approximately half of the mean task completion times from a prior study [5] where different participants used the same system to complete three of the same tasks without time limits. The system tracked the time, and after participants had been searching for 5 minutes, popped-up another message indicating time was up.

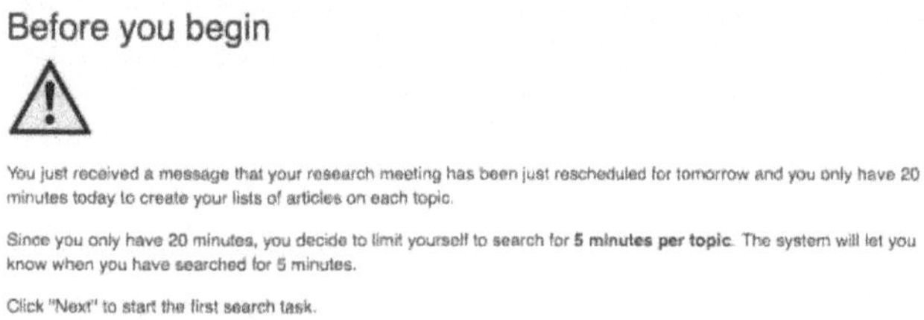

Figure 1: Task time limit instructions

Participants who were not given a task time limit were not provided with any instructions regarding the amount of time to spend on each task, although all participants were aware that the experimental session would last 1hr and 15min. If these participants were still searching after 1hr and 5min (i.e., with approximately 10 minutes remaining in the experimental session), we stopped them so they could complete the exit questionnaire and interview. Based on our previous experiences, we did not expect we would need to do this; however, this occurred in seven cases. To minimize time pressure caused by researcher presence [14], the researcher was stationed in an adjacent room while participants completed the study.

System response time was a within-subjects variable with two levels: delay and no delay. Participants completed two tasks in which we introduced 5 second delays after they submitted queries and clicked on SERP results and two tasks in which the system was not delayed. We selected a 5 second delay based on prior research which indicated that a delay of 4 seconds changed behaviors but not attitudes and is usually considered acceptable to users (delays of 7-10 seconds have been found to be unacceptable by users [15]). We presented delays in 2 orders: half of the participants experienced delays during their first and third tasks while the other half experienced delays during their second and fourth tasks.

The basic procedure was as follows. Participants were first shown the experiment instructions on screen including the simulated work task scenario and then completed a practice task to become familiar with the system; we did not impose a time limit or system delay during the practice task. Once participants completed the practice task, those with a task time limit were shown the instructions in Figure 1 before being presented with their first search task. For each search task, participants were shown the topic, completed a pre-search questionnaire, conducted their search and then completed a post-search questionnaire. After conducting all four searches, participants completed an exit questionnaire. Following this, the researcher returned to the room for a final interview and debriefing.

2.1 Scenario and Tasks

Following Borlund's [3] guidelines, search tasks were situated in the context of a project in which a research team needs to compare news coverage about four topics during the (consecutive) U.S. presidential terms of Clinton, Bush and Obama. Participants were told their job was to examine news during Clinton's second term, 1996-2000, which corresponded to the date range of the test collection [18]. We wanted the scenario to provide participants with a rationale for searching articles from this time period and to make this characteristic of the collection salient to help ground participants' relevance judgments. The scenario indicated that participants should find 8-12 articles per topic.

We selected topics from the collection with contemporary relevance where prior studies have reported that participants found the tasks at least moderately interesting and difficult [5]. We aimed to minimize potential variability in interest and difficulty in order to examine the impact of our independent variables. Four topics were used: wildlife extinction (347), journalist risks (354), piracy (367) and population growth (435). Participants were presented with the topic descriptions before each search.

To minimize order effects, we created a set of 24 topic rotations. We assigned the topic rotations to time limit and delay order combinations such that each topic rotation was used twice: once in each time limit condition and once in each delay order. We randomly assigned participants to time limit, delay order and topic rotation.

2.2 Search Questionnaires

Our search questionnaires measured several constructs including system usability, task difficulty, metacognitive actions and satisfaction. Several items functioned as manipulation checks to see if participants felt time pressure and noticed system delays (see Table 1). Participants responded to these items with a 7-point scale (1 = strongly disagree, 7 = strongly agree). In this paper, we only present items related to the manipulation checks and will analyze the additional measures in future work.

2.3 Search System

All participants used the same search system which resembled a standard search engine. The Whoosh IR Toolkit was used as the core of the retrieval system, with BM25 as the retrieval algorithm, using standard parameters, but with an implicit ANDing of query terms to restrict the retrieval set. Only a portion of the collection was indexed to ensure that the natural response time of the system was quick and constant. This was to control the effects of both the natural and experimental delays as much as possible. The documents included in the index consisted of all the TREC pooled documents for the given topics, along with the top 100 documents retrieved from the full index given a set of user generated queries from a past study (approximately 100-200 queries per topic). In total, over 200,000 documents were indexed. In all conditions, the search system displayed a spinning wheel when it was busy.

2.4 Participants

Forty-five people from a major research university participated including undergraduate students (n=13), graduate students (n=8) and staff (n=22) representing many different majors and occupations. Participants ranged in age from 18-59 years (M=32.1, SD=12.8) and 31 were female. Participants were compensated $20 USD.

3. RESULTS

We analyzed 163 tasks completed by 43 participants using a mixed ANOVA. We excluded data from 2 participants with no task time limit who spent most of the time completing a single search task, 7 tasks where participants with no task time limit were stopped in their third task or final task, and 2 tasks where participants accidentally ended the tasks by pressing the wrong button.

3.1 Time and Delay

We conducted a series of manipulation checks to make sure our experimental manipulations were successful. We found those with the task time limit reported feeling significantly more time pressure, a greater need to work fast and more rushed (Table 1). We found significant differences in perceived quickness of SERP and document display between the delay conditions. We found no interaction effects, but note a significant effect of delay on perceived time pressure.

We examined task completion times and found significant effects of task time limit and system delay on the total task time as shown in Table 1. The introduction of time limits and system delays complicates comparison of interaction measures as the total delay experienced by any one person is a function of the number of queries issued and documents viewed by this person. For this reason, we also examined adjusted task times where we subtracted the cumulative delay experienced by each participant for each task from the total task time; we found significant main effects of time limit and no main effect of delay. Interaction effects were significant ($F(2,118)=7.03$, $p<.01$).

To check the delay manipulation, we examined query and document processing times (in seconds). As expected, we found no significant differences in organic system response times and significant differences in the mean total processing time (organic + delay) according to delay condition. It took longer for the system to return requests for tasks with delay condition (query: M=5.92, SD=0.96; document: M=5.20, SD=1.16) than for tasks without delay (query: M=0.94, SD=0.84; document: M=0.29, SD=0.34). We found no main effect for time limit or interaction effects.

3.2 Search Behaviors

Table 1 shows the means and standard deviations of participants' search behaviors by time limit and response time condition. With one exception, there were no significant interaction effects, so we only report main effects. We normalized time-based measures to facilitate comparison. The adjusted rate-based measures reflect the number of queries, document views and documents marked relevant per minute using adjusted times; that is, total time minus time spent in delay as in Taylor, Dennis & Cummings [15]. While participants who experienced a task time limit had higher rates of querying, document viewing and marking documents as relevant, only the difference for query rate was significant. There were no significant differences according to whether or not participants experienced delays; in fact, these measures were very similar in these two conditions.

When we examine actions per query, we see those who experienced the task time limit examined search results more shallowly. They viewed fewer SERPs and documents and also did not navigate as deeply in the search results list. All of these differences were statistically significant. Participants with a task time limit also spent significantly less time viewing documents and SERPs. Although the trend was for participants to view fewer SERPs and documents per query when they experienced delays and not go as deeply in the search results list, these differences were not significant. Participants spent significantly more time viewing documents for delayed tasks, but they spent roughly equal amounts of time viewing SERPs for their delayed and non-delayed tasks.

With respect to performance, there were no differences in participants' save rates (% viewed marked relevant) according to time limit or response time conditions. Although we have not examined the content of the documents participants saved, we examined whether participants met the scenario goal of finding 8-12 relevant articles. This goal was achieved more often for tasks where no task time limit was present (96% vs. 84% of tasks) and for tasks where no delays were present (92% vs. 86% of tasks). Only 76% of tasks with both a delay and a task time limit had at least 8 pages marked relevant compared to 100% of tasks with no task time limit and delay.

4. DISCUSSION AND CONCLUSIONS

We investigated the impact of time pressure and system delays on search behaviors. Results showed participants who were given task time limits queried at a significantly higher rate, viewed significantly fewer documents per query, had significantly shallower hover and view depths, and spent significantly less time SERPs. They also spent significantly less time examining documents, and presumably, making judgments about which documents to save.

We did not find significant differences in search behavior with respect to system delays beyond the time spent completing the task (total and adjusted) and the time spent per document. While the delay was noticed by most participants, it did not significantly impact their search behaviors. These findings are consistent with other studies [1, 8]. Of course, it is likely that larger delay times would produce different results: Taylor et al. [15] found a tipping point between 7 and 11 seconds for behavioral impacts but some changes to satisfaction were observed at lower thresholds. Whether the delay is consistent or intermittent also seems to play a role [1]. Further analysis of the questionnaires and debriefings will likely provide additional insight about how time pressure and system delays impacted the user experience.

Interestingly, we found considerable variability in the task completion times for those without task time limits and two participants, whose data were excluded, used nearly the entire experimental session to search for a single task. For those tasks included in analyses, task completion times ranged from 1.76min to 36.27min. For 10 tasks, the total task completion time exceeded 15min. These variations surprised us because they differ considerably from what we have observed in previous laboratory studies, where the general challenge is often to create tasks that will require sustained interaction.

	Time Limit (main effects)			Response Time (main effects)		
	Session	Task	F	No Delay	Delay	F
Manipulation checks						
felt time pressure	3.43 (1.62)	5.25 (1.62)	15.27***	4.29 (1.90)	4.61 (1.80)	4.12*
needed to work fast	3.56 (1.56)	5.62 (1.50)	27.30***	4.70 (1.82)	4.71 (1.86)	0.00
felt hurried or rushed	3.03 (1.49)	4.91 (1.75)	17.93***	4.03 (1.96)	4.11 (1.82)	0.18
displayed search results quickly	4.31 (1.67)	4.65 (1.78)	0.99	4.96 (1.58)	4.01 (1.76)	19.73***
displayed articles quickly	4.39 (1.54)	4.68 (1.92)	0.63	5.00 (1.68)	4.09 (1.74)	17.72***
Interaction measures						
total task time (m)	9.04 (6.12)	4.60 (0.98)	21.82****	6.13 (4.00)	7.01 (5.27)	7.61**
adjusted task time (m)	8.25 (5.63)	4.08 (1.02)	21.29****	6.13 (4.00)	5.70 (4.67)	0.03
adjusted query rate	0.61 (0.44)	1.04 (0.61)	16.72***	0.85 (0.61)	0.85 (0.54)	0.03
adjusted view rate	2.28 (0.93)	2.63 (1.24)	2.55	2.52 (1.18)	2.42 (1.07)	1.60
adjusted mark relevant rate	1.64 (0.98)	2.05 (1.24)	3.22	1.85 (1.19)	1.89 (1.12)	0.00
SERPs viewed per q	2.25 (1.67)	1.64 (0.79)	5.36*	1.98 (1.54)	1.83 (0.96)	0.90
docs viewed per q	6.09 (5.75)	3.90 (3.47)	4.81*	5.08 (5.04)	4.65 (4.41)	0.71
hover depth per q	17.52 (16.70)	11.34 (8.78)	5.23*	14.77 (15.46)	13.34 (10.43)	0.77
view depth per q	14.88 (15.95)	8.89 (7.98)	6.51*	11.91 (14.46)	11.15 (10.11)	0.20
total time per doc (s)	14.05 (6.50)	8.82 (5.46)	17.26***	10.22 (5.54)	12.07 (7.23)	10.63***
total SERP time per q (s)	61.53 (60.35)	34.86 (23.44)	13.18***	46.73 (52.80)	46.55 (36.98)	0.00
save rate	0.70 (0.18)	0.73 (0.21)	0.64	0.69 (0.20)	0.74 (0.20)	2.30

Table 1: Manipulation check and interaction signals. Means (sd) and F-test results by time constraint (df= 1, 41) and response time (df=1,118), *p<0.05; **p<0.01; ***p<0.001; ****p<0.0001

While preliminary, our initial results open a new line of inquiry into how time pressure impacts search behaviors and how search tools might be designed to support people who are searching under time pressure. For example, interface features that make it easier for people to query, assess relevance and monitor progress might be especially beneficial. Displaying fewer results per SERP might also help keep people who are searching under time pressure stay focused.

5. REFERENCES

[1] I. Arapakis, X. Bai, and B. B. Cambazoglu. Impact of response latency on user behavior in web search. In *Proc. of the 37th ACM SIGIR conference*, pages 103–112, 2014.

[2] N. Bhatti, A. Bouch, and A. Kuchinsky. Integrating user-perceived quality into Web server design. *Computer Networks*, 33(1-6):1–16, 2000.

[3] P. Borlund. The IIR evaluation model: A framework for evaluation of interactive information retrieval systems. *Information Research*, 8(3):1–34, 2003.

[4] A. Crescenzi, R. Capra, and J. Arguello. Time pressure, user satisfaction and task difficulty. *Proc. of the American Society for Info. Sci. and Tech.*, 50(1):1–4, 2013.

[5] A. Edwards, D. Kelly, and L. Azzopardi. The impact of query interface design on stress, workload and performance. In *Proc. of the 37th ECIR Conference*, pages 691–702, Vienna, Austria, 2015.

[6] Y. Lee, A. N. K. Chen, and V. Ilie. Can online wait be managed? The effect of filler interfaces and presentation modes on perceived waiting time online. *MIS Quarterly*, 36(2):365–394, 2012.

[7] C. Liu, F. Yang, Y. Zhao, Q. Jiang, and L. Zhang. What does time constraint mean to information searchers? In *Proc. of the 5th IIIX Conference*, pages 227–230, 2014.

[8] D. Maxwell and L. Azzopardi. Stuck in traffic: How temporal delays affect search behavior. In *Proc. of the 5th IIIX Conference*, pages 155–164, 2014.

[9] R. B. Miller. Response time in man-computer conversational transactions. In *Proc. of the 1968 Fall Joint Computer Conference*, pages 267–277, 1968.

[10] N. Mishra, R. W. White, S. Ieong, and E. Horvitz. Time-critical search. In *Proc. of the 37th ACM SIGIR conference*, pages 747–756, 2014.

[11] R. Molich and J. Nielsen. Improving a human-computer dialogue. *Comm. of the ACM*, 33(3):338–348, 1990.

[12] J. W. Payne, J. R. Bettman, and E. J. Johnson. *The Adaptive Decision Maker.* Cambridge Uni. Press, 1993.

[13] R. Savolainen. Time as a context of information seeking. *Library & Info. Sci. Research*, 28(1):110–127, Mar. 2006.

[14] D. N. Stone and K. Kadous. The joint effects of task-related negative affect and task difficulty in multiattribute choice. *Organizational Behavior and Human Decision Processes*, 70(2):159–174, May 1997.

[15] N. J. Taylor, A. R. Dennis, and J. W. Cummings. Situation normality and the shape of search: The effects of time delays and information presentation on search behavior. *J. of the A. Soc. for Info. Sci. and Tech.*, 64(5):909–928, 2013.

[16] J. Teevan, K. Collins-Thompson, R. W. White, S. T. Dumais, and Y. Kim. Slow search: Information retrieval without time constraints. In *Proc. of the 7th HCIR Symposium*, pages 1–10, 2013.

[17] A. Tombros, I. Ruthven, and J. M. Jose. How users assess web pages for information seeking. *J. of the American Society for Info. Sci. and Tech.*, 56(4):327–344, 2005.

[18] E. M. Voorhees. Overview of the trec 2005 robust retrieval track. In *Proceedings of TREC-14*, 2006.

How Random Decisions Affect Selective Distributed Search

Zhuyun Dai, Yubin Kim, Jamie Callan
Language Technologies Institute
Carnegie Mellon University
Pittsburgh, PA 15213, USA
{zhuyund, yubink, callan}@cs.cmu.edu

ABSTRACT

Selective distributed search is a retrieval architecture that reduces search costs by partitioning a corpus into topical shards such that only a few shards need to be searched for each query. Prior research created topical shards by using random seed documents to cluster a random sample of the full corpus. The resource selection algorithm might use a different random sample of the corpus. These random components make selective search non-deterministic.

This paper studies how these random components affect experimental results. Experiments on two ClueWeb09 corpora and four query sets show that in spite of random components, selective search is stable for most queries.

Categories and Subject Descriptors

H.3.3 [**Information Search and Retrieval**]: Information Search and Retrieval

Keywords

distributed retrieval; selective search; variance

1. INTRODUCTION

A *selective search* architecture reduces search costs by organizing a large corpus into topical index *shards* and searching only the most likely shards for each query. As defined by prior research, selective search has several non-deterministic steps. Kulkarni [4] used sample-based k-means clustering to create topical shards, which is non-deterministic due to random sampling and cluster seeds. Some resource selection algorithms, such as Rank-S [5], use a random sample of the corpus to decide which shards to search for each query, which introduces additional non-determinism.

Prior research showed that selective search can be as accurate as a typical 'search all shards' distributed architecture but at a substantially reduced computational cost [1, 4, 5]. However, it was based on a single partitioning of the corpus. A different partitioning might yield different results.

We are not the first to notice this problem. Jayasinghe, et al. [3] proposed a linear model to statistically compare non-deterministic retrieval systems, using selective search as an example. Their model took into consideration the multi-dimensional variance in selective search. However, their work focused on testing whether selective search has equivalent mean effectiveness as a baseline search architecture. In our work, we focus on the variance itself.

This paper investigates the effect of random decisions on selective search accuracy by comparing results obtained with different partitionings of two ClueWeb datasets. It examines the variance of a system across four query sets (Section 3.1), and for individual queries (Section 3.2).

SIGIR'15, August 09 - 13, 2015, Santiago, Chile.

ACM 978-1-4503-3621-5/15/08 ...$15.00.
DOI: http://dx.doi.org/10.1145/2766462.2767796 .

2. EXPERIMENTAL METHOD

We define a *system instance* to be a partition of a corpus index and its corresponding resource selection database for algorithms such as Rank-S [5] or Taily [1]. Our system instances were defined by a slight adaptation of a process defined by Kulkarni [4]. First, 500K documents were randomly sampled from the corpus, k of those documents were selected to be seeds, and k-means clustering was used to form clusters. Second, the remaining documents were projected onto the most similar clusters to form index shards. Third, spam documents were removed and a resource selection index was constructed. The Rank-S resource selection index was formed from a 1% random sample of each cluster. The Taily resource selection index is created deterministically. Thus, each system instance involved 2-3 random processes.

The parameters used for Taily and Rank-S were suggested by Aly et al. [1] and Kulkarni et al. [5]. They were $n = 400$, $v = 50$ for Taily and $B = 5$, $CSI = 1\%$ for Rank-S.

The experiments also tested Relevance-Based Ranking (RBR), an oracle resource selection algorithm that ranks shards by the number of relevant documents that they contain. RBR makes it possible to distinguish between different types of variance. For query q, RBR searched the average number of shards that Rank-S and Taily searched for q.

Experiments were conducted on the ClueWeb09 Category A (*CW09-A*) corpus, which contains 500 million English web pages, and ClueWeb09 Category B (*CW09-B*), which contains 50 million English web pages. Queries were from the TREC 2009-2012 Web Tracks: 4 sets of 50 queries.

Parameters were set to produce shards of 500K documents on average. Each CW09-A system instance had 1000 shards; CW09-B system instances had 100 shards.

3. EXPERIMENT RESULTS

The effects of random decisions during partitioning and indexing can be measured across query sets or individual queries. Measuring across query sets provides information

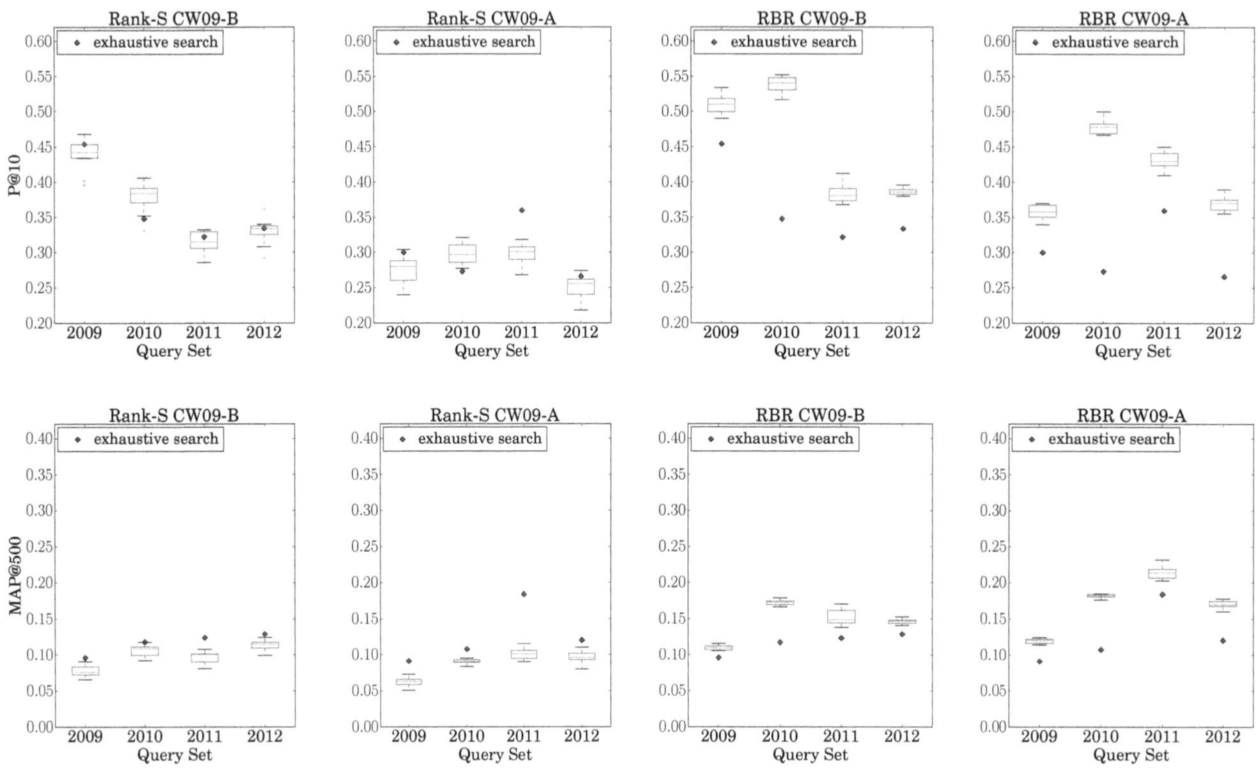

Figure 1: Accuracy distribution of Rank-S and RBR system instances. Mid line in boxes represents median. Outer edges of the boxes represent lower and upper quartiles, while whiskers indicate 1.5 interquartile range. + indicates outliers. Blue diamond is the performance of the typical 'search all shards baseline.

about the reliability of metrics such as MAP and NDCG that are typically reported in research papers. Measuring across individual queries provides information about the behavior that people will observe when they use the system. The experiments below provide both types of measurement.

3.1 Variability for Query Sets

The first experiment examined how random decisions affect the 'average case' metrics typically reported in research papers. It used three resource selection algorithms: Rank-S, which has a random component; Taily, which is deterministic; and RBR, the oracle algorithm. Ten random partitions were created for each dataset. Thus there were 2 datasets $\times$ 10 random partitions $\times$ 3 resource selection algorithms = 60 system instances. On average, Rank-S searched 3.91 CW09-A shards and 3.75 CW09-B shards; Taily searched 2.58 CW09-A shards and 2.53 CW09-B shards; and RBR searched 3.13 CW09-A shards and 2.80 CW09-B shards.

Retrieval accuracy was evaluated using three metrics: Precision at rank 10 (P@10), Normalized Discounted Cumulative Gain at rank 100 (NDCG@100), and Mean Average Precision at rank 500 (MAP@500) for compatibility with prior research [1]. Results for Taily and NDCG@100 were similar to results for Rank-S and other metrics, thus they are omitted due to space limitations.

The distributions of measurements over each type of system instance and the 'search all shards' baseline are shown in Figure 1. Tables 1 and 2 report the standard deviation and variance coefficient of Rank-S and RBR system accuracy scores. The standard deviation is a common measure, however it has two flaws: i) values produced by different metrics (e.g., P@10, MAP@500) cannot be compared because it is not dimensionless; and ii) the *importance* of a given level of deviation depends upon the value of the mean. The *variance coefficient* (VC) normalizes the standard deviation by the mean, thus eliminating these flaws.

The Relevance-Based Ranking (RBR) was generally more accurate and had lower variance across system instances than Rank-S and Taily, as expected. The one exception was the 2011 query set and the MAP@500 metric; Rank-S had lower variance than RBR under this condition. This exception was caused by a small set of queries. Rank-S had consistently poor accuracy on these queries, whereas RBR had greater accuracy but also greater variance.

The experimental results suggest that there are two sources of variance in selective search: Partitioning, and resource selection. RBR always selects the best shards, thus variance in RBR results is due to differences in partitioning effectiveness. Rank-S and Taily use models (resource selection indices) to make decisions about which shards to select for each query, however those models are necessarily incomplete. The increases in variance for Rank-S and Taily as compared to RBR are due to resource selection errors caused by weaknesses in the models of shard contents.

Selective search instances displayed differing levels of variability across different metrics. P@10 overall had a lower variance coefficient than MAP@500 (Tables 1 and 2). Similar behavior is observed for Taily instances. This behavior

Table 1: Standard Deviation (SD) and Variance Coefficient (VC) of accuracy scores for Rank-S instances.

a) P@10

Query Set	CW09-B		CW09-A	
	SD	VC	SD	VC
2009	2.22×10^{-2}	5.06%	2.00×10^{-2}	7.30%
2010	2.11×10^{-2}	5.57%	1.50×10^{-2}	4.90%
2011	1.52×10^{-2}	4.84%	1.51×10^{-2}	5.06%
2012	1.79×10^{-2}	5.44%	1.54×10^{-2}	6.14%

b) MAP@500

Query Set	CW09-B		CW09-A	
	SD	VC	SD	VC
2009	7.77×10^{-3}	10.04%	6.65×10^{-3}	10.65%
2010	7.56×10^{-3}	7.16%	3.31×10^{-3}	3.66%
2011	8.52×10^{-3}	8.89%	7.67×10^{-3}	7.62%
2012	7.17×10^{-3}	6.37%	7.96×10^{-3}	8.23%

indicates that selective search is more stable at the top of the ranking.

Rank-S is affected by one more random component than Taily, thus it might be expected to have greater variability across system instances. Table 3 shows the variance coefficient of MAP@500 for Rank-S and Taily across ten CW09-A system instances; similar behavior was observed across all metrics for both collections. Taily only had lower variance than Rank-S on 1 of the 4 query sets. These results might be considered surprising. The additional random component does not appear to cause greater instability in Rank-S results. As far as we know, prior research has not investigated the variability of results produced by document-based and model-based algorithms such as Rank-S and Taily.

3.2 Variability for Queries

Ideally selective search would provide similar results for a given query regardless of which system instance is used. The second experiment examined variability on a query-by-query basis.

We examined the variance of Average Precision of each query across Rank-S and Taily instances on CW09-A and observed some highly variant queries in both Rank-S and Taily. Rank-S had 14 queries with AP standard deviation higher than 0.1; Taily had 17 such high variance queries.

High variance could be due to errors from the partitioning process or errors from resource selection. To discover the source of the variance, a query-by-query experiment was conducted with RBR on the same partitions. RBR does not make resource selection errors but *is* affected by partitioning errors. Thus, if Rank-S, Taily, and RBR all have trouble with a query, the problem is likely to be partitioning.

Figure 2 shows the average precision (AP) of each query for ten RBR system instances. A notable observation is that most of the queries have stable AP; 177 of the 200 queries had a standard deviation of less than 0.05. However, there were a few queries with very high variance that contributed most of the average variance.

Whether the query is variable or stable remained mostly consistent across RBR, Rank-S, and Taily. While there were some highly variable queries in RBR that were not so in Taily and Rank-S, these were difficult queries (low 'search all shards' search accuracy), and had nearly zero MAP@500

Table 2: Standard Deviation (SD) and Variance Coefficient (VC) of accuracy scores for RBR instances.

a) P@10

Query Set	CW09-B		CW09-A	
	SD	VC	SD	VC
2009	1.38×10^{-2}	2.71%	1.05×10^{-2}	2.95%
2010	1.16×10^{-2}	2.15%	9.73×10^{-3}	2.04%
2011	1.36×10^{-2}	3.53%	1.31×10^{-2}	3.04%
2012	5.39×10^{-3}	1.39%	9.73×10^{-3}	2.63%

b) MAP@500

Query Set	CW09-B		CW09-A	
	SD	VC	SD	VC
2009	3.56×10^{-3}	3.25%	3.54×10^{-3}	2.97%
2010	3.87×10^{-3}	2.24%	2.46×10^{-3}	1.35%
2011	1.10×10^{-2}	7.21%	9.47×10^{-3}	4.40%
2012	3.53×10^{-3}	2.41%	4.97×10^{-3}	2.91%

Table 3: Comparison of MAP@500 scores (CW09-A) for Rank-S and Taily instances.

Query Set	Mean		Variance Coefficient	
	Rank-S	Taily	Rank-S	Taily
2009	0.062	0.065	10.65%	10.98%
2010	0.090	0.087	3.66%	6.89%
2011	0.101	0.084	7.62%	15.67%
2012	0.097	0.085	8.23%	5.36%

in Rank-S and Taily. All easy queries with high variance in RBR also had high variance in Rank-S and Taily. The consistency across RBR, Rank-S and Taily suggests that errors from the partitioning stage are a major source of variance of selective search accuracy; however, most of that variation comes from a small number of queries.

We investigated why some partitions performed much better than others on the high variance queries. One might expect that 'good' partitions group relevant documents into fewer shards. However, in all of our partitions, relevant documents were distributed across a small number of shards. Typically the 3 most relevant shards contained more than 60% of the relevant documents, which is consistent with the standards of most prior federated search research. Furthermore, in this experiment, all ten instances retrieved 100% of the relevant documents for 4 of the 5 most variant queries. However, these queries had AP values ranging from values similar to exhaustive search to as much as ten times *better* than exhaustive search.

An examination of the instances with unusually high AP in the RBR experiment revealed that the relevant documents and the most likely false positives were in different shards. Thus, the combination of partitioning and resource selection 'filtered out' non-relevant documents that otherwise would have been ranked highly. Although this behavior might seem desirable, it occurred because the partitioning process incorrectly assigned relevant documents to shards that contained documents that were largely dissimilar to the relevant documents. This poor clustering made it nearly impossible for Rank-S and Taily to identify which shards contained relevant documents due to the overwhelming number of dissimilar documents in the shard. RBR, which *knows* the number of relevant documents in each shard, had no such problem.

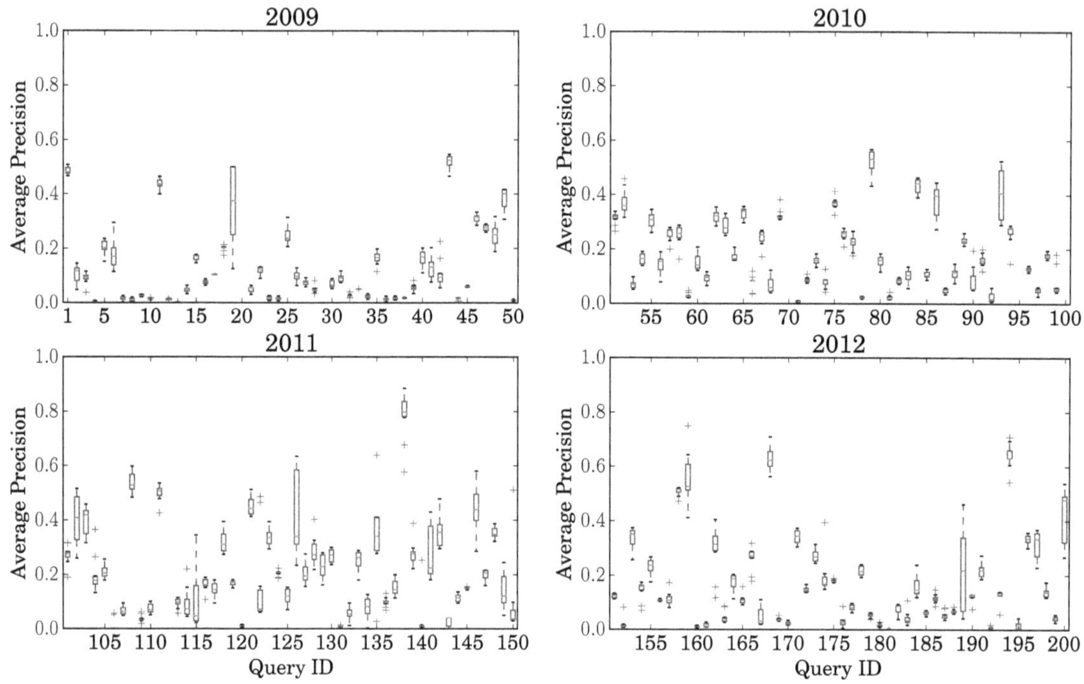

Figure 2: Query Average Precision of RBR instances. Each data point is a box and whisker plot with the edges of the boxes representing the upper and lower quantiles, the mid line the median, and the whiskers the 1.5 interquartile range. + are outliers.

Figure 2 also indicates that different query sets produced different levels of variability. The 2011 query set was notably more unstable than the others. Among the 24 queries with AP standard deviation higher than 0.05, 14 were from TREC 2011. We believe that this difference is due to the other three query sets using topics of medium-to-high frequency, while TREC 2011 used more obscure topics [2]. Our results indicate that the *type* of query has an impact on not only the average accuracy of a system, but also the variance of a system with random components. Topic-based partitioning may produce stable results for common topics, but may need improvement for queries about rare topics.

4. CONCLUSION

Understanding the variance of selective search effectiveness is critical for evaluating and improving selective search. This paper explores selective search variance and the effects of document collections, resource selection algorithms, and query characteristics. Partitioning and resource selection processes both introduce variance into search behavior, however in our experiments the effect on most queries was not large. Results were more stable at the top of the ranking, but variance at rank 500 was not unreasonable, especially for an architecture that avoids searching most of the index.

Rank-S and Taily produced nearly equal variance, which might be considered surprising given that Rank-S has one more random component than Taily.

Most of the variance observed in our per-query experiments was caused by a small number of queries – typically, rare queries. In some instances the partitioning process correctly grouped relevant documents together, but placed them in unrepresentative shards, which caused poor resource selection. This behavior may indicate the need for partitioning processes more sophisticated than simple k-means clustering.

5. ACKNOWLEDGMENTS

This research was supported by National Science Foundation (NSF) grant IIS-1302206 and Natural Sciences and Engineering Research Council of Canada (NSERC) Postgraduate Scholarship-Doctoral. Any opinions, findings, conclusions, and recommendations expressed in this paper are the authors' and do not necessarily reflect those of the sponsors.

6. REFERENCES

[1] R. Aly, T. Demeester, and D. Hiemstra. Taily: Shard selection using the tail of score distributions. In *Proceedings of SIGIR*, 2013.

[2] C. L. Clarke, N. Craswell, I. Soboroff, and E. M. Voorhees. Overview of the trec 2011 web track. In *Proceedings of TREC 2011*, 2011.

[3] G. K. Jayasinghe, W. Webber, M. Sanderson, L. S. Dharmasena, and J. S. Culpepper. Evaluating non-deterministic retrieval systems. In *Proceedings of SIGIR*, 2014.

[4] A. Kulkarni. *Efficient and Effective Large-scale Search*. PhD thesis, Carnegie Mellon University, 2013.

[5] A. Kulkarni, A. Tigelaar, J. Callan, and D. Hiemstra. Shard ranking and cutoff estimation for topically partitioned collections. In *Proceedings of CIKM*, 2012.

Comparing Approaches for Query Autocompletion

Giovanni Di Santo
giovi.disanto@gmail.com
Universitá degli studi dell'Aquila

Richard McCreadie, Craig Macdonald, and Iadh Ounis
{firstname.lastname}@glasgow.ac.uk
School of Computing Science
University of Glasgow
G12 8QQ, Glasgow, UK

ABSTRACT

Within a search engine, query auto-completion aims to predict the final query the user wants to enter as they type, with the aim of reducing query entry time and potentially preparing the search results in advance of query submission. There are a large number of approaches to automatically rank candidate queries for the purposes of auto-completion. However, no study exists that compares these approaches on a single dataset. Hence, in this paper, we present a comparison study between current approaches to rank candidate query completions for the user query as it is typed. Using a query-log and document corpus from a commercial medical search engine, we study the performance of 11 candidate query ranking approaches from the literature and analyze where they are effective. We show that the most effective approaches to query auto-completion are largely dependent on the number of characters that the user has typed so far, with the most effective approach differing for short and long prefixes. Moreover, we show that if personalized information is available about the searcher, this additional information can be used to more effectively rank query candidate completions, regardless of the prefix length.

Categories and Subject Descriptors: H.3.3 [Information Storage & Retrieval]: Information Search & Retrieval

Keywords: Query Completion, Information Retrieval

1. INTRODUCTION

Query auto-completion is a relatively recent functionality offered by search engines, which, given a prefix already typed by a user, tries to guess the final query the user is going to type. Using this functionality, the user does not need to type the whole query and in some cases the auto-completion suggestions may help the user formulate a more precise query. From an information retrieval perspective, this can be seen as a ranking task, where the aim is to rank all possible candidate (complete) queries given the current prefix typed by the user. The top ranked candidate queries will then be displayed as the user types. Figure 1 illustrates query auto-completion as implemented in a current search engine for the query 'information retrieval'.

SIGIR'15, August 09 - 13, 2015, Santiago, Chile.
© 2015 ACM. ISBN 978-1-4503-3621-5/15/08 ...$15.00.
DOI: http://dx.doi.org/10.1145/2766462.2767829 .

Figure 1: Illustration of query auto-completion for the query 'information retrieval'.

Importantly, query auto-completion is a challenging task. In particular, given only a few characters that can be quite ambiguous, there are potentially thousands of candidate queries that the user might type. To tackle this challenge, a variety of approaches have been proposed [1, 7, 8, 11]. Early works examined probability-based ranking, where queries are ranked by their occurrence probability within a background corpus [2]. Meanwhile, other studies have focused on leveraging evidence from query logs to rank the candidate queries. For instance, Bar-Yossef and Kraus [1] ranked the candidate queries by textual similarity to a user profile, while Shokouhi [8] leveraged user history and demographic features within a learning-to-rank model to rank the candidate queries. However, of important note is that these prior studies typically report performance using different proprietary datasets (e.g. for privacy reasons) and often do not share any common baselines. Hence, it is difficult to compare the wealth of approaches to query auto-completion to see which is the most effective, and, as a result, it is unclear what the state-of-the-art in query autocompletion is.

As a step toward tackling this knowledge gap, in this paper, we perform a comparison of 11 different approaches to rank query auto-completions, with the aim of determining those that are the most effective. In particular, using the same dataset comprised of medical articles and associated query/click logs from a commercial medical search engine, we perform a comparison of query auto-completion approaches taken from and inspired by the literature, covering both query-log independent approaches and personalized approaches that are primarily driven by query logs. From analysis of the results, we show that in general, approaches that personalize to the specific user outperform approaches that either do not use query-log evidence at all, or only consider past queries across multiple users in aggregate. Furthermore, we show that there is a dependence between the number of characters that the user has typed and the performance of the approaches tested - with the most effective approach changing based on the prefix length.

2. TASK DEFINITION

A query auto-completion engine takes as input a prefix p of length l typed by the user in the search engine box and a set of *candidate queries* Q_p to rank. A prefix p is a sequence of characters belonging to the query the user is about to submit. The candidate queries Q_p are a set of possible completions for the current prefix. These should be of high quality and represent the space of possible information needs that the user could have. The aim is to rank the candidate queries Q_p for a given prefix p, such that the query the user was typing appears within the top ranks.

Importantly, for the purposes of this paper, we assume that the set of candidate queries for each prefix are pre-provided. In this way, we can compare different query ranking strategies over the same set of candidate queries. We leave an examination of different approaches to generate these candidate queries to future work.

3. APPROACHES TO RANK CANDIDATE QUERIES

In this section, we summarize and formally define the 11 different candidate query ranking approaches that we compare in our subsequent experiments. In particular, we formalize each approach as a scoring function $score(q)$, where $q \in Q_p$. Note that we assume that we have access to a query-log containing past queries Q' and document clicks C' from which we can extract training evidence. We also naturally assume that we have access to the collection of documents D that the user is searching. Finally, for personalized approaches, we refer to all queries previously entered by the current user as the *user context.*

Most popular ranker (MP) is the ranking algorithm used as a *baseline* in the majority of the works present in the literature. Query candidates are ranked according to their past popularity, calculated as the query's frequency (cf) inside the query log. Usually, this frequency is normalized by the total sum of query frequencies. Notably, there are different variants of this approach. Shokouhi and Radinsky [9] replaced the query's actual frequency with a predicted frequency, while Strizhevskaya *et al.* [10] model the query frequencies using a time-series. We use the actual query frequency within the query-log.

$$MP(q) = \frac{cf(q)}{\sum_{i \in Q'} cf(i)} \quad (1)$$

Sentence occurrence ranker (SO) scores each query based upon the number of documents that match one or more of the query terms plus the number of documents that match all of the query terms. SO is inspired by [2].

$$SO(q) = \alpha \cdot |exactMatch(q, D)| + |termMatch(q, D)| \quad \alpha > 1 \quad (2)$$

Time ranker (TR) is a simple ranking algorithm that scores each candidate completion q by the time difference between the current time and the most recent past occurrence of it in the query log Q', thereby promoting queries that have been issued recently. LRD is the largest time difference between q and any query in Q'.

$$TR(q) = LRD - argmin_{q_i \in match(q,Q')} (date(q) - date(q_i)) \quad (3)$$

Most popular time ranker (MT) mixes *most popular ranker* and *time ranker* together, inspired by the *hybrid approach* in [1]. In our work, we set α to 0.7.

$$MT(q) = \alpha \cdot MP(q) + (1 - \alpha) \cdot TR(q) \quad (4)$$

Term occurrence ranker (TO) ranks candidate queries based on the background popularity of those candidate's terms. Term popularity is calculated as the mean of the frequency of the term inside the query log and the *TF-IDF* of the term within the corpus of documents being searched. The score for a candidate query is the mean of the scores for its terms.

$$TO(q) = \frac{\sum_{t \in q} \frac{(tfidf_{ql}(q) \cdot tfidf_c(q))}{2}}{|q|} \quad (5)$$

Near words (NW) takes into consideration the distance among the terms typed by the user in the candidate completions. It promotes completions where the query terms are next to one another. The *frequency difference (fd)* among the completions having the highest and lowest frequency in Q_p is calculated and divided by the number of terms present in the longest query, obtaining the *term difference (td)*. For each pair of user terms a value is assigned and summed to the overall score. That value is equal to the *fd* if one term directly follows the other and becomes lower as the distance increases. The *td* is subtracted from the *fd* for each term between the user terms pair. T_u in Equation (6) is defined as the set of terms typed by the user.

$$NW(q) = \frac{\sum_{(t_1,t_2) \in T_u} fd - td \cdot distance(t_1, t_2)}{|T_u|} \quad (6)$$

String similarity ranker (SS) scores a query based upon the similarity between that query and all previous queries issued by the user who submitted that query. The similarity measure used in this paper is the *Jaro Winkler edit distance* [13].

$$SS(q) = \frac{\sum_{q_i \in (Q')} JW(q, q_i)}{|Q'|} \quad (7)$$

WordNet similarity ranker (WR) uses *WordNet* [3] in order to capture semantic similarities between the query being ranked and the previous queries entered by the same user. The similarity is calculated for every pair of terms present in the completion being ranked and the user context. Mean similarity over the user's previous queries is used for scoring the completion. We use the Wu & Palmer [12] measure that calculates the relatedness of two terms by considering the depths of the two related synsets in the WordNet taxonomies.

$$WR(q) = \frac{\sum_{q_i \in (Q')} \sum_{(q_t, q_{it}) \in (q, q_i)} JW(q, q_i)}{|Q'|} \quad (8)$$

N-Gram similarity ranker (NR) scores a candidate query based upon the syntactic relation between it and the user context. In particular, we use the N-Gram similarity algorithm presented in [4]. We chose to use the *positional n-gram similarity* as the n-gram matching strategy.

$$NR(q) = \frac{\sum_{q_i \in (Q')} N - gramSim(q, q_i)}{|Q'|} \quad (9)$$

Kernel similarity ranker (KR) is based on the work presented in [5] and [6] that aims to estimate the similarity between two small strings by taking into account their semantic similarities. In particular, collection enrichment using the document corpus is applied to each candidate query and the user context. A candidate query is scored based upon the similarity between its expanded form and the expanded form of the user context (using the same kernel similarity measure as in [6]).

$$KK(q) = \frac{\sum_{q_u \in (C)} KernSim(q, q_u)}{|C|} \quad (10)$$

Clicked documents ranker (CR) models the user's interests as the content of documents previously clicked (D_c), where this set is represented by the terms present inside the document titles. The candidate query is represented in the same way, but considering all of the documents previously clicked for that candidate query in the query log (D_q) . The *cosine similarity* measure is used to score the candidate query representation by its similarity to the representation of the user's interests.

$$CR(q) = cosine(q_d, c_d) \quad q_d = \{t | t \in d_{title}, d \in D_q\}$$
$$c_d = \{t | t \in d_{title}, d \in D_c\} \quad (11)$$

The first three columns of Table 1 list the 11 approaches discussed above, highlighting whether each uses query-log information and/or the user context (e.g. queries previously entered by the user for personalization).

4. EXPERIMENTAL SETUP

Dataset: To evaluate query auto-completion, we use a sample of 1,417,880 unique queries issued by 37,806 different users between November 2010 to April 2013, provided by the *TRIPDatabase.com* medical search engine.[1] This dataset additionally contains 1,418,996 medical articles. Note that TRIP has basic in-built query suggestion based only on the corpus statistics, similar to SO approach.

Training/Testing Split: To facilitate experimentation, we divide the dataset into training and testing splits. In particular, all queries issued before April 2013 are used for training and extracting the user context information (past queries and clicks). For testing, we use a sub-set of the query sample, composed of 1405 queries by 968 users who had used TRIP for at least 3 months since March 2013 and had submitted at least one query during the month of April 2013.

Candidate Query Generation: To produce the candidate query set for a prefix, we use the query log from the TRIP medical search engine. Given a prefix, we first use a weighted compressed ternary search tree (WCT) that returns the first k most likely completions for the last term in the current prefix.[2] For instance, the prefix 'diab' might return 'diabetes' and 'diabetic' as term completions. We then use these terms to retrieve all queries, from the aforementioned search engine query-log, matching them and all the other terms already fully typed by the user.

Evaluation Metrics: As a ranking task, we evaluate query auto-completion performance in terms of the mean reciprocal rank (MRR) of the candidate query ranking produced by each approach over all of the test queries. To do so, we crop each query to the first k characters ($k \in \{2, 4, 6, 8$ and $10\}$), representing the user at different stages of typing that query. Only the final query that the user issued is considered the correct completion. We report MRR for all queries when concatenated to each of the target lengths.

5. QUERY AUTO-COMPLETION PERFORMANCES

In this section, we aim to answer the research question, 'RQ: which query auto-completion ranking approaches are the most effective?'. To do so, we compare the performance of each query auto-completion ranking approach described in Section 3. In particular, Table 1 reports the MRR performance of each of these approaches when ranking candidate query (completions) for prefixes of lengths {2,4,6,8,10}.

From Table 1, we observe the following. First, as a sanity check, comparing the 'sentence occurrence ranker' (SO) that does not use any query-log evidence to the other approaches that leverage query logs, we see that the query-log-based approaches all outperform the 'sentence occurrence ranker' (SO) for all prefix lengths. This confirms our expectations that approaches that rely on corpus statistics [2] are outperformed by query-log-based approaches [8].

Second, comparing the approaches that use query-log evidence without considering the current user in particular, we see that the most effective of these approaches when the user first starts typing (prefix length of 2), is the 'most popular ranker' (MP) approach. Recall that this approach simply chooses the most frequently occurring candidate query that starts with the target prefix. However, we also see that as the user continues to type (prefix lengths 4-10) the approach that combines query popularity with recency, i.e. the 'most popular time ranker (MT) becomes incrementally more effective. To explain this behaviour, it is first important to note that for all approaches, as the prefix length increases, the ranking performance of all approaches also increases. This is to be expected, since as the prefix becomes longer, there are less possible candidate queries that match the prefix. For a very short prefix, considering the candidate recency can be missleading, since there may be hundreds of candidate queries that were issued close to the current search time, but that are not likely to be good query candidates. Hence, the recency factor dilutes the more effective query frequency signal. However, as the candidate query set becomes smaller (due to a longer prefix length), the recency signal becomes more useful, as it down-weights candidate queries that have not been issued for months or years, and hence are not likely candidates.

Third, comparing the approaches that use the query-log evidence without considering the current user (MP,TR,MT, TO, and NW) to those approaches that additionally employ the query log to personalize to the current user (WR,NR, KR, CR and SS), we see that, in general, personalized approaches outperform unpersonalized approaches. For example, at prefix length 2, the approach that personalizes based on clicked documents ('clicked document ranker' (CR)) out-

[1]http://tripdatabase.com/

[2]Often the prefix will be only a single incomplete term, e.g. 'weig' but for longer prefixes it may be a second term that is incomplete, such as 'weight lo'.

Approaches			MRR				
Ranking	Query-log Evidence	Personalized	2	4	6	8	10
Sentence occurrence ranker (SO)	No	No	0.005▼	0.0456▼	0.0696▼	0.1003▼	0.1546▼
Most Popular ranker (MP)	Yes	No	0.0964	0.2146	0.2851	0.3248	0.3641
Time Ranker (TR)	Yes	No	0.0324▼	0.1236▼	0.1995▼	0.2707▼	0.3281▼
Most Popular Time ranker (MT)	Yes	No	0.0961	0.2249▲	0.3112▲	0.3684▲	0.4153▲
Terms occurrence ranker (TO)	Yes	No	0.0021▼	0.0326▼	0.0773▼	0.1163▼	0.1617▼
Near Words Ranker (NW)	Yes	No	0.0611▼	0.1576▼	0.2347▼	0.2972▼	0.3611
String Similarity Ranker (SS)	No	Yes	0.0137▼	0.0711▼	0.1628▼	0.1149▼	0.2069▼
WordNet Similarity Ranker (WR)	Yes	Yes	0.089▼	0.0302▼	0.0711▼	0.0908▼	0.1055▼
N-Gram Similarity Ranker (NR)	Yes	Yes	0.0837	0.2927▲	**0.3693▲**	**0.4207▲**	**0.4602▲**
Kernel Similarity Ranker (KR)	Yes	Yes	0.907	0.2876▲	0.3356▲	0.3923▲	0.4121▲
Clicked Documents Ranker (CR)	Yes	Yes	**0.1442▲**	**0.2952▲**	0.3462▲	0.3938▲	0.4183▲

Table 1: Query auto-completion performance over the queries issued during the month of April '13 in our dataset, using the 11 presented ranking approaches. Statistically significant improvements/reductions in performance over the Most Popular ranker (MP) ($p<0.05$ paired t-test) are denoted ▲ and ▼, respectively.

performs the query frequency-based ranker discussed earlier ('most popular ranker' (MP)) by a large and statistically significant margin (0.0964 MAP to 0.1442 MAP). This indicates that personalization to each individual user is preferable.[3] Next, comparing approaches within the class of personalized approaches, we see that for small prefix lengths (2-4) ranking the candidate queries via similarity to previously clicked documents by the user ('clicked documents ranker' (CR)) is the most effective. However, as the prefix length increases (6-10), the n-gram similarity approach that compares against the past queries issued by the user ('n-gram similarity ranker' (NR)) becomes more effective. These results indicate that for short prefix lengths, where a user has likely issued multiple queries that are valid candidates previously, using past queries is less effective as it is difficult to break ties between those candidates. On the other hand, as the prefix length increases, there is often only one previous candidate query that the user has entered that matches, which is likely to be the correct candidate (e.g. if the user is re-finding).

To answer our research question RQ, on our dataset there is no single approach that illustrates a top performance for all query lengths. Rather, the correct candidate query ranking approach is dependent on how many characters the user has typed so far. For short prefix lengths, simple past query frequency (MP ranker) is a good feature if no personalization information is available, while ranking based on the content of previously clicked documents is effective otherwise (CR ranker). For longer prefix lengths, mixing query candidate recency with its past usage frequency can result in performance gains (MT ranker) in the unpersonalized setting. Meanwhile. if personalized information is available to the search system, then ranking query suggestions by n-gram similarity to the users past queries is more effective (NR ranker).

6. CONCLUSIONS

In this paper, we presented a comparison study of current approaches to rank candidate query completions for the user query as they type. Using a query-log and document corpus from the *TRIP* medical search engine, we evaluated the performance of 11 candidate query ranking approaches from the literature and analysed where they are effective. From this analysis, we conclude that the most effective approach to query auto-completion is largely dependent on the number of characters that the user has typed so far and that personalized information can be used to more effectively rank the query candidate completions. This indicates selective approaches that apply different query-autocompletion models depending on the prefix length and user context are a promising direction for future work.

[3]Note that this information may not be available if users are searching anonymously however.

7. ACKNOWLEDGEMENT

We thank Jon Brassey from TRIPDatabase.com for providing the data used in this research.

8. REFERENCES

[1] Z. Bar-Yossef and N. Kraus. Context-sensitive query auto-completion. In *Proc. of WWW*, 2011.
[2] S. Bhatia, D. Majumdar, and P. Mitra. Query suggestions in the absence of query logs. In *Proc. of SIGIR*, 2011.
[3] C. Fellbaum. Wordnet and wordnets. Encyclopedia of Language and Linguistics, 2005.
[4] G. Kondrak. N-gram similarity and distance. In *Proc. of SPIRE*, 2005.
[5] M. Sahami and T. D. Heilman. Mining the web to determine similarity between words, objects, and communities. In *Proc. of FLAIRS*, 2006.
[6] M. Sahami and T. D Heilman. A web-based kernel function for measuring the similarity of short text snippets. In *Proc. of WWW*, 2006.
[7] C. Sengstock and M. Gertz. Conquer: A system for efficient context-aware query suggestions. In *Proc. of WWW*, 2011.
[8] M. Shokouhi. Learning to personalize query auto-completion. In *Proc. of SIGIR*, 2013.
[9] M. Shokouhi and K. Radinsky. Time-sensitive query auto-completion. In *Proc. of SIGIR*, 2012.
[10] A. Strizhevskaya, A. Baytin, I. Galinskaya, and P. Serdyukov. Actualization of query suggestions using query logs. In *Proc. of WWW*, 2012.
[11] S. Whiting and J. M Jose. Recent and robust query auto-completion. In *Proc. of WWW*, 2014.
[12] Z. Wu and M. Palmer. Verbs semantics and lexical selection. In *Proc. of ACL*, 1994.
[13] Winkler, William E String Comparator Metrics and Enhanced Decision Rules in the Fellegi-Sunter Model of Record Linkage, 1990.

Sign-Aware Periodicity Metrics of User Engagement for Online Search Quality Evaluation

Alexey Drutsa
Yandex
Moscow, Russia
adrutsa@yandex.ru

ABSTRACT

Modern Internet companies improve evaluation criteria of their data-driven decision-making that is based on online controlled experiments (also known as A/B tests). The amplitude metrics of user engagement are known to be well sensitive to service changes, but they could not be used to determine, whether the treatment effect is positive or negative. We propose to overcome this sign-agnostic issue by paying attention to the phase of the corresponding DFT sine wave. We refine the amplitude metrics of the first frequency by the phase ones and formalize our intuition in several novel overall evaluation criteria. These criteria are then verified over A/B experiments on real users of Yandex. We find that our approach holds the sensitivity level of the amplitudes and makes their changes sign-aware w.r.t. the treatment effect.

Categories and Subject Descriptions: H.1.2 [User/Machine Systems]: Human information processing; H.5.2 [User interface]: Evaluation/methodology

General Terms: Measurement, Experimentation

Keywords: User engagement; online controlled experiment; periodicity; DFT; sign-aware metric; A/B test

1. INTRODUCTION

Online controlled experiments, or A/B testing, have become the state-of-the-art technique of improving web services based on data-driven decisions [10, 7]. An A/B test compares two variants of a service[1] at a time by exposing them to two user groups and by measuring the difference between them in terms of a key metric (e.g., the revenue, the number of visits, etc.), also known as an overall evaluation criterion [8]. Many existing studies were devoted to an invention of new metrics [5, 9, 3] or to improvements of existing ones [2, 4] in order to make them more consistent with the long-term goals of the company [1, 6, 7] and to make their changes more detectable. The ability of the metric to detect the statistically significant difference when the treatment effect exists is referred to as the *sensitivity*.

User engagement metrics (e.g., the number of sessions per user [9], the absence time [5], etc.) are considered to be the best ones and are popular in the A/B testing practice of many companies, because user engagement reflects how often a user solves her needs (e.g., to search for something) by means of the considered service (e.g., a search engine) [6, 7]. Hence, on the one hand, these metrics are measurable in the short-term experiment period, and, on the other hand, they are predictive of long-term goals of the company [6, 7].

Recently, several metrics of user engagement periodicity were developed and were used in A/B experiments [3]. These metrics are *the amplitudes* of the discrete Fourier transform (DFT) of daily time series of several standard user engagement metrics (e.g., the daily number of sessions). On the one hand, the amplitude metrics were found to be more sensitive than the state-of-the-art ones, i.e., the average values of the time series (e.g., the number of sessions per day). However, on the other hand, the amplitudes (as considered in [3]) could not be used to determine, whether the treatment effect is positive or negative: if one of these metrics changes (increases or decreases) significantly, it just tells us that a user changes her behavior in response to the treatment variant with no insight on whether it is positive or negative for the user or for the service. Thus, these metrics are *sign-agnostic* with respect to an evaluated treatment effect.

In our work, we develop a novel approach, which improves several amplitude metrics by taking into account *the phases* of the DFT. We find that the DFT components with the first frequency detect signals of the UE measure trend along the experiment time period. Hence, these metrics could be profitable for delayed treatment effects (which are often caused by primacy and novelty effects [8, 6]). Our approach provides an experimenter with several intuitively clear guidelines (referred to as *symptoms*), that allow him to determine whether the treatment effect is positive or negative, when he or she observes changes in the periodicity components of a user engagement metric. Thus, *we overcome the sign-agnostic issue of the amplitudes.*

We reinforce our theoretical results by applying the proposed approach to evaluation of changes in a search engine. We considered 55 real large-scale online experiments (32 A/B tests and 23 A/A tests) run at Yandex, one of the popular search engines. We find that, on the one hand, *the novel approach is more sensitive* than the state-of-the-art user engagement metrics (it allows us to detect the treatment ef-

[1] e.g., a current version of the service (the control variant) and a new one (the treatment variant)

SIGIR'15, August 09 - 13, 2015, Santiago, Chile.
© 2015 ACM. ISBN 978-1-4503-3621-5/15/08 ...$15.00.
DOI: http://dx.doi.org/10.1145/2766462.2767814.

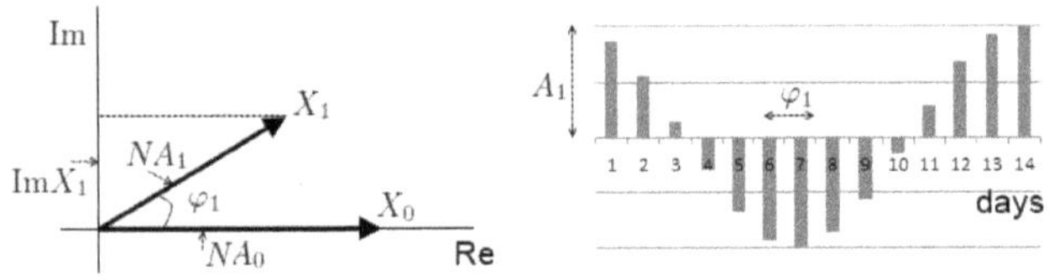

Figure 1: The amplitude A_1, the phase φ_1, and the sine wave $\mathbf{f}^1$.

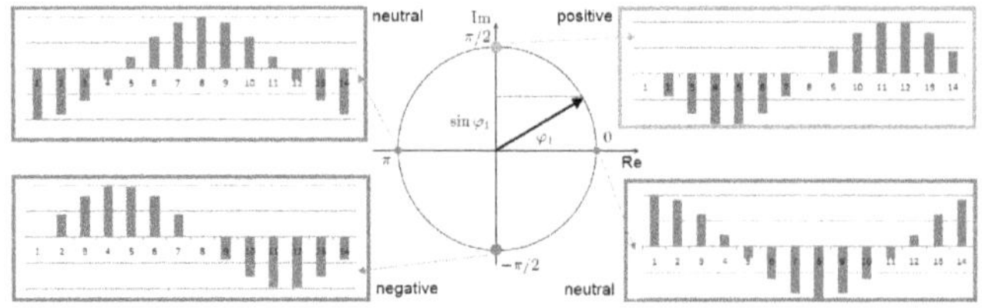

Figure 2: A positive, a negative, and neutral trends of the sine wave $\mathbf{f}^1$ w.r.t. the phase φ_1.

fect in more experiments). On the other hand, *the novel approach is sign-aware* (it allows us to understand, whether the detected treatment effect is positive or negative), while the classic amplitude metrics in [3] are sign-agnostic.

2. PERIODICITY METRICS

We briefly review the key points of the periodicity metrics, that were studied in [3]. Let us consider any user engagement (UE) measure calculated for an individual user, e.g., the number of sessions [9, 3]. Let $\mathbf{x} = (x_0, x_1, .., x_{N-1})$ be a daily time series of N numbers, that represent this UE measure calculated for N consecutive days (e.g., the daily number of sessions). Then, we apply the *discrete Fourier transform* (the *DFT*) to $\mathbf{x}$ and obtain the sequence of its coordinates in the harmonic basis $\{\mathbf{f}^k\}_{k=0}^{N-1}$:

$$X_k = \sum_{n=0}^{N-1} x_n e^{-\mathrm{i}\omega_k n}, \quad \omega_k = \frac{2\pi k}{N}, \quad k \in \mathbb{Z}_N,$$

where $\mathbf{f}^k = (e^{\mathrm{i}\omega_k n}/N)_{n\in\mathbb{Z}_N}$ is the sine wave (harmonic) with the frequency ω_k. From the polar form[2] of each complex number $X_k = |X_k|e^{\mathrm{i}\varphi_k}$, the *amplitude* $A_k = |X_k|/N$ and the *phase* φ_k are obtained, $k \in \mathbb{Z}_N$. The amplitude A_k represents *the magnitude* of the sine wave $\mathbf{f}^k$ with the frequency ω_k, presented in the series $\mathbf{x}$, whereas the phase φ_k represents how this wave is *shifted* (see Fig.1).

The amplitudes A_k and the normalized ones $A_k/A_0, k \in \mathbb{Z}_N$, are found to be considerably more sensitive to different changes in a search engine than the state-of-the-art baseline metric A_0[3]. However, these metrics do not determine the sign of the treatment effect: whether the evaluated service change is negative or positive for users (i.e., these metrics are *sign-agnostic*). In this study, we will show how several amplitudes could be refined in order to obtain *sign-aware* evaluation criteria, that will also be of high sensitivity.

3. CHANGE IN ENGAGEMENT TRENDS

In A/B testing practice, we are often faced with primacy and novelty effects [8, 6], that cause a delay in the treatment effect, which could not be easily detected by the state-of-the-art metrics. We supposed that the metrics aimed to detect changes in the trend of UE measures may be helpful in such and other cases. For instance, if a user is enjoyed with the treatment version, then the number of sessions should growth during the experiment. Otherwise, if the treatment harms user engagement, the number of sessions should decrease to the end of the period. Such UE measure changes along the whole experiment period should leave traces in the first frequency[4] (i.e., ω_1) of the DFT of the UE measure time series. Therefore, if the treatment effect stands out sharply in the UE trend, then the sine wave with this frequency should change. Moreover, the shift of this sine wave can help to determine the sign of the treatment effect (whether it is positive or negative).

From here on in this paper we will consider only the first amplitude A_1 and its normalized version A_1/A_0. In order to understand the meaning of a change in such amplitude, let us consider it together with the corresponding phase φ_1 of the sine wave $\mathbf{f}^1$ with the frequency ω_1. Let us consider the following cases (see Fig.2):

(a) if $\varphi_1 \approx \pi/2$ (or $\sin\varphi_1 \approx 1$), then the sine wave $\mathbf{f}^1$ oscillates in $\mathbf{x}$ with a positive trend;

(b) if $\varphi_1 \approx -\pi/2$ (or $\sin\varphi_1 \approx -1$), then the sine wave $\mathbf{f}^1$ oscillates in $\mathbf{x}$ with a negative trend;

(c) if $\varphi_1 \approx 0$ or π (or $\sin\varphi_1 \approx 0$), then the sine wave $\mathbf{f}^1$ oscillates in $\mathbf{x}$ with a neutral trend.

From these cases, we see that, for instance, an increase of the amplitude A_1 may led to both negative, and positive consequences. It depends on how the sine wave is shifted: if $\sin\varphi_1 < 0$, then the magnitude of the sine wave with a negative trend increases; on the contrary, if $\sin\varphi_1 > 0$, then the magnitude of the sine wave with a positive trend increases. Furthermore, even through the amplitude A_1 does not change at all, a change in the phase φ_1 could shift the type of the sine wave trend: make it more or less negative or positive. Therefore, we conclude that, *in order to understand the positiveness or negativeness of changes in the amplitudes A_1 and A_1/A_0 of the sine wave $\mathbf{f}^1$, we should pay attention to its phase φ_1.*

Before presenting in detail our evaluation criteria, let us dwell on two points. First, note that the equality $\mathrm{Im}X_1 = NA_1 \sin\varphi_1$ holds (see Fig.1). Therefore, from here on in this paper we will study the novel[5] metric $\mathrm{Im}X_1$ and its normalized version $\mathrm{Im}X_1/A_0$. Second, the straightforward approach to determine the trend of the N-day time series $\mathbf{x}$ is just a comparison of the first half of the series with the second one. Therefore, we will consider the difference D between the average value of the time series $\mathbf{x}$ over the last $[N/2]$ days $\mathrm{avg}_2\mathbf{x}$ and the one over the first $[N/2]$ days $\mathrm{avg}_1\mathbf{x}$ (i.e., $D = \mathrm{avg}_2\mathbf{x} - \mathrm{avg}_1\mathbf{x}$) as our baseline metric (besides the state-of-the-art metric A_0).

Growth and fall symptoms. We refer to a case in an A/B test, when the trend of a considered UE measure becomes more positive (or less negative), as *a growth symptom,* while we refer to a case, when the trend becomes more negative (or less positive), as *a fall symptom.* Let $\mathrm{avg}_A M$ and $\mathrm{avg}_B M$ be the average values of the metric M over the users, exposed to the variant A and B, respectively, and $\Delta M = \mathrm{avg}_B M - \mathrm{avg}_A M$ be the difference between the variants. Then, we summarize all symptoms under our study

[2] i.e., $z = re^{\mathrm{i}\varphi} = r\cos\varphi + r\sin\varphi\mathbf{i}$

[3] A_0 is the average value of the source time series $\mathbf{x}$ of the UE measure (e.g., the average number of sessions per day).

[4] The other frequencies (i.e., $\omega_k, k > 1$) are responsible for more frequent changes (e.g., the week periodicity, etc.).

[5] The authors of [3] considered only the amplitudes A_k and A_k/A_0, $k \in \mathbb{Z}_N$, as evaluation metrics.

Table 1: **The baseline (BASE) and the novel (DFT) growth and fall symptoms.**

	Growth symptoms				Fall symptoms			
Baseline (BASE):	$\mathbf{G_0}$	$\Delta D > 0$	$\mathbf{G_0^n}$	$\Delta D/A_0 > 0$	$\mathbf{F_0}$	$\Delta D < 0$	$\mathbf{F_0^n}$	$\Delta D/A_0 < 0$
Novel (DFT):	$\mathbf{G_1}$	$\Delta \mathrm{Im} X_1 > 0$ $\Delta A_1 = 0$	$\mathbf{G_1^n}$	$\Delta \mathrm{Im} X_1/A_0 > 0$ $\Delta A_1/A_0 = 0$	$\mathbf{F_1}$	$\Delta \mathrm{Im} X_1 < 0$ $\Delta A_1 = 0$	$\mathbf{F_1^n}$	$\Delta \mathrm{Im} X_1/A_0 < 0$ $\Delta A_1/A_0 = 0$
	$\mathbf{G_2}$	$\Delta\varphi_1 = 0$ $\mathrm{avg}_A \mathrm{Im} X_1 > 0$ $\Delta A_1 > 0$	$\mathbf{G_2^n}$	$\Delta\varphi_1 = 0$ $\mathrm{avg}_A \mathrm{Im} X_1/A_0 > 0$ $\Delta A_1/A_0 > 0$	$\mathbf{F_2}$	$\Delta\varphi_1 = 0$ $\mathrm{avg}_A \mathrm{Im} X_1 > 0$ $\Delta A_1 < 0$	$\mathbf{F_2^n}$	$\Delta\varphi_1 = 0$ $\mathrm{avg}_A \mathrm{Im} X_1/A_0 > 0$ $\Delta A_1/A_0 < 0$
	$\mathbf{G_3}$	$\Delta\varphi_1 = 0$ $\mathrm{avg}_A \mathrm{Im} X_1 < 0$ $\Delta A_1 < 0$	$\mathbf{G_3^n}$	$\Delta\varphi_1 = 0$ $\mathrm{avg}_A \mathrm{Im} X_1/A_0 < 0$ $\Delta A_1/A_0 < 0$	$\mathbf{F_3}$	$\Delta\varphi_1 = 0$ $\mathrm{avg}_A \mathrm{Im} X_1 < 0$ $\Delta A_1 > 0$	$\mathbf{F_3^n}$	$\Delta\varphi_1 = 0$ $\mathrm{avg}_A \mathrm{Im} X_1/A_0 < 0$ $\Delta A_1/A_0 > 0$

Table 2: **The studied user engagement measures.**

S	the number of sessions	PT	the presence time
Q	the number of queries	CpQ	the number of clicks per query
C	the number of clicks	ATpS	the absence time per session

in Table 1 (where all equalities and inequalities are treated as statistically significant). The growth (fall) symptoms are denoted by the letter **G** (**F**). The superscript n denotes the symptoms based on the normalized versions of the metrics.

We will describe only the growth non-normalized symptoms (all other cases are similar). The baseline symptom $\mathbf{G_0}$ is simple: the condition $\Delta D > 0$ means that the average value over the second part of the time period tends to growth w.r.t. the one over the first part. The novel DFT symptom $\mathbf{G_1}$: the condition $\Delta A_1 = 0$ means that the amplitude does not change, hence, the condition $\Delta \mathrm{Im} X_1 > 0$ infers that the phase φ_1 changes in the direction of $\pi/2$ (see Fig. 2), i.e., the sine wave shift changes in the positive direction. The symptom $\mathbf{G_2}$: the condition $\Delta\varphi_1 = 0$ means that the shift of the sine wave $\mathbf{f}^1$ does not change, the condition $\mathrm{avg}_A \mathrm{Im} X_1 > 0$ means that this shift is positive relating to the trend of $\mathbf{x}$, and $\Delta A_1 > 0$ means that the magnitude of this sine wave increases. The intuition of the symptom $\mathbf{G_3}$ is similar.

Note, that the sign of a symptom (growth or fall) is *the sign of a change in the trend* of the UE measure during an A/B test. Therefore, it should not be confused with *the sign of the treatment effect* (positiveness or negativeness). The latter one depends on the UE measure under consideration: whether its increase is preferable or not. For instance, the increase of the number of sessions is a positive effect, but increase in the absence time [5] is negative effect. Thus, the sign of the symptom ought to be properly translated into *the treatment effect sign* for each UE measure individually.

4. EXPERIMENTS

Experimental setup. In our paper, we consider 32 A/B and 23 A/A experiments conducted on *real users* of Yandex in order to validate our approach. Each experiment lasted *two weeks* ($N = 14$), the user samples used in the A/B tests were all uniformly randomly selected, and the control and the treatment groups were almost of the same sizes (at least, hundreds of thousands of users). Each A/B experiment compared a production version of the search engine with its *noticeable deterioration* or its *clear improvement*. We apply a commonly used two-sample t-test with the threshold $p_{\mathrm{val}} = 0.05$ for the p-value (as in [2, 9, 3]). We study the 6 main user engagement measures (Table 2) with the same definitions as in [9, 3, 4].

A/A tests. First of all, 23 control experiments (i.e., A/A tests) were conducted in order to check correctness of the experimentation [8, 1]. An A/A test, which compares the same versions of the service, should be failed about 5% of the time for our p-value threshold 0.05 [8, 1]. The number of failed A/A tests for each metric and each UE measure is reported in Table 3. We found that, first, the results for the metrics A_0, A_1, A_1/A_0, $\mathrm{Im}X_1$, and $\mathrm{Im}X_1/A_0$ are acceptable (the two latter ones have the borderline number of failed A/A tests). Second, the metrics D and D/A_0 (which correspond to the baseline symptoms) failed an unacceptable number of A/A tests for the vast majority of the UE measures.

Table 3: **The number of failed A/A tests (out of 23).**

Metric	A_0	D	D/A_0	A_1	A_1/A_0	$\mathrm{Im}X_1$	$\mathrm{Im}X_1/A_0$
S	0	1	2	1	1	2	2
Q	0	3	2	0	0	1	2
C	1	2	1	1	0	1	1
PT	1	2	3	1	2	2	2
CpQ	1	1	1	1	0	1	2
ATpS	0	2	2	1	1	1	1

Table 4: **The number of A/B tests (out of 32) with detected treatment effect (+ the number of those of them, where it is not detected by A_0).**

Metric	A_0	D	D/A_0	A_1	A_1/A_0	$\mathrm{Im}X_1$	$\mathrm{Im}X_1/A_0$
S	2	0 (+0)	1 (+1)	**3** (+2)	**3** (+2)	0 (+0)	1 (+1)
Q	1	2 (+2)	1 (+1)	**3** (+2)	**3** (+3)	1 (+1)	1 (+1)
C	8	2 (+1)	1 (+1)	**11** (+3)	2 (+1)	2 (+1)	1 (+1)
PT	**4**	1 (+1)	2 (+1)	**4** (+1)	1 (+1)	0 (+0)	2 (+1)
CpQ	**15**	1 (+1)	1 (+0)	12 (+1)	2 (+1)	1 (+1)	1 (+0)
ATpS	**4**	0 (+0)	0 (+0)	2 (+1)	3 (+2)	2 (+1)	0 (+0)

A/B tests. Table 4 summarizes the number of A/B experiments (out of 32) whose treatment effect is detected (i.e., $p_{\mathrm{val}} < 0.05$) by each metric and each UE measure (the best result in each row is highlighted in boldface). First, the measures C and CpQ demonstrate the highest sensitivity among all measures. Second, we see that the amplitude A_1 and sometimes the amplitude A_1/A_0 outperform the baseline metric A_0 by the number of A/B tests with detected treatment effect (i.e., they are more sensitive). Thus, we reproduce the findings of the study [3]. Moreover, we see that, in almost all cases of the UE measures, the metrics A_1 and A_1/A_0 detect the treatment effect in those A/B tests, where it is not detected by the baseline metric A_0 (see the values in brackets in Table 4). Unfortunately, it could be noted that the novel metrics $\mathrm{Im}X_1$ and $\mathrm{Im}X_1/A_0$ are worse than both the amplitudes A_1, A_1/A_0 and the average one A_0. Thus, these novel metrics do not improve noticeably the sensitivity, but the main benefit from them will be seen further in detection of the growth/fall symptoms.

Detected symptoms: examples. We start our study from consideration of two A/B experiments as examples. For these A/B tests, the differences of all studied metrics, as well

Table 5: Examples of A/B tests with detected symptoms (significant differences ($p_{\text{val}} < 0.05$) are highlighted).

#	UE meas.	ΔA_0	ΔD	ΔA_1	$\Delta \text{Im} X_1$	$\text{avg}_A \text{Im} X_1$	$\Delta D/A_0$	$\Delta A_1/A_0$	$\Delta \text{Im} X_1/A_0$	$\text{avg}_A \text{Im} X_1/A_0$	$\Delta \varphi_1$	Symptoms
1	CpQ	**0.0032**	−0.0009	**0.0004**	−0.0034	**−0.0119**	**−0.0039**	0.0009	**−0.0014**	**0.0055**	−0.003	$\mathbf{F_3}$ $\mathbf{F^n_0}$ $\mathbf{F^n_1}$
	ATpS	**1437**	23.3	−7.78	**144.37**	**−503.38**	0.0004	−0.0001	0.0002	**−0.0005**	**0.005**	$\mathbf{G_1}$
2	S	0.0493	0.0012	0.0001	0.0008	−0.0016	0.0057	**−0.0024**	0.0025	**0.0033**	−0.008	$\mathbf{F^n_2}$
	CpQ	−0.0012	0.0005	$3 \cdot 10^{-5}$	−0.0039	0.0085	0.0068	**−0.003**	0.0026	**0.0042**	−0.017	$\mathbf{F^n_2}$

Table 6: The number of growth and fall symptoms found in A/B tests (out of 32) for each UE measure and the number of A/B tests with detected treatment effect by symptoms from BASE, DFT, or ALL sets.

UE measure	$\mathbf{G_0}$	$\mathbf{G_1}$	$\mathbf{G_2}$	$\mathbf{G_3}$	$\mathbf{G^n_0}$	$\mathbf{G^n_1}$	$\mathbf{G^n_2}$	$\mathbf{G^n_3}$	$\mathbf{F_0}$	$\mathbf{F_1}$	$\mathbf{F_2}$	$\mathbf{F_3}$	$\mathbf{F^n_0}$	$\mathbf{F^n_1}$	$\mathbf{F^n_2}$	$\mathbf{F^n_3}$	# of A/B tests with BASE	DFT	ALL
S	0	0	0	0	1	1	1	0	0	0	0	**2**	0	0	1	0	1	**5**	5
Q	1	0	0	1	1	1	1	0	1	1	**2**	0	0	0	1	0	3	**7**	8
C	1	0	2	**3**	0	0	0	0	1	0	1	0	1	1	2	0	3	**9**	11
PT	1	0	0	1	1	1	0	0	0	0	1	**2**	1	1	1	0	3	**6**	7
CpQ	0	0	3	2	0	0	0	0	1	1	2	**5**	1	1	2	0	2	**14**	14
ATpS	0	1	1	1	0	0	1	1	0	1	0	0	0	0	1	0	0	**5**	5

as the average values of the metrics $\text{Im}X_1$ and $\text{Im}X_1/A_0$ over the control group A are presented in Table 5.

The first A/B test evaluates a treatment, which is an artificial deterioration of the ranking algorithm of the search engine. We consider this experiment regarding the clicks per query measure CpQ and the absence time measure ATpS. We see that, first, the state-of-the-art metric A_0 detects a significant increase of ATpS and CpQ for an average user (expected effects for this experiment). Second, for the measure CpQ, a statistically significant difference Δ is observed for several metrics: the baseline metric D/A_0, the amplitude A_1, and the novel Fourier coefficient $\text{Im}X_1/A_0$. These differences and the statistically significant positiveness of $\text{avg}_A\text{Im}X_1$ yields to a detection of three fall symptoms: $\mathbf{F_3}$, $\mathbf{F^n_0}$, and $\mathbf{F^n_1}$ (according to Table 1). Therefore, we conclude that the negative trend of the number of clicks per query per day stands out more sharply for an average user of the treatment variant B than of the control one. In this experiment, the novel growth symptom $\mathbf{G_1}$ is also observed for ATpS.

The second A/B test evaluates a deterioration of the user interface. The treatment effect of this experiment is not detected by the state-of-the-art metric A_0 both for the number of sessions measure S and for the clicks per query measure CpQ (their differences are not statistically significant). However, the amplitude A_1/A_0 detects (i.e., $p_{\text{val}} < 0.05$) the treatment effect in the both measures. The statistically significant positiveness of $\text{avg}_A\text{Im}X_1/A_0$ helps us to conclude that we observe the fall symptom $\mathbf{F^n_2}$ twice: both the trend of S, and the trend of CpQ are more negative in the treatment variant B than in the control one. Thus, we demonstrated how *the novel metrics helped us to understand the sign of the observed change in the amplitudes, even though the state-of-the-art metrics do not detect any treatment effect.*

Detected symptoms: overall. Finally, Table 6 summarizes the number of detected symptoms overall 32 A/B experiments. The last three columns of this table report the number of A/B tests, whose treatment effects were detected by one of the baseline symptoms (i.e., $\mathbf{G_0}$, $\mathbf{G^n_0}$, $\mathbf{F_0}$, or $\mathbf{F^n_0}$: the col. "BASE"), by one of the DFT symptoms (i.e., $\mathbf{G_k}$, $\mathbf{G^n_k}$, $\mathbf{F_k}$, or $\mathbf{F^n_k}$, $k = 1, 2, 3$: the col. "DFT"), or by any symptom (the col. "ALL"), respectively. We conclude that, first, *the novel symptoms allow us to detect noticeably more changes in the UE measure trends than the baseline symptoms*, i.e. they are more sensitive. Second, being based on the amplitudes A_1 and A_1/A_0, *the novel symptoms are more sensitive than the state-of-the-art metric A_0 (see Table 4), and, on the contrary to the single A_1 or A_1/A_0 usage, could explain whether the treatment effect is positive or negative.*

5. CONCLUSIONS AND FUTURE WORK

In this paper, we considered the problem of amplitude metrics that are well sensitive, but are not *sign-aware* w.r.t. an evaluated treatment effect. Since the DFT sine wave with the first frequency carries signals of the UE measure trend along the experiment time period, we found out that its phase could shed light on the correct understanding of changes of its amplitudes. We combined the amplitude metrics with the phase ones and formalized our intuition in several novel overall evaluation criteria (consisting of growth and fall symptoms of the UE measure trend). We verified our approach over 55 large-scale A/B experiments on real users of Yandex, one of the popular search engines. We found that, on the one hand, the most novel criteria outperformed the baseline and state-of-the-art metrics in terms of sensitivity. On the other hand, our approach refined the single amplitude metrics by making them sign-aware w.r.t. the treatment effect. As future work we can study the sign-awareness of the amplitudes with other frequencies.

6. REFERENCES

[1] T. Crook, B. Frasca, R. Kohavi, and R. Longbotham. Seven pitfalls to avoid when running controlled experiments on the web. In *KDD'2009*, pages 1105–1114. ACM, 2009.

[2] A. Deng, Y. Xu, R. Kohavi, and T. Walker. Improving the sensitivity of online controlled experiments by utilizing pre-experiment data. In *WSDM'2013*, pages 123–132. ACM, 2013.

[3] A. Drutsa, G. Gusev, and P. Serdyukov. Engagement periodicity in search engine usage: Analysis and its application to search quality evaluation. In *WSDM'2015*, pages 27–36, 2015.

[4] A. Drutsa, G. Gusev, and P. Serdyukov. Future user engagement prediction and its application to improve the sensitivity of online experiments. In *WWW'2015*, 2015.

[5] G. Dupret and M. Lalmas. Absence time and user engagement: evaluating ranking functions. In *WSDM'2013*, pages 173–182, 2013.

[6] R. Kohavi, A. Deng, B. Frasca, R. Longbotham, T. Walker, and Y. Xu. Trustworthy online controlled experiments: Five puzzling outcomes explained. In *KDD'2012*, pages 786–794. ACM, 2012.

[7] R. Kohavi, A. Deng, R. Longbotham, and Y. Xu. Seven rules of thumb for web site experimenters. In *KDD'2014*, 2014.

[8] R. Kohavi, R. Longbotham, D. Sommerfield, and R. M. Henne. Controlled experiments on the web: survey and practical guide. *Data Mining and Knowledge Discovery*, 18(1):140–181, 2009.

[9] Y. Song, X. Shi, and X. Fu. Evaluating and predicting user engagement change with degraded search relevance. In *WWW'2013*, pages 1213–1224, 2013.

[10] D. Tang, A. Agarwal, D. O'Brien, and M. Meyer. Overlapping experiment infrastructure: More, better, faster experimentation. In *KDD'2010*, pages 17–26. ACM, 2010.

Modelling Term Dependence with Copulas

Carsten Eickhoff
Dept. of Computer Science
ETH Zurich, Switzerland
ecarsten@inf.ethz.ch

Arjen P. de Vries
CWI Amsterdam
Amsterdam, The Netherlands
arjen@acm.org

Thomas Hofmann
Dept. of Computer Science
ETH Zurich, Switzerland
thomas.hofmann@inf.ethz.ch

ABSTRACT

Many generative language and relevance models assume conditional independence between the likelihood of observing individual terms. This assumption is obviously naïve, but also hard to replace or relax. There are only very few term pairs that actually show significant conditional dependencies while the vast majority of co-located terms has no implications on the document's topical nature or relevance towards a given topic. It is exactly this situation that we capture in a formal framework: A limited number of meaningful dependencies in a system of largely independent observations. Making use of the formal copula framework, we describe the strength of causal dependency in terms of a number of established term co-occurrence metrics. Our experiments based on the well known *ClueWeb'12* corpus and TREC 2013 topics indicate significant performance gains in terms of retrieval performance when we formally account for the dependency structure underlying pieces of natural language text.

Categories and Subject Descriptors

Information Systems [**Information Retrieval**]: Retrieval models

Keywords

Relevance models; Multivariate relevance; Ranking; Probabilistic framework; Language models.

1. INTRODUCTION & RELATED WORK

Generative n-gram language models are frequently used tools for representing document or collection vocabulary in the form of probability distributions over (spans of) textual tokens. They are popular for a wide array of tasks, including sentiment analysis, machine translation, content based classification and document retrieval. Most state-of-the-art models assume individual terms to be independently drawn from the underlying distribution. While this independence assumption greatly simplifies the computation of conditional probabilities, it is also rather naïve. It is easy to find examples of proper names such as "*Barack Obama*" or "*Hong Kong*", but also other fixed expressions ("*tax evasion*") as well as non-consecutive constructs ("*dollar*" , "*stock*"), that should benefit from an explicit model of term interdependency. It is easy to see that some of these examples go beyond the capabilities of mere higher-order language models. In the past, there have been a number of attempts to formally integrate term dependency structures into generative models.

Van Rijsbergen's early work on dependency trees [19] theoretically establishes the use of maximum spanning trees and term co-occurrence statistics in order to establish local term dependency structures. Yu et al. [20] present a comparison of tree and cluster-based methods for dependency modelling in information retrieval. Srikanth and Srihari [18] investigate dependency-aware relevance models by using higher order n-gram models and comparing to the unigram setting. They report consistent improvements for the dependency models. Croft et al. [7] propose the use of inference networks trained on the basis of term proximity information to model the relevance of entire phrases. In a related effort, Lossee [12] confirms the important role of proximity in dependency modelling. The author reports optimal performance using context windows of 3-5 terms surrounding each candidate term. In a comparison study of multiple dependency models, Bruza and Song [4] achieve best results using a matrix representation of co-occurrence contexts to describe terms. Gao et al. [11] explicitly decouple the dependency structure of a sentence from the concrete term generation probabilities in the form of linkages.

Nallapati and Allan [14] relax the independence assumption by modelling documents as groups of (still independent) sentences. Within each sentence, however, they condition the probability of observing a term on all previous terms in the same sentence. Their sentence model is based on the maximum spanning tree over the fully connected sentence graph. The individual strength of dependency within term pairs is measured in terms of the Jaccard coëfficient. They later refine this model by advancing from dedicated sentence trees to entire forests [15] of trees for each connected component in the sentence graph. Cao et al. [5] use Bayesian networks to combine two sources of term dependence: co-occurrence and semantic relatedness. The latter is expressed in terms of proximity in the WordNet graph. While most approaches define document language models and compare their respective likelihoods of having generated the query,

SIGIR'15, August 09 - 13, 2015, Santiago, Chile.
© 2015 ACM. ISBN 978-1-4503-3621-5/15/08 ...$15.00.
http://dx.doi.org/10.1145/2766462.2767831

Bai et al. [1] propose a term-dependency query model in order to account explicitly for query expansion. Metzler and Croft [13] learn Markov Random Fields that account for various forms of term dependence on the basis of arbitrary feature vectors. Bendersky et al. [3, 2] propose a learning to rank approach that accounts for higher order term and concept dependencies using hypergraphs. Shi and Nie [17] investigate different dependence weighting schemes based on the concept's utility in the respective retrieval task.

In this paper, we present the use of copulas, a robust statistical model family that is able to explicitly decouple marginal observations (i.e., the individual likelihoods of generating terms) from their underlying dependency structures. Comparing to a number of well-known baseline methods and evaluating on a large-scale standard dataset, we show the competitive performance of this novel approach to dependency modelling.

2. METHODOLOGY

In this section, we will give a brief overview of the formal copula framework, introducing the relevant notation and conventions. For a more comprehensive introduction to the topic, please refer to the previous IR applications by Eickhoff et al. [8, 9], or the surveys by Embrechts [10] and Schmidt [16].

Let X be a k-dimensional random vector of observations that we wish to use as input to our copula model:

$$X^k = (x_1, x_2, \ldots, x_k)$$

The copula allows us to model the likelihood of observing X by offering computationally efficient approximations to the true joint probability distribution in the high-dimensional space of cardinality k. As a first step, copulas require input scores U^k to be uniformly distributed in the $[0 \ldots 1]$ interval. We can achieve this by defining a set of transformations $F(X)$ between raw marginal observations X and their normalized equivalents on the unit cube U.

$$U^k = (u_1, u_2, \ldots, u_k) = F(X) = (f_1(u_1), f_2(u_2), \ldots, f_k(u_k))$$

An easy example of such a function is the empirical distribution function $\hat{f}$:

$$\hat{f}(t) = \frac{1}{n} \sum 1 \{x_i \leq t\}$$

The cumulative distribution function C for all copulas is fully defined in terms of a generator ψ and its inverse ψ^{-1}:

$$C(u_1, u_2, \ldots, u_k) = \psi^{-1}(\psi(u_1) + \psi(u_2) + \ldots + \psi(u_k))$$

There are many concrete instantiations of such copula functions. Each copula family defines their own generator and inverse. A previous study [8] compared a wide range of copula families for the task of Web retrieval, finding Gumbel copulas to be the most adequate choice in this setting. For reasons of space, this paper builds on the previous findings and concentrates exclusively on Gumbel copulas. Their generators are given in the following form:

$$\psi^{-1}(t) = exp(-t^{\frac{1}{\theta}})$$
$$\psi(t) = (-log(t))^{\theta}$$

The resulting distribution function for a 2-dimensional Gumbel copula is, for example:

$$C(u_1, u_2) = exp(-((-log(u_1))^{\theta} + (-log(u_2))^{\theta})^{\frac{1}{\theta}})$$

Once the choice of copula family is made, we are left with just a single parameter θ that allows us to control the strength of dependency between the individual marginal observations u. If we, for example, set $\theta = 1$, our distribution function defaults to the case of conditional independence:

$$C_{\theta=1} = exp(-(-log(u_1)) + (-log(u_2))) = u_1 * u_2$$

Any choice of $\theta > 1$ results in an increasing degree of conditional dependency between the k dimensions of our observation. At this point, we have introduced all relevant components for our original use case of statistical language modelling. A traditional unigram language model describes the likelihood of observing a string of text T under a given class c as the product of the individual likelihoods of each term:

$$P(T|c) = P(t_1|c)P(t_2|c) \ldots P(t_{|T|}|c)$$

The same can be achieved under the copula framework by considering the class-conditional probabilities of observing individual terms $t_1, t_2, \ldots$ as our marginal observations, making the dimensionality of our copula $k = |T|$:

$$P(T|c) = C_{\theta=1}(P(t_1|c), P(t_2|c), \ldots P(t_{|T|}|c))$$

By choosing $\theta = 1$, we ensure conditional independence between the marginal term observation likelihoods, giving us the standard unigram language model. As we however increase θ, the strength of dependency between the individual terms increases. This ability to account for term dependence makes the copula framework a powerful alternative to the standard language modelling scheme. At this point, any setting of θ globally describes the relationship between all terms. In practice, however, we much rather want a select few terms to depend on each other, while the majority of terms occur indeed independently.

This is easily achieved by using nested copulas. Instead of combining all dimensions in a single step as described earlier, they allow for a nested hierarchy of multiple copulas that estimate joint distributions for sub sets of the full term space and subsequently combine scores until one global model is obtained. Generally, an example of a fully nested copula with k dimensions is given by:

$$C_0(u_1, C_1(u_2, C_2(\ldots, C_{k-2}(u_{k-1}, u_k))))$$

By means of the structure of the nesting *"tree"*, nested copulas can explicitly model which dimensions depend on each other directly. Instead of the global θ parameter discussed earlier, each of the constituent copulas defines their respective θ_i, determining the strengths of these (per-dimension) dependencies. This mechanism gives nested copulas a theoretical advantage in flexibility over their non-nested counterparts. Effectively, this allows us to describe formally grounded probabilistic models under which select term pairs show dependencies ($\theta > 1$) while the majority of terms oc-

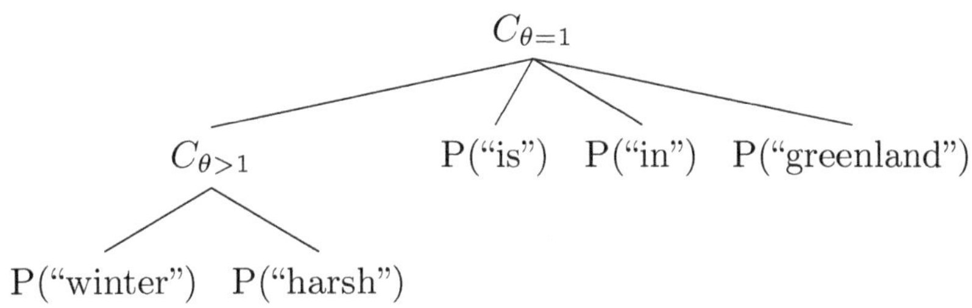

Figure 1: The copula dependence tree for the sentence "*Winter is harsh in Greenland.*" shows significant dependence between the terms "*winter*" and "*harsh*" while the remaining terms occur independently.

cur independently of each other ($\theta = 1$). Figure 1 shows an example of such a situation.

At this point, the final missing component in our language modelling scheme is a way to determine the concrete settings of θ for a pair of terms. To this end, we define conditional dependency in terms of frequency of co-occurrence in a document corpus and rely on two widely used co-occurrence metrics. The point-wise mutual information between terms t_1 and t_2 as well as their Jaccard coefficient measure in which fraction of sentences the terms co-occur.

$$PMI(t_1, t_2) = log_2 \frac{P(t_1,t_2)}{P(t_1)P(t_2)}$$

$$J(t_1, t_2) = \frac{|t_1 \cap t_2|}{|t_1 \cup t_2|}$$

Finally, the dependency parameter θ_{t_1,t_2} is defined on the basis of the concrete choice of metric $m \in \{PMI, J\}$ and its collection-wide metric mean (μ_{PMI}, μ_J) across all potential term pairs. All those pairs of higher-than-average co-occurrence frequency are assigned values of θ proportionally to their relative co-occurrence rate. Since θ is defined in the range $[1, \infty)$ and the resulting scores scale in a non-linear fashion, there is no need to further address or remove outlier pairs of extremely high frequency.

$$\theta_{m,t_1,t_2} = \begin{cases} \frac{m(t_1,t_2)}{\mu_m} & if\ m(t_1, t_2) > \mu_m \\ 1 & else \end{cases}$$

3. EXPERIMENTS

To empirically test the performance of the previously presented copula-based language modelling scheme, we investigate its performance at the task of adhoc document retrieval. Instead of modelling the likelihood of observing a given document under a topic specific language model, we will now establish one distinct model per document and compare their respective likelihoods of having generated the query q.

$$P(rel|q, d) \approx P(q|d)$$

$$P(q|d)_{indep} = \prod_{i=1}^{|q|} P(w_i|d)$$

$$P(q|d)_{cop} = C_d(w_1, w_2, \ldots, w_n)|w \in q$$

For our experimental comparison, we rely on the widely used ClueWeb'12 corpus, a collection of 730 million authentic Web documents. Our 50 topics originate from TREC's 2013 Adhoc retrieval task [6]. We contrast our method's performance with a number of established as well as state-of-the-art baselines such as standard unigram and bigram language models, Nallapati's sentence trees [14], as well as the Markov Random Field model [13] and apply Laplace smoothing to all LM variants in order to account for previously unseen query terms. Table 1 details the respective performances obtained by the various methods in terms of precision, recall, F_1 and MAP, each computed at a cut-off rank of 20 retrieved documents. Statistically significant improvements over all baseline methods are indicated by the asterisk character. Statistical significance was tested using a Wilcoxon signed-rank test at $\alpha \leq 0.05$-level. We can note that, due to their wider context, the classification performance of bigram language models significantly exceeds that of the lower-order model. SenTrees as well as the MRF model which explicitly capture term dependence show even higher classification performance. Finally, our copula language model yields significant performance improvements across most metrics and baselines. The improvements over the MRF model were only significant for some of the considered metrics.

Table 1: Retrieval performance on ClueWeb'12 and TREC 2013 Adhoc topics at a cut-off threshold of 20 retrieved documents.

Model	Precision	Recall	F_1	MAP
Unigram LM	0.31	0.22	0.26	0.41
Bigram LM	0.34	0.26	0.3	0.45
SenTree	0.35	0.28	0.31	0.47
MRF	0.38	0.31	0.34	0.51
Copula LM	**0.41***	**0.35***	**0.38***	**0.52**

4. CONCLUSION

In this paper, we demonstrated the use of the copula framework, a model family from the field of robust statistics, for representing term dependencies in language models. The main advantages of the proposed model are its formal rigour, the low model complexity in terms of training effort as well as disk space requirements and its high degree of flexibility. As an additional advantage, copulas have been previously shown [9] to be beneficial for qualitative manual inspection of results.

Our experiments, based on a sizeable document collection (ClueWeb'12) confirm the competitive performance of the proposed model in comparison with a number of state-of-the-art baselines.

The present paper describes early results of an ongoing body of research. Consequently, there are numerous directions for future work that are interesting to explore: **(1)** In this paper, we investigated "single-layer" dependency structures with a nesting depth of 1. The nested copula framework, however, is able to capture arbitrarily complex structures. Given a modified dependency estimation scheme, the model can easily account for cases of fine-grained multi-level dependencies. **(2)** Similarly, the current model regards only dependencies of degree 2. Since the copula framework is able to account for higher-degree dependencies (i.e., between three or more terms) this is another promising alley for continued research. **(3)** Previous work has investigated different forms of inter-term dependency, including, for example, semantic proximity. It would be easy to integrate such additional sources of evidence into our θ estimation step. **(4)** We would like to draw from the existing wealth of topic modelling techniques in order to describe not merely the dependency structure between individual terms but also between terms and more high-level (latent) concepts, allowing for exciting new insights. **(5)** Finally, we would like to explore means of representing local term context into the dependency model. Take for instance the two terms "new" and "york". In the query [affordable real estate on the US east coast] these terms clearly have some dependency, whereas they probably are less dependent when the query is [affordable real estate in yorkshire, UK]. The current paper highlights the applicability of the context invariant method for general queries. In the future we will additionally investigate the importance of the immediate context.

5. REFERENCES

[1] Jing Bai, Dawei Song, Peter Bruza, Jian-Yun Nie, and Guihong Cao. Query expansion using term relationships in language models for information retrieval. In *Proceedings of the 14th ACM international conference on Information and knowledge management*, pages 688–695. ACM, 2005.

[2] Michael Bendersky and W Bruce Croft. Modeling higher-order term dependencies in information retrieval using query hypergraphs. In *Proceedings of the 35th international ACM SIGIR conference*, pages 941–950. ACM, 2012.

[3] Michael Bendersky, Donald Metzler, and W Bruce Croft. Learning concept importance using a weighted dependence model. In *Proceedings of the third ACM international conference on Web search and data mining*, pages 31–40. ACM, 2010.

[4] Peter Bruza and Dawei Song. A comparison of various approaches for using probabilistic dependencies in language modeling. In *Proceedings of the 26th annual international ACM SIGIR conference*, pages 419–420. ACM, 2003.

[5] Guihong Cao, Jian-Yun Nie, and Jing Bai. Integrating word relationships into language models. In *Proceedings of the 28th annual international ACM SIGIR conference*, pages 298–305. ACM, 2005.

[6] Kevyn Collins-Thompson, Paul Bennett, Fernando Diaz, Charles LA Clarke, and Ellen M Voorhees. Trec 2013 web track overview. In *22nd Text REtrieval Conference, Gaithersburg, Maryland*, 2014.

[7] W Bruce Croft, Howard R Turtle, and David D Lewis. The use of phrases and structured queries in information retrieval. In *Proceedings of the 14th annual international ACM SIGIR conference*, pages 32–45. ACM, 1991.

[8] Carsten Eickhoff and Arjen P de Vries. Modelling complex relevance spaces with copulas. In *Proceedings of the 23rd ACM International Conference on Conference on Information and Knowledge Management*, pages 1831–1834. ACM, 2014.

[9] Carsten Eickhoff, Arjen P de Vries, and Kevyn Collins-Thompson. Copulas for information retrieval. In *Proceedings of the 36th international ACM SIGIR conference on Research and development in information retrieval*, pages 663–672. ACM, 2013.

[10] P. Embrechts, F. Lindskog, and A. McNeil. Modelling dependence with copulas and applications to risk management. *Handbook of heavy tailed distributions in finance*, 8(329-384):1, 2003.

[11] Jianfeng Gao, Jian-Yun Nie, Guangyuan Wu, and Guihong Cao. Dependence language model for information retrieval. In *Proceedings of the 27th annual international ACM SIGIR conference on Research and development in information retrieval*, pages 170–177. ACM, 2004.

[12] Robert M Losee. Term dependence: truncating the bahadur lazarsfeld expansion. *Information processing & management*, 30(2):293–303, 1994.

[13] Donald Metzler and W Bruce Croft. A markov random field model for term dependencies. In *Proceedings of the 28th annual international ACM SIGIR conference*, pages 472–479. ACM, 2005.

[14] Ramesh Nallapati and James Allan. Capturing term dependencies using a language model based on sentence trees. In *Proceedings of the eleventh international conference on Information and knowledge management*, pages 383–390. ACM, 2002.

[15] Ramesh Nallapati and James Allan. An adaptive local dependency language model: Relaxing the naıve bayes' assumption. 2003.

[16] T. Schmidt. Coping with copulas. *Risk Books: Copulas from Theory to Applications in Finance*, 2007.

[17] Lixin Shi and Jian-Yun Nie. Using various term dependencies according to their utilities. In *Proceedings of the 19th ACM international conference on Information and knowledge management*, pages 1493–1496. ACM, 2010.

[18] Munirathnam Srikanth and Rohini Srihari. Incorporating query term dependencies in language models for document retrieval. In *Proceedings of the 26th annual international ACM SIGIR conference*, pages 405–406. ACM, 2003.

[19] Cornelis Joost van Rijsbergen. A theoretical basis for the use of co-occurrence data in information retrieval. *Journal of documentation*, 33(2):106–119, 1977.

[20] Clement T Yu, Chris Buckley, K Lam, and Gerard Salton. A generalized term dependence model in information retrieval. Technical report, Cornell University, 1983.

Modeling Website Topic Cohesion at Scale to Improve Webpage Classification

Dhivya Eswaran*
CS Dept., IIT Madras
Chennai, India
dhivyae@cse.iitm.ac.in

Paul N. Bennett
Microsoft Research
Redmond, WA USA
pauben@microsoft.com

Joseph J. Pfeiffer III
CS Dept., Purdue University
West Lafayette, IN USA
jpfeiffer@purdue.edu

ABSTRACT

Considerable work in web page classification has focused on incorporating the topical structure of the web (e.g., the hyperlink graph) to improve prediction accuracy. However, the majority of work has primarily focused on relational or graph-based methods that are impractical to run at scale or in an online environment. This raises the question of whether it is possible to leverage the topical structure of the web while incurring nearly no additional prediction-time cost. To this end, we introduce an approach which adjusts a page content-only classification from that obtained with a global prior to the posterior obtained by incorporating a prior which reflects the topic cohesion of the site. Using ODP data, we empirically demonstrate that our approach yields significant performance increases over a range of topics.

Categories and Subject Descriptors

H.4 [**Information Systems Applications**]: Miscellaneous

Keywords

Text classification, large-scale, context-dependent priors

1. INTRODUCTION

Topical webpage classification has proven useful for a variety of information retrieval applications. For example, one of its most common applications is in building profiles for personalization [5, 7] including building short- and long-term topical profiles [1]. Additionally, topical classification has also been used for improving time-to-find information by organizing search results into a categorical display [3], detecting temporal shifts in query intent using changes in clicked URL and query topic distribution [9], and improving search relevance by matching query intent to topic intent [2]. Given the wide variety of applications for text classification in information retrieval, there remains interest in novel methods to improve text classification accuracy.

To this end, there has been considerable effort on incorporating the topical structure of the web (e.g., the hyperlink graph) to improve prediction accuracy [4, 6, 8]. Given both the size of the web and the frequently changing nature of web pages, production environments require efficient classifiers that can be updated with every re-crawl of a page while meeting very stringent performance demands. However, the majority of work has focused on relational or graph-based methods that are impractical to run at scale or in an online environment [4, 6, 8]. This raises the question of whether it is possible to leverage the topical structure of the web while incurring nearly no additional prediction-time cost.

Our key insight is to leverage the topical structure of the web. Namely, collections of webpages are typically organized into websites whose contents are topically related. For example, `www.espn.com` is a high-level web domain containing a collection of webpages centered around the *Sports* topic. More generally, each website tends to have a different topical focus that we view as a website-dependent prior over topics. In this paper, we demonstrate that these website-dependent priors can improve the accuracy of a classifier trained globally across all websites. Using this intuition, we develop a wrapper approach to incorporate website-dependent priors that can be used in conjunction with any probabilistic classifier.

Importantly, our method scales at a cost similar to the content-only classification of the webpage. That is, at training time we need only aggregate and estimate the priors for each website. For our purposes, a URL's corresponding 'website' is its top-level domain. Given this identification into website, it is straightforward to construct a mapping of website to distribution over topics using a map-reduce approach. Then, at prediction-time – the most computationally restrictive time in a production environment – incorporating website topical structure is a simple website look-up and a constant-time reweighting of the topical classification.

2. RELATED WORK

Here, we highlight previous work that has discussed adjusting posterior predictions when either the priors do not match [10] or attribute distributions vary [14]. Previous work discussing the priors mismatch assumes the corresponding correct priors cannot be directly estimated, leading to an iterative expectation-maximization solution. Similarly, modeling the distribution of covariates [14] for high dimensional text data would be difficult given the small sample

*Work performed while at Microsoft.

SIGIR '15, August 09-13, 2015, Santiago, Chile.

© 2015 ACM. ISBN 978-1-4503-3621-5/15/08... $ 15.00.

DOI: http://dx.doi.org/10.1145/2766462.2767834

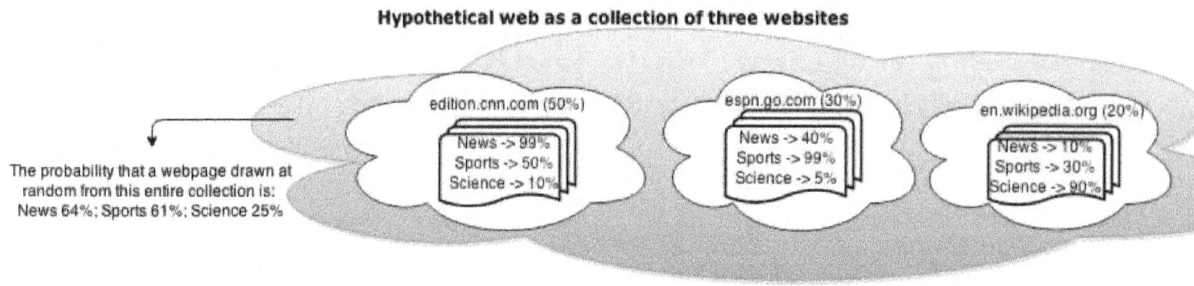

Figure 1: Example collection of three websites to demonstrate that the overall distribution of topics may vary greatly from that within website due to topical cohesion. Note that topic probabilities (over the web or within a website) need not sum to one, as we do not restrict a webpage to have only one category label.

sizes for the website-specific instances. In this work, we utilize the immediately available URL to group the items, allowing for a simpler approach to modeling the website-specific priors that is more suitable for online and time-constrained situations.

3. PROBLEM APPROACH

We hypothesize that the universe of webpages is not one homogeneous entity with a uniform distribution of labels, but is composed of many communities (websites[1]) each of which has its own prior distribution of class labels that can significantly differ from the global prior distribution of labels (Figure 1).

Ideally then, when a new webpage $\mathbf{x}$ is presented to the classifier, the model should make the class prediction c using both its content and its web domain w according to $P(c|\mathbf{x}, w)$. One way to approach this problem is to build a separate model for each website w; but this is not feasible due to limited labeled data. Alternatively, we can let all the websites share the same set of classifiers and incorporate the website specific class-distributional information in the priors alone. This is the key insight underlying our method.

3.1 Using a Website-specific Prior from a Generative Viewpoint

For explanatory purposes, it is useful to first approach how to incorporate website-specific priors from the viewpoint of a generative model. Consider Bayes' rule applied to the global distribution of the class (without using any web domain information) labels:

$$P_g(c|\mathbf{x}) \propto P(\mathbf{x}|c)P_g(c) \tag{1}$$

Here, we use a subscript g for the global prior, $P_g(c)$, but omit one on the class-conditional language model, $P(\mathbf{x}|c)$. This corresponds to the following hypothesized generative model for webpages: first, a class is picked from the global class distribution $P_g(c)$. Then, conditioned on the class, words are generated according to the language model, $P(\mathbf{x}|c)$. Assuming that the words are generated according to the same class-conditional language model, $P(\mathbf{x}|c) = P(\mathbf{x}|c, w)$, we can write:

$$\begin{aligned} P(c|\mathbf{x}, w) \propto& P(\mathbf{x}|c, w)P_w(c) \\ =& P(\mathbf{x}|c)P_w(c) \end{aligned} \tag{2}$$

While this assumption that the same class-dependent language model is used to generate content across websites may not hold in practice, it is a useful first-pass approximation. In the next section, we discuss how a similar approach can be taken with a discriminative classifier.

3.2 Discriminative Website-Specific Classifiers

Here, we wish to utilize a global discriminative classifier, $P_g(c|\mathbf{x})$, to make website-specific predictions of a webpage (i.e., $P(c|\mathbf{x}, w)$). We highlight that the conditional $P(\mathbf{x}|c)$ appears under our generative model for both the global class conditional and domain-specific conditional (i.e., Equations 1 and 2). Solving Equation 1 for $P(\mathbf{x}|c)$ and incorporating the normalization $P_g(\mathbf{x})$, we recover:

$$P(\mathbf{x}|c) = \frac{P_g(c|\mathbf{x})P_g(\mathbf{x})}{P_g(c)}$$

Inserting the above into Equation 2, we derive:

$$\begin{aligned} P(c|\mathbf{x}, w) &= \frac{P(\mathbf{x}|c)P_w(c)}{P_w(\mathbf{x})} \\ &= \frac{\frac{P_g(c|\mathbf{x})P_g(\mathbf{x})}{P_g(c)}P_w(c)}{P_w(\mathbf{x})} \\ &\propto P_g(c|\mathbf{x})\frac{P_w(c)}{P_g(c)} \end{aligned} \tag{3}$$

where in the last step we have simply dropped the variables that do not depend on the class c. The normalization of this last line can be marginalized over classes to write:

$$P(c|\mathbf{x}, w) = \frac{P_g(c|\mathbf{x})\frac{P_w(c)}{P_g(c)}}{\sum_c P_g(c|\mathbf{x})\frac{P_w(c)}{P_g(c)}} \tag{4}$$

Note the intuitive form of this conditional in Eq. 4. It only requires adjusting a classifier's prediction by the ratio of the website-specific to global prior. This process is summarized in Figure 2. Now, we turn to estimating the priors.

4. ESTIMATING PRIORS

We assume that we have a set of labeled data to both estimate the global priors and website-specific priors. While we leave the more general case of estimating website-specific priors from unlabeled data as future work, we do consider

[1]In this paper, we reserve the term "webpage" to refer to the content associated with a single URL and website to refer to a collection of webpages. For simplicity, we represent a website as the top-level domain of the URL although future work contemplates that improving identification of website-breaking of the URL may further improve our approach.

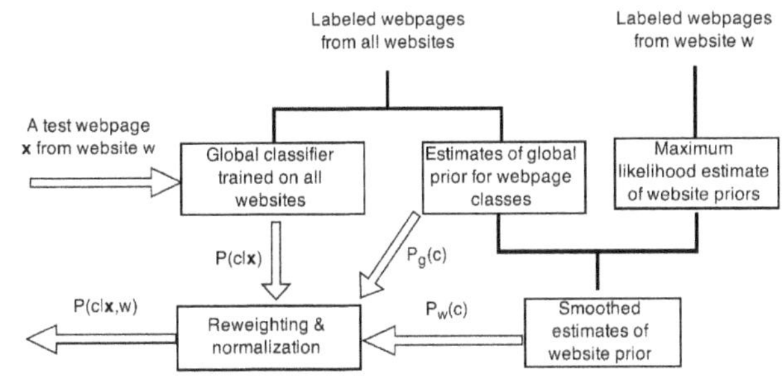

Figure 2: Overview of the proposed methodology.

how to smooth estimates to deal with the realistic conditions that labeled data for any particular website may be very sparse.

4.1 Estimating the Global Prior

The global prior can be estimated from the training set T or more generally any labeled dataset L drawn from the same distribution as T. $P_g(c)$ is obtained using the maximum likelihood estimate, i.e., the proportion of webpages in the labeled data that actually belong to the class. If $\mathcal{L}(\mathbf{x})$ denotes the set of classes (or labels) that a webpage $\mathbf{x}$ belongs to and $\mathbb{1}(\cdot)$ is the indicator function[2], the estimate for the global prior of a class c is the usual:

$$P_g^L(c) = \frac{\sum_{\mathbf{x}\in L} \mathbb{1}(c \in \mathcal{L}(\mathbf{x}))}{|L|}. \quad (5)$$

4.2 Estimating Website-Specific Priors

Using a website-conditioned counterpart of Eq. 5 directly to estimate $P_w(c)$ may result in overfitting the website-specific priors to the labeled set. To overcome this problem, we smooth the website-specific prior using a Bayesian m-estimate with the global prior. That is:

$$P_w^L(c) = \frac{\sum_{\mathbf{x}\in w} \mathbb{1}(c \in \mathcal{L}(\mathbf{x})) + m_{c,w} P_g^L(c)}{|w| + m_{c,w}}, \text{ where } m_{c,w} > 0 \quad (6)$$

Here, $m_{c,w}$ can be regarded as a virtual count of examples observed from the global distribution for this particular website and class. We focus on the case where there is a single value of m across all classes and websites, *i.e.*, $m = m_{c,w}$ for all c, w. By tying the parameter value across classes and websites in this way, the method is less prone to overfitting.

5. EMPIRICAL METHODOLOGY

As it is commonly used in many topic classification studies, we used the Open Directory Project (ODP, `dmoz.org`) ontology of the web to study the empirical effectiveness of our proposed approach. We crawled these web pages and randomly split them into 70% train, 15% validation, and 15% test. We chose to restrict the class set to focus on those categories with more than 1K positive training examples. This resulted in the 219 most frequent categories at the top two levels of the hierarchy. While still at a high-level of granularity, this is a similar number of categories shown to improve downstream applications such as personalization [1, 11]. Furthermore, like those works we choose to flatten the hierarchy and deal with the issue that a document can belong to multiple categories by training a binary classifier per class. We focus on the impact of predictive performance on the top category and the top three categories as use of the top three categories tend to be most common in the literature in downstream applications such as personalization. As standard in text classification, we examine the micro and macro averages of precision, recall, and F1 [13, 12].

Baseline

To create our baseline global classifier, we train a binary logistic regression classifier with L2 regularization on each of the classes. We use a tfidf representation where each feature vector is normalized to the unit sphere to deal with length variation. When optimized by a score cut threshold over the validation set, the micro-average F1 of the baseline is 0.60 which is a reasonably strong baseline whose performance is on a par with similar classifiers used in downstream applications [1, 11].

Cohesion

The *Cohesion* approach reported uses the labeled training data to estimate the website-specific priors according to Eq. 6 and incorporate them into the website specific posterior as in Eq. 4. Treating each binary classifier separately, we performed binary normalization in the denominator using its positive and negative examples. The final posteriors are used to rank the classes. A single value of the smoothing parameter m is chosen by doing a sweep over the validation data over $m \in \{0, 0.01, 0.025, 0.05, 0.075, 0.1, 0.25, 0.5, 0.75, 1, 2.5, 5, 7.5, 10, 25, 50, 75, 100, 250, 500, 750, 1000\}$ and selecting the value of m that yielded the best reduction in residual macro- and micro-F1 (equally weighting both).

6. RESULTS AND DISCUSSION

Table 1 presents the summary of each method when predicting the top category and top 3 categories for the value of m selected on the validation set. For the rank 3 cutoff, Figure 3 (left) shows the variation of residue with m while Figure 3 (right) shows a histogram of number of classes impacted versus the per-class change in F1 performance. First, we note in the table that the Cohesion method improves both macro and micro F1 at both rank 1 and rank 3 cutoffs. In fact, the Cohesion method improves every measure except for macro-precision at rank 1. Taken together with the improvement in micro-precision at rank 1, we see the Cohesion method hurts precision across a majority of classes although it improves for the more common classes (which have a larger impact on the micro-average). As the rank cutoff is increased to rank=3, we see that all measures improve – indicating that those categories that suffered at rank=1 still remain quite high in the ranks. At rank=3, Cohesion improves the precision/recall/F1 on 62%/77%/75% of classes, respectively. Thus, the gains are very robust over a large number of classes. Figure 3 (right) shows further detail on the distribution of gains/losses for F1 for rank=3.

To explain the trend observed in Figure 3 (left), as described earlier m indicates the pseudo count of webpages from the global distribution. Low values of m overfit the website-specific prior to the labeled set and a high residual F1 (error) is observed. As m is increased, the contribution from the global prior increases till m is just enough to offset the overfitting to training data. If m is increased beyond this value, the performance is again hurt as the topic cohesion of the websites are increasingly ignored.

[2]For a boolean variable y, $\mathbb{1}(y) = 1$ if y is true; else $\mathbb{1}(y) = 0$.

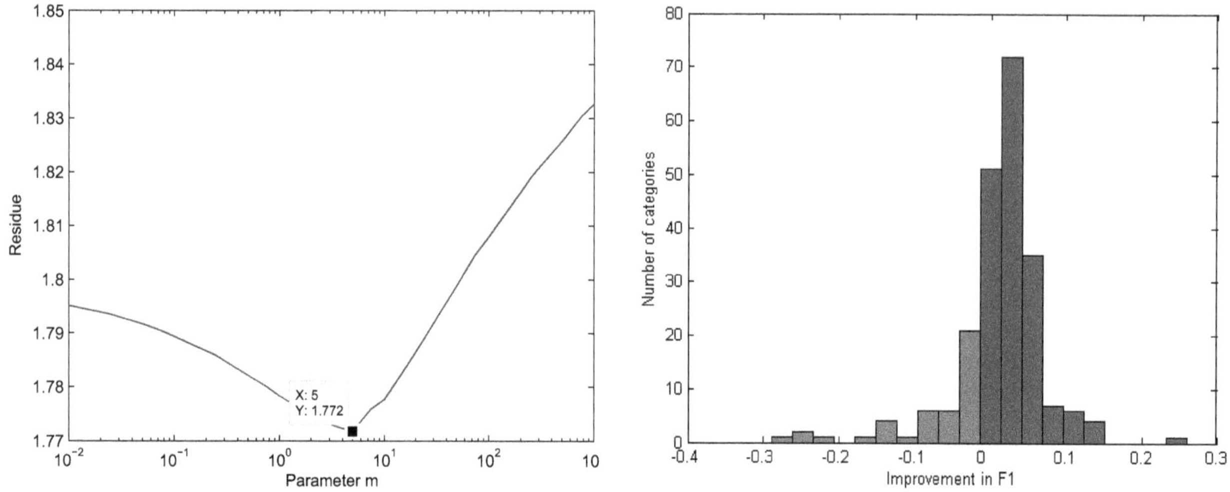

Figure 3: Predictions on the top three categories: variation of residual micro- and macro- F1 (left) and the distribution of absolute (right) improvement of the Cohesion model of the 165 improved categories (blue) and 54 hurt categories (red) (no categories tied).

	Method	Micro-Precision	Micro-Recall	Micro-F1	Macro-Precision	Macro-Recall	Macro-F1
Rank=1	Baseline	0.6509	0.3423	0.4487	**0.7683**	0.1623	0.2494
	Cohesion	**0.6923**	**0.3641**	**0.4772**	0.7328	**0.2006**	**0.2969**
Rank=3	Baseline	0.4180	0.6595	0.5117	0.4329	0.4423	0.4277
	Cohesion	**0.4353**	**0.6868**	**0.5328**	**0.4428**	**0.4718**	**0.4410**

Table 1: Predicting the top and top 3 categories for webpages in the test set. The best performer for each rank cutoff in each column is shown in bold. Underline indicates significant differences ($p \leq 0.05$) in macro-averages according to a two-sided macro-sign test [13].

7. CONCLUSION AND FUTURE WORK

In summary, we demonstrated how the topic cohesion of websites could be leveraged at scale to improve webpage classification through website-specific priors. Though our current approach is limited to the availability of labeled data for each domain, the significant overall gains we obtained in our experiments with a large majority of classes (75%) improving over the baseline as well demonstrate the effectiveness and robustness of our method. Future work in this area could investigate the amount of the labeled training data required for our approach and examine cautious techniques to learn website-specific priors from unlabeled data to generalize across websites where labeled data may be completely unavailable. In addition, we are also interested in methods that go beyond the top-level domain representation to model cohesion as a hierarchical relationship.

8. REFERENCES

[1] P. Bennett et al. Modeling the impact of short- and long-term behavior on search personalization. In *SIGIR '12*, 2012.

[2] P. N. Bennett, K. Svore, and S. T. Dumais. Classification-enhanced ranking. In *WWW '10*, 2010.

[3] S. Dumais, E. Cutrell, and H. Chen. Bringing order to the web: Optimizing search by showing results in context. In *CHI'01*, 2001.

[4] N. Friedman et al. Learning probabilistic relational models. In *In IJCAI '99*, 1999.

[5] S. Gauch, J. Chaffee, and A. Pretschner. Ontology-based user profiles for search and browsing. *WIAS*, 1(3-4):219–234, 2004.

[6] L. Getoor and B. Taskar. *Introduction to Statistical Relational Learning (Adaptive Computation and Machine Learning)*. The MIT Press, 2007.

[7] Z. Ma, G. Pant, and O. R. L. Sheng. Interest-based personalized search. *TOIS*, 25(1), Feb. 2007.

[8] X. Qi and B. D. D. 0001. Classifiers without borders: incorporating fielded text from neighboring web pages. In *SIGIR '08*, 2008.

[9] K. Radinsky et al. Modeling and predicting behavioral dynamics on the web. In *WWW '12*, 2012.

[10] M. Saerens, P. Latinne, and C. Decaestecker. Adjusting the outputs of a classifier to new a priori probabilities: A simple procedure. *Neural Computation*, 14(1):21–41, 2002.

[11] R. W. White, P. N. Bennett, and S. T. Dumais. Predicting short-term interests using activity-based search context. In *CIKM '10*, 2010.

[12] Y. Yang. An evaluation of statistical approaches to text categorization. *Inf. Retr.*, 1(1-2):69–90, May 1999.

[13] Y. Yang and X. Liu. A re-examination of text categorization methods. In *SIGIR '99*, 1999.

[14] B. Zadrozny. Learning and evaluating classifiers under sample selection bias. In *ICML '04*, 2004.

Topic-centric Classification of Twitter User's Political Orientation

Anjie Fang[1], Iadh Ounis[2], Philip Habel[2], Craig Macdonald[2] and Nut Limsopatham[2]
University of Glasgow, UK
[1]a.fang.1@research.gla.ac.uk, [2]{firstname.secondname}@glasgow.ac.uk

ABSTRACT

In the recent Scottish Independence Referendum (hereafter, IndyRef), Twitter offered a broad platform for people to express their opinions, with millions of IndyRef tweets posted over the campaign period. In this paper, we aim to classify people's voting intentions by the content of their tweets—their short messages communicated on Twitter. By observing tweets related to the IndyRef, we find that people not only discussed the vote, but raised topics related to an independent Scotland including oil reserves, currency, nuclear weapons, and national debt. We show that the views communicated on these topics can inform us of the individuals' voting intentions ("Yes"–in favour of Independence vs. "No"–Opposed). In particular, we argue that an accurate classifier can be designed by leveraging the differences in the features' usage across different topics related to voting intentions. We demonstrate improvements upon a Naive Bayesian classifier using the topics enrichment method. Our new classifier identifies the closest topic for each unseen tweet, based on those topics identified in the training data. Our experiments show that our Topics-Based Naive Bayesian classifier improves accuracy by 7.8% over the classical Naive Bayesian baseline.

1. INTRODUCTION

Both citizens and politicians are increasingly embracing social media to disseminate information, particularly during significant political events and campaigns. Twitter emerged as an especially popular platform during the recent IndyRef held in September 2014 a vote that, if successful, would have created an independent Scotland—a secession of the 300 years union with Great Britain. This critical event attracted unprecedented levels of political activity both offline and online. Social media usage was essential to both campaigns, with more than 5.8 million tweets using the *indyref* hashtag within the year leading up to the vote [6]. Therefore, we propose here a technique to analyse the voting intentions of users, based on data mining and machine learning approaches. Indeed, the general approach we advance could be used to understand vote intentions in other major elections.

SIGIR'15, August 09 - 13, 2015, Santiago, Chile.

ACM 978-1-4503-3621-5/15/08 ...$15.00
DOI: http://dx.doi.org/10.1145/2766462.2767833 .

To analyse voting intentions, we capture two months (August 1 to September 30, 2014) of Twitter data related to the IndyRef. To form a ground truth, we label users based upon hashtags appearing in their tweets, and we verify the reliability of this approach using the users' followee networks. Those in favour of an independent Scotland used hashtags such as *VoteYes* and *YesScotland*; those opposed used *BetterTogether* and *VoteNo*–which serves as our ground-truth. After removing the hashtags from these tweets, we then focus on the remaining terms, treating each term as a feature. However, the referendum created an evolving discourse, with different topical themes (such as *oil*, *currency*, and *debt*), which make the accurate classification of users' voting intentions more challenging. For instance, the word (feature) "change" is indicative of a "No" voter in the *currency* topic, and of a "Yes" voter in the *nuclear weapons* topic. That is, there was a significant discussion over whether Scotland would need to "change" its currency if it obtained independence, while the "Yes" camp purported that the nuclear arsenal base could "change" in an independent Scotland. The dichotomy of the term "change" in indicating voting intentions across different topics highlights the main benefit of our approach. Indeed, this paper contributes to the use of topical clusters to identify the topic of discussion in a tweet and subsequently to classify users' voting intentions. Our approach, called *Topics-Based Naive Bayesian* (TBNB) demonstrates marked improvements over a classical Naive Bayes (NB) classification baseline.

2. BACKGROUND AND RELATED WORK

Recently Al Zamal et al. [1] focused on the inference of latent attributes, such as age, gender and political orientation, based on textual and retweeting features. They achieved a high accuracy (90%); however, Raviv et al. [4] demonstrated that classification of political orientation was still a difficult problem and that the earlier result was exaggerated since it used easily classifiable political data. Conover et al. [5] showed that users' tweeting behaviours–such as the actions of re-tweeting, mentioning, and replying–can be used to classify the political polarization of users. In contrast, instead of leveraging the users' profile data or tweeting behaviours, we focus on the content of tweets to classify the users' voting intentions. We use as a starting point a classical Naive Bayesian (NB) classifier, which is an application of Bayes theorem within a probabilistic model to capture the conditional class probabilities of each feature. Since the number of features can be very large, it is common to use feature selection approaches to prune the features. For example, the following feature selection approaches are commonly

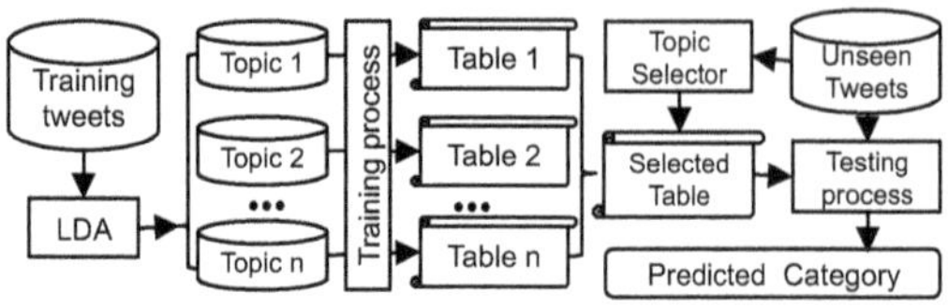

Figure 1: Data flow for TBNB.

used for the NB classifier: $Frequence(word)$ (denoted FR), $LogProbRatio(word)$ (LR), $ExpProbRatio(word)$ (ER), $OddsRatio(word)$ (OR) and $weightedOddsRatio(word)$ (WOR) (see [7]). OR is reported to obtain a high accuracy for the Naive Bayes classifier [7]. Each selection approach ranks and selects the F informative features (in our case we treat each term in a tweet as a feature) based on the training data (e.g., $F = 1000$). Of course, not every selected feature will appear in the unseen test tweets - we denote the number of such "activated" features as F_{test}. For instance, a testing tweet containing "Scotland has remained in the media spotlight throughout 2014" has 9 terms. If only "Scotland", "remained", "media" and "spotlight" were selected as features, the number of activated features is $F_{test} = 4$.

3. TOPICS-BASED NAIVE BAYESIAN

The IndyRef discussions on Twitter revolved around a number of topics, for which people's opinions usually reflected their vote intentions. For example, many "Yes" voters believed that revenues derived from the North Sea *oil* fields belonged to Scotland and could sustain it. On the other hand, many "No" voters argued that these sources were insufficient in the long run. A feature's **dissimilarity** represents the usage difference of this feature across topics, and the difference in usage of "oil" across different topics is therefore high. For a given topic, a feature's **variance** refers to the difference of the conditional probabilities of the occurrence of such a feature in different categories. For example, the conditional probability of "oil" in the "Yes" category is higher than in the "No" category. Typically, the feature selection approaches select features with higher variances between categories. Thus if a feature differs between topics, it will be treated as different features in the TBNB model. Thus TBNB can capture term dependencies between topic and user voting intentions. On the other hand, since the essence of the NB classifier is to learn those features with high variance from the categories, the TBNB classifier is believed to work better by leveraging both the features' dissimilarities across topics and their variances in the categories.

We assume that a single tweet involves a single topic. In the training step, the topics are first detected by Latent Dirichlet Allocation (LDA), a probabilistic graphical model introduced in [3]. For each topic, a corresponding probability table is produced, where each feature has two associated conditional probabilities related to the two possible voting intentions ("Yes"/"No"). Consequently, during the training step, we produce as many feature tables as the number of used topics. In the testing step, we treat a user as a virtual document and this document contains the users' tweets. For each tweet in the user's virtual document, the topic that is closest to the tweet's content is selected. As a topic can be represented by a mean vector of its tweets' vectors, the closest topic can be selected by computing the cosine similarity between the vector representation of the unseen tweet and the vector representations of the topics. We use standard TF vectors to represent both the tweets and topics. Terms in an unseen tweet are then examined using the probability table generated during the training step for the topic with which this tweet is associated. In this way, terms in different tweets are treated differently based on their associated topics, and the TNBN classifier applies, for each unseen tweet, those features that were learned from the corresponding topic. The detailed TBNB algorithm is presented in Algorithm 1. An overview of the whole TBNB classification process is shown in Figure 1. Note that the feature selection approaches can naturally be applied to the TBNB classifier. For example, if F (see Section 2) is set to 1000, the top 1000 features learned from each topic are selected.

Algorithm 1 Topics-Based Naive Bayesian (TBNB).

$topic_n, n = \{1, 2, .., N\} \leftarrow topic\_detection(tweets_{training})$
$n \leftarrow 1,\ c = \{\text{"}Yes\text{"}, \text{"}No\text{"}\}$
for $n \leq N, n{+}{+}$ **do**
  if w **in** $topic_n$ **then**
    $p(w|c_i) = \frac{number\ of\ the\ word\ w\ in\ topic_n\ in\ c_i}{total\ number\ of\ word\ w\ in\ topic_n}, \forall c$
    $probability\_table_n.add(p(w|c_i))$
  end if
end for
$ProbProduct_{c_i} \leftarrow 1$
for $tweet$ **in** $user_{testing}$ **do**
  $n \leftarrow topic\_selector(tweet_{testing})$
  for w **in** $tweet$ **do**
    if w **in** $probability\_table_n$ **then**
      $ProbProduct_{c_i} \times = p(w|c_i)$
    end if
  end for
end for
$p(c_i) = \frac{number\ of\ users\ belonging\ to\ c_i}{total\ number\ of\ users}$
$class(user) = argmax_{c_i}(p(c_i) \times ProbProduct_{c_i})$

Table 1: Topics and associated terms in the IndyRef.

Topic	Tweets%	Associated Terms
currency	20.25%	currency,money,change,pay,future
salmond	15.88%	salmond,alex,debate,audience,answer
glasgow	10.95%	glasgow,team,games,great,gold
women	9.82%	patronisingbtlady,women,undecided
oil	7.91%	oil,sea,privatisation,billion,gas,cuts
fear	7.87%	country,future,voting,fear,change
lastnight	7.32%	tonight,undecided,time,wearenational
debt	7.03%	scottish,debt,government,share,pay
weapon	6.84%	nuclear,weapon,clyde,year,glasgow
edinburgh	6.13%	edinburgh,johnjappy,minister,time

We use the LDA implemented in Mallet[1]. We investigate various topic numbers ($T = \{5, 10, 20, 30\}$). Table 1 shows the topic terms extracted using LDA for 10 topics. For readability purposes, the first column of Table 1 provides the general theme of the extracted topic[2]. For example, we can see that tweets related to *currency* and *oil* were common. Other oft-used topics and features included references to Alex Salmond, who was both the leader of the Scottish National Party (SNP) and the "Yes" campaign.

4. REFERENDUM DATA

The corpus pertaining to the Scottish Referendum event was collected from the Twitter network by searching for a number of referendum-specific hashtags (e.g. #IndyRef) and associated terms (e.g. 'vote', 'referendum') using the Twitter Streaming API[3]. The (uncompressed) 33GB dataset

[1] http://mallet.cs.umass.edu/ [2] These themes are manually annotated. [3] https://dev.twitter.com/

contains 6 million tweets from over 1 million users collected from August 1, 2014 to September 30, 2014.

In our dataset, 79.7% of users posting tweets with more than one. The most commonly used hashtags indicating the users' voting intentions are listed in Sets 1 and 2 below. As can be seen, certain hashtags were associated with a "Yes" vote, and others with a "No" vote. To reduce sparsity, we retain only users with more than 30 tweets posted during the timeframe of the collection. To generate our ground truth, we assume that if a user's tweets are only tagged by hashtags in Set 1, then this user is labeled as a "No" voter. Similarly, if a user's tweets contain only hashtags in Set 2, then the user is labeled as a "Yes" supporter, favoring independence.

Set 1: #NoBecause, #BetterTogther, #VoteNo, #NoThanks
Set 2: #YesBecause, #YesScotland, #YesScot, #VoteYes

Using this method, we find 5326 "Yes" users and 2011 "No" users. Together these 7337 users account for more than 420K tweets. After labelling, all hashtags in Set 1 and Set 2 are removed from their original tweet text. The resulting tweets constitute our classification dataset. We use this dataset to examine the usefulness of enriching the NB classifier with the extracted topics. Without the hashtags, the classification task is naturally more challenging, but importantly, the resulting generalisable classifier does not require the presence of hashtags.

Next, we verify our ground-truth's reliability using the users' followee networks. In particular, members of the Conservative Party (CONV) were staunchly opposed to independence, with post-election surveys showing that 95% of Conservatives voted "No"[4]. Thus, we argue that if a user mainly follows Conservative politicians, this person is likely to be a "No" voter. In contrast, 86% of SNP party voters favoured independence[4], and hence if a user follows SNP politicians, their vote intention is more likely to be "Yes"–in like manner to a previously used method to classify users' political orientation [2]. We then examined the networks of the 7337 users in our dataset, and used the Twitter REST API[3] to identify who these users follow among the 536 public Twitter accounts corresponding to Members of the British (MPs) or Scottish (MSPs) Parliaments. We use two verification approaches, denoted c_{V1} and c_{V2} for verifying the reliability of our ground truth: c_{V1} assumes an exclusive followee membership, while c_{V2} assumes a marked tendency to follow politicians of a given political party, namely:

$$c_{V1}(u) = \begin{cases} \text{``}Yes\text{''} & \text{if } n_{CONV}(u) = 0 \wedge n_{SNP}(u) > 0 \\ \text{``}No\text{''} & \text{if } n_{CONV}(u) > 0 \wedge n_{SNP}(u) = 0 \end{cases}$$

$$c_{V2}(u) = \begin{cases} \text{``}Yes\text{''} & \text{if } n_{SNP}(u) - n_{CONV}(u) > 20 \\ \text{``}No\text{''} & \text{if } n_{CONV}(u) - n_{SNP}(u) > 20 \end{cases}$$

where $n_p(u)$ is the number of times user u follows a politician (MPs/MSPs) of party p. We test our ground truth by comparing a user's label allocated using the hashtags versus that allocated using the two verification methods. If the two labels are concordant, then the user voting intention is said to be verified, i.e. it is likely to be correct. Table 2 reports the agreement statistics between our hashtag labelling method and the two verification methods. Comparing the hashtag labelling method with the two verifications, we find that c_{V1} verifies more users than c_{V2}, but shows lower agreement (c.f. Cohen's Kappa) than c_{V2}. Overall, we find, of the 6332 users verified by c_{V1} or c_{V2}, 87% can be verified into "Yes" or "No" voters, demonstrating that our ground-truth produced by the hashtags labeling method is reasonable and reliable.

[4] http://lordashcroftpolls.com/ 2014/09/scotland-voted/

Table 2: Ground-Truth agreement.

	Verified Users	Agreement Number	Agreement Precision	Kappa
c_{V1}	6339	5424	85.6%	66.2%
c_{V2}	684	619	90.5%	80.0%
$c_{V2} \cup c_{V2}$	6632	5770	87.0%	71.8%

5. EXPERIMENTS

We use the dataset described in Section 4 to compare the performances of the NB and TBNB classifiers. To assess the impact of parameters used in both classifiers, we vary the number of selected features F and the deployed feature selection approach for both NB and TBNB. We also vary the number of topics T in the TBNB classifier. Since the number of unique terms in our collection is 200K, we vary $F = \{5K, 10K, 20K, 50K, 100K, 120K, 150K, 180K\}$ for NB, while, for TBNB, as F depicts the number of features selected for each topic (i.e. the total number of features would be $F \times T$), we do not experiment with $F > 100K$[5].

We use a 10-fold cross validation process over the 7337 users of our dataset to evaluate the performances of the NB and TBNB classifiers. In particular, we use the following performance indicators:

Indicator 1: Accuracy, the standard classification accuracy measure.

Indicator 2: Average Number of Activated Features F_{test}. For an unseen Twitter user, we concatenate their posted tweets into a virtual document and count the number of selected features activated in the virtual document. We average these numbers across the 10 folds to obtain F_{test}. Intuitively, the higher F_{test}, the greater the confidence in the predicted category.

Indicator 3: Average Rank of the Activated Feature R_{test}. Each feature has a rank position ranked by the applied feature selection approach. This indicator represents the average rank position of all testing features of all users in the 10 folds. Intuitively, it reflects the average effectiveness level of the activated features.

We use the three indicators to investigate and explain the performances of the NB and TBNB classifiers, as well as to validate our hypothesis that the TBNB classifier will outperform NB on our IndyRef dataset. In particular, we answer the following related research questions: (i) how effective are the feature selection approaches on the used dataset?; (ii) what is the effect of F_{test} and R_{test} on the Accuracy performances of the classifiers?

Figure 2(a)-(g) shows the performances of the NB and TBNB classifier when varying the parameters of the classifiers. As a baseline, we use NB without feature selection (NB_NO). This baseline has at least a comparable performance to both Support Vector Machine (SVM) and Decision Tree-based (DT) classifiers. Both NB and TBNB perform poorly when F is low. However, all TBNB classifiers markedly outperform the NB_NO baseline when F ranges from 10K to 50K. The highest accuracy of TBNB (90.4%) is achieved when applying the WOR feature selection approach (TBNB_WOR) with T=10 and when the FR feature selection approach is deployed (TBNB_FR) with T= 5. This is a 7.8% improvement over the NB baseline (82.6%). When varying the number of used topics (T), we note that the performance of the TBNB classifier generally increases as T increases. However, once T reaches 30 topics (see Figure

[5] In our dataset, no topic has more than 100K features.

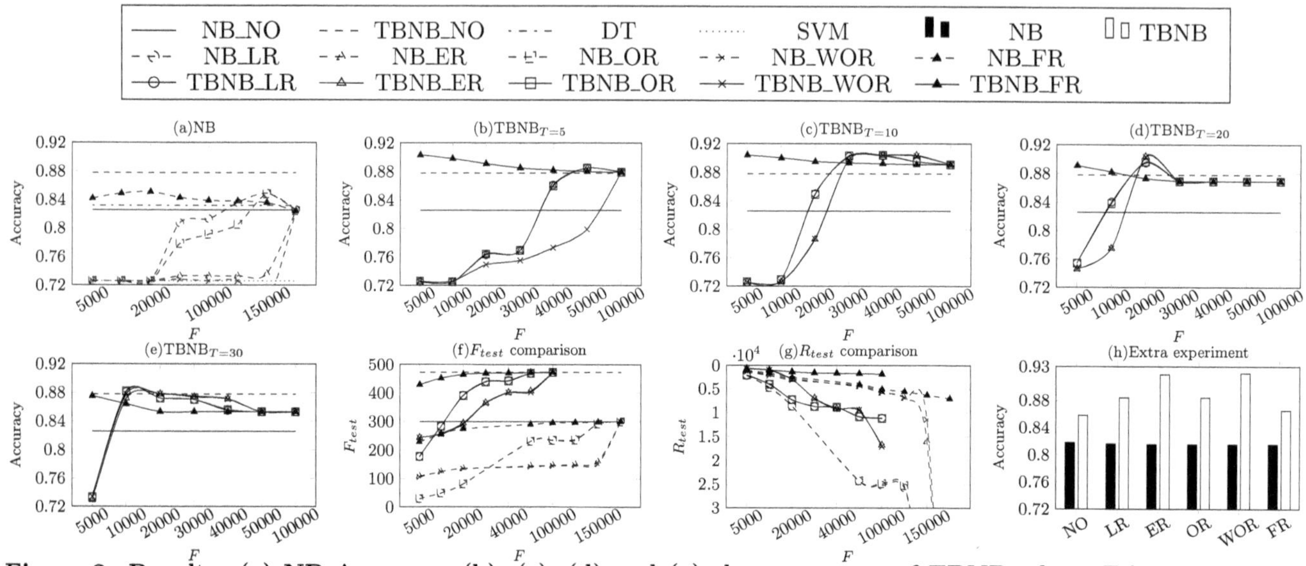

Figure 2: Results: (a) NB Accuracy; (b), (c), (d) and (e) show accuracy of TBNB where T is set to 5, 10, 20 and 30 separately; (f) and (g) show F_{test} & R_{test} for both NB & TBNB classifiers (T=10) while varying F; (h) shows an experiment on a 2nd dataset.

2(e)), the accuracy of TBNB starts decreasing while still outperforming the NB_NO baseline around the IndyRef. This suggests that the tweets corpus reflects 10-20 main discussion themes. On the other hand, each NB or TBNB classifier with feature selection approaches has an optimal F. For instance, the optimal F of NB_OR is 150K while that of TBNB_FR is 5K.

We first contrast the feature selection approaches for the NB and TBNB classifiers. Figure 2(f) shows that the average number of activated features (F_{test}) is lower for the NB classifier across all feature selection approaches than for TBNB with the same feature selection. This demonstrates that the TBNB classifier activates more features in the virtual document of the user, thereby improving its confidence in the voting intention classification. Unlike in previous work where the OR feature selection approach performs best (see Section 2), we found that the WOR and FR feature selection approaches are the most effective on our dataset.

Next, we consider the features selected and activated by each of the classifiers. Firstly, for NB, Figure 2(a) shows that increasing the number of features (F) increases the accuracy, until F reaches an optimal value, and decreases thereafter. The same conclusion is true for TBNB, e.g. for 10 topics (Figure 2(c)). However, contrasting Figures 2(a) & (c), we see that TBNB exhibits higher accuracy than NB, despite using less features (F). Indeed, we observe from Figure 2 (f) that the number of features activated in the unseen tweets (F_{test}) for a given F value is higher for TBNB than for NB - i.e. the classifier has more feature evidence to work with. Moreover, the average rank of those features selected (R_{test}, Figure 2(g)) increases as F increases. Hence, the relatively higher and stable F_{test} and R_{test} values observed for TBNB, in comparison to NB, are indicative of its higher accuracy. In summary, the advantage of TBNB over NB is that the topic-based features are more useful, leading to higher accuracies.

Finally, to show the generalisation of TBNB, we use a second dataset with 6234 labelled users, collected from an earlier period (i.e. July 25 to August 25 2014). For both NB and TBNB, we learn the parameters F and T from the first dataset with the 7337 users. We then use the learned parameters in a 10-fold cross validation on the second dataset. From Figure 2(h), we observe that the TBNB classifier outperforms NB in terms of accuracy, with and without the feature selection approaches, by up to 10.3%. Overall, our experiments validate our hypothesis in Section 5, namely that TBNB will outperform NB on the IndyRef dataset.

6. CONCLUSIONS

We classified the users' voting intentions on Twitter during the IndyRef. We noted that the users tended to focus their discussions on a specific set of topics, reflecting their voting intentions. As a consequence, we proposed to enrich the Naive Bayes classifier by leveraging the underlying topics covered in the tweets. Our proposed approach leverages the dissimilarity of the features across the topics, and their variance across the voting categories to increase the classification confidence. Our results demonstrate the effectiveness of our resulting TBNB classifier on two datasets with and without the use of feature selection approaches. In the future, we plan to analyse the effect of the evolving discussions on the users' voting intentions over time.

7. REFERENCES

[1] F. Al Zamal, W. Liu, and D. Ruths. Homophily and latent attribute inference: Inferring latent attributes of Twitter users from neighbors. In *ICWSM*, 2012.

[2] P. Barberá. Birds of the same feather tweet together: Bayesian ideal point estimation using Twitter data. *Political Analysis*, 23(1), 2015.

[3] D. M. Blei, A. Y. Ng, and M. I. Jordan. Latent dirichlet allocation. *the Journal of machine Learning research*, 3:993–1022, 2003.

[4] R. Cohen and D. Ruths. Classifying political orientation on Twitter: It's not easy! In *ICWSM*, 2013.

[5] M. Conover, J. Ratkiewicz, M. Francisco, B. Gonçalves, F. Menczer, and A. Flammini. Political polarization on Twitter. In *ICWSM*, 2011.

[6] L. Crossley. From Fife to Fiji: Amazing Twitter heatmap shows how the scottish independence referendum has been followed around the world in the past 30 days. *Daily Mail*, 18 Sep 2014.

[7] D. Mladenic and M. Grobelnik. Feature selection for unbalanced class distribution and naive bayes. In *ICML*, 1999.

A Word Embedding based Generalized Language Model for Information Retrieval

Debasis Ganguly
ADAPT Centre, School of Computing
Dublin City University
Dublin, Ireland
dganguly@computing.dcu.ie

Mandar Mitra
CVPR Unit
Indian Statistical Institute
Kolkata, India
mandar@isical.ac.in

Dwaipayan Roy
CVPR Unit
Indian Statistical Institute
Kolkata, India
dwaipayan_r@isical.ac.in

Gareth J.F. Jones
ADAPT Centre School of Computing
Dublin City University
Dublin, Ireland
gjones@computing.dcu.ie

ABSTRACT

Word2vec, a word embedding technique, has gained significant interest among researchers in natural language processing (NLP) in recent years. The embedding of the word vectors helps to identify a list of words that are used in similar contexts with respect to a given word. In this paper, we focus on the use of word embeddings for enhancing retrieval effectiveness. In particular, we construct a generalized language model, where the mutual independence between a pair of words (say t and t') no longer holds. Instead, we make use of the vector embeddings of the words to derive the transformation probabilities between words. Specifically, the event of observing a term t in the query from a document d is modeled by two distinct events, that of generating a different term t', either from the document itself or from the collection, respectively, and then eventually transforming it to the observed query term t. The first event of generating an intermediate term from the document intends to capture how well a term fits contextually within a document, whereas the second one of generating it from the collection aims to address the vocabulary mismatch problem by taking into account other related terms in the collection. Our experiments, conducted on the standard TREC 6-8 ad hoc and Robust tasks, show that our proposed method yields significant improvements over language model (LM) and LDA-smoothed LM baselines.

Categories and Subject Descriptors

H.3.3 [**INFORMATION STORAGE AND RETRIEVAL**]: Information Search and Retrieval—*Retrieval models, Relevance Feedback, Query formulation*

General Terms

Theory, Experimentation

SIGIR'15, Aug 9–13, 2015, Santiago, Chile.
Copyright 2015 ACM ISBN 978-1-4503-3621-5/15/08 ...$15.00.
http://dx.doi.org/10.1145/2766462.2767780 .

Keywords

Generalized Language model, Word Embedding, Word2Vec

1. INTRODUCTION

Word embedding as technique for representing the meaning of a word in terms other words, as exemplified by the *Word2vec* approach [7]. The embedding of the word vectors enables the identification of words that are used in similar contexts to a specufic word. a list of words that are used in similar contexts with respect to a given word. While word Embedding has gained significant interest among researchers in natural language processing (NLP) in recent years, there has to date been little exploration of the potential for use of these methods in information retrieval (IR).

This paper explores the use of word embeddings of enhance IR effectiveness. We begin with a brief introduction to word embedding techniques and then motivate how can these be applied in IR.

A brief introduction to word embedding. Word embedding techniques seek to embed representations of words. For example, two vectors $\vec{t}$ and $\vec{t'}$, corresponding to the words t and t', are close in an abstract space of N dimensions if they have similar contexts and vice-versa, (i.e. the contexts in turn having similar words) [4]. Use of a cosine similarity measure on this abstract vector space of embedded words can be used to identify a list of words that are used in similar contexts with respect to a given word. These semantically related words may be used for various natural language processing (NLP) tasks. The general idea is to train moving windows with vector embeddings for the words (rather than training with the more conventional word count vectors), and classify the individual windows [2]. This finds application for examples in applications such as POS tagging, semantic role labeling, named-entity recognition and other tasks. The state-of-the-art word embedding approaches involve training deep neural networks with the help of *negative sampling* [7]. It is reported that this process of negative sampling (commonly known as *word2vec*[1]) produces reliable word embeddings in a very efficient manner [7].

Potential use in IR. We now discuss how word embeddings can potentially be helpful in improving retrieval quality. In the context of IR, *vocabulary mismatch*, i.e. the inherent characteristic of using different but semantically similar terms across documents about

[1]The name *word2vec* comes from the name of the software tool released by Micholov et. al. (`https://code.google.com/p/word2vec/`

the same topic or between a query and its relevant documents, is a difficult problem to solve.

However, the working principle of most standard retrieval models in IR involves an underlying assumption of term independence, e.g. the vector space model (VSM) assumes that the documents are embedded in a mutually orthogonal term space, while probabilistic models, such as the BM25 or the language model (LM) assume that the terms are sampled independently from documents. Standard approaches in IR take into account term association in two ways, one which involves a *global* analysis over the whole collection of documents (i.e. independent of the queries), while the other takes into account *local* co-occurrence information of terms in the top ranked documents retrieved in response to a query. The latter approach corresponds to the relevance feedback step in IR which we do not investigate in this paper. Existing global analysis methods such as the latent semantic indexing (LSA) [3] or latent Dirichlet allocation (LDA) [1] only take into account the co-occurrences between terms at the level of documents instead of considering the context of a term. Since the word embedding techniques that we introduced in the beginning of this section, leverage the information around the local context of each word to derive the embeddings (two words have close vector representations if and only if they are used in similar contexts), we believe that such an approach can potentially improve the global analysis technique of IR leading to better retrieval effectiveness.

The rest of the paper is organized as follows. Section 2 discusses related work. In Section 3, we propose the generalized LM, which is evalaued in Section 4. Finally, Section 5 concludes the paper.

2. RELATED WORK

Latent semantic analysis (LSA) [3] is a global analysis technique in which documents are represented in a term space of reduced dimensionality so as to take into account inter-term dependencies. More recent techniques such as the latent Dirichlet allocation (LDA) represent term dependencies by assuming that each term is generated from a set of latent variables called the *topics* [1]. A major problem of these approaches is that they only consider word co-occurrences at the level of documents to model term associations, which may not always be reliable. In contrast, the word embeddings take into account the local (window-based) context around the terms [7], and thus may lead to better modeling of the term dependencies.

Moreover, most of these global analysis approaches, e.g. LDA, have been applied in IR in an ad-hoc way for re-assigning term weights without explicitly representing the term dependencies as an inherent part of an IR model. For example, an LDA document model (term sampling probabilities marginalized over a set of latent topic variables) is linearly added as a smoothing parameter to the standard LM probability [9], as a result of which the term dependencies are not clearly visible from the model definition. Contrastingly, in this paper, we intend to directly model the term dependencies as a part of an IR model.

3. A GENERALIZED LANGUAGE MODEL

In this section, we propose the generalized language model (GLM) that models term dependencies using the vector embeddings of terms.

3.1 Language Modelling

In LM, for a given query q, documents are returned as a ranked list sorted in decreasing order by the posterior probabilities $P(d|q)$. These posterior probabilities are estimated for each document d during indexing time with the help of the prior probability ($P(q|d)$) according to the Bayes rule [8, 6, 10].

$$P(d|q) = \frac{P(q|d).P(d)}{\sum_{d' \in C} P(q|d').(d')} \propto P(q|d).P(d) = P(d).\prod_{t \in q} P(t|d)$$
$$= \prod_{t \in q} \lambda \hat{P}(t|d) + (1-\lambda)\hat{P}(t|C) = \prod_{t \in q} \lambda \frac{tf(t,d)}{|d|} + (1-\lambda)\frac{cf(t)}{cs} \quad (1)$$

In Equation 1, the set C represents a universe of documents (commonly known as the *collection*), $\hat{P}(t|d)$ and $\hat{P}(t|C)$ denote the maximum likelihood estimated probabilities of generating a query term t from the document d and the collection respectively, using frequency statistics. The probabilities of these two (mutually exclusive) events are denoted by λ and $1-\lambda$ respectively. The notations $tf(t,d)$, $|d|$, $cf(t)$ and cs denote the term frequency of term t in document d, the length of d, collection frequency of the term t and the total collection size respectively.

3.2 Term Transformation Events

As per Equation 1, terms in a query are generated by sampling them independently from either the document or the collection. We propose the following generalization to the model. Instead of assuming that terms are mutually independent during the sampling process, we propose a generative process in which a noisy channel may transform (mutate) a term t' into a term t. More concretely, if a term t is observed in the query corresponding to a document d, according to our model it may have occurred in three possible ways, shown as follows.

- **Direct term sampling**: Standard LM term sampling, i.e. sampling a term t (without transformation) either from the document d or from the collection.
- **Transformation via Document Sampling**: Sampling a term $t'(t' \neq t)$ from d which is then transformed to t by a noisy channel.
- **Transformation via Collection Sampling**: Sampling the term t' from the collection which is then transformed to t by the noisy channel.

Transformation via Document Sampling. Let $P(t,t'|d)$ denote the probability of generating a term t' from a document d and then transforming this term to t in the query.

$$P(t,t'|d) = P(t|t',d)P(t'|d) \quad (2)$$

In Equation 2, $P(t'|d)$ can be estimated by maximum likelihood with the help of the standard term sampling method as shown in Equation 1. For the other part, i.e. transforming t' to t, we make use of the cosine similarities between the two embedded vectors corresponding to t and t' respectively. More precisely, this probability of selecting a term t, given the sampled term t', is proportional to the similarity of t with t'. Note that this similarity is independent of the document d. This is shown in Equation 3, where $sim(t,t')$ is the cosine similarity between the vector representations of t and t' and $\Sigma(d)$ is the sum of the similarity values between all term pairs occurring in document d, which being the normalization constant, can be pre-computed for each document d.

$$P(t|t',d) = \frac{sim(t,t')}{\sum_{t'' \in d} sim(t,t'')} = \frac{sim(t,t')}{\Sigma(d)} \quad (3)$$

Consequently, we can write Equation 2 as

$$P(t,t'|d) = \frac{sim(t',t)}{\Sigma(d)} \frac{tf(t',d)}{|d|} \quad (4)$$

Equation 4 favours those terms t's that are not only tend to co-occur with the query term t within d, but are also semantically related to

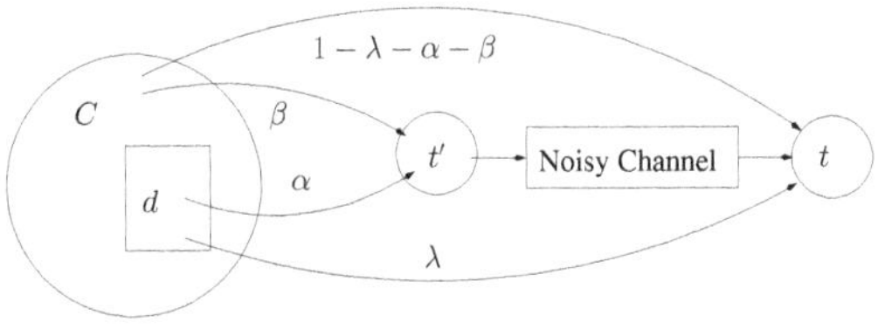

Figure 1: Schematics of generating a query term t in our proposed Generalized Language Model (GLM). GLM degenerates to LM when $\alpha = \beta = 0$.

it. Thus, words that are used in similar contexts with respect to the query term t over the collection, as predicted by the vector embeddings, are more likely to contribute to the term score of t. In other words, Equation 4 takes into account how well an observed query term t *contextually fits* into a document d. A term contextually fits well within a document if it co-occurs with other semantically similar terms. Terms, score high by Equation 4, potentially indicate a more relevant match for the query as compared to other terms with low values for this score.

Transformation via Collection Sampling. Let the complementary event of transforming a term t', sampled from the collection instead of a particular document, to the observed query term t be denoted by $P(t, t'|C)$. This can be estimated as follows.

$$P(t, t'|C) = P(t|t', C).P(t'|C) = P(t|t', C).\frac{cf(t')}{cs} \quad (5)$$

Now $P(t|t', C)$ can be estimated in a way similar to computing $P(t|t', d)$, as shown in Equation 3. However, instead of considering all (t, t') pairs in the vocabulary for computation, it is reasonable to restrict the computation to a small neighbourhood of terms around the query term t, say N_t because taking too large a neighbourhood may lead to noisy term associations. This is shown in Equation 6.

$$P(t|t', C) = \frac{sim(t, t')}{\sum_{t'' \in N_t} sim(t, t'')} = \frac{sim(t, t')}{\Sigma(N_t)} \quad (6)$$

While $P(t, t'|d)$ measures the contextual fitness of a term t in a document d with respect to its neighbouring (in the vector space of embedded terms) terms t' in d, $P(t, t'|C)$, on the other hand, aims to alleviate the vocabulary mismatch between documents and queries in the sense that for each term t in d it expands the document with other related terms t's. From an implementation perspective, $P(t, t'|d)$ reweights existing document terms based on their contextual fit, whereas $P(t, t'|C)$ expands the document with additional terms with appropriate weights.

Combining the Events. Finally, for putting all the events together in the LM generation model, let us assume that the probability of observing a query term t without the transformation process (as in standard LM) be λ. Let us denote the probability of sampling the query term t via a transformation through a term t' sampled from the document d with α, and let and the complementary probability of sampling t' from the collection be then β, as shown schematically in Figure 1. The LM term generation probability in this case can thus be written as shown in Equation 7. This is a generalized version of the standard LM, which we now henceforth refer to as generalized language model (GLM), that takes into account term relatedness with the help of the noisy channel transformation model, which in turn uses the word embeddings to derive the likelihood of term transformations. Note that the GLM degenerates to standard LM by setting α and β to zero, i.e. not using the transformation model in the term generation process.

Table 1: Dataset Overview

TREC disks	Qry set	Fields	Qry Ids	Avg. qry length	Avg. # rel. docs
4 & 5	TREC 6	title	301-350	2.48	92.22
	TREC 7	title	351-400	2.42	93.48
	TREC 8	title	401-450	2.38	94.56
	Robust	title	601-700	2.88	37.20

$$P(t|d) = \lambda P(t|d) + \alpha \sum_{t' \in d} P(t, t'|d)P(t') + \beta \sum_{t' \in N_t} P(t, t'|C)P(t') + (1 - \lambda - \alpha - \beta)P(t|C) \quad (7)$$

3.3 Implementation Outline

An efficient approach to get the neighbours of a given term is to store a pre-computed list of nearest neighbours in memory for every word in the vocabulary. After this step, for each document d in the collection, we iterate over term pairs (t, t') and assign a new term-weight to the term t representing the document sampling transformation according to Equation 4. Then we iterate again over every term t in d and use the pre-computed nearest neighbours of t (N_t) to compute a score for the collection sampling transformation, as shown in Equation 6. To account for the fact that these transformation probabilities are symmetrical, we add the term t' to d. Note that it is not required to add the term t' in case of the document sampling transformation event because t' is already present in d.

4. EVALUATION

Experimental Setup. Our experiments were conducted on the standard TREC ad hoc tasks from TREC 6, 7, 8 and the Robust track. Information about the document and the query sets is outlined in Table 1. We implemented GLM using the Lucene[2] IR framework. As one of our baseline retrieval models, we used standard LM with Jelinek Mercer smoothing [6, 10], which is distributed as a part of Lucene. Additionally, we also used LM with LDA smoothing [9] as our second baseline to compare against. In contrast to [9], which reports retrieval results with LDA smoothed LM (LDA-LM) on individual document subsets (and their corresponding relevance judgements) from the TREC collection as categorized by their sources, i.e. the "LA Times" and the "Financial Times", we instead executed LDA on the whole TREC collection. The rationale for using LDA as a baseline is that analogous to our model, LDA also attempts to model term dependencies by taking into account latent variables (called the topics). This baseline was also implemented in Lucene.

Parameters. The parameter λ of the LM baseline was empirically set to 0.2 (after varying it within a range of $[0.1, 0.9]$). This value of λ for the TREC collection agrees with the observations reported in [6]. According to the findings of [9], the number of topics in LDA, i.e. K, was set to 800. As prescribed in [5], we set the LDA hyper-parameters α and β (note that these are different from the GLM parameters) to $50/K$ and 0.01 respectively. Obtaining effective word embedding is an integral part of the GLM. The word embeddings for the experiments reported in this section were obtained on the TREC document collection with the parameter settings as prescribed in [7], i.e., we embedded the word vector in a 200 dimensional space, and used continuous bag-of-words

[2] `http://lucene.apache.org/core/`

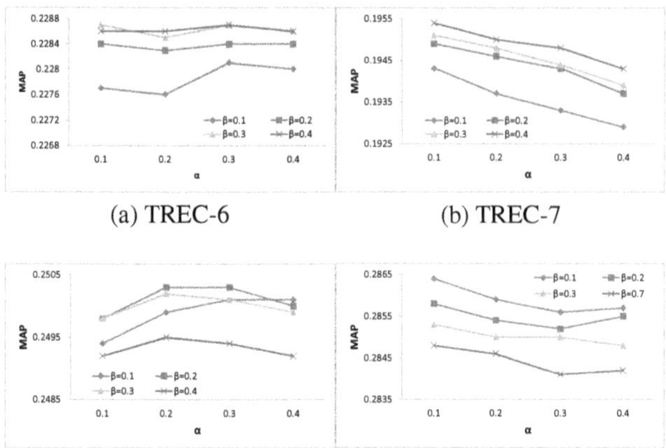

(a) TREC-6 (b) TREC-7

(c) TREC-8 (d) Robust

Figure 2: Effect of varying the GLM parameters α and β on the MAP values for the TREC query sets.

with negative sampling. The neighbourhood N_t of the GLM (see Equation 7) was set to 3, i.e., for each given term in a document, we consider adding at most 3 related terms from the collection.

Results. First, we varied the GLM parameters, namely α and β within the range $[0.1, 0.4]$ so as to ensure that $\alpha + \beta + \lambda < 1$ (λ being set to 0.2) for all the query sets used in our experiments. The results are shown in Figure 2. It can be seen that the optimal values of α and β depend on the query set, e.g. for the TREC 8 query set (Figure 2c, the optimal results are obtained for $(\alpha, \beta) = (0.3, 0.2)$, whereas this combination does not produce the optimal results for the other query sets. It can be observed that a reasonable choice for these parameters is in the range $[0.2, 0.3]$, which means imparting more or less uniform weights to all the term generation events, namely α, β and λ. In Table 2, we show the optimal results obtained with GLM for each individual query set and compare the results with the baselines, i.e. the LM and the LDA-LM. It can be observed that for each query set, GLM significantly[3] outperforms the baselines. It turns out that the LDA-LM (almost) consistently outperforms the standard LM. However, the results (as measured by the percentage gains in comparison to standard LM) do not seem to be as high as reported in [9] (about 3% as compared to about 8%). We believe that the reason for this is due to the diversity in the LDA topics caused by the news articles from different sources.

From Table 2, we observe that GLM consistently and significantly outperforms both LM and LDA-LM for all the query sets. Not only does it increase the recall values in comparison to LM, but it also increases precision at top ranks by always outperforming LDA in terms of MAP. Although LDA achieves higher recall than GLM in two cases (TREC-6 and Robust), the higher recall in the case of LDA does not significantly increase the MAP, which is indicative of the fact that the precision at top ranks does not improve. For GLM however, an increase in the recall value is always associated with a significant increase in MAP as well, which indicates that precision at top ranks remains relatively stable in comparison to LDA.

5. CONCLUSIONS AND FUTURE WORK

We proposed a generalized version of the language model for IR. Our model considers two possible cases of generating a term from either a document or the collection and then changing it to another term after passing it through a noisy channel. The term transformation probabilities of the noisy channel, in turn, are computed by making use of the distances between the word vectors embedded in an abstract space. We argue that this model has two fold advantage, firstly it is able to estimate how well a term fits in the context of a document, and secondly it is able to decrease the vocabulary gap by adding other useful terms to a document. Empirical evaluation shows that our method significantly outperforms the standard LM and LDA-LM. Possible future work will be to investigate compositionality of terms from the vector embeddings of words.

Acknowledgement. This research is supported by SFI through the CNGL Programme (Grant No: 12/CE/I2267) in the ADAPT Centre (www.adaptcentre.ie) at Dublin City University, and by a grant under the SFI ISCA India consortium.

[3]Measured by Wilcoxon statistical significance test with 95% confidence.

Table 2: Comparative performance of LM, LDA and GLM on the TREC query sets.

		Metrics		
Topic Set	Method	MAP	GMAP	Recall
TREC-6	LM	0.2148	0.0761	0.4778
	LDA-LM	0.2192	0.0790	**0.5333**
	GLM	**0.2287**	**0.0956**	0.5020
TREC-7	LM	0.1771	0.0706	0.4867
	LDA-LM	0.1631	0.0693	0.4854
	GLM	**0.1958**	**0.0867**	**0.5021**
TREC-8	LM	0.2357	0.1316	0.5895
	LDA-LM	0.2428	0.1471	0.5833
	GLM	**0.2503**	**0.1492**	**0.6246**
Robust	LM	0.2555	0.1290	0.7715
	LDA-LM	0.2623	**0.1712**	**0.8005**
	GLM	**0.2864**	0.1656	0.7967

6. REFERENCES

[1] D. M. Blei, A. Y. Ng, and M. I. Jordan. Latent Dirichlet Allocation. *Journal of Machine Learning Research*, 3:993–1022, March 2003.

[2] R. Collobert, J. Weston, L. Bottou, M. Karlen, K. Kavukcuoglu, and P. Kuksa. Natural language processing (almost) from scratch. *J. Mach. Learn. Res.*, 12:2493–2537, Nov. 2011.

[3] S. C. Deerwester, S. T. Dumais, T. K. Landauer, G. W. Furnas, and R. A. Harshman. Indexing by latent semantic analysis. *JASIS*, 41(6):391–407, 1990.

[4] Y. Goldberg and O. Levy. word2vec Explained: deriving Mikolov et al.'s negative-sampling word-embedding method. *CoRR*, abs/1402.3722, 2014.

[5] T. L. Griffiths and M. Steyvers. Finding scientific topics. *Proceedings of the National Academy of Sciences (PNAS)*, 101(suppl. 1):5228–5235, 2004.

[6] D. Hiemstra. *Using Language Models for Information Retrieval*. PhD thesis, Center of Telematics and Information Technology, AE Enschede, 2000.

[7] T. Mikolov, I. Sutskever, K. Chen, G. S. Corrado, and J. Dean. Distributed representations of words and phrases and their compositionality. In *Proc. of NIPS '13*, pages 3111–3119, 2013.

[8] J. M. Ponte and W. B. Croft. A language modeling approach to information retrieval. In *SIGIR*, pages 275–281. ACM, 1998.

[9] X. Wei and W. B. Croft. LDA-based document models for ad-hoc retrieval. In *SIGIR '06*, pages 178–185, 2006.

[10] C. Zhai and J. Lafferty. A study of smoothing methods for language models applied to information retrieval. *ACM Trans. Inf. Syst.*, 22(2):179–214, Apr. 2004.

A Head-Weighted Gap-Sensitive Correlation Coefficient

Ning Gao
College of Information Studies/UMIACS
University of Maryland, College Park
ninggao@umd.edu

Douglas W. Oard
College of Information Studies/UMIACS
University of Maryland, College Park
oard@umd.edu

ABSTRACT

Information retrieval systems rank documents, and shared-task evaluations yield results that can be used to rank information retrieval systems. Comparing rankings in ways that can yield useful insights is thus an important capability. When making such comparisons, it is often useful to give greater weight to comparisons near the head of a ranked list than to what happens further down. This is the focus of the widely used τ_{AP} measure. When scores are available, gap-sensitive measures give greater weight to larger differences than to smaller ones. This is the focus of the widely used Pearson correlation measure (ρ). This paper introduces a new measure, τ_{GAP}, which combines both features. System comparisons from the TREC 5 Ad Hoc track are used to illustrate the differences in emphasis achieved by τ_{AP}, ρ, and the proposed τ_{GAP}.

Categories and Subject Descriptors

H.3.4 [**Systems and Software**]: Performance evaluation

Keywords

Evaluation Metric; Rank Correlation Coefficient

1. INTRODUCTION

In information retrieval evaluation, we often wish to compare alternative systems based on some single-valued evaluation measures. For example, we might want to know whether comparing systems using relevance judgments created by one user (to whom we have access) can be used to compare systems in ways that are predictive of what we would have seen had some other user made the judgments [9]. Alternatively, we might want to know whether we can better approximate the system comparison results we could compute with very extensive relevance judgments on a large number of topics by reducing the number of topics or by reducing the number of judgments per topic [2]. In such cases, we can formulate our research question as asking about the correlation between two ranked lists of scores, where the scores result from some evaluation metric such as F_1, Expected Reciprocal Rank (ERR), Normalized Discounted Cumulative Gain (NDCG), or Mean Average Precision (MAP).

SIGIR'15, August 09 - 13, 2015, Santiago, Chile.
© 2015 ACM. ISBN 978-1-4503-3621-5/15/08 ...$15.00.
DOI: http://dx.doi.org/10.1145/2766462.2767793.

When making such comparisons, we focus on two desiderata. First, we prefer that those differences to be large, since small differences may not reflect any meaningful degree of impact on the user experience [3]. Second, we prefer that those differences be statistically significant, since unreliable measurements of differences could be misleading [7]. When extending our comparison from pairs to large sets of systems, as is common in shared-task evaluations such as TREC, CLEF, NTCIR and FIRE, we often care more about distinguishing systems that are very different from each other, which requires the evaluation metric to be gap-sensitive. We also care more about the comparisons among the best systems than we do about comparisons between, for example, the best and the worst systems, which requires the evaluation metric to be head-weighted.

Perhaps the most widely used measure of rank correlation in information retrieval research is Kendall's τ [4] in which swapping systems is penalized. Yilmaz et al. [10] introduced a head-weighted variant of τ that they call τ_{AP} that penalizes the misranking of the best systems (i.e., those near the head of the list), and that measure is now also often reported. Buckley and Voorhees have observed, however, that when systems receive very similar scores we should care less about swaps than when those scores are very different [1]. They therefore created a gap-sensitive measure by suppressing the effect of small swaps by treating any swap within a "fuzziness value" (e.g., 5% relative to the smaller value) as not being large enough to be counted. In this paper, we propose to generalize that approach to penalize swaps in proportion to the difference in scores, so that large swaps will gave the greatest influence on the measure, but small swaps are not completely ignored. This approach thus potentially offers greater insight, without the need to commit to a specific "fuzziness" threshold. Moreover, we combine this more nuanced approach with the head-weighted design of τ_{AP} to produce a new correlation measure for ranked lists of scores that is both head-weighted and gap-sensitive. We call our new measure τ_{GAP} (for Gap And Position).

The remainder of the paper is organized as follows, Section 2 reviews the prior work on the use of correlation measures for system comparison. Section 3 then define τ_{GAP} and establishes that it has a number of desirable properties. Section 4 complements this analytic perspective with empirical results for system scores from the TREC 5 Ad Hoc task, and then further analyses the focus of different correlation coefficient metrics through the heatmap of system pair weights. Section 5 concludes the paper with some remarks on limitations of the τ_{GAP} measure that may inspire further work on this important problem.

2. RELATED WORK

The Pearson correlation coefficient between two items is defined as the covariance of the two items divided by the product of their standard deviations:

$$\rho = \frac{E[(X-\mu_X)(Y-\mu_Y)]}{\sigma_X \cdot \sigma_Y} \tag{1}$$

where X and Y are the vectors of ranked lists; E is the expectation; σ is the standard deviation; and μ is the mean [6]. Given two ranked lists of items, the Spearman correlation coefficient [11] is defined as the Pearson correlation coefficient between the ranks (i.e., with the ranks used in place of scores). The most widely used measure in information retrieval research is neither Pearson nor Spearman correlation, however, but rather Kendall's τ [4]. Kendall's τ evaluates the correlation of two lists of items by counting their concordant and discordant pairs.

To fulfill the specific evaluation needs for different tasks, various definitions of correlation coefficients derived from Kendall's τ have been proposed. Kendall's tau rank distance [5] measures the disagreements between two ranking lists by counting the swaps that the bubble sort algorithm needed to sort one list in the same order as the other. The *AP Correlation* coefficient (τ_{AP}), proposed by Yilmaz et al. [10], focuses and penalizes more on the errors at high rankings. Given a ground-truth list and prediction list, τ_{AP} of the two lists is defined as:

$$\tau_{AP} = \frac{2}{(N-1)} \cdot \sum_{i=2}^{N} \frac{C_i}{i-1} - 1 \tag{2}$$

where N is the number of items in the list; C_i is the number of items above rank i in the prediction list and correctly ranked with respect to the item at rank i in the ground-truth list. For each item at rank i, τ_{AP} only checks the positions of the $i-1$ items with ranks above i, and calculates the proportion of the correctly ordered items with respect to the item at rank i. Finally, the value of τ_{AP} is a linear combination of all ranks i in the prediction list.

3. THE TAU GAP COEFFICIENT

τ_{GAP} is a non-parametric correlation coefficient, particularly sensitive to errors at high rankings and errors for item pairs with large score differences (gaps). In this section, we present the definition of τ_{GAP}. Since the definition of τ_{AP} and τ_{GAP} are both based on swapped item pairs counting, we further explore the mathematical properties of τ_{GAP} comparing with τ_{AP}.

$$\tau_{GAP} = \frac{2}{(N-1)} \cdot \sum_{i=2}^{N} \frac{\sum_{j<i}|CG_{ji}|}{\sum_{j<i}|G_{ji}|} - 1 \tag{3}$$

Given two ranked lists, a ground truth list and a prediction list, τ_{GAP} is defined as in Equation 3, where N is the number of items in the lists; i represents the item at rank i in the prediction list; j is the item ranked higher than i in the prediction list; G_{ji} is the gap between the item at rank j and item at rank i in ground-truth list; CG_{ji} returns the same value as G_{ji} when the item pair (j,i) in the prediction list are ranked in the same order as in the ground-truth list, otherwise, return 0. For each item at rank i in the prediction list, τ_{GAP} only considers the rank relation of the $i-1$ item pairs (j,i). $\sum_{j<i}|G_{ji}|$ is the sum of all the gaps for the $i-1$ item pairs, and $\sum_{j<i}|CG_{ji}|$ is the sum of the gaps for correctly ordered pairs.

THEOREM 1. *The value of τ_{GAP} is always between -1 and 1.*

PROOF. For each item at rank i, there will be $i-1$ pairs of items (j,i) taken into the consideration by τ_{GAP}. $\sum_{j<i}|G_{ji}|$ is the sum of the gaps of these $i-1$ pairs of items. $\sum_{j<i}|CG_{ji}|$ is the sum of the gaps that the prediction list ranks the two items (j,i) in the same order as the ground-truth list. Therefore, $\frac{\sum_{j<i}|CG_{ji}|}{\sum_{j<i}|G_{ji}|}$ is always between 0 and 1. Normalized across all ranks i, $\frac{1}{(N-1)} \cdot \sum_{i=2}^{N} \frac{\sum_{j<i}|CG_{ji}|}{\sum_{j<i}|G_{ji}|}$ is always between 0 and 1; $\frac{2}{(N-1)} \cdot \sum_{i=2}^{N} \frac{\sum_{j<i}|CG_{ji}|}{\sum_{j<i}|G_{ji}|}$ is always between 0 and 2. Then the value of τ_{GAP} is always between -1 and 1. □

THEOREM 2. *If the gaps between the items follow the uniform distribution, then τ_{GAP} is equal to τ_{AP}.*

PROOF. Let the uniform gap be g, then $\sum_{j<i}|G_{ji}| = (i-1)\cdot g$, and $\sum_{j<i}|CG_{ji}| = C_i \cdot g$. Therefore,

$$\begin{aligned}\tau_{GAP} &= \frac{2}{(N-1)} \cdot \sum_{i=2}^{N} \frac{C_i \cdot g}{(i-1)\cdot g} - 1 \\ &= \frac{2}{(N-1)} \cdot \sum_{i=2}^{N} \frac{C_i}{(i-1)} - 1 = \tau_{AP}\end{aligned} \tag{4}$$

Moreover, if the errors are uniformly distributed over the all the ranks in prediction list, then τ_{GAP}, τ_{AP} and τ are equivalent. □

THEOREM 3. *For two prediction lists with same number of items N and same number of errors located at the same ranks, if the errors of one list have large gaps and the errors of the other list have small gaps, then the value of τ_{GAP} for the list with large error gaps $\tau_{GAP-Large}$ will be smaller than the τ_{GAP} for the list with small error gaps $\tau_{GAP-Small}$.*

PROOF. If we define FG_{ji} as the gap between items at rank i and rank j when the item pair (j,i) in the prediction list are ranked in the converse order as in the ground-truth list, or otherwise 0, then τ_{GAP} could be represented as:

$$\tau_{GAP} = \frac{2}{(N-1)} \cdot \sum_{i=2}^{N} \frac{\sum_{j<i}|CG_{ji}|}{\sum_{j<i}|CG_{ji}| + \sum_{j<i}|FG_{ji}|} - 1 \tag{5}$$

If two prediction lists have the same number of errors located at the same ranks, then their will have the same N, i, j and CG_{ji}. The only difference between $\tau_{GAP-Large}$ and $\tau_{GAP-Small}$ is that $\tau_{GAP-Large}$ has larger values for FG_{ji}, so that the value of $\tau_{GAP-Large}$ will be always smaller than $\tau_{GAP-Small}$. □

THEOREM 4. *For a prediction list, if the swapped item pairs always have small gaps, then the value of τ_{GAP} is larger than τ_{AP}; if the swapped item pairs always have large gaps, then the value of τ_{GAP} is smaller than τ_{AP}.*

PROOF. The expectation of the difference between τ_{GAP} and τ_{AP} is:

$$\begin{aligned}E[\tau_{GAP} - \tau_{AP}] &= \frac{2}{N-1} \cdot \sum_{i=2}^{N} \left(\frac{\sum_{j<i} CG_{ji}}{\sum_{j<i} G_{ji}} - \frac{C_i}{i-1} \right) \\ &= \frac{2}{N-1} \cdot \sum_{i=2}^{N} \frac{(i-1)\sum_{j<i} CG_{ji} - C_i \sum_{j<i} G_{ji}}{(i-1)\sum_{j<i} G_{ji}}\end{aligned} \tag{6}$$

Let P_i be the probability that the items before item i in the prediction list are ranked as the same order as in ground-truth list, then we have

$$C_i = P_i \cdot (i-1) \tag{7}$$

Then

$$E[\tau_{GAP}-\tau_{AP}] = \frac{2}{N-1}\cdot\sum_{i=2}^{N}\frac{(i-1)(\sum_{j<i}CG_{ji}-P_i\sum_{j<i}G_{ji})}{(i-1)\sum_{j<i}G_{ji}}$$
$$= \frac{2}{N-1}\cdot\sum_{i=2}^{N}\left(\frac{1}{\sum_{j<i}G_{ji}}\cdot\left(\sum_{j<i}CG_{ji}-P_i\sum_{j<i}G_{ji}\right)\right) \quad (8)$$

The overall expectation of $E[\tau_{GAP}-\tau_{AP}]$ is a linear combination over all ranks $i \in [2,N]$. However, for each rank position i in the predict list, the expectation of the difference between τ_{GAP} and τ_{AP} is:

$$E_i[\tau_{GAP}-\tau_{AP}] = \frac{2}{\sum_{j<i}G_{ji}}\cdot\left(\sum_{j<i}CG_{ji}-P_i\sum_{j<i}G_{ji}\right) \quad (9)$$

Since $\sum_{j<i}G_{ji}$ is always positive, the relation between τ_{GAP} and τ_{AP} at rank i depends on $(\sum_{j<i}CG_{ji}-P_i\sum_{j<i}G_{ji})$. For rank i, there are $(i-1)$ pairs of items and their corresponding gaps in the prediction list taken into consideration, and there are $P_i(i-1)$ pairs ordered correctly. $\sum_{j<i}CG_{ji}$ is the sum of the gaps for these correct ordered pairs, and $P_i\sum_{j<i}G_{ji}$ is a definite proportion of the total gaps of the $(i-1)$ pairs. If the $P_i(i-1)$ correctly ordered pairs with large gaps, then $\sum_{j<i}CG_{ji} > P_i\sum_{j<i}G_{ji}$, and $E_i[\tau_{GAP}-\tau_{AP}] > 0$; if the $P_i(i-1)$ correctly ordered pairs focus on the pairs with small gaps, then $E_i[\tau_{GAP}-\tau_{AP}] < 0$; ideally, if the $P_i(i-1)$ correctly ordered pairs are distributed randomly across all levels of gaps, then $E_i[\tau_{GAP}-\tau_{AP}] = 0$. Since the expectation of $E[\tau_{GAP}-\tau_{AP}]$ is a linear combination over all $E_i[\tau_{GAP}-\tau_{AP}]$, we could conclude that if the error gaps of a prediction list are relatively small, then τ_{GAP} is larger than τ_{AP}; if the error gaps of a prediction list are relatively large, then τ_{GAP} is smaller than τ_{AP}. □

4. COMPARISON OF THE METRICS

In this section, we use 61 participating systems from TREC 5, ranked by MAP, as a case study to compare the different emphases of the correlation coefficients ρ, τ_{AP} and our proposed τ_{GAP}.

4.1 Correlation Scores for Prediction Lists

Figure 1 shows the result of a two-sided paired t-test for each pair of systems based on Average Precision (AP) scores for each of the 50 topics as samples, with both axes sorted in the same order. In that figure, system pairs with $p < 0.05$ are plotted as white (37%) and system pairs with $p > 0.05$ are plotted as black (63%). This illustrates clearly that swaps among many of the systems (near the main diagonal, where score differences are smallest) would offer little insight into whether one evaluation framework yielded system comparisons that we meaningfully different from another.

Figures 2 and 3 then each illustrate two ways of making ranked lists to compare. Each dot represents a system, with the true (TREC-5) rank of that system plotted on the X-axis, and a randomly permuted rank on the Y-axis. We produce the random permutations by randomly selecting five system pairs each time and swapping them. In Figure 2, we randomly select systems pairs that are statistically significantly different from each other (i.e., five of what were black dots in Figure 1). We do these five random draws 50 times (Figure 2 shows only one of the 50 times). The correlation coefficient metrics that result are $\rho = 0.70$; $\tau_{AP} = 0.68$; $\tau_{GAP} = 0.65$, averaging over 50 such random draws of five pairs to swap. In Figure 3, we randomly select system pairs from among the set of pairs that are not statistically significantly different from each other (i.e., five of what were white dots in Figure 1). We do this 50 times. The correlation coefficient metrics that result are $\rho = 0.99$; $\tau_{AP} = 0.92$; $\tau_{GAP} = 0.97$, averaging over 50 such random draws of pairs to swap. In general, we can see that swapping system pairs with large gaps yields lower correlation scores with any measure than swapping system pairs with small gaps. But the key observation to make is that, as proven in theorem 4, when the swapped system pairs have relative large gaps, $\tau_{GAP} = 0.65$ is lower than $\tau_{AP} = 0.68$; whereas when the swapped system pairs have relatively small gaps, $\tau_{GAP} = 0.97$ is larger than $\tau_{AP} = 0.92$.

4.2 Weights for System Pairs

Figures 4, 5 and 6 show the weight for each system pair in evaluating the correlation coefficient of two ranked lists under the measurement of ρ, τ_{AP} and τ_{GAP} respectively. The systems are also ranked by their ground truth MAP scores. So cell (1, 61) represents the weight of only swapping the systems at rank 1 and rank 61. In detail, taking τ_{GAP} in Figure 6 as example, the value of cell (1, 61) is calculated by: (1) produce the prediction list by only swapping the systems at rank 1 and 61 in ground truth list; (2) calculate the value of τ_{GAP} between the ground truth list and the prediction list; (3) fill the value of $(1-\tau_{GAP})$ to cell (1, 61); (4) after filling in all the cells, rescale the matrix to (0, 1) and build the heatmap. Therefore, in general, darker cells represent system pairs with higher weight in evaluating the correlation coefficient.

Figure 4 shows the heatmap of system pair weights by using ρ. Since ρ is only sensitive to the score difference, not the ranks of items, we can observe that the value of ρ is dominated by the swapping pairs with large differences, probably composed of a system at very high rank and a system at very low rank. The system pairs along the diagonal with non-significant difference get lower weights as expected. However, the swap of top ranked systems also get lower weights because of their relatively small difference. The heatmap of τ_{AP} in figure 5 shows a progressively decreasing from the top-left corner of (1, 1) to the bottom-right corner of (61, 61) due to its sensitivity over ranks. However, comparing Figure 5 with Figure 1, we can see that the 37% non-significant system pairs still get non-ignorable weights in calculating τ_{AP}. Figure 6 shows the heatmap using τ_{GAP}. Since τ_{GAP} is sensitive to both top ranked systems and the gap between system pairs, we can also observe a decreasing of weights for the system pairs from top-left corner to the bottom-right corner. At the same time, we can see a expansion of the lower weight area (bright-ish area) along the diagonal line comparing with the heatmap of τ_{AP}. This is due to τ_{GAP}'s sensitivity to the system pairs with small difference. Overall, the value of τ_{GAP} is dominated by the top ranked system pairs with large difference.

5. CONCLUSION

In this paper, we proposed a new metric τ_{GAP} for evaluating the correlation coefficient between two ranked lists of scores. We have shown that τ_{GAP} is sensitive to both top ranked items and to swapped item pairs that exhibit larger differences. Through analysis, we have shown that τ_{GAP} compares favorably with both ρ and τ_{AP}, and using the TREC 5 Ad Hoc track as a case study we have illustrated that the swaps that τ_{GAP} is most sensitive to the ones we have argued we should care the most about. Although we have introduced τ_{GAP} in the context of system comparison, it is of course a general correlation coefficient for ranked lists of scores that could be applied in any case in which both a head-weighted and gap-sensitive measure would be useful. There are, however, some characteristics of τ_{GAP} that might be further improved upon. For example, it might be useful to completely discount differences in scores that are not statistically reliable indicators of real differences in system behavior. As Figure 1 illustrates, such cases can

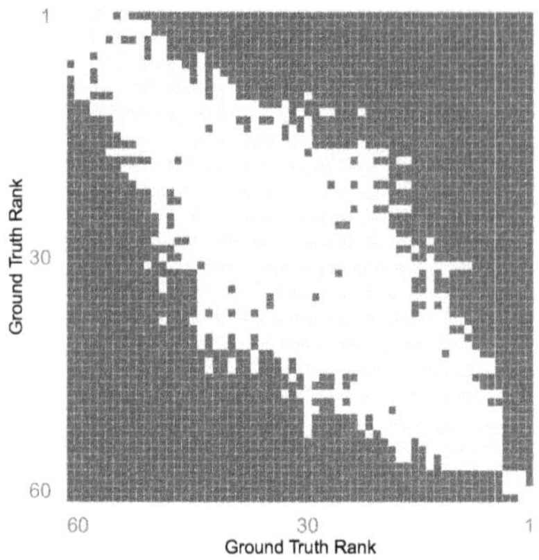

Figure 1: Significance of the MAP difference on TREC 5.

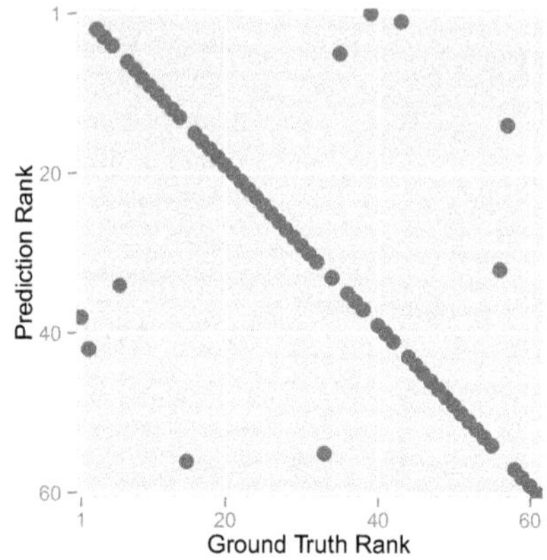

Figure 2: Significant difference between system pairs.

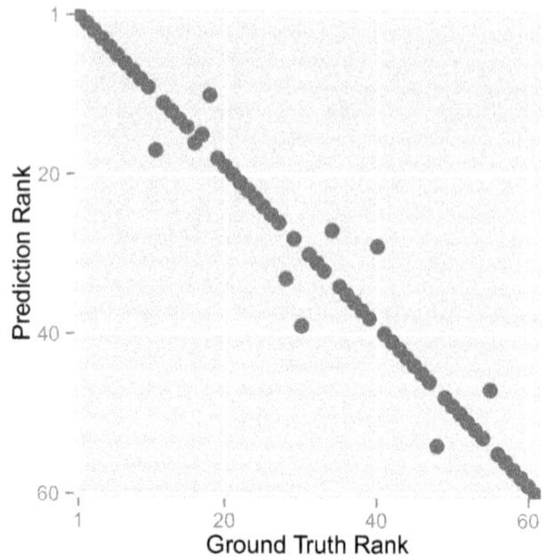

Figure 3: No significant difference between system pairs.

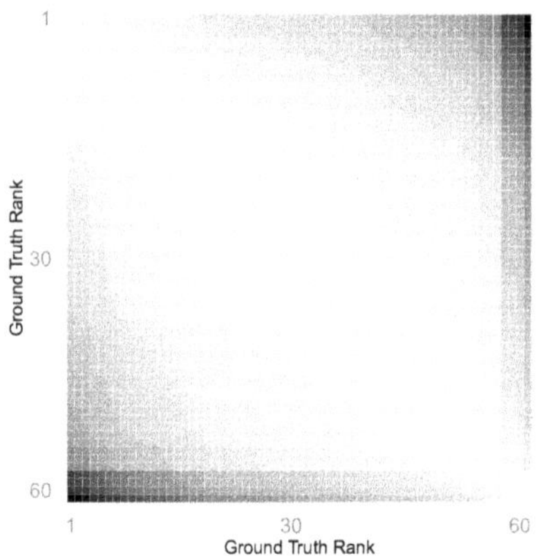

Figure 4: Gap-Sensitive: ρ

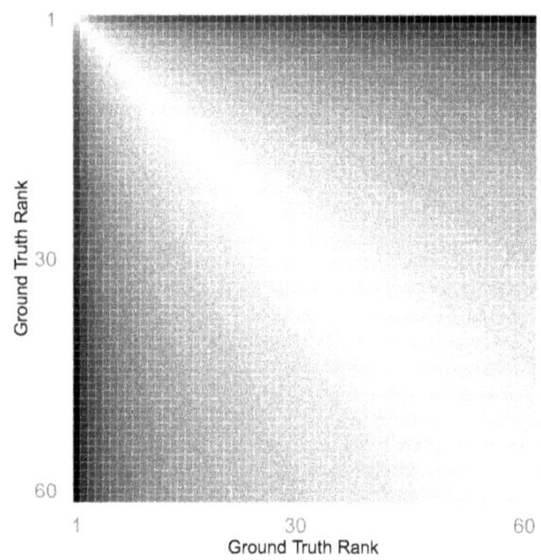

Figure 5: Head-Weighted: τ_{AP}

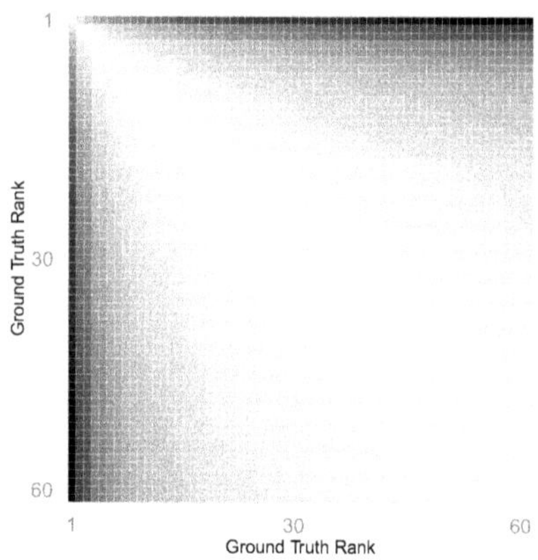

Figure 6: The proposed τ_{GAP}

be common. As another example, τ_{GAP} implicitly presumes that the scores are represented on a meaningful interval scale, meaning that (for example) a user would prefer a difference of 0.2 twice as much as they would prefer a difference of 0.1. User studies have shown that some current evaluation measures do not exhibit anywhere near this degree of correlation to extrinsic measures of success such as task completion rates [8]. Future extensions that more closely model extrinsic measures of satisfaction or success might therefore be useful. Nonetheless, we see the progression from τ to τ_{AP} and now to τ_{GAP} to be a useful one, and one that can perhaps serve as a basis for future extensions of these and other kinds.

6. ACKNOWLEDGEMENT

This work has been supported in part by NSF award 1065250. Opinions, findings, conclusions and recommendations are those of the authors and may not reflect NSF views.

References

[1] C. Buckley and E. M. Voorhees. Evaluating evaluation measure stability. In *SIGIR*, pages 33–40, 2000.

[2] N. Gao et al. Reducing reliance on relevance judgments for system comparison by using expectation-maximization. In *ECIR*, pages 1–12. 2014.

[3] K. S. Jones. Automatic indexing. *Journal of Documentation*, 30(4):393–432, 1974.

[4] M. G. Kendall. A new measure of rank correlation. *Biometrika*, pages 81–93, 1938.

[5] M. G. Kendall. *Rank correlation methods.* Griffin, 1948.

[6] K. Pearson. Note on regression and inheritance in the case of two parents. *Proceedings of the Royal Society of London*, 58(347-352):240–242, 1895.

[7] M. Smucker et al. A comparison of statistical significance tests for information retrieval evaluation. In *CIKM*, 2007.

[8] A. Turpin and W. R. Hersh. Why batch and user evaluations do not give the same results. In *SIGIR*, pages 225–231, 2001.

[9] E. M. Voorhees. Variations in relevance judgments and the measurement of retrieval effectiveness. *Inf. Process. Manage.*, 36(5):697–716, 2000.

[10] E. Yilmaz et al. A new rank correlation coefficient for information retrieval. In *SIGIR*, pages 587–594, 2008.

[11] G. U. Yule. *An introduction to the theory of statistics.* C. Griffin, limited, 1919.

On Term Selection Techniques for Patent Prior Art Search

Mona Golestan Far
NICTA & ANU
Canberra, Australia
mona.golestanfar@anu.edu.au

Scott Sanner
NICTA & ANU
Canberra, Australia
ssanner@gmail.com

Mohamed Reda Bouadjenek
INRIA & LIRMM, France
Montpellier, France
reda.bouadjenek@inria.fr

Gabriela Ferraro
NICTA & ANU
Canberra, Australia
gabriela.ferraro@nicta.com.au

David Hawking
Microsoft (Bing) & ANU
Canberra, Australia
david.hawking@acm.org

ABSTRACT

In this paper, we investigate the influence of term selection on retrieval performance on the CLEF-IP prior art test collection, using the Description section of the patent query with Language Model (LM) and BM25 scoring functions. We find that an oracular relevance feedback system that extracts terms from the judged relevant documents far outperforms the baseline and performs twice as well on MAP as the best competitor in CLEF-IP 2010. We find a very clear term selection value threshold for use when choosing terms. We also noticed that most of the useful feedback terms are actually present in the original query and hypothesized that the baseline system could be substantially improved by removing negative query terms. We tried four simple automated approaches to identify negative terms for query reduction but we were unable to notably improve on the baseline performance with any of them. However, we show that a simple, minimal interactive relevance feedback approach where terms are selected from only the *first* retrieved relevant document outperforms the best result from CLEF-IP 2010 suggesting the promise of interactive methods for term selection in patent prior art search.

Categories and Subject Descriptors: H.3.3 [Information Search and Retrieval]: Query Formulation

Keywords: Patent Search; Query Reformulation.

1. INTRODUCTION

Patent prior art search involves finding previously granted patents, or any published work, such as scientific articles or product descriptions that may be relevant to a new patent application. The objective and challenges of standard formulations of patent prior art search are different from those of standard text and web search since [8]: (i) queries are reference patent applications, which consist of documents with hundreds or thousands of words organized into several sections, while typical queries in text and web search constitute only a few words; and (ii) patent prior art search is a recall-oriented task, where the primary focus is to retrieve all relevant documents at early ranks, in contrast to text and web search that are precision-oriented, where the primary goal is to retrieve a subset of documents that best satisfy the query intent. Another important characteristic of patent prior art search is that, in contrast to scientific and technical writers, patent writers tend to generalize and maximize the scope of what is protected by a patent and potentially discourage further innovation by third parties, which further complicates the task of formulating queries.

In this work, we focus on the task of query reformulation specifically applied to patent prior art search [11, 16]. While prior work has largely focused on specific techniques for query reformulation, in Section 3, we first build an oracular query formed from known relevance judgments for the CLEP-IP 2010 prior art test collection [14] in an attempt to derive an upper bound on performance of standard Okapi BM25 and Language Models (LM) retrieval algorithms for this task. Since the results of this evaluation suggest that query reduction methods can outperform state-of-the-art prior art search performance, in Section 4.1 we proceed to analyze four simple automated methods for identifying terms to remove from the original patent query. Finding that none of these methods seems to independently yield promise for query reduction that strongly outperforms the baseline, in Section 4.2 we evaluate an alternative interactive feedback approach where terms are selected from only the first retrieved relevant document. Observing that such simple interactive methods for query reduction with a standard LM retrieval model outperform highly engineered patent-specific search systems from CLEF-IP 2010, we conclude that interactive methods offer a promising avenue for simple and effective term selection in patent prior art search.

2. BASELINE IR FRAMEWORK

We developed a baseline IR system for patent prior art search on the top of the Lucene search engine and LM (Dirichlet smoothing, and Jelinek-Mercer smoothing) scoring functions based on [2]. We used Lucene to index the English subset of the CLEF-IP 2010 dataset[1] that contains 2.6 million patent documents and a subset of 1281 topics (queries) in the English test set where we determined at least one valid, relevant English document was available. We used the default Lucene settings using the Porter stemming al-

[1]http://www.ifs.tuwien.ac.at/~clef-ip/

SIGIR'15, August 09 - 13, 2015, Santiago, Chile.

ACM 978-1-4503-3621-5/15/08 ...$15.00.
DOI: http://dx.doi.org/10.1145/2766462.2767801 .

gorithm and English stop-word removal. We also removed patent-specific stop-words as described in [8]. We indexed each section of a patent (title, abstract, claims, and description) in a separate field. However, when a query is processed, all indexed fields are targeted with an equal weight. We also used the International Patent Classification (IPC) codes assigned to the topics to filter the search results by constraining them to have common IPC codes with the patent topic as suggested in previous work [7]. Although this IPC code filter may prevent retrieval of relevant patents, we have chosen to keep it for the following reasons: (i) more than 80% of the patent queries share an IPC code with their associated relevant patents, and (ii) it makes the retrieval process much faster. System performance is evaluated using two popular metrics — Mean Average Precision (MAP) and Average Recall — on the top-100 results for each query, assuming that patent examiners are willing to assess the top 100 patents [5]. We achieved the best performance while querying with the Description section as in previous work [16] and using either the LM or the BM25 scoring functions. We call this the *Patent Query* and use it as our baseline.

In addition, we compare our results to *PATATRAS*, a highly engineered system developed by Lopez and Romary [7], which achieved the best performance in the CLEF-IP 2010 competition. This system uses multiple retrieval models and exploits patent metadata and citation structures. All results in the paper use the 1348 English topic subset as reported in the PATATRAS evaluation [14]. Since the evaluation of our systems used a slightly smaller subset of 1281 topics as noted previously, we assume no relevant results were found by our systems for the 67 remaining topics of the 1348 topic subset in order to ensure a fair comparison to PATATRAS.

3. ORACULAR TERM SELECTION

In this section we develop an *Oracular Query* to understand (a) the adequacy of the baseline *Patent Query*, (b) an upper bound on performance of the BM25 and LM models, and (c) the sufficiency of terms in the reference patent query.

3.1 Oracular Query Formulation

We begin by defining an oracular relevance feedback system, which extracts terms from the judged relevant documents. To this end, after an initial run of a given query, we calculate a Relevance Feedback (*RF*) score for each term t in the top-100 retrieved documents for query Q as follows:

$$RF(t,Q) = Rel(t,Q) - Irr(t,Q) \quad (1)$$
$$t \in \{\text{terms in top-100 retrieved documents}\}$$

where $Rel(t, Q)$ is the average term frequency in retrieved relevant patents and $Irr(t, Q)$ is the average term frequency in retrieved irrelevant patents. We assume that words with a positive score are *useful words* since they are more frequent in relevant patents, while words with negative score are *noisy words* as they appear more frequently in irrelevant patents. We empirically seek to evaluate the threshold τ on $RF(t, Q)$ (defined below) yielding the best oracular query.

We formulate two oracular queries. The first query is formulated by selecting terms in the top-100 documents:

$$Oracular\ Query = \{t \in \text{top-100} | RF(t,Q) > \tau\} \quad (2)$$

We formulate the second query by selecting terms that also occur in the reference patent query as follows:

$$Oracular\ Patent\ Query = \{t \in Q | RF(t,Q) > \tau\} \quad (3)$$

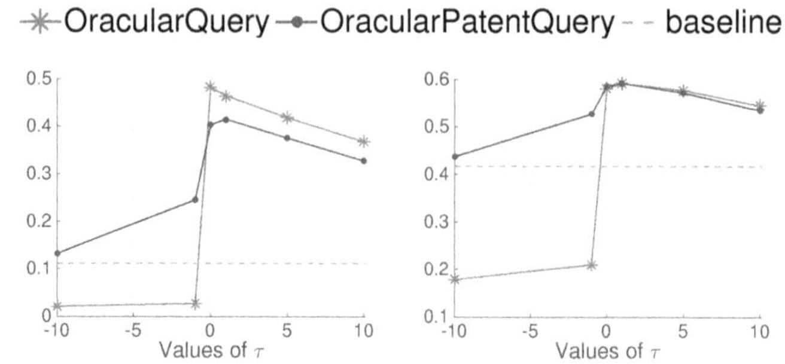

(a) Mean Average Precision. (b) Recall.

Figure 1: System performance vs. the threshold τ for Oracular Query and Oracular Patent Query.

Table 1: Performance for the *Patent Query* (baseline), two variants of the *Oracular Query*, and *Top CLEF-IP 2010 Competitor (PATATRAS)*.

		Baseline	PATATRAS	Oracular $\tau = 0$	Oracular (PQ), $\tau = 1$
LM	MAP	0.112	0.226	**0.482**	**0.414**
	Recall	0.416	0.467	0.582	0.591
BM25	MAP	0.123	0.226	**0.492**	**0.424**
	Recall	0.431	0.467	0.584	0.598

3.2 Baseline vs. Oracular Query

First, we investigate the ideal threshold setting τ for the oracular queries as shown in Figure 1. Notably, there is a rather unexpected steep drop-off in performance for both oracular queries when slightly noisy terms are included (i.e., τ just slightly less than 0). However, this dropoff is less pronounced for the *Oracular Patent Query* indicating that restriction to query terms in the reference patent may reduce the impact of the noisy terms that are present. While the *Oracular Query* and *Oracular Patent Query* peak at slightly different thresholds ($\tau = 0$ and $\tau = 1$, respectively), either value of τ yields good performance. However, values of $\tau > 1$ demonstrate a stronger relative decrease in performance due to the exclusion of a large number of useful terms.

In Table 1, we compare our best oracular relevance queries with both the baseline *Patent Query* and the PATATRAS system. In general we found BM25 and LM to offer very similar performance. Our subsequent results use only LM due to space limitations although results for BM25 are very similar. More importantly, the *Oracular Query* using $\tau = 0$ far outperforms the baseline and approximately performs twice as well on MAP as the PATATRAS system, the best competitor in CLEF-IP 2010. The MAP and the recall for the best *Oracular Patent Query* are respectively lower than the MAP and the recall for the best *Oracular Query*. However, the query reduction approach inherent in the *Oracular Patent Query* is still sufficient to achieve MAP performance appreciably better than PATATRAS (for $\tau \geq 0$) with reduced sensitivity to the inclusion of noisy terms (when $\tau < 0$).

Hence, our experiments related to oracular relevance feedback system suggest two important conclusions: (1) query reduction should suffice for effective prior art patent retrieval; and (2) very precise methods for eliminating poor query terms in the reduction process are needed.

4. QUERY REDUCTION: APPROXIMATING THE ORACULAR QUERY

The gain achieved using the Oracular Patent Query method motivates us to explore various methods to approximate the terms selected by this query without "peeking at the answers" provided by the actual relevance judgements. We first attempt this via fully automated methods and then proceed to evaluate semi-automated methods based on interactive relevance feedback methods.

4.1 Automated Reduction

We use the following four simple approaches to reduce the initial Patent Query:

(i) In standard IR approaches, removing terms appearing highly frequently across documents in the collection can improve retrieval effectiveness. Inspired by this fact, after an initial run of the query, we removed terms with a high average document frequency (DF) over the top-100 documents ($DF(t) > \tau$). As seen in Figure 2 (magenta line), such pruning hurts performance. DF pruning continues increasing and converges to the baseline as $\tau \to \infty$ (i.e., no pruning).

(ii) Frequent terms inside long and verbose queries are considered important [13]. Thus, we hypothesize that removing terms appearing infrequently in the Patent Query may help and hence propose to remove terms with query term frequency (QTF) below a threshold τ ($QTF(t) \leq \tau$). Results in Figure 2 (blue line) indicate the performance is slightly better than the baseline when removing low QTF terms. The best MAP is achieved when $\tau = 5$ and it meets the baseline when $\tau = 0$ (i.e., all terms retained).

(iii) We use Pseudo Relevance Feedback (*PRF*) to select query terms [13] — the same as we did for the Oracular Relevance Feedback system (Section 3). We assume that the top 5 retrieved documents are relevant and the rest are irrelevant (this performed best), then we calculate *PRF* score based on this assumption. Terms that have *PRF* score higher than the threshold τ ($PRF(t) > \tau$), are selected from the Patent Query to reformulate a reduced query. Figure 2 (red line) shows that this approach is also unsuccessful at achieving a notable improvement over the baseline.

(iv) The titles of IPC codes indicate the intended content of patents classified under that code by using a single phrase or several related phrases linked together. We used words in IPC code titles for each patent query as stopwords to reduce the query, based on the assumption that these terms are common to all patents having the same IPC code label. As it can be seen in Figure 2 (black line), this approach slightly helps the performance.

Figure 3 shows an anecdotal example for a sample query about an invention related to "emulsifier" to help explain why these four approaches *fail*. It shows the raw abstract of the invention, and the top 20 high-scoring terms (except for IPC Title Terms which are not scored, but simply displayed) and their associated *RF* scores for each approach. It can be seen that the four methods fail to clearly discriminate between useful and noisy terms. Important stemmed terms like "enzym" and "starch" would be pruned according to DF; in contrast, QTF and PRF both score "starch" highly and retain it, but also retain other noisy terms. Over half of the IPC Title Terms are noisy and appropriate to remove, but critical useful stemmed terms like "emulsifi" are also removed. Critically, all methods retain noisy terms (red/negative) and results from Section 3.2 showed that the inclusion of even slightly noisy terms can significantly hurt performance. Overall, all methods fail to retain only the oracular query terms (blue/positive) and do worse than PATATRAS.

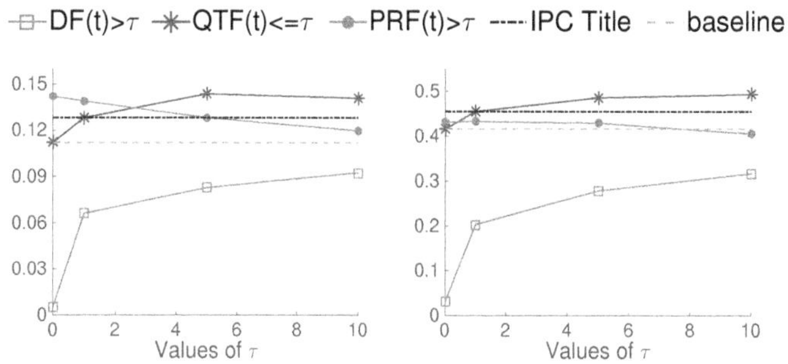

(a) Mean Average Precision. (b) Recall.

Figure 2: System performance vs. the threshold τ for four query reduction approaches.

```
(PAC-1293) - Abstract: The invention relates to an
emulsifier, a method for preparing said emulsifier,
and to its use in various applications, primarily
food and cosmetic applications.The invention also
relates to the use of said emulsifier for the
creation of an elastic, gelled foam.  An emulsifier
according to the invention is based on a starch
which is enzymatically converted, using a specific
type of enzyme, and modified in a specific
esterification reaction.

DF Terms:starch:14.6,enzym:29.5,amylos:-20.1,oil:8.6,
dispers:-8.7,ph:-4.6,dry:-6.2,heat:-2.3,product:-5.5,
slurri:-11,viscos:8,composit:-4,reaction:-2,food:-12,
agent:5,debranch:-11,reduc:-6,fat:-13,propar:-0.8,
hour:-5

QTF Terms:starch:14.6,emulsifi:6.7,succin:-3.5,
enzym:29.5,emuls:12.7,hydrophob:5.4,anhydrid:-5.5,
reaction:-2,octenyl:-0.7,stabil:3.6,alkenyl:0.06,
reagent:1.2,carbon:0.1,potato:3.7,alkyl:-0.3,wt:-4.6,
ether:2,enzymat:-3.4,convers:10.4,chain:-5.5

PRF Terms:starch:14.6,encapsul:17.5,chees:-4,oil:8.6,
hydrophob:5.4,agent:5,casein:-2.2,degrad:17,deriv:12,
tablet:5.3,debranch:-11,imit:-1,viscos:7.8,oxid:6,
activ:6,osa:9.3,funnel:2.7,amylas:26,amylopectin:-7,
maiz:20.6

IPC Title Terms:cosmet:3.8,toilet:0.2,prepar:-0.8,
caoc:0.5,accessori:-0.01,store:-0.4,handl:0.07,
pasti:-0.2,amylos:-20,fibrou:-0.01,pulp:-1.3,
constitut:-0.06,paper:1.3,impregn:-0.1,emulsifi:6.7,
wet:-0.3,dispers:-9,saccharid:-12,produc:-0.6,agent:5
```

Figure 3: The top 20 terms scored by each of four methods on a sample query (except for IPC Title Terms which are not scored); whether the term is pruned or retained depends on the approach, cf. (i)–(iv). Numerical oracular scores $RF(t, Q)$ are provided indicating whether the term was actually useful (blue/positive) or noisy (red/negative).

4.2 Semi-automated Interactive Reduction

Our sample analysis of specific queries and terms selected via our oracular approach suggests that automated methods fall far short of optimal term selection. This leads us to explore another approach of approximating the oracular query derived from relevance judgements by using a subset of relevance judgements through interactive methods. Specifically, to evaluate the impact of minimal user interaction, we next analyze the performance of an Oracular Patent Query

Table 2: System performance using minimal relevance feedback. τ is RF score threshold, and k indicates the number of top relevant patents.

	$k=1$ $\tau=0$	$k=1$ $\tau=1$	$k=3$ $\tau=0$	$k=3$ $\tau=1$
MAP	0.288	**0.289**	**0.369**	0.368
Recall	0.479	0.484	0.547	0.550

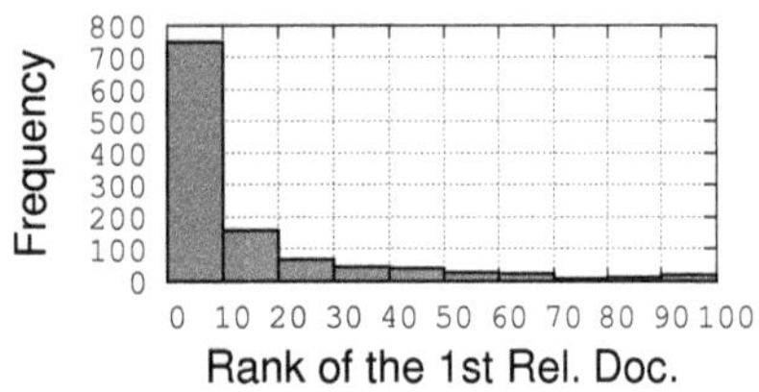

Figure 4: The distribution of the first relevant document rank over test queries.

(Equation 3) derived from *only* the top-k ranked relevant documents identified in the search results (for small k) — we assume that the remaining documents in the top-100 are irrelevant. Using this approach, Table 2 shows that we can double the MAP in comparison to our baseline and also outperform the PATATRAS system by identifying only the *first* relevant document.

Furthermore, to establish the minimal interaction required by this approach, Figure 4 indicates that the baseline methods return a relevant patent approximately 80% of the time in the first 10 results and 90% of the time in the first 20 results. Hence, such an interactive approach requires relatively low user effort while achieving state-of-the-art performance.

5. RELATED WORK

In this work, we focused on the development of an oracular query in order to address a number of fundamental questions regarding query reformulation and their efficacy in terms of approximating the oracular query. Previous works have not formulated such an oracular query, but nonetheless have inspired our investigation of query reformulation techniques. Bashir et al. [1] proposed query expansion with pseudo-relevance feedback that used machine learning for term selection. Verma and Varma [15] used IPC codes instead of using the patent text to query, which are expanded using the citation network. Itoh et al. [4] proposed a new term selection method using different term frequencies depending on the genre in the NTCIR-3 Patent Retrieval Task. Mahdabi et al. [12] used term proximity information to identify expansion terms. Ganguly et al. [3] adapted pseudo-relevance feedback for query reduction by decomposing a patent application into constituent text segments; the least similar segments to the pseudo-relevant documents are removed from the query. Kim et al. [6] provided diverse query suggestion using aspect identification from a patent query to increase the chance of retrieving relevant documents. Magdy et al. [9] and Bouadjenek et al. [2] studied different query expansion and reduction techniques for patent search on CLEF-IP 2010, and reported little improvement with automatic methods. Magdy et al. [10] further compare the best two systems in CLEF-IP 2010.

6. CONCLUSION

In this paper, we looked at the patent prior art search from a term selection perspective. While previous works proposed different solutions to improve retrieval effectiveness, we focused on term analysis of the patent query and top-100 retrieved patents. After defining an oracular query based on relevance judgements, we established both the sufficiency of the standard LM retrieval scoring models and query reduction methods to achieve state-of-the-art patent prior art search performance. After finding that automated methods for query reduction approaches fail to offer significant performance improvements, we showed that we can double the MAP with minimum user interaction by approximating the oracular query through a relevance feedback approach with a single relevant document. Given that such simple interactive methods for query reduction with a standard LM retrieval model outperform highly engineered patent-specific search systems from CLEF-IP 2010, we concluded that interactive methods offer a promising avenue for simple but highly effective term selection in patent prior art search.

Acknowledgments

NICTA is funded by the Australian Government as represented by the Department of Broadband, Communications and the Digital Economy and the Australian Research Council through the ICT Centre of Excellence program.

7. REFERENCES

[1] S. Bashir and A. Rauber. Improving retrievability of patents in prior-art search. In *ECIR*, 2010.
[2] M. R. Bouadjenek, S. Sanner, and G. Ferraro. A Study of Query Reformulation for Patent Prior Art Search with Partial Patent Applications. In *ICAIL*, 2015.
[3] D. Ganguly, J. Leveling, W. Magdy, and G. J. Jones. Patent query reduction using pseudo relevance feedback. In *CIKM*, 2011.
[4] H. Itoh, H. Mano, and Y. Ogawa. Term distillation in patent retrieval. In *ACL workshop on Patent corpus processing*, 2003.
[5] H. Joho, L. A. Azzopardi, and W. Vanderbauwhede. A survey of patent users: an analysis of tasks, behavior, search functionality and system requirements. In *IIiX*, 2010.
[6] Y. Kim and W. B. Croft. Diversifying query suggestions based on query documents. In *SIGIR*, 2014.
[7] P. Lopez and L. Romary. Experiments with citation mining and key-term extraction for prior art search. In *CLEF 2010-Conference on Multilingual and Multimodal Information Access Evaluation*, 2010.
[8] W. Magdy. *Toward higher effectiveness for recall-oriented information retrieval: A patent retrieval case study*. PhD thesis, Dublin City University, 2012.
[9] W. Magdy and G. J. Jones. A study on query expansion methods for patent retrieval. In *Proceedings of the 4th workshop on Patent information retrieval*, 2011.
[10] W. Magdy, P. Lopez, and G. J. Jones. Simple vs. sophisticated approaches for patent prior-art search. In *Advances in Information Retrieval*, pages 725–728. Springer, 2011.
[11] P. Mahdabi and F. Crestani. Patent query formulation by synthesizing multiple sources of relevance evidence. *ACM Transactions on Information Systems*, 2014.
[12] P. Mahdabi, S. Gerani, J. X. Huang, and F. Crestani. Leveraging conceptual lexicon: query disambiguation using proximity information for patent retrieval. In *SIGIR*, 2013.
[13] K. T. Maxwell and W. B. Croft. Compact query term selection using topically related text. In *SIGIR*, 2013.
[14] F. Piroi. Clef-ip 2010: Prior art candidates search evaluation summary. Technical report, IRF TR, Vienna, 2010.
[15] M. Verma and V. Varma. Patent search using IPC classification vectors. In *PaIR*, 2011.
[16] X. Xue and W. B. Croft. Transforming patents into prior-art queries. In *SIGIR*, 2009.

Automatic Feature Generation on Heterogeneous Graph for Music Recommendation

Chun Guo
School of Informatics and Computing
Indiana University Bloomington
Bloomington, IN, USA, 47405
chunguo@indiana.edu

Xiaozhong Liu
School of Informatics and Computing
Indiana University Bloomington
Bloomington, IN, USA, 47405
liu237@indiana.edu

ABSTRACT

Online music streaming services (MSS) experienced exponential growth over the past decade. The giant MSS providers not only built massive music collection with metadata, they also accumulated large amount of heterogeneous data generated from users, e.g. *listening history, comment, bookmark*, and *user generated playlist*. While various kinds of user data can potentially be used to enhance the music recommendation performance, most existing studies only focused on audio content features and collaborative filtering approaches based on simple user listening history or music rating. In this paper, we propose a novel approach to solve the music recommendation problem by means of heterogeneous graph mining. Meta-path based features are automatically generated from a content-rich heterogeneous graph schema with 6 types of nodes and 16 types of relations. Meanwhile, we use learning-to-rank approach to integrate different features for music recommendation. Experiment results show that the automatically generated graphical features significantly ($p < 0.0001$) enhance state-of-the-art collaborative filtering algorithm.

Categories and Subject Descriptors

H.3.3 [**Information Storage and Retrieval**]: Information Search and Retrieval

Keywords

Music Recommendation; Meta-Path; Feature Generation; Feature Selection

1. INTRODUCTION

In the past decade, online music streaming services (MSS), i.e., Pandora and Spotify, experienced exponential growth. The sheer volume of music collection makes music recommendation increasingly important and the related algorithms are well-documented. In prior studies, most algorithms employed content-based model (CBM) and collaborative filtering (CF) [8]. The former one focuses on acoustic/signal features extracted from audio content, and the latter one investigates music rating and user listening history. Actually, MSS generated user data present significant heterogeneity. Taking user-music relationship as an example, *comment, bookmark*, and *listening history* may potentially contribute to music recommendation in very different ways. Furthermore, user and music can be implicitly related via more complex paths, e.g., *user-play-artist-perform-music*. From this viewpoint, user-user, music-music or user-music relationship can be much more complex than the classical CF approach assumed.

In this paper, we propose a novel approach to address the music recommendation problem from the heterogeneous graph mining viewpoint, where 6 different types of nodes interact through 16 types of relationships. The recommendation problem, then, becomes a (supervised) random walk problem on the graph. Compared with earlier related studies, this study investigates the comprehensive relationships among different kinds of objects for music recommendation. Take [1] as an example, Bu et al., integrated acoustic features and CF information by using hypergraph mining approach. A number of hyperedges were proposed to address the user-music relationship. However, this study only focused on *user-tag-music* relationship (as a hyperedge), and other types of relations were not explored.

As Figure 1 shows, in this study, the constructed heterogeneous music graph is more complex than most existing graph mining studies, which challenges the classical approaches. For instance, Liu et al., [5] and Lao & Cohen [4] used relatively simple heterogeneous graph and manually generated meta-path features for scholarly recommendation, where each feature represents a ranking hypothesis. However, we can hardly use this approach for this study because of the complexity of the music graph schema. For example, if we restrict the path length to 4 or smaller, 259 candidate meta-paths between user and song nodes can be identified on this heterogeneous graph schema. With so many potential meta-paths, there is no guarantee that manually selected meta-path collection can optimize the recommendation performance. In this pilot study, we select a subset of meta-path features from the graph schema using the training data. Then, learning to rank method is utilized to generate the music recommendation model. Results show that the new method can significantly ($p < 0.0001$) enhance the recommendation performance.

SIGIR'15, August 09 - 13, 2015, Santiago, Chile.
© 2015 ACM. ISBN 978-1-4503-3621-5/15/08 ...$15.00.
DOI: http://dx.doi.org/10.1145/2766462.2767808.

2. LITERATURE REVIEW

Most previous music recommendation algorithms can be divided into two categories: content-based model (CBM) and collaborative filtering (CF).

Content-based music recommendation typically focuses on extracting acoustic features from music audio content. Then, it recommends music items based on the similarity between new items and items in the user's listening history. For example, Logan [6] in-

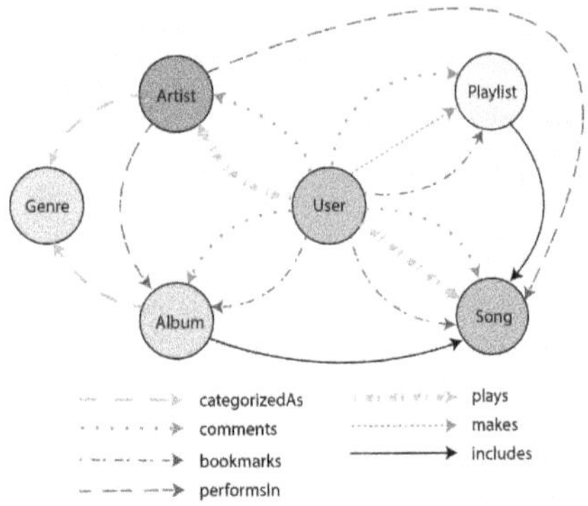

Figure 1: Heterogeneous Music Graph

vestigated Mel-frequency Cepstral Coefficients (MFCCs) as acoustic features and utilized Earth-Mover's distance to measure the similarity between songs for recommendation. More recently, Wang and Wang [10] used deep leaning techniques which perform feature learning from audio signals and music recommendation in a unified framework. Audio analysis extracts low-level acoustic features about music entities. However, they are not what causal users usually relate to in their music exploration.

Unlike CBM, collaborative filtering approach depends on user-music relationship, which has been proved to be one of the most effective recommendation techniques. There are two basic approaches towards collaborative filtering, memory-based and model-based. Memory-based CF algorithms derive item-to-item (item-based CF) or user-to-user (user-based CF) similarity from user rating/feedback matrices. Item-based CF recommends items similar to the user's favorite items, and user-based CF recommends items liked by similar users. Model-based CF typically utilizes matrix factorization techniques to predict user rating on his/her unseen items. CF approach has been proved to outperform other recommendation algorithms in KDD-Cup 2011 Yahoo! Music Recommendation challenge [2].

More recently, online music services have attracted large groups of users and collected rich context-based music information, e.g. comments, collaborative tags, user listening history, etc. Very heterogeneous relationships among different kinds of objects provide exciting opportunities for researchers to propose novel music recommendation algorithms. Symeonidis et al. [9], for example, employed collaborative tags from a social music website and proposed a personalized music recommendation system by applying latent semantic analysis and dimensionality reduction with the higher-order SVD technique to the *user-tag-item* tensor. Most previous context-based music recommendation systems use a single source of contextual information (e.g., music tags). In this paper, we propose an approach that takes advantage of the rich heterogeneous contextual information harvested from social music community.

3. RESEARCH METHODS

3.1 Graph Construction

Numerous studies have shown that one of the most effective channels for dissemination/recommendation of information is the network of community [3]. In this study, we verify this hypothesis for music recommendation by investigating very heterogeneous relationships among different kinds of objects. For example, for the case of Xiami[1], users can bookmark a song and come back to it later. Users can also comment on different music entities (artist, album, song, etc.), which gives them a way to publicly express their opinion, e.g., like/dislike about the music objects, or share their own emotions about the song. These all reveal user's preference about a candidate music track in terms of different relationships. Heterogeneous graph mining provides us a good way of modeling these relationships for recommendation tasks.

On this directed heterogeneous graph, $G = (\mathcal{V}, \mathcal{E})$, there are an object (node) type mapping function $\tau : \mathcal{V} \rightarrow \mathcal{A}$ and a link type mapping function $\phi : \mathcal{E} \rightarrow \mathcal{R}$, where each object $v \in \mathcal{V}$ belongs to one particular object type $\tau(v) \in \mathcal{A}$, each link $e \in \mathcal{E}$ belongs to a particular relation type $\phi(e) \in \mathcal{R}$, and if two links belong to the same relation type, the two links share the same starting object type as well as the ending object type. The types of nodes and edges used in our study are presented in Table 1.

Table 1: Nodes and Relations in Heterogeneous Music Graph

Node/Relation	Description
Ar	Artist
Al	Album
S	Music track
P	Playlist
G	Genre
U	User
$Ar \overset{cat}{\rightarrow} G$	Artist categorized as a genre
$Ar \overset{pIn}{\rightarrow} Al$	Artist performs in an album
$Al \overset{cat}{\rightarrow} G$	Album categorized as a genre
$Al \overset{i}{\rightarrow} S$	Album includes a music track
$Ar \overset{pIn}{\rightarrow} S$	Artist performs in a music track
$P \overset{i}{\rightarrow} S$	Playlist includes a music track
$U \overset{m}{\rightarrow} P$	User makes a playlist
$U \overset{pl}{\rightarrow} Ar$	User plays music track from an artist
$U \overset{pl}{\rightarrow} S$	User plays a music track
$U \overset{c}{\rightarrow} Ar$	User comments an artist
$U \overset{c}{\rightarrow} Al$	User comments an album
$U \overset{c}{\rightarrow} S$	User comments a music track
$U \overset{c}{\rightarrow} P$	User comments a playlist
$U \overset{b}{\rightarrow} Al$	User bookmarks an album
$U \overset{b}{\rightarrow} S$	User bookmarks a music track
$U \overset{b}{\rightarrow} P$	User bookmarks a playlist

Edge weights on the heterogeneous graph represent the transition probability from one node to another. For instance, $w(u_i \overset{pl}{\rightarrow} ar_j)$ represents the probability that user u_i plays the music from artist ar_j. For any node v on the graph, let O_v represents the set of its outgoing links. Then we have $\sum_{e \in O_v, \phi(e)=R_k} w(e) = 1$, where R_k is a particular relation type on the graph schema. That is to say, for any node on the graph, the sum of weights on the same type of outgoing links equals 1. For most relation types, weight is modeled as 1 divided by the number of its outgoing links of the same type. For example, an artist might be labeled with multiple genres. The weight of the link from artist a_i to genre g_j is defined as $w(a_i \overset{cat}{\rightarrow} g_j) = \frac{1}{d(a_i \overset{cat}{\rightarrow} G)}$, where $d(a_i \overset{cat}{\rightarrow} G)$ is the total number of genres that a_i is labeled with. For relation types that involve play counts and comments, weight modeling is different. For example, the weight of the link from user u_i to music track s_j is defined as $w(u_i \overset{pl}{\rightarrow} s_j) = \frac{d(u_i \overset{pl}{\rightarrow} s_j)}{d(u_i \overset{pl}{\rightarrow} S)}$, where $d(u_i \overset{pl}{\rightarrow} s_j)$ represents the number of times that s_j appears in user u_i's listening history and $d(u_i \overset{pl}{\rightarrow} S)$ represents the total play counts (for all the music tracks in the collection) in u_i's listening history.

3.2 Recommendation via Random Walk on Heterogeneous Graph

In this study, we take a ranking approach for music recommendation. For each query node on the graph, we retrieve a number of

[1]One of the largest online music streaming services (MSS) in China. Xiami.com has more than 20 million of active users.

candidate nodes and make recommendations based on their ranking scores. The ranking scores of each candidate node come from the meta-path based ranking features automatically generated from the heterogeneous graph schema. On the heterogeneous music graph, meta-path defines how the query node and result node are connected, which is an abstraction of the many path instances that follow the same pattern [5]. For the same recommendation task (e.g. recommend music tracks to a user), there are usually multiple possible meta-paths on the heterogeneous graph. For example, $U \xrightarrow{c} S$ is a simple meta-path, which denotes all the music tracks (S) that the user (U) have commented on. A meta-path can be represented as:

$$\dot{A}_Q \xrightarrow{R_1} \dot{A}_1 \xrightarrow{R_2} \dot{A}_2 \ldots \xrightarrow{R_l} \dot{A}_{l-1} \xrightarrow{R_l} \dot{A}_R$$

, where $\dot{A}_Q$ is the query node type, and $\dot{A}_R$ is the recommended node type. In this study, $\dot{A}_Q$ is the user node, and $\dot{A}_R$ is the music node. When we change the type of $\dot{A}_Q$ and $\dot{A}_R$, this method can be generalized to other recommendation tasks, e.g., recommending music to a playlist.

Previous research used manually selected meta-paths to solve different data mining tasks. However, there is no guarantee these selected meta-paths are the best performing ones. In this study, we exhaust all possible meta-paths from the heterogeneous graph schema (graph schema mining) and evaluate their performance individually. The first step is to derive the schema G_S of the heterogeneous music graph G. On G_S (as Figure 1 shows), each node is a unique object type on the original graph G, and each edge represents a unique relation type on G. Let $G_S = (\mathcal{V}_S, \mathcal{E}_S)$. Then we have $|V_S| = |A|$ and $|E_S| = |R|$. Given the query node v_Q and result node v_R on G_S, a depth first search is performed on G_S to locate all paths following the pattern $(v_Q, e_1, v_1, e_2, v_2, \ldots, e_k, v_R)$, where the length of this path k is always equal or smaller than a threshold l (maximum length of a potential meta-path). When l is large, more meta-paths will be generated, but the meta-path based features can be more noisy. For example, to perform the music track recommendation task, v_Q is the user node and v_R is the music node. On this graph schema, when $l = 3$, we have 49 features, and when $l = 4$, a total number of 259 features can be extracted.

After the meta-paths are identified from the graph schema, we define meta-path based ranking functions and the result nodes with the highest ranking scores are recommended. In this paper, we adopt a random walk based ranking function to calculate the ranking score for each candidate. We define the random walk based relevance measure between v_i and v_j as:

$$s(v_i, v_j|\mathcal{P}) = \sum_{t=v_i \rightsquigarrow v_j|\mathcal{P}} RW(t)$$

, where t is a tour from v_i to v_j following a specific meta-path $\mathcal{P}$, and $RW(t)$ is the random walk probability of the tour t. Suppose $t = (v_i, v_{i+1}, \ldots, v_{i+k}, \ldots, v_j)$, the random walk probability is then $RW(t) = \prod_{k=0}^{k=j-i-1} w(v_{i+k}, v_{i+k+1})$, where $w(v_{i+k}, v_{i+k+1})$ is the weight of edge $v_{i+k} \rightarrow v_{i+k+1}$. Alternatively, we can create a ranking model $\Phi(\mathcal{P}_1, \mathcal{P}_2 ..., \mathcal{P}_t)$, where $\mathcal{P}_i$ $(1 \le i \le t)$ is a meta-path based ranking feature. For this study, the ranking function Φ is derived using Coordinate Ascent [7], a learning to rank method.

3.3 Evaluation Method and Ranking Model Training

[Evaluation method]: For evaluation purpose, we randomly select a set of nodes $V^{(Q)}$ belonging to the query node type $\dot{A}_Q$ $(\forall v \in V^{(Q)}, \tau(v) = \dot{A}_Q)$. Then for $v_i^{(Q)} \in V^{(Q)}$, we locate the corresponding set of nodes $V_i^{(R)}$ that belong to the result node type $\dot{A}_R$ and are directly connected to $v_i^{(Q)}$ via a set of edges $E_i^{(Q)}$ of relation type R_Q. In order to evaluate the performance of the proposed approach, for $v_i^{(Q)} \in V^{(Q)}$, we randomly remove $p\%$ of edges in $E_i^{(Q)}$ from the graph. Different meta-path based ranking features and learning to rank model can be used to recommend nodes originally linked to $v_i^{(Q)}$ via these removed edges. Mean average precision (MAP), normalized discounted cumulative gain (NDCG), and Precision@10 are used as evaluation metrics. An importance score of 0-4 is assigned to each ground-truth query-result node pair for NDCG calculation. For music track recommendation task, if a music track is played more than 4 times by the query user, it is assigned an importance score of 4. A play count of 3 or 4 has an importance of 3. A music track played twice is assigned to 2, and once to 1. Score is 0 if the track is never played by query user.

[Learning to Rank model training]: The ranking performance of each meta-path is evaluated, and only the top t performing meta-paths are used to train the learning to rank model $\Phi(\mathcal{P}_1, \mathcal{P}_2 ..., \mathcal{P}_t)$. The dataset D used to train and test Φ is defined as $D_1 \cup D_2 \cup \cdots \cup D_t$, where D_i (1≤i≤t) is made up of the top k ranked items returned by $\mathcal{P}_i$. Each instance in D is a $(t+1)$ dimension tuple $(\vec{x}, y)$, where y is the ground-truth relevance judgment and the ith element of $\vec{x}$ is the ranking score derived from $\mathcal{P}_i$ or 0 if this item is not found by $\mathcal{P}_i$. The learning to rank model is evaluated using 5-fold cross-validation.

4. EXPERIMENT

In this section, we test the performance of the proposed approach on music track recommendation.

4.1 Data and Preprocessing

In order to build the heterogeneous music graph, we collected metadata and user generated data from xiami.com, a popular music social website in China. The website stores user-contributed and editor-curated metadata about different music entities (artist, album, song, etc.). It also allows users to build personal profile, record their listening history, create customized playlist, and socialize with other users within the community. For this study, the experiment dataset contains 56,055 artists, 43,086 albums, 1,233,651 songs, 633 genres, 677,275 users, and 305,916 playlists. As Table 1 shows, we also collected a large number of relationships among different objects. There are 15,929,369 edges in total created on the graph.

For evaluation, we randomly selected 1,000 users from the dataset whose listening history contains more than 50 different songs. We set up this filter to make sure there are enough training/test instances for each user. Then 40% of the "play" relationships originating from each of the 1000 selected users are removed for evaluation purpose.

We trained two learning to rank models, one with the top 10 performing meta-paths of length 4, and the other one with the top 10 performing meta-paths with length ≤ 3. For each meta-path, the top 1000 ranked results are kept to build the dataset for model training and test.

4.2 Result

We compare our algorithm with item-to-item based CF algorithm with jaccard similarity, which has been proved useful in [8].

Table 2 lists the evaluation results for different ranking algorithms. The first 10 rows list the 5 best-performing features whose length ≤ 3 and length = 4, ordered by MAP@10 decreasing. The best performing meta-path is $U \xrightarrow{pl} Ar \xrightarrow{pIn} Al \xrightarrow{i} S^?$. This meta-

Table 2: Evaluation Results

	Path	MAP@10	MAP@100	MAP@300	MAP	NDCG@10	NDCG@100	NDCG@300	NDCG	P@10
L≤3	$U \xrightarrow{pl} Ar \xrightarrow{pIn} Al \xrightarrow{i} S?$	0.0024	0.009	0.0145	0.0254	0.0852	0.0863	0.0944	0.1904	0.1135
L≤3	$U \xrightarrow{b} Al \xrightarrow{i} S?$	0.0016	0.0027	0.0029	0.003	0.0414	0.0211	0.0156	0.016	0.0648
L≤3	$U \xrightarrow{pl} Ar \xrightarrow{pIn} S?$	0.0015	0.0058	0.0092	0.0154	0.042	0.0461	0.0537	0.1179	0.0614
L≤3	$U \xrightarrow{c} Al \xrightarrow{i} S?$	0.0013	0.0021	0.0023	0.0023	0.0553	0.0236	0.0142	0.014	0.0733
L≤3	$U \xrightarrow{b} Al \xleftarrow{pIn} Ar \xrightarrow{pIn} S?$	0.0007	0.0018	0.0026	0.0037	0.0227	0.0187	0.0201	0.0354	0.0372
L=4	$U \xrightarrow{pl} S \xleftarrow{pIn} Ar \xrightarrow{pIn} Al \xrightarrow{i} S?$	0.0021	0.008	0.0131	0.0268	0.0717	0.0747	0.083	0.2063	0.0963
L=4	$U \xrightarrow{pl} S \xleftarrow{i} Al \xleftarrow{pIn} Ar \xrightarrow{pIn} S?$	0.0017	0.0069	0.0116	0.0242	0.0676	0.0642	0.0731	0.1937	0.0932
L=4	$U \xrightarrow{b} Al \xleftarrow{pIn} Ar \xleftarrow{pl} U \xrightarrow{pl} S?$	0.0013	0.0036	0.0057	0.0131	0.0551	0.0476	0.0522	0.1513	0.0747
L=4	$U \xrightarrow{pl} Ar \xrightarrow{pIn} S \xleftarrow{c} U \xrightarrow{pl} S?$	0.0009	0.0034	0.0058	0.0137	0.0538	0.0526	0.0551	0.1554	0.0797
L=4	$U \xrightarrow{pl} Ar \xrightarrow{pIn} S \xleftarrow{b} U \xrightarrow{pl} S?$	0.0009	0.0034	0.0057	0.014	0.0511	0.0525	0.0557	0.1587	0.075
CF	item similarity	0.0044	0.0085	0.0101	0.0122	0.1489	0.0735	0.0595	0.0919	0.1919
L2R	length≤3	0.0024	0.009	0.0144	0.0235	0.0887	0.0856	0.0925	0.168	0.1172
L2R	length=4	0.0022	0.0084	0.0144	0.0296	0.0845	0.0842	0.0957	0.2206	0.116
L2R	length≤3 + CF	0.0069***	0.0162***	0.0215***	0.0314***	0.2084***	0.1261***	0.1154***	0.1955***	0.2593***
L2R	length=4 + CF	0.0047*	0.0118***	0.017***	0.0314***	0.162**	0.0986***	0.0981***	0.2269***	0.2048**

*** Significant p <0.0001,** Significant p <0.001, * Significant p <0.01

path means we recommend music tracks from the albums released by artists in the user's listening history. Although it cannot outperform item-based CF algorithm for MAP@10, as rank goes up to 100, it gains higher MAP and NDCG scores. This finding indicates that single meta-path based ranking function can discover high quality music tracks based on the user's listening history. The best performing meta-path of length 4 is $U \xrightarrow{pl} S \xleftarrow{pIn} Ar \xrightarrow{pIn} Al \xrightarrow{i} S?$. It is not the best performing one across all meta-paths within length 4, but it still outperforms the second best meta-path within length 3. It means longer meta-paths are as competitive as, if not better than, the shorter ones. Note that the best performing meta-path of length 4 also outperforms the baseline collaborative filtering algorithm for MAP@300.

Collaborative filtering only takes advantage of user's listening/rating behavior. However, on the heterogeneous graph, music tracks are connected to the user via other types of relations as well (e.g. $U \xrightarrow{pl} Ar \xrightarrow{pIn} Al \xrightarrow{i} S?$). Meta-path based ranking functions can enhance collaborative filtering performance by providing additional information. To test this hypothesis, we tried two sets of experiments combining both meta-path features and the collaborative filtering feature. The last 2 rows of Table 2 show the results for the combination of CF ranking and rankings from the top 10 meta-paths with length ≤ 3 and length = 4. Both combined recommendation models significantly outperform the baseline CF algorithm and the meta-path ranking functions. It is also worth noting that the combination with meta-paths of length 4 does not perform as well as the one with shorter meta-paths. A good selection of meta-paths is critical for the performance.

5. ANALYSIS AND CONCLUSION

In this study, we propose a heterogeneous graph mining approach for music recommendation. Supervised random walk is used for music ranking (graph mining), and the meta-path based ranking features are identified from graph schema (schema mining). The best-performed features are used to train the recommendation model via learning to rank. Evaluation results show that: 1. for single meta-path ranking function, CF method works better for top ranked musics, but when rank is larger than 100, some meta-paths outperform CF approach. 2. After we applied learning to rank method, the recommendation performance significantly outperform all other methods, including the CF algorithm. 3. Some nodes and relationships can be more significant than others for music recommendation. For instance, the top ranked meta-paths are more likely to be related to artist (Ar), album (Al) and user (U), which can be important to locate the important music on the graph.

There are a couple of directions of research arising from this work which should be pursued. First, we will investigate more sophisticated feature selection methods to enhance the recommendation performance. Second, by using the constructed graph, we will explore other recommendation tasks, e.g., recommending music to playlist or recommending existing playlists to a user.

6. REFERENCES

[1] J. Bu, S. Tan, C. Chen, C. Wang, H. Wu, L. Zhang, and X. He. Music recommendation by unified hypergraph: combining social media information and music content. In *Proceedings of the international conference on Multimedia*, pages 391–400. ACM, 2010.

[2] G. Dror, Y. Labs, N. Koenigstein, Y. Koren, and M. Weimer. The yahoo! music dataset and kddcup'11. In *JMLR Workshop and Conference Proceedings: Proceedings of KDD Cup 2011 Competition*, pages 3–18, 2012.

[3] H. Kautz, B. Selman, and M. Shah. Referral web: combining social networks and collaborative filtering. *Communications of the ACM*, 40(3):63–65, 1997.

[4] N. Lao and W. W. Cohen. Relational retrieval using a combination of path-constrained random walks. *Machine Learning*, 81(1):53–67, Oct. 2010.

[5] X. Liu, Y. Yu, C. Guo, and Y. Sun. Meta-path-based ranking with pseudo relevance feedback on heterogeneous graph for citation recommendation. In *Proceedings of the 23rd ACM International Conference on Conference on Information and Knowledge Management*, CIKM '14, pages 121–130, New York, NY, USA, 2014. ACM.

[6] B. Logan. Music recommendation from song sets. In *5th International Society for Music Information Retrieval*, pages 425–428, 2004.

[7] D. Metzler and W. B. Croft. Linear feature-based models for information retrieval. *Information Retrieval*, 10(3):257–274, 2007.

[8] Y. Song, S. Dixon, and M. Pearce. A survey of music recommendation systems and future perspectives. In *9th International Symposium on Computer Music Modeling and Retrieval*, June 2012.

[9] P. Symeonidis, M. M. Ruxanda, A. Nanopoulos, and Y. Manolopoulos. Ternary semantic analysis of social tags for personalized music recommendation. In *11th International Society for Music Information Retrieval*, pages 219–224, 2008.

[10] X. Wang and Y. Wang. Improving content-based and hybrid music recommendation using deep learning. In *Proceedings of the ACM International Conference on Multimedia*, MM '14, pages 627–636, New York, NY, USA, 2014. ACM.

Differences in Eye-tracking Measures Between Visits and Revisits to Relevant and Irrelevant Web Pages

Jacek Gwizdka
School of Information
University of Texas at Austin
Austin, TX, USA
sigir2015@gwizdka.com

Yinglong Zhang
School of Information
University of Texas at Austin
Austin, TX, USA
yzhang@utexas.edu

ABSTRACT
This short paper presents initial results from a project, in which we investigated differences in how users view relevant and irrelevant Web pages on their visits and revisits. The users' viewing of Web pages was characterized by eye-tracking measures, with a particular attention paid to changes in pupil size. The data was collected in a lab-based experiment, in which users (N=32) conducted assigned information search tasks on Wikipedia. We performed non-parametric tests of significance as well as classification. Our findings demonstrate differences in eye-tracking measures on visits and revisits to relevant and irrelevant pages and thus indicate a feasibility of predicting perceived Web document relevance from eye-tracking data. In particular, relative changes in pupil size differed significantly in almost all conditions. Our work extends results from previous studies to more realistic search scenarios and to Web page visits and revisits.

General Terms
Experimentation, Human Factors, Measurement.

Keywords
H. Information Systems. H.3 INFORMATION STORAGE AND RETRIEVAL. H.3.3 Information Search and Retrieval. Subjects: Search process.

Author Keywords
Web search; relevance judgment; eye-tracking.

1. INTRODUCTION
Notwithstanding the large body of work on information relevance and relevance judgments, we still do not fully understand the process of how people judge relevance of documents. It is generally agreed that relevance judgment process is dynamic and multi-dimensional [3, 12], but we are only beginning to understand how the various relevance aspects might be applied by users in the process of assessing documents. A formal model of aggregating relevance aspects was proposed [6], but only few research projects attempted to deal with that process from the cognitive perspective [9]. Though, there is also a more recent work in which a cognitively-influenced two-stage model of document assessment was proposed [23].

SIGIR '15, August 09 - 13, 2015, Santiago, Chile

DOI: http://dx.doi.org/10.1145/2766462.27677950.

Given the notion of multi-stage relevance judgment process, we aim to investigate changes in cognitive processes as they are reflected in differences in how documents are viewed and read. In the current project we are looking for evidence of such differences in cognitive processing in Web information search that leads to finding one or more relevant documents. This type of investigation lends itself well to the application of eye-tracking as a data collection method. Eye-tracking helps to get insights into cognitive processes involved in assessing document relevance. Prior work that used eye-tracking in investigation of differences in user behavior between irrelevant and relevant documents tended to use simple documents (e.g., individual sentences or short paragraphs); work that used more realistic tasks and more complex documents (e.g., web pages) did not document visits and revisits, neither did it examine pupil dilation. Prior work tended to look at differences in eye measurements between levels of document relevance, but it did not examine differences at sequential stages in the information search process. Our goal in this short paper is to extend previous work by examining differences in eye-tracking derived measures on Web search tasks conducted on English Wikipedia on pages marked by users as relevant or irrelevant. We examine fixation durations and saccade-related measures, but focus mainly on pupil dilation. To investigate differences between stages of the search process, we operationalize them in a simple way as first visits and subsequent revisits to irrelevant and relevant pages. We formulated the following hypotheses:

H1. Pupil dilation and (some other) eye-tracking measures will differ between relevant and irrelevant pages.

H2. Pupil dilation and (some other) eye-tracking measures will differ between first and subsequent visits to Web pages.

H3. Pupil dilation and (some other) eye-tracking measures will differ between visits to relevant pages when a page relevance was decided compared to other visits to the same relevant pages, when the pages were not judged as relevant yet.

In the next section, we present related work to place our project in context and to motivate our hypotheses.

2. RELATED WORK
One reason why improved understanding of relevance judgment process from user's perspective is useful, is to better model differences between trained relevance judges and actual users. In the already mentioned work [23], Yilmaz et al. proposed a two-stage model of document assessment. The two stages are "1. initial assessment" and "2. extract utility". The authors used this model to explain disparities between judges and users relevance assessments. In addition to being motivated by the notion of stages in document assessment, our work draws on the authors' finding that effort plays an important role in user assessment of document relevance and their argument for including effort in modeling relevance judgment process. Other researchers also

postulated for including effort in modeling interactive information search; for example, using cost of search actions to explain some aspects of search behavior [1], or using search effort to explain search task success [2]. Furthermore, Villa and Halvey [21] showed a relationship between mental effort and relevance levels of judged documents. As we will explain later, pupil dilation, which is typically provided by eye-trackers, is related to mental effort.

Eye-tracking has received considerable attention as a data source useful in information retrieval research. Much of the work has concentrated on eye fixation patterns on ranked search results pages [4,7,14,19]. While this work brought an improved understanding of eye gaze on web pages in general, and on search engine results pages, specifically, it did not address how people view and read documents that differ in their degree of relevance to the user's information need. In other work, eye-tracking techniques have been used in research on relevance judgments. For example, Loboda et al. [16] focused at the word-level relevance and showed a relationship between eye fixation measures and the relevance of terminal words in sentences. Research presented in [20] and [5] demonstrated that user's eye movement behaviors would shift between scanning, reading, or deciding processes, and that reading and skimming behavior was heavily influenced by relevance (especially by topicality of text). In agreement with these findings, [8,10] reported that relevant and irrelevant paragraphs and short documents, respectively, could be discriminated based on gaze data and eye-movement patterns in reading experiments. Although eye-tracking derived measures were investigated in previous research, most of the above mentioned studies focused on fixation duration, fixation counts, and fixation locations; pupil dilation has been generally neglected. Cognitive psychology research informs us that under constant illumination pupil dilation is associated with mental effort and attention [18] and thus, plausibly, it may be related to cognitive processing of documents. Indeed, Gwizdka and Oliveira et al. [10,17] demonstrated that changes in pupil size are related to levels of relevance – pupil dilated for more relevant stimuli, both for text and images. In light of this evidence, it seems reasonable to incorporate pupilometry in interactive information retrieval research. The use of pupilometry is additionally corroborated by the relationship between pupil dilation and mental effort.

In summary, eye-tracking is a feasible approach to examining user's implicit relevance judgments. With the sizable body of prior work, there is still a need for more research conducted on more realistic search task scenarios and documents (e.g., on the live Web), and paying attention to sequential stages of search and to a wider range of eye-tracking measures. That's where we position our current work.

3. METHOD

We conducted a lab-based experiment of Web search on Wikipedia. 32 native English speakers (15 females) with a normal, to corrected-to-normal vision, attended individual experiment sessions held in the Information eXperience (IX) lab in the School of Information at University of Texas at Austin. Each session was completed within 1.5 hours; participants received $30 for their participation. Each participant was asked to complete four search tasks that were designed to differ in complexity (within-subject design). The searches were conducted on Wikipedia using a commercial test search engine created by Search Technologies Corp. We used the commercial search engine, because Wikipedia does not provide full-text search. Participants used a PC computer running Windows 7 that was equipped with Tobii T60 eye-tracker. The eye-tracking and interaction data was collected using Attention Tool software [13], while the task rotations and questionnaires were controlled by YASFIIRE software [22]. Task rotations were assigned to participants in a random order. In each task, participants read task description, completed pre- and post- task questionnaires, and searched Wikipedia. At the end of the session, they answered an exit questionnaire. There were no time limits set for search tasks. In this paper, our focus is on viewing behavior of Wikipedia pages. During a visit to a Wikipedia page, in addition to reading the page, a user could open a search task description on screen, bookmark the page and enter notes, edit the previously entered notes, and decide to complete the task by entering and editing the final notes about the results of their search. According to the instructions given to our participants, bookmarking a page signified that the page was perceived by a participant as relevant to the search task, thus the bookmarking events provided us with binary relevance judgments. Users were also able to delete any bookmark, if they decided that a page was not relevant any more. The visits to Wikipedia pages (relevant and irrelevant) were categorized into first visits and revisits. We further distinguished these visits to relevant pages when relevance judgments were made (these included first visits and revisits). We isolated time periods when a user was viewing a Wikipedia page (that is not reading task description nor entering notes) and considered each of them separately in our data analysis. We call user's activity during these time periods a *page viewing state* and emphasize that a visit to a Web page may contain one or more such states. Extraction of isolated page viewing states serves a purpose of separating cognitive activities related to document processing from other activities, and, thus, could be considered as contributing to eye-tracking data cleaning.

The perceived binary level of page relevance, page first visit, revisit, and visit with relevance judgment were factors used in data analysis. Table 1 shows eye-tracking derived variables.

Table 1. Eye-tracking measures

Variable	Description
Fixation duration	Duration of an eye fixation, in milliseconds
Saccade duration	Duration of a saccade, that is of a fast eye movement between eye fixations, in milliseconds
Saccade length	Length of a saccade, in pixels
Saccade angle	Angle of a saccade relative to the horizontal axis, in degrees
Relative pupil dilation	The relative change in pupil diameter: A difference between pupil size at a time *t* and the average pupil size for a participant, normalized by that average

4. DATA ANALYSIS AND RESULTS

We first removed page viewing states with few eye fixation data points by deleting states shorter than 6 seconds. This resulted in removing less than 6% of data. All further analyses were conducted after these short states were removed.

Table 2. Counts of page viewing states

Level	Page and visit types		Count	
1	Irrelevant page	first visit	306	215
2		revisit		91
n/a	Relevant page	first visit	765	358
n/a		revisit		407
3	Relevant page*	first visit*	697	323
4		revisit*		374
5	Rel. page visit with relevance judgment		68	

* shows counts after removing visits when relevance judgments were made, which are contained in level 5

Our data did not satisfy analysis of variance assumptions, therefore we performed non-parametric tests. We constructed a 5-level factor variable (shown in Table 2 & 3) from visits to irrelevant and relevant pages and different visit types (first visits, revisits, and visits to relevant pages with relevance judgment). The Kruskal-Wallis rank sum test conducted with this factor showed significant differences for fixation duration ($\chi(4)^2$=24.05, p<.001), pupil dilation ($\chi(4)^2$=891.33, p<<.0001), saccade duration ($\chi(4)^2$=171.3, p<<.0001), and saccade length ($\chi(4)^2$=41.15, p<.0001).

Table 3. Pupil dilation (mean(SD))

Level	Page and visit types		Pupil dilation	
1	Irrelevant page	first visit	-0.045 (0.054)	-0.0497 (0.053)
2		revisit		-0.0362 (0.054)
3	Relevant page*	first visit*	-0.036 (0.059)	-0.0428 (0.055)
4		revisit*		- 0.0319 (0.063)
5	Rel. page visit with relevance judgment		- 0.033 (0.059)	

* shows counts after removing visits when relevance judgments were made, which are contained in level 5

The post-hoc pairwise comparisons (all checked at p<.05) indicated significant differences in relative change in pupil size in almost all cases, except between revisits to irrelevant and relevant pages and visits when relevance judgment took place; pupil dilation was the largest on these visits, while the smallest dilation was on first visits to irrelevant pages. For other variables, the pairwise comparisons indicated significant differences in only in a few cases. A significantly longer fixation durations on revisits to relevant pages compared with revisits to irrelevant and first visits to relevant pages. Saccade duration on the first visits to relevant pages tended to be longer than on irrelevant pages. The slowest saccades were on relevance judgment visits to relevant pages. The pixel-length of saccades was significantly longer on all visits to irrelevant pages compared with first visits to relevant pages. The length of saccades was significantly shortest on first visits to relevant vs. revisits or relevance judgment visits to these pages. These results generally confirm our hypotheses, though, to a different extent for different variables; their pattern of significance is shown in Table 4.

Table 4. Summary of pairwise comparisons

	Comparisons between 5-level factor levels									
Variable	**1-2**	**1-3**	**1-4**	**1-5**	**2-3**	**2-4**	**2-5**	**3-4**	**3-5**	**4-5**
Fixation duration						+		+		
Saccade duration		|		+			+	+	+	+
Saccade length		+			+			+	+	
Saccade angle										
Relative pupil dilation	+	+	+	+	+	+		+	+	

+ indicates significant pairwise comparison.

For numbering of the 5-level factor levels please see Table 2.

One can expect significant cognitive processes to take place shortly before a decision is made. Therefore, we separately examined the last 2 seconds period of each page viewing state and compared differences between all visits with relevance judgment visits. The Wilcoxon rank sum test showed a significant difference for pupil dilation (W = 479178, p<<.0001). The same test also showed a significant difference between the first and the last two seconds of a visit to a relevant page during with relevance judgment (W = 45615.5, p<0.0001). Other variables were not significantly different. In both cases, pupil tended to be larger during the two second period before the relevance decision was made.

To further investigate how eye-tracking data reflects relevance judgments, we employed classification. In the analysis, we proposed two models to classify two different situations. The first model was used to classify first visits to relevant pages and visits to relevant pages during which participants judged relevance. The second one was used to classify visits to irrelevant pages and visits to relevant pages during which participants judged relevance. Because of the class imbalance in our datasets, we used up-sampling [15] to simulate additional data points, thereby improving balance across classes. For both models, we used flexible discriminant analysis (FDA) and all five variables were included as predictors (Table 1). The parameters of the two models were tuned to maximize Receiver Operating Characteristic (ROC) and cross-fold validation was used to evaluate the performance of the models. Outcomes of both our classification models showed that the relative pupil dilation was the most important predictor (Table 5). The models' performances are shown in Table 6.

Table 5. Variable importance for two classification models

Variable	Model 1	Model 2
Fixation duration	29.38	29.66
Saccade duration	81.27	59.94
Saccade length	46.70	0.00
Saccade angle	0.00	54.94
Relative pupil dilation	100.00	100.00

Table 6. Classification model performance

Model	Accuracy	Sensitivity	Specificity
Model 1	0.57	0.57	0.57
Model 2	0.61	0.57	0.62

5. DISCUSSION AND CONCLUSIONS

The findings show that several eye-tracking derived measures significantly differ between user visits and revisits to relevant and irrelevant Wikipedia pages.

In particular, a larger pupil dilation on visits to relevant pages indicates, in part, a higher mental effort and attention paid to relevant pages, and particularly so on revisits or when a relevance judgment was finally made. This result is inline with the results presented in [10, 21], but it also extends them, since our investigation distinguished first and subsequent visits to pages.

Average pupil dilation during page viewing states did not differentiate between revisits and relevance judgment visits to relevant pages. However, we showed that the significantly larger pupil dilation in the last 2 seconds before the relevance judgment was made, should enable one to differentiate the relevance judgment visits from any other visits to Web pages. This result can be plausibly explained by increased attention during relevance judgment.

Results with respect to fixation duration, saccade duration and length, generally confirm prior work. For example [5, 10], where a tendency for visual scanning of irrelevant pages and continuous reading of relevant pages was shown. Our results indicate that on revisits to relevant pages and when relevance judgments were made, the Web pages were read more carefully.

Previous studies that employed eye-tracking in characterization of text relevance were typically conducted under more constrained human-information interaction and, for example, examined only reading of prepared sentences [20], paragraphs [8] or short text documents [10] and not user-selected Web pages. Our work extends the prior research by investigating more realistic and complex interactive information retrieval scenarios on the Web and by conducting analysis at the level of page viewing states, which we constructed to isolate cognitive activities not related to document viewing/reading.

The classification results demonstrate a promise in using eye-tracking variables in predicting user's perceived relevance of Wikipedia pages. While accuracy of the two models shown in this paper is rather modest, it could be improved by combining with other interaction data and by applying further processing to pupil size, following, for example, approaches described in [11, 17].

One of the motivations of our work was the notion multi-stage of relevance judgment, the differences in variables between the visits and revisits provide some indirect support for it. Interestingly, patterns of pairwise comparison significance (Table 4) differ in all but two cases (1-3 and 3-5). Plausibly one could use different combinations of variables to infer different types of page viewing states (Table 2). This finding is a likely indication of differences in cognitive processes, such as shifts in mode of reading (e.g., scanning, skimming, and continuous reading) and levels of mental workload and attention changing between visits and revisits to pages at different levels of relevance.

A limitation of the current analysis is that we did not use time sequence analysis that would allow for more direct modeling of a sequence of stages in document assessment. In the future, we plan to apply techniques such as Hidden-Markov Modeling (HMM) to our data.

Other limitations include, a bias in our data towards relevance as well as use of only one web site, the English Wikipedia. We believe that our results should generalize to other text-heavy web pages and in our future work we plan to broaden the set of web pages we use and to address other limitations. In addition, our analysis was conducted at an aggregate level across all users and all tasks. In the follow up work, we will also examine data at an individual user and task levels.

6. ACKNOWLEDGMENTS
This research was supported, in part, by IMLS Career Development Grant #RE-04-11-0062-11A to Jacek Gwizdka.

7. REFERENCES
[1] Azzopardi, L. 2014. Modelling Interaction with Economic Models of Search. *Proceedings of SIGIR'2014* (New York, NY), 3–12.

[2] Bailey, E. and Kelly, D. 2011. Is amount of effort a better predictor of search success than use of specific search tactics? *Proceedings of the American Society for Information Science and Technology*. 48, 1, 1–10.

[3] Borlund, P. 2003. The concept of relevance in IR. *JASIST*. 54, 10, 913–925.

[4] Brumby, D.P. and Howes, A. 2008. Strategies for Guiding Interactive Search: An Empirical Investigation Into the Consequences of Label Relevance for Assessment and Selection. *Human–Computer Interaction*. 23, 1, 1–46.

[5] Buscher, G. et al. 2012. Attentive documents: Eye tracking as implicit feedback for information retrieval and beyond. *ACM Trans. Interact. Intell. Syst.* 1, 2, 9:1–9:30.

[6] Da Costa Pereira, C. et al. 2012. Multidimensional relevance: Prioritized aggregation in a personalized Information Retrieval setting. *Information Processing & Management*. 48, 2, 340–357.

[7] Cutrell, E. and Guan, Z. 2007. What are you looking for?: an eye-tracking study of information usage in web search. *Proceedings of the SIGCHI Conference on Human Factors in Computing Systems* (New York, NY), 407–416.

[8] Fahey, D. et al. 2011. Document Classification on Relevance: A Study on Eye Gaze Patterns for Reading. *Neural Information Processing*. B.-L. Lu et al., eds. Springer Berlin Heidelberg. 143–150.

[9] Greisdorf, H. 2003. Relevance thresholds: a multi-stage predictive model of how users evaluate information. *Information Processing & Management*. 39, 3, 403–423.

[10] Gwizdka, J. 2014. Characterizing Relevance with Eye-tracking Measures. *Proceedings of the 5th Information Interaction in Context Symposium* (New York, NY), 58–67.

[11] Hossain, G. and Yeasin, M. 2014. Understanding Effects of Cognitive Load from Pupillary Responses Using Hilbert Analytic Phase. *2014 IEEE Conference on Computer Vision and Pattern Recognition Workshops (CVPRW)* (Jun. 2014), 381–386.

[12] Huang, X. and Soergel, D. 2013. Relevance: An improved framework for explicating the notion. *JASIST*. 64, 1, 18–35.

[13] iMotions 2014. *Attention Tool Biometric Research Platform: Version*. iMotions, Inc.

[14] Joachims, T. et al. 2007. Evaluating the accuracy of implicit feedback from clicks and query reformulations in Web search. *ACM Trans. Inf. Syst.* 25, 2.

[15] Kuhn, M. and Johnson, K. 2013. *Applied Predictive Modeling*. Springer Science & Business Media.

[16] Loboda, T.D. et al. 2011. Inferring word relevance from eye-movements of readers. *Proceedings of the 16th international conference on Intelligent user interfaces* (New York, NY), 175–184.

[17] Oliveira, F.T.P. et al. 2009. Discriminating the relevance of web search results with measures of pupil size. *Proceedings of the 27th ACM international conference on Human factors in computing systems CHI'2009* (Boston, MA), 2209–2212.

[18] Onorati, F. et al. 2013. Characterization of affective states by pupillary dynamics and autonomic correlates. *Frontiers in Neuroengineering*. 6, 9.

[19] Pan, B. et al. 2004. The determinants of web page viewing behavior: an eye-tracking study. *Proceedings of the 2004 symposium on Eye tracking research & applications* (New York, NY), 147–154.

[20] Simola, J. et al. 2008. Using hidden Markov model to uncover processing states from eye movements in information search tasks. *Cognitive Systems Research*. 9, 4, 237–251.

[21] Villa, R. and Halvey, M. 2013. Is relevance hard work?: evaluating the effort of making relevant assessments. *Proceedings of SIGIR'2013* (New York, NY, US), 765–768.

[22] Wei, X. et al. 2014. YASFIIRE: Yet Another System for IIR Evaluation. *Proceedings of the 5th Information Interaction in Context Symposium* (New York, NY), 316–319.

[23] Yilmaz, E. et al. 2014. Relevance and Effort: An Analysis of Document Utility. *Proceedings of CIKM'2014* (New York, NY), 91–100.

Reducing Hubness: A Cause of Vulnerability in Recommender Systems

Kazuo Hara
National Institute of Genetics
Mishima, Shizuoka, Japan
kazuo.hara@gmail.com

Ikumi Suzuki
The Institute of Statistical Mathematics
Tachikawa, Tokyo, Japan
suzuki.ikumi@gmail.com

Kei Kobayashi
The Institute of Statistical Mathematics
Tachikawa, Tokyo, Japan
kei@ism.ac.jp

Kenji Fukumizu
The Institute of Statistical Mathematics
Tachikawa, Tokyo, Japan
fukumizu@ism.ac.jp

ABSTRACT

It is known that memory-based collaborative filtering systems are vulnerable to shilling attacks. In this paper, we demonstrate that *hubness*, which occurs in high dimensional data, is exploited by the attacks. Hence we explore methods for reducing hubness in user-response data to make these systems robust against attacks. Using the MovieLens dataset, we empirically show that the two methods for reducing hubness by transforming a similarity matrix—(i) centering and (ii) conversion to a commute time kernel—can thwart attacks without degrading the recommendation performance.

Categories and Subject Descriptors

H.4 [**Information Systems Applications**]: Miscellaneous

Keywords

Collaborative filtering; Shilling attack; Hubness

1. INTRODUCTION

Memory-based collaborative filtering (CF) is a type of recommendation system that predicts a user's response to unseen items by referencing past responses from the k-nearest neighbor (k-NN) users. A considerable drawback to memory-based CF is its vulnerability to *shilling attacks*. Shilling attacks inject recommendation systems with fake users in order to force the systems to generate biased recommendations [3, 1]. By design, memory-based CF issues recommendations based on the past responses to items by other users, rather than the individual to whom the recommendation is made. This design provides room for attackers to alter the system's decision by injecting fake users and forged ratings.

On the other hand, it has recently been found that *hubness* is subject to a form of the so-called curse of dimensionality [5]. That is, in higher dimensions, a small number of objects, called *hubs*, appear frequently in the k-NNs of other objects.

When k-NNs of users are computed in memory-based CF systems, hub users emerge because past user-response data is generally high dimensional [4, 2]. Because hub users contribute to the recommendation process, they can significantly influence recommendation systems.

We view shilling attacks as attacks that exploit hubness. The attacks inject fake users that are likely to become hubs, in order to gain maximum control over the output of the systems. To mitigate the effects of the attacks, we propose reducing hubness by transforming the similarity measure used in the k-NN computation. Because shilling attacks fabricate objects that are similar to the data centroid in an effort to maximize their influence, we transform similarity measure such that all objects, including the injected objects, are equally similar to the centroid. This transformation is achieved by computing a commute time kernel from a given similarity matrix [7], or more simply, by centering the similarity matrix [8]. Using the MovieLens dataset, we demonstrate that after such transformation, the hubness of fake users tends to be reduced. As a result, the transformation provides systems with tolerance to attacks, without degrading the accuracy of the predicted ratings.[1]

2. PRELIMINARY

2.1 Memory-Based Algorithm

We assume a set of observed responses is provided in a matrix R of size $N_{\text{user}} \times N_{\text{item}}$, where N_{user}, N_{item} is the number of users and items, respectively. A component value of R in the uth row and the ith column, $R(u, i)$, denotes the degree of preference of the uth user for the ith item. Matrix R may contain missing values, represented by *nil*; R is usually very sparse, in the sense that greater part of its components is nil. The goal of the system is to predict the value of each missing component in R, which corresponds to the future response from a user on an item. Using observed responses, memory-based algorithms predict missing values by interpolating the values of the k-NNs.

[1] Although this paper focuses solely on reducing hubness exploited by average attacks against user-based algorithms, the proposal can similarly be adopted for reducing hubness exploited by segment attacks against item-based algorithms.

SIGIR'15, August 09 - 13, 2015, Santiago, Chile.
© 2015 ACM. ISBN 978-1-4503-3621-5/15/08 ...$15.00.
DOI: http://dx.doi.org/10.1145/2766462.2767823.

Prediction Function.

Below, $Pred(u, i)$ denotes a function that predicts a future response of user u to item i.

$$Pred(u,i) = \frac{\sum_{n \in U} Sim(u,n)\{R(n,i) - \bar{R}(n)\}}{\sum_{n \in U} Sim(u,n)} + \bar{R}(u) \quad (1)$$

where $Sim(\cdot,\cdot)$ is a function that returns the similarity of two users, U is a set of the k most similar users to user u as measured by $Sim(\cdot,\cdot)$ that satisfies $R(n,i) \neq \text{nil}$ for $n \in U$, and

$$\bar{R}(u) = \frac{\sum_{i=1}^{N_{\text{item}}} R(u,i)\delta[R(u,i) \neq \text{nil}]}{\sum_{i=1}^{N_{\text{item}}} \delta[R(u,i) \neq \text{nil}]}$$

is the averaged response of user u to items. $\delta[\cdot]$ is the indicator function taking on 1 if the proposition in the brackets holds, or 0 otherwise.

Similarity Measure.

The appropriate selection of a similarity function, $Sim(\cdot,\cdot)$, is important, because the function determines the k-NNs (i.e., U), as well as their weighting, to compute a weighted sum of the k-NNs' responses according to (1). A popular similarity function calculates the cosine of the angles between row or column vectors of matrix R, after converting the nil components of R to zeros [6].

$$Sim(u,v) = Cos(u,v) = \frac{\langle x_u, x_v \rangle}{\sqrt{\langle x_u, x_u \rangle}\sqrt{\langle x_v, x_v \rangle}}, \quad (2)$$

where x_u is an N_{item} dimensional vector, the component of which is given as $x_u(i) = R(u,i)$ if $R(u,i) \neq \text{nil}$, $x_u(i) = 0$ otherwise. One disadvantage of using the above functions is that a bias caused by the difference in each user's mean response is ignored. Therefore, a popular correction is to subtract $\bar{R}(u)$ from each vector component [6, 4, 2]. The resulting similarity using corrected vectors is known as the Pearson correlation between users, as follows.[2]

$$Sim(u,v) = Pearson(u,v) = \frac{\langle x'_u, x'_v \rangle}{\sqrt{\langle x'_u, x'_u \rangle}\sqrt{\langle x'_v, x'_v \rangle}}, \quad (3)$$

where, if $R(u,i) \neq \text{nil}$ and $R(v,i) \neq \text{nil}$, then $x'_u(i) = R(u,i) - \bar{R}(u)$ and $x'_v(i) = R(v,i) - \bar{R}(v)$, if otherwise, then $x'_u(i) = 0$ and $x'_v(i) = 0$.

2.2 Average Attack

Memory-based CF determines recommendations based solely on users' responses (i.e., ratings) to items, and therefore, the recommendations can be changed by manipulating the matrix R stored in the systems. One such (malicious) manipulation, on which we focus in the following, is called *average attack* [3]. It injects fake users that pretend to prefer target items, as well as imitating genuine users' average behavior for other items. More precisely, fake users are tailored to give a high rating for target items, but average ratings for each of the remaining items. As a result, fake users that prefer target items become similar to any genuine users, and therefore, memory-based algorithms tend to falsely associate target items with all genuine users.

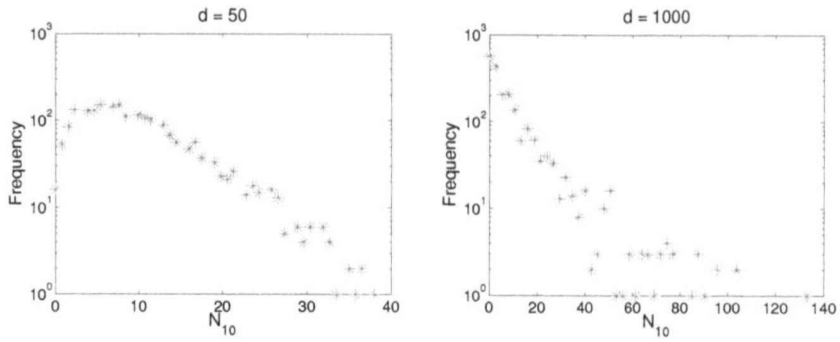

(a) Low dimension. (b) High dimension.

Figure 1: N_{10} distribution. Objects with large N_{10} values emerge in high dimension: *max* N_{10} is 38 in (a) but 133 in (b).

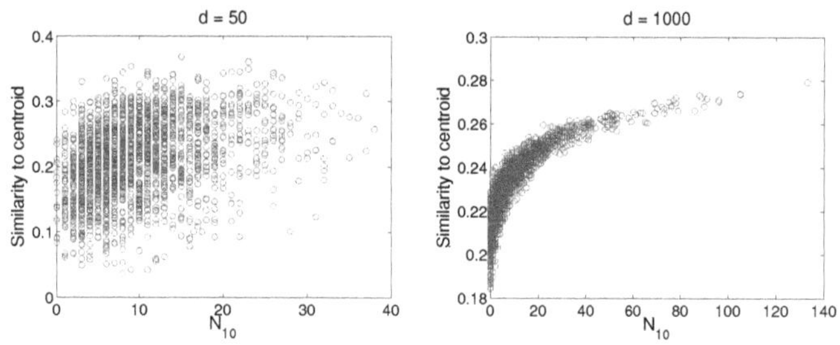

(a) Low dimension. (b) High dimension.

Figure 2: Scatter plot of objects for N_{10} values and similarity to data centroid. A strong correlation emerges in high dimension (b).

2.3 Hubness

Hubness is a new aspect of the curse of dimensionality [5]. Let D be a d-dimensional dataset and $N_k(x)$ denote the number of times an object $x \in D$ occurs in the k-NNs of other objects in D under some similarity measure. As the dimension d increases, the shape of the distribution of N_k changes to become right tail longer, or a small number of objects takes large N_k values. Such objects are called *hubs*, and the phenomenon is called *hubness*.[3]

We now review the emergence of hubness using synthetic data, as reported in [5]. To simulate situations of CF, where each user gives ratings to a few items and thus the rating matrix R is sparse, we produce a sparse dataset. The dataset consists of 2000 objects, each of which is a d-dimensional vector. For each dimension $i = 1, \cdots, d$, we draw a real number from $Lognormal(5; 1)$ distribution and compute its rounded integer n_i. We then choose n_i objects out of the

[2]As opposed to cosine similarity, user vector x'_u must be recomputed for each user it is paired with. Moreover, the number of nonzero elements of user vectors is determined by the number of items that are given a (non-nil) response by both paired users. For paired users giving responses to a few items in common, the number of non zero elements of vectors becomes small, and hence, the resulting Pearson correlation becomes less trustworthy. Therefore, we employ the shrunken variant $\frac{N_c}{N_c+\beta} Pearson(u,v)$, according to the number of non zero elements of paired vectors, N_c, with a positive valued parameter β [2].

[3]Following [5], we evaluate hubness by the skewness of the N_k distribution, defined as $S_{N_k} = E\left[(N_k - \mu_{N_k})^3\right]/\sigma^3_{N_k}$, where $E[\cdot]$ is the expectation operator, and μ_{N_k} and σ_{N_k} are the mean and the standard deviation of the N_k distribution, respectively. A large S_{N_k} means the emergence of hubness.

2000 uniformly at random, and assign a random number drawn uniformly from $[0, 1]$ to their ith component. We calculate the similarity between the objects using the cosine similarity.

To illustrate the emergence of hubness, we compare the distribution of N_{10} in two cases where the dimension is low ($d = 50$) and high ($d = 1000$). Figure 1 shows that, in high dimension, objects with large N_{10} values emerge, and as a result, the distribution of N_{10} becomes skewed to the right. We then compare a scatter plot of objects with respect to the N_{10} value and similarity to the data centroid, shown in Figure 2. We can see that a strong correlation arises in high dimension, and this indicates that the origin of hubness is an increased bias to the centroid caused by high dimensionality.

3. REMEDIES AGAINST ATTACK

3.1 Relation between Attack and Hubness

For memory-based CF, Nanopoulos et al. [4] and Knees et al. [2] reported that hubness emerges because k-NNs are computed in high dimensional spaces. Since the number of users and items are usually large, the feature spaces used for computing similarity, such as cosine and Pearson correlation, become high dimensional, and hence, hubness occurs. Hub objects very often appear in the k-NNs of other objects, and therefore, are responsible for determining many recommendations. However, hubs are not effectively similar to many objects. In other words, hub objects frequently occur in k-NNs only because they are similar to the data centroid in higher dimensions. In fact, according to [2], the performance of recommender systems is affected by the existence of hubs. In any case, because hubs are influential objects for recommender systems, manipulating hubs from outside the system can be effective for attacking the system.

Indeed, hubness renders memory-based recommender systems vulnerable to attacks. More precisely, fake users injected in the system during an average attack are more likely to constitute hubs and affect the system. Therefore, we expect that, by reducing hubness, attacks can be thwarted.

3.2 Reducing Hubness by Eliminating a Bias toward the Centroid

On the premise that specific objects become hubs because they are particularly similar to the data centroid, hubness can be reduced by transforming the similarity measures to make all objects equally similar to the data centroid. Such similarity measures can be obtained by computing a commute time kernel from a given similarity matrix [7], or more simply, by centering the similarity matrix [8].

Let N be the number of objects and $\mathbf{K}$ denote a similarity matrix of size N.[4] A commute time kernel $\mathbf{K}^{\mathrm{CT}}$ is given as

$$\mathbf{K}^{\mathrm{CT}} = \mathbf{L}^{+} \text{ (pseudo-inverse of } \mathbf{L}), \tag{4}$$

where $\mathbf{L} = \mathbf{D} - \mathbf{K}$ is called a *graph Laplacian* and $\mathbf{D}$ is a diagonal matrix with $\mathbf{D}_{ii} = \sum_j \mathbf{K}_{ij}$. Next, let $\mathbf{I}$ be an identity matrix and $\vec{1}$ be an N-dimensional all-ones vector. A centered similarity matrix is computed in the form

$$\mathbf{K}^{\mathrm{CENT}} = (\mathbf{I} - \frac{1}{N}\vec{1}\vec{1}^{\mathrm{T}})\mathbf{K}(\mathbf{I} - \frac{1}{N}\vec{1}\vec{1}^{\mathrm{T}}). \tag{5}$$

[4]When the algorithm (1) is used, $N = N_{\text{user}}$ and $Sim(u, v)$ in (2) or (3) gives the (u, v) component of $\mathbf{K}$.

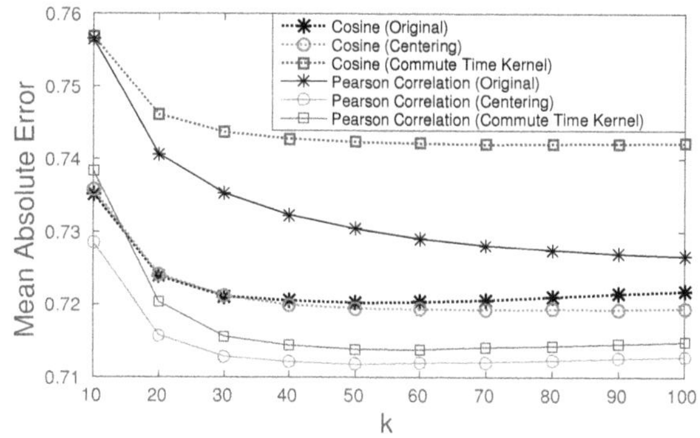

Figure 3: Prediction accuracy without attack using several similarity measures for different k.

4. EXPERIMENT

We used the MovieLens 1M dataset (`ml-1m`)[5] for evaluation. This dataset contains 1,000,209 ratings (i.e., integers from 1 to 5) from 6,040 users and 3,706 items, with every user rating at least 20 items. We examined the algorithm (1), which was combined with two similarity measures: cosine similarity (COS), and shrunken Pearson correlation (PEARSON).[6] The parameter β for PEARSON was set to $\beta = 100$, following [2]. To reduce hubness, we transformed the similarity matrix by converting it by (4) to obtain a commute time kernel (CT), or by (5) to center the similarity matrix (CENT). The main goal of this experiment is to compare the robustness of the system against attacks before and after the transformations.

4.1 Prediction Accuracy without Attack

Before investigating the robustness against attacks, we verified whether or not CENT and CT transformations affect the prediction accuracy when no attacks are present. To simulate a recommendation task, we divided 1,000,209 ratings in the dataset into 939,809 training data (observed ratings) and 60,400 test data (for prediction).[7] [8] We evaluated the prediction accuracy using *mean absolute error* (MAE), a common metric used for evaluating CF algorithms, calculated as $\mathrm{MAE} = 1/|T| \sum_{(u,i) \in T} |Pred(u, i) - R(u, i)|$, where T is the set of user-item pairs given as test data (here, $|T| = 60400$).

Figure 3 shows the MAE of the compared systems for various nearest neighbor parameter k. The figure indicates that CENT almost always decreases MAE (i.e., improves prediction accuracy), and CT also decreases MAE for PEARSON. For the evaluation of robustness below, we set $k = 50$, since these are the k values that achieved best MAE overall in the above experiment.

4.2 Robustness against Attack

[5]http://grouplens.org/datasets/movielens/

[6]We also tested unshrunken versions of Pearson correlation, but the results are not presented here because the prediction accuracy was inferior to that of the shrunken variants.

[7]We used the partition named `ra.train` and `ra.test` made from the whole dataset `ratings.dat` in `ml-1m.zip` by running a script `split_ratings.sh` distributed in `ml-10m.zip`.

[8]Test data is constructed by picking up 10 ratings randomly for each of 6040 users.

Table 1: Prediction shift caused by average attack and skewness of the N_k distribution ($k = 50$).

Similarity Measure	Transform	Skewness	PredShift
Cosine Similarity	(Original)	3.422	0.902
	CENT	1.629	0.319
	CT	1.526	0.205
Pearson Correlation	(Original)	6.389	1.542
	CENT	2.648	1.084
	CT	1.173	0.981

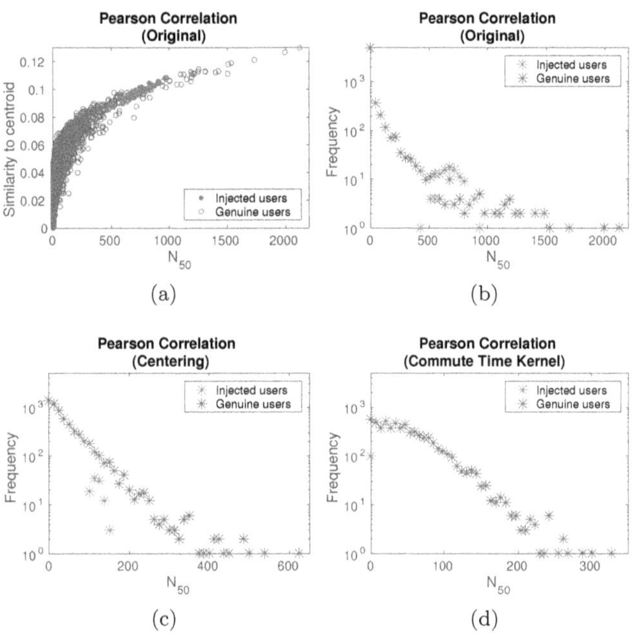

Figure 4: Behavior of injected users (red points).

We selected 21 movies as target items for average attack, such that the target movies are as close as possible to those presented in Lam et al. [3, Table 1, p. 397], a pioneer work of the average attack. For the setting of attack, we injected 100 fake users that were invented to introduce false ratings into systems. To raise the reputation of the target items, fake users assigned the highest rating (i.e., 5) to target items. For items other than target ones, fake users gave average ratings. That is, for each item, we generated a random number from Normal($\mu; \sigma$), where μ equals the average rating of genuine users who rated the item and $\sigma = 1.0$, and assigned the number after converting it to a nearest integer from 1 to 5. For evaluation, we used a metric called *prediction shift*, which measures the difference in the predicted rating before and after the attack. We calculated the prediction shift for each pair of genuine user and target item, except those belonging to the training data. We report the average over all target user-item pairs. Smaller the value of the shift, the better.

Table 1 shows the results of the prediction shift caused by the attack. The amount of prediction shift is reduced after the CENT or CT transformations are applied. This indicates that using the transformed similarity measures makes the recommendation system robust against the attack.

We now analyze why CENT and CT provided robustness against the attack, in terms of hubness. Figure 4(a) shows a scatter plot of users for PEARSON, where the horizontal axis is N_{50}, and the vertical axis represents similarity to the data centroid. The scatter plot indicates that a strong correlation was observed, and hence, hubness occurred. In addition, fake users injected by the average attack (displayed as red points) had a higher similarity to the centroid, because they were invented to imitate the average genuine user. Therefore, injected users became hubs that have large N_{50} values (*min* 465 and *max* 961) as compared to most genuine users, as seen from the N_{50} distribution in Figure 4(b). In contrast, hubness was reduced by CENT or CT transformations, resulting in a decrease in the N_{50} values of injected users between *min* 101 and *max* 156 using CENT, as shown in Figure 4(c), and a decrease between *min* 0 and *max* 4 using CT, as shown in Figure 4(d). It clearly shows that injected users appeared less frequently in k-NNs of other users by using CENT or CT than using original PEARSON. Thus, fake users became less influential in determining recommendations.

In total, applying transformations that reduce hubness, we can obtain the system with more robust against attacks as well as comparative or even better prediction accuracies than using the original similarity measures.

5. CONCLUSION

We have proposed a method for making memory-based CF robust against shilling attacks, by reducing the hubness that occurs in the user-response data. Our approach stands on the ground that hubness is one of the primary factors exploited by shilling attacks. We applied to the similarity matrix two transformations that are known to reduce hubness: centering and conversion to a commute-time kernel. Using the MovieLens dataset, we demonstrated that these transformations make the recommender system less susceptible to shilling attacks without degrading its recommendation accuracy.

6. REFERENCES

[1] R. Burke, B. Mobasher, R. Bhaumik, and C. Williams. Segment-based injection attacks against collaborative filtering recommender systems. In *ICDM '05*, pages 577–580, 2005.

[2] P. Knees, D. Schnitzer, and A. Flexer. Improving neighborhood-based collaborative filtering by reducing hubness. In *ICMR '14*, pages 161–168, 2014.

[3] S. K. Lam and J. Riedl. Shilling recommender systems for fun and profit. In *WWW '04*, pages 393–402, 2004.

[4] A. Nanopoulos, M. Radovanović, and M. Ivanović. How does high dimensionality affect collaborative filtering? In *RecSys '09*, pages 293–296, 2009.

[5] M. Radovanović, A. Nanopoulos, and M. Ivanović. On the existence of obstinate results in vector space models. In *SIGIR '10*, pages 186–193, 2010.

[6] B. Sarwar, G. Karypis, J. Konstan, and J. Riedl. Item-based collaborative filtering recommendation algorithms. In *WWW '01*, pages 285–295, 2001.

[7] I. Suzuki, K. Hara, M. Shimbo, Y. Matsumoto, and M. Saerens. Investigating the effectiveness of laplacian-based kernels in hub reduction. In *AAAI '12*, pages 1112–1118, 2012.

[8] I. Suzuki, K. Hara, M. Shimbo, M. Saerens, and K. Fukumizu. Centering similarity measures to reduce hubs. In *EMNLP '13*, pages 613–623, 2013.

Modularity-Based Query Clustering for Identifying Users Sharing a Common Condition

Maayan Harel
EE Department of Technion, Haifa, Israel
maayanga@tx.technion.ac.il

Elad Yom-Tov
Microsoft Research, Herzliya, Israel
eladyt@microsoft.com

ABSTRACT

We present an algorithm for identifying users who share a common condition from anonymized search engine logs. Input to the algorithm is a set of seed phrases that identify users with the condition of interest with high precision albeit at a very low recall. We expand the set of seed phrases by clustering queries according to the pages users clicked following these queries and the temporal ordering of queries within sessions, emphasizing the subgraph containing seed phrases. To this end, we extend modularity-based clustering such that it uses the information in the initial seed phrases as well as other queries of users in the population of interest. We evaluate the performance of the proposed method on two datasets, one of mood disorders and the other of anorexia, by classifying users according to the clusters in which they appeared and the phrases contained thereof, and show that the area under the receiver operating characteristic curve (AUC) obtained by these methods exceeds 0.87. These results demonstrate the value of our algorithm for both identifying users for future research and to gain better understanding of the language associated with the condition.

1. INTRODUCTION

A majority of internet users turn to the internet when they have a medical concern [7]. Data generated while people search for information on their medical concerns has been shown to be a fruitful source for insights on the health of large populations. The best known area where internet data was shown to provide medical insights is in influenza tracking [8, 10]. Other examples of such research include an examination of information needs of cancer patients [12], the links between media and the development of anorexia [15], and linking food-borne illnesses to specific restaurants [9].

One of the basic problems in conducting such research is identifying a relevant cohort for study, that is, given a medical condition, identify a group of (often anonymous) users who are likely to be suffering from this condition. A common method for identifying people suffering from a condition is thresholding the number of times a user asked about a specific medical topic [12]. Another approach is to find users who use a small set of highly indicative queries [15]. Both these methods provide a way to identify patients with a high precision, but at the cost of very low recall.

Here we propose a method for identifying users who likely share a medical condition. We begin with a small set of seed queries which are highly indicative of the population of interest. We apply graph-based clustering to the queries made by the target population, e.g., the population that makes use of the seed queries, giving a different weight (and thus emphasis) to the subgraph that includes the seed queries. Following query clustering, we use information on how users transition between clusters over time to find queries that are temporally close to the target queries. The list of extracted queries and clusters can be used as features for a classifier that identifies users that share the condition of interest.

The proposed method is not applicable solely to the medical domain. In online advertising, it is a common goal to find populations which may share a common interest, for example, motorcycles, so that ads for this interest can be shown to them. This is usually done implicitly though the users' demographics, queries, and site visits. However, click-through rates on ads are typically low, indicating that such fine-grained identification of interests is difficult to achieve. Wang et al. [13] have proposed related ideas for modeling users from search engine queries and clicked documents by development of a generative model.

Query clustering to identify topic queries has been a common topic for research, but is hampered by the fact that queries are usually very short. To overcome this limitation, several researchers have proposed to add the clicks on documents following the queries to the textual features (see, for example [3], [14] and [2]). Aiello et al. [1] added temporal and textual attributes to identify "missions", that is, activity fragments that express a coherent user intent, on the basis of their topical affinity. However, the goal of these algorithms is to identify related queries, not to identify a common trait of users issuing them.

2. METHODS

2.1 Clustering Algorithm

We begin by constructing a network of the users' queries. In this graph, nodes are queries and the edges are constructed according to the URLs clicked by users in response to the list of results presented by the search engine. Intuitively, if users click on the same URLs following two differ-

SIGIR'15, August 09 - 13, 2015, Santiago, Chile.

ISBN 978-1-4503-3621-5/15/08 ...$15.00.
DOI: http://dx.doi.org/10.1145/2766462.2767798.

ent queries, they are giving a strong indication that these two queries are similar. We construct a (sparse) representation of the number of times each URL is clicked in response to the query. The similarity between any two queries is computed as the cosine similarity between these representations.

To infer which of the queries form dense clusters in the graph we use the modularity index [11], a common quality index for a partition of a graph. Informally, for a given clustering of the graph, modularity quantifies the difference between the fraction of the edges in the clusters and the expected number of edges in the clusters if edges were randomly distributed. A clustering with high modularity indicates there are strong connections within the clusters – stronger than one would expect by mere randomness. Thus, a clustering of a graph can be found by maximizing the modularity on the graph.

In our query graph, only a few queries contain the original seed words. Therefore, their ability to induce clusters may be insufficient. That is, since the number of queries containing the seed words is minuscule compared to the total set of queries, we may only find clusters that reflect poorly the connections to the seed words and combine unrelated queries to them. The known resolution limit of the modularity index [6] also indicates that the modularity may fail to detect small clusters that reflect relations to the seed words.

To answer the need to focus on the subgraph with the seed queries without completely removing other queries, we extend the modularity maximization principle as follows. The graph is modified to have two edge types between the queries: *positive edges* and *negative edges*. We further denote a positive session as a session that contains a query with a seed word, and a negative session as one that does not contain such a query. Sessions comprise of all queries made by a user until a 30 minute or longer break. The weight of the positive (negative) edges is computed by the query-URL similarity of the queries in the positive (negative) sessions. Note that some queries appear in both positive and negative sessions. The resulting graph has the same query vertices as the original graph, but with different edge weights, where some pairs of query nodes have two types of edges.

We modify the modularity index such that it combines information on the two edge types by optimizing a convex combination of the modularity on the two edge sets. Finding the clustering with the maximal modularity is NP-hard [5], but there several ways to approximate it. Here we used the Louvain method [4], a greedy approach that evaluates the gain in moving vertices from one cluster to another, and iteratively builds new networks whose nodes are the clusters found by moving the vertices according to this measure.

We adapt the Louvain method to fit our implicit two graphs. Let $\Delta Q_P(i)$ and $\Delta Q_N(i)$ be the gain, computed on the set of positive and negative edges respectively, of moving node i to one of the clusters. Then, for a chosen rate $\alpha \in (0,1)$, we define the combined gain as

$$\Delta Q(i) = \alpha \Delta Q_P(i) + (1-\alpha)\Delta Q_N(i). \tag{1}$$

As in the Loavain method, the vertices are iteratively joined to clusters until there is no further gain in moving vertices. The only parameter in the extended method is the weight α; In Section 4 we explore the sensitivity of the algorithm to the choice of this parameter.

2.2 Transitions between Queries

Having obtained a clustering of the queries based on their proximity in clicked URLs, we apply a second phase of inference using the information in the proximity of queries in time. This phase is based on the notion that consecutive queries have a higher chance of being related to the same information need of a user.

Define a directed graph whose vertices, denoted by $\mathcal{V}$, are the clusters found by the modularity based optimization. A *transition* $T(C_A, C_B)$, from cluster $C_A \in \mathcal{V}$ to cluster $C_B \in \mathcal{V}$ is defined by the queries that constitute the clusters. Namely, a transition takes place whenever there is a crossing from query $q_{t_1} \in C_A$ to $q_{t_2} \in C_B$, for time stamps $t_1 < t_2$ that belong to the same session. Let $S = \{(C_A, C_B) : |T(C_A, C_B)| \geq 5, C_A, C_B \in \mathcal{V}\}$ define the set of all cluster pairs for which the number of transitions are at least 5.

The edge weights of the graph are a function of the transitions between the clusters, and are computed as follows: We define an *incoming query* to a cluster as the event of a transition that ends in a query that belongs to the cluster, and an *outgoing query* to a cluster as the event of a transition that begins in the cluster. For each pair $(C_A, C_B) \in S$ we compute the mutual information (MI) between the outgoing queries of cluster C_A and the incoming queries of cluster C_B. The MI encodes the association between the outgoing and incoming queries of the two clusters. Note that these are two discrete random variables, therefore, the observations of the data can be summarized in a contingency table, and the MI can be efficiently computed. To verify that a high MI is a result of a dependency in the right "direction", i.e. as a result of queries transitioning from cluster C_A to C_B, rather than transitioning from $\mathcal{V} \setminus C_A$ to C_B, we add a simple verification step. Namely, we check that the probability, $P(C_A \rightarrow C_B)$, of transitioning from cluster C_A to cluster C_B is grater than $P(C_i \in \mathcal{V} \setminus C_A \rightarrow C_B)$, the probability to transition to C_B from a cluster other than C_A. Finally, for all couples $(C_A, C_B) \in S$ for which the above condition holds, we add a final thresholding step to the MI value, and remove the edges whose weight is in the 5% quantile.

2.3 Extracted Query List (EQL)

The result of the above computation is a graph whose edges imply plausible crossings during a user's search from one cluster to another. We define the *zero-order* vertices on this graph as cluster vertices that contain queries with the seed terms, and *first-order* vertices as clusters that have incoming edges from first order clusters.

The queries that form all zero and first order clusters were taken as the Extracted Query List, denoted henceforce as EQL. This list will be used to identify users that share the condition of interest in Section 4. We note that we also looked at higher order connections and their propagation on the graph. However, we observed the existence of many transitions to unrelated popular queries (e.g. "Facebook"), and thus looking beyond first order clusters results in an overly noisy query list.

3. DATA SET DESCRIPTION

We analyzed two datasets which are comprised of browsing information of a major search engine[1].

[1]Name removed for anonymization.

Table 1: Example of words from the queries in the order-01 clusters with high positive weight in classification.

Dataset 1	skinny, weight, lose, diet, thin, fitspo, eating, nervosa, calorie, gap, bulimia, thigh, diet, bmi, fast, starve, tumblr.
Dataset 2	seroquel, zyprexa, effects, side, drugs, bipolar, icd, abilify, risperdal, anxiety, trazodone, lithium, disorder, seizures.

Dataset 1

Queries in this dataset were related to anorexia nervosa, an eating disorder. We extracted queries submitted to the search engine for a period of 6 months, beginning June 2013. We used the seed set of queries that included one of the following phrases: anorexia tips, how to anorexia, ana buddy, thinspo, and thinspiration. This list includes words that are likely to be used in anorexia related activity search. A total of 10,703 users and 5,566,611 queries were found in the period of the study. For each query of the selected users, we extracted the query text, time and date, a list of pages visited by the user as a result of the query (i.e. URLs clicked by the user), and an anonymized user identifier.

Dataset 2

Queries in Dataset 2 were related to mood disorders. The query data was comprised of 5 months of query data beginning March 2014. The list of terms used to select users that share this condition was comprised of drugs used to treat mood disorders, including: eskalith, lithobid, lithonate, lithotabs, valproic acid, divalproex, valproate, depakote, and depakene, as well as the term "mood stabilizing" (and its derivatives). We wanted to focus on users who are likely using mood stabilizing drugs, therefore we chose a threshold of 5 queries that contain one of the terms to identify users. A total of 3,101 users who made 1,009,642 queries were found in the data. The information extracted for each query was the same as in Dataset 1.

4. EVALUATION

Obtaining annotations of whether the users share the condition of interest without breaching privacy is difficult. This makes the validation of our algorithm challenging. In the following, we provide a validation that is based on the power of our extracted query list (EQL), that is, queries in zero and first order clusters, to predict whether a user is in the original condition group. That is, we check that the EQL can be useful for prediction of users for which we have high precision labeling (the seed phrases).

As an initial step for the quality assessment we extracted all the queries in a given month that have at least a 50% overlap of words with a query in the EQL. The data included all the searches in a three month period. Then, we selected users with at least 5 queries, and aggregated all the queries of each user. This process resulted in $\sim$20 million users for the anorexia condition and $\sim$ 10 million users for the mood disorder, for each month of the experiment. We conducted binary classification on intervals of one month, where in each month half the users were used for training and the other half for validation.

A positive label was given to users that have at least one query with a seed phrase, and a negative label to the rest of the users. Note that there are unavoidable false negatives in this list, as there are users that did not use a seed phrase but belong to the interest group. We also expect to have some false positives, namely, users that queried for a seed phrase, but whose remaining queries are unrelated to the interest group. Nonetheless, even with this noisy labeling, we expect a good predictive ability if the EQL reflects the interest group. Also note that the binary classification task is highly imbalanced: roughly 0.01% of the users of dataset 1 and 0.1% of users in dataset 2 were labeled as positive.

The aggregated queries of each user, *after excluding the ones with the seed phrases*, were used to construct features for classification. In our first experiment, we tested three types of features: (1) counts in zero-order clusters (order-0), (2) counts in zero- and first-order clusters (order-01), and (3) order-01 term counts (see Section 2.3 for definitions of zero and first order clusters). The cluster-based features are counts of how many queries of each user appeared in each cluster, to which we add five more features: the number of queries in the order-0 and order-1 clusters, and the number of unique order-0, order-1 and order-01 clusters visited. The word counts, in (3), are the number of times a user made use of a given word in their queries, where, by the manner the data was extracted, were only queries within order-0 and order-1 clusters. For each feature set we trained a linear classifier with Stochastic Gradient Decent with l_2 regularization. The regularization parameter was chosen as the default parameter[2]. Classifier performance was measured by the AUC.

The receiver operating characteristic curve (ROC) and AUC value for each of the feature types of dataset 1 is shown in Figure 1. The curves are averaged over the three months of the experiment. It is observed that there is a substantial gain in the quality of the classifier when using the information in the first order clusters in addition to the zero order clusters. The performance of the order-01 cluster-based features is similar to the performance of the features based on the terms in the queries in the order-01 clusters, with the cluster based features obtaining a better true positive rates at low false positive rates. This result validates that the clustering partition is highly representative of the condition, as it performed as well as the term features but with a reduced dimensionality (to less than 150 features). We also observed that the feature with the highest weight, when using our cluster based features, was the number of unique order-01 clusters visited by the user.

Our second experiment was done with the term counts features, namely, the counts of words within the queries that are in the order-01 clusters. The AUC values for the two datasets are shown in Table 2. A number of example words with high positive weight values are presented in Table 1. The main parameter of our proposed method is α in Equation (1), the weight given to the modularity of the graph with the positive edges. We tested three configurations of this parameter[3]. The AUC values for all the parameter values tested are high. While in some cases a specific choice of this selection gives superior performance, this choice is not

[2]Initially, we applied a grid search with cross validation, but the effect of the choice of the model parameter was found negligible on the large datasets.

[3]Note that setting $\alpha = 0.5$ is not equivalent to regular modularity maximization.

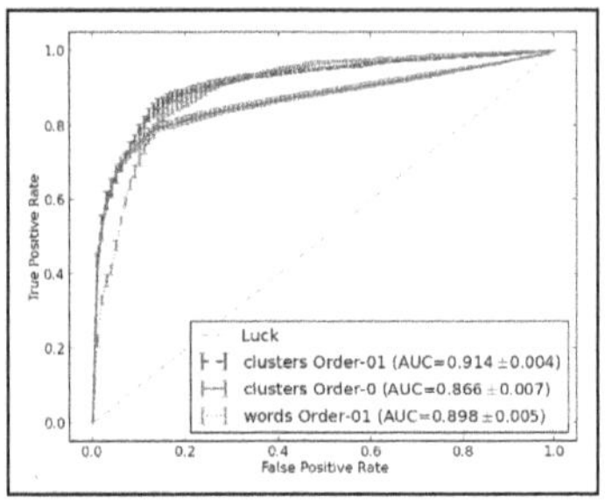

Figure 1: ROC curve - different features sets ($\alpha = 0.1$). See text for descreption of the three feature types.

Table 2: Prediction quality (AUC) of the extracted query list (EQL) with different convex weighting selection.

α	Anorexia	Mood disorder
0.1	0.876 (± .004)	0.877 (± .007)
0.5	0.817 (± .013)	0.874 (± .005)
0.9	0.813 (± .008)	0.879 (± .007)

consistent. Importantly, we observe that the algorithm is not highly sensitive to this choice.

For our third experiment we extracted *all* the queries of the users that were found by the EQL in dataset 1. We compared our ability to identify the positive users, using either the terms counts in the queries of the order-01 clusters, or the terms in all the queries (without the use of the clustering algorithm). We also applied two types of feature selection methods on the term count features of all the queries: recursive feature elimination (RFE), which recursively considers a smaller set of features by pruning the features with the lowest absolute weights of the trained classifier, and selection of the best features according to the chi-square statistic for each class-feature. Dimensionality was reduced to match the dimensionality of the term counts in queries of the order-01 clusters. These standard feature selection methods, as well as the prediction using the full term dictionary of the user queries broke down completly with a mean AUC value of 0.526 ± 0.003. The performance of the terms count of words in queries that belong to the order-01 clusters (on the same set of users) was 0.898 ± 0.005.

5. DISCUSSION

We presented an algorithm that uses a small set of seed terms for identifying users who share a common condition. While constructing a small set of terms that is highly associated with the interest group is a fairly simple task, performed, for example by extracting keywords from websites used by such groups or through consultations with a specialist, achieving higher recall is more difficult. We propose to infer a larger set of queries using the browsing information of users who use the seed terms in their queries. The difficulty of this task is to expand non trivially the seed terms, without adding too many irrelevant queries and reducing precision.

Our clustering algorithm is comprised of two phases, which utilize the two dimensions of the browsing information: the visited pages after a query, and the temporal ordering of queries made within a session. We evaluated the algorithm by testing the ability of the expanded query list to predict whether a user is in the interest group. The results show that the predictive power of both the extracted clusters and queries is high. This is in contrast with the use of the set of queries made by the users, even when coupled with feature selection, which achieves very poor performance. We suspect that the reason for this failure is the highly imbalanced nature of the data, which means that even though the training set is large, it includes a very small set of positive users and a very high initial dimensionality.

Our algorithm does not use any textual information. We assume that an additional phase of processing which will use the textual similarities, either to the initial queries or the final extended list, can further boost the performance. This is left for future research.

6. REFERENCES

[1] L. M. Aiello, D. Donato, U. Ozertem, and F. Menczer. Behavior-driven clustering of queries into topics. In *20th ACM international conference on Information and knowledge management*, pages 1373–1382, 2011.

[2] R. Baeza-Yates, C. Hurtado, and M. Mendoza. Query clustering for boosting web page ranking. In *Advances in Web Intelligence*, pages 164–175. Springer, 2004.

[3] D. Beeferman and A. Berger. Agglomerative clustering of a search engine query log. In *Proceedings of the sixth ACM SIGKDD international conference on Knowledge discovery and data mining*, pages 407–416. ACM, 2000.

[4] V. D. Blondel, J.-L. Guillaume, R. Lambiotte, and E. Lefebvre. Fast unfolding of communities in large networks. *Journal of Statistical Mechanics: Theory and Experiment*, 2008(10):P10008, 2008.

[5] U. Brandes, D. Delling, M. Gaertler, R. Gorke, M. Hoefer, Z. Nikoloski, and D. Wagner. On modularity clustering. *Knowledge and Data Engineering, IEEE Transactions on*, 20(2):172–188, 2008.

[6] S. Fortunato and M. Barthélemy. Resolution limit in community detection. *Proceedings of the National Academy of Sciences*, 104(1):36–41, 2007.

[7] S. Fox and M. Duggan. Health online 2013. *Health*, 2013.

[8] J. Ginsberg, M. Mohebbi, R. Patel, L. Brammer, M. Smolinski, and L. Brilliant. Detecting influenza epidemics using search engine query data. *Nature*, 457(7232):1012–1014, 2009.

[9] C. Harrison, M. Jorder, H. Stern, F. Stavinsky, V. Reddy, H. Hanson, H. Waechter, L. Lowe, L. Gravano, S. Balter, et al. Using online reviews by restaurant patrons to identify unreported cases of foodborne illness. *MMWR*, 63(20):441–445, 2014.

[10] V. Lampos and N. Cristianini. Tracking the flu pandemic by monitoring the social web. In *2nd International Workshop on Cognitive Information Processing*, pages 411–416. IEEE, 2010.

[11] M. E. Newman and M. Girvan. Finding and evaluating community structure in networks. *Physical review E*, 69(2):026113, 2004.

[12] Y. Ofran, O. Paltiel, D. Pelleg, J. M. Rowe, and E. Yom-Tov. Patterns of information-seeking for cancer on the internet: an analysis of real world data. *PloS one*, 7(9):e45921, 2012.

[13] H. Wang, C. Zhai, F. Liang, A. Dong, and Y. Chang. User modeling in search logs via a nonparametric bayesian approach. In *7th ACM international conference on Web search and data mining*, pages 203–212, 2014.

[14] J.-R. Wen, J.-Y. Nie, and H.-J. Zhang. Query clustering using user logs. *ACM Transactions on Information Systems*, 20(1):59–81, 2002.

[15] E. Yom-Tov and D. M. Boyd. On the link between media coverage of anorexia and pro-anorexic practices on the web. *International Journal of Eating Disorders*, 47:196–202, 2014.

Understanding Temporal Query Intent

Mohammed Hasanuzzaman
Normandie University
UNICAEN, GREYC CNRS, France
mohammed.hasanuzzaman@unicaen.fr

Sriparna Saha
IIT-Patna
Kurji, Patna, India
sriparna@iitp.ac.in

Gaël Dias
Normandie University
UNICAEN, GREYC CNRS, France
gael.dias@unicaen.fr

Stéphane Ferrari
Normandie University
UNICAEN, GREYC CNRS, France
stephane.ferrari@unicaen.fr

ABSTRACT

Understanding the temporal orientation of web search queries is an important issue for the success of information access systems. In this paper, we propose a multi-objective ensemble learning solution that (1) allows to accurately classify queries along their temporal intent and (2) identifies a set of performing solutions thus offering a wide range of possible applications. Experiments show that correct representation of the problem can lead to great classification improvements when compared to recent state-of-the-art solutions and baseline ensemble techniques.

Categories and Subject Descriptors

H.3.3 [**Information Storage and Retrieval**]: Information Search and Retrieval - Query Formulation

General Terms

Temporal IR, Ensemble learning, Multi-objective optimization

1. INTRODUCTION

As evidenced in [11], 1.5% of web search queries have explicit temporal intents (e.g. *fifa world cup 2014*) while the rate of implicit temporal queries (e.g. *history of coca-cola*) is more than 7%. Considering the large amount of queries issued everyday, recognizing the underlying temporal intent of a query is a crucial step towards improving the performance of search engines. For instance, this can be useful to select specific temporal retrieval models [10], temporally re-rank web results [9] or assess credible information [14].
Temporal query intent classification (TQIC), as first proposed in [8], seeks to determine whether users' information needs have a temporal dimension. This idea is pushed further in [6] and aims to determine whether the user is interested in information about the past, present or future when issuing a query or instead his information need has no temporal dimension.
Most recent works on TQIC have proposed supervised learning techniques based on the data set provided in NTCIR Temporalia [7]. Due to the small size of training data, best performing strategies have followed either the semi-supervised [16] or the ensemble learning paradigms [15, 5].
In this paper, we present an ensemble learning framework defined as a multi-objective optimization problem so to (1) obtain accurate classification results even when training evidences are limited and (2) identify different performing solutions thus offering a wide range of possible information access scenarios. Indeed, depending on the handled task, precise classification may be required (e.g. credible information assessment) or high recall may be preferred (e.g. temporal re-ranking).
Experiments over standard NTCIR data set show that great classification improvements (up to 16% accuracy) can be achieved compared to recent state-of-the-art solutions and baseline ensemble techniques, when a correct representation of the problem is proposed.

SIGIR'15 August 09 - 13, 2015, Santiago, Chile

DOI: http://dx.doi.org/10.1145/2766462.2767792.

2. RELATED WORK

The most influential attempt at temporal classification of queries comes from [8] who classify queries into three distinct classes: *atemporal*, *temporally unambiguous* and *temporally ambiguous*. In particular, they consider the distribution of retrieved documents over time and create meaningful features based on this distribution. Other ideas for implicit temporal queries have been developed by [11]. By analyzing query logs, they investigate the automatic detection of implicitly year qualified queries, i.e. queries that refer to an event in a specific year without containing the year in the query string. Following the same motivation, [1] proposed a solution based on content temporal analysis. In particular, they identify top relevant dates in web snippets with respect to a given implicit temporal query and temporal disambiguation is performed through a distributional metric called GTE.
Recently, the NTCIR Temporalia task [7] pushed further this idea and propose to distinguish whether a given query is related to *past*, *recency*, *future* or *atemporal*. Within this context, the most performing system is based on a SVM semi-supervised learning algorithm [16] and uses the AOL 500K User Session Collection [12] as unlabeled data. Two other competitive systems [15, 5] rely on ensemble learning (especially majority voting). Indeed, due to the small size of training data (only 100 queries distributed equally by class), classification results are weak if a single classifier is used in a traditional supervised way. To overcome this situation, we follow the ensemble learning paradigm defined as a multi-objective optimization problem in a similar way as [13].

3. LEARNING INSTANCES FOR TQIC

TQIC can be defined as follows. Given a web search query q and its issuing date d, predict its temporal class $c \in$ {*past*, *recency*, *future*, *atemporal*}. Based on this definition, [7] released a set of 100 training queries (25 queries for each class) and 300 testing queries (75 queries for each class). We will call this data set NTCIR-TQIC. Examples of the form $< q, d, c >$ are given as follows.

q	d	c
who was martin luther	Jan 1, 2013 GMT+0	*past*
amazon deal of the day	Feb 28, 2013 GMT+0	*recency*
release date for ios7	Jan 1, 2013 GMT+0	*future*
number of neck muscles	Feb 28, 2013 GMT+0	*atemporal*

3.1 External Resources

The NTCIR-TQIC data set evidences two crucial limitations. First, the training set is small. Second, the amount of literal features is limited as queries are short (between 3 and 4 words). The first case is a classical learning problem and it is discussed in section 4. As for the second case, external resources were used to expand the amount of query information [1].

So, for each query, we first collected the top K web snippets[1] returned by the Bing search API[2]. The underlying idea is that web snippets are likely to evidence temporal information if the query has a temporal dimension.

Then, for each query, we collected its most relevant year date along with its confidence value from the freely available web service GTE[3] proposed in [1]. In particular, given a temporally implicit query, GTE extracts from web snippets query-relevant year dates based on distributional similarity. Some examples of extracted year dates and confidence values are given as follows[4].

q	Most confident Year	Confidence value
who was martin luther	1929	0.944
amazon deal of the day	2015	0.760
release date for ios7	2013	0.893
number of neck muscles	2014	0.708

3.2 Features Definition

Most related works have proposed similar sets of features [7]. The most common are time gap, verb tense, named entities, lemmas and specific temporal words. Here, we identified 11 independent features from the query string, its issuing date and the extra data collected. In particular, we relied on previous studies and available tools and resources developed in our laboratory [1, 3]. Details of the different features are given as follows.

D_b_Dates: This feature aims to evaluate the time gap between the query and its issuing date. It is calculated as the difference between the year date explicitly mentioned in the query string q and the issue year date d_{year}. If there is no mention of a date inside q (timely implicit query), we consider the most confident year date obtained from GTE [1]. If no date is returned by GTE, this feature is given a null value.

C_o_Date: This feature aims to evidence the confidence value over the time gap definition. It is set to 1 when there is explicit mention of a year date inside q string (maximum confidence). Otherwise, it is set to the returned confidence value of GTE [1]. A 0 value is given if no date is returned by GTE.

[1]For computational reasons, we set $K = 10$.

[2]`https://datamarket.azure.com/dataset/bing/search`

[3]`http://wia.info.unicaen.fr/GTEAspNetFlatTempCluster_Server/`

[4]Extraction was processed April, 16th 2015 for illustration.

N_o_PW, N_o_RW and **N_o_FW:** These features aim to capture the query timeliness based on its temporal content words. They respectively represent the number of words in q belonging to past, present and future categories in TempoWordNet[5] [3].

N_o_PS, N_o_RS, N_o_FS and **N_o_AS:** This set of features aims to interpret the timeliness of the query q based on the temporality of its returned web snippets. The rationale is that if a query has a temporal dimension, web search results should evidence the same intent. So, for any q, these features are respectively the number of returned web snippets classified as past, recency, future and atemporal by the sentence temporal classifier (STC) defined in [3].

C_o_Q: The aim of this feature is to define the intrinsic temporality of a query (as if it was a sentence). So, this feature takes the value returned by STC [3] (i.e. past, recency, future or atemporal) when taking the query string q as input.

Q_S: The rationale of this feature is that specific (non-temporal) words may play an important role in temporal classification. As a consequence, each query string q is represented as its bag of unigrams where the presence of a word is associated to the value 1 and 0 when it is not present.

In order to better assess the importance of each individual feature, we present the top 5 features in terms of Information Gain (IG) in the following Table.

Feature	IG	Main resource/tool
D_b_Dates	0.245	GTE [1]
N_o_FW	0.219	TempoWordNet [3]
N_o_FS	0.135	STC [3]
C_o_Q	0.130	STC [3]
C_o_Date	0.114	GTE [1]

Results show that both the extra collected data (i.e. Bing web snippets and GTE year dates) and the different used resources and tools (i.e. TempoWordNet and STC) play an important role for the temporal query intent classification task.

4. LEARNING FRAMEWORK

An ensemble of classifiers is a set of classifiers whose individual decisions are combined in some way (typically by weighted or binary voting) to classify new examples [4]. In particular, ensemble learning is known to obtain highly accurate classifiers by combining less accurate ones thus allowing to overcome the training data size problem. Many methods for constructing ensembles have been developed in the literature [4]. In this paper, we propose to define ensemble learning as a multi-objective optimization (MOO) problem. Our motivations are two-fold. First, [13] showed that MOO strategies evidence improved results when compared to single objective solutions and state-of-the-art baselines. Second, MOO techniques propose a set of performing solutions rather than a single one. As TQIC can be thought as an intermediate module in some larger application (e.g. retrieval, ranking or visualization), offering different performing solutions can be a great asset to adapt to any kind of information access situation without loss of reliability.

4.1 MOO Problem Defintion

A definition of multi-objective optimization can be stated as follows: find the vector $\overline{x} = [x_1, x_2, \ldots, x_n]^T$ of decision variables that optimize O objective functions $\{O_1(\overline{x}), O_2(\overline{x}), \ldots, O_O(\overline{x})\}$ simultaneously which also satisfy user-defined constraints, if any. The concept of domination is also an important aspect of MOO. In case of maximization, a solution $\overline{x_i}$ is said to dominate $\overline{x_j}$ if both conditions (1) and (2) are satisfied.

[5]In particular, we used TWnL available at `https://tempowordnet.greyc.fr/`.

$$\forall k \in 1,2,\ldots,O, \quad O_k(\overline{x_i}) \geq O_k(\overline{x_j}) \quad (1)$$
$$\exists k \in 1,2,\ldots,O, \quad O_k(\overline{x_i}) > O_k(\overline{x_j}) \quad (2)$$

Finally, the set of non-dominated solutions of the whole search space S is called the Pareto optimal front, from which a single solution may be selected based on any suitable criterion.
Ensemble learning can be seen as a vote based problem. Suppose that one has a total number of N classifiers $\{C_1, C_2, ..., C_N\}$ trained for a M class problem. Then, the vote based classifier ensemble problem can be defined as finding the combination of votes V per classifier C_i, which will optimize a quality function $F(V)$. V can either represent a binary matrix (binary vote based ensemble) or a matrix containing real values (real/weighted vote based ensemble) of size $N \times M$. In case of binary voting, $V(i,j)$ represents whether C_i is permitted to vote for class M_j. $V(i,j) = 1$ is interpreted as the ith classifier is permitted to vote for the jth class else $V(i,j) = 0$ is interpreted as the ith classifier is not permitted to vote for the jth class. In case of real voting, $V(i,j) \in [0,1]$ quantifies the weight of vote of C_i for the class M_j. If a particular classifier is confident in determining a particular class, then more weight should be assigned for that particular pair, otherwise less weight should be attributed.
In terms of MOO formulation, the classifier ensemble problem at hand is defined as determining the appropriate combination of votes V per classifier such that objectives $O_1(V)$ and $O_2(V)$ are simultaneously optimized and O_1 = recall and O_2 = precision.

4.2 Evolutionary Procedure

The multi-objective methods used here are based on the search capabilities of the non-dominated sorting genetic algorithm [2].

String Representation: In order to encode the classifier ensemble selection problem in terms of genetic algorithms, we propose to study three different representations.
(1) Simple Classifier Ensemble (SCE): each individual classifier is allowed to vote or not. The chromosome is of length N and each position takes either 1 or 0 as value,
(2) Binary Vote based Classifier Ensemble (BVCE): each individual classifier is allowed to vote or not for a specific class M_j. The chromosome is of length $N \times M$ and each position takes either 1 or 0 as value,
(3) Real/weighted Vote based Classifier Ensemble (RVCE): all classifiers are allowed to vote for a specific class M_j with a different weight for each class. The chromosome is of length $N \times M$ and each position takes a real value.

Fitness: Each individual chromosome corresponds to a possible ensemble solution V, which must be evaluated in terms of fitness. Let the number of available classifiers be N and their respective individual F-measure values by class F_{ij}, $i = 1 \ldots N, j = 1 \ldots M$ (i.e. F_{ij} is the F-measure of C_i for class M_j). For a given query q, receiving class M_j is weighted as in Equation 3 where the output class assigned by C_i to q is given by $op(q, C_i)$. Note that in the case of SCE, $V(i,j)$ is redefined as $V(i,.)$ and F_{ij} as $F_{i.}$.

$$f(q, M_j) = \sum_{i=1:N \& op(q,C_i)=M_j} V(i,j) \times F_{ij}. \quad (3)$$

Finally, the class of the query q is given by $argmax_{M_j} f(q, M_j)$. As such, classifying all queries from a development set gives rise to two fitness (or objective) values, which are respectively recall (O_1) and precision (O_2) and must be optimized simultaneously.

Optimization and Selection: The multi-objective optimization problem is solved by using the Non-dominated Sorting Genetic Algorithm (NSGA-II) [2]. The most important component of NSGA-II is its elitism operation, where the non-dominated solutions present in the parent and child populations are moved to the next generation. The chromosomes present in the final population provide the set of different solutions to the ensemble problem and represent the Pareto optimal front.
It is important to note that all the solutions are important, representing a different way of ensembling the set of classifiers. But for the purpose of comparison with other methods, a single solution is required to be selected. For that purpose, we choose the solution that maximizes the F-measure based on its optimized sub-parts recall and precision as shown in equation 4.

$$F\text{-measure} = \frac{2 \times recall \times precision}{recall + precision}. \quad (4)$$

5. EXPERIMENTS

Experiments are run over a two-steps process. First, $N = 28$ individual classifiers are learned using 10-fold cross validation[6] over a subset of 80 training instances (20 examples for each of the $M = 4$ classes) randomly selected from the initial training set of NTCIR-TQIC containing 100 queries. For each classifier C_i, $F_{i.}$ (global F-measure) and F_{ij} (F-measure for class M_j) values are stored. All experiments were run over the Weka platform[7] with default parameters. Following Weka's denomination, the list of the 28 classifiers is as follows: NaiveBayes, NBTree, NNge, AdaBoostM1, Bagging, BayesNet, BFTree, ClassificationViaRegression, DecisionTable, FT, J48, JRip, IB1, IBk, Kstar, LWL, LMT, Logistic, LogitBoost, MultiBoostAB, MultilayerPerceptron, RandomCommittee, RandomForest, RBFNetwork, REPTree, RotationForest, SimpleLogistics and SMO. In order to assess the quality of each individual classifier, each one was tested on the NTCIR-TQIC test data set containing 300 unseen queries (75 for each class). Results of the top 5 classifiers are given in Table 1.

Classifiers	Precision	Recall	F-measure
Logistic	**82.9**	**75.0**	**78.8**
RandomForest	82.6	70.0	75.8
RotationForest	77.5	70.0	73.6
LMT	69.2	65.0	67.0
SimpleLogistics	69.2	65.0	67.0

Table 1: Results of single learning strategies.

The second step of the experiment is the optimization procedure. For that purpose, the remaining 20 query examples (5 for each class) from the NTCIR-TQIC training data set are used. We call it the development set. Based on the development set, the evolutionary optimization using NGSA-II is run for three representations (SCE, BVCE, RVCE) and the best solution is selected based on maximum F-measure as defined in equation 4. Performance results are presented in Table 2 and compared to two baselines ensemble techniques (BSL1, BSL2). BSL1 corresponds to Boosting with the single Logistic classifier and BSL2 is a SVM solution with 28 features each one corresponding to the output class (i.e. past, recency, future, atemporal) of each of the 28 classifiers.

As expected, our methodology outperforms BSL1 by 12.4% and BSL2 by 14.9% in terms of F-measure for the RVCE representation. In particular, BSL1 suffers from the use of a single classifier family while BSL2 can not generalize over the small amount of training data (only 20 examples). Moreover, the most fine tuned strategy in terms of ensemble learning evidences improved results

[6]Note that cross-validation is already an ensemble technique.
[7]http://www.cs.waikato.ac.nz/ml/weka/

Measures	RVCE	BVCE	SCE	BSL1	BSL2
Precision	**92.2**	85.1	86.0	82.9	77.5
Recall	**90.0**	85.0	83.7	75.0	75.0
F-measure	**91.1**	85.0	84.8	78.7	76.2

Table 2: Results of ensemble learning strategies.

when compared to coarse-grain solutions. Improvements of 6.1% and 6.3% are respectively shown against BVCE and SCE.

In order to understand the spectrum of the different solutions on the Pareto front, we present in Table 3 three different situations: the solution that maximizes precision (line 1), the solution that maximizes recall (line 2) and the solution that maximizes F-measure (line 3). Results show that high overall performances are provided by every solution. But, depending on the application at hand, one may expect to find a better tuned configuration.

Measures	Recall	Precision	F-measure
Max precision	88.7	**93.1**	90.9
Max recall	**90.8**	90.8	90.8
Max F-measure	90.0	92.2	**91.1**

Table 3: Precision and recall spectrum.

Finally, comparative accuracy results are given against state-of-the-art solutions from NTCIR-11 Temporalia TQIC in Table 4[8]. Our solution evidences highly improved results overall as well as for each individual class. In particular, accuracy improvements of 10% for past, 19% for recency, 9% for future, 10% for atemporal and 16% overall are achieved against best existing studies.

Classes	RVCE	#1 [16]	#2 [15]	#3 [5]
Past	**0.95**	0.85	0.75	0.79
Recency	**0.82**	0.48	0.56	0.63
Future	**0.94**	0.85	0.81	0.64
Atemporal	**0.89**	0.77	0.79	0.71
All	**0.90**	0.74	0.73	0.69

Table 4: Comparative accuracy results to state-of-the-art techniques presented in NTCIR-11 Temporalia task.

Note that all experimental results and data sets[9] of this paper are freely available at the following url `https://tempowordnet.greyc.fr` for reproducibility.

6. CONCLUSIONS AND FUTURE WORK

In this paper, we tackled the problem of identifying temporal intent of queries from a machine learning point of view. Due to the small amount of gold training data, we proposed an ensemble learning solution, whose underlying idea is to reduce bias by combining multiple classifiers instead of relying on a single one. In particular, recently developed multi-objective based ensemble techniques have been applied to improve overall accuracy. For our purpose, we made use of a set of features which can easily be extracted from different freely available resources to allow reproducibility.

Initial results are interesting to us and open new avenues for future research such as to bring on the intent of temporal query into the cluster of semantically related web search results for better user satisfaction. We are also investigating how to assign multiple temporal classes to web search queries especially for the implicit ones, in the line of the next NTCIR-12 Temporalia task.

[8]Results are taken from [7].

[9]Where copyright issues do not apply.

7. REFERENCES

[1] R. Campos, G. Dias, A. Jorge, and C. Nunes. Gte: A distributional second-order co-occurrence approach to improve the identification of top relevant dates in web snippets. In *Proceedings of the 21st ACM International Conference on Information and Knowledge Management (CIKM)*, pages 2035–2039, 2012.

[2] K. Deb, A. Pratap, S. Agarwal, and T. Meyarivan. A fast and elitist multiobjective genetic algorithm: NSGA-II. *IEEE Transactions on Evolutionary Computation*, 6(2):181–197, 2002.

[3] G. H. Dias, M. Hasanuzzaman, S. Ferrari, and Y. Mathet. Tempowordnet for sentence time tagging. In *Proceedings of the Companion Publication of the 23rd International Conference on World Wide Web Companion (WWW)*, pages 833–838, 2014.

[4] T. G. Dietterich. Ensemble methods in machine learning. In *Multiple classifier systems*, pages 1–15. Springer, 2000.

[5] Y. Hou, Q. Chen, J. Xu, Y. Pan, Q. Chen, and X. Wang. Hitsz-icrc at the ntcir-11 temporalia task. In *Proceedings of the NTCIR-11 Conference*, 2014.

[6] H. Joho, A. Jatowt, and R. Blanco. Ntcir temporalia: a test collection for temporal information access research. In *Proceedings of the Companion Publication of the 23rd International Conference on World Wide Web Companion (WWW)*, pages 845–850, 2014.

[7] H. Joho, A. Jatowt, R. Blanco, H. Naka, and S. Yamamoto. Overview of ntcir-11 temporal information access (temporalia) task. In *Proceedings of the NTCIR-11 Conference*, 2014.

[8] R. Jones and F. Diaz. Temporal profiles of queries. *ACM Transactions on Information Systems*, 25(3), 2007.

[9] N. Kanhabua and K. Nørvåg. Learning to rank search results for time-sensitive queries. In *Proceedings of the 21st ACM international conference on Information and knowledge management (CIKM)*, pages 2463–2466, 2012.

[10] X. Li and W. B. Croft. Time-based language models. In *Proceedings of the 12th International Conference on Information and Knowledge Management (CIKM)*, pages 469–475, 2003.

[11] D. Metzler, R. Jones, F. Peng, and R. Zhang. Improving search relevance for implicitly temporal queries. In *Proceedings of the 32nd international ACM SIGIR conference on Research and development in information retrieval*, pages 700–701. ACM, 2009.

[12] G. Pass, A. Chowdhury, and C. Torgeson. A picture of search. In *Proceedings of the 1st International Conference on Scalable Information Systems (InfoScale)*, 2006.

[13] S. Saha and A. Ekbal. Combining multiple classifiers using vote based classifier ensemble technique for named entity recognition. *Data Knowledge Engineering*, 85:15–39, 2013.

[14] J. Schwarz and M. Morris. Augmenting web pages and search results to support credibility assessment. In *Proceedings of the SIGCHI Conference on Human Factors in Computing Systems (CHI)*, pages 1245–1254, 2011.

[15] A. Shah, D. Shah, and P. Majumber. Andd7 @ ntcir-11 temporal information access task. In *Proceedings of the NTCIR-11 Conference*, 2014.

[16] H.-T. Yu, X. Kang, and F. Ren. Tuta1 at the ntcir-11 temporalia task. In *Proceedings of the NTCIR-11 Conference*, 2014.

On the Reusability of Open Test Collections

Seyyed Hadi Hashemi[1] Charles L.A. Clarke[2] Adriel Dean-Hall[2] Jaap Kamps[1] Julia Kiseleva[3]

[1]University of Amsterdam, Amsterdam, The Netherlands
[2]University of Waterloo, Waterloo, Canada
[3]Eindhoven University of Technology, Eindhoven, The Netherlands

ABSTRACT

Creating test collections for modern search tasks is increasingly more challenging due to the growing scale and dynamic nature of content, and need for richer contextualization of the statements of request. To address these issues, the TREC Contextual Suggestion Track explored an open test collection, where participants were allowed to submit any web page as a result for a personalized venue recommendation task. This prompts the question on the reusability of the resulting test collection: How does the open nature affect the pooling process? Can participants reliably evaluate variant runs with the resulting qrels? Can other teams evaluate new runs reliably? In short, does the set of pooled and judged documents effectively produce a post hoc test collection? Our main findings are the following: First, while there is a strongly significant rank correlation, the effect of pooling is notable and results in underestimation of performance, implying the evaluation of non-pooled systems should be done with great care. Second, we extensively analyze impacts of open corpus on the fraction of judged documents, explaining how low recall affects the reusability, and how the personalization and low pooling depth aggravate that problem. Third, we outline a potential solution by deriving a fixed corpus from open web submissions.

Categories and Subject Descriptors: H.3.3 [**Information Storage and Retrieval**]: Information Search and Retrieval—*Query formulation, Search process, Selection process*

General Terms: Algorithms, Measurement, Experimentation

1. INTRODUCTION

Controlled test collections remain crucial for evaluation and tuning of retrieval systems, both for offline testing in industry and for public benchmarks in academia. The TREC Contextual Suggestion Track experimented with an open test collection, where participants were allowed to submit any web page result for a personalized venue recommendation task. This option proved exceedingly popular amongst participants of the track, e.g., in 2014 the track received 25 open web submissions against 6 runs based on ClueWeb12. We focus here exclusively on the open web submissions, and investigate the reusability of the resulting open web test collection. There are at least three factors that may impede the reusability of the resulting test collection. First, the open nature may result in little to no overlap between the submissions, frustrating the pooling effect and limiting its evaluation power. Second, the track includes personalization of results to a specific user profile, hence a "topic" consists of the main statement of request (in this case a North American city) and a profile of the requester. Third, the resulting pooling depth over submissions per topic (i.e., a unique context and profile pair) are limited to rank 5. It is well known that low pool depth affects reusability [7]. The key factor in case of sparse judgments is the presence or absence of pooling bias [1].

SIGIR'15, August 09 - 13, 2015, Santiago, Chile.

ACM 978-1-4503-3621-5/15/08 ...$15.00.
DOI: http://dx.doi.org/10.1145/2766462.2767788.

In this paper, our main aim is to study the question: *How reusable are open test collections?* Specifically, we answer the following research questions:

1. *How does the open nature affect the evaluation of non-pooled systems?*
   (a) *What is the effect of leave out uniques on the score and ranking over all systems?*
   (b) *What is the effect of leave out uniques on the score and ranking over top ranked systems?*
2. *How does the open nature affect the fraction of judged documents?*
   (a) *What is the fraction of judged documents over ranks?*
   (b) *What is the effect of personalization on the fraction of judged documents?*

2. EXPERIMENTAL DATA

The TREC Contextual Suggestion Track asks participants to submit venue recommendations (in the form of a valid URL). We give some statistics of the open web submissions in 2014. There were a total of 25 submissions by 14 teams (with 11 teams submitting 2 runs). A topic consists of a pair of both a context (a North American city) and a profile of the requester (consisting of likes and dislikes of venues in another city). For example, to recommend venues to visit in the unknown city of Buffalo, NY, based on a profile with ratings of attractions in Chicago, IL. Runs were pooled at depth 5 and in total 299 context-profile pairs were judged, with an average of 28.2 unique judged venues per pair, hence 8,441 judgments in total. Details of the run and their P@5 scores are shown later in Table 2.

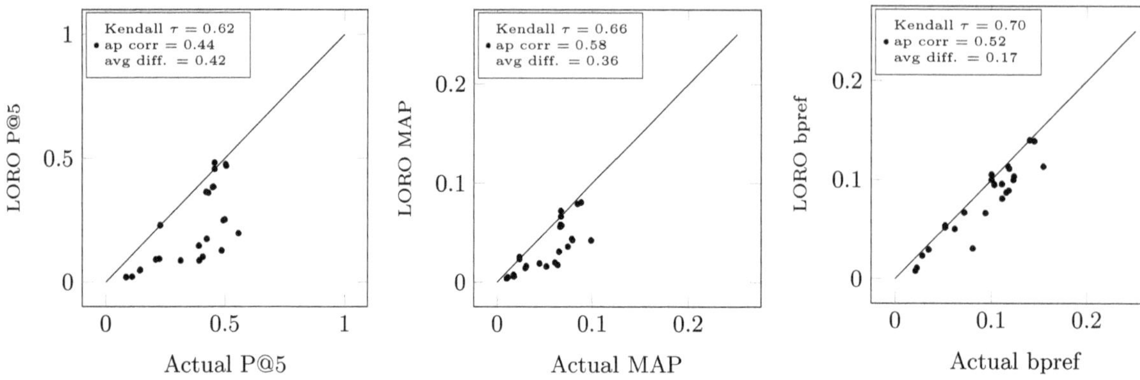

Figure 1: Difference in P@5, MAP, and bpref based on the leave one run out (LORO) test.

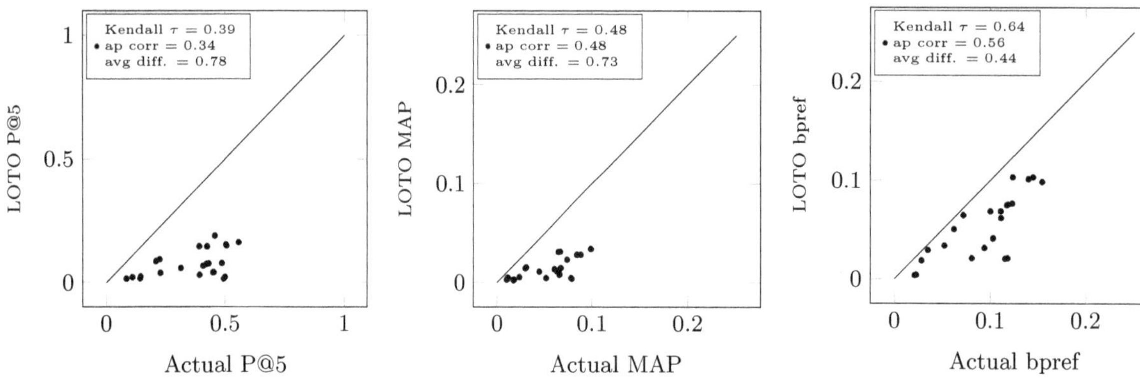

Figure 2: Difference in P@5, MAP, and bpref based on the leave one team out (LOTO) test.

3. IMPACT ON REUSABILITY

This section studies the reusability of the test collection, aiming to answer our first research question: *How does the open nature affect the evaluation of non-pooled systems?*

3.1 Leave Out Uniques Analysis

We first look at the question: *What is the effect of leave out uniques on the score and ranking over all systems?* Specifically, we perform both the leave-one-run-out [7] and leave-one-team-out [1] experiments to see what would have happened if a run had not contributed to the pool of judged documents. We also measure the effect on the runs' scores as well as their system ranking—as the main goal of a test collection is to determine the system ranking rather than absolute scores. The standard system rank correlation measure in IR research is Kendall's τ (i.e. $\tau = \frac{C-D}{N(N-1)/2}$), where C is the number of concordant pairs, D is the number of discordant pairs, and N is the number of systems in the given two rankings [6]. However, there are a number of researches studied that the Kendall's τ is not promising in some conditions [2, 3, 6]. In order to more precisely measure the test collection reusability, we also use AP Correlation Coefficient (i.e., $\tau_{AP} = \frac{2}{N-1} \cdot \sum_{i=2}^{n} (\frac{C(i)}{i-1}) - 1$), where $C(i)$ is the number of systems above rank i and correctly ranked [6].

Leave One Run Out.

In a leave-one-run-out (LORO) experiment, we exclude a pooled run's unique judgments from the test collection, and evaluate the run based on the new test collection in terms of P@5, MAP, or bpref metrics. This test is done for all of the pooled runs—hence for each run we obtain the score as if it had not been pooled and judged. Then, the ranking correlation of the official ranking of runs with the new one is estimated. In Figure 1, reusability of the test collection is evaluated based on the mentioned metrics. The Kendall's τ of this experiment based on P@5, MAP and bpref metrics are much lower than 0.9 that is the threshold usually considered as the correlation of two effectively equivalent rankings [4].

Moreover, difference of actual P@5, MAP and bpref and the ones based on LORO test is shown in Figure 1. As it is shown in this figure, average difference of MAP is 0.36 which is much higher than the ones reported for reusable test collections (e.g., from 0.5 to 2.2 [1, 5]). Figure 1 shows that bpref is a more reliable metric in comparison to (mean average) precision.

Leave One Team Out.

The LORO experiment can be biased in case teams' submit closely related runs containing many mutual venues. In reality, a non-pooled system might use completely different collection than the ones used by the pooled runs. Hence, we also conduct a leave-one-team-out (LOTO) experiment. Figure 2 demonstrates the same pattern as observed above for the LORO experiment, with somewhat lower rank correlations, and larger differences in scores. Again, bpref remains the most stable of the three measures.

Table 1: Reusability in top of the ranking

Metric	Depth 5	Depth All	P@5	MAP	bpref
Kendall τ	✓		0.800	0.800	0.000
Kendall τ_{sig}	✓		1.000	0.777	1.000
Bias	✓		0.000	0.111	0.000
Kendall τ		✓	0.393	0.480	0.646
Kendall τ_{sig}		✓	0.418	0.572	0.691
Bias		✓	0.290	0.213	0.154

3.2 Top Ranked Systems

The leave out uniques experiments give a clear call to caution on the reuse of the open web judgments, but we observe in the scatter plots that the top ranked runs seem to fare slightly better. Hence, we look at the question: *What is the effect of leave out uniques on the score and ranking over top ranked systems?* We look both at Kendall's τ and the τ_{sig}, which only consider significant inversions [3]. We also look at bias, which is the fraction of all significant pairs that are significant inversions [3]. We use a paired Student's t-test with $\alpha = 0.05$ is used to find significant inversions (i.e., $p < \alpha$). Table 1 reports the more critical LOTO test. Over all runs, we see that τ_{sig} is somewhat better than τ but still low enough to be very careful with using the resulting test collection for evaluating non-pooled runs. Over the top ranked systems (based on P@5 as reported in Table 2), the bias, τ and τ_{sig} correlations are substantially better.

In this section we looked at the leave out uniques analysis for the open test collection in both leave run and leave team out experiments. The outcome is mixed at best, while there is a strongly significant rank correlation, the effect of pooling is notable, and results in underestimation of score and hence affects the ranking. Although we observe a somewhat more reliable evaluation of the better scoring systems, this means that the judgments should be used with caution, and evaluating non-pooled systems requires great care.

4. IMPACT ON JUDGED DOCUMENTS

This section studies in more detail the factors contributing to the observed low reusability, trying to answer our second research question: *How does the open nature affect the fraction of judged documents?*

4.1 Fraction of Judged Documents

We first look at the question: *What is the fraction of judged documents over ranks?* We define *Overlap@N* as the fraction of the $top - N$ suggestions that is judged for the given set of topics:

$$Overlap@N(\langle C,P\rangle) = \frac{1}{|\langle C,P\rangle|} \sum_{\langle c,p\rangle \in \langle C,P\rangle} \frac{\#Judged@N(\langle c,p\rangle)}{N},$$

where $\#Judged@N(\langle c,p\rangle)$ corresponds to the count of judged suggestions for the given context and profile pair $\langle c,p\rangle$ in the top-N suggestions, and $\langle C,P\rangle$ is a set of judged context and profile pair. Table 2 shows the overlap@N of runs submitted to the contextual suggestion track in 2014. We see a significant drop after the pooling cut-off at rank 5, signaling that the recall base may be incomplete and the overlap between the different runs is relatively low. Clearly the lack of a fixed collection will have contributed to this.

Table 2: Overlap@N and P@5 of each pooled open web run based on the official TREC judgments

Run	Overlap@N (%) N=5	N=10	N=25	N=50	P@5 (%)
BJUTa	100.00	61.43	32.38	20.65	50.57
BJUTb	100.00	60.26	32.10	20.23	50.37
BUPT_PRIS_01	44.88	23.24	09.36	04.68	14.45
BUPT_PRIS_02	47.02	25.21	10.27	05.13	14.25
cat	99.93	59.06	31.90	19.83	20.94
choqrun	97.85	57.52	31.47	16.19	22.47
dixlticmu	100.00	59.49	32.33	21.46	39.13
gw1	97.99	51.97	24.98	14.21	10.99
lda	100.00	53.57	24.73	14.31	08.43
RAMARUN2	100.00	57.99	27.78	15.53	49.97
run_DwD	99.53	61.00	35.30	24.68	31.44
run_FDwD	99.59	79.79	37.61	23.68	42.41
RUN1	99.93	58.56	28.58	16.00	49.36
simpleScore	100.00	58.82	28.60	16.25	44.88
simpleScoreImp	100.00	59.43	28.86	16.34	45.22
tueNet	99.86	52.64	23.90	14.33	22.81
tueRforest	99.86	52.64	23.90	14.33	22.81
UDInfoCS2014_1	100.00	57.45	28.64	17.35	40.74
UDInfoCS2014_2	100.00	59.36	31.41	19.83	55.72
uogTrBunSumF	100.00	55.75	22.38	11.20	48.63
uogTrCsLtrF	100.00	55.75	27.30	16.40	39.26
waterlooA	99.79	64.28	31.10	19.67	42.21
waterlooB	99.79	59.53	30.50	19.36	43.08
webis_1	98.59	56.75	27.50	15.16	45.69
webis_2	98.59	56.75	27.50	15.16	45.69
Average	95.33	55.93	27.62	16.48	36.06

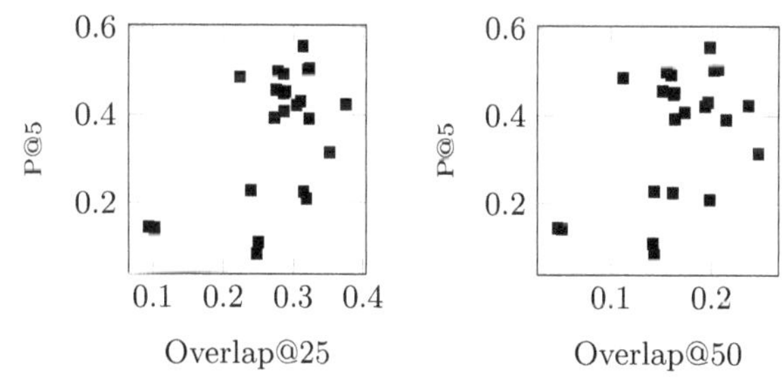

Figure 3: Overlap@N versus P@5 for open web runs.

In order to investigate the relation of the fraction of judged pages with the pooled runs' effectiveness, we plot Overlap@N vs. P@5 (i.e. the main official metric in this track) in Figure 3. Points in the graph represent pooled runs. Arguably, evaluating the best runs reliably is more important than separating the blatant failures. As it is shown in Figure 3, runs having higher P@5 usually have higher Overlap@N. This explains why for the evaluation is more reliable for the better performing runs. This figure also shows two runs that are outliers in terms of low fractions of judged documents. These two runs did usually provide fewer than 5 venues for the given topics.

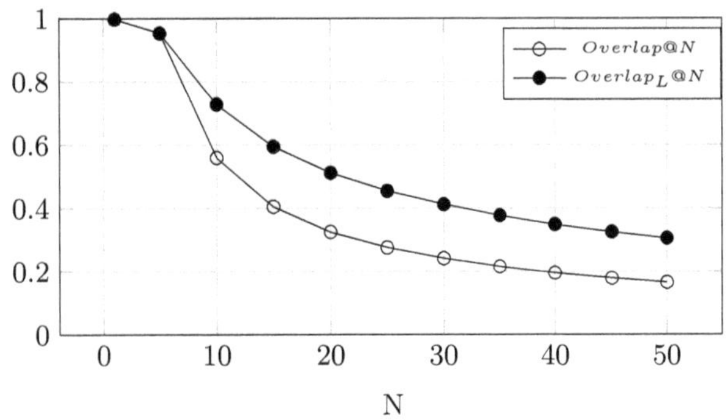

Figure 4: Effect of lenient judgments on Overlap@N.

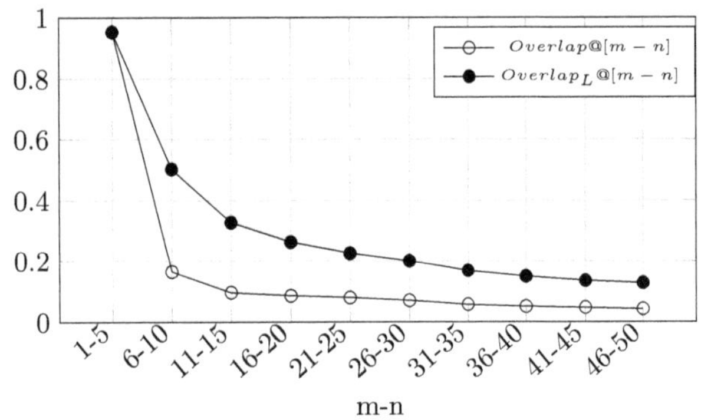

Figure 5: Overlap@N over rank intervals.

4.2 Impact of Personalization

We now look at the question: *What is the effect of personalization on the fraction of judged documents?* Specifically, we exploit the fact that contexts (i.e., cities) are judged for multiple profiles of the same (and other) submissions: in the case that the relevance of a venue to the given context is not judged for the given profile, judgments made for other profiles will be used. We define *Lenient Overlap* (i.e., $Overlap_L$@N) that is an instance of Overlap@N, in which *#Judged@N* is calculated by ignoring profile assumption. The results are shown in Figure 4, which shows that ignoring the exact profile substantially improves the fraction of judged pages.

To highlight the number of judged pages after the pooling depth, we show the same data in an interval level analysis in Figure 5. Obviously, for pooled runs, the Overlap@5 is guaranteed to be 1, making Overlap@10 guaranteed to be at least 0.5, etc. This shows the drop in fraction of judged paged for the personalized runs in an even more dramatic way. The lenient profile-ignorant overlap measure however remains more stable over the intervals. This signals that the relatively low fractions of judged pages can be attributed for some part to the low pool depth and personalization, rather than the open nature of the test collection.

This section looked at the fraction of judged pages in the open web submissions. The outcome clearly show the low recall: after the pooling depth the fraction plummets down, explaining the relatively low reusability of the open web judgments. We looked in the relative contribution of the open nature of the collection and the personalization and pool depth, which suggested that the latter play a major role in explaining the low fraction of overlap.

5. CONCLUSIONS

We have studied reusability of the TREC 2014 Contextual Suggestion open test collection in terms of the reusability of the judgments to evaluate non-pooled runs and in terms of fraction of judged venues. We analyzed the effectiveness of the pool for building a reusable test collection. Experimental results of leave out uniques (i.e., run or a team) tests based on various metrics, including Kendall's τ, AP correlation and average difference, showed that the test collection should be used with extreme care: non-pooled systems tend to be underestimated. However, for the high quality runs (i.e., top-5 of the ranking), the test collection performs somewhat better and had the highest correlation with the official ranking in terms of the τ based on significant inversions. Our empirical investigation has also shown that using an open collection tends to produce a diverse pool and consequently less fraction of judged venues at ranks deeper than the pool cut-off (e.g., only 16% overlap at ranks between 6 and 10). In addition, we looked at the role of personalization and low pooling depth, and showed that the lenient profile-ignorant fractions of judged page leads to considerable larger fractions of judged documents.

Our general observation is that the open collection leads to significantly lower recall, and low fraction of judged results, over individual runs. There are several ways in which this could be addressed. First, it is still an open question on whether we can derive a post hoc corpus and test collection from the open web submissions, by constructing a corpus based on the combined retrieved pages, and use this to evaluate runs over the combined set. We have done an initial analysis of this approach showing promising results. Second, the organizers of the TREC 2015 contextual suggestion track aim to collect open web results as a pre-task in early 2015, and use these submissions to construct a fixed open web collection shared to all track participants. The results of this paper give support to the creation of a fixed collection of open web results, and suggest that this will substantially increase the reusability of the benchmark for non-pooled runs in follow up experiments.

Acknowledgments This research is party funded by the European Community's FP7 (project meSch, grant # 600851).

References

[1] C. Buckley, D. Dimmick, I. Soboroff, and E. Voorhees. Bias and the limits of pooling for large collections. *Information retrieval*, 10(6):491–508, 2007.

[2] B. Carterette. On rank correlation and the distance between rankings. In *SIGIR*, pages 436–443, 2009.

[3] G. V. Cormack and T. R. Lynam. Power and bias of subset pooling strategies. In *SIGIR*, pages 837–838, 2007.

[4] E. M. Voorhees. Evaluation by highly relevant documents. In *SIGIR*, SIGIR '01, pages 74–82. ACM, 2001.

[5] E. M. Voorhees, J. Lin, and M. Efron. On run diversity in evaluation as a service. In *SIGIR*, pages 959–962, 2014.

[6] E. Yilmaz, J. A. Aslam, and S. Robertson. A new rank correlation coefficient for information retrieval. In *SIGIR*, pages 587–594, 2008.

[7] J. Zobel. How reliable are the results of large-scale information retrieval experiments? In *SIGIR*, pages 307–314, 1998.

Towards Vandalism Detection in Knowledge Bases: Corpus Construction and Analysis

Stefan Heindorf[1] Martin Potthast[2] Benno Stein[2] Gregor Engels[1]

[1]University of Paderborn
<last name>@upb.de

[2]Bauhaus-Universität Weimar
<first name>.<last name>@uni-weimar.de

ABSTRACT

We report on the construction of the Wikidata Vandalism Corpus WDVC-2015, the first corpus for vandalism in knowledge bases. Our corpus is based on the entire revision history of Wikidata, the knowledge base underlying Wikipedia. Among Wikidata's 24 million manual revisions, we have identified more than 100,000 cases of vandalism. An in-depth corpus analysis lays the groundwork for research and development on automatic vandalism detection in public knowledge bases. Our analysis shows that 58% of the vandalism revisions can be found in the textual portions of Wikidata, and the remainder in structural content, e.g., subject-predicate-object triples. Moreover, we find that some vandals also target Wikidata content whose manipulation may impact content displayed on Wikipedia, revealing potential vulnerabilities. Given today's importance of knowledge bases for information systems, this shows that public knowledge bases must be used with caution.

Categories and Subject Descriptors: H.3.2 [Information Storage and Retrieval]: Information Storage

General Terms: Documentation, Measurement

Keywords: Corpus; Data Quality; Knowledge Bases; Vandalism

1. INTRODUCTION

Information systems increasingly rely on structured knowledge to answer queries. This pertains particularly to question answering systems that reason about complex question queries, such as IBM Watson and Wolfram Alpha, but also to web search engines which display helpful information for all kinds of queries alongside the traditional "ten blue links." In fact, the additional information provided by the latter often suffices to answer many informational queries straight away, relieving users of browsing search results themselves. Given that, according to Broder [2], up to 48% of web search queries fall into this category, a lot depends on the accuracy of a search engine's knowledge base, or else users are misled.

Many search engines incorporate publicly available knowledge bases, which may be constructed, to various degrees, manually or automatically. Figure 1 overviews and organizes a selection of well-known knowledge bases in terms of their domain specificity and their primary construction principle. Both automatically and manually constructed knowledge bases face quality problems, albeit for different reasons. While automatically constructed knowledge bases solely rely on the validity of the heuristics applied for information extraction from their respective source of information, manually constructed knowledge bases rely on the trustworthiness of their volunteer contributors. Hence, the latter often impose rigid review processes to maintain integrity. Reviewing up to millions of changes every month is a tedious and time-consuming task, and if pending reviews are the reason for publication delays of new contributions, volunteers get discouraged. Not reviewing new contributions, however, may result in periods of time when vandalism, i.e., deliberate attempts to reduce data quality, is publicly visible.

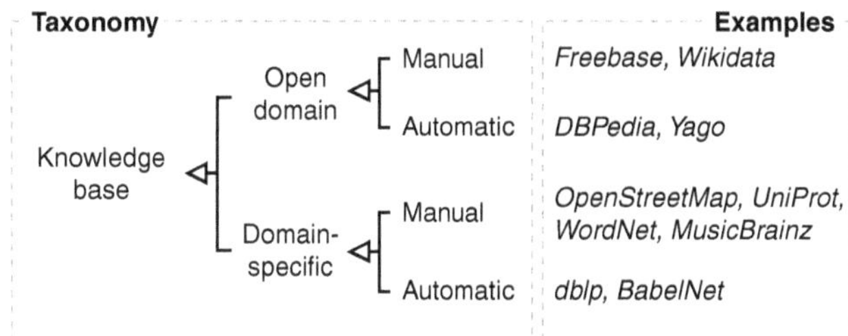

Figure 1: Taxonomy of knowledge bases with respect to their domain specificity and their primary construction principle along with well-known examples for each category.

An automatic solution to aid in reviewing would be of great benefit for the community of a knowledge base. However, vandalism in knowledge bases received little attention until now. The prevalence of the problem is unclear as well as what typical vandalism looks like. This gap of knowledge prevents in-depth research and development. To close this gap, we compile the first standardized vandalism corpus for structured knowledge bases and report on its analysis. As a basis for our corpus, we analyze Wikidata [11], the open-domain knowledge base of the Wikimedia Foundation which increasingly serves as a backend for Wikipedia. Despite its fairly recent launch, Wikidata attracts contributions from a large user base. Our contributions are twofold: (1) we compile the first large-scale corpus of Wikidata vandalism called Wikidata Vandalism Corpus WDVC-2015,[1] and, (2) we conduct a corpus analysis to investigate what content is vandalized and who are the vandals.

In what follows, Section 2 reviews related work, Section 3 gives a short introduction to Wikidata, Section 4 details the corpus construction methodology, and Section 5 reports on our corpus analysis. Section 6 concludes the paper.

SIGIR'15, August 09 - 13, 2015, Santiago, Chile.
© 2015 ACM. ISBN 978-1-4503-3621-5/15/08 ...$15.00.
DOI: http://dx.doi.org/10.1145/2766462.2767804.

[1] The corpus can be found at http://www.uni-weimar.de/medien/webis/corpora/

2. RELATED WORK

To the best or our knowledge, only two papers have tackled the detection of vandalism and low-quality content in *structured* knowledge bases so far: Neis et al. [4] develop a rule-based approach to detect malicious changes to OpenStreetMap, a domain-specific knowledge base for map data. For evaluation, a data set is constructed by analyzing whether or not OpenStreetMap users who have been blocked are vandals. The second paper by Tan et al. [9] focuses on Freebase, an open-domain crowdsourced knowledge base operated by Google. A machine learning-based approach to detect low-quality content is proposed, and for its evaluation, a data set is constructed using a so-called "test of time"-heuristic: basically, all additions that have been deleted within 4 weeks after their submission are considered low-quality. However, the authors of both papers provide little insight into the nature of low-quality content in their subjects of study, nor do the latter assess the performance of their heuristic. While the data sets are available to other researchers, they have not been published as dedicated corpora. Moreover, the usefulness of the Freebase data set may be diminished by the fact that Google is currently shutting down Freebase, whereas its contents will be transferred to Wikidata.

Besides structured knowledge bases, a large body of work can be found on detecting vandalism in what may be called an *unstructured* knowledge base, namely Wikipedia [1, 7, 10, 12, 13]. Many of these approaches have been proposed as a result of two shared tasks on Wikipedia vandalism detection [8, 6]. The evaluation corpus for these shared tasks has been constructed by Potthast [5] by means of manual annotation of a small sample of the revision history of Wikipedia via Amazon Mechanical Turk. The corpus is deemed high quality, yet, it comprises only 2400 revisions labeled vandalism. Therefore, Tran and Christen [10] as well as West et al. [13] construct their own evaluation data to achieve larger scales by means of automatic labeling methods. Both analyze the comments left by editors removing vandalism so as to identify prior revisions where vandalism has been introduced. Except West et al. [13], who analyze the spatio-temporal properties of vandalism, none of the above authors analyze their data sets in-depth. Our corpus complements theirs, but for the domain of structured knowledge bases, and, we provide a corpus analysis from the start.

3. WIKIDATA

Wikidata was launched in October 2012 by the Wikimedia Foundation. Based on the observation that a lot of factual knowledge appears redundantly throughout Wikimedia's projects, the goal of Wikidata is to collect and organize this knowledge in a central place [11]. Just like Wikipedia, anyone can edit Wikidata and the project quickly gained traction: since December 2013 there are constantly over 4000 editors with more than 5 edits per month [16].

Like other knowledge bases, Wikidata basically consists of subject-predicate-object triples. These triples are grouped by subject and each group is called an item. Currently, Wikidata stores about 17 million items and more than 50 million triples [17]. Every item is represented on its own Wikidata page which is divided into five parts: a unique label, a short plain text description, a set of aliases, a set of statements, and a set of sitelinks. For example, the item labeled "Barack Obama" is described as "44th President of the United States" and has aliases such as "Barack Hussein Obama II" and "Barack Obama II." Statements where this item forms the subject include "instance of: human" and "date of birth: 4 August 1961," and its sitelinks refer to all Wikipedia articles in different languages that cover Barack Obama.[2] Labels, descriptions, and aliases are multilingual and can have different values in every language. We refer to labels, descriptions, and aliases as textual content, whereas statements and sitelinks are structured content. Every edit of an item is recorded and assigned a unique ID within the revision history of Wikidata.

[2] http://www.wikidata.org/wiki/Q76

4. CORPUS CONSTRUCTION

Our corpus is designed with three goals in mind: it allows for the analysis of vandalism in knowledge bases, it allows for the evaluation of machine-learning approaches that detect vandalism, and it is as far as possible compatible to related corpora from the literature to allow for cross-domain evaluations (e.g., applying Wikipedia vandalism detection approaches to the structured data of Wikidata). In particular, we label revisions as vandalism or not. The following subsections detail the raw data of Wikidata, and how we apply an automatic labeling process based on the revision history.

4.1 Wikidata Database Dump

Our corpus is based on a database dump of the full revision history of Wikidata until November 7, 2014, which is provided by the Wikimedia Foundation free of charge [14]:

Revisions made on Wikidata	167,802,227	100 %
Revisions made on meta pages	1,211,628	1 %
Revisions made on special items	11,167	0 %
Revisions made automatically	142,574,999	85 %
Revisions made manually	24,004,433	14 %

Not all revisions enclosed in the dump are on Wikidata items, but on meta pages (e.g., user pages, discussion boards, etc.) and test items (sandbox items and Wikidata Tours items). We filter these revisions for their irrelevance to our corpus. From the remainder, about 85% of revisions are made automatically by bots approved by Wikidata's community. Basically, they are rule-based scripts that simplify tedious tasks. However, bots cannot fully replace the careful, manual curation of the data. As we are interested in detecting ill-intentioned contributions by humans, and not errors in bots, we base our corpus on the 24 million manual revisions.

4.2 Automatic Revision Labeling

Since vandalism detection is a classification task, we label all manual revisions as vandalism or not. While manually labeling such a large quantity of revisions is infeasible, we resort to automatic labeling and manual validity checks instead. The goal is to label as much vandalism as possible in a way that maintains precision, while being robust against vandal interference. Two of Wikidata's editing facilities are exploited for this purpose, namely *rollback* operations and *undo/restore* operations. While the former have previously been used by West et al. [13] to label vandalism in Wikipedia, neither has been manually validated until now.

Rollback. There are about 200 administrators and privileged users on Wikidata who are entitled to use the rollback facility: with a single click, a rollback reverts all consecutive revisions of the last editor of a given item. According to the Wikidata help, a "rollback should only be used to revert vandalism and test edits" [15]. Hence, all revisions that are reverted in a rollback can be considered vandalism. The use of the rollback facility is automatically logged in the comment of the resulting revision, so that identifying preceding revisions where vandalism was introduced is straightforward.

Undo/Restore. Like rollbacks, the undo/restore facility allows for reverts: the undo command reverts a single revision and the restore command restores an item to a previous state, undoing all intermediate revisions. Unlike rollbacks, however, the undo/restore facility is available to everyone, including unregistered users. The Wikidata help does not explicitly mention specific situations for which using this facility is reserved. Furthermore, users are free to change the automatically suggested comment. Hence, it is not possible to identify all undo/restore uses as reliable as rollbacks, however, users will often not bother to change the comment.

Of the 24 million manual revisions made on Wikidata, a total of 103,205 have been reverted via rollbacks, and 64,820 via undo/restore. Based on our below validity analysis, we label rollback revisions as vandalism, whereas this cannot be done with confidence for undo/restore revisions. Further, the natural level of granularity underlying Wikidata's database dumps is revisions, but vandals often strike the same item more than once in a row. Such events are quite different from isolated instances of vandalism by different users. Therefore, we also group consecutive revisions by the same user and annotate those revision groups. Nevertheless, our corpus keeps revisions as the level of granularity to maintain compatibility with related corpora from the literature.

4.3 Corpus Validity

To validate our labeling strategy, we manually review a random sample of 1000 rollback revisions, 1000 undo/restore revisions, and 1000 inconspicuous revisions. For each revision, the reviewer was presented with a visualization of the difference between the item states before and after the revision took place in the form of the well-known Wikipedia diff pages. To base the reviewer's decision solely on the content of a revision, meta information such as user names, IP addresses, dates, etc. were suppressed. We found 86%±3% (95% confidence level) of the rollback revisions to be vandalism, and 62%±3% of the undo/restore revisions. Furthermore, the reviewer annotated 4% (42) of the 1000 inconspicuous revisions as vandalism. We have analyzed these revisions more closely and found that only 1% (11) constitute actual vandalism. In many cases, only the context of a revision, which was invisible to our reviewer, reveals that it is not actually vandalism.

From a machine learning perspective, these results are encouraging: they show that, despite automatic labeling, the rollback revisions have a very low noise ratio, whereas the undo/restore revisions are on the borderline of being useful training data. For example, a biased SVM and weighted logistic regression can deal with up to 40% noisy labels [3]. Furthermore, the confidence in our labels is more easily obtained than that of Wikipedia vandalism corpora: more than 50% of revisions on Wikipedia require at least 9 reviewers to be labeled with a 2/3 majority vote [5]. In our case, two reviewers—the Wikidata admin and our reviewer—are sufficient to arrive at a reasonable quality. Altogether, the rollback revisions make up for a strong signal of vandalism on Wikidata, and this signal cannot be manipulated by vandals, unless they first infiltrate the senior staff of Wikidata. Regarding the undo/restore revisions, we leave denoising efforts, e.g., by means of statistical analyses and crowdsourcing, as future work.

5. CORPUS ANALYSIS

This section reports selected results of an exploratory analysis of our corpus. Particularly, we shed light on the following questions: (1) What is vandalized on Wikidata? (2) Who vandalizes Wikidata? But before going into details about these questions, we give key figures and statistics about our corpus, and Wikidata in general.

5.1 Corpus Statistics

Figure 2 visualizes the genesis of Wikidata in terms of manual revisions made per month from its launch in October 2012 until October 2014. Wikidata's growth rate significantly increased twice in March 2013 and again in May 2014. To determine the cause for these events, we analyzed all revisions with regard to the type of content affected. To determine the content type of a revision,

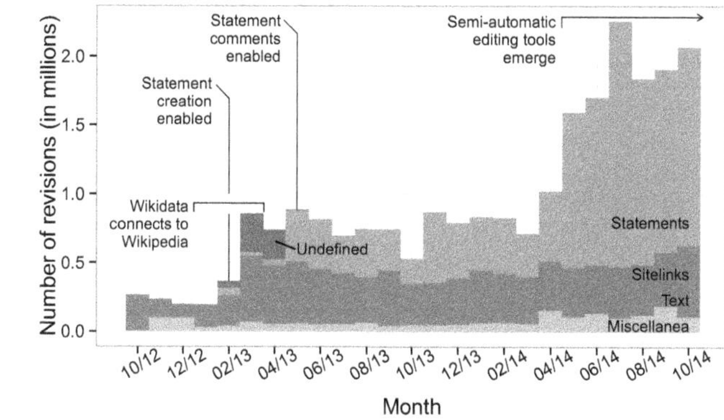

Figure 2: Manual revisions on Wikidata per month. Revisions affecting textual content (labels, descriptions, and aliases) are distinguished from revisions affecting structural content (statements and sitelinks). Major growth events are labeled.

we parse the automatically generated comments by the Wikibase software. The miscellaneous revisions includes merging of items, item creation and revisions with empty comments.

The first jump of growth rate was caused by enabling statement creation for first time. In the months around this event, Wikidata was connected to the Wikipedias in various languages, adding millions of statements and sitelinks. At that time, revisions affecting statements often had no automatically generated comment ("Undefined" in Figure 2). The second growth rate increase is due to the emergence of semi-automatic editing tools for Wikidata, most notably the Wikidata Game. This game with a purpose displays part of a Wikipedia page and asks the editor, for example, whether it is about a person and what their demographics are. In this way, editors can make a large amount of contributions in a short time.

5.2 What is vandalized on Wikidata?

Our answer to this question is twofold; we investigate (1) which categories of items are vandalized, and (2) which content types are vandalized (e.g., textual content or structural content).

Vandalized Item Categories. The distribution of vandalism on Wikidata is flat. Table 1 (left) shows the top vandalized items on Wikidata, where the top vandalized item accumulates only 47 of all vandalism cases (in terms of revision groups), whereas 70% (44,646 of 63,455) of the cases are the only ones in their items' revision histories. To learn which kinds of items are affected most by vandalism, we categorized the top 1000 vandalized items, and, the top 1000 items with the most revision groups (regardless whether they contain vandalism). Table 1 (right) contrasts the results. The distribution of attention over categories differs wildly when comparing vandals and all editors: disregarding categories with less than 1% share, the least vandalized category Places gets almost 4 times as much attention by all editors (31%), making it the most edited category. The categories People and Nature are on par, but the categories Culture, Society, Meta items, and Technology each get roughly double as much attention by vandals than overall. The focus of vandals deviates significantly from typical editors, giving rise to category-specific detection approaches.

The category Meta items comprises items that are used to automatically generate parts of important Wikipedia pages. By manipulating these items, a vandal may have tremendous impact. Apparently, many vandals attempt to exploit this potential vulnerability, since these items are otherwise of no particular interest (i.e., many contain only sitelinks). Moreover, while categorizing the revision samples, we noticed that 11% of the vandalized items concerned India, cross-cutting all categories, compared to 0.5% overall. The reason for this is still unclear, but merits further investigation.

Table 1: Top vandalized items (left); top vandalized categories and top edited categories in a sample of 1000 items each (right).

Cases	Item title
47	Cristiano Ronaldo
43	Lionel Messi
43	One Direction
41	Portal:Featured content
34	Justin Bieber
33	Barack Obama
29	English Wikipedia
29	Selena Gomez

Category	Vandalism	All
Culture	20%	12%
People	20%	21%
Society	16%	9%
Nature	14%	15%
Meta items	13%	8%
Technology	9%	4%
Places	8%	31%
Other	1%	1%

Vandalized Content Types. Table 2 (row 1) overviews which of the five content types of an item are most often vandalized. About 57% of the vandalism happens in textual content like labels, descriptions, and aliases; and about 40% happens in structural content like statements and sitelinks. The remaining 2% of miscellaneous vandalism includes merging of items and indecisive cases.

An explanation for the large portion of vandalism in textual content can be explained by the fact that textual content is more convenient to vandalize: it appears at the top of an item page and Wikibase allows for unrestricted plain text content. This renders the adaptation of Wikipedia vandalism detection approaches from the literature to detecting vandalism on Wikidata feasible. Nevertheless, up to 40% of vandalism can be found in structured contents of Wikidata items. Vandalism in these contents fulfills all the formatting constraints but still represents knowledge that must be considered malicious with regard to the item in question. Detecting such forms of vandalism requires the development of entirely new approaches to vandalism detection. A vandalism detection solution for Wikidata cannot work without also addressing this problem, since vandals are quick to notice weaknesses and they will adjust their behavior to exploit them.

5.3 Who vandalizes Wikidata?

About 86% (88,592 of 103,205) of vandalism on Wikidata originates from anonymous users. But simply considering all these revisions vandalism yields only 0.20 F_1 at 0.12 precision (88,592 of 768,027) and 0.86 recall—a baseline, but no justification to abolish anonymous editing. Only about 41% (35,979 of 88,592) of anonymous vandalism originates from an IP that has been previously used for vandalism. On average, one IP address is used for 1.7 (88,592 / 52,613) vandalism revisions. However, spot checks revealed that the IP addresses of some vandals on Wikidata also had a recent track record on Wikipedia, but a systematic analysis of cross-wiki vandalism is left for future work. For comparison, when vandals register before vandalizing, they tend to use their accounts an average 6.4 times (14,613 / 2,273) to vandalize and about 84% (12,340 of 14,613) of vandalism comes from accounts that have been previously used to vandalize. The available data does not reveal if vandals then switch accounts or just leave.

Finally, rows 2 and 3 of Table 2 break down vandalism from unregistered users and registered users by content type. Unregistered users primarily vandalize textual content and sitelinks, whereas registered users primarily vandalize statements and sitelinks. An explanation for this difference eludes our analysis so far, but it can be used to train different models via machine learning algorithm for each case, improving overall classification performance.

6. CONCLUSION AND OUTLOOK

In this paper, we report on the construction of a new resource for studying low-quality content in knowledge bases, namely vandalism. Vandalism has been one of the primary problems of Wikipedia, and with the growing success of Wikidata, this project will

Table 2: Vandalism by content type and user anonymity.

Vandalism	Item content type				Revisions
	Text	Statements	Sitelinks	Misc.	
Overall	57%	8%	32%	3%	103,205
Unregistered	63%	5%	31%	1%	88,592
Registered	19%	29%	39%	13%	14,613

become a bigger target for vandals as well. Vandalism in knowledge bases can have severe consequences, if information systems rely on its integrity and return facts extracted from the knowledge base without double-checking.

To enable future research in this domain, and to gain insights into the nature of vandalism in knowledge bases, we have compiled the first standardized corpus of knowledge base vandalism. Our corpus encompasses the entire history of Wikidata, and vandalism has been reliably identified using an automatic labeling strategy that cannot be easily manipulated. We have analyzed the vandalism found with regard to the mostly affected items, the affected types of content within items, and with regard to typical user behavior. Based on these insights, our future work will be the development a new approach to detect vandalism in knowledge bases.

Acknowledgement

This work was supported by the German Research Foundation (DFG) within the Collaborative Research Center "On-The-Fly Computing" (CRC 901).

References

[1] B. Adler, L. de Alfaro, S. M. Mola-Velasco, P. Rosso, and A. G. West. Wikipedia Vandalism Detection: Combining Natural Language, Metadata, and Reputation Features. CICLing 2011.

[2] A. Broder. A Taxonomy of Web Search. *SIGIR Forum* 36(2) 2002.

[3] N. Natarajan, I. S. Dhillon, P. K. Ravikumar, and A. Tewari. Learning with noisy labels. NIPS 2013.

[4] P. Neis, M. Goetz, and A. Zipf. Towards Automatic Vandalism Detection in OpenStreetMap. *ISPRS Int. J. Geo-Inf.* 1(3) 2012.

[5] M. Potthast. Crowdsourcing a Wikipedia Vandalism Corpus. SIGIR 2010.

[6] M. Potthast and T. Holfeld. Overview of the 2nd International Competition on Wikipedia Vandalism Detection. CLEF 2011.

[7] M. Potthast, B. Stein, and R. Gerling. Automatic Vandalism Detection in Wikipedia. ECIR 2008.

[8] M. Potthast, B. Stein, and T. Holfeld. Overview of the 1st International Competition on Wikipedia Vandalism Detection. CLEF 2010.

[9] C. H. Tan, E. Agichtein, P. Ipeirotis, and E. Gabrilovich. Trust, but Verify: Predicting Contribution Quality for Knowledge Base Construction and Curation. WSDM 2014.

[10] K.-N. Tran and P. Christen. Cross Language Learning from Bots and Users to detect Vandalism on Wikipedia. *IEEE TKDE* 27(3), 2014.

[11] D. Vrandečić and M. Krötzsch. Wikidata: A Free Collaborative Knowledgebase. *Commun. ACM* 57(10), 2014.

[12] W. Y. Wang and K. R. McKeown. "Got You!": Automatic Vandalism Detection in Wikipedia with Web-based Shallow Syntactic-semantic Modeling. COLING 2010.

[13] A. G. West, S. Kannan, and I. Lee. Detecting Wikipedia Vandalism via Spatio-temporal Analysis of Revision Metadata? EUROSEC 2010.

[14] Wikimedia Foundation. Wikidata XML Dump. http://dumps.wikimedia.org/wikidatawiki/20141106/wikidatawiki-20141106-pages-meta-history.xml.bz2, 2014.

[15] Wikimedia Foundation. Wikidata Rollbackers Help. http://www.wikidata.org/wiki/Wikidata:Rollbackers, 2015.

[16] Wikimedia Foundation. Wikidata Statistics. http://stats.wikimedia.org/wikispecial/EN/TablesWikipediaWIKIDATA.htm, 2015.

[17] Wikimedia Foundation. Wikidata Statistics. https://tools.wmflabs.org/wikidata-todo/stats.php, 2015.

About the 'Compromised Information Need' and Optimal Interaction as Quality Measure for Search Interfaces

Eduard Hoenkamp
Queensland University of Technology (QUT), Brisbane, Australia
Radboud University, Nijmegen, the Netherlands
hoenkamp@acm.org

"We have become the tool of our tools"

— Henry David Thoreau

ABSTRACT

Taylor's concept of *levels of information need* [16] has been cited in over a hundred IR publications since his work was first published. It concerns the phases a searcher goes through, starting with the feeling that information seems missing, to expressing a query to the system that hopefully will provide that information. As every year more IR publications reference Taylor's work, but none of these so much as attempt to formalize the concept they use, it is doubtful that the term is always used with the same connotation. Hence we propose a formal definition of levels of information need, as especially in IR with its formal underpinnings, there is no excuse to leave frequently used terms undefined.

We cast Taylor's informally defined levels of information need — and the transitions between them — as an evolving dynamical system subsuming two subsystems: the searcher and the search engine. This moves the focus from optimizing the search engine to optimizing the search interface. We define the quality of an interface by how much users need to compromise in order to fill their information need. We show how a theoretical optimum can be calculated that assumes the least compromise from the user. This optimum can be used to establish a base-line for measuring how much a search interface deviates from the ideal, given actual search behavior, and by the same token offers a measure of comparison among competing interfaces.

1. INTRODUCTION

Over the years, much work in information retrieval (IR) has focused on improving effectiveness and efficiency of search algorithms, notably encouraged by the TREC program and nourished by the SIGIR conferences. Early in the history of IR, however, several researchers emphasized that the function of IR systems is first and foremost, to quote Belkin [3] "...to help people solve problems, rather than directly to solve problems posed to them" (p. 42). This led to experiments aimed at helping searchers formulate their questions, such as suggesting suitable keywords [4], prompting them to be more talkative [14], or comparing the effects of written versus spoken queries [8]. The general finding is that if searchers could express their information need more in the way they would talk to a fellow-human, and in particular in everyday language, then this would benefit both the search results and the user satisfaction [12]. IR researchers recognized that the searcher's struggle to formulate a query has an obvious analog in a person browsing a library with only an approximate idea of the information needed. However, the librarian can assist a searcher with considerable more verve than we can expect from today's search interfaces. And thus the librarian as shining role model for future search interfaces explains the growing IR interest in the process of query formation. The latter process has been exemplary described in Taylor's [16] "The process of asking questions" which can be summarized with a direct quote from his abstract:

> Four levels of question formation may be isolated and analyzed: the actual, but unexpressed, need for information; the conscious within-brain description of the need; the formal statement of the question; and the question as presented to the information system (p. 391).

In his article the word 'information' in information retrieval denotes tangible things such as books, reports, and drawings, rather than information per se. In the case of IR we can take the images on a computer screen as perfect proxies for those books, reports etc. (printed on paper if necessary). And the analogy goes further. One could argue that in recents years IR has reached a phase of diminishing returns [11], as more and more effort is needed to achieve only a slight improvement in search performance. So further improvement can only be expected from improving the query, moving the onus from search engine back to the searcher. This is the point of Belkin's remark in the beginning of this section. That, in other words, means that IR should not be about getting the right answer, but about asking the right question. In the library context this is where the librarian steps in. This lead Taylor to write a follow-up article on question-negotiation for librarians [17]. In practice, though, IR researchers are still trying to push this part into the search engine, as we are about to see. Yet, it would be careless to write off Taylor's work as old hat, since bibliometric analysis shows [7] that the number of references to his approach increases each year, with IR notably occupying most of those references.

SIGIR'15, August 09 - 13, 2015, Santiago, Chile.

DOI: http://dx.doi.org/10.1145/2766462.2767800.

2. 'INFORMATION NEED' AND 'INTENT'

In Information Retrieval (IR) the term *information need* is ubiquitous, important, and intuitively clear. Surprisingly, attempts to *formally* define the notion are all but nonexistent [10]. Publications that tried a philosophical or sociological approach toward a definition got stuck in their attempts to cover everything that the term might connote. The last decade, following Broder's work [6] a movement is afoot to study the related notion of 'intent' instead. The suggestion is that if a search engine could infer the intent of the searcher, it would be better equipped to provide an optimal answer. There are, however, several issues with studying 'intent' in isolation:

- Early publications that studied 'intent' per se, sometimes lead to philosophical essays about all that could be understood by the term, but not applicable, formalizable, or amenable to empirical investigation.
- Conversely, pressed for an operational definition, as in patent applications, usually just one aspect of intent is selected and worked out (e.g. [15]).
- In dozens of experimental studies where intent was assessed on the basis of queries, the results were reliable but not valid [18].

The latter has serious consequences for the study of intent as a road to improve search, as we will see in a moment.

2.1 Reliability v. validity in appraising intent

About a century ago, it was common to assess a person's intelligence by measuring size and form of the skull. These measurements were extremely *reliable*: Someone who measured a second time would get the same answer, and someone else making the same measurement would get about the same answer as well. Yet, as Binet [5] showed at the time, these measurements had little to do with the 'intelligence' it was supposed to measure. Binet then introduced what became known as the Stanford-Binet test, which until today is considered a *valid* measurement, i.e. one that actually measures what it is supposed to measure (intelligence). Applying this distinction to the IR studies, it turns out that in the dozens of publications, the assessors of the query intent were different from the searcher who formulated the query. So, as with the studies of intelligence: even if the measurements were reliable, were they actually measuring the searcher's intent? To answer this question we carried out a careful meta-study of intent assessment: We recorded the interaction with a search engine from the participant's formulation of a query, the subsequent interaction with the search interface, and ending with the instruction to formulate the original intent. Afterwards the query and the interaction were presented to external assessors who were to guess the intent. What we found was a substantial discrepancy between the two [18]. That is, the measurements we found in the dozens of publications we studied, even if they were reliable, are not necessarily valid. It follows that:

- The word 'intent' may have different meanings in different publications,
- A score of publications may have studied something other than the searcher's intent, and therefore their advice about dealing with intent becomes dubious,
- Finally, if humans can not infer the intent from a fellow-human's query, how much hope is there that a search engine can achieve this feat?

The last point is bad news for search algorithms, obviously. The tension is located in the transition from Taylor's third level to his fourth level. That is, from the *formalized need* which is the searcher's expression of the information need that he hopes the system will answer, to the *compromised need*, which is the question asked in a way that the he thinks the system can answer (i.e. in a compromise to the system). This to us seems the main issue with the intent studies: they attempt to distill the third level from the fourth level. We are aware of many proposals to relax the compromise demanded from the user, such as making the interface more like a conversation between two humans [1, 12]. But in light of [18] it would be moot to try to push the envelope of studies of questionable validity. Instead, and at the same time to obviate the issues with defining 'intent,' we undertake a formalization of Taylor's levels of information need and *we shift attention from ranking the search engine to ranking the interface.* For this reason we need to dedicate a substantial part of this paper to the informal rendering.

3. QUERY AND SEARCH RESULT AS MEASUREMENTS

Taylor's informal definitions are rather verbose, so we extract the parts that are essential for our formalization. To formalize the different levels, we found the terminology from quantum mechanics (QM) most convenient. Hopefully this will not deter the reader, as the terminology fits like a glove, as we will see. (So keep in mind that we do not want to describe a physical system let alone a Schrödinger equation.) At the first level (the *visceral need*) we find:

> ...the conscious and unconscious need for information not existing in the remembered experience of the investigator [...] It may be only a vague sort of dissatisfaction [...] which would bring from the ideal system exactly what the inquirer needed, if he could state his need (p. 392).

Belkin [3] refers to this level as the *anomalous state of knowledge*. The correlate of the first level is the *observable* in QM, a superposition of states, in this case of mental states. The searcher is sitting and waiting for a query to come to the fore, no definite (mental) state exists at that time. After the searcher becomes aware of this, the first attempt at consciously describing what is missing arrives. This is what Taylor calls the second level (the *conscious need*):

> the conscious mental description of an ill-defined area of indecision [...] He qualifies his area of doubt by various oral and physical means.

This is the correlate of a measurement in quantum mechanics. Next comes the third level (the *conscious need*) at which the searcher forms:

> ...a rational and unambiguous description of his doubts. This question is what we like to believe the information system answers. It may not be, however, and probably is not, the question asked of the system.

This unambiguous description is the outcome of a measurement. In QM terminology: through the measurement the observable collapses into a query Q. The searcher could have come up with another query, assuming it is not a deterministic event but a probability distribution over queries $p(Q)$. Finally level four (the *compromised need*):

> The question is recast in anticipation of what the inquirer thinks he will get out of the system.

The searcher has made a compromise here, instead of his original query (the measurement) he expresses a query that he thinks the search engine is able to answer. In today's search technology, instead of using everyday language as he would do to another human, he uses the well-known terse query of two to three keywords. Only now the interaction with the search engine begins. We consider the state of the search engine as a second observable. Presumably there is a deterministic process underlying the search engine. But the links in it are updated, deleted, or created, in a way that for all intents and purposes is as opaque to us as the superposition of mental states that gave rise to a query. The first measurement, the query Q, is presented to the search engine, resulting in a set of documents R, which is a second measurement (a measurement of the search engine), governed by distribution $p(R)$. We are now ready to describe how the back and forth of the measurements can be described as the dynamics of the information need.

4. THE DYNAMICS OF AN INFORMATION NEED

We continue to denote the query and search results as the measurements Q and R with probability distributions $p(Q)$ and $p(R)$. So far we could have abstained from the QM terminology, as we have only used other names for undefined terms, e.g. by calling the visceral level an observable and the query a measurement. If we were not going to use the terms, this would only be window dressing. But we are going to exploit the QM model by looking at the observables as (Hermitian) operators. And more importantly as operators that do not commute. For this four page short paper there is not enough space to work out the constraints of how exactly the interaction between searcher and search engine could proceed. For example, there can be no way in which the searcher with just a feeling of missing information would cause the search engine to behave in a particular way. So what we will do is borrow from the insight of quantum systems and ask the reader to bear with us in the formal treatment. We may or may not presume an interaction between the two observables (the searcher and the search engine). And here is were we are going to use not just the QM terminology but the QM model. In that model we have to distinguish three cases:

1. Q and R belong to one system but they do not interact. That happens for example at the time when the searcher formulates the query, before sending it to the search engine. At that time, Q and R are independent processes, so their joint probability distribution is simply $p(Q,R) = p(Q) \times p(R)$,

2. They belong to two different systems.

3. They belong to one system but they do interact. This is a time of the back and forth between searcher and search engine, and there is obviously no way to measure one component independent of the other. (Note that during that time the operators do not commute, and so 'joint probability' has no meaning),

The first two cases are easy, so onwards with the last one: two systems, Q and R, that have some interaction. In the case of classical mechanics (commuting operators) we could consider a joint probability $p(Q,R)$, from which the marginal distributions can be computed. But the converse is not true: for a pair of marginals, many joint probabilities could give rise to these marginals. So suppose one samples distributions from the searcher and the search engine, *Is there a joint distribution given the marginals that deserves a special place?* The next section will point out that special place.

5. THE OPTIMAL SEARCH INTERFACE

The foregoing may remind the reader of approaches to compute the cost of searching, such as Azzopardi's using economic principles [2]. These can be used to explore optimal search strategies given a search interface. Here we explore the opposite however, optimality of interfaces given search behavior. It addresses the compromised information need: given a choice of interfaces, which one requires the fewest compromises? *The less searchers have to compromise to the technology, the less interaction they need to amend their query (in level 3) when the technology gets in the way.*

Suppose we can avail ourselves to a joint probability interaction between searcher and search engine, such as click traces or interactions accumulated from a number of users. A joint probability distribution can then be derived by sampling queries and search engine results. How can we, given the joint probabilities decide which one required the least interaction? Interestingly, this problem can be formally solved as we will do in a moment. For the reader not familiar with the mathematics in the next paragraph: what we derive is a formal criterion for the optimality of search interfaces, based on the interaction they demand from the user. More compromise requires more interaction to fulfill the information need. Therefore, *we propose to measure the quality of the search interfaces by the amount of interaction they demand.*

We are going to use a technique proposed by Jaynes [13] for statistical mechanics. Let us choose the distribution closest to the independent case (1) above [9]. As there is no weaker interaction than no interaction at all, this assumes the weakest interaction among the candidate distributions. In other words, we are looking for a distribution that is the most difficult to distinguish from the independent case (by the best test). So by definition of K-L divergence $KL(\cdot||\cdot)$, we need the joint probability with the smallest divergence from the independent case. That is, we are looking for a $p(x,y)$ that minimizes

$$KL(Q||R) = \sum_{Q}\sum_{R} \log p(x,y) \frac{p(x,y)}{p(x)\cdot p(y)}$$

constrained by what we know about $p(Q)$ and $p(R)$, such as their moments and, since they are probabilities, also the condition that $\sum_Q \sum_R p(x,y) = 1$. *This is a variational problem that can be solved using Langrange multipliers*, yielding the general form: $p(Q,R) = \frac{e^{-F(\lambda_1,\lambda_2,\lambda_3,\ldots)}}{G(\lambda_1,\lambda_2,\lambda_3,\ldots)}$ where the λ_i are the Langrange multipliers to be found for the F and G. For example if we would know the means of the query and search engine observables $\sum_Q x \cdot p(x)$ and $\sum_P y \cdot p(y)$, we would have:

$$\nabla KL(Q||R) = \sum_Q \lambda_1 \nabla x \cdot p(x) + \sum_R \lambda_1 \nabla y \cdot p(y)$$

with ∇ to abbreviate ∇_{x,y,λ_1}, and analogous expressions with λ_2 if the variances were known (and λ_i's for each additional constraint).

This model is ready for experiments to see how viable the technique is. This is imminent future work. Compare the design of it to TREC experiments where different search engines can be evaluated using a standardized corpus and topics, and precision and recall as metrics. In this vein we think of using one search engine and possibly similar standardized information needs to experiment with different search interfaces. This allows marginals over the queries to be computed and these can be compared to the marginals found by the proposed minimal interaction marginal. The interface nearest this minimum would then be counted as the best interface.

Of course this will be no sinecure, as no experimental work is. But the important message of this paper is: we now have a formal way to rank search interfaces, just as for years there has been wide consensus about how to rank search algorithms.

6. CONCLUSION AND FUTURE WORK

We showed how to formalize Taylor's levels of information as a quantum system. It contains two interacting subsystems, with query and search results as measurements of searcher and search engine. Presuming a quantum character, their statistical properties can be used to compute a parsimonious candidate for the minimal interaction needed to fulfill an information need during interaction.

Useful for future work are the manually constructed relevance data from the IR experiments of yesteryear. For example, the classical Cranfield paradigm provides correlations between query and relevant documents, $\rho(Q, R)$, that can be added as Lagrange constraint. The results will then serve as the base-line to compare the performance for different search interfaces, ranked according to their K-L divergence with the base-line.

Such work will tell if this is indeed a viable way to compare interfaces. But even if we are not immediately successful in applying this advice to IR, perhaps our operational definition of quality as optimal interaction may lead the way to investigate the necessity of evaluating search interfaces, in line with of Taylor's advice [16] that summarizes this goal:

> These areas of ignorance require discussion, experimentation, and analysis, not only for better design, but also to make the information system an effective and continuous element in the research process. The approach to such a Utopia will come only when we recognize that the inquirer is an integral part of the information system and not a stranger knocking at the door for directions (p. 396).

7. REFERENCES

[1] J. Allan, W. B. Croft, A. Moffat, and M. Sanderson. Frontiers, challenges, and opportunities for information retrieval. *SIGIR Forum*, 46(1):2–32, June 2012.

[2] L. Azzopardi. The economics in interactive information retrieval. In *Proceedings of SIGIR-11*, pages 15–24, New York, NY, USA, 2011. ACM.

[3] N. J. Belkin. Anomalous states of knowledge as a basis for information retrieval. *The Canadian Journal of Information Science*, 5:133–143, 1980.

[4] N. J. Belkin, P. Marchetti, and C. Cool. BRAQUE: Design of an interface to support user interaction in information retrieval. *Information Processing and Management*, 29(3):325–344, 1993.

[5] A. Binet. *The mind and the brain.* London: Kegan Paul, Trench, Trübner, 1907.

[6] A. Broder. A taxonomy of web search. *SIGIR FORUM*, 36(2):3–10, 2002.

[7] Y.-W. Chang. The influence of taylors paper, question-negotiation and information-seeking in libraries. *Information Processing and Management*, 49(5):983 – 994, 2013.

[8] F. Crestani and H. Du. Written versus spoken queries: A qualitative and quantitative comparative analysis. *JASIST*, 57(7):881–890, 2006.

[9] S. Guiasu. Joint probability distribution of composite quantum systems. *International Journal of Theoretical Physics*, 26(1):11–20, 1987.

[10] E. Hoenkamp. On the notion of "an Information Need". In L. Azzopardi, G. Kazai, S. Robertson, S. Ruger, M. Shokouhi, D. Song, and E. Yilmaz, editors, *Second International Conference on the Theory of Information Retrieval, ICTIR 2009*, pages 354–357, 2009.

[11] E. Hoenkamp. Taming the terabytes: a human-centered approach to surviving the information-deluge. In J. Strother, J. Ulijn, and Z. Fazal, editors, *Information Overload : A Challenge to Professional Engineers and Technical Communicators*, IEEE PCS professional engineering communication series, pages 147–170. John Wiley & Sons, Ltd, Hoboken, New Jersey, November 2012.

[12] E. Hoenkamp and P. Bruza. How everyday language can and will boost effective information retrieval. JASIST doi: 10.1002/asi.23279.

[13] E. T. Jaynes. Information theory and statistical mechanics. *Phys. Rev.*, 106:620–630, May 1957.

[14] D. Kelly, V. D. Dollu, and X. Fu. The loquacious user: a document-independent source of terms for query expansion. In R. A. Baeza-Yates, N. Ziviani, G. Marchionini, A. Moffat, and J. Tait, editors, *SIGIR*, pages 457–464. ACM, 2005.

[15] F. Radlinski, M. Szummer, and N. Craswell. *US Patent No. 20110289063.* Washington, DC: U.S. Patent and Trademark Office., 2011.

[16] R. S. Taylor. The process of asking questions. *American Documentation*, 13(4):391 – 396, 1962.

[17] R. S. Taylor. Question-negotiation and information seeking in libraries. *College and Research Libraries*, 29(3):178–194, 1968.

[18] S. Verberne, M. van der Heijden, M. Hinne, M. Sappelli, S. Koldijk, E. Hoenkamp, and W. Kraaij. Reliability and validity of query intent assessments. *JASIST*, 64(11):2224–2237, 2013.

I See You: Person-of-Interest Search in Social Networks

Hsun-Ping Hsieh
Grad. Inst. of Networking & Multimedia, National Taiwan University, Taipei, Taiwan
d98944006@csie.ntu.edu.tw

Cheng-Te Li
Research Center for IT Innovation, Academia Sinica, Taipei, Taiwan
ctli@citi.sinica.edu.tw

Rui Yan
Baidu Inc., Beijing, China
yanrui02@baidu.com

ABSTRACT

Searching for a particular person by specifying her name is one of the essential functions in online social networking services such as Facebook. So many times, however, one would like to find a person but what she knows is few social labels about the target, such as interests, skills, hometown, school, employment, etc. Assume each user is associated a set of social labels, we propose a novel search in online social network, *Person-of-Interest (POI) Search*, which aims to find a list of desired targets based on a set of user-specified query labels that depict the targets. We develop a greedy heuristic graph search algorithm, which finds the target who not only covers the query labels, but also either possesses better social interactions with peers or has higher social proximity towards the user. Experiments conducted on Facebook and Twitter datasets exhibit the satisfying accuracy and encourage more advanced efforts on POI search.

1. INTRODUCTION

In social networking services such as Facebook and LinkedIn, searching for a person of interest by her name is an essential function. Given the name of the target person specified by a user u, the goal of social search is usually to accurately find the target individual t who is what user u desires. So many times, however, the user may not know the name and just have limited information about the target from their past interaction experience, or just desires for finding persons who equip with some requirement specified (e.g. experts or celebrities). While a person can be depicted by a set of labels, such as her interests, gender, skills, hometown, favorite things, the activities they had ever participated together, and so on, it is potential to develop a system allowing person search without specifying names. In this paper, we propose a novel search, *Person-of-Interest (POI) Search*, which leverages the social connections as well as the labels associated on users to identify the desired targets for users in an online social network. By specifying a small set of labels that depicts the person of interest, instead of the name

SIGIR '15, August 9-13, 2015, Santiago, Chile

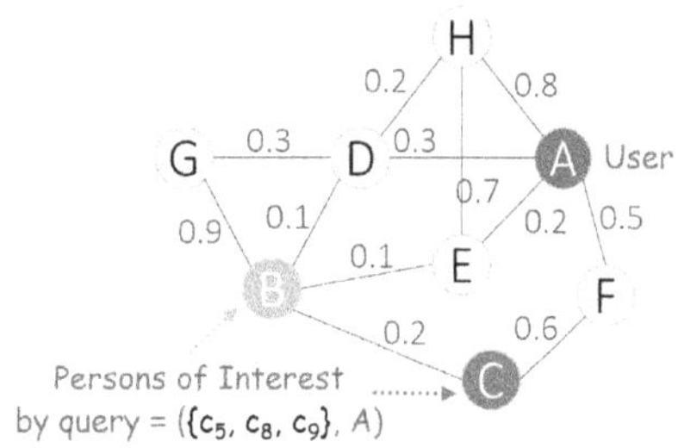

ID	Label Set
A	$\{c_1, c_2, c_3\}$
B	$\{c_8, c_9\}$
C	$\{c_4, c_5, c_8, c_{10}\}$
D	$\{c_4, c_6, c_7, c_9\}$
E	$\{\ \}$
F	$\{c_6, c_{10}, c_{11}, c_{12}\}$
G	$\{c_1, c_2, c_3, c_5\}$
H	$\{c_1, c_2, c_3, c_8, c_{12}\}$

Figure 1: A toy social network to elaborate POI Search, in which each node is associated with a set of labels, and each edge has an interaction cost.

information, POI Search will return a list of target persons that the user would like to find in mind.

The basic idea of the proposed *POI Search* lies in that there should be some relationship on either the input query labels or the social connections (in the network) between the user and the target. We use Figure 1 to elaborate the idea. Consider user A is searching for a person who possess query labels $\{c_5, c_8, c_9\}$. There are two individuals, B and C, who possess the most labels overlapped with the query and should be returned to A. Nevertheless, Nodes B and C play different roles if considering either their social interactions with nodes possessing similar labels or their structural proximity towards user A. Note that edge weights refer to the costs of interaction between individuals, lower weights indicate better interactions and higher proximity. Node B not only has lower interaction cost with those possessing some query labels, i.e., 0.4 to G (contains c_5), 0.1 to D (contains c_9), and 0.2 to C (contains c_5 and c_8) and 0.3 to H (contains c_8), but also has higher structural proximity towards user A (e.g. via paths A-D-B and A-E-B with costs 0.4 and 0.5 respectively). On the contrary, node C has higher interaction cost to D, E, G and H than node B and lower proximity towards A (via path A-F-C with cost 1.1). Therefore, in addition to satisfying the query labels, POI Search further allow users to specify the preference between the proximity towards the user and the minimization of interact cost with other nodes containing some of query labels.

We devise a graph search algorithm to fulfill *POI Search*. The basic idea is two-fold: (a) the target tends to have higher labels overlapped with the query labels, and either (b) the cost of interactions from the target to other nodes possessing some query labels is minimized, or (c) the proximity between the user and the target is maximized. The proposed method consists of three steps. We design and aim to optimize a *social cost* function that models part (b) and (c), and develop a greedy heuristic method to find a list of targets such that each target not only satisfies part (a) as much as possible, but also minimizes the social cost function.

Related Work. IR field focuses on optimizing Web search using social contents such as voting and tagging that are served as good summaries for web pages. Thus, social ranking methods, such as SocialPageRank [12] and HubRank [1], are validated to able to enhance the search quality. On the other hand, the viewpoint from J. Kleinberg [3], who defines it as searching over a social graph to find the set of individuals closest to a given user, is the most relevant to our POI search. Vieira et al. [11] modify the shortest paths between individuals as a structural ranking function to recommend friends for a single user. Though Schendel et al. [7] recommend items satisfying a given set of user-given query tags in a social tagging graph, social interactions are ignored. By using search log data in LinkedIn and Facebook, Huang et al. [2] and Spirin et al. [8] analyze the correlation between graph distance and various people search behaviors. In addition, Roth et al. [6] and McAuley and Leskovec [4] aims to group and recommend friends based on the social interactions between people. Though Mouratids et al. [5] use both graph and geographical distance for people search, labels that depict users are neglected.

2. PROBLEM STATEMENT

Definition 1: Social Network. A social network is an weighted graph $G = (V, E)$. Each node v has a set of labels. Each edge represents the interaction between two nodes. Edge weights refer to the interaction cost, where lower values indicate better interactions.

Definition 2: Person-of-Interest Query. A person-of-interest (POI) query consists of the user u who input such query and a set of query labels Q, in which $\forall c_i \in Q : c_i \in L$, where L is the universe set of labels.

Definition 3: Candidate Target. A candidate target v is a node whose label set L_v contain at least one query labels, i.e., $L_v \cap Q \neq \emptyset$.

The goal of person-of-interest search is to find a list of targets that not only cover the query labels as much as possible, but also have stronger relationships with respect to the user. For the latter part, considering the social interactions between the user and the *candidate targets* and the connections between candidate targets in the social network, we design the *social cost* to characterize various kinds of person-of-interest that allow a more flexible search. The intuition of the social cost is three-fold. First, it should consider the *proximity* between the user and the target. We exploit the technique of *Random Walk with Restart* (RWR) [10] to estimate such proximity. Second, we allow users to specify the *social vitality* of the target, in which targets with higher social vitality could be some celebrities while those with lower social vitality might or down-to-earth individuals or experts. To make the formulation simpler, we consider the number of the neighboring candidate targets of a target as the measure of social vitality. Third, we measure the cost of social interactions between candidate targets via the sum of weights of edges connecting them. We give the definition of social cost considering these three points.

Definition 3: Social Cost. Given a candidate target t, a set of other candidate targets U ($|U| = \pi$ and $t \notin U$), and the user $u \in V (u \notin U)$, the social cost $F(u, t)$ is defined as:

$$F(u,t) = \alpha \times (1 - RWR(u,t)) + (1-\alpha) \times \sum_{v \in U} dist(v,t), \quad (1)$$

where $\alpha = [0, 1]$ is the parameter that determines the preference between the proximity between u and t and the interaction cost between $v \in U$, π is the social vitality, $RWR(u,t)$ is the score of random walk restarting from u, and $dist(v,t)$ is the sum of edge weights in the shortest path between v and t. Note that in the execution of RWR, we use $1 - w_{u,v}$ as the edge weight since lower interaction cost means higher proximity.

Problem Definition. Given a social network G, the POI query (Q, u), and the parameters α and π, the task of person-of-interest (POI) search is to find a list of k targets S_k such that (a) the label set of each target $t \in S_k$, i.e., L_t, covers the set of query labels Q as much as possible, and (b) the social cost $F(u,t)$ is minimized. Note that we set $\alpha = 0.8$ and $\pi = 5$ by default.

THEOREM 1. *Person-of-Interest Search with the defined social cost is an NP-hard problem.*

The proof of Theorem 1 can be achieved by a reduction from *3-satisfiability* (3-SAT). Due to the page limit, however, we skip this proof.

3. THE PROPOSED METHOD

The proposed solution to person-of-interest search is a greedy heuristic method, consisting of four steps. The first is *Grouping-based Pruning* that aims to eliminate irrelevant nodes and keep the pathways with lower social costs for an efficient search. The second is to construct a *Query-Connected Graph* that combines both nodes and labels to facilitate the search. The third is *Greedy Search* that returns a list of k targets covering query labels and possessing lower social costs. The fourth is to find the *top-k targets* to be returned.

Step 1: Grouping-based Pruning. The first step is to prune irrelevant nodes that are impossible to be the targets. We group nodes containing any query label and extract the cost-effective pathways that connect the user to possible targets. A group, with respect to a query label $c_i \in Q$, is a set of connected subgraphs, in which each node contains at least c_i. After aggregating nodes into groups, we find the lowest-cost path (i.e., minimum sum of edge weights) between each pair of groups. Such paths will guide the following graph search to find the targets with lower costs. Finally, we restore the graph structure from purely the aggregated groups and the lowest-cost paths between them, and a pruned graph G' is derived.

Step 2: Query-Imposed Graph. Our approach is to find the targets satisfying the requirement of minimum cover of the query label set Q and lower social cost at the same time. Therefore, we impose query labels into G'. We create a new node for each label $c_q \in Q$, add the corresponding node v_{c_q} into G', and create edges to connect node v_{c_q} to those nodes possessing label c_q. Each newly-added edge is associated with a large positive value higher than the sum of all edge weights in G'. In the end a query-imposed graph H is constructed.

Step 3: Greedy Search. Given user u, the set of query-imposed nodes $v_{c_q} (c_q \in Q)$, and the query-imposed graph H, we develop a greedy algorithm to find the targets. We consider the set of nodes $X = \{u\} \cup \{v_{c_q} | c_q \in Q\}$ as seeds, and find a minimum-cost tree $T = (V_T, E_T)$ (from H) that connects all the seed nodes in X. The central procedure is to greedily select the next seed x^* from $X \setminus V_T$ with the least sum of edge weights to the current node set V_T in the growing T, and add the corresponding minimum-cost path $Path(x^*, V_T)$ (in H) into T. The tree T is derived when all the seed nodes in X are included.

Step 4: Top-k Targets. For each node $x \in V_T$ in T, we compute both the number of query labels that x possesses and the score of random walk with restart $RWR(u, x)$, and calculate the rank values of both parts (higher scores, higher rank values). By computing and using the average rank value for each $x \in V_T$, we pick k nodes x_t with higher average rank values as the targets to be returned. Note that the proposed algorithm can be shown to minimize the social cost function $F(u, t)$ with 2-approximation.

4. EVALUATION

We conduct experiments on Facebook and Twitter social network data provided by SNAP[1]. The data statistics are shown in Table 1, in which CC means clustering coefficient while APL refers to average path length. Labels in both data used include the categoies of school, hometown, employer, skill, gender, location, position, etc. In the social networks, we compute the edge weights (i.e., interaction costs) using the Jaccard coefficient: $w_{u,v} = 1 - (|L_u \cap L_v| / |L_u \cup L_v|)$, where L_u is the set of labels of node u. Our general aims to test whether or not the proposed *POI Search* can help users find the desired targets accurately.

Table 1: Statistics of Facebook and Twitter data.

	#nodes	#edges	CC	APL
Facebook	4,039	88,234	0.606	4.7
Twitter	81,306	1,768,149	0.565	4.5

POI Search is compared with three competitors: (a) *label matching* (LM): using the query label set Q to find a list of possible target nodes t such that the labels of t have the higher overlap with Q, $LM(t, Q) = \frac{|L_t \cap Q|}{|L_t|}$; (b) *Center-Piece Subgraph* (CePS) [9] with OR operation: consider those nodes that contain at least one label in Q as source nodes in CePS, run the CePS algorithm, and return a list of possible targets t with higher CePS scores $CePS(t, Q)$; and (c) *CePS+LM*: the selection procedure is similar as CePS but return the list of possible target nodes with toper average rank values of CePS and LM, $CePSLM(t, Q) = \frac{1}{2}(rank(CePS(t, Q)) + rank(LM(t, Q)))$.

In the evaluation setting, we first compile the universe set of all labels L, and then randomly select n labels from L to be the query set of labels Q, where $|Q| = n$ and $\forall c_q \in Q, freq(c_q) > \pi$ ($freq(c_q)$ is the number of nodes possessing label c_q). By randomly picking a node as the user u who is assumed to input a set of query labels Q, we perform an exhaustive search to find the list of top-θ optimal targets with the minimum scores of $F(u, t)$ and the maximum cover of query labels Q. The complexity exhaustive search is $O(|V|^2 \binom{|U|}{\pi} \log |V|)$ in the worst case. We utilize parallel programming to find the top-θ optimal targets for each pair of query Q and user u (we choose $\theta = 5$ here). To control the hardness of the problem, in the general evaluation, for each query Q, we select the user u whose top-k optimal targets locates within *3-degrees-of-separation* neighbors. We generate 5,000 pairs of query Q and user u possessing such requirement as the test data, i.e., $p_test = (Q, u) \in P, |P| = 5000$. Given the top-$k$ targets $S_k(Q, u)$ returned by a method and the ground-truth top-θ optimal targets $S^*_\theta(Q, u)$, we define the evaluation metric using accuracy: $accuracy = \sum_{(Q,u) \in P} hit(S_k(Q, u), S^*_\theta(Q, u)) / |P|$, where $hit(S_k(Q, u), S^*_\theta(Q, u)) = 1$ if $|S_k(Q, u) \cap S^*_\theta(Q, u)| \neq 0$; otherwise: $hit(S_k(Q, u), S^*_\theta(Q, u)) = 0$. It can be observed that given a fix number of θ, as k increases, the search task tends to be easier and will obtain a higher accuracy. That says, k determines the strictness of the evaluation.

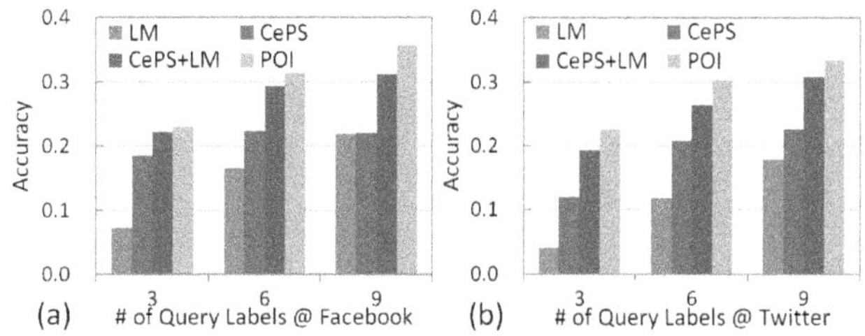

Figure 2: Accuracy scores by varying the number of query labels in Facebook ad Twitter data.

The evaluation plan consists of five parts: (a) general evaluation: varying the number of query labels $|Q|$ to show the performance of *POI Search*, larger set of Q means more specific search query; (b) varying the number of degrees of separation, a higher separation number refers to a harder search task; (c) varying the extent of *label rarity* in the query, defined by $LR(c_i) = 1 - \frac{|v \in V : c_i \in L_v|}{|V|}$, a query with higher label rarity indicates an easier search task; (d) varying the *top-k strictness* in the accuracy metric, a greater number of k means a loose accuracy definition; and (e) varying the parameter α in the objective function $F(u, t)$, a lower value of α leads to an easier search task because it tends to find the targets with higher proximity scores to user u.

Experimental results are shown in Figure 2-5. By varying the number of query labels, in Figure 2, we can find that the proposed POI search outperforms the other competitors, especially when the number of query labels increases. It is because more labels provide more evidences about the desired targets. LM cannot work well because it considers only the label matching while CePS uses only the structural connectivity. Though the integration of CePS and LM (CePS+LM) can boost the effectiveness to some extent, the accuracy scores are still lower than POI. Such results mean the heuristic of random walk cannot work well on finding the desired targets that minimize $F(u, t)$, and our POI search method is better to be closer the optimal solution.

Figure 3 reports the accuracy scores by varying the degree of separation of the ground-truth targets (selecting (Q, u) test pairs that satisfy a certain separation for the evaluation). As the degree of separation increases, the accuracy scores of all the methods get worse. We think it is because if the desired targets are farther from the users, the nodes satisfying query labels, the social costs incurred by the connections between nodes satisfying query labels, and their prox-

[1]http://snap.stanford.edu/data/egonets-Facebook.html
http://snap.stanford.edu/data/egonets-Twitter.html

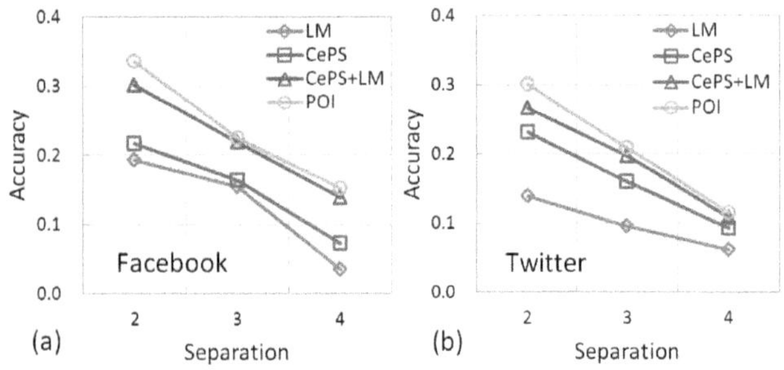

Figure 3: Accuracy scores by varying the degree of separation between user and target.

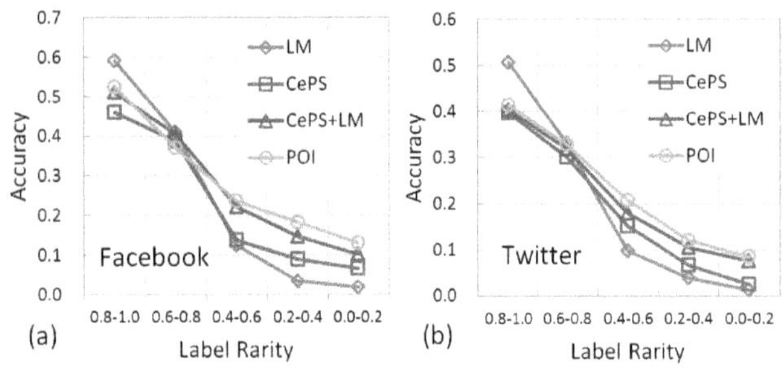

Figure 4: Accuracy scores by varying the label rarity of query labels.

imity to the users would increase accordingly. These factors lead to more candidate targets with lower social costs, and make the search task more challenging.

We shown the results of different extent of label rarity in Figure 4. We can find query labels with higher label rarity values lead to higher accuracy scores. As the label rarity of the query decreases, i.e., the query labels are frequently possessed by many nodes, the accuracy scores go down drastically. These results are reasonable since nodes whose labels with higher label rarity are essentially much less than those with lower label rarity. Therefore, it is natural to easily deal with query labels with higher rarity. Such results also suggest that when searching for desired targets, it would be beneficial for users to provide labels that tend to uniquely recognize the targets.

Figure 5 shows the results of sensitivity analysis for the parameters of (a) top-k strictness and (b) α in $F(u,t)$. A higher number of k in the accuracy metric, i.e., more targets are returned under a fixed number $\theta = 5$ of the ground-truth optimal targets, leads to a higher accuracy score, because the evaluation metric becomes looser. One can treat the top-k strictness as the number of returned targets that the users would view. If the users would like to explore more targets return, the possibility of finding the desired targets will be boosted. On the other hand, in Figure 5(b), a higher α value tends to guide the search to prefer the proximity between nodes possessing query labels and the user, and gets higher accuracy scores. An extreme case is to find the targets considering only the proximity part (i.e., $\alpha = 0.99$), which leads to high accuracy. On the contrary, lower α values shift the search to weight the social costs between the candidate targets, which could make the search towards a local optima, and thus result in lower accuracy.

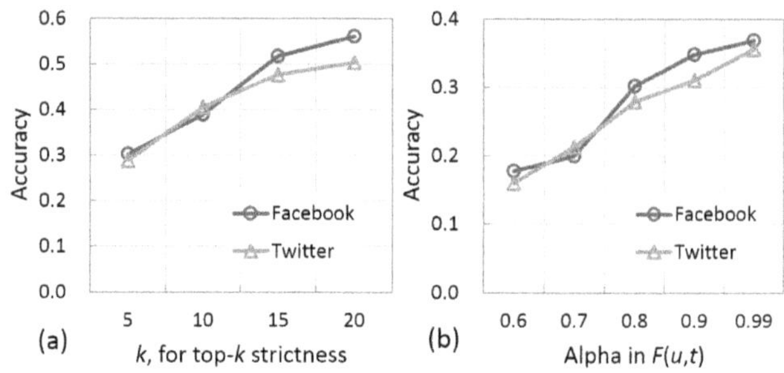

Figure 5: Accuracy by varying (a) top-k strictness, and (b) α parameter in the social cost function $F(u,t)$ using the proposed method.

5. CONCLUSIONS

This paper proposes *POI Search* to find persons of interest for users in online social networks. Considering the label cover, the structural proximity, and the social interaction between the query and the target, we devise a greedy heuristic algorithm to find a list of targets. Experimental results show the promising accuracy. Now we are evaluating POI Search using user study by a developed Facebook application. The future work is to extend POI Search into the realm of heterogeneous information networks.

6. REFERENCES

[1] S. Bao, G. Xue, X. Wu, Y. Yu, B. Fei, and Z. Su. Optimizing web search using social annotations. In *WWW*, 2007.

[2] S.-W. Huang, D. Tunkelang, and K. Karahalios. The role of network distance in linkedin people search. In *SIGIR*, 2014.

[3] J. Kleinberg. Social networks, incentives, and search. In *SIGIR*, 2006.

[4] J. McAuley and J. Leskovec. Learning to discover social circles in ego networks. In *NIPS*, 2012.

[5] K. Mouratidis, J. Li, Y. Tang, and N. Mamoulis. Joint search by social and spatial proximity. In *IEEE TKDE*, 2015.

[6] M. Roth, A. Ben-David, D. Deutscher, G. Flysher, I. Horn, A. Leichtberg, N. Leiser, Y. Matias, and R. Merom. Suggesting friends using the implicit social graph. In *KDD*, 2010.

[7] R. Schenkel, T. Crecelius, M. Kacimi, S. Michel, T. Neumann, and G. Weikum. Efficient top-k querying over social-tagging networks. In *SIGIR*, 2008.

[8] N. V. Spirin, J. He, M. Develin, K. G. Karahalios, and M. Boucher. People search within an online social network: Large scale analysis of facebook graph search query logs. In *CIKM*, 2014.

[9] H. Tong and C. Faloutsos. Center-piece subgraph: Problem definition and fast solutions. In *KDD*, 2006.

[10] H. Tong, C. Faloutsos, and J.-Y. Pan. Fast random walk with restart and its applications. In *ICDM*, 2006.

[11] M. V. Vieira, B. M. Fonseca, R. Damazio, P. B. Golgher, D. D. C. Reis, and B. Ribeiro-Neto. Efficient search ranking in social networks. In *CIKM*, 2007.

[12] Y. Yanbe, A. Jatowt, S. Nakamura, and K. Tanaka. Can social bookmarking enhance search in the web. In *JCDL*, 2007.

Towards Quantifying the Impact of Non-Uniform Information Access in Collaborative Information Retrieval

Nyi Nyi Htun
SEBE
Glasgow Caledonian University
Glasgow, G4 0BA, Scotland, UK
nyinyi.htun@gcu.ac.uk

Martin Halvey
Department of CIS
University of Strathclyde
Glasgow, G1 1XQ, Scotland, UK
martin.halvey@strath.ac.uk

Lynne Baillie
Department of CS
Heriot-Watt University
Edinburgh, EH14 4AS, Scotland, UK
lynne.baillie@hw.ac.uk

ABSTRACT

The majority of research into Collaborative Information Retrieval (CIR) has assumed a uniformity of information access and visibility between collaborators. However in a number of real world scenarios, information access is not uniform between all collaborators in a team e.g. security, health etc. This can be referred to as Multi-Level Collaborative Information Retrieval (MLCIR). To the best of our knowledge, there has not yet been any systematic investigation of the effect of MLCIR on search outcomes. To address this shortcoming, in this paper, we present the results of a simulated evaluation conducted over 4 different non-uniform information access scenarios and 3 different collaborative search strategies. Results indicate that there is some tolerance to removing access to the collection and that there may not always be a negative impact on performance. We also highlight how different access scenarios and search strategies impact on search outcomes.

Categories and Subject Descriptors

H.3.3 Information Search and Retrieval

General Terms

Measurement, Performance, Experimentation.

Keywords

Collaborative search; non-uniform access; effectiveness measures

1. INTRODUCTION

Collaborative Information Retrieval (CIR) involves people with common information needs working together, exploring and collecting useful information, and collectively making decisions that help them move toward their common goal. A simple example might be of a group of colleagues collaborating for a project where they may, individually or together, go through a number of information resources and then discuss their results, exchanging information and knowledge in order to contribute to the project.

A common assumption in much of the research in CIR is that all members of a team have equal access to the information sources, tools etc., and that they may share any relevant information they find with each other without any restriction [4, 5, 11]. However, in reality it may not always be the case that all searchers have equal information access. There are numerous situations where societal, legal or security reasons may prevent a searcher from sharing information within or out with a group. Handel and Wang [6] presented an example of such a scenario involving two intelligence analysts engaged in collaborative search, where one analyst is a signal intelligence specialist and the other a human intelligence specialist. Despite their unequal access to intelligence databases and underlying intelligence, as well as differing information needs and shareability, the two analysts must collaborate to achieve an outcome. This type of scenario was referred to as Multi-Level Collaborative Information Retrieval (MLCIR) [6]. Similar scenarios have been examined by other researchers who have looked at the effect of organisational structure in legal search [2], crisis management [3] and healthcare [10] to gain a better understanding of how these can impede collaboration. Others have considered how different roles within a search team might be leveraged to assist with CIR. For example, Pickens et al. [12] studied the impact of having two different roles in a collaborative exploratory search team, and looked into developing algorithms to support this. However, the main focus of these studies has been on the *division of labour* in CIR and although, to date, having different roles has been viewed as positive in collaborative search tasks, it might not always be. In fact, MLCIR is different from *division of labour* in that any system that supports MLCIR has to be aware of information flow, accessibility and shareability between collaborators [6]. Thus many of the concepts previously used to support CIR such as awareness, sense-making and persistence [4, 5, 11] may need to be revised.

Previous research [2, 3, 9, 10] has focused primarily on qualitative observations which may not be completely applicable in all non-uniform information access scenarios. To the best of our knowledge, there has yet to be a systematic evaluation on the impact of non-uniform information access within a team of searchers. We attempt to overcome this shortcoming by conducting a simulated user evaluation where we investigate the impact of two different kinds of non-uniformity in access, namely removing document access and search-term blacklisting for team members (Details are presented in Section 2.2). There are three main research questions that we attempt to answer in this paper:

1. What is the impact of non-uniform information access on the outcomes of CIR?
2. Do different types of non-uniformity have different impacts on CIR outcomes?
3. Are there scenarios where non-uniform access may be beneficial to CIR outcomes?

2. EXPERIMENTAL DESIGN

As there are a number of potential parameters for collaboration and non-uniformity in information access, we decided to use a simulated study. This approach means that we can more easily compare different variables and combinations than in a user evaluation. In future work, we anticipate exploring the findings from this study in more depth with a user evaluation.

SIGIR '15, August 09 - 13, 2015, Santiago, Chile
© 2015 ACM. ISBN 978-1-4503-3621-5/15/08...$15.00
DOI: http://dx.doi.org/10.1145/2766462.2767779

2.1 Data, Topic and Search Strategies

Our evaluation followed the same procedure as Joho et al.'s simulation of collaborative search [7], with some small changes as outlined below. We utilised the TREC HARD 2005 [1] collection (AQUAINT corpus) and topics. For their study, Joho et al. [8] generated a query pool through a user evaluation for 13 of the topics. We were provided with this query pool and thus use the same 13 topics (303, 344, 363, 367, 383, 393, 397, 439, 448, 625, 651, 658 689). The query pool has a total of 1157 queries across the 13 topics and each query contains up to 9 terms.

Joho et al. [7] simulated teams of searchers (of variable size from 2 to 5) to carry out collaborative search tasks. Each team had 20 search iterations per topic. During each iteration, a team member selected a random query from the query pool and was assumed to judge 20 documents per iteration. For simplicity in our evaluation we simulate a pair of users rather than vary team size, as this would introduce extra complexity, whereby combining a multitude of possible access combinations could become intractable. In other words, we assume that there are always 2 people in a search team for any given search session and the team performs 20 search iterations. Thus each individual in a team would judge a maximum of 400 documents per topic, with a team judging a maximum of 800 documents. One of the goals of Joho et al. was to compare a number of collaborative search strategies [7]; we utilise 3 of these search strategies for our study. These 3 strategies are:

1) *Independent Search (IS)*: team members judge documents independently without any interaction between each other, and have their results merged at the end of each search iteration.

2) *Independent Relevance Feedback (IRF)*: same as (1) but query expansion is performed based on their independent relevance feedback and then the expanded queries are resubmitted independently to the system. Team members do not share any knowledge on relevancy of documents.

3) *Shared Relevance Feedback (SRF)*: same as (2) but the query expansion is performed based on the relevance feedback of both members. Thus, team members share knowledge on relevancy of the documents.

For Joho et al. [7], *IS* was the most basic and simplest search strategy whereas the other two were the most effective. Due to its simplicity, *IS* is also the easiest to compare directly with any other search strategies in terms of performance, collection coverage, etc. The other two strategies chosen were the best performing in their experiments.

2.2 Access Scenarios and Combinations

We devised 4 scenarios to simulate non-uniform information access amongst team members completing a collaborative search task; these are summarised in Table 1 and outlined in detail below. For each scenario, we assumed that each of the two searchers have access to more or less of the collection relative to their search partner. For example, in one case, one searcher might be able to access only 10% of the collection while their partner can access 20% of the collection. Also, there is a possibility that one searcher cannot retrieve any documents that contain certain phrases or terms.

Therefore, starting with S1 (document removal), we began by indexing a random selection of 10% of the documents from the document collection. Then an iterative process was adopted whereby we increased the percentage of documents indexed by 10% until 100% of the collection had been indexed. This resulted in 10 different indexes for each person and 55 possible access combinations of indexes for two people (i.e. combinations of 10%-10%, 10%-20%, 10%-30%, 10%-40%; up to 100%-100%). This simulates a scenario laid out by Handel and Wang [6] where a person with higher security clearance may have access to more documents than a subordinate.

Table 1. Information access scenarios

Code	Scenario
S1	Remove access to documents from collection
S2	Term blacklisting – remove access to random terms from the collection
S3	Term blacklisting – remove access to terms based on their frequency in documents
S4	Term blacklisting - remove access to terms based on their frequency in query pool

Scenarios S2, S3 and S4 simulate term blacklisting, this is a major problem highlighted by Handel and Wang [6]. For S2, we began by analysing the collection for a list of terms. After that, we indexed the entire corpus meaning there is complete access. We then created other indexes by iteratively removing 10% of the terms randomly, until only 10% remained. This also resulted in 55 possible combinations of indexes for 2 individuals. Scenarios S3 and S4 took a more systematic approach. We analysed term frequencies in both collection and query pool, which contain 841498 and 591 unique terms respectively. We then followed the same procedure as S2 but instead of removing random terms we removed terms based on their frequencies in the collection and in the query pool respectively for S3 and S4. Therefore, for S3 the first 10% removed were the most frequent terms in the collection whereas for S4 those were the most frequent terms in the query pool. In each scenario we had 10 indexes for each team member and 55 different access combinations, although the indexes in S4 are of different size to S1, S2 and S3 because in S1, S2 and S3 we can theoretically exclude everything from the collection whereas for S4 this is dependent on the query pool.

Thus for each scenario, there are 55 possible combinations; for each of these combinations, we conducted each search simulation 10 times in order to reduce randomness and inconsistencies. In total, there were 1,716,000 search sessions performed by teams in our simulation (i.e. 3 search strategies x 4 access scenarios x 10 runs x 55 combinations x 13 topics x 20 iterations). For all of the indexing and retrieval, we used the Inverted File indexing method and BM25 retrieval algorithm, these were developed using the Terrier[1] library with out of the box settings.

2.3 Evaluation Measures

For the evaluation we utilised traditional IR evaluation metrics: recall, precision and f-measure in conjunction with specific metrics for CIR proposed by Shah and González-Ibáñez [13]: coverage, relevant coverage, unique coverage and unique relevant coverage. Coverage is the average number of distinct documents discovered by the team throughout the entire search session. Relevant coverage is the average number of documents in coverage that are actually relevant. Unique coverage is the average number of distinct documents that are only discovered in a given access combination, and not in any other. Unique relevant coverage is the average number of documents in unique coverage that are actually relevant.

[1] http://terrier.org

3. RESULTS

Table 2 shows the access combinations which yield the highest values for recall, precision and f-measure across all access scenarios and search strategies and Table 3 shows those for coverage, relevant coverage, unique coverage and unique relevant coverage. As our data was not normally distributed, for each measure across 4 access scenarios and 3 search strategies, we conducted a Friedman analysis to compare the 55 access combinations (i.e. 10-10, 20-10, 20-20, 30-10, etc.) and found that there was a statistically significant difference in every case. Post hoc analysis with Wilcoxon signed-rank tests was conducted with a Bonferroni correction applied, resulting in a significance level set at $p<0.00003367$. We present more detailed results of the pairwise comparisons in the following sub-sections. For reasons of space as there were many comparisons we do not present all of these comparisons.

3.1 Search Performance

Our first research question examined the impact of non-uniform information access on the outcomes of CIR. First of all, statistical analysis of recall, precision and f-measure values showed a number of access combinations that were not significantly different from the best performing access combinations. However, what was interesting among these is that for S1, S2 and S4, relevance feedback search strategies had a very high number of combinations that are not significantly different from their best performing access combinations (ranging from 50-20 to 90-60 for S1, 70-70 to 90-80 for S2, and 70-70 to 100-80 for S4) whereas the *IS* strategy had only a few (90-80, 90-90, 100-80, 100-100 for S1; 90-90, 100-10, 100-60 100-90 for S2; 90-90, 100-90 for S4). It suggests that in terms of recall, precision and f-measure non-uniform access for S1, S2 and S4 had very little effect when relevance feedback strategies were employed.

Table 2. Highest recall, precision and f-measure values with their respective access combinations. * indicates those values at full access (i.e. 100-100)

	Recall	Precision	F-measure
Independent Search			
S1	0.0859 (100-90) 0.0829*	0.2459 (100-90) 0.23898*	0.1270 (100-90) 0.1227*
S2	0.0813 (100-100)	0.2349 (100-100)	0.1204 (100-100)
S3	0.0818 (100-100)	0.2446 (100-20) 0.2353*	0.1210 (100-100)
S4	0.0830 (100-100)	0.2389 (100-100)	0.1228 (100-100)
Independent Relevance Feedback			
S1	0.1210 (90-90) 0.0383*	0.3576 (90-90) 0.1302*	0.1802 (90-90) 0.0604*
S2	0.1110 (90-90) 0.0376*	0.3273 (90-90) 0.1266*	0.1653 (90-90) 0.0588*
S3	0.1241 (90-90) 0.0370*	0.3931 (90-90) 0.1244*	0.1878 (90-90) 0.0572*
S4	0.0904 (90-90) 0.0376*	0.2711 (90-90) 0.1295*	0.1350 (90-90) 0.0580*
Shared Relevance Feedback			
S1	0.1001 (90-30) 0.0325*	0.3317 (80-70) 0.1756*	0.1502 (90-30) 0.0548*
S2	0.0836 (90-90) 0.0324*	0.4197 (90-90) 0.1748*	0.1391 (90-90) 0.0554*
S3	0.1006 (90-90) 0.0323*	0.5208 (90-90) 0.1745*	0.1683 (90-90) 0.0544*
S4	0.0762 (100-90) 0.0324*	0.3570 (90-90) 0.1748*	0.1173 (100-90) 0.0551*

Looking at Table 2, we found that when the *IS* strategy was employed for S1, the values of the 3 measures (recall, precision and f-measure) were highest at non-full access (i.e. 100-90) whereas for the rest of the scenarios (S2, S3 and S4) the values reached the highest at full access. When relevance feedback strategies were employed, however, it was found that the values reached the highest at non-full access (mostly at 90-90) for all 4 scenarios (S1, S2, S3 and S4). This suggests that there is some tolerance to removing access from the collection, and while it was expected that there would be a decrease in performance when access had been reduced, there were some cases which indicate that there may not always be a negative impact on performance. In addition, as mentioned earlier, our statistical test results revealed a number of combinations that are not significantly different from the best performing access combinations, which suggests that there are certain combinations that allow search performance to be comparable to the best performing access combination regardless of the users' unequal, or equal but not full (e.g. 90-90) access to the collection. This finding addresses our third research question. Moreover, the statistical test results also showed us that depending on the type of access scenario and search strategies being utilised, the resulting combinations were different, and thus resulted in different outcomes, addressing our second research question.

3.2 Collection Coverage

In terms of coverage for the document removing scenario (S1), statistical test results showed that in all 3 search strategies, there were many access combinations which were not significantly different from the best performing access combination and also represent the case where team members had access to a very diverse amount of the collection from each other (these are 50-10, 60-10, 70-10, 80-10, 80-20, 90-10, 90-20, 100-10, 100-20, 100-30). It appears that regardless of the search strategy, reducing access to documents for one member of the team means that a different member can make judgements about different parts of the collection thereby covering similar amount of documents as they would in the best performing access combinations. This finding is in contrast to term blacklisting scenarios (S2, S3 and S4) in which most combinations that are not significantly different from the best performing access combination represent the case where both team members had a higher access to the collection (e.g. 60-60, 100-80, etc.). Next, looking at coverage in Table 3, the fact that the highest values were obtained at non-full access again indicates that there may not always be a negative impact on performance when access has been reduced, addressing our third research question. In addition, statistical test results of coverage also showed that the resulting access combinations are different depending on the type of access scenario and search strategy being utilised which addresses our second research question.

In terms of relevant coverage, Table 3 indicates that when the *IS* strategy was utilised, the highest values were obtained at full access (100-100) for all of the term blacklisting scenarios (S2, S3 and S4). However, statistical test results also indicated that there were non-full-access combinations where relevant coverage was as high as the full access. Besides, it also showed that the resulting access combinations and their outcomes are different depending on the type of access scenario and search strategy being utilised, again addressing our second research question. With respect to unique coverage for S1, it can be seen in Table 3 that across all search strategies the access combination that has highest value is the lowest access (10-10), and this is opposite to S3 where the full access has the highest unique coverage. In addition, it is interesting to note that for all 4 scenarios (S1, S2, S3 and S4) the *SRF* strategy was able to obtain very high unique coverage in all access combinations compared to the other two strategies. Statistical test results showed that for S2, when the *IS* and *IRF* strategies were utilised, many of the access combinations ranging from 20-10 to 100-100 showed no significant difference from the best performing access combinations (i.e. 50-40 and 10-10 respectively). A similar outcome was also found for S4, but across all 3 search strategies. Unique relevant coverage in Table 3 shows that for all scenarios (other than for S3 of the *IS* strategy), the highest values were not obtained at full access. However, it appears that reducing access to the collection has little or no effect in terms of unique relevant coverage as statistical test results indicated that for almost every access scenario and search strategy, none of the access combinations showed any significant difference from the best performing access combinations.

Table 3. Highest values of different CIR measures with their respective access combinations. * indicates values of those measures at full access (i.e. 100-100)

	Coverage	Relevant Coverage	Unique Coverage	Unique Relevant Coverage
Independent Search				
S1	365.7769 (100-10) 297.7461*	44.6461 (100-80) 42.0769*	8.4923 (10-10) 2.0307*	0.0923 (80-20) 0.0461*
S2	355.7153 (80-80) 296.2615*	42.1615 (100-100)	14.7615 (50-40) 0.3769*	0.1923 (80-70) 0.0*
S3	304.2384 (100-90) 297.9615*	42.4769 (100-100)	9.8846 (100-100)	0.1615 (100-100)
S4	418.6461 (90-60) 296.1538*	42.4307 (100-100)	4.8461 (10-10) 1.8923*	0.1153 (100-30) 0.0538*
Independent Relevance Feedback				
S1	349.2769 (100-80) 290.8846*	48.3769 (90-60) 19.4846*	81.5231 (10-10) 12.4615*	0.3923 (10-10) 0.0*
S2	349.8692 (100-50) 292.4385*	47.5231 (90-80) 19.0538*	12.5923 (10-10) 7.9692*	0.3 (90-60) 0.0*
S3	326.6077 (100-90) 277.8692*	42.7538 (90-80) 18.2769*	17.1385 (100-100)	0.2231 (90-90) 0.0846*
S4	407.6769 (100-60) 281.6154*	40.3308 (90-90) 18.6*	8.7231 (100-100)	0.0846 (100-80) 0.0615*
Shared Relevance Feedback				
S1	353.6153 (100-10) 244.5308*	43.5 (90-40) 17.1*	133.3615 (10-10) 58.6692*	0.7923 (10-10) 0.0385*
S2	361.1615 (100-40) 241.3*	41.4308 (100-90) 17.2385*	74.7538 (40-40) 42.777*	1.2462 (80-20) 0.0769*
S3	304.0615 (100-90) 242.5308*	43.1615 (100-90) 17.0231*	67.2769 (100-100)	1.2692 (100-90) 0.2769*
S4	387.4077 (100-30) 249.3769*	40.1077 (100-90) 17.1308*	47.7692 (100-10) 45.7692*	0.4308 (100-90) 0.3077*

4. CONCLUSION AND FUTURE WORK

While a great deal of research has focused on CIR, only a few papers have considered the impact of non-uniform information access on CIR outcomes. This paper is one of the first attempts to quantify the impact of non-uniform information access on CIR outcomes. To that end, we conducted a simulated user evaluation using established scenarios [6] and search strategies [7].

In relation to our first research question it was found that in terms of recall, precision and f-measure that non-uniform access for S1, S2 and S4 had very little impact when relevance feedback strategies were employed. In addition, it was also found that in some cases, one member of the team having a high level of access can compensate for the other team member. Besides, our results have also highlighted that there is some tolerance to removing access from the collection and that there may not always be a negative impact on performance. This leads us into our second and third research questions. We have found that depending on the type of access scenario and search strategy, access combinations yield different outcomes. Removing access to documents and term blacklisting had different impacts in terms of coverage: for removing document access, coverage remained stable where at least one team member had high access, whereas for blacklisting both members needed high access to retain high coverage. We have also found that in some scenarios, performance is even increased due to non-uniformity. This may in part be because this ensures that parts of the collection which might otherwise be ignored due to overlap in retrieved documents are now examined. Thus, there can be some benefits to non-uniform access depending on the search task.

To address our research questions in this paper we used 3 search strategies, 4 access scenarios, 7 different measures and teams of 2 simulated users. We anticipate extending this study in various ways to be able to produce findings that greatly generalise to a number of real situations. Thus, we intend to look at more complex strategies and access scenarios, and incorporate more users within each team. Furthermore, the findings from this study will be examined further via a user evaluation. To conclude, our findings provide a better understanding on the impact of non-uniform information access amongst searchers in collaborative information retrieval, as well as a roadmap for further user studies.

5. REFERENCES

[1] Allan, J: HARD Track Overview in TREC 2005: High Accuracy Retrieval from Documents. *TREC 2005*, pp. 1-17

[2] Attfield, S., Blandford, A., Makri, S.: Social and interactional practices for disseminating current awareness information in an organisational setting. *IPM*, *46*(6), (2008)

[3] Bjurling, B., Hansen, P.: Contracts for Information Sharing in Collaborative Networks. ISCRAM 2010 (Vol. 1)

[4] González-Ibáñez, R., Shah, C.: Coagmento: A system for supporting collaborative information seeking. *JASIST*, *48*(1), 1-4 (2011)

[5] Halvey, M., Vallet, D., Hannah, D., Feng, Y., Jose, J. M.: An asynchronous collaborative search system for online video search. *IPM*, *46*(6), 733-748 (2010)

[6] Handel, M. J., Wang, E. Y.: I can't tell you what i found: problems in multi-level collaborative information retrieval. *3rd international workshop on Collaborative information retrieval*, pp. 1-6. ACM CIKM 2011

[7] Joho, H., Hannah, D., Jose, J. M.: Revisiting IR techniques for collaborative search strategies. ECIR 2009, pp. 66-77

[8] Joho, H., Hannah, D., Jose, J. M.: Comparing collaborative and independent search in a recall-oriented task. ACM IIiX, 2008 pp. 89-96

[9] Karunakaran, A., Reddy, M.: Barriers to collaborative information seeking in organizations. *JASIST*, *49*(1), (2012)

[10] Karunakaran, A., Reddy, M.: The Role of Narratives in Collaborative Information Seeking. ACM SIGGROUP 2012, pp. 273–276

[11] Morris, M. R., Horvitz, E.: SearchTogether: an interface for collaborative web search. ACM UIST 2007, pp. 3-12

[12] Pickens, J., Golovchinsky, G., Shah, C., Qvarfordt, P., Back, M.: Algorithmic mediation for collaborative exploratory search. ACM SIGIR 2008, pp. 315-322

[13] Shah, C., González-Ibáñez, R.: Evaluating the synergic effect of collaboration in information seeking. ACM SIGIR 2011, pp. 913-922

Features of Disagreement Between Retrieval Effectiveness Measures

Timothy Jones
RMIT University
timothy.jones@rmit.edu.au

Paul Thomas
CSIRO
paul.thomas@csiro.au

Falk Scholer
RMIT University
falk.scholer@rmit.edu.au

Mark Sanderson
RMIT University
mark.sanderson@rmit.edu.au

ABSTRACT

Many IR effectiveness measures are motivated from intuition, theory, or user studies. In general, most effectiveness measures are well correlated with each other. But, what about where they don't correlate? Which rankings cause measures to disagree? Are these rankings predictable for particular pairs of measures? In this work, we examine how and where metrics disagree, and identify differences that should be considered when selecting metrics for use in evaluating retrieval systems.

Categories and Subject Descriptors

H.3.4 [**Information Storage and Retrieval**]: Systems and software—*performance evaluation*

Keywords

IR evaluation; effectiveness measures; binary relevance

1. INTRODUCTION

Since information retrieval systems were first evaluated, system effectiveness measures have been a topic of discussion, study and controversy. When a new evaluation metric is introduced–or existing measures are criticised or praised–the discussion is usually motivated either by theoretical concerns with earlier metrics [5, 8, 9], or by user studies [1]. Sometimes, both approaches are combined [4].

Most IR effectiveness measures assume that the quality of results returned by a search engine can be calculated as a function of the gain vector inferred by a ranked list–sometimes also including additional knowledge such as the total number of relevant documents available [2]. In this paper we use:

SIGIR '15, August 09–13, 2015, Santiago, Chile

ACM 978-1-4503-3621-5/15/08 ... $15.00.
http://dx.doi.org/10.1145/2766462.2767824.

- k as the depth to which a particular effectiveness metric has been evaluated.
- R as the total number of relevant documents available.

In the case of binary relevance (where documents are assumed to either be relevant, or not), the gain vector can be represented as a bit string. In simple cases, it is easy to examine these bitstrings by eye and reason about which list should be preferred. For example, where $k = 3$, $\{1, 0, 0\}$ is almost always better than $\{0, 0, 1\}$.

However, some cases become more contentious. Consider two vectors with $k = 10$ and $R = 10$:

$$A = \{1100010000\}$$
$$B = \{1000101100\}$$

If asked which list is better, most researchers would say "it depends on the task". However, it's not always immediately clear whether particular effectiveness metrics would agree on which list is better. In this particular example, AP prefers ranking A over B, while DCG prefers ranking B over A. Put another way, it's not always clear which metric prefers which type of task, or whether particular metrics are consistent in their preferences. In this work, we perform an exhaustive search of the possible binary relevance vectors where $k = 10$, and investigate where the disagreement between metrics lies.

2. RELATED WORK

It's worth noting that many metric descriptions don't completely specify the details of implementation. For example, an implementation of DCG requires a selection of both a gain and a discount function. Similarly, an implementation of RBP requires a selection of the p parameter [9]. Kanoulas and Aslam examine several different possible choices for the gain and discount functions in NDCG [6]. They used a Generalisability Theory approach to find choices that produced a stable ranking of systems. In this environment, they show that the optimal discount function is less steep than previously thought, and also that the optimal gain function gives nearly equal weight to relevant and highly relevant documents.

Although producing a single score for a retrieved list is convenient, a single score is not a particularly effective way of capturing system performance [7]. One illustration of this is

Metric	Bounced	Monoton.	Converg.	Top-wgt	Localis.	Complete	Realis.
DCG	No	Yes	Yes	Yes	Yes	Yes	No
SP	No	Yes	Yes	Yes	Yes	Yes	No
RPrec	Yes	No	No	No	No	No	Yes
SN-DCG	Yes	No	No	Yes	Yes	No	Yes
SN-AP	Yes	No	No	Yes	Yes	No	Yes
Precision	Yes	No	Yes	No	Yes	Yes	No
NDCG	Yes	No	Yes	Yes	No	No	Yes
SDCG	Yes	No	Yes	Yes	Yes	Yes	No
RR/ERR	Yes	Yes	No	No	Yes	Yes	Yes
Recall	Yes	Yes	Yes	No	No	No	No
AP	Yes	Yes	Yes	Yes	No	No	No
RBP	Yes	Yes	Yes	Yes	Yes	Yes	No

Table 1: Properties of effectiveness metrics used (table reproduced and slightly modified from Moffat [8]. See original paper for footnotes and full discussion). All metrics are assumed to be an @k version.

the idea of 1-equivalence [10], which is the set of binary result vectors that receive the same score as a single document. The authors note that many 1-equivalent sets are contentious or at least counter-intuitive.

An interesting approach to measuring the quality of an effectiveness measure is to use the Maximum Entropy Method to infer the probabilities that each rank contains a relevant document, given the effectiveness score [2]. Once this probability vector is computed from the effectiveness score, a predicted precision–recall curve can be produced. The error between this and the actual precision–recall curve can be used to determine the quality of the metric. This approach asks the question "how good is the effectiveness score at inferring the original ranked list?".

Motivated by the wide variety of effectiveness metrics available, Moffat [8] introduces seven properties for describing and comparing metrics. They are:

- Boundedness: Whether the range of scores a metric can produce is bounded or not. For example, NDCG is bounded in the range 0–1, while DCG is unbounded in the upper range.
- Monotonicity: If extra documents are appended to the tail end of a ranking, the new score produced by a monotonic ranking is never less than the previous score. For example, Recall-at-k and DCG are monotonic, while AP is not.
- Convergence: If a document within the top k is swapped with a more relevant document outside the top k, then the score always increases if the metric is convergent. For example, DCG is convergent, while RR is not.
- Top-weighted: If a document within the top k is swapped with a more relevant document also within the top k but lower down the ranking, then the score always increases if the metric is top-weighted. For example, AP is top-weighted, while Precision-at-k is not.
- Localisation: If a score at depth k can be produced using only the information about the documents down to depth k, then a metric is localised. For example, RR is localised, while NDCG and AP both require additional information about the relevant documents that did not make it in to the ranking.
- Completeness: If a score can be produced when a query returns no relevant documents, then the metric is complete. For example, DCG is complete, while NDCG and AP both produce a division by zero when there are no relevant documents.
- Realisability: If a collection has any relevant documents, then a metric is realisable if it is possible to achieve the maximum value for that metric. For example, RR is realisable, but RBP is not.

Moffat notes that it is impossible for a metric to satisfy all seven properties, as some property combinations exclude others (for example, a metric that is monotonic and convergent cannot also be realisable if $k < R$).

3. METRIC DISAGREEMENT

Many previous comparisons between effectiveness metrics have looked at correlation between metrics. In this work, we are interested in the specific cases where metrics do not agree. That is, the cases where we have two binary relevance vectors A and B where–for example–AP says that A is the most effective result list, while DCG says that B is the most effective result list. In this work, we only focus on rankings where $k \leq 10$, since many of the metrics above include a user model, and it is common for users to only examine the first page of results in a web setting.

3.1 Method

We generate all possible combinations for binary relevance rankings where $1 \leq k \leq 10$ and $1 \leq R \leq 10$. This yields a total of 61,430 possible ranked lists. Since we are interested in the disagreement between metrics on specific (potentially) real queries, we only consider pairs of lists for comparison where both lists A and B have equal values of k and R. There are 32,062,341 such pairs. Each ranked list is evaluated for each metric, and for each pair of ranked lists and pair of metrics, agreement or disagreement is recorded. All metrics were computed using 64-bit floating point numbers, and equality was checked using an epsilon of 2^{-53}.

3.2 Metrics

We use the same metrics as Moffat [8], with the exception of HIT, which would receive the same score for every ranked list described above.

	DCG	RR	P@k	SDCG	NDCG	RBP85	RBP95	RBP50	ERR	R-Prec	SP	R@k	SN-AP	SNDCG
AP	1.32	30.10	20.62	1.32	1.32	2.13	3.51	8.67	30.10	20.62	0.01	20.62	31.20	31.68
DCG		29.38	20.80	0.00	0.00	2.83	3.91	8.06	29.38	20.80	1.31	20.80	31.11	31.07
RR			40.50	29.38	29.38	31.55	33.06	23.82	0.00	40.50	30.09	40.50	40.95	40.62
P@k				20.80	20.80	19.45	17.78	28.81	40.50	0.00	20.62	0.00	51.64	51.87
SDCG					0.00	2.83	3.91	8.06	29.38	20.80	1.31	20.80	31.11	31.07
NDCG						2.83	3.91	8.06	29.38	20.80	1.31	20.80	31.11	31.07
RBP85							1.85	10.15	31.55	19.45	2.12	19.45	32.68	33.15
RBP95								11.97	33.06	17.78	3.50	17.78	34.52	34.98
RBP50									23.82	28.81	8.67	28.81	26.08	24.80
ERR										40.50	30.09	40.50	40.95	40.62
R-Prec											20.62	0.00	51.64	51.87
SP												20.62	31.20	31.67
R@k													51.64	51.87
SN-AP														1.88

Table 2: Disagreement between metrics (%, lower is better).

Property	Has-prop	No-prop	Cross-prop
Bounded	24.38	1.31	15.43
Monoton.	22.25	26.11	20.68
Converg.	**18.75**	29.51	24.35
Top-wgt	18.77	26.46	**25.47**
Localis.	19.64	24.33	24.63
Complete	19.41	25.39	24.33
Realis.	20.01	**19.24**	24.69

Table 3: Disagreement between metrics with particular properties (%, lower is better). Bolded groups show significance.

Metric combination	Recall	First-rel	First-irrel
AP	52.41	4.07	65.53
DCG	22.10	71.63	14.34
DCG	33.24	62.38	11.27
RBP85	37.71	11.27	62.38
RBP85	0.00	75.00	1.38
RBP95	89.96	1.38	75.00
RBP50	0.00	70.24	0.00
RBP95	89.89	0.00	70.24

Table 4: Features of result lists where metric pairs disagree.

The metrics used are DCG, SP, R-Precision, SN-DCG [8], SN-AP [8], Prec@k, NDCG [6], SDCG [8], RR, Recall@k, AP [3] and RBP [9]. For RBP, 3 different values of p were used: 0.5, 0.85 and 0.95. As recommended by the authors [9], the lower bound of the score was taken to be the RBP score for this experiment. ERR was also implemented, but since it receives the same score as RR in binary relevance, the results are identical to RR [4]. See Table 1 for the breakdown of properties of each measure. Where choices for implementation were available, we implement the metric as described by Moffat [8].

4. RESULTS

The disagreement between each pair of measures can be seen in Table 2. In some cases (such as AP vs RR), the disagreement is not surprising, but in other cases where one would expect metrics to agree, they do not–such as the high disagreement with SNDCG and most other metrics. Also of note is the high disagreement between RBP variants–although this is not surprising, it is worth mentioning that simply changing the discount parameter dramatically affects the behaviour of the metric.

4.1 Realistic disagreement

The disagreement percentages shown in Table 2 are assuming that each possible ranking with $1 \leq k \leq 10$ can be returned by some system. However, retrieval systems aren't random; the results returned depend on collection statistics and other features which are not independent of relevance. To investigate whether these vectors are reasonable, we produced the $k = 10$ bitstrings for all runs submitted to the TREC4-8 adhoc tracks, and the 2005 and 2006 TREC robust tracks. All of the 1024 possible vectors were returned by real runs submitted to the track. This validates this exhaustive method of investigation.

4.2 Properties of metrics

To investigate whether the properties of effectiveness measures affect the disagreement between metrics, each disagreement score was sorted in to one of three buckets for each property: *has-prop*, where both metrics have the property; *no-prop*, where neither metric has the property, and *cross-prop*, where one metric has the property, and one does not. Table 3 shows the mean agreement between metrics in each bucket. Surprisingly, a single property is not enough to determine whether two metrics agree. Of note is the case of metrics which are not bounded, but as Table 1 shows, there are only two measures in the *no-prop* category for that property. With the exception of monotonicity, boundedness, and realisability, the *has-prop* category contains the lowest mean disagreement. However, a one way ANOVA test with a Tukey post-hoc analysis shows only the convergent/has-prop group and the realisable/no-prop group to be statistically significant predictors of agreement.

4.3 Task behaviour

To investigate whether metrics disagreed in a predictable way that might be correlated with a task goal, all disagreeing pairs of ranked lists from each pair of metrics were examined to find out which metric preferred: *recall*, the list with the most relevant documents (ignoring ties); *first-rel*, the list with the first relevant document (ignoring ties); and *first-irrel*, the list with the first irrelevant document (ignoring ties). Some selected results are in Table 4. Each pairing is divided by the space in the table. When AP and DCG disagree about which ranked list is better, this table shows that in 52.41% of disagreeing cases, AP will prefer the list with more relevant documents, while DCG prefers the higher recall list only 22.10% of the time. These numbers do not sum to 100%, as sometimes there is a tie in the recall between two ranked lists, and sometimes a disagreement means that one of the two metrics gives the same score to two ranked lists (as is the case with AP when comparing $\{1,0,0,0\}$ and $\{0,1,0,1\}$ when $R = 10$).

This approach provides an alternative way to think about metric selection. When choosing say between AP and DCG (two metrics with strong agreement), this approach allows us to drill down into the cases where they disagree, and decide what type of task we favour most. If we prefer finding a relevant document quickest, then Table 4 suggests that DCG is the metric to choose, with 71.63% of cases preferring the ranking with the highest ranked initial relevant document. Alternatively, if recall is preferred, then AP is the better metric. Note that although Table 2 shows only a 1.32% disagreement between AP and DCG, this is still over 42,000 pairs of ranked lists for different values of k and R.

The difference between the user model of RBP and DCG can also be seen in this data–DCG prefers the list with the earliest relevant document more often than RBP. And, as the weighting factor in RBP decreases, the metric prefers earlier relevant documents. Conversely, as the weight in RBP increases, the list with higher recall is preferred.

5. CONCLUSION

In this work we have introduced a novel strategy for investigating the disagreement between effectiveness metrics–by counting and examining the pairs of hypothetical rankings where the metrics disagree with each other. We validated our strategy by demonstrating that all possible rankings of 10 binary relevant documents have appeared in search results submitted to two of the TREC tracks, and we performed an initial investigation into whether the properties of effectiveness measures can be used to predict agreement. We found that two of the properties appeared to be weak predictors of agreement between metrics. Then, we used a feature-based approach to investigate whether the disagreement between a pair of metrics could be described in terms of task features. This approach allows statements like "if I select AP over DCG, I am preferring recall over highly ranked documents" to be made, allowing fine-grained selection between metrics.

6. FUTURE WORK

As mentioned above, search engines do not produce a random result set. Although all possible rankings for $k = 10$ did appear in real search results during the TREC adhoc and robust tracks, the frequency with which each ranking appears is not uniform. It would be valuable to examine the likelihood of disagreement that each result list has. It is possible that the gain vectors produced by systems could be used to determine how contentious they are–how sensitive evaluation would be to metric selection.

An obvious extension to Section 4.2 is to consider multiple groupings of properties. Although it seems that individual properties of effectiveness measures are not enough to predict agreement, perhaps some combination of the properties might be. In future work, we intend to include more variants of metrics, such as alternative discounts and gain functions. This may lead to discovery of further properties.

In Section 4.3, we only consider three features of ranked lists that map to task goals, but there are many more we could consider (such as longest consecutive run of relevant documents, or lowest ranked relevant document). Additionally, user preference experiments could be constructed using pairs of vectors where metrics disagree.

As noted in Section 4, many of the DCG variants completely agree on individual ranked lists, as all that changes is the normalisation. However, if multiple queries (and therefore multiple ranked lists) are used for evaluation–as in the case of TREC tracks–then different normalisation strategies may well cause further disagreement between metrics.

Finally, this work has only considered the binary relevance case. Many of these metrics behave differently when there are multiple grades of relevance. An important next step is to repeat this analysis using graded relevance.

7. REFERENCES

[1] A. Al-Maskari, M. Sanderson, and P. Clough. The relationship between IR effectiveness measures and user satisfaction. In *Proc SIGIR*, pages 773–774, 2007.

[2] J. A. Aslam, E. Yilmaz, and V. Pavlu. The maximum entropy method for analyzing retrieval measures. In *Proc SIGIR*, pages 27–34, 2005.

[3] C. Buckley and E. M. Voorhees. Evaluating evaluation measure stability. In *Proc SIGIR*, pages 33–40, 2000.

[4] O. Chapelle, D. Metlzer, Y. Zhang, and P. Grinspan. Expected reciprocal rank for graded relevance. In *Proc CIKM*, pages 621–630, 2009.

[5] K. Järvelin and J. Kekäläinen. Cumulated gain-based evaluation of IR techniques. *ACM Trans. Inf. Syst.*, 20(4):422–446, Oct. 2002.

[6] E. Kanoulas and J. A. Aslam. Empirical justification of the gain and discount function for nDCG. In *Proc. CIKM*, pages 611–620, 2009.

[7] S. Mizzaro. The good, the bad, the difficult, and the easy: Something wrong with information retrieval evaluation? In *Proc. ECIR*, volume 4956, pages 642–646, 2008.

[8] A. Moffat. Seven numeric properties of effectiveness metrics. In *AIRS*, volume 8281, pages 1–12, 2013.

[9] A. Moffat and J. Zobel. Rank-biased precision for measurement of retrieval effectiveness. *ACM Trans. Inf. Syst.*, 27(1):2:1–2:27, Dec. 2008.

[10] P. Thomas, D. Hawking, and T. Jones. What deliberately degrading search quality tells us about discount functions. In *Proc SIGIR*, pages 1107–1108, 2011.

Subsequence Search in Event-Interval Sequences

Orestis Kostakis
Aalto University
Espoo, Finland
orestis.kostakis@aalto.fi

Aristides Gionis
Aalto University
Espoo, Finland
aristides.gionis@aalto.fi

ABSTRACT

We study the problem of *subsequence search* in databases of event-interval sequences, or e-sequences. In contrast to sequences of instantaneous events, e-sequences contain events that have a duration. In Information Retrieval applications, e-sequences are used for American Sign Language. We show that the subsequence-search problem is **NP**-hard and provide an exact (worst-case exponential) algorithm. We extend our algorithm to handle different cases of subsequence matching with errors. We then propose the *Relation Index*, a scheme for speeding up exact retrieval, which we benchmark against several indexing schemes.

1. INTRODUCTION

Event-interval sequences, or *e-sequences*, are used in a plethora of real-world application domains, such as linguistics [2], sensor networks [6], and health informatics [7]. They are also used in information-retrieval applications for the American Sign Language (ASL) [5]. As a result, e-sequences have lately attracted considerable attention in both the database and knowledge-discovery communities.

An example of an e-sequence is shown in Figure 1. In contrast to instantaneous event sequences, events in e-sequences have a duration. Hence, e-sequences convey richer information than instantaneous event sequences. It can be shown that information contained in e-sequences cannot be represented by instantaneous event sequences. Such an example is shown in Figure 2, where mapping e-sequences to symbolic sequences of instantaneous events creates ambiguity. Our experiments demonstrate that this type of representation error occurs in practice.

In this paper we study the following problem: given a database $\mathcal{D}$ of e-sequences and a query e-sequence Q, find the e-sequences in $\mathcal{D}$ that contain Q.

This problem applies, among others, to searching for specific phrases or grammatical constructions, among transcriptions of American Sign Language. Similarly, in Heath Informatics, a professional needs to search among medical records for patients that exhibited symptoms in a specific combination; here we assume that event intervals are used to model conditions or medication states of patients.

SIGIR '15, August 09 - 13, 2015, Santiago, Chile

ACM 978-1-4503-3621-5/15/08 ...$15.00.
http://dx.doi.org/10.1145/2766462.2767778

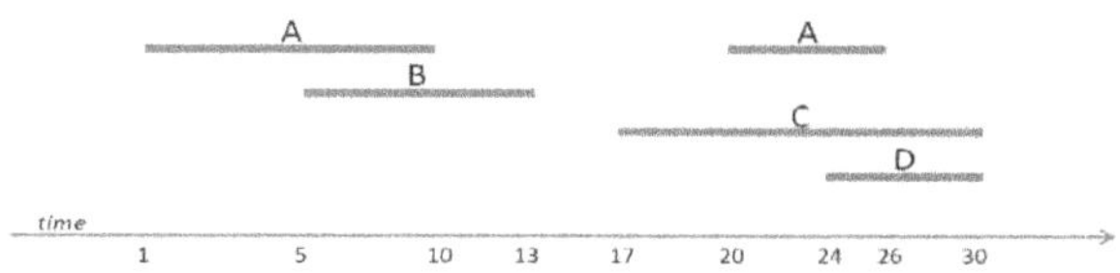

Figure 1: An event-interval sequence with 5 intervals.

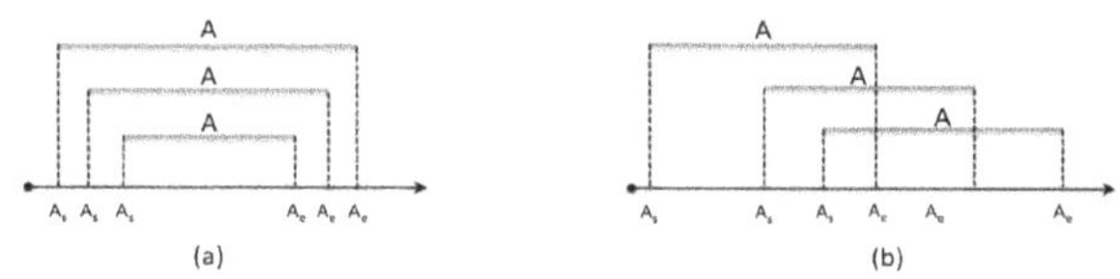

Figure 2: Event-interval sequences describe richer scenarios than symbolic sequences. Mapping event-interval sequences to symbolic sequences creates ambiguities.

In this paper we make the following contributions:

- We define the problem of subsequence matching, we prove that it is **NP**-hard, and we provide an exact algorithm.
- We extend our algorithm to handle different cases of approximate subsequence matching.
- We propose the *Relation Index*, a scheme for speeding up exact retrieval, which we benchmark against several indexing schemes.

2. BACKGROUND

An event-interval sequence, or e-sequence, $S = \{S_1, \ldots, S_{|S|}\}$ is a sequence of triples denoted $S_i = (S_i.E, t_{\text{start}}, t_{\text{end}})$. The coordinates of each triple denote the label, the start-time and end-time of each interval, respectively. For the example in Figure 1, the representation is $S = \{(A, 1, 10), (B, 5, 13), (C, 17, 30), (A, 20, 26), (D, 24, 30)\}$. We denote by $|S|$ the *length* of S, which is the number of its intervals. Note that it is also possible to have overlapping intervals with the same label.

Any pair of intervals in an e-sequence is characterized by a *relation*. The set of possible relations, based on Allen's model [1], are shown in Figure 3.

We only consider relations among intervals and ignore the absolute time durations. In American Sign Language, sentences are formed based on the combination of gestures not their duration: as with speaking, people may spend differ-

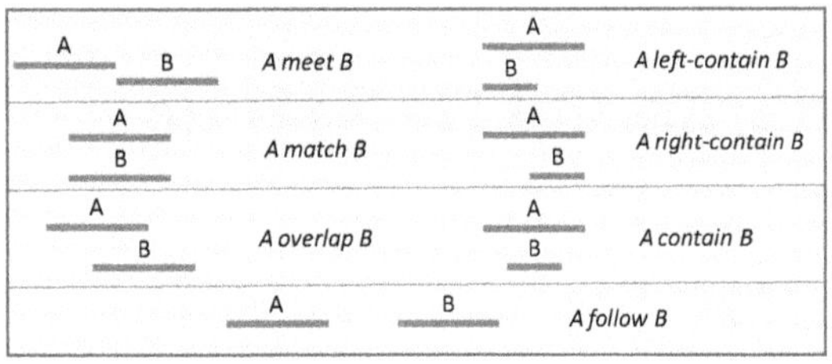

Figure 3: The 7 temporal relations between event-intervals that are considered in this paper.

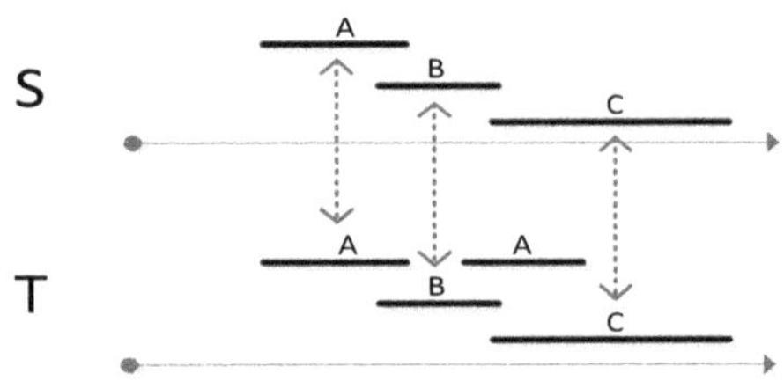

Figure 4: S is a subsequence of T.

ent time for gesturing the same phrase. Similarly, in robot sensor data, a high-level description of a situation is derived from the combination of relations of underlying events.

3. SUBSEQUENCE MATCHING

Problem definition: An e-sequence $S = \{S_1, \ldots, S_n\}$ is a *subsequence* of $T = \{T_1, \ldots, T_m\}$ if S is contained in T. S is contained in T if and only if there exists a sequence T' of intervals, $T' \subseteq T$, $T' = \{T'_1, \ldots, T'_n\}$, such that $T'_i.E = S_i.E, 1 \leq i \leq n$ and $R(S'_i, S'_j) = R(T'_i, T'_j), 1 \leq i < j \leq n$, where $R(\cdot, \cdot)$ returns the relation between two intervals.

Problem complexity: The subsequence matching problem (SSM) is **NP**-hard. This follows by a reduction from CLIQUE to SSM. The proof is omitted for space limitations.

THEOREM 1. *Subsequence matching is* **NP**-*hard.*

Note that in the special case that there is no overlap between intervals, the SSM problem can be solved in polynomial time, as it reduces to subsequence matching in strings.

Another special case is to require that, for a query Q, the matched intervals in S are contiguous. This is also a polynomial variant, which can be solved in time $\mathcal{O}(|S||Q|^2)$.

Algorithm: We present an exact algorithm, Algorithm 1, for determining if an e-sequence Q is a subsequence of S. The algorithm also returns the matching positions. It maintains a partial list that is used for backtracking.

The algorithm scans the larger e-sequence S to find the first interval that shares the same label with the first interval in Q (lines 4,5). If such an interval is never found, the procedure will terminate. Suppose that an interval is found. As it is the first pair matched, no further checks are needed. Then, another interval with the same label as that of the second interval in Q is searched for in S. Searching for succeeding intervals happens recursively (line 13), for the remainders of the S and Q. A variable list solSoFar keeps

Algorithm 1 SubsequenceMatch

```
1: procedure SSM(Q, qPtr, S, sPtr, solSoFar)
2:     if !S or !Q or sPtr > S.length() then
3:         return false, solSoFar
4:     for interval ∈ S[sPtr,...] do
5:         if Q[qPtr].label() = interval.label() then
6:             compatible ← check_relations(Q, qPtr, solSoFar, interval)
7:             if !compatible then
8:                 continue
9:             solSoFar.append(interval)
10:            if qPtr = Q.length()−1 then
11:                return true, solSoFar
12:            else
13:                (success,solSoFar) ← SSM(Q, qPtr, S, interval, solSoFar)
14:                if success then
15:                    return true, solSoFar
16:                else
17:                    solSoFar.pop()
18:    return false, solSoFar
```

the partial solution and is appended a new interval (line 9) or has an interval removed from the end (line 17); if Q is found in S, then upon termination solSoFar contains the corresponding intervals of S. Using this variable facilitates backtracking. Line 6 contains a check as to whether an interval in S, which has been found to have the same label as the next in Q, forms the same relations as those that are required by Q.

There exist $\binom{|S|}{|Q|}$ possible matchings between Q and S; when all interval labels are the same. However, different labels and the backtracking due to interval relations eliminate a large number of candidates and reduce the running time.

Problem variations: Algorithm 1 solves the problem of exact subsequence matching. However it can easily be modified to handle a number of variations, such as:

- The sets of labels are considered equivalent. In other words, we do not require strict matching of labels, but instead we allow substitutions. This is easily implemented by replacing the equality condition of line 5 with the desired equivalence function.
- A number of non-identical interval-relations are tolerated. In addition to solSoFar, we may use a second variable list that denotes how many relations with preceding intervals in solSoFar are violated when choosing solSoFar[i].
- A number of non-identical labels are tolerated. As above, we may use a variable list to maintain the errors.
- Pathological matchings are avoided. As with the Sakoe-Chiba Band [8] and the Itakura Parallelogram [4] for Dynamic Time Warping, we can force limits on the distance between consecutive intervals in S that get matched to Q. This is achieved by changing the limits of line 4.

4. INDEXING

When searching a very large dataset, sequential scan is prohibitive. An indexing scheme is required to improve the retrieval speed. We experiment with several approaches, each providing different trade-offs. We begin by describing the proposed indexing scheme, named Relation Index, while

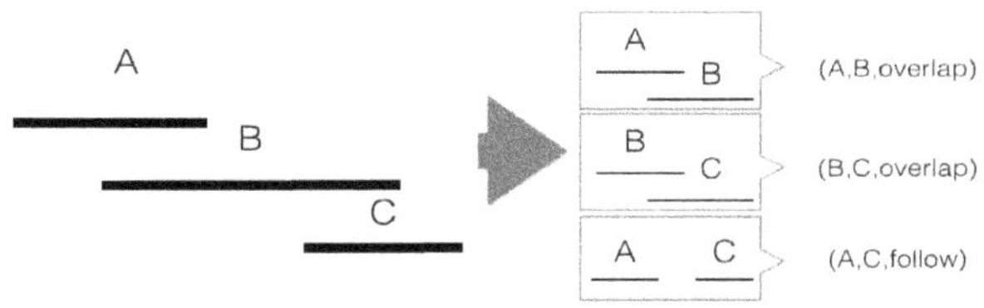

Figure 5: A query using Relation Index decomposes an e-sequence into 2-interval structures. *Linear* variation enumerates only the top two, *Quadratic* enumerates all of them.

the rest serve as baseline methods. All schemes guarantee a 100% recall rate: they return a superset of the valid result.

Relation Index: this approach decomposes each e-sequence into a set of 2-interval e-sequences. Then it relies on an inverted index for performing look-ups. The keys in this inverted index are triples of the form $(\Sigma_i, \Sigma_j, \text{rel}_k)$, with $\Sigma_i, \Sigma_j \in \Sigma$ and rel_k a type of relation. Each index key is associated with the list of e-sequence IDs that contain that specific combination.

In the *index-construction phase*, for each e-sequence $S \in \mathcal{D}$, we enumerate all $\binom{|S|}{2}$ pairs of intervals and obtain their relation. For each formed triple $(\Sigma_i, \Sigma_j, \text{rel}_k)$, the ID of that e-sequence is appended to the appropriate list in the index.

In the *retrieval phase*, a set of interval pairs of the query e-sequence Q is enumerated, and the set of triples $(\Sigma_i, \Sigma_j, \text{rel}_k)$ is produced. There are two approaches for choosing the set of interval pairs, as illustrated also in Figure 5:

1. *Quadratic*: all $\binom{|Q|}{2}$ pairs are enumerated.
2. *Linear*: only $|Q| - 1$ pairs are enumerated; those are extracted serially by examining only pairs of consecutive intervals, i.e. $(Q_i, Q_{i+1}), 1 \le i \le |Q| - 1$.

Given the set of produced triples, we first retrieve the cardinality of the index list of IDs for each key and we sort the keys in ascending order. The sorting helps speed-up the remainder of the process. Note that the set of values corresponding to the first key (the one with the fewer e-sequences containing that particular structure), is already a superset of the valid results for $|Q|$. Then, starting from the two smaller sets, we compute their intersection and then the intersection of the result with the third smallest set, etc. The process terminates when all intersections have been computed, or when the intersection contains at most one element.

Label Index: This approach is similar to the above, but it differs in the type of keys. Instead of having an inverted index for sub-structures of two intervals, we simply create an inverted index for the interval labels. The two aforementioned approaches demonstrate a trade-off between the size of the structures used as keys in the inverted index (the labels correspond to single intervals) and the index size.

Bitmap Index: E-sequences are represented only by the count of each label of the intervals they contain. In order for a query e-sequence Q to be a subsequence of an e-sequence S, it is a necessary, but not sufficient, requirement for S to contain at least as many intervals of each label as those contained in Q. In order to provide fast lookup for each label count, we use hash tables. When searching in the Bitmap Index, each hash table needs to be examined.

String Index: This is the baseline for indexing methods that map e-sequences to strings; each e-sequence in $\mathcal{D}$ is represented as a string. The tokens of the strings are the interval-labels, ordered in the same way as the intervals. For a query e-sequence Q to be a subsequence of an e-sequence S, it is a necessary, but not sufficient, requirement for the string representation of Q to be a subsequence of the string representation of S (easy proof omitted). All strings need to be examined, and the time complexity of each operation is $\mathcal{O}(|S|)$, hence the total time required for a single search is $\mathcal{O}(|\mathcal{D}||S|)$. We may also transform e-sequences into strings as in Figure 2, but it creates sequences of double length. We refer to this scheme as Cpoint Index.

Graph Indexing: We convert e-sequences to graphs, as described by Kostakis and Papapetrou [5], and then apply graph indexing techniques. We experimented with `gIndex` and `FG-Index` implementations provided by Han et al. [3].

Table 1: Dataset Summary.

Dataset	# of e-seq.	max e-seq time	e-seq. length min	e-seq. length max	# of classes
ASL	873	5957	4	41	9
Sensor Net	240	284	47	149	5
Hepatitis	498	7555	15	592	2

5. EXPERIMENTS

We evaluate the exact SSM algorithm and two of its variations on three real datasets, detailed in Table 1.

The variations of SSM that we evaluated are the following: (i) a number of non-identical interval relations are tolerated, and (ii) a number of non-identical interval labels are tolerated. The number of allowed errors takes values in $[0, \binom{|Q|}{2}]$ for the case of relations, and in $[0, |Q|]$ for the case of labels. In comparison to the exact SSM algorithm, these variations investigate more branches of the recursion tree, hence require longer run time. In addition, we expect a higher run time when we increase the number of allowed mismatches. Simply due to the fact that when the algorithm backtracks, this happens at a deeper stage. The expected size of the candidate set increases, too.

We employ a synthetic dataset generator to create very large datasets for benchmarking the indexing methods. We create datasets of one million e-sequences and alphabet size, $|\Sigma|$, equal to 5, 50 and 500. Each e-sequence has length 100. The indexing methods are benchmarked in terms of retrieval time and size of returned candidate set.

For all experiments, for each e-sequence in the dataset, we randomly select a number of intervals and query the dataset for the induced subsequence. The selected size ratios for $|Q|/|S|$, are 0.1, 0.2, 0.3, 0.5 and 0.99.

Results on matching variations: Approximate matching with allowed relation errors was faster than the one with allowed label errors; by several orders of magnitude in some cases. Both were slower than the exact algorithm. As expected, the approximate e-sequence matching variations returned larger candidate sets than the exact version. In addition, the size increased with the allowed error rate. The same holds for the run times. Figure 6 depicts the results for the ASL dataset. For the Hepatitis and sensor network datasets the increase in run times was more significant.

Indexing results: We witnessed that both `gIndex` and `FG-Index` are inefficient for the task at hand. Even for indexing a small dataset of 100 e-sequences with 100 intervals, both methods require over 1.5GB of memory. This is detrimental

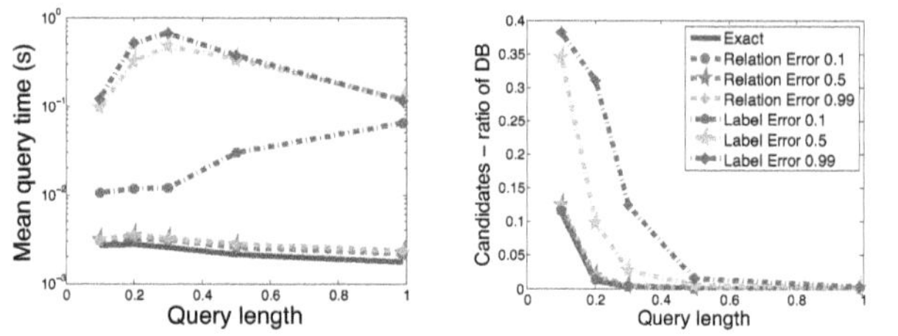

(a) Query runtimes (b) Candidates

Figure 6: Benchmark of SSM algorithm and variations for different values of allowed errors; ASL dataset. Same legend applies.

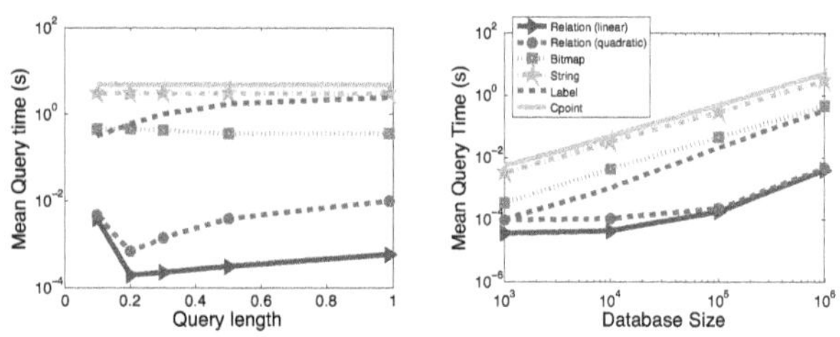

(a) Database size: 10^6 (b) Query length: 0.1

Figure 7: Mean query run time for synthetic dataset, $|\Sigma| = 500$, for variable (a) query e-sequence length and (b) database size.

for scaling up to one million e-sequences. The reason is that an e-sequence of 100 intervals corresponds to a complete graph of 100 vertices, and $\frac{100 \cdot 99}{2} = 4950$ edges. The number of edges is at least two orders of magnitude larger than those used by Han et al. [3]. Thus, we were unable to acquire any results for the datasets we experimented with.

In general, the query times for String, Cpoint and Bitmap Index increase linearly with respect to the size of the database. As expected, this is due to the fact that they perform a linear scan and need to check all instances in $\mathcal{D}$.

For $|\Sigma| = 500$, all methods managed to find the single correct counterparts in all cases; precision 100%. Figure 7 shows the run times. Relation Index is two orders of magnitude faster than Bitmap Index and three orders faster than String Index. Due to the large alphabet size, each combination of interval labels appears few times, hence few lookups in the inverted index suffice to identify the unique candidate.

For $|\Sigma| = 5$, for small query lengths the candidate sets are not singletons. In Figure 8 we notice that for query length ratio of 0.1, Bitmap and Label index compete in runtime with Relation Index but, including String and Cpoint Index, they are practically useless since they return the whole database. Only Relation Index is able to provide moderate pruning of the candidate set. The true candidate set is 27% of $\mathcal{D}$, while Relation Index returns 60% of the DB.

For $|\Sigma| = 50$, Relation Index remains at least an order of magnitude faster than the rest; Figure 9. Surprisingly, for small query lengths, it returns marginally more candidates than String Index. This is due to the fact that Relation Index retains no information on the location in the original e-sequence of the intervals involved in the relation. Hence, it may consider relations that do not correspond to the query's location in the e-sequence. On the other hand, its query time decreases significantly for larger query lengths, because it performs fewer intersections.

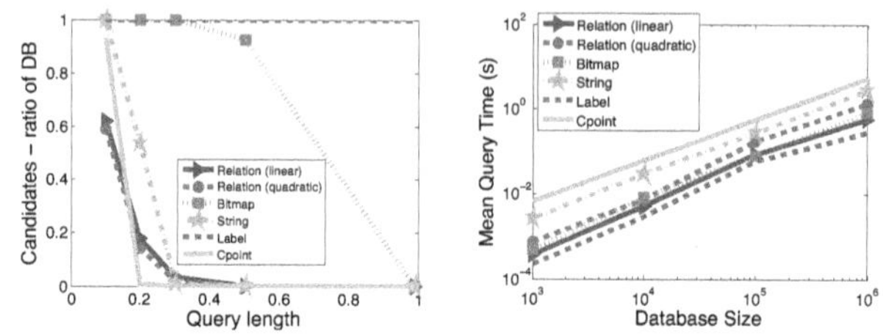

(a) Database size: 10^6 (b) Query length: 0.1

Figure 8: Synthetic dataset $|\Sigma| = 5$. (a) Candidates size for variable query length, (b) run times for variable database size.

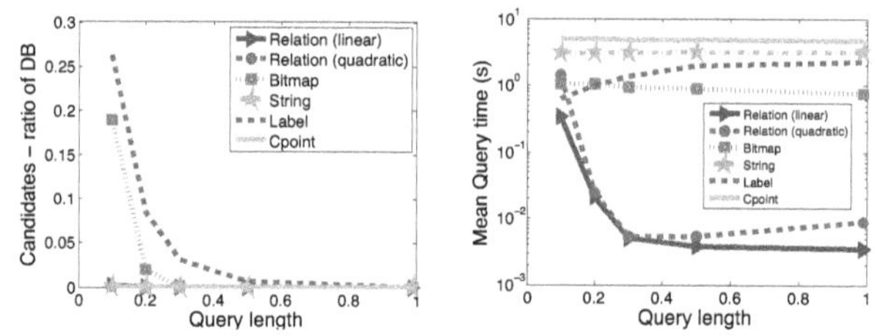

(a) Database size: 10^6 (b) Database size: 10^6

Figure 9: Synthetic dataset $|\Sigma| = 50$. (a) Candidates and (b) run times for variable query e-sequence length.

6. CONCLUSIONS

We studied the problem of subsequence search in databases of event-interval sequences, or e-sequences. We showed that the problem is **NP**-hard and provided an exact algorithm. We showed how to extend the exact algorithm to handle different cases of subsequence matching with errors. Finally, we proposed the Relation Index, a scheme that relies on decomposing e-sequences into pairs of intervals, for speeding up retrieval time. We benchmarked the proposed index against several baselines, including graph indexing schemes.

We witness that Relation Index is superior in terms of run time compared to the other methods. While string indexing methods can be applied, they are inefficient for cases of small alphabet size. Between the linear and quadratic variants of Relation Index, the first is usually faster but the later is more efficient in pruning, when the alphabet size is small.

References

[1] J. F. Allen. Maintaining knowledge about temporal intervals. *Communications of the ACM*, 26(11):832–843, 1983.

[2] B. Bergen and N. Chang. Embodied construction grammar in simulation-based language understanding. *Construction grammars*, pages 147–190, 2005.

[3] W.-S. Han, J. Lee, M.-D. Pham, and J. X. Yu. iGraph: a framework for comparisons of disk-based graph indexing techniques. *PVLDB*, 3(1-2):449–459, 2010.

[4] F. Itakura. Minimum prediction residual principle applied to speech recognition. *IEEE Transactions on Acoustics, Speech & Signal Processing*, 23(1):67–72, 1975.

[5] O. Kostakis and P. Papapetrou. Finding the longest common sub-pattern in sequences of temporal intervals. *Data Mining and Knowledge Discovery*, pages 1–33, 2015.

[6] F. Moerchen and D. Fradkin. Robust mining of time intervals with semi-interval partial order patterns. In *SDM*, 2010.

[7] D. Patel, W. Hsu, and M. Lee. Mining relationships among interval-based events for classification. In *SIGMOD*, 2008.

[8] H. Sakoe and S. Chiba. Dynamic programming algorithm optimization for spoken word recognition. *IEEE Transactions on Signal Processing*, 26(1):43–49, 1978.

Searcher in a Strange Land: Understanding Web Search from Familiar and Unfamiliar Locations

Elad Kravi[1,2], Eugene Agichtein[2,4], Ido Guy[2], Yaron Kanza[3], Avihai Mejer[2], Dan Pelleg[2]
[1] Technion, Israel [2] Yahoo Labs, Israel [3] Cornell Tech, USA [4] Emory University, USA
ekravi@cs.technion.ac.il, {agichtein,amejer}@yahoo-inc.com, {idoguy,pellegd}@acm.org, kanza@cornell.edu

ABSTRACT

With mobile devices, web search is no longer limited to specific locations. People conduct search from practically anywhere, including at home, at work, when traveling and when on vacation. How should this influence search tools and web services? In this paper, we argue that information needs are affected by the familiarity of the environment. To formalize this idea, we propose a new contextualization model for activities on the web. The model distinguishes between a search from a familiar place (*$\mathcal{F}$-search*) and a search from an unfamiliar place (*$\mathcal{U}$-search*). We formalize the notion of familiarity, and propose a method to identify familiar places. An analysis of a query log of millions of users, demonstrates the differences between search activities in familiar and in unfamiliar locations. Our novel take on search contextualization has the potential to improve web applications, such as query autocompletion and search personalization.

Keywords

Web search modeling; search personalization; query language modeling; location-based search

1. INTRODUCTION

Mobile devices have led to a paradigm shift from web search that is mainly conducted in specific locations to search that is being done virtually anywhere and is frequently related to the geographic environment. Consequently, many search engines provide a location-centric search, where the answer is affected by the location of the user, and it has been shown that this improves search results [1]. However, searches by residents and searches by infrequent visitors typically reflect different needs. For example, a search query "train dog", issued by a visitor, should refer to the regulations of traveling with a dog on a train. But for a local, it should relate to puppy training. As another example, in New York City, an obvious query auto-completion of "natural" is "natural history museum" for a tourist, but "natural gas" or "natural food" for residents.

SIGIR '15, August 09–13, 2015, Santiago, Chile.

http://dx.doi.org/10.1145/2766462.2767782.

To address this problem, we propose a new approach to geographical personalization—an approach that is *user*-centric and is based on how familiar the searcher is with the location. Previous studies along this line explored a functional typology, and in particular focused on a small set of labels ("home", "work", and sometimes "school") [10]. We argue that a complementary view revolves around the level of familiarity users have with their surroundings. In this respect, "home" would be considered a familiar place (as would "work" or "school"), *e.g.*, in contrast to a city that the user visits for the first time. The difference being that in a familiar place, basic needs of the user, such as food, transportation and place to live in, are generally part of a routine. In these familiar environments, constituting a user's "natural habitat", the user is likely to have prior knowledge for many basic needs, especially those related to the physical environment. As a result, in a familiar environment, the user may be free to focus on higher-level search activities that satisfy leisure needs and/or may require deeper level of involvement. We call a search in such environments *$\mathcal{F}$-search*, and argue that these environments result in a distinct set of information needs and search patterns.

The natural complement, still under the user-centric view, are unfamiliar places. This generally corresponds to an out-of-town scenario, but not always—a frequented location is considered "familiar", even if distant from the user's home. An unfamiliar place is simply a place that is seldom visited, or is visited for the first time, and we refer to a search in such places as *$\mathcal{U}$-search.*

In this work, we formally define a model that distinguishes between $\mathcal{F}$-search and $\mathcal{U}$-search and we apply it to a search query log on a large scale. We hypothesize that the information needs in unfamiliar locations are different from those in familiar locations and we show experimentally that familiarity affects the type of web searches users conduct.

Several studies compared information needs in mobile versus desktop search [2–4, 6]. Our distinction between search from familiar and unfamiliar locations is device-independent: while we expect more searches from mobile devices to be from unfamiliar locations, our model does not explicitly consider the device type and our findings suggest that both types of searches are conducted from both desktop and mobile devices. Yom-Tov and Diaz [9] showed that in a case of a natural disaster, the information needs considerably change based on the distance from the event's location. White and Buscher [8] compared searches of restaurants by local and non-local users and showed that local knowledge enabled finding venues of higher quality. None of these studies, however, propose or study the distinction between familiar and unfamiliar search locations.

The contributions of this paper include the following.

- A new characterization of search queries to distinguish between $\mathcal{F}$-search in "familiar" places versus $\mathcal{U}$-search in "unfamiliar" locations, defined on a per-user basis.
- Analysis of massive search logs, showing that the distinction provides useful information.
- Qualitative analysis that demonstrates the differences in language models and suggests potential applications, such as query auto-completion.

2. CONTEXTUALIZATION MODEL

We now formally define search familiarity. Let U be a set of users. Each user $u \in U$ is associated with a set of search activities S_u, where an activity is a query submitted to a search engine followed by a click on one of the results.

To each search activity s in S_u, we associate the time of the search and the location of the user at that time, denoted $t(s)$ and $l(s)$, respectively. An activity is also associated with the search query, the clicked link, and the type of the device on which the search was conducted.

The *search locations* of a user u is the set $L_u = \{l(s) \mid s \in S_u\}$ of all the locations of the activities of u. Our goal is to distinguish in L_u between familiar locations, in which u is regularly active, and the locations in which the activity is sporadic. In this research, we partition the geographical space into areas, according to zip-codes, and consider each area as a *place*. Each place is associated with the activities whose location is in this place, and for a specific user u and a place P, the set $S_u(P)$ is the set of searches of u within P.

When the user conducts many searches merely from a single place, we naturally assume that this place is familiar to the user. Next, we consider cases where the user performs searches from more than one place. Intuitively, we define a place as familiar if the search activities of the user reveal that the user has been active in this place during many days and in several occasions.

Formally, we define $Days_u(P)$ as the set of days on which u conducted a search from P, *i.e.*, all the days that contain a time $t(s)$ for some search activity $s \in S_u$ in place P. By $Days_u$, we denote all the days on which there is some search activity of u (in any place). We say that the *time spent* of u at P is the ratio $TS_u(P) = \frac{|Days_u(P)|}{|Days_u|}$. A *return* of user u to place P is a case where first, there is a search activity of u in P, then a search activity of u from at least one place different than P, and again, a search from P.

DEFINITION 2.1 ($\mathcal{F}$-SEARCH). *A place P is familiar to user u if one of the following two cases holds. (i) All the activities of u are in P. (ii) Given a time-spent ratio t and a return count r, P is familiar with respect to t and r, if* (1) *$TS_u(P) \geq t$, i.e. the time spent of u at P is at least t, and* (2) *the number of returns of u to P is at least r. A search activity of user u in a familiar place of u is considered an $\mathcal{F}$-search.*

A place P that is not familiar to user u is considered *unfamiliar* to u and we refer to a search activity of u at such place as *$\mathcal{U}$-search*.

In our experiments, we opted to set r to 2, requiring that a user will return at least twice to a place in order for it to become a familiar place for the user (unless it is the sole search place). Parameter t was set to be 10%, because this balanced between the two conditions, giving them a roughly equal weight. That is, inspecting all pairs (u, P), such that user u conducted a search activity in place P, applying merely Condition 1 with $t = 10\%$ deemed 53.6% of the places in these pairs as familiar, while applying merely Condition 2 with $r = 2$ deemed 53.3% of the places as familiar, causing both conditions to be almost equally selective. With both of these parameters jointly applied, 51.4% of the places were considered familiar to their corresponding user.

3. SEARCH CHARACTERISTICS

In this section, we analyze the different aspects of search activities in familiar and unfamiliar places. First, we present our experimental setup and provide some statistics regarding users and their searches.

Our dataset includes more than a billion search actions sampled from the logs of a popular commercial search engine during a period of six months. These queries were posted by more than 35 million unique users from about 30,000 US zip codes. The dataset includes only users with at least 20 recorded search activities and at least 20 days of activity. On average, during the inspected time period, each of these users performed search activities from 9.15 different places (stdev: 12.79, median: 4). For places, the average number of users per place was 3887 (stdev: 5123.91, median 235).

Distribution of time spent: Obviously, search activities are not conducted everywhere and all the time. So, how are they distributed? There are many places in which people are only seldom active and only a few places in which people are active during many days. To illustrate this, we calculated the distribution of activity days per places and the results are depicted in Fig. 1. A point (d, p) on the graph indicates that in p percent of the search places, the user was active during at least d percent of the days. While 69.3% of the places account for at least 1% of the activity days, only 19.2% of the places account for at least 5% of the days; 11.0% account for at least 10% of the days, and in 6.4% of the places, the activity spanned more than 20% of the user's activity days. This shows the effect of changing t in Definition 2.1—increasing t will reduce the number of places that are deemed familiar, roughly following a power-law distribution.

Home as a familiar place: As a first step of verifying our model, we examined how often the defined home of a user u is deemed a familiar place of u. To this end, we define the *minimum $\mathcal{F}$-search distance from home* as the minimal distance between the location of an $\mathcal{F}$-search and the location of the declared home of the user (for users with at least one familiar place and a declared home). Fig. 2 shows the percentage of users whose minimum $\mathcal{F}$-search distance from home was smaller than a given distance d. For 53.9% of these users, the distance was smaller than 20 kilometers and for 75.4% of the users it was smaller than 100 kilometers. This result agrees with prior work which analyzed all page views, rather than just search actions [7]. Overall, this confirms that in many cases the home of the user is a familiar place, but not always, since the declared home is not always the actual home of the user (e.g., a fake or obsolete address).

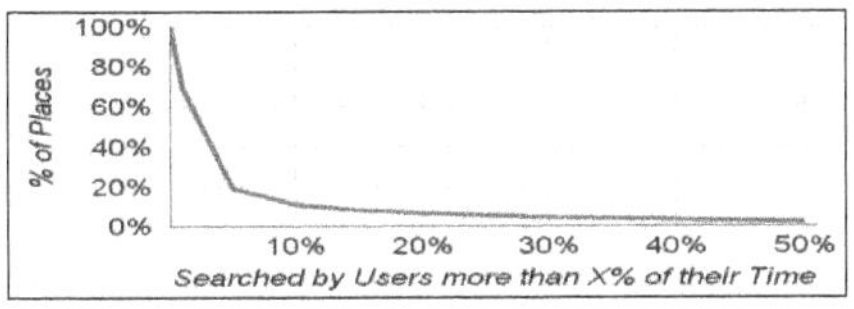

Figure 1: Distribution of activity time in places.

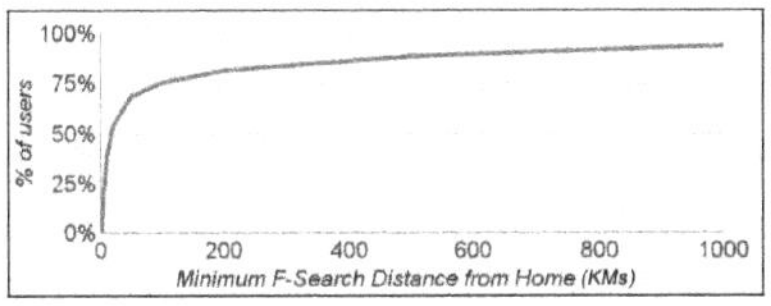

Figure 2: Distribution of the minimum $\mathcal{F}$-search distance from home.

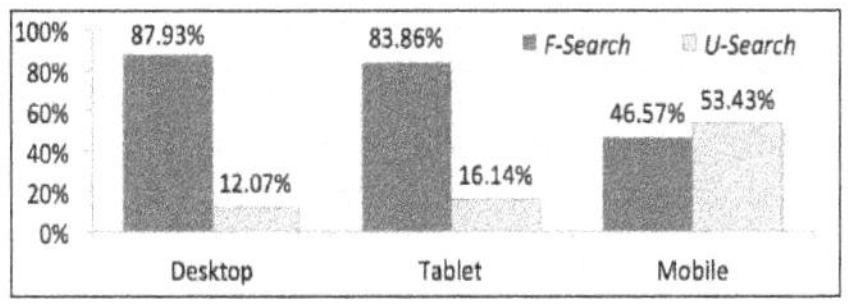

Figure 3: Percentage of $\mathcal{F}$-search and $\mathcal{U}$-search for different devices.

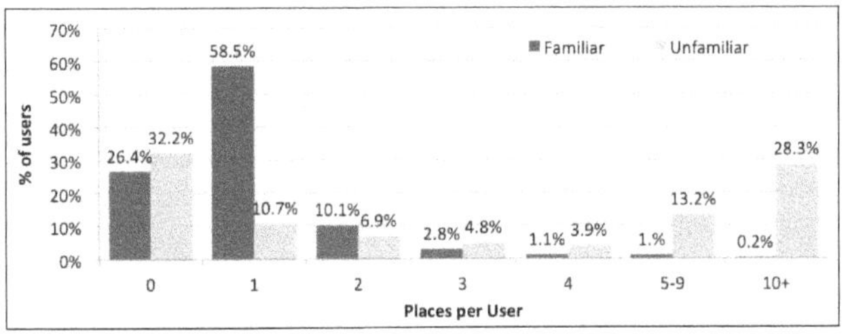

Figure 4: Distribution of the number of familiar and unfamiliar places per user.

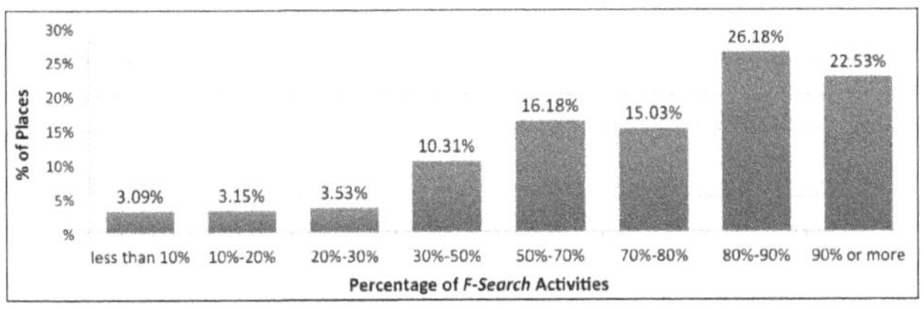

Figure 5: $\mathcal{F}$-search portion per place.

Familiar and unfamiliar places: Fig. 4 presents the distribution of the number of familiar and unfamiliar places per user, according to Definition 2.1. About a quarter of the users do not have familiar places at all; the majority of the users (58.5%) have one familiar place, while a little over 15% of the users have two or more familiar places. As for unfamiliar places, while 32.2% of the users have no $\mathcal{U}$-search activities at all, for the remaining users, the number of unfamiliar places in which they were active is typically much higher than the number of familiar places: only 10.7% of the users have exactly one unfamiliar place in which they posed a query, while 28.3% of the users have ten or more unfamiliar places and 13.7% have 20 or more unfamiliar places.

$\mathcal{F}$-Search and $\mathcal{U}$-search activities per place: Fig. 5 presents the distribution of the portion of $\mathcal{F}$-searches per place. In only 3.1% of the places, less than 10% of the searches were $\mathcal{F}$-searches. In almost 80% of the places (16.2+15.0+26.2+22.5), there are more $\mathcal{F}$-searches than $\mathcal{U}$-searches. In nearly 50% of the places (26.2 + 22.5), over 80% of the search activities were $\mathcal{F}$-searches.

The effect of the device: In Fig. 3, we see that the device affects the percentage of $\mathcal{F}$-searches. As expected, on desktops and on tablets, almost all the searches are $\mathcal{F}$-searches, whereas on mobile phones, slightly more than 50% of the searches are $\mathcal{U}$-searches. Surprisingly, in this measure, tablets are more similar to desktops than to mobile phones.

$\mathcal{F}$-Search vs. $\mathcal{U}$-search query language: To gain better intuition into the differences between $\mathcal{F}$-searches and $\mathcal{U}$-searches, we investigated which keywords characterize queries sent from familiar places as compared to queries sent from unfamiliar places. To this end, we built two specialized language models (LMs)—one for $\mathcal{F}$-searches and one for $\mathcal{U}$-searches. To build language models that would scale to the large query log volume, we used the Berkeley LM library [5], which provides an efficient and scalable implementation of n-gram LMs. For unknown terms we used standard Laplace smoothing with ϵ of 1 over the size of the vocabulary in the training data. After creating the LMs, we set out to identify the terms with the highest divergence between the familiar and unfamiliar models. Specifically, Table 1 presents the top 12 uni-grams and bi-grams with the highest Kullback-Leibler (KL) divergence scores between the two models, after stop-word removal.

Uni-grams		Bi-grams	
$\mathcal{F}$-Search	$\mathcal{U}$-Search	$\mathcal{F}$-Search	$\mathcal{U}$-Search
facebook	google	for sale	new york
sale	restaurant	how to	phone number
free	schedule	facebook login	google search
games	football	to make	new jersey
ebay	ny	homes for	high school
how	lyrics	cool math	how many
login	ct	you tube	hobby lobby
online	store	sales in	in new
craiglist	movie	funeral home	football schedule
recipes	hours	real estate	r us
porn	locations	black friday	movie theater
tube	mall	for kids	nfl scores

Table 1: The top 12 distinctive query terms of $\mathcal{F}$-searches and $\mathcal{U}$-searches.

It can be seen that the $\mathcal{F}$-search lists consist of activities related to shopping, social networks, games, knowledge seeking and adult content. The $\mathcal{U}$-search lists, in contrast, are focused on searching for location or schedule of restaurants, movies, malls, cities, institutes, and sport events. The top word in the uni-gram lists reflect the fundamental difference between the two types of information needs: it is "google" for $\mathcal{U}$-searches and "facebook" for $\mathcal{F}$-searches. Both are the two most popular sites on the web (according to Alexa.com). The first is focused on search and the second on social networking, indicating general information needs while in unfamiliar places, compared to stronger social information needs in familiar places.

Inspecting the main categories of the top 100 uni-grams and bi-grams, we found similar trends. The top $\mathcal{F}$-search queries included keywords that relate to the following categories: `shopping` (15%), e.g., 'sales' and 'amazon'; `social media` (10%), e.g., 'twitter', 'tumblr' and 'youtube'; `multi-media` (9%), e.g., 'video', 'photos', 'netflix', 'watch'; `adult content` (6%), e.g., 'porn', 'pornhub', 'sex'; `news` (6%), e.g., 'news', 'yahoo', and 'msn'; `email` (5%), e.g., 'gmail', 'hotmail'; `games` (4%), e.g., 'angry birds', 'games'; `family` (4%), e.g., 'wife', 'children'; `healthcare` (4%), e.g., 'medicine', 'symptoms', 'pregnant'.

Category	Prefix	Familiar	Unfamiliar
Food	coffee	table:2, shop:4	shop:2, table:5
	steak	marinade:1, house:2	house:1, marinade:4
	pizza	dough:3, places:5	places:3, dough:5
Travel	gas	fireplace:3, station:6	station:3, fireplace:8
	train	crash:1, schedule:7	schedule:2, crash:6
	car	games:2, wash:6	wash:2, games:7
Local	court	cases:1, house:4	house:1, cases:2
	science	news:4, museum:10	museum:3, news:7
	police	scanner:2, department:9	department:2, scanner:4
Leisure	wild	rice:2, horse:5	horse:2, rice:4
	soccer	drills:4, scores:13	scores:5, drills:7
	piano	sheet:2, bar:8	bar:2, sheet:4

Table 2: Sample word completion patterns reporting the first word (prefix), and example completions, excluding stop words, with rank, sorted by decreasing completion frequency for the familiar and unfamiliar settings, respectively.

The top $\mathcal{U}$-searches included keywords related to the following categories: `entertainment` (25%), e.g., 'restaurant', 'movie', 'mall', 'club'; `tourism` (16%), e.g., 'airport', 'weather', 'los angeles', 'texas'; `navigation` (15%), e.g., 'directions', 'location', 'street'; `sports` (5%), e.g., 'nfl', 'espn', 'scores'.

Overall, in familiar places, people search for more profound information that requires time (and state-of-mind) exploring, watching, reading and interacting. In unfamiliar places, on the other hand, there is a greater need for quick lookups for more "touristic" information needs such as food and entertainment, with focus on navigation, directions, and opening times.

4. DISCUSSION

We defined and demonstrated some of the differences between $\mathcal{F}$-search and $\mathcal{U}$-search. This distinction can be of value in practical applications for personalization of search results, news-feed items, or recommendations. Specifically, we now demonstrate how $\mathcal{F}$-search/$\mathcal{U}$-search distinction can be useful for query auto-completion.

4.1 Query Auto-Completion

In query auto-completion, the user types a few characters or the first word of the search query, and the system predicts potential queries. Based on the observations above and on our analysis of familiar and unfamiliar query patterns, we propose to use this information to improve query auto-completion. Specifically, we propose to use different completions for familiar versus unfamiliar places. To gain some intuition into the different completions, we present examples of different completions for common query categories in Table 2. For these examples, we report the initial word of the query, in the dataset described above, together with excerpts from the query completion lists, ranked in decreasing order by completion frequency (in the format of '<completion word>:<rank>'). For example, in the "Food" category, the $\mathcal{F}$-searches focus on aspects more likely to be performed in one's home, such as marinading a steak or buying a coffee table. In contrast, in unfamiliar places, food aspects more likely to focus on immediate needs, such as pizza places (higher on the list for unfamiliar places) or steak houses. A similar effect can be observed in the "Travel", "Local", and "Leisure" categories. For example, for the term "train", the completion "crash" is the first ranked in familiar places, while less frequent (6th) at unfamiliar places, whereas "schedule" is ranked high (2nd) in unfamiliar places, but lower (7th) in familiar places; for the term "court", "cases" is the top completion in familiar places, as users may have more time for looking into these, while "house" is the top completion in unfamiliar places, reflecting more ad-hoc needs. These results suggest that for popular query categories, search suggestions ranking should take user's location familiarity into account.

4.2 Other Applications

Different applications can benefit from a new contextualization model that distinguishes between familiar and unfamiliar locations of search. Obviously, and based on our preliminary results, in web search it is beneficial to provide different results to $\mathcal{F}$-searches and to $\mathcal{U}$-searches. A natural extension is to use the proposed distinction in web advertising and recommender systems: for unfamiliar places, touristic services would be suggested, but in $\mathcal{F}$-search, daily needs will populate the ads and recommendations. Even navigation systems may benefit from the suggested distinction—in an unfamiliar surrounding, people prefer the simplest routes to follow. But locals will take the fastest (traffic-adjusted) way, however convoluted. We are exploring these topics for follow-up works.

5. REFERENCES

[1] P. N. Bennett, F. Radlinski, R. W. White, and E. Yilmaz. Inferring and using location metadata to personalize web search. In *Proc. of SIGIR*, 2011.

[2] K. Church and B. Smyth. Understanding the Intent Behind Mobile Information Needs. In *International Conf. on Intelligent User Interfaces*, 2009.

[3] M. Kamvar and S. Baluja. A Large Scale Study of Wireless Search Behavior: Google Mobile Search. In *Proc. of SIGCHI*, 2006.

[4] M. Kamvar, M. Kellar, R. Patel, and Y. Xu. Computers and Iphones and Mobile Phones, Oh My!: A Logs-based Comparison of Search Users on Different Devices. In *Proc. of WWW*, 2009.

[5] A. Pauls and D. Klein. Faster and smaller n-gram language models. In *Proc. of the 49th Annual Meeting of the Association for Computational Linguistics: Human Language Technologies-Volume 1*, 2011.

[6] D. Pelleg, D. Savenkov, and E. Agichtein. Touch Screens for Touchy Issues: Analysis of Accessing Sensitive Information from Mobile Devices. In *ICWSM*, 2013.

[7] D. Pelleg, E. Yom-Tov, and Y. Maarek. Can you believe an anonymous contributor? on truthfulness in Yahoo! answers. In *SocialCom*, 2012.

[8] R. White and G. Buscher. Characterizing Local Interests and Local Knowledge. In *SIGCHI*, 2012.

[9] E. Yom-Tov and F. Diaz. Out of Sight, Not out of Mind: On the Effect of Social and Physical Detachment on Information Need. In *SIGIR*, 2011.

[10] H. Zang and J. Bolot. Anonymization of location data does not work: A large-scale measurement study. In *Proc. of MobiCom*, 2011.

Evaluating Retrieval Models through Histogram Analysis

Kriste Krstovski[†,§]
kriste@cs.umass.edu

David A. Smith[‡]
dasmith@ccs.neu.edu

Michael J. Kurtz[§]
kurtz@cfa.harvard.edu

[†]College of Information and Computer Sciences
University of Massachusetts Amherst
Amherst, MA, 01003

[‡]College of Computer and Information Science
Northeastern University
Boston, MA, 02115

[§]Harvard-Smithsonian Center for Astrophysics
Cambridge, MA, 02138

ABSTRACT

We present a novel approach for efficiently evaluating the performance of retrieval models and introduce two evaluation metrics: **Distributional Overlap** (DO), which compares the clustering of scores of relevant and non-relevant documents, and **Histogram Slope Analysis** (HSA), which examines the log of the empirical distributions of relevant and non-relevant documents. Unlike rank evaluation metrics such as mean average precision (MAP) and normalized discounted cumulative gain (NDCG), DO and HSA only require calculating model scores of queries and a fixed sample of relevant and non-relevant documents rather than scoring the entire collection, even implicitly by means of an inverted index. In experimental meta-evaluations, we find that HSA achieves high correlation with MAP and NDCG on a monolingual and a cross-language document similarity task; on four ad-hoc web retrieval tasks; and on an analysis of ten TREC tasks from the past ten years. In addition, when evaluating latent Dirichlet allocation (LDA) models on document similarity tasks, HSA achieves better correlation with MAP and NCDG than perplexity, an intrinsic metric widely used with topic models.

Categories and Subject Descriptors: H.3.3 [Information Search and Retrieval]: Retrieval models, Selection process

Keywords: efficient evaluation; retrieval models; topic models

1 Introduction

Evaluating retrieval models with ranking metrics, such as mean average precision (MAP) and normalized discounted cumulative gain (NDCG), requires computing, in the worst case, the relevance score of each query against each member of a collection of n documents and then sorting the results. In practice, of course, most retrieval systems achieve vastly better performance by: exploiting inverted indices containing sufficient statistics on features such as terms and n-grams; by performing lossless or lossy pruning of posting lists; and by keeping track of only the top k documents for each query. For large collections, however, building even one index can be costly, and evaluating multiple models may require the creation of multiple indices. Reindexing can become even more common when working with continuous representations, as in image retrieval or in using topic models for text.

Before building new indices and tuning other efficiency parameters of an IR system, researchers may want some validation that a new feature, such as skip n-grams or LDA [1] topics, will positively impact effectiveness on the target task. *Rescoring* ranked lists generated by a baseline system provides one such check on model validity; however, new models will be most useful when they identify relevant results outside the output of the baseline system.

To alleviate these drawbacks, this paper proposes a novel approach for efficiently evaluating retrieval models by analyzing the relationship between histograms computed over the empirical distribution of relevance scores of query relevant and non-relevant documents. We analyze the performance of two metrics based on these histograms—**Distributional Overlap** (DO) and **Histogram Slope Analysis** (HSA)—in three different settings: monolingual and cross-language document-similarity retrieval; ad-hoc web retrieval; and a meta-evaluation of the ranked lists of ten TREC tracks from the past ten years. HSA achieves better correlation with MAP and NDCG on full collections than does MAP or NCDG on the subcollections used by HSA. In addition, when evaluating LDA models on document similarity tasks, HSA achieves better correlation with MAP and NCDG than perplexity, an intrinsic metric widely used with topic models.

SIGIR'15, August 09 - 13, 2015, Santiago, Chile.
© 2015 ACM. ISBN 978-1-4503-3621-5/15/08 ...$15.00.
DOI: http://dx.doi.org/10.1145/2766462.2767821.

2 Histogram Analysis

Our evaluation approach is based, first of all, on the simple notion that a good retrieval model should cluster relevant documents together with higher scores than non-relevant documents (We discuss below the relation to other such "cluster hypotheses".). Better retrieval models, under this hypothesis, will have a relatively small overlap between the scores of relevant and non-relevant documents. We use the volume of the distributional overlap between the histograms of query relevant and non-relevant documents to define our first evaluation metric—Distributional Overlap (DO).

Computing the log ratio between the histograms of the query relevant and non-relevant documents gives us the proportion of relevant documents that we would expect to find at certain relevance values. Across different retrieval models, as the performance of the model improves, the proportion of relevant documents found at higher relevance scores should increase thus making the slope of the histogram analysis steeper going down from higher to lower values on the relevance scale. We define this slope as an evaluation metric that we call Histogram Slope Analysis (HSA).

By computing DO and HSA from the full set of relevant documents and a relatively small sample of non-relevant documents, we are able to evaluate retrieval models much more efficiently than with metrics computed over ranked lists of documents. We simply need to summarize the empirical distribution of relevant and non-relevant documents using histograms with some fixed number of bins.

3 Computing DO and HSA

For a test collection of k queries $Q = q_1, q_2, q_3, ...q_k$ and sets of query relevant $R_{q_i} = r_1^i, r_2^i, r_3^i, ...r_m^i$ and non-relevant $NR_{q_i} = nr_1^i, r_2^i, r_3^i, ...r_n^i$ documents, we evaluate retrieval model's scoring function $Score_f$ to get $V_R = Score_f(q_i, R_{q_i})$ and $V_{NR} = Score_f(q_i, NR_{q_i})$. Relevance scores have range of values that vary depending on the scoring function of the retrieval model. Different retrieval models generate relevance values on different scales. In order to compare and rank their performance, relevance values generated by each model are normalized to a range of [0,1].

Using a set B of equally spaced bins, histograms are computed over the two sets of relevance scores to give $H_R = [h_1^r, h_2^r, h_3^r, ..., h_{|B|}^r]$ and $H_{NR} = [h_1^{nr}, h_2^{nr}, h_3^{nr}, ..., h_{|B|}^{nr}]$. The h_b^r and h_b^{nr} are the counts of the number of times relevant and non-relevant scores fall within the bin centered at b: $h_b^r = \#(V_R \in b)$, $h_b^{nr} = \#(V_{NR} \in b)$. Since in typical real document collections the portion of query relevant documents is significantly smaller than non-relevant documents, we use log scale for the frequency axis when creating the two histograms. We further define a set of supported bins $B' = \{b' : h_{b'}^r, h_{b'}^{nr} \neq 0\}$. Distributional Overlap measures the volume of the overlap between the two histograms:

$$DO = \sum_{b' \in B'} \log(\min(h_{b'}^r, h_{b'}^{nr})) \qquad (1)$$

Figure 1 illustrates an example of computing DO. In this figure we show the joint histogram plots across two different document similarity models on the task of finding document translation pairs. Both similarity models are based on the Polylingual Topic Model (PLTM) [5] configured with number of topics T=50 and 500. We detail this experimental setup in §5.1.

For HSA, we take the log ratio of the two histograms for the bins $b' \in B'$ where they are both observed $O_{b'} = \log(\frac{H_{R_{b'}}}{H_{NR_{b'}}})$ and then fit a linear function $O_{b'} = \alpha + \beta b' + \epsilon_{b'}$ using linear least squares regression. We define HSA to be the estimated slope:

$$HSA \ = \ \hat{\beta} = \frac{\sum_{b' \in B'}(b' - \bar{B}')(O_{b'} - \bar{O})}{\sum_{b' \in B'}(b' - \bar{B}')^2} \qquad (2)$$

Figure 2 shows an example of computing HSA across two retrieval models on the TREC Web Track 2009. In this example we compute HSA over the relevance scores of query relevant and non-relevant web pages obtained using BM25, which gave the worst NDCG, and the sequential dependence model (SDM), which achieved the highest NDCG. See §5.2 for experimental details. The first two subplots show the log histograms of the query relevant (R) and non-relevant documents (NR). The bottom two subplots show the log ratio of the empirical distributions of R and NR scores $O_{b'}$ along with the linear fit $\hat{O}_{b'}$.

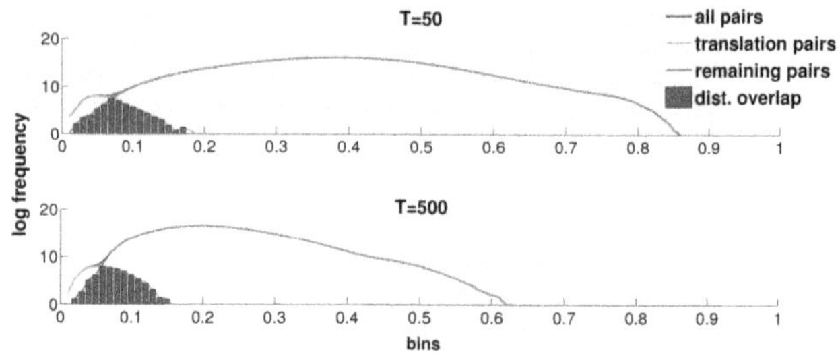

Figure 1: Computing DO to evaluate PLTM models on the task of retrieving document translation pairs. PLTM with 50 topics: acc.=94.3%; with 500 topics, acc.=99.3%.

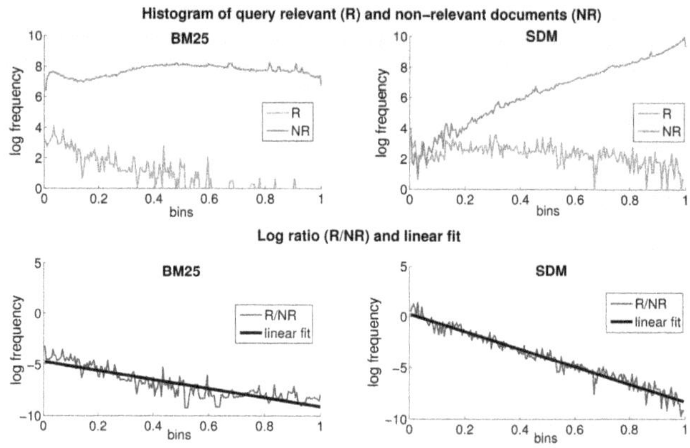

Figure 2: Computing HSA to evaluate ad-hoc retrieval models on the TREC Web Track 2009. NDCG(BM25)=0.106, NDCG(SDM)=0.293.

4 Previous Work

In their original work, Jardine and van Rijsbergen [3] used histograms to define one of the prominent concepts in information retrieval: the cluster hypothesis, which states that "closely associated documents tend to be relevant to the same requests". The hypothesis introduced the cluster based retrieval [8] and many of its variants [2]. To measure the potential of the cluster based retrieval on a particular document collection, Jardine and van Rijsbergen [3] proposed the cluster hypothesis test. For a given collection and a set of queries the test measures the similarity between all query relevant documents and between all query relevant and non-relevant documents. Aside from the cluster hypothesis test, researchers have proposed other measures of the cluster hypothesis [7, 9]. More recently, Raiber and Kurland [6] analyzed how these measures correlate with the performance of cluster based retrieval. While different measures exist for the cluster hypothesis they have not found their use in evaluating the performance of different retrieval models.

Although developed independently, the DO metric is consistent with the cluster hypothesis. Unlike cluster hypothesis tests, which asks whether two relevant documents are similar to each other, with DO we analyze the similarity of relevance scores between query relevant and non-relevant documents. Since DO is reflecting on the cluster hypothesis one may also consider DO as an intuitive implementation of the cluster hypothesis test in the space of query relevance values. As we shall see, however, HSA is better correlated with established ranking metrics than DO.

5 Experimental Results

The purpose of developing DO and HSA was to be able to evaluate and predict the performance of retrieval models. To demonstrate this ability we compare the values of DO and HSA with existing IR metrics and evaluate their predictive power by performing linear correlation using Pearson correlation coefficient (R). Using Spearman's rank correlation coefficient (ρ) we compute the correlation between the ranked list of models' performance sorted by existing IR metrics and the ranked list obtained using DO and HSA. We demonstrate the generality of our evaluation approach across different retrieval tasks, models, and scoring functions, which we group into three experimental setups: (1) document similarity models where the scoring function computes similarity between two documents, (2) ad-hoc retrieval where the scoring functions represents the relevance score of the document given a query, and (3) a meta-evaluation of ranked lists submitted to ten TREC tracks in the past ten years. With our last experimental setup, we also demonstrate that DO and HSA can be computed using the ranks of the retrieved documents as relevance values.

5.1 Document Similarity Tasks

We first showcase DO and HSA on two document similarity tasks: prior-art patent search [10] and the cross-language IR (CLIR) task of finding document translations [4]. Both tasks use topic models to retrieve similar documents. Experiments were performed with 7 different topic configurations. More specifically, the prior-art patent search task uses LDA with number of topics set to T=50, 100, 200, 500, 1k, 2k and 5k. While on the CLIR task PLTMs were configured with T=100, 200, 300, 400, 500, 700 and 1k. On the patent retrieval task, following the experimental setup of [10], model performance was evaluated using MAP computed over 372 queries and a test collection of 70k patents. In [4], performance of PLTMs was evaluated on a test collection of ~14k English-Spanish Europarl speeches based on the percentage of true document translation pairs (out of the whole test set) that the model ranked as most similar. This metric is referred to as "percentage at rank one" (P@1).

Table 1 shows the correlation coefficients computed between our evaluation metrics and MAP and P@1. Topic models are typically evaluated intrinsically using perplexity

Correlation	MAP(LDA)			P@1(PLTM)		
	DO	HSA	Perp.	DO	HSA	Perp.
R	-0.75	0.92	-0.84	0.00	0.71	-0.63
ρ	0.64	0.93	0.89	0.11	0.64	0.25

Table 1: Predicting document similarity model performance using DO, HSA and perplexity: Pearson (R) and Spearman's (ρ) coef. computed over MAP and P@1.

Model	MAP[s]	DO[s]	HSA[s]	Perplexity[s]
LDA T=50	288.1	28.2	28.2	11.1
LDA T=100	224.8	33.0	33.0	27.2
LDA T=200	240.1	47.5	47.6	53.6
LDA T=500	345.9	99.2	99.2	143.1
LDA T=1k	405.6	176.3	176.3	3166.7
LDA T=2k	559.5	333.6	333.6	32930.0
LDA T=5k	1037.4	816.2	816.2	46340.0

Table 2: Absolute computation time for MAP, DO, HSA and perplexity for evaluating patent retrieval.

on held-out data, which is considered as a good predictor of the model performance on an extrinsic task. Correlation coefficients were also computed for this metric in order to compare its predictive power with DO and HSA.

On both retrieval tasks, HSA exhibits better linear and rank correlation compared to perplexity, while the linear and rank correlation of all three metrics is higher with MAP compared to P@1. In practice this allows us to compute HSA only on the set of query relevant and non-relevant patents and predict the performance of the document similarity model without the need of processing all patents in the collection.

Table 2 shows the absolute computation times for each evaluation metric when computed on the patent search task across different LDA model configurations. Computation time between DO and HSA differs in the second step where computing the volume requires ~10ms while computing the slope takes ~60ms. It is evident from this table that, both DO and HSA, are the most efficient metrics to compute compared to MAP and perplexity. On the CLIR task, due to the nature of the evaluation metric, the computation time for MAP, DO and HSA, while being different for each metric, is equal across the different model configurations. While perplexity, as in the case with LDA, grows linearly with the number of topics. Computing DO and HSA on the PLTM model we achieve a relative speed improvement of 5.12 times over MAP.

5.2 Ad-Hoc Retrieval Tasks

We conducted experiments using query sets from 4 previous TREC Web Tracks (2009-2012). Experiments were performed on the ClueWeb09 Category-B with spam filtering (a threshold of 60 using the Waterloo spam scores) collection using the open source retrieval engine Galago[1] with 7 different retrieval models: BM25, BM25RF, RM, SDM and three QL models with various parameter settings. Table 3 and Table 4 show the correlation coefficient values for DO and HSA computed across three IR metrics: MAP, precision at ten (P@10), and NDCG. All evaluation metrics were

[1]http://www.lemurproject.org/galago.php

Web Track	HSA			DO		
	MAP	P@10	NDCG	MAP	P@10	NDCG
2009	0.89	0.91	0.95	0.84	0.88	0.94
2010	0.88	0.71	0.93	0.64	0.60	0.79
2011	0.91	0.93	0.99	0.77	0.81	0.92
2012	0.89	0.87	0.97	0.79	0.79	0.92

Table 3: Evaluating ad-hoc retrieval models using DO and HSA: Pearson (R) coef. computed across MAP, P@10 and NDCG.

Web Track	HSA			DO		
	MAP	P@10	NDCG	MAP	P@10	NDCG
2009	0.82	0.86	0.86	-0.86	-0.89	-0.89
2010	0.93	0.79	0.96	-0.46	-0.68	-0.50
2011	1.00	0.96	1.00	-0.82	-0.79	-0.82
2012	0.71	0.82	0.75	-0.46	-0.61	-0.39

Table 4: Evaluating ad-hoc retrieval models using DO and HSA: Spearman's (ρ) coef. computed across MAP, P@10 and NDCG.

computed using the top 10k retrieved documents and their relevance scores.

Across all evaluation sets, HSA has a high linear and rank correlation with all three IR metrics. While DO has a high linear correlation, its rank correlation is negative, since a large overlap between the distributions of relevant and non-relevant documents is undesirable.

5.3 TREC Ranked Lists

So far in our experiments, we have computed DO and HSA using a relatively large set of query based relevance scores (e.g. 70k patents and 10k ClueWeb documents). However, typical IR systems, across various tasks, are configured to return the top k documents, which is usually a relatively smaller percentage of all the documents in the collection. For example, across different TREC tracks, ranked lists submitted by participants typically consist of the top 1k retrieved documents. Relevance values obtained from such ranked lists are a very small subset on the values across the whole collection. To measure the correlation when DO and HSA are computed over such small sample sets of relevance values we used ranked lists submitted on ten TREC tracks from the past ten years (2004-2013). From each year's TREC we randomly picked a track and for the selected track we randomly chose 7 submitted ranked lists. Unlike previous experimental settings where we computed DO and HSA using the relevance values generated by the retrieval models, in this experimental setup we compute DO and HSA over the normalized values of the document ranks. This is due to the fact that in some instances the relevance scores in the ranked lists are not properly formatted or missing and moreover there is no information on the relevance function used. Table 5 and Table 6 show the linear and rank correlation coefficients computed across various TREC tracks. Results in these tables shown that over all ten tracks HSA has a high linear and rank correlation with MAP and NDCG.

TREC Track	HSA			DO		
	MAP	P@10	NDCG	MAP	P@10	NDCG
Microblog '13	0.98	0.95	0.93	-0.82	-0.80	-0.70
Medical '12	0.90	0.84	0.94	0.30	0.10	0.50
Web '11	0.75	0.86	0.79	0.80	0.51	0.90
Session '10	0.82	0.75	0.84	0.46	0.27	0.68
Chemical '09	0.85	0.95	0.82	0.66	0.84	0.65
Enterprise '08	0.93	-0.14	0.93	0.99	0.21	0.99
Million '07	0.85	0.93	0.88	0.87	0.89	0.94
Terabyte '06	0.97	0.98	1.00	0.94	0.97	0.97
Robust '05	0.75	0.60	0.74	0.82	0.83	0.91
Web '04	0.87	0.63	0.88	-0.41	-0.02	-0.36

Table 5: Evaluating TREC track submissions using DO and HSA: Pearson (R) coef. computed across MAP, P@10, and NDCG.

TREC Track	HSA			DO		
	MAP	P@10	NDCG	MAP	P@10	NDCG
Microblog '13	0.82	0.79	0.86	-0.53	-0.64	-0.51
Medical '12	0.96	0.82	0.96	-0.32	-0.14	-0.32
Web '11	0.71	0.86	0.75	-0.68	-0.43	-0.71
Session '10	0.71	0.86	0.64	-0.54	-0.32	-0.75
Chemical '09	0.82	0.86	0.79	-0.96	-0.89	-0.93
Enterprise '08	0.86	-0.14	0.75	-0.86	-0.04	-0.89
Million '07	0.86	0.68	0.86	-0.89	-0.89	-0.89
Terabyte '06	0.86	0.43	0.86	-0.18	-0.29	-0.12
Robust '05	0.78	0.57	0.79	-0.67	-0.54	-0.68
Web '04	0.68	0.39	0.71	0.00	-0.07	-0.07

Table 6: Evaluating TREC track submissions using DO and HSA: Spearman's (ρ) coef. computed across MAP, P@10, and NDCG.

6 Conclusion and Future Work

We presented two evaluation metrics, DO and HSA, that use a novel approach for evaluating retrieval models performance through histogram analysis. We showed that HSA has a high linear and rank correlation with MAP and NDCG while being more efficient to compute. These metrics can predict the performance of document retrieval models without the need for indexing and searching entire collections. In the future, we plan to explore the relationship between the number of query relevant and non-relevant score values used to compute HSA and its effect on the correlation coefficients.

References

[1] D. M. Blei, A. Y. Ng, and M. I. Jordan. Latent Dirichlet allocation. *JMLR*, 3:993–1022, 2003.

[2] W. Croft. A model of cluster searching based on classification. *Information Systems*, 5(3):189–195, 1980.

[3] N. Jardine and C. J. van Rijsbergen. The use of hierarchical clustering in information retrieval. *Information Storage and Retrieval*, 7:217–240, 1971.

[4] K. Krstovski and D. A. Smith. Online polylingual topic models for fast document translation detection. In *WMT'11*, pages 252–261, 2013.

[5] D. Mimno, H. Wallach, J. Naradowsky, D. A. Smith, and A. McCallum. Polylingual topic models. In *EMNLP'09*, pages 880–889, 2009.

[6] F. Raiber and O. Kurland. The correlation between cluster hypothesis tests and the effectiveness of cluster-based retrieval. In *SIGIR '14*, pages 1155–1158, 2014.

[7] M. D. Smucker, J. Allan, and B. Carterette. A comparison of statistical significance tests for information retrieval evaluation. In *CIKM '07*, pages 623–632, 2007.

[8] C. van Rijsbergen. *Automatic Information Structuring and Retrieval*. PhD thesis, University of Cambridge, 1972.

[9] E. M. Voorhees. The cluster hypothesis revisited. In *SIGIR '85*, pages 188–196, 1985.

[10] X. Xue and W. B. Croft. Transforming patents into prior-art queries. In *SIGIR '09*, pages 808–809, 2009.

Inter-Category Variation in Location Search

Chia-Jung Lee[†], Nick Craswell[‡] and Vanessa Murdock[‡]
[†]College of Information and Computer Sciences, University of Massachusetts Amherst, MA, USA
[‡]Microsoft, Redmond, WA, USA
cjlee@cs.umass.edu, {nickcr, vanmur}@microsoft.com

ABSTRACT

When searching for place entities such as businesses or points of interest, the desired place may be close (finding the nearest ATM) or far away (finding a hotel in another city). Understanding the role of distance in predicting user interests can guide the design of location search and recommendation systems. We analyze a large dataset of location searches on GPS-enabled mobile devices with 15 location categories. We model user-location distance based on raw geographic distance (kilometers) and intervening opportunities (nth closest). Both models are helpful in predicting user interests, with the intervening opportunity model performing somewhat better. We find significant inter-category variation. For instance, the closest movie theater is selected in 17.7% of cases, while the closest restaurant in only 2.1% of cases. Overall, we recommend taking category information into account when modeling location preferences of users in search and recommendation systems.

Categories and Subject Descriptors

H.3.3 [**Information Storage and Retrieval**]: Information Search and Retrieval

Keywords

Mobile local search; category; rank distance; cross entropy

1. INTRODUCTION

Users interested in finding a location entity are increasingly using mobile devices to search, rather than desktop machines[1]. On mobile devices, the user's location context is available with greater precision[2], allowing it to answer questions such as *What is the closest movie theater?* By contrast, the location of a desktop machine is inferred from its IP address, giving a city-level estimate. This would allow us to list which movie theaters are in the city, but not which is closest to the user. Given this improved location context, it is possible to study specific scenarios such as reranking search results [7] or identifying the specific place a user is currently visiting [12]. While such advances in specific problem areas are valuable, they do not give us an overview of location intent on these new devices. Insights into location intent can guide our design for location-based applications, machine learning systems and evaluation metrics.

Geolocated mobile search logs from a general-purpose search engine provide an opportunity to study what types of location entities users find and select, and how this relates to their location context. Location context includes the location of the user, the distance of the user from the relevant entity, and the density of alternative entities near the user. The relationship between these aspects is complex, and may vary according to the category of entity. For example, if the density of nearby hotels and nearby ATMs is similar, that does not mean that users who search for the nearest ATM will also search for the nearest hotel. Motivated by this intuition, this study focuses on modeling user-entity distance and inter-category differences in location preference.

Our predictive models are based on raw geographic distance (*How many meters is the ATM from me?*), and intervening opportunities (*How many other ATMs are closer?*). We make minimal assumptions about how an end-to-end system would work, by for example using querying, mapping and ranking interfaces to narrow down the search. We analyse user needs in a system-agnostic manner.

Aggregating data on local intent is a challenging problem. Our dataset is from the general-purpose Bing search engine. During the time of our data collection, the system returns up to three location results in the first instance, then the user can opt to view more. We do not employ human relevance assessors to judge the quality of the results, because we do not wish to rely on a third party to understand location intent. Instead we employ information on which results were selected in the touch-based interface, on the assumption that selected results are of interest. Unlike previous studies [7] we do not simply rerank the results to put the clicked item higher. Although reranking offers some benefit to users, it does not give a clear picture of location intent characterization and in-context information needs. For these reasons, we aggregate over queries for studying distance and category, and use cross entropy to evaluate predicted click distributions over location entities.

[1]`http://searchengineland.com/study-consumers-increasingly-turn-mobile-varied-media-combinations-last-mile-200283` visited February 2015
[2]A median accuracy of 75 meters is reported in [12]

SIGIR'15, August 09 - 13, 2015, Santiago, Chile

ACM 978-1-4503-3621-5/15/08 ...$15.00
DOI: http://dx.doi.org/10.1145/2766462.2767797.

Cross entropy has been used to characterize the amount of information in personalized search signals [9], and to evaluate click position bias in search results [3]. Similarly, we use cross entropy to measure the predictability of distance models for different business categories. Our results suggest significant inter-category variation, with the intervening opportunity model performing better in most cases.

2. RELATED WORK

Mobile search is a relatively new field because mobile phones were not as commonly used for search prior to 2007. There are some early studies of mobile information seeking behavior [2, 4], but they do not relate directly to distance modeling or evaluation. Lymberopoulos et al. [8] predicted user clicks on mobile devices by incorporating location at different levels of granularity (e.g., zip code or state), and suggested the state-level models achieves higher accuracy than a US-wide model. Lv et al. [7] noted that the click-through rate of a business in local search sublinearly decreases with the distance to the user, which is evaluated using a click-based reranking framework. Berberich et al. [1] leveraged direction requests from an online mapping service to determine a reasonable travel distance for a user to a business, along with the business density in the area surrounding the business. We consider a superset of these scenarios, since we gather data from a general-purpose system that allows for driving directions, phone calls and informational intent.

One key exploration is to study the notion of intervening opportunities in the context of local search on mobile devices. In 1940, Stouffer [13] proposed that whether a person is willing to move to another place is dependent not on the geographic distance, but on the number of comparable alternatives along the way. This mobility model explained user movements from one neighborhood to another in the city of Cleveland. Our work does not make claims about the movements of people in a city; rather we reference his characterization to patronize a business or visit a point of interest. We adopt Stouffer's proposal that a person's willingness to visit a business is related to the number of comparable intervening businesses available to that person, which we denote as *rank distance*. Noulas et al. [10] used intervening opportunities to model Foursquare check-ins, finding that the probability of transitioning to a new location is inversely proportional to a power of its rank. Kumar et al. [5] used a combination of distance and rank distance to model geographic choice. They tested this using driving directions data with a source and destination address, taking cases where the destination address is a restaurant and interpreting the source address as the user's location.

We base our evaluation approach on cross entropy. Entropy has been used widely to measure the degree of predictability of a probability distribution. Mei and Church [9], for instance, estimated the size of the search space of the web using entropy, and further computed the conditional entropy to characterize the contribution of personalization in web search. Craswell et al. [3] compared cross entropy among various models of click position bias in a manner that is agnostic to the model itself.

3. EVALUATING DISTANCE MODELS

Raw distance model. Given GPS coordinates, the most intuitive model is to directly measure the raw physical distance between users and places. We compute this using the great circle distance[3]. To avoid false assumptions, we opt for a non-parametric approach that counts the number of times entities are clicked given they were x kilometers away from users. In the training data, we discretize the raw distance and record the probability of click at each tick. We test different bucketing sizes including 1, 5 and 10 kilometers.

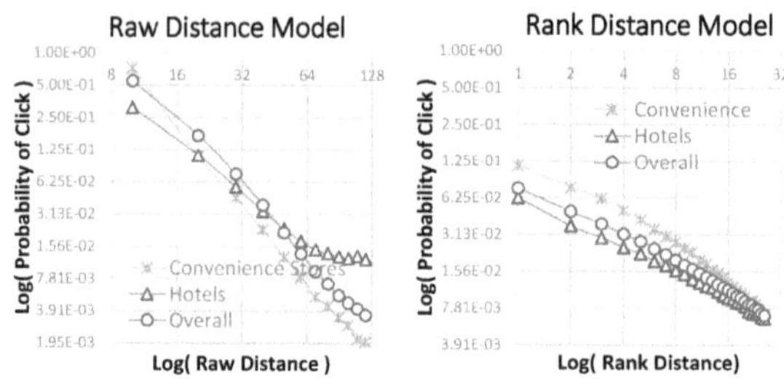

Figure 1: The log-log plot for the probability distribution of clicks as a function of raw (left) and rank (right) distance. The distributions of categories Hotels and Convenience stores differ more in the raw distance model than the rank distance model.

Rank distance model. For a place v, we define its rank distance as the number of places w that are in the same category as v but are closer to a user u than v is. That is, $rank_u(v) = |w : d(u,w) < d(u,v)| + 1$. We count the number of times an entity is clicked at each rank, based on which the probability of click is calculated.

An important difference between rank distance and raw distance is related to business density. Users in a dense area, with many in-category alternatives, may tend to have lower raw distance and users in a sparse area will have higher raw distance. This makes it difficult for a single raw distance model to explain users in both areas. By contrast, a rank distance model naturally predicts lower distances in dense areas because there are many nearby intervening opportunities. For both models, we consider all nearby entities in the same category as alternatives[4], not just those that were retrieved by the engine. We build both models in a per-category manner. Figure 1 shows the resulting distance models for two example categories. In the raw distance model, the difference in click distributions is evident where we see the probability mass spreads out for the hotel entities, implying that distance may play a less critical role for hotel selection. Interestingly, such variation in categories appears less obvious in the rank distance model, suggesting that rank distance is more invariant of categories, resembling the findings of human mobility in cities [10].

Cross Entropy. Evaluating local search is a challenging problem. The existing Cranfield style evaluation [11] is less appropriate in local search. Unlike web documents, local businesses are represented by metadata, which is sparse. The location relevance heavily depends on various contextual factors such as current user location or time [6, 8], making the assessment non-trivial to recover for offline judges.

Another popular approach to evaluation is to utilize click data in a reranking experiment, where clicks are approxi-

[3]`http://en.wikipedia.org/wiki/Great-circle_distance` visited February 2015

[4]We take into account entities within an area of $9 \cdot 10^4$ km^2 for a better trade-off between efficiency and coverage.

Category	Uniform	$TopUni_{50}$	$RawD_{10}$	$RawD_5$	$RawD_1$	RankD	Δ_{RankD}
Movie Theater	13.33	7.54	5.78	5.74	5.73	5.61	57.92%
Convenience Store	16.49	9.87	8.02	7.70	7.58	7.18	56.46%
Department Store	15.84	9.64	7.48	7.38	7.35	7.14	54.90%
ATM	16.84	10.56	8.40	8.15	8.09	7.65	54.56%
Grocery	15.37	9.59	7.60	7.45	7.41	7.11	53.70%
Furniture Store	15.77	10.62	7.85	7.79	7.77	7.61	51.72%
Elementary School	16.08	11.87	8.53	8.37	8.30	8.05	49.94%
Auto Maintenance Repair	17.13	15.93	9.94	9.88	9.87	9.77	42.98%
Healthcare	16.49	15.38	9.72	9.68	9.67	9.68	41.28%
Apartment	16.48	15.05	10.23	10.09	9.96	9.81	40.48%
Government Office	16.68	15.42	10.02	9.98	9.97	9.94	40.40%
Church	17.28	17.02	10.95	10.89	10.88	10.76	37.72%
Lawyer	15.95	15.66	10.08	10.05	10.05	10.14	36.41%
Restaurant	19.23	20.67	14.23	14.08	14.01	13.93	27.53%
Hotels	15.89	16.86	13.39	13.34	13.30	13.28	16.41%
Mean-Model	16.32	13.45	9.48	9.37	9.33	9.18	43.77%

Table 1: Cross entropy results for different categories and distance models. $RawD_x$ denotes raw distance model with bucket size x and RankD is rank distance model. Δ_{RankD} shows the reduction in cross entropy when using RankD compared to the uniform model. RankD performs the best by reducing the most uncertainty.

mated as relevance judgments [1, 8]. The general goal is to improve retrieval metrics such as nDCG@10 or MAP by reranking top results [7]. One problem with this is that the collected responses are biased towards the design of search systems (e.g., ranking or display algorithms). For mobile search, this becomes more of a concern since only a small number of local entities are shown to users. At the time of our data collection, users were presented with three or fewer results in 97% of cases, making most clicks land on only the top three results. Indeed, if we compute MAP as in [7], we get 0.84 for our log sample, leaving it unclear if reranking and evaluating using clicks on top results truly reflects systems' retrieval ability.

To address these difficulties, we look to an information-theoretic approach to evaluation. In information theory, entropy refers to the average amount of information contained in a sample, while cross entropy measures the average number of bits needed to identify an event when a given distribution P' is assumed rather than the true distribution P. We use cross entropy to measure how well the distance models learned from historical data predict users' responses in the test set. That is, to measure the quality of distance models, we compare, for a test query, the test distribution P against the distribution estimated from the training data P' based on the formula $H_c = -\sum_e p(e) \log p'(e)$, where e denotes a local entity. Thus, cross entropy favors a model if P and P' are more similar. Although click data is still inherently biased by the user's choice of query and the ranking of the search system, by aggregating over many such queries and incorporating all nearby opportunities, we hope to better represent the distribution of possible clicks for a given user location and business category.

We assemble a test query to be a tuple containing a user u, a clicked entity e of category c, all surrounding entities e' of the same category c (e is considered as in e'), and the geo-information of u and e'. Given such tuple, we are able to compute the raw and rank distances from the current user to the clicked entity in a test case. This requirement of exact one clicked entity ensures that we hold no assumptions about the probability of click in the test set (i.e., P). That is, the test distribution will assign probability 1 to the clicked entity and 0 to the rest. Since our evaluation is based on the clicked entity, we must use the distance model to predict which entity will be clicked. We do this separately for each test case, using either the raw or rank distance model to firstly assign a probability to each entity in e' based on its distance from the user, then renormalizing to give a probability distribution over the set of those entities (i.e., e').

4. EXPERIMENTAL RESULTS

4.1 Experimental Setup

Data Collection. We evaluate using Bing mobile search log of users in the U.S. The training data for building the distance models is sampled from a period of four months in 2014, and the evaluation set is sampled from the following two months. We complement the mobile search data with an entity repository that includes location information (i.e., latitude and longitude) and category information (i.e., whether an entity is a hotel or a convenience store etc). Our resulting test set contains approximately 1.1 million queries.

Baseline Approaches. The naive baseline assumes that no distance information is given between a place and a user, as is the case when users do not allow their location to be known. In this case, a uniform model assigns equal probability to every in-category place entity (Uniform in Table 1). To improve the pure uniformity, the second baseline assigns equal probability to the user's k closest in-category entities with a total probability mass 0.99, with the remaining 0.01 uniformly distributed to the much larger number of more distant alternatives. We denote this as a top k uniform model, and we report the results for the 50 closest entities ($TopUni_{50}$ in Table 1). These two approaches are used as comparison basis for the raw and rank distance models.

4.2 Cross Entropy Results

We take the average of the cross entropy of test queries in each category and show the results in Table 1. The naive uniform model gives an average cross entropy of 16.32, meaning that the search space for a category is approximately 2^{16} when given no distance information. Under the top 50 nearby places, the average number of bits needed is reduced to 13.45, shrinking the search space about 8 times. The average cross entropy for user clicks is approximately 9.48

if we bucket the physical distance by 10 kilometers, which is a huge improvement compared to the top uniform model. The quantity becomes 9.37 and 9.33 respectively when using bucket sizes of 5 and 1 kilometers. This suggests that a finer granularity may lead to lower entropy but the improvement may saturate quickly. Finally, predicting user clicks with the rank distance model performs the best with the lowest cross entropy 9.18, which is a 10% reduction in the search space compared to the best performing raw distance model (i.e., at 1 km granularity). This suggests that using rank distance can explain users' selections towards local places better in our test set, despite that the notion of rank distance, in fact, discards the geographic distance information.

In addition to distance, the categories of entities play an important role for predicting user clicks. The cross entropy H_c of the uniform model is directly influenced by the number of entities in a category. The more entities a category contains, the higher H_c is since it is harder to predict which entities users may click without prior knowledge. In our dataset, the size of Restaurant category is the largest, resulting in the largest H_c 19.23 compared to others.

Table 1 shows interestingly that H_c for the Hotel category drops, at relatively smaller scale, from 15.89 in the uniform model to 13.28 in the rank distance model, resulting only a reduction of 16.41% in uncertainty. On the contrary, when the searches were intended for entities of ATMs or Convenience stores, H_c drops significantly with more than 50% reduction in the rank distance model. This suggests that although the distance factor plays a strong role in predicting ATMs searches, the clicks on hotel entities are less explainable using only distance from the searching user.

For categories such as Department store or Furniture store, the reduction in H_c is evident in the rank distance model. This implies for queries with shopping intent, users may have a tendency to click entities that are closer to them. Entities of these categories may be more replaceable when the store items are not significantly different for the users[5]. People also have a tendency to search for nearby movie theaters, where using rank distance can account for 57.92% uncertainty. The category Elementary school is another example where the closer entities seem preferable, consistent with our intuition that children go to the elementary school in their neighborhood in most districts.

When are users more willing to travel farther even in the presence of entities that are nearby? Relatively speaking, for categories such as Healthcare, Lawyer and Auto Maintenance, the entropy reduction degree is smaller compared to ATM or Convenience store, but not as small as in Hotel. People may skip closer places and seek their more desired choices in the cost of travel. This can be because these entities usually provide services that require specific professional knowledge, and nearby places might not meet a user's exact need. As the cost increases, the overhead of travel may suppress the desire, which is different from the case of Hotel where distance plays even a less important role. Interestingly, we observe that searchers skipped closer intervening opportunities and clicked restaurants farther away. Indeed, people go to restaurants not only for food, but also for factors such as the atmosphere, the chef and nearby attractions or friends. The results for categories such as Church, Apartment and Government office also imply that using distance alone is not sufficient for predicting user clicks.

So far we focus our discussion on the comparison *within* the rank distance model. Similar trends can be observed if we compare results within the top uniform or the raw distance model, with varying degree in entropy reduction. It is interesting to note that in the top 50 uniform model, the assumption that closer entities should receive more clicks fails for the case of hotels and restaurants; the uncertainty in fact increases compared to pure uniformity.

[5]We note that there should be exceptions when users look for things only available in specific stores.

5. CONCLUSION

This paper explored several ways that distance can be modeled in the context of mobile local search. Rather than merely reranking the top results, we considered intervening entities that were physically near the users, shedding light on user choices beyond those on the result page. The cross entropy results suggest that raw geographic and rank distance are both helpful, with the rank distance model outperforming in most cases. This suggests that the task of mobile local search resembles general human mobility in that it is influenced by intervening opportunities. Our analysis identifies significant inter-category variation. We find that locations that are highly replaceable (e.g., convenience stores) are more predictable based solely on distance, whereas user clicks on categories such as hotels and restaurants are dependent on complex factors. Overall, we recommend taking category information into account when modeling location preferences of users in search and recommendation systems.

6. REFERENCES

[1] K. Berberich, A. C. Koenig, D. Lymberopoulos, and P. Zhao. Improving local search ranking through external logs. In *Proc. of SIGIR*, 2011.

[2] K. Church, B. Smyth, P. Cotter, and K. Bradley. Mobile information access: A study of emerging search behavior on the mobile internet. *ACM Trans. Web*, 1(1), 2007.

[3] N. Craswell, O. Zoeter, M. Taylor, and B. Ramsey. An experimental comparison of click position bias models. In *Proc. of WSDM*, 2008.

[4] M. Kamvar and S. Baluja. Deciphering trends in mobile search. *Computer*, 40(8):58–62, 2007.

[5] R. Kumar, M. Mahdian, B. Pang, A. Tomkins, and S. Vassilvitskii. Driven by food: Modeling geographic choice. In *Proc of WSDM*, 2015.

[6] N. D. Lane, D. Lymberopoulos, F. Zhao, and A. T. Campbell. Hapori: Context-based local search for mobile phones using community behavioral modeling and similarity. In *Proc. of UbiComp*, 2010.

[7] Y. Lv, D. Lymberopoulos, and Q. Wu. An exploration of ranking heuristics in mobile local search. In *Proc. of SIGIR*, 2012.

[8] D. Lymberopoulos, peixiang Zhao, C. Koenig, K. Berberich, and J. Liu. Location-aware click prediction in mobile local search. In *Proc. of CIKM*, 2011.

[9] Q. Mei and K. Church. Entropy of search logs: How hard is search? with personalization? with backoff? In *Proc. of WSDM*, 2008.

[10] A. Noulas, S. Scellato, R. Lambiotte, M. Pontil, and C. Mascolo. A tale of many cities: Universal patterns in human urban mobility. *PLoS One*, 7(5), 2012.

[11] M. Sanderson. Test collection based evaluation of information retrieval systems. *Foundations and Trends in Information Retrieval*, 4(4):247–375, 2010.

[12] B. Shaw, J. Shea, S. Sinha, and A. Hogue. Learning to rank for spatiotemporal search. In *Proc. of WSDM*, 2013.

[13] S. A. Stouffer. Intervening opportunities: A theory relating mobility and distance. *American Sociological Review*, 5(6), 1940.

Reachability based Ranking in Interactive Image Retrieval

Jiyi Li
Department of Social Informatics, Graduate School of Informatics, Kyoto University
Yoshida-Honmachi, Sakyo-ku, Kyoto 606-8501, JAPAN
garfieldpigljy@gmail.com

ABSTRACT

In some interactive image retrieval systems, users can select images from image search results and click to view their similar or related images until they reach the targets. Existing image ranking options are based on relevance, update time, interestingness and so on. Because the inexact description of user targets or unsatisfying performance of image retrieval methods, it is possible that users cannot reach their targets in single-round interaction. When we consider multi-round interactions, how to assist users to select the images that are easier to reach the targets in fewer rounds is a useful issue. In this paper, we propose a new kind of ranking option to users by ranking the images according to their difficulties of reaching potential targets. We model the interactive image search behavior as navigation on information network constructed by an image collection and an image retrieval method. We use the properties of this information network for reachability based ranking. Experiments based on a social image collection show the efficiency of our approach.

Categories and Subject Descriptors

H.3.3 [**Information Storage and Retrieval**]: Information Search and Retrieval—*Retrieval models*

Keywords

Interactive Image Retrieval; Information Network; Ranking

1. INTRODUCTION

When users search images in an image collection, they first input some queries, which can be keywords or images, to get some initial image search results. When the initial results are not satisfied, some image retrieval systems provide interfaces of user interactions, e.g, relevance feedback, to gather additional information for refining the search results.

They allow users to click images to view other similar or related images until they reach the targets. For example, Figure 1 shows an example of Google image search [1]. After a user inputs "Kyoto" as the keyword for search, Google returns the initial image search results. There is a link of "search by image" for each image in the search results. The user can click these links to reach further results until he finds satisfied results. After several rounds, this user finally finds his target image which may be about the cherry-blossom at Arashiyama in Kyoto in spring.

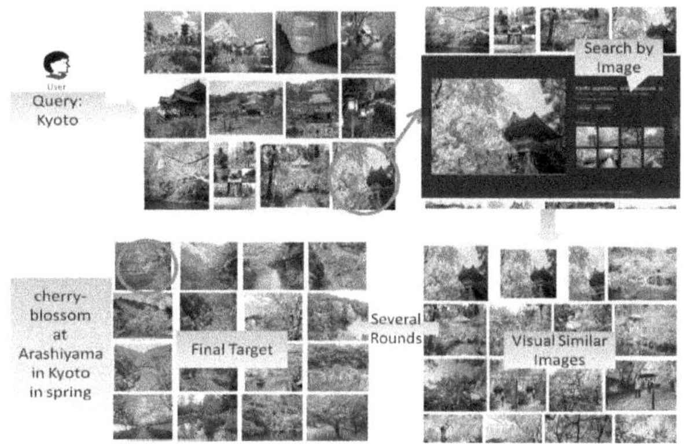

Figure 1: Example of Interactive Image Retrieval

Existing image ranking options are based on content or context relevance, update time, interestingness and so on. They concentrate on initial image search results or refined results of the single-round interaction. They do not consider the possible results in subsequent multi-round interactions. However, some reasons can lead to users' failures on reaching the targets in the initial or refined results. For example, users do not exactly describe their specific targets in the queries and single-round interactions because it is a difficult or boring task; users' targets may be still not clear when they start their searches, because they are just seeking the information they are interested in; the performance of image retrieval methods are still not good enough to return results which can match the query topics or detect user intentions for personalized search results.

If we can assist users to select the images that are easier to reach the targets, users can cost fewer interactions and spend less time in search sessions. For this purpose, we need to consider what kind of results can be returned after multi-round interactions. In this paper, we propose a new kind

[1] http://images.google.com

SIGIR'15, August 09 - 13, 2015, Santiago, Chile.

ACM 978-1-4503-3621-5/15/08 ...$15.00.
DOI: http://dx.doi.org/10.1145/2766462.2767777 .

of ranking option by ranking the images, according to their difficulties of reaching the potential targets.

The image search behavior with multi-round interactions in a search session can be regarded as navigation on the information space of an image collection. A query image or the first clicked image in the search results of a query keyword can be the start of this navigation. The end of this navigation can be some images which may contain the final target images. The user may find the targets or fail to find the targets in current search session and give up at the end of this navigation. We thus construct an image information network for interactive image retrieval on a given image collection based on a specific image retrieval method. The nodes in the network are images, and the edges in the network depend on the image retrieval method which can return top k search results from the image collection for a given image.

We leverage the properties of this information network which can indicate the difficulty of reaching target images from start images to propose our ranking method. Note that our work of ranking by reachability is used as a ranking option on the image search results, like ranking by relevance, update time, and so on. It is independent on the image retrieval methods which are used to generate the search results and construct the information network. It can be integrated with these methods.

The contributions of this paper are as follows.

First, we propose a novel kind of image ranking option based on the ideal reachability of images to other images. It is able to reduce the rounds of user interactions and accelerate the processes of reaching the targets in search sessions.

Second, we construct image information network for a given image collection based on a specific image retrieval method to reflect user navigation behavior on the images. The properties of this information network are used for our image ranking approach.

The remainder of this paper is organized as follows. In Section 2 we list some related work. In section 3 we propose our image ranking approach. We report the experimental results in Section 4 and give a conclusion in Section 5.

2. RELATED WORK

On one hand, Datta et al. [1] list many works on image retrieval. Many of them focus on the issue of one query and its direct image search results without further interactions.

On the other hand, Relevance feedback (RF) has been widely used in image re-ranking in supervised scenarios and is an important solution in interactive image retrieval. Rui et al. [2] and Porkaew et al. [3] proposed query re-weighting, reformulation, modification, point movement and expansion approaches. Tang et al. [4] used one click relevance feedback which only required the user to click only one query image to minimize the effort of relevance feedback instance selection.

The ranking methods used in all above-mentioned related work are relevance based while our work is reachability based. They mainly consider only single-round user interaction and the corresponding ranking results. They do not consider the scenario of multi-round interactions in the search sessions.

3. OUR RANKING APPROACH

In this section, we introduce our detailed reachability based ranking approach. After modeling our scenario of interactive image retrieval, we first construct the information network for a given image collection based on a specific image retrieval method. After that, we rank the images in the search results of the image retrieval method based on the properties of image nodes in the information network.

3.1 Interactive Image Retrieval

Our model of interactive image retrieval is as follows. We define an image as a_i in a given image collection C. In a search session, the queries that user input can be images or keywords. In the case of query by image, the start image is the query; in the case of query by keyword, the start image is the clicked image in the initial search result. The start image can also be any clicked image which is not the target in the search session. This definition of start image can simplify the constructed information network with only one type of nodes. Each node in this graph represents an image. There is no node representing other types of objects such as text. It can simplify the analysis on the graph when using it for various applications.

It may be boring for users to input too many additional actions in user interactions, and users may prefer succinct and convenient interfaces. Therefore, in our scenario of interactive image retrieval, in each round of user interaction, a user selects and clicks only one image. After the user clicks, a specific image retrieval method F is used to return top k image search results by using this clicked image as query. This image retrieval method can use either visual content information or textual context information of the clicked image. Such one click interface is used in recent image search engine like Google image search. There are several rounds of user interactions in a search session. The images clicked in all rounds construct a navigation sequence on the graph. In addition, even if multiple images are clicked in one round, we can regarded that there is a unique path from the start to the target and one of the clicked images is on this path.

The definition of search session is somewhat different from existing work in the areas like web page search. We assume that when a user modifies his original query, the current search session is regarded as finished, no matter whether the user reaches his targets. There are no jumps from one image node to another image node between which there is no edge because such a jump is regarded as a new session. In this way, the navigation behavior on the image information network in a search session is continuous by following the edges on the graph.

3.2 Information Network Construction

The steps of image information network construction for an image collection C based on an image retrieval method F are as follows.

1. Create a node for each image a_i in C.

2. For each image a_i, compute its top k image search results A_i from the image collection by using the image retrieval method F.

3. Create an edge from a_i to each image a_j in A_i. This image information network G_k is thus a directed graph.

Because we assume that users only view and click the images from the top k ranked images in the search engine results page (SERP). The out degree of nodes in this constructed information network is at most k. This constraint is able to control the number of edges of the graph and the time cost when computing the graph properties for analysis.

In addition, the relevance score or similarity score between a_i and each image a_j in A_i can be stored as the weights of the edges. Because it is not necessary in this paper, we still use same weights (equal to 1) for all edges.

3.3 Reachability Based Image Ranking

This constructed information network has various potential applications, for example, global performance evaluation of image retrieval methods on data collections, user intention detection in a search session and final user targets prediction. In this paper, we use it to rank images based on reachability to potential targets. Our ranking approach provides a different ranking option by reachability. It can be integrated with various image retrieval methods which are used to generated the search results.

In the communities of graph theory and social network analysis, many metrics have been proposed for analyzing various properties of graph and information network, e.g., average shortest path, diameter, centrality and so on. The length of shortest path of two images on information network can show the difficulty of reaching the target image from the start image in ideal. Some centrality measures of nodes are defined based on shortest path, for example, betweenness centrality and closeness centrality.

Betweenness centrality of an image node is defined as the number of shortest paths from all nodes to all others that pass through this node. Closeness centrality of an image node is defined as the inverse of the sum of the length of the shortest path of this node to all other nodes. They can indicate the reachability of the nodes to potential targets, and we will use them to provide two alternatives for our ranking approach. For the given image collection C, specific image retrieval method F and information network G_k, we rank these top k images based on one of the centrality measures.

These two centrality measures represent different assumptions on user behaviors. Betweenness centrality assumes that from start node a_s to target node a_t a user selects the shortest path p_{st}, and the evaluated node a_i is on the shortest path. Closeness centrality assumes that from the evaluated node a_i to the target node a_t a user selects the shortest path p_{it}. Both of these two assumptions are ideal because of using shortest paths. Users may not select the ideal shortest paths to reach the targets. West et al. [5] made an analysis of human wayfinding in entity information network. They find that human wayfinding is different from shortest paths but is still very efficient. Our ranking method is to assist users to select the paths more close to ideal ones if users select the top ranked results by our ranking method.

These two centrality measures are global and computed based on the whole image information network G_k. We use Gephi [7] to compute the centralities. The information network construction and computation of centrality for a large graph are time-consuming. It results in the dynamic problem and scalability problem. Current implementation of our approach needs offline pre-computation and is proper for static image collection which does not update frequently and is not too large. In the experiments, we use a public social image collection with tens of thousands of images.

To solve the dynamic problem, a solution is to do the offline pre-computation at some timestamps. To solve the scalability problem, in the future work, we can use the approximate algorithms in the existing work such as [6] for centrality computation, so that our approach can handle large scale image collections.

Furthermore, the ranking approach provides general ranking results and does not consider specific user intention, for the future work, we will focus on how to detect specific user intention and predict personalized targets by utilizing the graph model and partial navigation sequence.

4. EXPERIMENT

4.1 Experimental Settings

The dataset we use for our experiments is MIRFlickr 25000 [8] which is constructed by images and tags downloaded from Flickr. It contains 25,000 images and provides the raw tags of these images on Flickr. We use two kinds of visual features as two different content based image retrieval approaches. One is a color feature. The feature descriptor is a 1024-Dimension color histogram on the HSV color space. The other one is the SIFT feature with the bags of words model and 1000 visual words in the codebook.

We generate the top k similar images of an image by computing the distance of visual feature vectors. There are various visual distance measures and we arbitrarily use the Pearson correlation distance in these experiments. The visual distance between image a_i and a_j is defined as $s(a_i, a_j) = \sum_x (\mathcal{H}'_i(x) * \mathcal{H}'_j(x))/\sqrt{(\sum_y \mathcal{H}'_i(y)^2) * (\sum_y \mathcal{H}'_j(y)^2)}$, $\mathcal{H}'_i(x) = \mathcal{H}_i(x) - \sum_y \mathcal{H}_i(y)/\mathcal{N}$, where $\mathcal{H}_i$ and $\mathcal{H}_j$ are visual feature vectors. $\mathcal{N}$ is the size of the visual feature vector.

We also use a textual based image retrieval approach which searches textual related images to the query image. The textual information in the dataset is social tags. We use the tag list of an image as its textual feature vector, and generate the top k relevant images of an image by computing the cosine distance of textual feature vectors. The textual distance between image a_i and a_j is defined as, $t(a_i, a_j) = |\mathcal{T}_i \cap \mathcal{T}_j|/\sqrt{|\mathcal{T}_i| * |\mathcal{T}_j|}$, where $\mathcal{T}_i$ and $\mathcal{T}_j$ are textual feature vectors, and $|\cdot|$ is the number of tags. The images without textual information have no related images.

In our experiments, we first use one of the given image retrieval methods F to generate top k (k=50) image search results which are regarded as "original" ranking results. After that, we construct the information network G_k and rank these top k image results with our approach using the properties of G_k. The new results are regarded as "betweenness" and "closeness" ranking results respectively.

To evaluate the performance of the ranking results based on different ranking options, we assume that users only select the images from the top r ($r \leq k$) images in the search results in their interactive image search sessions. We respectively construct new information network with the top r images in the ranking results for each ranking option. After that, on one hand, we use the average shortest path length (ASPL) in these new information networks as the evaluation metric. This metric reflects ideal multi-round global performance of an image retrieval method by using all rounds of user interactions in a search session and considering the images in the whole data collection, though not all start and target image pairs included in this evaluation metric are meaningful enough. Note that when $r = k$, the performance of different ranking options are same because the nodes and edges of the information network are same.

On the other hand, we also evaluate the average diversity (AD) in the single-round image search results. The diversities of multi-round image search results can be computed by averaging the single-round diversities of images on the paths. Higher diversity means that it can provide more diverse candidates in a limited number of top search results and thus assist users to reach the targets easier.

4.2 Experimental Results

Table 1: Comparison of Average Shortest Path Length (ASPL) and Average Diversity (AD) between Original Ranking Results of Image Retrieval Methods and Reachability based Ranking Results

Method	Ranking Option	ASPL		AD	
		top r		top r	
		10	25	10	25
HSV	Original	12.73	7.25	0.2129	0.2541
	Betweenness	8.11	6.14	0.2795	0.2854
	Closeness	10.03	6.26	0.3048	0.2991
SIFT	Original	11.21	6.68	0.4264	0.4623
	Betweenness	6.35	5.45	0.4918	0.4890
	Closeness	7.96	5.63	0.5311	0.5166
Text	Original	10.30	5.37	0.2513	0.3250
	Betweenness	6.30	4.65	0.4322	0.4275
	Closeness	9.30	4.98	0.3648	0.3861

Table 1 lists the experimental results. We respectively evaluate the performance on $r = 10$ and $r = 25$. The results on metric ASPL illustrate that our ranking approach based on different centrality measures have smaller ASPL than the original ranking results, which means our approach can assist users to reach the targets more quickly and with fewer rounds of interactions in ideal. In addition, the ASPL based on closeness centrality is higher than that based on betweenness centrality. It is because closeness centrality allows users to select non-shortest paths between the start and the target images. Note that an ASPL with value l does not mean that a user needs l-round interactions to reach a reasonable target. All images on a path can be reasonable targets.

The results on metric AD in Table 1 illustrate that our ranking approach can generate results with higher diversities and thus can accelerate the processes of reaching the targets in search sessions.

Figure 2 shows the shortest paths between a pair of start and target images based on different ranking options. It uses the textual based method and a user is assumed to be enjoying various "pet" images. The start image is a "dog" image and the target image is a "cat" image. Such a pair of start and target concepts is reasonable while a user is viewing "dog" images and changes his interest to "cat" images. The start concepts and target concepts can be more different. For example, the example used in [5] for navigation in entity information network of an information seeker is from "Dik-dik" to "Albert Einstein" on Wikipedia pages.

Because betweenness centrality indicates the property associated with the shortest path between start and target images, we use it as the sample here. In this example, our ranking approach uses fewer steps to reach the targets. Because the dog and cat in some images of this example are very small, we mark them in the figure with yellow circles. This example also shows that our approach is possible to provide reasonable paths. For these start and target images, the possible path of our approach may only contain images with concepts of "pet" or "animal". The path of the original ranking results may be not reasonable for user selection because a "dog" image is connected with a "boat" image through the concepts in the background. In this example, a user may tend to use the path provided by our results.

Furthermore, there are some pairs of start and target image that have no path in the information network constructed by the top r ranking results. In such case, after increasing the value of r and k, these pairs can finally have paths. If the path is very long, it means that the target image is difficult to reach from the start image by the given image retrieval method.

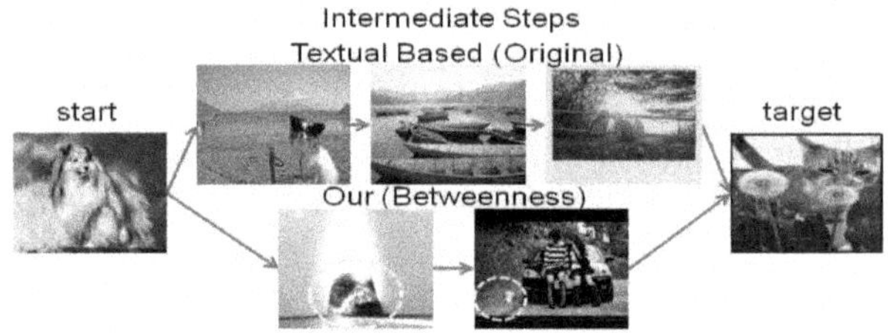

Figure 2: Sample Results

5. CONCLUSION

In this paper, we propose a new kind of ranking option by ranking the images according to their reachability to potential targets. We model the image search behavior with user interaction as navigation on an image information network. We use the properties of this network for reachability based ranking. This ranking approach provides ideal and general results without considering specific user intentions. In future work, we will focus on predicting personalized targets.

6. REFERENCES

[1] R. Datta, D. Joshi, J. Li, and J.Z. Wang. Image retrieval: Ideas, influences, and trends of the new age. *ACM Computing Surveys (CSUR)*, 40(2):1–60, 2008.

[2] Y. Rui, T.S. Huang, M. Ortega, and S. Mehrotra. Relevance feedback: a power tool for interactive content-based image retrieval. *IEEE Trans. on CSVT*, 8(5):644–655, 1998.

[3] K. Porkaew, S. Mehrotra, and M. Ortega. Query reformulation for content based multimedia retrieval in MARS. In *ICMCS'99*, pp. 747-751, 1999.

[4] X.O. Tang, K. Liu, J.Y. Cui, F. Wen, X.G. Wang. IntentSearch: Capturing User Intention for One-Click Internet Image Search. *IEEE Trans. on PAMI*, 34(7):1342–1353, 2012.

[5] R. West and J. Leskovec. Human wayfinding in information networks. In *WWW'12*, pp.619–628, 2012.

[6] M. Riondato and E.M. Kornaropoulos. Fast approximation of betweenness centrality through sampling. In *WSDM'14*, pp.413-422, 2014.

[7] M. Bastian, S. Heymann, and M. Jacomy. Gephi: an open source software for exploring and manipulating networks. In *ICWSM'09*, 2009.

[8] M.J. Huiskes and M.S. Lew. The MIR Flickr Retrieval Evaluation. In *MIR'08*, pp.39–43, 2008.

Modeling Multi-query Retrieval Tasks Using Density Matrix Transformation

Qiuchi Li[1,2], Jingfei Li[1], Peng Zhang[1], Dawei Song [*1,3]
[1]School of Computer Science and Technology, Tianjin University, China
[2]Department of Electronic Engineering, Tsinghua University, China
[3]The Computing Department, The Open University, United Kingdom
liqiuchi2015@gmail.com, jingfl@foxmail.com,
{pzhang, dwsong}@tju.edu.cn

ABSTRACT

The quantum probabilistic framework has recently been applied to Information Retrieval (IR). A representative is the Quantum Language Model (QLM), which is developed for the ad-hoc retrieval with single queries and has achieved significant improvements over traditional language models. In QLM, a density matrix, defined on the quantum probabilistic space, is estimated as a representation of user's search intention with respect to a specific query. However, QLM is unable to capture the dynamics of user's information need in query history. This limitation restricts its further application on the dynamic search tasks, e.g., session search. In this paper, we propose a Session-based Quantum Language Model (SQLM) that deals with multi-query session search task. In SQLM, a transformation model of density matrices is proposed to model the evolution of user's information need in response to the user's interaction with search engine, by incorporating features extracted from both positive feedback (clicked documents) and negative feedback (skipped documents). Extensive experiments conducted on TREC 2013 and 2014 session track data demonstrate the effectiveness of SQLM in comparison with the classic QLM.

Categories and Subject Descriptors

H.3.3 [**Information Search and Retrieval**]: Query formulation, Relevance feedback, Retrieval Models

Keywords

Quantum Language Model, Session Search, Density Matrix Transformation

1. INTRODUCTION

Recently, various quantum theory (QT) based IR models are developed under the inspiration of the pioneering work of van Rijsbergen [8], which draws a clear connection between the QT and IR. Piwowarski et al. [5] proposed that queries and documents can be modeled as density operators and subspaces respectively, but the tensor space based representation method has not led to good performance. The advent of Quantum Language Model (QLM) [7] , a representative QT-based IR model, successfully solved this issue. In QLM, both single terms and compound term dependencies are represented as projectors in a vector space, while queries and documents are represented as density matrices defining a quantum probability distribution in the space. An EM-based training method for the estimation of density matrix is then devised [7]. The advantages of QLM over traditional language models have been demonstrated from both theoretical and experimental perspectives.

Despite its success in the ad-hoc retrieval, QLM (referred to as classical QLM in the rest of the paper) is solely targeted on single ad-hoc queries. It is insufficient to capture the dynamics of users' information need in response to the user's interaction with the search engine. As a result, it is difficult for the classical QLM to be applied in more complex search tasks, such as multi-query session search.

To address this challenge, we propose to integrate user' short-term interaction information into the estimation of QLM for the current query, and correspondingly a novel Session-based QLM (SQLM) is proposed. The evolution of the user's information need within a search session is modeled by the density matrix transformation, i.e., transforming the original density matrices (for single queries) by some principled rules based on user interactions (e.g., the click and dwell time). We also put forward the concepts of positive projectors and negative projectors extracted from the positive feedback documents (clicked documents) and negative feedback documents (skipped documents), respectively, to enhance the representation ability of the QLM. Specially, a novel training algorithm for QLM with different projectors is devised. Although there exists a body of related work [3][9] for integrating users' interaction information in IR models, they did not model term dependencies in queries and documents, compared with the SQLM proposed in this paper.

2. QLM PRELIMINARIES

2.1 Quantum Probability

In the field of IR, the quantum probability is defined on a real finite space $\mathbf{R}^n$ [7] for simplicity (originally, defined on the infinite Hilbert space). In this paper, we use

*Corresponding Author: Dawei Song, Email: dwsong@tju.edu.cn

SIGIR'15, August 09 - 13, 2015, Santiago, Chile.

ACM 978-1-4503-3621-5/15/08 ...$15.00.
DOI: http://dx.doi.org/10.1145/2766462.2767819 .

the Dirac's notation to represent a unit column vector $\vec{u} \in \mathbf{R}^n$ as $|u\rangle$ and its transpose $\vec{u}^T$ as $\langle u|$, respectively. An *elementary quantum event* can be uniquely represented by a projector onto a 1-dimensional subspace of $\mathbf{R}^n$. For a unit vector $|u\rangle$, the corresponding elementary quantum event, or the projector, is denoted as $|u\rangle\langle u|$. Suppose $|e_1\rangle$,$|e_2\rangle$,...,$|e_n\rangle$ forms an orthonormal basis for $\mathbf{R}^n$, then each unit vector $|v\rangle$ can be uniquely expressed as the *superposition* of $|e_i\rangle$: $|v\rangle = \sum_i v_i|e_i\rangle$, where $\sum_i v_i^2 = 1$.

A measure μ is introduced to define the quantum probability on $\mathbf{R}^n$. It satisfies two conditions: (I) for every projector $|v\rangle\langle v|$, $\mu(|v\rangle\langle v|) \in [0,1]$ and (II) for any orthonormal basis $\{|u_i\rangle\}$ for $\mathbf{R}^n$, we have $\sum_{i=1}^n \mu(|u_i\rangle\langle u_i|) = 1$. The Gleason's Theorem [2] can prove the existence of a mapping function $\mu_\rho(|v\rangle\langle v|) = tr(\rho|v\rangle\langle v|)$ for any vector v given a density matrix $\rho \in S^n$ (S^n is the density matrix space containing all n-by-n positive semi-definite matrices with trace 1, i.e., $tr(\rho) = 1$). Formally, any density matrix ρ assigns a quantum probability for each quantum event in vector space $\mathbf{R}^n$, thereby uniquely determining a quantum probability distribution over the vector space.

2.2 Classical Quantum Language Model

The classical Quantum Language Model(QLM) aims at modeling term dependencies in the principled quantum theory formulation. Different from traditional language models, QLM extracts term dependencies in each document as projectors in the quantum probabilistic space. The single words correspond to projectors $|e_i\rangle\langle e_i|$, and the compound terms (with two or more words for each term) correspond to projectors $|v\rangle\langle v|$ (refer to Section 2.1). The projectors are used to estimate density matrices ρ_q and ρ_d for a query and each document by maximizing a likelihood function with the EM-based iterative approach, i.e., $R\rho R$ algorithm [7]. Then, the top retrieved documents in the initial search results returned by the traditional language model are re-ranked according to the negative VN-Divergence between ρ_q and ρ_d. For details of the classical QLM, please refer to [7].

3. SESSION QUANTUM LANGUAGE MODEL (SQLM)

3.1 Framework

In QLM, a single query can be represented by a density matrix ρ over a vector space for a certain vocabulary. The positive definite matrix with unitary trace can be decomposed as follows:

$$\rho = \sum_{i=1}^{n} \lambda_i(|u_i\rangle\langle u_i|) \tag{1}$$

where $|u_i\rangle$ is a eigenvector, and λ_i is the eigenvalue. Correspondingly, $\Pi_i = |u_i\rangle\langle u_i|$ can be interpreted as an elementary quantum event or projector, and λ_i is the corresponding quantum probability for the elementary event ($\sum_{i=1}^n \lambda_i=1$). By obtaining a density matrix, we actually obtain a set of mutually orthogonal quantum elementary events along with the corresponding discrete probability distribution, and vice versa. In a real search scenario, a user often interacts with the search engine many times before achieving his/her actual information need. We propose a density matrix transformation framework to model the interaction process, which is mathematically formulated as a mapping function T in the density matrix space S^n.

$$T : S^n \to S^n \tag{2}$$

In session search, we assume that there exists an "ideal" transformation T for density matrices which can model dynamic query intention in the historical interactions. Specifically, T is a transformation that for any two consecutive queries q_{i-1} and q_i, the estimated density matrix $\hat{\rho_i}= T\rho_{i-1}$ represents the user's information need for q_i, where ρ_{i-1} is a representation of q_{i-1}. This implies we further make a 1st order Markov assumption that a query is dependent solely on its last previous query. This assumption is reasonable because the dependency can continuously back-propagate in the session.

Theoretically, from Eq.(1), we can easily find that T can be divided into two separate transformation process: $T = T_1T_2$. T_1 is the transformation operator for quantum events $|u_i\rangle$. Since $|u_i\rangle$ forms an orthogonal basis, T_1 can be any standard transition matrix. T_2 changes the original probability distribution for the events (namely, change the values of λ_i), and it is be a diagonal matrix. In this sense, the transformation of density matrix is basically a transformation of main quantum events, and a reallocation of quantum probability for each event.

In practice, however, this consideration seems infeasible due to its high degree of freedom. Suppose a vocabulary $\mathcal{V}$ with $|\mathcal{V}|$ distinct words, T_1 will have a freedom of $O(|\mathcal{V}|^2)$, and T_2 will have a freedom of $O(|\mathcal{V}|)$. Thus the model is prone to be overfiting and computationally expensive. Moreover, it is hard to draw a clear and reasonable connection from the training of T_1 and T_2 to the extraction of projectors. Therefore, we propose an iterative training approach to represent the transformation process, inspired by the updating method of the classical QLM. Specially in this paper, we use the density matrix ρ_{i-1} for query q_{i-1} as the initial density matrix to train the density matrix ρ_i for query q_i.

To facilitate subsequent discussions, we define notations for the session search. In a search session, we have a set of historical interaction units $\{Q_i, R_i, C_i\}_{i=1}^{N-1}$, where Q_i, R_i and C_i represent the query, returned documents and clicked documents for the ith interaction unit respectively. We need to use the historical interaction information to retrieve documents for the current query Q_N. To this end, we first obtain the top N retrieved documents returned by the traditional language model (LM), denoted as R_N. $\{\rho_i\}_{i=1}^{N-1}$ denote a set of $|\mathcal{V}|$-order density matrices representing user's information need for each historical query, where $|\mathcal{V}|$ is the size of the vocabulary containing all distinct terms in the historical queries and the current query.

3.2 Modeling a Single Query

For a historical interaction of a search session, the first clicked document of the query is not always the first one in the search results list. In other words, users often skip some irrelevant results before clicking the first assumingly relevant document. Therefore, we assume that the "skip" behavior is a strong negative feedback signal of users, since the user would have otherwise clicked them. In our assumption, some extreme cases are neglected. For example, the user may gain the right information only by reading the snippets without detecting any click behaviors. Based on this point, we form a positive documents set $R_{pos}(i)$ with all clicked documents as well as a negative set $R_{neg}(i)$ with all skipped documents in R_i for each query q_i. Note that, $R_{pos}(i)$ is equivalent to C_i, and $R_{neg}(i)$ is null for the queries whose first returned document is clicked.

From $R_{pos}(i)$ and $R_{neg}(i)$, positive projectors $\mathcal{P}_{pos} = \{\Pi_i\}_{i=1}^{M_{pos}}$ and negative projectors $\mathcal{P}_{neg} = \{\Pi_j\}_{j=1}^{M_{neg}}$ are extracted using the method discussed in Section 2.2, where M_{pos} and M_{neg} is the number of positive and negative projectors respectively. Note that some details when extracting projectors: i) only single words, bi-grams and tri-grams are considered as possible compound dependencies, since otherwise the computational complexity will be exponential to the vocabulary size; ii) we use TFIDF to assign the superposition weight v_i rather than the IDF or UNIFORM weights introduced in the original paper [7], since TFIDF is a document specific measure and has better distinguishability across documents. In order to maximize the probability that all positive events happen while all negative events not happen with respect to the quantum probability distribution (i.e., the density matrix ρ), the Maximum Likelihood Estimation (MLE) problem can be formulated as

$$\hat{\rho} = argmax(\sum_{i=1}^{M_{pos}} \log tr(\rho\Pi_i) \sum_{j=1}^{M_{neg}} \log(1 - tr(\rho\Pi_j))) \quad (3)$$

where Π_i and Π_j denote a positive projector and a negative projector. Since

$$\begin{aligned} 1 - tr(\rho\Pi_j) &= tr(\rho(I - \Pi_j)) \\ &= (|\mathcal{V}| - 1) * tr(\rho\widehat{\Pi_j})) \end{aligned} \quad (4)$$

where $\widehat{\Pi_j} = \frac{I-\Pi_j}{|\mathcal{V}|-1}$ is also a legal density matrix and $|\mathcal{V}| - 1$ is a constant. Then Eq.(3) can be rewritten as

$$\hat{\rho} = argmax(\sum_{i=1}^{M_{pos}} \log tr(\rho\Pi_i) \sum_{j=1}^{M_{neg}} \log tr(\rho\widehat{\Pi_j})) \quad (5)$$

Eq.5 is similar to the objective function in classical QLM. Thus we can apply the similar updating method used in [7] to update the density matrix ρ. Since the $R\rho R$ algorithm in [7] dose not guarantee convergence, we revise it by utilizing the updating method in [4]:

$$\tilde{\rho}_{(m+1)} = (1 - \zeta)\hat{\rho}_{(m)} + \zeta\frac{\hat{\rho}_{(m)}R(\hat{\rho_{(m)}}) + R(\hat{\rho_{(m)}})\hat{\rho}_{(m)}}{2} \quad (6)$$

It can be strictly proved in [4] that for a sufficiently small value of ζ, Eq.(6) guarantees global convergence. Although this updating method guarantees the global convergence theoretically, it requires a sufficiently small value of parameter ζ, resulting in a slow training speed. Therefore, in this paper we do not target on training the density matrix to its convergence, but control an appropriate iterative steps (will be discussed in Section 3.3).

In SQLM, we also model the dwelling time and click sequence for each clicked document. The assumption is that a longer dwelling time and an earlier click mean that the document is more likely to be relevant. Specifically, the weight for a clicked document d is calculated as

$$W_d = e^{\frac{t_d}{t_{all}}} * c^{Seq_d - 1} \quad (7)$$

where t_d is the dwelling time for the document d, t_{all} is the lasting time of the whole interaction, Seq_d denotes the rank of d in the returned document list, and c is a decaying parameter in [0,1], which we will further discuss in Section 4.2. The objective function (3) can therefore be updated as

$$\mathcal{L}_{\mathcal{P}}(\rho) = \sum_{i=1}^{M_{pos}} W_{D(i)} \log tr(\rho\Pi_i) \sum_{j=1}^{M_{neg}} \log tr(\rho\widehat{\Pi_j}) \quad (8)$$

where $D(i)$ is the document containing the projector Π_i. The new objective function is similar to Eq.5, and the only difference is that the new one multiplies each projector in clicked documents by a weight $W_{D(i)}$. Thus the updating methods discussed for Eq.6 can still be applied to the new objective function in Eq.8.

3.3 Density Matrix Transformation

In this paper, we do not train the quantum events transformation operator T_1 and the quantum probability change operator T_2 for density matrix transformation operator T, because of the high freedom. Instead, we propose an iterative training algorithm to approximate the process of density matrix transformation between two subsequent queries:

Algorithm 1 : Density Matrix Transformation.

1: $\rho_0 \leftarrow diag(LM)$; // Initiate the density matrix ρ_0 with the traditional unigram language model.
2: **for** $k = 1$; $k \leq N - 1$; $k += 1$ **do**
3: Extract projectors from ${R_k}^{pos}, {R_k}^{neg}$ (Section 3.2);
4: Estimate ρ_k with initial density matrix ρ_{k-1} with $TrainingSteps(k) = \mathcal{S}\gamma^{k-1}$ iterative steps;
5: **end for**
6: Return the desired density matrix for interactions ρ_{N-1}.

The training steps are different for different queries, since we believe nearer queries to the current query will have stronger influence on the estimation of current query. The initial training steps $\mathcal{S}$ and the discount factor γ are free parameters which need to be further discussed. The more steps the density matrix is trained, the closer it moves towards the current query density matrix and away from the initial matrix. Thus, gaining an appropriate training steps can achieve a balance between the current query information and historical interaction information.

3.4 Ranking

We use the top K (we set $K = 50$ in this paper) retrieved documents (pseudo feedback documents) returned by traditional LM to train a pseudo feedback QLM ρ_N^p for current query. The representation of user's search intention can be formulated as the linear combination of ρ_{N-1} and ρ_N^p:

$$\hat{\rho} = \alpha\rho_N^p + (1 - \alpha)\rho_{N-1} \quad (9)$$

where α controls the extent to which the history influence on the query representation. After obtaining $\hat{\rho}$, it can be used to re-rank the retrieved documents following the same method in [7].

4. EMPIRICAL EVALUATION

4.1 Experimental Setup

Empirical evaluations are conducted on the TREC 2013 and 2014 session track data shown in Table 1. The corpus

Table 1: Statistics For TREC 2013 and 2014 Datasets (TREC 2014's official ground truth only contains the first 100 sessions).

Items	TREC 2013	TREC 2014
#Sessions	87	100
#Queries	442	453
#Avg. session length	5.08	4.53
#Max. session length	21	11

Table 2: Performance on TREC 2013 and 2014.

TREC2013	NDCG@10	chg%	MAP	chg%
QLM	0.0763	+0.00	0.01708	+0.00
SQLM	0.0847	+11.01	0.01799	+5.32
SQLM+LM	0.0967	+26.74	0.01994	+16.74
TREC2014	NDCG@10	chg%	MAP	chg%
QLM	0.0909	+0.00	0.0164	+0.00
SQLM	0.0950	+4.51	0.0170	+3.66
SQLM+LM	0.1033	+13.64	0.0180	+9.76

used in our experiments is the ClueWeb12 full corpus[1] which consists of 733,019,372 English webpages collected from the Internet. We index the corpus with Indri search engine[2]. In the indexing process, we filtered out all documents with Waterloo's spam scores [1] less than 70, removed the stop words and stemmed all words with Porter stemmer [6].

To verify the effectiveness of the proposed model, we compared the following models: (i) **QLM**, the classic quantum language model which is regarded as the baseline model; (ii) **SQLM**, the proposed session-based quantum language model; (iii) **SQLM+LM**, the combination model of SQLM and traditional language model (LM), which takes the feature of LM into consideration (the linear combination parameter is β). We employ the official evaluation metrics MAP and NDCG@10 to evaluate the models.

A number of parameters are involved in the proposed models, and they are summarized as follows: c in Eq.7, $\mathcal{S}$ and γ in Algorithm 1, α in Eq.9, and β in model $SQLM+LM$. For the global setup, we select $\zeta = 0.01$ in Eq.6. The selection of best parameters will be discussed in next section.

4.2 Results and Discussion

Table 2 reports the experimental results for TREC 2013 and 2014 datasets respectively. In the tables, "chg%" means the improvement percentage over the baseline, i.e., QLM.

Since the modeling process of SQLM only involves matrix addition and multiplication, the computing complexity is low, allowing us to conduct a grid search to find the best parameter configuration. For TREC 2013, the best parameter configuration is $\{c = 0.95, \mathcal{S} = 10, \gamma = 1.05, \alpha = 0.7\}$ for SQLM; and $\{c = 0.95, \mathcal{S} = 30, \gamma = 1.05, \alpha = 0.6, \beta = 0.9\}$ for SQLM+LM. For TREC 2014, the best parameter configuration is $\{c = 0.95, \mathcal{S} = 30, \gamma = 1.0, \alpha = 0.7\}$ for SQLM, and $\{c = 0.95, \mathcal{S} = 30, \gamma = 1.15, \alpha = 0.9, \beta = 0.9\}$ for SQLM+LM.

The results indicate that the proposed SQLM achieves improvements over the classical QLM, on both TREC 2013 (11.01% improvement for NDCG and 5.33% for MAP), and TREC 2014 Session data (4.51% relative improvements for NDCG and 3.66% for MAP). Moreover, a linear combination of SQLM and LM can further enhance the performance of SQLM, suggesting that SQLM is adaptive to other features such as the traditional LM. It also indicates that SQLM has a large potential for further improvements.

[1]http://www.lemurproject.org/clueweb12/index.php
[2]http://www.lemurproject.org

5. CONCLUSION AND FUTURE WORK

In this paper, we present a novel quantum theory based probabilistic framework for multi-query retrieval task, i.e., session search. By extending the classical Quantum Language Model (QLM), our proposed Session-based Quantum Language Model (SQLM) incorporates the sound mechanism of the density matrix transformation to approximate the dynamics of information need entailed in historical interactions, for re-ranking the initial results generated by the search engine. At the operational level, we utilise the information from both clicked documents and top unclicked documents, and devise a new training algorithm. Extensive experiments on both TREC 2013 and 2014 Session track datasets demonstrate that SQLM does perform better than classical QLM for multi-query retrieval systems, and also show its potential of being further improved for session search.

Therefore, it is safe and reasonable to conclude that the proposed Session-based Quantum Language Model(SQLM) is a feasible expansion of classical Quantum Language Model(QLM) on the multi-query session search tasks. As for future work, we believe that a better retrieval result could be achieved if one can find a better realization of density matrix transformation based on the quantum inference, and incorporate more features into the framework. We will also apply the model to data closer to real-time retrieval systems.

6. ACKNOWLEDGMENTS

This work is supported in part by them Chinese National Program on Key Basic Research Project (973 Program, grant No.2013CB329304, 2014CB744604), the Chinese 863 Program (grant No. 2015AA015403), the Natural Science Foundation of China (grant No. 61402324, 61272265), and the Research Fund for the Doctoral Program of Higher Education of China (grant no. 20130032120044). Any comments from anonymous reviewers are appreciated.

7. REFERENCES

[1] G. V. Cormack, M. D. Smucker, and C. L. A. Clarke. Efficient and effective spam filtering and re-ranking for large web datasets. *Inf. Retr.*, 14(5):441–465, 2011.

[2] A. M. Gleason. Measures on the closed subspaces of a hilbert space. *J. Math. Mech*, 6(6):885–893, 1957.

[3] D. Guan, S. Zhang, and H. Yang. Utilizing query change for session search. In *SIGIR*, pages 453–462. ACM, 2013.

[4] M. G. A. Paris and J. Rehĺćcek. Quantum State Estimation. 649, 2004.

[5] B. Piwowarski, I. Frommholz, M. Lalmas, and K. Van Rijsbergen. What can quantum theory bring to information retrieval. In *CIKM*, pages 59–68. ACM, 2010.

[6] M. F. Porter. An algorithm for suffix stripping. *Program: electronic library and information systems*, 14(3):130–137, 1980.

[7] A. Sordoni, J.-Y. Nie, and Y. Bengio. Modeling term dependencies with quantum language models for ir. In *SIGIR*, pages 653–662. ACM, 2013.

[8] C. J. Van Rijsbergen. *The geometry of information retrieval.* Cambridge University Press, 2004.

[9] S. Zhang, D. Guan, and H. Yang. Query change as relevance feedback in session search. In *SIGIR*, pages 821–824. ACM, 2013.

Predicting User Behavior in Display Advertising via Dynamic Collective Matrix Factorization

Sheng Li*
Northeastern University
Boston, MA, USA
shengli@ece.neu.edu

Jaya Kawale
Adobe Research
San Jose, CA, USA
kawale@adobe.com

Yun Fu
Northeastern University
Boston, MA, USA
yunfu@ece.neu.edu

ABSTRACT

Conversion prediction and click prediction are two important and intertwined problems in display advertising, but existing approaches usually look at them in isolation. In this paper, we aim to predict the conversion response of users by jointly examining the past purchase behavior and the click response behavior. Additionally, we model the temporal dynamics between the click response and purchase activity into a unified framework. In particular, a novel matrix factorization approach named dynamic collective matrix factorization (DCMF) is proposed to address this problem. Our model considers temporal dynamics of post-click conversions and also takes advantages of the side information of users, advertisements, and items. Experiments on a real-world marketing dataset show that our model achieves significant improvements over several baselines.

Categories and Subject Descriptors

H.3.3 [**Information Search and Retrieval**]: Information filtering

Keywords

Conversion prediction; matrix factorization; temporal dynamic

1. INTRODUCTION

With the proliferation of the Internet and online shopping websites, digital marketing has become an effective way to reach out to consumers. Typically consumers can be influenced via targeted advertisements (ads) on the web to make purchases. Display advertising is a popularly used medium for targeting users and allows advertisers to place graphical ads on the publishers' web pages. Most of the ads aim to create an impulse leading to a sale. Traditionally, the *click-through rate* (CTR) has been used as a central measure for evaluating the performance of a direct response ad campaign. An alternate strategy that has gained attention in the recent past is to maximize the *conversion rate* (CVR) instead of just ad-clicks, as many advertisers would prefer not to pay for an ad impression unless it leads to a conversion. The conversion could either imply revenue generated via buying a product or could mean account creation. In both strategies it is critical to understand the user behavior and predict the response so as to have better targeting of the ads and as a result higher conversions.

So far, the problem of click prediction and conversion prediction has mainly been studied in isolation. Researchers have successfully applied novel strategies for click prediction and there has been significant work in the area [1]. Recently the problem of conversion prediction has been studied by [2] to analyze the ad campaigns. However, the objectives of the two problems are often intertwined together and there is a need to study the two problems in conjunction with each other. With the notable exception of [3], there is not much work analyzing the two objectives together to understand the user purchase behavior better. Jointly studying the two problems can help us understand the pathway leading to conversion and can provide answers to several questions. For example, *What ads should be shown to a particular user so that he generates revenue?* and *Will a given user generate revenue?*

In this paper, we propose a novel approach called as dynamic collective matrix factorization (DCMF) to jointly examine the user click behavior and the purchase activity. The DCMF model is a substantial extension of the collective matrix factorization model used to jointly factorize multiple matrices [4]. Apart from considering the two matrices of click and purchase behavior together as in a CMF model, our model also takes into account the temporal influence of an ad impression/click on conversion. We model the time dependency into the matrix factorization framework to account for the decay in the influence of an ad. An efficient optimization algorithm is devised to solve the problem. Our approach is well suited for an interactive setting where the user preferences and behavior change over time.

Our key contributions can be summarized as follows:

- We propose a dynamic collective matrix factorization (DCMF) approach for conversion prediction, which jointly models the temporal relationships between click events and purchase events in display advertising. It also incorporates the side information of users, ads and items via regression.

*This work was completed during Sheng Li's internship at Adobe Research.

SIGIR'15, August 09 - 13, 2015, Santiago, Chile.
© 2015 ACM. ISBN 978-1-4503-3621-5/15/08 ...$15.00.
DOI: http://dx.doi.org/10.1145/2766462.2767781.

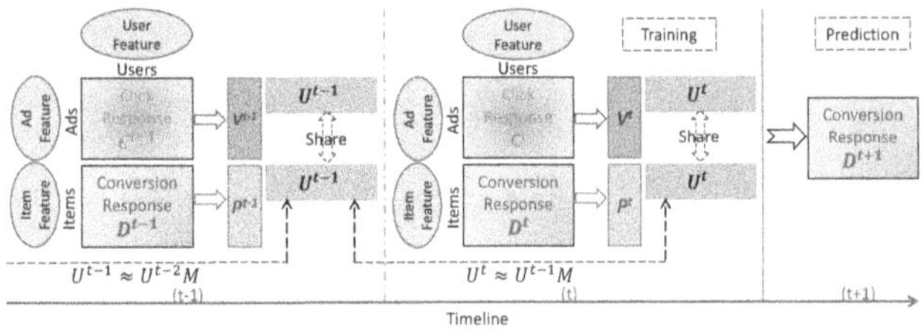

Figure 1: Framework of DCMF approach.

- Our framework is based upon examining the data in time slices to account for the decayed influence of an ad and we use stochastic gradient descent for optimization. This makes the framework well suited for interactive settings as well as large datasets.
- We evaluate the conversion prediction performance of our approach on real-world datasets and show that our model performs better as compared to the several baseline methods.

2. RELATED WORK

Response Prediction. Response prediction in digital marketing has been widely studied in recent years. Most of the prior work focuses on predicting the click-through-rate (CTR) of online ads or other contents [1]. The ultimate goal of display advertising is conversion. However, there are only a few works that investigate the conversion prediction problem [2]. For example, Lee *et al.* estimated the conversion rate by using the past performance observations along with user, publisher and advertiser data hierarchies [2]. Unlike the existing conversion prediction methods, our approach takes advantage of the click response and side information via the collective matrix factorization technique. The most relevant method in the literature is the hierarchical multi-task learning algorithm presented in [3]. It jointly models the conversion, click and unattributed-conversion problems. There are significant differences between [3] and our work. First, we make use of the explicit temporal relationship between click and purchase events, which is ignored in [3]. Second, unlike the multi-task learning model used in [3], we develop a matrix factorization approach.

Temporal Prediction Models. The prediction model considering temporal dynamics was first developed for collaborative filtering in [5]. The idea of using temporal dynamics has been explored in online advertising. Barajas *et al.* proposed a time series approach for evaluating the effectiveness of display advertising [6]. Most recently, Oentaryo *et al.* designed a hierarchical importance-aware factorization machine (HIFM) for click response prediction in mobile advertising [7]. It is able to handle the temporal ad response data. Unlike HIFM, our approach aims to tackle the conversion prediction problem, and to model the temporal relationships between click and purchase events.

3. APPROACH

3.1 Modeling Temporal Dynamics

We deal with the conversion prediction problem using the collaborative filtering (CF) technique. The fundamental intuition behind CF is that the "similar" users will have "similar" preferences. There has been work on applying the CF technique to conversion prediction [8], but it models the interactions between pages and ads. In our paper, we directly model the relationships between users and ads/items, which enables us to predict the user behaviors. The intuition is that "similar" users are very likely to click "similar" ads and purchase "similar" items. Figure 1 shows our framework.

First, we want to jointly analyze the relational data, i.e., the click response and purchase activities of users. Inspired by the collective matrix factorization (CMF) [4], we factorize the click response matrix (User$\sim$Ads) and the purchase activity matrix (User$\sim$Item) simultaneously.

Secondly, we aim to model the temporal information, which is critical in attributing the conversions to the ad clicks. A key observation is that, *the behavior of users may change over time*. For example, if a user has already purchased an item in the previous week, it is unlikely that he/she will purchase the same item again in the next week. Therefore, we incorporate temporal information into CMF.

Thirdly, we need to ensure that the latent features of users do not dramatically change in a short period of time, as in reality the user preferences would evolve smoothly. To address this concern, we leverage the latent features of the users learned in time $t-1$.

Given T pre-defined time slices $t \in \{1, 2, \cdots, T\}$, we use $C^t \in \mathbb{R}^{N_u \times N_a}$ and $D^t \in \mathbb{R}^{N_u \times N_p}$ to denote the click responses and purchase activities from N_u users to N_a ads (or N_p items) in the time slice t, respectively. By exploiting the temporal relationships between click response and purchase events, we notice that the purchase events in time $t+1$ are mainly related to the click events in time t and hence our model needs to account for that. The objective function is:

$$\begin{aligned} \arg\min_{\substack{U^t,V^t,\\ P^t,M}} \quad & f(U^t, V^t, P^t, M) = \alpha \|W^{Ct} \odot (C^t - U^t V^{t\mathrm{T}})\|_{\mathrm{F}}^2 \\ & +(1-\alpha)\|W^{Dt} \odot (D^t - U^t P^{t\mathrm{T}})\|_{\mathrm{F}}^2 \\ & +\lambda_1 \|U^t - U^{t-1}M\|_{\mathrm{F}}^2 \\ & +\lambda_2(\|U^t\|_{\mathrm{F}}^2 + \|V^t\|_{\mathrm{F}}^2 + \|P^t\|_{\mathrm{F}}^2 + \|M\|_{\mathrm{F}}^2), \end{aligned} \tag{1}$$

where W^{Ct} and W^{Dt} are boolean matrices that indicate the training samples in C^t and D^t, respectively. U^t, V^t and P^t are latent factors; M is a transition matrix; $\odot$ denotes the entry-wise product; α, λ_1 and λ_2 are trade-off parameters.

The first two terms in (1) denote the approximation errors, and the last four terms are regularizations used to prevent overfitting. In (1), the smooth transition of user latent factors are modeled based on the assumption:

$$U^t \approx U^{t-1} M, \tag{2}$$

where U^{t-1} is the latent features of users learned from the previous time slice $t-1$. We assume that the latent features in time t are closely related to the feature in time $t-1$, which is reasonable in real applications. M is a transition matrix of users' behavior, which tries to capture the mappings between users' behavior in two successive time slices. The intuition is that users' intention on purchasing items should be smoothly transited over time.

3.2 Modeling Side Information

So far, we have seen that the model in (1) is not aware of side information, i.e., the features of users, ads, and items. We can further exploit the additional information to improve the prediction performance. The side information are also particularly useful as the data in conversion and click prediction problems are generally sparse. For example, we do not have any click responses or conversion responses of some new users, which lead to the *cold-start* problem. In this case, the latent features of new users estimated by (1) are not reliable anymore. However, side information provide useful cues from another perspective, and make it possible to learn robust latent features in the cold-start scenario. In this section, we incorporate the side information into (1), and present the DCMF method.

Let X, Y and Z denote the feature matrices for users, ads and items, respectively. We assume that the click response and purchase activity are generated by the inner product of latent factors, and the side information via linear regression. Thus, the matrix approximation can be written as:

$$\begin{aligned} C^t &\approx U^t V^{t\mathrm{T}} + \hat{U}^t Y^{\mathrm{T}} + X\hat{V}^{t\mathrm{T}}, \\ D^t &\approx U^t P^{t\mathrm{T}} + \hat{U}^t Z^{\mathrm{T}} + X\hat{P}^{t\mathrm{T}}, \end{aligned} \tag{3}$$

where $\hat{U}^t$, $\hat{V}^t$ and $\hat{P}^t$ are regression coefficients on user features, ad features and item features, respectively. We treat the three terms used to approximate C^t (or D^t) equally for simplicity. The performance can be enhanced by assigning different weights for them.

By replacing the matrix approximations in (1) with (3), we can then rewrite the objective function as:

$$\begin{aligned} \arg \min_{\substack{U^t,V^t,P^t,M,\\ \hat{U}^t,\hat{V}^t\hat{P}^t}} \; & \alpha\|W^C \odot (C^t - U^t V^{t\mathrm{T}} - \hat{U}^t Y^{\mathrm{T}} - X\hat{V}^{t\mathrm{T}})\|_{\mathrm{F}}^2 \\ & +(1-\alpha)\|W^D \odot (D^t - U^t P^{t\mathrm{T}} - \hat{U}^t Z^{\mathrm{T}} - X\hat{P}^{t\mathrm{T}})\|_{\mathrm{F}}^2 \\ & +\lambda_1\|U^t - U^{t-1}M\|_{\mathrm{F}}^2 + \lambda_2(\|U^t\|_{\mathrm{F}}^2 + \|V^t\|_{\mathrm{F}}^2 + \|P^t\|_{\mathrm{F}}^2 \\ & +\|\hat{U}^t\|_{\mathrm{F}}^2 + \|\hat{V}^t\|_{\mathrm{F}}^2 + \|\hat{P}^t\|_{\mathrm{F}}^2 + \|M\|_{\mathrm{F}}^2). \end{aligned} \tag{4}$$

With the learned latent factors, we can predict the conversion score of user m for item n at time $t+1$ as:

$$Score(m, n, t+1) = u_m^t p_n^{t\mathrm{T}} + \hat{u}_m^t z_n^{\mathrm{T}} + x_m \hat{p}_n^{t\mathrm{T}}, \tag{5}$$

where u_m^t and $\hat{u}_m^t$ are the m-th row of U^t and $\hat{U}^t$, p_n^t and $\hat{p}_n^t$ are the n-th row of P^t and $\hat{P}^t$, respectively.

3.3 Optimization

As the stochastic gradient descent (SGD) algorithm is efficient in practice, we utilize SGD to solve (4).

First, we fix M, and update other variables, $U^t = \{u_1^t, \cdots, u_r^t\}$, $V^t = \{v_1^t, \cdots, v_r^t\}$, $P^t = \{p_1^t, \cdots, p_r^t\}$, $\hat{U}^t = \{\hat{u}_1^t, \cdots, \hat{u}_r^t\}$, $\hat{V}^t = \{\hat{v}_1^t, \cdots, \hat{v}_r^t\}$, and $\hat{P}^t = \{\hat{p}_1^t, \cdots, \hat{p}_r^t\}$. For simplicity, we use f to denote the objective in (4). After selecting a pair of random training points C_{ij}^t and D_{ik}^t, we only need to update u_i^t, v_j^t, p_k^t, $\hat{u}_i^t$, $\hat{v}_j^t$ and $\hat{p}_k^t$ using:

$$\begin{aligned} u_i^t = u_i^t - \gamma\tfrac{\partial}{\partial u_i^t} f, v_j^t = v_j^t - \gamma\tfrac{\partial}{\partial v_j^t} f, p_k^t = p_k^t - \gamma\tfrac{\partial}{\partial p_k^t} f, \\ \hat{u}_i^t = \hat{u}_i^t - \gamma\tfrac{\partial}{\partial \hat{u}_i^t} f, \hat{v}_j^t = \hat{v}_j^t - \gamma\tfrac{\partial}{\partial \hat{v}_j^t} f, \hat{p}_k^t = \hat{p}_k^t - \gamma\tfrac{\partial}{\partial \hat{p}_k^t} f, \end{aligned} \tag{6}$$

where γ is the learning rate. The detailed gradients for each variable are omitted here due to the space limit.

Next, we fix all the other variables, and update M. By ignoring all the irrelevant terms with respect to M, the objective (4) reduces to:

$$\arg\min_M f(M) = \lambda_1\|U^t - U^{t-1}M\|_{\mathrm{F}}^2 + \lambda_2\|M\|_{\mathrm{F}}^2. \tag{7}$$

We can then update M using:

$$M = M - \gamma\tfrac{\partial}{\partial M} f(M), \tag{8}$$

where gradient is $\frac{\partial f}{\partial M} = -\lambda_1 U^{(t-1)\mathrm{T}}(U^t - U^{t-1}M) + \lambda_2 M$. The above process is repeated until convergence.

4. EXPERIMENTS

In this section, we evaluate the performance of our approach and baselines on a marketing dataset.

4.1 Data and Settings

To evaluate the performance on conversion prediction, we examine a subset of the marketing data from Oct. 1, 2013 ~ Nov. 30, 2013. The dataset constitutes of behavioral characteristics of 448,158 number of users and 737 ads. Along with the impression records, we also have click and purchase activity information for all the users. We empirically choose one week as the time window t in our model. To construct the binary response tables, we denote the click events and purchase events as positive responses, and the impressions (without any following events) as negative responses. All the other entries are treated as missing values. As the click and purchase are rare events in reality, our data set is extremely sparse. To collect the side information, we select some features of users, ads and items, respectively. For each user, we encode the demographic information (e.g., country, state, domain) into a binary valued vector. The attributes of ads (e.g., advertiser, ad size) and items (e.g., type, price) are also encoded into binary vectors, respectively. To conduct fair comparisons, we set up 5 different training/test cases along the timeline. Each training set consists of a click events table and a purchase events table. Each test set only contains a table of purchase events, as our goal is to predict the conversions.

We compare our approach with the following baselines: PMF [9], LIBMF [10], SVDFeature [11], HBMFSI [12], and CMF [4]. For PMF, LIBMF, SVDFeature and HBMFSI, we only use the purchase data for training, due to the intrinsic limitation of these methods. For CMF and our approach, we use both the click data and purchase data for training. In particular, we use the click events and purchase events at time t to predict the purchase events in time $t+1$ (i.e., D^{t+1}). Following [3], we use the ROC curve and the area under ROC (AUC-ROC) as our evaluation metrics.

For SGD based matrix factorization methods (e.g., PMF, LIBMF, SVDFeature and CMF), the major parameters are the learning rate γ and the trade-off parameter λ for regularization terms. For Bayesian method HBMFSI, we follow the settings in [12]. We sample a validation set from the training data, and tune these parameters empirically. The parameters γ, λ_1 and λ_2 are set to 0.003, 0.001 and 0.02, respectively. In CMF and our approach, another important parameter is α. To understand its sensitivity, we observe the AUC-ROC of CMF and DCMF approach with various choices of α. Figure 2(a) shows the AUC-ROC values in Case-3. We can observe that our approach is not sensitive to the values of α. We achieve better performance when α falls into the range $[0.5, 0.8]$. In the following experiments, α is set to 0.6. In addition, the dimension of latent features is set to 20 for each method. To initialize our approach in Case-1, we borrow the latent factors of CMF learned from Oct. 1~Oct. 7 as the input U^{t-1}.

4.2 Results and Discussions

We evaluate the performance of each compared method in 5 training/test splits. Figure 2(b) shows the ROC in

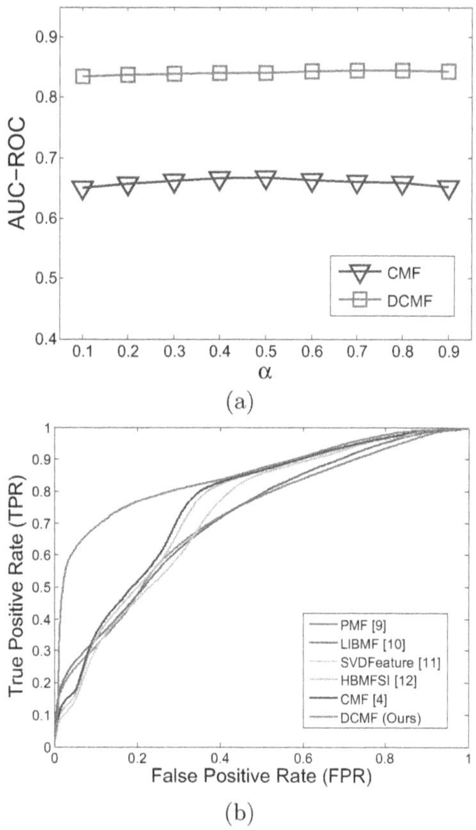

Figure 2: (a): AUC-ROC of CMF and DCMF in Case-3 with different α. (b): ROC curves in Case-1.

Table 1: AUC-ROC of each methods on marketing data.

Method	Case 1	Case 2	Case 3	Case 4	Case 5
PMF [9]	0.729	0.718	0.645	0.712	0.714
LIBMF [10]	0.731	0.719	0.653	0.726	0.723
SVDFeature [11]	0.742	0.729	0.661	0.731	0.732
HBMFSI [12]	0.750	0.737	0.669	0.739	0.741
CMF [4]	0.751	0.746	0.668	0.736	0.737
DCMF (**Ours**)	**0.850**	**0.851**	**0.841**	**0.832**	**0.837**

Case-1, and Table 1 lists the AUC-ROC of all cases. Form Figure 2 and Table 1, we make the following observations: (1) Incorporating side information improves the prediction results significantly. SVDFeature and HBMFSI employ the features of users and items, they achieve much better performance than PMF and LIBMF, which do not utilize any side information. Similarly, our DCMF approach performs very well by virtue of the side information. (2) Modeling click response is helpful in predicting purchase events. CMF and our approach take advantages of the click response information, and they outperform PMF and LIBMF in each case. (3) Temporal dynamics is critical in conversion prediction. Our approach obtains better results than CMF, indicating that the latent features learned from previous time slice are very useful. (4) Our DCMF approach achieves the best results in each case, compared to the baselines. It demonstrates that the side information and temporal information could be complementary to each other in predicting user behaviors such as conversion.

5. CONCLUSIONS

In this paper, we presented a novel matrix factorization approach DCMF for conversion prediction in display advertising. DCMF jointly examines the click events and purchase events in an online learning fashion by leveraging the temporal information and side information. Extensive experimental results on a real-world marketing dataset demonstrate the superiority of our approach over existing methods.

Acknowledgements

This research is supported in part by the NSF CNS award 1314484, ONR award N00014-12-1-1028, ONR Young Investigator Award N00014-14-1-0484, and U.S. Army Research Office Young Investigator Award W911NF-14-1-0218.

6. REFERENCES

[1] Deepak Agarwal, Bo Long, Jonathan Traupman, Doris Xin, and Liang Zhang. Laser: a scalable response prediction platform for online advertising. In *WSDM*, pages 173–182, 2014.

[2] Kuang chih Lee, Burkay Orten, Ali Dasdan, and Wentong Li. Estimating conversion rate in display advertising from past performance data. In *KDD*, pages 768–776, 2012.

[3] Amr Ahmed, Abhimanyu Das, and Alexander J. Smola. Scalable hierarchical multitask learning algorithms for conversion optimization in display advertising. In *WSDM*, pages 153–162, 2014.

[4] Ajit Paul Singh and Geoffrey J. Gordon. Relational learning via collective matrix factorization. In *KDD*, pages 650–658, 2008.

[5] Yehuda Koren. Collaborative filtering with temporal dynamics. In *KDD*, pages 447–456, 2009.

[6] Joel Barajas, Ram Akella, Marius Holtan, Jaimie Kwon, and Brad Null. Measuring the effectiveness of display advertising: a time series approach. In *WWW (Companion Volume)*, pages 7–8, 2011.

[7] Richard Jayadi Oentaryo, Ee-Peng Lim, Jia-Wei Low, David Lo, and Michael Finegold. Predicting response in mobile advertising with hierarchical importance-aware factorization machine. In *WSDM*, pages 123–132, 2014.

[8] Aditya Krishna Menon, Krishna Prasad Chitrapura, Sachin Garg, Deepak Agarwal, and Nagaraj Kota. Response prediction using collaborative filtering with hierarchies and side-information. In *KDD*, pages 141–149, 2011.

[9] Ruslan Salakhutdinov and Andriy Mnih. Probabilistic matrix factorization. In *NIPS*, 2007.

[10] Yong Zhuang, Wei-Sheng Chin, Yu-Chin Juan, and Chih-Jen Lin. A fast parallel sgd for matrix factorization in shared memory systems. In *RecSys*, pages 249–256, 2013.

[11] Tianqi Chen, Weinan Zhang, Qiuxia Lu, Kailong Chen, Zhao Zheng, and Yong Yu. Svdfeature: a toolkit for feature-based collaborative filtering. *Journal of Machine Learning Research*, 13:3619–3622, 2012.

[12] Sunho Park, Yong-Deok Kim, and Seungjin Choi. Hierarchical bayesian matrix factorization with side information. In *IJCAI*, 2013.

Zero-shot Image Tagging by Hierarchical Semantic Embedding

Xirong Li, Shuai Liao, Weiyu Lan, Xiaoyong Du, Gang Yang*
Key Lab of Data Engineering and Knowledge Engineering, Renmin University of China, 100872, China
Multimedia Computing Lab, School of Information, Renmin University of China, 100872, China
{xirong,leoshine,weiyu,duyong,yanggang}@ruc.edu.cn

ABSTRACT

Given the difficulty of acquiring labeled examples for many fine-grained visual classes, there is an increasing interest in zero-shot image tagging, aiming to tag images with novel labels that have no training examples present. Using a semantic space trained by a neural language model, the current state-of-the-art embeds both images and labels into the space, wherein cross-media similarity is computed. However, for labels of relatively low occurrence, its similarity to images and other labels can be unreliable. This paper proposes **Hier**archical **S**emantic **E**mbedding (HierSE), a simple model that exploits the WordNet hierarchy to improve label embedding and consequently image embedding. Moreover, we identify two good tricks, namely training the neural language model using Flickr tags instead of web documents, and using partial match instead of full match for vectorizing a WordNet node. All this lets us outperform the state-of-the-art. On a test set of over 1,500 visual object classes and 1.3 million images, the proposed model beats the current best results (18.3% versus 9.4% in hit@1).

Categories and Subject Descriptors

I.4.8 [**Image Processing and Computer Vision**]: Scene Analysis—*Object recognition*

Keywords

Image tagging, zero shot learning, semantic embedding

1. INTRODUCTION

People use tags to find specific images in social media. As user-contributed tags tend to be overly personalized and incomplete, automated image tagging that can predict labels relevant with respect to the visual content is crucial for image search. The state-of-the-art approach to image tagging employs a deep convolutional neural network [6], trained on millions of manually labeled examples. However, such a supervised approach cannot handle novel labels that have no training examples available.

Since acquiring training examples by expert labeling is costly, one might consider to automatically harvest training examples from many user-tagged images online. Indeed, this line of research has produced encouraging results for generic visual classes such as 'beach', 'animal', and 'car' [5, 11]. A prerequisite for their success is that there need to be sufficient, say thousands of, candidate examples for a specific class. However, for many classes, in particular for those fine-grained subclasses, even the candidate examples are scarce, as tagging images with these classes is nontrivial for users without domain-specific knowledge.

To bypass training example acquisition, zero shot learning has been introduced to handle novel labels [1,3,7,9]. Instead of finding a direct mapping between images and target labels, the key idea of zero shot learning is to introduce an intermediate layer between images and labels such that a novel label can also be represented in this layer, even when no example of this label is supplied. In the seminal work by Lampert *et al.* [7] for animal object recognition, this layer is implemented as a set of human-specified high-level attributes, e.g., shape and color, of animals. By exploiting the relative strength of association between attributes and classes, the authors extrapolate attribute-level prediction to novel classes. In a follow-up work [1], the intermediate layer is constructed by embedding image feature vectors and labels into a common Euclidean space such that cross-media relevance can be computed. The attributes are used as side information for label embedding. Although the use of attributes makes the intermediate layer more interpretable, specifying a proper set of attributes suitable for interpreting thousands of visual classes is challenging.

We are interested in zero-shot image tagging that works with no need of manually specifying attributes or other knowledge about the novel labels. In a related work [3], a deep learning based semantic embedding method is proposed. In particular, by training a neural language model [8] on millions of Wikipedia documents, the authors first construct a semantic space where semantically close words are mapped to similar vector representations. Consequently, label embedding is achieved by a table lookup in the model vocabulary. Images are mapped into the same space, by linearly transforming the corresponding visual feature vectors. The transformation is optimized on a set of training labels such that the product similarity between the embedding vectors of an image and its correct label is higher than between the

*Corresponding author.

SIGIR'15, August 09 - 13, 2015, Santiago, Chile

ACM 978-1-4503-3621-5/15/08 ...$15.00.
DOI: http://dx.doi.org/10.1145/2766462.2767773.

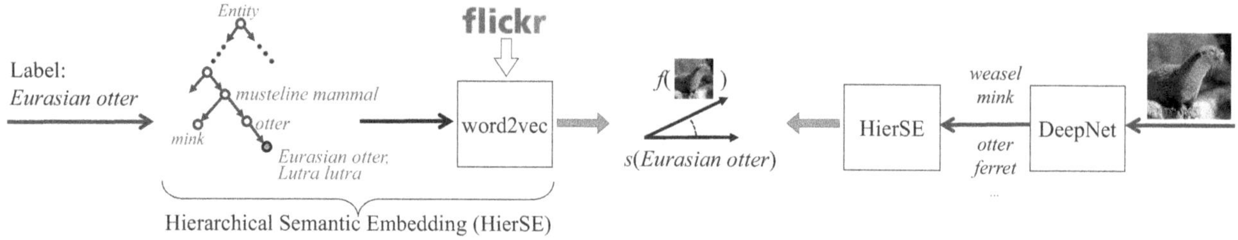

Figure 1: Zero-shot image tagging by hierarchical semantic embedding. Cross-media relevance between an unlabeled image and a test label is computed by cosine similarity between their embedding vectors.

image and other randomly chosen words. More recently, Norouzi *et al.* propose a simpler yet more effective solution for image embedding [9]. Given an unlabeled image, they use an existing m-way image classification system (whose labels have no overlap with target labels) to predict a few most relevant labels, and build the embedding vector of the given image by convex combination of the label embedding vectors. With this solution, they achieve the state-of-the-art results on the ImageNet zero-shot learning task.

We argue that several issues are overlooked in the semantic embedding method [9]. First, since the neural language model essentially exploits word co-occurrence in a text corpus, for a label of relatively low occurrence, its embedding vector could be unreliable for computing its similarity to images and other labels. On the other hand, it is this kind of label that we want to tackle via zero shot learning (otherwise we could choose to harvest training examples from the Internet). Second, how to deal with labels that are out of the language model vocabulary is unclear. Moreover, while Wikipedia articles have been the default source for deducing the semantic space [3,9], Flickr might be a better source, as its tag co-occurrence statistics better reflect a label's visual context. By addressing the above issues, this paper improves on the semantic embedding method, and eventually contributes a new model, as illustrated in Fig. 1, that outperforms the state-the-art for zero-shot image tagging.

2. ZERO-SHOT IMAGE TAGGING

2.1 Problem Statement

Given an unlabeled image, the goal of zero-shot image tagging is to automatically tag the image with labels that have no training examples available. This is approached by embedding both the image and the novel labels into a common semantic space such that their relevance can be estimated in terms of the distance between the corresponding vectors in the space. More formally, let x be an image, y be a label, and $p(y|x)$ be a classifier which estimates the relevance of the label y with respect to the image x. Given a set of m_0 training labels $\mathcal{Y}_0$, we have access to n training examples $\mathcal{D}_0 = \{(x_i, y_i)\}_{i=1}^n$, where $y_i \in \mathcal{Y}_0$. Consequently, let $p_0(y|x)$ be a m_0-way classifier learned from $\mathcal{D}_0$. We use $\mathcal{Y}_1$ to denote a set of m_1 test labels, which have no training examples in the zero-shot learning setting, i.e., $\mathcal{Y}_0 \cap \mathcal{Y}_1 = \emptyset$. With the help of $\mathcal{D}_0$ and some semantic knowledge, we aim to build a classifier $p_1(y|x)$ that can perform reasonably well for $\mathcal{Y}_1$.

Our work improves on the semantic embedding model [9], so we first describe it in Section 2.2, and subsequently introduce our model in Section 2.3.

2.2 The Semantic Embedding Model

For the ease of consistent description, we borrow some notation from [9]. The semantic embedding model assumes each label $y \in \mathcal{Y}_0 \cup \mathcal{Y}_1$ is associated with a semantic embedding vector $s(y) \in \mathcal{S}$, where $\mathcal{S}$ is a real coordinate space of q dimensions. The semantic space is formed such that two labels are similar if and only if their corresponding vectors are close. In [9], $\mathcal{S}$ is instantiated by training the skip-gram model [8] using Wikipedia documents. Each $s(y)$ is obtained by matching the label with words in the skip-gram model.

By projecting images into $\mathcal{S}$, cross-media relevance can be computed. To do so, the model leverages the existing classifier $p_0(y|x)$, and create the semantic embedding vector of x as a convex combination of semantic vectors of the most relevant training labels. In particular, let $y(x,t)$ be the t-th most likely training label for x according to $p_0(y|x)$. Then, the semantic embedding vector of x, denoted by $f(x) \in \mathcal{S}$, is defined as

$$f(x) := \frac{1}{Z}\sum_{t=1}^{T} p_0(y(x,t)|x) \cdot s(y(x,t)), \qquad (1)$$

where T is the maximum number of training labels to be employed, and $Z = \sum_{t=1}^{T} p_0(y(x,t)|x)$ is a normalization factor. The classifier for the novel label set $\mathcal{Y}_1$ is defined as

$$p_1(y|x) := cos(f(x), s(y)), \qquad (2)$$

where cos is the cosine similarity.

Due to potential mismatch between the vocabulary of the skip-gram model and the labels, $s(y)$ could be null. For some successfully matched labels, their relatively low occurrence in the training corpus makes the similarity measurement unreliable. Next, we present a remedy to these issues.

2.3 Hierarchical Semantic Embedding

The proposed method is to construct label embedding and consequently image embedding by exploiting the hierarchical structure defined in the WordNet. We presume that each label has a corresponding node in the WordNet. The WordNet hierarchy allows us to trace from a specific label back to the root, obtaining all its ancestors, denoted as $super(y)$. In contrast to [9] that uses y alone, we utilize both y and $super(y)$. Intuitively, nodes that are more close to y shall contribute more. Putting all this together, we define a hierarchically embedded vector $s_{hi}(y)$ as

$$s_{hi}(y) = \frac{1}{Z_{hi}} \sum_{y' \in \{y\} \cup super(y)} w(y'|y) \cdot s(y'), \qquad (3)$$

where $w(y'|y)$ is a weight subject to exponential delay with respect to the minimal path length from y to y', and Z_{hi} is a normalization factor given by $Z_{hi} = \sum_{y' \in \{y\} \cup super(y)} w(y'|y)$. As shown in Eq. (3), the use of $super(y)$ always allows y to be mapped into $\mathcal{S}$, while the convex combination makes the similar measure more reliable for rare labels. Moreover, for a label of multiple senses, e.g., 'mouse', it will have distinct embedding vectors depending on its given sense. In contrast, in previous embedding models the label will always be represented by the same vector regardless of its senses.

For some WordNet nodes, they consist of multiple phrases, e.g., 'book jacket' and 'dust cover'. To represent a specific node in $\mathcal{S}$, previous work tries to find matches in the skip-gram model for every phrase, and average the corresponding vectors [9]. Since we are interested in learning the skip-gram model from Flickr tags, which are however mostly single words instead of phrases, we consider a less strict rule that makes matches in terms of single words. As opposed to the previous full match, we term this rule as partial match.

Putting $s_{hi}(y)$ into Eq. (1), we obtain $f_{hi}(x)$ as the hierarchically embedded semantic vector of an image. Accordingly, we get a new classifier as $cos(f_{hi}(x), s_{hi}(y))$. The hyper-parameter T is set to be 10, according to [9]. An overview of the proposed model is visualized in Fig. 1.

3. EMPIRICAL EVALUATION

This section presents an evaluation to verify our proposal, compared with the baseline model [9]. For reproducibility, the evaluation is based on public data.

3.1 Setup

Training Label Set $\mathcal{Y}_0$. Following [9], we use the ImageNet 1K label set as $\mathcal{Y}_0$, including 1,000 visual object classes defined in the Large Scale Visual Recognition Challenge 2012 [10]. A pre-trained DeepNet model provided by Caffe [4] is used as $p_0(y|x)$. It is a stacked convolutional neural network [6], consisting of five convolutional layers followed by two fully connected layers and a softmax output layer. The model is learned from over 1m labeled examples.

Test Label Set $\mathcal{Y}_1$. Following [9], the test label set consist of labels within 2 tree hops of $\mathcal{Y}_0$, namely their direct parent and child nodes, resulting in 1,548 novel labels in total. The ground-truthed test images are from ImageNet [2], with the number of relevant images per label ranges from 1 to 2,330, with an average number of 846. The total number of test images is 1.3m.

Semantic Space $\mathcal{S}$. Similar to [9], $\mathcal{S}$ in this work is also trained by a skip-gram model, using the word2vec software [8]. We train a 500-D model with 2.2m words using the latest Wikipedia dump. Another 500-D model with 382k words is learned from user tags of 4 million Flickr images. Additionally, we experiment with a pre-trained model with 3m words [8], trained on a Google News dataset.

Performance Metric. We report hit@k, which is the percentage of test images for which the true label is among the top-k predicted tags.

3.2 Experiments

In order to study 1) which resources to use for constructing the semantic space, 2) how to convert a WordNet node to a semantic embedding vector, and 3) if adding the hierarchy in the embedding process is helpful, we conduct the following three experiments. For the ease of comparison, we abbreviate the proposed model as HierSE, and name the baseline model [9] as FlatSE.

Table 1: Performance of different models. Numbers marked with star (*) are taken from [9]. Bold font indicates the top performer in different settings.

Model	Resource for word2vec	hit@k (%) 1	2	5	10
FlatSE [9]	Wikipedia	*9.4	*15.1	*24.7	*32.7
Full match:					
FlatSE	Wikipedia	7.5	12.1	19.4	25.3
FlatSE	Google	7.5	11.7	18.8	24.9
FlatSE	Flickr	9.3	14.7	22.6	29.1
HierSE	Wikipedia	14.5	23.1	36.4	45.1
HierSE	Google	15.6	24.4	38.3	48.2
HierSE	Flickr	**16.2**	**25.0**	**40.7**	**52.0**
Partial match:					
FlatSE	Wikipedia	13.5	20.8	32.7	40.6
FlatSE	Google	14.3	22.1	33.6	41.5
FlatSE	Flickr	15.7	24.7	39.4	49.9
HierSE	Wikipedia	17.3	26.4	39.8	48.9
HierSE	Google	16.9	26.2	40.2	49.9
HierSE	Flickr	**18.3**	**27.9**	**42.9**	**54.1**

Table 2: Nearest terms to 'grass' and 'hair', measured using cosine distance in the semantic spaces that are learned from Google News (by [8]) and Flickr tags (by this work), respectively.

Tag	Resource for word2vec	The 10 nearest terms
grass	Google	bermuda_grass, rye_grass, lawns, fescue, zoysia_grass, kikuyu, kikuyu_grass, tall_fescue_grass, buffalograss, zoysia
	Flickr	greengrass, tree, leaf, hedge, fence, pasture, lawn, meadow, graze, field
hair	Google	curly_hair, tresses, mane, hairdo, blonde_hair, blond_hair, gray_hair, wavy_hair, hairstyle, blonde_locks
	Flickr	hairstyle, hairdo, curl, haircare, blackhair, curlyhair, forehead, facial, hairspray, updo

Experiment 1. Which resource for training the semantic space? As shown in Table 1, the Flickr-based word2vec model consistently outperforms its Wikipeida and Google counterparts under varied settings. For a more intuitive understanding, Table 2 shows tags closest, in terms of cosine similarity, to 'grass' and 'hair' in the Google based and Flickr based semantic spaces, respectively. While subspecies of grass is retrieved in the Google based space, tags depicting the visual context of grass, e.g., 'tree', 'hedge', and 'pasture', are deemed to be more relevant to 'grass' in the Flickr based space. Hence, among the three resources compared, we conclude that Flickr is most suited for learning word2vec models for zero-shot image tagging.

Experiment 2. Partial Match or Full Match? We see from Table 1 that given the same embedding model and the same word2vec model, partial match results in a higher hit rate than full match. While full match is more precise, the number of labels that cannot be matched is much larger than its counterpart in partial match. Consider the Flickr based semantic space for instance. The number of test labels that cannot be matched in FlatSE is 749, which is reduced to only 54 when using partial match instead. Also notice that with

Table 3: Top-5 predicted tags, with the correct prediction marked by *italic* (blue) font. Test images are hand-picked to illustrate the cases that the HierSE performs well, and a failure case.

Test Image	Ground truth	$p_0(y\|x)$ by Caffe	$p_1(y\|x)$ by FlatSE	$p_1(y\|x)$ by HierSE
	entellus	gibbon langur Saluki patas spider monkey	crab-eating macaque vervet tamarin guereza striped hyena	*entellus* vervet crab-eating macaque Barbary ape rhesus
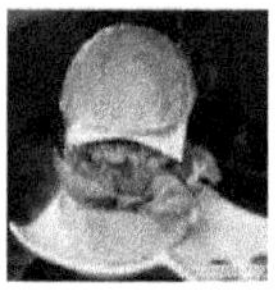	hamburger	cheeseburger bagel potpie French loaf burrito guacamole meat loaf	pepperoni pizza sausage pizza anchovy pizza cheese pizza *hamburger* sandwich spaghetti sauce	*hamburger* sandwich sausage pizza pepperoni pizza anchovy pizza cheese pizza quesadilla
	weight	dumbbell barbell sunglass lab coat sunglasses	shoulder holster toy box spiral ratchet screwdriver carpenter's hammer flat tip screwdriver	*weight* lifting device airfoil gymnastic apparatus fastener
	dune buggy	thresher go-kart harvester racer lawn mower	car farm machine refrigerator car bicycle machine	farm machine car machine textile machine bulldozer

partial match, our implementation of FlatSE outperforms its original implementation (13.5% versus 9.4% in hit@1).

Experiment 3. HierSE or FlatSE? As Table 1 shows, HierSE beats FlatSE. In particular, when used in combination with the Flickr based semantic space, HierSE almost achieves a doubled accuracy when compared to the number reported in [9] (18.3% versus 9.4% in hit@1). Notice that our implementation of FlatSE scores lower than the original paper. One possible reason is that we use an off-the-shelf DeepNet, which might be less effective than its counterpart in [9]. Some tagging results are provided in Table 3.

4. CONCLUSIONS

This paper contributes to zero-shot image tagging by introducing the WordNet hierarchy into a deep learning based semantic embedding framework. The proposed hierarchical semantic embedding model is found to be effective. In addition, we identify two good practices which further improve the tagging accuracy. That is, using Flickr tags to train the semantic space, and using partial match to embed a WordNet node into the space. Code is available at `https://github.com/li-xirong/hierse`

Acknowledgements. This work was supported by NSFC (No. 61303184), the Fundamental Research Funds for the Central Universities and the Research Funds of Renmin University of China (No. 14XNLQ01).

5. REFERENCES

[1] Z. Akata, F. Perronnin, Z. Harchaoui, and C. Schmid. Label-embedding for attribute-based classification. In *CVPR*, 2013.

[2] J. Deng, W. Dong, R. Socher, L.-J. Li, K. Li, and L. Fei-Fei. ImageNet: A large-scale hierarchical image database. In *CVPR*, 2009.

[3] A. Frome, G. Corrado, J. Shlens, S. Bengio, J. Dean, M. Ranzato, and T. Mikolov. DeViSE: A deep visual-semantic embedding model. In *NIPS*, 2013.

[4] Y. Jia, E. Shelhamer, J. Donahue, S. Karayev, J. Long, R. Girshick, S. Guadarrama, and T. Darrell. Caffe: Convolutional architecture for fast feature embedding. In *ACMMM*, 2014.

[5] S. Kordumova, X. Li, and C. Snoek. Best practices for learning video concept detectors from social media examples. *MTAP*, 74(4):1291–1315, 2015.

[6] A. Krizhevsky, I. Sutskever, and G. Hinton. ImageNet classification with deep convolutional neural networks. In *NIPS*, 2012.

[7] C. Lampert, H. Nickisch, and S. Harmeling. Learning to detect unseen object classes by between-class attribute transfer. In *CVPR*, 2009.

[8] T. Mikolov, K. Chen, G. Corrado, and J. Dean. Efficient estimation of word representations in vector space. In *ICLR*, 2013.

[9] M. Norouzi, T. Mikolov, S. Bengio, Y. Singer, J. Shlens, A. Frome, G. Corrado, and J. Dean. Zero-shot learning by convex combination of semantic embedding. In *ICLR*, 2014.

[10] O. Russakovsky, J. Deng, H. Su, J. Krause, S. Satheesh, S. Ma, Z. Huang, A. Karpathy, A. Khosla, M. Bernstein, A. Berg, and L. Fei-Fei. ImageNet Large Scale Visual Recognition Challenge. *arXiv:1409.0575*, 2014.

[11] S. Zhu, Y.-G. Jiang, and C.-W. Ngo. Sampling and ontologically pooling web images for visual concept learning. *TMM*, 14(4):1068–1078, 2012.

Using Term Location Information to Enhance Probabilistic Information Retrieval

Baiyan Liu, Xiangdong An, Jimmy Xiangji Huang
Information Retrieval and Knowledge Management Research Lab
School of Information Technology
York University, Toronto, ON M3J 1P3, Canada
{baiyan, xan, jhuang}@yorku.ca

ABSTRACT

Nouns are more important than other parts of speech in information retrieval and are more often found near the beginning or the end of sentences. In this paper, we investigate the effects of rewarding terms based on their location in sentences on information retrieval. Particularly, we propose a novel Term Location (TEL) retrieval model based on BM25 to enhance probabilistic information retrieval, where a kernel-based method is used to capture term placement patterns. Experiments on f ve TREC datasets of varied size and content indicate the proposed model signif cantly outperforms the optimized BM25 and DirichletLM in MAP over all datasets with all kernel functions, and excels the optimized BM25 and DirichletLM over most of the datasets in P@5 and P@20 with different kernel functions.

Categories and Subject Descriptors

H.3.3 [**Information Systems**]: Information Search and Retrieval

Keywords

Term location, probabilistic information retrieval, noun

1. INTRODUCTION

English has 5 basic sentence patterns [1, 10]: (1) Subject + Verb (e.g., Joe swims); (2) Subject + Verb + Object (e.g., Joe plays the guitar); (3) Subject + Verb + Complement (e.g., Joe becomes a doctor); (4) Subject + Verb + Indirect Object + Direct Object (e.g., I give her a gift); and (5) Subject + Verb + Object + Complement (e.g., We elect him president). Most English simple sentences follow these 5 patterns and exceptions are rare (compound and complex sentences can be split into simple sentences) [10], where nouns and noun-phrases are mostly located in the beginning or the end of sentences. On the other hand, past research has indicated that nouns and noun-phrases are more information-bearing than the other parts of speech in information retrieval (IR) [6, 3, 8, 12]. Therefore, integrating term location information into IR may help improve retrieval performances.

Two illustrative experiments are conducted to verify the hypothesis. The f rst illustrative experiment on WT2g dataset (247,491 web documents, TREC'99 Web track) indicates nouns do concentrate on both ends of sentences as shown in Table 1, where $AvgDis$ is the average of the normalized distances of a set T of nouns from the middle of their sentences as def ned by Eq. 1. In Eq. 1, $|T|$ means the cardinality of set T (In this paper, except as explicitly noted, |x| means absolute value of x).

$$AvgDis = \frac{\sum_{t \in T} avg(|Mid(t) - Pos(t)|/Mid(t))}{|T|} \quad (1)$$

where $Mid(t)$ is the middle position of the sentence that noun t is in, $Pos(t)$ is the position of t, and T is the set of nouns. Since a term may appear in a document more than once, average function $avg(.)$ is used. $AvgDis$ has a range of [0, 1], and is closer to 0 if all nouns are gathered in the middle of sentences.

Table 1 shows that $AvgDis > 0.5$ on both halves of the sentences, which means that the nouns are nearer to the beginning or the end of sentences than to the middle of sentences.

Table 1: Noun placement in sentences

End	AvgDis	# Nouns	Avg. sent. len.	# Sentences
Left	0.5901	24,918,926	10.5619	14,360,676
Right	0.613	26,286,542		

Table 2: Relevant noun placement in sentences

Term	Score	Term	Score
louisa	43	head	-24
gradgrind	27	ladi	-17
tom	23	hand	-16
bounderbi	22	countri	-16
slackbridg	15	time	-16

The second illustrative experiment on *Hard Times* by Charles Dickens [2] illustrates that relevant terms are more likely located in the beginning or the end of than in the middle of sentences as shown in Table 2, where $Score > 0$ if a term is more often found near the beginning or the end of sentences, and $Score < 0$ otherwise. To obtain $Score$ of a term t in a document D, sentences in D are each partitioned into three parts, $\{p_1\ p_2\ p_3\}$, where $|p_1| = |p_3|$ and $|p_2| = |p_1| + |p_3|$, and a score to t for its each occurrence in D is assigned by Eq. 2:

$$Score(t) = \begin{cases} 1 & \text{if t } \in p_1 \cup p_3 \\ -1 & \text{if t } \in p_2 \end{cases} \quad (2)$$

Then $Score$ of t for all of its occurrences in D is given by Eq. 3:

$$Score(t, D) = \sum_{t_i \in D} Score(t_i) \quad (3)$$

where t_i is the ith occurrence of t in D.

Table 2 shows that the highest scoring terms "louisa", "gradgrind", "bounderbi", "tom", and "slackbridg" turn out to be the

SIGIR'15, August 09 - 13, 2015, Santiago, Chile.
© 2015 ACM. ISBN 978-1-4503-3621-5/15/08 ...$15.00.
DOI: http://dx.doi.org/10.1145/2766462.2767827.

main or minor characters in the book, whereas the lowest scoring terms are not particularly related with the novel.

The results from the two illustrative experiments above indicate the hypothesis deserves a deeper investigation. The main contributions of this paper are as follows:

- We extend BM25 naturally with term location information to enhance probabilistic information retrieveal;
- In order to reward terms that are more likely to be nouns, we propose a novel kernel-based Term Location (TEL) retrieval model to capture term placement patterns;
- Experiments on f ve TREC datasets of varied size and content indicate the proposed model is highly promising.

2. RELATED WORK

Jing and Croft [6] proposed PhraseFinder to automatically construct collection-dependent association thesauri, and then used the association thesauri to assist query expansion and found that nouns and noun-phrases were most effective in improving IR. Liu et al. [8] classif ed noun-phrases into four types – proper names, dictionary phrases, simple phrases, and complex phrases – and ranked documents based on phrase similarity. Zheng et al [17] used noun-phrases and semantic relationships to represent documents in order to assist document clustering, where noun-phrases were extracted with the assistance of WordNet. Yang et al [14] used a parse tree to transform the sentences in legal agreements into subject-verb-object (SVO) representations, which are then used in conjunction with cue terms to identify the provisions provided by the sentences. However, they found that provision extraction using the SVO representation resulted in high precision but low recall, which could be due to the specif city of SVO sentence patterns and the diff culty in parsing complex sentences. Hung et al. [4] used syntactic pattern matching to extract syntactically complete sentences that express event-based commonsense knowledge from web documents, and then semantic role labeling was used to tag the semantic roles of the terms in the sentences, such as the subject and the object. Ibekwe-SanJuan et al. [5] built f nite state automaton with syntactic patterns and synonyms from WordNet, which was used to tag the sentences in scientif c documents according to its category. It is diff cult to f nd syntactic patterns that are effective in all the documents of a single corpus, and rule-based part-of-speech taggers are less effective in unseen text [7]. Terms were rewarded based on their locations in a document in [15, 16].

3. OUR APPROACH

3.1 Term Location

We assume that the most important terms in the documents are near the beginning or the end of the sentences. We determine the importance (relevancy) of a term t by examining its distance from the middle of its sentence in document D as def ned by Eq. 4:

$$q(t, D) = |Mid(t, D) - Pos(t, D)| \tag{4}$$

$$\text{where } Mid(t, D) = (SL(t, D) - 1)/2,$$

$SL(t, D)$ is the length of the sentence in D that contains t, and $Pos(t, D)$ is the location of t in the sentence. We use the average distance of t from the middle of its sentences in D if t appears more than once in D, which is def ned as $r(t, D)$ by Eq. 5:

$$r(t, D) = (\sum_{t_i \in D} q(t_i, D))/tf(t, D) \tag{5}$$

where t_i is the ith occurrence of t in D and $tf(t, D)$ is the term frequency of t in D. We def ne $m(t, D)$ to be the average length of the sentence(s) that contain t in D as Eq. 6:

$$m(t, D) = \frac{\sum_{t_i \in D} SL(t_i, D)}{\beta * tf(t, D)} + \gamma \tag{6}$$

where parameter β has a larger effect for longer sentences since it is proportional to the lengths of the sentences, and parameter γ has a proportionally smaller effect for longer sentences since it is the same for all sentences. These two parameters are used to balance term weights in particularly short or long sentences.

3.2 Kernel Functions

In order to measure the distances of the terms from the middle of their sentences, we f t a kernel function over each sentence. We adjust the weight of each term based on its average distance to the middle of its sentences. In this paper, we explore the following kernel functions for our location based reward function $RN(t, D)$ used in Eq. 9:

$$\text{Gaussian - } Kernel(r, m) = 1 - e^{\frac{r^2}{-2m^2}}$$

$$\text{Triangle - } Kernel(r, m) = \frac{r}{m}$$

$$\text{Cosine - } Kernel(r, m) = 1 - \frac{1 + \cos \frac{r\pi}{m}}{2}$$

$$\text{Circle - } Kernel(r, m) = 1 - \sqrt{1 - \left(\frac{r}{m}\right)^2}$$

$$\text{Quartic - } Kernel(r, m) = 1 - \left(1 - \left(\frac{r}{m}\right)^2\right)^2$$

$$\text{Epanechnikov - } Kernel(r, m) = \left(\frac{r}{m}\right)^2$$

$$\text{Triweight - } Kernel(r, m) = 1 - \left(1 - \left(\frac{r}{m}\right)^2\right)^3$$

Among them, Gaussian kernel is widely used in statistics and machine learning such as Support Vector Machines, Triangle kernel, Circle Kernel, and Cosine Kernel are applied to estimate the proximity-based density distribution for the positional language model [9]. Since the kernel functions are not maturely applied in IR, we also explore Quartic kernel, Epanechnikov kernel and Triweight kernel in this work. In these kernel functions, r and m are def ned by Eqs. 5 and 6, respectively. With these kernel functions, the number of terms that are given maximum reward decreases as $m(t, D)$ increases.

3.3 Integration into BM25

In this experiment, we use the BM25 weighting model as our base weighting model. BM25 is def ned as follows:

$$Score(t, D) = TF(t, D) * IDF(t) \tag{7}$$

$$\text{where } TF(t, D) = \frac{(k_3 + 1) * tf(t, D) * qtf(t)}{(k_3 + qtf(t)) * K},$$

$$IDF(t) = log_2 \frac{N - n(t) + 0.5}{n(t) + 0.5},$$

$$K = k_1 * \left(1 - b + \frac{b * |D|}{AvgDL}\right) + tf(t, D),$$

k_1, k_3, and b are tuning parameters for BM25, $qtf(t)$ is the frequency of t in the query, $|D|$ is the number of terms in D, $AvgDL$ is the average length of the documents in the collection, N is the number of documents in the collection, and $n(t)$ is the number of documents in the collection that contain t. We modify $TF(t, D)$ to account for the reward given to the terms based on their locations in the sentences. We def ne the Term Location score (TL) as follows:

$$TL(t, D) = \frac{(k_3 + 1) * RN(t, D) * tf(t, D) * qtf(t)}{(k_3 + qtf(t)) * K_{TL}} \tag{8}$$

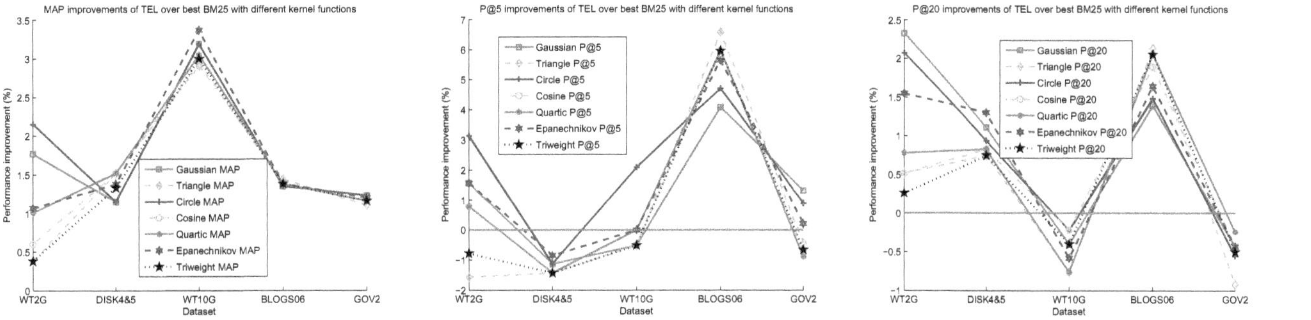

Figure 1: Performance improvements of TEL over best BM25 with different kernel functions.

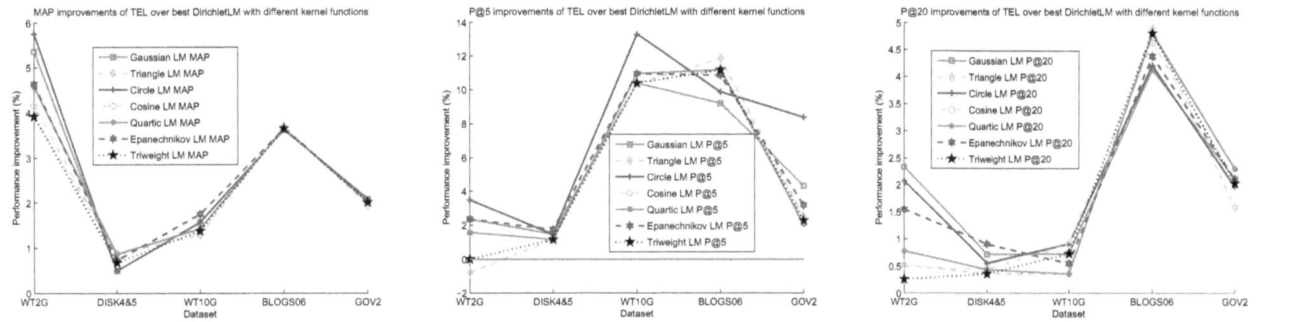

Figure 2: Performance improvements of TEL over best DirichletLM with different kernel functions.

where

$$K_{TL} = k_1 * \left(1 - b + \frac{b * |D|}{AvgDL}\right) + RN(t, D) * tf(t, D) \quad (9)$$

We integrate our model into BM25 to form the Term Location Score (TEL) as follows:

$$TEL(t, D) = ((1 - \alpha) * TF(t, D) + \alpha * TL(t, D)) * IDF(t) \quad (10)$$

where α controls the contribution of our model.

4. EXPERIMENTAL RESULTS

We conduct experiments on f ve standard TREC collections: WT2G, DISK4&5, WT10G, BLOGS06, and GOV2. These datasets vary in both size and content, where WT2g contains 247,491 general Web documents (TREC'99 Web track), DISK4&5 is comprised of 528,155 newswire documents from sources such as the Financial Times and the Federal Register (TREC'97-99 Ad hoc track), WT10G has 1,692,096 general web documents (TREC'00-01 Web track), BLOGS06 consists of 3,215,171 feeds from late 2005 to early 2006 with associated permalink and homepage documents (TREC'06-08 Blog track), and GOV2 holds 25,178,548 documents crawled from .gov sites (TREC'04-06 Terabyte track).

We compare our model against the following weighting models when they perform best on each dataset with parameters obtained as follows:

1. BM25, with $k_1 = 1.2$ and $k_3 = 8$. We adjust b in the range of [0.1, 0.9] in steps of 0.1 for each dataset to f nd the value of b that gives the best MAP for that dataset.
2. DirichletLM. We adjust μ in the range of [100, 3000] in steps of 100. We f nd the optimal value of μ for each dataset.

The proposed model TEL uses the same values as BM25 for k_1, k_3, and b, and sets $\alpha = 0.2$, $\beta = 3$, and $\gamma = 3$ for all datasets. In the future, we would study the optimal values of the model parameters and their relations with the characteristics of the datasets. We use the TREC off cial evaluation measures in our experiments, namely the topical MAP on BLOGS06 [11], and Mean Average Precision (MAP) on all the other datasets [13]. To stress the top retrieved documents, we also include P@5 and P@20 as the evaluation measures. All statistical tests are based on Wilcoxon Matched-pairs Signed-rank test.

The experimental results are presented in Table 3. To illustrate the performance differences graphically, we plot the results in Figures 1 and 2. As shown by the two f gures, our model TEL outperforms optimized BM25 and DirichletLM in MAP over all datasets with all kernel functions, and outperforms the two optimized baseline models over most of the datasets in $P@5$ and $P@20$ with different kernel functions. The performance improvements of our model TEL against DirichletLM are greater than those against BM25. According to the two f gures, each kernel function has its advantage on some datasets. There is no single kernel function that outperforms others on all the datasets.

5. CONCLUSIONS AND FUTURE WORK

In this paper, we extend BM25 and reward the terms based on their locations in the sentences with kernel functions. Experimental study shows that the proposed model performs signif cantly better than BM25 and DirichletLM on MAP over all datasets, and signif icantly better on P@5, p@10, and p@20 over most datasets.

In the future, more experiments will be conducted to further investigate the proposed model. We would investigate non-symmetric kernel functions and kernel functions with negative values since the placement of the terms at the beginning of the sentences is different from that at the end of the sentences as indicated in the f rst illustra-

Model	Eval Metric	WT2G	DISK4&5	WT10G	BLOGS06	GOV2
$BM25$	MAP	0.3167	0.2176	0.2134	0.3195	0.3008
	$P@5$	0.5120	**0.4680**	0.3918	0.6380	0.6094
	$P@20$	0.3870	0.3613	**0.2776**	0.6095	**0.5406**
$DirichletLM$	MAP	0.3059	0.2190	0.2168	0.3125	0.2983
	$P@5$	0.5080	0.4560	0.3531	0.6080	0.5919
	$P@20$	0.3870	0.3627	0.2745	0.5935	0.5272
TEL Gaussian	MAP	0.3223*+ (+1.77%,+5.36%)	0.2201 (+1.15%,+0.50%)	0.2202* (+3.19%,+1.57%)	0.3238+ (+1.35%,+3.62%)	**0.3045*+** (+1.23%,+2.08%)
	P@5	0.5200* (+1.56%,+2.36%)	0.4627+ (-1.13%,+1.47%)	0.3898+ (-0.51%,10.39%)	0.6640* (+4.08%,+9.21%)	**0.6174*+** (+1.31%,+4.31%)
	P@20	**0.3960** (+2.33%,+2.33%)	0.3653* (+1.11%,+0.72%)	0.2765 (-0.40%,+0.73%)	0.6180 (+1.39%,+4.13%)	0.5383 (-0.43%,+2.11%)
TEL Triangle	MAP	0.3179 (+0.38%,+3.92%)	**0.2209*** (+1.52%,+0.87%)	0.2196* (+2.91%,+1.29%)	**0.3241*+** (+1.44%,+3.71%)	0.3041*+ (+1.10%,+1.94%)
	P@5	0.5040 (-1.56%,-0.79%)	0.4613+ (-1.43%,+1.16%)	0.3898+ (-0.51%,+10.39%)	**0.6800*** (+6.58%,+11.84%)	0.6067+ (-0.44%,,+2.50%)
	P@20	0.3890* (+0.52%,+0.52%)	0.3640*+ (+0.75%,+0.36%)	0.2755+ (-0.76%,+0.36%)	**0.6225** (+2.13%,+4.89%)	0.5356 (-0.92%,+1.59%)
TEL Circle	MAP	**0.3235*+** (+2.15%,+5.75%)	0.2201 (+1.15%,+0.50%)	0.2202* (+3.19%,+1.57%)	0.3238+ (+1.35%,+3.62%)	**0.3045*+** (+1.23%,+2.08%)
	P@5	**0.5280*** (+3.13%,+3.49%)	0.4627+ (-1.13%,+1.47%)	**0.4000*** (+2.09%,+13.28%)	0.6680* (+4.70%,+9.87%)	0.6148*+ (+0.89%,+8.37%)
	P@20	0.3950 (+2.07%,+2.07%)	0.3647* (+0.94%,+0.55%)	0.2770 (-0.22%,+0.91%)	0.6185 (+1.48%,+4.21%)	0.5376 (-0.55%,+1.97%)
TEL Cosine	MAP	0.3186 (+0.60%,+4.15%)	**0.2209*** (+1.52%,+0.87%)	0.2197* (+2.95%,+1.43%)	0.3239*+ (+1.38%,+3.65%)	0.3043*+ (+1.16%,+2.01%)
	$P@5$	0.5160* (+0.78%,+1.57%)	0.4613+ (-1.43%,+1.16%)	0.3898+ (-0.51%,+10.39%)	0.6760* (+5.96%,+11.18%)	0.6054+ (-0.66%,+2.28%)
	$P@20$	0.3890* (+0.52%,+0.52%)	0.3643*+ (+0.83%,+0.44%)	0.2770+ (-0.22%,+0.91%)	0.6210 (+1.89%,+4.63%)	0.5383 (-0.43%,+2.11%)
TEL Quartic	MAP	0.3199*+ (+1.01%,+4.58%)	**0.2209*** (+1.52%,+0.87%)	0.2199* (+3.05%,+1.43%)	0.3239*+ (+1.38%,+3.65%)	0.3043*+ (+1.16%,+2.01%)
	P@5	0.5160* (+0.78%,+1.57%)	0.4613+ (-1.43%,+1.16%)	0.3918+ (+0.00%,+10.96%)	0.6760* (+5.96%,+11.18%)	0.6040+ (-0.89,+2.04%)
	P@20	0.3900* (+0.78%,+0.78%)	0.3643*+ (+0.83%,+0.44%)	0.2755 (-0.76%,+0.36%)	0.6220 (+2.05%,+4.80%)	0.5393 (-0.24%,+2.30%)
TEL Epanechnikov	MAP	0.3201*+ (+1.07%,4.64%)	0.2206 (+1.38%,+0.73%)	**0.2206*** (+3.37%,+1.75%)	0.3239+ (+1.38%,+3.65%)	0.3044*+ (+1.20%,+2.04%)
	P@5	0.5200* (+1.56%,+2.36%)	0.4640+ (-0.85%,1.75%)	0.3918+ (+0.00%,+10.96%)	0.6740* (+5.64%,+10.86%)	0.6107*+ (+0.21%,+3.18%)
	P@20	0.3930 (+1.55%,+1.55%)	**0.3660*** (+1.30%,0.91%)	0.2760 (-0.58%,+0.55%)	0.6195 (+1.64%,+4.38%)	0.5383 (-0.43%,+2.11%)
TEL Triweight	MAP	0.3179 (+0.38%,+3.92%)	0.2205* (+1.33%,+0.68%)	0.2198* (+3.00%,+1.38%)	0.3239*+ (+1.38%,+3.65%)	0.3043*+ (+1.16%,+2.01%)
	P@5	0.5080 (-0.78%,0.00%)	0.4613+ (-1.43%,+1.16%)	0.3898+ (-0.51%,+10.39%)	0.6760* (+5.96%,+11.18%)	0.6054+ (-0.66%,+2.28%)
	P@20	0.3880* (+0.26%,+0.26%)	0.3640*+ (+0.75%,+0.36%)	0.2765+ (-0.40%,+0.73%)	0.6220 (+2.05%,+4.80%)	0.5379 (-0.50%,+2.03%)

Table 3: Comparison between TEL and two baselines BM25 and DirichletLM with different kernel functions: Parameter b of BM25 and parameter μ of DirichletLM are obtained and set individually for each dataset for their best performances, and "*" and "+" denote statistically signif cant improvements over BM25 and DirichletLM (Wilcoxon signed-rank test with $p < 0.05$), respectively. The best result obtained on each dataset is in bold. The two percentages below each value are the percentage improvement of TEL over BM25 and DirichletLM, respectively.

tive experiment. It is also worthwhile to analyze the optimal values of the model parameters and their relations with the characteristics of the datasets. Different term proximity measures would also be explored to improve the performance of our model.

6. ACKNOWLEDGMENTS

This research is supported by the research grant from the Natural Sciences & Engineering Research Council (NSERC) of Canada and NSERC CREATE Award. We thank anonymous reviewers for their thorough review comments on this paper.

7. REFERENCES

[1] H. Ann. *The Essentials of English — a writer's handbook*. New York, Pearson Education, 2003.

[2] C. Dickens. *Hard Times*. Bradbury & Evans, 1854.

[3] D. A. Evans and C. Zhai. Noun-phrase analysis in unrestricted text for information retrieval. In *ACL 1996*, pages 17–24.

[4] S.-H. Hung, C.-H. Lin, and J.-S. Hong. Web mining for event-based commonsense knowledge using lexico-syntactic pattern matching and semantic role labeling. *Expert Systems with Applications*, 37(1):341–347, 2010.

[5] F. Ibekwe-SanJuan and et al. Annotation of scientif c summaries for information retrieval. *CoRR*, 2011.

[6] Y. Jing and W. B. Croft. An association thesaurus for information retrieval. In *RIAO'94*, pages 146–160.

[7] K. Liu and et al. Effectiveness of lexico-syntactic pattern matching for ontology enrichment with clinical documents. *Meth. of info. in med.*, 50(5):397, 2011.

[8] S. Liu, F. Liu, C. Yu, and W. Meng. An effective approach to document retrieval via utilizing wordnet and recognizing phrases. In *SIGIR'04*, pages 266–272.

[9] Y. Lv and C. Zhai. Positional language models for information retrieval. In *SIGIR'09*, pages 299–306.

[10] C. F. Meyer. *Introducing English Linguistics*. Cambridge University Press, 2010.

[11] I. Ounis and et al. Overview of the TREC-2006 blog track.

[12] O. Vechtomova. Noun phrases in interactive query expansion and document ranking. *Info. Retrieval*, 9:399–420, 2006.

[13] E. Voorhees and D. Harman. *TREC: Experiment and evaluation in information retrieval*. MIT Press, 2005.

[14] D. Yang and et al. A natural language processing and semantic-based system for contract analysis. In *ICTAI 2013*, pages 707–712.

[15] J. Zhao, X. Huang, and S. Wu. Rewarding term location information to enhance probabilistic information retrieval. In *SIGIR'12*.

[16] J. Zhao, X. Huang, and Z. Ye. Modeling term associations for probabilistic information retrieval. *ACM Trans. Inf. Syst.*, 32(2), 2014.

[17] H.-T. Zheng and et al. Exploiting noun phrases and semantic relationships for text document clustering. *Info. Sci.*, 179(13):2249–2262, 2009.

Learning Context-aware Latent Representations for Context-aware Collaborative Filtering

Xin Liu
Institute for Infocomm Research
Singapore
liu-x@i2r.a-star.edu.sg

Wei Wu
Institute for Infocomm Research
Singapore
wwu@i2r.a-star.edu.sg

ABSTRACT

In this paper, we propose a generic framework to learn context-aware latent representations for context-aware collaborative filtering. Contextual contents are combined via a function to produce the context influence factor, which is then combined with each latent factor to derive latent representations. We instantiate the generic framework using biased Matrix Factorization as the base model. A Stochastic Gradient Descent (SGD) based optimization procedure is developed to fit the model by jointly learning the weight of each context and latent factors. Experiments conducted over three real-world datasets demonstrate that our model significantly outperforms not only the base model but also the representative context-aware recommendation models.

Categories and Subject Descriptors

H.3.3 [**Information Search and Retrieval**]: Information filtering; H.4 [**Information Systems Applications**]: Miscellaneous

General Terms

Algorithms, Performance

Keywords

Context-aware; collaborative filtering; recommendation; latent factor models

1. INTRODUCTION

Rich contextual information that is pervasively available in many online applications provides an important information source to accurately model users' preference for collaborative filtering (CF) tasks such as rating prediction and top-N recommendation [1, 11, 5, 8, 3, 2]. For instance, in Point-of-Interest (POI) recommendation, the information such as time, weather and emotion may influence a user's preference on a certain POI, and hence influences the recommendations generated for this user.

SIGIR'15, August 09 - 13, 2015, Santiago, Chile.
© 2015 ACM. ISBN 978-1-4503-3621-5/15/08 ...$15.00.
DOI: http://dx.doi.org/10.1145/2766462.2767775.

Conventional context-aware CF models either separately process contexts, e.g., using contexts to partition input data (pre-processing) or adjust the order of recommended item list (post-processing) [1, 8] or jointly learn the context influence and other parameters during model building [10, 14, 13]. In this work, we follow the joint learning approach, which provides strong mathematical foundation for context modeling. Recent such models are designed based on latent factor models such as Matrix Factorization (MF). However, most of these approaches assume users, items and contexts share the same latent space (i.e., the relations among the three entities are captured by the inner product of their latent factors), which may not always make sense in complex real-world applications. Moreover, treating users, items and contexts as the same level entities may over-estimate the influence of contextual information, thus weakening the impacts of other latent aspects.

In order to address these issues, we propose a generic context-aware framework for latent factor models. The contextual information is firstly processed to generate user-related and item-related context influence factors. Such influence factors are then directly combined with users' and items' latent factors to derive the context-aware latent representations, which can be used to calculate users' context-aware preference on items. Such an approach not only handles user-related and item-related contexts for users' and items' latent factors respectively, but also properly integrates context influence into latent factors to balance the impacts of contexts.

We instantiate the proposed framework using biased MF model, a popular MF based model for rating prediction. We develop a Stochastic Gradient Descent (SGD) based optimization procedure to learn the context-aware latent representations by jointly estimating context related parameters and users' and items' latent factors. Experiments using three real-world datasets demonstrate that our context-aware biased MF evidently outperforms the conventional biased MF, as well as a representative context-aware model called Factorization Machines (FM) [11].

2. RELATED WORK

Recent research focuses on integrating contexts into latent factor models. By modeling feedback information as a user-item-context tensor, Karatzoglou et al. [5] proposed a multiverse recommendation model, where tucker decomposition is applied to factorize the tensor. However, the type of contexts is restricted to be categorical. Similar ideas are presented in [15], which was particularly designed for top-N recommendation by directly optimizing Mean Average Precision (MAP). Another line of research focuses on Factorization Machines [11, 13], which can handle diverse types of contexts for context-aware CF. The basic idea is to assign same dimension latent vectors to users, items and contexts and model all interactions between pairs of the three entities with respect to the target. An improvement that selects useful contexts for FM using gradient booting was introduced in [4]. In [10], the authors improve FM by breaking the limits of linearly combining latent factors. A non-linear probabilistic algorithm for context-aware recommendation was proposed using Gaussian processes. As mentioned in introduction section, such approaches suffer from the issue that restricts users, items and contexts to share the same latent space, which may not capture the real relations among the three entities.

There are also some models proposed to handle specific types of context such as social information [9] or time [7]. However, these methods cannot be directly applied to process general contextual information.

3. A GENERIC CONTEXT-AWARE FRAMEWORK

In this section, we present a generic framework for context-aware collaborative filtering. We denote user set by $\mathcal{U} = \{u_1, u_2, ...\}$, where the real-valued latent factor vector (with the dimensionality of D) of user u is represented by $\mathbf{u}$, and item set by $\mathcal{V} = \{v_1, v_2, ...\}$, where the real-valued latent factor vector (with the dimensionality of D) of item v is represented by $\mathbf{v}$. The outcome of the interaction between user u and item v is denoted by $y_{u,v}$, which can be explicit (e.g., 5-point scale rating) or implicit (e.g., clicked an advertisement). Tensor $Y \in \mathcal{R}^{|\mathcal{U}|\times|\mathcal{V}|\times K}$ records all observed interactions between users and items under the corresponding K types of contexts.

The research problem of context-aware collaborative filtering is formulated as *given observed users' feedback to items and the associated contextual information, model the interaction between feedback data and context data to predict users' feedback to unobserved items under certain context situations.* Mathematically, we want to find context-aware latent representations φ for user u and item v to derive u's feedback to v:

$$y_{u,v} = f(\varphi(\mathbf{u}, \theta_u), \varphi(\mathbf{v}, \theta_v)), \quad (1)$$

where θ_x ($x = u$ or v) denotes the context influence factor derived for the user or the item. $\varphi(.,.)$ is a function that combines the user's or item's latent factor and the corresponding context influence factor for latent representations. $f(.,.)$ is a function that formulates users' and items' latent representations for predicting users' feedback score to items[1].

The framework is generic from two aspects: (1) any form of function (linear or non-linear) $\varphi(.,.)$ can be applied to combine latent factor and context influence factor to derive context-aware latent representations, and (2) the idea can be applied to any latent factor model such as basic MF, SVD++ [6], even social recommendation models like SoReg [9]. In the next section, we instantiate this generic framework using biased MF to demonstrate how it works.

[1]For most latent factor models like MF, such a function calculates the inner product of the latent factors of the corresponding user and item

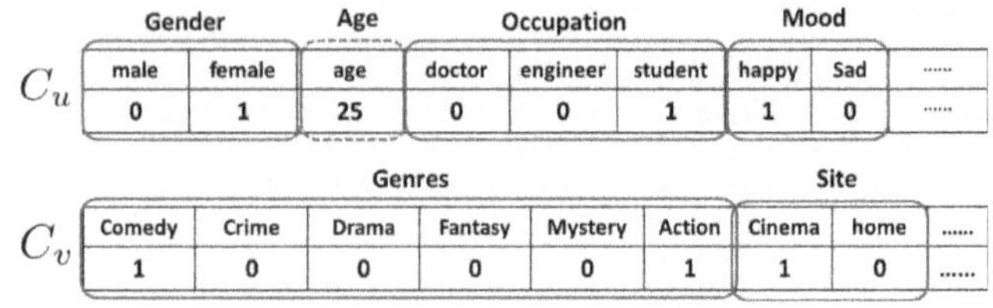

Figure 1: An example of user-related and item-related contextual information in the context of movie recommendation. Dashed rectangle indicates continuous-valued context and regular rectangle indicates categorical-valued context (binary variable where 1 indicates "belong to" and 0 otherwise).

4. CONTEXT-AWARE BIASED MATRIX FACTORIZATION

In order to better model the influence of contexts on users' and items' latent factors, we divide all contexts into user-related contexts that may influence users' behavior (e.g., in movie recommendation, users' age, gender, time of watching, mood, etc.) and item-related contexts that may characterize items (e.g., in movie recommendation, movies' genres, showed in cinema or on TV, etc.). For an interaction between user u and item v, the associated user-related contextual information is denoted by C_a which consists of K_a types of contexts[2]. Similarly, the associated item-related contextual information, which consists of K_b types of contexts, is denoted by C_b. To support both continuous valued contexts and categorical valued contexts, following FM [11], C_a/C_b is represented as a real-valued variables vector (see Figure 1 as an example).

We use a sigmoid function to linearly combine contexts to derive the context influence factor:

$$\theta_{x,d} = \frac{1}{1 + e^{-(\eta_{x,d} + \sum_{i=1}^{|C_x|} w_{i,d}\gamma_i)}}, \quad (2)$$

where $x = a$ or b, indicating the context influence factor is derived for users or items, and d denotes the index of the latent factor in the vector. γ_i denotes the ith context value and w_i is the corresponding weight, η is the bias to adjust the context influence to the corresponding latent factor. Intuitively, each latent factor of each user or item expects a unique influence factor (i.e., the unique context influence parameters including the bias and context weights for contexts combination) for context-aware latent representation. However, this significantly increases model complexity in terms of parameter update computation and storage. To make the model applicable in practice, we propose to maintain D sets of context influence parameters for the D latent factors of *all* users and *all* items respectively, that is, we introduce totally $2 \times D \times (|C_a| + |C_b| + 1 + 1)$ context influence parameters. We argue that the introduced complexity is minor in that it won't increase with the increasing number of observations but only rely on latent vector dimensionality and the size of the context variable vector, which are typically small (compared to the number of latent factors) in most application scenario.

[2]Note that user-related contexts and item-related contexts may overlap.

We can then derive the latent representations that combine[3] latent factors and context influence factors for user u and item v:

$$\varphi_{u,d} = \mathbf{u}_d + \theta_{u,d}, \tag{3}$$

$$\varphi_{v,d} = \mathbf{v}_d + \theta_{v,d}, \tag{4}$$

where d indicates the dth latent factor of u's or v's latent vector. After obtaining latent representations, following the design of biased MF, user u's feedback to item v can be predicted as:

$$\hat{y}_{u,v} = \mu + b_u + b_v + \sum_{d=1}^{D} \varphi_{u,d}\varphi_{v,d}, \tag{5}$$

where μ is the global mean, b_u and b_v are user bias and item bias respectively. The loss function is formulated as:

$$L = \frac{1}{2}\sum_{(u,v)\in\Omega}(y_{u,v} - \hat{y}_{u,v})^2 + \frac{\lambda_1}{2}(\sum_u \parallel \mathbf{u} \parallel^2 + \sum_v \parallel \mathbf{v} \parallel^2 + \sum_u b_u^2 + \sum_v b_u^2) + \frac{\lambda_2}{2}\sum_{d=1}^{D}(\eta_{a,d}^2 + \sum_{i=1}^{|C_a|} w_{i,d}^2 + \eta_{b,d}^2 + \sum_{j=1}^{|C_b|} w_{j,d}^2), \tag{6}$$

where Ω indicates the training set. The second and third terms are used to avoid overfitting, where λ_1 and λ_2 are regularization terms for latent factors (and biases), and context influence parameters respectively, d indicates the dth latent factor of latent vector.

To fit the proposed context-aware biased MF, we develop a SGD based optimization procedure which iteratively updates all parameters until the loss converges or pre-defined iterations have reached:

$$\Theta_f \leftarrow \Theta_f - \alpha_f \frac{\partial L}{\partial \Theta_f}, \tag{7}$$

$$\Theta_c \leftarrow \Theta_c - \alpha_c \frac{\partial L}{\partial \Theta_c}, \tag{8}$$

where Θ_f indicates latent factors, users' and items' biases, and Θ_c indicates context influence parameters (i.e., context weights and biases). α_f and α_c are the corresponding learning rates. The gradient of L with respect to each user's or item's latent factor as well as the bias is computed as follows:

$$\frac{\partial L}{\partial \mathbf{u}_d} = (\hat{y}_{u,v} - y_{u,v})(\mathbf{v}_d + \theta_{v,d}) + \lambda_1 \mathbf{u}_d. \tag{9}$$

$$\frac{\partial L}{\partial \mathbf{v}_d} = (\hat{y}_{u,v} - y_{u,v})(\mathbf{u}_d + \theta_{u,d}) + \lambda_1 \mathbf{v}_d. \tag{10}$$

$$\frac{\partial L}{\partial b_u} = (\hat{y}_{u,v} - y_{u,v}) + \lambda_1 b_u. \tag{11}$$

$$\frac{\partial L}{\partial b_v} = (\hat{y}_{u,v} - y_{u,v}) + \lambda_1 b_v. \tag{12}$$

The gradient of L with respect to each context influence parameter (i.e., the weight of each context and context bias for users and items) is computed as follows:

[3]We also tried other combination methods such as multiplication, but experimental results show that addition generates better performance.

$$\frac{\partial L}{\partial w_{i,d}} = (\hat{y}_{u,v} - y_{u,v})(\mathbf{v}_d + \theta_{v,d})\theta_{u,d}(1 - \theta_{u,d})\gamma_i + \lambda_2 w_{i,d}, \tag{13}$$

where i indicates the ith context value in the user-related context vector C_a.

$$\frac{\partial L}{\partial w_{j,d}} = (\hat{y}_{u,v} - y_{u,v})(\mathbf{u}_d + \theta_{u,d})\theta_{v,d}(1 - \theta_{v,d})\gamma_j + \lambda_2 w_{j,d}, \tag{14}$$

where j indicates the jth context value in the item-related context vector C_b.

$$\frac{\partial L}{\partial \eta_a} = (\hat{y}_{u,v} - y_{u,v})(\mathbf{v}_d + \theta_{v,d})\theta_{u,d}(1 - \theta_{u,d}) + \lambda_2 \eta_a. \tag{15}$$

$$\frac{\partial L}{\partial \eta_b} = (\hat{y}_{u,v} - y_{u,v})(\mathbf{u}_d + \theta_{u,d})\theta_{v,d}(1 - \theta_{v,d}) + \lambda_2 \eta_b. \tag{16}$$

Once all parameters have been learned, user u's feedback to item v can be predicted by using Eq. 5.

5. EVALUATION

5.1 Experimental setup

We evaluate the performance of the proposed model using three real-world datasets: (1) Movielens-100K[4], which consists of 100,000 ratings (ranging from 1 to 5) from 943 users on 1682 movies. The user-related contexts include age, gender, occupation; the movie-related contexts include genres. (2) Douban[5] book data [16], which records 1,097,148 ratings from 33,523 users on 381,767 books. The user-related contexts include the number of friends, the number of "wish[6]" issued and the number of ratings provided; the book-related contexts include the number of "wish" received and the number of ratings got. (3) Douban music data [16], which records 1,387,216 ratings from 29,287 users on 257,288 music items. The user-related and item-related contexts are the same with those used in Douban book data.

We compare the proposed context-aware biased MF with conventional biased MF and a representative context-aware model FM. Note that FM and our model share the same context set. The latent factors are initialized following uniform distribution [0 , 1E-4]. The parameters of latent factor models such as latent vector dimensionality, regularization term, learning rate, etc. are determined by cross-validation.

We randomly divide each dataset into training set that consists of 80% data and test set that contains 20% data. We measure the performance using Mean Absolute Error (MAE) and Root Mean Squared Error (RMSE), which are conventional metrics for measuring rating prediction accuracy. Each experiment is conducted 10 times, and we report the averaged results. Standard errors are shown (in Table 1) to indicate the confidence of the results.

5.2 Experimental results

Figure 2 shows when Movielns-100K data is used, how the performance of our model varies with different latent

[4]http://grouplens.org/datasets/movielens/

[5]Douban (http://www.douban.com/) is one of the largest Chinese based social platforms for sharing reviews and recommendations for books, movies and music. A social network is also provided to connect users.

[6]A user, although has not read a book, may still express her interest by indicating "wish"

Table 1: Performance comparison

	MovieLens-100K		Douban book		Douban music	
	MAE	RMSE	MAE	RMSE	MAE	RMSE
Our model	$0.7020_{\pm 0.0012}$	$0.8993_{\pm 0.0015}$	$0.5782_{\pm 0.0010}$	$0.7378_{\pm 0.0013}$	$0.5163_{\pm 0.0011}$	$0.6588_{\pm 0.0016}$
Biased MF	$0.7245_{\pm 0.0015}$	$0.9185_{\pm 0.0014}$	$0.6045_{\pm 0.0013}$	$0.7733_{\pm 0.0016}$	$0.5401_{\pm 0.0014}$	$0.6911_{\pm 0.0016}$
FM	$0.7160_{\pm 0.0010}$	$0.9112_{\pm 0.0013}$	$0.5886_{\pm 0.0012}$	$0.7584_{\pm 0.0014}$	$0.5342_{\pm 0.0014}$	$0.6755_{\pm 0.0017}$

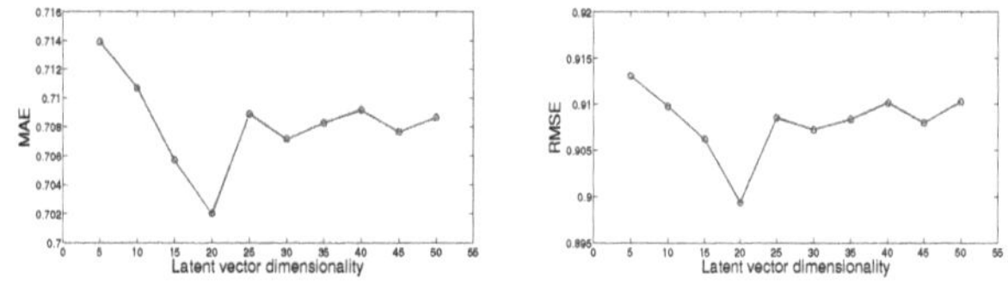

(a) MAE. (b) RMSE.

Figure 2: Performance with different latent dimensionality.

vector dimensionality. We set $\alpha_f = 0.012$, $\alpha_c = 0.0016$, $\lambda_1 = 0.0125$, $\lambda_2 = 0.000003$. We observe that MAE and RMSE are improved when the latent vector dimensionality increases. The best results are achieved when the dimensionality is 20, after which MAE and RMSE increase and become relatively stable. In the same way, we set latent dimensionality to 30 for Douban data ($\alpha_f = 0.005$, $\alpha_c = 0.00005$, $\lambda_1 = 0.01$, $\lambda_2 = 0.0001$), and 35 for Douban music data ($\alpha_f = 0.005$, $\alpha_c = 0.00005$, $\lambda_1 = 0.04$, $\lambda_2 = 0.0001$).

Table 1 summarizes the performance of all models when different datasets are used. By modeling pair-wise interactions among contexts, users and items, which are all represented by latent vectors, FM evidently outperforms biased MF, indicating the importance of contextual information in collaborative filtering. In all cases, our context-aware model outperforms FM (and biased MF), demonstrating the advantage of directly integrating contextual information into latent factors to learn context-aware latent representations. The results also reveal the limitation of restricting contexts to share the same latent space with users and items.

6. CONCLUSION

In this paper, we propose a generic framework to integrate contextual information into latent factor models. Context influence factor, which is derived by combining contexts, is directly combined with latent factor to generate content-aware latent representations. Such a framework is instantiated by using biased MF model. SGD based optimization procedure is developed to fit the context-aware biased MF model. Experimental results demonstrate the advantages of our model by comparing with the base model and FM.

An immediate next step is to instantiate the generic framework by using CF models for implicit feedback data such as Bayesian Personalized Ranking (BPR) [12] to provide context-aware top-N recommendation, which is useful in more application scenarios. Another direction is to investigate more sophisticated ways (e.g., non-linear methods) to combine contexts to better model context influence factor.

7. REFERENCES

[1] Gediminas Adomavicius, Ramesh Sankaranarayanan, Shahana Sen, and Alexander Tuzhilin. Incorporating contextual information in recommender systems using a multidimensional approach. *ACM Trans. Inf. Syst.*, 23(1):103–145, 2005.

[2] Deepak Agarwal, Bee-Chung Chen, and Bo Long. Localized factor models for multi-context recommendation. In *Proceedings of the 17th SIGKDD*, 2011.

[3] Tianqi Chen, Hang Li, Qiang Yang, and Yong Yu. General functional matrix factorization using gradient boosting. In *Proceedings of the 30th ICML*, 2013.

[4] Chen Cheng, Fen Xia, Tong Zhang, Irwin King, and Michael R. Lyu. Gradient boosting factorization machines. In *Proceedings of the 8th RecSys*, 2014.

[5] Alexandros Karatzoglou, Xavier Amatriain, Linas Baltrunas, and Nuria Oliver. Multiverse recommendation: n-dimensional tensor factorization for context-aware collaborative filtering. In *Proceedings of the 4th RecSys*, 2010.

[6] Yehuda Koren. Factorization meets the neighborhood: A multifaceted collaborative filtering model. In *Proceedings of the 14th SIGKDD*, 2008.

[7] Yehuda Koren. Collaborative filtering with temporal dynamics. In *Proceedings of the 15th SIGKDD*, 2009.

[8] Xin Liu and Karl Aberer. Soco: A social network aided context-aware recommender system. In *Proceedings of the 22nd WWW*, 2013.

[9] Hao Ma, Dengyong Zhou, Chao Liu, Michael R. Lyu, and Irwin King. Recommender systems with social regularization. In *Proceedings of the 4th WSDM*, 2011.

[10] Trung V. Nguyen, Alexandros Karatzoglou, and Linas Baltrunas. Gaussian process factorization machines for context-aware recommendations. In *Proceedings of the 37th SIGIR*, 2014.

[11] Steffen Rendle. Factorization machines with libFM. *ACM Trans. Intell. Syst. Technol.*, 3(3):57:1–57:22, May 2012.

[12] Steffen Rendle, Christoph Freudenthaler, Zeno Gantner, and Lars Schmidt-Thieme. Bpr: Bayesian personalized ranking from implicit feedback. In *Proceedings of the 25th UAI*, 2009.

[13] Steffen Rendle, Zeno Gantner, Christoph Freudenthaler, and Lars Schmidt-Thieme. Fast context-aware recommendations with factorization machines. In *Proceedings of the 34th SIGIR*, 2011.

[14] Yue Shi, Alexandros Karatzoglou, Linas Baltrunas, Martha Larson, and Alan Hanjalic. Cars2: Learning context-aware representations for context-aware recommendations. In *Proceedings of the 23rd CIKM*, 2014.

[15] Yue Shi, Alexandros Karatzoglou, Linas Baltrunas, Martha Larson, Alan Hanjalic, and Nuria Oliver. Tfmap: Optimizing map for top-n context-aware recommendation. In *Proceedings of the 35th SIGIR*, 2012.

[16] Erheng Zhong, Wei Fan, Junwei Wang, Lei Xiao, and Yong Li. Comsoc: Adaptive transfer of user behaviors over composite social network. In *Proceedings of the 18th SIGKDD*, 2012.

Exploiting User and Business Attributes for Personalized Business Recommendation

Kai Lu, Yi Zhang, Lanbo Zhang
School of Engineering
University of California, Santa Cruz
{kailu, yiz, lanbo}@soe.ucsc.edu

Shuxin Wang
Institute of Computing Technology
Chinese Academy of Sciences
wangshuxin@ict.ac.cn

ABSTRACT

Data sparsity and cold-start are two major problems in personalized recommendation. They are especially severe in business recommendation, because business transactions are usually completed offline and customers generally do not provide ratings after a transaction. Due to these two problems, matrix factorization (MF) models, which are shown to be effective in many recommendation tasks, are likely to fail on business recommendation tasks, especially for new users and new items. In this paper, we propose an Integrated Bias and Factorization Model (IBFM), which exploits user and business attributes. The user attributes include demographic information, vote information, point-of-interests; the business attributes include check-in information, locations, business names, categories, etc. To handle the cold-start problem, we employ a sampling strategy to generate the latent factor vectors for new users and new businesses based on similar users/businesses. Our methods are evaluated on the data set used in the RecSys 2013 Yelp business rating prediction challenge. Experimental results show that our proposed methods significantly outperform several existing state-of-the-art methods. In particular, the single model IBFM performs the best in this challenge on both public and private leaderboards.

Categories and Subject Descriptors

H.3.3 [**Information Search and Retrieval**]: Information Filtering

Keywords

Collaborative Filtering; Data Sparsity; Cold-start; Context Information; Matrix Factorization

1. INTRODUCTION

Collaborative Filtering (CF) based recommender systems provide an effective way to solve the information overload problem. In general, CF approaches can be divided into two categories: neighborhood models and matrix factorization (MF) models [1]. Neighborhood models capture the similarities between the neighbors of users (or items). However, this approach performs poorly when the data is sparse. MF maps users and items into comparable latent factors and can handle the data sparsity problem better.

SIGIR'15, August 09 - 13, 2015, Santiago, Chile.

ACM 978-1-4503-3621-5/15/08 ...$15.00.
DOI: http://dx.doi.org/10.1145/2766462.2767806.

There are two major problems which affect the performances of recommendation models: data sparsity and the cold-start (i.e. new user or new item) problem. In business recommendation, these two problems are more severe. As business transactions are usually completed offline, user ratings are extremely sparse, e.g., each user has very few ratings. For example, 50% of the users have only 1 rating in the training data released in RecSys13 Yelp business recommendation challenge. Traditional MF models often fail for two reasons: 1) existing user and business latent factor vectors over fit as each user/business has too few ratings in the training data; 2) predictions for new users or new businesses are very unreliable and introduces much uncertainty into the latent space.

To overcome the weakness of MF, we propose an Integrated Bias and Factorization Modeling approach (IBFM) which can mitigate both problems. IBFM overcomes the data sparsity and cold-start problem simultaneously in a framework through three major components. First, IBFM incorporates multiple user and business features into an integrated framework, which can mitigate the data sparsity, and enable the model to learn hidden representations of users and items more reliably with augmented information. Second, IBFM utilizes a sampling strategy to generate the new uers' (businesses') latent factor vectors. Instead of random sampling, IBFM considers user and business attributes, and uses the trained latent vectors of a new user/business's nearest existing users/businesses to generate their latent vector. Third, IBFM also incorporates user's potential interests in businesses they are not aware of before.

2. RELATED WORK

Variations of MF models are becoming very popular for their good performances on standard rating prediction tasks such as Netflix challenge. An SVD model with alternating least square optimization was proposed in [5]. Stochastic gradient descent based approaches for basic MF and Regular SVD were discussed [7]. SVD ++ [4] and Factorization Machine [8] which use Bayesian inference and MCMC sampling are now two of the state-of-the-art models in rating prediction tasks. However, these methods do not work well in the cold-start scenarios.

To solve the cold-start problems, many methods have been tried. [11, 2, 10] asked new users for several interviews to capture their preferences, and deployed latent factor models to provide recommendations for new users. [9] and [3] utilized content information to solve the new item recommendation problem, while their methods require a long training time and are not suitable for new users.

Compared with the methods mentioned above, our approaches can mitigate the data sparsity and cold-start problem for both new user and new business together. They are also more efficient and scalable to large data.

3. PROPOSED APPROACH

To solve the data sparsity and cold-start problems simultaneously, we propose an integrated single model, which we call Integrated Bias and Matrix Factorization Model, to incorporate user and business's various attributes together. The model contains three major components: user bias (i.e. preferences) model, business bias (i.e. preferences) model and latent factor space. We introduce each part step by step in the following sub sections.

3.1 User and Business Bias Model

To illustrate our idea, let's start with a baseline rating bias model proposed by [4], which is represented as: $\hat{r}_{ui} = \mu + b_u + b_i$. Where μ is the global average rating value, b_u is user's rating bias and b_i is business's rating bias.

3.1.1 User Attributes

We argue that a user's bias is related to his demographic information, his point-of-interests, and other users' voting information (e.g., funny, useful, cool) for his ratings. First, users who have the same gender might have similar rating tendency. Gender bias can be seen as the shared component for all the ratings by users with the same gender. Second, we assume if users have similar vote patterns, they share similar rating bias. Thus we can employ the user's vote information to infer his bias. Third, a user's rating bias is also related to his point-of-interests. Therefore we try to model user's bias/preference as follows:

$$b'_u = b_u + b_{gender(u)} + b_{vote(u)} + b_{u,lct(i)} \tag{1}$$

In this equation, $gender(u) = \{0, 1\}$, $vote(u) = \{0, 1, 2\}$. i.e., based on all the votes u gets, we choose the largest number as his vote classifier (i.e. funny, useful, cool). $b_{u,lct(i)}$ represents u's point-of-interests and $b_{u,lct(i)} = \alpha_{u,lct(i)} \cdot \omega_{u,lct(i)}$. We represent the business's location using its zip code, thus $lct(i)$ is the location (i.e. zip code) of business i. $\alpha_{u,lct(i)}$ is user u's bias for location of business i (i.e. zip code) and $\omega_{u,lct(i)}$ is the location weights, which is calculated as follows:

$$\omega_{u,lct(i)} = \frac{\log(1 + R_{u,lct(i)})}{1 + \log(1 + R_u)}$$

Where R_u is u's total ratings, $R_{u,lct(i)}$ is u's rating number of the businesses whose zip code is $lct(i)$.

3.1.2 Business Attributes

On the business side, we can also collect various features. These features can be categorized into three categories: check-in information, location information and content information.

Checkin: For the check-in information, we think that a business's rating bias is related to the businesses whose check-in patterns are close to it. Thus the business rating bias can be represented as follows:

$$c_i = \frac{\sum_{j \in C(i)} b_j \cdot csim(i \parallel j)}{\sum_{j \in C(i)} csim(i \parallel j)} \tag{2}$$

where $C(i)$ are the businesses with check-in patterns similar to i. We measure $csim(i \parallel j)$ using KL-divergence:

$$KL(p_i \parallel p_j) = \sum_{k=0}^{P} p_i(k) \log \frac{p_i(k)}{p_j(k)}$$

$$csim(i \parallel j) = 1 - \frac{KL(p_i \parallel p_j)}{max\{KL(p_i \parallel p_x) : x \in X\}}$$

where p_i and p_j denote business i and j's check-in distributions in different hours of weekdays, P is the vector length, and X denotes all businesses with check-in information.

Location: Based on a business's location information, we propose a location bias model that incorporates the business's zip code, street, city, longitude and latitude. The model is:

$$l_i = b_{zip\_code(i)} + b_{street(i)} + b_{city(i)} + \frac{\sum_{j \in G(i)} b_j \cdot gsim(i, j)}{\sum_{j \in G(i)} gsim(i, j)} \tag{3}$$

In the location bias, $zip\_code(i)$, $street(i)$ and $city(i)$ are business i's zip code, street and city information respectively. $G(i)$ are the nearest businesses in terms of geolocation. $\frac{\sum_{j \in G(i)} b_j \cdot gsim(i,j)}{\sum_{j \in G(i)} gsim(i,j)}$ is other closest businesses' bias affect for i's bias. We use longitude and latitude to measure the similarities between two businesses:

$$gsim(i, j) = 1 - \frac{distance(i, j)}{max\{distance(i, l) : l \in L\}}$$

In this equation, $distance(i, j)$ is calculated by the longitude and latitude of i and j, L denotes all the businesses with location information.

Name and Category: Two types of business content information are considered: name and category taxonomy. A specific company may have multiple stores in different places; e.g., in Yelp review data, there are over 30 different "CVS pharmacy" stores in Arizona. Assuming businesses with the same name are similar, we introduce a name based bias to capture the similarities between stores of similar names. There are over 2,000 different categories in the Yelp business data set, among which 25 are first level categories. We use the first level category which each business is classified into. We also consider that the business's bias is related to other businesses' bias in the same category. Thus the content bias model is:

$$t_i = b_{u,rtc(i)} + b_{cg(i)} + \frac{1}{|Name(i)|} \sum_{j \in Name(i)} b_j + \frac{1}{|CG(i)|} \sum_{j \in CG(i)} b_j \tag{4}$$

where $CG(i)$ contains all the businesses in the same category as business i. $Name(i)$ are the set of businesses with the same name as business i. $b_{u,rtc(i)}$ is user u's bias for business i's root category (i.e. $rtc(i)$).

3.1.3 Unified Bias Model

By integrating all the aspects of business features mentioned in Equation (2), (3) and (4), we get the business's new rating bias $b_i' = b_i + c_i + l_i + t_i$.

Integrating user and business attributes together, we get the full bias model as follows:

$$r'_{ui} = \mu + b'_u + b'_i \tag{5}$$

3.2 Integrated Bias and Factorization Model

In the basic MF model, a user is modeled by a hidden vector p_u and a business is modeled by a hidden vector q_i. The prediction is calculated as the inner product of the two user and business latent factor vectors: $\hat{r}_{ui} = p_u^T q_i$.

After integrating the full bias model (Equation (5)), we get the final Integrated Bias and Factorization Model (IBFM) as follows:

$$\hat{r}_{ui} = r'_{ui} + q_i^T \Big(p_u + |N(u)|^{-\frac{1}{2}} \sum_{j \in N(u)} y_j + |C(u)|^{-\frac{1}{2}} \sum_{j \in C(u)} c_j + |G(u)|^{-\frac{1}{2}} \sum_{j \in G(u)} g_j \Big) \tag{6}$$

where $N(u)$ represents the set of all businesses user u has rated. $C(u)$ and $G(u)$ are the business sets user u is interested in and has not rated. y_j, c_j and g_j are parameters to be estimated and they are used to capture the user's implicit feedback. $C(u)$ is calculated based on the category information associated with the businesses u has rated. $G(u)$ is calculated based on the zip code associated with the businesses u has rated. The businesses in $C(u)$ and $G(u)$ are sorted by their popularity, and only the top 20 businesses are considered.

New users/businesses: Each unrated user-business pair falls into one of the following scenarios: existing user and existing business, existing user and new business, new user and existing business, new user and new business. New users and new businesses pairs do not have related training data, thus their latent vectors are unknown, which introduces huge uncertainty in the prediction stage. To reduce uncertainty, we use user and business features to compensate the disadvantages of traditional MF models as follows:

1) New user u: we use u's gender to find the *top-k* most popular existing users with the same gender. Then we fit a Gaussian distribution to the hidden representation of those users, and sample from this distribution to generate u's latent vector p_u.

2) New business i: Based on i's location information, content information and check-in information, we find the *top-k* closest existing businesses using the similarity measure described in 3.1. Then we fit a Gaussian distribution to the hidden representation of those businesses, and sample from this distribution to generate p_u.

4. EXPERIMENT

To test the performance of the proposed methods, we carried out extensive experiments on the Yelp business review data. RMSE is used to evaluate the models' performance.

4.1 Datasets and Experimental Settings

The Yelp business data set is a publicly available benchmark data set shared on Kaggle [1]. The data set includes rating data, business check-in data, user profile data and business profile data. There are 60,692 users and 15,040 businesses in the ratings, and the training data contains 230,000 ratings and test data has 36,404 ratings. The objective is to predict user-business ratings on the test data.

[1]`http://www.kaggle.com/c/yelp-recsys-2013`

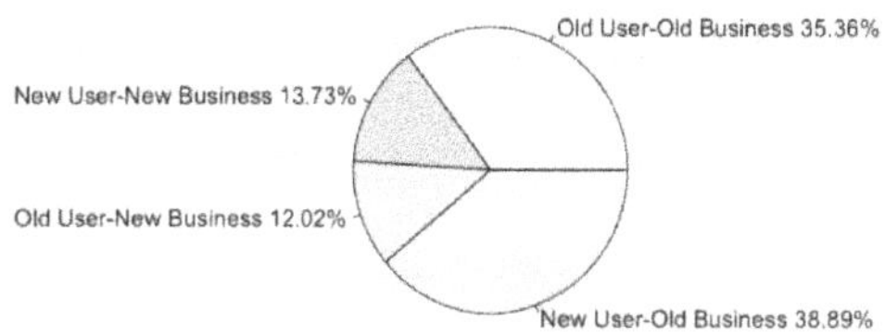

Figure 1: The ratings' distribution in the test data

This data set has several unique characteristics. First of all, rating density is only 0.03%, which means the data sparsity issue is much more serious than that of the Yahoo! Music rating data set (0.4%) released in KDD-Cup 2011 and Netflix movie rating data set(1.1%). Second, about 49.65% users have only 1 rating in the training data, 16.15% users have 2 ratings, and only 8.23% users have more than 10 ratings. In addition, the cold-start problem is more serious as well. The rating distribution of the test data is shown in Figure 1. We can see only 35.36% ratings are warm ratings. In the test data set, about 52.6% users are new users and about 25.75% businesses are new businesses without training data. Therefore, all the problems mentioned above cause huge difficulty to make accurate rating predictions.

Meanwhile, there is rich information in user profiles, business profiles and business check-in data. For users, their names and other users' vote distributions for their ratings are given. Each user gender is inferred based on a male/female name dictionary. For each business, its name, category, address, city, longitude and latitude are available. The check-in data contains each business's check-in times in different time periods.

We use several state-of-the-art rating prediction models as our baselines, including SVD with alternating least-square optimization (ALS-SVD) [5], basic MF [7], RSVD [7], rating bias [4], SVD ++ [4] and Factorization Machine (FM) model [8]. To learn the factorization models, we randomly generate a validation data based on the cold-start rating distributions of the test data from the original Yelp competition training data, so that the validation data's cold-start rating distributions are close to that of the test data. There are 32,020 ratings in the validation data, where 37.85% ratings are warm ratings, 37.20% ratings are new users and old businesses, 20.55% ratings are new users and new businesses, and 4.5% ratings are existing users and new businesses. In addition, there are 53.50% new users and 16.03% new businesses. The remaining data are used for training.

Without lose of generality, we set k to 100 in our experiments. The latent factor dimensions of all factorization models are set as 50. To learn the model parameters $(b_*, y_i, c_i, g_i, p_u, q_i)$, we minimize the mean square error of the predicted ratings on the training data using a stochastic gradient descent method and the validation data is used for early stopping to avoid over fitting. To tune the relevant hyper-parameters, i.e., learning rate and regularization, we use Nelder-Mead simplex search algorithm [6] with the initial learning rate as 0.001 and regularization value as 0.01.

Table 1: Performance (RMSE) of relevant models

Method	Validation	Public LB	Private LB
ALS-SVD	1.27046	1.31063	1.31572
BasicMF	1.26489	1.30671	1.31370
RSVD	1.21214	1.25138	1.25543
SVD++	1.19324	1.24473	1.24971
FM	1.19298	1.24311	1.24870
RatingBias	1.19404	1.24291	1.24912
UserFeature	1.19107	1.23837	1.24012
CheckinFeature	1.19221	1.2401	1.24419
ContentFeature	1.18076	1.22701	1.23010
LocationFeature	1.17518	1.22424	1.22282
UnifiedBiasModel	1.14003	1.19171	1.19780
IBFM *	1.12691	1.17858	1.18389

4.2 Experimental Results

The ratings of the test data are unknown, and they are randomly divided into two parts in the yelp competition. 20% ratings are used in the public leaderboard evaluation and the left 80% ratings are used in the private leaderboard evaluation. The results can be known through submitting the results in Kaggle.

The experimental results of all models are shown in Table 1. We have the following findings:

1) Both of the BasicMF and ALS-SVD perform poorly on this data set. RSVD, which incorporates user and business rating bias, greatly improve prediction accuracy compared with MF and ALS-SVD. RatingBias model performs much better than RSVD, and has a similar performance as SVD++ and FM. The reason is that when users have too few ratings on the training data, the user and business latent vectors have big variance. In addition, the cold-start ratings in the test data make user and business latent vectors very unreliable for predictions.

2) By incorporating user's attributes (gender, vote information and point-of-interests), business's features (check-in, name and category and location information), all the models (UserFeature, CheckinFeature, ContentFeature and LocationFeature) significantly improve the recommendation performance. Among all the four features, the location feature is most effective. This makes sense, because locations play an important role in business recommendations. By combining user and business attributes together, the UnifiedBiasModel further improves performance significantly. This demonstrates that the user and businesses features are complementary, and using appropriate feature learning methods can effectively mitigate the data sparsity and cold-start problem.

3) Furthermore, after adding the sampling method for generating new user and new business latent vectors based on user and business attributes, IBFM shows the best performance on all three data sets. Compared with the state-of-the-art models (SVD++ and FM) on prediction problems, IBMF increases the prediction accuracy by **5.15%**. It shows that our sampling method can effectively generate reasonable initial hidden representations for new users and new businesses.

5. CONCLUSION

In this paper, we propose an integrated bias and factorization model (IBFM) which has two advantages. First, it utilizes user's demographic information, votes and point-of-interests, business check-in information, content information, and location information seamlessly. Second, it uses sampling method to generate latent factor vectors for new users and new businesses, which enables IBFM to make reasonable predictions in cold-start scenarios. Our experimental results show that IBFM can significantly outperform the traditional state-of-the-art models on benchmark business rating prediction tasks. In addition, our single model IBFM performs the best on both the public and private leaderboard of RecSys 2013 Yelp business challenge, which demonstrate it can effectively take advantages of user and businesses attributes and the superiority of factorization model.

6. ACKNOWLEDGMENTS

This work was funded by National Science Foundation ICES-1101741 and IIS-0953908. Any opinions, findings, conclusions or recommendations expressed in this paper are the authors, and do not necessarily reflect those of the sponsors.

7. REFERENCES

[1] G. Adomavicius and A. Tuzhilin. Toward the next generation of recommender systems: A survey of the state-of-the-art and possible extensions. *IEEE Trans. on Knowl. and Data Eng.*, 17(6):734–749, June 2005.

[2] N. Golbandi, Y. Koren, and R. Lempel. Adaptive bootstrapping of recommender systems using decision trees. In *Proceedings of the Fourth ACM International Conference on Web Search and Data Mining*, 2011.

[3] A. Gunawardana and C. Meek. Tied boltzmann machines for cold start recommendations. In *Proceedings of the 2008 ACM Conference on Recommender Systems*, 2008.

[4] Y. Koren. Factorization meets the neighborhood: a multifaceted collaborative filtering model. In *Proceedings of the 14th ACM SIGKDD Conference*, 2008.

[5] Y. Koren, R. Bell, and C. Volinsky. Matrix factorization techniques for recommender systems. *Computer*, 42(8):30–37, 2009.

[6] J. A. Nelder and R. Mead. A simplex method for function minimization. *Computer journal*, 7(4):308–313, 1965.

[7] A. Paterek. Improving regularized singular value decomposition for collaborative filtering. In *Proceedings of KDD cup and workshop*, volume 2007, pages 5–8, 2007.

[8] S. Rendle. Factorization machines with libFM. *ACM Trans. Intell. Syst. Tech.*, 3(3):57:1–57:22, May 2012.

[9] L. Zhang and Y. Zhang. Discriminative factored prior models for personalized content-based recommendation. In *Proceedings of the 19th ACM CIKM Conference*, CIKM '10, 2010.

[10] L. Zhang and Y. Zhang. Interactive retrieval based on faceted feedback. In *Proceedings of the 33rd International ACM SIGIR Conference*, SIGIR'10, 2010.

[11] K. Zhou, S.-H. Yang, and H. Zha. Functional matrix factorizations for cold-start recommendation. In *Proceedings of the 34th International ACM SIGIR Conference*, 2011.

Speeding up Document Ranking with Rank-based Features

Claudio Lucchese
ISTI–CNR, Pisa, Italy
c.lucchese@isti.cnr.it

Franco Maria Nardini
ISTI–CNR, Pisa, Italy
f.nardini@isti.cnr.it

Salvatore Orlando
Univ. di Venezia, Italy
orlando@unive.it

Raffaele Perego
ISTI–CNR, Pisa, Italy
r.perego@isti.cnr.it

Nicola Tonellotto
ISTI–CNR, Pisa, Italy
n.tonellotto@isti.cnr.it

ABSTRACT

Learning to Rank (LtR) is an effective machine learning methodology for inducing high-quality document ranking functions. Given a query and a candidate set of documents, where query-document pairs are represented by feature vectors, a machine-learned function is used to reorder this set. In this paper we propose a new family of *rank-based* features, which extend the original feature vector associated with each query-document pair. Indeed, since they are derived as a function of the query-document pair and the full set of candidate documents to score, rank-based features provide additional information to better rank documents and return the most relevant ones. We report a comprehensive evaluation showing that rank-based features allow us to achieve the desired effectiveness with ranking models being up to 3.5 times smaller than models not using them, with a scoring time reduction up to 70%.

Categories and Subject Descriptors

H.3.3 [**Information Storage and Retrieval**]: Information Search and Retrieval—*Search process*

Keywords

Learning to Rank; Efficiency; Meta-Features

1. INTRODUCTION

The problem of ranking documents in response to a user's query is particularly challenging in Web search. Hence most of the search engines exploit document ranking pipelines based on *Learning-to-Rank* (LtR) techniques [4, 9]. In a LtR framework, a machine learning algorithm is used to derive a model from a training set of labeled documents [12]. Search engines usually exploit LtR models within a two-stage ranking architecture: (i) candidate retrieval and (ii) candidate re-ranking. The first stage retrieves from the inverted index a set $\mathcal{C}_q$ of (possibly relevant) candidate documents matching a user query q, where $|\mathcal{C}_q| \gg k$ and k is the number of relevant url's to include in the return page. This preliminary filtering is usually achieved by a simple and fast base ranker, e.g., BM25 plus some document features. In the second stage, the LtR model is used to score and re-rank the documents in $\mathcal{C}_q$. Finally, the top k documents in $\mathcal{C}_q$ are returned to the user.

SIGIR '15, August 09 - 13, 2015, Santiago, Chile

ACM 978-1-4503-3621-5/15/08 $15.00
DOI: http://dx.doi.org/10.1145/2766462.2767776.

In this scenario, the efficiency of the second LtR-based stage is crucial. It clearly impacts on the response time of the system. In addition, a more efficient ranker allows us to score more candidate documents: this is a very important property, since when larger sets of candidate documents are retrieved during the first step, we observe a better recall and a better overall quality of the final result list [10].

The efficiency of machine-learned rankers have recently attracted increasing interest, since state-of-the-art LtR algorithms induce models that are indeed very complex and expensive at scoring time, and may become a bottleneck in a two-stage ranking pipeline [4, 14, 16, 15, 1, 2]. Most of the work published so far focused primarily on the optimization techniques that can be adopted to make the second-stage ranker faster. Our approach is orthogonal to such optimization techniques. Indeed, we address the problem of improving the efficiency of a ranking model by *extending* the feature set used to represent a query-document pair with additional *rank-based features*. Since they are a function of the query-document pair and the full set of candidate documents $\mathcal{C}_q$, rank-based features provide additional information to better score documents. We show that these rank-based features, when used to extend the original feature vectors, are able to improve the learning process and achieve the desired ranking quality with learned models of reduced complexity.

Specifically, we propose to extend the feature set associated with each document in $\mathcal{C}_q$ as follows. For each original feature considered, we add four *rank-based* variants, named Dist-Min, Dist-Max, Rank, and Rev-Rank. The goal of rank-based features is to provide additional information about some ordering properties of a document compared with the others in $\mathcal{C}_q$. For example, given a feature $f \in \mathcal{F}$, where $\mathcal{F}$ is the feature set characterizing a generic document $c \in \mathcal{C}_q$, its Rank_f variant is equal to the *rank* of c in $\mathcal{C}_q$, where $\mathcal{C}_q$ is ordered in decreasing order of f. Indeed, each rank-based feature turns out to be a function of the query and the full candidate results set, rather than just of a query-document pair, thus providing a richer information.

We focus on the two state-of-the-art rankers, i.e., Gradient-Boosted Regression Trees (GBRT) [7] and λ-MART [3], as they have been proved to be the most effective in the recent Yahoo! learning to rank challenge [5]. We experimentally show that the use of *rank-based* features can reduce the number of regression trees generated by gradient boosting

Table 1: **A small example of golden set for learning to rank.**

q_1			q_2			q_3		
rel	BM25	PR	*rel*	BM25	PR	*rel*	BM25	PR
1	.80	.20	1	.60	.50	1	.65	.45
1	.75	.15	1	.60	.47	1	.67	.40
0	.65	.05	1	.50	.45	0	.60	.35
0	.65	.05	0	.45	.40	0	.40	.15

approaches up to 3.5 times and they provide a scoring time reduction up to 70%.

2. RANK-BASED FEATURES

To introduce the new set of *rank-based* features, let us consider the example in Table 1. The table illustrates a small training set of query-document feature vectors. It is made up of three queries with four candidate results each. For each document associated with a query, a binary relevance label *rel* and two well-known features – BM25 and PageRank (PR) – are listed. During learning, a tree-based algorithm should find the rules that best separate relevant from irrelevant results. A simple decision stump – i.e., a tree with one node and two leaves – is not sufficient in this case, since a "minimal" classification tree with perfect accuracy is the following:

```
if BM25 ≥ .75 then 1 else
    if PR ≥ .45 then 1 else
        if BM25 ≥ .67 then 1 else 0
```

Simpler but still effective trees can be obtained if we enrich the feature set associated with each pair (q, c), $c \in \mathcal{C}_q$, with new *rank-based* features. In our toy example, an optimal decision tree that achieves perfect accuracy is the one that classifies as relevant the documents with a PR score being at most 0.05 less than the best PR score in the same candidate set, that is:

```
if Dist-Max_PR ≤ 0.05 then 1 else 0
```

where $\textsf{Dist-Max}_{\text{PR}}$ measures the difference between each value of PR and the largest value assumed by PR in $\mathcal{C}_q$. This last classifier does not improve the quality of the first one. On the other hand, it is much simpler and its evaluation requires much less time if *rank-based* features are available.

We propose four construction strategies to build new *rank-based features* for a given feature $f \in \mathcal{F}$, occurring in the feature vector representing each pair (q, c), where $c \in \mathcal{C}_q$:

- $\textsf{Rank}_f$. Feature $\textsf{Rank}_f \in \{1, 2, \ldots, |\mathcal{C}_q|\}$ corresponds to the *rank* of c after sorting $\mathcal{C}_q$ in *descending order* of f.
- $\textsf{Rev-Rank}_f$. The same as $\textsf{Rank}_f$, but $\mathcal{C}_q$ is ordered in *ascending order* of f.
- $\textsf{Dist-Min}_f$. Feature $\textsf{Dist-Min}_f \in \mathbb{R}$ is given by the absolute value of the difference between the value of f and the *smallest value* of f in $\mathcal{C}_q$.
- $\textsf{Dist-Max}_f$. The same as $\textsf{Dist-Min}_f$, but we consider the difference with the *largest value* of f in $\mathcal{C}_q$.

We expect that these new features can improve the scoring ability of the learned models since they contribute to give information about the whole set of candidates C_q, while other features give information limited to the single pairs (q, c) with respect to the entire collection of indexed documents. We claim that they can capture *relatively better* or *relatively worse* concepts over the current candidate set. It is worth noting that $\textsf{Rank}_f$ and $\textsf{Rev-Rank}_f$ are not mutually exclusive. If higher values of f are better, the former could promote good documents, while the latter should demote bad documents. Moreover, the proposed *rank-based features* are orthogonal to other meta-level features and query-level normalization techniques, as some *rank-based features* can be built on top of normalized ones. We also compared *rank-based features* against query-level z-score normalization, with the latter showing very poor performance. Due to space constraints, these experiments are not reported.

Rank-based feature generation. It is possible to apply the four *rank-based* feature construction strategies to every feature $f \in \mathcal{F}$. This would multiply by five the size of the input dataset, making the learning process very expensive. In order to save space and time, we apply our feature construction methodology to a limited subset of the original features, using this subset to generate the new ranked-based ones. Specifically, we adopt a greedy approach exploiting a feature evaluation technique to choose which subset of features to enrich with the new rank-based ones:

1. We train a ranker on a given training dataset (golden set) by exploiting the full feature set $\mathcal{F}$.
2. We run a feature ranking method, aiming at identifying the 10 best performing features.
3. We create a new dataset, where the original features $\mathcal{F}$ are accompanied by 40 additional features, generated by applying the four *rank-based* construction strategies to the best 10 features. The resulting feature set is denoted by $\mathcal{F}^{+40}$.
4. A new ranker is trained on the new data, and the $\mathcal{F}^{+40}$ feature are evaluated and ranked as above.
5. Finally, we create an smaller dataset that contains all the original features $\mathcal{F}$, but only the best 10 *rank-based* features found in the previous step. The resulting dataset is denoted by $\mathcal{F}^{+10}$.

We show that the rankers derived using $\mathcal{F}^{+40}$ or $\mathcal{F}^{+10}$ can improve over the ranker built on the original feature set $\mathcal{F}$.

As previously stated, we focus on two state-of-the-art tree-based ranking algorithms: namely GBRT [7] and λ-MART [3]. Both generate large forests of additive regression trees. Our objective is thus to exploit the feature sets $\mathcal{F}^{+40}$ and $\mathcal{F}^{+10}$ to reduce the number of trees without hindering the ranking quality. Feature importance in these rankers can easily be estimated as described in the following section.

Feature importance evaluation. Several approaches have been proposed to evaluate the goodness of a feature in a ranking model [17, 11, 8]. Since both GBRT and λ-MART rankers are based on boosted regression trees, we borrow a method for feature evaluation from the original work on GBRTs by J. Friedman [7]. During the construction of each tree t in set of trees of the GBRT model T, for each feature we compute a measure similar to the *least square improvement measure* proposed in [7]. Since each tree split node improves the objective function, the *gain* g_i for each $f_i \in \mathcal{F}$ can be estimated by summing up the gains across all the split nodes $n \in t$ for all the trees $t \in T$ where feature f_i is used. We thus have:

$$g_i = \sum_{t \in T} \sum_{n \in t} \hat{i}_n^2 \; 1(v_n = f_i)$$

where v_n is the splitting feature used in node n, $1()$ is the indicator function, and $\hat{i}_n^2$ is the empirical improvement in

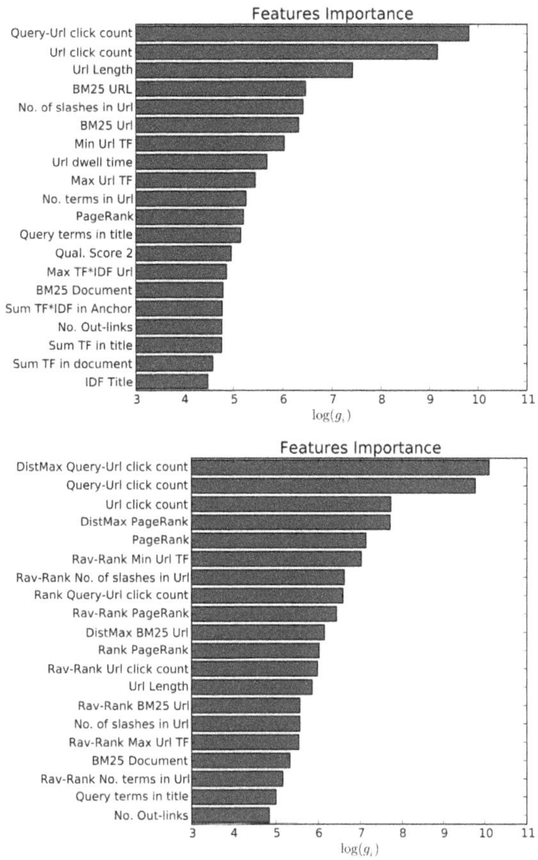

Figure 1: Features importance averaged over 5 folds of the MSN dataset: $\mathcal{F}$ (above) and $\mathcal{F}^{+40}$ (below).

the squared error as a result of the split. More specifically, according to [7], we have:

$$\hat{i}_n^2 = \frac{n_l n_r}{n_l + n_r} (\overline{y}_l - \overline{y}_r)^2$$

where n_l (n_r) is the number of instances in the left (right) child of the splitting node n, and $\overline{y}_l$ ($\overline{y}_r$) is the mean value assumed by the relevance label in the left (right) child of n.

Note that g_i measures exactly the improvement provided by f_i on the basis of the squared error reduction that was observed in the training set.

3. EXPERIMENTS

In our experiments we use the MSN learning to rank[1] datasets. It consists of vectors of 136 features extracted from query-url pairs. This dataset is partitioned into five subsets for five-fold cross validation. For each fold, we employ the validation set to fine-tune the number of trees of the generated models to avoid overfitting. In the following, we denote these folds by MSN/Fold i, $i \in \{1, 2, 3, 4, 5\}$. The MSN dataset provides relevance judgment labels ranging from 0 (irrelevant) to 4 (perfectly relevant). We use RankLib[2], an open-source implementation of the GBRT and λ-MART algorithms to learn our models. We then evaluate

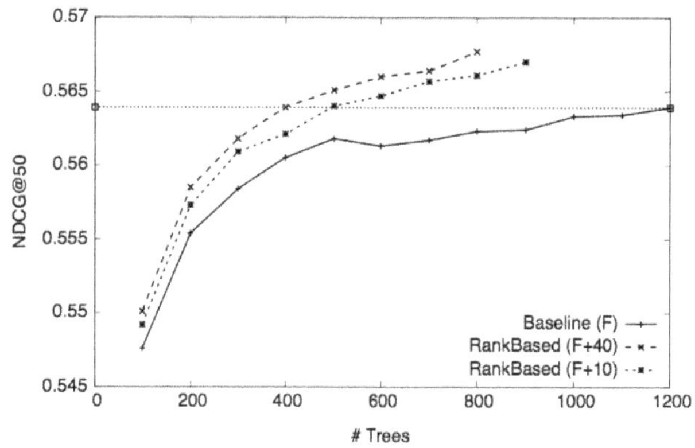

Figure 2: Effectiveness with features sets $\mathcal{F}^{+40}$, $\mathcal{F}^{+10}$, and $\mathcal{F}$ on MSN/Fold 1.

the effectiveness of the ranking models by using NDCG@k, $k \in \{10, 25, 50, 100\}$.

Assessment of feature importance. Feature importance is measured by gain g_i as defined above. We report results regarding the MSN dataset, averaged over 5 folds, on which we trained λ-MART rankers by optimizing NDCG@50. The results achieved at different NDCG cut-offs show a similar trend. Figure 1 plots the importance of the top-20 features according to gain g_i (log scale) for λ-MART trained on $\mathcal{F}^{+40}$. Our experiments confirm that a few features contribute to the largest part of the cost function optimization. This motivated our choice of applying the proposed feature construction strategies to the best 10 features of $\mathcal{F}$ only, thus obtaining the new feature set $\mathcal{F}^{+40}$. Figure 1 shows that the most important feature in $\mathcal{F}^{+40}$ is a rank-based one, and that 12 out of the top-20 features are rank-based.

We also notice that in most cases the rank-based features become more important than the original one. Consider for example feature f = PageRank: it was the 11th most important feature in $\mathcal{F}$, but its variant Dist-Max$_f$ is the 4th and precedes in $\mathcal{F}^{+40}$ the original feature f.

We conclude that GBRT and λ-MART models largely use the new rank based features as they were considered more informative than others. We also find out that rank-based features are not a replacement of original features, but they rather provide complementary information.

Efficiency of learned models. Figure 2 illustrates the quality in terms of NDCG of the λ-MART models trained on MSN/Fold 1 by using $\mathcal{F}$, $\mathcal{F}^{+40}$, and $\mathcal{F}^{+10}$. We report the values of NDCG@50 obtained on the test set of MSN/Fold 1 as a function of the number of trees of the generated model. Note that the three curves stops in correspondence of a different number of trees: this is because the validation set is used to choose the number of trees in the final model.

The benefit of our rank-based features shows up very early in the learning process. First, we note that the new feature sets $\mathcal{F}^{+40}$ and $\mathcal{F}^{+10}$ always produce models that are more effective than the one obtained by using the original feature set $\mathcal{F}$ at smaller ensemble sizes. More importantly, the maximum quality of the model trained on $\mathcal{F}$ requires a number of trees that is about three times larger than the number of trees of the models trained on either $\mathcal{F}^{+40}$ or $\mathcal{F}^{+10}$ to obtain the same NDCG@50. This behaviour is very significant, since the number of trees directly impacts ranking

[1] `http://research.microsoft.com/en-us/projects/mslr/`
[2] `http://sourceforge.net/p/lemur/wiki/RankLib/`

Table 2: Scoring time performance at the best NDCG@50 provided by $\mathcal{F}$.

Dataset	Features	λ-MART				GBRT			
		# Trees	Time μs.	Δ Time	NDCG@50	# Trees	Time μs.	Δ Time	NDCG@50
MSN / Fold 1	$\mathcal{F}$	1163	29.337		0.5640	833	21.094		0.5581
	$\mathcal{F}^{+40}$	500	14.529	-50%	0.5651	300	9.533	-54%	0.5605
	$\mathcal{F}^{+10}$	500	13.464	-54%	0.5640	300	8.303	-60%	0.5608
MSN / Fold 2	$\mathcal{F}$	898	22.717		0.5645	708	17.971		0.561
	$\mathcal{F}^{+40}$	400	12.031	-47%	0.5656	400	12.031	-33%	0.5623
	$\mathcal{F}^{+10}$	400	11.468	-49%	0.5652	300	8.303	-53%	0.5614
MSN / Fold 3	$\mathcal{F}$	750	19.020		0.5659	915	23.142		0.5623
	$\mathcal{F}^{+40}$	400	12.031	-36%	0.5678	300	9.533	-58%	0.5646
	$\mathcal{F}^{+10}$	400	10.634	-44%	0.5675	300	8.303	-64%	0.5637
MSN / Fold 4	$\mathcal{F}$	1420	35.757		0.5648	942	23.816		0.5613
	$\mathcal{F}^{+40}$	400	12.031	-66%	0.5657	400	12.031	-49%	0.5629
	$\mathcal{F}^{+10}$	400	10.467	-70%	0.5657	300	8.469	-64%	0.5613
MSN / Fold 5	$\mathcal{F}$	581	14.799		0.5705	990	25.015		0.5696
	$\mathcal{F}^{+40}$	300	9.533	-35%	0.5715	400	12.031	-51%	0.5703
	$\mathcal{F}^{+10}$	300	8.304	-43%	0.5715	400	10.967	-56%	0.5717

efficiency. Document scoring requires in fact the traversal of all the trees of the model, and its cost is thus linearly proportional to their number.

In order to evaluate the benefits of the proposed models at scoring time, we have to consider both the time needed to generate the rank-based features, and the time for traversing the forest of trees. In fact, the use of rank-based features should reduce the number of trees at least as much as to cover the cost of generating them.

Table 2 reports the scoring time of the best GBRT and λ-MART model in terms of NDCG@50 built with $\mathcal{F}$. We also measured the quality of the models exploiting rank-based features by adding 100 trees at a time, and we selected the smallest forest of trees achieving at least the same quality as the best model build using the original feature set. For such model, we also measured and reported the per-document scoring time, which *includes* the feature generation time.

It is apparent that the rank-based features allows to achieve the same or better performance than using $\mathcal{F}$, with a much smaller number of trees, thus resulting in a significantly smaller scoring time. We observe that the scoring time can be reduced up to a 70% factor. The time needed to extract the rank-based features is thus rewarded with a strongly reduced scoring time. For the sake of completeness, we measured the quality of the complete forests (results are not reported here) and we observed a statistically-significant improvement in NDCG with both proposed features sets with a p-value always smaller than 0.01 under randomization test with 100,000 permutations [13].

4. CONCLUSIONS AND FUTURE WORK

We proposed a novel feature construction strategy to enrich a feature set with new *rank-based* features in a learning-to-rank framework. The exploitation of *rank-based* features allows us to generate significantly faster rankers, i.e., with less trees, without any quality loss. Experiments proved that our proposed features can reduce the number of regression trees generated by gradient boosting approaches up to 3.5 times and they provide a speed-up in the scoring time up to 70%. In addition, results shown that *rank-based* features can provide statistically-significant improvements in the effectiveness of the generated ranking models.

We envision several open research directions. We apply the rank-based feature construction only to a subset of the whole set $\mathcal{F}$. We intend to study the impact of feature selection techniques for rank-based feature enhancement. Moreover, we will investigate the impact of our rank-based features on other, non tree-based (LtR) algorithms. We also intend to study the performance of a multi-stage ranking pipeline [6, 4] exploiting our rank-based features.

Acknowledgements. We acknowledge the support of Tiscali S.p.A. In particular, we wish to warmly thank Domenico Dato and Monica Mori (Istella) for fruitful discussions and valuable feedbacks helping us in concretizing this paper.

5. REFERENCES

[1] N. Asadi and J. Lin. Training efficient tree-based models for document ranking. In *Proc. ECIR*, pages 146–157, 2013.

[2] N. Asadi, J. Lin, and A. P. de Vries. Runtime optimizations for prediction with tree-based models. *IEEE TKDE*, 99:1, 2013.

[3] C. J. Burges, K. M. Svore, P. N. Bennett, A. Pastusiak, and Q. Wu. Learning to rank using an ensemble of lambda-gradient models. *Journal of Machine Learning*, 14:25–35, 2011.

[4] B. B. Cambazoglu, H. Zaragoza, O. Chapelle, J. Chen, C. Liao, Z. Zheng, and J. Degenhardt. Early exit optimizations for additive machine learned ranking systems. In *Proc. WSDM*, pages 411–420. ACM, 2010.

[5] O. Chapelle and Y. Chang. Yahoo! learning to rank challenge overview. *J. of Machine Learning Research*, 14:1–24, 2011.

[6] V. Dang, M. Bendersky, and W. B. Croft. Two-stage learning to rank for information retrieval. In *Advances in Information Retrieval*, pages 423–434. Springer, 2013.

[7] J. H. Friedman. Greedy function approximation: a gradient boosting machine. *Annals of Statistics*, pages 1189–1232, 2001.

[8] X. Geng, T.-Y. Liu, T. Qin, and H. Li. Feature selection for ranking. In *Proc. SIGIR'07*, ACM.

[9] T.-Y. Liu. Learning to rank for information retrieval. *Found. and Trends in Information Retrieval*, 3(3):225–331, 2009.

[10] C. Macdonald, R. L. Santos, and I. Ounis. The whens and hows of learning to rank for web search. *Information Retrieval*, 16(5):584–628, 2013.

[11] F. Pan, T. Converse, D. Ahn, F. Salvetti, and G. Donato. Feature selection for ranking using boosted trees. In *Proc. CIKM'09*, pages 2025–2028, ACM.

[12] I. Segalovich. Machine learning in search quality at yandex. *Invited Talk, SIGIR*, 2010.

[13] M. D. Smucker, J. Allan, and B. Carterette. A comparison of statistical significance tests for information retrieval evaluation. In *Proc. CIKM '07*, pages 623–632. ACM, 2007.

[14] L. Wang, J. J. Lin, and D. Metzler. Learning to efficiently rank. In *Proc. SIGIR*, pages 138–145. ACM, 2010.

[15] L. Wang, J. J. Lin, and D. Metzler. A cascade ranking model for efficient ranked retrieval. In *Proc. SIGIR*, pages 105–114. ACM, 2011.

[16] L. Wang, D. Metzler, and J. J. Lin. Ranking under temporal constraints. In *Proc. CIKM*, pages 79–88. ACM, 2010.

[17] L. Yu, H. Liu, and I. Guyon. Efficient feature selection via analysis of relevance and redundancy. *Journal of Machine Learning Research*, 5:1205–1224, 2004.

Mining Measured Information from Text

Arun S. Maiya, Dale Visser, and Andrew Wan
Institute for Defense Analyses — Alexandria, VA, USA
{amaiya, dvisser, awan}@ida.org

ABSTRACT

We present an approach to extract *measured information* from text (*e.g.,* a 1370 $°C$ melting point, a BMI greater than 29.9 kg/m^2). Such extractions are critically important across a wide range of domains — especially those involving search and exploration of scientific and technical documents. We first propose a rule-based entity extractor to mine *measured quantities* (*i.e.,* a numeric value paired with a measurement unit), which supports a vast and comprehensive set of both common and obscure measurement units. Our method is highly robust and can correctly recover valid measured quantities even when significant errors are introduced through the process of converting document formats like PDF to plain text. Next, we describe an approach to extracting the *properties* being measured (*e.g.,* the property *pixel pitch* in the phrase "a pixel pitch as high as 352 μm"). Finally, we present MQSEARCH: the realization of a search engine with full support for *measured information.*

Categories and Subject Descriptors

I.2.7 [**Artificial Intelligence**]: Natural Language Processing—*Text Analysis*; H.3.3 [**Information Storage and Retrieval**]: Information Search and Retrieval—*Search Process*

Keywords

text mining, information retrieval, information extraction, measured quantities, numerical queries

1. INTRODUCTION AND MOTIVATION

Scientific and technical documents describe methods and results using *measured quantities*: a numeric value paired with a unit of measurement. Examples of text snippets containing such measured quantities include:

- *average gravity curvature* $\zeta = (1.3999 \pm 0.003) \times 10^{-5} s^{-2} m^{-1}$
- 12 $°C$ *melting point*
- *distance from Earth to the Sun is* 9.3×10^7 *miles*
- *average responsivity as low as* 6.2 pA/K

Note that these measured quantities (*e.g.,* 6.2 pA/K) are typically associated with a specific *measured property* (*e.g.,* average responsivity). In this paper, we study ways in which to extract these kinds of *measured information* from documents.[1] The mining of such information is critically important across many domains — especially those involving search and exploration of scientific and technical articles. For instance, an optics researcher may wish to know if the performance of Nd:YAG laser-pumped KTP parametric oscillators has ever been tested at wavelengths longer than 2.4 μm. Full-text search engines using inverted indexes allow ad hoc queries on terms such as "KTP parametric oscillator", but the ability to further filter search results based on wavelengths greater than 2.4 μm is *not* typically supported. To accomplish this, one must first identify and extract valid *measured quantities* (*e.g.,* 2.4 μm) in unstructured text and, then, identify and extract the *properties* being measured (*e.g., wavelength*). These extractions could then be stored in the index of a search engine in a way that supports subsequent document queries on measured information (*e.g.,* faceted navigation, numeric range queries).

Surprisingly, there is very little existing work on how best to realize this process. Lines of research most closely related to the present work include extracting numerical attributes (*e.g.,* [1,4]), supporting numerical document queries (*e.g.,* [5,12]), and formula identification (*e.g.,* [7]). However, none of these existing works address the comprehensive extraction of and search for measured information in document data, as described above. Indeed, numerous challenges exist in such scenarios. Many widely-used, full-text search engines (*e.g.,* Apache Solr) convert the original document format to *plain text* prior to indexing and storage — an *extremely* error-ridden process. For instance, in the extracted text, exponents are typically lost (*e.g.,* 10^5 becomes 105, s^{-2} becomes s–2). Moreover, the conversion of some characters can be highly inconsistent and unpredictable. A simple minus sign can be converted to a range of different dash characters or even "garbage" characters. The same is true for other symbols such as μ, multiplication signs, and degree symbols. It is this inconsistent and error-ridden text, then, that is ultimately stored in the index of the search engine making it virtually impossible to adequately locate documents by measured quantities. Without the correct identification of measured quantities, it is virtually impossible to identify *properties* being measured, which are critical in efficiently

SIGIR '15, August 9–13, 2015, Santiago, Chile.

ACM 978-1-4503-3621-5/15/08...$15.00
DOI: http://dx.doi.org/10.1145/2766462.2767789.

[1]We define *measured information* as *measured quantities* and the *measured properties* to which they are associated.

navigating scientific and technical articles for state-of-the-art information. In general, there is a great deal of heterogeneity in how *measured quantities* and *measured properties* appear in text – both naturally and through corruption. This, then, motivates the current investigation of how best to extract such information.

Recent studies [3, 6] have revealed that rule-based approaches to information extraction tend to be more effective, interpretable, and customizable than state-of-the-art machine learning approaches. We employ rule-based extraction methods in this work. Our contributions are as follows:

- We propose and describe a rule-based entity extractor to identify *measured quantities* in unstructured text documents. Our method includes an error-correcting procedure that recovers from aforementioned text conversion errors by 1) *reverse engineering* the corrupted and mangled measured quantities back to their original, correct form and 2) *standardizing* this form for storage in an inverted index and subsequent query processing.
- Using these extracted measured quantities, we show how to further extract the *measured properties* to which they are associated.
- Finally, we present MQSEARCH: the realization of a search engine with full support for *measured information*. MQSEARCH is a facet-based navigation system that allows users to navigate large document sets based on measured quantities, measured properties, and the topics and themes to which they are associated. To the best of our knowledge, no other search engine in existence fully supports such a capability.

We begin with describing the extraction of *measured quantities*.

2. MEASURED QUANTITIES

We view *measured quantities* as a 5-tuple of the form: (*sign*, *number*, *error*, *scientific notation*, *units*), where underlined elements are mandatory and others are optional. As an example, a team of researchers in Italy recently reported the first direct measurement of gravity's curvature as $(1.3999 \pm 0.003) \times 10^{-5} s^{-2} m^{-1}$ [10]. The corresponding 5-tuple representation of this[2] is:

$$(\text{<empty>}, 1.3999, 0.003, 10^{-5}, s^{-2}m^{-1}).$$

5-tuples such as this are populated using a series of extraction rules that operate on individual sentences. These rules fall into four broad categories: 1) pre-processing, 2) units, 3) quantities, and 4) post-processing. Simplified forms of some of the rules for units and quantities are shown in Table 1.[3] We refer to the algorithm implementing such rules as *Measured Quantity Extractor* or **MQE**. We begin with pre-processing rules.

Pre-Processing. As mentioned previously, when extracting text from various document formats (*e.g.,* PDF, MS Office), characters often appear inconsistently. Minus signs, multiplication signs (*e.g.,* $\times$, $\cdot$), equal-like symbols (*e.g.,* $\approx$, $\simeq$, $\cong$), degree symbols, and the μ character can appear in a variety of ways or, in some cases, as "garbage" characters. For instance, minus can appear as the *en dash* character or appear corrupted as â€. Pre-processing rules identify these variations in text and perform the necessary normalization for accurate extraction of units and quantities.

Units. A *measurement unit* preceded by a numeric string conforming to the 5-tuple structure is the base indicator of a *measured quantity*. Thus, to identify valid *measured quantities*, we require a comprehensive ontology of units. We obtained an initial units ontology from the OBO Foundry,[4] but this was quite incomplete. We, then, expanded the ontology using largely public sources (*e.g.,* `convert-me.com`, DoD technical reports, Physical Review, Nature Communications). Each unit has an associated rule. An example rule for m (*i.e.,* symbol for meters) is shown in Rule 5 of Table 1. Note that such rules include optional prefixes for submultiples and multiples (*e.g.,* μ before m, *kilo* before *meter*). Unit rules, when combined with pre-processing rules described previously, can accurately extract units under a range of noisy conditions. For instance, the corrupted unit mâ€1 is correctly recovered as m^{-1} by MQE. Finally, as shown in Rules 6 and 7, compound units are also supported (*e.g.,* km/h, kilometer per hour, $s^{-2} \cdot m^{-1}$).

Quantities. Like units, quantities (*i.e.,* numbers with optional error ranges and scientific notation) can appear in a range of ways due to both corruptions and natural variation. These variations are collectively captured by rules such as those shown in Table 1 (*i.e.,* Rules 1-4), which populate the remainder of the 5-tuple structure. As shown in Table 1, such rules capture a wide range of quantity formats (*e.g.,* 10,000 with a comma, $1.3999 \pm 0.003 \times 10^{-5}$ with both an error range and scientific notation, 1.23×105 with lost exponent in 10^5). To support numeric range queries, extracted quantities are standardized prior to storage in a search engine index (*e.g.,* the extracted quantity $1.3999 \pm 0.003 \times 10^{-5}$ is stored simply as 0.000013999) [11].

Post-Processing. We have already seen that text extracted from various document formats can be noisy. For instance, information from tables, headers, and figures can sometimes result in seemingly random sequences of numbers and letters in extracted text. In some cases, such information can erroneously be picked up by aforementioned rules as *measured quantities*. This is especially true for single letter units (*e.g.,* m for meters, A for Ampere, etc.). Post-processing rules are employed to reject such extractions and minimize false positives. Examples of such rejection rules include context-based rules (*e.g.,* reject when preceded by "Table" or "Figure"), repetition-based rules such as rejecting compound units consisting of repeated single letter units (*e.g.,* 3 AJmm), and allowing a dash only between certain quantities and units (*e.g.,* *10-cm* is okay but not *10-A*).

As we will show in Section 4, when used in combination, these rules collectively enable highly accurate extractions of *measured quantities* – which, in turn, can be exploited to extract the *properties* being measured, as described next.

[2]Since there is no explicit sign in this example, the first element is left empty.

[3]Rules are shown in Perl-like syntax, the de facto standard for regular expressions.

[4]`http://www.obofoundry.org/`

<table>
<tr><th>Rule</th><th>Pattern</th><th>Example Matches</th></tr>
<tr><td>1) number</td><td>[+−]?(\d((\d?\d?[,]\d{2,3}([,]\d{2,3})*)|\d*))(\.(\d[\d\s]*\d|\d))?</td><td>1000.05, +5, -0.2, and 1,000</td></tr>
<tr><td>2) number (leading point)</td><td>[+-]?\.\d(\d\d(\s\d{3})+(\s\d{1,3})?|\d*)</td><td>-.98, .04, +.755</td></tr>
<tr><td>3) error</td><td>(\s{0,2} ± \s{0,2}[\d.]+)?</td><td>±0.003 in "1.3999 ± 0.003"</td></tr>
<tr><td>4) sci. notation.</td><td>(\s*[eE]|\s*([xX×])\s*10 *\^? [+-]?\d+)?</td><td>e.g., forms of $\times 10^{-5}$: ×105, e-5, E-5</td></tr>
<tr><td>5) unit</td><td>e.g., [fpnμmcdk]?m([\^]?[2-6] | [\-][1-6]) — $m^{\#}$ normalized to m^#</td><td>μm, m–1 (m^{-1}), $cm2$ (cm^2), cm^2</td></tr>
<tr><td>6) connector</td><td>(\s?/\s? | [Pp]er |-per-| [-\s× ·*])?</td><td>per, /, ·, ×</td></tr>
<tr><td>7) compound unit</td><td><unit>(<connector><unit>)+</td><td>km/h, kilometer per hour,km·h^{-1}</td></tr>
</table>

Table 1: **[MQE Rules.]** Simplified forms of some rules for extraction of *measured quantities.*

<table>
<tr><th>Pattern</th><th>Example Matches (two examples shown for each rule)</th><th></th></tr>
<tr><td>NP SYM{0,2} EQ mq</td><td>1) gravity curvature <u>$\zeta =$</u> $1.4 \times 10^{-5} s^{-2} m^{-1}$</td><td>2) floor area <u>$\approxeq$</u> $32m^2$</td></tr>
<tr><td>mq IN? NP</td><td>1) a 352 μm pixel pitch</td><td>2) $50mL$ <u>of</u> 30% fuming sulfuric acid</td></tr>
<tr><td>NP IN DT? NP VP+ (TO|IN|RB|JJ)* mq</td><td>1) strength of panel <u>was set to</u> 9 ksi</td><td>2) freq. of scans <u>was roughly</u> 300 Hz</td></tr>
<tr><td>NP (IN DT? NP)* VP+ (IN|TO|RB|JJ)* mq</td><td>1) pixel pitch <u>employed was</u> 352 μm.</td><td>2) panel strength <u>was recorded at</u> 9 ksi.</td></tr>
<tr><td>NP (CC|IN|TO|RB|JJ)* \(?mq\)?</td><td>1) wavelengths <u>of at least</u> 2.4 μm</td><td>2) panel strength (9 ksi)</td></tr>
</table>

Table 2: **[MPE Rules.]** Simplified forms of some syntactic patterns to extract *measured properties.*

3. MEASURED PROPERTIES

We now turn our attention to the extraction of *measured properties.* To better illustrate the problem, we show several example snippets containing measured quantities. In each example, the *measured quantity* is shown in blue, the *property* being measured is highlighted in red, and the characters connecting them are underlined:

- *a pixel pitch* <u>*as high as roughly*</u> 352 μm
- *a* 352 μm *pixel pitch*
- *The pixel pitch* <u>*employed was*</u> 352 μm.
- *average gravity curvature* <u>$\zeta =$</u>$(1.3999 \pm 0.003) \times 10^{-5} s^{-2} m^{-1}$
- *with* $50mL$ <u>*of*</u> *30% fuming sulfuric acid*
- *size* $\cong 0.1m^2$
- *frequency of longitudinal scan* <u>*was approximately*</u> *300 Hz.*
- *a nominal current density* <u>*of*</u> *1.3* A/cm^2 <u>*to*</u> *0.03* A/cm^2
- *panel strength* <u>*lower than*</u> *8.90 ksi (61.4 MPa)*
- *wavelengths* <u>*at least*</u> 2.4 μm
- *large fields* <u>*of about, or above*</u> *10 kV/cm*

From just the examples shown, it is easy to see that there is an extremely high degree of variability in the words connecting a *measured property* with a *measured quantity.* These examples represent just a small sample of the many possible variations. However, upon closer inspection, we find that this variability can be reduced to a small number of syntactic patterns based on part-of-speech (POS) that capture most scenarios. Table 2 shows some syntactic patterns that we employ to extract *measured properties.* We refer to the extractor applying such syntactic rules as *Measured Property Extractor* or **MPE**.

In Table 2, noun phrases shown in red (*i.e.,* NP) are extracted and taken as the *measured property.* Measured quantities are represented in blue by mq. The EQ tag represents all symbols related to '=' (*e.g.,* ≈, ≃). The SYM tag matches one or two character symbols (*e.g.,* a greek letter). Other symbols (*e.g.,* JJ, RB, IN, CC, VP) are part-of-speech tags in Penn Treebank format. Note that tags such as RB (*i.e.,* an adverb) should be taken to include variations such as the comparative and superlative forms. This is not explicitly shown for reasons of brevity. This small set of patterns matches a very wide range of possible phrase combinations for *measured properties* and are executed sequentially in the order shown. We implemented MPE using the Brill part-of-speech tagger [2]. As we will show in the next section, the accuracy with which our algorithms are able to extract measured properties and measured quantities is remarkable — especially given the aforementioned issues with noisy and corrupted input text.

4. EXPERIMENTAL EVALUATION

Since our research is sponsored by the U.S. Department of Defense (DoD), we evaluate our approach on a text corpus consisting of 40,807 unclassified research reports published in the 2008-2010 time frame and hosted by the Defense Technical Information Center (DTIC). This rich collection describes a wide range of research funded by the DoD spanning numerous fields from engineering and physical science to biomedical research and social science. The DTIC documents considered in this paper have been approved for public release and unlimited distribution. All documents are in PDF format, and text was extracted from them using the `pdftotext` utility.[5] From this collection, we generated samples using the following procedure. To evaluate the ability of MQE to extract measured quantities, we sampled uniform random sentences from the population of all sentences containing a numeric value. By examining sentences with a number (but not necessarily a measurement unit), we are able to accurately identify false negatives in addition to false positives. Next, to evaluate the ability of MPE to extract measured properties, we generated a random sample of sentences from the population of all sentences containing a measured quantity, as identified by MQE. We employed sample sizes of 1000 and 500 for MQE and MPE, respectively. This produced sufficient 95% confidence bounds on our estimates for precision and recall over the entire corpus. Different fields employ different measures in different ways. By considering sentences sampled randomly in this fashion, we are able to evaluate our methods on text data that capture the diverse ways in which measured information is reported across different fields. To the best of our knowledge, no other approaches exist for extracting such *measured information* from scientific and technical documents. Thus, there are no appropriate baselines against which our meth-

[5] `http://www.foolabs.com/xpdf/home.html`

ods can be compared. Table 3 shows the precision and recall estimates for both the measured quantity extractor and the measured property extractor over the entire corpus.

Extractor	Precision	Recall
MQE	(0.93, 0.99)	(0.92, 0.99)
MPE	(0.93, 0.97)	(0.88, 0.94)

Table 3: **95% Confidence Intervals** for precision and recall when extracting *measured quantities* (using MQE) and *measured properties* (using MPE) from the DTIC corpus.

As can be seen in the table, both MQE and MPE perform extraordinarily well in extracting *measured quantities* and the *properties* they describe from documents across disparate fields. Having demonstrated the success with which *measured information* can be mined, we now demonstrate how these extractions can be exploited in novel search applications.

5. AN APPLICATION: MQSEARCH

Here, we present MQSEARCH: a realization of a search engine with full support for *measured information.* MQSEARCH is implemented using Apache Solr[6] and AJAX Solr[7], both of which support full-text search, faceted navigation, and numeric range queries. During the process of indexing and ingesting the DTIC document set into our search engine, we apply our extractors to encountered text and store both *measured quantities* and *measured properties* in the search engine index. In addition, the search engine performs keyphrase extraction on documents using the KERA algorithm described in [8]. Using Solr filter queries, extracted keyphrases can be used to produce a tag cloud for any subset of the document set. Figure 1 shows the faceted navigation panel of MQSEARCH, which allows users to filter documents based on discovered measurement units, quantity ranges, and measured properties. In Figure 1, the measurement unit *U/mL* is selected. We see that there are 153 documents (out of roughly 40,000) mentioning this unit with quantities ranging from 0.001 U/mL to 10,000 U/mL. The property most frequently measured in *U/mL* is *penicillin.* From the tag cloud, we see that documents containing quantities measured in *U/mL* tend to cover topics such as breast cancer and prostate cancer research.[8] The search results can be filtered further along any of these dimensions. Filtering by LDA-discovered topics is also supported but not shown in the figure [9]. To the best of our knowledge, ours is the first search engine with such support for *measured information.*

6. CONCLUSION

In this paper, we have proposed a demonstrably effective approach to extracting *measured information* from unstructured text data. We showed both how to extract *measured quantities* and the *properties* being measured. We further demonstrated how such extractions might be used in a search engine for documents rich in measured information. To the best of our knowledge, no other search engine in existence supports such functionality. Our extraction methods have the potential to substantially improve search, navigation, and exploratory analysis of large or even massive collections of scientific and technical articles. For future work, we plan on marrying our proposed approaches with other well-studied techniques for exploratory search.

[6]`http://lucene.apache.org/solr/`

[7]`https://github.com/evolvingweb/ajax-solr`

[8]This cancer research was funded by U.S. Army MRMC through a congressionally directed research program.

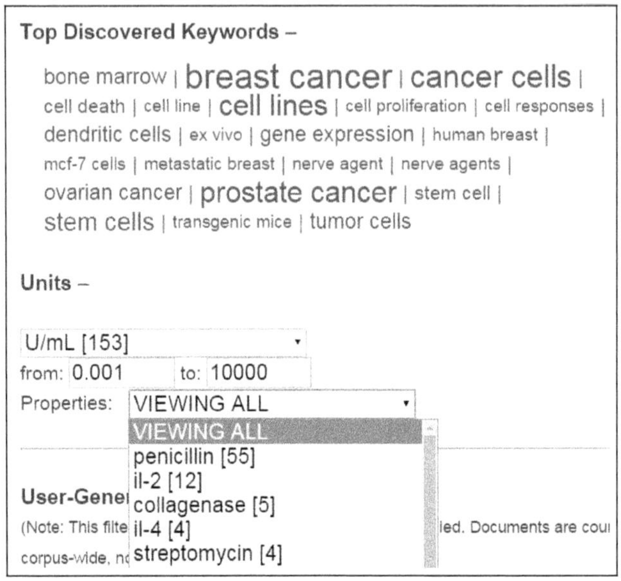

Figure 1: [MQSEARCH.] The measurement unit *U/mL* is selected, which reveals the associated topics (*e.g.,* breast/prostate cancer), associated measured properties (*e.g.,* concentrations of *penicillin*), and associated quantity ranges (*i.e., 0.001* to *10,000*).

7. REFERENCES

[1] A. Bakalov, A. Fuxman, P. P. Talukdar, and S. Chakrabarti. Scad: collective discovery of attribute values. In *WWW '11.*

[2] E. Brill. A Simple Rule-based Part of Speech Tagger. In *ANLC '92.*

[3] L. Chiticariu, Y. Li, and F. R. Reiss. Rule-based Information Extraction is Dead! Long Live Rule-based Information Extraction Systems! In *EMNLP '13.*

[4] D. Davidov and A. Rappoport. Extraction and Approximation of Numerical Attributes from the Web. In *ACL '10.*

[5] M. Fontoura, R. Lempel, R. Qi, and J. Zien. Inverted Index Support for Numeric Search. *Internet Math.*, 3(2):153–186, 2006.

[6] S. Gupta and C. Manning. SPIED: Stanford Pattern based Information Extraction and Diagnostics. In *Proc. 2014 Workshop on Interactive Language Learning, Visualization, and Interfaces.*

[7] X. Lin, L. Gao, Z. Tang, X. Lin, and X. Hu. Mathematical Formula Identification in PDF Documents. In *ICDAR '11.*

[8] A. S. Maiya, J. P. Thompson, F. L. Lemos, and R. M. Rolfe. Exploratory Analysis of Highly Heterogeneous Document Collections. In *KDD '13.*

[9] A. K. McCallum. MALLET: A Machine Learning for Language Toolkit, 2002.

[10] G. Rosi, L. Cacciapuoti, F. Sorrentino, M. Menchetti, M. Prevedelli, and G. M. Tino. Measurement of the Gravity-Field Curvature by Atom Interferometry. *Physical Review Letters*, 114(1), Jan. 2015.

[11] U. Schindler and M. Diepenbroek. Generic XML-based Framework for Metadata Portals. *Comput. Geosci.*, 34(12):1947–1955, Dec. 2008.

[12] H. Seidl, F. I. Informatik, T. Schwentick, and A. Muscholl. Numerical Document Queries. In *PODS 2003.* ACM, June 2003.

An Initial Investigation into Fixed and Adaptive Stopping Strategies

David Maxwell and Leif Azzopardi
School of Computing Science
University of Glasgow
Glasgow, Scotland
d.maxwell.1@research.gla.ac.uk
Leif.Azzopardi@Glasgow.ac.uk

Kalervo Järvelin and Heikki Keskustalo
School of Information Sciences
University of Tampere
Tampere, Finland
kalervo.jarvelin@uta.fi
heikki.keskustalo@uta.fi

ABSTRACT

Most models, measures and simulations often assume that a searcher will stop at a predetermined place in a ranked list of results. However, during the course of a search session, real-world searchers will vary and adapt their interactions with a ranked list. These interactions depend upon a variety of factors, including the content and quality of the results returned, and the searcher's information need. In this paper, we perform a preliminary simulated analysis into the influence of stopping strategies when query quality varies. Placed in the context of ad-hoc topic retrieval during a multi-query search session, we examine the influence of fixed and adaptive stopping strategies on overall performance. Surprisingly, we find that a fixed strategy can perform as well as the examined adaptive strategies, but the fixed depth needs to be adjusted depending on the querying strategy used. Further work is required to explore how well the stopping strategies reflect actual search behaviour, and to determine whether one stopping strategy is dominant.

Categories and Subject Descriptors: H.3.3 [**Information Storage and Retrieval**]: Information Search and Retrieval:Search Process H.3.4 [**Information Storage and Retrieval**]:Systems and Software:Performance Evaluation

Keywords Search Strategies; Search Behaviour; Stopping Strategies; Evaluation

1. INTRODUCTION

Most models, simulations and measures that examine or evaluate searcher interaction typically rely on the assumption that searchers will reach a fixed depth, with *precision-at-n (P@n)* being a prime example. In practice, this assumption is unlikely to hold. Indeed, searchers are likely to vary their interaction and the depth to which they inspect snippets and documents, depending on the performance of the system, their information need/task, and the amount of time they have available [4, 17, 18, 20, 22]. For example, a searcher may issue a query that does not return any relevant documents (i.e. a *'dud'* query). It is then likely that once the searcher inspects a few snippets and/or documents, (s)he will conclude that the issued query was unsuccessful. In this case, the searcher is then likely to issue a new query rather than continue down the current results list. This intuition has been confirmed by empirical analysis, where research shows that searchers examined significantly fewer documents when the search system failed to retrieve any relevant material in the top ten results, in contrast to when it did [1]. Thus, real searchers are inherently adaptive, and their behaviour is conditioned on the quality of the ranked lists that they interact with. In this paper, we examine the aforementioned fixed depth assumption, and perform a preliminary analysis to determine the impact of assuming a fixed depth when interacting with a search system over the course of a session. To this end, we will propose two adaptive stopping strategies - motivated by various stopping rules - and compare them to the fixed depth stopping strategy.

While we assume that adaptive approaches may perform better, we hypothesise that this depends on the quality of the queries issued. For example, if all queries issued by a searcher are 'duds', then the stopping strategy may be irrelevant. However, what if all their queries are successful, or if their queries are of varying quality? What then is the influence of the stopping strategy on overall performance?

SIGIR'15, August 09 - 13, 2015, Santiago, Chile

ACM 978-1-4503-3621-5/15/08 ...$15.00
DOI: http://dx.doi.org/10.1145/2766462.2767802

2. RELATED WORK

Knowing when to stop is considered a fundamental aspect of human thinking [15]. Consequently, IR researchers have examined stopping behaviours in a bid to understand why, and when, searchers stop. Many studies investigating when people stop searching have concluded that the decision was mainly based on intuition, or the subjective notion of *"feeling good enough"* [22] - often termed *satisficing* [9, 21, 22]. Furthermore, decisions have also been shown to be highly dependent upon the task type being undertaken, time constraints, and various actions that the searcher performs [4, 17, 20, 22]. However, in this work, we are interested in the stopping rules and heuristics that have been proposed [5, 6, 7, 11, 15] and how to operationalise them.

When formulating such rules, researchers have considered stopping behaviours with respect to the overall search task (e.g. ceasing the search when enough information has been acquired to meet some threshold, or satisfy some task or goal) [5, 6, 15]. For example, Nickles et al. [15] proposed a number of rules investigating the sufficiency of information: the *mental list rule*, where searchers construct a mental list of criteria about a given item (such as a car) that must be satisfied before stopping; the *representational stability rule*, where a searcher continues to examine information until the underlying mental model that they possess of the topic begins to stabilise; the *difference threshold rule*, where a searcher sets an *a priori* difference level to gauge when he or she is not learning anything new; and the *magnitude threshold rule*, where a searcher has a cumulative amount of information that must be reached before he or she stops.

Other work focuses on stopping behaviour at the query level (e.g. whether the searcher continues to examine documents, or decides to submit a new query) [7, 11]. For example, Cooper [7] devised two stopping rules for examining a list of ranked results: the *frustration point rule*, where a searcher stops after a certain number of non-relevant documents are encountered; and the *satisfaction stopping rule*, where searchers would stop when a certain number of relevant documents were obtained. Later, Cooper [8] developed rules using *utility theory*, positing that searchers stop examining documents once the effort of examining another document outweighs the benefit of moving to a new results list. Similar rules can be obtained from *Search Economic Theory* [1] and *Information Foraging Theory* [16].

In this work, we focus on query level stopping rules and implement two variations of the frustration point rule to explore the relationship between stopping strategies and query performance. This rule was also implemented by Lin and Smucker [12]. When navigating similar documents, their simulated searchers stopped after seeing two contiguous non-relevant documents. Our work however considers different implementations, and explores a range of stopping thresholds for ad-hoc topic retrieval.

3. EXPERIMENTAL METHOD

To explore the influence of the stopping strategy on overall performance, we conducted a number of simulations where we varied the stopping strategy and querying strategy. This was to determine which stopping strategy achieved the best performance when the quality of queries was varied. Our simulations consisted of 'searchers' performing ad-hoc topic retrieval over a series of topics on two TREC collections.

Corpora, Topics and System: We used two test collections: *TREC AQUAINT* with the *TREC 2005 Robust Track* topics, and *TREC WT2g* with the *TREC Ad-Hoc and Small Web* topics. Both topic sets were comprised of 50 topics. Each collection was indexed using the Whoosh IR toolkit[1], where stopwords[2] were removed and Porter stemming applied. The retrieval model used was PL2 ($c = 10.0$).

3.1 Simulations

While various methods have been proposed to model or simulate session-based retrieval [2, 3, 14, 19], we utilise an adaption of the method proposed by Baskaya et al. [3] as follows. A searcher ***(1)*** issues a query to the system, and then ***(2)*** proceeds to examine the first/next result snippet, or decides to issue a new query (back to *(1)*). If a given snippet is considered relevant, ***(3)*** the document is examined. If said document is considered relevant, ***(4)*** it is marked as such, and the searcher returns to *(2)*. If either a snippet or document are considered non-relevant, the searcher returns to *(2)* - with the document remaining unmarked.

Experimental Setup: At *(2)*, Baskaya et al. [3] assumed in one of their baselines a fixed depth of ten. In this paper, we consider a range of fixed depths n. In addition, we also include two adaptive stopping strategies (see Section 3.2). To generate queries of varying quality, we will employ a range of strategies as suggested by Keskustalo et al. [10] (see Section 3.3). To determine the relevance of a document, the corresponding TREC relevance assessments are typically used. Here, the action/decision of clicking on a relevant snippet or marking a relevant document is determined in a probabilistic manner. In this work, we used the probabilities of clicking on a (non)relevant snippet and the probabilities of marking a document as (non)relevant from the study performed by Smucker and Clarke [18]. In previous work, for each run, whether a document is examined or marked relevant is determined on the fly. This means that for the same query (or even a different query), the same snippet/document can be considered relevant and then non-relevant, or vice versa. In this paper, we pre-compute whether a document is considered relevant or not *a priori*, so that for different thresholds, depths and other factors, the same judgements are made for each run. This means we can perform a pairwise comparison, thus reducing the total number of simulations required.

Finally, the goal of the search task is to find as many relevant documents in a fixed time period of 1200 seconds (20 minutes). For each action performed during the simulation, the times in Table 1 were used. The estimates for each action were obtained from a user study we performed with 48 subjects over the TREC 2005 Robust Track [13].

Table 1: Summary of interaction times (in seconds) used for the simulations in this study.

Time Required to...	Seconds
...issue a query	15.1
...undertake an initial results page examination	1.1
...examine an individual snippet	1.3
...examine a document	21.45
...mark a document as relevant	2.57

3.2 Stopping Strategies

We considered three stopping strategies - the default fixed depth strategy (***SS1***), and two other strategies based on the frustration point rule (***SS2*** & ***SS3***) [7].

SS1 (Fixed Depth): This fixed stopping strategy encodes the heuristic that a searcher will stop examining a results list after they have viewed x_1 snippets, regardless of their relevance to the given topic.

SS2 (Total Non-Relevant): Under this stopping strategy, the searcher will stop once they have observed x_2 non-relevant snippets. If a snippet has been previously seen and was considered non-relevant, it is included in the count.

SS3 (Contiguous Non-Relevant): Similar to ***SS2*** above, the searcher will stop using this strategy when they observe x_3 non-relevant documents *in a row*. As above, previously seen non-relevant snippets are included in the count.

For this analysis, we set the thresholds (x_1, x_2 & x_3) to be 1-20 in steps of 1, and 25-50 in steps of 5. The final value of 50 was sufficiently deep enough such that if a simulated

[1]`https://pypi.python.org/pypi/Whoosh/`

[2]Fox's classical stopword list was used. Refer to `http://git.io/vT3So` for the complete list.

searcher only issued one query and examined all documents, they would run out of time. Note that for ***SS1***, x_1 corresponds to the maximum depth per query, whereas for ***SS2*** and ***SS3***, x_2 and x_3 represent the minimum depth per query. For example, when $x_2 = 3$, a searcher is willing to tolerate three non-relevant snippets. However, they may see two relevant snippets in the process, and thus stop at a depth of five. In our results, we will report the average depth per query for each x_i. This will therefore allow us to compare across the three implemented stopping strategies.

3.3 Querying Strategies and Selection

Keskustalo et al. [10] define and analyse a number of different querying strategies. For the purposes of this paper, we have selected the best performing querying strategy (referred to as ***QS3***, consisting of two *pivot terms* and one other term), and the worst performing querying strategy (referred to as ***QS1***, consisting of a series of single terms) [3]. These querying strategies were used to determine how the different stopping strategies performed when combined with differing querying quality. We also implemented a blended querying strategy ***QS1+3***, which interleaved the queries generated by ***QS1*** and ***QS3***. ***QS1+3*** was implemented to determine how robust the different stopping strategies were against poor performing (or 'dud') queries.

Queries were generated as follows. For each topic, the title and description were used to create a *Maximum Likelihood Estimate (MLE)* language model, i.e. $p(term|topic)$. For ***QS1***, we then extracted a list of all single terms, ranking them according to this probability. For ***QS3***, we took all two term combinations of the title terms, and selected the pair with the highest joint probability as the pivot. A list of three term candidate queries q was then constructed by appending another term from the topic to the pivot. These were then ranked according to $p(q|topic)$.

4. RESULTS

Figure 1 plots the mean depth per query[3] versus the rate of gain per second (averaged over all sessions and topics), given each threshold value for the AQUAINT collection[4]. All nine combinations of the aforementioned querying strategies (***QS1***, ***QS1+3*** & ***QS3***) and stopping strategies (***SS1***, ***SS2*** & ***SS3***) are shown. From the plots, we can see that the adaptive stopping strategies (***SS2*** & ***SS3***) generally outperformed the fixed depth strategy (***SS1***), regardless of the querying strategy employed, or the depth attained.

Table 2 reports the maximum gain attained across each of the stopping and querying strategies for both AQUAINT and WT2g, together with the thresholds (x_i) and mean depth per query (d). To determine whether one stopping strategy outperformed another, we performed a series of paired t-tests comparing each stopping strategy with a given querying strategy (e.g. ***SS1*** & ***QSx*** vs. ***SS2*** & ***QSx***). We found that there were no significant differences at $p = 0.05$.

To examine why this was the case, given that adaptive strategies should be intuitively more successful, we evaluated the retrieval performance of the queries that were issued during the simulation. Table 3 reports the mean retrieval performance metrics ($P@5$, $P@10$ & $P@20$) for

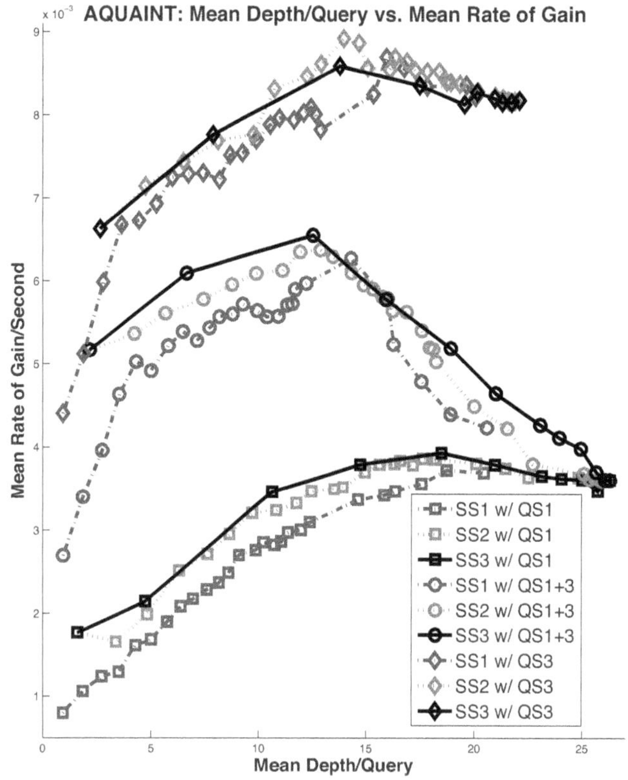

Figure 1: The mean depth per query versus the mean rate of gain per second for the AQUAINT collection, for each query and stopping strategy. Each point represents a particular threshold value, i.e. x_i.

both collections and for each of the three querying strategies used (***QS1***, ***QS1+3*** & ***QS3***). In line with previous work, the three-term querying strategy (***QS3***) outperformed the single-term strategy (***QS1***) [10], while blended ***QS1+3*** queries performed better than those generated by ***QS1***, but worse than ***QS3*** queries. Notably, each querying strategy had a high variance. This resulted in 35-40% of queries issued under ***QS1*** achieving $P@10 = 0$ ('dud' queries), while approximately 25% of queries under ***QS1+3*** and ***QS3*** were 'duds'. This suggests that our manipulation provided a mixture of highly performing and underperforming queries, yet the performance of the best cases for the fixed strategy were similar in overall gain to the adaptive strategies. This may be an artefact of the simulation as fixed interaction probabilities were used, whereas searchers may be more or less likely to click depending on the quality of the list (and the information scent [21]). In future work, we will examine how the behaviour of a searcher changes given the quality of the ranked list to provide a more grounded simulation.

When we examined the threshold for the fixed depth stopping strategy (***SS1***), we observed that it was quite high, ranging from 25-50. This range is much deeper than inspecting ten results per query, which is typically assumed in simulations [3]. Furthermore, real searchers are unlikely to know in advance the average performance of their queries or adopt only one particular querying strategy, so it is unlikely that a real searcher would subscribe to a fixed depth strategy. Similarly to ***SS1***, ***SS2*** also requires a range of thresholds in order to achieve maximum gain. In contrast, ***SS3*** is more consistent, where thresholds range from three to five over both collections, depending on the querying strategy used.

[3] The depth for a query is the lowest item in the results list for which a simulated searcher examined the associated snippet of. Mean depth is averaged for all simulated searchers over each query issued.

[4] Similar plots were obtained for the WT2g collection.

Table 2: Maximum cumulative gain values with corresponding thresholds and depths for each stopping and querying strategy for AQUAINT and WT2g. Significance tests indicate that there are no differences between stopping strategies.

		QS1	*QS1+QS3*	*QS3*
AQUAINT	*SS1*	4.5 ± 1.1 $x_1 = 45, d = 18.7$	7.6 ± 1.1 $x_1 = 25, d = 14.3$	10.6 ± 1.8 $x_1 = 30, d = 15.9$
	SS2	4.7 ± 0.9 $x_2 = 19, d = 17.9$	7.8 ± 1.1 $x_2 = 9, d = 12.8$	10.9 ± 0.9 $x_2 = 9, d = 13.9$
	SS3	4.7 ± 0.7 $x_3 = 5, d = 18.5$	8 ± 1.1 $x_3 = 3, d = 12.5$	10.5 ± 0.7 $x_3 = 3, d = 13.7$
WT2g	*SS1*	3.9 ± 1 $x_1 = 45, d = 18.2$	4.9 ± 0.9 $x_1 = 25, d = 13.6$	6.6 ± 1.4 $x_1 = 50, d = 18.9$
	SS2	3.9 ± 0.7 $x_2 = 17, d = 17$	5 ± 0.7 $x_2 = 9, d = 12.8$	6.7 ± 0.9 $x_2 = 30, d = 19.6$
	SS3	3.8 ± 0.6 $x_3 = 5, d = 19$	4.9 ± 0.6 $x_3 = 3, d = 12.2$	6.6 ± 0.8 $x_3 = 4, d = 16.9$

Table 3: Means (and standard deviations) of the queries issued during the simulation for each querying strategy, both for AQUAINT (AQ.) and WT2g.

		QS1	*QS1+3*	*QS3*
AQ.	***P@5***	0.2 ± 0.27	0.32 ± 0.31	0.41 ± 0.31
	P@10	0.21 ± 0.26	0.31 ± 0.29	0.41 ± 0.28
	P@20	0.13 ± 0.18	0.2 ± 0.2	0.32 ± 0.25
WT2g	***P@5***	0.19 ± 0.26	0.25 ± 0.29	0.32 ± 0.33
	P@10	0.19 ± 0.22	0.26 ± 0.25	0.35 ± 0.29
	P@20	0.15 ± 0.21	0.18 ± 0.21	0.29 ± 0.25

This strategy is also more in line with intuition. Here, the searcher moves to the next query after encountering three to five contiguous non-relevant documents. This suggests that ***SS3*** is more robust across query performance, but further research is required to confirm this.

5. SUMMARY AND FUTURE WORK

In this paper, we used simulations to examine different stopping strategies. Overall, the adaptive stopping strategies tend to outperform the fixed stopping strategy. However, to our surprise, this was not significantly so. The caveat being that for the fixed stopping strategy to provide similar performance, the right threshold needs to be chosen. In practice, this would require a different type of adaptive behaviour, where the searcher changes the depth they are willing to go to based on their querying strategy. This seems unlikely. The most robust stopping strategy appeared to be ***SS3*** (contiguous non-relevant), with a threshold of around three to five non-relevant documents. This stopping strategy seems to match better with intuition, but whether real searchers adopt such a strategy is an open question. In future work, we will examine a greater variety of querying strategies/selection methods (such as lower and higher precision) to determine whether the adaptive strategies result in greater gains. We shall also explore which strategy, if any, best characterises real searcher stopping behaviour, and explore whether there is a relationship between results list quality and interaction probabilities. Other adaptive stopping strategies will be examined, as well as comparing proposed strategies against observed stopping behaviours.

Acknowledgments: We would like to thank the ESF-funded MUMIA COST Action (ref. ECOST-STSM-IC1002-080914-049840). We would also like to thank Horaţiu Bota, Sean McKeown, Alastair Maxwell and Paul Thomas for their input.

References

[1] L. Azzopardi. Modelling interaction with economic models of search. In *Proc. 37th ACM SIGIR*, pages 3–12, 2014.
[2] F. Baskaya, H. Keskustalo, and K. Järvelin. Time drives interaction: Simulating sessions in diverse searching environments. In *Proc. 35th ACM SIGIR*, pages 105–114, 2012.
[3] F. Baskaya, H. Keskustalo, and K. Järvelin. Modeling behavioral factors in interactive information retrieval. In *Proc. 22nd ACM CIKM*, pages 2297–2302, 2013.
[4] M. J. Bates. The fallacy of the perfect thirty-item online search. *RQ*, 24(1):pp. 43–50, 1984.
[5] G. Browne, M. Pitts, and J. Wetherbe. Stopping rule use during web-based search. In *38th HICSS*, page 271, 2005.
[6] G. J. Browne, M. G. Pitts, and J. C. Wetherbe. Cognitive stopping rules for terminating information search in online tasks. *MIS Quarterly*, 31(1):89–104, 2007.
[7] W. S. Cooper. On selecting a measure of retrieval effectiveness part ii. implementation of the philosophy. *J. of the American Society for Info. Sci.*, 24(6):413–424, 1973.
[8] W. S. Cooper. The paradoxical role of unexamined documents in the evaluation of retrieval effectiveness. *Info. Processing and Management*, 12(6):367 – 375, 1976.
[9] M. Dostert and D. Kelly. Users' stopping behaviors and estimates of recall. In *Proc. 32nd ACM SIGIR 2009*, pages 820–821, 2009.
[10] H. Keskustalo, K. Järvelin, A. Pirkola, T. Sharma, and M. Lykke. Test collection-based ir evaluation needs extension toward sessions — a case of extremely short queries. In *Proc. 5th AIRS*, pages 63–74, 2009.
[11] D. Kraft and T. Lee. Stopping rules and their effect on expected search length. *IPM*, 15(1):47 – 58, 1979.
[12] J. Lin and M. D. Smucker. How do users find things with pubmed?: Towards automatic utility evaluation with user simulations. In *Proc. 31st ACM SIGIR*, pages 19–26, 2008.
[13] D. Maxwell and L. Azzopardi. Stuck in traffic: How temporal delays affect search behaviour. In *Proc. 5th IIiX*, pages 155–164, 2014.
[14] A. Moffat, P. Thomas, and F. Scholer. Users versus models: What observation tells us about effectiveness metrics. In *Proc. 22nd ACM CIKM*, pages 659–668, 2013.
[15] K. R. Nickles, S. P. Curley, and P. G. Benson. Judgment-based and reasoning-based stopping rules in decision making under uncertainty. Technical report, U. of Minnesota, 1995.
[16] P. Pirolli and S. Card. Information foraging. *Psychological Review*, 106:643–675, 1999.
[17] C. Prabha, L. S. Connaway, L. Olszewski, and L. R. Jenkins. What is enough? Satisficing information needs. *J. of Documentation*, 63(1):74–89, 2007.
[18] M. D. Smucker and C. L. Clarke. Time-based calibration of effectiveness measures. In *Proc. 35th ACM SIGIR*, pages 95–104, 2012.
[19] P. Thomas, A. Moffat, P. Bailey, and F. Scholer. Modeling decision points in user search behavior. In *Proc. 5th IIiX*, pages 239–242, 2014.
[20] E. G. Toms and L. Freund. Predicting stopping behaviour: A preliminary analysis. In *Proc. 32nd ACM SIGIR*, pages 750–751, 2009.
[21] W. C. Wu, D. Kelly, and A. Sud. Using information scent and need for cognition to understand online search behavior. In *Proc. 37th ACM SIGIR*, pages 557–566, 2014.
[22] L. Zach. When is "enough" enough? modeling the information-seeking and stopping behavior of senior arts administrators: Research articles. *J. of the American Society for Info. Sci. and Tech.*, 56(1):23–35, 2005.

Regularised Cross-Modal Hashing

Sean Moran
School of Informatics
The University of Edinburgh
EH8 9AB, Edinburgh, UK
sean.moran@ed.ac.uk

Victor Lavrenko
School of Informatics
The University of Edinburgh
EH8 9AB, Edinburgh, UK
vlavrenk@inf.ed.ac.uk

ABSTRACT

In this paper we propose Regularised Cross-Modal Hashing (RCMH) a new cross-modal hashing model that projects annotation and visual feature descriptors into a common Hamming space. RCMH optimises the hashcode similarity of related data-points in the annotation modality using an iterative three-step hashing algorithm: in the first step each training image is assigned a K-bit hashcode based on hyperplanes learnt at the previous iteration; in the second step the binary bits are smoothed by a formulation of graph regularisation so that similar data-points have similar bits; in the third step a set of binary classifiers are trained to predict the regularised bits with maximum margin. Visual descriptors are projected into the annotation Hamming space by a set of binary classifiers learnt using the bits of the corresponding annotations as labels. RCMH is shown to consistently improve retrieval effectiveness over state-of-the-art baselines.

Categories and Subject Descriptors

H.3.3 [**Information Storage and Retrieval**]: Information Search and Retrieval

Keywords

Locality Sensitive Hashing, Cross-Modal Retrieval

1. INTRODUCTION

Hashing-based approximate nearest neighbour (ANN) search has emerged as an effective technique for efficiently finding nearest neighbours in large multimedia data collections. Data-points are transformed into compact binary codes via projection [6] and quantisation [7] operations that ensure similar data-points are assigned hashcodes with low Hamming distance. Hashcodes of length K are generated by learning K hyperplanes within the data-space. Depending on which side of a hyperplane a data-point falls its hashcode is appended with a 1 or 0. Each subspace formed by the K hyperplanes constitutes the bucket of a hashtable. Similarity preserving hashcodes can therefore be used as the indices into the buckets of a hashtable for constant time search: a given query need only be compared to data-points falling within the same bucket vastly cutting down the search space.

Most previous hashing research has focused on generating binary codes for data-points within the same modality, for example, a text query executed against a database consisting of textual documents. However it is frequently the case that similar data-points exist in different modalities, for example a Wikipedia page discussing Einstein and an associated image of the scientist. An interesting research question is whether an effective hashing scheme can be constructed to learn hashcodes that are also similar *across* disparate modalities - in this case the Einstein Wikipedia article will ideally be assigned a similar hashcode to the relevant embedded image. Hashing methods that effectively bridge the cross-modal gap will enable the efficiency of ANN search to be expanded to cross-modal data.

In this paper we propose Regularised Cross-Modal Hashing (RCMH), an extension of the *unimodal* hashing model Graph Regularised Hashing (GRH) [6]. RCMH employs a three-step iterative scheme to learn a set of K hash functions: in the first step hashcodes are assigned to the training images using K learnt hyperplanes from the last iteration; in the second step a formulation of graph regularisation [2] refines the distribution of annotation binary bits so that annotations from neighbouring images are assigned similar bits. In the third step K binary classifiers are trained to predict the regularised bits with maximum margin. RCMH forms a cross-modal bridge by subsequently projecting visual descriptors into the learnt annotation Hamming space: this is achieved by learning K binary classifiers in visual space with the bits of the associated annotations as labels.

SIGIR'15, August 09 - 13, 2015, Santiago, Chile.

ACM 978-1-4503-3621-5/15/08 ...$15.00.
DOI: http://dx.doi.org/10.1145/2766462.2767816.

2. RELATED WORK

Cross-modal hashing research has received increased interest over the past several years due to the recent emergence of large freely available cross-modal datasets from sources such as Flickr. Existing cross-modal hashing schemes seek to jointly preserve the within-modality and between-modality similarities of related data-points in a shared Hamming space. This requirement is frequently solved by learning two sets of K hyperplanes that partition each space into buckets in a manner that yields similar hashcodes for similar data-points both within and across modalities.

Cross-Modal Semi-Supervised Hashing (CMSSH) [1] integrates eigendecomposition and boosting to learn a common multi-modal space for hashing. Cross-View Hashing (CVH)

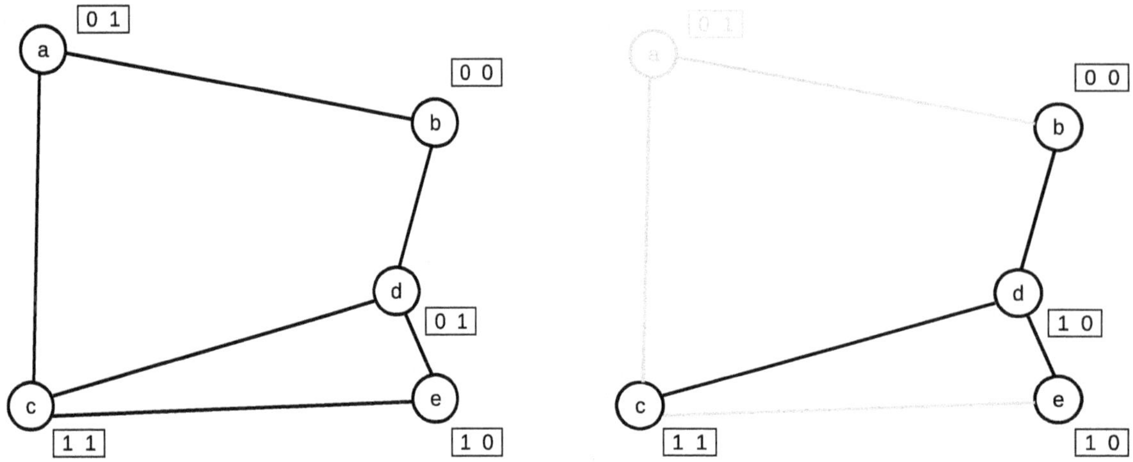

Figure 1: Regularisation step: the hashcode for node d is updated to be more similar with its neighbours (c,b,e)

[5] employs Canonical Correlation Analysis (CCA) [4] to learn a shared latent space from two modalities. The authors of [10] proposed Co-Regularised Hashing (CRH) that learns hash functions for each bit by solving DC (difference-of-convex function) programs, with multiple bits learnt via boosting. Inter-Media Hashing (IMH) [9] minimises a loss function consisting of graph Laplacian terms for intra-modal similarity, a trace minimisation term for inter-modal similarity and linear regression for out-of-sample prediction.

The closest related work to RCMH is Predictable View Hashing (PDH) [8]. PDH employs an iterative scheme for hashcode learning: the annotation bits are used to learn K hyperplanes for the image modality, while the image bits are used to learn K hyperplanes for the annotation modality. RCMH is different to PDH in several aspects, including our novel method of bridging the modalities, our integration of graph regularisation [2] and the lack of an eigendecomposition step. We show that RCMH is much more effective.

3. REGULARISED CROSS-MODAL HASHING (RCMH)

3.1 Problem definition

Let $\mathbf{D} = \{(\mathbf{a}_i, \mathbf{v}_i) : i = 1 \ldots N\}$ denote a collection of N annotated images. Each image is represented by two components: the annotation $\mathbf{a}_i$, and the visual descriptor $\mathbf{v}_i$. The annotation $\mathbf{a}_i$ is a vector over textual features. Visual descriptor $\mathbf{v}_i$ is a vector of real-valued visual features. Our goal is to learn a pair of hash functions F, G that map annotations and visual descriptors into binary hashcodes consisting of K bits. We impose two constraints on our hash functions: **(i)** the annotation hashcode $F(\mathbf{a}_i)$ should be similar to the visual hashcode $G(\mathbf{v}_i)$ of the same image; and **(ii)** the annotation hashcodes $F(\mathbf{a}_i)$ and $F(\mathbf{a}_j)$ should be similar whenever images i and j are considered *neighbours*. The neighbourhood structure for the collection is dictated by an affinity matrix $\mathbf{S}$, where $S_{ij} = 1$ indicates that i and j are neighbours, and $S_{ij} = 0$ indicates they are not.

3.2 The algorithm

Our approach is based on a unimodal method GRH [6]. GRH is restricted to a single modality, while we propose a method that learns a pair of hash functions across two separate modalities: text annotations $\mathbf{a}_i$ and visual descriptors $\mathbf{v}_i$. The hash functions F, G are based on K hyperplanes each: $\mathbf{f}_1 \ldots \mathbf{f}_K$ for the space of words and $\mathbf{g}_1 \ldots \mathbf{g}_K$ for the space of visual features. The hyperplane $\mathbf{f}_j$ is used to assign the j'th bit in the annotation hashcode, while $\mathbf{g}_j$ determines the j'th bit in the visual hashcode. We initialise all hyperplanes randomly, and iteratively perform the following steps: **(1) hashing**, where the hyperplanes $\mathbf{f}_1 \ldots \mathbf{f}_K$ are used to assign hashcodes $\mathbf{b}_1 \ldots \mathbf{b}_N$ to the training images, **(2) regularisation**, where the hashcodes $\mathbf{b}_1 \ldots \mathbf{b}_N$ are made more consistent with the affinity matrix S and **(3) partitioning**, where we adjust the hyperplanes $\mathbf{f}_j, \mathbf{g}_j$ to be consistent with the j'th bit of the hashcodes from step (2).

3.2.1 *Step 1: Hashing*

We start by assigning a K-bit binary hashcode $\mathbf{b}_i$ to each training image i. Each of the K bits in $\mathbf{b}_i$ is based on a dot product between the image annotation $\mathbf{a}_i$ and one of the hyperplanes $\mathbf{f}_1 \ldots \mathbf{f}_K$:

$$\mathbf{b}_i = F(\mathbf{a}_i) = H\left[\mathbf{a}_i^\intercal \mathbf{f}_1 \ldots \mathbf{a}_i^\intercal \mathbf{f}_K\right] \tag{1}$$

Here $H(x)$ is the Heaviside step function that returns 0 for negative x and 1 otherwise. At test time, hashcodes of visual features $G(\mathbf{v}_i)$ can be computed in the same manner, but using the visual hyperplanes $\mathbf{g}_1 \ldots \mathbf{g}_K$.

3.2.2 *Step 2: Regularisation*

The aim of this step is to make the hashcodes we obtained in step 1 more consistent with the affinity matrix $\mathbf{S}$. Specifically, whenever images i and j are neighbours, we would like the hashcodes $\mathbf{b}_i$ and $\mathbf{b}_j$ to be similar in terms of their Hamming distance. We achieve this by interpolating the hashcode of image i with the hashcodes of all *neighbouring* images j for which $S_{ij} = 1$. Our approach is similar to the *score regularisation* method of [2]. Formally, we regularise the hashcodes via the following equation:

$$\mathbf{B} \leftarrow H\left(\alpha\ \mathbf{S}\mathbf{D}^{-1}\mathbf{B} + (1{-}\alpha)\ \mathbf{B} - 0.5\right) \tag{2}$$

Here $\mathbf{S}$ is the affinity matrix and $\mathbf{D}$ is a diagonal matrix containing the number of neighbours for each image. The matrix $\mathbf{B} \in \{0,1\}^{N \times K}$ represents the hashcodes assigned to every image in step 1 of the algorithm and α is a free parameter that specifies how aggressively we regularise the

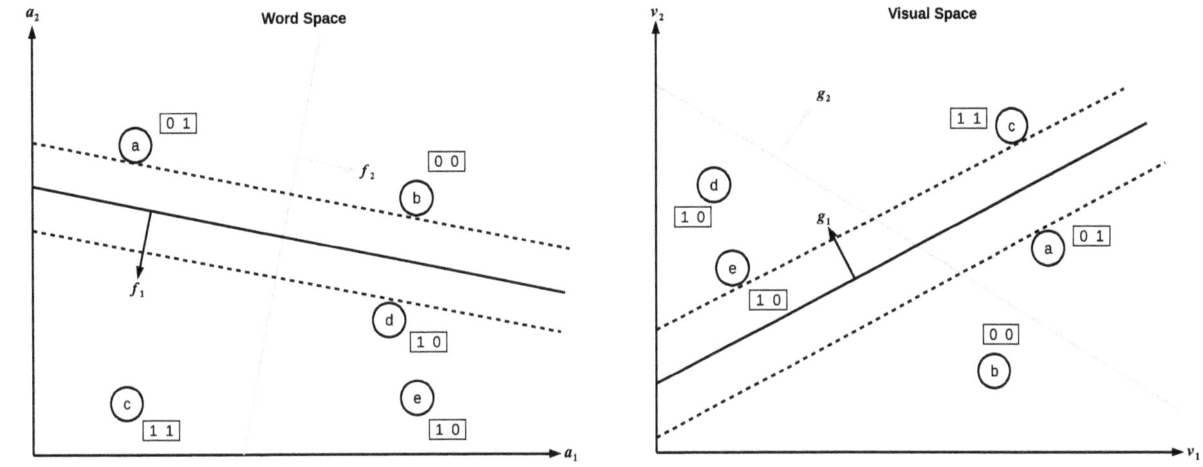

Figure 2: Partitioning step: hyperplanes are learnt in the annotation and visual space using annotation bits as labels.

bits. We show our approach intuitively in Figure 1. In the left side we show 5 images $a \dots e$ with their initial hashcodes (K=2 bits for this example). The lines between images reflect the neighbourhood structure encoded in the affinity matrix $\mathbf{S}$. Image d has a hashcode 01, but its neighbours b, c, e have hashcodes 00, 11 and 10 respectively. The right side of Figure 1 shows the effect of equation (2) for image d: its hashcode changes to 10, which is more consistent with neighbouring hashcodes (on average).

3.2.3 *Step 3: Partitioning*

In the final step of the algorithm, we re-estimate the hyperplanes $\mathbf{f}_1 \dots \mathbf{f}_K$ and $\mathbf{g}_1 \dots \mathbf{g}_K$ to make them consistent with the regularised hashcodes from step 2 of the algorithm. For each bit $j = 1 \dots K$, we treat the values $b_{1j} \dots b_{Nj}$ as the training labels. Specifically, if $b_{ij} = 1$ then the annotation vector $\mathbf{a}_i$ constitutes a positive example for the hyperplane $\mathbf{f}_j$, and the visual vector $\mathbf{v}_i$ is a positive example for $\mathbf{g}_j$. If $b_{ij} = 0$ then $\mathbf{a}_i$ and $\mathbf{v}_i$ are negative examples for $\mathbf{f}_j$ and $\mathbf{g}_j$. Each hyperplane is learned using `liblinear` [3] to maximise the margin between positive and negative examples.

The approach is illustrated in Figure 2. We show five images $a \dots e$ in two sets of coordinates: the word space on the left and the visual feature-space on the right. Each image is associated with a 2-bit hashcode, and each bit is used to learn a maximum-margin hyperplane that bisects the corresponding space. For example, the first bit has value 0 for images a, b and value 1 for images c, d, e, giving rise to hyperplanes $\mathbf{f}_1$ and $\mathbf{g}_1$, shown as dark lines on the left and the right parts of Figure 2. Note that $\mathbf{f}_1$ and $\mathbf{g}_1$ look very different, because they are defined over two completely different modalities: words on the left and visual features on the right. Similarly, the second bit results in the hyperplanes $\mathbf{f}_2$ and $\mathbf{g}_2$, shown in lighter colour.

3.3 Iteration and constraints

We repeat steps 1-3 above for a small number of iterations M. We briefly describe how the steps enforce the two constraints we imposed on our hash functions in section 3.1. Constraint (i) is enforced in step 3 of the algorithm, when we use the same bit values b_{ij} as targets for the word hyperplanes $\mathbf{f}_j$ and visual hyperplanes $\mathbf{g}_j$. Any image i will either be a positive example for both hyperplanes, or it will be negative for both, so at test time we can expect $\mathbf{a}_i^\intercal \mathbf{f}_j$ to yield the same bit value as $\mathbf{v}_i^\intercal \mathbf{g}_j$. Constraint (ii) is enforced in step 2 of our procedure, where the hashcode for image i is moved towards the centroid hashcode of its neighbours. The centroid (before it is binarised) is a point that minimizes aggregate Euclidean distance to the neighbours, so after step 2 hashcodes $\mathbf{b}_1 \dots \mathbf{b}_N$ are expected to be more consistent with the neighbourhood structure $\mathbf{S}$.

4. EXPERIMENTS

4.1 Datasets

We evaluate RCMH on two publicly available benchmark datasets: Wiki[1] and NUS-WIDE[2]. Wiki is generated from 2,866 Wikipedia articles. Each article is described with text and an associated image. The visual modality is formed from 128-bit SIFT descriptors, while the annotation modality is represented as 10-dimensional probability distribution over LDA topics. NUS-WIDE is a web image dataset consisting of 269,648 images downloaded from Flickr. We keep the image-text pairs associated with the most frequent 10 classes and perform PCA on the tag co-occurrence features to form a 1,000-dimensional annotation feature set [10] . Each image is represented as a 500-D bag-of-words vector derived from SIFT descriptors. The ground truth nearest neighbours are based on the semantic labels supplied with the datasets, that is, if two images share a class in common they are regarded as true neighbours [10, 9]. Following previous work [10, 9] we randomly select 20% (Wiki) and 1% (NUS-WIDE) of the data-points as queries with the remainder forming the database over which our retrieval experiments are performed. We randomly sample 20% (Wiki) and 1% (NUS-WIDE) of the data-points from the database to form the training dataset (T) to learn the hash functions.

4.2 Baselines

CVH [5], CMSSH [1], CRH [10], IMH [9] and PDH [8].

4.3 Evaluation Protocol

We evaluate RCMH based on two cross-modal retrieval tasks: 1) *Image query vs. text database:* an image is used to

[1]`http://www.svcl.ucsd.edu/projects/crossmodal/`
[2]`http://lms.comp.nus.edu.sg/research/NUS-WIDE.htm`

Task	Method	Code Length		
		K=24	K=48	K=64
Image Query vs. Text Database	CRH	0.1632	0.1752	0.1698
	CVH	0.1570	0.1519	0.1538
	CMSSH	0.1439	0.1501	0.1420
	IMH	0.1881	0.1892	0.1897
	PDH	0.2109	0.2186	0.2266
	RCMH	**0.2439†**	**0.2463†**	**0.2590†**
Text Query vs. Image Database	CRH	0.1266	0.1239	0.1267
	CVH	0.1284	0.1176	0.1185
	CMSSH	0.1119	0.1123	0.1124
	IMH	0.1507	0.1514	0.1491
	PDH	0.1790	0.1860	0.1902
	RCMH	**0.2066†**	**0.1918†**	**0.2201†**

Table 1: mAP scores for Wiki ($T = 574$). † indicates statistical significance vs. PDH (Wilcoxon: p-value < 0.01).

Task	Method	Code Length		
		K=24	K=48	K=64
Image Query vs. Text Database	CRH	0.3536	0.3539	0.3588
	CVH	0.3397	0.3436	0.3412
	CMSSH	0.3429	0.3386	0.3382
	IMH	0.4022	0.4019	0.4040
	PDH	0.4217	0.4245	0.4272
	RCMH	**0.4605†**	**0.4719†**	**0.4649†**
Text Query vs. Image Database	CRH	0.3495	0.3427	0.3481
	CVH	0.3394	0.3435	0.3410
	CMSSH	0.3429	0.3377	0.3492
	IMH	0.3926	0.3960	0.3997
	PDH	0.4053	0.4081	0.4096
	RCMH	**0.4325†**	**0.4380†**	**0.4350†**

Table 2: mAP scores for NUS-WIDE ($T = 1866$). † indicates statistical significance vs. PDH (Wilcoxon: p-value < 0.01).

retrieve the most related text in the text database; 2) *Text query vs. image database:* a text query is used to retrieve the most similar images from the image database. Retrieval accuracy is measured using *Hamming ranking* [10, 9]: binary codes are generated for both the query and the database items and the database items are then ranked in ascending order of the Hamming distance. We evaluate using mean average precision (mAP). Results are the average over 10 random query/database partitions.

4.4 Parameter Optimisation

RCMH has three meta-parameters: the number of iterations M, the amount of regularisation α and the flexibility of margin C. We optimise all meta-parameters via grid search on the validation dataset. Holding the margin parameter constant at $C = 1$, we perform a grid search over $M \in \{1 \dots 5\}$ and $\alpha \in \{0.1, \dots, 0.9, 1.0\}$. We then hold M and α constant at their optimised values, and sweep $C \in \{0.01, 0.1, 1.0, 10, 100\}$. We equally weigh both classes (0 and 1). The IMH β and λ parameters are set via grid search over the range $\{10^{-6}, 10^{-3}, 1, 10^3, 10^6\}$. The CRH λ_x and λ_y parameters are tuned over the range $\{0.001, 0.01, 0.1, 1\}$ and $\{0.01, 0.1, 1.0, 10, 100, 1000\}$ for γ. We sweep C for PDH in an identical manner to RCMH.

4.5 Results

Our cross-modal retrieval results are presented in Tables 1-2. We observe that RCMH outperforms the baseline systems on both datasets and across all hashcode lengths. For example, for image-text retrieval, RCMH outperforms PDH by a substantial 16% relative mAP at 24 bits on the Wiki dataset and 9% on the NUS-WIDE dataset. We test the statistical significance of the gain in mAP vs. PDH using a Wilcoxon signed rank test on the mAP scores resulting from each random query/database partition: the difference is statistically significant for $p < 0.01$. This is an encouraging result: RCMH is devoid of a computationally expensive eigendecomposition step as most baselines [9, 8, 5], relying instead on graph regularisation to maintain the neighbourhood structure.

5. CONCLUSIONS

In this paper we introduced Regularised Cross-Modal Hashing (RCMH). RCMH employs an iterative three-step scheme to learn a shared multi-modal Hamming space: in the first step hashcodes are assigned to images based on learnt hyperplanes; in the second step hashcodes within the annotation space are refined by updating a node's hashcode to be the average of the hashcodes of its nearest neighbours. In the third step RCMH learns a set of hyperplanes to partition the annotation space into buckets using the bits from the previous step as labels. Visual descriptors are projected into the annotation Hamming space by learning a set of hyperplanes in the visual space using the associated annotation bits as labels. RCMH outperforms a set of strong cross-modal hashing baselines.

6. REFERENCES

[1] M. M. Bronstein, A. M. Bronstein, F. Michel, and N. Paragios. Data fusion through cross-modality metric learning using similarity-sensitive hashing. In *CVPR*, pages 3594–3601, 2010.

[2] F. Diaz. Regularizing query-based retrieval scores. In *IR*, pages 531–562, 2007.

[3] R.-E. Fan, K.-W. Chang, C.-J. Hsieh, X.-R. Wang, and C.-J. Lin. Liblinear: A library for large linear classification. In *JLMR*, pages 1871–1874, 2008.

[4] D. R. Hardoon, S. R. Szedmak, and J. R. Shawe-taylor. Canonical correlation analysis: An overview with application to learning methods. In *NC*, pages 2639–2664, 2004.

[5] S. Kumar and R. Udupa. Learning hash functions for cross-view similarity search. In *IJCAI'11*, pages 1360–1365, 2011.

[6] S. Moran and V. Lavrenko. Graph regularised hashing. In *ECIR*, pages 135–146, 2015.

[7] S. Moran, V. Lavrenko, and M. Osborne. Neighbourhood preserving quantisation for LSH. In *SIGIR*, pages 1009–1012, 2013.

[8] M. Rastegari, J. Choi, S. Fakhraei, H. D. III, and L. S. Davis. Predictable dual-view hashing. In *ICML*, pages 1328–1336, 2013.

[9] J. Song, Y. Yang, Y. Yang, Z. Huang, and H. T. Shen. Inter-media hashing for large-scale retrieval from heterogeneous data sources. In *SIGMOD*, pages 785–796, 2013.

[10] Y. Zhen and D. yan Yeung. Co-regularized hashing for multimodal data. In *NIPS*, pages 1385–1393, 2012.

Adapted B-CUBED Metrics to Unbalanced Datasets

Jose G. Moreno
Normandie University
UNICAEN, GREYC CNRS
F-14032 Caen, France
jose.moreno@unicaen.fr

Gaël Dias
Normandie University
UNICAEN, GREYC CNRS
F-14032 Caen, France
gael.dias@unicaen.fr

ABSTRACT

B-CUBED metrics have recently been adopted in the evaluation of clustering results as well as in many other related tasks. However, this family of metrics is not well adapted when datasets are unbalanced. This issue is extremely frequent in Web results, where classes are distributed following a strong unbalanced pattern. In this paper, we present a modified version of B-CUBED metrics to overcome this situation. Results in toy and real datasets indicate that the proposed adaptation correctly considers the particularities of unbalanced cases.

Categories and Subject Descriptors

H.3.3 [**Information Storage and Retrieval**]: Information search and retrieval—*clustering*

Keywords

Evaluation, Search results clustering, Unbalanced datasets

1. INTRODUCTION

Evaluation of partitions obtained as a result of clustering algorithms is a challenging task. Two main kinds of metrics can be identified: supervised and unsupervised metrics. In this paper, we will deal with the former. In the information retrieval area, a recent study proposed the use of a family of metrics known as B-CUBED [1], which is used when clusters of documents are evaluated. These new metrics successfully satisfy a set of formal constraints that include problematic situations such as *Cluster Homogeneity*, *Cluster completeness*, *Rag Bag*, and finally, *Cluster size vs. quantity*. Each of these constraints evaluate a different situation that must be solved with a good evaluation metric. However, in the particular case of unbalanced datasets, these metrics fail to identify the correct solution [4]. The particularity of an unbalanced dataset is that one of the classes covers most of the document collection. Namely, this is the case when the set of documents to be clustered is dominated by one class, e.g., one of the classes covers a high percentage of documents and the remaining documents belong to many small classes. This is not a strange situation. Indeed, this is a recurrent case when the Web Search Results Clustering (SRC) problem is studied. SRC consists in grouping Web results in meaningful clusters where each cluster should "hopefully" correspond to a unique topic. Moreover, it is often the case that topics are not equally distributed in Web results. For example, consider the results obtained with a search engine and presented in Figure 1. Note that mainly two topics can be found in the results, the animal and the car. The total number of images related to the animal is almost 5 times the number of images related to the car[1]. This example clearly illustrates the existence of unbalance between the two classes[2]. In general, this behaviour can be observed in several Web SRC datasets including ODP239 [3], MORESQUE [7] and WEBSRC401 [6]. For this reason, the use of clustering evaluation metrics must be verified in unbalanced cases. This is recurrently present in the SRC problem as well as in other clustering problems.

SIGIR'15 August 09 - 13, 2015, Santiago, Chile
©2015 ACM ISBN 978-1-4503-3621-5/15/08 ...$15.00
DOI: http://dx.doi.org/10.1145/2766462.2767836.

Figure 1: Commercial search engine results for the query "jaguar". 57 Web image results visualized, 47 of which are related to the animal and only 10 to the car.

In this paper, we present an evaluation of the B-CUBED metrics family using SRC datasets. Our results support the idea that B-CUBED give high scores to algorithms that follow similar distributions to the topics and otherwise, low scores even when cluster are randomly assigned. This can be explained by saying that B-CUBED metrics were also designed to penalize the erroneous links created between two classes more than putting documents in the wrong class [2]. Finally, we show how B-CUBED metrics can be modified to consider the evaluation of datasets that present the unbalanced issue. The remainder of this paper includes a description of B-CUBED clustering metrics and their modifications in Section 2. Experiments and results are presented in Section 3 and finally, discussion and conclusions are presented in Sections 4 and 5.

[1] Surrounded by the dotted blue rectangle.

[2] Many reasons could explain this distribution, however, how it affects user interaction with Web results is out of the scope of this paper.

2. ADAPTED B-CUBED FOR SRC

SRC algorithms have been evaluated with several supervised and unsupervised clustering metrics. In the former category, B-CUBED metrics have received a lot of attention in recent years. Similarly, SRC has also privileged these metrics but their impact in this particular problem is not clearly discussed. The particularities of the SRC problem motivate our efforts to develop an adapted version of these metrics.

2.1 B-CUBED metrics

B-CUBED metrics were originally proposed in [2], but exhaustively studied in [1] where it is shown that they can successfully evaluate partitions in situations included in defined formal constraints. Full comparison with illustrated examples can be found in [1]. B-CUBED F-measure (F_{b^3}), Precision (P_{b^3}) and Recall (R_{b^3}) are defined in Equations 1, 2 and 3.

$$\frac{1}{F_{b^3}} = \frac{\alpha}{P_{b^3}} + \frac{1-\alpha}{R_{b^3}} \tag{1}$$

$$\begin{aligned} P_{b^3} &= \frac{1}{N}\sum_{i=1}^{k}\frac{1}{|\pi_i|}\sum_{x_j\in\pi_i}\sum_{x_l\in\pi_i} g_0^*(x_j,x_l) \\ R_{b^3} &= \frac{1}{N}\sum_{i=1}^{k}\frac{1}{|\pi_i^*|}\sum_{x_j\in\pi_i^*}\sum_{x_l\in\pi_i^*} g_0(x_j,x_l) \end{aligned} \tag{2}$$

$$\begin{aligned} g_0(x_i,x_j) &= \begin{cases} 1 \iff \exists l : x_i \in \pi_l \land x_j \in \pi_l \\ 0, otherwise \end{cases} \\ g_0^*(x_i,x_j) &= \begin{cases} 1 \iff \exists l : x_i \in \pi_l^* \land x_j \in \pi_l^* \\ 0, otherwise \end{cases} \end{aligned} \tag{3}$$

where π_i is the cluster solution i and π_i^* is the gold standard of the category i and N is the total number of documents.

2.2 Adapted B-CUBED metrics

Two main parameters of B-CUBED metrics can be modified. First, the α parameter in Equation 1 can vary to alter the importance of P_{b^3} and R_{b^3}. This issue will be discussed in section 3. Second, the number of elements considered to calculate the Precision or Recall, i.e., the number of inputs received by $g_0(\cdot,\cdot)$ and $g_0^*(\cdot,\cdot)$ can be extended to three or more elements. The new formulation to allow the use of several elements[3] is presented in Equation 4.

$$\begin{aligned} g_0(\vec{x}) &= \begin{cases} 1 \iff \exists l : \forall x_i \in \vec{x}, x_i \in \pi_l \\ 0, otherwise \end{cases} \\ g_0^*(\vec{x}) &= \begin{cases} 1 \iff \exists l : \forall x_i \in \vec{x}, x_i \in \pi_l^* \\ 0, otherwise \end{cases} \end{aligned} \tag{4}$$

Note that because more possible combinations are considered, the normalization factors in Equation 2, $\frac{1}{|\pi_i|}$ or $\frac{1}{|\pi_i^*|}$ must be modified. After mathematical factorization, the normalization value is cancelled by the modified Precision ($P_{b^3}^{mod}$) and it is factorized in terms of R_{b^3} by the modified Recall ($R_{b^3}^{mod}$). Factorized versions of the adapted B-CUBED metrics are presented in Equation 5.

$$P_{b^3}^{mod} = P_{b^3} \land R_{b^3}^{mod} = R_{b^3}^{|\vec{x}|-1} \Rightarrow \frac{1}{F_{b^3}^{mod}} = \frac{\alpha}{P_{b^3}} + \frac{1-\alpha}{R_{b^3}^{|\vec{x}|-1}} \tag{5}$$

[3]The number of elements will be determined by the size of $\vec{x}$.

Note that, when the number of elements considered by the g_0 functions is equal to 2, i.e. $|\vec{x}| = 2$, then the $F_{b^3}^{mod} = F_{b^3}$. In particular, the new $F_{b^3}^{mod}$ tends to give less importance to partitions with high Recall and benefits Precision preserving the α parameter.

3. EXPERIMENTS AND RESULTS

3.1 Datasets

In our experiments, we use a total of five toy examples that include four classical clustering situations as well as one situation that represents the unbalanced case. These toy examples are included in the first row of Table 1. Note that for each example, a left and right partition is included. In all cases, the right partition is considered a more adequate solution. Finally, in order to show the impact in real situations, we perform experiments in three SRC datasets: ODP239 [3], MORESQUE [7] and WEBSRC401 [6].

3.2 Clustering algorithms

SRC ALGORITHMS: A host of classical and recent algorithms were used: LINGO, STC and CascadeSRC. LINGO is based on the spectral decomposition of a term-document matrix to define the respective clusters. Finally, labels are assigned by choosing the best representative for each found cluster. STC clusters documents based on a suffix tree. Clusters are determined from the tree by selecting the longest set of strings which are used as labels. CascadeSRC [5] is a two level combination algorithm that preserves the quality in terms of intra-document similarity offered by LINGO and the compactness offered by STC.

RANDOM ALGORITHMS: Two random algorithms are studied to verify the impact of document distribution in the obtained partitions. First, the UniformRand algorithm assigns documents to each cluster in such a way that, in the end, each partition contains equally sized clusters. Secondly, the UltraShapedRand algorithm imitates the unbalanced SRC distribution. In this case, if k clusters are required, then for the clusters $c_1,..,c_{k-1}$ only one document is randomly assigned and the remaining documents are assigned to cluster c_k. Note that this distribution is an extreme case of SRC but allows to show the difference from a uniform distribution.

3.3 Formal Constraints

The formal constraints are listed as *Cluster Homogeneity*, *Cluster completeness*, *Rag Bag* and *Cluster size vs. quantity*. *Cluster Homogeneity* consists in giving a higher score to partitions where clusters contain elements of only one class, *Cluster completeness* gives higher scores to partitions where classes are represented by few clusters, *Rag Bag* gives higher scores to partitions where only one cluster contains different classes than to several clusters containing different classes. Finally, *Cluster size vs. quantity* gives higher scores to partitions where few clusters are provided but separates most classes. In addition to these formal constraints, the *Unbalanced* constraint was recently added by [4] and evaluates if a misclassification is present in a big class or in a small one. This constraint gives better scores when the incorrect classified element is from the biggest class. Results using the examples proposed by [1] and [4][4] are shown in Table 1[5]. For each example, the first column shows the value obtained with the metric for the left partition, the second column shows the result for the right partition and the third column indicates if the formal constraint is satisfied (✓) or

[4]The original example was slightly modified to put only one misclassified document in each evaluated partition.
[5]All metrics can be found in [7] and [1].

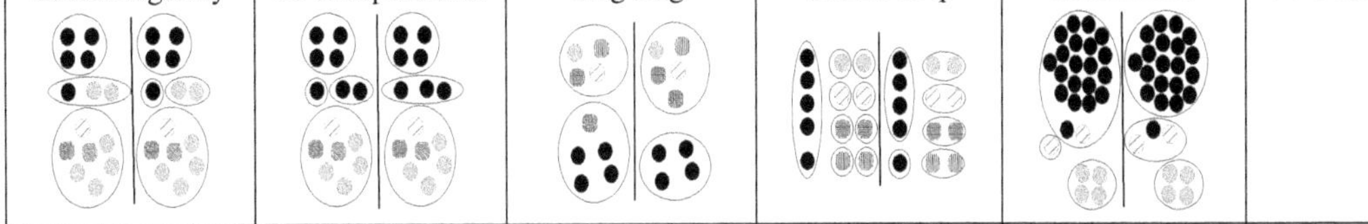

	C. Homogenity			C. Completeness			Rag Bag			C. size vs q.			Unbalanced			4 + 1 F.C.
Purity	0.71	0.79	✓	0.79	0.79	✗	0.56	0.56	✗	1.00	1.00	✗	0.96	0.96	✗	✖
Inv. Purity	0.79	0.79	✗	0.79	0.79	✗	1.00	1.00	✗	0.69	0.92	✓	0.96	0.96	✗	✖
F&M	0.47	0.49	✓	0.47	0.53	✓	0.61	0.61	✗	0.85	0.85	✗	0.95	0.94	✗	✖
RandIndex	0.68	0.70	✓	0.68	0.70	✓	0.72	0.72	✗	0.95	0.95	✗	0.94	0.94	✗	✖
Adj.RandIndex	0.25	0.28	✓	0.24	0.31	✓	0.40	0.40	✗	0.80	0.80	✗	0.79	0.79	✗	✖
Jaccard	0.31	0.33	✓	0.31	0.36	✓	0.38	0.38	✗	0.71	0.71	✗	0.90	0.89	✗	✖
F-measure	0.71	0.79	✓	0.79	0.79	✗	0.56	0.56	✗	1.00	1.00	✗	0.96	0.96	✗	✖
P_{b^3}	0.60	0.69	✓	0.69	0.69	✗	0.49	0.56	✓	1.00	1.00	✗	0.93	0.95	✓	✖
R_{b^3}	0.70	0.70	✗	0.71	0.76	✓	1.00	1.00	✗	0.69	0.88	✓	0.96	0.93	✗	✖
F_{b^3}	0.64	0.69	✓	0.70	0.72	✓	0.55	0.71	✓	0.82	0.93	✓	0.94	0.93	✗	✖
$P_{b^3}^{mod}$	0.60	0.69	✓	0.69	0.69	✗	0.49	0.56	✓	1.00	1.00	✗	0.93	0.95	✓	✖
$R_{b^3}^{mod}$ $(\|\vec{x}\| = 3)$	0.45	0.45	✗	0.56	0.57	✓	1.00	1.00	✗	0.46	0.77	✓	0.93	0.86	✗	✖
$F_{b^3}^{mod\&0.9}$	0.58	0.66	✓	0.67	0.68	✓	0.52	0.58	✓	0.90	0.97	✓	0.93	0.95	✓	✔
$F_{b^3}^{0.9}$	0.61	0.70	✓	0.69	0.70	✓	0.52	0.58	✓	0.96	0.99	✓	0.93	0.94	✓	✔

Table 1: Satisfaction of formal constraints with common SRC metrics: Examples.

not (✗). Finally, the column "4+1 F.C." indicates if the five formal constraints are satisfied simultaneously.

Note that none of current metrics can satisfy all constraints. Indeed, F_{b^3} satisfies the first 4 F.C., but misses the correct identification of the best partition for the unbalanced case as reported by [4]. However, the proposed modifications $F_{b^3}^{mod\&0.9}$ (with $|\vec{x}| = 3$) and $F_{b^3}^{0.9}$ manage to correctly classify all the formal constraints using the parameter $\alpha = 0.9$. Indeed, positive values are obtained starting from $\alpha = 0.7$, but to achieve a more general solution $\alpha = 0.9$ was selected. Our choice is motivated by the reduction of the bias generated by unbalanced datasets namely for the SRC task. It is important to remark that when $\alpha > 0.5$, Precision receives more importance than Recall.

3.4 Results in SRC datasets

A total of 10 runs were performed for each random algorithm. $F_{b^3}^{mod\&0.9}$ and $F_{b^3}^{0.9}$ average values of the two random algorithms are presented in Table 2 for different k values (from 2 to 20) and using the three SRC datasets. The UltraShapedRand algorithm behaves better than the UniformRand when evaluated with both metrics using the mentionned datasets[6]. Although when $k = 2$ both algorithms score similarly, the differences get larger as the number of k partitions grows. This was observed for both metrics in the three datasets. However, when $k = 20$, the differences are larger for $F_{b^3}^{mod\&0.9}$ than $F_{b^3}^{0.9}$. It is because $F_{b^3}^{0.9}$ gives high importance to Precision allowing to get good performance by just getting more clusters. Indeed, when the number of clusters is increasing, the number of elements by cluster must be reduced. This situation reduces the chances of putting together elements from different classes which implicitly increases Precision.

When using MORESQUE and ODP239, $F_{b^3}^{0.9}$ gives better scores to the UltraShapedRand algorithm as the number of k partitions increases. Again, this situation is given by the parameter $\alpha = 0.9$, which gives higher importance to Precision than Recall. However, this situation is not the same for $F_{b^3}^{mod\&0.9}$. This metric does not always give better scores to this situation and partitions with higher numbers of clusters may not be preferred. This is an important issue, because results suggest that $F_{b^3}^{0.9}$ will prefer partitions with clusters that contain a unique document which is not the case in any of the used datasets.

		F_{b^3}	$F_{b^3}^{0.9}$	$F_{b^3}^{mod\&0.9}$
MORESQUE	STC	**0.4602**	0.5715	**0.4186**
	LINGO	0.3989	**0.5784**	0.3497
	CascadeSRC	0.4602	0.4386	0.3874
ODP239	STC	0.4027	0.4369	**0.3410**
	LINGO	0.3461	**0.5162**	0.2902
	CascadeSRC	**0.4229**	0.3463	0.3303
WEBSRC401	STC	0.4293	0.6135	0.3618
	LINGO	0.3095	0.5758	0.2279
	CascadeSRC	**0.6665**	**0.6349**	**0.5955**

Table 3: F_{b^3}, $F_{b^3}^{0.9}$ and $F_{b^3}^{mod\&0.9}$ results for partitions obtained with STC, LINGO and CascadeSRC using real datasets. In bold the best score by metric and dataset.

A summary of three SRC algorithms (LINGO, STC, CascadeSRC) using F_{b^3}, $F_{b^3}^{0.9}$ and $F_{b^3}^{mod\&0.9}$ is presented in Table 3. Note that for MORESQUE and ODP239, $F_{b^3}^{0.9}$ and $F_{b^3}^{mod\&0.9}$ give better scores to the SRC algorithms than to the random strategies, as it is expected for a good evaluation metric[7]. Unfortunately, the behaviour is different for WEBSRC401, where none of the metrics manages to correctly assign the scores when compared with the random strategies. However, as shown in [6], WEBSRC401 is a hard SRC dataset. But this still raises discussion.

4. DISCUSSION

Although many clustering evaluation metrics exist, none of them can consider all possible situations. Indeed, new metrics could be

[6]This situation was also observed for the F_{b^3} metric.

[7]This is not an evident situation. Remember that, as shown by [4], F_{b^3} can not select the correct partition in unbalanced datasets.

			k									
			2	4	6	8	10	12	14	16	18	20
$F_{b^3}^{0.9}$	MORESQUE	UniformR.	**0.3282**	0.3179	0.3103	0.3105	0.3081	0.3102	0.3097	0.3135	0.3134	0.3184
		UltraSh.R.	0.3483	0.3586	0.3706	0.3814	0.3940	0.4028	**0.4049**	0.4048	0.3992	0.3812
	ODP239	UniformR.	0.2534	0.2567	0.2617	0.2702	0.2752	0.2826	0.2908	0.2975	0.3053	**0.3112**
		UltraSh.R.	0.2601	0.2745	0.2885	0.3042	0.3162	0.3276	0.3383	0.3448	**0.3497**	0.3464
	WEBSRC401	UniformR.	**0.5921**	0.5422	0.5097	0.4850	0.4574	0.4451	0.4330	0.4208	0.4139	0.3994
		UltraSh.R.	**0.6453**	0.6393	0.6407	0.6381	0.6472	0.6380	0.6402	0.6393	0.6438	0.6432
$F_{b^3}^{mod\&0.9}$	MORESQUE	UniformR.	**0.2700**	0.1672	0.1248	0.1138	0.1096	0.1095	0.1105	0.1113	0.1079	0.1114
		UltraSh.R.	0.3479	0.3568	0.3666	0.3727	**0.3775**	0.3724	0.3489	0.3154	0.2590	0.1890
	ODP239	UniformR.	**0.2298**	0.1721	0.1355	0.1129	0.0972	0.0894	0.0798	0.0747	0.0683	0.0638
		UltraSh.R.	0.2599	0.2739	0.2870	0.3005	0.3091	**0.3134**	0.3119	0.2947	0.2573	0.1940
	WEBSRC401	UniformR.	**0.4614**	0.2144	0.1350	0.1079	0.0871	0.0782	0.0875	0.0722	0.0702	0.0649
		UltraSh.R.	0.6108	0.6040	0.6053	0.6029	**0.6119**	0.6030	0.6048	0.6039	0.6079	0.6081

Table 2: $F_{b^3}^{mod\&0.9}$ and $F_{b^3}^{0.9}$ results for partitions obtained with different k clusters of the UltraShapedRandom (UltraSh.R.) and the UniformRandom (UniformR.) algorithms using real datasets. In bold the best score for each random algorithm.

proposed to simultaneously deal with the formal constraints as well as adapt to the specific task. However, as shown in Table 1, this is a hard task. Moreover, we have presented $F_{b^3}^{mod\&0.9}$ which is a modified version of the B-CUBED metrics. Our proposal manages to correctly classify the examples used to validate the initial 4 formal constraints and the case for unbalanced datasets. Note that a simple α parameter modification (the $F_{b^3}^{0.9}$ metric) also manages to correctly classify the examples, but fails when it is evaluated in real datasets. It is mainly due to the fact that too much importance to Precision is given thus privileging partitions with many clusters formed by few documents. On the other hand, the $F_{b^3}^{mod\&0.9}$ not only deals with the formal constraints but is also not disoriented by the random algorithms. Note from Table 2 that for the UniformRandom, $F_{b^3}^{mod\&0.9}$ reduces the assigned score as the number of clusters increases. On contrary, for the UltraShapedRand, it increases until a certain point from which it starts to decrease. These behaviours were observed for both algorithms in the three datasets.

These results could inspire the development of (1) new analysis to identify more cases (such as the unbalanced) that must be considered in the SRC problem, (2) new metrics or adaptations of existing ones to satisfy the 4+1 studied formal constraints and (3) SRC strategies that consider adapted optimization functions to obtain the satisfaction of the formal constraints. Regarding the last one, some of the existing algorithms implicitly capture these characteristics, i.e., classical SRC algorithms, such as LINGO and STC, generate shapes similar to UltraShapedRand without explicitly including it in their algorithm. This situation could explain why these are hard to beat algorithms. Indeed, the classical K-means algorithm generates partition shapes similar to the UniformRand algorithm and usually its performance is under what is obtained with LINGO or STC.

5. CONCLUSIONS

This paper presents a study about B-CUBED metrics and proposes an non-trivial adaptation of the F_{b^3} to be used in the SRC problem. Unbalanced datasets are implicitly used in the SRC problem and it is a frequently ignored issue in recent studies. Several experiments were performed in toy examples and real datasets. Main findings indicate that our proposed metric ($F_{b^3}^{mod\&0.9}$ with $|\vec{x}| = 3$) is the only one to correctly classify the toy examples in the evaluation of the formal constraints including the unbalanced case, and at the same time, able to give adequate scores when comparing SRC algorithms against random algorithms with unbalanced shapes. New research in SRC must consider the effect of using unbalanced datasets by using adapted metrics to achieved more adequate results. Similarly, existing metrics based on F_{b^3} must reconsider the unbalanced effect in the datasets. Our immediate work consists in the exploration of bigger sizes for $|\vec{x}|$ that will help in the understanding of this parameter.

6. REFERENCES

[1] E. Amigó, J. Gonzalo, J. Artiles, and F. Verdejo. A comparison of extrinsic clustering evaluation metrics based on formal constraints. *Information Retrieval*, 12(4):461–486, 2009.

[2] A. Bagga and B. Baldwin. Entity-based cross-document coreferencing using the vector space model. In *Proceedings of the 36th Annual Meeting of the Association for Computational Linguistics - Volume 1*, ACL '98, pages 79–85, 1998.

[3] C. Carpineto and G. Romano. Optimal meta search results clustering. In *33rd International ACM SIGIR Conference on Research and Development in Information Retrieval (SIGIR)*, pages 170–177, 2010.

[4] M. C. P. de Souto, A. L. V. Coelho, K. Faceli, T. C. Sakata, V. Bonadia, and I. G. Costa. A comparison of external clustering evaluation indices in the context of imbalanced data sets. In *Proceedings of the 2012 Brazilian Symposium on Neural Networks (BSNN)*, SBRN '12, pages 49–54, 2012.

[5] J. G. Moreno and G. Dias. Easy web search results clustering: When baselines can reach state-of-the-art algorithms. 14th Conference of the European Chapter of the Association for Computational Linguistics (EACL), pages 1–5, 2014.

[6] J. G. Moreno, G. Dias, and G. Cleuziou. Query log driven web search results clustering. In *Proceedings of the 37th International ACM SIGIR Conference on Research & Development in Information Retrieval (SIGIR)*, pages 777–786, 2014.

[7] R. Navigli and D. Vannella. Semeval-2013 task 11: Word sense induction & disambiguation within an end-user application. In *Proceedings of the International Workshop on Semantic Evaluation (SEMEVAL)*, pages 1–9, 2013.

A Time-aware Random Walk Model for Finding Important Documents in Web Archives

Tu Ngoc Nguyen, Nattiya Kanhabua, Claudia Niederée and Xiaofei Zhu

L3S Research Center / Leibniz Universität Hannover, Germany
{tunguyen, kanhabua, niederee, zhu}@L3S.de

ABSTRACT

Due to their first-hand, diverse and evolution-aware reflection of nearly all areas of life, web archives are emerging as gold-mines for content analytics of many sorts. However, supporting search, which goes beyond navigational search via URLs, is a very challenging task in these unique structures with huge, redundant and noisy temporal content. In this paper, we address the search needs of expert users such as journalists, economists or historians for discovering a *topic in time*: Given a query, the top-k returned results should give the best representative documents that cover most interesting time-periods for the topic. For this purpose, we propose a novel random walk-based model that integrates relevance, temporal authority, diversity and time in a unified framework. Preliminary experimental results on a large-scale, real-world web archival collection shows that our method significantly improves the state-of-the-art algorithms (i.e., PageRank) in ranking temporal web pages.

Categories and Subject Descriptors

H.3.3 [**Information Storage and Retrieval**]: Information Search and Retrieval—*Retrieval models*

General Terms

Algorithms, Experimentation, Performance

Keywords

Temporal Ranking, Web Archive, Authority, Diversity

1. INTRODUCTION AND BACKGROUND

Web archives reflect nearly all types of social cultural, societal and everyday processes of our lives in the web as well as the exponential growth and continuous change in content and structure of the world wide web. Therefore, web archives from organizations such as the Internet Archive have the potential of becoming invaluable gold-mines for temporal content analytics of many kinds (e.g., politics and social issues, economics or media). First hand evidences about such processes are of great benefit for expert users such as journalists, economists, or historians. However, support for navigational search as it is, for example, offered by the Wayback machine[1], is not sufficient for tapping the full potential of web archives. Instead, search results should provide a good coverage of the query topic over time for enabling exploration of the topic and its evolution. Therefore, content relevance is not the only driver: time relevance and impact are other key factors. Further aspects, which make web archive search very different from web search are the high redundancy (pages of near-identical content are crawled all over again) and the special role that time/crawling time is playing in the web archive structure.

In this paper, we tackle the problem of discovering important documents along the time-span of the web archives by a ranking approach. The intuition is that the impact/authority of a document in the web archives with regards to a query is strongly influenced by time. Hence, the temporal authority of a document should be accumulated over a surrounding time window (instead of considering only one or all temporal snapshots).

Temporal link analysis for web search improvement has been studied in previous work [1, 4, 9, 10]. Their common goal is to improve state-of-the-art link-based algorithms (i.e., PageRank [8]) in favoring new web pages, instead of old, stale pages (that often ranked high due to its accumulated in-links). The most advanced approach in this direction is described in [4], where they track the authority of a page over multiple historical (past) web snapshots. This allows the incorporation of web freshness into authority propagation, and hence, boosts the authority of fresh (new) page at the querying time. In estimating the temporal authority along the time dimension, we adapt their strategy by propagating the authority of *past* and *future* snapshots. This backward propagation (from future snapshots) accounts for the 'lagging' time a new document needs to gather in-links. For example, a document about health care reform issued in March, 2010 is more relevant with the time point than April, 2010, where it has more number of in-links.

Graph-based diversity for ranking based on random walk are addressed in [2, 5, 11]. The first two utilized a greedy algorithm in transforming a picked node into an absorbing state. This punishes neighboring nodes but the random walk still lingers at away nodes, hence increases diversity. Mei et al. [5] introduce a vertex- reinforcement base on the intuition that nodes are visited many times tend to be more likely to be re-visited. This reinforcement on the transition

SIGIR'15, August 09 - 13, 2015, Santiago, Chile.
© 2015 ACM. ISBN 978-1-4503-3621-5/15/08 ...$15.00.
DOI: http://dx.doi.org/10.1145/2766462.2767832.

[1]http://archive.org/web/

probability has a strong theoretical foundation, brings less complexity and can be improved towards scalability in large graphs.

For temporal ranking in the web archive, we are the first ones to combine the problems of relevance, temporal authority, diversity and time in a unified framework. In more detail, we construct a temporal graph over the web archive. Using time preference and relevance as priors, in Section 2.1, we propose a novel random walk model on the temporal graph. The model accounts for the in-link and natural time lagging in the web archive in mining the temporal authority. We present two ways of injecting time preference in Section 2.2. Further more, we introduce a novel diversity mechanism that penalizes both neighbors in the same web snapshots and *across* snapshots in Section 2.3. Our experiments are conducted on a large-scale, real-world web archival dataset, which is further explained in Section 3.

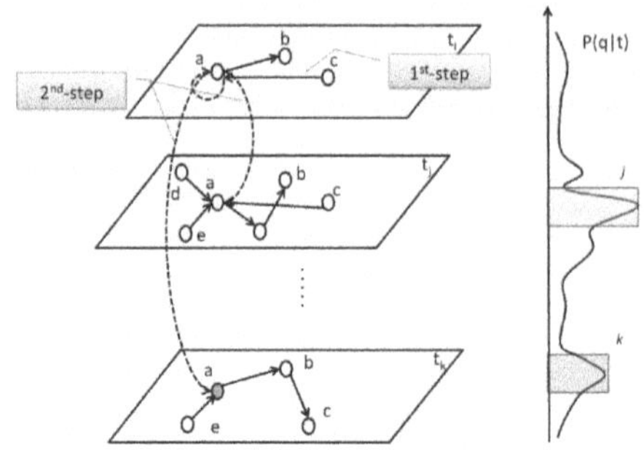

Figure 1: Time-travel web archive surfer. Solid lines indicate *within*-snapshot transitions, and dashed lines indicate the *across*-snapshot teleporting

2. METHODOLOGY

2.1 Temporal Ranking Model

In this work, we re-design the traditional PageRank (at document/page level) to more precisely measure the temporal authority of the documents. We propose a new time-aware random surfer model, with the intuition that instead of jumping to a random node with equal probability, this traveler favors jumping to a node at a time period of interest.

Temporal Graph Model A temporal graph $\mathcal{G}$ consists of multiple graphs at different time points, called graph snapshots (snapshots for short). A snapshot G is a directed graph with time annotation, $G_t = (V_t, E_t, t)$, with $t \in T$, $V_t \in V$ and $E_t \in E$. A vertex $v \in V$ can belong to multiple snapshots $\{V_t\}$. A vertex $v \in V_{t_i}$ is connected with $v \in V_{t_j}$ by an inter-link $\{v_{t_i}, v_{t_j}\} \in \mathcal{I}$. In the web archive context, each vertex v in a graph snapshot is a revision of a document d, identified by an unique URL. The vertex is time-stamped by the crawling time. The edge between two vertices is the hyper-link between two revisions. It is time-stamped as the time of the source vertex.

Temporal Random Surfer Model We describe a 'time travel random surfer model', which redefines how an web archive searcher (so-called *time traveler*) surfs in the web archive. The 'time travel random surfer model' is initiated by the 'random surfer model', which explains underlying PageRank [8]. The original model describes the surfing behavior of a web surfer that after following the link structure starting from a page for several steps and then jump to a random page. However, this surfer model does not well-captured the temporal nature of a longitudinal web archive. Surfing in the web archive, we assume that a user prefers search results from interesting time points. Hence, the surfing behaviour of a time traveler should be adapted to incorporate this temporally important aspect.

In this work, we model a time-travel surfing as in moves that consist of two distinct steps (i.e., non-temporal and temporal, as illustrated in Figure 1). At each move, a traveler starts with a *non-temporal* step. A searcher chooses to either follow the out-links of a page or jump to a remote page. In order to achieve the precise temporal authority of a page at a time point, we employ the fresh favoring mechanism as in [4], so that old pages are degraded. A traveler in our model prefers a new/fresh page. As contrast to [4], we do not consider the editorial behaviour of the page because we focus on *informational* queries, where the content of a document is nearly *static* over time. In order that, we take into account the freshness linked with the age of a document a at time t_i, $\mathcal{F}(a, t_i)$, which is quantified as:

$$\mathcal{F}(a, t_i) = e^{-\beta_1 (t_i - \mathcal{T}(a))} \tag{1}$$

where $\mathcal{T}$ denotes the first time a page appears in the collection. In the second (temporal) step, a traveler jumps to a snapshot of the page at different time points. To capture the temporal authority, we model the authority propagation flow among nodes at nearby time points. Here, we introduce two kinds of propagations: *forward-* (authority is propagated by past snapshots) and *backward-* (authority is propagated by future snapshots). The propagation is modeled in a decay fashion, and hence, in a time window with length controlled by a decay parameter. This authority propagation is different from [4] in the sense that, it helps capturing the precise temporal authority of a document at a given time point (instead of using for smoothing purpose). We model the length of the temporal propagation as controlled by the decay parameter β_2 (further explained in Section 2.2), that we model as a global parameter in this work.

2.2 Time-sensitive PageRank

In this section, we explain two novel methods to inject time preference into the PageRank: (1) the jumping probability at the 1st step, so that the jumping scope is not restricted to within current snapshot but other snapshots and (2) via the transition probability between snapshots, at the 2nd step.

In the normal case where no preferences are defined, the vector $\vec{v}$ which presents the jumping probability from node a to all the nodes N in the temporal graph is uniformly distributed ($= [\frac{1}{N}]N \times 1$). However, different from this ordinary behavior, we present a *query-dependent*, time-aware vector $\vec{v}_{temp}$ over the temporal graph as follows:

Time-aware Teleportation Instead of limiting the jumping scope in within a web snapshot, the traveler in this case can jump to any snapshot with a time preference. The probability of jumping from q to p at time t_i, $P_{t_i}(p|q, Jump)$, is dependent on the preference score of time t_i, $I(t_i)$. The probability that a traveler reaches the page p at snapshot t_i can be written as[2]:

$$\pi_{p,i} = \sum_{t_j \in T_i} P_{t_i|t_j}(p) \sum_{q:q\rightarrow p|t_j} P_{t_j}(Follow|q) P_{t_j}(p|q, Follow) + \sum_{\forall q} P(Jump|q) I(t_i) \quad (2)$$

Time-aware Transition Probability For this second type of embedding time preference into the model, we modify the transition probability across time snapshots. Intuitively, a snapshot at time t_i with high time preference will have higher transition probability. In this case, the jumping scope is restricted within the time snapshot. The probability that a traveler reaches the page p at snapshot t_i can be written as:

$$\begin{aligned}\pi_{p,i} &= \begin{array}{l}\sum_{t_j \in S_i} P_{t_i|t_j}(p) \sum_{q:q\rightarrow p|t_j} P_{t_j}(Follow|q) P_{t_j}(p|q, Follow) \\ \quad + \sum_{t_j \in S_i} P_{t_i|t_j}(p) \sum_{q|t_j} P_{t_j}(Jump|q) P_{t_j}(p|q, Jump)\end{array} \\ &= \sum_{t_j \in S_i} P_{t_i|t_j}(p) \cdot \left[(1-\alpha) \sum_{q:q\rightarrow p|t_j} F_{t_j}(p,q) \cdot \pi_{q,j} + \alpha \sum_{q|t_j} \frac{\pi_{q,j}}{N_{t_j}}\right]\end{aligned}$$

where S_i is the set of snapshots which can directly distribute authority to t_i within one step. Even though presenting a similar generalization of the propagation model to us, the results in [4] indicate that the decay propagation is not most suitable for their task (normal web ranking). In our case, instead this transition probability (propagation) is strongly time-influenced. A node most propagates its authority to the time of interest (to help the time-aware ranking) that most near its time snapshot. The transition probability $P_{t_i|t_j}(p)$ is derived from the interestingness measure of the two time points and is calculated as:

$$P_{t_i|t_j}(p) = \frac{I(t_j)}{\sum_{\forall t_k} I(t_k)} \cdot w(t_i, t_j) \quad (4)$$

where $w(t_i, t_j) = e^{\beta_2 |t_i - t_j|}$. Hence the propagation scope is restricted to a time window $\mathcal{W}$ with the size (also size of S) is controlled by β_2. Within the time window $\mathcal{W}$, one with high time preference will be more likely to be propagated.

2.3 Time-based Diversity in Temporal Graph

In this section, we target another issue of the ranking problem, the time-based diversification of the top-k results.

Reinforcement in Random Walk

Mei et al. [5] introduce the integration of the vertex-reinforced random walk (VRRW) into the conventional PageRank to address the diversity ranking in graphs. Their intuition follows the 'rich gets richer' phenomenon, which specifically, the node that has been visited many times will have higher probability to be revisited again. Hence, the transition probability in the Markov random walk (to a state from others) is reinforced by the number of previous visits to that state. Our time-based diversity model follows the same intuition.

[2]One can introduce a parameter α in the formula so that $\sum_p \pi_{p,i} = 1$. However, to simplify the problem, we omit the parameter.

The vertex reinforcement is applied within each snapshot, so that the *within*-snapshot neighbors of a popular node (visited many times) are penalized. For the authority propagation across time snapshots, however, this mechanism cannot be integrated directly. Instead, we follow a *voting* propagation mechanism. For every step, we check for the node snapshot with maximum number of visits over the propagation time window, and only this node snapshot got propagated from others. The other nodes receive no propagation from other nodes. Hence, this approach allows a partial *across*-snapshot penalty and helps the time-based diversity.

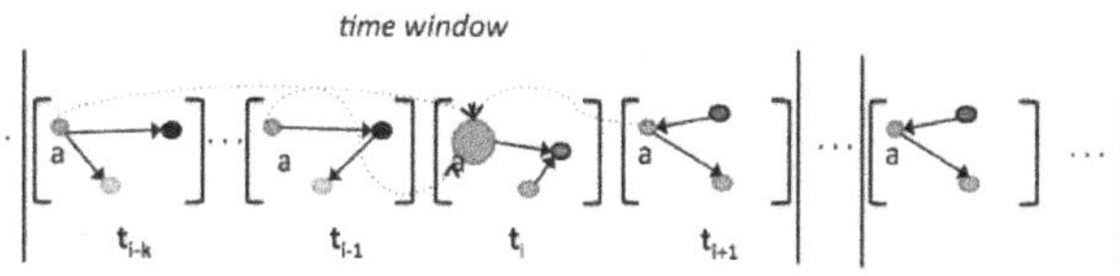

Figure 2: Reinforced/dynamic propagation over a time window. There is only one node gets all the propagations.

In a similar fashion to [5], the time-variant transition probability from q to p at step T (of the random walk) within a time snapshot t_i is defined as:

$$P^T_{t_i}(p,q) = (1-\alpha) \cdot s(p_{t_j}) + \alpha \cdot \frac{P^0_{t_i}(p,q) \cdot N^T_{t_i}(q)}{D^T_{t_i}(p)} \quad (5)$$

where $N^T_{t_i}(q)$ is the number of visits to q at step T. $D^T_{t_i}(p) = \sum_{q \in t_i} P^0_{t_i}(p,q) N^T_{t_i}(q)$. The cross snapshot- transition probability $P_{t_i|t_j}(p)$ at step T is:

$$P_{t_i|t_j}(p) = \begin{cases} \text{calculated as Equation 4} & if \\ \quad p = \text{argmax}_{\forall t_i \in \mathcal{W}_{t_j}} N^T_{t_i}(p), & \\ 0 & otherwise. \end{cases} \quad (6)$$

where $\mathcal{W}_{t_j}$ is the time window of t_j, such that $\forall t_i \in \mathcal{W}_{t_j}$, $w(t_i, t_j) > 0$.

3. EXPERIMENTS

In this section, we evaluate the performances of 5 different methods: temp-BM25, temp-PageRank[3](baseline), our approach with time-aware teleportation (ours), our approach with vertex-reinforcement random walk (ours+div) and our approach with time-aware vertex-reinforcement random walk (ours+tempdiv).

3.1 Experiment settings

Dataset We utilize a corpus of archival web pages in .gov domain collected by the Internet Archive from January 1995 to September 2013. The corpus contains over 900 million of text captures and over 58.8 billion temporal links. In order to shrink down the huge collection to extract a subset/subgraph of interest, we follow the idea of recent work that exploiting the value of anchor text. First, we achieve over 60 related long-term controversial political topics from the debate website[4]. We then look into the document linking graph and extract the links with anchor text reflecting any of the topics (both lexicographically and semantically). We

[3]To incorporate temporal prior, we apply PageRank and BM25 at each time snapshot and then multiply them with the corresponding time preference score.

[4]http://www.debate.org/big-issues/

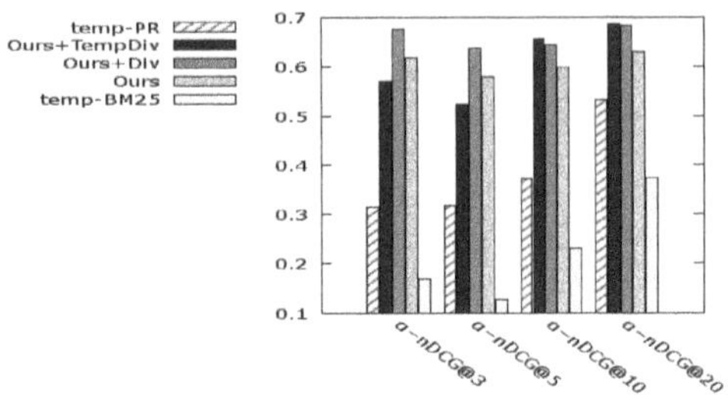

Figure 3: Performance of time-based subtopic diversity.

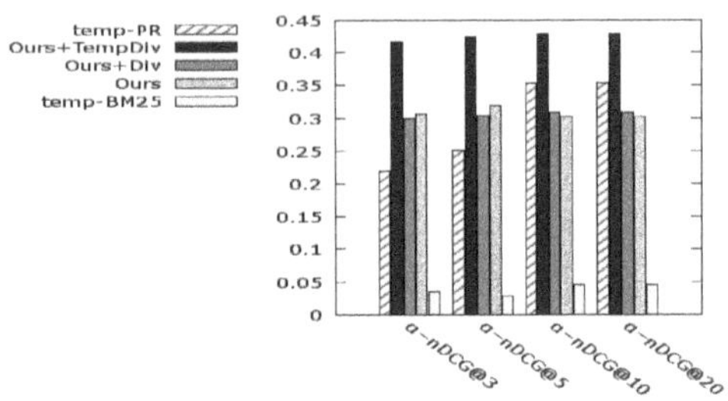

Figure 4: Performance of content-based subtopic diversity.

then captured the source and destination web pages of these links and treat them as the document seeds. We further capture the in-pages pointing to source pages and out-pages (which the destinations point to) to achieve a substantially large collection of over 100 million document revisions (approx. 40 million unique documents). We then picked 20 controversial/informational queries to conduct the experiment.

Ground Truth and Metrics Since there is no publicly available gold standard for our work, we rely on manual annotation for the 20 queries. For each document, we asked human experts, whether it is relevant to (1) one of the time-points and (2) any of the content-based subtopics. The scale for time is binary, whereas to account for authority, we use a scale from 0 (not related) to 4 (highly relevant) for the subtopic relevance judgment. A document with score larger than 2 is considered as relevant. For evaluation, follow the adopted setting of recent TREC web tracks (diversity task) as presented in [6], we use a generalization of a well-known result diversification metric (that accounts for both diversity and relevance), α-$nDCG$ [3] (so that it takes into account the subtopic weights). We consider two different subtopic dimensions, (1) *time* - with associated weight mined from the anchor-text distribution and (2) subtopics mined from *content* - equally weighted.

Priors and Parameter Tuning For the temporal prior, we mined from the anchor text frequency distribution (to mimic the query logs, following [7]). For the relevance prior, we utilize the scores from the BM25 retrieval model. For the random walk parameters, we set the jumping probability to be the default 0.15. All decay parameters are set to 0.4. All algorithms are run over Apache Giraph[5].

3.2 Experiment results

Figures 3 and 4 show the *time* and *subtopic* diversification results of the compared models respectively. For the *time* diversity, our models outperform the baseline significantly ($p < 0.05$) at $k = 3$ and $k = 5$. It is empirically found that, our propagation method helps identifying the temporal authority with regards to the relevant time more precisely. For example, given the query electoral college and a time period February 2009, a document issued in September 2008 has a high score for the traditional PageRank. However, our propagation accounts for both *freshness* and *lagging* ranks another document issued in February 2009 higher (that is more time relevant). The good performance of our approach shows that we capture better the temporal authority of documents with regards to the time preference. Our temporal diversity method also shows that it diversifies time effectively. The results for *content*-based subtopic diversity measurement also indicate a good performance of our method. Ours+tempdiv best performs (significant with $p < 0.05$) for all cases. This rather shows the effectiveness of our time-aware diversity approach.

[5]http://giraph.apache.org/

4. CONCLUSIONS

In this paper, we have studied the problem of finding important document in the web archive and address it in a unified framework that integrates relevance, temporal authority, diversity and time together. In detail, we proposed a novel random walk model incorporating time and the link structure of the web archive. Our model is shown to outperform PageRank for both relevance and diversity tasks. For future work, we would like to investigate the application of the novel model on different open challenges of web archive, i.e., time-aware summarization. Scalability issues will also be another target.

Acknowledgments The work was partially funded by the European Commission for the ERC Advanced Grant ALEXANDRIA under grant No. 339233 and the FP7 project ForgetIT under grant No. 600826. We thank the Internet Archive and Altiscale for providing access to the archived data.

References

[1] K. Berberich, M. Vazirgiannis, and G. Weikum. Time-aware authority ranking. *Internet Mathematics*, 2(3):301–332, 2005.
[2] X.-Q. Cheng, P. Du, J. Guo, X. Zhu, and Y. Chen. Ranking on data manifold with sink points. *Knowledge and Data Engineering, IEEE Transactions on*, 25(1):177–191, 2013.
[3] C. L. Clarke, M. Kolla, G. V. Cormack, O. Vechtomova, A. Ashkan, S. Büttcher, and I. MacKinnon. Novelty and diversity in information retrieval evaluation. In *Proceedings of SIGIR'2008*, pages 659–666.
[4] N. Dai and B. D. Davison. Freshness matters: in flowers, food, and web authority. In *Proceedings SIGIR'2010*, pages 114–121.
[5] Q. Mei, J. Guo, and D. Radev. Divrank: the interplay of prestige and diversity in information networks. In *Proceedings of SIGKDD'2010*, pages 1009–1018.
[6] T. N. Nguyen and N. Kanhabua. Leveraging dynamic query subtopics for time-aware search result diversification. In *Proceedings of ECIR'2014*, pages 222–234.
[7] T. N. Nguyen, N. Kanhabua, W. Nejdl, and C. Niederée. Mining relevant time for query subtopics in web archives. In *Proceedings of WWW'2015 companion*, pages 1357–1362.
[8] L. Page, S. Brin, R. Motwani, and T. Winograd. The pagerank citation ranking: Bringing order to the web. 1999.
[9] L. Yang, L. Qi, Y.-P. Zhao, B. Gao, and T.-Y. Liu. Link analysis using time series of web graphs. In *Proceedings of CIKM'2007*, pages 1011–1014.
[10] P. S. Yu, X. Li, and B. Liu. On the temporal dimension of search. In *Proceedings of WWW'2004*, pages 448–449.
[11] X. Zhu, A. B. Goldberg, J. Van Gael, and D. Andrzejewski. Improving diversity in ranking using absorbing random walks. In *Proceedings of HLT-NAACL'2007*, pages 97–104.

A Test Collection for Spoken Gujarati Queries

Douglas W. Oard
University of Maryland
College Park, MD USA
oard@umd.edu

Rashmi Sankepally
University of Maryland
College Park, MD USA
rashmi@umd.edu

Jerome White
New York University
Abu Dhabi, UAE
jerome.white@nyu.edu

Aren Jansen
Johns Hopkins HLTCOE
Baltimore, MD USA
aren@jhu.edu

Craig Harman
Johns Hopkins HLTCOE
Baltimore, MD USA
craig@craigharman.net

ABSTRACT

The development of a new test collection is described in which the task is to search naturally occurring spoken content using naturally occurring spoken queries. To support research on speech retrieval for low-resource settings, the collection includes terms learned by zero-resource term discovery techniques. Use of a new tool designed for exploration of spoken collections provides some additional insight into characteristics of the collection.

Categories and Subject Descriptors

H.3 [**Information Storage and Retrieval**]: Information Search and Retrieval

General Terms

Experimentation, Measurement

Keywords

speech retrieval; relevance judgment; test collection

1. INTRODUCTION

Like many sciences, information retrieval must accommodate some differences between what can be studied in the lab and what naturally occurs in practice. Information retrieval in general, and speech retrieval in particular, relies on test collections in which researchers can test and compare their ideas in a setting that is reproducible. For results obtained using such test collections to be transferable, we need collections that reflect the characteristics of specific settings. For research in speech retrieval, striking this balance can be particularly challenging. The difficulty lies in *what* speech is being used for testing, and *how* that speech is indexed. In an ideal situation, studies would cover speech that occurs naturally in the intended application setting, indexed in a manner that is practical for that setting. There are now several test collections that model high-resource settings fairly well (e.g., retrieval of English-language news broadcasts [5, 3]), but we are not aware of other test collections that model search by low-literacy users, our focus in this paper. In such cases both spoken content and spoken queries are required; we only know of one present test collection (for retrieval of Japanese technical talks) with such a structure [1].

It has been repeatedly shown that Large-Vocabulary Continuous Speech Recognition (LVCSR) can produce useful features on which ranked retrieval can be based, but creating robust LVCSR systems with current techniques is an expensive undertaking, costing on the order of $100,000 U.S. dollars or more. For that reason, sufficiently accurate LVCSR systems are presently available for just a few dozen languages. An alternative is to bypass pronunciation and language models altogether and focus on terms identified in some acoustic or phonetic feature space. This approach to "zero-resource term discovery" has been shown to be effective in text clustering and classification experiments when applied to English [4], and in detection of single terms in several languages for which information retrieval test collections are not yet available [2]. Extending the application of zero-resource term discovery to more complex queries requires the development of new test collections. This paper describes the construction of one such test collection.

2. TEST COLLECTION FRAMEWORK

We often think of test collections as containing documents, topics, and relevance judgments. This, however, may be too narrow a view when evaluation of the test collection is the main goal. Thinking somewhat more comprehensively, test collections can include:

Content: The content to be searched, in its original form. In a test collection, this is often a combination of words and structure; in a multimedia collection, this is typically digital content or some digitization of the original artifact.

Representation(s): Additional representations of the content that can be used as a basis for search. Such representations are typically included to foster specific ways of using the collection, or to facilitate certain comparisons. For the test collection in this paper, we use terms that are discovered automatically from acoustic features based on detectable repetition of relatively long acoustic units.

Targets: What is sought. In a text collection, this is often documents, which are an implicit packaging of the content into units that serve as the target for retrieval. For rela-

SIGIR'15, August 09 - 13, 2015, Santiago, Chile.

ACM 978-1-4503-3621-5/15/08 ...$15.00.
DOI: http://dx.doi.org/10.1145/2766462.2767791 .

tively long spoken content, this could be the point where replay should begin. For the test collection described in this paper, the target is a relatively short recording that we call a "response."

Queries: The basis for search. For fully automated evaluations, it is common to specify one or more standard query forms (e.g., TREC "title queries") so as to enhance comparability across systems. In our collection, we use a complete spoken voice forum post as the query.

Topics: The basis for relevance judgment. Topics and queries are often confused: topics are a mental state of the assessor; topics can be summarized in writing, but the assessor's opinion, not the summary, is the basis for each judgment. We provide written summaries of each topic.

Relevance Judgments: Human-generated encoding of the degree to which each target satisfies a topic. It is typically not possible to judge every target for relevance to every topic, so some sampling is required. For our collection, we sample by pooling highly ranked targets from several systems for each query, a common design.

Evaluation Measures: A characterization of experiment results. Although rarely made explicit, test collections are generally designed with some class of evaluation measures in mind. Our test collection is intended for use with ranked retrieval measures such as Normalized Discounted Cumulative Gain (NDCG), Mean Average Precision (MAP), and Mean Reciprocal Rank (MRR), and with measures such as bPref and xinfAP which are designed to be relatively robust to incomplete relevance judgments [10].

3. THE TEST COLLECTION

Queries and responses in our collection were formulated using recorded spoken content from the Avaj Otalo "speech forum," an information service that was regularly used by farmers in Gujarat, India [8]. The goal was to provide a resource for the local farming community to exchange ideas and have their questions answered. To this end, farmers would call into the system and peruse answers to existing questions, or would pose their own questions for the community. Other farmers could call into the system to leave answers to those questions. On occasion, there were also a small group of system administrators who would periodically call in to leave announcements that they expected would be of interest to the broader farming community. The system was completely automated—no human intervention was involved. Avaj Otalo's recorded speech was divided into 50 *queries* and 2,999 *responses*. Queries were intended to be statements on a particular topic, sometimes phrased as a question, sometimes phrased as an announcement. As an example, consider an English translated summary of Query 6: *"This question is about the crop of "jeera" (cumin). Medicine Pento Methyl was provided at some first stage to prevent growing of "nindaman" but yet it has grown. Then can the medicine be provided at the second stage too?"* The 2,999 responses varied between answers to questions, additions to announcements, and new questions on similar topics. Very short recordings were omitted, as were those in which little speech activity was automatically detected. The average length of a query was approximately 70 seconds (SD = 14.40s), or approximately 61 seconds (SD = 15.76s) after silence was automatically removed. Raw response lengths averaged 110 seconds (SD = 88.80s), or 96.52 seconds (SD = 82.75s) after silence was removed.

	Round 1			Round 2			Round 3		
	A	B	C	A	B	C	A	B	C
A	-	0.41	0.39	-	0.28	0.32	-	×	×
B		-	0.62		-	0.87		-	0.85

Table 1: Inter-assessor agreement (κ).

3.1 Representation

Audio was processed using a zero-resource term discovery system described by Dredze et al. [4]. The system detects repetitions of similar speech patterns, assigning a unique (and arbitrary) term identifier to each set of similar patterns. Because the system lacks knowledge of word, syllable, or phoneme boundaries, several terms of different temporal scope can be co-active; it is not uncommon to have a dozen or more such terms overlapping. The resulting terms can be indexed by any information retrieval system, although systems that model term length and term overlap have been shown to yield better results than systems that treat all terms similarly [7].

3.2 Relevance Judgments

Judgment pools were formed by combining top-ranked results from several ranked retrieval systems developed by White et al. [9]. Three native speakers of Gujarati performed relevance assessment; none had any role in system development. Assessment was performed by listening to the audio and making a graded relevance judgment. Assessors could assign one of the following judgments to each response: 1) unable to assess, 2) not relevant, 3) relevant, or 4) highly relevant. To support computation of NDCG, the relevant and highly relevant categories were coded as 1 and 2, respectively; non-relevant judgments were coded as 0. For evaluation measures such as Mean Average Precision (MAP) that require binary judgments, and for evaluating annotator agreement, relevance judgments were subsequently binarized by collapsing highly relevant and relevant responses to relevant. Three rounds of assessments were conducted.

The first 20 queries were used for Round 1 of relevance judgments. For each query, the top 10 responses retrieved by each of three basic systems [7] were judged. All assessors judged each pooled response. As outlined in Table 1, assessors B and C were largely in agreement ($\kappa > 0.6$), while Assessor A was an outlier. The assessors then met to discuss the assessment process. To facilitate this discussion, specific cases of disagreement were randomly sampled for each assessor pair and used to seed the discussion.

The second set of judgments were created by pooling the top 10 responses for all 50 queries from 21 more sophisticated systems [9], most of which used term length and term overlap as features. Assessor A judged queries 1–15, Assessor B judged queries 16–30, and Assessor C judged queries 31–45. All assessors independently judged queries 46–50. Agreement between assessors B and C improved from Round 1 ($\kappa > 0.8$), while Assessor A remained an outlier. Assessor A's judgments of queries 1–15 were retained, as those judgments had been discussed with assessors B and C. Assessor C's judgments for queries 46–50 were retained.

During the first two rounds of judging, assessors occasionally mentioned that some queries were difficult to assess

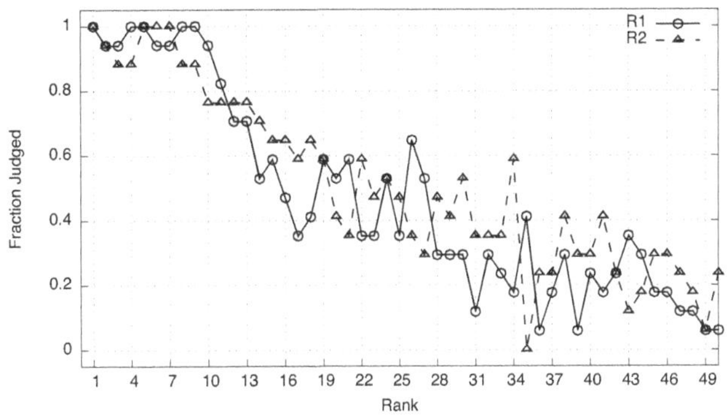

Figure 1: Judged responses by rank.

because they did not clearly express an information need. To help clarify the issue, assessors wrote brief English summaries of each query after the second round. Based on these summaries, and further discussion with assessors, 33 queries that did not pose a clear information need were removed from the collection. The final round of judgment pools were then constructed by pooling the top 10 responses from 15 sophisticated systems. The 17 retained queries were assessed as follows: Assessor C judged queries 1, 2, 6, 9, 11, 12, 23, 44, 48, and 50; Assessor B judged queries 24, 26, 28, 30, 38, 42–44, 48, and 50. The multiple judgments for queries 44, 48, and 50 were used to measure inter-annotator agreement ($\kappa > 0.8$). Assessor C's judgments were used for these cases.

Because pools from Rounds 2 and 3 differed somewhat, the completeness of the assessments was enriched by combining judgments from those pools as follows: 1) if only one judgment is available, keep it; 2) if judgments from two rounds are the same, keep it; 3) if one marked "highly relevant" and the other marked "relevant", keep it "highly relevant". 4) if only one marked "unable to assess", keep the other; 5) remove cases of clear disagreement (e.g, one marked "non-relevant," the other marked "relevant").

The test collection was designed to support three principal evaluation measures: NDCG, MAP, and MRR. MRR can be computed for all 17 topics. MAP yields the same result as MRR for the seven topics for which only one relevant response is known, so MAP is best used for the other 10 topics (each having three or more relevant responses). There are a total of 61 relevant responses for those 10 topics, an average of 6.1 responses per topic ($SD = 2.13$).

4. UTILITY OF THE TEST COLLECTION

It can be useful when introducing a new test collection to review characteristics that assess its utility—aspects that make it effective and generalizable. Although not a complete list, there are at least three such characteristics that deserve attention, and in which this test collection is couched:

Insightfulness: Ultimately test collections are built in order to answer questions, so the degree of insight that a test collection offers is a key criterion. On the positive side, this test collection includes real content, both as queries and as responses. It also includes relevance judgments made by native speakers of Gujarati, whose judgments exhibit good inter-annotator agreement. On the negative side, relevance judgments were not made by actual users of the system, and removal of non-topical queries late in the process resulted in a query set that is too small to reliably support statistical significance testing. Further, the number of responses within the collection is at the low end of what is typically expected of a real-world application.

Affordability: Acquiring content, creating representations, constructing queries, generating documentation, and sharing the collection all incur some cost. Those costs, however, are often dwarfed by the costs of creating relevance judgments. The design of the relevance assessment process is thus often the central focus of affordability concerns, so affordability and insightfulness are invariably in some tension. In this case, the two were balanced by using pooling to produce incomplete but useful relevance judgments, and by making judgments directly on the audio.

Reusability: The reuse of relevance judgments can enhance affordability by amortizing assessment costs over multiple future uses. Reuse also benefits insightfulness by eliminating otherwise uncontrolled differences in assessor opinions. Reusability thus receives special attention in test collection design. Reusability and insightfulness are sometimes in tension, however, as newly designed systems may find responses that are unlike those that have been previously assessed. Speech retrieval test collections are particularly vulnerable to this effect, since changes in either the speech processing or the retrieval algorithms could result in new systems returning results from previously unassessed parts of the collection. Figure 1 shows the fraction of responses placed at a given rank, across all 17 queries. When this fraction is high, every evaluation measure can reasonably be compared. As the fraction decays, the attention should shift to measures such as bPref and xinfAP that can accommodate a moderate level of missing judgments. Notably, the robustness of such measures is typically assessed using random ablation of a rich set of judgments, and there is no assurance that the missing judgments in any specific case are well modeled by random selection. Nonetheless, in the absence of evidence to the contrary, use of measures that are designed to be robust to missing judgments would be a reasonable choice when the ranks of interest exhibit moderate judged fractions (e.g., 0.3 to 0.7). The example shown in Figure 1 is for the best system (by MAP) that contributed to the judgment pools (R1) and for an intentionally somewhat different system that did not contribute to the judgment pools (R2). In the case of R1, most of the top 10 responses have been judged for relevance, as would be expected given our assessment methodology. The observed exceptions are the few responses that were determined by the assessor to be unjudgable. Although R2 exhibits a larger drop-off by rank 10 than R1, that drop-off is moderate: 76% of the responses have been judged. Overall, the fraction of judged responses for R2 maintains a strong correlation to R1 throughout the ranked range ($r(998) = 0.91, p < 0.001$). While it is necessary to look at such plots on a case-by-case basis, such a result is evidence for collection reusability.

5. EXPLORING THE COLLECTION

Unlike text retrieval, where visualizing representations can be straightforward, conventional ways of exploring untranscribed speech rely on listening. We therefore developed VaporEngine, a collection browsing and annotation tool.[1] In

[1] https://vapor.umiacs.umd.edu

Figure 2: Using VaporEngine to explore a response.

VaporEngine's term-centric view, waveforms for several occurrences of the term are displayed and the user can play those examples in quick succession. As each occurrence plays, the link to the response in which the term was found is highlighted. Following a link shows the corresponding response-centric view. Text entry fields are available in either view for a user to provide an English gloss translation for the term. In the response-centric view shown in Figure 2, a term cloud is shown, where each term initially has a generic identifier (e.g., "pt8834"), sized by the term frequency in the response. As English gloss translations are provided by the user, generic identifiers are replaced with the corresponding English term, both in this term cloud and in term clouds for every other response. Thus, as the user annotates terms, the generic clouds progressively transform into English term clouds. In this way, the response-centric view supports efficient collection browsing with a relatively modest annotation effort.

State-of-the-art zero resource term discovery systems are most easily able to detect repetitions of longer terms that are spoken by speakers with similar vocal characteristics. We found, from a bilingual annotator who used VaporEngine to browse the Avaj Otalo collection, that an unexpectedly large number of such terms arose from speaking conventions used in announcements; which consistently included long salutations, and which were recorded by a relatively small number of speakers (e.g., agricultural outreach agents). Such insights could help with the design of retrieval systems for this type of content.

We therefore generated six term importance criteria that could be used to prioritize the annotation effort for any language, each combining document frequency and median term duration in some way. The top 50 terms by each criterion were then pooled to form a single set and presented to the annotator in VaporEngine. The annotator was able to translate 200 terms in four hours, which covered the top 50 terms of each term ranking. Each translation was then manually labeled as a "content term" if the assessor felt it was indicative of the content of the response in which it was found. For each criterion, two evaluation measures were computed for each ranking: 1) term precision (the fraction of the 50 annotated terms that were labeled as content-bearing), and 2) collection coverage (a recall-like measure computed as the fraction of responses that contain at least one term annotated as content-bearing). At one end of the spectrum, emphasizing document frequency resulted in 11/50 content terms that together covered 16% of the collection. At the other end, emphasizing duration resulted in 28/50 content terms that covered only 2% of the collection. Balancing the two yielded a term precision of 25/50 terms as content-bearing that covered 8% of the collection. From this we conclude that the collection is sufficiently rich in content-bearing terms to be used in retrieval experiments, that visualization systems such as VaporEngine that leverage repetition in speech are potentially useful tools when designing ranking functions, and that additional work on optimizing the design of such systems is therefore called for.

6. CONCLUSION AND FUTURE WORK

We have built a test collection for zero-resource ranked retrieval of spoken Gujarati content based on spoken Gujarati queries. Our experience has highlighted the difficulty of topic selection when the researchers themselves do not know the language, the practicality of performing relevance judgments directly on the audio, and unusual characteristics of voice forum content that have implications for retrieval system design. Our evaluation of the collection shows a balance between insightfulness, affordability, and reusability that is suitable for formative evaluation of ranked-retrieval methods for the type of zero-resource features provided. The test collection, which is available for research use, has been used in Forum for Information Retrieval Evaluation (FIRE) shared tasks [6, 7].[2]

7. ACKNOWLEDGMENTS

We would like to thank Komal Kamdar, Dhwani Patel, and Yash Patel for performing relevance assessments. This work has been supported in part by NSF award 1218159.

References

[1] T. Akiba et al. Overview of the NTCIR-11 spoken query and doc task. In *NTCIR-11*, 2014.
[2] X. Anguera et al. The spoken web search task. In *MediaEval*, 2013.
[3] P. Comas et al. Sibyl, a factoid question-answering system for spoken documents. *ACM TOIS*, 30(3):19, 2012.
[4] M. Dredze et al. NLP on spoken documents without ASR. In *EMNLP*, 2010.
[5] J. Garofolo et al. The TREC spoken document retrieval track: A success story. In *RIAO*, 2000.
[6] H. Joshi and J. White. Document silmilarity amid automatically detected terms. In *FIRE*, 2014.
[7] D. Oard et al. The FIRE 2013 question answering for the spoken web task. In *FIRE*, 2013.
[8] N. Patel et al. Avaaj Otalo: A field study of an interactive voice forum for small farmers in rural India. In *CHI*, 2010.
[9] J. White et al. Using zero-resource spoken term discovery for ranked retrieval. In *NAACL-HLT*, 2015.
[10] E. Yilmaz et al. A simple and efficient sampling method for estimating AP and NDCG. In *SIGIR*, 2008.

[2]http://www.umiacs.umd.edu/~oard/qasw/

Discovering Experts across Multiple Domains

Aditya Pal
IBM Almaden Research
San Jose, CA, USA
apal@us.ibm.com

ABSTRACT

Researchers have focused on finding experts in individual domains, such as emails, forums, question answering, blogs, and microblogs. In this paper, we propose an algorithm for finding experts across these different domains. To do this, we propose an expertise framework that aims at extracting key expertise features and building an unified scoring model based on SVM ranking algorithm. We evaluate our model on a real World dataset and show that it is significantly better than the prior state-of-art.

Categories and Subject Descriptors

H.3.3 [**Information Storage and Retrieval**]: Information Search and Retrieval

General Terms

Algorithms, Experimentation, Theory

Keywords

Expertise finding; Social media; Enterprise search

1. INTRODUCTION

The existing efforts on expertise discovery have targeted a specific data source for finding experts, such as emails [4], question answering [11], blogs [7] and microblogs [9]. There is little prior work (except [5]) that models expertise by combining data from these web sources - primarily because of challenges in gathering such data and disambiguating users across website (e.g. finding Twitterers on Facebook) can be impossible. Prior work [5] considered data within an Enterprise that allows its employees to publish documents in several data sources internally. They proposed an expertise model that indexes all the content in Lucene and uses the relevant documents retrieved through Lucene to compute users' expertise. There are several shortcomings of this approach. First it assumes that all documents are reflective of the expertise of its authors, which need not be the case. Second, it uses a weighted sum of document relevance and popularity to compute users' expertise. This aggregation strategy can bias the model towards authors that have large number of less relevant documents.

Our expertise framework systematically addresses the shortcomings of prior work. It first analyses documents on various aspects, such as *language*, *questions*, *topics*, *indicator of expertise* with a goal of extracting key features from the expertise documents of an author. We then propose IR techniques (such as a proximity based document relevance computation, concept filtering based) beyond a basic Lucene search to retrieve highly relevant documents. Finally, we propose a sophisticated rank aggregation framework that takes the relevant documents as input and computes the expertise score of their authors. Evaluation over a large real World dataset shows the improved performance of our approach in comparison to prior methods.

SIGIR'15, August 09 - 13, 2015, Santiago, Chile.
© 2015 ACM. ISBN 978-1-4503-3621-5/15/08 ...$15.00.
DOI: http://dx.doi.org/10.1145/2766462.2767774.

2. RELATED WORK

Expertise discovery is a heavily researched area (see [1] for a comprehensive overview). Dom et al. [4] considered an email network for expertise identification. They evaluated several graph based algorithms and found PageRank algorithm to outperform HITS. Zhang et al. [11] presented an expertise discovery algorithm to rank experts in a question answering website by examining the number of questions answered by the user along with the number of persons that were answered by the user. They showed that a simple model could outperform classical expert finding models like PageRank and HITS in the QA domain. Java et al. [7] modeled the spread of influence in the blogosphere in order to select an influential set of bloggers such that they would maximize the spread of information in the blogosphere. Pal et al. [9] proposed a feature-based algorithm for finding topical authorities in microblogs. They proposed features to capture topical interest and prominence for users and showed that their model out-performs graph based models.

There is little work on expert finding across different web-based data sources, with a notable exception of [5]. Guy et al. [5] proposed a Lucene based model to index multi-domain documents and combined document relevance, and popularity to compute user expertise. While somewhat similar to this prior work, our approach differs in important ways. First, we incorporate a number of components and algorithms with the goal of extracting key features (topics, language) from *documents that are indicative of users' expertise*. Then we systematically improve the retrieval engine

Employees	Blogs	Wikis	Forum Posts	Microblogs
20,000	38,675	87,301	44,794	160,484

Table 1: Dataset statistics.

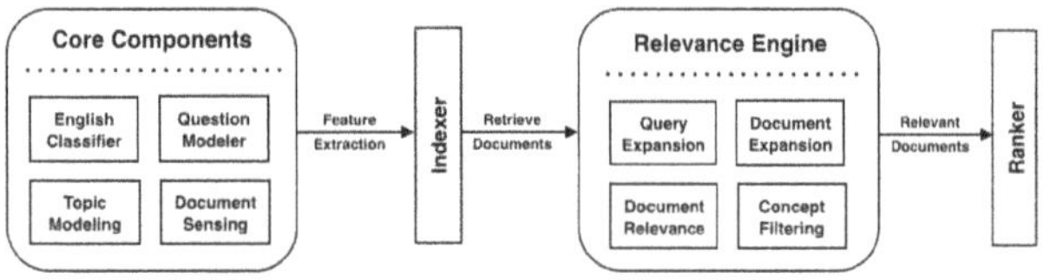

Figure 1: Expertise framework.

Algorithm 1 DocSense(D_u)

Require: $keywords, \gamma = 0.7, \alpha, \beta$
for $d \in D_u$ **do**
  Mark d if
    $|d[:1] \cap keywords| > 0$ {non-relevant}
    d has $P, |d \cap P| \geq \gamma|d|$ or $|d| < 20$ {url summary}
    $\max_{d' \in D_u \setminus d} \{|d \cap d'|\} \geq \gamma|d|$ {duplicate}
end for
$D'_u \leftarrow \{d \in D_u : d \text{ is not marked}\}$
for $d \in D'_u$ **do**
  Mark d if $|\{d' \in D'_u : JS_{d,d'} \geq \beta\} \setminus d| \leq \alpha$ {non-topical}
end for
return $\{d \in D'_u : d \text{ is not marked}\}$

through key modules such as, proximity based document relevance computation and rank aggregation.

3. DATASET

We crawled online participation data of employees within IBM. We selected 20,000 employees randomly and crawled their complete online activity which includes publishing blogs, microblogs, wikis, forum posts. Additionally we crawled the profiles of the employees which includes their job title, role and self-reported expertise and past experience. Table 1 presents the summary statistics of the crawled dataset.

4. EXPERTISE FRAMEWORK

Fig. 1 presents an overview of our expertise framework. It consists of several core components that are geared towards extracting key features, relevance engine that aims at picking the relevant documents to a query, and a ranking component to select top experts.

4.1 Core Components

We describe the core components that are used for extracting key features from user documents.

Language Detection: Our dataset consists of documents written in several languages. However the technical jargon (such as products, tools) are shared across all languages. Ignoring this multi-lingual aspect of the documents could retrieve experts versed in different languages - thereby confusing the end users. We use *ngram* based classifier [3] to select only the documents written in English as it is the most predominant language of our dataset (80%).

Topic Estimation: We use the Latent Dirichlet Allocation algorithm (LDA) [2] to estimate the documents' topics. To estimate the number of topics for LDA, we use Bayesian Information Criteria (BIC). We use Jensen-Shannon divergence [8] to compute the similarity between the documents.

Question Modeler: Users employ ingenious methods to ask questions in different data sources, e.g. a user can create a wiki page with a question and the users can answer by editing the wiki. We trained a linear SVM classifier over the *ngrams* of a set of labeled documents (question or not a question). Only the first four sentences of a document are considered for feature extraction as beyond that several documents have questions that do not merit any answer, e.g. *if you have further questions, please contact the author.*

Document Sensing: A crucial component for expertise discovery is identifying documents that reflect expertise of their authors. E.g. talk announcements, webpage summary, scribe notes, financial reports, can provide misleading indicators for users' core expertise. For filtering such documents, we propose DocSense algorithm that takes documents authored by a user as input and filters them on 4 criteria: 1) *non-relevance*: document contains specific keywords (summary, announcement, call for) in its opening paragraph, 2) *url summary*: document summarizing a url, 3) *duplicate*: document matching other documents of the author (useful for filtering financial reports, reminders, etc.), and 4) *non-topical*: document not pertinent to user's core interest area.

4.1.1 Document Features

Table 2 lists the document features. Most of these features are common across the different document types. Since we treat an user's information such as role, bio, etc as a user document, so some of the content features are relevant to it.

We carried out language analysis using Linguistic Inquiry and Word count (LIWC) tool. LIWC provides scores on 80-90 features for the input text. We used *JS* divergence to compute the similarity between a post and its replies.

Type	Features
Content	document length, publish date, #referenced url, similarity with referenced urls' content, presence of smiles and greetings, #referenced entities, #hashtags, #technical jargons, topic distribution, language analysis
Social	#reply, #view, #recommendation, #share, #vote
Processed	is a question?, document marking (DocSense)
Reply	*processed features* of parent, similarity with parent doc., responsiveness (how soon reply was posted), relative content features (compared to other replies on the same parent)

Table 2: List of document features.

4.2 Retrieval Engine

We use Apache Lucene to index the documents. Separate indexes are maintained for each domain; ensuring that the retrieval engine doesn't get biased towards any specific data source (such as microblogs, which typically have shorter length). It also provides a flexibility of picking same number of documents per source irrespective of their relevance. We propose several components besides Lucene that are aimed towards improving the relevance of the retrieved documents.

Query Expansion: Before a query is passed to Lucene, we first use the probabilistic query expansion model [10] to expand it by adding relevant terms. This is done so that all the topically-relevant documents are retrieved. The query expansion model depends on a word-word similarity thesaurus which we build using the *JS* divergence over the

Algorithm 2 DocRel(d – document, Q – expanded query)

Require: $\alpha \in [0.5, 1)$, $\beta \in (1, \infty)$
  $R^\star \leftarrow 0; n \leftarrow 0$
  for $i \leftarrow 1$ *to* $|d|$ and $w \leftarrow d[i]$ **do**
    continue if $\nexists W \in Q$, s.t. $w \in W$ {w not a query keyword}
    $P[W[1]] \leftarrow i$ {Set/Update w's root's position}
    $R \leftarrow \max\left\{0, 1 - \frac{i+1-min(P)-|P|}{10}\right\}$ {current relevance}
    if $|P| < |Q|$ **then**
      $R \leftarrow R\left\lceil \frac{|P|}{|Q|} - \frac{1}{2}\right\rceil \log(\frac{1}{2} + \frac{|P|}{|Q|})$ {partial match penalty}
    end if
    if $n < |P|$ *or* $\{n = |P|$ *and* $rel^\star < rel\}$ **then**
      $R^\star \leftarrow R; n \leftarrow |P|$ {Update global best relevance}
    end if
  end for
  return $R^\star$

words' topical distribution. The model ensures that the terms that bind closely with the query keywords are selected. The expanded query is then used to retrieve 1000 documents per data source.

Document Relevance: Lucene's relevance scores are based on tf-idf normalized weights of the query terms in the documents. This scheme is not ideal for two reasons: (1) restriction on the length of documents differ for different data sources, which could bias this relevance, and (2) it does not consider the proximity of the query keywords within the documents - altering the context of the documents altogether. E.g. a document containing *machine* and *learning* far apart, might pertain to systems domain and not artificial intelligence. We propose DocRel algorithm that takes into consideration the minimum distance between query keywords (vector of vector due to query expansion) in the documents to compute the document relevance. The algorithm also takes care of the scenario where not all query keywords are present in the document.

Concept Filtering: A user query partitions the documents into relevant and non-relevant bucket. The relevant documents can be further partitioned into *concepts* buckets. E.g. a query *machine learning* might draw documents from concepts, such as finance, math and statistics, computer science, software engineering. The idea here is to eliminate concepts that are not well represented by examining the underlying topic distribution of the document. We use Gaussian Mixture Model (GMM) over the document topics for partitioning them into concept space and discard document that belong to low frequency clusters.

4.3 Expertise Model

Let the set of relevant documents provided by the retrieval engine be $\mathcal{D} = \{D^{wiki}, D^{microblogs}, \ldots\}$. Let $d \in D^s$ indicate document d's features (Table 2). First we estimate the relative expertise score (R^s_d) of the documents given all other relevant document from the same source.

$$R^s_d = \left\{\prod_{i=1}^{n(d)} \left\{\int_{-\infty}^{d_{(i)}} \mathcal{N}(x; \mu^s_i, \sigma^s_i)\, dx\right\}^{w^s_i}\right\} \quad (1)$$

where $n(d)$ is the number of features in d, $d_{(i)}$ indicates the ith component of d, $\mathcal{N}$ is a Gaussian distribution and w^s_i is the weight on the ith feature. The model parameters μ^s, σ^s are estimated using the observed D_s. We get,

$$\mu^s_i = \frac{\sum_{d \in D^s} d_{(i)}}{|D^s|} \qquad \sigma^s_i = \sqrt{\frac{\sum_{d \in D^s} (d_{(i)} - \mu^s_i)^2}{|D^s| - 1}}$$

Weights over individual features in R^s_d is computed through a Gaussian CDF function which is a monotonically increasing function and hence well suited to our scoring problem as we prefer a higher value for all features. If a lower value is preferred, then negation can be applied to that feature before applying the above formula.

In order to learn the weights w_i on different features, we consider a training dataset with $\bar{R}^s_d$ as the true score of the document. Following optimization is used to get optimal w.

$$\arg\min_{w^s} \left\{\sum_{d \in D_s} (\bar{R}^s_d - \ln R^s_d)^2 + \lambda_1 ||w^s||^1_1 + \lambda_2 ||w^s||^2_2\right\} \quad (2)$$

The above optimization problem is quadratic in w^s and hence can be computed using ElasticNet regression. It leads to shrinking in the values of w as well as induces sparsity. Another advantage is that amongst a block of highly correlated features - only few features have non-zero weights.

Once we have relative expertise of documents, we can compute users' expertise per data source. Let $u(D) \subseteq D$ indicate the documents in D authored by u. Then we compute the source specific expertise (E^s_u) of a user as follows.

$$E^s_u = \frac{\sum_{d \in u(D^s)} R^s_d \cdot \text{DocRel}(d, q)}{|u(D^s)|} \quad (3)$$

We get expertise score for each user per data source. To combine these scores, we use SVM rank aggregation algorithm [6]. Let $E_u = [E^{wiki}_u \ldots]^T$ be the vector of expertise score of the user u. Let $(u, v) \in \mathcal{R}$ be the ranked set of the users, indicating that user u has higher expertise than user v. The rank aggregation problem can be written as:-

$$\begin{aligned} &minimize: && \frac{1}{2}a^T a + \lambda \sum \xi_{u,v} \\ &subject\ to: && \\ &\forall (u,v) \in \mathcal{R}: && a^T(E_u - E_v) \geq 1 - \xi_{u,v} \\ &\forall (u,v) \in \mathcal{R}: && \xi_{u,v} \geq 0 \end{aligned} \quad (4)$$

The constraints are geared towards finding a ranking function that is consistent with the ranked set $\mathcal{R}$. ξ indicates soft-margin penalties to the separation constraints, without which the minimization problem might be infeasible (in case of non-linearly separability). The optimal weights $a^\star$ are used to sort the users in decreasing order of $a^T E_u$ value.

5. RESULTS AND EVALUATION

We compared our model with several baseline models:

B1: This model uses the prior state-of-art approach [5] for discovering experts across multiple domains.

B2: This model adapts $B1$ to use the several components proposed in our framework. The final expertise of users is aggregated the same way as suggested by $B1$.

B3: This model uses the document retrieval technique proposed by our expertise framework. Then users are selected with probability proportional to the relevance of the documents published by them.

All the models were trained using a small labeled dataset of the experts for two hand picked queries. In order to evaluate our approach, we conducted a user study in which results from our model were compared to those from three baseline models. We selected a set of 10 popular queries (such as *Distributed Scrum*, *Commercial Finance*, *Topic Modeling*) and picked top 10 authors per model per query. Then 40 authors per query (usually less due to some commonality) are shown to five coders in a random order. The coders were shown authors' profile and the relevant documents published by them and they were asked to rate on a 5-point Likert scale, the expertise of the authors on the query. Inter rater agreement between the coders was 0.6, indicating moderate agreement.

5.1 Model Performance

Table 3 shows the average survey rating received by the top 10 authors. We note that the authors discovered by our model received 37% higher rating than the prior work ($B1$). It also performed 10% better than $B2$ indicating the effectiveness of our expertise framework in comparison to a simple aggregation technique. *All improvements were statistically significant using one-sided t-test with 95% CI.*

Our	B1	B2	B3
3.40	2.48	3.10	2.84

Table 3: Average ratings of the models.

Table 4 shows the discounted cumulative gain (DCG)[1] of the four models. We note that the DCG of our model is statistically significantly better for all queries, indicating that it surfaced top experts at a higher position in the ranked list, in comparison to the baselines.

Our	B1	B2	B3
24.51	17.49	21.14	19.85

Table 4: Discounted cumulative gain of the models.

5.2 Model Performance using Best Rating

In practice, an end-user is looking for connecting with one expert and hence they would be satisfied if the model recommends at least one expert that matches their requirements. To compare the models in this practical setting, we consider the ratings given to the best-rated author per model by each coder (Table 5). We observe that authors of our model received heist ratings – indicating that an end-user would be most satisfied with our model. Additionally we see that the best author is surfaced within top 2 of the ranked list, which makes it easier for an end-user to locate the top expert.

Our		B1		B2		B3	
a	r	a	r	a	r	a	r
4.2	**1.8**	3.8	1.9	4.1	1.9	3.9	2.1

Table 5: (a) Best ratings and (r) rank of best author.

5.3 Model Component Analysis

The previous results show that our expertise framework improves over the baselines, which is primarily due to the various components proposed in this paper. Here we estimate the exact contribution of the different components towards model performance.

[1]DCG works in our case as we are retrieving equal number of experts from each model

Component	DCG loss (%)
Language Classification	6.9
Question Classification	10.0
Document Sensing	17.1
Query Expansion	4.0
Document Relevance	9.7
Concept Filtering	2.1

Table 6: Drop in DCG by removing a component.

Recall that the authors retrieved by the full model are coded for expertise. We consider the rank of these authors and their ordering when computing the DCG of the model. In this case, we consider the DCG of the full model and consider the drop in DCG for the partial models.

Table 6 shows the drop in average DCG received by our model without a specified component. We note that a component can affect the model performance in several ways. E.g. if the language analysis component is turned off, then several non-English documents would be retrieved at the cost of relevant English documents. These documents could reduce the score of top experts, thereby reducing their ranks and giving prominence to sub-par authors. We observe that the document sensing is in particular the most effective component of the model, without which the model would retrieve authors with 17% less ratings. We note that document sensing, question classification and document sensing contribute substantially towards improving the model performance.

6. CONCLUSION

This paper presents a framework for expertise finding that aggregates content from several data sources. We introduced several novel components pivotal for building an effective expertise search engine, such as language classifier, question classifier, concept filtering scheme, and expertise rank aggregation. Our experiments show improved performance in comparison to models that ignores these aspects.

References

[1] K. Balog, Y. Fang, M. de Rijke, P. Serdyukov, and L. Si. Expertise retrieval. *FTIR*, 6(2-3):127–256, 2012.

[2] D. M. Blei, A. Y. Ng, and M. I. Jordan. Latent dirichlet allocation. *JMLR*, 2003.

[3] W. B. Cavnar and J. M. Trenkle. N-gram-based text categorization. In *SDAIR*, 1994.

[4] B. Dom, I. Eiron, A. Cozzi, and Y. Zhang. Graph-based ranking algorithms for e-mail expertise analysis. In *DMKD*, 2003.

[5] I. Guy, U. Avraham, D. Carmel, S. Ur, M. Jacovi, and I. Ronen. Mining expertise and interests from social media. In *WWW*, 2013.

[6] T. Joachims. Optimizing search engines using clickthrough data. In *KDD*, 2002.

[7] A. Kale, A. Karandikar, P. Kolari, A. Java, T. Finin, and A. Joshi. Modeling trust and influence in the blogosphere using link polarity. In *ICWSM*, 2007.

[8] J. Lin. Divergence measures based on the shannon entropy. *IEEE Transactions on Information Theory*, 2006.

[9] A. Pal and S. Counts. Identifying topical authorities in microblogs. In *WSDM*, 2011.

[10] Y. Qiu and H.-P. Frei. Concept based query expansion. In *SIGIR*, 1993.

[11] J. Zhang, M. S. Ackerman, and L. A. Adamic. Expertise networks in online communities: structure and algorithms. In *WWW*, 2007.

Using Key Concepts in a Translation Model for Retrieval

Jae Hyun Park and W. Bruce Croft
Center for Intelligent Information Retrieval
University of Massachusetts Amherst, Amherst, MA 01003
{ jhpark, croft } @cs.umass.edu

ABSTRACT

Many queries, especially those in the form of longer questions, contain a subset of terms representing *key concepts* that describe the most important part of the user's information need. Detecting the key concepts in a query can be used as the basis for more effective weighting of query terms, but in this paper, we focus on a method of using the key concepts in a translation model for query expansion and retrieval. Translation models have been used previously in community-based question answering (CQA) systems in order to bridge the semantic gap between questions and the corresponding answer documents. Our method uses the key concepts of a question as the translation context and selectively applies the translation model to the secondary (non-key) parts of the question. We evaluate the proposed method using a CQA collection and show that selectively translating key and secondary concepts can significantly improve the retrieval performance compared to a baseline that applies the translation model without considering key concepts.

Categories and Subject Descriptors

H.3.3 [**Information System**]: Information Search and Retrieval

Keywords

translation model; query term classification; query expansion; answer passage retrieval

1. INTRODUCTION

Statistical translation models have been used for query term expansion in a number of previous studies (e.g., [2, 10]) and have been shown to be particularly effective for retrieving answer passages in collaborative question answering (CQA) systems [12, 11]. One of the challenging issues in using translation models for expansion is incorporating more of the query context into the translation process. For example, Figure 1 shows two example questions that include the word "*grow*". The first question is about growing hair while the other question is about growing flowers. The expansion words generated from the translation for "*grow*" should be different in these two contexts.

SIGIR'15, August 09 - 13, 2015, Santiago, Chile.
© 2015 ACM. ISBN 978-1-4503-3621-5/15/08 ...$15.00.
DOI: http://dx.doi.org/10.1145/2766462.2767768.

The hypothesis that we study in this paper is that the most important, *key concepts* in a query should be treated differently in the translation model compared to secondary concepts. The key concepts of queries represent the main topics of users' information needs [1]. For example, "*hair*" and "*Columbine flower*" in Figure 1 are the key concepts. We propose a translation model for expansion that estimates the translation probabilities of query terms given the key concept of a query as the context. This will result in the translation results (and query expansions) for "*grow*" being different depending on whether "*hair*" or "*Columbine flower*" is the key concept.

In addition to the key concepts of queries, we also identify the secondary (non-key) parts of queries. In our approach, these concepts are the focus of translation (expansion) since translating the key concept may significantly change the meaning of the query. Lee et al. [10] describe an approach to identifying important terms in documents for training the translation model. In contrast, we focus on using query analysis to affect the translation results. We use the secondary concepts of queries as the focus for translation and the key concepts as context for the translation.

The rest of the paper is organized as follows. In Section 2, we describe the key concept-based translation model. Section 3 describes a method for classifying question terms for the proposed translation model. In Section 4, we show experimental results.

Q: How do you get your *hair* to **grow** faster?

A: Supposedly this works but never tried it. prenantal vitamins. they're just vitimans so they're not going to make u grow ...

Q: How to **grow** *Columbine flowers*?

A: Plant outside in sun or light shade, they will grow in both places. Scratch or loosen the soil lightly with a garden claw or rake. Sprinkle your seeds on and cover with the loose soil. You just cover with enough ...

Figure 1: Example questions containing "*grow*" in different contexts.

2. A KEY CONCEPT-BASED TRANSLATION MODEL

Translation models have been used as a query term expansion method for both document and answer passage retrieval [7, 11, 12]. The models estimate probabilities that terms in documents are translated into terms in queries. We employ Xue et al's translation model [12] for CQA retrieval as follows:

$$P(q_i|D) = (1-\beta_1-\beta_2)\cdot P(q_i|D) + \beta_1 \cdot \sum_{t_j\in D, t_j\neq q_i} P(q_i|t_j)P(t_j|D) + \beta_2 \cdot \sum_{t_j\in D, t_j\neq q_i} P(t_j|q_i)P(t_j|D), \quad (1)$$

where t_j is a term in a document D, $P(t_j|D)$ represents the probability that a term t_j is generated by a document D and $P(t_j|q_i)$ and $P(q_i|t_j)$ represent the translation probability that a document term t_j is translated into a query term q_i and vice versa. Note that, since we are focusing on CQA, we use "question" instead of "query" in the rest of the paper.

In this translation model, Xue et al investigated the issues of self-translation and bi-directional translation. In a translation model for a single language, every word has some probability to translate into itself. In order to prevent low self-translation probabilities from assigning low weights to matching terms and high self-translation probabilities from nullifying the effect of the translation approach, Xue et al separate self-translation from the general translation model and use the parameter β to control the impact of self-translation. They use different parameter values β_1 and β_2 according to the directions of translation $P(t_j|q_i)$ and $P(q_i|t_j)$.

In order to estimate the translation probabilities $P(t_j|q_i)$ and $P(q_i|t_j)$, IBM model 1 was used. Higher-order versions of the IBM model were proposed to take into account other features such as the order of words, the length of aligned words in source and target expressions, etc. Because the number of sentences in questions and answer passages (or documents) vary widely and the goal of the translation is to generate expansion terms, these higher-order IBM models are not appropriate for this study.

Instead of using the higher-order models, some previous studies [8, 11] have used a simpler approach in which a sentence is converted to a sequence of term pairs. For example, a sentence "*A helicopter gets its power from rotors or blades*" is converted to *(helicopter-gets) (gets-power) (power-rotors) (rotors-blades)* to estimate the translation probabilities between adjacent term pairs. Without formulating translation models for specific types of linguistic features, Surdeanu et al. model translation between different types of text representations such as bags of words, n-grams, syntactically dependent pairs of terms and predicate-argument pairs of semantic labels. We use this approach to generate a key concept-based translation table. For a given question, we assume one of the terms is the key concept of the question. We generate a set of term-pair sequences in which we treat each term in a question as the key concept of the question. For example, for a question "*A* ***helicopter*** *gets its* ***power*** *from* ***rotors*** *or* ***blades***", we generate four pair sequences in which each one of the question terms is used as the key concept of the question as follows:

grow	**hair**–*grow*	**PLANT**–*grow*
make	hair	plant
plant	growth	soil
healthy	biotin	cut
take	long	make
month	take	water
hair	healthy	garden
help	supplement	fruit
biotin	take	start
fast	grow	good
water	microgram	concrete

Table 1: The translation results of "*grow*" with different contexts. PLANT represents a WordNet category.

Q1: *helicopter*-helicopter *helicopter*-power *helicopter*-rotors *helicopter*-blades
Q2: *power*-helicopter *power*-power *power*-rotors *power*-blades
Q3: *rotors*-helicopter *rotors*-power *rotors*-rotors *rotors*-blades
Q4: *blades*-helicopter *blades*-power *blades*-rotors *blades*-blades

In these pair sequences, each term is concatenated with a key concept (shown in italics). From a question with n terms, we produce n pairs. Using these pair-sequence representations of questions and the original answers, we estimate the key concept-based translation table. Table 1 shows the top 10 translation terms for *grow* with different contexts. The terms in the first column, where *grow* is translated without considering context, are a mixture of terms related to various topics. The second column uses *hair* as the key concept context and contains more specific terms.

We use WordNet senses and named-entity labels to substitute for words to generate additional data to address the data sparseness problem [11, 13]. The idea is to replace terms by their categories so that we can generate more samples per category and thus obtain better estimations. For example, *Columbine* is used once in our test collection, but the WordNet sense *PLANT* is used more frequently. We can then estimate translation probabilities for *PLANT-grow* instead of *Columbine-grow*. The third column of Table 1 is the translation terms for *grow* using *PLANT* as the key concept.

We use the key concept-based translation table for the translation probability $p(t_j|q_i)$ in Eq. 1 as follows:

$$P_{mx}(q_i|D) = (1-\beta_1-\beta_2)\cdot P(q_i|D) + \beta_1\cdot\varphi(q_i)\cdot \sum_{t_j\in D, t_j\neq q_i} P((\kappa_Q, q_i)|t_j)P(t_j|D) + \beta_2\cdot\varphi(q_i)\cdot \sum_{t_j\in D, t_j\neq q_i} P(t_j|(\kappa_Q, q_i))P(t_j|D), \quad (2)$$

in which κ_Q represents the key concept of a query Q and $\varphi(q_i)$ is the binary function that is 1 when q_i is a secondary concept and 0 otherwise. The translation probability with key concepts $P((\kappa_Q, q_i)|t_j)$ can be interpreted in two ways. We translate a question term q_i given the key concept of a question κ_Q. Or, we repeatedly interpret the key concept of a question κ_Q for each term in the question. The binary function for secondary concepts $\varphi(q_i)$ is used to selectively apply the translation model to question terms. In the next section, we will explain how to predict κ_Q and $\varphi(q_i)$ in detail.

3. IDENTIFYING KEY AND SECONDARY CONCEPTS

In our approach, we classify question terms as key concepts and secondary concepts. Key concepts are used as the context of translation and secondary concepts are used to selectively apply the translation model for query term expansion. For this purpose, we use a machine learning method to classify question terms [6]. For the classifier, training data consists of triplets as follows:

$$(q_1, k_1, s_1), (q_2, k_2, s_2), \ldots, (q_n, k_n, s_n),$$

in which n is the number of question terms. k_i and s_i are the labels of a question term q_i for key concepts and secondary concepts, respectively.

The definition of key concepts can differ according to their intended use. Bendersky and Croft [1] annotated the key concepts of queries to assign higher weight to the most important terms in queries. Lee et al. [10] used the TextRank algorithm in which the importance of terms is measured by the PageRank scores of terms. Lee et al [9] proposed a method to empirically select important query terms that maximizes the mean average precision of retrieval results. In our case, for the training labels of key concepts, we select k_i values according to the effectiveness of the translation model when we use q_i as the key concept of a question κ_Q. The training label of secondary concepts s_i is selected according to the improvement in retrieval effectiveness when we apply the translation model to q_i. We select only one key concept per question, although there can be more than one term which can improve the effectiveness of the key concept-based translation model.

We use three types of features for identifying key concepts and secondary concepts: lexical features, syntactic features and semantic features. The aim is to estimate how likely a given term is to be a key concept or a secondary concept given these syntactic and semantic characteristics.

Lexical Features. Lexical features are used to take account of the characteristics of an individual term.

- **Is Capitalized**: This feature is a Boolean indicator that is set to TRUE iff the first character is capitalized.
- **All Capitalized**: This feature is a Boolean indicator that is set to TRUE iff all characters are capitalized.
- **Clarity score**: This feature is the relative entropy between a term in the query language model and the collection language model [5], which indicates how important the term is in describing the topic of the query.
- **OddRatio**: The odds ratio between a given term being used in a question and the term being used in an answer. This feature is motivated by the observation that some terms in questions such as commonly-used verbs do not occur in answers.
- **Unseen**: This feature is a Boolean indicator that is set to TRUE iff a term is not observed in the top 15 retrieved documents.

Syntactic Features. Syntactic features are used to consider the role of a given term in a question.

	Prec@1	Recall@5	MRR
Baseline	0.476	0.774	0.612
TM	0.492(3.4%)	0.794(2.6%)	0.628(2.6%)
Secondary	$0.515^{\dagger}_{\ddagger}$(8.2%)	$0.818^{\dagger}_{\ddagger}$(5.7%)	$0.650^{\dagger}_{\ddagger}$(6.2%)
Key+ Secondary	$0.537^{\dagger}_{\ddagger}$(12.8%)	$0.837^{\dagger}_{\ddagger}$(8.1%)	$0.669^{\dagger}_{\ddagger}$(9.3%)

Significant differences relative to *Baseline* and *TM* are marked by † and ‡, respectively (using the two-tailed Wilcoxon test with $p < 0.05$).

Table 2: The experimental results of answer retrieval using the CQA collection. MRR represents Mean Reciprocal Rank.

- **Phrase Label**: This feature is the types of phrase that contains a given term.
- **Part-of speech (POS) tags**: Four Boolean features represent whether a question term is a noun, verb, adjective, or proper noun.
- **Depth in a parse tree**: The distance from root node to a given term in the parse tree of a question.

Semantic Features. We use WordNet sense classes and the named-entity classes of terms as semantic features [3].

4. EXPERIMENTS AND ANALYSIS

4.1 Experimental Setup

We evaluate the key concept-based translation model using the Yahoo! Answers Comprehensive Questions and Answers test collection (version 1.0[1]). We are interested in questions containing multiple concepts for which we can classify the role of these concepts for the proposed translation model. Therefore, we follow the same refinement process as [11]. Briefly, we select how-to questions containing more than four content words. Among selected 148,102 question-answer pairs, we used 30,761 question answer pairs for which the baseline system retrieved answers within the top 15 retrieval results.

We used 60% of these question-answer pairs for training, 20% for development, and 20% for testing. The training data is used to estimate the translation probabilities and to train the key concept classification method. The development data is used to select optimal parameter settings of β_1, β_2 in Eq 2. We indexed answers as documents. Then, we retrieved answers by submitting the questions as queries, using the Galago toolkit [4] for indexing and retrieval, and the sequential dependence model as the baseline. The SuperSenseTag software [3] was used to annotate WordNet categories for question terms.

4.2 Experimental Results

Our experiments evaluated the effectiveness of using key concepts and secondary concepts in a translation model for query expansion in answer retrieval. Table 2 shows the experimental results for precision at rank 1, recall at rank 5 and the Mean Reciprocal Rank (MRR) of answers in retrieval results. The baseline is the sequential dependence model without query expansion. Among 8,715 question-answer pairs in

[1]http://webscope.sandbox.yahoo.com/

	Unchanged	Improved	Decreased
Secondary	6,759	1,521	435
Key+ Secondary	5,307	2,646	762

Table 3: The number of question-answer pairs for which retrieval results are unchanged, improved, and decreased by the translation-based model with key and secondary concepts.

the test data, the baseline system retrieved the answers at the first rank for 4,150 (47.6%) of questions. As another baseline, we use the translation-based model from Eq. 1 (*TM*) that does not use key concepts. We do not have a pseudo-relevance feedback baseline (such as the RM3 model provided in Galago) because the Xue et al model has already been shown to be superior to pseudo-relevance feedback for this type of data [12].

Secondary is the experimental results of the translation-based model that applies the translation only for the secondary concepts of question terms. By translating only secondary keywords in questions, we potentially reduce the number of non-relevant translation results. *Key+ Secondary* shows the results when we translate the secondary concepts of questions using the key concepts as context.

As we can see, considering key concepts as the context for translation significantly improves the performance of the system. To analyze this further, we compare the experimental results of the baseline system and the translation-based model for individual questions. Table 3 shows the number of question-answer pairs for which retrieval results are unchanged, improved and decreased by using key concepts and secondary concepts for the translation model. The translation-based model without the key concepts affects fewer retrieval results. This model introduces expansion terms related to a range of possible contexts, which consequently has less effect on ranking. Using the predicted key concepts as context, the translation model generates more precise translation results. However, the ratio of questions for which results were decreased by the translation-based model with key and secondary concepts is also higher than when only using the secondary concepts. This shows that, if the selection of key concepts is inaccurate, using them as context can have a negative impact on effectiveness.

5. CONCLUSIONS AND FUTURE WORK

In this paper, we proposed the key concept-based translation model for query expansion. Key concepts represent the most important part of the users' information needs. We use the key concepts of questions as the context of translation. In addition, we also classify question terms as secondary concepts to selectively apply the translation model. Key concepts can improve the effectiveness of the query expansion by constraining the translations of question terms within the contexts of questions. By translating only secondary concepts, we can also reduce the non-relevant translation results. The key concept-based translation model significantly improved the effectiveness of translation-based query expansion for finding answers in a CQA collection.

For future work, we plan to apply the proposed method to passage retrieval in documents. Because of the lack of training data, previous work on using a translation model for retrieval has used pseudo data such as synthesized queries for given documents [7].

6. ACKNOWLEDGMENTS

This work was supported in part by the Center for Intelligent Information Retrieval and in part by NSF Grant IIS-1419693. Any opinions, findings and conclusions or recommendations expressed in this material are those of the authors and do not necessarily reflect those of the sponsor.

7. REFERENCES

[1] M. Bendersky and W. B. Croft. Discovering key concepts in verbose queries. In *Proceedings of the ACM SIGIR conference*, pages 491–498. ACM, 2008.

[2] A. Berger, R. Caruana, D. Cohn, D. Freitag, and V. Mittal. Bridging the lexical chasm: statistical approaches to answer-finding. In *Proceedings of the 23rd annual international ACM SIGIR conference on Research and development in information retrieval*, pages 192–199. ACM, 2000.

[3] M. Ciaramita and Y. Altun. Broad-coverage sense disambiguation and information extraction with a supersense sequence tagger. In *Proceedings of EMNLP*, pages 594–602, 2006.

[4] W. B. Croft, D. Metzler, and T. Strohman. *Search engines: Information retrieval in practice*. 2010.

[5] S. Cronen-Townsend and W. B. Croft. Quantifying query ambiguity. In *Proceedings of HLT*, pages 104–109, 2002.

[6] T. Joachims. *Learning to classify text using support vector machines: methods, theory and algorithms*. Kluwer Academic Publishers, 2002.

[7] M. Karimzadehgan and C. Zhai. Estimation of statistical translation models based on mutual information for ad hoc information retrieval. In *Proceedings of the ACM SIGIR conference*, pages 323–330. ACM, 2010.

[8] K. Kishida and E. Ishita. Translation disambiguation for cross-language information retrieval using context-based translation probability. *Journal of Information Science*, 2009.

[9] C.-J. Lee, R.-C. Chen, S.-H. Kao, and P.-J. Cheng. A term dependency-based approach for query terms ranking. In *Proceedings of the CIKM*, pages 1267–1276. ACM, 2009.

[10] J.-T. Lee, S.-B. Kim, Y.-I. Song, and H.-C. Rim. Bridging lexical gaps between queries and questions on large online q&a collections with compact translation models. In *Proceedings of EMNLP*, pages 410–418. Association for Computational Linguistics, 2008.

[11] M. Surdeanu, M. Ciaramita, and H. Zaragoza. Learning to rank answers to non-factoid questions from web collections. *Computational Linguistics*, 37(2):351–383, 2011.

[12] X. Xue, J. Jeon, and W. B. Croft. Retrieval models for question and answer archives. In *Proceedings of the ACM SIGIR conference*, pages 475–482. ACM, 2008.

[13] G. Zhou, Y. Liu, F. Liu, D. Zeng, and J. Zhao. Improving question retrieval in community question answering using world knowledge. In *Proceedings of the IJCAI*, pages 2239–2245. AAAI Press, 2013.

On the Cost of Phrase-Based Ranking

Matthias Petri Alistair Moffat
Department of Computing and Information Systems
The University of Melbourne
matthias.petri, ammoffat@unimelb.edu.au

ABSTRACT

Effective postings list compression techniques, and the efficiency of postings list processing schemes such as WAND, have significantly improved the practical performance of ranked document retrieval using inverted indexes. Recently, suffix array-based index structures have been proposed as a complementary tool, to support phrase searching. The relative merits of these alternative approaches to ranked querying using phrase components are, however, unclear. Here we provide: (1) an overview of existing phrase indexing techniques; (2) a description of how to incorporate recent advances in list compression and processing; and (3) an empirical evaluation of state-of-the-art suffix-array and inverted file-based phrase retrieval indexes using a standard IR test collection.

Categories and Subject Descriptors

H.3.1 [**Information Storage and Retrieval**]: content analysis and indexing—*indexing methods*; H.3.4 [**Information Storage and Retrieval**]: systems and software—*performance evaluation.*

1. INTRODUCTION

Postings list processing schemes such as WAND [2] have greatly decreased the cost of similarity computations for bag-of-words retrieval; and postings list storage schemes such as Elias-Fano codes have also reduced the cost of manipulating document-level postings lists [12]. But phrases are sometimes a further part of similarity computations such as BM25 and language models, and including them in similarity computations requires additional information, which must be either explicitly stored in the index, or computed at query time. A range of storage schemes have been proposed that provide different query time, storage space, and retrieval effectiveness trade-offs [4, 11, 19]. Of especial interest is the relative performance of traditional inverted index-based schemes and suffix array-based indexes. The latter have received significant recent attention because they support arbitrary phrase searching.

We compare storage schemes that support phrases as part of ranked queries, when evaluated via list processing schemes such as WAND. Specifically, we define a collection $\mathcal{D}$ of N documents $\mathcal{D} = d_0, \ldots, d_{N-1}$. Each document consists of a non-empty string of symbols drawn from an alphabet Σ of size σ consisting of the parsed word tokens of the collection. We additionally define a sequence $\mathcal{C} = d_0\$d_1\$d_2 \ldots d_{N-1}\$$ consisting of the concatenation of the documents in $\mathcal{D}$, separated by a symbol $\$ \notin \Sigma$. The length of $\mathcal{C}$ is given by n. A phrase $\mathcal{P}$ consists of a pattern $\mathcal{P}[0 \ldots m-1]$ drawn from Σ, where $m \geq 2$. The frequency of $\mathcal{P}$ in document d_i is denoted by $f_{i,\mathcal{P}}$. We seek to address the following requirement:

Sorted Document Listing with Frequencies – Preprocess a document collection $\mathcal{D}$ such that, given an arbitrary phrase $\mathcal{P}$, an increasing sequence of $N_{\mathcal{P}}$ document identifiers $\langle i, \ldots, j \rangle$ can be efficiently computed, together with the frequencies $f_{i,\mathcal{P}}, \ldots, f_{j,\mathcal{P}}$, where $d_k \in \mathcal{D}$ and $f_{k,\mathcal{P}} > 0$ for each $k \in \langle i, \ldots, j \rangle$.

The sorted document listing can then be used as a component in a similarity computation using algorithms such as WAND, exactly as if it had been drawn directly from a pre-computed phrase index.

SIGIR'15, August 09-13, 2015, Santiago, Chile.

ACM 978-1-4503-3621-5/15/08 ...$15.00.
http://dx.doi.org/10.1145/2766462.2767769.

2. PHRASE INDEXING SCHEMES

Five broad categories of phrase indexing scheme have been proposed, with combinations providing other trade-offs.

Positional. A list of term positions is stored, relative to the start of each document (hierarchical), or as absolute positions within $\mathcal{D}$ [17]. The relative representation requires less space, but at the cost of increased run-time performance, since intersection has to be performed both at the document and at the positional level. To answer phrase queries using absolute positions, the positional lists of the terms are intersected using an algorithm such as SvS [4], then converted to an increasing list of document identifiers and frequencies by mapping each position to a corresponding document number.

Pre-computation. Instead of performing list intersection at query time, the final set of $\langle i, f_{i,P} \rangle$ pairs can be stored in the index and accessed when needed by queries. Storage limits mean that pre-computing postings lists for all phrases is impossible, and techniques have been explored to choose lists to be computed, including analyzing query logs [3, 19] and using collection statistics [13]. Indexing only a subset of the phrases implies that either other ways of creating lists at query time must be provided too, or that retrieval effectiveness must be sacrificed.

Suffix-Array. Suffix arrays and suffix trees have primarily been used to support regular pattern searches over a continuous text; but suffix array-based structures can also be used for the sorted document listing problem [10, 11]. All suffix array-based indexes are structured as follows. First, a suffix array $SA[0 \ldots n-1]$ over $\mathcal{C}$ is constructed. Then an array $DA[0 \ldots n-1]$ is added, to store the document number in which each suffix appears. To compute a document listing, the interval $SA[sp, ep]$ containing all suffixes prefixed by $\mathcal{P}$ is determined, by searching the suffix array. The unique document identifiers and their frequencies in *DA*[*sp*, *ep*] are then determined, using one of several possible methods. In this work we compare three suffix array-based indexes that provide a range of time-space trade-offs.

As a suffix array baseline we use the SORT [6] index. It replaces *SA* by a compressed suffix array (CSA) [14], which reduces the space required; and stores *DA* as an array using $n\lceil\log_2 N\rceil$ bits. To determine document identifiers and frequencies for a range *DA*[*sp*, *ep*], it is copied to a temporary vector and sorted using a standard integer sorting algorithm. One additional pass produces the list of all $N_{\mathcal{P}}$ pairs $\langle i, f_{i,\mathcal{P}}\rangle$ matching $\mathcal{P}$. The second option, Sadakane's (SADA) index [15] also uses a CSA to find $\langle sp, ep\rangle$. But instead of storing *DA* explicitly, it is emulated using a bitvector of length n that marks the document boundaries. Two range minimum query (RMQ) data structures are used, and each unique document identifier in the range is processed only once. In addition, for each document d_i a separate CSA is stored, to determine $f_{i,\mathcal{P}}$. The third variant (WT) stores *DA* using a wavelet tree [5]. After determining *DA*[*sp*, *ep*], the wavelet tree supports retrieval of the $N_{\mathcal{P}}$ pairs $\langle i, f_{i,\mathcal{P}}\rangle$ in sorted order in $O(N_{\mathcal{P}} \log \sigma)$ time [16].

Navarro [11] provides details of these mechanisms.

Next Word Indexing. Instead of storing position lists for all unique terms in Σ, positions for all unique bi-grams in $\mathcal{C}$ can be stored [19]. This requires additional space, but intersection of long phrases can be performed efficiently, as the bi-gram lists are shorter than the corresponding term lists. Williams et al. [19] explore additional trade-offs where only some bi-gram lists are stored explicitly, based on common phrases identified in a query log.

Document Surrogates. Direct sequential search for phrases can be carried out in parsed documents if a small number of candidates is identified via an initial document-level search process. These methods make use of the "direct" file that is maintained by some search systems. Other indexes tailored towards proximity queries also cannot efficiently be used to answer phrase queries [1, 20].

3. LISTS AND INTERSECTION

Indexes that make use of postings lists store sorted sequences of integers, both as part of the underlying document level inverted index, and as part of the positional index. Compression techniques such as OptPforDelta [4] and representations based on Elias-Fano codes [12, 18] allow compact storage of sorted lists, and support fast execution. One of our purposes in this work is to explore the benefits of these new structures in the context of phrase processing.

Packed Binary. One of the most effective encoding schemes for postings lists is OptPforDelta [21], which compresses blocks of integers using a fixed width b, storing values larger than $2^b - 1$ as exceptions using a secondary codec. The underlying structure of the code, and the availability of SIMD instructions to assist the process [9], means that implementations can be very fast, and well-suited to hierarchical indexes. On the other hand, absolute positional indexes require encoding schemes which support large integers, and while all of the methods described can be adapted to support 64-bit values, underlying SIMD instructions may not be available, and decoding may be slower. Similarly, compression schemes tuned for positional information may be slower than document level compression codecs [20].

Bitvector Hybrids. Kane and Tompa [7] combine bitvector representations and standard compression techniques. Each postings list in the index is either stored completely as a bitvector; partially using a bitvector for the first part and then a compressed representation for the tail; or fully compressed. But bitvectors are only viable if the set being represented is dense across the domain. For example, a bitvector representing a domain of $N \approx 25$ million documents requires ≈ 3 MiB. The domain is much sparser when storing positional information; and for a collection containing $n \approx 23$ billion words, a bitvector would be 2.8 GiB. That is, the methods of Kane and Tompa (and the earlier work of Culpepper and Moffat [4]) are not suited to storing positional information.

Elias-Fano Codes. The Elias-Fano (EF) representation for increasing sequences has been rediscovered recently and applied to postings lists [18]. Elias-Fano codes provide a principled way of including bitvectors into postings list representations. Each number is split up into low and high parts. The high parts of the numbers in a sequence are stored as unary encoded differences in a bitvector; the low parts in binary using a fixed number of bits. Ottaviano and Venturini [12] show that a block-partitioned two-level EF representation can compete in both space and time with other forms of posting list compression. Like some other coding methods, the partitioned EF scheme exploits locality within postings lists. Document reordering, typically based on source URLs, produces clusters of similar documents and hence non-uniform postings lists, and can improve compression effectiveness and list processing speed by up to 40% [7]. However, these clusterings schemes are not applicable to improving compression for lists of term positions [20].

Intersection. Conjunctive bag-of-words queries and phrase searching using positional indexes both rely on list intersection, with skip information or bitvectors used to improve intersection speed [4, 7]. Elias-Fano codes directly include bitvectors, and Vigna [18] demonstrates how the bitvector representing the high parts of the sequence can be used as part of the compressed representation of the sequence, as well as an auxiliary structure to support fast skipping. Ottaviano and Venturini [12] show that Boolean conjunctive queries using EF codes outperform OptPforDelta schemes, support 64-bit integers, and are competitive to other representations optimized to support fast list intersection.

4. EXPERIMENTS

Dataset and Methodology. We use the standard GOV2 test collection of the TREC 2004 Terabyte Track, stored in URL-sort order. To ensure reproducibility we extract the integer token sequence $\mathcal{C}$ from Indri[1] using default parameters without removing stop-words. We index sequences of length $|\mathcal{C}| = n = 23{,}468{,}782{,}575$ consisting of $N = 25{,}205{,}179$ documents and $\sigma = 39{,}177{,}922$ unique word tokens. The raw collection uses ≈ 426 GiB, which is reduced to 71 GiB of 26-bit binary term identifiers after tokenization. All experiments were run on a server equipped with 148 GiB of RAM and two Intel Xeon E5640 processors each with a 12 MiB L3 cache.

To evaluate query performance, we traverse the suffix tree over $\mathcal{C}$ and assign phrases according to: a band $1 \le b \le 5$ where $10^b \le N_{\mathcal{P}} < 2 \times 10^b$; a band $b \le l \le 7$, where the phrase's least frequent term occurs between 10^l and 2×10^l times in $\mathcal{C}$; and by phrase length $2 \le m \le 6$. Each bucket was capped at 1,000 phrases; because of the three dimensional nature of the categorization, some had fewer. All reported timings are median per-query elapsed times, with all index components fully memory-resident.

Index Sizes and Implementation. Figure 1 shows space use. The suffix array-based indexes are roughly the size of $\mathcal{C}$, or larger. The CSA shared by all suffix array methods requires 21 GiB. The SORT method adds an uncompressed *DA* array of 70 GiB, whereas the WT method uses a wavelet tree over *DA* (WTD), which is stored

[1] `http://www.lemurproject.org/indri/`

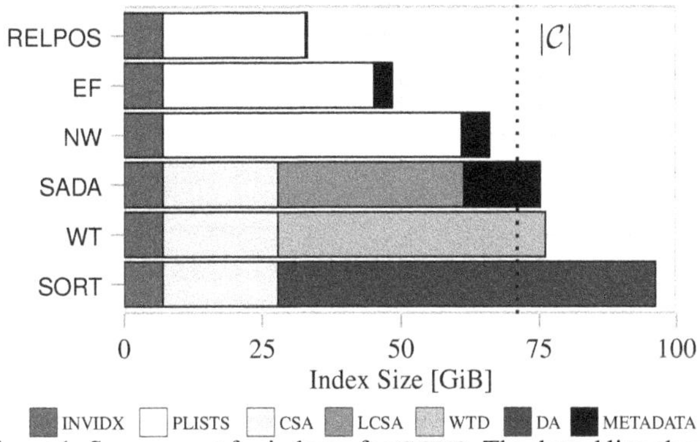

Figure 1: Space usage for indexes for GOV2. The dotted line shows the size of the tokenized collection.

using hybrid bitvectors [8], and requires only 49 GiB. The SADA method uses a local CSA (denoted LCSA in Figure 1) for each document; these are implemented using the method described by Gog et al. [6]. The metadata for SADA includes the two RMQ structures. These index arrangements reflect the current (practical) state-of-the-art for succinct indexes for the sorted document listing with frequencies problem. The components were partially provided by and implemented using the current version of the sdsl library [6]; our additional code is also available.[2]

The three inverted file-based indexes share the same document-level inverted index (INVIDX), implemented with uniform partitioned EF lists (UEF) with blocksize 128. The document identifiers and frequencies require 5.5 GiB, matching the values reported by Ottaviano and Venturini [12][3]. The inverted indexes additionally require 2 GiB metadata used for list offsets, document permutations, and WAND list max scores. The positional data is represented using absolute offsets, but for comparison we also include the size of an positional index that uses relative positions (RELPOS). This approach reduces the size significantly, but is slower than the absolute positional index [17]. The absolute index requires additional metadata to map absolute position offsets in $\mathcal{C}$ to document identifiers, implemented using a uncompressed bitvector of length n which marks each document boundary in $\mathcal{C}$. Constant time rank operations are used to achieve the mapping [11]. The nextword index (NW) stores absolute positions for all 473,366,430 bi-grams in GOV2. While there are techniques that only partially store lists [3, 13, 19], we measure the exhaustive case in which all bi-grams are indexed. The position lists of NW are stored using UEF codes, and require 55 GiB, still less than the three suffix-based indexes.

Document Level Retrieval. As a preliminary, we compare the performance of suffix array and inverted file-based methods in the context of bag-of-words conjunctive Boolean queries. Four indexes are used: the UEF and WT methods already described; plus regular Elias-Fano (EF) and OptPforDelta (OP4) encoded postings lists. The latter two require indexes of 8.3 GiB and 5.7 GiB respectively; and in the EF, UEF, and OP4 methods, intersection is achieved via the set-versus-set (SvS) approach. The WT index supports conjunctive queries by performing *intersection* operations, as described by Gagie et al. [5]. For each query term, the range $SA[sp, ep]$ is determined. These are then processed simultaneously using the wavelet tree over *DA*, to determine document identifiers which contain all terms. This approach has not yet been compared empirically to inverted file-based intersection approaches, hence our interest.

[2] `https://github.com/mpetri/pos-cmp`

[3] Yan et al. [21] report 4.1 GiB but the basis of this is unclear, and may involve stopping or other index reduction techniques.

Queries	EF	UEF	OP4	WT
TREC 2005	0.92	1.51	1.28	77.78
TREC 2006	2.32	3.71	3.12	148.90

Table 1: Median conjunctive Boolean bag-of-words retrieval times, in milliseconds, over GOV2.

Band	EF	NW	SORT	WT	SADA
$b = 1$	0.09	0.08	0.11	0.37	0.37
$b = 2$	0.69	0.38	0.12	1.59	2.65
$b = 3$	6.43	1.20	0.22	9.09	25.36
$b = 4$	62.69	2.09	1.34	34.36	222.41
$b = 5$	522.20	52.66	13.61	226.17	1922.13

Table 2: Median phrase materialization times, in milliseconds, over GOV2, using 1,000 queries in each bucket except when $b = 5$ (421 queries), with $10^b \le N_{\mathcal{P}} < 2 \times 10^b$ in the bth band. The pattern length is fixed at $m = 3$, and the smallest list size band at $l = b+2$ for queries in the bth band.

All queries of length $m \ge 2$ in the TREC 2005 and 2006 Terabyte Track efficiency tasks are used in this experiment, 34,495 and 94,253 queries respectively. Table 1 shows median query times, in milliseconds. The relative times of the inverted file-based indexes are broadly similar to those reported in recent studies [7, 12], except that our OP4 index is faster than the UEF index. This is in contrast to what was reported by Ottaviano and Venturini [12], a difference that we attribute to optimizations done in the NEQ skip method they used. All studies to date agree that EF is faster than OP4, but requires more space.

The three inverted file-based indexes outperform the WT index by a considerable margin. This is a consequence of the random memory accesses required to work the wavelet tree, compared to fast sequential processing of postings lists in the inverted file indexes. That is, the WT index is not competitive in either space or time. However, the WT index can also answer phrase queries, whereas additional positional information is required before inverted file indexing schemes can do the same (Figure 1).

Phrase Materialization. We turn to our main interest – the query-time generation of postings lists for phrases, ready for incorporation in ranked retrieval such as WAND-based evaluation of the BM25 scoring regime. Similarity computations using WAND can be performed efficiently, meaning that materializing additional postings lists must also be fast if it is not to dominate execution times. For example, Ottaviano and Venturini [12] report average BM25 computation times of ≈ 9 milliseconds for GOV2.

Table 2 shows median query times to materialize phrase lists for synthetic queries of length $m = 3$, categorized according to the band corresponding to the result size $N_{\mathcal{P}}$. For each band b, we fix the smallest position list size l to be $b + 2$. That is, the smallest postings list for each query is $\approx$ 100 times larger than $N_{\mathcal{P}}$ for that query. For small b, the cost of phrase materialization using all methods is within the cost of performing a WAND computation. As b becomes larger, the WT method becomes uncompetitive; once $b = 5$, both SADA and EF require too much time to be included in a similarity computation. The simple SORT method and NW index remain competitive. Surprisingly, the fastest index for bands $b \ge 2$ is the simple SORT index, which copies and sorts parts of *DA*. Unlike SADA and WT, the performance of SORT is dependent on $ep - sp$, which can be much larger than $N_{\mathcal{P}}$. But SORT does not perform random accesses, and instead makes use of fast localized

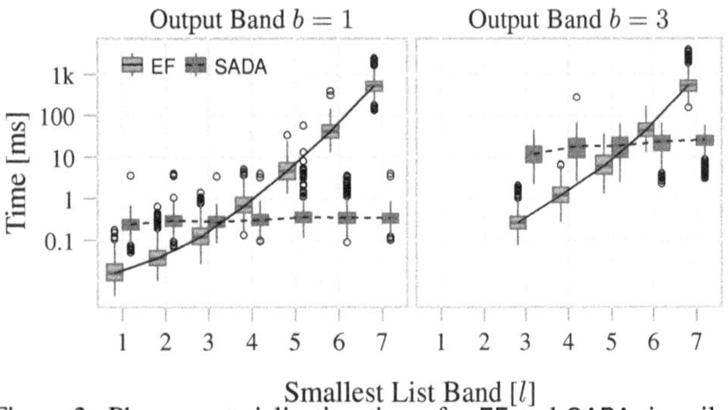

Figure 2: Phrase materialization times for EF and SADA, in milliseconds over GOV2, for queries where $10^b \leq N_{\mathcal{P}} < 2 \times 10^b$ for $b = 1$ and $b = 3$ for smallest list sizes $l \in b \ldots 7$. Patterns lengths are in the range $m \in 2 \ldots 6$.

integer sorting. Its drawback is the space required – 98 GiB, more than the other indexes.

In the previous experiment the size of the input for EF is fixed to be a constant ratio of the output size. The performance of list intersection-based methods depends on the size of the smallest list to be intersected, whereas all suffix array based methods only depend on the size of $N_{\mathcal{P}}$. Figure 2 shows the phrase materialization cost for patterns with $b = 1$ and $b = 3$, varying l, the minimum list length band, over $b \leq l \leq 7$. The time to process a phrase query using SADA depends primarily on the output size, rather than the lengths of the terms' position lists. In contrast, the EF run time significantly increases as l grows. In particular, EF is faster than SADA for small l (for example, for $b = 3$ and $l = 4$, EF takes 1.22 milliseconds, compared to 18.16 for SADA), but is more than an order of magnitude slower for phrases containing no infrequent terms.

Additional Trade-offs. We have evaluated a selection of index types in our phrase list comparison. Other combinations have also been proposed, with different time and space trade-offs. The nextword index (NW) in our experiments stores positional lists for all unique word bi-grams in $\mathcal{C}$. Williams et al. [19] examine hybrid schemes, in which only certain bi-gram lists are stored, reducing the space required. Similarly, Petri et al. [13] propose a mixed arrangement which pre-computes document/frequency lists up to a certain size threshold. Smaller lists are materialized at query time by processing *DA*, similar to the SORT index. A nextword index could also be used to materialize missing lists in this scheme. Another option is to avoid storing *DA* explicitly, and extract document numbers from the CSA by storing an additional bitvector marking document boundaries. This change would greatly reduce the storage cost of the index, but would add $ep - sp$ calls to suffix array values and rank operations, adversely affecting query time. That is, this method can only be viable for small $\langle sp, ep \rangle$ ranges.

Construction Cost. Our primary focus has been on phrase list materialization times. But construction costs are also a factor to be considered when choosing an index. The cost of building the suffix array-based indexes is an order of magnitude higher than inverted file-based indexing methods [6], and constructing *SA* for large parsings requires RAM not available in commodity hardware.

5. CONCLUSION

We compare inverted file indexes to suffix-based alternatives. The WT index is uncompetitive in both time and space for conjunctive Boolean retrieval; and all suffix-based indexes are larger than their inverted file-based counterparts. For phrase components, the SADA and WT methods are fast to materialize short lists, but slow considerably when there are many answers. Regular positional list intersection can produce phrase lists efficiently if the smallest intersected list is short. The nextword index (NW) is smaller than all suffix array indexes, and provides materialization times which are reasonably fast. The simple SORT index processes phrase queries rapidly even for large b, but uses nearly 100 GiB RAM. These various relativities are determined by the number of answers and the frequency of the smallest input term, and in future work we will more fully categorize the respective zones of applicability.

Acknowledgment. This work was funded by the Australian Research Council's *Discovery Project* scheme (project DP140103256), and by the Victorian Life Sciences Computation Initiative (grant VR0052), an initiative of the Victorian Government, Australia.

References

[1] D. Arroyuelo, S. González, M. Marín, M. Oyarzún, and T. Suel. To index or not to index: Time-space trade-offs in search engines with positional ranking functions. In *Proc. SIGIR*, pages 255–264, 2012.

[2] A. Z. Broder, D. Carmel, H. Herscovici, A. Soffer, and J. Zien. Efficient query evaluation using a two-level retrieval process. In *Proc. CIKM*, pages 426–434, 2003.

[3] A. Broschart and R. Schenkel. High-performance processing of text queries with tunable pruned term and term pair indexes. *ACM Trans. Inf. Sys.*, 30(1):5, 2012.

[4] J. S. Culpepper and A. Moffat. Efficient set intersection for inverted indexing. *ACM Trans. Inf. Sys.*, 29(1):1, 2010.

[5] T. Gagie, G. Navarro, and S. J. Puglisi. New algorithms on wavelet trees and applications to information retrieval. *Theor. Comp. Sc.*, 426-427:25–41, 2012.

[6] S. Gog, T. Beller, A. Moffat, and M. Petri. From theory to practice: Plug and play with succinct data structures. In *Proc. SEA*, pages 326–337, 2014.

[7] A. Kane and F. W. Tompa. Skewed partial bitvectors for list intersection. In *Proc. SIGIR*, pages 263–272, 2014.

[8] J. Kärkkäinen, D. Kempa, and S. J. Puglisi. Hybrid compression of bitvectors for the FM-index. In *Proc. DCC*, pages 302–311, 2014.

[9] D. Lemire and L. Boytsov. Decoding billions of integers per second through vectorization. *Soft. Prac. & Exp.*, 45(1):1–29, 2015.

[10] S. Muthukrishnan. Efficient algorithms for document retrieval problems. In *Proc. SODA*, pages 657–666, 2002.

[11] G. Navarro. Spaces, trees and colors: The algorithmic landscape of document retrieval on sequences. *ACM Comp. Surv.*, 46(4.52), 2014.

[12] G. Ottaviano and R. Venturini. Partitioned Elias-Fano indexes. In *Proc. SIGIR*, pages 273–282, 2014.

[13] M. Petri, A. Moffat, and J. S. Culpepper. Score-safe term-dependency processing with hybrid indexes. In *Proc. SIGIR*, pages 899–902, 2014.

[14] K. Sadakane. New text indexing functionalities of the compressed suffix arrays. *J. Alg.*, 48(2):294–313, 2003.

[15] K. Sadakane. Succinct data structures for flexible text retrieval systems. *J. Disc. Alg.*, 5(1):12–22, 2007.

[16] T. Schnattinger, E. Ohlebusch, and S. Gog. Bidirectional search in a string with wavelet trees. In *Proc. CPM*, pages 40–50, 2010.

[17] D. Shan, W. X. Zhao, J. He, R. Yan, H. Yan, and X. Li. Efficient phrase querying with flat position index. In *Proc. CIKM*, pages 2001–2004, 2011.

[18] S. Vigna. Quasi-succinct indices. In *Proc. WSDM*, pages 83–92, 2013.

[19] H. E. Williams, J. Zobel, and D. Bahle. Fast phrase querying with combined indexes. *ACM Trans. Inf. Sys.*, 22(4):573–594, 2004.

[20] H. Yan, S. Ding, and T. Suel. Compressing term positions in web indexes. In *Proc. SIGIR*, pages 147–154, 2009.

[21] H. Yan, S. Ding, and T. Suel. Inverted index compression and query processing with optimized document ordering. In *Proc. WWW*, pages 401–410, 2009.

Location-Aware Model for News Events in Social Media

Mauricio Quezada, Vanessa Peña-Araya, and Barbara Poblete
PRISMA Research Group
Department of Computer Science
University of Chile, Santiago, Chile
{mquezada, vpena, bpoblete}@dcc.uchile.cl

ABSTRACT

Nowadays, social media services are being used extensively as news sources and for spreading information on real-world events. Several studies have focused on detecting those events and locating them geographically. However, in order to study real-world events, for example, finding relationships between locations or detecting high impact events based on their coverage, we need more suitable models to represent events. In this work we propose a simple model to represent real-world news events using two sources of information: the locations that are mentioned in the event (where the event occurs), and the locations of users that discuss or comment on it. We then characterize a country based on the amount of events in which that country is mentioned and also participates on the event. We show some applications of the model: we find clusters of news events based on the level of participation of countries, identifying global and impactful events in certain areas. Also, we show groups of similar countries, finding promising insights about their relationships. This model can be useful at finding unsuspected relations among countries based on the news coverage and country participation, identifying different levels of news coverage in the world, and finding bias in international news sources.

Categories and Subject Descriptors

H.3.3 [**Information Search and Retrieval**]: Information filtering

General Terms

Design, Experimentation

Keywords

Event modeling; localized events; knowledge discovery

SIGIR '15, August 09 - 13, 2015, Santiago, Chile

ACM 978-1-4503-3621-5/15/08 $15.00
DOI: `http://dx.doi.org/10.1145/2766462.2767815`.

1. INTRODUCTION

Online Social Networks (OSN) such as Twitter[1], Facebook[2], and Sina Weibo[3] have become important sources of news. In particular, Twitter is nowadays a central part of information spread, as one of its main functions is to pass along information as news stories develop. When a breaking news event happens, Twitter users react to it by posting messages about the subject and quickly broadcasting the information to other users.

Twitter is an OSN and social media service that enables users to post messages of 140 characters. These messages, called *tweets*, can also include hyperlinks and can be geotagged with exact coordinates, depending on the location of the user. Even if the location is not provided, it is possible to infer an approximate location by analyzing the text of the tweets, or the location included in the author's profile description.

Also, with the increasing amount of GPS-enabled devices, OSN have enabled the ability of *geotagging* messages according to the location from they were posted. Even without these capabilities, users can assign a location to a message, or the location can be inferred from the message's text, etc. In particular, this allows researchers to study the interactions on OSN by looking at the spatial dimension. By examining the geotagged messages, it is possible to study information propagation, event detection, visualization of trends, etc.

It is necessary to model events accordingly in order to gain valuable insights about them. Placing the events in a map is useful for understanding *what* is happenning and *where*, but we need more suitable tools to study general trends about news events (*how* it is happening) and the role the geographical locations play in the propagation and impact of the events (*why* it is happening), especially on a large scale. For example, we would want to answer queries such as: which news events and which countries where these news events occurred are currently impacting Southeast Asia, or which countries are being impacted by news events taking place in Spain.

Our main goal is to find a representation of news events that allows us to answer the following research questions:

1. Can we identify groups of news that have similar properties in terms of the countries that they impact and in terms of the places where they occur? What other

[1]`https://twitter.com`
[2]`https://facebook.com`
[3]`http://weibo.com`

interesting insights can we gain from these relationships?

2. Which news is truly *global* in terms of the locations impacted by its occurrence?

3. Which news is causing high impact to certain locations, in terms of the reactions of the users from these locations?

4. How biased are certain news sources according to the locations covered in news reports?

We propose a model for news events disseminated in OSN streams that considers the geographical location information of an event. This information comes from two sources: the locations of places where the event occurs, and the locations of users that participate in the event in the social network.

Our model is a simple way to represent news events based on the location data extracted from the social media messages related to them. With this representation in mind, we show that we can find relationships between sources of information and the impacted locations, in terms of the messages posted in those locations. This can be useful in finding relations of causality between news events, identifying different levels of news coverage in the world (finding biases or the influence of news media in certain places), tracking news events in social media streams, and discovering unsuspected relationships among countries or conflicts, etc.

We show some applications of the model using a dataset of news events collected from Twitter. We show clusters of locations where events took place and users participate in them, illustrating that we can find high impact events based on news coverage, or to study the bias or the influence of a certain news source using these locations. Also, we compare some selected countries based on the events that took place in these locations, discovering relationships between countries. In terms of Information Retrieval applications, with this kind of model it would be possible to find events similar to a given event, to retrieve events based on certain given features, or to rank events and countries based on the level of participation of users on OSN.

2. RELATED WORK

As social networks have grown in popularity, several research studies have focused on event detection and characterization in social media streams, in particular, on detecting and geotagging events. For example, localized [9, 1, 8], global [7], or critical [4, 5] events. However, they do not place much attention on the representation of events in order to perform more in-depth studies of the events identified. We did not find many studies related to event modeling or event representation from social media messages.

Regarding models of social media data, in the work of Kamath et al. [3], the authors carried out a large-scale study of the spatio-temporal dynamics of Twitter *hashtags* (a hashtag is a user-generated string prefixed by # that users can include in a tweet as a way to associate it with an event or to a topic). They represented a hashtag as a tuple consisting in the location coordinates of the hashtag. A simple model is used to find interesting insights about social media memes. However, these memes may not necessarily correspond to real-world events.

Our work does not focus on the event detection problem, but rather on the event representation, to gain insight from events, where it is not possible to do so in other models.

3. LOCATION-AWARE EVENT MODEL

We propose a novel and simple way to represent an event based on the location data extracted from social media messages that cover the topic. We identify two dimensions of the problem: first, the countries where the news originated (*protagonist countries*), and secondly, the countries from where users talk about the news (*participating countries*). Using both concepts we define a matrix that characterizes the locations based on the level of protagonism and participation of them in the events. We can represent an event by the protagonist countries, the participating countries, or both.

Let $\mathcal{E} = \{e_1, e_2, \ldots, e_N\}$ be a set of events. Each news event e is defined as a tuple $e = (C_{\text{protagonist}}, C_{\text{participating}})$, where $C_{\text{protagonist}}$ is the set of protagonist countries and $C_{\text{participating}}$ is the set of participating countries in the event. By also having the total amount of messages posted from each participating country, $C_{\text{participating}}$ can be defined as the set of pairs $(c, \text{total\_messages}_c)$, storing the total message information for country c.

We now define a matrix M which we call *protagonism-participation matrix*. Each cell M_{ij} contains the amount of events from $\mathcal{E}$ which contain the country c_i as a protagonist country and the country c_j as a participation country, $1 \leq i, j \leq \text{total\_countries}$. Each row of the matrix is called *protagonism-participation vector*, $\mathbf{v}_i$, which characterizes a particular country c_i. By also having the amount of messages associated with each participating country in an event, we can extend the definition of the matrix by weighting each cell by the average amount (or any other suitable function) of messages posted from country c_j in all the corresponding events. We leave this extension to the matrix as future work.

Formally, each cell of the matrix is defined as follows:

$$M_{ij} = \left|\{e \in \mathcal{E} \mid c_i \in C_{\text{protagonist}} \wedge c_j \in C_{\text{participating}}\}\right|$$

And the protagonism-participation vector $\mathbf{v}_i$ is defined as follows:

$$\mathbf{v}_i = (v_1, v_2, \ldots, v_{\text{total\_countries}}),$$

where v_j is the the total amount of events which have country c_i as protagonist country and country c_j as participation country, $1 \leq j \leq \text{total\_countries}$.

The idea behind the model is that we represent a country c by the level of participation that other countries have on the events that took place in c. With this, we can find relationships between countries. Also, we consider an event as the tuple consisting on the protagonist and participating countries, so we can not only locate events in a map, but also we can find the countries which participate in the event. For example, to assess the impact of events based on their coverage.

4. EXPLORATORY STUDY

Using a dataset of news events collected from Twitter, we computed the event representation described in the previous section, and the protagonism-participation matrix. We show that we can identify global and impactful events in terms of

(a) Indonesia and the United States. (b) United States, Indonesia and United Kingdom. (c) Indonesia. (d) United States, Indonesia and United Kingdom.

Figure 1: Clusters of participation countries across all events. Each map shows one cluster of participation countries. The size of a bubble in a country is proportional to the square root of the average amount of tweets posted from that country of all the events. The caption in each subfigure contains the name or names of the most prominent countries in each cluster.

their coverage using cluster analysis, and that we can find similar countries based on the countries that participate in the news that mention the similar ones, using Euclidean distance between protagonism-participation vectors.

4.1 Dataset Description

We used a dataset of approximately 18,000 news events collected from Twitter dating from August 2013 until May 2014. Each event consists of a set of tweets describing or commenting the occurrence. Using manually selected verified Twitter news accounts (such as CNN, BBC, AP, etc.), we collected news headlines, identified recurring words in the headlines, and then used these words to perform searches in Twitter to retrieve tweets that cover each news, using the Twitter REST API [2]. An observation worth noting is that most of the news accounts correspond to American or English sources, so the dataset is biased to news events from these sources.

We employed an open source library for geotagging text, CLAVIN [6] (Cartographic Location And Vicinity INdexer) to identify locations from the tweets. We geotagged each tweet alone by looking at its text and its author's information (discarding the messages to which it was not possible to associate with a location), yielding the participating countries for every event. On the other hand, we considered the text of all the tweets belonging to an event as a single document, and then we identified the protagonist countries for that event, by choosing the most mentioned locations in the tweets.

4.2 Participation Clusters

We first performed a cluster analysis of the participating countries of the events. Recall that the participating countries are the countries from where users post messages about the event. Using the number of tweets as the amount of messages for each country, we used the k-means clustering algorithm with parameter $k = 4$ to identify clusters of vectors representing the most common participating countries across the events. Figure 1 shows the clusters in maps with the four participation clusters. Figure 1a shows a higher coverage in Indonesia, followed by the United States, while Figure 1b shows coverage world-wide, notoriously in the United States, the United Kingdom (recall that most of the news sources are from these locations), and Indonesia. Figure 1c shows participation only from Indonesia, while Figure 1d is similar to Figure 1b, but with lesser participation from the United States. We consider a higher level of coverage as the result of high impact news to these locations, allowing us to identify critical events on the social network.

	Brazil	Germany	Ukraine	Russia	Israel
Germany	**4.7648**				
Ukraine	13.1369	12.4971			
Russia	12.8379	12.0232	**4.4605**		
Israel	7.5124	7.4612	11.6408	11.4627	
Palestine	7.0845	6.8949	12.9251	12.8307	**3.4988**

Table 1: Euclidean distance between protagonism-participation vectors corresponding to selected countries. Lower value means higher similarity.

4.3 Protagonism-Participation Clusters

Using the protagonism-participation vectors, we find similar groups of countries through hierarchical cluster analysis. We compare countries using a simple visual approach by representing the countries by their corresponding protagonism-participation vectors as heatmaps. In this article we only illustrate selected examples from the resulting clustering solution.

Table 1 shows the computed Euclidean distance between the protagonism-participation vectors corresponding to Brazil, Germany, Ukraine, Russia, Israel and Palestine, based on the news events in the dataset. The resulting pairs of similar countries can be explained by the recurring news events related to them (e.g., the conflict in Ukraine, or the soccer match between Germany and Brazil in the 2014 FIFA World Cup).

Figures 2a, 2b, and 2c show heatmaps of pairs of countries in the same cluster: Russia and Ukraine, Israel and Palestine, and Germany and Brazil, while Figure 2d shows two dissimilar countries, the United States and the United Kingdom. It can be seen that the pairs of heatmaps are visually similar, and different from the other pairs (also documented in Table 1 using Euclidean distance). Russia and Ukraine share the most similar heatmaps, followed by Israel and Palestine. This can be explained by the recurring events concerning these countries. The case of Germany and Brazil can be explained by the events triggered in the 2014 FIFA World Cup. The similarity between the vectors corresponding to Germany and Brazil is not as low compared to the other pairs (as shown in Table 1), and this could be reflecting the fact that the corresponding news events happened in a short time interval (days), as opposed to the events concerning the other countries (months). Finally, the last heatmap (Figure 2d) shows two dissimilar countries, illustrating that the method is useful to find relationships between countries based on the news events that took place in these locations.

This approach shows that the countries share properties related to the news events that happened in these locations.

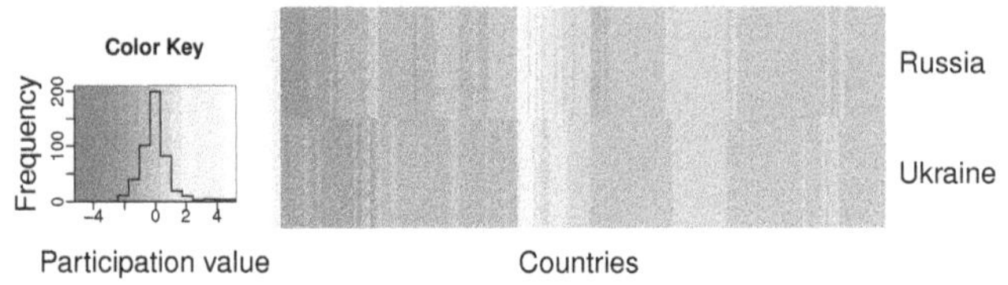

(a) Russia and Ukraine

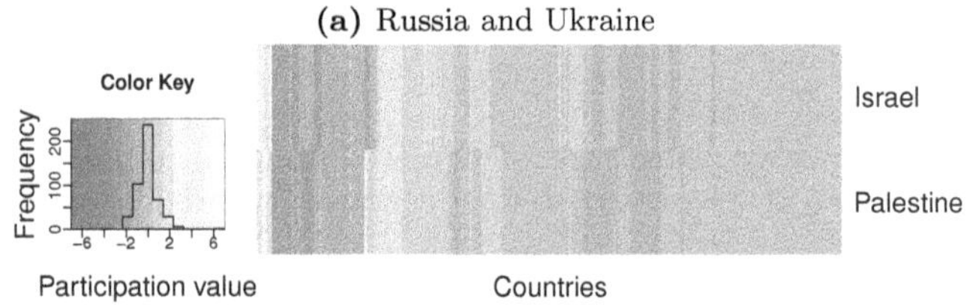

(b) Israel and Palestine

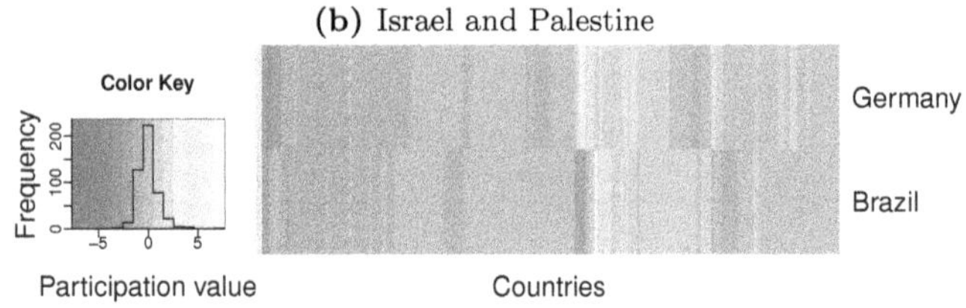

(c) Germany and Brazil

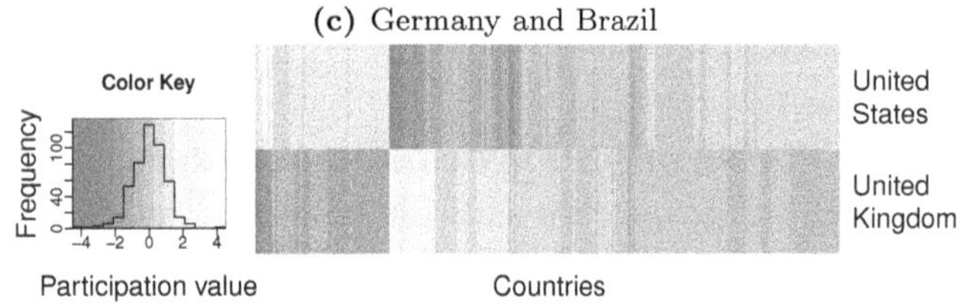

(d) United States and United Kingdom

Figure 2: Heatmaps comparing protagonism-participation vectors between pairs of selected countries. The x-axis of the heatmap corresponds to the countries (country names were omitted for clarity), and the color (participation value) corresponds to the scaled (zero mean and unit variance) amount of events in which the countries participate in the events in which the given country is protagonist.

Also, it is possible to recognize the most participating countries by looking at the heatmap (country labels were removed from the figures for the sake of readability). We can find unexpected relationships between countries using this approach by just inspecting the resulting heatmaps.

5. CONCLUSIONS AND FUTURE WORK

We proposed a simple model to represent events from social media, using the location information included in the messages related to the events. Using two dimensions of the problem (the locations where the event occurred and the locations of users who participate in the event), we define a matrix of the amount of events participating in a certain country, characterizing countries based on the corresponding events. We conducted a cluster analysis of the resulting vectors, showing that it is possible to find global and impactful events based on the coverage of news, and relationships between countries based on their participation in news events, using a visual approach.

Future work includes extending the model, considering the level of participation of countries in the analysis, performing a large scale study of news events, and formalizing the kind of queries that can be done to the model in terms of a event search engine system. In particular, by clustering participation countries we can find biases of news sources by analyzing only news of selected sources. Also, by comparing different countries using protagonism-participation vectors we can find unsuspected relationships based on several news events involving these countries. We expect to extend these analyses to show even more promising results.

6. ACKNOWLEDGMENTS

The authors were partially supported by FONDECYT Grant 11121511 and the Millennium Nucleus Center for Semantic Web Research[4] under Grant NC120004.

7. REFERENCES

[1] H. Abdelhaq, C. Sengstock, and M. Gertz. EvenTweet: Online Localized Event Detection from Twitter. *Proceedings of the VLDB Endowment*, 6(12):1326–1329, Aug. 2013.

[2] T. Inc. Twitter Developers. `https://dev.twitter.com/`. Accessed: 2015-01-30.

[3] K. Y. Kamath, J. Caverlee, K. Lee, and Z. Cheng. Spatio-temporal Dynamics of Online Memes: A Study of Geo-tagged Tweets. In *Proceedings of the 22Nd International Conference on World Wide Web*, WWW '13, pages 667–678, Republic and Canton of Geneva, Switzerland, 2013. International World Wide Web Conferences Steering Committee.

[4] A. MacEachren, A. Jaiswal, A. Robinson, S. Pezanowski, A. Savelyev, P. Mitra, X. Zhang, and J. Blanford. SensePlace2: GeoTwitter analytics support for situational awareness. In *2011 IEEE Conference on Visual Analytics Science and Technology (VAST)*, pages 181–190, Oct 2011.

[5] T. Sakaki, M. Okazaki, and Y. Matsuo. Earthquake Shakes Twitter Users: Real-time Event Detection by Social Sensors. In *Proceedings of the 19th International Conference on World Wide Web*, WWW '10, pages 851–860, New York, NY, USA, 2010. ACM.

[6] B. Technologies. CLAVIN: Cartographic Location And Vicinity INdexer. `http://clavin.bericotechnologies.com/`, 2012–2013.

[7] B. E. Teitler, M. D. Lieberman, D. Panozzo, J. Sankaranarayanan, H. Samet, and J. Sperling. NewsStand: A New View on News. In *Proceedings of the 16th ACM SIGSPATIAL International Conference on Advances in Geographic Information Systems*, GIS '08, pages 18:1–18:10, New York, NY, USA, 2008. ACM.

[8] M. Walther and M. Kaisser. Geo-spatial Event Detection in the Twitter Stream. In *Advances in Information Retrieval*, pages 356–367. Springer Berlin Heidelberg, Berlin, Heidelberg, Jan. 2013.

[9] K. Watanabe, M. Ochi, M. Okabe, and R. Onai. Jasmine: A Real-time Local-event Detection System Based on Geolocation Information Propagated to Microblogs. In *Proceedings of the 20th ACM International Conference on Information and Knowledge Management*, CIKM '11, pages 2541–2544, New York, NY, USA, 2011. ACM.

[4]`http://ciws.cl`

Exploring Opportunities to Facilitate Serendipity in Search

M. Ataur Rahman
School of Computer Science
University of Nottingham, UK
shuvo.2007@gmail.com

Max L. Wilson
School of Computer Science
University of Nottingham, UK
max.wilson@nottingham.ac.uk

ABSTRACT

Serendipitously discovering new information can bring many benefits. Although we can design systems to highlight serendipitous information, serendipity cannot be easily orchestrated and is thus hard to study. In this paper, we deployed a working search engine that matched search results with Facebook 'Like' data, as a technology probe to examine naturally occurring serendipitous discoveries. Search logs and diary entries revealed the nature of these occasions in both leisure and work contexts. The findings support the use of the micro-serendipity model in search system design.

Categories and Subject Descriptors

H.3.3 [**Information Search and Retrieval**]: Relevance Feedback; H.5.2 [**User Interfaces**]: Screen Design

Keywords

Serendipity; design; web search

1. INTRODUCTION

Serendipity is a naturally occurring phenomenon in our daily life, and has been proven to be valuable in many domains, including: medicine [18], business [8], creative thinking [2], as well as simply discovering new songs, good movies, or even useful literature in a library. Fine & Deegan [12] proposed the definition of serendipity as *"the unique and contingent mix of insight coupled with chance"*, which sums prior definitions by saying that a successful serendipitous encounter requires both a prepared mind and an accidental occurrence, to create a new insight.

To deliberately support serendipitous discoveries, research has tried to deconstruct serendipity and identify design opportunities [1]. In this project, we suggest that user interests, gathered from social media profiles, can be used in web search to facilitate serendipity: 1) users might select partially relevant or less directly relevant search results, when seeing information is related to other interests, and 2) users can identify valuable ways to connect new interesting information to existing ideas.

The subjective and individual nature of serendipity, however, makes it very difficult to perform a controlled user study to examine the impact of potentially serendipitous user interface designs [13]: 1) Serendipitous searches must be personally relevant, rather than from fictional tasks, 2) users cannot be tasked with being serendipitous, and 3) the discovery must also be personally valuable to make the connection. Consequently, rather than perform a controlled laboratory experiment, we chose to deploy a live system, named Feegli (Figure 1), which used real profile data from users' social media profiles. We asked participants to use this as their primary search engine for 7 consequetive days, which allowed us to explore the potential of encountering serendipitous information in real contexts, and to investigate participants' experiences. This paper, therefore, describes a lightweight naturalistic study of serendipity in web search happening in the wild, insights into its nature and frequency of it happening, and presents findings that support the notion of micro-serendipity as a relevant model for web search.

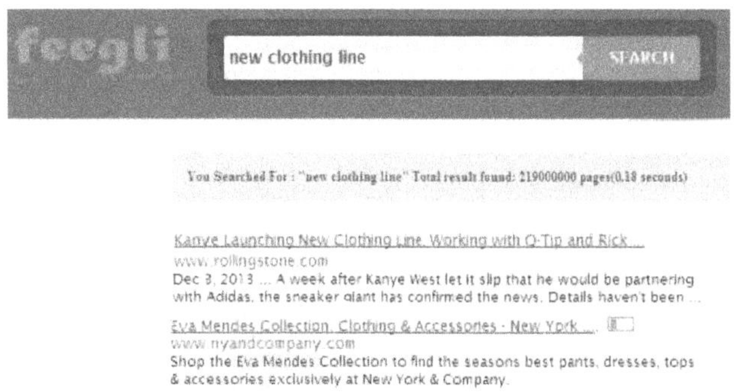

Figure 1: Feegli highlights interest topics, gathered from social media profiles, within search results

2. RELATED WORK

The definition of serendipity is both unclear and disputed [21, 15], with many researchers from various disciplines, having invested a great amount of time to study it [1, 5, 7, 9, 8, 16, 20]. Beyond simply encountering new information [11], McCay-Peet & Toms [17] describe serendipity as an event involving unexpectedness and a bi-sociation (mental connection). Conversely, Rubin et al. [20] described serendipity as happening when 1) someone is prepared to see cues, 2)

SIGIR'15, August 09 - 13, 2015, Santiago, Chile.

ACM 978-1-4503-3621-5/15/08 ...$15.00.
DOI: http://dx.doi.org/10.1145/2766462.2767783

an unexpected event occurs, and 3) a connection leads to a fortuitous outcome.

Makri & Blandford [16] focused on the stages of connection, realisation, and reflection that lead people to retrospectively consider an event serendipitous. They also highlight that most serendipitous events lead to a *macro*-serendipity tangible benefit, but that outcomes may also simply be an advancement of knowledge or understanding. Bogers & Bjorneborn further focused on these as micro-serendipity events, which were valuable even without clear tangible outcomes [5].

Andre et al [2] found that serendipity happens in web search, where interesting and both partially relevant or completely irrelevant search results have the potential for serendipity. Letizia [14], a browser agent, analysed web histories to recommend potentially interesting items to the user, but aimed to recommend interesting pages rather than highlight serendipity during normal web search. Similarly, a system called Max [7] sent recommendations to users via email after analysing two months of browsing data. Evaluations revealed that of 100 recommendations, 7 were found to be valuable by users. Mitsikeru [4] did try to highlight serendipitous results during search, but was not studied.

3. RESEARCH APPROACH

As serendipity cannot be simulated within a lab study, we chose, like others [2], to use investigative methods to explore naturally occuring examples of serendipity. Unlike prior work, however, we built a custom working search engine, Feegli, which uses real social media data to highlight results from normal searches that might also relate to one of their interests. As found with the design of PIM tasks [10], the individual nature of serendipity requires the use of real personal data. This personal nature of serendipity, however, precludes the creation of a comparable control group. Feegli, as a technology probe, however, allowed us to study naturally occurring serendipitous occasions, using event logs and insights from a longditudinal diary study.

3.1 Feegli: a serendipitous search engine

Feegli was built using the Google Custom Search REST API, and extracted interest data, as JSON files, from the Facebook Graph API v1.0, as soon as they signed up using their Facebook account. Further, participants added additional interests within a settings page for the Feegli system. When users issued a query, the titles and snippets of the search results were matched against the recorded Like data, as exact strings and whole words. Partial matches were not highlighted to avoid matches like 'cha**IR**'. Unlike typical personalisation systems, we did not re-rank results based on these interests. Instead, we highlighted results, leveraging the Restorff Isolation Effect [22] to provide a secondary notion of potential relevance to ranking.

Several indicators of interest-relevance were considered during the design phase: 1) interest matched, 2) intensity of match, and 3) source of interest. After discussing several alternatives for such indicators during focus groups, the last of these was not included in the design: social media icons were presumed to be for sharing results on social networks, and listing the source network provided less value than including more results before the fold.

Matched interests were highlighted in place, with a yellow background as seen in Figure 1, rather than being listed separately. For intensity of match, we chose to indicate *number* of matched interests, rather than estimating from the snippets an *amount* of relevance. Consequently, as shown in Figure 2, we designed a glyph (like [3]) to show up to three matches with increasing intensity.

Each query and all presented search results were logged by the system, including whether each result was highlighted as being related to an interest. Consequently, we could tell from the logs every potentially seredipitous result shown, for which query and which interest, and where in the results list it was presented. Further, each clicked result was logged by the system. We also wanted to gather at-the-time judgements about results, but with minimal interruption to their normal search behavior. Consequently, each time, but only when, a highlighted link was clicked on by a participant, Feegli asked for the primary reason, as per Figure 3. A popup was not shown if they did not click on a visible highlight, as we did not want to artificially drive click through towards such results. Further, we wanted to reduce the impact of the popups on normal web search behaviour.

Figure 2: Interest glyph shows number of interests

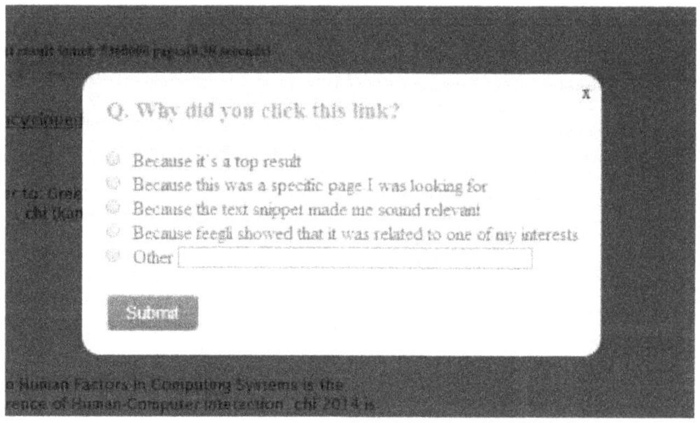

Figure 3: Popup when a highlighted link was clicked

3.2 Participants - Daily Diary Entries

Study participants were recruited primarily from the Universty of Nottingham, UK. In total, 14 active facebook users, with 'Like' data, were recruited. 9 were male, 5 were female. 12 already had an undergraduate degree. The study was approved by the school's ethics board and participants were entered into a draw to win $100.

To learn about the potentially serendipitous events experienced by our participants, we asked them to fill in a daily structured diary entry. The diary began with an open-ended request to describe any serendipitous experiences they had with Feegli during that day. Then, to support participants in recalling events, participants were presented with illustrated examples of their queries from that day. If a user clicked on the highlighted serendipitous results, they were asked to briefly explain the reason for clicking on it, and whether their information goal was met or not. Alternatively, when a user *did not* click on a highlighted result, they were asked about whether they had seen it, considered clicking on it, and so on. The daily diary was manually constructed by the experimenter to include the daily examples, and sent to the participants as a word document via email. Diary entries were returned in the same way.

4. RESULTS

Each participant used Feegli as their primary search engine between 25th April to 4th May, 2014. During these 11 days, participants made 506 queries in total (avg. 46 queries per day). Feegli returned 5380 search results during the study. Of these, Feegli highlighted 445 (8%) to be potentially serendipitous. Of these, 57 were clicked on by participants. From the immediate popup feedback, 35.1% were chosen because the text snippet made them seem relevant and 26.6% because the link was the top result. 17.5% of results were clicked because the user was specifically looking for the link. 22.8%, however, were clicked because Feegli highlighted them.

Commonly there are three types of queries people make in search engines: Navigational (to get to a certain website), Transactional (e.g. to buy, download, or retrieve something) and Informational (to resolve an information need) [6]. 84% of the queries were classified as informational; navigational and transactional counted for 8% each. Of the 445 highlighted results, 96% were shown for informational queries, and 4% for navigational queries. Using proportion of queries as an expected ratio, a chi-squared analysis showed that highlights were significantly more likely to be shown for informational queries ($\chi^2(2) = 49.826, p < 0.0001$). Of the 57 highlighted results clicked on by users, 98% were for informational queries. Using proportion of highlights shown as an estimated ratio, a chi-squared analysis showed that this was not significantly more than would be expected. All of the occasions where a user indicated that they clicked on the highlighted result because of the potentially serendipitous content were from these informational queries.

We also analysed the likely work or leisure focus of the queries. 52% were related to work and 40% of the queries are related to leisure search; 8% could not be easily classified. 64% of the highlighted, potentially serendipitous, results were shown for work queries, while only 34% were for social. Using proportion of classifiable queries submitted as an estimated ratio, a chi-squared analysis showed that significantly more highlights were shown for work-oriented queries than expected ($\chi^2(1) = 11.352, p < 0.001$). Of the 57 actually clicked, 60% were for work queries, while the remaining 40% were for leisure queries. Using proportion of highlights shown as an estimated ratio, a chi-squared analysis showed that highlights were not significantly more likely to be clicked in either work or leisure searches. The clicks that users said were because of the potentially serendipitous highlight were present in both groups. Perhaps surprisingly, these results indicate that there is opportunity and reason to support serendipitous discoveries in focused work tasks too, as well as when more casually searching.

4.1 Diary Entries

Diary entires confirmed that users did experience serendipity while using Feegli, primarily for informational needs, but also for both leisure and work searches.

4.1.1 Macro- vs Micro-serendipity

Following a recommendation, Feegli helped P3 to stumble upon unexpected link and later helped to find serendipitous results, for example: *"I clicked it because the green icon suggested that it had information I needed. After looking at closer look I found out the paper has a lot details about designing a mobile communication system and it had information on different generation of systems, which helped me. I found serendipitous information [about] a comparison between different modulation techniques and it led to me change my initial plan and gave me a series of new ideas about designing the system."* (P3)

The intensity glyph helped P3 to experience serendipitous information that was not among the top results; rather it was positioned seventh. This indicates that Feegli helped users to examine more results below the top, most frequently clicked search results. Perhaps interestingly, however, the user saw the glyph as being information they *needed*, rather than being related to an interest. In this case, the result led to a serious change in a work product, consistent with the macro-view of serendipity.

Highlighted interest keywords also helped to draw attention, as P5 said *"Well, the search engine showed me that the link is of my interest and that's why I clicked it. I was randomly searching and looking for if there is a new brand in clothing. It was the fifth link which highlighted Eva Mendes in the text, I was curious to know more and later found out Eva Mendes has a clothing line. It is difficult for me to answer whether it met my information need or not however it was nice to know that she has a clothing line. I would call this serendipitous [...] I am not sure if it was valuable to me or not but it definitely satisfied my curiosity."* (P5)

P5's experience is a good example of a leisure search, but also of micro-serendipity as the user was not sure if the new information was fulfilling the original information goal but it was serendipitous. This user may also have been more open to serendipitous recommendations, given the undirected nature of the query.

4.1.2 Serendipitous Discovery vs. Directed Search

Highly directed search may reduce serendipity, as when a user is focused on finding specific information, serendipitous recommendations were ignored: *"I did not click any of those because I did not look that far down; I found my target website within first few top results."* (P8)

Users also reported either looking at the type of link or reading the snippet to understand what type of information the link can offer: *"I did not click because I was looking for the information regarding old Robocop TV series and I went to see at first IMDB link to check it and I found it from there."* (P11). Instead, P11 utilized the highlight when goal was vague in nature: *"... first link was a Wikipedia link and of second and third, only 3rd link was highlighted so I thought it would may be important. I was looking for alternative models for kuznet curve and after a while I found it..."*.

5. DISCUSSION

Participants in our study described serendipitous encounters for both work and leisure related searches. Perhaps surprisingly, work related queries drove serendipitous encounters more than for leisure search, despite both Facebook and Feegli data showing the 'interests' of the users to be more hobby and leisure related. It is possible that there is less chance for leisure searches to only partially overlap with leisure interests, where as work overlapping with leisure interests are more serendipitous. One observation from the data, is that people who inserted more data in the profile, and had more Facebook Likes, received more serendipitous results than others. Future work may wish to examine optimal levels of interest modeling to support serendipity.

5.1 Models and Theories of Serendipity

Our study data loosely supports both main perspectives on serendipity: the unexpected encounter [17], and the purposeful awareness of cues [20]. In both cases, however, there was element of 'surprise' in the process and also there was presence of 'insight' where user made the connection [16]. More notably, however, it is evident that some of the serendipitous events helped our participants in some less outcome-oriented ways, but still described as valuable to them. These findings further support the focus on occasions of micro-serendipity [5], which were notably present in participants' diary entries.

5.2 Recommendations

Several key recommendations for designing systems can be drawn from our exploratory investigation: 1) evidence suggests that the model of microserendipity is worth following in design, 2) rich interest profiles are likely to highlight more potentially serendipitous results, 3) capturing work 'interests' may be equally as important as everyday interests, and 4) serendipitous design may be better if focused towards informational queries.

Future work may wish to focus on the influence of different design decisions on these encounters, or by integrating other sources of interest data. Unfortunately, we were not able to compare a range of possible user interface designs in our study (e.g. like [19]). Systems like Google, however, have a notable potential to examine this issue by combining topical content from +1 data, rather than specific pages, with search results. Likewise, Bing could examine this issue using their integration with Facebook. Further, Feegli used only a relatively simple technique to model and match user interests, and so much smarter methods, including those used in prior work, could be used to examine more design opportunities.

6. CONCLUSIONS

To investigate naturally occurring serendipity in web search a technology-probe search engine, Feegli, was deployed that highlighted Google API search results that related to their Facebook 'Like' data. Feegli was deployed to 14 people to use as their primary search engine for 7 days. 506 search queries were made by the user during the diary study and 445 results were recommended by the search engine as serendipitous. 57 distinct events were found where users clicked on the serendipitous search results. Whilst generally confirming empirically grounded models of serendipity [16], the logged behaviours, and insights from the diary entries, support Bogers & Bjorneborn's model of microserendipity [5].

7. ACKNOWLEDGMENTS

Thanks to our participants, and the support from EPSRC Grants EP/L019981/1 and EP/M000877/1.

8. REFERENCES

[1] P. André, J. Teevan, and S. T. Dumais. From x-rays to silly putty via uranus: serendipity and its role in web search. In *Proc. CHI*, pages 2033–2036. ACM, 2009.

[2] P. André, J. Teevan, S. T. Dumais, et al. Discovery is never by chance: designing for (un) serendipity. In *Proc. C&C*, pages 305–314. ACM, 2009.

[3] S. S. Bateman, C. A. Gutwin, and G. I. McCalla. Social navigation for loosely-coupled information seeking in tightly-knit groups using webwear. In *Proc. ACM CSCW 2013*, pages 955–966. ACM, 2013.

[4] R. Beale. Supporting serendipity: Using ambient intelligence to augment user exploration for data mining and web browsing. *IJHCS*, 65(5):421–433, 2007.

[5] T. Bogers and L. Björneborn. Micro-serendipity: Meaningful coincidences in everyday life shared on twitter. In *Proc. iConference 2013*, pages 196–208, 2013.

[6] A. Broder. A taxonomy of web search. In *ACM Sigir forum*, volume 36, pages 3–10. ACM, 2002.

[7] J. Campos and A. d. Figueiredo. Searching the unsearchable: Inducing serendipitous insights. In *Proc. ICCBR-2001*, 2001.

[8] S. R. Clegg, S. Mendonça, et al. On serendipity and organizing. *European Management Journal*, 28(5):319–330, 2010.

[9] E. B. Cooksey. Too important to be left to chance-serendipity and the digital library. *Science & Technology Libraries*, 25(1-2):23–32, 2004.

[10] D. Elsweiler and I. Ruthven. Towards task-based personal information management evaluations. In *Proc. SIGIR '07*, pages 23–30. ACM, 2007.

[11] S. Erdelez. Information encountering: It's more than just bumping into information. *ASIST Bulletin*, 25(3):26–29, 1999.

[12] G. A. Fine and J. G. Deegan. Three principles of serendip: insight, chance, and discovery in qualitative research. *IJQSE*, 9(4):434–447, 1996.

[13] A. Foster and N. Ford. Serendipity and information seeking: an empirical study. *Journal of Documentation*, 59(3):321–340, 2003.

[14] H. Lieberman et al. Letizia: An agent that assists web browsing. *IJCAI*, 1995:924–929, 1995.

[15] S. Makri. Serendipity is not bullshit. In *Proc. EuroHCIR2014*, 2014.

[16] S. Makri and A. Blandford. Coming across information serendipitously–part 1: a process model. *Journal of Documentation*, 68(5):684–705, 2012.

[17] L. McCay-Peet and E. G. Toms. The process of serendipity in knowledge work. In *Proc. IIiX 2010*, pages 377–382. ACM, 2010.

[18] M. A. Meyers. Science, creativity, and serendipity. *AJR*, 165(4):755–764, 1995.

[19] A. Muralidharan, Z. Gyongyi, and E. Chi. Social annotations in web search. In *Proc. ACM CHI 2012*, pages 1085–1094. ACM, 2012.

[20] V. L. Rubin, J. Burkell, and A. Quan-Haase. Facets of serendipity in everyday chance encounters: a grounded theory approach to blog analysis. *Information Research*, 16(3), 2011.

[21] A. Singh. Serendipity is bullshit. *The Stanford Daily*, 2014.

[22] H. Von Restorff. Uber die wirkung von bereichsbildungen im spurenfeld. *Psychologische Forschung*, 18(1):299–342, 1933.

Combining Orthogonal Information in Large-Scale Cross-Language Information Retrieval

Shigehiko Schamoni
Department of Computational Linguistics
Heidelberg University
69120 Heidelberg, Germany
schamoni@cl.uni-heidelberg.de

Stefan Riezler
Department of Computational Linguistics
Heidelberg University
69120 Heidelberg, Germany
riezler@cl.uni-heidelberg.de

ABSTRACT

System combination is an effective strategy to boost retrieval performance, especially in complex applications such as cross-language information retrieval (CLIR) where the aspects of translation and retrieval have to be optimized jointly. We focus on machine learning-based approaches to CLIR that need large sets of relevance-ranked data to train high-dimensional models. We compare these models under various measures of orthogonality, and present an experimental evaluation on two different domains (patents, Wikipedia) and two different language pairs (Japanese-English, German-English). We show that gains of over 10 points in MAP/NDCG can be achieved over the best single model by a linear combination of the models that contribute the most orthogonal information, rather than by combining the models with the best standalone retrieval performance.

Categories and Subject Descriptors

H.3.3 [**Information Storage and Retrieval**]: Information Search and Retrieval; I.2.7 [**Artificial Intelligence**]: Natural Language Processing

General Terms

Algorithms, Experimentation

Keywords

Machine translation, cross-lingual retrieval, patent search

1. INTRODUCTION

Cross-Language Information Retrieval (CLIR) needs to jointly optimize the tasks of translation and retrieval, however, it is standardly approached with a focus on one aspect. For example, the industry standard leverages state-of-the-art statistical machine translation (SMT) to translate the query into the target language, in which standard retrieval is performed [4]. Most research approaches start from a retrieval perspective [13], or, more recently, from a machine learning direction [11]. Besides two different tasks, CLIR also needs to incorporate different languages and specialized domains. Thus, techniques that combine specialized systems into an improved joint system are a promising research direction. In this paper we show that a linear system combination can yield improvements of more than 10 MAP/NDCG points over the best single system, if the combined systems represent orthogonal information. We focus on machine learning-based approaches to CLIR that need large sets of relevance-ranked data to train high dimensional models. The systems investigated in this paper are systems based on direct use of SMT technology, systems that apply learning-to-rank techniques, systems based on probabilistic neural networks, and methods that incorporate domain-specific meta-information into linear learners. We present various measures of correlation/orthogonality on the level of scores (Pearson's correlation coefficient and principal component analysis), ranks (Kendall's rank correlation coefficient), and retrieved documents (Jaccard coefficient), and show on two different domains (patents, Wikipedia) and two different language pairs (Japanese-English, German-English) that the contribution of a single system to the combination is best determined by the orthogonality of the information it represents, rather than by its standalone retrieval performance.

SIGIR '15, August 09-13 2015, Santiago, Chile

DOI: http://dx.doi.org/10.1145/2600428.2609539

2. RELATED WORK

Various publications have investigated different methods of system combination for CLIR, including logical operations on retrieved sets [3], voting procedures based on retrieval scores [1], or machine learning techniques that learn combination weights directly from relevance rankings [14]. The focus of this paper is on machine learning-based CLIR approaches and on metrics to measure orthogonality between these systems. Since all of our models require large sets of relevance-ranked training data, e.g. for learning high-dimensional cross-lingual word matrices, we cannot use standard CLIR datasets from CLEF or TREC campaigns that consist of a few hundred queries with precomputed features. Instead, we use specialized domains such as patents or Wikipedia where relevance information can be induced from the citation or link structure.

3. CLIR MODELS

Translation Models. SMT-based models translate a query and then perform monolingual retrieval. Our first model is called *Direct Translation (DT)* and uses the SMT framework `cdec` [5] to generate a single best query translation.

A second model is called *Probabilistic Structured Queries*

(PSQ). The central idea of this approach is to project query terms into the target language by probabilistically weighted translations from the n-best list of a full SMT system [17].

In both models, we use the Okapi BM25 scoring scheme for document retrieval.

Ranking Models. Let $\mathbf{q} \in \{0,1\}^Q$ be a query and $\mathbf{d} \in \{0,1\}^D$ be a document where the nth vector dimension indicates the occurrence of the nth word for dictionaries of size Q and D. A linear ranking model is defined as

$$f(\mathbf{q},\mathbf{d}) = \mathbf{q}^\top W \mathbf{d} = \sum_{i=1}^{Q}\sum_{j=1}^{D} q_i W_{ij} d_j,$$

where $W \in \mathbb{R}^{Q\times D}$ encodes a matrix of ranking-specific word associations [2, 14] . We optimize this model by pairwise ranking, which assumes labeled data in the form of a set $\mathcal{R}$ of tuples $(\mathbf{q},\mathbf{d}^+,\mathbf{d}^-)$, where $\mathbf{d}^+$ is a relevant (or higher ranked) document and $\mathbf{d}^-$ an irrelevant (or lower ranked) document for query $\mathbf{q}$. We compare two methods to find a weight matrix W such that an inequality $f(\mathbf{q},\mathbf{d}^+) > f(\mathbf{q},\mathbf{d}^-)$ is violated for the fewest number of tuples from $\mathcal{R}$.

The first method uses the *Vowpal Wabbit (VW)* toolkit [6] to optimize the following ℓ_1-regularized hinge loss objective:

$$\mathcal{L}_{hng} = \sum_{(\mathbf{q},\mathbf{d}^+,\mathbf{d}^-)\in\mathcal{R}} \left(f(\mathbf{q},\mathbf{d}^+) - f(\mathbf{q},\mathbf{d}^-)\right)_+ + \lambda||W||_1,$$

where $(x)_+ = \max(0, m-x)$ with margin m and λ is the regularization parameter. VW was run on a data sample of 5M to 10M tuples from $\mathcal{R}$. On each step, W is updated with a scaled gradient vector $\nabla_W \mathcal{L}_{hng}$ and clipped to account for ℓ_1-regularization.

The second method is a *boosting model (BM)* that optimizes an exponential loss [16]:

$$\mathcal{L}_{exp} = \sum_{(\mathbf{q},\mathbf{d}^+,\mathbf{d}^-)\in\mathcal{R}} \mathcal{D}(\mathbf{q},\mathbf{d}^+,\mathbf{d}^-)e^{f(\mathbf{q},\mathbf{d}^-)-f(\mathbf{q},\mathbf{d}^+)},$$

where $\mathcal{D}(\mathbf{q},\mathbf{d}^+,\mathbf{d}^-)$ is a non-negative importance function on tuples. The algorithm combines batch boosting with bagging over independently drawn bootstrap data samples of 100k instances each from $\mathcal{R}$. In every step, the single word pair feature is selected that provides the largest decrease of $\mathcal{L}_{exp}$. The final scoring function comprises the averaged resulting models. For regularization we rely on early stopping.

Neural Network Models. These models utilize the bilingual compositional vector model (biCVM) of [9] to train a retrieval system based on a bilingual autoencoder. The training task is to learn two functions $f: Q \to \mathbb{R}^d$ and $g: D \to \mathbb{R}^d$, which map a query $\mathbf{q}$ and a relevant document $\mathbf{d}$ from a corpus C onto a distributed semantic representation in $\mathbb{R}^d$. The energy of a query-document pair $(\mathbf{q},\mathbf{d})$ is defined by $E_{bi}(\mathbf{q},\mathbf{d}) = ||f(\mathbf{q}) - g(\mathbf{d})||^2$. Introducing a large margin m into the noise-contrastive update prevents the model from degenerating. This results in the following regularized hinge-loss objective:

$$\mathcal{H} = \sum_{(\mathbf{q},\mathbf{d}^+)\in C}\left(\sum_{i=1}^{k}\left(m + E_{bi}(\mathbf{q},\mathbf{d}^+) - E_{bi}(\mathbf{q},\mathbf{d}^-)\right)_+\right) + \frac{\lambda}{2}||\theta||^2,$$

where we treat less relevant documents $\mathbf{d}^-$ as noise samples during training. θ represents the model parameters.

While [9] train their system exclusively on parallel data on sentence and document level, we examine different training setups where we let the architecture learn distributed representations from: (a) data based on expert translations (family patents) and comparable data (Wikipedia articles on the same topic in different languages), which we call CVM_{FM}, and, (b) generally relevant documents (cited patents, linked Wikipedia articles), which we refer to as CVM_R.

Domain Knowledge Model. The final model (DK) for comparison uses highly informative dense features which capture similar aspects of e.g. patents or Wikipedia articles. Domain knowledge features for patents were inspired by [8]: a feature fires if two patents share similar aspects, e.g. a common inventor, similar number of claims, or common patent classes in the IPC hierarchy.

For Wikipedia, we implemented features that compare the relative length of documents, number of links and images, the number of common links and common images, and Wikipedia categories (hypernym and hyponym relations).

4. MEASURES OF ORTHOGONALITY

Jaccard similarity coefficient. This coefficient measures the percentage of overlap between two sets. In the retrieval setup, we limit our attention to the *relevant documents* within the top-k results for each query. The overlap metric expressing the similarity of two candidate systems is then:

$$J@k_{s_i\cap s_j} = \frac{|retrieved@k_{s_i} \cap retrieved@k_{s_j}|}{|retrieved@k_{s_i} \cup retrieved@k_{s_j}|},$$

where *retrieved@k* are the relevant documents retrieved within the top-k results. We report the pairwise overlap of two systems s_i and s_j for $k = 100$.

Pearson's ρ and Kendall's τ. The Pearson product-moment correlation coefficient, Pearson's ρ, is used to measure the linear correlation between the scores assigned to each retrieved relevant document. Kendall's τ works directly on the ranks and is insensitive to the absolute score values.

We calculate the metrics on a per-query basis and report the arithmetic mean. Again, we discard all irrelevant documents from the retrieved results by assigning them a score of 0. Then for each pair of systems, we select the queries which have at least 3 data points (i.e. relevant documents) in common, as 2 data points are always correlated. On average, this method selects about 75% of the queries for evaluation.

Principal Component Analysis (PCA). PCA is a method to find the set of n principal components (PC) that span the subspace of the data where most of the data variance resides. The straightforward approach would be to identify all the PCs (or eigenvectors) describing the retrieved data and to compare them. Our experiments showed that at least 850 PCs are required to capture more than 90% of the data variance, making a thorough comparison infeasible. Thus, we opt for a simplified approach where we consider only a small subset of the most important PCs.

We start by creating $|q| \times |d|$ matrices of retrieval scores for each system, where $|q|$ and $|d|$ are the numbers of queries and documents. PCA returns the first k principal components for each system. By calculating their dot products we obtain a sequence of values, or a k-dimensional vector, which describes the difference between the retrieval results of two candidate systems. To further reduce this vector to a single value, we report the normalized ℓ_2-norm of this vector of the top-k PC's similarity. This reflects our requirement

		#q	#d	#d+/q
Patents (JP-EN)	train	107,061	888,127	13.28
	dev	2,000	100,000	13.24
	test	2,000	100,000	12.59
Wikipedia (DE-EN)	train	225,294	1,226,741	13.04
	dev	10,000	113,553	12.97
	test	10,000	115,131	13.22

Table 1: Ranking data statistics: number of queries and documents, and average number of relevant documents per query.

that only the *dimension* of variance is of interest:

$$||PC||@k_{s_i,s_j} = \sqrt{\frac{1}{k}\sum_{n=1}^{k}\langle \mathbf{b}_i^n, \mathbf{b}_j^n\rangle^2}$$

The vector $\mathbf{b}_i^n$ represents the nth normalized PC describing the space of relevant documents retrieved by system s_i, thus the range of values for $||PC||@k$ lies between 0 (all orthogonal) and 1 (all similar). In this sense, our PCA-based analysis is directly connected to the notion of orthogonality. We used $k = 10$ principal components in our experiments.

5. EXPERIMENTS

Patent Prior-art Search. Our first dataset consists of a Japanese-English (JP-EN) corpus of patent abstracts from the MAREC and NTCIR data.[1] It contains automatically induced relevance judgments for patent abstracts [7]: EN patents are regarded as relevant to a JP query patent with level (3) if they are in a family relationship (e.g., same invention), (2) if cited by the patent examiner, or (1) if cited by the applicant. On average, queries and documents contain about 5 sentences. Table 1 shows the size of the dataset, consisting of over 100k queries and nearly 1M documents, with approximately 13 relevant documents per query.

Wikipedia Article Retrieval. Our second dataset consists of relevance-linked Wikipedia pages.[2] Relevance judgments were extracted by aligning German (DE) queries with their English (EN) counterparts ("mates") via the graph of inter-language links available in articles and Wikidata. The highest relevance level is assigned to the EN mate, the next relevance level to all other EN articles that link to the mate, *and* are linked to by the mate. Instead of using all outgoing links from the mate, only articles with bidirectional links are used. EN documents are restricted to the first 200 words to reduce the number of features for *BM* and *VW* models. To avoid rendering the task too easy for literal keyword matching of queries about named entities, title words are removed from German queries. Data statistics are given in Table 1.

Parallel Data for SMT Models. *DT* and *PSQ* require an SMT system trained on parallel corpora. A JP-EN system was trained on 1.8M parallel sentences from the NTCIR-7 JP-EN PatentMT subtask. For Wikipedia, we trained a DE-EN system on 4.1M parallel sentences provided by WMT[3].

System Combination. We reapply the *VW* ranking approach described in Section 3 on dev set data for system combination. This method shows stable gains over three different IR-metrics: the precision-based MAP [11] and NDCG [10], where the latter considers relevance levels, and the recall-oriented PRES [12]. All scores were computed on the top 1,000 retrieved documents.

[1] www.cl.uni-heidelberg.de/boostclir

[2] www.cl.uni-heidelberg.de/wikiclir

[3] www.statmt.org/wmt11/translation-task.html

	models	MAP	NDCG	PRES
Patents (JP-EN)	DT	0.2554	0.5397	0.5680
	PSQ	0.2659	0.5508	0.5851
	VW	0.2205	0.4989	0.4911
	BM	0.1730	0.4335	0.5431
	CVM_{FM}	0.2504	0.5399	0.6104
	CVM_R	0.1767	0.4229	0.6121
	DK	0.2203	0.4874	0.5171
Wikipedia (DE-EN)	DT	0.3678	0.5691	0.7219
	PSQ	0.3642	0.5671	0.7165
	VW	0.1249	0.3389	0.6466
	BM	0.1386	0.3418	0.6145
	CVM_{FM}	0.1467	0.3326	0.5584
	CVM_R	0.1686	0.3515	0.6178
	DK	0.1824	0.3393	0.4937

Table 2: Test results for *standalone* CLIR models using direct translation (*DT*), probabilistic structured queries (*PSQ*), sparse ranking model (*VW*), sparse boosting model (*BM*), compositional vector model trained on parallel/comparable documents (CVM_{FM}) and on all relevant documents (CVM_R), and dense domain knowledge features (*DK*).

Results. Table 2 shows the performance of single retrieval systems according to MAP, NDCG, and PRES. SMT-based CLIR-methods clearly outperform all others. Only on specialized domains like patent-prior-art-search and by training on very clean data (expert translations), the neural network-based CVM_{FM} model is competitive. On the task of Wikipedia article retrieval, SMT-based methods outperform other approaches by a large margin.

Our hypothesis is that rather than combining the systems with the best standalone retrieval performance, the best overall system is gained by combining systems that are least similar and contribute orthogonal information to the combination. Table 3 lists all possible pairwise system combinations, together with their retrieval performance and their orthogonality/correlation.

An inspection of the patents in Table 3 shows that all measures of orthogonality/correlation capture the high similarity of the two SMT-based methods, *DT* and *PSQ*. Combining these two models results only in a small improvement in retrieval performance. Similar relations are found for all pairs of systems from same groups: ranking-based approaches such as *VW* and *BM* or neural network approaches such as CVM_{FM} and CVM_R are similar according to all measures of orthogonality/correlation, and lead to small improvements in retrieval performance in combination. Picking the least similar systems among the four groups, irrespective of their standalone retrieval performance, yields much higher improvements in combination. This is very pronounced for the *DK* system that is orthogonal to all other models. The biCVM-models also seem to contribute new information, where the gains are mostly higher for combinations with CVM_R despite its lower performance as a standalone model compared to CVM_{FM}. The last row in the Patents section presents the best performing combination of the four groups' systems, showing that the improvements by orthogonal combinations add up.

On Wikipedia data, shown in the lower part of Table 3, we find similar relations. The lower similarity between CVM_R and CVM_{FM} can be explained by training data dif-

combination	MAP	NDCG	PRES	J	ρ	τ	$\|\|PC\|\|$
Patents (JP-EN)							
PSQ + DT	^{L}.2707	.5578	.5941	.7318	.7488	.7591	.4717
PSQ + VW	.2912	.5862	.6286	.5077	.4475	.5387	.2590
PSQ + BM	^{L}.2661	.5611	.6257	.5358	.4964	.5413	.2541
PSQ + CVM_{FM}	.3071	.6105	.6808	.5528	.4336	.5154	.2359
PSQ + CVM_R	.3095	.6140	.7059	.4666	.3139	.3806	.2342
PSQ + DK	.3554	.6560	.7320	.3893	.2001	.3081	.1018
DT + VW	.2799	.5742	.6095	.5345	.4682	.5574	.3129
DT + BM	^{L}.2523	^{L}.5472	.6114	.5485	.5041	.5537	.2707
DT + CVM_{FM}	.3068	.6108	.6804	.5357	.4109	.5036	.1470
DT + CVM_R	.3084	.6139	.7071	.4560	.3082	.3730	.1651
DT + DK	.3515	.6530	.7295	.3870	.2026	.3084	.1147
VW + BM	.2389	.5324	.5985	.4802	.4139	.4899	.2163
VW + CVM_{FM}	.2923	.5970	.6623	.4729	.3880	.4832	.2380
VW + CVM_R	.2883	.5983	.6912	.3853	.2850	.3584	.2237
VW + DK	.3283	.6366	.7104	.3677	.1942	.2998	.0890
BM + CVM_{FM}	.2739	.5708	.6490	.4929	.4018	.4607	.3047
BM + CVM_R	.2402	.5222	.6630	.4290	.3197	.3694	.3567
BM + DK	.3083	.6167	.7092	.3461	.1627	.2500	.1454
DK + CVM_{FM}	.3388	.6443	.7493	.3667	.1931	.2919	.1379
DK + CVM_R	.3169	.6241	.7487	.3217	.1439	.2133	.1505
CVM_{FM}+CVM_R	^{L}.2529	^{L}.5407	.6608	.5787	.5149	.5098	.5358
PSQ+VW +CVM_R+DK	.3834	.6860	.7804	–	–	–	–
Wikipedia (DE-EN)							
PSQ + DT	.3724	.5758	.7258	.8445	.8535	.8110	.7202
PSQ + VW	^{L}.3623	.5935	.7857	.4092	.2630	.2452	.3054
PSQ + BM	.2908	.5106	^{L}.7207	.4956	.4224	.3949	.2850
PSQ + CVM_{FM}	.3718	.5840	.7467	.4017	.2866	.2923	.2061
PSQ + CVM_R	.3843	.6006	.7888	.3841	.1299	.1376	.1298
PSQ + DK	.3894	.6110	.7772	.3309	.0617	.1207	.0221
DT + VW	^{L}.3714	.5997	.7888	.4042	.2551	.2406	.2985
DT + BM	.2993	.5170	^{L}.7243	.4899	.4119	.3894	.2965
DT + CVM_{FM}	.3770	.5873	.7521	.3926	.2711	.2806	.1941
DT + CVM_R	.3870	.6021	.7911	.3809	.1258	.1345	.1621
DT + DK	.4009	.6186	.7814	.3275	.0557	.1168	.0168
VW + BM	^{R}.1337	.3559	.6792	.3805	.2831	.2446	.2981
VW + CVM_{FM}	.1652	.3922	.6952	.3547	.2492	.2079	.2154
VW + CVM_R	^{R}.1663	.3929	.7189	.3618	.1701	.1300	.2890
VW + DK	.2239	.4616	.7331	.2930	.0918	.1119	.0202
BM + CVM_{FM}	.1024	.3006	^{L}.6093	.3648	.2321	.2064	.2097
BM + CVM_R	.1315	^{L}.3372	.6546	.3546	.1541	.1371	.2390
BM + DK	.1893	.4031	.6669	.2804	.0314	.0772	.0211
DK + CVM_{FM}	^{L}.1856	.4023	.6780	.2803	.0267	.0694	.0141
DK + CVM_R	.2243	.4455	.7226	.2785	.0339	.0550	.0073
CVM_{FM}+CVM_R	.1880	.3905	.6652	.3652	.2224	.1986	.2379
DT+VW +CVM_R+DK	.4009	.6352	.8312	–	–	–	–

Table 3: Test results for *combined* CLIR models (see Table 2). Jaccard index J@100, Pearson's ρ, Kendall's τ, and the PCA-based $||PC||$@10 show correlation/orthogonality of a system pair. Preceding superscript letters indicate non-significant difference of the combined system to the ^{L}eft or ^{R}ight component at $p = .001$ using the paired randomization test described in [15].

ferences: the latter expects pairs of comparable documents, thus we employed the first 200 *unfiltered* article words as queries for training. As a result, both models are less similar and the combination shows notable gains compared to the patent task. The similarity measures between *VW* and *BM* on Wikipedia are blurred for an analogous reason: *BM* is trained on the full vocabulary, while *VW* uses correlated feature hashing to lower the memory footprint [2].

6. CONCLUSION

We presented an empirical validation of the conjecture that best results in CLIR system combination are achieved by combining systems that comprise orthogonal information. We measured correlation/orthogonality on various levels, and identified the groups of translation-based models agnostic of ranking, direct ranking optimizers unapt for translation, distributed semantic representations by neural networks, and linear learners based on meta-information. We showed experimentally that combining models from these orthogonal groups outperforms standalone models or combinations of best-performing models.

Acknowledgments. This research was supported in part by DFG grant RI-2221/1-2 "Weakly Supervised Learning of Cross-Lingual Systems".

7. REFERENCES

[1] J. A. Aslam and M. Montague. Models for metasearch. In *SIGIR*, 2001.

[2] B. Bai, J. Weston, D. Grangier, R. Collobert, K. Sadamasa, Y. Qi, O. Chapelle, and K. Weinberger. Learning to rank with (a lot of) word features. *Information Retrieval Journal*, 13(3), 2010.

[3] N. J. Belkin, P. Kantor, E. A. Fox, and J. A. Shaw. Combining the evidence of multiple query representations for information retrieval. *Inf. Process. Manage.*, 31(3):431–448, 1995.

[4] J. Chin, M. Heymans, A. Kojoukhov, J. Lin, and H. Tan. Cross-language information retrieval. Patent Application, 2008. US 2008/0288474 A1.

[5] C. Dyer, A. Lopez, J. Ganitkevitch, J. Weese, F. Ture, P. Blunsom, H. Setiawan, V. Eidelman, and P. Resnik. cdec: A decoder, alignment, and learning framework for finite-state and context-free translation models. In *ACL*, 2010.

[6] S. Goel, J. Langford, and A. L. Strehl. Predictive indexing for fast search. In *NIPS*, 2009.

[7] E. Graf and L. Azzopardi. A methodology for building a patent test collection for prior art search. In *EVIA Workshop*, 2008.

[8] Y. Guo and C. Gomes. Ranking structured documents: A large margin based approach for patent prior art search. In *IJCAI*, 2009.

[9] K. M. Hermann and P. Blunsom. Multilingual models for compositional distributed semantics. In *ACL*, 2014.

[10] K. Järvelin and J. Kekäläinen. Cumulated gain-based evaluation of IR techniques. *ACM Transactions in Information Systems*, 20(4):422–446, 2002.

[11] H. Li. *Learning to Rank for Information Retrieval and Natural Language Processing.* Morgan & Claypool, 2014.

[12] W. Magdy and G. J. Jones. PRES: a score metric for evaluating recall-oriented information retrieval applications. In *SIGIR*, 2010.

[13] J.-Y. Nie. *Cross-Language Information Retrieval.* Morgan & Claypool, 2010.

[14] S. Schamoni, F. Hieber, A. Sokolov, and S. Riezler. Learning translational and knowledge-based similarities from relevance rankings for cross-language retrieval. In *ACL*, 2014.

[15] M. D. Smucker, J. Allan, and B. Carterette. A comparison of statistical significance tests for information retrieval evaluation. In *CIKM*, 2007.

[16] A. Sokolov, L. Jehl, F. Hieber, and S. Riezler. Boosting cross-language retrieval by learning bilingual phrase associations from relevance rankings. In *EMNLP*, 2013.

[17] F. Ture, J. Lin, and D. W. Oard. Looking inside the box: Context-sensitive translation for cross-language information retrieval. In *SIGIR*, 2012.

Tailoring Music Recommendations to Users by Considering Diversity, Mainstreaminess, and Novelty

Markus Schedl
Department of Computational Perception
Johannes Kepler University
Linz, Austria
markus.schedl@jku.at

David Hauger
Department of Computational Perception
Johannes Kepler University
Linz, Austria
david.hauger@jku.at

ABSTRACT

A shortcoming of current approaches for music recommendation is that they consider user-specific characteristics only on a very simple level, typically as some kind of interaction between users and items when employing collaborative filtering. To alleviate this issue, we propose several user features that model aspects of the user's music listening behavior: diversity, mainstreaminess, and novelty of the user's music taste. To validate the proposed features, we conduct a comprehensive evaluation of a variety of music recommendation approaches (stand-alone and hybrids) on a collection of almost 200 million listening events gathered from *Last.fm*. We report first results and highlight cases where our diversity, mainstreaminess, and novelty features can be beneficially integrated into music recommender systems.

Categories and Subject Descriptors

Information systems [**Information retrieval**]: Music recommendation

Keywords

Music Information Retrieval, Music Recommendation, Recommender Systems, User Modeling, Evaluation

1. MOTIVATION AND RELATED WORK

Music recommendation has become a popular research and business topic over the past few years [3, 10]. While the importance of incorporating user characteristics and contextual aspects into recommender systems has been acknowledged many times, among others in [12, 14, 1], work that looks into this matter in the domain of music recommendation is still scarce.

Baltrunas et al. [2] focus on music recommendation in cars, taking into account traffic, road, driver, and weather conditions. Cheng and Shen [4] propose a music recommender that exploits location, listening history, music descriptors, and music popularity trends. Wang et al. [13] propose a mobile music recommender that predicts user activity from time, acceleration, and ambient noise, and selects music from a set of tracks that have been labeled in advance by the user to fit a certain activity. A similar approach is taken by Park et al. [8] who learn emotional states from weather, light level, and temporal data, and again recommend music by matching with pre-labeled tracks. These works concentrate on factors other than the previous music listening behavior when modeling the user, ignoring the potential usefulness of decent features that describe aspects of the listeners' music consumption.[1]

We already investigated in [11] a variety of user demographics to filter results of different music recommendation algorithms. We found significant improvements when tailoring music recommendations to users of similar age, living in the same country (in particular, for the US and Russia), and enjoying either folk, blues, or jazz music. In the work at hand, we develop more elaborate listening-specific user attributes and center our recommendation models around these. We further investigate a content-based recommender and a variety of hybrids and provide detailed results.

In the remainder of the paper we first present the employed music recommendation approaches (Section 2). We then introduce the proposed user characteristics (Section 3), before detailing the used dataset and experimental setup, and discussing the results (Section 4). Conclusions and possible extensions round off this paper (Section 5).

2. RECOMMENDATION APPROACHES

We investigate stand-alone approaches as well as hybrids, which are detailed in the following. Each user u has a listening profile L_u which contains all items listened to — artists in our case. Furthermore, u is assigned a normalized playcount vector $\vec{p}_u$ containing the number of listening events over all items I in the corpus. This vector is normalized so that its Euclidean norm equals 1. For the content-based approaches, each item i is assigned a TF·IDF vector $\vec{w}_i$ which we construct by (i) gathering all *Last.fm* tags and tag weights of i, (ii) treating the tags of i as a document and the corresponding tag weights as term frequencies, (iii) filtering tags that occur for less than 100 items (i.e. $< 0.01\%$ of all

SIGIR'15, August 09 - 13, 2015, Santiago, Chile.

ACM 978-1-4503-3621-5/15/08 ...$15.00.
DOI: http://dx.doi.org/10.1145/2766462.2767763 .

[1] We do not consider as decent features the result of feeding the listening histories of users into a collaborative filtering approach, which has been done before of course.

artists in the corpus), and (iv) computing the ltc variant [6] of TF·IDF based on the described vector space model.

2.1 Stand-alone Approaches

PB: A popularity-based recommender that returns the N items listened to most frequently by the entirety of users in the dataset, irrespective of time.

CF: A user-based collaborative filtering approach that recommends N items listened to by u's nearest neighbors in terms of listening histories; neighbors are identified by computing the Inner product between $\vec{p}_u$ and $\vec{p}_v \; \forall v \in V$, where V is the set of all users excluding u.[2]

IB: A content-based (instance-based) approach that identifies for each training item in L_u its nearest neighbors via maximizing cosine similarity between $\vec{w}_i$ and $\vec{w}_j \; \forall j \in J$, where J is the set of all items excluding i.

LB: An extension to **CF** in that we consider as nearest neighbors of u only users that are located in the same country as u. Although this seems to be only a rough description of user location, **LB** turned out to frequently improve performance when integrating such a location component in a hybrid approach.

RB: A baseline that randomly picks users and recommends N artists they listened to.

For **CF**, **IB**, and **LB**, we investigate two aggregation functions to fuse the recommendations contributed by the nearest neighbors,[3] in case they are overlapping: arithmetic mean or maximum between the similarity scores of each item that is recommended by more than 1 neighbor.

2.2 Hybrid Approaches

Leaving aside **RB**, we create hybrid systems that integrate combinations of **PB**, **CF**, **IB**, and **LB**. Fusing the results of all recommenders involved in such a hybrid system is performed by rank aggregation applying Borda counts [5] on the similarity scores of items recommended by each involved approach.[4] This fusion technique has already proven successful for multimodal music recommendation [7]. In total, we investigate the following 14 approaches, again, focusing on algorithmic combinations that performed superior in preliminary experiments:
RB, **PB**, $\mathbf{CF_{mean}}$, $\mathbf{CF_{max}}$, $\mathbf{IB_{mean}}$, $\mathbf{IB_{max}}$, $\mathbf{LB_{mean}}$, $\mathbf{PB{+}CF_{mean}}$, $\mathbf{PB{+}CF_{max}}$, $\mathbf{PB{+}IB_{mean}}$, $\mathbf{PB{+}LB_{mean}}$, $\mathbf{CF_{mean}{+}IB_{mean}}$, $\mathbf{CF_{mean}{+}LB_{mean}}$, and $\mathbf{PB{+}CF_{mean}{+}IB_{mean}}$.

3. USER CHARACTERISTICS

In the following, we define the proposed listening-centric user features, we base our experiments on. We also indicate how we split the users in the dataset according to their feature values.

3.1 Diversity

We define diversity of a user's music taste in two ways: based on how often the user listens to each track in her collection on average and based on the distinct number of genre tags in a user's listening profile. The former variant is computed as $D\_PC_u = P_u / |L_u|$ where P_u denotes the total number of playcounts of u and L_u refers to the set of unique items u listened to. We create two user sets `US_D_PC_[l|h]` by splitting users at their median D_PC value of 2.93 into showing low or high taste diversity, respectively. To compute diversity based on the second definition, we first index all *Last.fm* tags assigned to the items in L_u through a dictionary of almost 2,000 genres fetched from *Freebase*. This naturally results in a set of unique genre tags G_u that describes u's music taste. Diversity is then simply computed as $D\_genres_u = |G_u|$. Users are split into 3 categories `US_D_genres_[l|m|h]`, the borders between them being defined at thirds of accumulated D_genres values.

3.2 Mainstreaminess

We also describe users in terms of the degree to which they prefer music items that are currently popular or rather ignore such trends. We hence coin the term "mainstreaminess" and define the respective user feature as follows. We first define the "mainstream" as a distribution of relative item frequencies among the global set of listening events. To this end, a global playcount vector $\vec{p}$ is defined analogously to $\vec{p}_u$ in Section 2, but on the overall set of listening events and normalized by the sum P of all listening events. The mainstreaminess M_u of a user u then relates the user playcounts to these global playcounts: $M_u = \sum_{p_i \in \vec{p}} \sqrt{\frac{P_{up_i}}{P_u} \cdot \frac{P_{p_i}}{P}}$, where P_{up_i} is the frequency user u listens to each item p_i in vector $\vec{p}$, P_u and P_{p_i} is the total playcount of user u and item p_i, respectively. To account for temporal dynamics in the mainstream and measure to which extent users follow current trends, we introduce a time window which we set to 6 months in our experiments.[5] Considering only listening events within the current window t naturally extends the definition of M_u to M_{ut} of user u in time window t. Shifting t along the temporally ordered listening events of user u and computing the arithmetic mean over all M_{ut} values yields again a scalar value describing u's mainstreaminess. For our experiments, users are categorized into 3 classes for each definition (global and 6-month-average): `US_M_global_[l|m|h]` and `US_M_avg_6m_[l|m|h]`; the borders between them are again defined at thirds of accumulated mainstreaminess values.

3.3 Novelty

This feature models the inclination of user u to listen to unknown music. Splitting u's listening history into time slots of again 6 months, we calculate the percentage of new items listened to, i.e. items appearing for the first time in u's listening history. The novelty N_{ut} of u's listening events in time window t is defined as $N_{ut} = \frac{|\{l \in L_{ut} \wedge l \notin L_{ux} \forall x < t\}|}{|L_{ut}|}$, where L_{ut} is the entirety of items u listened to in time window t, including duplicates, and $l \notin L_{ux} \forall x < t$ denotes all listening events not listened to by u at any time before t. Averaging over all time slots user u was active in, we obtain u's overall novelty score N_u. We again investigate user sets

[2] As a matter of fact, we omit from $\vec{p}(u)$ the items that occur in the test set.

[3] In case of **CF** and **LB**, nearest neighbors refer to users; in case of **IB**, they refer to items.

[4] We also investigated maximum, mean, sum, and product, but Borda outperformed these in the majority of cases in preliminary experiments.

[5] Preliminary analyses of the data evidenced that a time window of 6 months represents a good trade-off between computational complexity and stability, still incorporating important music trends.

categorized at accumulated thirds into low, medium, and high novelty: US_N_avg_6m_[l|m|h].

4. EVALUATION

To investigate if tailoring music recommendations to listeners within a certain group according to our diversity, mainstreaminess, and novelty definitions improves recommendation results, we perform the following experiments.

4.1 Dataset and Experimental Setup

The used dataset covers 191,108,462 listening events by 16,429 active *Last.fm* users, who listened to 9,163,123 unique tracks from 2,372,601 unique albums by 1,140,014 unique artists. The average number of listening events per user is 11,603 ± 7,130. We investigate 14 recommendation methods (7 stand-alone and 7 hybrids, cf. Section 2) and 14 user categories (cf. Section 3). For each combination of recommendation approach and user category, we perform 5-fold cross-validation on a per-user basis. To this end, we split the entire listening history of each user into a training set containing 80% unique artists and a test set containing the remaining 20%, and perform five experiments, iterating over all five permutations.

4.2 Results and Discussion

We compute average precision, recall, and F1-score as performance measures, where we compute the arithmetic mean over all users. We obtain precision at different recall levels by varying the number of recommended artists between 1 and 1000. Note that the highest achievable recall for **PB** and **CF** is roughly 39%, because of the frequent case that some artists are listened to by only a single user, are hence never correctly recommended. In the following tables, we show for all user categories the best performing approaches in terms of precision, recall, and F1-score.[6] Tables 1 and 2 show the results for the two diversity definitions, Tables 3 and 4, respectively, for the global and 6-month-average of the mainstreaminess definition, and Table 5 for the novelty using a 6-month-window. Statistically significant results, identified by employing the Mann-Whitney U test for equal means of samples [9], are marked with asterisks. For comparative reasons, Table 6 shows the performance measures for all approaches and the entire user set. Comparing the results over all user sets and methods, we make the following observations:

- Grouping users according to the introduced features and performing recommendations within these groups generally tends to outperform recommenders working on the entire user set, in particular, in terms of recall (12 out of 14 cases).

- For all user categories, recommendations based on popularity (**PB**) seem to play a crucial role; however, solely when combined with other approaches. The only case where **PB** alone performs roughly on par is for the user group with high global mainstreaminess, which is trivial to explain.

- The content-based recommender (**IB**) alone performs poorly, independent of user set and performance measure. In contrast, an **IB** component is integrated in the top performing recommenders in terms of recall, in 50% of the user groups. When combined with other methods, it seems that **IB** nicely diversifies the recommendations. This becomes especially evident for users with medium and high inclination to explore novel music, in contrast to low-novelty-users for whom **IB** does not improve results.

- While in general no substantial difference in results could be identified between the two mainstreaminess definitions (M_global and M_avg_6m), all investigated recommendation methods underperform for users with low mainstreaminess, most of which not even beat the **RB** baseline.

- The genre-based diversity definition (D_genres) outperforms the playcount-based one (D_PC) in terms of F1-score, except for very low levels of diversity. By far the highest recall levels could be achieved for users with low diversity.

- Integrating location information (**LB**) only yields an improvement for users with a high global mainstreaminess. In combination with the popularity-based recommender (**PB**), these users seem to largely enjoy music currently popular among other users in the same country.

[6] Results for all approaches are available on request.

Table 1: Mean average precision, recall, and F-score for (significantly) best performing stand-alone and hybrid methods on user categories US_D_PC.

US_D_PC_h			
Method	Precision	Recall	F-score
RB	1.34	6.35	1.85
$PB + CF_{max}$	3.80	17.38	∗**5.82**
$PB + LB_{mean}$	2.86	∗**18.91**	4.46
$CF_{mean} + IB_{mean}$	∗**6.18**	2.43	2.80

US_D_PC_l			
Method	Precision	Recall	F-score
RB	1.78	5.05	2.36
CF_{max}	**10.23**	2.33	2.95
$PB + CF_{mean} + IB_{mean}$	3.54	∗**23.30**	**5.60**

Table 2: Results for user categories US_D_genres.

US_D_genres_h			
Method	Precision	Recall	F-score
RB	2.62	2.95	1.94
$PB + CF_{max}$	∗**9.83**	4.93	4.99
$PB + CF_{mean} + IB_{mean}$	6.08	∗**13.65**	∗**7.75**

US_D_genres_m			
Method	Precision	Recall	F-score
RB	1.86	2.29	1.38
CF_{max}	∗**6.43**	4.10	3.92
$PB + CF_{max}$	4.18	15.84	∗**6.50**
$PB + CF_{mean} + IB_{mean}$	3.28	∗**21.06**	5.56

US_D_genres_l			
Method	Precision	Recall	F-score
RB	0.76	2.83	0.84
CF_{max}	**4.17**	8.12	3.65
$PB + IB_{mean}$	1.32	∗**31.20**	2.50
$PB + CF_{mean}$	3.32	16.03	∗**4.41**

5. CONCLUSIONS AND OUTLOOK

We proposed three computational features that describe a user's music taste: diversity, mainstreaminess, and novelty. We performed first experiments investigating to which

Table 3: Results for user categories US_M_global.

US_M_global_h			
Method	Precision	Recall	F-score
RB	3.78	8.35	4.86
PB	10.35	* **14.62**	7.59
CF_{max}	* **13.28**	3.90	5.61
$PB + LB_{mean}$	8.72	13.20	* **9.66**

US_M_global_m			
Method	Precision	Recall	F-score
RB	1.37	2.58	1.21
$PB + IB_{mean}$	2.00	* **26.00**	3.58
$PB + CF_{mean}$	4.93	12.70	* **5.12**
$PB + CF_{mean} + IB_{mean}$	* **8.25**	0.86	1.48

US_M_global_l			
Method	Precision	Recall	F-score
RB	**5.15**	5.83	**4.56**
$PB + LB_{mean}$	1.74	**10.67**	2.25

Table 4: Results for user categories US_M_avg_6m.

US_M_avg_6m_h			
Method	Precision	Recall	F-score
RB	3.60	3.82	2.54
CF_{max}	* **10.14**	10.94	6.27
$PB + CF_{max}$	7.53	* **18.73**	* **9.93**

US_M_avg_6m_m			
Method	Precision	Recall	F-score
RB	1.50	5.79	2.18
PB	**5.93**	10.07	3.26
$PB + CF_{max}$	3.56	* **18.89**	5.51
$PB + CF_{mean} + IB_{mean}$	5.03	8.90	**5.55**

US_M_avg_6m_l			
Method	Precision	Recall	F-score
RB	**3.02**	7.83	**3.42**
$PB + LB_{mean}$	2.23	**14.77**	2.87

Table 5: Results for user categories US_N_avg_6m.

US_N_avg_6m_h			
Method	Precision	Recall	F-score
RB	1.12	4.57	1.30
PB	**3.89**	10.28	**3.40**
$PB + CF_{mean} + IB_{mean}$	3.51	* **11.96**	3.30

US_N_avg_6m_m			
Method	Precision	Recall	F-score
RB	1.78	2.66	1.34
CF_{max}	* **6.58**	4.96	3.73
$PB + CF_{mean} + IB_{mean}$	3.60	* **23.31**	* **5.83**

US_N_avg_6m_l			
Method	Precision	Recall	F-score
RB	3.66	6.54	3.51
PB	**4.27**	9.48	3.91
$PB + CF_{mean}$	4.00	12.64	**3.97**
$PB + LB_{mean}$	3.66	**13.38**	3.97

Table 6: Results for all approaches on the entire user base.

Method	Precision	Recall	F-score
RB	1.55	4.49	1.58
PB	4.82	11.83	4.26
CF_{mean}	5.41	9.26	4.42
CF_{max}	5.22	9.03	4.20
IB_{mean}	1.82	5.09	1.45
IB_{max}	0.44	3.25	0.55
LB_{mean}	2.59	4.74	2.22
$PB + IB_{mean}$	3.95	11.30	3.71
$PB + CF_{mean}$	**6.35**	10.00	**5.14**
$PB + CF_{max}$	6.34	9.70	4.96
$PB + LB_{mean}$	4.58	9.38	4.02
$CF_{mean} + IB_{mean}$	4.51	10.74	4.13
$CF_{mean} + LB_{mean}$	4.91	8.52	4.01
$PB + CF_{mean} + IB_{mean}$	4.99	**13.85**	4.75

extent music recommendations can be tailored when categorizing users according to these features. Comparative experiments on a variety of stand-alone and hybrid recommendation algorithms identified several algorithms that should be preferred when addressing certain user groups. Summarizing our findings, we conclude that hybrid methods generally outperform stand-alone recommenders, irrespective of user group. For users with high mainstreaminess, a popularity component is particularly important, ideally coupled with location-based filtering. Content-based recommenders should not be used as stand-alone, but recommendations benefit when they are integrated with collaborative filtering or popularity recommenders.

While most results may not seem too surprising, the presented experiments serve as a good starting point for further investigations on tailoring music recommendations according to user characteristics. We noticed that the used dataset is biased towards frequent users of *Last.fm*. We will thus assess if results generalize to less active listeners. In addition, we plan to directly integrate diversity, mainstreaminess, and novelty as user factors into matrix factorization algorithms.

Acknowledgments

This research is supported by the EU-FP7 project no. 601166 and by the Austrian Science Fund (FWF): P25655.

6. REFERENCES

[1] G. Adomavicius and A. Tuzhilin. *Recommender Systems Handbook*, chapter Context-Aware Recommender Systems, pages 217–253. Springer, 2011.

[2] L. Baltrunas, M. Kaminskas, B. Ludwig, O. Moling, F. Ricci, K.-H. Lüke, and R. Schwaiger. InCarMusic: Context-Aware Music Recommendations in a Car. In *Proc. EC-Web*, 2011.

[3] O. Celma. *Music Recommendation and Discovery – The Long Tail, Long Fail, and Long Play in the Digital Music Space*. Springer, 2010.

[4] Z. Cheng and J. Shen. Just-for-Me: An Adaptive Personalization System for Location-Aware Social Music Recommendation. In *Proc. ICMR*, Glasgow, UK, April 2014.

[5] J.-C. de Borda. Mémoire sur les élections au scrutin. *Histoire de l'Académie Royale des Sciences*, 1781.

[6] F. Debole and F. Sebastiani. Supervised Term Weighting for Automated Text Categorization. In *Proc. SAC*, 2003.

[7] M. Kaminskas, F. Ricci, and M. Schedl. Location-aware Music Recommendation Using Auto-Tagging and Hybrid Matching. In *Proc. RecSys*, Hong Kong, China, 2013.

[8] H.-S. Park, J.-O. Yoo, and S.-B. Cho. A context-aware music recommendation system using fuzzy bayesian networks with utility theory. In *FSKD. LNCS (LNAI)*, pages 970–979. Springer, 2006.

[9] B. Prajapati, M. Dunne, and R. Armstrong. Sample Size Estimation and Statistical Power Analyses. *Optometry Today*, 16(7), 2010.

[10] M. Schedl, E. Gómez, and J. Urbano. Music information retrieval: Recent developments and applications. *Foundations and Trends in Information Retrieval*, 8(2–3):127–261, 2014.

[11] M. Schedl, D. Hauger, K. Farrahi, and M. Tkalčič. On the Influence of User Characteristics on Music Recommendation. In *Proc. ECIR*, Vienna, Austria, 2015.

[12] Y. Shi, M. Larson, and A. Hanjalic. Collaborative Filtering Beyond the User-Item Matrix: A Survey of the State of the Art and Future Challenges. *ACM Comput. Surv.*, 47(1):3:1–3:45, May 2014.

[13] X. Wang, D. Rosenblum, and Y. Wang. Context-aware mobile music recommendation for daily activities. In *Proc. ACM Multimedia*, 2012.

[14] Yuan Cao Zhang, Diarmuid O Seaghdha, Daniele Quercia, Tamas Jambor. Auralist: Introducing Serendipity into Music Recommendation. In *Proc. WSDM*, 2012.

Challenges of Mathematical Information Retrieval in the NTCIR-11 Math Wikipedia Task

Moritz Schubotz
Database Systems and Information Management Group, TU Berlin, Germany
schubotz@tu-berlin.de

Volker Markl
Database Systems and Information Management Group, TU Berlin, Germany
volker.markl@tu-berlin.de

Abdou Youssef
Department of Computer Science, The George Washington University, USA
ayoussef@gwu.edu

Howard S. Cohl
Applied and Computational Mathematics Div., National Inst. of Standards and Technology, USA
howard.cohl@nist.gov

ABSTRACT

Mathematical Information Retrieval concerns retrieving information related to a particular mathematical concept. The NTCIR-11 Math Task develops an evaluation test collection for document sections retrieval of scientific articles based on human generated topics. Those topics involve a combination of formula patterns and keywords. Another task in NTCIR-11 is the optional Wikipedia Task, which provides a test collection for retrieval of individual mathematical formula from Wikipedia based on search topics that contain exactly one formula pattern. We developed a framework for automatic query generation and immediate evaluation. This paper discusses our dataset preparation, our topic generation and evaluation methods, and summarizes the results of the participants, with a special focus on the Wikipedia Task.

1. INTRODUCTION

Math Information Retrieval (MIR) is a growing field. Recent publications (e.g., [1, 6, 10]) show that there is a significant demand for enhancement in Mathematical Knowledge Management. In order to compare different approaches and measure their performance, test collections are needed. At the CICM 2012 conference in Bremen, Germany, the first "MIR happening" took place with two participants, 10,000 arXiv documents and a dataset size of 293 MB. In 2013, the NTCIR-10 Math pilot task [2] for MIR attracted 6 participants and used 100,000 arXiv documents with a dataset size of 63GB. Based on the gathered experience, MIR qualified for a main task at NTCIR-11 [3] which took place in 2014 with 8 participants and 8 million document sections of 174GB in total. Additionally, the newly introduced Wikipedia Task was appreciated by the participants. We expect that the automated feedback and evaluation framework will lower the entrance level for participants and attract even more participants in the future. In this first section, we provide a general introduction to MIR, list some applications of MIR, and explain why MIR is fundamentally different from other IR tasks, such as text retrieval and XMLretrieval. In Section 2, we describe how the Wikipedia dataset was prepared and augmented. In Section 3 and 4, we describe the query design and evaluation process respectively. In Section 5, we present the participating teams and the performance their MIR systems. In Section 6 we give a future outlook for the Wikipedia Task.

Publication rights licensed to ACM. ACM acknowledges that this contribution was authored or co-authored by an employee, contractor or affiliate of the US Government. As such, the Government retains a nonexclusive, royalty-free right to publish or reproduce this article, or to allow others to do so, for Government purposes only.
SIGIR'15, August 09-13, 2015, Santiago, Chile.

ACM 978-1-4503-3621-5/15/08.
DOI: http://dx.doi.org/10.1145/2766462.2767787.

Introduction to Math Information Retrieval

The use cases for MIR are diverse. They include applicable theorem search, plagiarism detection, related work search, patent search, and search in Excel spreadsheets [5]. Some of the fundamental concepts that relate back to tree structure search can be used for code-search or search for chemical formulae.

For the Wikipedia Task, the focus is on information needs that involve mathematics that is naturally expressed using mathematical expressions. With regard to the aforementioned applications, those information needs can be expressed as mathematical expressions, combination of expressions and keywords, or keywords only. While the main task uses all of these combinations to retrieve documents, the Wikipedia Task provides exactly one formula per topic to describe an information need.

2. DATASET & FEEDBACK TO WIKIPEDIA

The test collection used at NTCIR-10 in 2013 was based on a random selection of arXiv articles converted via LaTeXML to HTML5 [8]. The arXiv is a vast and expanding source of knowledge for researchers and experts in highly specialized domains. However, neither math search engine developers (participants) nor the assessors that evaluate the search engine results usually are domain experts in all the topics addressed in the arXiv publications. Some topics discussed in the research papers are so specialized that it becomes impossible for participants to get even a preliminary idea of the content and to decide on the relevance of a formula with respect to a topic (i.e., the underlying information need). This fact adds additional complexity to debugging and testing of the Math search engines. In contrast to the arXiv

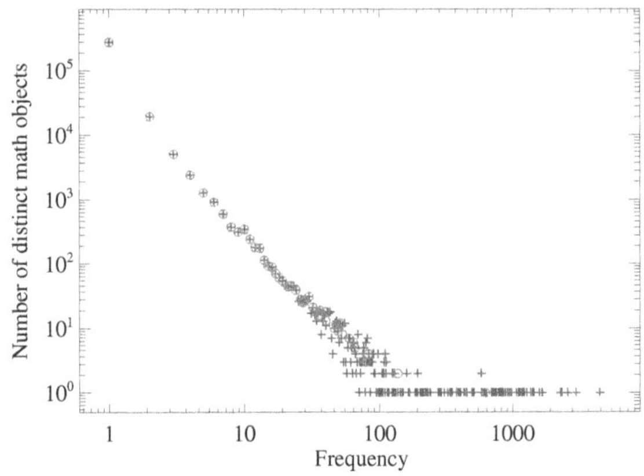

Figure 1: Distribution (blue "+") and mean (red "o") of the number of distinct formulae and their frequencies. For example the expression n occurs 2988 times and there are about 280 000 formulae that occur only once.

Figure 2: Density of the topics with regard to the frequency of seed formula $f(t)$ and the number of query variables in the topic $q(t)$. The blackest box corresponds to the highest count (up to 41 topics) and the lightest grey corresponds to only 1 topic.

dataset, the Wikipedia encyclopaedia contains most of the mathematical world knowledge explained in simple terms. While this knowledge is not sufficient for new research, it is perfectly suitable as a test corpus for math search competitions. This knowledge simplifies debugging and testing of the math search engines and enables the participants to test their systems on a dataset that is easier to understand and contains all formulae they are already familiar with. The English Wikipedia contains about 30k encyclopaedic articles with mathematical formula. Those are written using the TeX-like input format texvc. Even though the syntax in texvc is restricted and does not allow to write Turing complete programs, as it is possible with TeX, TeX is neither the optimal way to represent Mathematics on the web nor to search for formula. In contrast, MathML was designed to serve the aforementioned purposes.

Schubotz and Wicke [7] compare different conversion methods and identify the LaTeXML converter as the most reasonable solution with content MathML support for Wikipedia. A majority of the participating systems use content for the search task. Therefore, both tasks (arXiv and Wikipedia) use LaTeXML to convert the original user input to MathML with parallel content and presentation markup and the original input as annotation.

In order to generate stable and unique references to each individual formula used in Wikipedia, we created an unique index, from which one can derive many interesting statistics about the usage of mathematics within Wikipedia. For example, Figure 1 shows the frequency distributions of the formulae. One use case we published at `formulasearchengine.com` is an auto-completion list for TeX commands based on the usage statistics that we gathered by tokenizing the frequency ordered formulae. People editing Wikipedia articles about math with mobile devices will benefit from this feature.

3. TOPIC DESIGN

From our experience with the Math pilot task at NTCIR-10, we draw the following conclusions: 1) for each query there should be at least one relevant hit in the dataset; 2) the semantics of query variables should be well-defined; 3) only the information that would be exposed to a MIR system should be communicated to the participants; 4) the relevance criteria for each topic should be independent of the topic author and assessor. While the main task addressed these issues with human intuition, we chose a different approach for the Wikipedia Task that does not involve humans.

We developed a program that generates queries in three simple steps. At first, the so called seed formula is chosen based on random selection from our mathindex. In a second step, we inject query variables. In contrast to the main task, where humans chose a meaningful name for the query variable, we call our query variables $x_0, x_1, \ldots$. Finally, we generate the NTCIR-11 XML Topics [1] using LaTeXML. Our relevance criterion is to find a formula similar to the seed. By our naming convention for the query variable and the absence of a topic title we ensure that no information is exposed to the participants that is not intended to be used according to the topic specification, i.e., MIR systems cannot use the name of query variables for relevance ranking. Our method generates two meta-information pieces $f(t)$ and $q(t)$ for each topic t. Here, $f(t)$ is the frequency, that indicates how many exact matches (based on exact matches on the original TeX input) for each seed are contained in the dataset, and $q(t)$ is the number of query variables used. This allows for an *a priori* classification of the search topics based on f and q. For simplicity, we partition the set of generated topics T (Figure 2) into the 4 following groups: *Easy topics* without query variables and exactly one precise match $E = \{t \in T : f(t) = q(t) - 1 = 1\}$; *variable topics* with query variables but only one exact match for the underlying seed $V = \{t \in T : f(t) = 1 \land q(t) > 0\}$; *frequent topics* without query variables but with non-unique seeds $F = \{t \in T : q(t) = 0 \land f(t) > 1\}$ and *hard topics* that contain query variables and non-unique seeds $H = \{t \in T : f(t) > 1 \land q(t) > 0\}$. For the set of queries used in NTCIR-11 the following cardinalities were given: $|E| = 41, |V| = 27, |F| = 24, |H| = 8 \Rightarrow |T| = 100$.

4. EVALUATION PROCESS

For retrieval tasks with one known good result, a typical evaluation measure is the mean reciprocal rank (mrr) [9]. In addition, our automatic evaluation software calculates mean average precision in the first k hits for different levels of k, and counts the *number of found seeds* referred to as *success*

Participant	runs total	runs distinct	page total	page easy	page frequent	page variable	page hard	formula total	formula easy	formula frequent	formula variable	formula hard
TUB Technische Universität Berlin (Germany)	4	4	**91**	100	96	74	87	**87**	100	92	70	63
			73	94	30	90	46	**68**	87	25	86	30
KWARC Jacobs University Bremen (Germnay)	1	1	**75**	83	75	70	50	-	-	-	-	-
			82	95	44	97	67	-	-	-	-	-
RMHS Richard Montgomery High School (USA)	1	1	**48**	54	46	40	50	-	-	-	-	-
			02	01	00	03	01	-	-	-	-	-
RIT Rochester Institute of Technology (USA)	17	4	**88**	98	79	89	63	**78**	95	50	81	63
			80	96	31	92	83	**86**	94	47	96	83
MIAS Masaryk University (Czech republic)	19	4	**65**	97	92	15	-	**63**	95	83	15	13
			76	93	46	83	-	**81**	91	71	83	01
TUW Vienna University of Technology (Austria)	5	3	**97**	100	100	93	88	**93**	100	96	89	63
			82	97	50	96	54	**88**	96	72	94	71
NII National Institute of Informatics (Japan)	9	4	**97**	98	100	93	100	**94**	98	96	89	88
			76	99	49	82	67	**77**	89	92	78	48

Table 1: This table lists the best performing runs, with regard to (success upper number in %) and mrr (lower number in %) with page and formula-centric evaluation methods. Furthermore, we have displayed the individual results with respect to the query categories *easy*, *frequent*, *variable* and *hard*.

in the rest of this paper, which corresponds to the recall for $k \to \infty$. The evaluation tool performs two types of evaluations, a *page-centric* evaluation that regards a hit as correct if the seeding page was found, and the *formula-centric* evaluation, which assumes that a hit is correct, if a formula with exactly the same TeX input was found. To avoid over-fitting, only aggregated results are displayed as feedback to the participants. Thus the participants get feedback on how their systems performed on average for all topics, but they do not know how the systems performed on an individual topic or on a topic category. We observed that the intermediate feedback feature was highly appreciated by the participants, because it helped them to identify and fix bugs in their software. We observed that participants submitted 3 to 5 times until they were satisfied with the results. Some participants submitted subsequent runs under different names. This justifies the reports by the participants that the submission system helped to improve MIR systems. Some teams have improved their mrr by 50% or more.

5. PARTICIPANTS AND EVALUATION RESULTS

We had seven participants from five countries and in total 56 runs with about 2 million hits. The results of the evaluation described in the former section are listed in Table 1. A detailed overview of the participants and their MIR approaches can be found in [3]. The best result with regard to success was submitted by TUW and NII. Both runs found 97% of the topics according to the page-centric evaluation. With mrr = 82% the ranking of TUW is slightly better compared to Nii (74.5%). For the formula-centric evaluation Nii has the best success with 94% and mrr = 82%. The best TUW run achieves a mrr value of 88% at a sucess rate of 93%. Table 1 shows that there is a high correlation between the topic category and the system performance. Furthermore, all teams that submitted more than one run got very good results for the easy topics. The difference between page and formula exact evaluation is not significant.

As shown in Figure 3, the performance results from different teams vary more than different runs submitted by the same team. The MIaS team runs (circles) show the well known behavior that mrr (or precision) decays with growing success (or recall respectively).

We observe that all topics except one were found by two or more participants, even if the formula exact evaluation method is used. The known good result for query 99 $\frac{?x_0}{?x_1}$ that can be verbalized as "any fraction", was found only by one team at rank 8983. More interesting is that 4 teams assigned a high rank to the result $\frac{\frac{x}{y}}{\frac{y+z}{y}}$ from the Harmonic progression page in contrast to the first mathematical expression $\frac{1}{2}$ from the Wikipedia article titled fraction that was not ranked very high.

6. CONCLUSION

We discussed the NTCIR-11 Math Wikipedia Task that lowers the entrance barrier for new participants to Math Information Retrieval and broadens the scope of NTCIR Math tasks to encyclopedic applications. We presented three main technology contributions, integrated in the MediaWiki MathSearch extension. First, we developed methods to convert Wikipedia dumps (in any language) to the main task data format including content and presentation MathML. Second, we developed a method for automated search pattern generation with example hits. Third, our extension provides a fully automated evaluation framework with real time feedback at submission time and a comparative evaluation for multiple submissions including hit pooling.

For the future, we plan to continue development and improvement of the platform with regard to the following aspects. We will allow for user feedback for results with regard to relevance for the entries submitted by the systems. While it's questionable that volunteers can be found to evaluate the results, participants can evaluate their own results which will be helpful for system tuning. Furthermore, we will display some basic similarity scores for each hit and will allow users to create their own search topics. The queries used for NTCIR-11 will stay available for training and testing. A query exact feedback will be displayed for new submissions for the old topics. We intend to attract more participants and found a Math Search interest group made of mathematicians, scientists and people from the traditional information retrieval community. Due to the continuously available por-

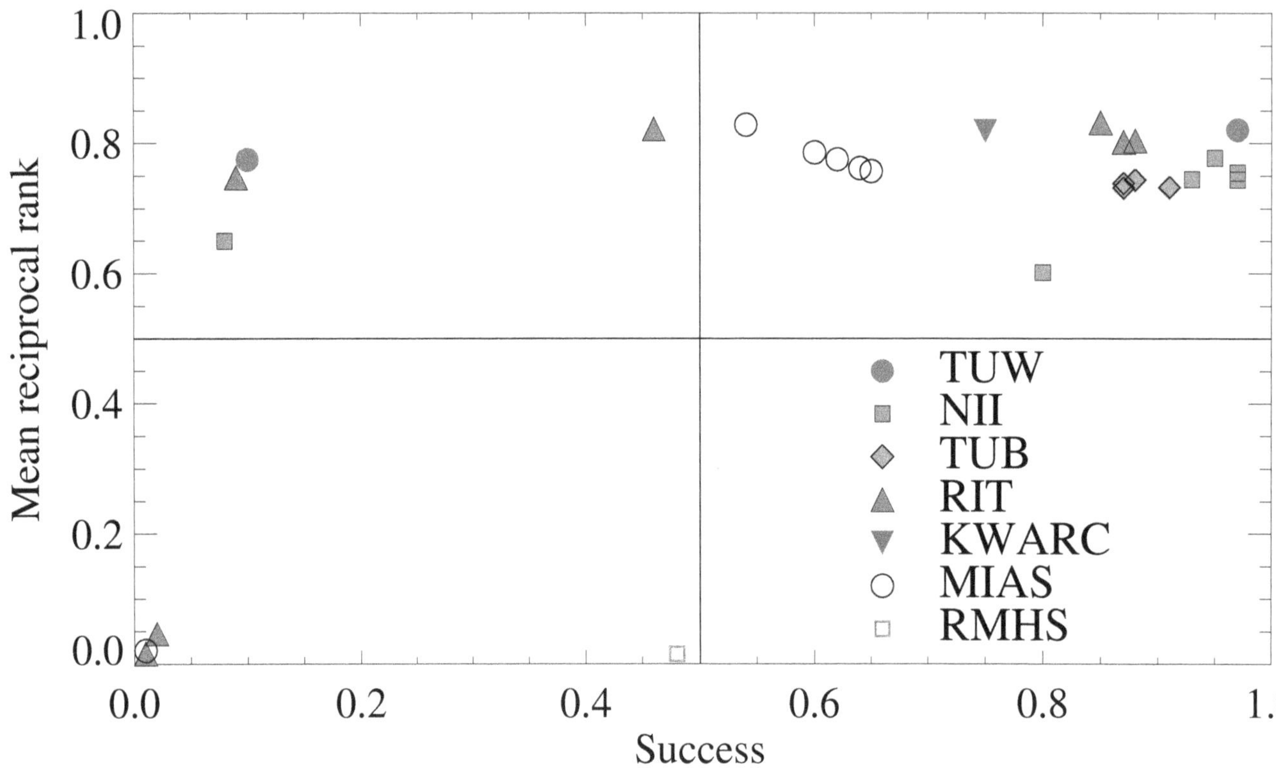

Figure 3: Page-centric evaluation: The Figure shows all runs with regard to mean reciprocal rank and sucess. For example, the runs of the MIAS team show a typical trade-off between mean reciprocal rank and success. Other teams reported that they used the automated feedback from the submission system to fix implementation problems. This increased mrr and sucess at the same time.

tal, participants will be able to test new features whenever they are ready. We will publish new queries on demand, and synchronize participants with the NTCIR events.

Acknowledgments. The authors acknowledge the help and support of Akiko Aizawa, Michael Kohlhase, Goran Topic and Marcus Leich. This work has been supported through grants by the German Science Foundation (DFG) as FOR 1306 Stratosphere and by the German Ministry for Education and Research as Berlin Big Data Center BBDC (funding mark 01IS14013A).

7. REFERENCES

[1] Formats for topics and submissions for the math2 task at ntcir-11. Technical report, NTCIR, 2014.

[2] Akiko Aizawa, Michael Kohlhase, and Iadh Ounis. NTCIR-10 Math Pilot Task Overview. In *Proceedings of the 10th NTCIR Conference on Evaluation of Information Access Technologies*, pages 654–661, Tokyo, Japan, 2013.

[3] Akiko Aizawa, Michael Kohlhase, Iadh Ounis, and Moritz Schubotz. NTCIR-11 Math-2 Task Overview. In *Proceedings of the 11th NTCIR Conference on Evaluation of Information Access Technologies*, pages 88–98, 2014.

[4] Michael Kohlhase, Helena Mihaljevic-Brandt, Wolfram Sperber, and Olaf Teschke. Mathematical Formula Search. pages 56–57, September 2013.

[5] Michael Kohlhase, Corneliu Prodescu, and Christian Liguda. Xlsearch: A search engine for spreadsheets. In Simon Thorne et. al, editor, *Proceedings of the EuSpRIG 2013 Conference "Spreadsheet Risk Management". July 4-5, London, United Kingdom*, pages 47–58. Five Star Printing Ldt, Claydon, 2013.

[6] Matthias S. Reichenbach, Anurag Agarwal, and Richard Zanibbi. Rendering expressions to improve accuracy of relevance assessment for math search. *Proceedings of the 37th international ACM SIGIR conference on Research & development in information retrieval - SIGIR '14*, pages 851–854, 2014.

[7] Moritz Schubotz and Gabriel Wicke. Mathoid: Robust, scalable, fast and accessible math rendering for wikipedia. In Stephen Watt et al., editor, *Intelligent Computer Mathematics*, volume 8543 of *Lecture Notes in Computer Science*, pages 224–235. Springer International Publishing, 2014.

[8] Heinrich Stamerjohanns, Michael Kohlhase, Deyan Ginev, Catalin David, and Bruce Miller. Transforming large collections of scientific publications to xml. *Mathematics in Computer Science*, 3(3):299–307, 2010.

[9] Ellen M. Voorhees. The TREC-8 Question Answering Track Report. *TREC*, 1999.

[10] Keita Del Valle Wangari, Richard Zanibbi, and Anurag Agarwal. Discovering real-world use cases for a multimodal math search interface. *Proceedings of the 37th international ACM SIGIR conference on Research & development in information retrieval - SIGIR '14*, pages 947–950, 2014.

Probabilistic Multileave for Online Retrieval Evaluation

Anne Schuth[1] Robert-Jan Bruintjes[2] Fritjof Büttner[2] Joost van Doorn[2]
Carla Groenland[2] Harrie Oosterhuis[2] Cong-Nguyen Tran[2] Bas Veeling[2]
Jos van der Velde[2] Roger Wechsler[2] David Woudenberg[2] Maarten de Rijke[3]

[1]anne.schuth@uva.nl [2]firstname.lastname@student.uva.nl [3]derijke@uva.nl

University of Amsterdam, Amsterdam, The Netherlands

ABSTRACT

Online evaluation methods for information retrieval use implicit signals such as clicks from users to infer preferences between rankers. A highly sensitive way of inferring these preferences is through interleaved comparisons. Recently, interleaved comparisons methods that allow for simultaneous evaluation of more than two rankers have been introduced. These so-called multileaving methods are even more sensitive than their interleaving counterparts. Probabilistic interleaving—whose main selling point is the potential for reuse of historical data—has no multileaving counterpart yet. We propose *probabilistic multileave* and empirically show that it is highly sensitive and unbiased. An important implication of this result is that historical interactions with multileaved comparisons can be reused, allowing for ranker comparisons that need much less user interaction data. Furthermore, we show that our method, as opposed to earlier sensitive multileaving methods, scales well when the number of rankers increases.

Categories and Subject Descriptors

H.3 [**Information Storage and Retrieval**]: H.3.3 Information Search and Retrieval

Keywords

Information retrieval; Evaluation; Interleaved comparisons; Multileaved comparisons

1. INTRODUCTION AND RELATED WORK

Search engines are constantly being improved upon. Engineers may propose changes to a ranker and such changes need be evaluated. Evaluation should not only compare alternative rankers against the current best ranker, but also against each other as these comparisons are important for guiding ranker development efforts. Pairwise preferences between rankers can be obtained in several ways. Traditional offline metrics based on relevance assessments can be computed [2] in a TREC-style evaluation setting [20].

Besides being expensive and time consuming, assessors' judgments do not necessarily agree with actual users' preferences [16]. In contrast, online metrics infer preferences directly from user interactions [12]. Interleaved comparison methods do so while being one to two orders of magnitude more sensitive than A/B testing [1, 9, 10, 15]. An interleaving method presents a user with a ranked result list that contains documents from two rankers and estimates user preferences by interpreting interactions with the interleaved list. Many variations of interleaving methods exist. *Balanced interleave* (BI) [11] randomly selects a ranker to start with and then, alternatingly, documents that have not been picked are picked from the two input rankings. BI can result in a preference for a ranker irrespective of where a user clicks. This bias is corrected in *team draft interleave* (TDI) [15]. More recent methods include *document constraints* (DC) [4] and *optimized interleave* (OI) [14]. Recently, interleaving outcomes were made to agree with A/B tests [19].

Interleaving methods have an important disadvantage: they can only evaluate two rankers at a time. When the number of rankers that have to be compared increases, this quickly becomes infeasible. Schuth et al. [18] have proposed multileaved comparison methods as a way of directly inferring preferences among a set of rankers. Instead of requiring rankers to be compared pairwise, their method allows for a single comparison of multiple rankers at once. Multileaved comparison methods produce a list that contains results from multiple rankers and use clicks on this list to infer a ranking over rankers. Schuth et al. [18] propose extensions of TDI and OI to *team draft multileave* (TDM) and *optimized multileave* (OM), respectively. Both learn preferences much faster than interleaving methods. Each has its own merit: TDM learns slightly slower but results in more accurate preferences while OM initially learns faster and scales better when the number of compared rankers goes up.

The interleaving and multileaving methods listed so far can only infer preferences among rankers based on interaction data that is generated using those very same rankers, thus preventing generalizations to new and unseen rankers. *Probabilistic interleave* (PI), however, is a recent interleaving method that can reuse *historical interaction data* collected using other rankers than the ranker being evaluated to infer preferences between rankers [6, 7]. This allows for comparisons that are more efficient in terms of how many user impressions are required for reliable comparisons.

We propose an extension of PI to *probabilistic multileave* (PM): a multileaving method that is able to reuse historical interaction data. An evaluation method is *sensitive* if it quickly detects differences in the quality of rankings. That is, if rankers are of different quality, the evaluation method should detect those differences with the least number of comparisons. An evaluation method is *unbiased* if all the rankers are equal in expectation when clicks are random. That is, the method should evaluate rankers fairly and only on the basis of their actual performance. We show experimentally: (1) that PM is at least as sensitive as TDM (which in turn is more sensitive than OM); (2) that PM is unbiased; and (3) that PM scales well when the number rankers that are compared increases. An important implication of our results is that historical interactions with multileaved comparisons

SIGIR'15, August 09 - 13, 2015, Santiago, Chile.

ACM 978-1-4503-3621-5/15/08 ...$15.00.
DOI: http://dx.doi.org/10.1145/2766462.2767838.

Algorithm 1 Creating a multileaved list in PM.

1: **Input**: rankers $\mathcal{R}$, size k.
2: $L \leftarrow []$ *// initialize interleaved list*
3: **while** True **do**
4: $\quad \mathcal{R}' \leftarrow \mathcal{R}$
5: $\quad$ **while** $|\mathcal{R}'| > 0$ **do**
6: $\quad\quad \mathcal{R}_j \leftarrow$ draw from uniform distribution over $\mathcal{R}'$
7: $\quad\quad \mathcal{R}' \leftarrow \mathcal{R}' \setminus \{\mathcal{R}_j\}$
8: $\quad\quad d \leftarrow$ draw from $\mathcal{R}_j$ with $P(d|\mathcal{R}_j)$ *// see (1)*
9: $\quad\quad L.append(d)$
10: $\quad\quad$ **if** $|L| = k$ **then**
11: $\quad\quad\quad$ **return** L
12: $\quad\quad$ **for** $\mathcal{R}_j \in \mathcal{R}$ **do**
13: $\quad\quad\quad \mathcal{R}_j.remove(d)$ *// renormalize $P(d|\mathcal{R}_j)$*

can be reused, allowing for ranker comparisons that need much less user interaction data. This, in turn, means that users are exposed less often to inferior rankers and that more rankers can be compared with the same number of user interactions.

2. METHOD

In this section we derive *probabilistic multileave* (PM), a multileaving version of *probabilistic interleaving* (PI). Extending PI to multiple rankers is non-trivial due to three challenges. First, the interleaving method, which combines multiple rankings to one list, must be extended to accommodate more than two rankers in a probabilistic way; see Section 2.1. Secondly, we need to represent the outcomes of a multileaved comparison such that it allows for more than two rankers. Lastly, we need to extend the marginalization over all assignments[1] to the multileave setting without increasing the number of possible assignments beyond what we can reasonably handle.

2.1 Constructing multileaved lists

Probabilistic interleaving [6] constructs interleaved lists in a way similar to TDI. For each rank in the interleaved list a coin is flipped to decide which ranker assigns the next document. Instead of picking the top document from that ranking, like in TDI, the document is drawn from a softmax distribution. After a document has been chosen it is removed from all rankings it occurs in and all softmax distributions are renormalized. An extension of this approach to the setting with r rankers can be found in Algorithm 1. As in TDM, and unlike PI, we choose to introduce the notion of rounds on line 5: in each round *all* rankers are chosen at random to contribute a document. This way we increase the change of the multileaved list to include documents from the top of each ranker that is to be compared while ensuring non-zero probability for all possible multileavings.

Documents d are drawn from ranker $\mathcal{R}_j$ with probability

$$P(d|\mathcal{R}_j) = \frac{\frac{1}{r_j(d)^\tau}}{\sum_{d' \in D} \frac{1}{r_j(d')^\tau}}, \tag{1}$$

where $r_j(d)$ denotes the rank of the document in ranker $\mathcal{R}_j$. When documents are removed from $\mathcal{R}_j$, as is done on line 13, this changes the distribution. The softmax decay is controlled by τ which we set to 3, following PI [6].

2.2 Inferring preferences

Once the multileaved list has been created, shown to a user, and once the user has clicked on zero or more documents, these clicks can be interpreted as preferences for rankers.

[1]Following TDM and PI, documents in a multileaved list are assigned to a rankers' teams in order to distribute credit from clicks.

Algorithm 2 Inferring preferences in PM.

Input: multileaved list L, rankers $\mathcal{R}$, clicks C.
$A \leftarrow \{\}$ *// assignment tree keeps track of outcome and probabilities*
$A' \leftarrow \{\langle o \leftarrow [0, ..., 0], p \leftarrow 0\rangle\}$ *// init assignment tree, $|o| = |\mathcal{R}|$*
for $d \in L$ **do**
$\quad A \leftarrow A', A' \leftarrow \{\}$ *// next layer in assignment tree*
$\quad$ **for** $\mathcal{R}_j \in \mathcal{R}$ **do**
$\quad\quad p_j \leftarrow P(d|\mathcal{R}_j)$ *// see (1)*
$\quad\quad \mathcal{R}_j.remove(d)$ *// renormalize $P(d|\mathcal{R}_j)$*
$\quad$ **for** $\langle o, p\rangle \in A$ **do**
$\quad\quad$ **for** $\mathcal{R}_j \in \mathcal{R}$ **do**
$\quad\quad\quad$ **if** $random() > \frac{1}{|\mathcal{R}|} \cdot n^{\frac{1}{|L|}}$ **then**
$\quad\quad\quad\quad$ **continue** *// sample, skip branch*
$\quad\quad\quad p' \leftarrow p + \log(\frac{p_j}{2})$ *// log probability of assigning d to $\mathcal{R}_j$*
$\quad\quad\quad o' \leftarrow o$ *// copy outcome vector from parent*
$\quad\quad\quad$ **if** $d \in C$ **then**
$\quad\quad\quad\quad o'_j \leftarrow o'_j + 1$ *// click on d, increment outcome for $\mathcal{R}_j$*
$\quad\quad\quad A' \leftarrow A' \cup \{\langle o', p'\rangle\}$ *// append to next layer*
$o \leftarrow [0, ..., 0]$ *// init outcome, $|o| = |\mathcal{R}|$*
for $\langle o', p'\rangle \in A'$ **do**
$\quad o \leftarrow o + o' \cdot e^{p'}$ *// aggregate outcome vector o weighted with $e^{p'}$*
return o

Hofmann et al. [6] proposes an unbiased estimator of the expected outcome of a comparison outcome over many such query impressions as

$$E[o(C, A)] \approx \frac{1}{|Q|} \sum_{q \in Q} o(c_q, a_q). \tag{2}$$

Here, Q denotes a given set of queries, with clicks c_q and assignments a_q. In the PI implementation, $o(c, a) \in \{-1, 0, 1\}$ is used to denote the outcome of a comparison, which we change to $o_j(c, a) \in \mathbb{N}$ to denote the outcome (credit) for a single ranker $\mathcal{R}_j$. This outcome simply counts how many clicked documents were assigned to this ranker, as in TDI or TDM. Changing the outcome notation leads us to also compute the expected outcome per ranker $\mathcal{R}_j$ as

$$E[o_j(C, A)] \approx \frac{1}{|Q|} \sum_{q \in Q} o_j(c_q, a_q). \tag{3}$$

The PI algorithm then proposes a marginalization over all possible assignments. The intuition behind why this is a good idea for both PI and PM is that through a single interaction with users, inferences can be performed as if the $\mathcal{R}$ rankers were multileaved many more times. This allows for highly sensitive comparisons.

We follow the marginalization of PI closely, and marginalize over all possible assignments as

$$E[o_j(C, A)] \approx \frac{1}{|Q|} \sum_{q \in Q} \sum_{a_q \in \tilde{A}_q} o_j(c_q, a_q) \cdot P(a_q|L_q, q). \tag{4}$$

In this equation, $P(a_q|l_q, q)$ denotes the probability of an assignment a_q occurring given the interleaved list L_q for query q. We borrow this probability directly from the PI implementation.

A major difference with PI, however, is that we can no longer consider all possible assignments A as there are generally too many of them, namely $|\mathcal{R}|^{|L|}$, which, even with a small amount of rankers, is prohibitively large. Instead, we limit the number of assignments by taking an, in expectation, random and uniform sample from them. We denote the sample as $\tilde{A}$, and control the size $n \approx |\tilde{A}|$ by, deciding with probability $\frac{1}{|\mathcal{R}|} \cdot n^{\frac{1}{|L|}}$ whether we consider a *branch* of assignments in a *tree* of assignments not. This sampling happens on line 11 in Algorithm 2 which lists our method for inferring preferences in PM. The algorithm builds a tree of assignments by considering assigning each document $d \in L$ (line 4) to all possible rankers $\mathcal{R}_j \in \mathcal{R}$ (line 10) with the probability mentioned before (line 11). The algorithm keeps track of the outcome for each ranker for each assignment branch (line 16). It also tracks the probability of each such assignment (line 13). Once the outcomes $o_j(c_q, a_q)$ have been computed for all assignments $a_q \in A'$, we aggregate them weighted with their assigned probabilities on line 20 into a single outcome. From this outcome we construct the preference matrix $\hat{P}_{ij}$ just as is done in TDM.

Note that in our implementation, just as in PI, we use log probabilities and sums to avoid buffer underflow. Also following PI, as an optmization, we only actually compute assignments and probabilities up to the lowest clicks.

3. EXPERIMENTS

Our implementation of probabilistic multileaving, PM, is evaluated experimentally for sensitivity, bias, and scalability using the experimental setup detailed below.

The methodology used to evaluate the different interleaving and multileaving methods is borrowed from [18]. Several features (i.e., BM25, LMIR.JM, Sitemap, PageRank, HITS, and TF.IDF) from the NP2003 and NP2004 dataset [13] are used as different rankers. These rankers can then be evaluated against each other using the aforementioned interleaving and multileaving methods. Evaluation is done by simulating users interacting with the interleaving and multileaving methods. In this setup, described by Hofmann [5], clicks are produced based on a *cascade click model* (CCM) [3] with four instantiations.

	$P(click = 1 \mid R)$		$P(stop = 1 \mid R)$	
Relevance R	$R = 0$	$R = 1$	$R = 0$	$R = 1$
perfect	0.0	1.0	0.0	0.0
navigational	0.05	0.95	0.2	0.9
informational	0.4	0.9	0.1	0.5
random	0.5	0.5	0.0	0.0

Queries are sampled from training data, clicks are generated based on relevance labels for each query. We use 1000 queries per run. Results are averaged over 25 repetitions over 5 folds for 2 datasets. We sample $|\mathcal{R}| = 5$ features as rankers for each run.

Ground truth NDCG [8] is computed for each ranker on held out test data. Then, just as in [18], a matrix P is defined using the difference in expected NDCG between the separate rankers:

$$P_{ij} = 0.5(NDCG(R_i) - NDCG(R_j)) + 0.5. \qquad (5)$$

Any interleaving or multileaving method tries to estimate this matrix P. Interleaving methods do this by iterating over all pairs of rankers $i, j \in \mathcal{R}$, while multileaving methods compare all rankers $\mathcal{R}$ at once. To measure performance, we follow [18] and use a *binary error metric* to evaluate the correctness of this estimated matrix $\hat{P}$:

$$E_{bin} = \frac{\sum_{i,j \in \mathcal{R} \wedge i \neq j} sgn(\hat{P}_{ij} - 0.5) \neq sgn(P_{ij} - 0.5)}{|\mathcal{R}| \cdot (|\mathcal{R}| - 1)}.$$

After every simulated query this error can be computed for each interleaving and multileaving method.[2] We test significance with a two tailed student-t test.

To evaluate the *sensitivity* of PM, it is compared to TDM and PI. A multileaving method should be more sensitive than an interleaving method as it can compare more than two rankers at the same time. For this evaluation, we use the *perfect*, *navigational*, and *informational* instantiations. It is hypothesized that multileaving will need fewer impressions to converge than interleaving.

To assess the *bias* of all of the interleaving and multileaving methods mentioned above, we observe the error under a *random* clicking user. The error, in this case, is not based on ground truth NDCG matrix P_{ij} as in (5) but instead on a ground truth $P_{ij} = 0.5$ for all pairs of rankers i, j.

Lastly, we look into *scaling up* the number of rankers. The experiments listed above are all run using $|\mathcal{R}| = 5$ rankers; we also investigate what happens when $|\mathcal{R}| = 20$ for the navigational click model and with the sample size of PM fixed to $n = 10^4$.

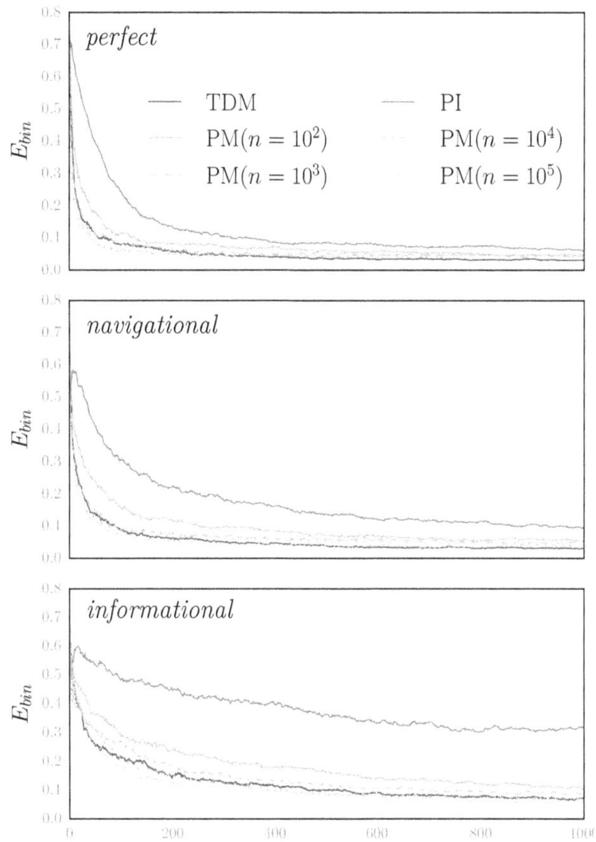

Figure 1: The binary error E_{bin} is plotted against the number of queries on which the error was evaluated for interleaving and multileaving methods. Clicks are generated by a *perfect*, *navigational*, and *informational* instantiations of CCM [3].

4. RESULTS AND ANALYSIS

In Figure 1 we see that for impressions from all three click models, TDM performs similar to PM with a large number of samples n, although TDM performs slightly (but not significantly) better in the long run for the (unrealistic) *perfect* click model. The multileaving methods both perform much better than PI, as expected since the latter can only compare two rankers at a time.[3]

The binary error for both probabilistic multileaving quickly goes down to almost zero. Performance after 500 queries for the same experiments is found in Table 1 where we also perform statistical significance testing. In the table we see that PM always has a

[2]All code is open source and available at `https://bitbucket.org/ilps/lerot` [17].

[3]The bump for PI in the first few query impressions, that is mostly visible under *informational* feedback, is due to the fact that it takes a while for PI to have preferences for all pairs of rankers.

Table 1: Mean E_{bin} scores after 500 impressions for PM and SPM compared to baselines PI (first symbol) and TDM (second symbol). The symbol ▲ means statistically better with $p < 0.01$ and △ for $p < 0.05$, whereas ▼ and ▽ are their inverses.

	perfect	*navigational*	*informational*
PI	0.085 (0.08)	0.137 (0.11)	0.363 (0.15)
TDM	0.037 (0.06)	0.038 (0.05)	0.099 (0.09)
PM($n = 10^2$)	0.062 (0.07) ▲▼	0.073 (0.07) ▲▼	0.162 (0.10) ▲▼
PM($n = 10^3$)	0.054 (0.05) ▲▼	0.060 (0.06) ▲▼	0.117 (0.09) ▲▽
PM($n = 10^4$)	0.046 (0.05) ▲-	0.054 (0.05) ▲▼	0.090 (0.08) ▲-
PM($n = 10^5$)	0.046 (0.05) ▲-	0.039 (0.05) ▲-	0.087 (0.08) ▲-

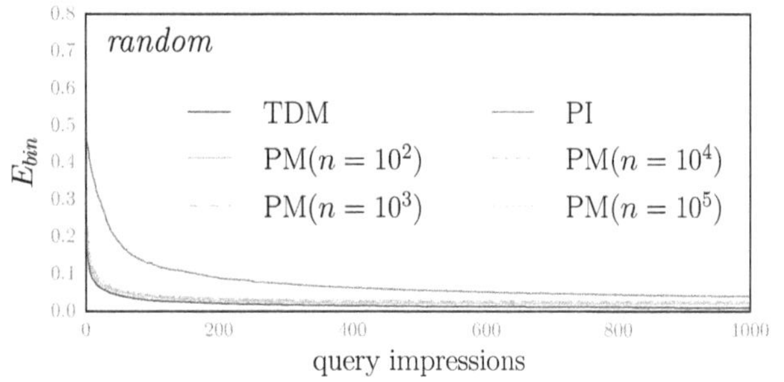

Figure 2: The error is plotted against the number of queries. The error was evaluated by comparing to a ground truth of *no preferences* (i.e., $P_{ij} = 0.5$ for all i, j). Clicks are generated by a *random* instantiation of CCM [3].

lower error than PI and when there are enough samples ($n \geq 100$) statistically significantly so. However, when the number of samples is too small, PM is outperformed significantly by TDM. When the number of samples increases sufficiently, PM is on par with TDM in terms of sensitivity. Interestingly, when noise increases, performance of PM decreases less compared to TDM.

In terms of bias, we see in Figure 2 that PM is on par with TDM. Both methods only need about 100 impressions from a random user to conclude that no preferences between rankers can be inferred. Again naturally, PI needs much more query impressions to draw the same conclusion because it needs to compare all pairs of rankers. PM is as unbiased as TDM, irrespective of the number of samples.

Lastly, we investigate what happens when the number of rankers $|\mathcal{R}|$ that are being compared increases from the five rankers used until now. We test this with $|\mathcal{R}| = 20$ and find that after 500 navigational query impressions for PI, $E_{bin} = 0.56$, for TDM $E_{bin} = 0.15$, and for PM($n = 10^4$) we find $E_{bin} = 0.13$. The advantage of multileaving over interleaving is clearly shown by these numbers. But moreover, PM clearly outperforms TDM when the number of rankers increases. We confirm a finding from Schuth et al. [18] who showed this to be an inherent disadvantage of TDM as it needs to represent al rankers with teams in the multileaving. PM, because it marginalizes over all possible team assignments, does not have this drawback and still performs well when the number of rankers goes up.

5. CONCLUSION

We have introduced a new method for online ranker evaluation called *probabilistic multileave* (PM). PM extends *probabilistic interleave* (PI) such that it can compare more than two rankers at once, while keeping PI's characteristic of being able to reuse historical interaction data. We empirically compared PM to PI as well as an earlier multileaving method called *team draft multileave* (TDM). The new method infers preferences between rankers by marginalizing over a *sample* of possible team assignments. We use a sample of controlled size to keep the computation tractable and show experimentally that given a large enough sample, our method is both as sensitive and as unbiased as TDM and more so than PI. That is, PM is capable of quickly finding meaningful differences between rankers and it does not infer preferences where it should not.

An important implication of this work is that historical interactions with multileaved comparisons can be reused, allowing for ranker comparisons that need much less user interaction data. Furthermore, we show that our method, as opposed to earlier sensitive multileaving methods, scales well when the number of rankers increases.

Acknowledgements. This research was partially supported by the European Community's Seventh Framework Programme (FP7/2007-2013) under grant agreement nr 312827 (VOX-Pol), the Netherlands Organisation for Scientific Research (NWO) under project nrs 727.011.005, 612.001.116, HOR-11-10, 640.006.013, 612.066.930, CI-14-25, SH-322-15, Amsterdam Data Science, the Dutch national program COMMIT, the ESF Research Network Program ELIAS, the Elite Network Shifts project funded by the Royal Dutch Academy of Sciences (KNAW), the Netherlands eScience Center under project number 027.012.105, the Yahoo! Faculty Research and Engagement Program, the Microsoft Research PhD program, and the HPC Fund.

REFERENCES

[1] O. Chapelle, T. Joachims, F. Radlinski, and Y. Yue. Large-scale validation and analysis of interleaved search evaluation. *ACM Trans. Inf. Syst.*, 30(1), 2012.

[2] C. W. Cleverdon, J. Mills, and M. Keen. Factors determining the performance of indexing systems. Aslib cranfield project, Cranfield: College of Aeronautics, 1966.

[3] F. Guo, C. Liu, and Y. M. Wang. Efficient multiple-click models in web search. In *WSDM '09*. ACM, 2009.

[4] J. He, C. Zhai, and X. Li. Evaluation of methods for relative comparison of retrieval systems based on clickthroughs. In *CIKM '09*. ACM, 2009.

[5] K. Hofmann. *Fast and Reliably Online Learning to Rank for Information Retrieval*. PhD thesis, University of Amsterdam, 2013.

[6] K. Hofmann, S. Whiteson, and M. de Rijke. A probabilistic method for inferring preferences from clicks. In *CIKM '11*. ACM, 2011.

[7] K. Hofmann, A. Schuth, S. Whiteson, and M. de Rijke. Reusing historical interaction data for faster online learning to rank for IR. In *WSDM '13*. ACM, 2013.

[8] K. Järvelin and J. Kekäläinen. Cumulated gain-based evaluation of IR techniques. *ACM Trans. Inf. Syst.*, 20(4):422–446, 2002.

[9] T. Joachims. Optimizing search engines using clickthrough data. In *KDD '02*. ACM, 2002.

[10] T. Joachims. Evaluating retrieval performance using clickthrough data. In *Text Mining*. Physica/Springer, 2003.

[11] T. Joachims, L. A. Granka, B. Pan, H. Hembrooke, F. Radlinski, and G. Gay. Evaluating the accuracy of implicit feedback from clicks and query reformulations in Web search. *ACM Trans. Inf. Syst.*, 25(2), 2007.

[12] R. Kohavi, R. Longbotham, D. Sommerfield, and R. M. Henne. Controlled experiments on the web: survey and practical guide. *Data Mining and Knowledge Discovery*, 18(1):140–181, 2009.

[13] T.-Y. Liu, J. Xu, T. Qin, W. Xiong, and H. Li. LETOR: Benchmark dataset for research on learning to rank for information retrieval. In *LR4IR '07*, 2007.

[14] F. Radlinski and N. Craswell. Optimized interleaving for online retrieval evaluation. In *WSDM '13*. ACM, 2013.

[15] F. Radlinski, M. Kurup, and T. Joachims. How does clickthrough data reflect retrieval quality? In *CIKM '08*. ACM, 2008.

[16] M. Sanderson. Test collection based evaluation of information retrieval systems. *Found. & Tr. Inform. Retr.*, 4(4):247–375, 2010.

[17] A. Schuth, K. Hofmann, S. Whiteson, and M. de Rijke. Lerot: An online learning to rank framework. In *LivingLab '13*. ACM, 2013.

[18] A. Schuth, F. Sietsma, S. Whiteson, D. Lefortier, and M. de Rijke. Multileaved comparisons for fast online evaluation. In *CIKM '14*, pages 71–80. ACM, 2014.

[19] A. Schuth, K. Hofmann, and F. Radlinski. Predicting search satisfaction metrics with interleaved comparisons. In *SIGIR'15*. ACM, 2015.

[20] E. M. Voorhees and D. K. Harman. *TREC: Experiment and Evaluation in Information Retrieval*. MIT Press, 2005.

Twitter Sentiment Analysis with Deep Convolutional Neural Networks

Aliaksei Severyn*
Google Inc.
aseveryn@gmail.com

Alessandro Moschitti†
Qatar Computing Research Institute
amoschitti@qf.org.qa

ABSTRACT

This paper describes our deep learning system for sentiment analysis of tweets. The main contribution of this work is a new model for initializing the parameter weights of the convolutional neural network, which is crucial to train an accurate model while avoiding the need to inject any additional features. Briefly, we use an unsupervised neural language model to train initial word embeddings that are further tuned by our deep learning model on a distant supervised corpus. At a final stage, the pre-trained parameters of the network are used to initialize the model. We train the latter on the supervised training data recently made available by the official system evaluation campaign on Twitter Sentiment Analysis organized by Semeval-2015. A comparison between the results of our approach and the systems participating in the challenge on the official test sets, suggests that our model could be ranked in the first two positions in both the phrase-level subtask A (among 11 teams) and on the message-level subtask B (among 40 teams). This is an important evidence on the practical value of our solution.

Categories and Subject Descriptors

I.5.1 [**Pattern Recognition**]: Models—*Neural nets*

Keywords

Convolutional neural networks; twitter sentiment analysis

1. INTRODUCTION

In this work we describe our deep convolutional neural network for sentiment analysis of tweets. Its architecture is most similar to the deep learning systems presented in [2, 3] that have recently established new state-of-the-art results on various NLP sentence classification tasks also including sentiment analysis. Convolutional neural networks have been also successfully applied in various IR applications, e.g., [8, 9]. While already demonstrating excellent results, training a convolutional neural network that would beat hand-engineered approaches that also rely on multiple manual and automatically constructed lexicons, e.g. [5, 11], requires careful attention. This becomes an even harder problem especially in cases when the amount of labelled data is relatively small, e.g., thousands of examples.

It turns out that providing the network with good initialisation parameters can have a significant impact on the accuracy of the trained model. To address this issue, we propose a three-step process to train our deep learning model for sentiment classification. Our approach can be summarized as follows: (i) word embeddings are initialized using a neural language model [4, 7], which is trained on a large unsupervised collection of tweets; (ii) we use a convolutional neural network to further refine the embeddings on a large distant supervised corpus [1]; (iii) the word embeddings and other parameters of the network obtained at the previous stage are used to initialize the network with the same architecture, which is then trained on a supervised corpus from Semeval-2015.

We apply our deep learning model on two subtasks of Semeval-2015 Twitter Sentiment Analysis (Task 10) challenge: phrase-level (subtask A) and message-level (subtask B). Our system achieves high results on the official tests sets of the phrase-level and on the message-level subtasks. In addition to the above test sets, we also used the so-called progress test set, which consists of five test sets, where our system again outperforms most of the systems participated in the challenge. In particular, if we ranked all systems (including ours) according to their accuracy on each of the six test sets and compute their average ranks, our model would be ranked first in both subtasks, A and B.

2. OUR DEEP LEARNING MODEL FOR SENTIMENT CLASSIFICATION

The architecture of our convolutional neural network for sentiment classification is shown on Fig. 1. It is mainly inspired by the architectures used in [2, 3] for performing various sentence classification tasks. Given that our training process (described in Sec. 3.3) requires to run the network on a rather large corpus, our design choices are mainly driven by the computational efficiency of our network. Hence, different from [2], which presents an architecture with several layers of convolutional feature maps, we adopt a single level architecture. Nevertheless, single-layer architectures have been shown in [3] to perform equally well.

Our network is composed of a single convolutional layer followed by a non-linearity, *max* pooling and a soft-max classification layer.

In the following, we give a brief explanation of the main components of our network: sentence matrix, activations, convolutional, pooling and softmax layers. We also describe how to adapt the network for predicting sentiment of phrases inside the tweets.

*This work was carried out at University of Trento.
†Professor at University of Trento, DISI.

SIGIR'15, August 09 - 13, 2015, Santiago, Chile.
 ISBN 978-1-4503-3621-5/15/08 ...$15.00.
DOI: http://dx.doi.org/10.1145/2766462.2767830.

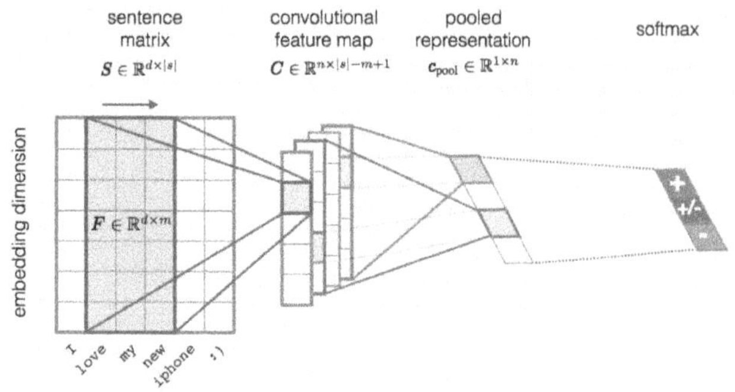

Figure 1: The architecture of our deep learning model for sentiment classification.

2.1 Sentence matrix

The input to our model are tweets each treated as a sequence of words: $[w_i, .., w_{|s|}]$, where each word is drawn from a vocabulary V. Words are represented by distributional vectors $\mathbf{w} \in \mathbb{R}^{1 \times d}$ looked up in a word embeddings matrix $\mathbf{W} \in \mathbb{R}^{d \times |V|}$. This matrix is formed by simply concatenating embeddings of all words in V. For convenience and ease of lookup operations in $\mathbf{W}$, words are mapped into indices $1, \ldots, |V|$.

For each input tweet $\mathbf{s}$, we build a sentence matrix $\mathbf{S} \in \mathbb{R}^{d \times |s|}$, where each column i represents a word embedding $\mathbf{w}_i$ at the corresponding position i in a sentence (see Fig. 1). To learn to capture and compose features of individual words in a given sentence from low-level word embeddings into higher level semantic concepts, the neural network applies a series of transformations to the input sentence matrix $\mathbf{S}$ using convolution, non-linearity and pooling operations, which we describe next.

2.2 Convolutional feature maps

The aim of the convolutional layer is to extract patterns, i.e., discriminative word sequences found within the input tweets that are common throughout the training instances.

More formally, the convolution operation, $*$, between an input matrix $\mathbf{s} \in \mathbb{R}^{d \times |s|}$ and a filter $\mathbf{F} \in \mathbb{R}^{d \times m}$ of width m results in a vector $\mathbf{c} \in \mathbb{R}^{|s|+m-1}$, where each component is computed as follows:

$$\mathbf{c}_i = (\mathbf{S} * \mathbf{F})_i = \sum_{k,j} (\mathbf{S}_{[:,i-m+1:i]} \otimes \mathbf{F})_{kj}, \quad (1)$$

where $\otimes$ is the element-wise multiplication and $\mathbf{S}_{[:,i-m+1:i]}$ is a matrix slice of size m along the columns. Note that the convolution filter is of the same dimensionality d as the input sentence matrix. As shown in Fig. 1, it slides along the column dimension of $\mathbf{S}$ producing a vector $\mathbf{c} \in \mathbb{R}^{1 \times (|s|-m+1)}$ in output. Each component c_i is the result of computing an element-wise product between a column slice of $\mathbf{S}$ and a filter matrix $\mathbf{F}$, which is then summed to a single value.

So far we have described a way to compute a convolution between the input sentence matrix and a single filter. To form a richer representation of the data, deep learning models apply a set of filters that work in parallel generating multiple feature maps (also shown on Fig. 1). A set of filters form a filter bank, $\mathbf{F} \in \mathbb{R}^{n \times d \times m}$, sequentially convolved with the sentence matrix $\mathbf{S}$ and producing a feature map matrix $\mathbf{C} \in \mathbb{R}^{n \times (|s|-m+1)}$.

In practice, we also need to add a bias vector $\mathbf{b} \in \mathbb{R}^n$ to the result of a convolution – a single b_i value for each feature map $\mathbf{c}_i$. This allows the network to learn an appropriate threshold.

2.3 Activation units

To enable the learning of non-linear decision boundaries, each convolutional layer is typically followed by a non-linear activation function, $\alpha()$, applied element-wise. Among the most common choices of activation functions are: sigmoid (or logistic), hyperbolic tangent *tanh*, and a rectified linear (ReLU) function defined as simply $max(0, \mathbf{x})$ to ensure that feature maps are always positive.

We use ReLU in our model since, as shown in [6], it speeds up the training and sometimes produces more accurate results.

2.4 Pooling

The output from the convolutional layer (passed through the activation function) is then passed to the pooling layer, whose goal is to aggregate the information and reduce the representation. The result of the pooling operation is:

$$\mathbf{c}_{\text{pooled}} = \begin{bmatrix} \text{pool}(\alpha(\mathbf{c}_1 + b_1 * \mathbf{e})) \\ \ldots \\ \text{pool}(\alpha(\mathbf{c}_n + b_n * \mathbf{e})) \end{bmatrix},$$

where $\mathbf{c}_i$ is the ith convolutional feature map with added bias (the bias is added to each element of $\mathbf{c}_i$ and $\mathbf{e}$ is a unit vector of the same size as $\mathbf{c}_i$) and passed through the activation function $\alpha()$.

The most popular choices for pooling operation are: max and average pooling. Recently, *max* pooling has been generalized to k-max pooling [2], where instead of a single max value, k values are extracted in their original order. We use *max* pooling in our model, which simply returns the maximum value. It operates on columns of the feature map matrix $\mathbf{C}$ returning the largest value: $\text{pool}(\mathbf{c}_i) : \mathbb{R}^{1 \times (|s|+m-1)} \rightarrow \mathbb{R}$ (also shown schematically in Fig. 1).

The convolutional layer utilizing the activation function and the pooling layer acts as a non-linear feature extractor. Given that multiple feature maps are used in parallel to process the input, deep learning networks are able to build rich feature representations of the input.

2.5 Softmax

The output of the penultimate convolutional and pooling layers $\mathbf{x}$ is passed to a fully connected softmax layer. It computes the probability distribution over the labels:

$$\begin{aligned} P(y = j|\mathbf{x}, \mathbf{s}, \mathbf{b}) &= \text{softmax}_j(\mathbf{x}^T\mathbf{w} + \mathbf{b}) \\ &= \frac{e^{\mathbf{x}^T\mathbf{w}_j + b_j}}{\sum_{k=1}^{K} e^{\mathbf{x}^T\mathbf{w}_k + b_k}}, \end{aligned}$$

where $\mathbf{w}_k$ and b_k are the weight vector and bias of the k-th class.

2.6 Phrase-level sentiment analysis

To perform phrase-level sentiment analysis, we feed the network with an additional input sequence indicating the location of the target phrase in a tweet. The elements are encoded using only two word types: the tokens spanning the phrase to be predicted are encoded with 1s and all the others with 0s. Each word type is associated with its own embedding. So, when tackling the phrase-level sentiment classification, we form a sentence matrix $\mathbf{S}$ as follows: for each token in a tweet, we have to look up its corresponding word embedding in the word matrix $\mathbf{W}$, and the embedding for one of the two word types. Hence, the input sentence matrix is augmented with an additional set of rows from the word type embeddings. Other than that, the architecture of our network remains unchanged.

3. OUR APPROACH TO TRAIN THE NETWORK

Convolutional neural networks can be tricky to train as are often severely subject to overfitting when trained on small datasets. In the following, we describe our approach to train our deep learning model.

3.1 Network Parameters and Training

We use stochastic gradient descent (SGD) to train the network and use backpropogation algorithm to compute the gradients. We opt for the *Adadelta* [12] update rule to automatically tune the learning rate.

3.2 Regularization

While neural networks have a large capacity to learn complex decision functions they tend to easily overfit especially on small and medium sized datasets. To mitigate the overfitting issue, we augment the cost function with l_2-norm regularization terms for the parameters of the network.

We also use another popular and effective technique to improve regularization of the neural networks — dropout [10]. Dropout prevents feature co-adaptation by setting to zero (dropping out) a portion of hidden units during the forward phase when computing the activations at the softmax output layer.

3.3 Initializing the model parameters

Convolutional neural networks are trained with non-convex function optimization algorithms, which typically lead to locally optima. Hence, starting the optimization from *a good point* can be crucial to train an accurate model. We propose the following 3-step process to initialize the parameter weights of the network:

1. Given that the largest parameter of the network is the word matrix $\mathbf{W}$, it is crucial to feed the network with the high quality embeddings. We use a popular `word2vec` neural language model [4] to learn the word embeddings on an unsupervised tweet corpus. For this purpose, we collect 50M tweets over a two-month period. We perform a minimal preprocessing, tokenizing the tweets, normalizing the URLs and author ids. To train the embeddings, we use a skipgram model with window size 5 and filter words with frequency less than 5.

2. When dealing with small amounts of labelled data, starting from pre-trained word embeddings is a large step towards successfully training an accurate deep learning system. However, while the word embeddings obtained at the previous step should already capture important syntactic and semantic aspects of the words they represent, they are completely clueless about their sentiment behaviour. Hence, we use a distant supervision approach [1] using our convolutional neural network to further refine the embeddings. More specifically, (i) we collected 10M tweets treating tweets containing positive emoticions, which can be used as distantly supervised labels; and (ii) we used such noisy label to train our embeddings. This step required a few days.

3. Finally, we take the the parameters θ of the network obtained at the previous step and use it to initialize the network which is trained on the supervised training corpus from Semeval-2015.

Table 1: Semeval-2015 data.

Dataset	Subtask A	Subtask B
Twitter'13-train	5,895	9,728
Twitter'13-dev	648	1,654
Twitter'13-test	2,734	3,813
LiveJournal'14	660	1,142
SMS'13	1,071	2,093
Twitter'14	1,807	1,853
Sarcasm'14	82	86
Twitter'15	3,092	2,390
# Teams	11	40

4. EXPERIMENTS AND EVALUATION

4.1 Data and setup

We test our model on two subtasks from Semeval-2015 Task 10: phrase-level (subtask A) and message-level (subtask B)[1]. The datasets used in Semeval-2015 are summarized in Table 1. We use train and dev from Twitter'13 for training and Twitter'13-test as a validation set. The other datasets are used for testing, whereas Twitter'15 is used to establish the official ranking of the systems. For evaluation we use the official scorers from Semeval 2015, which compute the average between F-measures for the positive and negative classes.

To pre-train the weights of our network, we use a large unsupervised corpus containing 50M tweets for training the word embeddings and a 10M tweet corpus for distant supervision. The latter corpus was built similarly to [1], where tweets with positive emoticons, like ':)', are assumed to be positive, and tweets with negative emoticons, like ':(', are labeled as negative. The dataset contains equal number of positive and negative tweets.

The parameters of our model were (chosen on the validation set) as follows: the width m of the convolution filters is set to 5 and the number of convolutional feature maps is 300. We use ReLU activation function and a simple max-pooling. The dimensionality of the word embeddings d is set to 100. For the phrase-level subtask the size of the word type embeddings, which encode tokens that span the target phrase or not, is set to 10.

4.2 Pre-training the network

To train our deep learning model, we follow our 3-step process as described in Sec. 3.3. We report the results for training the network on the official supervised dataset from Semeval'15 using parameters that were initialized: (i) completely at random (`Random`); (ii) using word embeddings from the neural language model trained on a large unsupervised dataset (`Unsup`) with the `word2vec` tool and (iii) initializing all the parameters of our model with the parameters of the network that uses the word embeddings from the previous step and are further tuned on a distant supervised dataset (`Distant`).

Table 2 summarizes the performance of our model on five test sets using three parameter initialization schemas.

We note that: first, training the network with all parameters initialized completely at random results in a rather mediocre accuracy. This is due to a small size of the training set.

[1] the test datasets of SemEval'15 subsume the test sets from previous editions of Semeval, i.e., Semeval'13 and Semeval'14, so our results directly apply to those of the previous years.

Table 2: **Testing the model on the progress test sets from Semeval-2015 with different parameter initializion schemes: `Random` (random word embeddings); `Unsup` (word2vec embeddings); `Distant` (all parameters from a network trained on a distant supervised dataset).**

Dataset	Random	Unsup	Distant
LiveJournal'14	63.58	73.09	72.48
SMS'13	58.41	65.21	68.37
Twitter'13	64.51	72.35	72.79
Twitter'14	63.69	71.07	73.60
Sarcasm'14	46.10	52.56	55.44

Secondly, using embeddings pre-trained by a neural language model considerably boosts the performance.

Finally, using a large distant supervised corpus to further tune the word embeddings to also capturing the sentiment aspect of the words results in a further improvement across all test sets (except for a small drop on LiveJournal'14).

4.3 Official rankings

The comparison of our system performance with the official system rankings from Semeval'15 for both subtasks A and B are summarized in Table 3. As we can see our system performs particularly well on subtask A, it would be ranked 1st on the official Twitter'15 test set, while also showing excellent accuracy on all other test sets.

On subtask B our system would rank 2nd also showing high results on the other test sets (except for the LiveJournal'14). In fact, no single system at Semeval-2015 performed equally well across all test sets. For example, a system that ranked 1st on the official Twitter'15 dataset performed much worse on the progress test sets ranking, i.e., $\{14, 14, 11, 7, 12\}$ on {`LiveJournal'14`, `SMS'13`, `Twitter'13`, `Twitter'14`, and `Sarcasm'14`}, respectively. This results on an AveRank of 9.8, which is only at the 6th position if systems were ranked according to this average rank metric. In contrast, our system shows high robustness as its results, across all tests, would provide the AveRank of 4.3, which is the top-score according to this metric among all 40 submissions.

5. CONCLUSIONS

We described our deep learning approach to sentiment analysis of tweets for predicting polarities at both message and phrase levels. We give a detailed description of our 3-step process to train the parameters of the network that is the key to our success. The resulting model sets a new state-of-the-art on the phrase-level and is 2nd on the message-level subtask. Considering the average rank across all test sets our system is 1st on both subtasks.

Our network initialization process includes the use of distant supervised data (noisy labels are inferred using emoticons found in the tweets) to further refine the weights of the network passed from the completely unsupervised neural language model. Thus, our solution successfully combines together two traditionally important aspects of IR: unsupervised learning of text representations (word embeddings from neural language model) and learning on weakly supervised data. In the future we plan to apply deep learning approach to other IR applications, e.g., learning to rank for Microblog retrieval and answer reranking for Question Answering.

Acknowledgments. This work has been supported by the EC project CogNet, 671625 (H2020-ICT-2014-2). The first author was supported by the Google Europe Doctoral Fellowship Award 2013.

Table 3: Results on Semeval-2015 for phrase and tweet-level subtasks. Rank shows the absolute position of our system on each test set. AveRank is the averaged rank across all test sets.

Dataset	Score	Rank
Phrase-level subtask A		
LJournal'14	84.46	2
SMS'13	88.60	2
Twitter'13	90.10	1
Twitter'14	87.12	1
Sarcasm'14	73.65	5
Twitter'15	**84.79**	**1**
AveRank	2.0	1
Message-level subtask B		
LJournal'14	72.48	12
SMS'13	68.37	2
Twitter'13	72.79	3
Twitter'14	73.60	2
Sarcasm'14	55.44	5
Twitter'15	**64.59**	**2**
AveRank	4.3	1

REFERENCES

[1] A. Go, R. Bhayani, and L. Huang. Twitter sentiment classification using distant supervision. In *CS224N Project Report, Stanford*, 2009.

[2] N. Kalchbrenner, E. Grefenstette, and P. Blunsom. A convolutional neural network for modelling sentences. In *ACL*, 2014.

[3] Y. Kim. Convolutional neural networks for sentence classification. In *EMNLP*, 2014.

[4] T. Mikolov, I. Sutskever, K. Chen, G. S. Corrado, and J. Dean. Distributed representations of words and phrases and their compositionality. In *NIPS*, 2013.

[5] S. M. Mohammad, S. Kiritchenko, and X. Zhu. Nrc-canada: Building the state-of-the-art in sentiment analysis of tweets. In *Semeval*, 2013.

[6] V. Nair and G. E. Hinton. Rectified linear units improve restricted boltzmann machines. In *ICML*, 2010.

[7] J. W. Ronan Collobert. A unified architecture for natural language processing: deep neural networks with multitask learning. In *ICML*, 2008.

[8] Y. Shen, X. He, J. Gao, L. Deng, and G. Mesnil. A latent semantic model with convolutional-pooling structure for information retrieval. *CIKM*, 2014.

[9] Y. Shen, X. He, J. Gao, L. Deng, and G. Mesnil. Learning semantic representations using convolutional neural networks for web search. In *WWW*, 2014.

[10] N. Srivastava, G. Hinton, A. Krizhevsky, I. Sutskever, and R. Salakhutdinov. Dropout: A simple way to prevent neural networks from overfitting. *Journal of Machine Learning Research*, 15:1929–1958, 2014.

[11] S. M. M. Xiaodan Zhu, Svetlana Kiritchenko. Nrc-canada-2014: Recent improvements in sentiment analysis of tweets, and the Voted Perceptron. In *SemEval*, 2014.

[12] M. D. Zeiler. Adadelta: An adaptive learning rate method. *CoRR*, 2012.

Anchoring and Adjustment in Relevance Estimation

Milad Shokouhi
Microsoft
Cambridge, United Kingdom
milads@microsoft.com

Ryen W. White
Microsoft
Redmond, Washington
ryenw@microsoft.com

Emine Yilmaz
University College London
London, United Kingdom
e.yilmaz@cs.ucl.ac.uk

ABSTRACT

People's tendency to overly rely on prior information has been well studied in psychology in the context of *anchoring and adjustment*. Anchoring biases pervade many aspects of human behavior. In this paper, we present a study of anchoring bias in information retrieval (IR) settings. We provide strong evidence of anchoring during the estimation of document relevance via both human relevance judging and in natural user behavior collected via search log analysis. In particular, we show that sequential relevance judgment of documents collected for the same query could be subject to anchoring bias. That is, the human annotators are likely to assign different relevance labels to a document, depending on the quality of the last document they had judged for the same query. In addition to manually assigned labels, we further show that the implicit relevance labels inferred from click logs can also be affected by anchoring bias. Our experiments over the query logs of a commercial search engine suggested that searchers' interaction with a document can be highly affected by the documents visited immediately beforehand. Our findings have implications for the design of search systems and judgment methodologies that consider and adapt to anchoring effects.

Categories and Subject Descriptors

Information Systems [**Information Retrieval**]: Evaluation of retrieval results—*Relevance assessment*

1. INTRODUCTION

Consider a simple experiment; which involves estimating the total value of the following mathematical equation in five seconds:

$$1 \times 2 \times 3 \times 4 \times 5 \times 6 \times 7 \times 8$$

What was your estimate? Now, how about the following equation?

$$8 \times 7 \times 6 \times 5 \times 4 \times 3 \times 2 \times 1$$

It is immediately apparent that the second equation is the same as the first but in reverse order, thus the estimate should not change.

SIGIR'15, August 09 - 13, 2015, Santiago, Chile.
 ISBN 978-1-4503-3621-5/15/08 ...$15.00.
DOI: http://dx.doi.org/10.1145/2766462.2767841.

In 1974, Tversky and Kahneman [12] conducted the same experiment and presented the first sequence to a group of subjects and the second to another group. They noted that the median estimate was 512 for the subjects in the first group and 2250 for those in the second.[1] This drastic difference between the median estimates of the two groups can be explained by the *anchoring effect* – also referred to as *anchoring bias* [12]. Anchoring – or focalism – is a cognitive bias that explains the human tendency to rely heavily on first presented information (*anchor*) when making decisions. In the example above, given the short amount of time permitted for calculation, the subjects were subconsciously biased by the first few numbers in equations and reached significantly different estimates across the two groups. Anchoring effects have been studied in a range of settings. Northcraft and Neale [7] showed that the listed price of a property affects how much people – including experts – are willing to pay for it despite having access to comprehensive information about the quality factors. Wansink et al. [14] demonstrated that consumers are likely to purchase more products when they are presented in multiple-unit prices and purchase limits (e.g., "On sale – 6 cans for $3" versus "On sale – 50¢"). Here, the number of units acts as the anchor and biases consumer behavior.

In this paper, we study the anchoring effect in IR. In particular, we focus on how anchoring affects the *relevance* ratings of documents. Relevance labels for documents are usually obtained either (1) in a batch form by soliciting explicit judgments from human assessors with respect to a query, or (2) in an online form where the document relevance is inferred by using implicit feedback e.g., time spent on a document (dwell time) from search log data. We first demonstrate that the relevance label of a document is affected by the judgment that was made on an immediately preceding document. We further focus on relevance inferred from dwell time and show that the relevance of the previously-clicked document can also have a significant impact on the time searchers spend on the current document, which could significantly affect relevance inferred via dwell time. While the notion of relevance in IR has been studied for decades [8], we believe that our study is the first investigation of anchoring bias on implicitly inferred relevance labels.

Our results suggest that (1) the biases introduced by the relevance of the last labeled/clicked document should be considered both for batch and online evaluation, (2) that dwell time estimates should be used with caution as proxy for relevance, in particular for the documents that are presented towards the bottom of a ranked list (which are likely to be considered only after higher-ranked alternatives), and (3) the models that infer relevance from dwell time could be improved by incorporating the relevance label (or dwell time) of the previously judged/clicked document, if available.

[1] The correct value is 40320.

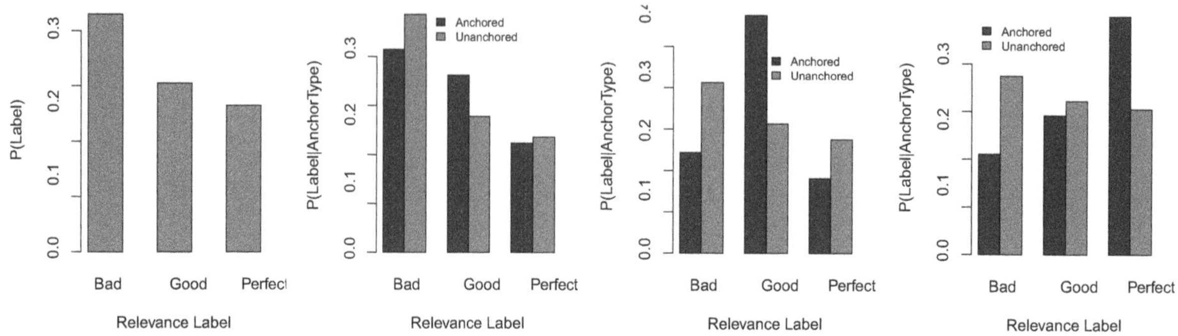

(a) Anchor-Type: None (b) Anchor-Type: Bad (c) Anchor-Type: Good (d) Anchor-Type: Perfect

Figure 1: Conditional probability of observing a relevance label for a document given the relevance label assigned to its anchor. (a) probability distribution when the document labels are collected in the absence of anchors. (b-d) the dark blue bars show the labels assigned to anchored documents separately for each class of anchor. In each plot, the red columns depict the label distribution over the same subset of documents based on the unanchored judgments.

2. ANCHORED RELEVANCE RATINGS

Relevance judgments for a query are typically collected in batches where each assessor may rate multiple documents for the same query [13]. The problem with this common practice is that the document(s) judged early for a given query can *anchor* judges' remaining judgments on that topic. Carterette and Soboroff [1] were the first to report that sequential labeling of documents may affect the assigned relevance label. They observed that sequentially judged documents tend to receive the same labels, and referred to this phenomenon as "autocorrelation". However, the authors did not provide any explanation for their observations nor compare their results with unanchored datasets to establish a ground truth.

Scholer et al. [9] performed the first analysis of anchoring in relevance assessments by measuring the "priming effect" in relevance judgments.[2] They used the relevance of the top k labeled documents by an assessor as the anchor and analyzed how the relevance of these documents may affect the labels assigned to the documents judged subsequently. They showed that if the judges are presented with many documents of high relevance when they start assessing for a query, they tend to assign lower relevance labels to documents labeled later on (and vice versa). In our work, part of our focus is to analyze how the relevance of the previously-labeled document can affect the relevance label assigned to the current document. In contrast to Scholer et al. [9], our results show that when labeling a document, judges tend to assign the same label as the previous document they have labeled.

Our conclusions do not necessarily reject those reached by Scholer et al. [9]. The differences are caused by the type of anchoring that is considered in the two studies. Scholer et al. focus on long-term anchoring (top k labeled documents as the anchor) and analyze how this affects the relevance labels assigned to the documents judged later. In our work, we focus on the short-term anchoring (last labeled document as the anchor) and analyze how this affects the relevance labels assigned to the document judged immediately after. The relevance of a single document is unlikely to have a significant effect on judges' overall expectation of relevance. However, having seen a document of a certain relevance level, the judges might subconsciously expect the relevance level of the next document judged to be similar, and hence their judgments may be affected.

For our experiments, we sampled 400 queries from a ranker training dataset of the Bing search engine. For each query in this dataset there are tens of documents from which we randomly selected three. The first two documents are used as anchors ($\mathcal{A}_1$, $\mathcal{A}_2$) and the last document is used as the target (anchored) (τ) document to measure the impact of the anchoring effect. We hired three mutually exclusive groups of professional relevance assessors from the crowdsourcing platform of the Bing search engine, and provided them with an identical judging guidelines for rating the relevance of documents in three levels (Bad, Good, Perfect). In total we collected our judgments from 220 assessors. We used the first group of judges (81 assessors) to collect *unanchored* relevance labels for our target documents. Each document is judged by three different assessors from this group and is annotated based on the majority vote (although other consensus models can be also used instead). In 8.5% of cases (34 queries) there were ties, which were broken by selecting one of the labels at random. Figure 1(a) depicts the distribution of relevance labels for target documents assigned by these judges.

The assessors in the other two groups are used to collect anchored judgments. We refer to these assessors as *anchored judges*. The anchored judges first rate an anchor document ($\mathcal{A}_1$ or $\mathcal{A}_2$ depending on the group) and then rate the target document (τ) for a query. Therefore, the target documents are rated by both groups of anchored judges, while the anchor documents are different across the two groups. Again, each anchor and target document is rated by three different judges in each group, and the final label is determined by the majority vote and tie-breaking as with the unanchored set. Judges rated a maximum of 20 (query, anchor, target) tuples. They always judged an anchor document ($\in \mathcal{A}_1$ or $\mathcal{A}_2$) then the target (anchored) document ($\in \tau$). For each task, a tuple was randomly sampled, without replacement, from the pool of 400 total. To ensure that there are no systematic differences between the anchored groups we compared the overall distribution of labels. An unpaired t-test found no statistically significant differences ($p = 0.979$).

The first question that we investigate is if relevance judgments are subject to anchoring effects. That is: *Does anchor quality affect the labels assigned to target documents?* We grouped the anchored judgments collected for the target documents according to the labels assigned to their anchor documents. The dark blue bars in Figure 1 represent the probability of observing a relevance label for

[2] There is a subtle difference between the anchoring and priming paradigms; in the latter, the priming information (or anchor) is often externally provided by the experimenter, while in the former it is internally generated by the participants themselves [11].

a target document, depending on the rating assigned to its anchor. For instance, Figure 1(b) includes only cases where the target document was judged immediately after an anchor page which was rated as *Bad* by the assessor. Figure 1(c-d) are generated in a similar manner but for *Good* and *Perfect* anchors respectively. The red bars in Figure 1(b-d) represent the distribution of labels assigned to the same set of documents but by unanchored judges. It is clear from these graphs that the anchored and unanchored judgments have different distributions despite the fact that they are computed over the same set of target documents. We applied Chi-squared tests to compare the label distributions for each of the three anchor types in Figure 1(b-d). The results confirm that the differences between the anchored and unanchored groups are statistically significant (Bad anchor: $\chi^2(2) = 8.91, p = 0.0028$; Good anchor: $\chi^2(2) = 80.49, p < 0.0001$; Perfect anchor: $\chi^2(2) = 6.76, p = 0.0093$). This provides supporting evidence for the presence of anchoring biases that can be introduced in collecting sequential relevance judgments from human assessors. Overall, there is a stronger anchoring effect for Good and Perfect judgments. This is expected as Good and Perfect documents both represent relevant documents and are more similar to each other than to Bad documents, which are irrelevant. The next question that naturally arises from these findings is: *Can the anchoring direction be predicted?* That is, given the label of the anchor document can one make any predictions about the label that will be assigned to the target (anchored) document? The conditional probabilities in Figure 1(c-d) clearly suggest that the most likely label for a relevant (Good, Perfect) target document is the rating assigned to its anchor. In other words, the anchoring direction is *towards* the anchor. However, Figure 1(b) shows that non-relevant anchors (Bad) have the opposite effect, with anchored judges being observed to be less likely to select a rating of Bad. Understanding all factors that affect the anchoring direction in relevance judgments is an interesting direction for future research.

3. ANCHORED CLICK BEHAVIOR

Search result clickthrough rate was once commonly used to infer the relevance of documents [3]. Subsequently, it has been shown that clickthrough statistics are often highly affected by issues such as presentation bias and perceived relevance of the documents. The perceived relevance of a document is mainly based on the summary (snippet) of the document presented on the result page, and can be different than the actual relevance of the document; hence, searchers may end up clicking on a document and discover that it is not relevant [2]. In order to overcome this problem, dwell time, the time spent examining a document, has been proposed as an implicit signal of relevance. Dwell time has been examined in a number of previous studies to infer searcher satisfaction [4, 6] and relevance [5] from observed search behavior. Over many years, a dwell time of 30 seconds has become a standard threshold from which to infer document relevance from document examination behavior [10]. Document visits with dwell times exceeding that threshold have been regarded as implicit indications of relevance.

Beyond controlled experimental settings, such as that employed in the previous section, we were also interested in whether there was any evidence of anchoring effects in the wild, in naturalistic search settings such as Web search. In such settings, anchoring might affect relevance labels inferred implicitly from search behaviors. We used six weeks of search logs from the Bing search engine. These logs contained millions of query-URL pairs on which to perform our study. To remove geographic and linguistic variations we focused on queries generated by searchers within the United States geographic locale. The logs contained queries, the time-ordered sequence of result clicks for each query, and dwell time on each of the landing pages reached through a result click.

In this analysis, we focused on the effects of anchoring on landing page dwell time. We calculated dwell time based on the time between subsequent search engine interactions, including re-visits to the search result page and query reformulations. Dwell times could not be computed for the last clicks for impressions (since there was no subsequent event on which to base dwell time estimates), and these clicks were ignored in our analysis. We divided the landing page dwell times into two groups: (i) Quickback: Dwell time of 15s or less, and (ii) Satisfied: Dwell time of 30s or more. These thresholds were derived from previous research on implicit feedback and satisfaction modeling in Web search settings [4]. Documents with dwell times ranging from 16-29s (inclusive) were excluded in order to simplify our analysis since it is less clear whether such dwell times are associated with satisfaction or dissatisfaction.

We utilize similar terminology as used in the previous section. For queries with multiple clicks, we define the set of *anchor* clicks as the first clicks and the set of *target* clicks as the second clicks. Note that we may observe separate instances of the same (query, clicked URL) pair in both sets depending on search activity, e.g. for a given query q, a searcher may click on a document d and terminate the search session (unanchored), while another searcher may click on a few documents first before clicking on d (anchored). The average rank position (r) of the anchor clicks and the target click is significantly different (anchor click: r = 2.28, target (anchored) click: r = 4.15, independent measures t-test: $p < 0.001$), signaling that searchers often adhere to a top-down examination strategy.

The first question that we sought to answer was whether there were differences in the dwell times for the target clicks given the nature of the anchor. Since we consider clicks within a query, we could be more confident that the searcher had the same intention with each observed click. Table 1 shows the distribution of dwell times (as percentages of the total count of query-click pairs in the four groups) across the four combinations of dwell times assigned to the first and the second click for a query. The table shows that in this analysis, consistent satisfaction (i.e., pairs of *Satisfied* clicks) is observed most frequently, whereas decreased satisfaction (i.e., transitions from *Satisfied* to *Quickback* clicks) occurs least often.

Given the raw counts that are used in computing the percentages reported in Table 1, we can also compute the extent to which they deviate from expected given independence between the first and second click. The numbers in brackets present the percentage deviations from the *expected* values given independence between the dwell time groups (i.e., for each cell, expected = (sum of row × sum of column) / overall total). It is clear that there is a significant deviation from the expected dwell time in the distribution of dwell times on the second (target) click for a query given the dwell time of the first (anchor) click (Chi-squared test over the frequency counts for the cells in Table 1 produces $\chi^2(1) = 3139222.15, p < .0001$). This suggests that there is a strong association between the nature of the dwell time on an anchor click and the dwell time on the target (anchored) click that follows. However, this analysis is only for queries with multiple clicks, and there may be limitations in considering such situations alone. For instance, low quality documents—that tend to have high Quickback rate—are more likely to appear in low quality search results. That is, if there is a low-relevance document returned in the top results, there might be a higher chance that the other top results are also low quality. To help address this concern, we identified a set of *unanchored* clicks comprising those with no preceding clicks (i.e., the first click for queries) from the same six weeks of data used in our log-based analysis. We then investigated the dwell times of the same query-URL pairs when

Table 1: Distribution of dwell times across all combinations of the two dwell time groups (Quickback ($\leq$ 15s), Satisfied ($\geq$ 30s)). Values in brackets denote percentage deviations from expected given independence between dwell time bucket groups of first and second clicks. Arrows denote direction of the deviation (up=higher than expected, down=lower than expected).

		2nd click	
		Quickback	**Satisfied**
1st click	**Quickback**	19.74% [▲46.32%]	25.51% [▼19.68%]
	Satisfied	10.08% [▼38.28%]	44.68% [▲16.26%]

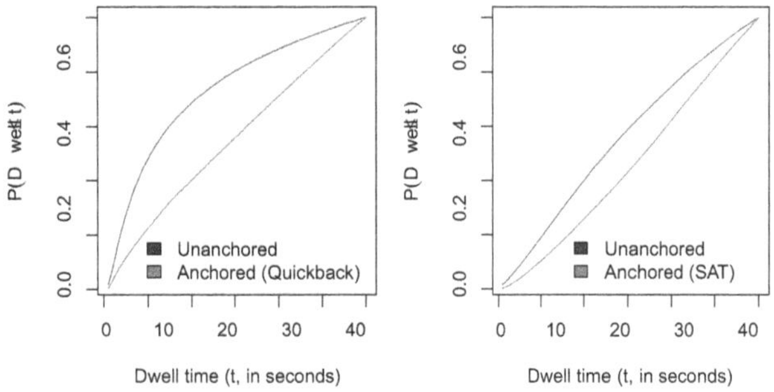

Figure 2: Cumulative dwell time distributions for anchored and unanchored clicks, per anchor type (Quickback and Satisfied).

they appear in our anchored sets. For each of the two anchor types (*Quickback* and *Satisfied*) we then computed the distribution of median dwell times for the anchored clicks, and compared it against the distribution of median dwell times from the unanchored clicks.

Figure 2 shows the cumulative distribution of median dwell times across the 60 seconds immediately following the page load (including the region from 16-29s that excluded in the earlier analysis), grouped by anchor type. At any point on the x-axis of the figure, the value on the y-axis reflects P(Dwell) $\leq t$, where t denotes the dwell time in seconds.

From Figure 2 we can observe clear differences in dwell time distributions between the documents in the anchored and unanchored sets. These differences are significant according to the Kolmogorov Smirnov test within each anchor type (Quickback Anchor: $\mathcal{D} = 0.6333$, $p < 0.001$; SAT Anchor: $\mathcal{D} = 0.2833$, $p = 0.0162$). This demonstrates that the dwell time on the anchor document is related to the dwell time on the target page. Research on dwell time typically considers the time spent on each document independently for applications such as satisfaction modeling, e.g., [6]. Our findings in this section suggest that models that interpret dwell times of a document from median dwell time across all searchers may be affected by anchoring biases. These models also need to consider the dwell time of any anchor that may be present when making inferences about the target (anchored) click, for applications such as relevance and satisfaction estimation.

The trends in our findings are clear and we analyze the aggregate behavior of millions of searchers, improving our confidence in the robustness of our conclusions. However, we should also acknowledge that there are other factors that may influence the dwell time beyond the nature of the anchor, such as those associated with searcher traits (e.g., people with a tendency to review pages quickly) or task constraints (e.g., pressing deadlines leading to the rapid review of content). Further work is required to understand the significance of these additional factors on the generalizability of our conclusions about anchoring effects and dwell times.

4. CONCLUSIONS

Anchoring is a cognitive bias that explains the human tendency to rely heavily on first presented information (*anchor*) when making decisions. In this paper, we studied how anchoring may affect human perception of relevance during relevance judging and in the examination of search results in naturalistic search settings. In particular, we focused on (1) relevance labels obtained from relevance assessors by obtaining explicit judgments, and (2) relevance labels inferred from dwell time, the time spent on a document. We showed that relevance of the last labeled document can have a significant effect on the relevance label assigned to the current document during relevance assessment. Our results demonstrate that judges tend to assign different labels depending on the relevance of the previously labeled document. We showed that the impact of short-term anchoring based on preceding documents could be different to those reported previously based on the longer term anchoring [9]. Determining the point where one effect diminishes and the other becomes dominant is an interesting future direction. We further demonstrated that the time searchers spend dwelling on a document is highly related to the amount of time they have spent on the last document that they clicked on, which can lead to significant biases on relevance labels inferred from dwell time.

Our findings can significantly impact the evaluation of retrieval systems and the training of learning-to-rank algorithms. Our results suggest that when human generated or implicit relevance labels are used, labels assigned to previous documents need to be considered.

References

[1] B. Carterette and I. Soboroff. The effect of assessor error on ir system evaluation. In *SIGIR*, 2010.

[2] G. Dupret and C. Liao. A model to estimate intrinsic document relevance from the clickthrough logs of a web search engine. In *WSDM*, 2010.

[3] G. Dupret and B. Piwowarski. A user browsing model to predict search engine click data from past observations. In *SIGIR*, 2008.

[4] S. Fox, K. Karnawat, M. Mydland, S. Dumais, and T. White. Evaluating implicit measures to improve web search. *ACM Trans. Inf. Syst.*, 23(2):147–168, Apr. 2005.

[5] D. Kelly and N. J. Belkin. Display time as implicit feedback: Understanding task effects. In *SIGIR*, 2004.

[6] Y. Kim, A. Hassan, R. W. White, and I. Zitouni. Modeling dwell time to predict click-level satisfaction. In *WSDM*, 2014.

[7] G. B. Northcraft and M. A. Neale. Experts, amateurs, and real estate: An anchoring-and-adjustment perspective on property pricing decisions. *Organizational behavior and human decision processes*, 39(1):84–97, 1987.

[8] T. Saracevic. Relevance: A review of the literature and a framework for thinking on the notion in information science. part ii: nature and manifestations of relevance. *JASIST*, 58(13):1915–1933, 2007.

[9] F. Scholer, D. Kelly, W.-C. Wu, H. S. Lee, and W. Webber. The effect of threshold priming and need for cognition on relevance calibration and assessment. In *SIGIR*, 2013.

[10] D. Sculley, R. G. Malkin, S. Basu, and R. J. Bayardo. Predicting bounce rates in sponsored search advertisements. In *SIGKDD*, 2009.

[11] F. Strack and T. Mussweiler. Explaining the enigmatic anchoring effect: Mechanisms of selective accessibility. *Journal of Personality and Social Psychology*, 73(3):437, 1997.

[12] A. Tversky and D. Kahneman. Judgment under uncertainty: Heuristics and biases. *Science*, 185(4157):1124–1131, 1974.

[13] E. M. Voorhees, D. K. Harman, et al. *TREC: Experiment and evaluation in information retrieval*. MIT Press, 2005.

[14] B. Wansink, R. J. Kent, and S. J. Hoch. An anchoring and adjustment model of purchase quantity decisions. *Journal of Marketing Research*, pages 71–81, 1998.

Cognitive Activity during Web Search

Md. Hedayetul Islam Shovon[1], D (Nanda) Nandagopal[1], Jia Tina Du[1], Ramasamy Vijayalakshmi[2], and Bernadine Cocks[1]
[1]Cognitive Neuroengineering Laboratory,
School of Information Technology and Mathematical Sciences,
University of South Australia, Adelaide, Australia
[2]Department of Applied Mathematics and Computational Sciences,
PSG College of Technology, Coimbatore, Tamil Nadu, India
shomy004@mymail.unisa.edu.au,nanda.nandagopal@unisa.edu.au

ABSTRACT
Searching on the Web or Net-surfing is a part of everyday life for many people, but little is known about the brain activity during Web searching. Such knowledge is essential for better understanding of the cognitive demands imposed by the search system and search tasks. The current study contributes to this understanding by constructing brain networks from EEG data using normalized transfer entropy (NTE) during three Web search task stages: query formulation, viewing of a search result list and reading each individual content page. This study further contributes to the connectivity analysis of the constructed brain networks, since it is an advanced quantitative technique which enables the exploration of brain function by distinct and varied brain areas. By using this approach, we identified that the cognitive activities during the three stages of Web searching are different, with various brain areas becoming more active during the three Web search task stages. Of note, query formulation generated higher interaction between cortical regions than viewing a result list or reading a content page. These findings will have implications for the improvement of Web search engines and search interfaces.

Categories and Subject Descriptors
H.3.3 [**Information Search and Retrieval**]: Search process

General Terms
Measurement, Design, Experimentation

Keywords
Information seeking; cognitive load; interactive information retrieval (IIR); EEG; normalized transfer entropy; graph theoretical analysis

1. INTRODUCTION
Interactive information retrieval is cognitive in nature [1, 2]. To understand the search process, it is necessary to understand individual users' cognitive activity or load during information interaction [3]. Previous research by Kim and Rieh [4], used the dual-task method for assessing mental effort during Web searching, finding significant differences in user mental effort between viewing search results and reading contents pages. Similarly, Gwizdka [5] used dual-task method to demonstrate dynamic changes in cognitive load in the task stage level of Web searching, reporting significantly higher average cognitive load during query formulation. Cole, Gwizdka, Lui and Belkin [6] further measured dynamic cognitive load during Web searching using eye movement patterns. They found that cognitive effort increases as the task difficulty increases. The dual-task method which is based on users' performance and reaction time to a secondary task, does not, however, directly measures brain activity. Similarly, eye tracking does not measure brain activity effectively; it is assumed that the captured indicators are closely related to the nervous system. As previous studies have relied on these inferential methods, how brain regions connect during effective Web searching, and which region acts as an information convergence region or hub remain unknown. Neuroimaging techniques such as EEG can, however, provide more direct measures of users' cognitive activity and recent studies have also highlighted the potential of neuroscience to contribute in interactive information retrieval [7]. The current study aims to capture the dynamic interactions between neuronal elements of the human brain during Web search task stages by constructing functional brain networks (FBNs) from time series observations of EEG signals using NTE [8]. We selected EEG for measuring cognitive load during Web search interactions because it is an inexpensive and non-invasive technology with high temporal resolution, and allows easy setup of a Web search experiment in a user-friendly environment. The rest of the paper is structured as follows: Section 2 will discuss the current literature on NTE; Section 3 will describe the methodology. The discussion of results will be presented in Sections 4, followed by a brief conclusion and future research directions in Section 5.

SIGIR '15, August 9-13, 2015, Santiago, Chile.
© 2015 ACM. ISBN 978-1-4503-3621-5/15/08…$15.00
DOI: http://dx.doi.org/10.1145/2766462.2767784

2. NORMALIZED TRANSFER ENTROPY
Transfer Entropy (TE) is an information theoretical measure which determines the direction and quantifies the information transfer between two processes [9]. TE estimates the amount of activity of a system which is not dependent on its own past activity but on the past activity of another system. Given two processes x and y, the TE from y to x is shown in equation 1:

$$TE_{y\to x} = \sum_{x_{n+1},x_n,y_n} p(x_{n+1}, x_n, y_n) \log\left(\frac{p(x_{n+1}, x_n, y_n).p(x_n)}{p(x_n, y_n).p(x_{n+1}, x_n)}\right) \quad (1)$$

Here, x_n denotes the status (value) of signal/system x at time n, y_n denotes the status of signal y at time n and x_{n+1} denotes the status of signal x at time $n+1$. Due to the finite size and non-stationarity of data, TE matrices usually contain much noise. In the existing literature, noise/bias has been removed from the estimate of TE by subtracting the average transfer entropy from y to x using shuffled version of y denoted by $< TE_{y_{shuffle} \to x} >$, over several shuffles. $y_{shuffle}$ contains the same symbol as in y but those symbols are rearranged in a randomly shuffled order. The normalized TE is calculated from y to x with respect to the total information in sequence x itself. This will represent the relative amount of information transferred by y. The NTE is shown in equation 2 as follows [10]:

$$NTE_{y \to x} = \frac{TE_{y \to x} - < TE_{y_{shuffle} \to x} >}{H(x_{n+1}|x_n)} \qquad (2)$$

In equation 2, $H(x_{n+1}|x_n)$ represents the conditional entropy of process x at time $n+1$ given its value at time n as shown in equation 3.

$$H(x_{n+1}|x_n) = -\sum_{x_{n+1}, x_n} p(x_{n+1}, x_n) \log \frac{p(x_{n+1}, x_n)}{p(x_n)} \qquad (3)$$

NTE is in the range $0 \leq NTE_{y \to x} \leq 1$. NTE is 0 when y transfers no information to x, and is 1 when y transfers maximal information to x. In the present study, the FBNs are constructed by computing the NTE between EEG channels.

3. METHODS

3.1 Participants and EEG Data Acquisitions

Ten healthy, right-handed adult (seven males, three females; age range 22-59) academic/professional staff and students of the University of South Australia volunteered to participate in this study. The experiments were conducted at the Cognitive Neuroengineering Laboratory of the University of South Australia. All participants reported normal hearing, normal or corrected-to-normal vision without any history of psychological, neurological or psychiatric disorders. EEG data were acquired at a sampling rate of 1000 Hz through a 40 channel Compumedics Neuroscan Nuamps amplifier using Curry 7 software. Prior to data collection, each participant was fitted with an appropriate sized 32 channels Quikcap. The 30 electrode sites used were based on the international 10-20 convention: FP1, FP2, F7, F3, Fz, F4, F8, FT7, FC3, FCz, FC4, FT8, T3, C3, Cz, C4, T4, TP7, CP3, CPz, CP4, TP8, T5, P3, Pz, P4, T6, O1, Oz and O2 with the average of two earlobes (A1, A2) used as the reference. Continuous EEG data were collected during three different brain states: eyes open (baseline), visual search and Web search interaction conditions. All stimulus onsets and participant responses were time-marked on the EEG record using Compumedics Neuroscan STIM 2 software and with the help of interaction logs from screen capture software Camtasia Studio.

3.2 Cognitive Tasks

Continuous EEG data was recorded while participants undertook the following computer-based experimental tasks. Stimuli were presented via STIM software for the first two tasks (i.e. 3.2.1 and 3.2.2 discussed below). For task 3.2.3, participants were provided with an Internet-connected computer. Users' Web search interaction sequences (e.g. mouse and keyboard activity; visited and bookmarked URLs) were recorded using Camtasia Studio software.

3.2.1 Eyes Open/Eyes Closed (2 minutes each)

To obtain baseline brain activity in Eyes Open (EOP) state, participants were asked to stare at a blue color fixation star comfortably on the STIM computer monitor for 2 minutes. They were then asked to close their eyes and sit calmly for a further two minutes. In the current study, only the EOP data were used for analysis and comparison with the search related brain activity.

3.2.2 Visual Search (VS) Task (approx. 2 minutes)

In this task, participants were asked to identify a target object from an array of distractor targets. For example, in Figure 1, the top red letter is the primary target. The participants would be required to press 'y' if the target is present amongst the black distractor array, or 'n' if the target is absent.

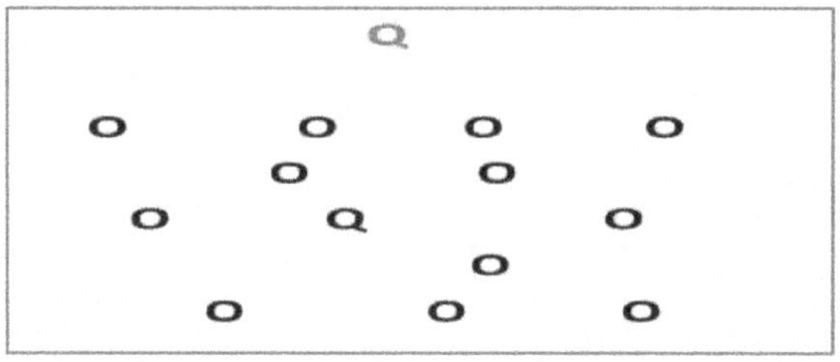

Figure 1. An example of visual search

3.2.3 Web Search Task (approx. 5-10 minutes)

The participants were instructed to search information on the Web based on three provided topic areas. They were free to use any Web browser (e.g. Internet Explorer, Google Chrome, Mozilla Firefox) and any search engine (e.g. Google, Yahoo). Participants were also free to choose the source of information. The search questions provided for the three different scenarios are given below:

Scenario 1: *Your employer has just told you that he is going to give you a new company car and asked you to choose one. The only restrictions are that the car must be red and be reasonably fuel efficient but it cannot be a European brand.*

Scenario 2: *While walking in the scrub in the Adelaide Hills you get bitten by what appears to be a tick. Should you go to the hospital Emergency Department ASAP? YES/NO and WHY?*

Scenario 3: *You've decided that you want to see a movie at the cinema. What movie do you decide to see, which session, which cinema and why?*

3.3 EEG Signal Pre-processing

From the collected EEG recordings of ten participants, two were excluded based on excessive residual artifacts such as muscle movements. Pre-processing of the remaining eight participants' EEG data was done by applying 1-70 Hz band pass filter and a notch filter at 50 Hz. To detect eye blinks, one of the typical eye blinks was selected by visual inspection and the remaining eye blinks detected using Curry 7 template matching. These eye blink artifacts were then removed using principal component analysis (PCA). Bad blocks were removed manually.

3.4 Analysis Framework

In the Web search interaction, the tasks were divided into three subtasks: Query formulation (Q), viewing of search result List (L) and reading the each individual Content page (C) as shown in Figure 2. Subtasks were time marked on the EEG signals using the captured interaction logs (key and mouse strokes) of Camtasia Studio software, although we did not distinguish between the subtasks of each individual task. EEG data were then divided into 2 second epochs for each subtask (if greater than 2 seconds). Those epochs were then averaged for each subtask level to produce one epoch of averaged data level. In order to compare search features with the baseline (EOP), 50 chunks of EEG data of two seconds duration were randomly selected from the EOP data, and then averaged. Visual search data was also considered as baseline search activity by making 2 second epochs from the stimulus onsets, then averaging into a single 2 second averaged data epoch. Averaged EEG data epoch during EOP, VS, Q, L and C were then used for the computation of NTE matrices, where each cell of the NTE matrices represents the NTE value from one electrode to another. In the case of FBNs, scalp electrodes are considered as vertices/nodes and the connections/links between electrodes are measured using NTE [8]. The constructed NTE matrices were then binarized for the analysis using different types of complex network metrics. The following complex network metrics were used: connectivity density representing the actual number of edges as a proportion to the total number of possible edges [11] which is the simplest estimator of physical cost of a network and basically used to find the global interaction pattern/magnitude of the network; node degree of directed network represents the total of incoming and outgoing edges [11] which is basically used to find hub node/region of a network. The data, information processing and associated computational steps are illustrated in Figure 2.

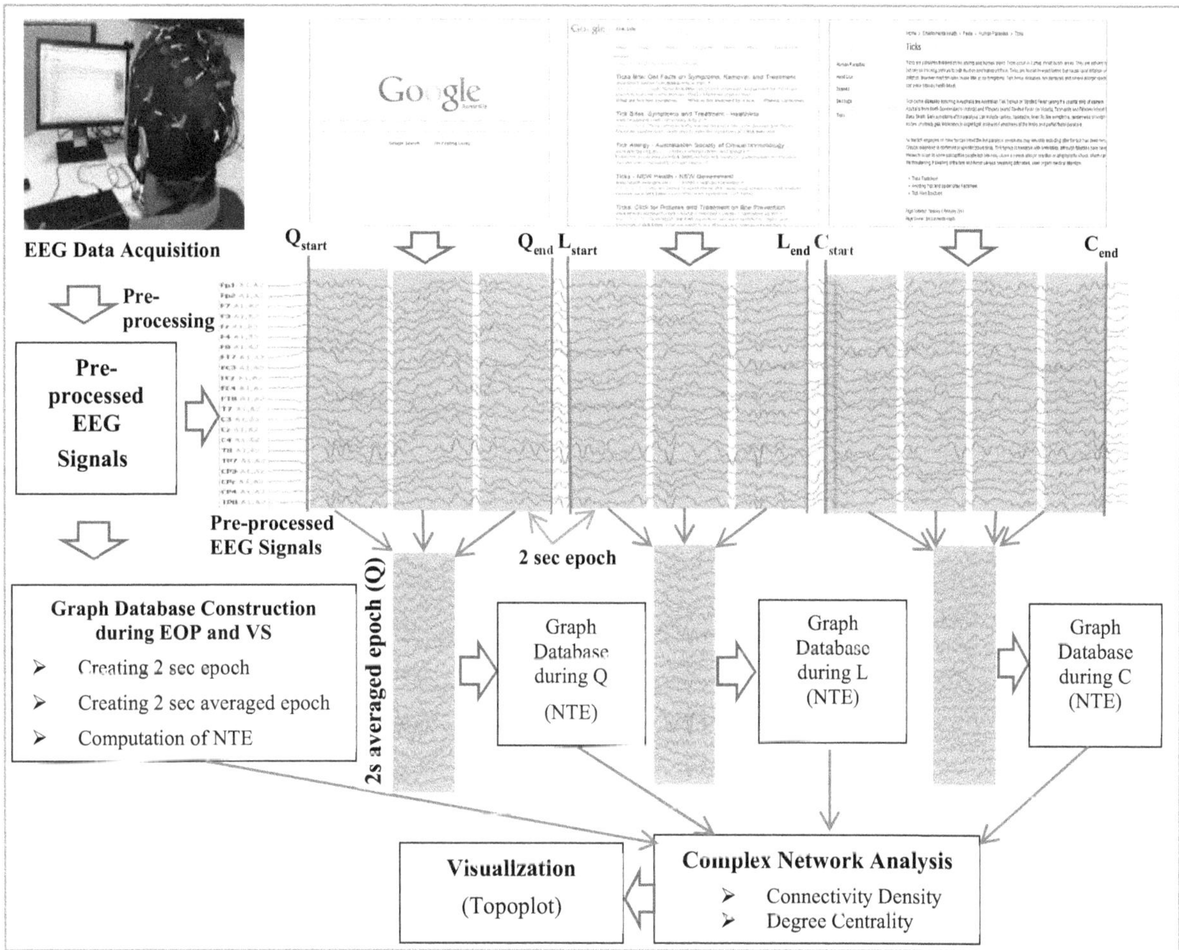

Figure 2. Transfer Entropy Analysis Framework for Web Search (TEAF-WS)

4. RESULTS AND DISCUSSION

4.1 Connectivity Density

The group averaged connectivity density of different brain states (EOP, VS, Q, L and C) was calculated and shown in Figure 3. To calculate the group averaged connectivity density, connectivity density of each individual participant was calculated then averaged across participants. As EOP was the baseline cognitive state, it had the least connectivity density compared to Web search task stages (Q, L, and C). This suggests that higher connectivity density during Q, L and, C is directly task related. That Q has higher connectivity density than L or C further supports this given that query formulation requires the execution of a number of simultaneous processes (e.g. defining query terms, viewing search interface, typing etc.).

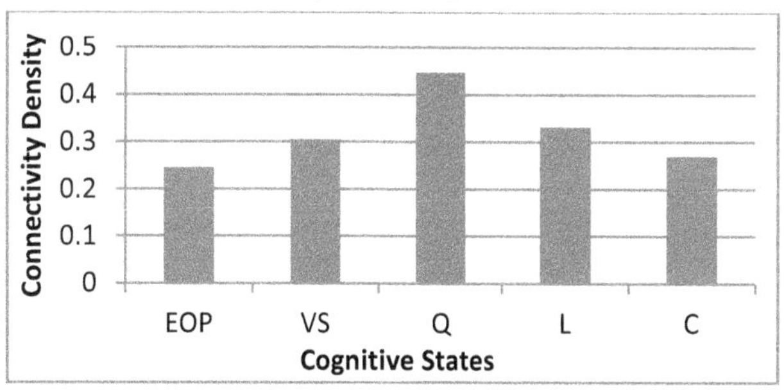

Figure 3. Connectivity density during different brain states

4.2 Topoplot using Degree Centrality

The group averaged degree centrality of all electrodes for each brain state was plotted and displayed in Figure 4 using the

EEGLAB Topoplot function [12]. Topoplot function visualizes a topographic map of a scalp data field in a 2-D circular view. To visualize the subtle variation of degree centrality value in different brain states, the color map scale of Topoplot was customized such that a color map scale is used from minimum degree centrality value to maximum degree centrality value among the degree centrality value of all the electrodes of all the brain states [12]; thus blue represents the minimum degree centrality value and red the maximum degree centrality value. Of note, all topoplots showed clear activity which is reflective of the degree of engagement for each task; that is, the visual search condition shows greater engagement than the eyes open condition, while the list reading condition shows greater engagement than the content reading condition. In the case of eyes open versus visual search, this is easily explainable – a visual search task requires focused, more intense visual attention than simply staring at a fixation star. Similarly, the button press response requirement of the visual search task elicited higher activity in motor areas (FCz, Cz, C4) than the eyes open condition. The differences between list and content reading are also explainable, albeit conjecturally, on an attentional/focus basis; that is, content reading has been "filtered" via the list process, therefore is focused externally by this process such that content reading requires less internal focus through reduced decision-making requirements. Interestingly, the similarities in processing between the visual search and contents reading tasks suggest that the two tasks share common cortical regions in the execution of those tasks. There are, however, some obvious differences between content and list reading, with list reading eliciting higher activity at CP4 and TP8 whereas content reading exhibited higher midline activity at CPz and Pz. However, in the case of the query formulation task, the high activity is most likely a reflection of multiple processes contaminating the averaging process. Further work is currently being conducted to divide this task into smaller sub-tasks so that movement, language, decision-making, and attentional processes can be further delineated during this query formation phase.

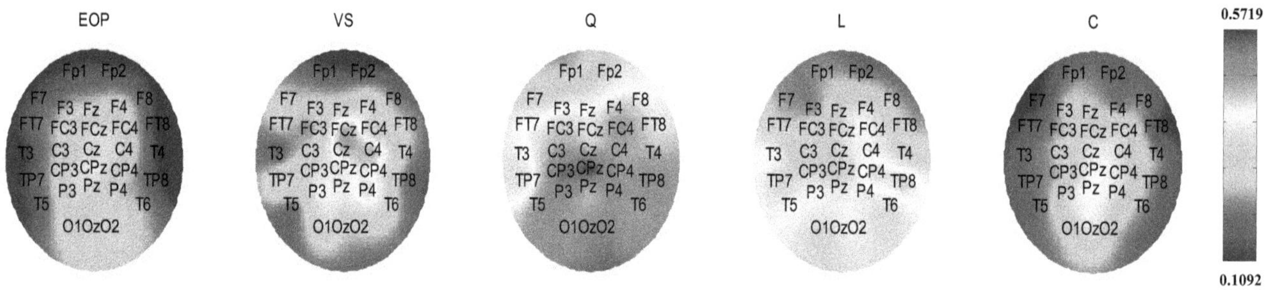

Figure 4. Topoplot during different brain states using degree centrality

5. CONCLUSION

The key contribution of this study is the construction of functional brain networks using NTE during different stages of Web searching which enabled detailed investigation of brain function during Web searching. This study quantitatively identified that during Web searching the information transfer increases in brain networks when compared to baseline. This study also demonstrated that brain activity during different Web search task stages is not the same. This study may have implications to examine the effects of cognitive abilities on information search behaviour/processes and search task performance/outcomes, thus it could allow an adaptive information retrieval system to better personalize its interaction with users. Future work will increase the sample size and consider the effect of task complexity in the experimental design.

6. REFERENCES

[1] Du, J.T.: Cognitive coordinating behaviors in multitasking web search. Proceedings of the 34th international ACM SIGIR conference on Research and development in Information Retrieval, pp. 1117-1118. ACM (2011)

[2] Du, J.T., Spink, A.: Toward a web search model: Integrating multitasking, cognitive coordination, and cognitive shifts. Journal of the American Society for Information Science and Technology 62, 1446-1472 (2011)

[3] Scholer, F., Kelly, D., Wu, W.-C., Lee, H.S., Webber, W.: The effect of threshold priming and need for cognition on relevance calibration and assessment. Proceedings of the 36th international ACM SIGIR conference on Research and development in information retrieval, pp. 623-632. ACM (2013)

[4] Kim, Y.M., Rieh, S.Y.: Dual task performance as a measure for mental effort in library searching and web searching. In Proceeding of the 68th Annual Meeting of the American Society for Information Science & Technology 42 (2005)

[5] Gwizdka, J.: Distribution of Cognitive Load in Web Search. Journal of the American Society for Information Science and Technology 61, 2167-2187 (2010)

[6] Cole, M.J., Gwizdka, J., Lui, C., Belkin, N.J.: Dynamic Assesment of Information Acquisition Effort During Interactive Search. Proceedings of the American Society for Information Science and Technology 48, 1-10 (2011)

[7] Gwizdka, J., Mostafa, J., Moshfeghi, Y., Bergman, O., Pollick, F.E.: Applications of neuroimaging in information science: Challenges and opportunities. Proceedings of the American Society for Information Science and Technology 50, 1-4 (2013)

[8] Shovon, M.H.I., Nandagopal, D.N., Vijayalakshmi, R., Du, J.T., Cocks, B.: Transfer Entropy and Information Flow Patterns in Functional Brain Networks during Cognitive Activity. In Neural Information Processing, Lecture Notes in Computer Science (LNCS 8834), Part I, 1-10 (2014)

[9] Schreiber, T.: Measuring information transfer. Physical review letters 85, 461-464 (2000)

[10] Gourévitch, B., Eggermont, J.J.: Evaluating information transfer between auditory cortical neurons. Journal of Neurophysiology 97, 2533-2543 (2007)

[11] Rubinov, M., Sporns, O.: Complex network measures of brain connectivity: uses and interpretations. Neuroimage 52, 1059-1069 (2010)

[12] Delorme, A., Makeig, S.: EEGLAB: an open source toolbox for analysis of single-trial EEG dynamics including independent component analysis. Journal of neuroscience methods 134, 9-21 (2004).

Personalized Semantic Ranking for Collaborative Recommendation

Song Xu
Institute of Automation,
Chinese Academy of Sciences
Beijing, China
song.xu@nlpr.ia.ac.cn

Shu Wu
Institute of Automation,
Chinese Academy of Sciences
Beijing, China
shu.wu@nlpr.ia.ac.cn

Liang Wang
Institute of Automation,
Chinese Academy of Sciences
Beijing, China
wangliang@nlpr.ia.ac.cn

ABSTRACT

Recently a ranking view of collaborative recommendation has received much attention in recommendation systems. Most of existing ranking approaches are based on pairwise assumption, i.e., everything that has not been selected is of less interest for a user. However it is usually not proper in many cases. To alleviate the limitation of this assumption, in this work, we present a unified framework, named Personalized Semantic Ranking (PSR). PSR models the personalized ranking and the user-generated content (UGC) simultaneously, and the semantic information extracted from UGC can make a remedy for the pairwise assumption. Moreover, utilizing the semantic information, PSR can capture the more subtle information of the user-item interaction and alleviate the overfitting problem caused by insufficient ratings. The learned topics in PSR can also serve as proper explanations for recommendation. Experimental results show that the proposed PSR yields significant improvements over the competitive compared methods on two typical datasets.

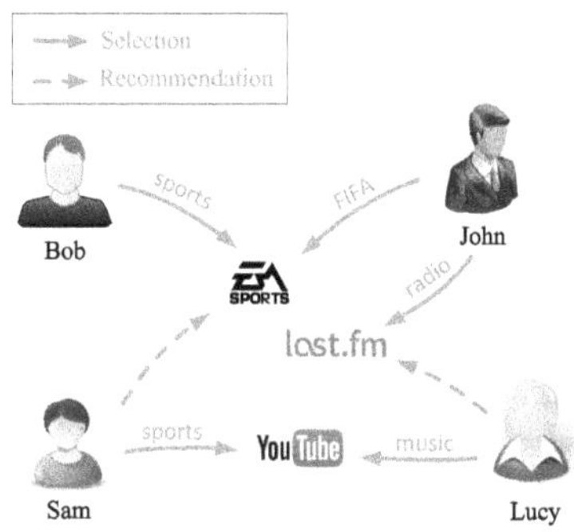

Figure 1: An illustration of user-generated content in website recommendation system. All the three websites, YouTube.com, last.fm and EASports.com, are represented by their logos respectively. The green solid lines represent "Selection", and the orange dashed lines denote "Recommendation". For example, Sam tags the website "YouTube" with "sports" and is recommended with "EASports".

Categories and Subject Descriptors

H.3.3 [**Information Storage and Retrieval**]: Information Search and Retrieval—*Information Filtering*

Keywords

Learning to rank; recommendation; user-generated content

1. INTRODUCTION

In recent years there have been growing concerns over the problem of information overload. To cater the users' needs for finding right information, a lot of researches have been done on recommender systems (RS). Personalized recommendation involves a process of learning users' preferences by analyzing their feedback, either in explicit or implicit form, and delivering the right items to each user. As one of the most well-known approaches in RS, collaborative filtering (CF) exploits the similarity among users and recommend items the similar users liked.

In most of real-world circumstances, implicit feedback, such as clicks, purchases, is more frequently available. A characteristic of implicit feedback is that it is one-class, i.e., only positive examples are observed. Motivated by the work in the domain of learning-to-rank, a ranking view to recommendation [4, 7] provides us a good way to handle the implicit feedback. One of the most successful methods is Bayesian Personalized Ranking (BPR), which assumes that everything that has not been selected is of less interest for a user [7]. However this assumption is usually not proper in many cases. In order to overcome the limitation mentioned above, we utilize semantic information extracted from UGC to construct personalized ranking for better recommendation. In the recommendation scenarios, the user-generated content is assigned by certain user to certain item in the process of user-item interaction (such as rating, purchasing, etc.). In these scenarios, UGC provides us a further clue not only on the user interest but also on the item characteristic. By incorporating UGC, recommendation systems have the potential to generate more meaningful and effective recommendations for users.

SIGIR'15, August 09 - 13, 2015, Santiago, Chile.
© 2015 ACM. ISBN 978-1-4503-3621-5/15/08 ...$15.00.
DOI: http://dx.doi.org/10.1145/2766462.2767772.

For ease of explanation, we take the tags in website recommendation systems (e.g. Delicious[1]) as a specific example to illustrate some benefits of UGC. (1) As shown in Figure 1, we may infer that Bob prefers "EASports" over "Lastfm" following the pairwise assumption in BPR. Nevertheless it is obviously unreasonable to making a judgment that Bob prefers "EASports" over "YouTube". The semantic similarity (e.g. common tags) between "EASports" and "YouTube" can make a remedy for the pairwise assumption, whereas the semantic difference between "EASports" and "Lastfm" strengthen the pairwise hypothesis. (2) Utilizing the UGC is a good choice to solve the rating sparsity problem. In Figure 1, both Sam and Lucy have selected the website "YouTube". Merely from this behavior, we may infer that they have the same interest. However, through further observation of their tags on "YouTube", we realize Sam prefers "sports" video while Lucy prefers "music" video. These behaviors cannot differentiate users' interests or item properties while the UGC can. From the above example, we notice that UGC is capable to reflect more subtle information, which may not be revealed by very sparse rating behavior. (3) As the UGC captures both the user interest and item characteristic explicitly, it can help us understand user preferences explicitly, which makes a great difference in recommendation systems. After capturing the user preference, RS can demonstrate the topics user interested in, rather than describe redundantly and blindly with a lot of annoying details. In the case described in Figure 1, we can recommend Sam "EAsports" with proper explanation, such as, "it is a popular sports site". This adequate and persuasive explanation would make the recommendation more acceptable.

In this paper, we present a novel probabilistic framework, named Personalized Semantic Ranking (PSR), which jointly modeling the personalized ranking and UGC in a common subspace. It alleviates the rigid pairwise assumption in BPR by seamlessly incorporating semantic information for recommendation. Our method captures both the collaborative preference and the content-based preference, whick can also alleviate the overfitting problem caused by sparse rating data. PSR can also exhibit the user interests and item characteristics in an explicit manner, which can be interpreted as a vector of topics discovered from UGC.

2. RELATED WORK

Collaborative filtering with implicit feedbacks has been steadily receiving more attention. For item prediction, [3] and [5] propose a regularized least-square optimization with case weights (WR-MF). The case weights can be used to reduce the impact of negative examples. Despite its popularity, the above approaches often performs poorly compared to more recent models based on ranked loss minimization. The main reason is that all these approaches focus on the task of accurately predicting the exact rating values, while ranked loss minimization focus on accurately picking the top N recommended items, which is a more practical goal. As one of the most popular methods, Bayesian Personalized Ranking (BPR) is still under a rigid assumption, that everything that has not been selected is of less interest for a user [7]. Besides, all the above approaches suffer from the problem of poor explanation for recommendation.

There are several methods which integrate attribute information about users and items into recommender systems. For example fLDA [1] and CTR [9] utilize topic models [2] for recommendation. Instead of learning one representation from a single document in these methods, PSR learns each user/item latent vector from all the relevant documents, which is more appropriate for UGC. Even some general frameworks like [6] can not well utilize the UGC.

3. PRELIMINARY

Notations In our scenario, all the observations can be denoted by $\mathcal{G} = (\mathcal{U}, \mathcal{V}, \mathcal{E}^+, \mathcal{W})$, where $\mathcal{U} = \{u_1, ..., u_N\}$ is the user set, $\mathcal{V} = \{v_1, ..., v_M\}$ is the item set. The positive feedback is given by user-item interaction set $\mathcal{E}^+ \subseteq \mathcal{U} \times \mathcal{V}$, and the element $(u, i) \in \mathcal{E}^+$ represents that user $u \in \mathcal{U}$ has purchased/clicked on item $i \in \mathcal{V}$. All the UGC is a collection of documents denoted by $\mathcal{W} = \{\mathbf{w}_{u,i} | u \in \mathcal{U}, i \in \mathcal{V}\}$. The document $\mathbf{w}_{u,i}$ is the content posted by user u to item i, and its t-th word is $W_{u,i,t}$, where $t \in \{1, ..., T_{u,i}\}$. If there is no content between user u and item i, word count $T_{u,i} = 0$.

Personalized Ranking from Implicit Feedback For each user, we transform the implicit feedback $\mathcal{E}^+$ to personalized ranking $\mathcal{R}$. Instead of modeling the implicit feedback $\mathcal{E}^+$ directly, we adopt a popular pairwise approach mentioned in BPR [7]. The idea is to discriminate the positive items $\mathcal{V}_u^+ = \{i | (u, i) \in \mathcal{E}^+\}$ from the remaining items $\mathcal{V} \backslash \mathcal{V}_u^+$ for each user u. Let "user u prefers item i to item j" be specified as $i \succ_u j$. If an item i has been selected by user u, then we assume that the user prefers this item over all other non-observed items. This property is formulated as follows:

$$\forall i, j \in \mathcal{V} : i \in \mathcal{V}_u^+ \wedge j \in \mathcal{V} \backslash \mathcal{V}_u^+ \Leftrightarrow i \succ_u j. \quad (1)$$

For convenience, we employ a random variable $R_{u,i,j}$ to denote the above pairwise property

$$R_{u,i,j} = \begin{cases} 1 & \text{if } i \succ_u j \\ 0 & \text{else} \end{cases} \quad (2)$$

For any two different items $i, j \in \mathcal{V}$, we have $R_{u,i,j} = 1 \Leftrightarrow R_{u,j,i} = 0$ (or $R_{u,i,j} = 0 \Leftrightarrow R_{u,j,i} = 1$). In our experiments, we just take the $R_{u,i,j} = 1$ ($R_{u,j,i} = 0$) into consideration. The set of all pairwise preferences can be represented as $\mathcal{T} = \{(u, i, j) | i \in \mathcal{V}_u^+ \wedge j \in \mathcal{V} \backslash \mathcal{V}_u^+\}$, and the ranking set is $\mathcal{R} = \{R_{u,i,j} | (u, i, j) \in \mathcal{T}\}$. Our model is expected to accurately preserve the ranking order.

4. PERSONALIZED SEMANTIC RANKING

Probabilistic Framework PSR maps both users and items to a common latent factor space $\mathbb{R}^K$ (each dimension represents a latent factor). Each user u is associated with a factor vector $\mathbf{U}_u \in \mathbb{R}^K$, which encodes the user preferences, and each item i is associated with a factor vector $\mathbf{V}_i \in \mathbb{R}^K$, representing the item characteristics. Both $\mathcal{W}$ and $\mathcal{R}$ can be generated from the latent factors.

For constructing the ranking $\mathcal{R}$, we first assume that each user-item pair has a rating score, which reflects the preference degree. Thus we have a preference score $x_{u,i}$ for user-item pair (u, i) and another score $x_{u,j}$ for a different pair (u, j). The probability that user u prefers item i to item j is $p(R_{u,i,j} = 1)$, which is parameterized by the relative score $x_{u,i,j} = x_{u,i} - x_{u,j}$. Here, we adopt a scoring function, which is widely used in factor models, $x_{u,i} = \mathbf{U}_u^T \mathbf{V}_i$.

[1]http://www.delicious.com

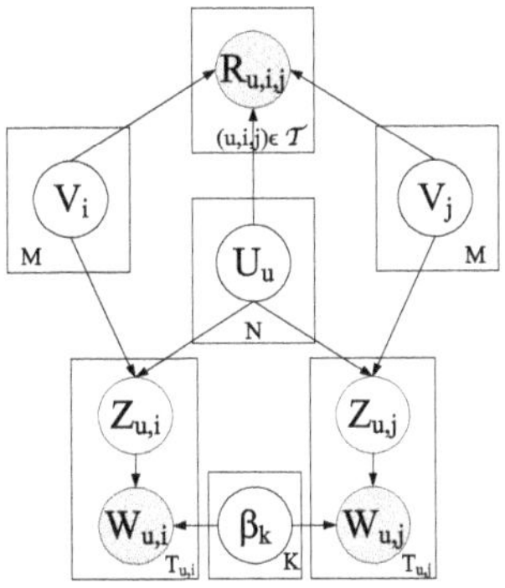

Figure 2: Graphical model of PSR. There are N users and M items. R is the personalized ranking. For some of the user-item pairs, there are documents extracted from the UGC. The Gaussian prior parameters for U and V have been omitted for simplicity in this figure.

For constructing the content $\mathcal{W}$, a latent representation for $\mathbf{w}_{u,i}$ is introduced as $\boldsymbol{\theta}_{u,i}$. It is also called topic proportions in topic models [2], where $\mathbf{z}_{u,i}$ is the topic assignments for each word in document $\mathbf{w}_{u,i}$ and each topic $\boldsymbol{\beta}_k$ is a distribution over words. $\boldsymbol{\theta}_{u,i}$ encodes not only the latent semantic of document $\mathbf{w}_{u,i}$, but also the user u's topic preferences on item i. Each component of $\boldsymbol{\theta}_{u,i}$ is expected to be positively correlated with both the corresponding user factor and item factor. That is, if an item has higher value of a certain factor, or a user values higher on a certain topic, the corresponding topic is more likely to appear in the UGC. In order to preserve such dependent correlation, we introduce a simple way to build a direct connection between the user-item pair and document, $\boldsymbol{\theta}_{u,i} = \pi(\mathbf{U}_u + \mathbf{V}_i)$. For a K-dimensional vector $\mathbf{x}$, $\pi(\mathbf{x})$ is logistic transformation function $\pi(\mathbf{x}) = \exp(\mathbf{x})/\sum_k \exp(x_k)$, which makes it possible to bound $\mathbf{x}$ within the range $[0, 1]$.

In order to balance the model's complexity against overfitting on the training data, Gaussian priors are also imposed on the factors $\mathbf{U}$ and $\mathbf{V}$. The graphical model is depicted in Figure 2. The generative process for all the textual documents $\mathcal{W}$ and personalized ranking $\mathcal{R}$ is as follows:

1. For each user u, draw user factors $\mathbf{U}_u \sim \mathcal{N}(\boldsymbol{\mu}_U, \boldsymbol{\Sigma}_U)$
2. For each item i, draw item factors $\mathbf{V}_i \sim \mathcal{N}(\boldsymbol{\mu}_V, \boldsymbol{\Sigma}_V)$
3. For each word $W_{u,i,t}$ / $W_{u,j,t}$
   (a) Draw topic assignment $Z_{u,i,t}|\mathbf{U}_u, \mathbf{V}_i \sim Mult(\boldsymbol{\theta}_{u,i})$
   (b) Draw word $W_{u,i,t}|Z_{u,i,t} \sim Mult(\boldsymbol{\beta}_{Z_{u,i,t}})$
4. For each triplet $(u, i, j) \in \mathcal{T}$, draw the ranking $R_{u,i,j} \sim Ber(1/(1 + \exp(-x_{u,i,j})))$

For ease of exposition, let $\Theta = [\boldsymbol{\mu}_U, \boldsymbol{\mu}_V, \boldsymbol{\Sigma}_U, \boldsymbol{\Sigma}_V, \boldsymbol{\beta}]$ denote the model parameters, $\Delta = [\mathbf{U}, \mathbf{V}, \mathbf{Z}]$ denote the latent variables. The joint probability distribution for the observed variables can be written as

$$p(\mathcal{R}, \mathcal{W}|\Theta) = \iint p(\mathbf{U})p(\mathbf{V})p(\mathcal{R}|\mathbf{U}, \mathbf{V})p(\mathcal{W}|\mathbf{U}, \mathbf{V})d\mathbf{U}d\mathbf{V}, \quad (3)$$

where Θ is omitted in the right for brevity.

Maximum A Posterior The objective of our model is to find the optimal latent factors $\mathbf{U}$ and $\mathbf{V}$ for accurately modeling ranking and UGC. Maximum a posterior (MAP) estimation can be used to obtain a point estimate of the posterior based on the observed data, $[\hat{\mathbf{U}}, \hat{\mathbf{V}}] = \arg\max_{\mathbf{U},\mathbf{V}} p(\mathbf{U}, \mathbf{V}|\mathcal{W}, \mathcal{R}; \Theta)$. The negative log likelihood can be used as loss function

$$\mathcal{L}_{MAP} = -\log p(\mathbf{U}, \mathbf{V}|\mathcal{W}, \mathcal{R}; \Theta) = \overbrace{-\log p(\mathcal{R}|\mathbf{U}, \mathbf{V})}^{\mathcal{L}_R} \quad (4)$$
$$\underbrace{-\log p(\mathcal{W}|\mathbf{U}, \mathbf{V})}_{\mathcal{L}_W} \underbrace{- \log p(\mathbf{U}) - \log p(\mathbf{V})}_{\mathcal{L}_{reg}}.$$

In Equation (4), we notice that loss function consists of three parts, ranking loss $\mathcal{L}_R$, content loss $\mathcal{L}_W$ and regularization loss $\mathcal{L}_{reg}$. The ranking loss $\mathcal{L}_R$, which ensures successfully preserving the ranking, will be discussed in the next section. The content loss can be denoted by $\mathcal{L}_W = -\sum_{u,i}\sum_{t} n_{u,i,t} \sum_{k} \log \theta_{u,i,k}\beta_{k,W_{u,i,t}}$, where $n_{u,i,t}$ denotes how often the word $W_{u,i,t}$ occurred in document $\mathbf{w}_{u,i}$. If we place zero-mean spherical Gaussian priors on $\mathbf{U}$ and $\mathbf{V}$, $\mathcal{L}_{reg}$ works like $L2$ regularization which prevent models from overfitting [8]. Given the model parameters Θ, the optimal factors $[\mathbf{U}, \mathbf{V}]$ should be obtained by minimization of all three losses. Then each score $x_{u,i}$ can be predicted by $\mathbf{U}_u^T\mathbf{V}_i$. After sorting all the scores for each user, the top N items will be recommended to the user.

5. EXPERIMENTS

Datasets and Settings We evaluate our model on two published datasets: social bookmarking dataset from Delicious and scientific literature from Citation-network. In Delicious dataset, each user bookmarks a set of webpages which can be regarded as positive examples of the user's interests. Here, the bookmark is a kind of UGC, and the task is to recommend webpages to users. In our experiments, we draw a subsample such that each user has bookmarked at least 5 webpages, each webpage has been selected by at least 3 users and each bookmark appears at least 5 times. Citation-network $V1$ is a dataset released by Arnetminer. In this circumstance, we treat the paper title as a kind of UGC between the author and the publication, and our task is to recommend publications to authors. Removing papers which have no publication information, we obtain a subset of papers published from 2001 to 2010.

Baselines and Evaluation Metric We conduct comparisons with several state-of-the-art methods, including SVD, WR-MF [3, 5], BPR-MF [7] and FM [6]. In SVD, the missing is treated as negative examples. In FM, the UGC are directly treated as additional dimension in feature vector. In order to evaluate the qualities of the recommendations, we randomly select 20% of the implicit ratings to be the test set, and use the remaining entries for training. Two metrics, F1-score and Mean Average Precision (MAP), which are widely used for recommendation evaluation, are adopted here.

Result Analysis Table 1 gives the performance comparison with a variety of dimensionalities on the Delicious and the Citation-network datasets. From that we can see, under different settings of K, our models consistently outperform the compared methods. Figure 3a is the precision-recall curve on Delicious dataset. From the results we notice that the personalized ranking methods have great superiority over rating prediction methods. Owing much to the se-

Table 1: **Performance comparison on the Delicious and Citation-network datasets with three different factor dimensionalities $K = 10, 30, 50$. The predictive accuracy is measured by MAP and F1-score. The values are under the percentage scale.**

Method	Delicious						Citation-network					
	F1@10			MAP@10			F1@10			MAP@10		
	K=10	K=30	K=50	K=10	K=30	K=50	K=10	K=30	K=50	K=10	K=30	K=50
SVD	2.52	2.73	2.73	1.91	2.24	1.99	0.91	0.91	1.07	3.17	3.33	3.42
WR-MF	3.03	3.17	4.34	2.65	2.90	2.97	1.27	1.28	1.32	4.02	4.15	4.80
BPR-MF	3.35	3.50	3.57	2.54	2.87	2.71	1.53	1.51	1.57	6.08	5.80	6.12
FM	5.57	5.52	5.61	4.43	4.63	4.72	1.72	1.75	1.74	7.82	7.67	7.88
PSR	6.12	6.35	6.41	4.72	4.93	5.23	2.39	2.26	2.50	11.4	11.2	12.2

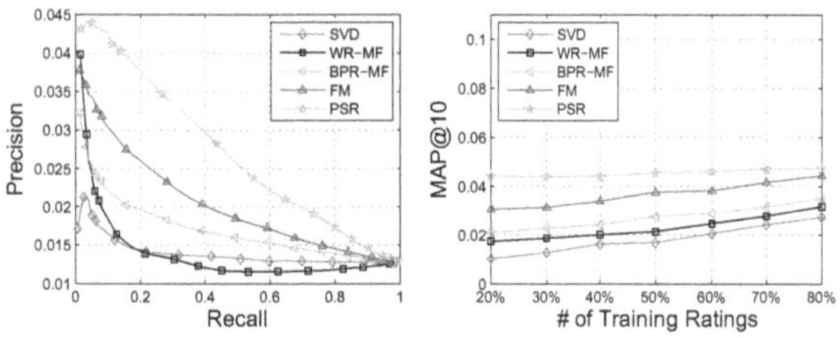

(a) (b)

Figure 3: Left panel: precision-recall curves of the Delicious dataset. Right panel: MAP with different amounts of training ratings on Delicious dataset. (K=30)

Table 2: Five topics discovered by PSR on the Citation-network dataset. Each topic is shown with the top 8 words, top 4 authors and top 5 publications. (K=30)

topic 00 "CV"	Topic 02 "Wireless"	topic 05 "Education"	topic 013 "Graphics"	topic 020 "Grid Computing"
learning	network	computer	motion	grid
analysis	sensor	science	surface	control
recognition	wireless	teaching	interactive	access
image	hoc	student	simulation	web
algorithm	routing	design	dynamic	computing
neural	energy	education	texture	resource
classification	mobile	assessment	mesh	management
face	protocol	study	human	composition
Jennifer C.	Joseph P.	Brian H.	Andrew S.	Chunlin L.
Guoliang X.	Sha L.	Jorma S.	Bryan E.	Layuan L.
Radha P.	Ajit W.	Marja K.	Eran G.	Brahim M.
Loukas L.	Antonio G.	Raymond L.	Yiying T.	Steve B.
ACCV	IJSNet	ICER	SIGGRAPH	IJWGS
SSVM	TOSN	ACE	I3D	CCGrid
PR	EWSN	SIGCSE	SGP	HPDC
TIP	SECON	JERIC	SPM	JSSPP
IJCV	WiSec	FECS	TOG	AusGrid

mantic analysis from UGC, PSR increases the performance by more than 20% compared to SVD and WR-MF. PSR achieves great improvement even compared with BPR-MF, which largely due to the semantic offset from naive pairwise assumption in BPR-MF. PSR works better than the general framework FM for well utilizing the UGC.

We further evaluate the ability of compared methods in handling different amount of training ratings (20% – 80%). The performance comparison with $K = 30$ on the Delicious dataset is shown in Figure 3b. The experimental results indicate that PSR can obtain the best performance with varying amounts of training ratings. These improvements are largely due to the incorporation of UGC. Moreover, our method outperforms other methods more significantly when fewer ratings are provided. When we use 80% of the ratings as training set, PSR increases the performance of SVD with 130%, while given 20% ratings, PSR enhances the performance by more than 360%. The evidences show that when the rating matrix is sparse, the impact of UGC is very significant in PSR.

Another advantage of PSR is that it can explain the user and item latent space using the topics discovered from the user-generated content. For user u, we can find the top matched topics by ranking the entries of factor vector $\mathbf{U}_u$. For item i, we also can rank the entries of factor vector $\mathbf{V}_i$. The top matched topics serve as an explanation of user interest and item characteristic. Some of the topics discovered in the Citation-network are displayed in Table 2. For example, the table illustrates that the top words in topic 02 are "network" , "sensor" etc., the most related authors of this topic are "Joseph P.", "Sha L. " etc, and the most related publications are "IJSNet", "TOSN" etc. Owing to the good properties of interpretation, user experience would be greatly improved in real-world recommender systems.

6. ACKNOWLEDGMENTS

This work is jointly supported by National Basic Research Program of China (2012CB316300) and National Natural Science Foundation of China (61403390, 61175003, 61135002, U1435221).

7. REFERENCES

[1] D. Agarwal and B.-C. Chen. flda: Matrix factorization through latent dirichlet allocation. In *WSDM*, 2010.

[2] D. M. Blei, A. Y. Ng, and M. Jordan. Latent dirichlet allocation. *JMLR*, 2003.

[3] Y. Hu, Y. Koren, and C. Volinsky. Collaborative filtering for implicit feedback datasets. In *ICDM*, 2008.

[4] J. Lee, S. Bengio, S. Kim, G. Lebanon, and Y. Singer. Local collaborative ranking. In *WWW*, 2014.

[5] R. Pan, Y. Zhou, B. Cao, N. N. Liu, R. Lukose, M. Scholz, and Q. Yang. One-class collaborative filtering. In *ICDM*, 2008.

[6] S. Rendle. Factorization machines. In *ICDM*, 2010.

[7] S. Rendle, C. Freudenthaler, Z. Gantner, and L. Schmidt-Thieme. Bpr: Bayesian personalized ranking from implicit feedback. In *UAI*, 2009.

[8] R. Salakhutdinov and A. Mnih. Probabilistic matrix factorization. In *NIPS*, 2007.

[9] C. Wang and D. M. Blei. Collaborative topic modeling for recommending scientific articles. In *ACM SIGKDD*, 2011.

Active Learning for Entity Filtering in Microblog Streams

Damiano Spina[†]
damiano.spina@rmit.edu.au

Maria-Hendrike Peetz[‡, *]
mariahendrike.peetz@gmail.com

Maarten de Rijke[‡]
derijke@uva.nl

[†] RMIT University, Melbourne, Australia
[‡] University of Amsterdam, Amsterdam, The Netherlands

ABSTRACT

Monitoring the reputation of entities such as companies or brands in microblog streams (e.g., Twitter) starts by selecting mentions that are related to the entity of interest. Entities are often ambiguous (e.g., "Jaguar" or "Ford") and effective methods for selectively removing non-relevant mentions often use background knowledge obtained from domain experts. Manual annotations by experts, however, are costly. We therefore approach the problem of entity filtering with active learning, thereby reducing the annotation load for experts. To this end, we use a strong passive baseline and analyze different sampling methods for selecting samples for annotation. We find that margin sampling—an informative type of sampling that considers the distance to the hyperplane used for class separation—can effectively be used for entity filtering and can significantly reduce the cost of annotating initial training data.

Categories and Subject Descriptors

H.3.3 [**Information Search and Retrieval**]: Information filtering

Keywords

Text classification; Entity filtering; Active learning; Twitter

1. INTRODUCTION

With increasing volumes of social media data, monitoring and analyzing this data is a vital part of the marketing strategy of businesses. The extraction of topics, conversations, and trends around an entity (such as a company, organization, celebrity) allows analysts to understand and manage the entity's reputation. It is infeasible to manually process every single tweet or blogpost that may have been written about an entity. Since entity names are often ambiguous, filtering social media for relevant information—that is, Entity Filtering (EF)—saves tedious work and is a vital preprocessing step for further automation of Online Reputation Monitoring (ORM) [8, 12, 13]. If the performance of the EF module decreases, the performance of all subsequent modules is harmed [13]. EF on social media is therefore an active field of research and has previously been considered in various settings: at the WePS-3 evaluation effort [1] and as part of the RepLab 2012 and 2013 challenges [2, 3]. Missing important tweets and news items about an entity of interest can be disastrous and expensive [9]. An entity may need to react immediately to avoid long-lasting harmful publicity. The ORM industry therefore seeks to find a balance between manual and automatic filtering.

Our approach to EF is based on active learning [11], a semi-automatic machine learning process interacting with the user for updating the classification model. It selects instances that are meant to maximize the classification performance with minimal annotation effort. Active learning is especially attractive in the setting of EF for ORM as it promises to (a) use the analysts' background knowledge and understanding to improve performance, and (b) capture new topics and problems without exhaustive annotation effort. Active learning has been widely used in information access tasks [10, 16] and text categorization [7]. Below, we present an active learning framework for EF.[1] We start from simple but competitive passive baselines and then examine alternative strategies for sampling examples for learning and their applicability for EF.

2. APPROACH

In this section we elaborate our active learning approach to EF. Briefly, (1) instances are represented as feature vectors; (2) instances from the training dataset are used for building the initial classification model; (3) test instances are automatically classified using the initial model; (4) we sample candidates for additional labeling; this step is performed by margin sampling: the instance closest to the class separation is selected; and (5) the user manually inspects the instance and labels it; the labeled instance is then considered when updating the model. The active learning process is repeated until a termination condition is satisfied.

We use a Support Vector Machine[2] (SVM) classifier. Our active learning approach can be split into the *selection of candidates* for active annotations, *annotation of the candidates* and *updating the model*. Therefore, one iteration of our learning model follows the following three steps: (1) select the best candidate x from the test set T; (2) annotate the candidate x; and (3) update the model.

If the resources are available, the training data used to initialize the model can be a large manually annotated (bulk) set of tweets published before the test set. Below we detail the candidate selection, candidate annotation, and model updating steps.

2.1 Candidate selection and annotation

Candidate selection is the process of sampling candidates that are used for annotation. A successful selection approach selects candi-

*Now at Google Switzerland.

SIGIR '15, August 09–13, 2015, Santiago, Chile.

ACM 978-1-4503-3621-5/15/08 ... $15.00.
DOI: http://dx.doi.org/10.1145/2766462.2767839

[1]The code is available at http://damiano.github.io/al-ef
[2]http://scikit-learn.org/stable/modules/svm.html

dates that, when annotated, improve the model. Standard baseline approaches are: *passive learning* without sampling, which is identical to non-active learning, *random sampling*, which samples randomly from the pool, and *margin sampling*, which samples close to the margin of the classification boundary. We also propose two further approaches to improve margin sampling. For *reranking*, we rerank the list of samples based on density.

Passive learning. Passive learning does not use any active learning at all. We only initialize the model without retraining it, therefore skipping the candidate selection, training, and updating phase.

Random sampling. Here, the candidate instance is sampled without replacement from the training set. There is no informed prior on the instances. Random sampling has proven to be effective for other tasks, e.g., building dependency treebanks [5], or clinical text classification [6].

Margin sampling. The most commonly used sampling method in binary classification problems is uncertainty sampling [11]. We consider a specific uncertainty sampling method especially suitable for support vector machines [15]: *margin sampling*. We measure the uncertainty of a candidate x based on the distance to the margin:

$$\text{Uncertainty}(x) = 1 - \left|P(C_1 \mid F_x) - P(C_2 \mid F_x)\right|, \quad (1)$$

where $P(C_1 \mid F_x)$ and $P(C_2 \mid F_x)$ are the probabilities that the candidate x, as represented by the feature vector F_x, generates the classes C_1 and C_2, respectively.

Candidates are sampled based on the classification difficulty, thereby selecting candidates where the classifier is less confident. Following this, the candidate x to be annotated from the test set T is selected as follows:

$$x = \arg\max_{x_i \in T} \text{Uncertainty}(x_i). \quad (2)$$

This candidate x is then annotated and used to update the model. For a linear kernel of the SVM this means: instances (tweets here) that are closest to the class separation are selected.

*Margin*Density.* Following [17], we incorporate the density of a candidate into the maximization criterion of a candidate ranker. Intuitively, while outliers may be difficult to predict, they are also not very helpful in improving the classifier:

$$\text{K-Density}(x) = \textstyle\sum_{x_i \in \text{KNN}(x,T,K)} \frac{\text{sim}(x,x_i)}{K}, \quad (3)$$

where $\text{KNN}(x, T, K)$ are the K most similar instances to x in the test set T. The similarity $\text{sim}(x, x_i)$ between two instances x, x_i is based on the Jaccard similarity. We say that the $\text{K-Density}(x)$ is the $\text{Density}(x)$, if K is dynamically set to $|T|$.

In the Margin*Density setting, the candidate x to be annotated from the test set T is selected as follows:

$$x = \arg\max_{x_i \in T} \text{Uncertainty}(x_i) \cdot D(x_i), \quad (4)$$

where $D(x_i)$ is a placeholder for $\text{K-Density}(x)$ or $\text{Density}(x)$.

Once the candidates are selected, the algorithm collects annotations from the user. Section 3.2 details how we simulate the user input.

2.2 Model updating

The training of the model is fast.[3] We therefore decided to *retrain* the model with *every* freshly annotated instance. The instance and its annotation are added to the training set and the model is retrained. As commonly done, the weights for both training and new instances are uniform.

[3] In our experiments, a few dozen seconds on a workstation with 16 cores, 2.6GHz, and 96GB RAM workstation. In the ORM scenario, the training set is entity-oriented and would typically not include more than a thousand tweets.

3. EXPERIMENTAL SETUP

We aim to analyze the effectiveness of active learning for EF. Below, we describe the dataset, the feedback scenario, and how we evaluate.

3.1 Data

We use the RepLab2013 [3] dataset, which is, to our knowledge, the largest dataset available for the EF task in microblog posts.[4] The dataset comprises a total of $142,527$ tweets in two languages: English and Spanish. The dataset consists of 61 entities in four domains: automotive, banking, universities and music. For every company, 750 $(1,500)$ tweets were used as training (test) set, on average, with the beginning of the training and test set being six months apart. Crawling was performed from June 1, 2012 to December 31, 2012 using each entity's canonical name as query (e.g., "stanford" for Stanford University).

Tweets are represented as set-of-words: bag-of-words with binary occurrence (1 if the word is present in the tweet, 0 if not). We removed punctuation, lowercasing, tokenizing by white spaces, reducing multiple repetitions of characters (from n to 2), and stopwords.

3.2 Scenario

Without direct users, the usual approach to model an active learning setting is to take the annotations from the test set. This simulates the user feedback; this is also what we do. We therefore train on the dedicated training set and sample from the entire test set.

For our experiments we use Support Vector Machines, using a linear kernel.[5] The penalty parameter C is automatically adjusted by weights inversely proportional to class frequencies. We use the default values for the rest of parameters.

We compare the effectiveness using different N_{test} of sampled tweets with the effectiveness of two passive supervised learning approaches: the initial model and the best approach at RepLab2013. We compare random sampling, margin sampling, and the diverse instantiations of density sampling methods listed in the previous section. Table 1 provides an overview over the acronyms used for the runs that we consider. The *passive* run is the underlying baseline for active learning; it is based on the training set. The *best* run is the score for the best performing system at RepLab2013. *RS* and *MS* are active learning runs, using random and margin sampling,

Table 1: Runs used in our experiments. MSD and MS-RRD can be combined with a K for K-Density.

Acronym	Active	Description
passive	no	Passive learning, lower bound
best	no	Best RepLab2013 system
RS	yes	Random sampling
MS	yes	Margin sampling
MSD	yes	Margin*Density sampling
MS-RRD	yes	Reranking MS based on density

[4] http://nlp.uned.es/replab2013

[5] We tested different algorithms (Naïve Bayes, Decision Trees) and this is the one that obtained the best results in terms of the initial (passive learning) model.

respectively. *MSD* combines margin with density sampling, based on the candidate set. Finally, *MS-RRD* reranks margin sampling based on density.

3.3 Evaluation

Unless stated otherwise, we use the official evaluation metrics from the RepLab2013 Filtering Subtask: accuracy and the harmonic mean of reliability and sensitivity $\left(F_1(R,S)\right)$ [4]. We use the Student's t-test to evaluate the significance of observed differences, using Bonferroni normalization where appropriate. We denote significant improvements with $^\blacktriangle$ and $^\vartriangle$ ($p < 0.01$ and $p < 0.05$, respectively). Likewise, $^\blacktriangledown$ and $^\triangledown$ denote declines.

4. RESULTS AND ANALYSIS

We analyze the passive baseline in Section 4.1. We then discuss the performance of margin sampling and random sampling in Section 4.2 and the impact of training in Section 4.3. Section 4.4 analyses the performance of density sampling.

4.1 Passive baseline

In order to establish our passive baseline as state of the art for EF, we compare it with the best performing system at RepLab.

Table 2: Performance of *passive* baseline and *best* RepLab2013 system.

Run	Accuracy	$\mathbf{F_1(R,S)}$
best	0.91	0.49
passive	0.92	0.42

Table 2 compares the effectiveness of *best* and *passive* runs in terms of accuracy and $F_1(R,S)$. A number of observations are worth making. First, in terms of accuracy, the effectiveness of all the runs is above 0.9, leaving little room for improvement. The *passive* run outperforms the *best* run, but the difference is not statistically significant. In contrast, $F_1(R,S)$ reveals more differences between the runs. Taking into account that our *passive* approach that relies on sets-of-words is more efficient than the approach used in *best*—which makes use of external knowledge bases—, we conclude that *passive* is a suitable starting point to use for active learning of EF.

4.2 Margin sampling vs. random sampling

We compare the effectiveness of two candidate selection methods for active learning, random and margin sampling. We also compare our active learning approach to EF against the state-of-the-art in the EF task and against our *passive* learning baseline.

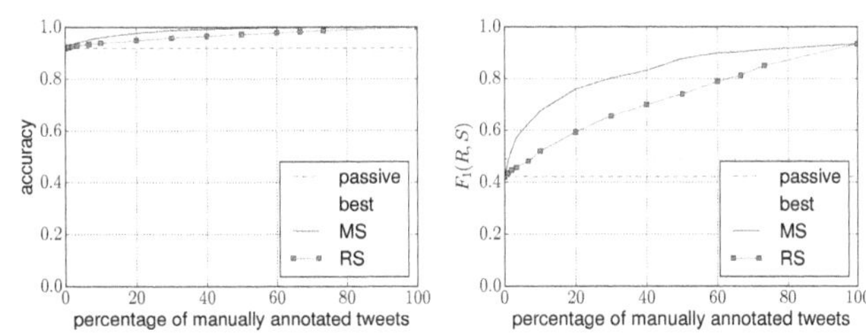

(a) Accuracy (b) $F_1(R,S)$

Figure 1: Accuracy (1a) and $\mathbf{F_1(R,S)}$ (1b) vs. percentage of manually annotated tweets $\mathbf{N_{test}}$.

Fig. 1 compares the *MS* and *RS* runs with the passive runs in terms of accuracy (1a) and $F_1(R,S)$ (1b). *MS* outperforms *passive* and *best* after inspecting only 2% of the test data (which, on average, corresponds to 30 tweets per entity), obtaining a $F_1(R,S)$-score of 0.52 (vs. 0.49). Using $N_{\text{test}} = 5\%$, *MS* significantly outperforms *best*, obtaining an $F_1(R,S)$-score of $0.63^\blacktriangle$. On the other hand, *RS* needs more feedback to be able to reach *best*. Using $N_{\text{test}} = 5\%$ it achieves an $F_1(R,S)$-score of 0.48, while using 10% of sampled tweets achieves a score of 0.52. The graphs also show *MS* outperforming *RS* consistently. Here, differences begin to be statistically significant from 3%–5%, with $F_1(R,S)$-scores of $0.57^\vartriangle$, $0.63^\blacktriangle$. Interestingly, while *RS* shows a linear behavior, *MS* starts with an exponential gain of effectiveness in terms of $F_1(R,S)$. In terms of $F_1(R,S)$, the effectiveness reached by *RS* after inspecting 10% of the test data can be achieved by *MS* considering only 2%. This amounts to an 80% reduction in cost.

In sum, our active learning approach requires small amounts of feedback to outperform state-of-the-art passive EF systems. Additionally, margin sampling significantly outperforms random sampling.

4.3 Initial training reduction

We examine to which degree active learning can reduce the cost of the initial training phase. Initializing any supervised approach—whether passive or active—to EF has a cost derived from annotating the initial training data. We look at different percentages of training data used to initialize the model.

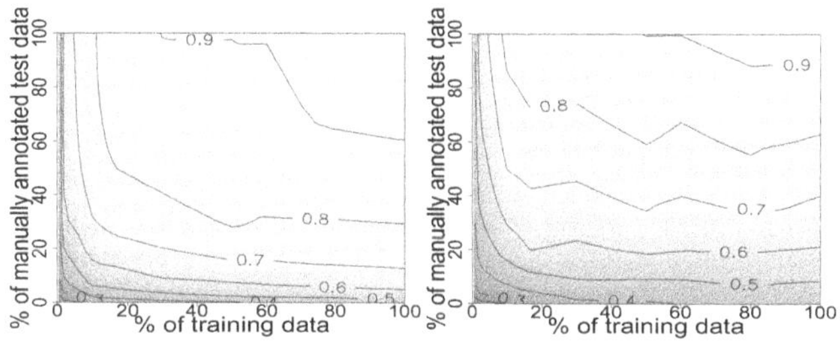

(a) Margin Sampling (b) Random Sampling

Figure 2: $\mathbf{F_1(R,S)}$-scores with different percentages of training data for the initial model (x-axis) and different percentages of test data for manually inspection during the active learning process (y-axis), using margin (2a) or random (2b) sampling. Red/dark and yellow/light correspond to lower and higher $\mathbf{F_1(R,S)}$ values, respectively.

Fig. 2 shows heat maps representing the evolution of $F_1(R,S)$ for different percentages of training data (x-axis) and sampled test data (y-axis), for *MS* (2a) and *RS* (2b). Red/dark and yellow/light correspond to lower and higher $F_1(R,S)$ values, respectively. *MS* needs less training data to obtain competitive $F_1(R,S)$-scores than *RS*. For instance, initializing the model with 10% and inspecting 10% of test data using *MS* achieves an $F_1(R,S)$-score of 0.55, while *RS* achieves only 0.44. Considering only 10% (i.e., 75 tweets) as the initial training set, the effectiveness of *best* can be reached after 100 tweets ($N_{\text{test}} < 7\%$) using *MS*. In terms of annotation cost, this corresponds to a 75% reduction.

In sum, the cost of training the initial model can be substantially reduced by using active learning, especially with margin sampling.

4.4 Dealing with outliers

We compare the effectiveness of favoring samples that are close to the margin and similar to other, unknown, samples in the candidate set. Fig. 3a compares margin*density sampling (*MSD*) for

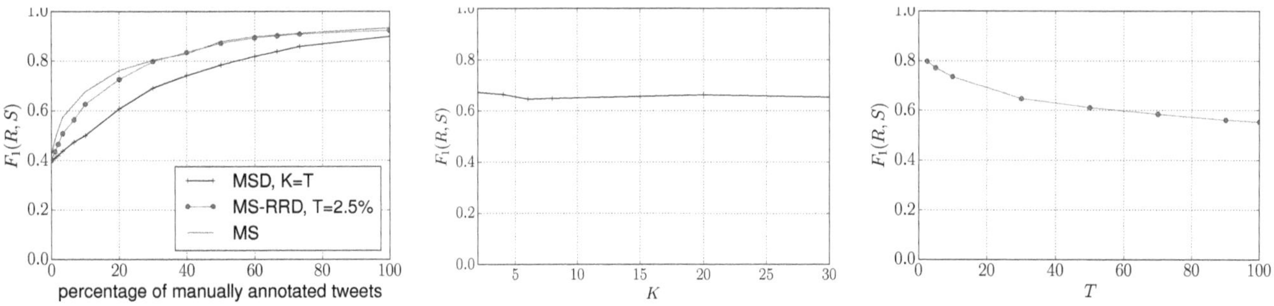

(a) *MSD* and *MS-RRD* vs. *MS*. (b) K for *MSD*, considering $N_{\text{test}} = 28\%$. (c) T for *MS-RRD*, considering $N_{\text{test}} = 28\%$.

Figure 3: $\mathbf{F_1(R,S)}$-scores for the two approaches of density sampling, *MSD* and *MS-RRD*. Fig. 3a shows the development for different percentages of annotated tweets, Fig. 3b and Fig. 3c show the difference in $\mathbf{F_1(R,S)}$-scores for $\mathbf{28\%}$ of manually annotated tweets over different K and K, for *MSD* and *MS-RRD*, respectively.

$K = T$ and the best performing MSD reranking (*MS-RRD*, $T = 3$) in terms of $F_1(R,S)$ with margin sampling (*MS*). Both approaches to *MSD* performs worse than *MS*. Experiments that consider different numbers of instances K to compute the density (Fig. 3b) show that the performance is quite constant over K.

The performance of reranking based on density highly depends on the quantity of items of the initial ranking that are being considered (Fig. 3c). The performance drops significantly with the number of candidates used to rerank. While the performance of *MS-RRD* is closer to *MS* than *MSD*, vanilla *MS* performs significantly better than all density approaches.

One entity, however, stands out: *Chrysler* reaches an $F_1(R,S)$ of 1 using *MSD* and an $F_1(R,S)$ of 0 for normal margin sampling.[6] This entity has very clear topical clusters, about *winning prizes*, *chrysler 300*, *chrysler building*, and *union rights*. Manually classifying one of the elements in a cluster automatically classifies all the other elements. The other entity, *Bankia*, where *MSD* performs much better than *MS*, features a similar topical distribution.

We can conclude that unlike what was found in previous work, for EF density usually does not provide complementary information to margin sampling on this dataset.

5. CONCLUSION

We have examined the feasibility of using active learning for entity filtering on tweets. We have shown that much less annotation is needed when annotation is done on the fly, i.e., using active learning with 10% of the initial training set can lead to a 75% reduction of costs. We have contrasted several state-of-the-art sampling methods and have shown that margin sampling works best.

Future work should focus on entity filtering specific sampling algorithms and exploring the task in streaming scenarios. Since entity filtering is a daily task, an active learning streaming scenario simulates the ORM process even better.

Acknowledgments. This research was supported by the European Community's Seventh Framework Programme (FP7/2007-2013) under grant agreement nr 312827 (VOX-Pol), the Netherlands Organisation for Scientific Research (NWO) under project nrs 727.011.005, 612.001.116, HOR-11-10, 640.006.013, 612.066.930, CI-14-25, SH-322-15, Amsterdam Data Science, the Dutch national program COMMIT, the ESF Research Network Program ELIAS, the Elite Network Shifts project funded by the Royal Dutch Academy of Sciences (KNAW), the Netherlands eScience Center under project nr 027.012.105, the Yahoo! Faculty Research and Engagement Program, the Microsoft Research PhD program, and the HPC Fund.

[6]Note that $F_1(R,S)$ tends to zero when the system displays a non-informative behavior [4, 14].

6. REFERENCES

[1] E. Amigó, J. Artiles, J. Gonzalo, D. Spina, B. Liu, and A. Corujo. WePS-3 evaluation campaign: Overview of the online reputation management task. In *CLEF '10 (Online Working Notes/Labs/Workshop)*, 2010.

[2] E. Amigó, A. Corujo, J. Gonzalo, E. Meij, and M. de Rijke. Overview of RepLab 2012: Evaluating online reputation management systems. In *CLEF '12 (Online Working Notes/Labs/Workshop)*, 2012.

[3] E. Amigó, J. Carrillo de Albornoz, I. Chugur, A. Corujo, J. Gonzalo, T. Martín, E. Meij, M. de Rijke, and D. Spina. Overview of RepLab 2013: Evaluating online reputation monitoring systems. In *CLEF '13 (Online Working Notes/Labs/Workshop)*, pages 333–352, 2013.

[4] E. Amigó, J. Gonzalo, and F. Verdejo. A general evaluation measure for document organization tasks. In *SIGIR '13*, pages 643–652, 2013.

[5] J. Atserias, G. Attardi, M. Simi, and H. Zaragoza. Active learning for building a corpus of questions for parsing. In *LREC '10*, 2010.

[6] R. L. Figueroa, Q. Zeng-Treitler, L. H. Ngo, S. Goryachev, and E. P. Wiechmann. Active learning for clinical text classification: is it better than random sampling? *Journal of the American Medical Informatics Association*, 19(5):809–816, 2012.

[7] R. Hu. *Active Learning for Text Classification.* PhD thesis, Dublin Institute of Technology, 2011.

[8] M.-H. Peetz. *Time-Aware Online Reputation Analysis.* PhD thesis, University of Amsterdam, 2015.

[9] E. Pilkington. Unsold H&M clothes found in rubbish bags as homeless face winter chill. http://bit.ly/theguardian2010HM, January 2010.

[10] M. Sassano. An empirical study of active learning with support vector machines for Japanese word segmentation. In *ACL '02*, 2002.

[11] B. Settles. Active learning literature survey. Computer Sciences Technical Report 1648, University of Wisconsin–Madison, 2009.

[12] D. Spina. *Entity-Based Filtering and Topic Detection for Online Reputation Monitoring in Twitter.* PhD thesis, UNED, 2014.

[13] D. Spina, J. Carrillo de Albornoz, T. Martín, E. Amigó, J. Gonzalo, and F. Giner. UNED Online Reputation Monitoring Team at RepLab 2013. In *CLEF '13 (Online Working Notes/Labs/Workshop)*, 2013.

[14] D. Spina, J. Gonzalo, and E. Amigó. Discovering filter keywords for company name disambiguation in Twitter. *Expert Systems with Applications*, 40(12):4986–5003, 2013.

[15] S. Tong and D. Koller. Support vector machine active learning with applications to text classification. *Journal of Machine Learning Research*, 2:45–66, Mar. 2002.

[16] Z. Xu, R. Akella, and Y. Zhang. Incorporating diversity and density in active learning for relevance feedback. In *ECIR '07*, 2007.

[17] J. Zhu, H. Wang, and B. Tsou. A density-based re-ranking technique for active learning for data annotations. In *ICCPOL '09*, 2009.

Relevance-aware Filtering of Tuples Sorted by an Attribute Value via Direct Optimization of Search Quality Metrics

Nikita Spirin[1], Mikhail Kuznetsov[2], Julia Kiseleva[3], Yaroslav Spirin[4], Pavel Izhutov[5]
[1]UIUC, Urbana IL, USA; [2]MIPT, Dolgoprudny, Russia; [3]Eindhoven University of Technology, Eindhoven, Netherlands; [4]Datastars, Moscow, Russia; [5]Stanford University, Palo Alto CA, USA
spirin2@illinois.edu[1], mikhail.kuznecov@phystech.edu[2], j.kiseleva@tue.nl[3], izhutov@stanford.edu[5]

ABSTRACT

Sorting tuples by an attribute value is a common search scenario and many search engines support such capabilities, e.g. price-based sorting in e-commerce, time-based sorting on a job or social media website. However, sorting purely by the attribute value might lead to poor user experience because the relevance is not taken into account. Hence, at the top of the list the users might see irrelevant results. In this paper we choose a different approach. Rather than just returning the entire list of results sorted by the attribute value, additionally we suggest doing the relevance-aware search results (post-)filtering. Following this approach, we develop a new algorithm based on the dynamic programming that directly optimizes a given search quality metric. It can be seamlessly integrated as the final step of a query processing pipeline and provides a theoretical guarantee on optimality. We conduct a comprehensive evaluation of our algorithm on synthetic data and real learning to rank data sets. Based on the experimental results, we conclude that the proposed algorithm is superior to typically used heuristics and has a clear practical value for the search and related applications.

Keywords

Search Metric; Attribute; Filtering; Dynamic Programming

Categories and Subject Descriptors

H.3.3 [**Information Search and Retrieval**]: Information filtering, Retrieval models, Search process, Selection process

1. INTRODUCTION

Many search engines support sorting of the search results by an attribute value, e.g. sort items by price in e-commerce or sort resumes by the update time on the job websites. A similar scenario exists in the social domain when the goal is to construct a chronologically sorted social feed, e.g. Twitter, Facebook. However, sorting purely by the attribute value might not be the best approach since at the top of the list users might find irrelevant results. For example, see the screenshots of the search user interfaces for Indeed.com and Amazon.com on Figure 1. In both cases the results sorted by the attribute values are hardly relevant for the queries.

To evaluate how such search scenarios are supported today, we conducted the ad hoc evaluation of ten popular search engines from the e-commerce and job industries[1]. For each search engine we submitted 25 queries (different queries for different industries), applied the sorting based on one of the attributes (relevance, date, price), and judged the quality of results[2]. The ranking by relevance is of very high quality. The average Precision@10 is 0.86. On the other hand, we found that the search results are far from relevant when the attribute-based sorting is done. For instance, across the sites the average Precision@1 is 0.44, Precision@5 is 0.45, and 61% of queries have the Precision@10 below 0.5. We think that it is mainly due to the relevance not being taken into account when the attribute-based sorting is requested. Therefore, our research questions are: (RQ1) Can the quality of results sorted by the attribute value be improved by incorporating the relevance into the ranking process? (RQ2) What is the best way to accomplish it?

In this paper we propose a new principled approach to perform relevance-aware search results (post-)filtering via *direct optimization of a given search quality metric*. Our algorithm uses the ideas from dynamic programming and is guaranteed to deliver the optimal solution. The algorithm is presented in Section 3. The experiments on synthetic and real learning to rank (L2R) data sets are described in Section 4.

2. RELATED WORK

This work is related to the research on search user behavior analysis, search metrics, and learning to rank. The proposed algorithm is based on the dynamic programming [1].

Researchers studied the way people interact with search engines by analyzing mouse movements, eye-tracking and click logs. Joachims et al. [9] discovered the *position bias* phenomenon, i.e. the results at the first two positions receive most attention, and then it quickly drops. Plus, on average users tend to read the results in a linear order from top to bottom. Craswell et al. [4] explored how the position bias might arise and proposed four hypotheses and the corresponding probabilistic click models. They found that the "cascade" model, where users view results from top to bottom and leave as soon as they see a worthwhile document, is

[1]Amazon, Walmart, Target, Etsy, BestBuy, NewEgg for products and Indeed, LinkedIn, SuperJob, Monster for jobs.
[2]we don't describe the exact setup due to the page limit.

SIGIR'15, August 09 - 13, 2015, Santiago, Chile.
 ISBN 978-1-4503-3621-5/15/08 ...$15.00.
DOI: http://dx.doi.org/10.1145/2766462.2767822.

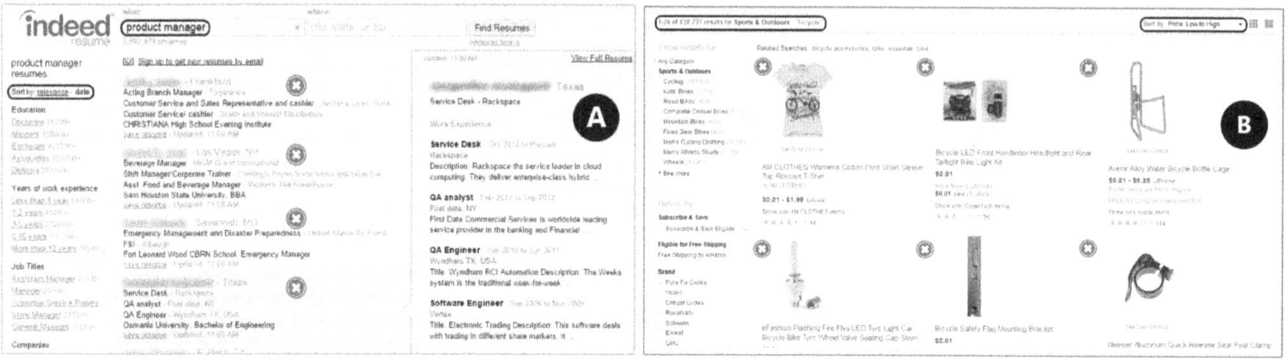

Figure 1: *(A)* Indeed.com resume search results for the query *"product manager"* sorted by *"date"* and *(B)* Amazon.com search results for the query *"bicycle"* sorted by *"price"*. While sorting by relevance is accurate, the results sorted by the attribute value are hardly relevant for the query, which leads to poor user experience.

the best explanation for position bias in early ranks. Dupret et al. [5] generalized this model by allowing for the possibility that a user skips a document without examining it.

Complementary to the work on search models, a lot of attention has been devoted to the design and analysis of search metrics. Thus, in addition to the traditional metrics, like the Precision and the Recall, Järvelin and Kekäläinen proposed the (Normalized) Discounted Cumulative Gain (*DCG*) [8], Chapelle et al. — the Expected Reciprocal Rank (*ERR*) [2], to name just a few. Recently, Chuklin et al. [3] developed a unified framework to convert any click model into the evaluation metric. Essentially, all search metrics model the position bias and penalize the top ranked irrelevant results.

Numerous ranking algorithms have been developed to accurately predict the relevance of documents. Typically, these algorithms are based on machine learning and find the optimal parameters by optimizing the "surrogate" objective function. However, the solution to the approximation is not always optimal for the original ranking problem. Therefore, recently several approaches have been proposed that directly optimize a given search metric. For instance, Xu et al. [12] focus on the algorithms that optimize the objectives upper-bounding the original non-smooth search metrics. Tan et al. [11] proposed *DirectRank*, which is based on the iterative coordinate ascent with the smart line search procedure.

Attribute-based ranking, however, has been handled very differently. Rather than taking the relevance into account, search engines return the list of results sorted by the attribute value or suboptimal heuristics are used (Section 4.1). Inspired by the recent advancements in L2R, in this work we bridge the gap between the relevance-based ranking and the attribute-based ranking by proposing to do relevance-aware search results filtering, which directly optimizes a given search metric, when the sorting by the attribute value is requested. It is worth highlighting the difference between the proposed algorithm and a famous TA algorithm by Fagin et al. [6]. While TA algorithm finds the top-k most relevant tuples by scoring them *individually*, we return the tuples, which *cumulatively* optimize a given search quality metric. The ordering of the tuples is as crucial as their relevance.

3. OUR APPROACH

We consider the scenario when a user requests the sorting of the search results by the attribute value, e.g. by date (Figure 1, A) or by price (Figure 1, B). Our goal is to produce the final ranking that both satisfies the strict ordering constraints and optimizes a given search quality metric (in turn it minimizes the user's effort on finding relevant results). We only focus on the results filtering and assume that the relevance scores are already predicted by the ranking algorithm. Therefore, the formalization of our problem looks as follows.

Input: *a list of tuples* $\{(t_i, r_i)\}_{i=1}^{l}$*, where* t_i *is the attribute value and* $r_i \in \mathbb{R}+$ *is the relevance score predicted by the ranking algorithm; a search quality metric* Q*.*
Output: *a (sub)list of indices* J *delivering the maximum to the metric* Q *and totally ordered based on the attribute value, i.e.* $J = \arg\max Q(r_{j_i}|j_i \in J)$*, s.t.* $t_{j_1} < ... < t_{j_l}$*.*

Throughout the paper, we consider the *DCG* as the search quality metric (although *ERR* or other metric can be used), date as the attribute, and the input sorted chronologically. It is worth mentioning that the formalization above covers the post-filtering scenarios as well, i.e. the input might consist of tuples that passed some other filtering algorithm.

Currently, this problem is solved heuristically. Mainly there are two approaches built around the same idea of thresholding. We can take only the results that have the relevance score above the threshold. We can also sort the results by the relevance score, take the top-k elements, and finally re-sort the list by date. While these approaches are easy to implement, they have two major drawbacks. First, it is not clear how to set the threshold. Second, the described approaches are the approximate solutions of our problem. Even the result set constructed from the top-k tuples sorted by relevance, being re-sorted by the attribute value, gets ordered randomly if we look at the relevance component.

The solution that guarantees optimality is to enumerate all possible subsequences, compute the metric for each one, and take the best one. However, this approach is not tractable as the number of subsequences is exponential. We propose a polynomial algorithm based on the dynamic programming [1]. There are three key observations behind our algorithm: (1) natural enumeration order for subsequences; (2) additivity of the metric; (3) optimality of subproblems.

First, all subsequences can be partitioned into the factor classes based on their length, i.e. in each factor class there will be the subsequences of the same length. To enumerate all subsequences, we can iterate over the factor classes and

Algorithm 1 (A1) Relevance-aware filtering of totally ordered set via direct optimization of a search quality metric

Input: DCG and $\{(t_i, r_i)\}_{i=1}^{l}$, s.t. $t_i < ... < t_l$ and $r_i \in \mathbb{R}+$
Output: $J = \arg\max DCG(r_{j_i} | j_i \in J)$, s.t. $t_{j_1} < ... < t_{j_l}$
1: $M \leftarrow Matrix(l+1, l+1); M(:,0) \leftarrow 0; M(0,:) \leftarrow 0;$
2: $Path \leftarrow Matrix(l+1, l+1);$ *# to recover max sequence*
3: **for** i in $1, \dots, l$
4:   **for** j in $1, \dots, i$
5:     $gain \leftarrow \frac{2^{r_i}-1}{\log(j+1)};$
6:     **if** $M(i-1, j-1) + gain > M(i-1, j)$
7:       $M(i,j) \leftarrow M(i-1, j-1) + gain;$
8:       $Path(i,j) \leftarrow (i-1, j-1);$
9:     **else**
10:       $M(i,j) \leftarrow M(i-1, j);$
11:       $Path(i,j) \leftarrow (i-1, j);$
12: $(i,j) \leftarrow \arg\max M(l,:);$ *# last element of solution*
13: $J \leftarrow List(); J.append(j);$
14: **while** $i > 1$ and $j > 1$
15:   **if** $P(i,j).last < j$
16:     $J.append(P(i,j).last);$
17:   $(i,j) \leftarrow P(i,j);$ *# jump to shorter subsequence*
18: **return** $J.reverse()$

within each factor class enumerate all subsequences. Second, the search metrics are additive and can be computed in linear time from the beginning of the list to the end [2]. It means that having a partial metric value for the prefix, we can compute the new metric value by simply adding the gain/utility provided by the current element. Third, the optimal subsequence for the prefix of length k is one of the optimal subsequences from each of the factor classes for the prefix of length $k-1$ with or without the current element appended (proof by induction for the prefix length).

Combining the observations above, we present our algorithm and its analysis. It starts by initializing the memoization matrix to store the optimal DCG values for subproblems and the transition matrix to reconstruct the optimal subsequence. Then, it iterates over the prefixes of the input sequence in the outer loop and over the factor classes in the inner loop. The cell (i,j) is for the optimal subsequence of length j for the prefix of length i. At each step we decide whether we should append the current element of the input sequence i to the optimal subsequence of length $j-1$ for the prefix of length $i-1$ (the recursion on lines 6-11). If we append the current element, we go diagonal. If we don't append, we keep the existing optimal subsequence of length j and stay on the same column. A legal evaluation order and the dependencies between the cells are shown in Figure 2, A. Finally, to reconstruct the optimal subsequence, we find the maximum in the last row (the last element is always "in" since the elements are non-negative) and go backwards in the $Path$ matrix. If the line is diagonal, we take the element in the next cell. Otherwise, we skip. The $Path$ matrix is depicted in Figure 2, B. The complexity (both time and space) of the algorithm is $O(l^2)$ because we have two nested loops, costing us $O(1)$ time at each iteration, and the square memoization matrices. It is guaranteed to deliver the optimum because we "virtually" enumerate all subsequences within the dynamic programming framework. For a toy example problem $\{(0,0),(1,3),(2,1),(3,2),(4,1),(5,3))\}$ the optimal solution is $\{1,3,4,5\}$ with the DCG equal to 12.40.

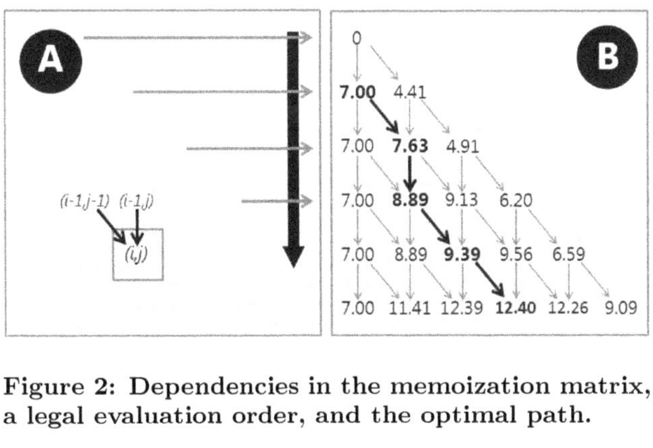

Figure 2: Dependencies in the memoization matrix, a legal evaluation order, and the optimal path.

4. EXPERIMENTS AND RESULTS

In this section we study how our approach contributes to the ranking quality using two real LETOR [10] (MQ2007, MSLR-WEB10K) and synthetically generated data sets.

4.1 Learning to Rank Data Sets

To answer our research questions, we do the simulations using the real learning to rank data sets. We extend MQ2007 and MSLR-WEB10K data sets by assigning a random timestamp to each document to model the sorting by the attribute value. Scikit-learn[3] implementation of the Gradient Boosted Regression Trees ($GBRT$) [7] is used to predict the relevance scores. The optimal parameters for the final $GBRT$ model are picked using cross validation for each data set. We use the 5-fold cross validation partitioning from LETOR [10].

Three popular baselines are considered, which are typically used to perform the filtering of the search results:
Baseline 1 (B1): sort by the attribute value, no filtering;
Baseline 2 (B2): sort by the attribute value, keep the results with the predicted relevance scores above the threshold (we normalized the scores to [0,1] and set the threshold=0.5);
Baseline 3 (B3): sort results by the predicted relevance score, take the top-k (where k is the cutoff point for the metric value calculation), and re-sort by the attribute value.

The evaluation procedure works as follows. First, we train the $GBRT$ on the training folds. Second, we predict the relevance scores using the trained $GBRT$ model for the documents in the testing fold. Third, we apply a baseline filtering algorithm to the documents in the testing fold by working with the relevance scores from the step two and the randomly generated timestamps. Fourth, we apply our filtering algorithm to the tuples that passed the baseline filtering. Finally, knowing the true relevance labels, we calculate the $NDCG@k$ for the filtered result list sorted by the timestamp. To make sure that the conclusions are not due to randomness, we average the results from 1000 runs.

The results of the experiment are presented in Table 1 and 2. We can see that the output (post-)filtered with our algorithm is regularly better than the baselines. We applied the binomial test and found that almost all differences in the $NDCG$ values are statistically significant (marked in bold), p-value is below 0.001. One average the increase in the metric value is around 2-4%. Moreover, since the data sets used have very different characteristics (e.g. the average query

[3] `http://scikit-learn.org/stable/index.html`

NDCG	*@1*	*@5*	*@10*	*@20*	*@40*
B1 only	0.226	0.245	0.273	0.336	0.496
A1 ∘ *B1*	**0.299**	**0.287**	**0.304**	**0.363**	**0.511**
B2 only	0.289	0.318	0.357	0.448	0.450
A1 ∘ *B2*	**0.315**	**0.326**	**0.364**	**0.453**	**0.454**
B3 only	0.433	0.417	0.418	0.451	0.498
A1 ∘ *B3*	0.433	0.417	**0.420**	**0.455**	**0.512**

Table 1: The demonstration of effectiveness of the proposed approach on MQ2007 data set.

NDCG	*@1*	*@5*	*@10*	*@20*	*@40*
B1 only	0.131	0.161	0.190	0.236	0.309
A1 ∘ *B1*	**0.173**	**0.183**	**0.208**	**0.250**	**0.321**
B2 only	0.170	0.208	0.244	0.300	0.379
A1 ∘ *B2*	**0.192**	**0.215**	**0.250**	**0.304**	**0.383**
B3 only	0.390	0.362	0.365	0.380	0.418
A1 ∘ *B3*	0.390	0.362	**0.366**	**0.382**	**0.421**

Table 2: The demonstration of effectiveness of the proposed approach on MSLR-WEB10K data set.

length for MQ2007 is 40 and for MSLR-WEB10K — 120), the experiment suggests that the algorithm achieves good performance for a wide range of input problems. Yet, one should note that the increase in the ranking quality comes with the extra computational cost because the complexity of our algorithm is $O(\frac{l}{\log l})$ times larger than for the baselines.

4.2 Synthetic Data Sets

In this section we focus on the filtering only (both relevance labels and timestamps are generated) and study how the algorithm behavior changes for different input sizes and relevance label distributions. We consider the following four label distributions modeling the real situations: (a) uniform integer in the range $[0, 5]$; (b) uniform real in the range $[0, 5]$; (c) power law, the slope $\alpha = 2.0$; (d) $\frac{3x^2}{125}$ with the support in the range $[0, 5]$. We generate the input lists for the filtering algorithm by sampling from the corresponding distribution. Similarly to the previous experiment, we simulate each combination of conditions 1000 times and average the runs. Only the Baseline 1 is used in this experiment for simplicity. The data from the simulation is presented in Figure 3.

There are several observations that could be made with the help of this figure. First, the output size is linearly proportional to the input size (Figure 3, C). *DCG* also grows linearly with the growth of the input size (Figure 3, A). Second, the proposed algorithm always outperforms the Baseline 1 (Figure 3, B), which is expected because we do the filtering directly optimizing a given search quality metric. Third, both the graph for the ratio of the *DCG* values and the graph for the ratio of the output sequence lengths for the proposed algorithm and the baseline monotonically converge for the longer input lists (Figure 3, B and D). This means

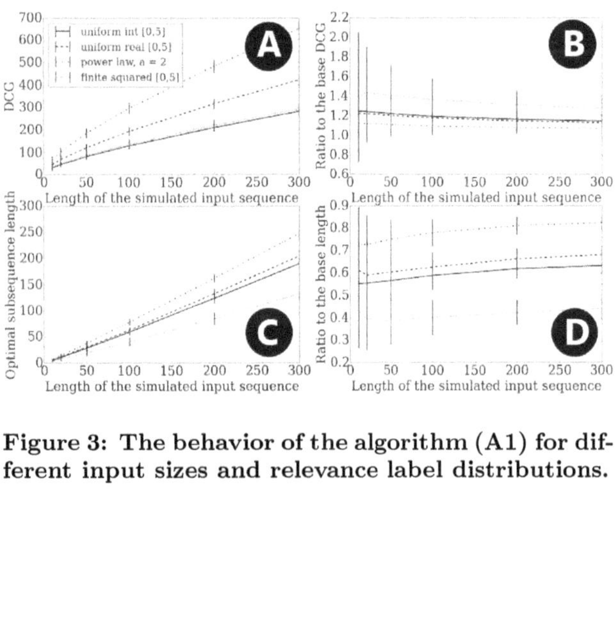

Figure 3: The behavior of the algorithm (A1) for different input sizes and relevance label distributions.

that our algorithm works better when the original hit list is shorter. Fourth, higher gains in *DCG* over the baseline are characteristic for the relevance label distributions, where relevant results are more probable (Figure 3, B). The observations above are valid for non-degenerate cases, e.g. not all labels are the same or sorted in a special order.

5. CONCLUSIONS AND FUTURE WORK

In this paper we addressed the important problem in search, that is, how to increase the relevance of the search results sorted by an attribute value. Our solution is based on the idea to perform relevance-aware search results filtering by directly optimizing a given search quality metric. We developed a simple, yet effective algorithm based on the dynamic programming, which consistently outperforms typically used heuristic approaches and is guaranteed to deliver the optimal solution. In the future, we plan to integrate the proposed algorithm in a real search engine and instrument an A/B test to see how such a modification will affect the user engagement and satisfaction with the search results.

6. ACKNOWLEDGEMENTS

We thank Karrie Karahalios, ChengXiang Zhai, and anonymous reviewers for their valuable comments and suggestions.

7. REFERENCES

[1] R. Bellman. *Dynamic Programming.* Dover Books on Computer Science, USA, 2003.

[2] O. Chapelle, D. Metlzer, Y. Zhang, and P. Grinspan. Expected reciprocal rank for graded relevance. CIKM'09.

[3] A. Chuklin, P. Serdyukov, and M. de Rijke. Click model-based information retrieval metrics. SIGIR'13.

[4] N. Craswell, O. Zoeter, M. Taylor, and B. Ramsey. An experimental comparison of click position-bias models. In *Proceedings of Web Search and Data Mining 2008.*

[5] G. E. Dupret and B. Piwowarski. A user browsing model to predict search engine click data from past observations. In *Proceedings of ACM SIGIR 2008.*

[6] R. Fagin, A. Lotem, and M. Naor. Optimal aggregation algorithms for middleware. In *Proceedings of PODS '01.*

[7] J. H. Friedman. Greedy function approximation: A gradient boosting machine. *Annals of Statistics*, 29(5), 2001.

[8] K. Järvelin and J. Kekäläinen. Cumulated gain-based evaluation of ir techniques. *ACM Trans. Inf. Syst.*, 20(4).

[9] T. Joachims, L. Granka, B. Pan, H. Hembrooke, and G. Gay. Accurately interpreting clickthrough data as implicit feedback. SIGIR'05.

[10] T. Qin, T.-Y. Liu, J. Xu, and H. Li. LETOR: A benchmark collection for research on learning to rank for information retrieval. *Inf. Retr.*, 13(4).

[11] M. Tan, T. Xia, L. Guo, and S. Wang. Direct optimization of ranking measures for learning to rank models. KDD'13.

[12] J. Xu, T.-Y. Liu, M. Lu, H. Li, and W.-Y. Ma. Directly optimizing evaluation measures in L2R. SIGIR'08.

Multi-source Information Fusion for Personalized Restaurant Recommendation

Jing Sun
Shanghai Key Laboratory of Data Science
School of Computer Science
Fudan university
jingsun@fudan.edu.cn

Yun Xiong
Shanghai Key Laboratory of Data Science
School of Computer Science
Fudan university
yunx@fudan.edu.cn

Yangyong Zhu
Shanghai Key Laboratory of Data Science
School of Computer Science
Fudan university
yyzhu@fudan.edu.cn

Junming Liu
Rutgers Business School
Rutgers University
liujm000@gmail.com

Chu Guan
University of Science and Technology of China
guanchu0329@gmail.com

Hui Xiong
Rutgers Business School
Rutgers University
xionghui@gmail.com

ABSTRACT

In this paper, we study the problem of personalized restaurant recommendations. Specifically, we develop a probabilistic factor analysis framework, named RMSQ-MF, which has the ability in exploiting multi-source information, such as the users' task, their friends' preferences, and human mobility patterns, for personalized restaurant recommendations. The rationale of this work is motivated by two observations. First, people's preferences can be affected by their friends. Second, human mobility patterns can reflect the popularity of restaurants to a certain degree. Finally, empirical studies on real-world data demonstrate that the proposed method outperforms benchmark methods with a significant margin.

Categories and Subject Descriptors

H.3.3 [**Information Search and Retrieval**]: Information filtering

Keywords

Restaurant Recommendation, Matrix Factorization, Bayesian models, Mobile Computing

1. INTRODUCTION

Recent years have witnessed a rapid development on restaurant recommendation and advertisements. With the emergence of social media and mobility applications, a more comprehensive and effective restaurant recommendation strategy provides the opportunity to offer convenience to customers as well as to improve profits for restaurants. The largest social media of restaurant, Yelp,[1] have provided a set of benchmark 5-point rating for restaurants in US, expressing the extent of the customers' favors on each restaurant. Previous work [3] exploited the multi-aspect ratings of restaurant to uncover the user preference. However, without considering the social factor and mobility factor, the recommendation accuracy is not high enough and need further improvement.

Indeed, traditional recommender systems usually assume that the user and the item data are independent and identically distributed, which ignores the interrelationships among items. As users' preferences are not actually binary decisions and have a certain granularity, manually specifying personal preferences is obstructive and usually bring a biased recommendation to users. To the best of our knowledge, limited efforts have been made for understanding customers' preferences for restaurants. Indeed, the tradition personalized ranking targets at building ranking models to disclose the user interests from profiles of rating event, such as user-dependent features, item-dependent features, and shared features. Also, filtering based methods can be divided into two categories: collaborative filtering and content-based filtering. Collaborative filtering recommends items to the users whose tastes are similar whereas content-based filtering recommends items similar to those the user has liked in the past. Recently, matrix factorization models in collaborative filtering become more and more popular. Matrix factorization assumes users' preferences can be generated by user latent factors and item latent factor in a latent space.

However, restaurants interact with people through daily dining. There are several unique characteristics of restaurant review systems, which make traditional matrix factorization techniques difficult to be adapted for restaurant recommendation. In fact, the decision process of a user choosing a restaurant is more complicated because of so many influence factors: 1) users tend to check around several centers, where the check-in locations follow Gaussian distribution at each center for a typical user's rating behavior. Second, users can be easily influenced by the friends they trust, and prefer their friends' recommendations. 2) two restaurants with similar or the same semantic topics can have different popularities if they are located in different regions. 3) popularity affects purchase behaviors. The probability of a

[1] http://www.yelp.com

SIGIR '15 August 09 - 13, 2015, Santiago, Chile

DOI: http://dx.doi.org/10.1145/2766462.2767818.

user choosing a restaurant is partly affected by the traffic conditions around the restaurant. 4) the users have dynamic mobility behaviors, which impose the challenges on the modeling of restaurant decision. While there are some studies on restaurant recommendations [3, 2], it is necessary to build an integrated analysis of the joint effect of the factors mentioned above. Intuitively, if a flexible method is utilized to collect more information, then better performance may be achieve. Therefore, we need a model that jointly encodes the user ratings, social factors, region topic and mobility factors into the user decision process to learn user preferences for effective recommendation recommendations.

In this paper, a Bayesian graphical model taking account of both collaborative filtering latent factors, the social factor and mobility factor is proposed to learn the user preferences. We carried out the experiments to show the efficiency and effectiveness of the proposed approach with real world data evaluations.

2. RELATED WORK

Content-based approaches and collaborative filtering (CF) approaches have been the prevailing recommendation strategies. Content-based algorithms are based on a description of the item and profile of the user's preference, which try to recommend items according to a user's historical preference. CF algorithms assume that people's behavior is affected by someone with similar preferences, and user's ratings are adjusted by his neighbors' ratings or recommendation. CF approaches can be categorized into two classes: memory-based CF and model-based CF. Memory-based CF algorithms first search for neighbors who have similar rating histories to the target user. Then the target user's rating histories can be predicted according to his neighbors' ratings. Model-based CF algorithms use various models and machine learning techniques such as clustering algorithms or Bayesian networks to discover latent factors that account for the observed ratings. A particular type of CF algorithm uses matrix factorization, a low-rank matrix approximation technique [4].

In contrast, restaurant recommender systems can also be developed in terms of users' past preferences via matrix factorization (MF), such as SVD++ [8], PMF [6], NMF [1]. One drawback of MF is the so-called ramp-up problem, in which MF performs poorly when the recommender system is not initialized with a sufficient number of ratings. Therefore, more studies such as BiasedMF [8] and SocialMF [5] incorporated side and prior information into latent factor models by exploring users' and items' observable features. The work [7] studied on restaurant recommendation relied on knowledge about users and restaurants to generate recommendations. However, previous studies in restaurant recommendation still have several limitations: they lack of integrated modeling of the joint influence of personalization in user ratings, social factors, geographic interrelationship between users and restaurants, bias effect and profile similarity.

3. PROPOSED MODEL

3.1 Problem Definition

The problem of restaurant recommendation is to recommend restaurant to a user based on ratings and other side information (e.g.,user profile, social factor and mobility factor information) collected from a web site. Let $U = \{u_1, u_2, \cdots, u_u, \cdots, u_p\}$ be a set of users, where each user has a user profile (e.g.location, yelping time). Let $V = \{v_1, v_2, \cdots, v_i, \cdots, v_q\}$ be a set of restaurants, where each restaurant has a location $l_i = \{lon_i, lat_i\}$ in terms of longitude and latitude, and observable restaurant-dependent features (e.g.business hours, cuisine categories, etc.) which describe the restaurant features. We denote the rating as R_{ui} for the pair of user u and restaurant i. We also have social influence weight between two friends that is based on both of their social connections and similarity of their visiting activities. $S_{uf} = \delta \frac{|\tau(u) \cap \tau(f)|}{|\tau(u) \cup \tau(f)|} + (1-\delta)\frac{|A_u \cap A_f|}{|A_u \cup A_f|}$, where δ is a tuning parameter ranging within [0,1], and $\tau(u)$ and A_u denote the friend set and visiting restaurants set of user u, respectively. Also, we refer u as user and i as restaurant in the following unless otherwise specified.

3.2 Model specification

Figure 1 shows the decision process of user u to choose restaurant i in a generative way. RSMQ-MF model fuses personal interest in restaurants(Q), personal interest in the area around restaurants(M) and social influence(S). The main contribution of the approach is that we fuse the information of the region around the restaurants and use the taxi drop-off as the popularity of the region. Here, we firstly infer the proposed personalized recommendation model to predict users' ratings. And then, we show the training method of our approach. For the user and restaurant latent feature on

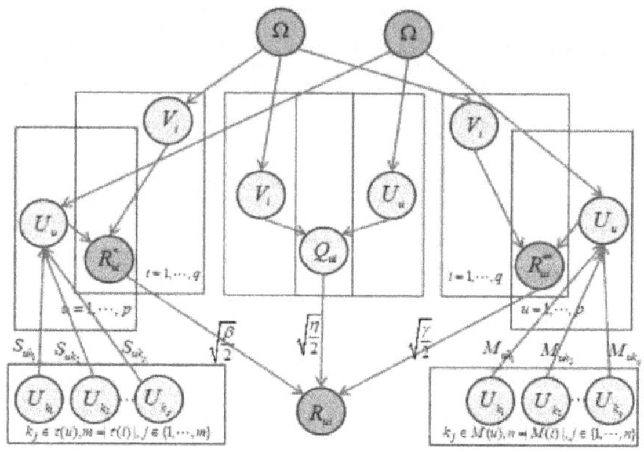

Figure 1: The graphical representation of the proposed RSMQ-MF model.

the personal interest, we have the conditional distribution according to:

$$p(Q|U,V,\Omega) = \prod_u \prod_i [\mathcal{N}(Q_{u,i}|U_u, V_i^\top, \Omega)]^{I_{u,i}^R} \quad (1)$$

where $\mathcal{N}(|\mu,\Omega)$ is the gaussian distribution with mean μ and variance Ω. $I_{u,i}^R$ is the indicator function which is equal to 1 if user u has rated restaurant i and equal to 0 otherwise. Note that the condition distribution based on the users' ratings is similar with the conditional probability based on personal latent interest:

$$p(R|U,V,\Omega) = \prod_u \prod_i [\mathcal{N}(R_{u,i}|U_u, V_i^\top, \Omega)]^{I_{u,i}^R} \quad (2)$$

Given the latent features on the topic interest of his friends, for the user latent feature based on interest topic, we have the conditional distributions as follows:

$$p(U|M,\Omega) = \prod_u \mathcal{N}(U|\sum_{f\in U} M_{u,f}U_f,\Omega) \tag{3}$$

Here, f is a friend of user u. As mentioned above, there are three main aspects influencing personalized recommendation in our model: 1) social influence $S_{u,f}$, which means you would trust your friends; 2) interest topic $M_{u,f}$, which means your region interest topic is similar with your friends', which is probability affected by the taxi drop-off information (see in the Experiment section); 3) personal interest $Q_{u,i}$, which means the effect on the restaurants you are interested based on user and restaurant profiles. Thus, by combining the social influence S, interest similarity M of the friends and user personal interest Q with the observed ratings R, the proposed RSMQ-MF model decreases the training error. According to the basic MF model, through bayesian inference, the posterior probability of our model is as follows:

$$\begin{aligned}
&p(U,V|R,S,M,Q,\omega) \propto p(R|U,V,\Omega)p(U|S,\Omega)p(U|M,\Omega)\\
&p(Q|U,V,\Omega)\\
&p(U|\Omega)p(V|\Omega) = \prod_u\prod_i[\mathcal{N}(R_{u,i}|U_u,V_i^\top,\Omega)]^{I^R_{u,i}}\times\\
&\prod_u \mathcal{N}(U|\sum_{f\in U} S_{u,f}U_f,\Omega)\times\prod_u \mathcal{N}(U|\sum_{f\in U} M_{u,f}U_f,\Omega)\\
&\prod_u\prod_i[\mathcal{N}(Q_{u,i}|U_u,V_i^\top,\Omega)]^{I^R_{u,i}}\times\\
&\prod_u \mathcal{N}(U_u|0,\Omega)\times\prod_i \mathcal{N}(V_i|0,\Omega)
\end{aligned} \tag{4}$$

Keeping the prior variance and observation noise fixed, we have the loss function:

$$\begin{aligned}
&\mathcal{L}(R,U,V,S,M,Q) = \frac{1}{2}\sum_{u,i}(R_{u,i}-\hat{R}_{u,i})^2 + \frac{\lambda}{2}(\|U\|_F^2+\\
&\|V\|_F^2) + \frac{\beta}{2}\Sigma_u((U_u-\Sigma_f S_{u,f}U_f)(U_u-\Sigma_f S_{u,f}U_f)^\top)\\
&+\frac{\gamma}{2}\Sigma_u((U_u-\Sigma_f M_{u,f}U_f)(U_u-\Sigma_f M_{u,f}U_f)^\top)\\
&+\frac{\eta}{2}\Sigma_{u,i}(Q_{u,i}-U_uV_i^\top)^2
\end{aligned} \tag{5}$$

Here, $\hat{R}_{u,i}$ is the predicted rating. $\|.\|_F^2$ denotes Frobenius norm. λ is regularization weight, and β, γ and η are iteration step size. In Eq.(5), the idea of social influence is the second term, which means that user personal interest would be similar with the friends latent interest. The third term is enforced as the similarity of the interest topic. And the factor of user personal interest is the last term which means that users would be interested with several restaurant. To obtain a local minimum of the objective function given by Eq.(5), we perform gradient descent in U_u and V_i:

$$\begin{aligned}
&\frac{\partial\mathcal{L}}{\partial U_u} = \sum_i I^R_{u,i}(\hat{R}_{u,i}-R_{u,i})V_i + \lambda U_u + \beta(U_u-\\
&\Sigma_v S_{u,f}U_f) - \beta\Sigma_{f:u\in F_f}S_{u,f}(U_f - \Sigma_{\omega\in F_f}S_{v,w}U_w)+\\
&\gamma(U_u-\Sigma_{f\in F_u}M_{u,f}U_f) - \gamma\Sigma_{f:u\in F_f}M_{f,u}(U_f-\\
&\Sigma_{\omega\in F_f}M_{f,\omega}U_\omega) + \eta\Sigma_i I^R_{u,i}(U_uV_i^\top - Q_{u,i})V_i
\end{aligned} \tag{6}$$

(a) restaurants (b) taxis

Figure 2: A demonstration of restaurants and taxis drop-off points in the dataset.

$$\begin{aligned}
\frac{\partial\mathcal{L}}{\partial V_i} &= \sum_u I^R_{u,i}(\hat{R}_{u,i}-R_{u,i})U_u + \lambda V_i\\
&+\eta\sum_u I^R_{u,i}(U_uV_i^\top - Q_{u,i})U_u
\end{aligned} \tag{7}$$

where $I^R_{u,i}$ is the indicator function that is equal to 1 if user u has rated restaurant i, and 0 otherwise. The initial values of U and V are sampled from the Gaussian distribution with zero mean. The latent feature matrix learning was empirically affected. We adjust the step size based on the previous values of the two latent feature matrix U and V in each iteration.

4. EXPERIMENTS

4.1 Date set and Evaluation Metrics

Data set. We crawled the data from yelp.com site covering Manhattan district. We collect a complete snapshot, including users' profile, user's rating, users' friend list, and restaurants' profile, from Yelp. The total number of restaurant is 7,115. In order to easy to do experiments to validate the performance of our model. We positively pick the restaurant to limit other type of potential impact. And we select 1,000 restaurants using a greedy algorithm with max distance, which keep we don't have nearest restaurants. The detailed statistics of the final dataset are shown in Table 1. Density is the percentage of entries in the user-restaurant matrix that have ratings.

Moreover, to measure the popularity in Manhattan, we adopt the taxi drop-off information from New York City taxi Data[2] which was collected from Jan. 2013 to Jun. 2013. Setting lunch time period as 11:00-13:30, and dinner time period as 17:30-20:00 in Manhattan. Then, match the restaurant location and taxi customer drop-off longitude and latitude distance, select those restaurant recently and the distance between two is less than 10 meters. Get 21,684,273 taxi drop-off records related to the 1000 restaurants. Figure 2

[2]https://uofi.box.com/NYCtaxidata

Table 1: Size of dataset

# Users	# Restaurants	# Ratings	% Density
1500	1000	33720	2.248%

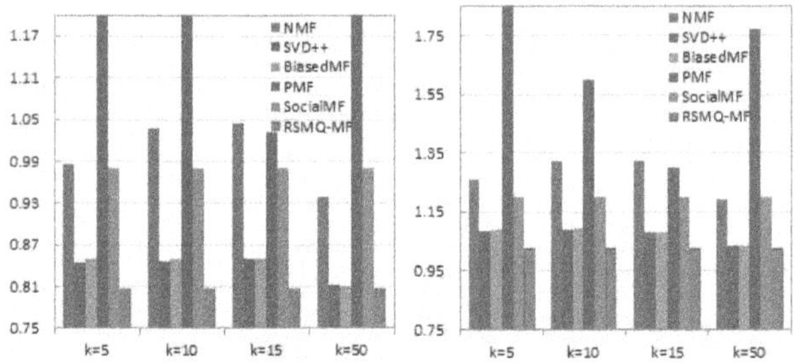

(a) MAE (b) RMSE

Figure 3: The average MAE and RMSE values at different latent dimensions k.

is a map illustration of restaurants and taxis in Manhattan Area. Each black point representing one restaurant in Figure 2(a) or one taxi drop-off location in Figure 2(b). This map shows there are lots of taxi drop-off behaviors around the restaurant of Manhattan.

Evaluation Metrics. We use the following two metrics for evaluation.

(1) the Mean Absolute Error,

$\text{MAE} = \sum_{u,i} |r_{ui} - \hat{r}_{ui}|/N$,

(2) the Root Mean Square Error,

$\text{RMSE} = \sqrt{\sum_{u,i} (r_{ui} - \hat{r}_{ui})^2/N}$,

where r_{ui} and $\hat{r}_{ui}$ denote the observed rating and the predicted rating, and N denotes the total number of the tested data. The smaller the value of MAE or RMSE, the more precise a recommendation.

4.2 Performance Comparison

To show the effectiveness of the proposed RSMQ-MF model, we compare the performances of our model against the following baseline algorithms: 1)Nonnegative Matrix Factorization (NMF) [1]. 2)SVD++ [8], which directly incorporates implicit feedback into the singular value decomposition (SVD) model. 3)BiasedMF [8], which is a multifaceted collaborative filtering model. 4)Probabilistic Matrix Factorization (PMF)[6]. 5)SocialMF [5], which is a matrix factorization technique with trust propagation for recommendation in social networks. We randomly selected 80% of data from our dataset as training data and different number of latent factors (k=5,10,15,50) to test all the methods. We set learning rate as 0.01, regularization $\lambda_U = 0.01$ and $\lambda_V = 0.05$ for all methods. For our approach, we set $\beta = 20$, $\gamma = 20$,$\eta = 20$.

From the Figure 3(a), it is clear that our approach outperforms the other methods on different number of latent factors (k). The MAE values of our approach (with average 0.79) are lower than the MAE values of SVD++, BiasedMF, NMF, SocialMF or PMF (with average 1.03). In addition, in all the baselines, BiasedMF and SVD++ works better than NMF, SocialMF and PMF in all k value settings. PMF gives comparatively low performance with 2.219 MAE(k=5), since the model is a pure probabilistic factor model and does not take advantage of social or mobility factors.

Figure 3(b) shows the RMSE comparisons: our approach outperforms all the completing models. For example, the average RMSE of five baselines is about 1.28 whereas the RMSE of our method is only 0.98. SocialMF works better than NMF and PMF because of its aggregation of user social links. The present method not only consider social factors, but also incorporates taxi drop-off information, which makes our approach performing more effective recommendation method.

5. CONCLUSION

In this paper, in order to provide more accurate and efficient restaurant recommendation, we propose a novel fused matrix factorization framework to take into account multi-source information. To incorporate the side information, we explored the bias effect which was regressed from user profiles and restaurant characteristics, as well as exploited the similarity from social factors and mobility factors between users and restaurants. Our model not only discovered the social influence of user by flexibly collecting information from user's social network, but also incorporates the taxi drop-off information into the user preference indices. Experimental results on real-world data shows the proposed RSMQ-MF model can achieve significantly better performance than other state-of-the-art methods.

6. ACKNOWLEDGEMENTS

This work was supported in part by grants from the National Natural Science Foundation of China under Grant No.61170096,71331005.The work was also partially supported by grants from Shanghai Foundation for Development of Science and Technology under Grant No.13dz2260200 13511504300, 14511107302.

7. REFERENCES

[1] D.D.Lee and H. Seung. Algorithms for non-negative matrix factorization. *In Advances in Neural Information Processing Systems*, 20:1257–1264, 2001.

[2] F.Yanjie, L.Bin, G.Yong, and X.Hui. User preference learning with multiple information fusion for restaurant recommendation. In *SDM2014 Conference Proceedings*, pages 470–478, April 2014.

[3] H.H.Lee and G.W.Teng. Incorporating multi-criteria ratings in recommendation systems. In *IRI2007 Conference Proceedings*, pages 273–278, August 2007.

[4] I.Markovsky. *Low-Rank Approximation: Algorithms, Implementation, Applications.* Springer ISBN 978-1-4471-2226-5, 2012.

[5] M.Jamali and M.Ester. A matrix factorization technique with trust propagation for recommendation in social networks. In *RecSys2010 Conference Proceedings*, pages 135–142, Septmber 2010.

[6] R.Salakhutdinov and A.Mnih. Probabilistic matrix factorization. *In Advances in Neural Information Processing Systems*, 13:556–562, 2008.

[7] S.Trewin. Knowledge-based recommender systems. *Encyclopedia of Library and Information Science*, 69(32):180–200, 2000.

[8] Y.Koren. Factorization meets the neighborhood: a multifaceted collaborative filtering model. In *KDD2008 Conference Proceedings*, pages 426–434, August 2008.

Joint Matrix Factorization and Manifold-Ranking for Topic-Focused Multi-Document Summarization

Jiwei Tan, Xiaojun Wan* and Jianguo Xiao
Institute of Computer Science and Technology, Peking University, Beijing 100871, China
The MOE Key Laboratory of Computational Linguistics, Peking University, Beijing 100871, China
{tanjiwei, wanxiaojun, xiaojianguo}@pku.edu.cn

ABSTRACT

Manifold-ranking has proved to be an effective method for topic-focused multi-document summarization. As basic manifold-ranking based summarization method constructs the relationships between sentences simply by the bag-of-words cosine similarity, we believe a better similarity metric will further improve the effectiveness of manifold-ranking. In this paper, we propose a joint optimization framework, which integrates the manifold-ranking process with a similarity metric learning process. The joint framework aims at learning better sentence similarity scores and better sentence ranking scores simultaneously. Experiments on DUC datasets show the proposed joint method achieves better performance than the manifold-ranking baselines and several popular methods.

Categories and Subject Descriptors

H.3.1 [**Information Storage and Retrieval**]: Content Analysis and Indexing—*abstracting methods*

Keywords

Multi-document summarization; matrix factorization; manifold-ranking

1. INTRODUCTION

Multi-document summarization (MDS) aims at producing a summary of the major information from a set of documents. Topic-focused multi-document summarization is a task which requires the generated summary to be biased to a given topic. As topic-focused MDS can provide a personalized profile, it is useful in news services, QA systems and search engines. Manifold-ranking based summarization method [13] has proved useful to deal with the topic-focused MDS task. It makes uniform use of the sentence-to-sentence relationships and sentence-to-topic relationships in a manifold-ranking process, and does not need a training procedure or subtle parameter tuning, which makes it more appropriate for practical application.

*Xiaojun Wan is the corresponding author.

SIGIR'15, August 09 - 13, 2015, Santiago, Chile.
© 2015 ACM. ISBN 978-1-4503-3621-5/15/08 ...$15.00.
DOI: http://dx.doi.org/10.1145/2766462.2767765.

However, the basic manifold-ranking summarization method constructs the relationships of sentences simply by the bag-of-words cosine similarity, which cannot faithfully capture the semantic similarity among sentences. We believe a better similarity metric will further improve the performance of the manifold-ranking based summarization method. In this paper, we propose a Joint Matrix Factorization and Manifold-Ranking (JMFMR) framework for topic-focused multi-document summarization, which aims at learning better sentence similarity scores and better sentence ranking scores simultaneously.

In the following parts of this paper, we first summarize related works, and then introduce the manifold-ranking framework and the matrix factorization framework. Then we propose our approach and the experiments. At last is the conclusion of this paper.

2. RELATED WORK

There have been quite a lot works on multi-document summarization and in this section we mainly focus on the unsupervised topic-focused extractive-based summarization task. Some methods treat summarization as a ranking task and apply graph-based ranking algorithms. [13] propose to use manifold-ranking to make uniform use of sentence-to-sentence and sentence-to-topic relationships. [12] extend a multi-modality manifold-ranking by considering the within-document sentence relationships and the cross-document sentence relationships as two modalities. [1] further improve the manifold-ranking based relevance propagation via mutual reinforcement between sentences and theme clusters.

Matrix factorization technique has been applied to summarization tasks in several works. For example, [8] propose using nonnegative matrix factorization to extract the query relevant sentences. [9] use nonnegative matrix factorization and K-means clustering for sentence clustering and extraction. [14] propose using sentence-level semantic analysis and symmetric nonnegative matrix factorization to factorize the sentence-sentence similarity matrix.

3. PRELIMINARIES

In this section we first introduce the framework of manifold-ranking based multi-document summarization in [13]. Then we will introduce the matrix factorization technique for latent semantic similarity learning in our approach.

3.1 Manifold-Ranking Method

Given a set of data points as $\chi = \{s_1, s_2, \ldots, s_N\}$, representing sentences to be ranked including the pseudo-sentence as s_1, let $\Gamma : \chi \rightarrow R$ denotes a ranking function which assigns each point s_i $(1 \leq i \leq N)$ with a ranking value f_i. Γ can be viewed as a vector $F = [f_1, \ldots, f_N]^T$. Define a prior vector $Y = [y_1, \ldots, y_N]^T$, in which $y_1 = 1$ because s_1 is a topic description pseudo-sentence and $y_i = 0$ $(2 \le i \le N)$ for all the remaining sentences to be ranked. The adjacency matrix of the graph can be denoted as $\mathbf{W} = \{W_{ij}\}$ $(1 \le i, j \le N)$, with each element W_{ij} corresponding to the similarity between s_i and s_j (W_{ii} is forced to 0 to avoid self-reinforcement). Then the manifold-ranking algorithm can be formulized as a regularization framework of minimizing:

$$\varphi(F) = \sum_{i,j=1}^{N} W_{ij} \left| \frac{1}{\sqrt{D_{ii}}} f_i - \frac{1}{\sqrt{D_{jj}}} f_j \right|^2 + \mu \sum_{i=1}^{N} |f_i - y_i|^2 \quad (1)$$

where $\mathbf{D}$ is a diagonal matrix with its (i, i)-element equals to the sum of the i-th row of $\mathbf{W}$. Let F^* denotes the solution of minimizing $\varphi(F)$, and F^* can be solved by iterating (2) until convergence:

$$F^{(t+1)} = \alpha \mathbf{S} F^{(t)} + (1 - \alpha) Y \quad (2)$$

where $\mathbf{S} = \mathbf{D}^{-1/2}\mathbf{W}\mathbf{D}^{-1/2}$ and $\alpha = 1/(1 + \mu)$.

3.2 Matrix Factorization

We introduce a Weighted Textual Matrix Factorization (WTMF) model [3] for assessing latent semantic text similarity. Given a $M \times N$ co-occurrence matrix $\mathbf{X}$, where the row number M corresponds to M words in the corpus, and the column number N corresponds to N sentences. Each cell X_{ij} contains the TF-IDF value of word w_i in the sentence s_j. The WTMF framework aims at factorizing matrix $\mathbf{X}$ into two matrices such that $\mathbf{X} \approx \mathbf{P}^{\mathrm{T}}\mathbf{Q}$, where $\mathbf{P}$ is a $K \times M$ matrix, and $\mathbf{Q}$ is a $K \times N$ matrix. K is the dimension of latent vectors. The main difference between WTMF and LSA [7] is that WTMF allows for direct weight control on each matrix cell X_{ij}. The model variables to be solved (vectors in $\mathbf{P}$, $\mathbf{Q}$) are optimized by minimizing:

$$\sum_{i=1}^{M} \sum_{j=1}^{N} W_{ij} \left(P_{\cdot,i} \cdot Q_{\cdot,j} - X_{ij}\right)^2 + \lambda \left\|\mathbf{P}\right\|_2^2 + \lambda \left\|\mathbf{Q}\right\|_2^2 \quad (3)$$

where λ is a free regularization factor to control the regularization term, and the weight matrix $\mathbf{W}$ defines a weight for each cell in $\mathbf{X}$. $P_{\cdot,i}$ is a K-dimensional latent semantic vector profile for word w_i and $Q_{\cdot,j}$ is the K-dimensional vector profile that represents sentence s_j. Then the similarity of two sentences s_j and $s_{j'}$ can be calculated by the cosine similarity of $Q_{\cdot,j}$ and $Q_{\cdot,j'}$. The weight matrix $\mathbf{W}$ is defined as:

$$W_{ij} = \begin{cases} 1, & if\ X_{ij} \neq 0 \\ \omega_m, & if\ X_{ij} = 0 \end{cases} \quad (4)$$

ω_m is a very small weight for penalty. The intuition of a small ω_m when $X_{ij} = 0$ in WTMF is to diminish the influence where word w_i is missed in the sentence s_j, and the weighted matrix factorization is argued to yield better latent vectors than traditional matrix factorization [3].

4. OUR PROPOSED METHOD

4.1 Overview

We propose a joint approach of matrix factorization based manifold-ranking, to learn the similarity metric and sentence ranking scores in a framework simultaneously. The underlying idea is that a better similarity metric will help improve the manifold-ranking process; meanwhile information from the manifold-ranking process can also help learn a better similarity metric. In this section we first introduce the objective function of our proposed joint approach, and then we discuss how to solve the minimization problem and the inner weighted nonnegative matrix factorization problem.

4.2 Joint Learning Objective

In the joint framework, we adopt a weighted **nonnegative** matrix factorization technique similar to WTMF, to learn sentence similarity. Specifically, we integrate similarity learning and sentence score learning into one optimization objective, as minimizing Φ:

$$\begin{aligned} \Phi = & \sum_{i,j=1}^{N} W'_{ij} \left| \frac{1}{\sqrt{D_{ii}}} f_i - \frac{1}{\sqrt{D_{jj}}} f_j \right|^2 + \mu \sum_{i=1}^{N} |f_i - y_i|^2 \\ & + \sum_{i=1}^{M} \sum_{j=1}^{N} W''_{ij} (P_{\cdot,i} \cdot Q_{\cdot,j} - X_{ij})^2 + \lambda \|\mathbf{P}\|_2^2 + \lambda \|\mathbf{Q}\|_2^2 \\ & s.t.\ P_{ki} \ge 0,\ Q_{kj} \ge 0,\ f_i \ge 0.\ (1 \le k \le K) \end{aligned} \quad (5)$$

where $W'_{ij} = \cos(Q_{\cdot,i}, Q_{\cdot,j})$ represents the cosine value of the angle between latent semantic vectors $Q_{\cdot,i}$ and $Q_{\cdot,j}$, intuitively representing the cosine similarity of sentence s_i and s_j after matrix factorization. $\mathbf{D}$ is a diagonal matrix with its (i, i)-element equals to the sum of the i-th row of $\mathbf{W}'$. Y is same as in Section 3.1. $\mathbf{X}$ is same as in WTMF, representing the word-sentence co-occurrence matrix. $\mathbf{W}''$ here is defined as:

$$W''_{ij} = \begin{cases} e^{f_j}, & if\ X_{ij} \neq 0 \\ \omega_m, & if\ X_{ij} = 0 \end{cases} \quad (6)$$

In the objective function (5), $\mathbf{P}$, $\mathbf{Q}$ and F are to be optimized, and constrained to be nonnegative. μ and λ are free parameters to control the regularization terms. By optimizing the objective function, similarity measurements of the sentences will be got from $\mathbf{Q}$, as $\mathrm{sim}(s_i, s_j) = \cos(Q_{\cdot,i}, Q_{\cdot,j})$; simultaneously the ranking scores of sentences will be got from F. We will explain the idea underlying the objective function as follows. We define the following two sub-objective functions:

$$\phi_1 = \sum_{i,j=1}^{N} W'_{ij} \left| \frac{1}{\sqrt{D_{ii}}} f_i - \frac{1}{\sqrt{D_{jj}}} f_j \right|^2 + \mu \sum_{i=1}^{N} |f_i - y_i|^2 \quad (7)$$

$$\phi_2 = \sum_{i=1}^{M} \sum_{j=1}^{N} W''_{ij} (P_{\cdot,i} \cdot Q_{\cdot,j} - X_{ij})^2 + \lambda \|\mathbf{P}\|_2^2 + \lambda \|\mathbf{Q}\|_2^2 \quad (8)$$

Sub-objective function (7) corresponds to the objective function of manifold-ranking. The only difference is that $\mathbf{W}$ in the objective function of manifold-ranking is now replaced by $\mathbf{W}'$, a function of an optimization variable $\mathbf{Q}$. Sub-objective function (8) corresponds to the objective function of matrix factorization, which is similar to the WTMF framework, and we call it Weighted Textual Nonnegative Matrix Factorization (WTNMF). Besides the nonnegative constraints, the main difference between WTNMF and WTMF is that when $X_{ij} \neq 0$, W''_{ij} is changed from 1 to e^{f_j}. The change aims to strengthen the influence of the terms in the important sentences which have high ranking scores obtained by manifold-ranking. This aim is achieved by forcing $P_{\cdot,i} \cdot Q_{\cdot,j}$ closer to X_{ij} if sentence s_j is more important. In the joint objective function, manifold-ranking is affected by similarity measurements from matrix factorization, and matrix factorization is affected by sentence importance scores from manifold-ranking. This co-effect will lead to a different convergence state from separate matrix factorization and manifold-ranking objective functions, which we believe will help improve the results.

4.3 Approximate Optimization Algorithm

In this section, we discuss how to minimize objective function (5). Gradient based optimization algorithms can be used, but they are too time-consuming for this task. To solve this problem, we explore an alternating strategy to find an approximate solution to the optimization problem. The approximate algorithm optimizes $\mathbf{P}$, $\mathbf{Q}$ and F alternately. When optimizing $\mathbf{P}$ and $\mathbf{Q}$, F is treated as fixed, and in this step $\mathbf{P}$ and $\mathbf{Q}$ are optimized to convergence, by minimizing ϕ_2 to convergence. After the optimization of $\mathbf{P}$ and $\mathbf{Q}$, an adjacency matrix for manifold-ranking can be calculated from $\mathbf{Q}$. Then it is turn to fix $\mathbf{P}$, $\mathbf{Q}$ and optimize F to convergence, by minimizing ϕ_1 with (2) to convergence. Then a new F is achieved and the alternating procedure can be restarted to optimize $\mathbf{P}$ and $\mathbf{Q}$ again. This alternating optimization is repeated several times, and an approximate solution will be achieved. The entire procedure is shown in Algorithm 1. The underlying idea of the alternating strategy is that in the matrix factorization procedure, a new similarity metric is learned, and a better similarity metric will help the manifold-ranking procedure learn better sentence importance scores; at next step, better sentence importance scores will further help improve matrix factorization results. After several repeats, an approximate stable state will be reached and better similarity measurements and ranking scores of sentences will be achieved.

Algorithm 1 Approximate optimization algorithm

Input: $\mathbf{X}$, Y, μ, λ, K and ω_m
Initialization: Set $t = 0$, initialize $\mathbf{P}^t = \mathbf{Q}^t = \mathbf{1}$, $F^t = \mathbf{0}$
repeat
  Update $\mathbf{W}''^t$ according to F^t.
  Minimize ϕ_2 to convergence. Get $\mathbf{P}^{t+1}$ and $\mathbf{Q}^{t+1}$.
  Update $\mathbf{W}'^t$ and $\mathbf{D}^t$ according to $\mathbf{Q}^{t+1}$.
  Minimize ϕ_1 to convergence. Get F^{t+1}.
  $t = t + 1$.
until convergence **or** the iteration number reaches a predefined number
Output: F^* and $\mathbf{Q}^*$.

4.4 Weighted Nonnegative Matrix Factorization

In this section we discuss how to optimize $\mathbf{P}$, $\mathbf{Q}$ in (8). In WTMF [3] without nonnegative constraints, $\mathbf{P}$, $\mathbf{Q}$ are computed iteratively by the following equations:

$$\begin{aligned} P_{\cdot,i} &= \left(\mathbf{Q}\tilde{\mathbf{W}}^{(i)}\mathbf{Q}^T + \lambda\mathbf{I}\right)^{-1}\mathbf{Q}\tilde{\mathbf{W}}^{(i)}X_{i,\cdot}^T \\ Q_{\cdot,j} &= \left(\mathbf{P}\tilde{\mathbf{W}}^{(j)}\mathbf{P}^T + \lambda\mathbf{I}\right)^{-1}\mathbf{P}\tilde{\mathbf{W}}^{(j)}X_{\cdot,j} \end{aligned} \tag{9}$$

where $\tilde{\mathbf{W}}^{(i)} = \text{diag}(W''_{i,\cdot})$ is an $N \times N$ diagonal matrix containing the i-th row of weight matrix $\mathbf{W}''$ and $\tilde{\mathbf{W}}^{(j)} = \text{diag}(W''_{\cdot,j})$ is an $M \times M$ diagonal matrix containing the j-th column of $\mathbf{W}''$. The derivation of (9) can be found in [10].

Inspired by the alternating nonnegative least squares algorithm used in [6], we apply the nonnegative least squares algorithm to solve (9) by solving the reformed alternating least squares problem (10). We used a C++ implement of nonnegative least squares tool called *tsnnls*[1] in the experiment to solve (10).

$$\begin{aligned} &\min_{P_{\cdot,i}} \left\| \left(\mathbf{Q}\tilde{\mathbf{W}}^{(i)}\mathbf{Q}^T + \lambda\mathbf{I}\right)P_{\cdot,i} - \mathbf{Q}\tilde{\mathbf{W}}^{(i)}X_{i,\cdot}^T \right\|_2^2 \\ &\min_{Q_{\cdot,j}} \left\| \left(\mathbf{P}\tilde{\mathbf{W}}^{(j)}\mathbf{P}^T + \lambda\mathbf{I}\right)Q_{\cdot,j} - \mathbf{P}\tilde{\mathbf{W}}^{(j)}X_{\cdot,j} \right\|_2^2 \\ &\quad s.t.\ P_{ki} \geq 0,\ Q_{kj} \geq 0.\ (1 \leq k \leq K) \end{aligned} \tag{10}$$

[1]http://www.jasoncantarella.com/wordpress/software/tsnnls/

5. EXPERIMENTS AND EVALUATIONS

5.1 Dataset and Evaluation Metric

We conducted experiments on the widely used Document Understanding Conference (DUC) datasets, with DUC 2005 as the development set to determine the parameters and DUC 2006 as the test set. We used the popular ROUGE toolkit[2] for evaluation.

5.2 Experiment Setup

We conducted the experiments similarly to [13]. For every topic and its related documents, we first constructed the word-sentence co-occurrence matrix $\mathbf{X}$, and initialize all elements of $\mathbf{P}$, $\mathbf{Q}$ and F with 1. $Y = [1, 0, \ldots, 0]^T$, and parameters μ, λ, K and ω_m are set before the optimization procedure starts.

After the optimization procedure in Algorithm 1 is finished, the ranking scores and similarity measurements of sentences can be got from F^* and $\mathbf{Q}^*$, respectively. Then the greedy algorithm in [13] is applied to remove redundancy between sentences. A final summary is formed with the highest overall ranking score sentences.

5.3 Results

To prove the effectiveness of the proposed method (JMFMR), we implemented two baselines of the basic manifold-ranking method (MR Baseline) [13] and a strong baseline (WTNMF-MR). WTNMF-MR replaces the bag-of-words similarity in the basic manifold-ranking method with latent semantic similarity learned with WTNMF. The main difference between WTNMF-MR and JMFMR is that WTNMF-MR does not consider the mutual effect of the manifold-ranking process and matrix factorization process. The comparison intends to test the effectiveness of the joint model. Parameters of WTNMF-MR are the same with JMFMR. The ROUGE scores of recall are shown in Table 1. Two-tailed t-tests showed that the improvements of JMFMR to the two baselines are all statistically significant ($p \ll 0.001$).

We also compared our method (JMFMR) with several representative unsupervised MDS methods, including 1) manifold-ranking based methods: Multi-modality manifold-ranking (MM-MR) [12], Mutually reinforced manifold-ranking (RDRP-AP) [1]; 2) matrix factorization based methods: Latent Semantic Analysis (LSA) and Symmetric Nonnegative Matrix Factorization (SNMF) [14]; 3) other typical methods: query Latent Dirichlet Allocation (qLDA) and Topic Modeling with Regularization (TMR) [11], Multi-objective Optimization model (MO-LEX) [5], Document Summarization based on Data Reconstruction (DSDR-non) [4]. Results of these methods for comparison are directly borrowed from respective papers as shown in Table 1 and Table 2. As we cannot get the summary-level scores for each document set, we are unable to perform t-test between our results with the results directly copied from published papers. However, we can see the large performance gap between our results and these results.

Tables 1 and 2 show the results over ROUGE recall and F-measure scores on the DUC 2006 dataset [2]. The parameters of our model are tuned on DUC 2005 dataset and set as follows: $\mu = 0.1$, $\lambda = 0.09$ and 6 iterations. We also set $K = 100$, $\omega_m = 0.0005$ which are the same with WTMF [3]. As we can see from Tables 1 and 2, the proposed joint optimization method achieves significant improvement over the MR Baseline and WTNMF based manifold-ranking method. Compared with other unsupervised methods, the proposed method also achieves better results over most metrics,

[2]http://haydn.isi.edu/ ROUGE/
The entire ROUGE command used is "ROUGE-1.5.5.pl -n 2 -m -x -2 4 -u -c 95 -r 1000 -f A -p 0.5 -t 0 -a -d -l 250".

Method	ROUGE-1	ROUGE-2	ROUGE-SU4
JMFMR	0.41482	0.08921	0.14671
RDRP-AP	0.39615	0.08975	0.13905
MO-LEX	0.4030	0.0913	0.1449
TMR	0.41176	0.08759	0.14213
qLDA	0.40211	0.08687	0.14419
WTNMF-MR	0.40908	0.08744	0.14404
MR Baseline	0.40552	0.08374	0.14169
NIST Baseline	0.30217	0.04947	0.09788

Table 1: ROUGE Recall scores on DUC 2006

Method	ROUGE-1	ROUGE-2	ROUGE-SU4
JMFMR	0.41244	0.0887	0.14585
MM-MR	0.40306	0.08508	0.13997
SNMF	0.39551	0.08549	0.13981
LSA	0.33087	0.05022	0.10226
DSDR-non	0.33168	0.06047	———
NIST Baseline	0.32082	0.05267	0.10408

Table 2: ROUGE F-measure scores on DUC 2006

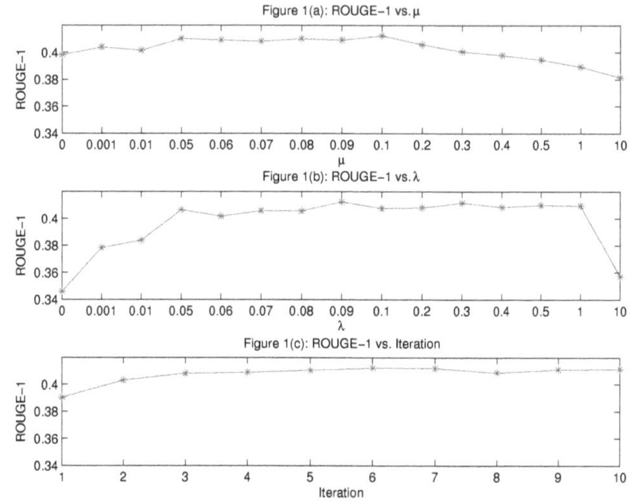

Figure 1: Parameter Sensitivity

which demonstrates the effectiveness of the proposed joint matrix factorization and manifold-ranking method.

5.4 Parameter Sensitivity Study

In this section we explore how the proposed optimization model is influenced by different parameter values on F-measure scores of ROUGE-1. When tuning one parameter, we fixed other parameters at the initial values in the experiments introduced in Section 5.3.

It can be seen from Figure 1(a) that the model gets best results around $\mu = 0.1$, and the overall results are good when $\mu \leq 0.1$, and fall down rapidly when μ is too large. The reason can be got from the iteration equation (2), that when μ is too large, $\alpha = 1/(1+\mu)$ becomes too small, and F is mainly determined by the initial score vector Y with most elements being 0. In Figure 1(b) the results are relatively good around $\lambda = 0.05$ to $\lambda = 1$, showing that the model is not fiercely influenced by the matrix factorization regularization parameter λ. In Figure 1(c) the results achieve a relatively stable state after 4 iterations, so after 6 times of iteration the optimization procedure can be viewed as convergent.

6. CONCLUSION AND FUTURE WORK

In this paper, we propose a joint optimization framework to integrate the manifold-ranking process and the similarity metric learning process simultaneously. In the future work, we will explore more syntactic and semantic information of the documents to further improve the similarity metric learning.

7. ACKNOWLEDGMENTS

This work was supported by National Hi-Tech Research and Development Program (863 Program) of China (2015AA015403, 2014AA015102) and National Natural Science Foundation of China (61170166, 61331011).

8. REFERENCES

[1] Xiaoyan Cai and Wenjie Li. Mutually reinforced manifold-ranking based relevance propagation model for query-focused multi-document summarization. *Audio, Speech, and Language Processing*, 20(5):1597–1607, 2012.

[2] Hoa Trang Dang. Overview of duc 2006. In *Document Understanding Conference. New York City*, 2006.

[3] Weiwei Guo and Mona Diab. Modeling sentences in the latent space. In *ACL*, pages 864–872. Association for Computational Linguistics, 2012.

[4] Zhanying He, Chun Chen, Jiajun Bu, Can Wang, Lijun Zhang, Deng Cai, and Xiaofei He. Document summarization based on data reconstruction. In *AAAI*, 2012.

[5] Lei Huang, Yanxiang He, Furu Wei, and Wenjie Li. Modeling document summarization as multi-objective optimization. In *IITSI*, pages 382–386. IEEE, 2010.

[6] Yong-Deok Kim and Seungjin Choi. Weighted nonnegative matrix factorization. In *Acoustics, Speech and Signal Processing, 2009.*, pages 1541–1544. IEEE, 2009.

[7] Thomas K Landauer, Peter W Foltz, and Darrell Laham. An introduction to latent semantic analysis. *Discourse processes*, 25(2-3):259–284, 1998.

[8] Sun Park, Ju-Hong Lee, Chan-Min Ahn, Jun Sik Hong, and Seok-Ju Chun. Query based summarization using non-negative matrix factorization. In *Knowledge-Based Intelligent Information and Engineering Systems*, pages 84–89. Springer, 2006.

[9] Sun Park, Ju-Hong Lee, Deok-Hwan Kim, and Chan-Min Ahn. Multi-document summarization based on cluster using non-negative matrix factorization. In *SOFSEM 2007: Theory and Practice of Computer Science*, pages 761–770. Springer, 2007.

[10] Nathan Srebro, Tommi Jaakkola, et al. Weighted low-rank approximations. In *ICML*, volume 3, pages 720–727, 2003.

[11] Jie Tang, Limin Yao, and Dewei Chen. Multi-topic based query-oriented summarization. In *SDM*, volume 9, pages 1147–1158. SIAM, 2009.

[12] Xiaojun Wan and Jianguo Xiao. Graph-based multi-modality learning for topic-focused multi-document summarization. In *IJCAI*, pages 1586–1591, 2009.

[13] Xiaojun Wan, Jianwu Yang, and Jianguo Xiao. Manifold-ranking based topic-focused multi-document summarization. In *IJCAI*, volume 7, pages 2903–2908, 2007.

[14] Dingding Wang, Tao Li, Shenghuo Zhu, and Chris Ding. Multi-document summarization via sentence-level semantic analysis and symmetric matrix factorization. In *SIGIR*, pages 307–314. ACM, 2008.

Towards Understanding the Impact of Length in Web Search Result Summaries over a Speech-only Communication Channel

Johanne R. Trippas
johanne.trippas@rmit.edu.au

Damiano Spina
damiano.spina@rmit.edu.au

Mark Sanderson
mark.sanderson@rmit.edu.au

Lawrence Cavedon
lawrence.cavedon@rmit.edu.au

School of Computer Science and Information Technology
RMIT University, Melbourne, Australia

ABSTRACT

Presenting search results over a speech-only communication channel involves a number of challenges for users due to cognitive limitations and the serial nature of speech. We investigated the impact of search result summary length in speech-based web search, and compared our results to a text baseline. Based on crowdsourced workers, we found that users preferred longer, more informative summaries for text presentation. For audio, user preferences depended on the style of query. For single-facet queries, shortened audio summaries were preferred, additionally users were found to judge relevance with a similar accuracy compared to text-based summaries. For multi-facet queries, user preferences were not as clear, suggesting that more sophisticated techniques are required to handle such queries.

Categories and Subject Descriptors

H.5.1 [**Multimedia Information Systems**]; H.3.3 [**Information Search and Retrieval**]

Keywords

Spoken Retrieval; Search Result Summarisation; Crowdsourcing

1. INTRODUCTION

Speech-based web search (i.e., posing search queries using voice rather than a keyboard/touchscreen interface) is increasingly ubiquitous, particularly through the use of mobile devices. Several systems (e.g., Siri, Google Now, Cortana) can speak a reply to "factoid"-style search queries (e.g., "How high is Everest?"). If no factoid answer exists, the systems revert to displaying a ranked list of results on screen. However, there are situations where a full speech-only interface is preferable, such as while driving a car [6, 7], when there is no screen or keyboard available [20], when users are mobile [12, 16, 18], or when using wearable devices [4].

SIGIR'15, August 09–13, 2015, Santiago, Chile.

DOI: http://dx.doi.org/10.1145/2766462.2767826.

Moreover, visually presented results may be inaccessible for certain populations, such as visually impaired users [14, 17] or people with limited literacy skills.

Presenting lists of search results over a speech-only communication channel presents a number of challenges; in particular, simply speaking the textual component of a standard search results list has been shown to be ineffectual [17]. The serial nature of the speech/audio channel makes it difficult for users to "skim" back and forth over a list of results (a standard process in browsing a visual list).

Few studies have investigated techniques for effective presentation of web search results via a speech-only communication channel (hereafter referred to as audio) [7]. The present study seeks to address this. In particular, we seek a better understanding of how to present search results over audio while not overwhelming the users with information [18], nor leaving users uncertain as to whether what they heard covered the information space [19].

The length of a spoken search result summary plays a crucial role in the success or failure of presenting search results over audio. A short summary might not yield enough information to judge whether the retrieved document is relevant or not; in contrast, a more descriptive summary might take too long to be played and thereby diminish user experience. Thus a trade-off is necessary between a short summary and a longer, more descriptive summary.

The present study investigated these trade-offs via a crowdsource-based interactive experimental design. The aim of the study was to develop a baseline of understanding about the audio result summary length users prefer. This study aimed to answer the following research questions:

- What is the impact of search result summary length in a spoken retrieval scenario?
- Do users prefer a longer or shorter summary?

2. METHODOLOGY

Our experiments used a crowdsourcing platform to present queries and search results to users. Result summaries of various length were presented in text or audio form. Summary length was either a *full* Google-length summary or a *truncated* version extracted from the original summary. Users were asked to select a result that best addressed the query, and were also presented with post-task and exit questionnaires. The present study used the CrowdFlower crowdsourcing tool [9, 10] to provide user data for the tasks and questionnaires.

Table 1: Examples of full and truncated summaries for faceted and single-faceted queries.

Query	Type	Full Summary	Truncated Summary
`old town scottsdale`	faceted	Downtown Scottsdale / Old Town Scottsdale. Downtown Scottsdale pulses with a vibrant energy all its own. By day, shopping, gallery-hopping and dining...	and residents alike to enjoy art galleries, specialty retail...
Find restaurants in Old Town Scottsdale, AZ.		Where the Old West Meets the New West. Downtown Scottsdale is the ultimate destination for visitors and residents alike to enjoy art galleries, specialty retail...	all its own. By day, shopping, gallery-hopping and dining...
`what was the name of elvis presley's home`	single-facet	The unique association between Elvis Presley and Graceland, his home in Memphis, ... Early on, Elvis became known around the world by his first name alone...	Elvis Presley and Graceland, his home in Memphis, ... Early
What was the name of Elvis Presley's home?		Graceland? Learn fun Graceland facts, and get the official answers to common questions about the home of Elvis Presley! ... How did Graceland get its name?	Graceland facts, and get the official answers to common

2.1 Experimental Design

We first describe the task users undertook, followed by the queries, search engine results summaries, post-task and exit questionnaires, and use of text as a baseline for audio. The crowdsourcing setup for presenting results lists to users and collecting judgements is also described.[1]

Users were presented with a task which consisted of three queries, corresponding lists of result summaries, a post-task questionnaire, and an exit questionnaire. Users were asked to read three query descriptions and read/listen to the summaries, before stating their preferred result description in the questionnaires. One set of summaries was the full length, one set was truncated.

2.1.1 *Queries*

The task was designed to reflect common search tasks on the Web: query topics from the Text REtrieval Conference (TREC) 2013 Web Track were used [5]. The queries in the track were manually selected from logs of a commercial search engine [5]. Since this was a preliminary study, a subset of twenty queries from the TREC 2013 Web Track dataset were used. An assessment of the queries indicated two categories, *single-facet queries* (queries with a clear intent) and *faceted queries* (typically broader in intent and represented with subtopics). It was decided to investigate whether these categories impacted on result summary preference.

The present study included seven single-facet and thirteen faceted queries. Table 1 shows an example for each type of query. Only informational subtopics were selected for the present study, since they have a primary interpretation which is reflected in the description field.

2.1.2 *Search Engine Results Summaries*

Each query was sent to the Google search engine and Google-generated text summaries were extracted for the top five search results.[2] The summaries were converted into a spoken synthetic voice (audio). Instructions were added to each summary set: *These are summaries of the top results. Select the summary that leads to the information you are looking for.* A list-rank number was added to the front of each summary to allow easy identification of the users' selection. Table 1 shows a sample summary before and after the conversion for the task.

Truncated versions of the original Google-generated summaries were created manually. Here, a contiguous subset of nine words was selected from each full summary. Nine was found to be a little less than half the length of a standard Google-generated summary. For this initial work, manual summaries were created to avoid bias introduced by poor automatic truncation, which may negatively impact user perception. Human judgement was assumed to be the best way to preserve the meaning of the summary.

The presentation of the twenty search queries was randomized with the use of a Latin square design. Each user saw three queries per task. The order in which the users were presented with the result description (original summary vs. truncated summary) was rotated. These steps were implemented to avoid learning effects triggered by usage order and by users becoming accustomed to a synthetic voice [1, 11].

A problem reported with crowdsourcing is that users try to receive payment without completing the task properly [3]. Therefore, every task was populated with a *Gold Question* to help with data integrity and to detect if the participant was paying attention to the task [2]. The Gold Questions in this study used queries with clear pre-determined answers. Users were presented with three query descriptions and corresponding summaries. However, one of these summaries was populated with unrelated summary results. A user that was not able to identify that the summaries were not related to the query had their judgements discarded.

Though crowdsourcing provides a significant and easily accessible sample, we discovered that despite the precaution of releasing the tasks at different times and on different days, the results showed that many users completed every task. As a result, a modification was made and instead of running a new task for every set of queries, the queries were grouped into batches of ten and restrictions placed on how many batches users could judge.

2.1.3 *Post-task and Exit Questionnaires*

Post-task questionnaires are frequently implemented to assess the system–task interaction and gather user feedback on their experiences with using a particular system to complete a particular task [11]. Since no validated questionnaire has been published for studying user reaction to audio summaries, we used questionnaires adapted from previous studies.

Users completed the post-task questionnaire three times for each of the queries given. The post-task questionnaire (see Table 2) consisted of five questions on a five-point Likert scale (1–5); one question on query judgement with multiple choice answers (6); one question on how the participant listened to the audio with tick boxes (7); and a text box for further comments (8).

In addition, [11] suggests conducting a questionnaire at the end of the completed task to capture comparisons for within-subjects studies. Thus users were also presented with an exit questionnaire. Using a dynamic panel, the exit questionnaire was available only to users who were successful in answering a Gold Question. The exit questionnaire was used to measure users' preferences for information exploration using different result description configurations.

[1]All experiments were performed under Ethics Application BSEH 10-14 at RMIT University.

[2]Only the top five were presented to keep the audio task manageable.

Table 2: Post-task questionnaire questions.

Post-task Questionnaire
1. The search results I heard are informative.
2. The search results give me a good overview of the available options.
3. The search results give me enough information to select the most relevant result.
4. The search results are presented in a way that is easy to understand.
5. I am confident I can recall the search results that I heard.
6. Which search result would you select to hear further information for?
7. Which statement describes how you listened to the audio?
8. Further comments.

Table 3: Exit questionnaire results for preferences in the search engine result summaries. ▲$p < .01$.

Exit Question	Text Summary		Audio Summary	
	Full	Truncated	Full	Truncated
Recommend to a friend	572▲(57%)	434 (43%)	529 (51%)	512 (49%)
Easier to find relevant result	548▲(54%)	458 (46%)	514 (49%)	527 (51%)
Gave better result	576▲(57%)	430 (43%)	539 (52%)	502 (48%)
More efficient to use	529 (53%)	477 (47%)	499 (48%)	542 (52%)

The exit questionnaire was analysed with the help of responses from the post-task questionnaire.

2.1.4 *Using Text as Baseline for Audio*

Tasks were paired, whereby one task's summaries were audio and the other's were text. The text output was used to create a baseline measure of the system, facilitating analysis of the difference in preference between audio and text [11], enabling us to compare audio against the text baseline.

2.2 Users

CrowdFlower allows *contributors* (users who submit tasks to CrowdFlower) to place constraints on the users assigned to a task. The following constraints were put in place for the present study:

- Only users with an IP address from Australia, Ireland, New Zealand, the UK, and the USA were allowed to participate in order to maximise the likelihood that users were native English speakers or or had a high level of English.
- Users were able to participate only once in a particular task to maximise the worker pool.
- Users who took less than sixty seconds to complete the whole task were discarded on the basis that it would take users more than sixty seconds to listen to/read the summaries.

Although users were not permitted to participate more than once in a task which had the same set of queries, they were allowed to participate in tasks with different queries. A minimum of 36 users were recruited for each given task [13].

When a participant did not answer the Gold Question successfully, that participant's submission was discarded. These users were also not allowed to participate in later tasks. It was found that 11.8% of all users did not answer the Gold Question successfully, their submissions were discarded.

3. RESULTS

The exit questionnaire was analyzed using the χ^2 goodness-of-fit test to compare the distribution of scores across two levels. Results are shown in Table 3.

The χ^2 goodness-of-fit test [11] was used to assess whether changing the result summary had an effect on user preference.

Users were asked (in the post-task questionnaire) which summary made the users want to know more about the underlying document.[3] These judgements were analysed with the two-sample Kolmogorov-Smirnov test (*KS test*) to determine whether two given samples follow the same distribution [15]. The tasks compared the result 'click' distributions where the length of the summary was manipulated. The tasks were conducted in pairs: audio and text [11].

The KS test showed that for truncated summaries, only two out of twenty queries were there different distributions for audio-based versus text-based summaries. For full-length summaries and three out of twenty summaries resulted in different distributions for audio versus text. In general, the same distribution was found for query judgements between the text baseline and audio indicating that users made similar query judgements regardless of the presentation style being audio or text.

3.1 Preferred Length of Text Summaries

Table 3 shows that users tend to prefer full text summaries rather than their truncated counterpart. For instance, 57% of users would recommend full text summaries to a friend and 57% indicated that full summaries gave better results. The χ^2 goodness-of-fit tests were statistically significant ($p < .01$) for three exit questions in relation to the use of the original summary for presenting text results, indicating that this information exploration style was preferred.

3.2 Preferred Length of Audio Summaries

Results in audio summaries do not indicate a clear preference between full and truncated (preferences differ at most by only 2%). The χ^2 goodness-of-fit tests were not statistically significant ($p > .05$) for any of the exit questions about presenting audio results. No statistically significant difference were found for faceted queries. However, for single-facet queries using audio, all exit questions where statistically significant ($p < .05$) with a user preference for truncated summaries.

The KS test revealed that only one out of seven single-facet queries judgements was statistically significant ($p < .05$) when comparing truncated audio to the truncated text baseline. The KS test was not statistically significant for any faceted queries in audio, with one exception.

Users reported that overall it was easier to recall truncated audio summaries (54.4%) than full audio summaries (49.9%). Moreover, fewer users reported that they had to listen to the audio more than once (16.8%) for truncated summaries than for full-length audio summaries (23.7%). Only three users reported that they stopped the audio for truncated summaries, possibly indicating that both the information presented and the length of the information were short enough to avoid cognitive overload.

4. DISCUSSION

The present study investigated whether summaries of shorter length would be preferred for audio presentation as they could avoid overloading users' memory [20]. The exit questionnaire responses demonstrated that, for text summaries, full-length were preferred. However, for audio, no significant length preference was found.

[3]This is equivalent to asking which result they would *click* in a traditional search engine result page (SERP).

Users reported that truncated summaries for single-facet queries were preferred. Thus for simpler, less ambiguous queries, shorter audio summaries were both effective and preferred. However, for faceted queries, users may have benefited from a more informative audio response even at the cost of listening time.

The single-facet query judgement distribution for both audio and text followed the distribution reported in past work [8] where query results ranked first and second receive most user attention. However, this expected distribution was not reflected in the faceted query judgements; rather, summaries ranked first and last obtained the most attention. This is also of interest: the serial nature of audio seems to lead to a bias towards most-recently-heard results, a behavior not found in visual presentation.

Users left comments in questionnaires. For summaries of faceted queries, they indicated that the summaries were missing key information. This suggests that the way of presenting summaries may differ depending on query intent: short audio summaries may be appropriate for clear intent queries (single-facet), whereas broader intent queries (faceted) may need more complex techniques (e.g., interactive/conversational approaches).

5. CONCLUSIONS

The present paper describes an initial investigation into result summaries for audio-based search. This study aimed to answer the following research questions:

- What is the impact of search result summary length in a spoken retrieval scenario?
- Do users prefer a full or truncated summary?

Differences were observed when result summary lengths were presented in the spoken retrieval scenario. In general, there was no preference for fuller descriptive summaries or for truncated summaries. However, results revealed that different kinds of queries (single-facet vs. faceted) benefited from an optimised summary depending on the type of query.

Extensions of the research include testing based on a larger number of queries and using automated techniques for truncating summaries for audio presentation. (The current method used manual truncation to avoid poor truncation from confounding the results.) More significantly, the results suggest a need for developing more sophisticated approaches to handling result-presentation over audio for faceted queries.

Acknowledgments

This research was partially supported by Australian Research Council Project LP130100563 and Real Thing Entertainment Pty Ltd. The authors wish to thank Bruce Croft who provided valuable feedback.

6. REFERENCES

[1] W. Albert, T. Tullis, and D. Tedesco. *Beyond the Usability Lab: Conducting Large-Scale Online User Experience Studies*. Morgan Kaufmann, 2009.

[2] S. Buchholz, J. Latorre, and K. Yanagisawa. Crowdsourced assessment of speech synthesis. *Crowdsourcing for Speech Processing*, pages 173–216, 2013.

[3] C. Callison-Burch and M. Dredze. Creating speech and language data with amazon's mechanical turk. In *Proc. of NAACL HLT CSLDAMT'10 Workshop*, 2010.

[4] E. Chang, F. Seide, H. M. Meng, C. Zhuoran, S. Yu, and L. Yuk-Chi. A system for spoken query information retrieval on mobile devices. *Transactions on Speech and Audio Processing*, 10(8):531–541, 2002.

[5] K. Collins-Thompson, P. Bennett, F. Diaz, C. L. Clarke, and E. M. Voorhees. TREC 2013 Web Track Overview. In *TREC'13*, 2014.

[6] V. Demberg and A. Sayeed. Linguistic cognitive load: implications for automotive uis. In *Proc. of AutomotiveUI 2011*, 2011.

[7] V. Demberg, A. Winterboer, and J. D. Moore. A strategy for information presentation in spoken dialog systems. *Computational Linguistics*, 37(3):489–539, 2011.

[8] T. Joachims, L. Granka, B. Pan, H. Hembrooke, and G. Gay. Accurately interpreting clickthrough data as implicit feedback. In *Proc. of SIGIR '05*, 2005.

[9] G. Jones. An introduction to crowdsourcing for language and multimedia technology research. *Information Retrieval Meets Information Visualization*, 7757:132–154, 2013.

[10] F. Jurčíček, S. Keizer, M. Gašic, F. Mairesse, B. Thomson, K. Yu, and S. Young. Real user evaluation of spoken dialogue systems using amazon mechanical turk. In *Proc. of INTERSPEECH'11*, 2011.

[11] D. Kelly. Methods for evaluating interactive information retrieval systems with users. *Foundations and Trends in Information Retrieval*, 3(1–2):1–224, 2009.

[12] S. R. Klemmer, A. K. Sinha, J. Chen, J. A. Landay, N. Aboobaker, and A. Wang. Suede: a wizard of oz prototyping tool for speech user interfaces. In *Proc. of UIST'00*, 2000.

[13] B. P. Knijnenburg, M. C. Willemsen, and A. Kobsa. A pragmatic procedure to support the user-centric evaluation of recommender systems. In *Proc. of RecSys'11*, 2011.

[14] J. Lai and N. Yankelovich. *Speech Interface Design*. Elsevier, 2006.

[15] F. J. Massey. The Kolmogorov-Smirnov test for goodness of fit. *Journal of the American Statistical Assoc.*, 46(253):68–78, 1951.

[16] L. J. Najjar, J. J. Ockerman, and J. C. Thompson. User interface design guidelines for speech recognition applications. In *Proc. of VRAIS '98*, 1998.

[17] N. G. Sahib, D. Al Thani, A. Tombros, and T. Stockman. Accessible information seeking. In *Proc. of Digital Futures'12*, 2012.

[18] M. Turunen, J. Hakulinen, N. Rajput, and A. A. Nanavati. Evaluation of mobile and pervasive speech applications. In *Speech in Mobile and Pervasive Environments*, pages 219–262. 2012.

[19] S. Varges, F. Weng, and H. Pon-Barry. Interactive question answering and constraint relaxation in spoken dialogue systems. In *Proc. of ACL'06*, 2006.

[20] N. Yankelovich, G.-A. Levow, and M. Marx. Designing speechacts: Issues in speech user interfaces. In *Proc. of the SIGCHI'95*, 1995.

Early Detection of Topical Expertise in Community Question Answering

David van Dijk[†‡]
d.v.van.dijk@hva.nl

Manos Tsagkias[§]
manos@904labs.com

Maarten de Rijke[‡]
derijke@uva.nl

[†]Create-IT, Amsterdam University of Applied Sciences, Amsterdam, The Netherlands
[‡]University of Amsterdam, Amsterdam, The Netherlands
[§]904Labs, Amsterdam, The Netherlands

ABSTRACT

We focus on detecting potential topical experts in community question answering platforms early on in their lifecycle. We use a semi-supervised machine learning approach. We extract three types of feature: (i) textual, (ii) behavioral, and (iii) time-aware, which we use to predict whether a user will become an expert in the longterm. We compare our method to a machine learning method based on a state-of-the-art method in expertise retrieval. Results on data from Stack Overflow demonstrate the utility of adding behavioral and time-aware features to the baseline method with a net improvement in accuracy of 26% for very early detection of expertise.

Categories and Subject Descriptors

H.3 [**Information Storage and Retrieval**]: H.3.3 Information Search and Retrieval

Keywords

Community question answering; User profiling; Expertise finding

1. INTRODUCTION

Community Question Answering (CQA) sites such as Stack Overflow[1] provide a growing resource of information. Users contribute and interact by posting questions, answers and comments, and provide feedback by voting on questions and answers and by selecting the best answer to their question. Key to the success of CQA platforms are the users that can provide high quality answers to the more difficult questions posted, however, this type of user is scarce [10, 11]. In this setting, it becomes important to stimulate the growth of the group of users who provide the most useful answers. There are several methods for doing so; applying gamification methods on the website for incentivizing users to contribute their expertise is one [2]. Another angle to this challenge is to detect and nurture users with topical expertise early enough so we can recommend questions relevant to their expertise [7]. Central here, and our aim, is to identify users with a strong potential to become prolific users on a subject, i.e., potential topical experts, from their first interactions with the platform. The main challenge here lies in inherent data sparsity issues: how to profile an expert given only a handful of data points, i.e., questions, answers and comments.

Detecting topical expertise is a well-studied problem, which relates to expertise finding and retrieval [3]. Common to all methods is the profiling of a user and a topic for generating candidate matches. In our scenario, a user's expertise manifests itself via multiple channels, e.g., comments, questions, answers, accepted answers. Our hypothesis is that when we combine information from these channels, we can accurately detect early expertise even in scenarios where data is sparse. Focusing on early expert detection in CQA, Pal et al. [5] apply a machine learning approach to identify general experts during the first few weeks after their first answer. Bouguessa and Romdhane [4] propose a parameter-free mixture model-based approach for identifying of authorities in online communities. Pal et al. [6] observe how behavioral signals evolve over time for grouping experts. Our work differs from previous work on early expertise discovery in two ways: (i) in how we define early expertise, and (ii) we study and report on the importance of combining a large number of textual, behavioral and time-aware signals for detecting early expertise.

We cast the task of early detection of topical expertise as a classification problem: to decide whether a user will be an expert in the long-term by using evidence from increasingly long timespans of a user's early behavior. We define early expertise based on the number of best answers given by a user. A best answer is the one answer that gets accepted by a question poster as a the most useful. Users with ten or more best answers on a topic are considered experts on the topic. We engineer three feature sets to capture early expertise: (i) textual, (ii) behavioral, and (iii) time-aware. We seek to answer the following research questions: (RQ1) What is the impact on classification effectiveness when we use each feature set individually and in combination over a baseline based on a state-of-the-art method in expertise finding? Does performance remain stable over time? (RQ2) What is the most important feature set for early detection of topical expertise among: textual, behavioral, and temporal feature sets? (RQ3) What is the most important individual feature within and across feature sets? To answer these questions we use data from Stack Overflow, a CQA platform for programming-related topics.[2] Our experimental results show significant improvements over the baseline and validate the utility of

[1]http://stackoverflow.com

[2]Our dataset is publicly available from http://ilps.science.uva.nl/resources

SIGIR'15, August 09 - 13, 2015, Santiago, Chile.

ACM 978-1-4503-3621-5/15/08 ...$15.00.
DOI: http://dx.doi.org/10.1145/2766462.2767840 .

using behavioral and time-aware features from multiple behavioral channels. Results also show we can achieve high accuracy in early detection of topical expertise at relatively early stages of a user's lifespan, i.e., F_1 score 0.75 at user's first best answer.

2. APPROACH

Our approach for early discovery of potential experts is based on a semi-supervised machine learning method. We extract a set of features indicative of a user's expertise on a topic, which we use to train a classifier that learns whether a user shows signals of early expertise given a topic. We cater for early expertise by carefully crafting the training data used to train the classifier. Our method is semi-supervised because we automatically generate training data, by labeling experts in a data-driven manner; see Section 3.

We first need to define early expertise. Although time is a natural way for separating early from seasoned experts, the diverse behavioral patterns among experts make it hard to define early expertise using time in an experimental setting [6, 8, 9]. One future expert might submit ten best answers within two days after joining while another may post one comment during their entire first week. We define expertise based on best answers. Here, a *best answer* is one that gets accepted by the question poster. The more best answers a user gives, the more expert they are. We took as experts those users with one standard deviation number of best answers larger than the average user. On our dataset (see below) this translates into people with more than nine best answers on a topic. *Early expertise* is defined as the expertise shown by a user between the moment of joining and becoming an expert, based on the best answers provided. We interpret the values of the selected features between the moment of joining and becoming an expert as the strength of a user's early expertise, and predict future expertise based on it.

Table 1 provides a summary of the features we use.

Textual features. We build on prior work on expertise retrieval by [3]. It aggregates a user's textual relevance scores of answers as an indication of expertise. We start with generating a profile per topic—here, a topic is a tag associated with a question on Stack Overflow—by retrieving all questions that are associated with the topic along with all comments, answers, and comments to answers associated with the question. We profile terms by ranking them using tf.idf scoring and select the top-100 terms for a topic's profile. For profiling users we retrieve all answers that are posted by a certain user that are associated with the topic. Once we have topic and user profiles, we apply Model 2 [3] to determine the user's textual relevance to the topic. In particular,

$$p(q|ca) = \sum_{d \in D_{ca}} f(d, ca) \cdot p(d|ca), \qquad (1)$$

where q is a topic, ca is a candidate expert, d is a document (i.e., question, answer, comment), $f(d, ca)$ is a function denoting the textual similarity between the textual profiles of a document and a candidate user, and D_{ca} stands for the documents of the candidate, in our case the answer history of the user. We consider three readily used textual similarity functions as individual features: (i) language modeling (LM), (ii) BM25 (BM25), and (iii) tf.idf (TFIDF).

Behavioral features. On top of our textual features based on expertise retrieval, we mine a user's posting behavior to extract nine features that are indicative of their expertise. We extract these features per topic. Below, we describe them shortly.

Number of questions, answers and comments are used based on intuitions, such as that an expert is likely to ask fewer questions on his field of expertise and could be selective in what questions to answer or comment on. Z-Score, a measure to quantify expertise, is defined as $z = \frac{a-q}{\sqrt{a+q}}$ [11] and combines the number of answers and the number of questions into one score. Similarly to z-score, we engineer features that combine different behavioral signals as ratios between the number of different types of post: Nr. of questions divided by nr. of answers., Nr. of answers divided by nr. of comments and Nr. of comments divided by nr. of questions. First and timely answers a have a higher chance of becoming accepted by a questioner. Users that show timely answering behaviour are more likely to get their answers accepted by users.

Table 1: Summary of the three types of feature we consider: (i) textual, (ii) behavioral, and (iii) time-aware, 25 in total.

ID	Feature	Gloss
Textual features		
1	LM	Model 2 using language modeling scoring
2	BM25	Model 2 using BM25 scoring
3	TFIDF	Model 2 using tf.idf scoring
Behavioral features		
4	Question	Number of questions by a user
5	Answer	Number of answers by a user
6	Comment	Number of comments by a user
7	Z-Score	Question-answering ratio
8	Q.-A.	Nr. of questions divided by nr. of answers
9	A.-C.	Nr. of answers divided by nr. of comments
10	C.-Q.	Nr. of comments div. by nr. of questions
11	First Answer	Number of first answers a user has posted
12	Timely Answer	Nr. of answers posted within 4h by a user
Time-aware features		
13	Time Interval	Days between joining and N-th best answer
14	LM/T	LM / Time interval
15	BM25/T	BM25 / Time interval
16	TFIDF/T	TFIDF/ Time interval
17	Question/T	Question / Time interval
18	Answer/T	Answer / Time interval
19	Comment/T	Comment / Time interval
20	Z-Score/T	Z-Score / Time interval
21	Q.-A./T	Q.-A. / Time interval
22	A.-C./T	A.-C. / Time interval
23	C.-Q./T	C.-Q. / Time interval
24	First Answer/T	First Answer / Time interval
25	Timely Answer/T	Timely Answer / Time interval

Time-aware features. We also include features with a focus on expert's activity patterns over time. We consider the time interval between a user's best answers, and we measure it as the number of days between the moment a user joined the forum and when the posted his N-th best answer ($1 \leq N \leq 9$). Our hypothesis here is that an expert is likely to take less time between posting best answers than a non-expert user. We create a time-aware version for each of the textual and behavioral features we discussed above, by dividing the respective feature value by the time interval. This provides us, e.g., with the number of answers per day. As the time interval can substantially vary between users, we expect time-aware features to be more indicative than their non-time-aware variants.

3. EXPERIMENTAL SETUP

In addressing the early detection of topical expertise problem, we concentrate on developing features and combinations of features that can be used for early detection of expertise. In this respect, our goals are comparable to those of [1, 5]. In particular, we want to know the effectiveness of our complete set of features, and of individual feature sets, for classifying users as experts and non-experts; see Table 2 for a summary of systems we consider.

Table 2: **Summary of the systems we consider, and the individual features they consist of.**

ID	Type	Feature	ID	Feature
A	Textual	1–3	E	C + D
B	Behavioral	4–12	F	A + B
C	Time-aware 1	13–25	G	A + B + C + D
D	Time-aware 2	1–25 per bin		

Table 3: Dataset statistics over 100 topics and 90,486 experts. A user can be expert in more than one topic, contributing more than one expert.

X per topic	Mean	Std.Dev	Min	Max
Users	16,279	15,171	2,485	79,211
Experts	905	1,383	68	6,622
Questions	108,532	150,549	26,624	700,175
Answers	192,920	277,471	37,596	1,328,446
Comments	205,115	309,620	31,580	1,422,483

Our dataset comes from Stack Overflow,[3] covers the period August 2008–mid-September 2014, and consists of 6,044,028 questions, 10,794,654 answers and 24,708,671 comments. We select the 100 most active topic tags in terms of number of questions and answers to maximize the number of experts we can use for training and testing. Highly semantically related topic tags are grouped together. We mark users as experts on a topic when they have ten or more of their answers marked as best by the question poster, which is one standard deviation larger than the average number of answers over all users and topics. Table 3 lists statistics for our dataset.

Machine learning. Our semi-supervised machine learning method starts out with unlabeled data and adopts a data-driven approach to labels users who provide above average best answers on a topic as topical experts. Training data for users is generated on the period between joining and becoming an expert. To prevent classification bias in the training set, we balance the number of experts and non-experts per topic by down-sampling non-experts uniformly over the number of best answers. We divide this dataset into two: we hold out 10% for feature engineering and development, and 90% for testing. We choose to evaluate the effectiveness of three classifiers: Gaussian Naive Bayes, Linear Support Vector Classification and Random Forest (RF); no parameter optimization is performed. In preliminary experiments, RF, as implemented in Scikit,[4] outperformed the other two classifiers, hence we use it for our main experiments. We use Apache Lucene[5] for extracting textual features.

We report on F1 scores over each best answer of a user starting from their first best answer and going up to their ninth answer, i.e., one best answer before they are deemed experts. At each step, we perform 10-fold cross validation on our test set. We use a two-tailed paired T-test to determine statistical significance and report on significant differences for $\alpha = .05$ and $\alpha = 0.01$.

4. RESULTS AND ANALYSIS

Our first experiment aims at answering RQ1: What is the impact on classification effectiveness when we use each feature set individually and in combination over a baseline based on a state-of-the-art method in expertise finding? Does performance remain stable over time? Among individual feature sets, the textual feature set (system A) outperforms the behavioral one (system B) up to best answer three, and after that we see the reverse, i.e., the behavioral feature set outperforming the textual one, possibly due to aggregation of more behavioral data. The combination of all features sets (system G) shows the best performance among all systems peaking F1 at 0.7472, and outperforms the baseline (system A) in statistically significant way. The performance of time-aware feature sets (systems D and E) hovers around that of system G. They all include D, which holds all features normalized by time. In general, we find that incremental combinations of feature sets improve performance over the baseline in a statistically significant way (i.e., $G \geq E > F$). Fig. 1 illustrates the performance of all systems over time. Common to all systems is a big leap in performance between best answer one and two, which is likely caused by data sparsity at the first best answer.

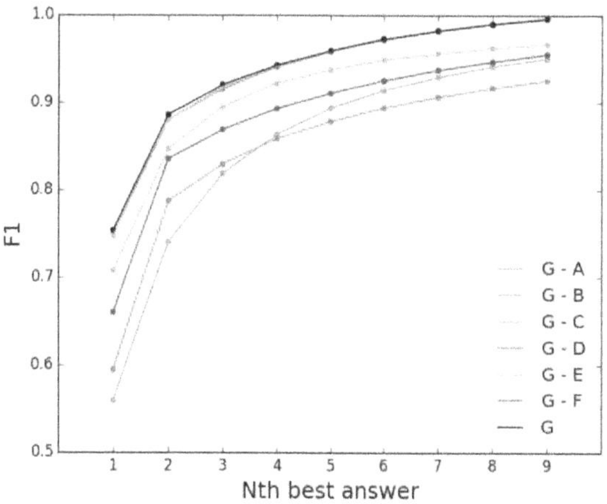

Figure 1: System performance in F1 using individual feature sets and their combination.

Turning to our next two research questions, RQ2 and RQ3: What is the most important feature set among textual, behavioral, and temporal feature sets, and the most important features within and across feature sets? We perform an ablation study, where we remove one feature set at a time from our best performing system (system G); see Fig. 2. The removal of the two time-aware feature sets leads to the largest drop in effectiveness. This shows that normalizing features by time helps detecting early expertise in a statistically significant way. Next, we aim to find out what individual features in our feature sets have the largest impact in performance. By incrementally removing individual features, we found a small set of features that when combined, they perform similarly to our best system (G): TFIDF (feature 3 in Table 1), Answer (feature 5), BM25/T (feature 15), TFIDF/T (feature 16), Answer/T (feature 18), Time Interval (Time-Aware 2, feature 13). This optimal feature set is a combination of textual features, time-aware features, and behavioral features; the kappa-statistic over all best answers is 0.8705, which supports the strong predictive power of this optimal set of features. An interesting finding is that the z-score, a widely-used measure for quantifying expertise, although it has performed well in similar tasks [4–6], in our setting was not selected as an important individual feature.

To better understand our results, we perform an analysis of the performance of our best system (G). First, we look at the time difference between a user's first best answer and their tenth best answer. Fig. 3 (left) shows that a large number of users become experts within the same month they post their best answer but there is also a long tail of users who become experts many months later. Second, we plot system performance, on the first best answer, on the selected feature set, over the time difference between a user's

[3]https://archive.org/details/stackexchange
[4]http://scikit-learn.org
[5]http://lucene.apache.org

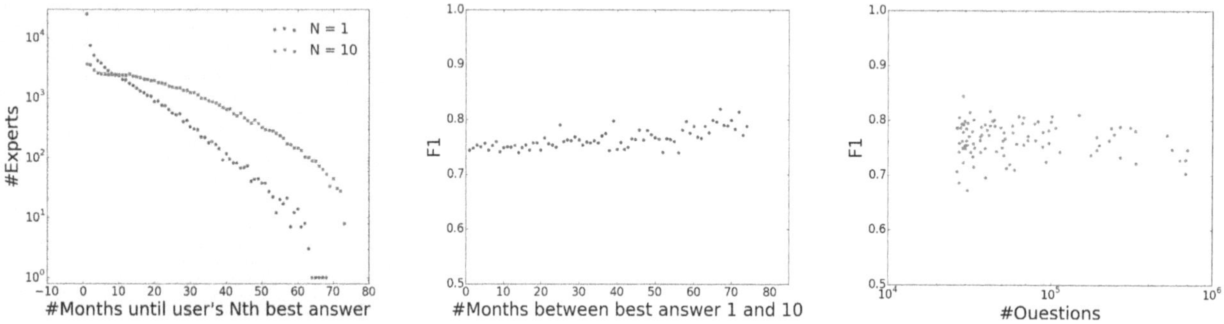

Figure 3: Number of experts that provided their N-th best answer before month X (left). Performance in F1 over experts binned per time between first and tenth best answer (middle). Performance in F1 over size of topics on first and second best answer (right).

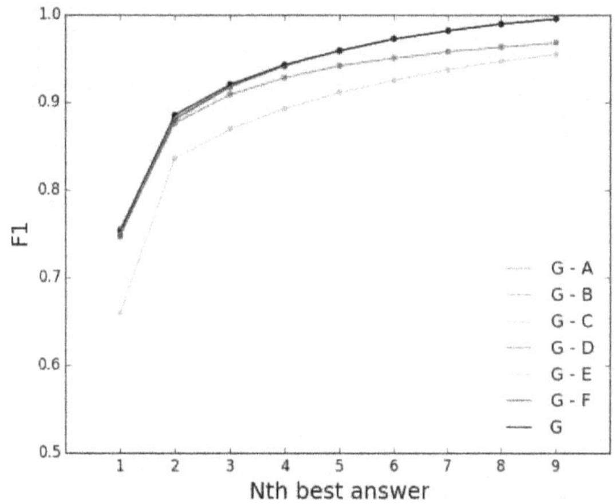

Figure 2: Ablation study on feature sets.

first and tenth best answer in Fig. 3 (middle). System performance is stable over all time bins, suggesting that our classifier is not overfitting for users who become experts in short time, and also performance increases for users who become experts many months after their first best answer. This fact provides evidence that we can accurately detect experts early on (e.g., from 10 to 70 months in advance). Finally, we look at system performance with regards to the size of a topic in terms of number of questions for the first best answer. Fig. 3 (right) illustrates that sparser topics have a larger variance in performance, which is likely due to data sparsity itself. However, an interesting finding is that our system performs on average better on sparser topics than on non-sparse ones. This may be attributed to that topics with many answers may contain more noise than sparse ones. In sum, we find that topic size has little influence on system effectiveness, which provides evidence that our system can effectively detect experts for both popular and non-popular topics at an early stage.

5. CONCLUSIONS

We addressed the task of early detection of topical expertise. We proposed a robust way for defining early expertise based on the number of a user's best answers rather than time, catering for different user activity behaviors. We presented a semi-supervised approach using textual, behavioral and temporal feature sets, and demonstrated the effectiveness of our method over a machine learning method based on a state-of-the-art method in expertise retrieval. We found that behavioral and temporal features when combined with textual features significantly boost effectiveness peaking F1-score at 0.7472; an 26% improvement over the baseline method. Results demonstrated that our system can accurately predict whether a user will become an expert from a user's first best answer; projected in time, our system makes correct predictions even in 70 months before a user becomes an expert. Although the features to be used may vary, accepted answers are a common phenomenon in QA sites. We therefore expect the method to generalise well within this domain. In future work, we plan to evaluate our method on other corpora as well as extend our features to capture more aspects of early expertise, e.g., answer quality, diversity, novelty, and also track how a user's expertise evolves from one topic to another over time, which can yield a strong predictor of early expertise.

Acknowledgments. This research was supported by the European Community's Seventh Framework Programme (FP7/2007-2013) under grant agreement nr 312827 (VOX-Pol), the Netherlands Organisation for Scientific Research (NWO) under project nrs 727.011.005, 612.001.116, HOR-11-10, 640.006.013, 612.066.930, CI-14-25, SH-322-15, Amsterdam Data Science, the Dutch national program COMMIT, the ESF Research Network Program ELIAS, the Elite Network Shifts project funded by the Royal Dutch Academy of Sciences (KNAW), the Netherlands eScience Center under project nr 027.012.105, the Yahoo! Faculty Research and Engagement Program, the Microsoft Research PhD program, and the HPC Fund.

REFERENCES

[1] E. Agichtein, C. Castillo, D. Donato, A. Gionis, and G. Mishne. Finding high-quality content in social media, with an application to community-based question answering. In *WSDM '08*, pages 183–194. ACM, 2008.

[2] A. Anderson, D. Huttenlocher, J. Kleinberg, and J. Leskovec. Steering user behavior with badges. In *WWW '13*, pages 95–106. ACM, 2013.

[3] K. Balog, Y. Fang, M. de Rijke, P. Serdyukov, and L. Si. Expertise retrieval. *Foundations and Trends in Information Retrieval*, 6(2–3): 127–256, August 2012.

[4] M. Bouguessa and L. B. Romdhane. Identifying authorities in online communities. *TIST*, 6(3), 2015.

[5] A. Pal, R. Farzan, J. Konstan, and R. Kraut. Early detection of potential experts in question answering communities. In *ICUMAP '11*, pages 231–242, 2011.

[6] A. Pal, S. Chang, and J. A. Konstan. Evolution of experts in question answering communities. In *ICWSM '12*. AAAI, 2012.

[7] J. San Pedro and A. Karatzoglou. Question recommendation for collaborative question answering systems with rankslda. In *RecSys '14*, pages 193–200. ACM, 2014.

[8] G. Szabó and B. A. Huberman. Predicting the Popularity of Online Content. *Communications of the ACM*, 53(8):80–88, 2010.

[9] M. Tsagkias, W. Weerkamp, and M. de Rijke. News comments: Exploring, modeling, and online prediction. In *ECIR '10*, pages 191–203. Springer, 2010.

[10] J. Yang, K. Tao, A. Bozzon, and G.-J. Houben. Sparrows and owls: Characterisation of expert behaviour in stackoverflow. In *UMAP '14*, volume 8538, pages 266–277. Springer, 2014.

[11] J. Zhang, M. S. Ackerman, and L. Adamic. Expertise networks in online communities: Structure and algorithms. In *WWW '07*, pages 221–230. ACM, 2007.

LBMCH: Learning Bridging Mapping for Cross-modal Hashing

Yang Wang[†‡], Xuemin Lin[†], Lin Wu[♯], Wenjie Zhang[†] and Qing Zhang[‡†]
[†]The University of New South Wales, Kensington, Sydney, Australia
[♯]Australian Centre for Visual Technologies, The University of Adelaide, SA, Australia
[‡]Australian E-Health Research Centre, Brisbane, Australia
{wangy,lxue,zhangw}@cse.unsw.edu.au, lin.wu@adelaide.edu.au, qing.zhang@csiro.au

ABSTRACT

Hashing has gained considerable attention on large-scale similarity search, due to its enjoyable efficiency and low storage cost. In this paper, we study the problem of learning hash functions in the context of multi-modal data for cross-modal similarity search. Notwithstanding the progress achieved by existing methods, they essentially learn only one common hamming space, where data objects from all modalities are mapped to conduct similarity search. However, such method is unable to well characterize the flexible and discriminative local (neighborhood) structure in all modalities simultaneously, hindering them to achieve better performance.

Bearing such stand-out limitation, we propose to learn heterogeneous hamming spaces with each preserving the local structure of data objects from an individual modality. Then, a novel method to learning bridging mapping for cross-modal hashing, named LBMCH, is proposed to characterize the cross-modal semantic correspondence by seamlessly connecting these distinct hamming spaces. Meanwhile, the local structure of each data object in a modality is preserved by constructing an anchor based representation, enabling LBMCH to characterize a linear complexity w.r.t the size of training set. The efficacy of LBMCH is experimentally validated against real-world cross-modal datasets.

Categories and Subject Descriptors

H.3.3 [**Information Storage and Retrieval**]: Information Search and Retrieval

Keywords

Hashing; Multi-modal Data; Bridging Mapping

1. INTRODUCTION

Hashing is dramatically efficient for approximate nearest neighbor search while enjoying the low storage cost of loading low dimensional hash codes. It, hence, inspired numerous hashing methods over *single-modal* data, which is described within only one feature space.

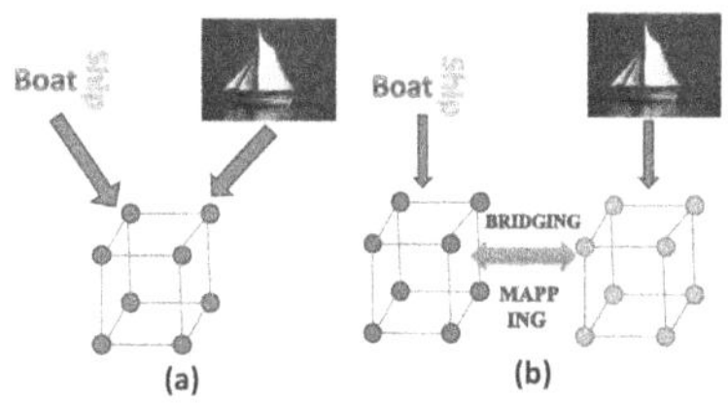

Figure 1: (a) Conventional methods learn the hashing functions to map all modalities into one common hamming space (b) Our proposed technique learns individual hamming space to well preserve the local structure for each modality.

With the rapid growth of information technology, significant efforts are shifted to learning hashing functions from single-modal hashing to *Cross-modal* hashing, which is more widely seen in real-life application over multiple data sources as multi-modalities [9, 10, 8, 11, 12, 7], while characterize the same semantics, with each individual data source corresponding to one modality, where a query from one modal is issued to search semantically relevant results from another modal [14]. Typical example is image search via a text query to return the images characterizing the similar semantics as text query. There have been a lot of approaches, where the basic idea of learning cross-modal hashing functions is relying on canonical correlation analysis (CCA) [4]. Specifically, [5] extended conventional spectral hashing [13] from single modality to multi-modal data, and learnt a common hamming space in which the local structure of all modalities can be well preserved. Motivated by anchor graph hashing [6], Zhu *et al.* [16] proposed a linear cross-modal hashing method against anchor based representation regarding each modality. To effectively preserve local structure, [15] proposed a novel parametric method to learn an individual projection matrix for each data object.

Despite the progress achieved by these approaches, one fundamental limitation is that they learn only *one* common hamming space, which is unable to *simultaneously* characterize the flexible and discriminative local structure of each individual modal, or even ignore the local structure preservation, hindering them to achieve better performance.

Bearing the limitation above, we propose a novel technique aimed at Learning Bridging Mapping for Cross-modal Hashing, named LBMCH, to learn an individual hamming

SIGIR'15, August 09 - 13, 2015, Santiago, Chile.
 ISBN 978-1-4503-3621-5/15/08 ...$15.00.
DOI: http://dx.doi.org/10.1145/2766462.2767825.

space adaptive to local structure of each modal, while automatically learn a bridging mapping to preserve cross-modal semantic correspondence by seamlessly connecting distinct hamming spaces.

Our proposed method is orthogonal to recent state-of-the-arts with featured contributions summarized below

- We adaptively learn distinct hamming spaces to characterize discriminative local structure for each modal. The bridging mapping is automatically learned to characterize the cross-modal semantic correlation by connecting these hamming spaces.
- We formulate the problem of learning bridging mapping for cross-modal hashing, and propose a novel two-stage optimization technique to achieve the goal, featured with a sub-linear time complexity with respect to the size of training samples.
- Extensive experiments are conducted over real-world datasets, which demonstrate the superiority of LBMCH over state-of-the-art methods.

2. LEARNING BRIDGING MAPPING FOR CROSS-MODAL HASHING

In this section, we focus on two modalities, which can be easily extended to multiple modalities.

2.1 Problem Definition

Assume N_q is the number of training data in the qth modal, denoted as $X^{(q)} \in \mathbf{R}^{N_q \times d_q}$, where d_q is the dimensions for q^{th} modal. $x_i^{(q)}$ is the ith training data object from the qth modal. N_{pq} is the number of observed semantic correspondence between training data objects in the pth and q^{th} modalities. Without relying on semantic labels of training data, we study a more practical case with training data unlabeled. Unless otherwise specified, given any matrix $\mathbf{A}$, $\mathbf{A}_{ij}$ represents the entry at the ith row and j^{th} column of $\mathbf{A}$. Given $x_i^{(q)}$, we map it to k-dimensional representation $z_i^{(q)}$, with its jth dimension encoding the Euclidean distance between $x_i^{(q)}$ and the jth anchor, $a_j^{(q)}$ $(j = 1, \ldots, k)$, denoted as $z_{ij}^{(q)}$. We make this fit Gaussian distribution, formulated as

$$p_{ij}^{(q)} = \frac{exp(-z_{ij}^{(q)}/\sigma)}{\sum_{l=1}^{k} exp(-z_{il}^{(q)}/\sigma)}, \tag{1}$$

where $p_{ij}^{(q)}$ represents the refined representation based on $z_{ij}^{(q)}$, σ is the bandwidth parameter controlling the decay rate of $z_{ij}^{(q)}$, which can be defined as the largest distance to all its k anchors. We further represent $x_i^{(q)}$ as $\rho_i^{(q)} = [p_{ij}^{(q)}, \cdots, p_{ik}^{(q)}]$. We only keep the value for the s nearest anchors ($s \ll k$) with others being 0, then we can normalize s positive values to refine the representation. Collecting all $\rho_i^{(q)} (i = 1, \cdots, N_q)$ to be the columns of $Z^{(q)}$, we have $Z^{(q)} \in \mathbf{R}^{k \times N_q}$.

Instead of learning only one common hamming space, LBMCH is to learn hashing functions characterized by W_p and W_q for the pth and q^{th} modalities, which can map training data objects into distinct hamming spaces with m_p and m_q dimensions *i.e.*, code length, respectively, such that m_p and m_q may be different. A bridging mapping matrix *i.e.*, $\mathbf{M} \in \mathbf{R}^{m_p \times m_q}$, is learnt to map the hash code of query from the pth modal to search semantically relevant result within the hamming space from q^{th} modal.

2.2 Learning Bridging Mapping to Preserve Cross-modal Semantic Correlation

We rewrite two hashing projection matrices W_p and W_q to be $W_p = [w_p^1, \cdots, w_p^{m_p}]^T$ and $W_q = [w_q^1, \cdots, w_q^{m_q}]^T$, where each column of W_p and W_q generates one bit of hash code for the pth and q^{th} modal. Then we attempt to learn a bridging mapping matrix, $\mathbf{M}$, to map the hash codes from m_p-dimensional hamming space to m_q-dimensional hamming space or vice versa, by utilizing the cross-modal semantic correlation as provided by training data objects. That is, the cross-modal semantically related data objects should have similar hash codes after mapping. Besides, we expect the bridging mapping matrix to have a good generalization capacity simultaneously. Then we propose to minimize the following objective function

$$\sum_{i,j}^{N_{pq}} S_{ij}^{(pq)} \sum_{h=1}^{m_q} \left(\sum_{l=1}^{m_p} \mathbf{M}_{hl} (w_p^l)^T \rho_i^{(p)} - (w_q^h)^T \rho_j^{(q)} \right)^2 + \lambda ||\mathbf{M}||_F^2, \tag{2}$$

where $\mathbf{M}_{hl}$ is the l^{th}entry of the hth row of $\mathbf{M}$. S^{pq} encodes the semantic correlation between training data objects from two modalities. $S_{ij}^{pq} = 1$ indicates that $x_i^{(p)}$ is semantically similar to $x_j^{(q)}$, it is 0 otherwise. The regularization term $||\mathbf{M}||_F^2$ is leveraged into Eq. (2) to achieve the good generalization power.

Now we are ready to propose the overall objective function to learn hash functions W_p and W_q, for both modalities and the bridging mapping $\mathbf{M}$, simultaneously.

2.3 Overall Objective Function

Given the pth and q^{th} modality, we propose to learn W_p,W_q, and $\mathbf{M}$ by minimizing the objective function below.

$$\begin{aligned} \boldsymbol{F}(W_p, W_q, \mathbf{M}) = & \sum_{j \in \{p,q\}} Tr(W_j Z^{(j)} L^{(j)} (Z^{(j)})^T W_j^T) \\ & + \frac{\mu}{2} \sum_{i,j}^{N_{pq}} S_{ij}^{(pq)} \sum_{h=1}^{m_q} \left(\sum_{l=1}^{m_p} \mathbf{M}_{hl} (w_p^l)^T \rho_i^{(p)} - (w_q^h)^T \rho_j^{(q)} \right)^2 \\ & + \frac{\lambda}{2} ||\mathbf{M}||_F^2 \\ & s.t. \;\; W_p Z^{(p)} (Z^{(p)})^T W_p^T = N_p I_{m_p} \\ & \quad\;\; W_q Z^{(q)} (Z^{(q)})^T W_q^T = N_q I_{m_q}, \end{aligned} \tag{3}$$

where μ and λ are trade-off parameters, m_p and m_q denote the hash code length for the pth and q^{th} modal. I_{m_p} and I_{m_q} represent the identity matrix with the size of $m_p \times m_p$ and $m_q \times m_q$. Unlike existing methods that narrowly consider only one hamming space, we account for a generalized case adaptive to different modalities, while bridged by mapping $\mathbf{M}$. Next, we will discuss the optimization solution to Eq. (3).

2.4 Two-Stage Sequential Optimization Strategy

Minimizing Eq. (3) is not jointly convex to W_p, W_q and $\mathbf{M}$. Hence, we turn to propose a gradient descent method [2] to minimize Eq. (3), seeking the local optimization for each variable while fixing others.

Motivation. Unlike conventional methods [15] by conducting **one-to-one** bit of hash code learning fashion (*e.g.*, learning *only* the pth bit for *two* modalities at each iteration) alternatively for two modalities regarding one common hamming space, we consider a more generalized case of learning heterogeneous hamming spaces via **many-to-many** bit relationship, characterized by bridging mapping $\mathbf{M}$, which is more practical yet challenging. As we observed, the *second term* in Eq. (3) indicates that one bit of hash code from the pth modal is related to all bits from the qth modal, and vice versa. Hence, without loss of generality, we first initialize all m_q bits from q^{th} by using spectral hashing [13], while initializing all M_{hl} to be 1. Particularly, we conduct a sequential optimization strategy, which comprises of two stages below.

- Sequentially learn each hash bit for the pth modal.
- Sequentially learn each bit of hash code for the qth modal, and each entry $\mathbf{M}_{hl}$ in $\mathbf{M}$ based on all the m_p hash bits from the pth modal learned in the first stage

Why learn all bits from q^{th} modal and $\mathbf{M}_{hl}$ at the second stage? To answer this question, we first derive the gradient descent for M_{hl} by calculating $\frac{\partial F}{\partial \mathbf{M}_{hl}}$, formulated as

$$\frac{\partial F}{\partial \mathbf{M}_{hl}} = \mu \sum_{i,j}^{N_{pq}} S_{ij}^{(pq)} (w_p^l)^T \rho_i^{(p)} (\sum_{l=1}^{m_p} \mathbf{M}_{hl} (w_p^l)^T \rho_i^{(p)} - (w_q^h)^T \rho_j^{(q)}) + \lambda \mathbf{M}_{hl}. \quad (4)$$

Then we update $\mathbf{M}_{hl}$ by one step gradient descent. Remarkably, $\frac{\partial F}{\partial \mathbf{M}_{hl}}$ relies on all hash bits from the pth modal and the hth hash bit from the qth modal, implied by $(w_q^h)^T \rho_j^{(q)}$. Thus, we can learn each entry $\mathbf{M}_{hl}$ upon the hth bit *i.e.*, w_q^h from the qth modal, and all m_p bits of hash code at the *second stage*.

2.4.1 *Sequentially learning each bit from the pth modal*

Assume we have learned the previous $l-1$ bits, then we can learn the lth bit by calculating the derivative with respect to w_p^l, that is,

$$E_l^{(p)} w_p^l + \mu \sum_{i,j}^{N_{pq}} S_{ij}^{(pq)} \sum_{h=1}^{m^q} M_{hl} \rho_i^{(p)} (\rho_i^{(p)})^T w_p^l = \mu \sum_{i,j}^{N_{pq}} S_{ij}^{(pq)} \sum_{h=1}^{m_q} \rho_i^{(p)} (\rho_j^{(q)})^T w_q^h + \lambda_p \mathbf{K}_l^{(p)} w_p^l, \quad (5)$$

where

- $E_l^{(p)} = Z_l^{(p)} L_l^{(p)} (Z_l^{(p)})^T \in \mathbf{R}^{k \times k}$, $L_l^{(p)} = D_l^{(p)} - S_l^{(p)}$ and $S_l^{(p)} = (Z_l^{(p)})^T (Z_l^{(p)})$.
- $Z_l^{(p)} = Z^{(p)} - \sum_{k=1}^{l-1} w_p^k (w_p^k)^T Z^{(p)}$ and $\mathbf{K}_l^{(p)} = Z_l^{(p)} (Z_l^{(p)})^T$.

Remarkably, all the above variables are updated and determined by $Z_l^{(p)}$, and $Z_l^{(p)} = Z^{(p)} - \sum_{k=1}^{l-1} w_p^k (w_p^k)^T Z^{(p)}$ is formed by removing the projections of $Z^{(p)}$ on the subspace spanned by $w_p^k (k = 1, \cdot\cdot, l-1)$, thus to encourage bits decorrelation. To learn the optimum w_p^l w.r.t. the lth bit of hash code, we have

$$w_p^l = (E_l^{(p)} + \mu \sum_{i,j}^{N_{pq}} S_{ij}^{(pq)} \sum_{h=1}^{m^q} \mathbf{M}_{hl} \rho_i^{(p)} (\rho_i^{(p)})^T - \lambda_p \mathbf{K}_l^{(p)})^{-1} H_q, \quad (6)$$

where $H_q = \mu \sum_{i,j}^{N_{pq}} S_{ij}^{(pq)} \sum_{h=1}^{m_q} \rho_i^{(p)} (\rho_j^{(q)})^T w_q^h$.

2.4.2 *Sequentially learning each bit from the qth modal and $\mathbf{M}$*

Assume we have learned the previous $h-1$ bits, and we are ready to learn the hth bit by calculating the derivative with respect to w_q^h, then we have

$$E_h^{(q)} w_q^h + \mu \sum_{i,j}^{N_{pq}} S_{ij}^{(pq)} \rho_j^{(q)} (\rho_j^{(q)})^T w_q^h = \mu \sum_{i,j}^{N_{pq}} S_{ij}^{(pq)} \sum_{l=1}^{m_p} \mathbf{M}_{hl} \rho_j^{(q)} (\rho_i^{(p)})^T w_p^l + \lambda_q \mathbf{K}_h^{(q)} w_q^h, \quad (7)$$

where

- $E_h^{(q)} = Z_h^{(q)} L_h^{(q)} (Z_h^{(q)})^T$, $L_h^{(q)} = D_h^{(q)} - S_h^{(q)}$ and $S_h^{(q)} = (Z_h^{(q)})^T (Z_h^{(q)})$.
- $Z_h^{(q)} = Z^{(q)} - \sum_{k=1}^{h-1} w_q^k (w_q^k)^T Z^{(q)}$ and $\mathbf{K}_h^{(q)} = Z_h^{(q)} (Z_h^{(q)})^T$.

The variables above are updated due to $Z_h^{(q)}$, and $Z_h^{(q)} = Z^{(q)} - \sum_{k=1}^{h-1} w_q^k (w_q^k)^T Z^{(q)}$ is formed by removing the projections of $Z^{(q)}$ on the subspace spanned by $w_q^k (k = 1, \cdot\cdot, h-1)$, to encourage bits de-correlation. To learn the optimum w_q^h w.r.t. the hth bit of hash code, we have

$$w_q^h = (E_h^{(q)} + \mu \sum_{i,j}^{N_{pq}} S_{ij}^{(pq)} \rho_j^{(q)} (\rho_j^{(q)})^T - \lambda_q \mathbf{K}_h^{(q)})^{-1} H_p, \quad (8)$$

where $H_p = \mu \sum_{i,j}^{N_{pq}} S_{ij}^{(pq)} \sum_{l=1}^{m_p} \mathbf{M}_{hl} \rho_j^{(q)} (\rho_i^{(p)})^T w_p^l$. Meanwhile, we learn $\mathbf{M}_{hl}$ via one step gradient descent by Eq. (4) based on w_q^l and all m_p hash bits from the pth modal.

3. COMPLEXITY ANALYSIS AND DISCUSSIONS

The time complexity of learning each bit *e.g.*, w_p^l, from the pth modal of running Eq. (6) comes from the inverse computation, which costs $\mathcal{O}(k^3)$. The same cost holds for learning each bit *e.g.*, w_q^h, from q^{th} modality by the inverse computation from running Eq. (8). The cost for updating $\mathbf{M}_{hl}$ is $\mathcal{O}(m_p N_{pq} k)$ by implementing Eq. (4). Therefore, the total complexity is $\mathcal{O}((m_p + m_q)k^3 + m_p m_q k N_{pq} + kN_p + kN_q) = \mathcal{O}(\max\{kN_p, kN_q, (m_p + m_q)k^3, m_p m_q N_{pq} k\})$, where k is the number of anchors. As $k \ll N_p$ and $k \ll N_q$, while m_p and m_q are the length of hash codes for p^{th} and q^{th} modalities, such that $m_p \ll k$ and $m_q \ll k$.

Therefore, we expect $m_{j(j=p,q)}^2 < \min\{N_p, N_q, N_{pq}\}$ and $k^2 < \min\{N_p, N_q, N_{pq}\}$, which leads to $m_p m_q k < k^3 < \min\{kN_p, kN_{pq}, kN_q\} < \max\{kN_p, kN_q\}$. Having k as a constant, the time complexity can be rewritten as $\mathcal{O}(\max\{N_p, N_q\})$, which is linear to the number of training samples on both modalities.

4. EXPERIMENTS

We use **Wiki** [1] and **NUS-WIDE** [2] for cross-modal hashing with two tasks: retrieving relevant texts by using images as queries and retrieving images by using texts as queries.

The **Wiki** dataset consists of 2,866 Wikipedia documents, each of which contains one text-image pair. All documents

[1] http://www.svcl.ucsd.edu/projects/crossmodal/
[2] http://lms.comp.nus.edu.sg/research/NUS-WIDE.htm

are labeled by one of 10 semantic categories. Each image is represented by a 128-dimensional bag-of-visual SIFT feature vector and each text is encoded by a 10-dimensional feature vector generated by Latent Dirichlet Allocation (LDA) [1]. Following [16], 2173 documents are partitioned as training pairs and remaining 693 documents form query set.

The **NUS-WIDE** database contains 269,648 labeled images crawled from Flickr, and is manually annotated with 81 categories. We prune it via selecting 186,577 image-tag pairs that belong to the ten largest concepts. The images are represented by 500-dimensional bag-of-visual words (BoVW) and the tags are represented by 1000-dimensional tag occurrence feature vectors. We randomly select $300 \times 300 = 90,000$ image-tag pairs to be training pairs, with remaining to be query set for two tasks. Besides the training and query set, we also conduct out-of-sample experiments by randomly selecting the 2000 images from the remaining to be query set to search tag modal.

Following [16], we set 300 and 600 anchors *i.e.*, $k = 300$ and $k = 600$ in Eq. (1), for both modalities on **Wiki** and **NUS-WIDE** datasets. Among k centroids, we set $s = 3$ nearest anchors to encode the local structure of each data object for both modalities. We set $\lambda = 0.01$ in Eq. (3).

4.1 Competitors

We consider three state-of-the-art competitors: (1) Cross-Modal Similarity-Sensitive Hashing (**CMSSH**) [3] tackles cross-modal hashing by using Adaboost to sequentially construct hash function for each modality whilst only considering cross-modal similarity in one common hamming space without preserving local structures. (2) Cross-View Hashing (**CVH**) [5] extends spectral hashing to cross-modal hashing via CCA (Canonical Correlation Analysis) in one common hamming space. (3) Linear Cross-Modal Hashing (**LCMH**) [16] propose a cross-modal hashing using different anchor graphs, while preserving both intra-and-inter modal similarity in one common hamming space.

4.2 Performance Comparison

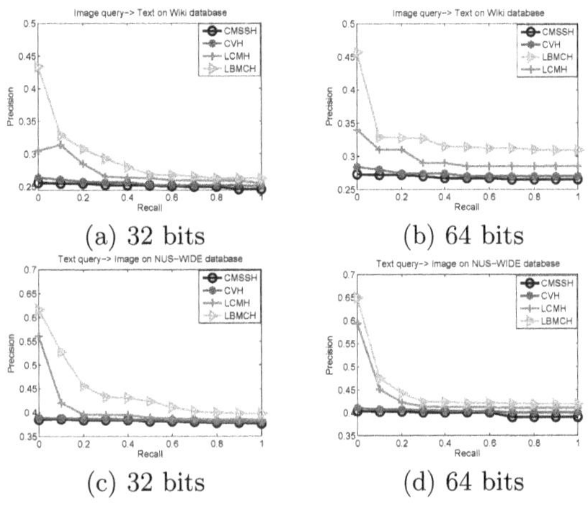

(a) 32 bits (b) 64 bits (c) 32 bits (d) 64 bits

Figure 2: Precision-recall curve on Wiki dataset ((a),(b)) and NUS-WIDE dataset ((c),(d)) over searching text modality via image query and searching image modality via text query.

Results on NUS-WIDE Dataset. We show the result of two tasks on NUS-WIDE in Fig.2 (c)-(d). Obviously, we can see the advantage of LBMCH by flexibly learning the bridging mapping for various hamming spaces instead of only one common space characterized by other methods.

Time complexity against training size. We evaluate the time complexity with varied training size on two databases, and report the results in Fig.3. It can be seen that the time cost of our method grows linearly with increasing training samples, which demonstrates the efficiency of **LBMCH**.

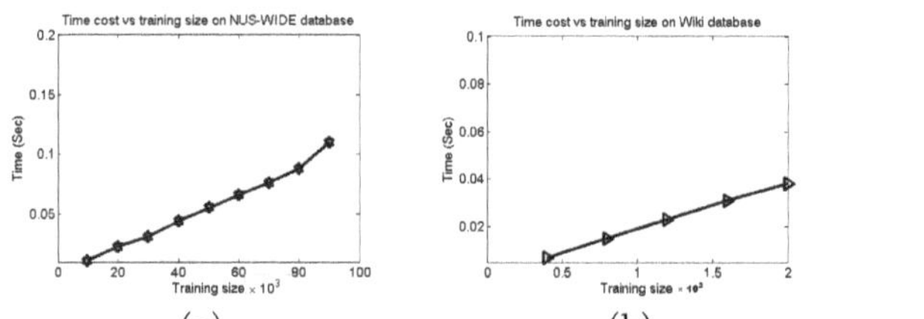

(a) (b)

Figure 3: Time complexity against training size over two databases.

5. CONCLUSIONS

In this paper, we propose a novel technique by learning distinct hamming space so as to well preserve the flexible and discriminative local structure of each modality. Based on that, a bridging mapping is learned to seamlessly connect these individual hamming spaces for cross-modal hashing. Extensive experimental results over real-world datasets demonstrate the effectiveness and efficiency of our method.

Acknowledgements. Xuemin Lin is supported by NSFC61232006, ARC DP120104168, ARC DP140103578, and ARC DP150102728. Wenjie Zhang is supported by ARC DP150103071 and ARC DP150102728.

6. REFERENCES

[1] D. M. Blei, A. Y. Ng, and M. I. Jordan. Latent dirichlet allocation. In *NIPS*, 2001.

[2] S. Boyd and L. Vandenberghe. *Convex Optimization*. Cambridge University Press, 2004.

[3] M. Bronstein, A. Bronstein, F. Michel, and N. Paragios. Data fusion through cross-modality metric learning using similarity-sensitive hashing. In *CVPR*, 2010.

[4] H. Hotelling. Relations between two sets of variables. *Biometrika*, 28(3/4):321–377, 1936.

[5] S. Kumar and R. Udupa. Learning hash functions for cross-view similarity search. In *IJCAI*, 2011.

[6] W. Liu, J. Wang, S. Kumar, and S. Chang. Hashing with graphs. In *ICML*, 2011.

[7] Y. Wang, M. A. Cheema, X. Lin, and Q. Zhang. Multi-manifold ranking: Using multiple features for better image retrieval. In *PAKDD*, 2013.

[8] Y. Wang, X. Lin, L. Wu, Q. Zhang, and W. Zhang. Shifting multi-hypergraphs via collaborative probabilistic voting. *Knowledge and Information Systems, DOI 10.1007/s10115-015-0833-8*.

[9] Y. Wang, X. Lin, L. Wu, W. Zhang, and Q. Zhang. Exploiting correlation consensus: Towards subspace clustering for multi-modal data. In *ACM Multimedia*, 2014.

[10] Y. Wang, X. Lin, and Q. Zhang. Towards metric fusion on multi-view data: a cross-view based graph random walk approach. In *ACM CIKM*, 2013.

[11] Y. Wang, X. Lin, Q. Zhang, and L. Wu. Shifting hypergraphs by probabilistic voting. In *PAKDD*, 2014.

[12] Y. Wang, J. Pei, X. Lin, Q. Zhang, and W. Zhang. An iterative fusion approach to graph-based semi-supervised learning from multiple views. In *PAKDD*, 2014.

[13] Y. Weiss, A. Torralba, and R. Fergus. Spectral hashing. In *NIPS*, 2008.

[14] L. Wu, Y. Wang, and J. Shepherd. Efficient image and tag co-ranking: a bregman divergence optimization method. In *ACM Multimedia*, 2013.

[15] D. Zhai, H. Chang, Y. Zhen, X. Liu, X. Chen, and W. Gao. Parametric local multimodal hashing for cross-view similarity search. In *IJCAI*, 2013.

[16] X. Zhu, Z. Huang, H. T. Shen, and X. Zhao. Linear cross-modal hashing for efficient multimedia search. In *ACM Multimedia*, 2013.

Gibberish, Assistant, or Master? Using Tweets Linking to News for Extractive Single-Document Summarization

Zhongyu Wei
University of Texas at Dallas
800 W. Campbell Road, Richardson
Texas 75080-3021, USA
zywei@hlt.utdallas.edu

Wei Gao
Qatar Computing Research Institute
Qatar Foundation
Doha, Qatar
wgao@qf.org.qa

ABSTRACT

Single-document summarization is a challenging task. In this paper, we explore effective ways using the tweets linking to news for generating extractive summary of each document. We reveal the very basic value of tweets that can be utilized by regarding every tweet as a vote for candidate sentences. Base on such finding, we resort to unsupervised summarization models by leveraging the linking tweets to master the ranking of candidate extracts via random walk on a heterogeneous graph. The advantage is that we can use the linking tweets to opportunistically "supervise" the summarization with no need of reference summaries. Furthermore, we analyze the influence of the volume and latency of tweets on the quality of output summaries since tweets come after news release. Compared to truly supervised summarizer unaware of tweets, our method achieves significantly better results with reasonably small tradeoff on latency; compared to the same using tweets as auxiliary features, our method is comparable while needing less tweets and much shorter time to achieve significant outperformance.

Categories and Subject Descriptors

H.3 [**Information Storage and Retrieval**]: Miscellaneous

Keywords

Single-document summarization; tweets; highlights

1. INTRODUCTION

Single-document summaries are also known as story highlights of an article, which are provided by only a few news website such as CNN.com. A summary typically consists of three or four succinct itemized texts for readers to quickly capture the gist of the document. The highlights can dramatically reduce reader's information load, which can be seen as an example in Table 1.

Table 1: An CNN news article with story highlights

Story highlights • A third person has died from the bombing, Boston Police Commissioner Ed Davis says • An 8-year-old boy was one of those killed • The bombs were small, with no initial sign of high-grade explosive material, an official tells CNN • Obama vows those guilty "will feel the full weight of justice"
(CNN)– ......*Boston Police Commissioner Ed Davis said Monday night that the death toll had risen to three.* Scores were injured at the scene. ...... *One of the dead was an 8-year-old boy, according to a state law enforcement source.* Hospitals reported at least 144 people are being treated, with at least 17 of them in critical condition and 25 in serious condition. ...... *In Washington, President Barack Obama vowed, "Any responsible individuals, any responsible groups, will feel the full weight of justice."* ...... *A federal law enforcement official told CNN that both bombs were small, and initial tests showed no C-4 or other high-grade explosive material, suggesting that the packages used in the attack were crude explosive devices.* ......

Although practically very useful, generating such abstractive summaries is technically challenging due to the ultimate need for language understanding capability [17]. In practice, most summarizers are based on extractive approach [8, 1, 14, 10, 17, 5]. The extractive summarization task aims at selecting a subset of textual units of the documents such as sentences, clauses and phrases that can optimize an objective for sentence scoring and satisfy a length constraint. Sentence scoring can be done by learning from various statistical and linguistic features [14, 17, 16], or by graph-based centrality method for capturing the relative importance of textual units [1, 10]. Another school of research intends to identify novel features for improving summary quality based on external data sources such as Web search results [7], click-through data [13], query logs and Wikipedia [14], comments from news readers [6], and recently tweets corpus [18, 3, 16].

Nowadays it becomes more and more common that users share interested news content via Twitter. Intuitively, the more often some part of the story is tweeted, the more salient it might be. Previous work assumed that such socially focused sentences might be closely related to the reference summary [18, 3, 16]. However, there are some important questions left unanswered. Tweets content is notoriously informal and noisy, and Twitter users' elusive posting behavior can hardly be related to summarization in the first place. Meanwhile, as a kind of third-party data source, tweets are

SIGIR'15, August 09 - 13, 2015, Santiago, Chile.

DOI: http://dx.doi.org/10.1145/2766462.2767835.

inevitably subject to latency as tweets linking to a news come after the news exposure, which might drag the summarization performance.

In this paper, we intend to address three major concerns about using relevant tweets for single-document summarization: (i) Are the linking tweets largely gibberish or useful for producing summaries? (ii) If being useful, do they play assistant or master roles? (iii) Is the latency of tweets a major setback or a reasonable tradeoff regarding the quality of summaries? For these questions, we first conduct empirical analysis on a public tweets-news-highlights tripling corpus to reveal the very basic value of tweets that was not discovered before; Then we naturally come with unsupervised models that leverage the linking tweets to opportunistically "supervise" the sentence scoring. Furthermore, by comparing with state-of-the-art baselines, we examine how the volume and latency of tweets influence the summaries to provide deeper insight into the practicality and usefulness of using tweets linking to news for single-document summarization.

2. THE BASIC VALUE OF TWEETS

Recently, much attention was paid to connecting news and microblogs for content enrichment [12, 3, 4, 15, 16]. Particularly, a corpus containing news-tweets-highlights triplings based on CNN/USAToday news was used to enrich the features based on the tweets linking to news for highlights extraction in [16]. This public corpus contains 121 documents, 455 highlights and 78,419 linking tweets regarding 17 world news events during July 2012-July 2013. Tweets were collected using Topsy search API[1], and then the retrieved tweets containing URLs that point to CNN and USAToday news documents are gathered together with the documents and the associated story highlights. The corpus was preprocessed by removing the extremely short tweets and those tweets suspected duplicating the reference highlights.

We look into this data more deeply for revealing the basic relation among the highlights, tweets and news sentences. Our goal is to answer what exact basic value tweets can provide. Figure 1 exhibits some interesting findings:

– Figure 1a[2] shows the positions of sentences that are most similar[3] to each of the reference highlights. Figure 1b[4] demonstrates the positions of sentences that receive the top-four largest number of "votes" from tweets, where *vote* means that a tweet finds the sentence at that position as the best match. We observe that most of these important positions are located within the first 20 sentences. Considering average document length (which is 54 sentences long), highlights are most likely originated from anterior part of an article.

– The more anterior a sentence's position, the more probable it is selected as the source of highlights, and likewise the more likely it is caught attention and tweeted by users. This can be seen in Figure 1c where the probability of sentences hit by highlights and tweets along their positions in documents appear very close except for the first sentence position, at which the probability hit by highlights (0.52) is much larger than hit by tweets (0.13).

– Figure 1d shows that there is extremely rare case in the corpus that the tweets copy or nearly duplicate the reference highlights, which indicates that the corpus was cleansed to avoid the tweets that are biased towards the highlights already shown in the webpages.

Therefore, the basic value of tweets linking to news lies in the fact that they tend to pick out sentences in similar positions of articles as reference highlights do. So, the next question is if they can only serve as auxiliary features as suggested in [16] or master the selection of sentences directly.

3. METHODS

Most successful single-document summarizers are trained by using reference summaries and other precious resources for feature generation [14, 17, 5, 16]. Generally, this makes it impractical to adapt the model to *new domains or languages* where such required data resources are not available. Particularly, tweets can only play less important role as assistant features in some approaches [14, 16]. Following our findings, we naturally come up with two unsupervised models that allow tweets to directly locate the salient sentences without the need of reference summaries.

– **Social Vote (SociVote):** In this model, we directly utilize the votes (or hits) of every document sentences received from all its linking tweets. Given a tweet, we say it *hits* a sentence when the tweet is more similar to the sentence than any other sentences in the document. Then we can simply rank the sentences according to their *hit counts* and extract the top-four sentences as a summary. This model, although simple, makes use of the very basic value of relevant tweets as described in Section 2.

– **Heterogeneous Graph Random Walk (HGRW):** In this model, we create an undirected similarity graph which is inspired by LexRank [1]. However, our graph is heterogenous, thus becomes a joint model, where the nodes are of two types including news sentences and tweets, and the edge weights (i.e., node similarity) are defined as follows:

$$sim(x,y) = \begin{cases} \beta * \text{idf-modified-cosine}(x,y) & \text{, if } x.t \neq y.t; \\ (1-\beta) * \text{idf-modified-cosine}(x,y), & \text{otherwise} \end{cases}$$

where the coefficient β is used to control the contribution of sentence-tweet cross-type similarity ($.t$ indicates the type of node). With β, we encourage the voting effect between heterogeneous nodes to be mutually reinforced during random walk; Varying β also affects the overall ranking via the relation among homogenous nodes.

The node scores are updated by random walk over the heterogeneous graph based on the above modified edge weights: while computing the score for a sentence, we make its centrality balance the effect from other sentences and that from the linking tweets with the similarity function; for a tweet, its centrality is determined by balancing its affinity to the centroid sentences and centroid tweets. We configure the system to output a summary with only sentences, a summary with only tweets or a joint summary containing both.

3.1 Baselines

– **Lead Sentences (Lead):** This model simply extracts the first four sentences from each document, which was a well-known strong baseline adopted in DUC single-document summarization task [11].

– **LexRank:** The original LexRank [1] algorithm that takes as input the homogenous type of texts, i.e., either news sentences or tweets separately.

[1]`http://topsy.com`
[2]Highlight1-4: the highlights in reference summary
[3]IDF-modified-cosine [1] is used to calculate similarity
[4]Tweet1-4: the four largest number of "votes" from tweets

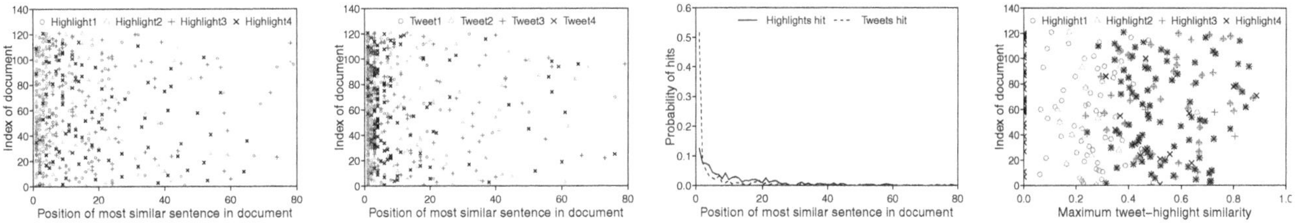

(a) highlights hit (b) tweets hit (c) highlights vs. tweets hit (d) max tweet-highlight sim.

Figure 1: (a) Position of highlights hits in the documents; (b) Top-4 tweets hits in the documents; (c) The probability of highlights hit vs. tweets hit in the documents; (d) The maximum similarity between highlights and tweets per document

Table 2: Results on CNN/USAToday corpus. **Bold**: best score; Underline: $p<0.05$ as to the baselines except for CrossL2R based on paired two-tailed t-test; The suffixes **-S**, **-T** and **-ST**: output contains sentences, tweets and both, respectively; *: supervised models

	Method	ROUGE-1 F-score	ROUGE-1 precision	ROUGE-1 recall	
Baseline	Lead-S	0.263	0.211	0.374	Homo-type
	LexRank-S	0.259	0.206	0.376	
	LexRank-T	0.250	0.254	0.259	
	*L2R-S	0.256	0.214	0.345	
	*L2R-T	0.264	0.280	0.274	
	*CrossL2R-S	0.292	0.239	0.398	Cross-type
	*CrossL2R-T	0.295	**0.320**	0.295	
Ours	SociVote-S	0.282	0.236	0.376	
	HGRW-S	0.292	0.237	**0.403**	
	HGRW-T	0.293	0.279	0.324	
	HGRW-ST	**0.298**	0.258	0.376	

– **Learning to Rank (L2R):** The supervised summarizer based one RankBoost [2] with 27 local and cross-type features described in [16]. For training, the pairwise orders are derived from the largest ROUGE-1 F-score [9] of each instance between the instance and the reference highlight sentences. The model is configured to (1) take either sentences or tweets as input only, denoted as **L2R**; (2) take both to incorporate cross-type features, referred to as **CrossL2R**. We conducted 5-fold cross-validation and used 3-1-1 split among the five folds for training, development and test.

4. EVALUATION AND ANALYSIS

Comparison results

We use ROUGE-1 F-score rather than recall alone as main evaluation metric [9] because the output summaries in this task are *limited as four sentences and/or tweets* but have no length constraint. Table 2 shows the results. Our unsupervised models outperform the baselines most of time including L2R unaware of tweets and perform comparably well as CrossL2R using tweets as auxiliary features. Paired two-tailed t-test shows that the F-scores of HGRW-S/-T/-ST are significantly better than most of the baselines except for CrossL2R (which is comparable). Even our simplest model SociVote performs comparably well as L2R. It implies that the linking tweets are strongly indicative of candidate sentences, being an effective *opportunistic* master.

Our method performs comparably well as CrossL2R according to t-test and sometimes with even higher F-score. This is because the similarity between different type of instances can be directly utilized in the graph, but CrossL2R has to transform such correlation into high-level features that may not be expressive enough to capture the salient correlations.

The impact of β in HGRW

Figure 2a shows the impact of β. It is clear that larger β, i.e., giving higher weights to cross-type similarity, is generally helpful. When β increases, the joint ranking benefits from the addition of cross-type voting effect until some turning point. In fact, the turning points usually come late when β close to 1, which is a good property since there is no training data for officially tuning β, and therefore one can basically use relatively large β to safeguard good performance. In our case, we empirically set β as 0.8. An exception is that the performance of HGRW-S drops quickly when $\beta>0.85$. This is because excessive involvement of similarity from tweets allows noise dominating the sentence scoring.

The impact of tweets volume and latency

One of the general issues using third-party data source is caused by the volume and latency originated from the nature of the source used. Tweets are characterized by their instantaneity and large quantity obtainable quickly. In this section, we examine how the volume and latency of tweets can influence the performance of summarization on the news.

Preprocessing: We first acquired the timestamps of the news and the associated tweets which were not provided in the original corpus [16]. We accomplished this by two steps: (1) we downloaded the news articles and captured the exact publish time of the webpages indicated by the proper meta tag, such as <meta content="2012-07-20T09:14:52Z" itemprop="datePublished" name="pubdate" property="og:pub date">, which was then transformed into the timestamp in milliseconds; (2) we re-downloaded the tweets according to tweet IDs together with their timestamps in milliseconds. Then we ranked the tweets of each article by their timestamps to compare with the article timestamp.

The impact of tweets volume: Figure 2b shows that our three HGRW variants reach plateau with 250+ tweets, and HGRW-S performs better initially with fewer tweets while HGRW-T and HGRW-ST catch up later with more number of tweets added. Therefore, more tweets are clearly advantageous. SociVote seem a little unstable with small tweets volume because there is lack of focus with not many posts, while such shortage can be compensated by HGRW with the participation of news sentences. At most of time, CrossL2R has lower performance than HGRW under differ-

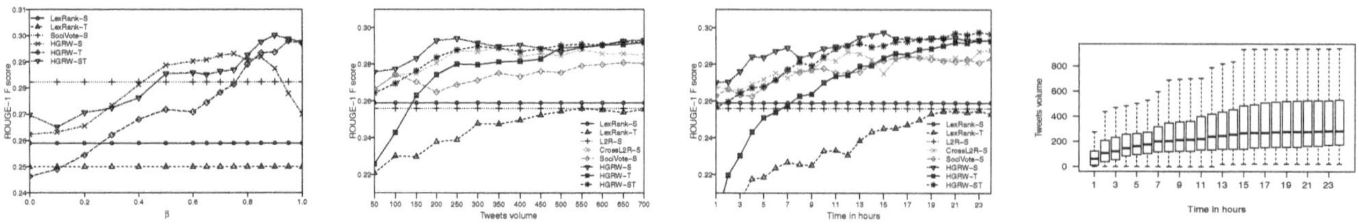

(a) Impact of β (b) Impact of tweets volume (c) Impact of tweets latency (d) time vs. tweets volume

Figure 2: The influence and relation of some major factors, i.e., the coefficient β, tweets volume, and tweets latency

ent tweets volumes. This confirms that the cross-type similarity from tweets plays a master role with HGRW more than just assisting CrossL2R as features.

The impact of tweets latency: We examined the performance of different systems based on one-hour interval for 24 hours starting from the publish times of articles. Figure 2c shows that latency of tweets indeed influences the results. With reference to Figure 2d that displays the box plot of the tweets volume at each given time, during the first hour, tweets-aware systems have only limited number of tweets (with around 100 tweets per article in average). Under such a case very close to cold start, two of our four models, i.e., HGRW-S and SociVote-S, still outperform the two LexRank baselines and L2R, where the real cold-start performance is guaranteed as effective as the best system not using tweets. Also, we find that HGRW-S and HGRW-ST reached significantly better performance over the baselines that ignore the tweets much more quickly than CrossL2R-S did. It took HGRW-S and HGRW-ST only 7 and 11 hours respectively, whereas CrossL2R-S needed 23 hours. By referring to the tweets volume in Figure 2d, the mean number of tweets required is 399 for HGRW-S and 469 for HGRW-ST, but CrossL2R needs around 577 tweets in average. We believe that such relatively small cost that one needs to tolerate some 7-11 hour latency yet with significant gains, is a generally reasonable tradeoff for most news summarization applications.

5. CONCLUSION AND FUTURE WORK

In this paper, we explored to use tweets linking to news articles for improving extractive single-document summarization without resorting to the reference summaries. We revealed the very fundamental merit of tweets that offers a voting effect on the important news sentences. Based on this finding, we present a heterogeneous graph model, which is simple but very effective, leveraging the linking tweets to opportunistically "supervise" sentences and tweets scoring. We also evaluated the influence of tweets volume and latency on the performance of summarization. Compared to the truly supervised summarizer unaware of tweets, our method achieves significantly better results with a reasonably small trade-off on latency; compared to the same that uses tweets as auxiliary features, our method is comparable but needs less amount of tweets and much shorter time.

There are some interesting future directions. For example, we can study how the relevant tweets can be used to generate news summary even before the news were massively reported so that other reporters can compose articles that more intentionally favor to or deepen the content on the already known focus of the online readers; A challenging problem is that we can search for the relevant tweets that are potentially massive but not linking to the articles directly for reducing or even eliminating the latency; Also, we may cross-lingually summarize an article using relevant tweets of other languages for those who are not familiar with the original language of the news article.

6. REFERENCES

[1] G. Erkan and D. R. Radev. Lexrank: Graph-based lexical centrality as salience in text summarization. *Journal of Artificial Intelligence Research*, 22:457–479, 2004.

[2] Y. Freund, R. Iyer, R. E. Schapire, and Y. Singer. An efficient boosting algorithm for combining preferences. *Journal of Machine Learning Research*, 4:933–969, 2003.

[3] W. Gao, P. Li, and K. Darwish. Joint topic modeling for event summarization across news and social media streams. In *CIKM*, pages 1173–1182, 2012.

[4] W. Guo, H. Li, H. Ji, and M. Diab. Linking tweets to news: A framework to enrich short text data in social media. In *ACL*, pages 239–249, 2013.

[5] T. Hirao, Y. Yoshida, M. Nishino, N. Yasuda, and M. Nagata. Single-document summarization as a tree knapsack problem. In *EMNLP*, pages 1515–1520, 2013.

[6] M. Hu, A. Sun, and E.-P. Lim. Comments-oriented document summarization: understanding documents with readers' feedback. In *SIGIR*, pages 291–298, 2008.

[7] J. Jagarlamudi, P. Pingali, and V. Varma. Query independent sentence scoring approach to DUC 2006. In *Proceedings of the Document Understanding Conference (DUC)*, 2006.

[8] P. Lal and S. Ruger. Extract-based summarization with simplification. In *Proceedings of the ACL 2002 Automatic Summarization / DUC 2002 Workshop*, 2002.

[9] C.-Y. Lin. ROUGE: A package for automatic evaluation of summaries. In *Text Summarization Branches Out: Proceedings of the ACL-04 Workshop*, pages 74–81, 2004.

[10] M. Litvak and M. Last. Graph-based keyword extraction for single-document summarization. In *Proceedings of the workshop on multi-source multilingual information extraction and summarization*, pages 17–24, 2008.

[11] A. Nenkova. Automatic text summarization of newswire: Lessons learned from the document understanding conference. In *AAAI*, pages 1436–1441, 2005.

[12] O. Phelan, K. McCarthy, M. Bennett, and B. Smyth. Terms of a feather: Content-based news recommendation and discovery using Twitter. In *ECIR*, pages 448–459. 2011.

[13] J.-T. Sun, D. Shen, H.-J. Zeng, Q. Yang, Y. Lu, and Z. Chen. Web-page summarization using clickthrough data. In *SIGIR*, pages 194–201, 2005.

[14] K. M. Svore, L. Vanderwende, and C. J. Burges. Enhancing single-document summarization by combining RankNet and third-party sources. In *EMNLP-CoNLL*, pages 448–457, 2007.

[15] M. Tsagkias, M. de Rijke, and W. Weerkamp. Linking online news and social media. In *WSDM*, pages 565–574, 2011.

[16] Z. Wei and W. Gao. Utilizing microblog for automatic news highlights extraction. In *COLING*, pages 872–883, 2014.

[17] K. Woodsend and M. Lapata. Automatic generation of story highlights. In *ACL*, pages 565–574, 2010.

[18] Z. Yang, K. Cai, J. Tang, L. Zhang, Z. Su, and J. Li. Social context summarization. In *SIGIR*, pages 255–264, 2011.

Context-aware Point-of-Interest Recommendation Using Tensor Factorization with Social Regularization

Lina Yao, Quan Z. Sheng, Yongrui Qin, Xianzhi Wang, Ali Shemshadi, and Qi He
School of Computer Science, The University of Adelaide
Adelaide, SA 5005, Australia
{firstname.lastname}@adelaide.edu.au

ABSTRACT

Point-of-Interest (POI) recommendation is a new type of recommendation task that comes along with the prevalence of location-based social networks in recent years. Compared with traditional tasks, it focuses more on personalized, context-aware recommendation results to provide better user experience. To address this new challenge, we propose a Collaborative Filtering method based on Nonnegative Tensor Factorization, a generalization of the Matrix Factorization approach that exploits a high-order tensor instead of traditional User-Location matrix to model multi-dimensional contextual information. The factorization of this tensor leads to a *compact* model of the data which is specially suitable for context-aware POI recommendations. In addition, we fuse users' social relations as regularization terms of the factorization to improve the recommendation accuracy. Experimental results on real-world datasets demonstrate the effectiveness of our approach.

Categories and Subject Descriptors

H.2.8 [**Data Management**]: Database Applications—*Data mining*; H.3.5 [**Information Storage and Retrieval**]: General

Keywords

Tensor factorization; social regularization; location based social networks; recommendation

1. INTRODUCTION

With the popularization of mobile devices, wireless networks and location-enabling techniques, location-based social networks (LBSNs), such as Foursquare, Gowalla, and Brightkite, have been attracting millions of users. People are increasingly using LBSNs services to connect with friends, explore places (e.g., restaurants, shops, cinemas etc.), and share their locations via check-in activities, which contain rich clues of users' preference on locations [5, 2, 6]. We take Brightkit check-in data[1] as an example to show some key patterns:

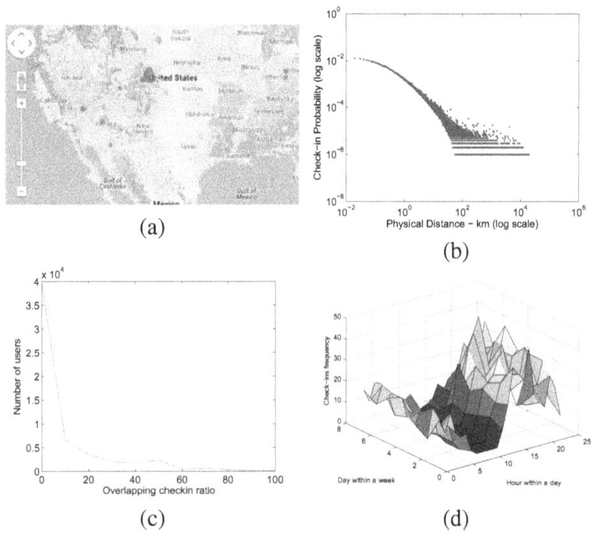

Figure 1: Illustration of check-in patterns in terms of geographical pattern (a) and (b), friendship impact (c) and temporal pattern of one specific user (d) over Brightkit

- Check-in activities have shown some interesting geographical characteristics such as spatial clustering patterns (as shown in Figure 1 (a)). Generally, people tend to visit nearby locations of their homes or offices, which are their POIs, and may also be interested in visiting the nearby locations of these POIs, even if they become far away from their homes [3, 11]. In addition, the majority of POIs checked in by the same users tend to aggregate within a certain range of short distances (as shown in Figure 1 (b));

- Users' social relationships have shown impact on checking-in activities. A dominant percentage of users have less than 10% overlapping locations with their friends (as shown in Figure 1 (c));

- Check-in data also show the periodical features depending on the type of POIs. For example, restaurants' peak time may be in the lunch hours, yet nightclubs or cinemas are most probably during nights and weekends (Figure 1 (d)).

Such availability of check-in data with rich spatial-temporal-social information makes it possible to design the context-aware location recommendation applications. In view of such informative patterns in check-in information, many significant works have been con-

[1]http://snap.stanford.edu/data/loc-brightkite.html

SIGIR'15 August 09 - 13, 2015, Santiago, Chile
©2015 ACM ISBN 978-1-4503-3621-5/15/08 ...$15.00
DOI: http://dx.doi.org/10.1145/2766462.2767794.

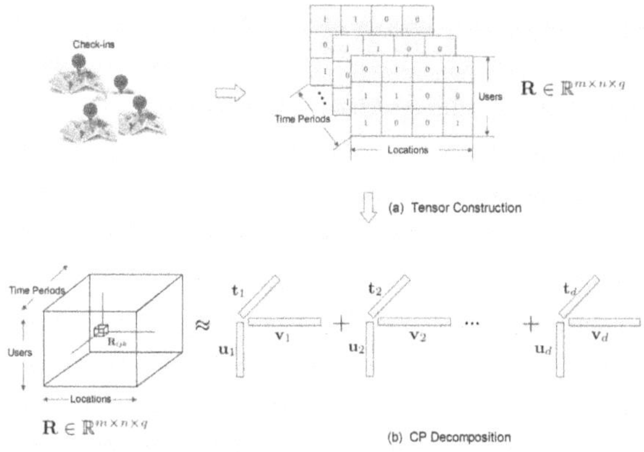

Figure 2: (a) Tensor Construction; (b) CP Decomposition

ducted on POI recommendation by analyzing users' check-in history and social constraints patterns [3, 12, 5]. In particular, Ye et al. [11] apply a power-law probabilistic model to capture the geographical influence among users' check-ins. Zhang et al. [13] consider social and geographical influence from both user and location perspectives, and develop a recommendation model by fusing Kernel density estimation into the matrix factorization framework. Yuan et al. [12] propose a collaborative recommendation model by incorporating temporal information. In a very recent work, Hu et al. [6] propose to improve the recommendation accuracy by incorporating the geographical neighborhood information.

Instead of modeling check-ins as a traditional two-dimensional user-location matrix, in this paper, we address the POI recommendation problem by incorporating the multi-dimensional contextual information of check-in data with high order tensor factorization to uncover the hidden dependency of multi-dimensional contextual information. Karatzoglou et al. [7] also propose a tensor-based context-aware recommendation framework using tucker decomposition. However, they did not consider the internal correlations among the contextual entities. In contrast to their work, we employ three order tensor to uncover the hidden dependency of multi-dimensional contextual information, and further explore the social influence among users, to support more accurate POI recommendation.

This paper makes the following contributions:

- We propose using high order tensor to interpret the multi-dimensional contextual information of check-in data in a compact manner. In particular, we further impose users' social connections as an extra regularization to improve recommendation accuracy.
- We evaluate our proposed method using real datasets, and the experimental results demonstrate the effectiveness of our approach.

Notations. In the rest of this paper, scalars will be denoted by lowercase letters, (e.g., m), vectors by boldface lowercase letters (e.g., $\mathbf{u}$), matrices by boldface capital letters (e.g., $\mathbf{U}$), and tensors by Calligraphy (e.g., $\mathcal{R}$). We will use $\circ$ to denote the outer product, $\odot$ the Khatri-Rao operation, and $||\cdot||_F$ the Frobenius norm.

2. PROPOSED METHOD

The POI recommendation problem in this paper can be defined as: given the historical check-in records of m users $\{u_i\}_{i=1}^m$ on n locations $\{v_j\}_{j=1}^n$ and q timeframes $\{t_k\}_{k=1}^q$, recommending the target users a set of locations that they might be interested in. We model the check-in tensor $\mathcal{R} \in \mathbb{R}^{m\times n\times q}$ via third order tensor, where each $\mathcal{R}_{ijk}$ quantifies users' preference in terms of frequency, i.e., the times that user u_i visits location v_j within time slice t_k. The tensor construction from check-in records $\mathcal{R} \in \mathbb{R}^{m\times n\times q}$ can be defined as the check-in frequency of if user u_i visits location v_j within time frame t_k, where $\mathcal{R}_{ijk}$ denotes user u_i checks in at location v_j within time period t_k (Figure 2 (a)). To address the temporal dependency of users' dynamic check-ins over time, the third order tensor $\mathcal{R}$ can be estimated from check-in records using tensor decomposition techniques, such as the High Order Singular Value Decomposition (HOSVD) and CANDECOMP/PARAFAC (CP) decomposition [4]. In this paper, we employ CP decomposition D-component of rank 1 tensors [8] to characterize the three dimensional check-in records (Figure 2 (b)), the preference of user u_i on location l_j in time frame t_k can be approximated as: $\hat{\mathcal{R}} \approx \sum_{d=1}^{D} \mathbf{u}_d \circ \mathbf{v}_d \circ \mathbf{t}_d$ where $\hat{\mathcal{R}}$ denotes the predicted approximation of $\mathcal{R}$; $\mathbf{u}_d \in \mathbb{R}^m$, $\mathbf{v}_d \in \mathbb{R}^n$ and $\mathbf{t}_d \in \mathbb{R}^q$. We aim at finding the decomposition $\hat{\mathbf{R}}$ that best approximates the original tensor $\mathcal{R}$ to achieve best recommendation results. In particular, we solve the optimization problem by minimizing the squared loss as follows.

$$\begin{aligned} L(\mathbf{U},\mathbf{V},\mathbf{T}) &= \frac{1}{2}\min_{\mathbf{U},\mathbf{V},\mathbf{T}} ||\mathcal{R}-\hat{\mathcal{R}}||_F^2 \\ &= \frac{1}{2}\min_{\mathbf{U},\mathbf{V},\mathbf{T}} ||\mathcal{R}-\sum_{d}^{D}\mathbf{u}_d\circ\mathbf{v}_d\circ\mathbf{t}_d||_F^2 \end{aligned} \tag{1}$$

where $\mathbf{U} = [\mathbf{u}_1, ..., \mathbf{u}_D] \in \mathbb{R}^{m\times D}$, $\mathbf{V} = [\mathbf{v}_1, ..., \mathbf{v}_D] \in \mathbb{R}^{n\times D}$, and $\mathbf{T} = [\mathbf{t}_1, ..., \mathbf{t}_D] \in \mathbb{R}^{q\times D}$ are all factor matrices. To avoid overfitting, the regularization terms associated with $\mathbf{U}$, $\mathbf{V}$ and $\mathbf{T}$ are introduced into Equation 1 as:

$$\min_{\mathbf{U},\mathbf{V},\mathbf{T}} \frac{1}{2}||\mathcal{R}-\hat{\mathcal{R}}||_F^2 + \frac{\lambda}{2}(||\mathbf{U}||_F^2+||\mathbf{V}||_F^2+||\mathbf{T}||_F^2) \tag{2}$$

where λ is the regularization parameter. We further consider users' explicit social friendships to improve recommendation accuracy, which has been widely used in two-dimensional matrix factorization based recommendation frameworks [9]. The social regularization term can constrain the matrix factorization objective function and indirectly propagate users' preferences.

The Equation 2 can be reformulated as:

$$\begin{aligned} L(\mathbf{U},\mathbf{V},\mathbf{T}) &= \min_{\mathbf{U},\mathbf{V},\mathbf{T}} \frac{1}{2}||\mathcal{R}-\hat{\mathcal{R}}||_F^2 + \frac{\lambda}{2}(||\mathbf{U}||_F^2+||\mathbf{V}||_F^2+||\mathbf{T}||_F^2) \\ &\quad + \frac{\alpha}{2}\sum_{i,j=1}^{s}\mathbf{A}_{i,j}\sum_{d}^{D}([\mathbf{U}_{i,d}]-[\mathbf{U}_{j,d}])^2 \\ &= \min_{\mathbf{U},\mathbf{V},\mathbf{T}} \frac{1}{2}||\mathcal{R}-\hat{\mathcal{R}}||_F^2 + \frac{\lambda}{2}(||\mathbf{U}||_F^2+||\mathbf{V}||_F^2+||\mathbf{T}||_F^2) \\ &\quad + \frac{\alpha}{2}\sum_{d}^{D}\mathbf{U}_{*d}{}^T\mathbf{L}\mathbf{U}_{*d} \\ &= \min_{\mathbf{U},\mathbf{V},\mathbf{T}} \frac{1}{2}||\mathcal{R}-\hat{\mathcal{R}}||_F^2 + \frac{\lambda}{2}(||\mathbf{U}||_F^2+||\mathbf{V}||_F^2+||\mathbf{T}||_F^2) \\ &\quad + \frac{\alpha}{2}\mathrm{tr}(\mathbf{U}^T\mathbf{L}\mathbf{U}) \\ &= \min_{\mathbf{U},\mathbf{V},\mathbf{T}} \frac{1}{2}||\mathcal{R}-\hat{\mathcal{R}}||_F^2 + \frac{1}{2}\mathrm{tr}[\mathbf{U}^T(\lambda\mathbf{I}+\alpha\mathbf{L})\mathbf{U}] + \frac{\lambda}{2}(||\mathbf{V}||_F^2+||\mathbf{T}||_F^2) \\ &= \min_{\mathbf{U},\mathbf{V},\mathbf{T}} \frac{1}{2}||\mathcal{R}-\hat{\mathcal{R}}||_F^2 + \frac{1}{2}\mathrm{tr}[\mathbf{U}^T(\lambda\mathbf{I}+\alpha\mathbf{L})\mathbf{U}] + \frac{\lambda}{2}\mathrm{tr}[\mathbf{V}\mathbf{V}^T+\mathbf{T}\mathbf{T}^T] \end{aligned} \tag{3}$$

where $\mathbf{A}_{i,j}$ indicates the similarity between user i and j, $\mathbf{L}$ is the Laplacian matrix induced from users' social networks matrix $\mathbf{A} \in \mathbb{R}^{m \times m}$; $\mathbf{L} = \mathbf{D} - \mathbf{A}$, where $\mathbf{D}$ is the diagonal matrix whose i-th diagonal element is the sum of all the elements in the i-th row of $\mathbf{A}$, i.e., $\mathbf{D}_{ii} = \sum_j \mathbf{A}_{ij}$.

$$\nabla_{\mathbf{U}} L(\mathbf{U}, \mathbf{V}, \mathbf{T}) = \nabla_{\mathbf{U}} ||\mathcal{R}_{(1)} - \hat{\mathbf{U}}(\mathbf{V} \odot \mathbf{T})^T||_F^2 + \frac{\lambda}{2}\mathbf{I} + \frac{\alpha}{2}\mathbf{L}$$
$$\nabla_{\mathbf{V}} L(\mathbf{U}, \mathbf{V}, \mathbf{T}) = \nabla_{\mathbf{V}} ||\mathcal{R}_{(2)} - \hat{\mathbf{V}}(\mathbf{U} \odot \mathbf{T})^T||_F^2 + \frac{\lambda}{2}\mathbf{I}$$
$$\nabla_{\mathbf{T}} L(\mathbf{U}, \mathbf{V}, \mathbf{T}) = \nabla_{\mathbf{T}} ||\mathcal{R}_{(3)} - \hat{\mathbf{T}}(\mathbf{U} \odot \mathbf{V})^T||_F^2 + \frac{\lambda}{2}\mathbf{I} \quad (4)$$

where $\mathcal{R}_{(1)} \approx \mathbf{U}(\mathbf{V} \odot \mathbf{T})^T$, $\mathcal{R}_{(2)} \approx \mathbf{V}(\mathbf{U} \odot \mathbf{T})^T$ and $\mathcal{R}_{(3)} \approx \mathbf{T}(\mathbf{U} \odot \mathbf{V})^T$. As Equation 3 is not convex, we adopt the alternating optimization strategy to solve the objective function. In particular, we alternately optimize each of the three parameters $\mathbf{U}$, $\mathbf{V}$ and $\mathbf{T}$, while fixing the other two until convergence to find the optimal solution using Equation 4.

3. EXPERIMENTS

3.1 Experimental Settings

Dataset. We select the check-in occurred during January 2010 to September 2010 from the original Brightkite [3], we remove users whose checked-in records are fewer than 5 POIs, and then removed POIs with fewer than 5 users checked in. For each user, we randomly mark off another 20% of POIs as testing data to evaluate the effectiveness of the recommendation methods. We use *Precision@x* and *Recall@x* to evaluate our proposed method (x= 5, 10, 15, 20).

Comparison Methods. We compare the proposed models **TenInt** with the following other methods, which basically consist of two categories: (1) *Non-contexts*: we implement basic non-negative matrix factorization (**NMF**), user-based collaborative filtering (**UCF**) and item-based collaborative filtering (**ICF**) [10]; (2) *Partial contexts*: we develop three models by taking into geographical influence, temporal information and friendship into account, respectively.

- **NMF.** It only considers the 2D user-location matrix. It applies non-negative matrix factorization on user-location matrix to predict the possibility of check-in. The user-location matrix can be decomposed into two lower dimension matrices in this method:

$$\min_{\mathbf{U},\mathbf{V}} \frac{1}{2} \sum_{i=1}^{m} \sum_{j=1}^{n} (r_{ij} - \mathbf{u}_i^T \mathbf{v}_j)^2 \quad (5)$$

- **User-CF (UCF).** It predicts a user's preferences by taking the preferences of other similar users into account and use *Jacaard similarity* for similarity computation.

- **Item-CF (ICF).** It predicts a user's preferences on a target location by taking his preferences on similar locations into account [10] and *Jaccard similarity* is used for similarity computation.

- Friendship-aware CF (**FA**). The probability of user i checks in location k can be calculated as:

$$R_{ik}^f = \frac{\sum_{j \in F_i} s_{ij}^f \cdot c_{jk}}{\sum_{j \in F_i} s_{ij}} \quad (6)$$

where $c_{jk} = 1$ if user i checked in location k, otherwise 0. s_{ij}^f is computed as:

$$s_{ij}^f = \lambda \frac{|F_i \cap F_j|}{|F_i \cup F_j|} + (1 - \lambda) \frac{|L_i \cap L_j|}{|L_i \cup L_j|} \quad (7)$$

where $F_.$ denotes user's friendship set and $L_.$ denotes the locations checked in by each user. λ is used to balance the importance of friend impact and impact of shared checked in locations [11]. $\lambda = 0.4$ is the best setting based on our empirical study in this work.

- Geographic-aware CF (**GA**). We use Gaussian Mixture Model (GMM) to capture the geographical clustering influence, where Gaussian center could be user's home, office, or entertainment places like shopping malls or restaurants [1]. The probability that user i visits location k is modeled as below:

$$R_{ik}^g = \sum_{m=1}^{M} \pi_m N(l_k | \mu_m, \sum_m) \quad (8)$$

where l_k denotes location k, which is represented by longitude and latitude coordinates, and m is the number of Gaussian clusters.

- **Time-aware.** To address the temporal influence in users' check-in behaviors, we decompose the time over two dimensions of day (Mon. to Sun.) and hour (1 to 24). The probability of check-in is computed as:

$$R_{ik}^t = \frac{\sum_{l=1}^{L} \mathbb{I}(i, l) \cdot sim(l, k) \cdot f(T)}{\sum_{l=1}^{L} sim(l, k) \cdot f(T)} \quad (9)$$

where l denotes a subset closely associated with user i according to his historical check-in records. $sim(l, k)$ can be computed using Jaccard similarity. $f(T)$ is a temporal adjustment function for each user, which can be computed by using:

$$f(T) = \eta \cdot Pr(k|h) + (1 - \eta) \cdot Pr(k|d) \quad (10)$$

where $Pr(k|h)$ is the probability of check-in at location k, given the h-hour within a day (24 hours one day). $Pr(k|d)$ is the probability of check-in at location k, given the d th day within a week (7 days one week).

We also compare with a linear model (**LIM**) by integrating these three partial contextual models together. The overall probability that user i would visit location k can be obtained:

$$R_{ik} = \alpha R_{ik}^t + \beta R_{ik}^f + (1 - \alpha - \beta) R_{ik}^g \quad (11)$$

$\alpha = 0.1$ and $\beta = 0.6$ are the best settings based on our empirical study.

3.2 Results

3.2.1 Overall Comparison

The overall comparison results are shown in Figure 3, from which we summarize two main observations. First, our tensor-based recommendation method significantly outperforms all compared methods (including both non-context aware methods and context-aware methods) in terms of top 5 to top 20 validations. Our method obtains better prediction than the linear model, mostly because the tensor-based factorization can better reveal the hidden information. Second, all context-aware methods (e.g., the linear model fully combined with friendship, spatial and temporal influence) have better performance than the ones without or with only partial context-awareness. The basic matrix factorization method has the worst accuracy, as it only works on user-location matrix and does not integrate any contextual information. To sum up, the results demonstrate the effectiveness of incorporating multi-dimensional contextual information in a unified tensor based approach in improving the recommendation performance.

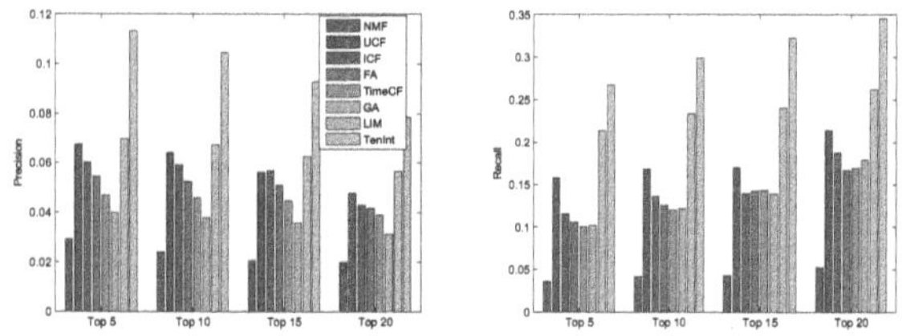

(a) Precision@x (x = 5, 10, 15, 20) (b) Recall@x (x = 5, 10, 15, 20)

Figure 3: Precision and recall over all methods

3.2.2 *Impact of Tensor Dimensionality*

As the parameter dimensionality fundamentally determines the number of latent factors involved in the tensor factorization, in this section, we investigate the impact of the dimensionality by varying the value of dimensionality from 5 to 60 with a step size 5. Figure 4 shows the precision and recall at top 5, 10, 15 and 20 under different tensor dimensionality. We observe that the precision and recall keep increasing with larger dimensionality, however they slightly drop when dimensionality reaches around 55. The results reveal a larger dimensionality can effectively uncover information of check-ins and improve the recommendation performance. But when the dimensionality exceeds certain threshold, the performance may degrade because of over-fitting. Larger dimensionality also requires more computational cost. Based on our results, we have set the dimensionality as 50 in above comparison.

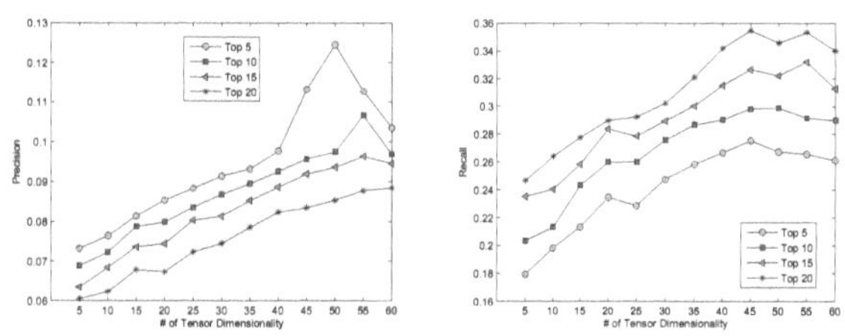

(a) Precision@x (x = 5, 10, 15, 20) (b) Recall@x (x = 5, 10, 15, 20)

Figure 4: Impact of tensor dimensionality

4. CONCLUSION

In this paper, we propose a tensor non-negative decomposition based Point-of-Interest (POI) recommendation approach using users' social constraints as regularization. We model the check-in records as three dimensional tensor and employ the non-negative tensor factorization method to enable effective POI recommendation in a higher dimensional space. Specially, we propose to impose users' social constraints as regularization terms on tensor non-negative factorization to improve the recommendation accuracy. Our proposed method achieves better performance than seven standard baselines in our experimental study.

5. REFERENCES

[1] C. Cheng, H. Yang, I. King, and M. R. Lyu. Fused matrix factorization with geographical and social influence in location-based social networks. In *Twenty-Sixth AAAI Conference on Artificial Intelligence*, 2012.

[2] C. Cheng, H. Yang, M. R. Lyu, and I. King. Where you like to go next: Successive point-of-interest recommendation. In *Proceedings of the Twenty-Third international joint conference on Artificial Intelligence*, pages 2605–2611. AAAI Press, 2013.

[3] E. Cho, S. A. Myers, and J. Leskovec. Friendship and mobility: user movement in location-based social networks. In *Proceedings of the 17th ACM SIGKDD international conference on Knowledge discovery and data mining*, pages 1082–1090. ACM, 2011.

[4] D. M. Dunlavy, T. G. Kolda, and E. Acar. Temporal link prediction using matrix and tensor factorizations. *ACM Transactions on Knowledge Discovery from Data (TKDD)*, 5(2):10, 2011.

[5] H. Gao and H. Liu. Data analysis on location-based social networks. In *Mobile Social Networking*, pages 165–194. Springer, 2014.

[6] L. Hu, A. Sun, and Y. Liu. Your neighbors affect your ratings: on geographical neighborhood influence to rating prediction. In *Proceedings of the 37th international ACM SIGIR conference on Research & development in information retrieval*, pages 345–354. ACM, 2014.

[7] A. Karatzoglou, X. Amatriain, L. Baltrunas, and N. Oliver. Multiverse recommendation: n-dimensional tensor factorization for context-aware collaborative filtering. In *Proceedings of the fourth ACM conference on Recommender systems*, pages 79–86. ACM, 2010.

[8] T. G. Kolda and B. W. Bader. Tensor decompositions and applications. *SIAM review*, 51(3):455–500, 2009.

[9] H. Ma, D. Zhou, C. Liu, M. R. Lyu, and I. King. Recommender systems with social regularization. In *Proceedings of the fourth ACM international conference on Web search and data mining*, pages 287–296. ACM, 2011.

[10] B. Sarwar, G. Karypis, J. Konstan, and J. Riedl. Item-based collaborative filtering recommendation algorithms. In *Proceedings of the 10th international conference on World Wide Web*, pages 285–295. ACM, 2001.

[11] M. Ye, P. Yin, W.-C. Lee, and D.-L. Lee. Exploiting geographical influence for collaborative point-of-interest recommendation. In *Proceedings of the 34th international ACM SIGIR conference on Research and development in Information Retrieval*, pages 325–334. ACM, 2011.

[12] Q. Yuan, G. Cong, Z. Ma, A. Sun, and N. M. Thalmann. Time-aware point-of-interest recommendation. In *Proceedings of the 36th international ACM SIGIR conference on Research and development in information retrieval*, pages 363–372. ACM, 2013.

[13] J.-D. Zhang and C.-Y. Chow. igslr: personalized geo-social location recommendation: a kernel density estimation approach. In *Proceedings of the 21st ACM SIGSPATIAL International Conference on Advances in Geographic Information Systems*, pages 334–343. ACM, 2013.

Adaptive User Engagement Evaluation via Multi-task Learning

Hamed Zamani, Pooya Moradi, and Azadeh Shakery
School of Electrical and Computer Engineering, College of Engineering,
University of Tehran, Tehran, Iran
{h.zamani, po.moradi, shakery}@ut.ac.ir

ABSTRACT

User engagement evaluation task in social networks has recently attracted considerable attention due to its applications in recommender systems. In this task, the posts containing users' opinions about items, e.g., the tweets containing the users' ratings about movies in the IMDb website, are studied. In this paper, we try to make use of tweets from different web applications to improve the user engagement evaluation performance. To this aim, we propose an adaptive method based on multi-task learning. Since in this paper we study the problem of detecting tweets with positive engagement which is a highly imbalanced classification problem, we modify the loss function of multi-task learning algorithms to cope with the imbalanced data. Our evaluations over a dataset including the tweets of four diverse and popular data sources, i.e., IMDb, YouTube, Goodreads, and Pandora, demonstrate the effectiveness of the proposed method. Our findings suggest that transferring knowledge between data sources can improve the user engagement evaluation performance.

Categories and Subject Descriptors

H.2.8 [**Database Management**]: Data Mining; J.4 [**Computer Applications**]: Social and Behavioral Sciences

Keywords

User engagement; transfer learning; multi-task learning; adaptive model

1. INTRODUCTION

Micro-blogging platforms such as Twitter have become tremendously popular in the past few years. These platforms let people express their opinions and thoughts as fast as possible and this fact makes them a rich source of information about people's everyday lives. Due to the high speed of information diffusion, several web applications have been integrated with Twitter to let people share their opinions about items (e.g., movies in IMDb) [7, 11].

Tweets containing the opinions of users about items (or products) could be used to improve the performance of recommender systems. It is shown that the total number of users' interactions on tweets can represent the satisfaction of users. In other words, the value of achieved engagements is correlated with the interest of users in the received messages [7]. In addition, Uysal and Croft [10] have investigated an important usage of engagement evaluation, which is designing personalized content filters. It is notable that the problem of engagement prediction or online participation has been extensively studied in news websites, social networks, and discussion forums. Petrovic et al. [8] have tried to predict the number of retweets or to detect the tweets that will be retweeted. Note that the aforementioned methods have investigated tweets with arbitrary content, while we are interested in predicting the engagement of tweets with predefined content. This characteristic of tweets eliminates the influence of textual features in our task.

According to the importance of user engagement evaluation and its influences on recommender systems, ACM Recommender Systems Challenge 2014[1] focused on ranking IMDb tweets of each user based on their engagements. Similar to this challenge, in this paper the "*engagement*" is computed as the total number of retweets and favorites that a tweet has gained.

In this paper, we try to answer two crucial research questions in user engagement evaluation. (1) Do tweets of various web applications differ with each other in terms of being engaging? (2) Is there any commonality among tweets of different web applications, which could be used to improve engagement evaluation? And how to benefit from these commonalities? To answer these questions, we focus on the problem of *detecting the tweets with positive engagement*. We first create a dataset containing tweets about items of four popular web applications in completely different domains: IMDb (movies), YouTube (Video clips), Goodreads (books), and Pandora (musics). By analyzing these datasets as well as performing in-domain and cross-domain experiments, we investigate the first question. We further propose an adaptive method based on multi-task learning, a transfer learning technique, to share knowledge between these domains. Since the data is highly imbalanced, we modify the loss function of multi-task learning algorithms by adding an instance weighting matrix to the loss function formulation. To the best of our knowledge, this is the first work that has focused on adaptive models for user engagement evaluation. The experiments demonstrate that the proposed method outperforms the baselines and in most cases, the improvements are statistically significant.

[1]`http://2014.recsyschallenge.com/`

SIGIR'15, August 09 - 13, 2015, Santiago, Chile.
 ISBN 978-1-4503-3621-5/15/08 ...$15.00.
DOI: http://dx.doi.org/10.1145/2766462.2767785.

2. ADAPTIVE USER ENGAGEMENT EVALUATION

In this section, we first briefly introduce the employed multi-task learning algorithms and describe how we deal with the imbalanced data in multi-task scenarios. Then, we introduce our features for user engagement evaluation.

2.1 Multi-task Learning

The problem of dealing with different distributions between training and test data has been extensively studied in the literature [2, 3, 4]. Various transfer learning approaches have been so far proposed to share knowledge between data with different distributions. In this paper, we use *multi-task learning* (MTL) [3], an inductive transfer learning technique whose goal is to improve the generalization performance by leveraging the domain-specific signals of related tasks.

We first introduce our notation. Let T be a set of t tasks and each task i has n_i training instances $\{(x_{i1}, y_{i1}), \cdots, (x_{in_i}, y_{in_i})\}$ in which $y_{ij} \in \mathbb{R}$ and $x_{ij} \in \mathbb{R}^d$ respectively denote the label and the features vector, where d is the number of features. The input features and labels can be stacked together as $X_i = \{x_{i1}, \cdots, x_{in_i}\}$ and $Y_i = \{y_{i1}, \cdots, y_{in_i}\}$, respectively. The weight of features are represented in matrix $W \in \mathbb{R}^{d \times t}$. We consider the logistic loss function which is widely used for linear classification. The logistic loss function in multi-task learning algorithms is defined as follows:

$$\mathcal{L}(W, X, Y) = \sum_{i=1}^{t} \sum_{j=1}^{n_i} \ln\left(1 + \exp\left(-Y_{ij}(W_i^T X_{ij} + c_i)\right)\right)$$

where c_i is the bias term for task i. Since the distribution of data in our problem is highly skewed, we assign higher weights to the instances from the minority class and vice versa. To this aim, for each task i we define an instance weighting matrix $\Lambda_i \in \mathbb{R}^{n_i \times 1}$ whose elements correspond to the weight of task i training instances. The elements of Λ is computed as:

$$\Lambda_{ij} = \frac{1/n_i^{(j)}}{\sum_{k=1}^{n_i} 1/n_i^{(k)}} \tag{1}$$

where $n_i^{(j)}$ denotes the number of training instances in task i with label y_{ij}. A similar idea for coping with imbalanced data in single-task classification problems has been previously proposed in [1]. In Equation (1), the weights of instances in each task are normalized to make the influence of all tasks equal in the total loss function. We redefine the logistic loss function for MTL as follows:

$$\mathcal{L}(W, X, Y) = \sum_{i=1}^{t} \sum_{j=1}^{n_i} \Lambda_{ij} \ln\left(1 + \exp\left(-Y_{ij}(W_i^T X_{ij} + c_i)\right)\right)$$

There are a number of MTL methods with different learning strategies and different assumptions. In this paper, we consider two linear MTL algorithms as follows:

MTL Trace [4]. This MTL method assumes that all tasks are related to each other and it tries to transfer knowledge between all tasks. The objective function in MTL Trace considers the trace-norm of matrix W for regularization.

MTL CASO [5]. This MTL method uses a convex relaxed alternative structured optimization (CASO) in its computations which decomposes the model of each task into two components: task-specific and task-shared feature mappings. It has been shown that there is an equivalence relationship between CASO and clustered MTL (CMTL) which assumes that tasks have group structure and thus, all tasks in each cluster are related to each other.

Table 1: Dataset Characteristics

	IMDb	YouTube	Goodreads	Pandora
Items type	movie	video clip	book	music
# of tweets	100,206	239,751	65,445	98,212
# of users	6,852	6,480	3,813	3,312
# of items	13,502	154,041	31,558	32,321
Avg eng.	0.1097	0.4737	0.1632	0.0778
% of tweets with eng>0	4.139	14.193	6.931	6.285

2.2 Features

In this task, each tweet is tweeted by a user about an item (e.g., movie). For each tweet, we extract 23 features partitioned into three categories: user-based, item-based, and tweet-based. Since the contents of tweets are predefined by the web applications and users usually do not edit tweets contents, we do not consider textual features. More details about the exact definition of features can be found in [11].[2]

User-based features. Number of followers, Number of followees, Number of tweets, Number of tweets about domain's items, Number of liked tweets, Number of lists, Tweeting frequency, Attracting followers frequency, Following frequency, Like frequency, Followers/Followees, Followers-Followees.

Item-based features. Number of tweets about the item.

Tweet-based features. Mention count, Number of hashtags, Tweet age, Membership age at the tweeting time, Hour of tweet, Day of tweet, Time of tweet, Holidays or not, Same language or not, English or not.

3. EXPERIMENTS

3.1 Dataset

In this paper, we investigate the tweets of four diverse and popular web applications (hereafter, called domains): IMDb, YouTube, Goodreads, and Pandora which contain movies, video clips, books, and musics, respectively. These applications let people express their opinions about items in Twitter. Tweets contents are predefined, but can be edited by users.

Recently, Dooms et al. [6] created a similar dataset by collecting recent tweets. Since their dataset is very sparse, we expand their approach by also gathering all related tweets of new users. Therefore, our created dataset is more realistic. Statistics of our created dataset are reported in Table 1. The dataset is freely available for research purposes.[3]

3.2 Experimental Setup

To decrease the effect of having considerably different amounts of training data in different domains and to equally weight the contribution of each domain in the learning process, we train all models using the same number of instances from each domain. Hence, we select 65,445 instances (size

[2]A few number of features employed in [11] which cannot be applied for all the domains are ignored. Note that the baseline results with and without using these features are approximately equal. Designing an adaptive model to handle different features in each domain will be considered in the future.

[3]Available at `http://ece.ut.ac.ir/node/100770`

Table 2: F1-measure and BA achieved by in-domain and cross-domain experiments.

Train \ Test		IMDb	YouTube	Good-reads	Pandora
IMDb	F1	0.1206	0.3696	0.2033	0.1661
	BA	**0.5948***	0.6679	0.5851	0.5667
You-Tube	F1	**0.1406**	**0.3932***	0.1970	0.1350
	BA	0.5470	**0.6975***	0.5596	0.5387
Good-reads	F1	0.1288	0.3317	**0.2175***	0.1572
	BA	0.5732	0.6633	**0.6353***	0.5774
Pan-dora	F1	0.1304	0.3329	0.2050	**0.1741**
	BA	0.5732	0.6639	0.6109	**0.5899***

of the smallest domain) for each domain and cut it in half to create training and test sets. We repeat this process 30 times by shuffling the data of each domain randomly. Average of the results obtained on 30 shuffles are reported.

As expected and shown in Table 1, percentage of data with positive engagement is by far lower than percentage of those with zero engagement. This makes our data highly imbalanced and thus, accuracy could not be a proper evaluation metric for this task. We consider two widely used evaluation metrics for classification in imbalanced environments: F1-measure and balanced accuracy (BA) [9].[4]

In all experiments, the instance weighting technique is applied for both baselines and the proposed method.[5] For hyper-parameter optimization in all methods, we perform stratified k-fold cross validation over training data and find the optimum parameters using grid search. Moreover, statistical t-test with 95% confidence is used to find the significant differences between results. The experiments are done using Scikit-learn[6] and MALSAR[7] packages.

3.3 Results and Discussion

In this section, we try to experimentally answer the two research questions mentioned in Section 1.

3.3.1 Exploring Gaps Between Domains

The statistics in Table 1 demonstrate several differences among different domains. According to this table, average engagement of tweets varies a lot between different domains. For instance, average engagement in YouTube tweets is six times higher than that in Pandora tweets. These differences might be related to different functionalities of these applications and also their popularity. Similar differences can be captured by considering number of tweets with positive engagement in the domains.

In addition to the different nature of the domains explained above, we design a set of experiments to investigate differences between the distributions of data in various domains. To this end, we train an SVM classifier with linear kernel on the training data of each domain and test it on the test data of all domains. The results in terms of F1-measure and BA are reported in Table 2. In each target domain (each column), the result which is significantly higher than its corresponding values is marked by "*". Table 2 shows that in all target domains, BA obtained by in-domain (training and test data from the same domain) experiment is significantly higher than all the cross-domain experiments (training and test data are from different domains). Except for IMDb, there is a similar pattern for F1-measure, i.e., in-domain result is higher than cross-domain results in each test set. In IMDb, all the cross-domain experiments achieve higher F1-measure compared to the in-domain experiment, although the improvements are not significant. The reason could be that IMDb is the most sparse dataset among other domains (see Table 1) and because of this highly imbalanced situation, the learning models cannot create a proper model using the IMDb training data and the learned model is biased towards the majority class. That is why F1-measure (which considers the precision and recall of the positive class) for cross-domain experiments are higher, but BA (which considers both classes equally) are not.

3.3.2 Analysis of the Adaptive Model

In the second set of experiments, to evaluate the performance of MTL methods, we compare them with two baselines: (1) STL: a single-task classifier which is trained on in-domain data, and (2) STL-Pooling: a single-task classifier which is trained on the data of all domains. We employ SVM as a single-task classifier in our experiments, which has been shown to be highly effective in different tasks. Since the mentioned MTL methods are linear, we also consider linear kernel for SVM to have a fair comparison.

To evaluate the methods with different amounts of training data, we consider 10 subsets of the created training set for each domain in each random shuffle with different sizes ranging from 10% to 100% of the instances. Figure 1 shows the learning curves on the four target domains in terms of F1-measure and BA.

According to Figure 1, the results of MTL methods in each domain are very close to each other. The reason is that all domains are related and the group structured assumption in MTL CASO does not affect the results, significantly. In the following, we analyze the results for each target domain separately and then, provide a general analysis.

IMDb. The results show that STL always performs better than STL-Pooling in terms of BA, but there is not a similar observation in terms of F1-measure; the reason could be that based on Table 1, IMDb domain is the most sparse domain and with the limited amount of training data, STL cannot create a proper model for detecting positive instances. Therefore, pooling the domains can help to improve the results in terms of F1-measure which combines the precision and recall of the positive class. Note that since the distributions of data in different domains vary a lot, by increasing the number of instances the performance of STL is also increased, but the STL-Pooling's performance is not. In other words, distribution of all the training data together differs with the distribution of the IMDb test data. The results also show that MTL methods outperform the baselines, in particular when the portion of training data is more than 50%. Statistical test shows that these improvements are statistically significant.

YouTube. Since other domains are more sparse than YouTube domain, pooling the domains can be effective in detecting the tweets with zero engagement. That is why the BAs achieved by STL-Pooling in beginning of the learning curve are higher than those obtained by the other methods. As expected, STL-pooling could not perform well in terms

[4]BA is computed as the mean of accuracy in each class.

[5]For the sake of space, the results without instance weighting which are far below the reported results are not reported.

[6]`http://scikit-learn.org/`

[7]`https://github.com/jiayuzhou/MALSAR`

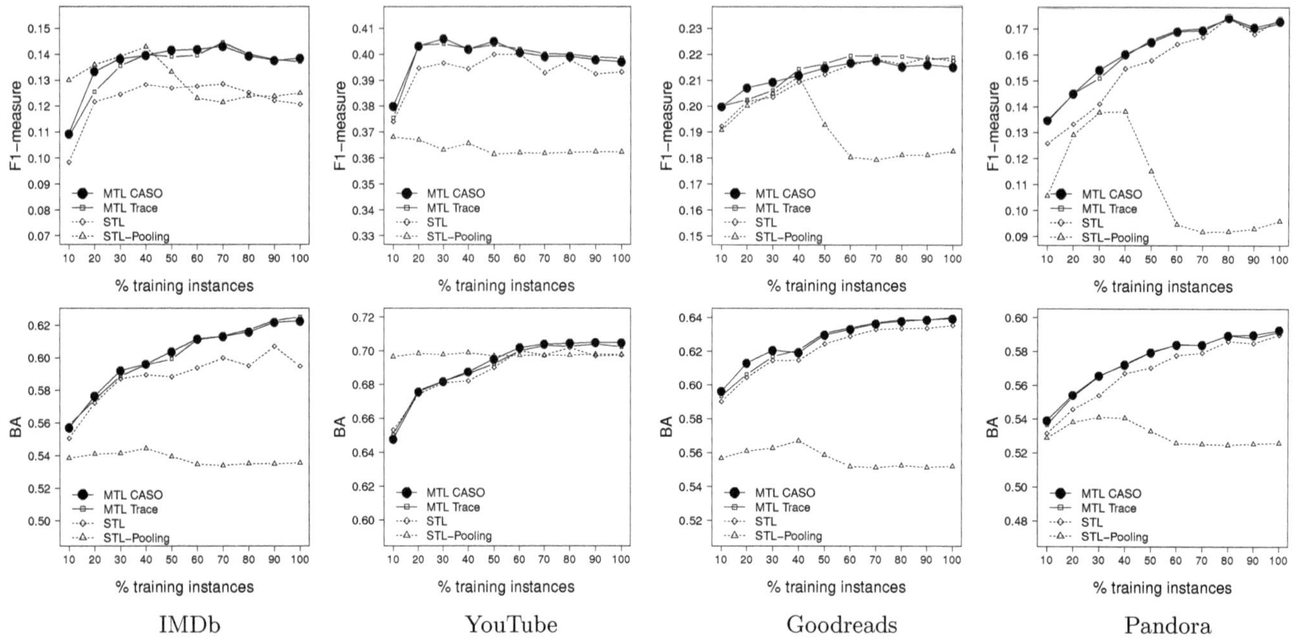

Figure 1: Learning curve of STL, STL-Pooling, and MTL methods over four domains in terms of F1-measure and BA.

of F1-measure; because, pooling with more sparse data reduces the accuracy of SVM to classify positive instances. By increasing the amounts of data, MTL methods outperform both STL methods. In addition, since YouTube domain is more balanced than the other domains, the results obtained on YouTube are higher than the others.

Goodreads and Pandora. The results of these two domains show that MTL methods outperform the baselines. The BA improvements are always significant, but the F1-measure improvements usually are not. This shows that transferring the knowledge helps more to correctly classify the zero engagement instances in these two domains. Because of the differences between training data in different domains, STL-Pooling could not perform well.

Considering the results of all domains, by increasing the number of training instances from 10% to 100%, the results of MTL methods vary from 4% to 6% in terms of F1-measure and from 3% to 5% in terms of BA. The learning curves in terms of BA become stable earlier than that of F1-measure. To wrap it up, when enough amount of training data is available, STL in general performs better than STL-Pooling and MTL methods perform better than STL. Conversely, if limited amount of training data is available, STL-Pooling may perform better than STL and again, MTL methods usually perform better than the baselines. Therefore, we can conclude that multi-task learning can transfer knowledge between these domains to improve the performance.

4. CONCLUSIONS AND FUTURE WORK

In this paper, we proposed an adaptive method based on multi-task learning technique for user engagement evaluation. To be able to cope with imbalanced data, we modified the logistic loss function in the mutli-task learning methods by adding an instance weighting matrix to its formulation. We considered four popular web applications in our experiments: IMDb, YouTube, GoodReads, and Pandora. The experimental results showed that distributions of data in these domains are different and multi-task learning methods can transfer knowledge between the domains to improve user engagement evaluation performance. A direction for future work is to recognize which domains can affect a given target domain. Other user engagement evaluation problems, such as ranking the tweets based on their engagements, could also be studied in the future.

5. REFERENCES

[1] R. Akbani, S. Kwek, and N. Japkowicz. Applying support vector machines to imbalanced datasets. In *ECML*, pages 39–50, 2004.

[2] J. G. C. de Souza, H. Zamani, M. Negri, M. Turchi, and D. Falavigna. Multitask learning for adaptive quality estimation of automatically transcribed utterances. In *NAACL-HLT*, pages 714–724, 2015.

[3] R. Caruana. Multitask learning. *Machine Learning*, 28(1):41–75, 1997.

[4] J. Chen, J. Liu, and J. Ye. Learning incoherent sparse and low-rank patterns from multiple tasks. *ACM Trans. Knowl. Discov. Data*, 5(4):22:1–22:31, 2012.

[5] J. Chen, L. Tang, J. Liu, and J. Ye. A convex formulation for learning shared structures from multiple tasks. In *ICML*, pages 137–144, 2009.

[6] S. Dooms, T. De Pessemier, and L. Martens. Mining cross-domain rating datasets from structured data on twitter. In *MSM@WWW*, 2014.

[7] D. Loiacono, A. Lommatzsch, and R. Turrin. An analysis of the 2014 recsys challenge. In *RecSysChallenge*, pages 1–6, 2014.

[8] S. Petrovic, M. Osborne, and V. Lavrenko. Rt to win! predicting message propagation in twitter. In *ICWSM*, pages 586–589, 2011.

[9] D. Powers. Evaluation: From precision, recall and f-measure to roc, informedness, markedness & correlation. *J. Mach. Learn. Tech.*, 2(1):37–63, 2011.

[10] I. Uysal and W. B. Croft. User oriented tweet ranking: A filtering approach to microblogs. In *CIKM*, pages 2261–2264, 2011.

[11] H. Zamani, A. Shakery, and P. Moradi. Regression and learning to rank aggregation for user engagement evaluation. In *RecSysChallenge*, pages 29–34, 2014.

Compact Snippet Caching for Flash-based Search Engines

Rui Zhang[1†] Pengyu Sun[1,2†] Jiancong Tong[1,2]
Rebecca J. Stones[1] Gang Wang[1‡] Xiaoguang Liu[1‡]

[1]College of Computer and Control Engineering & College of software, Nankai University, China
[2]Baidu, Inc
{zhangruiann, sunpengyu, jctong, becky, wgzwp, liuxg}@nbjl.nankai.edu.cn

ABSTRACT

In response to a user query, search engines return the top-k relevant results, each of which contains a small piece of text, called a snippet, extracted from the corresponding document. Obtaining a snippet is time consuming as it requires both document retrieval (disk access) and string matching (CPU computation), so caching of snippets is used to reduce latency. With the trend of using flash-based solid state drives (SSDs) instead of hard disk drives for search engine storage, the bottleneck of snippet generation shifts from I/O to computation. We propose a simple, but effective method for exploiting this trend, which we call fragment caching: instead of caching the whole snippet, we only cache snippet metadata which describe how to retrieve the snippet from the document. While this approach increases I/O time, the cost is insignificant on SSDs. The major benefit of fragment caching is the ability to cache the same snippets (without loss of quality) while only using a fraction of the memory the traditional method requires. In our experiments, we find around 10 times less memory is required to achieve comparable snippet generation times for dynamic memory, and we consistently achieve a vastly greater hit ratio for static caching.

Categories and Subject Descriptors

H.3.3 [**Information Storage and Retrieval**]: Information Search and Retrieval-Search process

Keywords

Cache; Snippet; Solid State Drive

1. INTRODUCTION

Caching is an important method for reducing query latency in search engines. A large-scale search engine typically consists of three sets of servers [2, 5]: (a) web servers, which interact with users and coordinate the whole query processing, utilizing a query result cache (QRC), (b) index servers, which match top-k documents that are most related to the query, and (c) document servers, which generate the query result pages, which include the title, URL, and a snippet for each of the top-k documents.

For a given query, a snippet is the portion of a document which matches the query best and the query terms are highlighted. In order to alleviate query latency, frequently requested documents and snippets are cached. These two in-memory caches are called *document cache* (DC) [10] and *snippet cache* (SC) [3], respectively. DC stores document pages to decrease disk accesses when generating snippets, while SC stores snippets for documents to avoid repeated computation and disk access.

Recently, solid state drives (SSDs) have been increasingly used by the industries as a secondary storage medium. Many companies are replacing their hard disk drives (HDDs) by SSDs. SSDs have properties such as fast read (10 to 100 times faster than HDD) and write, lower power consumption, and better shock resistance [4].

Snippet generation is an expensive process in terms of both disk access and CPU computation [10]. In traditional HDD-based search engines, the latency of snippet processing is dominated by disk access operations (i.e., I/O). As SSD has faster read (especially random read), snippet calculation time becomes the bottleneck in snippet processing [11]. In this context, techniques for increasing caching efficiency will have changed.

To address this hardware difference, we adopt a relative location representation, motivated by Hoobin *et al.* [6], which allows more snippets to be cached, and so fewer snippets need to be generated on the fly. Instead of caching the full snippet, we cache the snippet metadata, indicating how to retrieve the snippet, along with the text that needs highlighting, from the document; the idea being to increase the number of queries that can be cached within a limited memory space.

To the best of our knowledge, this is the first study that takes advantage of SSDs to improve the efficiency of snippet caching (although Tong *et al.* [8] used SSDs to improve list caching).

2. RELATED WORK

Snippet generation is one of the most time-consuming processes in document servers. The problem of reducing snippet processing latency has been studied from different

---

†The authors contributed equally to this work.
‡Corresponding authors.

SIGIR'15, August 09 - 13, 2015, Santiago, Chile.
 ISBN 978-1-4503-3621-5/15/08 ...$15.00.
DOI: http://dx.doi.org/10.1145/2766462.2767764.

directions. Liu *et al.* [7] used a CPU-GPU hybrid system to accelerate snippet generation. Ceccarelli *et al.* [3] introduced an effective "supersnippet" method, but this method may degrade the accuracy of snippet. Turpin *et al.* [10] used zlib to compress documents and reduced snippet generation latency by 58%; their method can dramatically reduce I/O cost in HDD-based search engine. Tsegay *et al.* [9] stored "surrogates" instead of the whole document to reduce I/O time.

Once SSDs are used to replace HDDs, methods which aim to reduce I/O time may not be of significant benefit. To illustrate, Wang *et al.* [11] found that document caching, which may significantly reduce the I/O of a document server, is not as effective on SSD-based search engines.

3. FRAGMENT CACHE

The use of SSDs dramatically reduces the disk accessing time of snippet processing. As a result, the CPU computation time plays a proportionally larger role in snippet generation. Thus, we will present a snippet caching model with this in mind.

For a given snippet, we define its *fragment* to be the data structure

$$\langle \text{docID}, \text{Frag}_s, \text{Frag}_e, \text{Highlight}_s, \text{Highlight}_e \rangle$$

where docID denotes the ID number of the corresponding document, Frag_s and Frag_e record the start and end points of the snippet to be returned, respectively, and Highlight_s and Highlight_e are two arrays which record the start and end points of the highlighted terms. A fragment records where on the document the relevant snippet data can be found.

Figure 1 depicts what is recorded in a toy example. In it, we have $\text{Frag}_s = \text{offset}$, $\text{Frag}_e = \text{offset}+\text{length}$, $\text{Highlight}_s = [\text{offset}_1, \text{offset}_2]$, and $\text{Highlight}_e = [\text{offset}_1+\text{length}_1, \text{offset}_2+\text{length}_2]$.

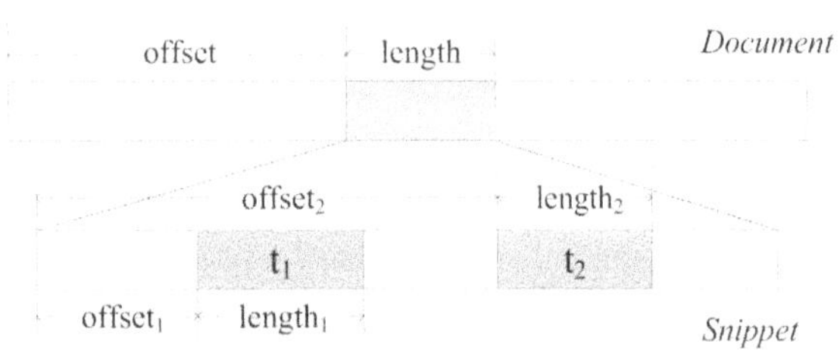

Figure 1: Illustrating the snippet structure. The top image shows the full document stored on the SSD (and possibly also in the document cache). The zoomed in image shows the snippet to be returned, along with which parts of it need highlighting.

This method of generating fragments is independent of the snippet generation algorithm used, so any snippet generation method can be used while utilizing fragment caching. Caching fragments instead of the full snippets will reduce the size of cached items, thereby increasing the number of snippets represented in the cache and increasing the cache hit ratio.

Figure 2 depicts the snippet processing and the fragment processing methods on document servers. The cache stores fragments instead of snippets is called *fragment cache* (FC).

We can model the snippet generation time mathematically. For a random query q for which the snippet for the document d = docID is required, we define the following variables:

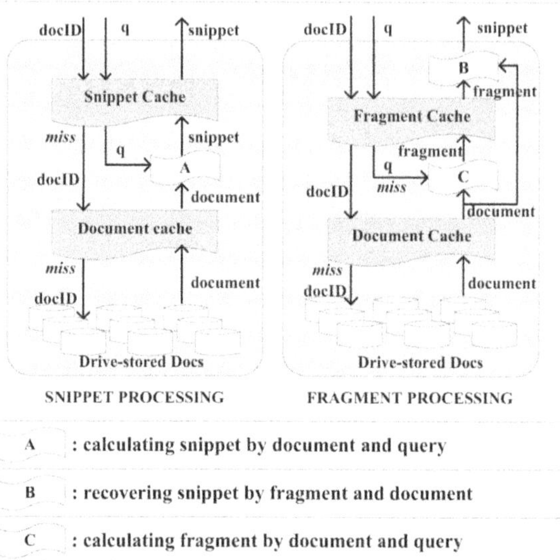

Figure 2: An outline of the workflow in snippet processing and fragment processing. The query q and document ID docID will be sent from the web server. Both methods return exactly the same snippet.

- $C^{(\text{sn})}_{(q,d)}$ and $C^{(\text{fr})}_{(q,d)}$ are the total times of processing (q, d) using snippet caching and fragment caching, respectively;
- $\overline{C}_{\text{drive}}$ is the average time it takes to retrieve a document from the drive;
- $p^{(\text{sn-miss})}$ and $p^{(\text{fr-miss})}$ are the probabilities of a snippet cache miss or a fragment cache miss, respectively;
- r is the probability a document is not represented in the document cache;
- $C_{\text{doc-cache}}$ is the time it takes to check the document cache for a document;
- $C_{\text{sn-cache}}$ and $C_{\text{fr-cache}}$ are the respective times it takes to check the snippet cache and fragment cache;
- $\overline{C}_{\text{sn-gen}}$ and $\overline{C}_{\text{fr-gen}}$ are the respective average times it takes to generate the snippet or fragment from (q, d);
- In the case of fragment caching, $\overline{C}_{\text{fr-sn-rec}}$ is the average time it takes to recover the snippet, given the fragment and document.

In snippet processing, we always check the snippet cache. If we hit the snippet cache, we're done, otherwise we check the document cache (which occurs with probability $p^{(\text{sn-miss})}$). If we miss the document cache (which occurs with probability r), we also check the disk, and in either case, we generate the snippet from the document and the query.

In fragment processing, we always check the fragment cache, and if we miss, we will need to generate the fragment from the query and the document. Whether or not we hit the fragment cache, we search for the document in the document cache, and if we miss the document cache (which occurs with probability r), we also check the drive. When the document is found after a fragment cache miss, we generate the fragment, and subsequently the snippet from the fragment.

As a result of the above discussion, the expected runtimes for snippet processing and fragment processing can be modelled as follows (using linearity of expectation):

$$\mathrm{E}(C^{(\mathrm{sn})}_{(q,d)}) = C_{\text{sn-cache}} + p^{(\text{sn-miss})}(C_{\text{doc-cache}} + r\,\overline{C}_{\text{drive}} + \overline{C}_{\text{sn-gen}}),$$

$$\mathrm{E}(C^{(\mathrm{fr})}_{(q,d)}) = C_{\text{fr-cache}} + C_{\text{doc-cache}} + r\,\overline{C}_{\text{drive}} + \overline{C}_{\text{fr-sn-rec}} + p^{(\text{fr-miss})}\,\overline{C}_{\text{fr-gen}}.$$

For SSD-based search engines, these equations are dominated by the $p^{(\text{sn-miss})}\overline{C}_{\text{sn-gen}}$ and $p^{(\text{fr-miss})}\overline{C}_{\text{fr-gen}}$ terms, respectively (i.e., computation time). Since $\overline{C}_{\text{sn-gen}} \approx \overline{C}_{\text{fr-gen}}$, when $p^{(\text{fr-miss})} < p^{(\text{sn-miss})}$ (i.e., the hit ratio of fragment caching is higher than the hit ratio of snippet caching), we can expect fragment caching to perform better than snippet caching.

This mathematical model also predicts that on HDD-based systems, where these equations are instead dominated by $p^{(\text{sn-miss})} r\,\overline{C}_{\text{drive}}$ and $r\,\overline{C}_{\text{drive}}$, respectively, fragment caching will perform worse than snippet caching.

4. PERFORMANCE EVALUATION

We evaluate the proposed fragment caching by comparing it vs. traditional snippet caching. We test both static and dynamic cache strategies. For static caching, we use MFU (Most Frequently Used) [1], and for dynamic caching, we use LRU (Least Recently Used). We control the hit ratio of the query result cache (in the web server) as 30% in order to keep the workload of document server realistic during the experiments.

4.1 Experimental setup

In our experiments, we use a collection of 12 million webpages crawled by Sogou Labs[1]. The experiments are performed by replaying real queries from the Sogou search engine. The query log contains 2M queries. The first half is used as the training set to "warm" the cache and the second half is used as the test set. We deploy a Lucene[2] based search engine, in which we implement fragment caching. The server is a Intel Xeon E5645 (2.4GHz) machine, with 12GB of main memory and Windows 7 SP1. We carry out experiments on a 120GB OCZ Vertex-3 SSD.

4.2 Experimental results

In our experiments, we find the average snippet size is 937 bytes while the average fragment size is only 61 bytes, which implies an average increase in the number of items cached by factor of approximately 15.

The total snippet generation time is given by $C_{\text{snip}} + C_{\text{doc}}$, where C_{doc} denotes the overhead of document retrieval, and C_{snip} denotes the remaining time (i.e., the snippet calculation time for snippet caching (A in Figure 2), and the sum of the fragment calculation time and snippet recovering time for fragment caching (B and C in Figure 2)).

Figures 3 and 4 compare the average snippet generation time for snippet caching and fragment caching using both static and dynamic cache strategies (split into C_{snip} and C_{doc}). Tables 1 and 2 list the hit ratios of snippet caching and fragment caching with different cache sizes under MFU and LRU, respectively. In Figures 3 and 4 and Tables 1 and 2, by "Snippet/fragment cache size" of size X, we mean, of the total memory (shared by SC/FC and DC), the portion reserved for snippet caching or fragment caching is approximately equal to the memory required to store $1000X$ snippets.

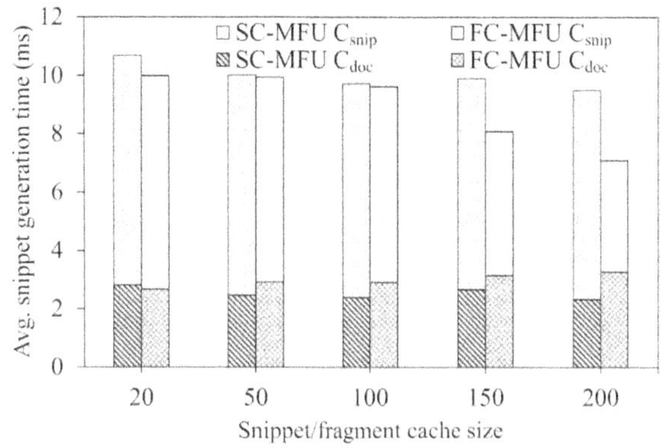

Figure 3: The latency of snippet processing and fragment processing under static caching (MFU).

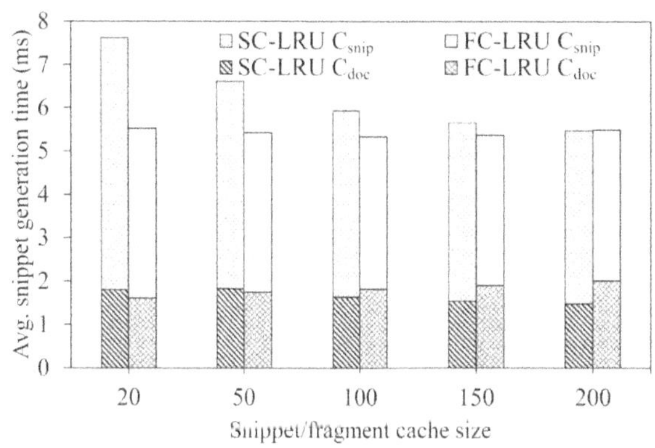

Figure 4: The latency of snippet processing and fragment processing under dynamic caching (LRU).

Table 1: The cache hit ratio for snippet caching and fragment caching under static caching (MFU).

Snippet/fragment cache size	20	50	100	150	200
Snippet (%)	24.8	29.9	33.8	35.9	37.4
Fragment (%)	39.9	45.5	51.3	68.2	77.7

4.3 Discussion

In static caching, we fill the caches in the document server using MFU according to the training set. As snippets can not be cached if the cache space is already filled during the training phase, the constrained cache size restricts the performance of snippet caching. The use of fragment caching decreases the probability of a cache miss substantially (see Table 1), which leads to a reduction of C_{snip}. And due to the fast read of SSD, the increase of C_{doc} is not substantial. As a result, we see better performance by fragment processing than snippet processing, particularly for larger memory sizes. E.g., when we allocate a snippet/fragment cache size of 200, fragment processing is 25% faster than snippet processing (see Figure 3).

We observe that fragment caching can also perform better than snippet caching with dynamic caching (see Figure 4). Using fragment caching, we only need a fragment cache size of 20 to get the similar snippet generation time as snippet

[1]http://www.sogou.com/labs/resources.html?v=1
[2]http://lucene.apache.org

Table 2: The cache hit ratio for snippet caching and fragment caching under dynamic caching (LRU).

Snippet/fragment cache size	20	50	100	150	200	550
Snippet (%)	38.5	52.8	59.8	62.9	64.8	70.7
Fragment (%)	67.5	72.2	75.9	77.5	77.7	77.7

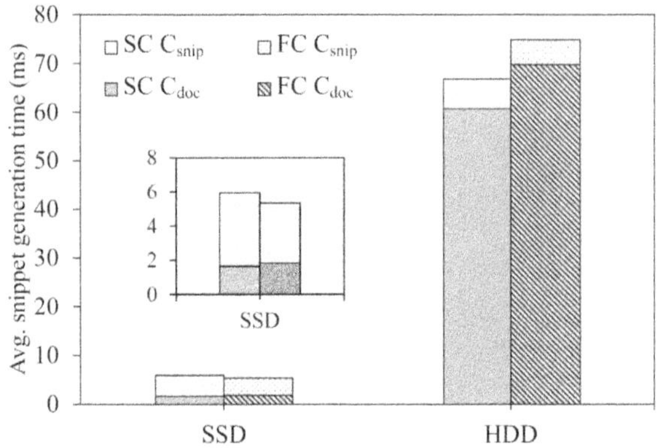

Figure 5: The latency of snippet processing and fragment processing under dynamic caching (LRU) on HDD-based and SSD-based search engine (cache size is 100).

caching with a snippet cache size of 200, i.e., 10 times as large. For snippet caching, snippet generation latency decreases when more memory is used to cache snippets. However the situation changes if fragment caching is used. The cached fragments occupy so much less memory space that even a substantially smaller fragment cache can cache most of the popular fragments. Consequently, allocating more memory to the fragment cache does not decrease C_{snip} significantly, but results in more document cache misses (due to document cache memory being reallocated as fragment cache memory) which results in an increased C_{doc}. Therefore, when the fragment cache size exceeds 100, we see the snippet generation latency increasing slightly as the fragment cache size increases. We conclude that when the query stream contains many distinct snippets that can not be held completely by the snippet/fragment cache, fragment caching will show its performance advantage.

Table 2 lists the cache hit ratios for snippet caching and fragment caching under dynamic caching with different snippet/fragment cache sizes. The hit ratio for snippet caching increases rapidly as more memory space is allocated to the snippet cache, whereas fragment caching achieves a high hit ratio even for substantially smaller cache sizes (a factor of 10 smaller). After the popular fragments have been cached in the fragment cache, increasing the cache size further does not improve its hit ratio substantially. With a fragment cache size of 200, fragment caching achieves the highest possible hit ratio, which indicates all the fragments except the unique ones have been cached. By contrast, snippet caching does not achieve this hit ratio even when the snippet cache size is 550. We conclude that fragment caching can achieve a high hit ratio while using a greatly smaller space than snippet caching.

We also briefly test these caching strategies on a 500GB WDC HDD (5400rpm). As expected, (a) regardless of the caching method used, we found a drastic reduction in latency in SSDs vs. HDDs, and (b) fragment caching results in far more document accessing than snippet caching, and performs worse (see Figure 5).

5. CONCLUSION

Many search engines servers are moving from hard disk drives (HDDs) to solid state drives (SSDs) to store masses of documents, largely due to SSDs massive advantage in I/O speed. In this work, we present a simple, yet effective caching method for compactly caching snippets, called fragment caching, which takes advantage of SSD-based hardware. Instead of caching whole snippets in memory, we instead cache snippet metadata which are used to retrieve the snippets from documents when required. This greatly reduces the memory required for caching, while the increased I/O is not a major concern on SSDs (as it is for HDDs).

6. ACKNOWLEDGEMENTS

This work is partially supported by NSF of China (61373018, 11301288, 11450110409), Program for New Century Excellent Talents in University (NCET130301) and the Fundamental Research Funds for the Central Universities (65141021).

7. REFERENCES

[1] R. A. Baeza-Yates, A. Gionis, F. Junqueira, V. Murdock, V. Plachouras, and F. Silvestri. The impact of caching on search engines. In *Proc. SIGIR*, pages 183–190, 2007.

[2] L. A. Barroso, J. Dean, and U. Hölzle. Web search for a planet: The google cluster architecture. *IEEE Micro*, 23(2):22–28, 2003.

[3] D. Ceccarelli, C. Lucchese, S. Orlando, R. Perego, and F. Silvestri. Caching query-biased snippets for efficient retrieval. In *Proc. EDBT*, pages 93–104, 2011.

[4] F. Chen, D. A. Koufaty, and X. Zhang. Understanding intrinsic characteristics and system implications of flash memory based solid state drives. In *Proc. SIGMETRICS*, pages 181–192, 2009.

[5] J. Dean. Challenges in building large-scale information retrieval systems: invited talk. In *Proc. WSDM*, page 1, 2009.

[6] C. Hoobin, S. J. Puglisi, and J. Zobel. Relative Lempel-Ziv factorization for efficient storage and retrieval of web collections. *Proc. VLDB Endowment*, 5(3):265–273, 2011.

[7] D. Liu, R. Li, X. Gu, K. Wen, H. He, and G. Gao. Fast snippet generation based on CPU-GPU hybrid system. In *Proc. ICPADS*, pages 252–259, 2011.

[8] J. Tong, G. Wang, and X. Liu. Latency-aware strategy for static list caching in flash-based web search engines. In *Proc. CIKM*, pages 1209–1212, 2013.

[9] Y. Tsegay, S. J. Puglisi, A. Turpin, and J. Zobel. Document compaction for efficient query biased snippet generation. In *Advances in Information Retrieval, ECIR*, pages 509–520, 2009.

[10] A. Turpin, Y. Tsegay, D. Hawking, and H. E. Williams. Fast generation of result snippets in web search. In *Proc. SIGIR*, pages 127–134, 2007.

[11] J. Wang, E. Lo, M. L. Yiu, J. Tong, G. Wang, and X. Liu. The impact of solid state drive on search engine cache management. In *Proc. SIGIR*, pages 693–702, 2013.

When Personalization Meets Conformity: Collective Similarity based Multi-Domain Recommendation

Xi Zhang[1], Jian Cheng[1], Shuang Qiu[1], Zhenfeng Zhu[2], Hanqing Lu[1]
[1]National Laboratory of Pattern Recognition, Institute of Automation, Chinese Academy of Sciences
[2]Institute of information Science, Beijing Jiaotong University
{xi.zhang, jcheng, shuang.qiu, luhq}@nlpr.ia.ac.cn, zhfzhu@bjtu.edu.cn

ABSTRACT

Existing recommender systems place emphasis on personalization to achieve promising accuracy. However, in the context of multiple domain, users are likely to seek the same behaviors as domain authorities. This conformity effect provides a wealth of prior knowledge when it comes to multi-domain recommendation, but has not been fully exploited. In particular, users whose behaviors are significant similar with the public tastes can be viewed as domain authorities. To detect these users meanwhile embed conformity into recommendation, a domain-specific similarity matrix is intuitively employed. Therefore, a collective similarity is obtained to leverage the conformity with personalization. In this paper, we establish a Collective Structure Sparse Representation(CSSR) method for multi-domain recommendation. Based on adaptive k-Nearest-Neighbor framework, we impose the lasso and group lasso penalties as well as least square loss to jointly optimize the collective similarity. Experimental results on real-world data confirm the effectiveness of the proposed method.

Categories and Subject Descriptors

H.3.3 [**Information Search and Retrieval**]: Information Filtering

Keywords

Multiple Domains; Recommendation; Conformity

1. INTRODUCTION

The fast growth of Web 2.0 technologies facilitates and encourages various online user behaviors, meanwhile brings tremendous information to the public. Personalized recommendation, as critical methods to push the right information to the right users, have attracted large amounts of research in both industry and academia. Among these methods, Collaborative Filtering(CF) has superior performance than other methods via an underlying assumption about entity similarity. Namely, users with common interests in the past would behave much more similarly on items in the future. Traditionally, CF approaches regard mining distinct types of user behavior as a task within a single domain. Nevertheless, in many real applications, multiple behaviors ranging from reading books, favoring music, to watching videos can reflect the characteristics of users together, and thus training a group of predictors in a unified manner would enhance accuracy for all the domains.

To cope with multi-domain recommendation, a straightforward scheme is to extend the CF algorithms into a multi-task learning problem solved by propagating similarities among domains [4, 2]. However, somewhat surprisingly, the context of multi-domain often introduces *conformity*[1] to online user behaviors, which cannot be ignored. In particular, the public are inclined to conform to the choices or beliefs of domain authorities [6]. For example, comments from well-known movie critics would be likely to affect the trend of box offices while reading lists of celebrated writers would probably receive admiration. That is to say, compared with ordinary users, opinions of these domain elites are more representative and thus have considerable influence on recommendation results. Unfortunately, this effect has not been fully exploited in existing multi-domain approaches.

The key problem becomes how to detect the domain authorities and integrate the conformity effect into recommendation. To simplify this problem, we concern that the elites are users whose past behaviors can largely reflect the public tastes. In fact, if a user has significant similar behaviors to a large number of other users, she/he is probably the elite user who can represent others. To this end, a domain-specific user similarity matrix based on observed behaviors is built to embody conformity. On the other hand, since users' intrinsic preferences over domains are also decisive, a domain-shared user similarity matrix is utilized to profile users globally. Therefore, a collective similarity combining the effect of conformity with the original personalization is established.

In this paper, we propose a Collective Structured Sparse Representation(CSSR) method to optimize the collective similarity for a top-N multi-domain recommendation task. The CSSR is on the basis of the adaptive k-Nearest-Neighbor framework. To learn ranked item lists under each domain for users, a least square regression loss of feedback representation is employed. To encode personalization and confor-

[1]The general conformity is a social phenomenon of matching attitudes, beliefs, and behaviors to group norm. Here we narrow the concept to achieving same behaviors as elites.

SIGIR'15, August 09 - 13, 2015, Santiago, Chile.
© 2015 ACM. ISBN 978-1-4503-3621-5/15/08 ...$15.00.
DOI: http://dx.doi.org/10.1145/2766462.2767810.

mity, regularization with lasso and group lasso are adopted. Also, we show how to use the Alternating Direction Method of Multipliers(ADMM) [1] to efficiently optimize the parameters. Experiments show that our method consistently achieves more accurate results than other state-of-the-arts.

2. THE PROPOSED APPROACH

2.1 Notation and Background

Suppose that there are a set of users $\mathcal{U} = \{u_1, \cdots, u_n\}$ and D types of domains. Let the matrix $\mathbf{X}_d \in \mathbb{R}^{m_d \times n}$ record the interactions between the overall user set and item set $\mathcal{V}_d$ for the d-th domain, where $d = 1, \cdots, D$ and m_d is the size of the item set. Then if a user has any behavior on item, the element entry of $\mathbf{X}_d$ could be 1 or a positive value, otherwise the entry is set as 0. Note that implicit feedback such as clicks, purchases and posts are easier to obtain than rating records in real-world scenarios. Thus we assume that the multiple feedback matrices are binary.

For a multiple domain recommendation, given a series of user-item feedback matrices $\{\mathbf{X}_1, \cdots, \mathbf{X}_D\}$, our goal is to recommend a personalized ranking list of the potential enjoyed items under each domain for users.

Here we introduce a general similarity based framework for recommendation without multi-domain. Normally, preference scores are estimated by a function of $f(\mathbf{X}, \Theta)$, where $\mathbf{X}$ is the feedback matrix and Θ is the model parameter. The adaptive k-Nearest-Neighbor(kNN) method, which is very popular for collaborative filtering, has been shown its simpleness but effectiveness in top-N recommendation [3]. We establish our model based on the adaptive kNN technique in this paper. Consider a user based kNN problem, the parameter Θ is set as matrix $\mathbf{W} \in \mathbb{R}^{n \times n}$, and the prediction function $f(\cdot)$ could be presented as an aggregation of the feedback values of k nearest neighbors. Mathematically, $\widehat{x}_{ij} = \mathbf{x}_i^T \mathbf{w}_j$, where $\widehat{x}_{ij}$ is the predicted scores, $\mathbf{x}_i \in \mathbb{R}^n$ denotes the feedback indicator of item v_i, and $\mathbf{w}_j \in \mathbb{R}^n$ denotes a similarity coefficients of user u_j. The parameter $\mathbf{W}$ can be regarded as the similarity between user pairs, which can be optimized by the following problem

$$\widetilde{\mathbf{W}} = \arg\min_{\mathbf{W}} \mathcal{L}(\mathbf{W}) + \Omega(\mathbf{W}) \tag{1}$$

where $\mathcal{L}$ is a loss function usually defined as least squares or logistic regression, and Ω is a regularization penalty to enforce parameter with specific structures. Ridge, lasso, or elastic net regularization has been used in previous methods.

2.2 Collective Similarity

Now we consider the problem of multi-domain recommendation. As the user set is common across domains, the user based similarity is exploited. The interpretation behind the idea is simple. That is, to learn a set of nearest neighbors who are sufficiently similar with the user in terms of multiple behaviors over domains. In other words, a user's interests can be represented by the set of her/his neighbors. The usual approach assumes that all users are ordinary with the comparative ability of representation and thus the personalized neighbors are mined for each users independently. Nevertheless, conformity always occurs in the context of multi-domain. Under a specific domain, elite users' favorites are more acceptable to the public during recommendation. This indicates that the similarity coefficients between these

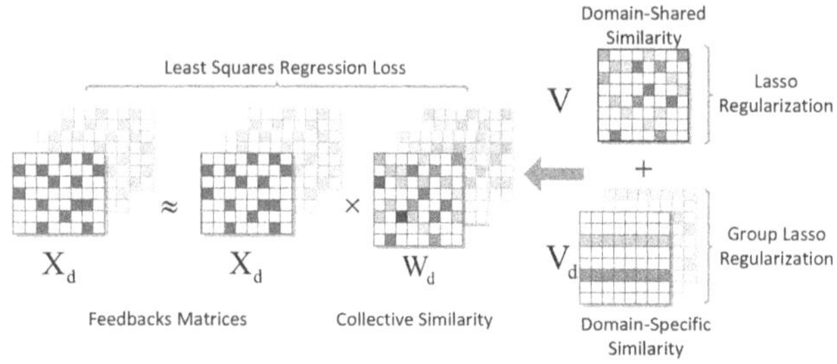

Figure 1: Illustration of the CSSR Model

representative elite users and others tend to be significant. Hence, we propose a collective similarity as

$$\mathbf{W}_d = \mathbf{V} + \mathbf{V}_d \tag{2}$$

where $d = 1, \cdots, D$. Parameter matrix $\mathbf{V} \in \mathbb{R}^{n \times n}$ indicates the personalized neighbors with intrinsic similar interest across domains, which is a domain-shared component. Parameter matrix $\mathbf{V}_d \in \mathbb{R}^{n \times n}$ embodies the representative of elite neighbors in the domain, which is a domain-specific component.

Next, we seek to explore the conformity by regularizing the structure of the parameter set $\{\mathbf{V}_1, \cdots, \mathbf{V}_D\}$ with group lasso. On the one hand, the domain-specific elite users can largely represent other users, which results in more dense for the corresponding rows in $\mathbf{V}_d$. On the other hand, the fact that elite users are always the minority leads to the sparsity in columns. Hence, the above structure serves to define a group lasso regularization term

$$\Omega_{glas}(\mathbf{V}_d) = \beta_d \|\mathbf{V}_d\|_{2,1} = \sum_{i=1}^{n} \beta_d \|\mathbf{v}_d^i\|_2 \tag{3}$$

where $\|\mathbf{v}_d^i\|_2$ is the ℓ_2-norm for each row of $\mathbf{V}_d$. $\ell_{2,1}$-norm encourages the row sparsity with jointly selecting the significant rows as elite users. β_d encodes the contributions of group lasso for each domain. Without loss of generality, we assume $\forall d, \beta_d = \beta$.

Furthermore, users' personalized neighbors are also sparse in the overall user set. A lasso constraint is utilized to filter out noised coefficients in $\mathbf{V}$, which is

$$\Omega_{las}(\mathbf{V}) = \lambda \|\mathbf{V}\|_1 = \sum_{i=1}^{n} \sum_{j=1}^{n} \lambda |v_{ij}| \tag{4}$$

With above discussion, the collective similarity can be incorporated into a loss function with a least square loss as $\mathcal{L}(\mathbf{W}_d) = \frac{1}{2}\|\mathbf{X}_d - \mathbf{X}_d\mathbf{W}_d\|_F^2$. Following the general framework in Eq. (1), we propose a CSSR model for adaptive kNN problem in multiple domains as

$$\begin{aligned} &\min_{\Theta} \sum_{d=1}^{D} \alpha_d \left(\mathcal{L}(\mathbf{W}_d) + \Omega_{glas}(\mathbf{V}_d)\right) + \Omega_{las}(\mathbf{V}) \\ &s.t. \mathbf{W}_d = \mathbf{V} + \mathbf{V}_d, \mathbf{W}_d \geq 0, \mathbf{diag}(\mathbf{W}_d) = 0 \\ &\quad \forall d, \quad d = 1, \cdots, D \end{aligned} \tag{5}$$

The parameter set Θ is written as $\{\mathbf{W}_d, \mathbf{V}_d, \mathbf{V}\}$ for succinct. And α_d balances the effect of different domain. In addition, the non-negative constraint is used on similarity for a more interpretable consideration, while $\mathbf{diag}(\mathbf{W}_d) = 0$ ensures that the trivial solution of identity matrix is avoided. From the unified objective function, information of feedback matrices can be transferred among domains by $\mathbf{V}$ and distinctions can be captured by $\mathbf{V}_d$. The entire model is depicted in Figure 1.

2.3 Optimization

Although non-smooth terms are introduced, our approach maintains convexity of the objective function. We propose to apply the ADMM [1] to split the original problem into several subproblems which can be handled in alternating directions.

To solve the problem in Eq. (5), we first obtain the augmented Lagrangian as

$$\min_{\Theta, \mathbf{Y}_d} \sum_{d=1}^{D} \alpha_d \left(\mathcal{L}(\mathbf{W}_d) + \mathcal{I}_+(\mathbf{W}_d) + \Omega_{glas}(\mathbf{V}_d)\right) + \Omega_{las}(\mathbf{V}) + \sum_{d=1}^{D} \left(tr(\mathbf{Y}_d^T(\mathbf{W}_d - \mathbf{V} - \mathbf{V}_d)) + \frac{\rho}{2}\|\mathbf{W}_d - \mathbf{V} - \mathbf{V}_d\|_F^2 \right) \tag{6}$$

where $\mathbf{Y}_d$ is Lagrangian multiplier of the d-th domain, $\mathcal{I}_+(\cdot)$ is the indicator function for the non-negative constraint, and $\rho > 0$ is a penalty parameter. For the given domain d, optimizing $\{\mathbf{W}_d, \mathbf{V}_d, \mathbf{Y}_d\}$ are independent with optimizing the set of variables in other domains, thus ADMM proceeds by solving following problems alternately until convergence

$$\min_{\mathbf{W}_d \geq 0} \alpha_d \mathcal{L}(\mathbf{W}_d) + \frac{\rho}{2}\|\mathbf{W}_d - \mathbf{V} - \mathbf{V}_d + \mathbf{U}_d\|_F^2 \tag{7a}$$

$$\min_{\mathbf{V}_d} \alpha_d \Omega_{glas}(\mathbf{V}_d) + \frac{\rho}{2}\|\mathbf{W}_d - \mathbf{V} - \mathbf{V}_d + \mathbf{U}_d\|_F^2 \tag{7b}$$

$$\min_{\mathbf{V}} \Omega_{las}(\mathbf{V}) + \frac{\rho}{2}\sum_{d=1}^{D} \|\mathbf{W}_d - \mathbf{V} - \mathbf{V}_d + \mathbf{U}_d\|_F^2 \tag{7c}$$

$$\mathbf{U}_d = \mathbf{U}_d + \mathbf{W}_d - \mathbf{V} - \mathbf{V}_d \tag{7d}$$

where $\mathbf{U}_d = \frac{1}{\rho}\mathbf{Y}_d$ leads to a scaled form. Then we provide closed-form solutions of the subproblems for Eq.(7a), Eq.(7b) and Eq.(7c) as below.

Update for $\mathbf{W}_d$. We first rewrite the problem into an unconstrained problem as

$$\min_{\mathbf{W}_d} \alpha_d \mathcal{L}(\mathbf{W}_d) + \frac{\rho}{2}\|\mathbf{W}_d - \mathbf{V} - \mathbf{V}_d + \mathbf{U}_d\|_F^2 - tr(\Phi_d^T \mathbf{W}_d) \tag{8}$$

Since Eq.(7a) is smooth, the solution can be found by taking its derivative and set it to be zero

$$\left(\mathbf{X}_d^T \mathbf{X}_d + \rho \mathbf{I}\right) \mathbf{W}_d + \rho(\mathbf{U}_d - \mathbf{V} - \mathbf{V}_d) - \mathbf{X}_d^T \mathbf{X}_d - \Phi_d = 0 \tag{9}$$

Using the Karush-Kuhn-Tucker complementary condition for the nonnegativity of $\mathbf{W}_d$, $[\Phi_d]_{ij}[\mathbf{W}_d]_{ij} = 0$, we get

$$[\mathbf{W}_d]_{ij} = [\mathbf{W}_d]_{ij} \sqrt{\frac{\left[\mathbf{X}_d^T \mathbf{X}_d + \rho(\mathbf{U}_d - \mathbf{V} - \mathbf{V}_d)^-\right]_{ij}}{\left[(\mathbf{X}_d^T \mathbf{X}_d + \rho \mathbf{I})\mathbf{W}_d + \rho(\mathbf{U}_d - \mathbf{V} - \mathbf{V}_d)^+\right]_{ij}}} \tag{10}$$

To guarantee the nonnegativity, we decompose matrices with any signs as $\mathbf{A} = \mathbf{A}^+ - \mathbf{A}^-$, where $\mathbf{A}_{ij}^+ = (|\mathbf{A}_{ij}| + \mathbf{A}_{ij})/2$ and $\mathbf{A}_{ij}^- = (|\mathbf{A}_{ij}| - \mathbf{A}_{ij})/2$.

Update for $\mathbf{V}_d$. For each row of $\mathbf{V}_d$, the optimization problem in Eq.(7b) comes to

$$\min_{\mathbf{v}_d^i} \beta\|\mathbf{v}_d^i\|_2 + \frac{\rho}{2}\|\mathbf{v}_d^i - (\mathbf{w}_d^i - \mathbf{v}^i + \mathbf{u}_d^i)\|_2^2 \tag{11}$$

where i is the row index of parameter matrices. Let $\mathbf{z}_d^i = \mathbf{w}_d^i - \mathbf{v}^i + \mathbf{u}_d^i$. This problem can be solved by a proximal operator of group lasso to each row vector as

$$\mathbf{v}_d^i = S_{glas, \frac{\beta}{\rho}}(\mathbf{z}_d^i) = \begin{cases} 0, & \text{if } \|\mathbf{z}_d^i\|_2 \leq \frac{\beta}{\rho} \\ \frac{\|\mathbf{z}_d^i\|_2 - \frac{\beta}{\rho}}{\|\mathbf{z}_d^i\|_2}\mathbf{z}_d^i, & \text{otherwise.} \end{cases} \tag{12}$$

Update for $\mathbf{V}$. Optimizing the second term with respect to $\mathbf{V}$ in Eq.(7c) equals to optimizing $\frac{\rho}{2}\|\mathbf{V} - \frac{1}{D}\sum_{d=1}^{D}(\mathbf{W}_d - \mathbf{V}_d + \mathbf{U}_d)\|_F^2$ which can be substituted into Eq.(7c). Then we have the element-wise optimal solution as

$$[\mathbf{V}]_{ij} = S_{\text{las}, \frac{\lambda}{\rho}}\left(\left[\frac{1}{D}\sum_{d=1}^{D}(\mathbf{W}_d - \mathbf{V}_d + \mathbf{U}_d)\right]_{ij}\right) \tag{13}$$

where $S_{\text{las},\varepsilon}(\cdot)$ is the soft-thresholding operator

$$S_{\text{las},\varepsilon}(x) = \begin{cases} x - \varepsilon, & \text{if } x > \varepsilon \\ x + \varepsilon, & \text{if } x < -\varepsilon \\ 0, & \text{otherwise.} \end{cases} \tag{14}$$

3. EXPERIMENTS

3.1 Experiment Settings

To empirically study the effectiveness of our method, we perform experiments on a multi-domain dataset crawled from the publicly available site Douban[2]. It is a famous Web2.0 website containing rating behavior of users, scaled from 1 to 5 stars, on books, music and movies. As we face with a top-N recommendation task, we use the implicit feedback instead of rating scores. For a sufficient evaluation of each user, we filtering out users with less than 10 feedbacks on the three domains and obtained a dataset of 5,916 users. The detailed description is presented in Table 1.

Table 1: Description of Douban Dataset

Domain	#Items	%Sparsity	#Ratings per User
Book	14,155	99.85	22
Music	15,492	99.75	38
Movie	7,845	98.87	88

For personalized item recommendation, we analyze performance of the model by comparing the top suggestions to the true behaviors taken by a user. We adopt two widely used evaluation metrics in top-N recommendation: MAP(Mean Average Precision), NDCG(Normalized Discounted Cumulative Gain) with the setting $N = 5$. Higher values on the metrics imply better recommendation results.

We compare the proposed CSSR with several popular baseline methods: PopRank, NCDCF_U, NCDCF_I [5], mrBPR [2], mrSLIM. Here we extend SLIM [3] to mrSLIM by constructing a feedback matrix that takes all items in three domains as rows. For a comprehensive comparison, performances of CSSRsh and CSSRsp are shown. They merely consider the domain-shared or domain-specific similarity in Eq. (2), and utilize lasso constrains.

In our experiments, we randomly pick 80% observed feedbacks for each user to form the training set in each domain and the rest of 20% is test set. The random sampling is repeated 10 times and the average performance are reported. We set the weights combination of domains in CSSR as

[2]http://www.douban.com

Table 2: Prediction performance(mean ± std.) of three variants of CSSR and PopRank, NCDCF_U, NCDCF_I, mrSLIM, mrBPR on three domains of Douban dataset. Results in bold indicate the best ones.

Methods	Params		Book		Music		Movie	
			MAP	NDCG	MAP	NDCG	MAP	NDCG
PopRank		N/A	$0.1370_{\pm 0.0039}$	$0.0619_{\pm 0.0014}$	$0.1879_{\pm 0.0029}$	$0.0922_{\pm 0.0014}$	$0.3784_{\pm 0.0031}$	$0.2249_{\pm 0.0017}$
NCDCF_U	-	100	$0.1826_{\pm 0.0033}$	$0.0813_{\pm 0.0013}$	$0.2647_{\pm 0.0035}$	$0.1325_{\pm 0.0015}$	$0.4982_{\pm 0.0038}$	$0.3159_{\pm 0.0024}$
NCDCF_I	-	50	$0.1864_{\pm 0.0029}$	$0.0835_{\pm 0.0011}$	$0.2668_{\pm 0.0016}$	$0.1341_{\pm 0.0007}$	$0.5049_{\pm 0.0047}$	$0.3230_{\pm 0.0027}$
mrSLIM	5	0.1	$0.2014_{\pm 0.0035}$	$0.0906_{\pm 0.0013}$	$0.2861_{\pm 0.0028}$	$0.1453_{\pm 0.0022}$	$0.5115_{\pm 0.0040}$	$0.3241_{\pm 0.0023}$
mrBPR	0.01	1e-3	$0.2333_{\pm 0.0035}$	$0.1071_{\pm 0.0019}$	$0.3180_{\pm 0.0037}$	$0.1554_{\pm 0.0021}$	$0.5206_{\pm 0.0039}$	$0.3377_{\pm 0.0025}$
CSSRsh	-	0.01	$0.2217_{\pm 0.0023}$	$0.1013_{\pm 0.0010}$	$0.2949_{\pm 0.0028}$	$0.1453_{\pm 0.0011}$	$0.4952_{\pm 0.0055}$	$0.3106_{\pm 0.0026}$
CSSRsp	-	0.01	$0.2348_{\pm 0.0041}$	$0.1070_{\pm 0.0019}$	$0.3020_{\pm 0.0046}$	$0.1539_{\pm 0.0022}$	$0.5052_{\pm 0.0029}$	$0.3241_{\pm 0.0020}$
CSSR	0.5	0.01	$\mathbf{0.2746}_{\pm 0.0032}$	$\mathbf{0.1241}_{\pm 0.0013}$	$\mathbf{0.3345}_{\pm 0.0037}$	$\mathbf{0.1703}_{\pm 0.0014}$	$\mathbf{0.5341}_{\pm 0.0030}$	$\mathbf{0.3471}_{\pm 0.0015}$

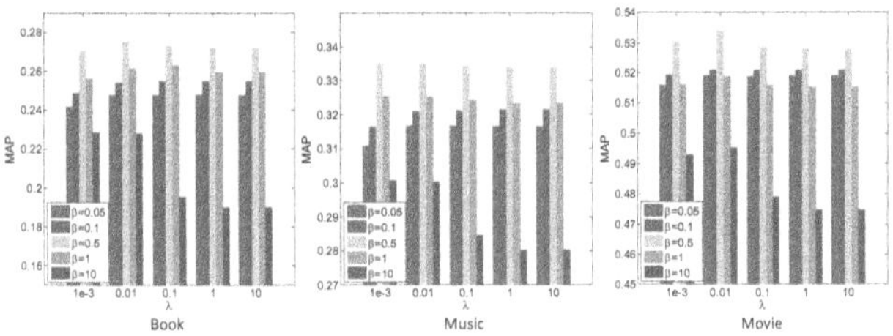

Figure 2: Performance variation of CSSR with respect to β and λ on three domains.

$\{\alpha_1 = 0.2, \alpha_2 = 0.3, \alpha_3 = 0.5\}$ based on the MAP performance on the test set. The impact of group lasso parameter β and lasso parameter λ will be further studied.

3.2 Results and Analysis

Experimental results of above baselines and three variants of the proposed CSSR are shown in Table 2. The optimal parameters we obtained for CSSR are $\beta = 0.5, \lambda = 0.01$. From Table 2 we observed that, our full model CSSR consistently outperforms all the other baselines. Specifically, for the reason that PopRank is not a personalized algorithm and only recommends items based on their popularity, all other baselines can beat it. This proves the importance of personalization in recommender systems. By comparing the results along with three domains, we discover that recommending movies is a relatively easier task as all the approaches except PopRank perform well on this domain. Thereby, transferring knowledge from movie domain would benefit the other two tasks. Lacking of a properly designed mechanism for multi-task learning, NCDCF_U and NCDCF_I (with the number of nearest neighbors $k = 100$ and $k = 50$) cannot achieve satisfying results in book and music domains. We implement mrSLIM by setting the weights of elastic net as $\beta = 5$ and $\lambda = 0.1$ to find an optimal performance. With the learned item similarity matrix, mrSLIM behaves better than its simple version NCDCF_I. Moveover, CSSR surpasses the state-of-the-art ranking method mrBPR with the learning rate as 0.01 and the weights of ℓ_2-norm as $1e-3$. mrBPR focuses on studying the domain consistency to model a sharing component, but ignores the heterogeneous part which might be different in domains, in particular, conformity.

To evaluate the effectiveness of collective similarity, we compare the three variants of CSSR. CSSRsh and CSSRsp encode consistency and heterogeneous among domains under the adaptive kNN settings, separately. However, the results show that they obtain improvement on Book and Music domains but fail to outperform previous methods in Movie domain. Integrating different aspect of the two variants, our method yields the best performance in multiple domains.

Finally, to understand the influence of regularization terms, we analyze the performance variations with respect to λ and β. As illustrated in Fig.2, by fixing α, the performance first increases when β gets larger. This verifies our conformity assumption that some users are representative and could be detected by enforcing a group lasso structure. But overwhelmingly large β would cause information loss in domains and result in the accuracy declining. By fixing β, we can see that the α is less sensitive. Another interesting observation is when β is improperly large($\beta = 10$), decreasing α can upgrade results to some extent. This indicates some missing information of domain-specific component could be compensated by domain-shared component.

4. CONCLUSIONS

In this paper, we propose a novel CSSR method for multi-domain recommendation, which integrates personalization with conformity effect to construct a collective similarity parameter. By applying the least square loss, ranking scores can be predicted by the optimized neighbors. To model the different kind of neighbors, lasso and group lasso constraints are used. Experiments on multi-domain dataset show our method outperforms baselines for top-N recommendation.

5. REFERENCES

[1] S. Boyd, N. Parikh, E. Chu, B. Peleato, and J. Eckstein. Distributed optimization and statistical learning via the alternating direction method of multipliers. *Found. Trends Mach. Learn.*, 2011.

[2] A. Krohn-Grimberghe, L. Drumond, C. Freudenthaler, and L. Schmidt-Thieme. Multi-relational matrix factorization using bayesian personalized ranking for social network data. In *WSDM*, 2012.

[3] X. Ning and G. Karypis. SLIM: Sparse linear models for top-n recommender systems. In *ICDM*, 2011.

[4] A. P. Singh and G. J. Gordon. Relational learning via collective matrix factorization. In *KDD*, 2008.

[5] T. Yuan, J. Cheng, X. Zhang, S. Qiu, and H. Lu. Recommendation by mining multiple user behaviors with group sparsity. In *AAAI*, 2014.

[6] X. Zhang, J. Cheng, T. Yuan, B. Niu, and H. Lu. Toprec: domain-specific recommendation through community topic mining in social network. 2013.

Sub-document Timestamping of Web Documents

Yue Zhao and Claudia Hauff
Web Information Systems, Delft University of Technology, The Netherlands
{y.zhao-1,c.hauff@tudelft.nl}

ABSTRACT

Knowledge about a (Web) document's creation time has been shown to be an important factor in various *temporal information retrieval* settings. Commonly, it is assumed that such documents were created at a single point in time. While this assumption may hold for news articles and similar document types, it is a clear oversimplification for general Web documents. In this paper, we investigate to what extent (i) this simplifying assumption is violated for a corpus of Web documents, and, (ii) it is possible to accurately estimate the creation time of individual Web documents' components (so-called *sub-documents*).

Categories and Subject Descriptors: H.3.3 Information Storage and Retrieval: Information Search and Retrieval
Keywords: timestamping; sub-documents; Web archiving

1. INTRODUCTION

Accurately estimating at what point in time a (Web) document has originally been created is of importance for a number of applications, including the tracking of ideas over time, the detection of copied content, and temporal information retrieval (IR) — for some topics users might prefer to be served older Web documents, while for others users may prefer more recently created content.
Current research in Web-document based temporal IR usually considers either the documents' creation timestamp (i.e. when the document first appeared on the Web) or the extracted content timestamps (i.e. which time periods the document contains information about) as a raw signal to be included in retrieval models [2]. In this work we focus on the creation time of Web documents. Previous work, e.g. [9, 5, 8], has made the simplifying assumption that each Web document d_i has been created at one moment in time t_i and t_i can either be approximated by the first time the document (its URL) was crawled or by the first/oldest timestamp appearing in the document content. On the Web this is a highly unrealistic assumption — documents are constantly altered and updated, a classic example being blogs, which contain many different "sub-documents" (blog entries) created at different points in time. While the different sub-documents of a blog page may be easy to timestamp, for many other types of Web documents this is harder.
Thus, in this work, we aim to arrive at a first understanding of *sub-document timestamping*. Specifically, we empirically investigate the following two research themes:

RT1: To what extent do Web documents consist of sub-documents created at different times? What kind of documents contain two or more sub-documents? What is the timespan between the oldest and most recent sub-document of a document?

RT2: To what extent are we able to classify each sub-document as either having been created within the past month (relative to the document crawl time), within the past year or more than m years ago? What document features are most useful in the classification? Which type of sub-documents can we most accurately identify?

We investigate a subset of documents from the ClueWeb12 corpus[1] and date each document's paragraphs (a paragraph is a sub-document) individually based on historic Web crawl data collected from the Internet Archive[2] (IA).

Having dated all sub-documents, we first analyse this corpus of sub-documents before turning towards estimating the creation time of each sub-document with a standard machine learning pipeline.
We find that **two thirds** of the investigated Web documents (66.5%) do indeed contain sub-documents created at different points in time. More importantly, we also find a large gap between the oldest and most recently created sub-document (**1052 days on average**), indicating that relying on a single creation timestamp per document provides at best a very distorted picture of the true creation times. Classifying sub-documents according to their creation time using only sub-document internal features is possible with more than 66% of instances correctly classified.

2. RELATED WORK

Document creation timestamps are used in different temporal IR settings, such as timeline construction [11, 5], improving retrieval relevance [10, 8] and the estimation of a document's focus time [7].
A few existing works aim to infer the creation timestamps of document. De Jong et al. [4] built temporal language mod-

[1] `http://www.lemurproject.org/clueweb12.php/`
[2] `https://archive.org/`

SIGIR'15, August 09 - 13, 2015, Santiago, Chile.
© 2015 ACM. ISBN 978-1-4503-3621-5/15/08 ...$15.00.
DOI: http://dx.doi.org/10.1145/2766462.2767803.

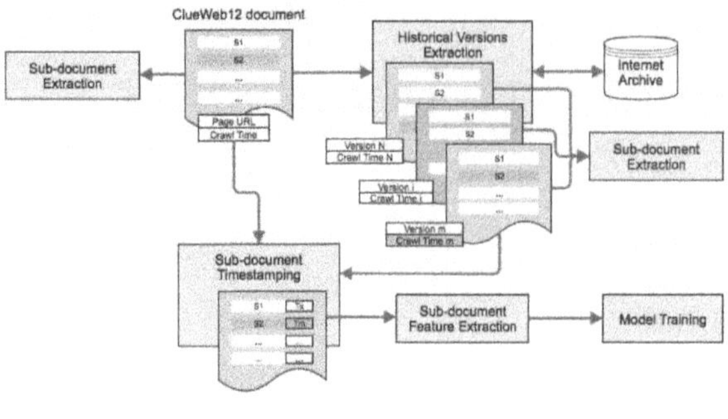

Figure 1: Overview of our processing pipeline for sub-document timestamping.

els from existing newspaper articles across a range of years and tagged non-timestamped articles based on the likelihood of being generated by a particular model. Kanhabua et al. [9] improve the temporal language model by using word interpolation, temporal entropy and external search statistics. They rely on documents recorded on the IA for their experiments, with the document's creation time being the first recorded crawl within the IA. Chambers et al. [3] use machine learning to infer documents' cration timestamps based on the temporal expressions by leveraging the MaxEnt model and additional time constraints. Ge et al. [6] propose an event-based time label propagation model by using the relationship between events and documents (exploiting the fact that news articles are often about events).
All these works infer a single creation time per document. In fact, most works [4, 9, 3, 6] rely on news corpora, which by design are rarely (or never) updated and usually contain an easily accessible creation timestamp. For *general Web documents*, there is little research work on inferring the sub-document creation timestamps. We attempt to fill this gap with our work.

3. APPROACH

To investigate our research questions we require a set of Web documents for which to determine the sub-document creation times. Instead of randomly sampling Web documents, we rely on the 11,075 relevant documents D_{rel} available for the ClueWeb12 corpus (topics topics 201-300), which consists of more than 700 million English Web documents and was crawled between 02/2012 and 05/2012. We thus investigate documents that are at least relevant to some information needs based on their textual content, avoiding Web spam documents and Web documents that contain very little to no text in the process.

Historical Versions Extraction In Fig. 1 we present an overview of our pipeline. For each document in D_{rel} (identified through its URL), we retrieve all available historic versions from the IA, which began archiving Web documents in 1996. 7118 of the documents in D_{rel} contain at least one historic version. We continue our processing with those documents only ($D_{rel}^{archived}$). On average we are able to identify 17 historic versions per document in $D_{rel}^{archived}$.

Sub-document Extraction In the second step we identify the different sub-documents of each document $d_i \in D_{rel}^{archived}$ as well as the sub-documents of d_i's m historic versions $Hist_i = \{d_i^{h_1}, d_i^{h_2}, ..., d_i^{h_m}\}$ where h_1 is the most recent archived version of d_i (most recent but older than d_i's crawl date) and h_m is the oldest available version. In order to split a Web document d_i into k sub-documents $d_i = \{s_{1,i}, s_{2,i}, .., s_{k,i}\}$, we parse d_i's HTML. A sub-document is then a fraction split by tags `<p>` or `<div>`, which contains at least 50 non-markup characters. We empirically found this process to be a simple but robust mechanism to identify sub-documents. The number of sub-documents identified are on average 39 per document (median 21).

Sub-document Timestamping Let $Hist_i^{subdocs}$ be the set of all sub-documents created across *all* historic versions of document d_i. Then, for each sub-document $s_{i,j}$ of d_i we determine all matching (using approximate string matching) elements in $Hist_i^{subdocs}$ and assign to $s_{i,j}$ the creation timestamp of the oldest historic sub-document we found.

F1	Starting position of $s_{k,i}$ within d_i
F2	Number of terms in $s_{k,i}$
F3	Relative length of $s_{k,i}$: $\frac{\text{length of } s_{k,i}}{\text{length of } d_i}$
F4	Character distance between last position of $s_{k-1,i}$ and starting position of $s_{k,i}$
F5	Character distance between last position of $s_{k,i}$ and starting position of $s_{k+1,i}$
F6	Number of sentences in $s_{k,i}$
F7	Number of terms in the longest sentence in $s_{k,i}$
F8	Number of terms in the shortest sentence in $s_{k,i}$
F9	Average sentence length in $s_{k,i}$
F10	Number of temporal expressions in $s_{k,i}$
F11	Number of temporal expressions appearing before $s_{k,i}$
F12	Number of *Dates* in $s_{k,i}$
F13	Number of *Durations* in $s_{k,i}$
F14	Number of *Times* in $s_{k,i}$
F15	Number of *Sets* in $s_{k,i}$
F16	Difference in days between 1/1/1996 and the earliest temporal expression in $s_{k,i}$
F17	Difference in days between 1/1/1996 and the most recent temporal expression in $s_{k,i}$
F18	Difference in days between 1/1/1996 and the temporal expression in $s_{k,i}$ being closest to d_i's crawl time
F19	Difference in days between the earliest and most recent temporal expressions in $s_{k,i}$
F20	Average number of characters between the appearance of temporal expressions in $s_{k,i}$
F21	Longest character distance between the appearance of temporal expressions in $s_{k,i}$

Table 1: Features derived for sub-document $s_{k,i} \in d_i$. All features are based on the non-markup content.

Model Training Having identified for each sub-document its creation time, we now derive a set of 21 features in order to investigate **RQ2**. We restrict ourselves to document-internal features only.
The features are listed in Tab. 1. All features are based on the non-markup content extracted for a particular sub-document. While features F1 to F9 gather basic paragraph and sentence statistics, features F10 to F21 are based on the temporal expressions (TEs) we extract from a sub-document[3]. TEs can be classified into four different categories, depending on the specificity of the information: [F12] *Date* (e.g. *Feb. 18, 2015*), [F13] *Duration* (e.g. *from 1996 to 2012*), [F14] *Time* (e.g. *1pm*) and [F15] *Set* (e.g. *every weekend*). Since the focus of our work is an exploratory analysis of sub-document timestamping, we chose an established classifier with fixed parameter settings (Random Forest [1] with 5 features per tree and 100 trees in total) instead of experimenting with different algorithms and configurations.
We train & test the classifier on the 277K pairs of (*sub-document, sub-document creation timestamp*). We distinguish 5 classes and annotate each pair accordingly depending on the difference between a sub-document $s_{k,i}$'s creation time and the

[3]TEs are extracted with the SUTime tagger: `http://nlp.stanford.edu/software/sutime.shtml`.

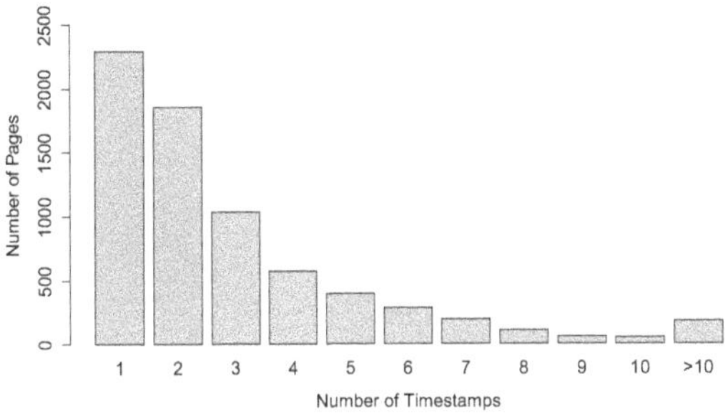

Figure 2: Overview of the number of documents containing content created at different points in time.

page crawl time of d_i[4]. We use the following five intervals: $A = [0, 20.5], B = (20.5, 311.5], C = (311.5, 973.5], D = (973.5, 2183.5]$ and $E = (2183.5, \infty)$. That is, class A contains those sub-documents created within the first 20 days of the page crawl time, while class E contains those sub-documents created more than 6 years before the page was actually crawled. We chose these interval settings to create a balanced data-set: each class has ~55K instances.

In a second set of experiments we consider a subset of all instances, namely those 120K in which each sub-document contains at least one TE, as we aim to investigate the effect TEs have on the accuracy of the classification.

We employed the classifier to predict into which class a particular sub-document falls in a 10-fold cross-validation setup.

4. RESULTS

Sub-document timestamps.

Let us first consider **RT1** and the question to what extent sub-document timestamping is actually an issue on the Web. In Fig. 2 we plot the number of documents within $D_{rel}^{archived}$ and the number of *different* timestamps we assigned to their respective sub-documents. Overall, 62.5% of documents have between 2 and 8 creation timestamps; very few documents contain content created at eight or more different times (4%).

Since not only the number of different creation timestamps a document possesses, but also the time interval between the timestamps is important, in Fig. 3 we present the average difference (in days) between the oldest and most recent creation timestamp of a document, with the document set partitioned according to the total number of creation timestamps found in a document. For documents with two creation timestamps, the median difference is 400 days, i.e. 50% of those documents contain content created more than one year apart.

Considering these numbers we next investigate how much content is created at different points in time. For each document $d_i = \{s_{1,i}, s_{2,i}, .., s_{k,i}\} \in D_{rel}^{archived}$ with 2, 3 or 4 creation timestamps we determined what fraction of document content was created when. The results are shown in Fig. 4. Here, we consider all sub-documents (i.e. the non-markup text) of d_i as 100% of the content and compute what percentage of text was existing at each creation timestamp.

[4]We assume that in practice a page's crawl time is usually available (as is the case for the ClueWeb12 corpus)

This is a simplification of how Web documents are maintained (content might also be updated, deleted and added again over time). However, since we use the content of d_i as our starting point, we are only interested in the time a particular sub-document of d_i was first created. The graph shows that most content is created initially — for documents with 2 creation timestamps, on average 78% of the content is available after the first version of the document. For documents with 3 and 4 creation timestamps, 68% and 55% of content are created initially. Interestingly, the amount of content added in subsequent creation timestamps is roughly the same.

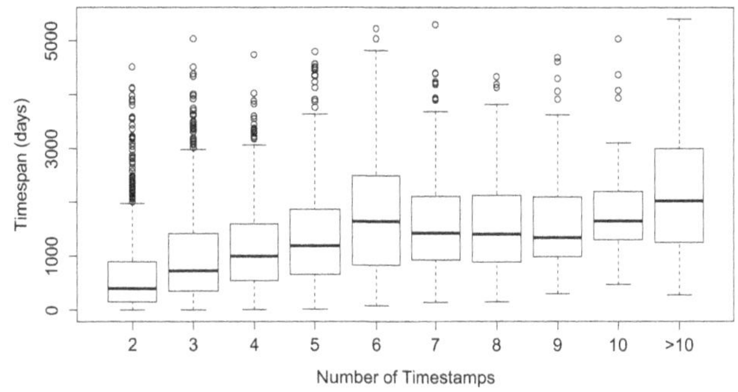

Figure 3: The document set $D_{rel}^{archived}$ is partitioned according to the number of creation timestamps (documents with a single creation timestamp are ignored). Shown is the difference (in days) between the oldest and most recent creation timestamp.

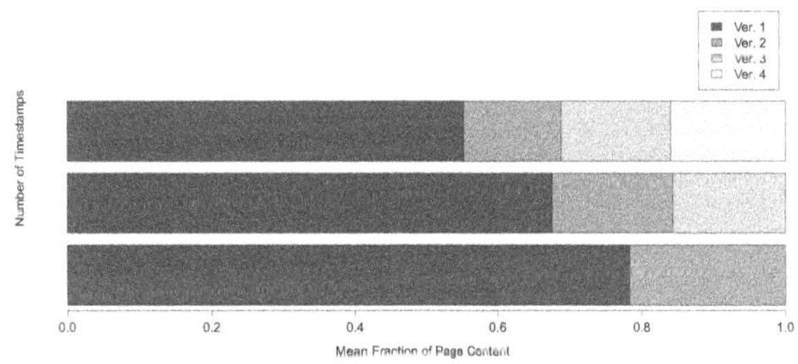

Figure 4: The document set $D_{rel}^{archived}$ is partitioned according to the number of creation timestamps (documents with a single creation timestamp are ignored). A bar shows the mean fraction of content available at each creation timestamp for documents with 2, 3 and 4 creation timestamps. *Ver. 1* indicates the content created at the oldest timestamp, *Ver. 2* the content created at the second oldest timestamp and so on.

Finally, we consider whether or not different information needs (topics) attract different kinds of documents, i.e. documents with few or many creation timestamps. Fig. 5 shows the distribution of documents with differing creation times for the 25 ClueWeb12 TREC adhoc topics with the largest number of relevant documents (the median number of relevant documents is 126). The results show that for most topics a relatively large percentage of relevant documents contain two or more creation timestamps. If we were able to predict what type of topics favour what kind of documents (a single creation time vs. several) we could employ these

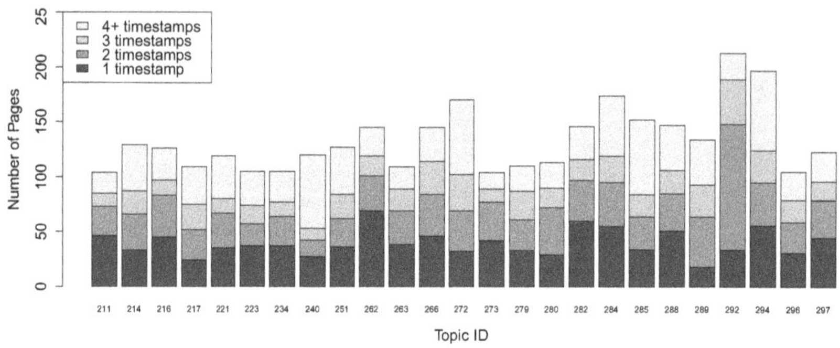

Figure 5: Overview of the relevant documents per TREC topic and the amount of creation timestamps.

	#Instances	Method	Misclassified	F-Measure / Class A	B	C	D	E
Entire Data Set	277,973	RF	33.73%	0.68	0.61	0.60	0.64	0.76
Data Set with TEs only	120,620	RF	33.12%	0.69	0.59	0.58	0.63	0.79
Data Set with TEs only	120,620	BL: earliest TE	60.90%	0.42	0.28	0.21	0.36	0.56
Data Set with TEs only	120,620	BL: latest TE	63.76%	0.33	0.29	0.19	0.36	0.50

Table 2: Effectiveness of our sub-document timestamp classification pipeline. ***RF*** **refers to the Random Forest setup, while** ***BL*** **indicates the baseline, using a single feature only (oldest/most recent temporal expression appearing in the sub-document).**

creation time-based signals in a retrieval ranking function (a direction of future work).

Predicting Sub-document Timestamps.

Our vision is to eventually develop techniques that are reliably able to tag any Web page's sub-documents with an accurate estimate of their creation time. To answer the questions raised in **RT2**, we consider the results of the creation timestamp classification experiments in Tab. 2. The Random Forest (RF) classifier classifies ~65% of the instances correctly, independent of the existence of TEs in a sub-document (rows 1 & 2). Instances of class E (i.e. those sub-documents created 6+ years before the page crawl time) can be classified with highest accuracy. We also present the results of two baselines for those instances that contain one or more TEs: using as single feature either the oldest or most recent TE for classification purposes only. About two thirds of the instances are not correctly classified showing that TEs alone are not sufficient in this setup and additional features (which on first sight may not always be pertinent to creation timestamps) are required.

5. CONCLUSIONS

Our work shows that sub-document timestamping is an issue which should be considered when employing document creation timestamps in IR applications. Not only the amount of documents containing content created at several points in time is significant, but also the interval between the changes is considerable.

One of the limitations of our work is the fact that we relied on the Internet Archive and its historic versions of a document to determine each sub-document's creation time. While this approach yields very precise results for documents archived often by the Internet Archive, for less well-archived documents the temporal resolution is limited[5]. For this reason we resorted to a classification setup with five classes instead of estimating the exact creation time.

In future work we will (i) investigate the impact of sub-document timestamps on retrieval applications, and (ii) experiment with document-external features to increase the classification accuracy.

6. REFERENCES

[1] L. Breiman. Random forests. *Machine learning*, 45(1):5–32, 2001.

[2] R. Campos, G. Dias, A. M. Jorge, and A. Jatowt. Survey of temporal information retrieval and related applications. *ACM Computing Surveys (CSUR)*, 47(2):15, 2014.

[3] N. Chambers. Labeling documents with timestamps: Learning from their time expressions. In *ACL '12*, pages 98–106, 2012.

[4] F. de Jong, H. Rode, and D. Hiemstra. Temporal language models for the disclosure of historical text. Royal Netherlands Academy of Arts and Sciences, 2005.

[5] L. Döhling and U. Leser. Extracting and aggregating temporal events from text. In *WWW '14*, pages 839–844, 2014.

[6] T. Ge, B. Chang, S. Li, and Z. Sui. Event-based time label propagation for automatic dating of news articles. In *EMNLP '13*, pages 1–11, 2013.

[7] A. Jatowt, C.-M. Au Yeung, and K. Tanaka. Estimating document focus time. In *CIKM '13*, pages 2273–2278, 2013.

[8] R. Jones and F. Diaz. Temporal profiles of queries. *ACM Transactions on Information Systems*, 25(3):14, 2007.

[9] N. Kanhabua and K. Nørvåg. Using temporal language models for document dating. In *Machine Learning and Knowledge Discovery in Databases*, pages 738–741. 2009.

[10] X. Li and W. B. Croft. Time-based language models. In *CIKM '03*, pages 469–475. ACM, 2003.

[11] R. Swan and D. Jensen. Timemines: Constructing timelines with statistical models of word usage. In *KDD Workshop on Text Mining*, pages 73–80, 2000.

[5]Note though, that this has only a very limited effect on the number of creation timestamps. Correlating the number of records of documents with the number of creation timestamps found in them, yields $r = 0.37$.

DINFRA: A One Stop Shop for Computing Multilingual Semantic Relatedness

Siamak Barzegar*, Juliano Efson Sales*, Andre Freitas†, Siegfried Handschuh†, Brian Davis*
* Insight Centre for Data Analytics, NUI Galway, Ireland
Firstame.Lastname@insight-centre.org
† Department of Computer Science and Mathematics, University of Passau, Germany
Firstame.Lastname@uni-passau.de

ABSTRACT

This demonstration presents an infrastructure for computing multilingual semantic relatedness and correlation for twelve natural languages by using three distributional semantic models (DSMs). Our demonsrator - DInfra (Distributional Infrastructure) provides researchers and developers with a highly useful platform for processing large-scale corpora and conducting experiments with distributional semantics. We integrate several multilingual DSMs in our webservice so end user can obtain a result without worrying about the complexities involved in building DSMs. Our webservice allows the users to have easy access to a wide range of comparisons of DSMs with different parameters. In addition, users can configure and access DSM parameters using a easy to use API.

Categories and Subject Descriptors

H.1.0 [**Information Systems**]: MODELS AND PRINCIPLES.

Keywords

Distirbutional Infrastructure, Multilingual Semantic Relatedness, Distributional Semantic Models

1. INTRODUCTION

Dinfra is an implementation of Explicit Semantic Analysis (ESA), Latent Semantic Analysis (LSA) and Random Indexing based on the EasyESA [4] and S-Space [7] . It runs as a JSON[1] webservice, which allows users to submit queries for similar terms in a multilingual fashion bases on a semantic relatedness measure which use Spearman's correlation to test relatedness scores.

The Dinfra webservice allows the user to obtain semantic similarity using Spearman correlation for **12** natural languages[2]. Our service can be tested online[3]. It includes **two** components: 1- Semantic Relatedness (Figure 1) that calculates the words similarity, 2- Correlation (Figure 2) that calculates the spearman's rank correlation.

2. RELATED WORK

Ferret [5] tested corpust-based approaches for measuring semantic similarity. He also chose to use limited means because of deficit of linguistic tools are not, or at least freely available, for all popular languages. Bullinaria et al. [3, 2] have built semantic vectors from very small co-occurrence windows, together with a cosine distance measure, stopwords, word stemming, and dimensionality reduction using singular value decomposition to improve performance. The BNC and (British National Corpus)[4] and ukWaC[5] corpus were used In [2] and [3], respectively.

3. SYSTEM DEMONSTRATION

Three word similarity datasets WordSim353 (W353), the Rubenstein & Goodenough (RG) (1965) and Miller & Charles (MC) (1991) have been used in Dinfra. All these datasets consist of human similarity ratings for word pairings. We also consider Wikipedia[6] corpus the years (2006, 2008, 2014) and ukWaC [1] corpus from which to build the vectors.

In Dinfra, three DSMs were instantiated. Latent Semantic Analysis (LSA) [9], Random Indexing (RI) [10] and Explicit Semantic Analysis (ESA) [6]. The different combinations of DSMs and corpora were evaluated for the computation of semantic similarity and relatedness measures.

For the semantic relatedness component (Figure 1), four *parametrs* such as main term, target set, language and similarity measure are used. The user can compare target words to main word with three similarity measures in **twelve** different languages. For the example, we compared (*Wife*, *Child* and *love*) with *mother*, also we used the *Correlation*[7] measure, Figure 1 shows the results that is returned by our

[1]JSON - Java Script Object Notation

[2]English, Portuguese, German, Spanish, French, Swedish, Italian, Dutch, Chinese, Russian, Arabic and Persian

[3]http://vmdgsit04.deri.ie:8008

[4]http://www.natcorp.ox.ac.uk/

[5]2 billion word corpus constructed from the Web limiting the crawl to the .uk domain and using medium-frequency words from the BNC

[6]http://en.wikipedia.org/wiki/Wikipedia:Database_download

[7]A mean-adjusted version of Cosine as defined in [8]

SIGIR'15, August 09-13, 2015, Santiago, Chile.
ACM 978-1-4503-3621-5/15/08.
DOI: http://dx.doi.org/10.1145/2766462.2767870 .

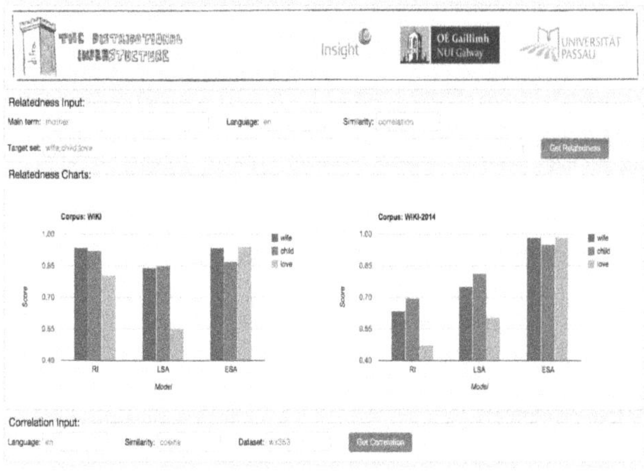

Figure 1: Semantic Relatedness Component

webservice. The semantic relatedness measure is a real number within the [0,1] interval, representing the degree of semantic proximity between two terms. Semantic relatedness can be used for semantic matching in the context of the development of semantic systems such as question answering, text entailment, event matching and semantic search[4] and also for entity/word sense disambiguation tasks.

The correlation component (Figure 2) calculates the Spearman's rank correlation for the three similarity datasets, twelve different languages and three similarity measures (Cosine, Euclidean distance, Correlation)[8].

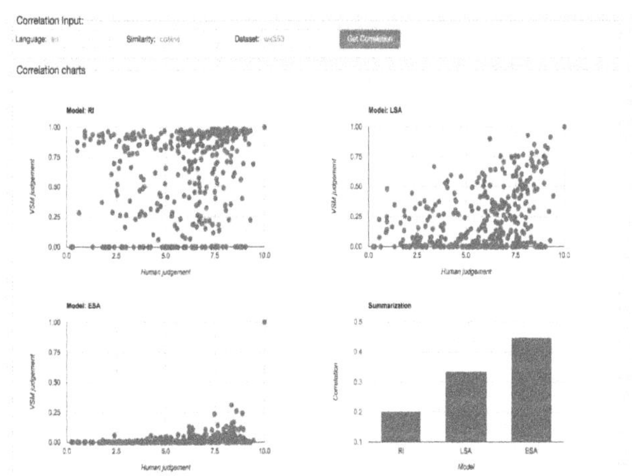

Figure 2: Correlation Component

All three datasets WS353, RG and MC were translated and localised by native speakers for each of the target 11 languages. More importantly the localised datsets for each language underwent a linguistic quality assurance by a well know localisation company. Hence, we are confident that our localised datasets per language are of high translated quality.

[8]See [8] page 3 for definitions of these similarity measures.

4. ACKNOWLEDGMENTS

This publication has emanated from research conducted with the financial support of Science Foundation Ireland (SFI) under Grant Number SFI/12/RC/2289.

We would like in particular to thank Alexandros Poulis and Juha Vilhunen from the Lionbridge Natural Language Solutions ensuring the production word of high quality translations for our similarity datasets.

5. REFERENCES

[1] M. Baroni, S. Bernardini, A. Ferraresi, and E. Zanchetta. The wacky wide web: a collection of very large linguistically processed web-crawled corpora. *Language resources and evaluation*, 43(3):209–226, 2009.

[2] J. A. Bullinaria and J. P. Levy. Extracting semantic representations from word co-occurrence statistics: A computational study. *Behavior research methods*, 39(3):510–526, 2007.

[3] J. A. Bullinaria and J. P. Levy. Extracting semantic representations from word co-occurrence statistics: stop-lists, stemming, and svd. *Behavior research methods*, 44(3):890–907, 2012.

[4] D. Carvalho, C. Callı, A. Freitas, and E. Curry. Easyesa: A low-effort infrastructure for explicit semantic analysis. In *Proceedings of the 13th International Semantic Web Conference (ISWC)*, 2014.

[5] O. Ferret. Testing semantic similarity measures for extracting synonyms from a corpus. In *LREC*, volume 10, pages 3338–3343, 2010.

[6] E. Gabrilovich and S. Markovitch. Computing semantic relatedness using wikipedia-based explicit semantic analysis. In *IJCAI*, volume 7, pages 1606–1611, 2007.

[7] D. Jurgens and K. Stevens. The s-space package: an open source package for word space models. In *Proceedings of the ACL 2010 System Demonstrations*, pages 30–35. Association for Computational Linguistics, 2010.

[8] D. Kiela and S. Clark. A systematic study of semantic vector space model parameters. In *Proceedings of the 2nd Workshop on Continuous Vector Space Models and their Compositionality (CVSC) at EACL*, pages 21–30, 2014.

[9] T. K. Landauer, P. W. Foltz, and D. Laham. An introduction to latent semantic analysis. *Discourse processes*, 25(2-3):259–284, 1998.

[10] M. Sahlgren. Vector-based semantic analysis: Representing word meanings based on random labels. In *In ESSLI Workshop on Semantic Knowledge Acquistion and Categorization.* Citeseer, 2001.

VenueMusic: A Venue-Aware Music Recommender System

Zhiyong Cheng
School of Information Systems
Singapore Management University
Singapore, 178902
zy.cheng.2011@smu.edu.sg

Jialie Shen
School of Information Systems
Singapore Management University
Singapore, 178902
jlshen@smu.edu.sg

ABSTRACT

Users' music preferences can be greatly influenced by their location and environment nearby. In this demonstration, we present an intelligent music recommender system, called VenueMusic, to automatically identify suitable music for various popular venues in our daily lives. VenueMusic enjoys a set of nice features: i) music concept sequence generation scheme and Location-aware Topic Model (LTM) are proposed to map the characteristics of venues and music into a latent semantic space, where suitability of music for a venue can be directly measured, ii) a smart interface enabling user to smoothly interact with VenueMusic, and iii) high quality music playlist. The demonstration will show several interesting use-cases of VenueMusic, and illustrate its superiority on recommending music based on where user presents.

Categories and Subject Descriptors

H.3.3 [**Information Search and Retrieval**]: Query formulation, Search process; H.5.5 [**Sound and Music Computing**]: Systems

Keywords

Music Recommendation, Context-Aware, Topic Model

1. INTRODUCTION

Mobile devices have increasingly become significant mediums for enjoying music anywhere and anytime. It is well known that users' music preferences can be greatly influenced by where they are and surrounding environment. Therefore, how to leverage venue related information is a key issue towards effective location based music recommendation. Different venues usually have different atmosphere and ambience. Accordingly, different music contents are suitable for different venues in general. For example, energetic music is popular in gym, while love songs fit a romantic restaurant well. Recent physiological study [3] shows that human judges the suitability of a music for a place based on various

SIGIR'15, August 09-13, 2015, Santiago, Chile.
ACM 978-1-4503-3621-5/15/08.
DOI: http://dx.doi.org/10.1145/2766462.2767869.

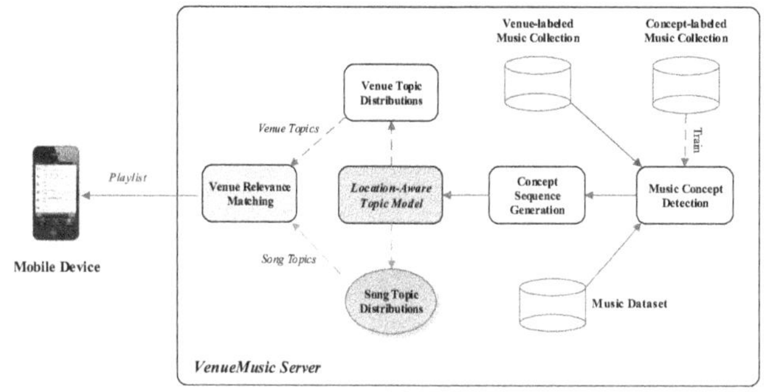

Figure 1: System architecture.

music semantics (e.g., genre and mood). However, it is very difficult to apply low level acoustic features to explicitly describe those semantics due to the well-known "semantic gap". Besides, the acoustic contents of music belonging to same or similar concepts could be highly diverse [4]. In the demonstration, we present an intelligent music recommender system, called VenueMusic, to automatically identify suitable music for various popular venues in our daily lives [2]. Towards this goal, a novel topic model called Location-aware Topic Model (LTM) is proposed to measure the suitability of music for venues in a latent semantic space. Besides, music concept sequence generation scheme is developed to represent each track as a set of music concepts. The demonstration also focuses on a few interesting use-cases, and illustrates the superiority of VenueMusic on recommendation accuracy and robustness at various venues.

2. SYSTEM OVERVIEW

VenueMusic's architecture comprises two major components: (1) Music Concept Sequence Generation (MCSG) and (2) Location-aware Topic Model (LTM). Main functionality of MCSG is to detect music concepts (e.g., *instrument*, *genre*, and *mood*) to represent audio contents of the music tracks. Figure 1 illustrates the detail architecture of VenueMusic. Specifically, when receiving a music track, VenueMusic partitions it into multiple short segments, from which different concepts (i.e., genres and moods) are extracted based on their audio contents using automatic concept detectors (trained based on concept-labeled data). To improve the quality of the detected concepts for a segment, concepts with low detected probabilities or causing rare concept co-occurrence patterns are removed via Infrequent Concept Pattern Filtering (ICPF). For a track, its music concept sequence is the concatenation of the concepts of all segments. Serving as the second component, LTM extracts the latent topics from location-labeled music tracks and uses them to represent the characteristics of the location and the music content with the probabilistic distributions of the mined topics. When the new tracks (unlabeled-tracks) are available, we fit them into the model by fixing the topics and obtain their topic distributions. Through characterizing the location and music tracks by probability distributions of the same topics, the suitability score of a music track m for a venue v is estimated using Kullback-Leibler (KL) distance as,

$$KL(v||m) = \sum_i v(i)ln(\frac{v(i)}{m(i)}) \quad (1)$$

3. DEMONSTRATION

In the demonstration, we show a few nice features of the VenueMusic including good usability, effectiveness and robustness.

3.1 Good Usability

VenueMusic has a simple but effective interface alongside with intelligent recommendation engine at backend. The design of the interface is to facilitate the easy use of the system, and the intelligent backend enables flexible recommendation to satisfy different music needs and personal preferences. The demo will focus on several nice characteristics of VenueMusic's user interface.

- **Simplicity**: To simplify the process of finding suitable music tracks in different venues, VenueMusic only needs users to select the venue where they are currently present, then a suitable playlist for the venue will be presented to the users. Meanwhile, the songs having a good matching to different venues are periodically generated and updated based on users' listening records.
- **Flexibility**: Users might have different preferences for the songs listened in a venue according to their activities or other factors (e.g., mood and event). To better satisfy their needs, in addition to the selection of venue type, the system also allows users to input several keywords to describe their specific music needs. Based on the input keywords (query), songs are recommended based on their relevances to the query and suitability to the given venue type.
- **Adaptivity:** Although users share common interest on the *features* of music they prefer in a certain venue, different users typically favor different songs due to their unique personalities and tastes. To providing better personal service, VenueMusic is adapted for personalization with the use of personal listening records, such as played and skipped times of different songs, and other listening contexts (e.g., time). The listening history is recorded automatically and implicitly with the permission of users. Besides, users can also construct their own profiles by creating a personal account and providing additional information for better personal service, such as demographic information and favorite songs.

3.2 Effectiveness and Robustness

In order to validate the effectiveness and robustness of the system, a user study was conducted using large scale test collection including 10,000 songs. In the test, the system was applied to recommend suitable music tracks to *eight* common venues (as shown in Table 1) and compared with several competitors. Due to the space limitations, the results of three competitors are presented:

- Audio-Based Content Filtering (**ABCF**) - this method recommends music based on the audio content. Each venue is represented by several representative audio feature vectors, which are generated from the labeled tracks using K-means method.
- Concept-Based Content Filtering (**CBCF**) - in this method, tracks and venues are described using generated concept histograms.
- Concept-based LTM (**CLTM**) - comparing to VenueMusic, this method does not use ICPF in the concept generation process.

Totally 29 music concepts (5 moods, 12 genres and 12 instruments) are used in the experiments. 7 human subjects are recruited to evaluate the recommendation results of each method. The evaluation procedure is the same to the user study in [1]. Table 1 presents the mean P@20 of all subjects over the eight venues. The comparisons with ABCF and CBCF demonstrate the superiority of using semantic topic representations for venues and music; and the comparison with CLTM verify the usefulness of using ICPF in the generation of music concept sequences for music tracks. VenueMusic outperforms the competitors across the eight venues *significantly* and *consistently*, which demonstrates its *effectiveness* and *robustness* on location-aware music recommendation.

Table 1: Precision@20 comparison over different venues.

Venue	ABCF	CBCF	CLTM	VenueMusic
Bar	**0.95**	0.85	**0.95**	**0.95**
Bedroom	0.25	0.45	0.55	**0.65**
Gym	0.40	0.45	0.55	**0.65**
Library	0.35	0.60	0.60	**0.65**
Office	0.40	0.45	0.45	**0.50**
Restaurant	**0.30**	0.20	**0.30**	**0.30**
Mall	0.15	0.35	0.30	**0.45**
Bus/Train	0.20	0.50	0.45	**0.55**

4. ACKNOWLEDGEMENTS

This research is supported by Singapore Ministry of Education under Academic Research Fund Tier-2 (MOE Ref: MOE2013-T2-2-156) and the Microsoft Research Grant (FY14-RES-OPP-048).

5. REFERENCES

[1] Z. Cheng and J. Shen. Just-for-me: An adaptive personalization system for location-aware social music recommendation. In *ACM ICMR*, 2014.

[2] Z. Cheng and J. Shen. On effective location-aware music recommendation. *Submitted to ACM TOIS*, 2015.

[3] S. Hallam, I. Cross, and M. Thaut. *Oxford Handbook of Music Psychology*. Oxford University Press, 2009.

[4] J. Shen, H. Pang, M. Wang, and S. Yan. Modeling concept dynamics for large scale music search. In *ACM SIGIR*, 2012.

Shiny on Your Crazy Diagonal

Giorgio Maria Di Nunzio
Department of Information Engineering
University of Padua
Via Gradenigo 6/a, 35131 Padua, Italy
dinunzio@dei.unipd.it

ABSTRACT

In this demo, we present a web application which allows users to interact with two retrieval models, namely the Binary Independence Model (BIM) and the BM25 model, on a standard TREC collection. The goal of this demo is to give students deeper insight into the consequences of modeling assumptions (BIM vs. BM25) and the consequences of tuning parameter values by means of a two-dimensional representation of probabilities. The application was developed in R, and it is accessible at the following link: `http://gmdn.shinyapps.io/shinyRF04`.

Categories and Subject Descriptors

H.3.3 [[**Information Search and Retrieval**]: Retrieval Models; D.2.8 [**Software Engineering**]: Metrics—*complexity measures, performance measures*

General Terms

Theory, Algorithms, Experimentation

Keywords

Probabilistic Models, Bayesian Inference, Text Retrieval

1. INTRODUCTION

The Binary Independence Model (BIM) has been one of the most influential models in the history of Information Retrieval [3]. It is a probabilistic model that considers documents as binary vectors and ranks them in order of their probability of relevance given a query according to the Probability Ranking Principle [2]. The Okapi BM25 model goes one step further by taking into account the frequencies of the terms and the length of the documents. These two models are easy to train and reach satisfactory results even with standard default parameters. The optimisation of the parameters can be performed by means of machine learning approaches; nevertheless, this process may be computationally demanding and only lead to partial improvements [6].

SIGIR'15, August 09-13, 2015, Santiago, Chile.
ACM 978-1-4503-3621-5/15/08.
DOI: http://dx.doi.org/10.1145/2766462.2767867 .

In this demo, we want to study the problem of the optimisation of the parameters of the two BIM and BM25 models by means of an interactive visualisation approach based on the idea of Likelihood Spaces [5], a two-dimensional representation of probabilities. We have developed a web application which allows users to be directly involved into the process of the optimisation of the retrieval function in a real machine learning setting. The goal of this demo is to give students deeper insight in the consequences of modeling assumptions (BIM vs. BM25) and the consequences of tuning parameter values. As a showcase, we used the TREC2004 Robust test collection (528,155 documents and 250 topics). [1] We added to the original collection a pseudo-relevance feedback set constituted by the top 100 documents obtained by a 'standard' BM25 approach for each query. For the online version of this demo, we used a sample of the collection in order to make the application usable. In particular, we built the training/validation sets by using all the pseudo-relevant feedback documents of the BM25 and the test set with all the relevant documents of the pool.

2. MATHEMATICAL BACKGROUND

The BIM ranks documents according to the probability of relevance ($R = 1$) given a document d and a query q, $P(R = 1|d, q)$. The logarithm of this probability can be approximated by (see [4] for the details of all the passages):

$$\log\left(P(R = 1|d, q)\right) \approx \sum_{t_i \in d \cap q} w_i \qquad (1)$$

where w_i is the relevance score of the term t_i, defined as

$$w_i = log \frac{p_i}{(1 - p_i)} \frac{(1 - q_i)}{q_i} \,, \qquad (2)$$

where p_i is the probability that a relevant document contains the term t_i, while q_i is the probability that a non-relevant document contains the term t_i. The estimates of p_i and q_i are smoothed with two parameters α and β to avoid zero probabilities (by default, $\alpha = \beta = 0.5$, see [1]). The BM25 model has the same form of Eq.1 by replacing w_i with w'_i:

$$w'_i = \frac{tf_i}{tf_i + k_1 * ((1 - b) + b * dl/\Delta)} \cdot w_i \qquad (3)$$

where tf_i is the frequency of the term t_i in the document, k_1 and b are two parameters (usually set to 1.2 and 0.75, respectively), dl is the length of document d, and Δ is the

[1] `http://trec.nist.gov/data/t13_robust.html`

average document length. Eq. 3 derives from [4] (in this formulation, $(k_1 + 1)$ is not present in the numerator).

In the two-dimensional representation of probabilities, we keep $P(R = 1|d, q)$ distinct from the probability of a document being not relevant $P(R = 0|d, q)$, and we order documents according to the difference:

$$\sum_{t_i} \log\left(\frac{p_i}{1-p_i}\right) - \sum_{t_i} \log\left(\frac{q_i}{1-q_i}\right) \qquad (4)$$

With two more parameters M and Q, we define a decision line $y = Mx + Q$ (see the details in [1]):

$$\underbrace{M\sum_{t_i} \frac{p_i}{1-p_i}}_{x} + Q - \underbrace{\sum_{t_i} \frac{q_i}{1-q_i}}_{y} \qquad (5)$$

This formulation allows us to study the problem on a two-dimensional space where documents are represented by two coordinates x and y and ranking is performed by the line $Mx + Q - y$.

3. SHINY WEB APPLICATION

The application has been developed in R using the Shiny package, an R package that makes it easy to build interactive web applications straight from R. [2] The main window of the application is split into two parts, see Fig. 1: on the left side, the user can interact with the retrieval models and see the results on the right side in terms of both the performance of the retrieval and the visualisation of the coordinates.

Interaction: (1) The user chooses the topic of interest from the drop-down menu, and the query is shown in the text area. (2) The user selects the retrieval model (if BM25 is not selected, the BIM is on), the pseudo-relevance feedback is used (default is on), and whether the sum of Eq. 5 of the probabilities is computed over the selected features (4) or over the query terms. If BM25 is selected, the parameters k_1 and b can be adjusted. (3) The parameters α and β are used to smooth the probabilities p_i and q_i. (4) The fourth part focuses on the machine learning approach to the problem: select the number of folds k and the number of features we need to train the retrieval model. By default we have a five-cross validation and the top 50 features selected according to the difference $p_i - q_i$. The user can change the ranking line by adjusting the two sliders *Angular coefficient* M and *Intercept* Q. The default values are 1 and 0, respectively, which correspond to a zero-one loss function. When these parameters are changed, a green line remain fixed in the position of the zero-one loss function for comparison.

Visualization: The right panel is divided into two columns: (6) shows the results on the validation set, (7) the results on the test set. Both columns contain the following pieces of information (from top to bottom): (i) The text box shows the total number of objects used for validation and the number of positive examples (red points, the pseudo-relevant documents of the chosen topic). The box in the validation column also tells the user in what fold we are validating. (ii) The table shows performance measures in terms of precision-at-j (j = 5, 10, 20, 100, 500, 1000). (iii) The two-dimensional plot shows in red the relevant documents of the chosen topic (pseudo-relevant for the validation fold, true relevant for test set) and in black all the other documents of the collection.

[2] `http://shiny.rstudio.com/`

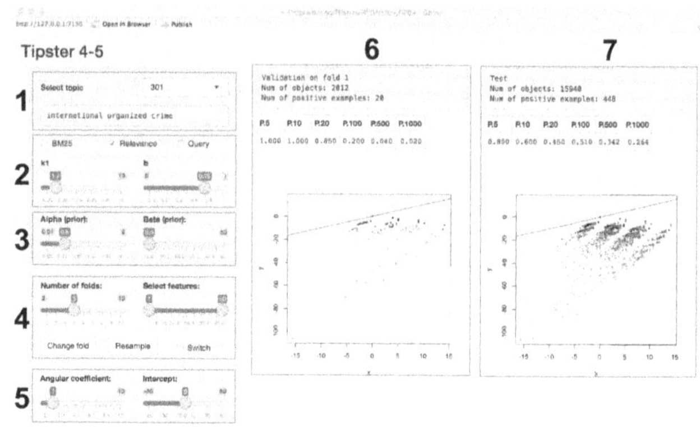

Figure 1: Web application developed in Shiny.

The blue line changes according to the parameters selected in (5) while the green line remains fixed to the bisecting line of the third quadrant.

4. CONCLUSIONS

In this demo, we have presented a Web application developed in R which allows users to interact with two retrieval models, the BIM and the BM25 models, on a standard TREC collection. The probabilistic models are visualised on a two-dimensional space based on the idea of Likelihood spaces. The interactive application shows, in a real machine learning setting, how the human pattern recognition capabilities can immediately detect whether the model is close to the optimal solution or not. In theory, a classical fully-automatic machine learning approach that searches the best combination of parameters can find the optimal solution [6]. However, the number of possible combinations of the values of the parameters grows exponentially with the number of the parameters; consequently, this interactive approach may be a crucial step in setting the initial parameters of the function that optimises these parameters automatically.

5. REFERENCES

[1] Giorgio Maria Di Nunzio. A new decision to take for cost-sensitive naïve bayes classifiers. *Information Processing & Management*, 50(5):653 – 674, 2014.

[2] S. E. Robertson. The Probability Ranking Principle in IR. *Journal of Documentation*, 33(4):294–304, 1977.

[3] Stephen E. Robertson and Karen Sparck Jones. Relevance weighting of search terms. In Peter Willett, editor, *Document retrieval systems*, pages 143–160. Taylor Graham Publishing, London, UK,, 1988.

[4] Stephen E. Robertson and Hugo Zaragoza. The probabilistic relevance framework: BM25 and beyond. *Foundations and Trends in Information Retrieval*, 3(4):333–389, 2009.

[5] Rita Singh and Bhiksha Raj. Classification in likelihood spaces. *Technometrics*, 46(3):318–329, 2004.

[6] Andrew Trotman, Antti Puurula, and Blake Burgess. Improvements to bm25 and language models examined. In *Proceedings of the 2014 Australasian Document Computing Symposium*, ADCS '14, pages 58:58–58:65, New York, NY, USA, 2014. ACM.

CricketLinking: Linking Event Mentions from Cricket Match Reports to Ball Entities in Commentaries

Manish Gupta
Microsoft, India
gmanish@microsoft.com

ABSTRACT

The 2011 Cricket World Cup final match was watched by around 135 million people. Such a huge viewership demands a great experience for users of online cricket portals. Many portals like espncricinfo.com host a variety of content related to recent matches including match reports and ball-by-ball commentaries. When reading a match report, reader experience can be significantly improved by augmenting (on demand) the event mentions in the report with detailed commentaries. We build an event linking system *CricketLinking* which first identifies event mentions from the reports and then links them to a set of balls. Finding linkable mentions is challenging because unlike entity linking problem settings, we do not have a concrete set of event entities to link to. Further, depending on the event type, event mentions could be linked to a single ball, or to a set of balls. Hence, identifying mention type as well as linking becomes challenging. We use a large number of domain specific features to learn classifiers for mention and mention type detection. Further, we leverage structured match, context similarity and sequential proximity to perform accurate linking. Finally, context based summarization is performed to provide a concise briefing of linked balls to each mention.

Categories and Subject Descriptors

H.2.8 [**Information Systems**]: Database Applications—*Data Mining*; H.4.0 [**Information Systems Applications**]: General

Keywords

Cricket data analysis, Event linking, Article-Commentary linking, Mention type detection, Entity linking

1. INTRODUCTION

Cricket is one of the most popular sports with a large amount of related content published online. For each match, online portals publish ball-by-ball commentaries. These commentaries describe what happened when a ball was bowled including the name of the bowler, the batsman, number of runs scored, the type of the ball delivered, the type of shot, and sometimes comments on the form of the bowler or the batsman. Thus, every match has this detailed description of the match in the form of a maximum of 600 balls (plus the extras). Besides this, multiple experts write articles (or reports) describing the events that occurred during the match. The articles summarize the match in a concise way but miss out on interesting details due to lack of space. In this demo, we focus on providing an ability to the user to zoom in on particular event mentions from the match reports and read about a few ball commentaries most relevant to the event.

Figure 1 shows an example user interaction. When reading a match report, the user selected a phrase "The loss of Ahmed Shehzad followed by Sohaib Maqsood in the space of three balls from Umesh" and is shown ball commentary relevant to the event mentioned in the phrase. Given a match report and the corresponding ball commentaries, we focus on the problem of linking phrases from the match report with balls in the commentary. Linking could be done to a single ball, to a set of balls, or to the entire innings.

SIGIR'15, Aug 09-13, 2015, Santiago, Chile.
© 2015 ACM. ISBN 978-1-4503-3621-5/15/08 ...$15.00.
http://dx.doi.org/10.1145/2766462.2767865.

2. RELATED WORK

There is little work in the field of sports data analysis. To the best of our knowledge, this is the first work in the IR community focused on applying entity linking methods in the domain of sports. Shen et al. [3] provide a thorough overview of the main approaches to entity linking. A typical entity linking system consists of mention detection, candidate entity generation and candidate entity ranking. Entity linking has been found to be useful for information extraction, information retrieval, content analysis [1], question answering and knowledge base population [2]. We model the event mention linking problem to cricket commentary balls as an entity linking problem where entities are balls or sets of balls.

3. COMPONENTS OF CRICKETLINKING

Figure 2 shows a system diagram for `CricketLinking`. The system has three main components: Pre-processing, Mention Detection and Ball Linking.

3.1 Pre-processing Commentaries and Reports

The ball commentaries are available in a semi-structured form. For accurate linking, first we obtain a structured representation of each ball which contains the following fields: ball number, bowler name, bowler country, batsman name, batsman country, non-striker batsman name, runs scored, aggregate runs scored, current run rate, required run rate, previous bowler, event (out, four, six), striker statistics (runs, strike rate, fours, sixes), runner name, type of ball (short, yorker, etc.), type of shot, number of balls played by batsman till this ball, comment for batsman or bowler. Further, beyond the 600 ball entities, we also obtain linkable derived entities as follows: all balls faced by a batsman, balls that denote partnership between two batsmen, all balls bowled by a bowler, all balls bowled by a bowler and faced by a batsman, all balls on which a four was hit in the first/second innings, all balls on which a six was hit in

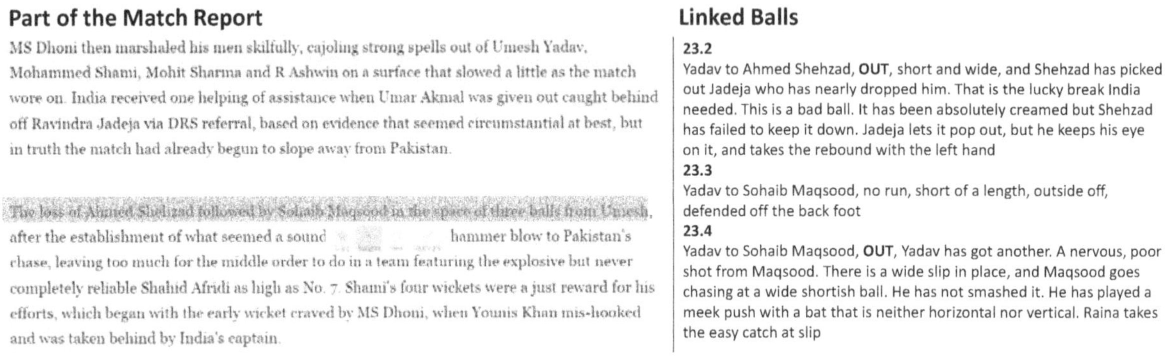

Figure 1: Screenshot of the *CricketLinking* System

the first/second innings, etc. Besides these, anomalous set of balls are also identified as derived entities. Anomalies in cricket include the following: very low runs conceded by a bowler, high number of wickets by a bowler, very high runs by a batsman, high strike rate, quick wickets, large number of fours in an over, etc.

Match reports are completely unstructured. We annotate them by performing co-reference resolution at a paragraph level, parse tree construction, and dependency analysis.

3.2 Mention Detection

This stage consists of two main parts: Event Mention Detection and Mention Type Detection. The event mention detection part identifies linkable phrases (or 'mentions'). Parse tree annotations help us to identify phrases which are classified using a large number of domain specific features. We create cricket dictionaries for cricket terms, words to indicate specific events like a wicket, a boundary or a six, etc. The features used for mention detection include number of batsman names, number of bowler names, event words, maximum similarity score with any ball, number of batsman action words, number of bowler action words, number of partnership action words, number of words found in a list of words found frequently in mentions, position of mention in the report, contains score, number of words denoting extra balls, etc. The second part identifies the type of the mention: single ball, batsman innings, all balls by a bowler, partnership, spells, powerplay, inning, extras, anomaly, etc. This also uses a classifier trained using similar features as the ones used for mention detection.

3.3 Ball Linking

In this stage, we link the mentions discovered in the previous stage to a set of balls. The first step involves identification of temporal clues like: "in the 42nd over", "first 10 overs", "last 3 balls of the tenth over." Such clues help us to link the mention to the right set of balls accurately. If there are no temporal clues, we find all balls or derived entities whose structured representation contains words from the phrase. These words could include player names, number of wickets so far, runs, run rate, a particular event, etc. Such entities form candidates that can be linked to the mention. Further, the candidates are ranked based on the Jaccard Similarity between the candidate and the mention. The similarity is computed only with respect to words in the cricket terms dictionary (around 250 words). Given a paragraph, it is necessary to maintain consistency across all entities linked to mentions within the paragraph. Usually mentions in a paragraph follow a temporal order. Thus, the entities for every mention are re-ranked based on the sequential proximity of the linked set of balls. Finally, some derived entities (like all balls faced by a player) could contain a large number of balls. Such entities are then summarized by picking eventful balls and using them to show a concise summary. The user is also given an option to see all the related balls.

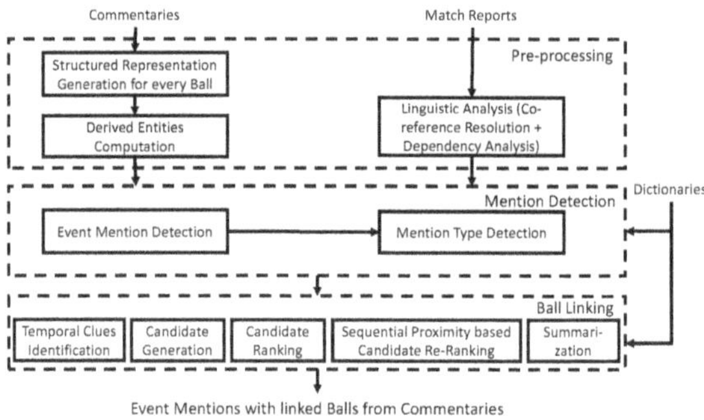

Figure 2: `CricketLinking`: System for Linking Event Mentions with Cricket Match Commentaries

4. DEMONSTRATION

We will demonstrate the capabilities of `CricketLinking` as described in Section 3. We crawled match reports and commentaries for 421 matches from 2009 to 2014 from espncricinfo[1]. The demo will allow the users to select any commentary file and a match report file and see the mentions detected from the match report. The users can also select particular phrases and look for linked balls as well as a concise summary when the number of linked balls is large. There are no specific demo requirements.

5. CONCLUSION

We present the system `CricketLinking` which takes a cricket match report and commentary as input and outputs detected mentions from the report and links them to the commentary balls. The system goes beyond traditional entity linking by considering the sequential nature of both the reports as well as the entities (balls). This is the first system that applies the concept of entity linking to the sports domain. The system can be very useful for quick referencing of commentary balls when reading match reports on various cricket portals.

6. REFERENCES

[1] Abhishek Gattani, Digvijay S Lamba, Nikesh Garera, Mitul Tiwari, Xiaoyong Chai, Sanjib Das, Sri Subramaniam, Anand Rajaraman, Venky Harinarayan, and AnHai Doan. Entity Extraction, Linking, Classification, and Tagging for Social Media: A Wikipedia-based Approach. *PVLDB*, 6(11):1126–1137, 2013.

[2] Johannes Hoffart, Fabian M Suchanek, Klaus Berberich, and Gerhard Weikum. YAGO2: A Spatially and Temporally Enhanced Knowledge Base from Wikipedia. In *IJCAI*, pages 3161–3165, 2013.

[3] Wei Shen, Jianyong Wang, and Jiawei Han. Entity Linking with a Knowledge Base: Issues, Techniques, and Solutions. *TKDE*, Jun 2014.

[1]http://www.espncricinfo.com/

An Aspect-driven Social Media Explorer

Nedim Lipka
Adobe Research
lipka@adobe.com

W. Bruce Croft
University of Massachusetts
croft@cs.umass.edu

ABSTRACT

We demonstrate an exploration tool that organizes social media content under diverse aspects enabling comprehensive explorations. Unlike existing approaches that group content by trending topics, we present a holistic view of diverse and relevant content with respect to a given query.

Categories and Subject Descriptors: H.4 Information Systems: Information Systems Applications; H.5 Information Systems: Information Interfaces and Presentation

General Terms: Computer Applications.

Keywords: Information Retrieval; Term Diversity; Social Media Content

1. INTRODUCTION

Communities within social networks that intersect with a company's targeted audience enable the assessment of brand perception, customer satisfaction, and consumer needs and therefore go beyond marketers' standard key performance indicators. The amount and diversity of information in social networks is challenging and relevance-based exploration tools are needed.

We introduce a tool for marketers that organizes social media content by employing methods for term level search result diversification enabling the comprehensive exploration of diverse and relevant content. Existing listening and monitoring tools suggest a content categorization into trending topics based on the volume, the recency or the burstiness of keywords, which lacks of the capability to identify aspects with low popularity, ongoing and non-volatile aspects, and a notion of relevance for better exploration.

Retrieval Method. Our approach is based on concepts used for term level search result diversification by Dang and Croft [8]. A ranking becomes more diverse the more novelty each document introduces to the higher ranked content. Common diversification frameworks, such as xQuAD [13] or PM-2 [7] which are either considering redundancy or proportionality for computing a diverse ranking, are given a set of aspects A that is used for sub-queries and a probabilistic notion of relevance. Dang and Croft [8] propose to adapt the summarization algorithm DSPApprox [10] to determine A for a so-called *term level* diversification, which treats words, phrases, or hashtags as candidates for A. For diversification under the xQuAD and the PM-2 framework, this approach outperforms topic level diversification with aspects A generated by LDA [3] and KNN [5].

The variant of DSPApprox [8] greedily removes in each iteration the term from a set of candidates that has the maximum utility score and adds it to A. The utility of a term t is the product of its topicality and predictiveness, whereby the predictiveness of the remaining candidate terms is recomputed in each iteration. The *topicality* of t assesses

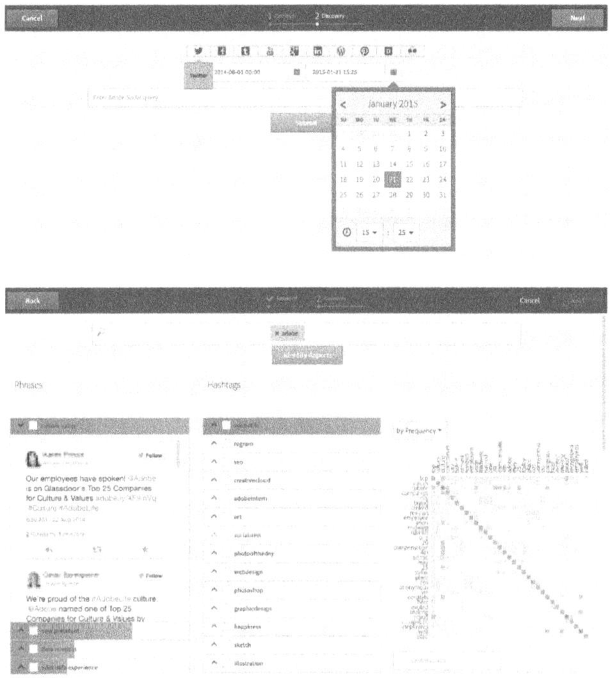

Figure 1: (*Top*) Specification of time period, social media sources, and optionally keywords in order to retrieve the data set of interest from a NoSQL database. (*Bottom*) Search results for phrases and hashtags after diversification and ranking wrt. a given query. For a selected aspect, the expanded block in the ranking shows the corresponding content and the right sidebar renders a word co-occurrence matrix sorted by frequency or sentiment.

SIGIR'15, August 09-13, 2015, Santiago, Chile.
ACM 978-1-4503-3621-5/15/08.
http://dx.doi.org/10.1145/2766462.2767864

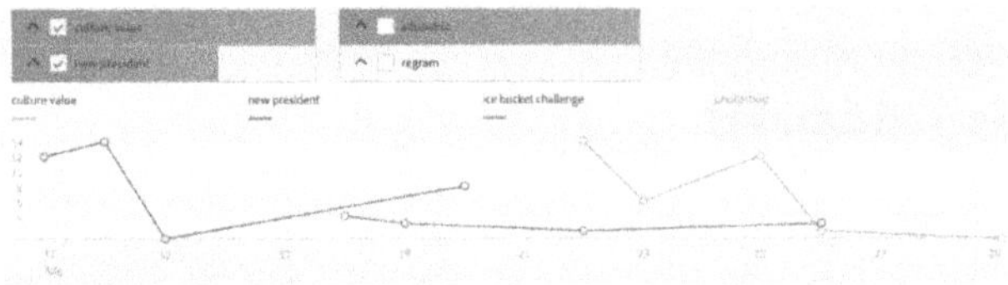

Figure 2: Time series of the volume of selected aspects.

t's power to discriminate between relevant and non-relevant documents, weighted by the relevance of each document to the initial query q. The *predictiveness* of t aggregates the probabilities that t's co-occurring terms always co-occur with t in a given proximity window.

For our exploration tool, the DSPApprox variant identifies and ranks aspects associated with a given query q. Each aspect is used to categorize and re-rank social media content by using it as a sub-query. The algorithm outputs aspects that are diverse, represent superior sub-queries, and are relevant to q in order to surface documents that are representative for the particular aspects. Here, aspects are either words, phrases, or hashtags that also function as readable and meaningful category descriptors.

Related Work. TweetMotif by Krieger and Ahn [9] identifies topic phrases (aspects) by computing a likelihood ratio similar to our topicality score and merges redundant aspects as diversification approach. Our method differs as it additionally considers a relevance model. Furthermore, we achieve diversity by the scoring the predictiveness of terms after each iteration of selecting and removing a term from a candidate set.

Other related approaches such as trend detection based on the burstiness of keywords [11] or event summarization [12] are likely to ignore aspects with low popularity or volatility. Additionally, general multi-document summarization algorithms have the disadvantage that they require a post-processing step to consider diversification.

Aspects can also be understood as a non-exclusive document partitioning computed by a clustering or topic modeling algorithm. These approaches require the number of topics as a parameter and their output is not providing readable descriptors.

2. ARCHITECTURE

A three-tier architecture balances the amount of data and the provided functionalities. At the first level, a Cassandra database stores the content from a variety of social networks. The data stems from owned social accounts as well as GNIP [1], a third-party social data provider, and is enhanced with extracted meta data, such as spam, sentiment, or emotion scores.

At the second level, an Apache Tomcat container uses the open source search engine Galago [6], which implements the ranking functionality including a language model and a relevance model. Galago operates on an global index for reference statistics and on an ad-hoc index of the social data retrieved from the first tier. The DSPApprox algorithm and also the computation of word co-occurrences are implemented here. The results are materialized and stored in the requested HTML document.

The third level is the user's Web-browser. It enables the rendering of content according to the style of particular social networks, information visualizations such as word co-occurrences, and interaction mechanisms. The Web UI is implemented with an internal touch-first, front-end framework used for Adobe Cloud experiences.

Our tool currently works in two phases: In phase one, the user specifies the time frame, the social data sources, and optionally filtering keywords in order to stream the respective content from the Cassandra database to the Galago indexing engine. In phase two, the user specifies the initial query and the tool computes related aspects, their utility, and the rankings.

3. USER EXPERIENCE

- **Querying.** A search bar lets the user specify the initial query q. Once the corresponding aspects are displayed, they can be added to q via a drag and drop mechanism in order to create more specific queries.
- **Ranking of aspects.** The main view, Figure 1 (bottom), renders two columns with ranked aspects based on phrases and on hashtags. A blue filling visualizes the utility score on an aspect.
- **Ranking of content under aspects.** Aspects and their corresponding content are displayed under the accordion paradigm [2]. Upon a click, an aspect block expands and unveils its ranked content, which is scrollable. Not more than one aspect per column can be expanded at the same time.
- **Co-occurrence matrix.** The right sidebar shows the co-occurrences of words associated with a selected aspect. It is employing Mike Bostock's D3 matrix implementation [4], where a dark shade of a field indicates a strong degree of co-occurrence of a word pair. Green, red, and orange indicate a positive, negative, or neutral sentiment; word pairs with different sentiments are colored in gray.
- **Aspect time series.** Multiple aspects can be selected to visualize their frequency of occurrence over time, see Figure 2.

4. REFERENCES

[1] www.gnip.com.

[2] www.w3.org/TR/wai-aria-practices/#accordion.

[3] D. M. Blei, A. Y. Ng, and M. I. Jordan. Latent dirichlet allocation. *J. Mach. Learn. Res.*, 3, 2003.

[4] M. Bostock, V. Ogievetsky, and J. Heer. D3: Data-driven documents. *IEEE Trans. Visualization & Comp. Graphics*, 2011.

[5] B. Carterette and P. Chandar. Probabilistic models of ranking novel documents for faceted topic retrieval. In *Proc. of CIKM*, 2009.

[6] B. Croft, D. Metzler, and T. Strohman. *Search Engines: Information Retrieval in Practice.* Addison-Wesley, 2009.

[7] V. Dang and W. B. Croft. Diversity by proportionality: An election-based approach to search result diversification. In *Proc. of SIGIR*, 2012.

[8] V. Dang and W. B. Croft. Term level search result diversification. In *Proc. of SIGIR*, 2013.

[9] M. Krieger and D. Ahn. TweetMotif: exploratory search and topic summarization for Twitter. In *Proc. of ICWSM*, 2010.

[10] D. Lawrie, W. B. Croft, and A. Rosenberg. Finding topic words for hierarchical summarization. In *Proc. of SIGIR*, 2001.

[11] M. Mathioudakis and N. Koudas. TwitterMonitor: Trend detection over the Twitter stream. In *Proc. of SIGMOD*, 2010.

[12] A. J. McMinn, D. Tsvetkov, T. Yordanov, A. Patterson, R. Szk, J. A. Rodriguez Perez, and J. M. Jose. An interactive interface for visualizing events on Twitter. In *Proc. of SIGIR*, 2014.

[13] R. L. Santos, C. Macdonald, and I. Ounis. Exploiting query reformulations for web search result diversification. In *Proc. of WWW*, 2010.

ERICA: Expert Guidance in Validating Crowd Answers

Nguyen Quoc Viet Hung, Duong Chi Thang, Matthias Weidlich[†], Karl Aberer
École Polytechnique Fédérale de Lausanne and [†]Humboldt-Universität zu Berlin

ABSTRACT

Crowdsourcing became an essential tool for a broad range of Web applications. Yet, the wide-ranging levels of expertise of crowd workers as well as the presence of faulty workers call for quality control of the crowdsourcing result. To this end, many crowdsourcing platforms feature a post-processing phase, in which crowd answers are validated by experts. This approach incurs high costs though, since expert input is a scarce resource. To support the expert in the validation process, we present a tool for *ExpeRt guidance In validating Crowd Answers (ERICA)*. It allows us to guide the expert's work by collecting input on the most problematic cases, thereby achieving a set of high quality answers even if the expert does not validate the complete answer set. The tool also supports the task requester in selecting the most cost-efficient allocation of the budget between the expert and the crowd.

Categories and Subject Descriptors: H.1.2 [User/Machine Systems]: Human information processing
Keywords: crowdsourcing; validation; guiding user feedback

1. INTRODUCTION

Crowdsourcing has been established as an efficient and scalable approach to overcome problems that are computationally expensive or unsolvable for machines, but rather trivial for humans [6]. In essence, crowdsourcing enables users to post tasks in the form of questions, which are then answered by crowd workers for financial rewards. Crowd workers, however, have different backgrounds and wide-ranging levels of expertise and motivation [3], so that the obtained answers are not necessarily correct. Even aggregation of answers from multiple workers to a single question cannot guarantee result correctness. Platforms for crowdsourcing, such as Amazon Mechanical Turk (AMT), aim at including the answer trustworthiness by including a validation phase. That is, the obtained crowd answer are checked against expert answers that are supposedly correct. Involving an expert incurs high costs, though. Hence, only a fraction of the obtained crowd answers can be considered in the validation phase, which raises the question of how to involve experts effectively and efficiently.

This demo presents ERICA: a tool for *ExpeRt guidance In validating Crowd Answers*. Its functionalities are summarized as follows:

SIGIR'15, August 09-13, 2015, Santiago, Chile.
ACM 978-1-4503-3621-5/15/08.
http://dx.doi.org/10.1145/2766462.2767866 .

(1) *Minimizing expert efforts*: ERICA guides experts during the whole validation process. By exploiting the fact that some validations are more beneficial than others, it reduces the cost of expert validation.
(2) *Handling faulty workers*: Faulty workers, such as spammers or sloppy workers, can increase the cost of acquiring correct answers. By detecting them, ERICA improves the quality of the crowdsourcing result.
(3) *Estimating quality*: During the validation process, ERICA maintains an *aggregated answers set* which are the answers considered to be correct together with various statistics related to this set. These statistics support the expert in deciding when to end the validation.
(4) *Optimizing overall cost*: ERICA enables crowdsourcing users to determine the best budget allocation between a validating expert and the crowd w.r.t a budget and a crowdsourcing setup.
(5) *Detecting expert mistakes*: In practice, expert input may contain mistakes that are not caused by the lack of knowledge, but stem from the interaction as part of the validation [5]. ERICA supports the detection of such mistakes, so that they can be fixed by the expert themselves.

To the best of our knowledge, ERICA is the first system to provide such comprehensive support for expert-based validation of crowdsourcing results, thereby providing a valuable add-on to existing crowdsourcing services. In contrast to related approaches to the detection of faulty workers, quality estimation or cost optimization, all our techniques are grounded in expert feedback, which results in higher quality and better performance [5]. In the remainder, we first discuss the implementation of these functionalities in Section 2. Next, Section 3 demonstrates the ERICA by means of an example scenario, before Section 4 closes the paper with a summary.

2. IMPLEMENTATION

This section discusses how ERICA handles large amounts of crowd answers and implements the above functionalities. The underlying theory of the respective techniques is discussed in detail in our earlier work [5].

Functionality

Minimizing expert efforts. To guide the expert validation, ERICA selects and ranks questions for which expert feedback should be sought based on their expected benefit. The expected benefit of a validation question is measured using an information theoretic model. Then, the question with the highest information gain is shown first for expert feedback elicitation [5].

Handling faulty workers. To detect faulty workers, ERICA computes the likelihood of a worker to be spammer (*spammer score*) [5]. To this end, confusion matrices are constructed based on the ex-

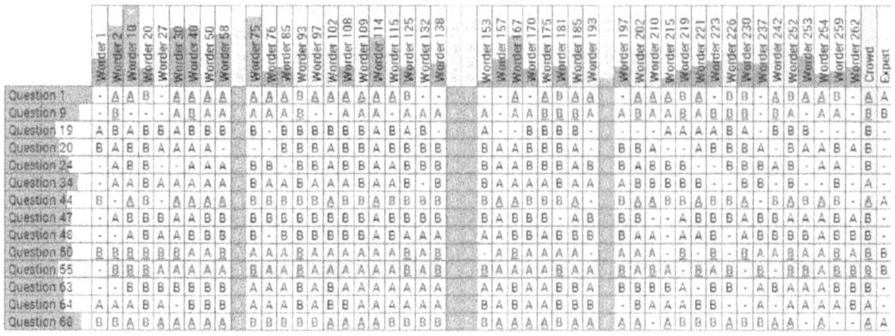

Figure 1: An answer matrix

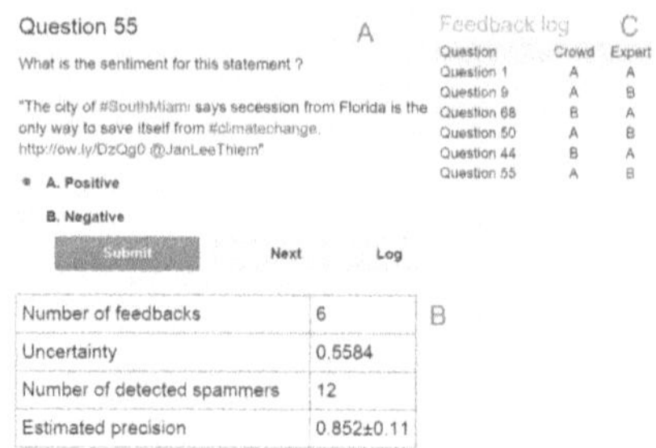

Figure 2: Expert feedback view

pert feedback obtained so far. Answers from workers with a high likelihood to be a spammer are removed by ERICA.

Estimating quality. The quality of the aggregated answers is measured using k-fold cross validation [4]. That is, ERICA arbitrarily partitions the expert feedback into test and training sets. Then, the training set is used to compute the aggregated answers for the test set and the similarity between two aggregated answers sets (one created using only the training set, one using the whole feedback set) is measured. Repeating this procedure k times, ERICA estimates the quality of the aggregated answers.

Optimizing cost. ERICA helps to find the optimal distribution of a pre-defined budget between an expert and the crowd based on characteristics of the crowd. Since these characteristics are not known beforehand, it samples the crowd with a few test questions and simulates the crowd to decide on the best budget distribution [5].

Detecting expert mistakes. ERICA also uses k-fold cross validation to detect expert mistakes. Here, k is fixed to 1, though, in order to detect incorrect feedback. Then, the aggregated answer for the question in the test set is compared with the feedback by the expert. If they are different, the expert is encouraged to revisit the respective question and reconsider the answer.

Scalability

To achieve an efficient implementation for large-scale data, ERICA employs two techniques: *parallelization* and *partitioning*. First, since the computations of the information gain and the spammer score are independent for different questions, they are executed in parallel concurrently for all questions. Second, common answer matrices are sparse [1]. Therefore, ERICA uses sparse matrix partitioning [2] to divide a large answer matrix into smaller dense ones that fit for human interactions and can be handled more efficiently.

Technicality

ERICA is implemented as a web service. The back-end is written in Python and Java. The front-end is an HTML5 website communicating with the server using Javascript and jQuery.

3. DEMONSTRATION

To demonstrate the application of ERICA, we first present its user interface before we turn to an example scenario.

User interface. ERICA offers a rich user interface (see Figure 1,2), which consists of 2 main components:

- *Answer matrix:* contains all the questions and crowd answers. Each row is a question, each column is a worker and a cell denotes the respective answer. The workers and the questions are color-coded to reflect their reliability and difficulty, respectively. The aggregated answers, considered to be correct according to the crowd answers and the expert feedback, are shown in a separate column.
- *Expert feedback view:* contains three panels that present additional information during the validation. Panel A shows the content of the currently-selected question that requires expert input. Various statistics are provided in Panel B for the expert's consideration. Further, the history of expert feedback is visualized in Panel C.

Demonstration scenario. We use the example from Figure 1 to demonstrate how to use ERICA to analyze and validate the answer matrix (a screencast of the demonstration is publicly available [1]).

Before posting a task to a crowdsourcing platform, a user may compute the budget allocation between an expert and the crowd. First, a user posts a set of test questions to study the characteristics of the crowd. Based on the answers, ERICA will simulate the crowd and compute the best budget allocation. Then, the user decides how many questions are posted to the crowd.

After all answers have been collected for the crowdsourcing task, the expert starts the validation. First, ERICA will select the question, for which the feedback is most beneficial. The question and its possible answers are shown in Panel A. Once the expert has submitted their answer, ERICA will recompute the aggregated answers and the reliability of the workers. After several feedback iterations, the expert can remove the answers of a worker, if the estimated reliability of the worker is too low. ERICA will measure the effect of this removal and recompute the result accordingly. The expert can stop the validation process when the estimated precision shown in Panel B is high or the aggregated answers and the feedback are similar for a consecutive number of times, as shown in Panel C.

4. SUMMARY

This paper presented ERICA: a tool for expert guidance in validating crowd answer. Unlike traditional tools for crowdsourcing, ERICA is the first to streamline the validation process by an expert for crowd answers. The expert feedback provides a reliable means to detect and remove faulty workers, which can improve the quality of the result significantly. ERICA helps crowdsourcing users by computing the best budget allocation between the expert and the crowd. As such, ERICA serves not only as a tool to reduce the validation effort, but also acts as a decision-support system to achieve a reduction of validation cost and an improvement of result quality.

Acknowledgment. The research has received funding from the EU-FP7 EINS project (grant 288021) and the ScienceWise project.

5. REFERENCES

[1] H. J. Jung et al. Improving quality of crowdsourced labels via probabilistic matrix factorization. In *HCOMP*, 2012.

[2] G. Karypis et al. Metis-unstructured graph partitioning and sparse matrix ordering system. *Technical Report*, 1995.

[3] G. Kazai et al. Worker types and personality traits in crowdsourcing relevance labels. In *CIKM*, 2011.

[4] B. Mozafari et al. Scaling up crowd-sourcing to very large datasets: A case for active learning. In *VLDB*, 2014.

[5] Q. V. H. Nguyen et al. Minimizing efforts in validating crowd answers. In *SIGMOD*, 2015.

[6] A. J. Quinn et al. Human computation: a survey and taxonomy of a growing field. In *CHI*, 2011.

[1] `https://code.google.com/p/crowdvalidator/`

Large-scale Image Retrieval using Neural Net Descriptors

David Novak
Masaryk University
Brno, Czech Republic
david.novak@fi.muni.cz

Michal Batko
Masaryk University
Brno, Czech Republic
batko@fi.muni.cz

Pavel Zezula
Masaryk University
Brno, Czech Republic
zezula@fi.muni.cz

Categories and Subject Descriptors

H.3.1 [**Information Storage and Retrieval**]: Content Analysis and Indexing; H.3.3 [**Information Storage and Retrieval**]: Information Search and Retrieval

Keywords

metric indexing; deep convolutional neural network; content-based image retrieval; k-NN search

1. ONLINE IMAGE RETRIEVAL SYSTEM

One of current big challenges in computer science is development of data management and retrieval techniques that would keep pace with the evolution of contemporary data and with the growing expectations on data processing. Various digital images became a common part of both public and enterprise data collections and there is a natural requirement that the retrieval should consider more the actual visual content of the image data. In our demonstration, we aim at the task of retrieving images that are visually and semantically similar to a given example image; the system should be able to online evaluate k nearest neighbor queries within a collection containing tens of millions of images. The applicability of such a system would be, for instance, on stock photography sites, in e-shops searching in product photos, or in collections from a constrained Web image search.

A successful content-based image retrieval system must stand on two pillars: *effective* image-processing technique to achieve high-quality retrieval, and *efficient* search techniques to make the system work in real time and on a large scale. Our demonstration uses the cutting edge approach of deep convolutional neural networks [4] to obtain powerful visual features that carry a certain semantic footprint of the image content. These descriptors compared by a distance function seem to very well correspond to the human perception of general visual similarity. Our main contribution is the search engine that can organize large volumes of these complex descriptors so that the similarity queries can be evaluated efficiently. The engine exploits our recent distance-based index PPP-Codes [5] which organizes 320 GB of neural network descriptors extracted from a collection of 20 million images; given a query image, the memory part of the index is able to identify a relatively small candidate set of descriptors that is loaded from the disk and refined to obtain the final result of the similarity query.

Figure 1: Examples of visual queries in the demo.[1]

One of the main objectives of our demonstration is to share the unique user experience of online search powered by neural networks on a large collection of high-quality images. Figure 1 shows examples from the demo, which is available at `http://disa.fi.muni.cz/demos/profiset-decaf/`.

2. SYSTEM ARCHITECTURE

Let us describe in detail the components and overall architecture of the demonstrated system.

2.1 Visual Search with Deep Neural Networks

Recently, the successful application of deep convolutional neural networks revolutionized the area of image and video recognition. Our system exploits the breakthrough image classifier by Krizhevsky et al. [4] that gained significant attention by winning the 2012 ImageNet challenge, defeating other approaches by a significant margin. This neural network was trained on about 1.2M images classified into 1000 categories. Moreover, it was soon observed that intermediate outputs of hidden layers of the network can be used as *features* for assessment of general mutual similarity of various types of images – even without any need of retraining the neural network [2, 4].

[1]The copyright of the images belongs to their authors; they are used for research purposes according to *Profiset usage agreement* at `http://disa.fi.muni.cz/profiset/`

SIGIR'15, August 09-13, 2015, Santiago, Chile.
ACM 978-1-4503-3621-5/15/08.
DOI: http://dx.doi.org/10.1145/2766462.2767868.

Specifically, we use the $DeCAF_7$ feature produced by the last hidden layer of the neural network model provided by Caffe[2] [3], which has been trained by the procedure described in the original paper [4]. We have extracted these features from a collection of 20 million images (see Section 2.3 for details). The extraction process consists of image normalization to 256×256 pixels, generation of ten overlapping patches of 224×224, and a forward feed of these patches through the network [4]. The resulting $DeCAF_7$ feature of an image is the average of the last-but-one layer outputs for the ten image patches. Such extraction takes about 100 ms on our GPU (30 days for the 20M collection). One $DeCAF_7$ feature is a 4096-dimensional vector taking 16 KB on the disk; the whole 20M dataset has thus some 320 GB of uncompressed data. Given a query image, the same extraction procedure generates feature $q \in DeCAF_7$, where $DeCAF_7$ denotes the 4096-dimensional feature space; this is schematically depicted in the top part of Figure 2.

2.2 Distance Indexing for Similarity Search

In our system, we adopt a broad similarity model based on mutual object distances, specifically, $\mathbb{D}$ is a *domain of data* and δ is a total *distance* function $\delta : \mathbb{D} \times \mathbb{D} \longrightarrow \mathbb{R}_0^+$; we assume that this space $(\mathbb{D}, \delta)$ satisfies metric postulates of *identity*, *symmetry* and *triangle inequality* [6]. In our specific case, domain $\mathbb{D}$ is the 4096-dimensional $DeCAF_7$ space and δ is Euclidean distance, as proposed in the image recognition papers [4, 2]. The actual set of 20M features is denoted as $\mathbb{X} \subseteq \mathbb{D}$; the search is modeled by the *nearest neighbors query* k-NN(q) returning the k objects from $\mathbb{X}$ with the smallest distances to given $q \in \mathbb{D}$: $\delta(q, x)$, $x \in \mathbb{X}$.

Our PPP-Codes index uses multiple *recursive Voronoi partitioning* of the metric space; in this way, each object $x \in \mathbb{X}$ is mapped onto its $PPP(x)$ code, which carries information about location of x in these Voronoi diagrams [5]. A memory index is then created on $PPP(x)$ codes, $\forall x \in \mathbb{X}$; each object x is identified by its ID. Given a query k-NN(q), $q \in \mathbb{D}$, this index determines a set $C(q) \subseteq \mathbb{X}$ of candidate objects, or rather object IDs. Objects from $C(q)$ are read from an ID-object disk store and are refined by evaluation of $\delta(q, x)$, $\forall x \in C(q)$ in order to obtain final answer for k-NN(q); this process is sketched in the lower part of Figure 2.

The result of this search process is an approximation of the precise k-NN(q) answer. The precision of the answer depends on the size of the candidate set and so does the response time, because the search costs mainly consist of (1) CPU costs of $C(q)$ generation, (2) I/O costs of reading $C(q)$ objects from the disk and (3) CPU costs of $C(q)$ refinement. Because we work with complex and bulky features, the I/O costs are important, even though we compress the features down to 1/3 of their original size. The PPP-Codes index has about 1 GB in memory and it is designed to provide a very accurate candidate set; for instance, refining 5000 candidate objects results in 80% average recall for 10-NN queries with average response time around 400 ms.

2.3 Dataset and Demo Description

Our demonstration uses a unique collection Profiset[3] consisting of 20 million high quality images provided for research purposes by a stock photography company [1]. The search engine is running on a commodity machine with 8 GB of

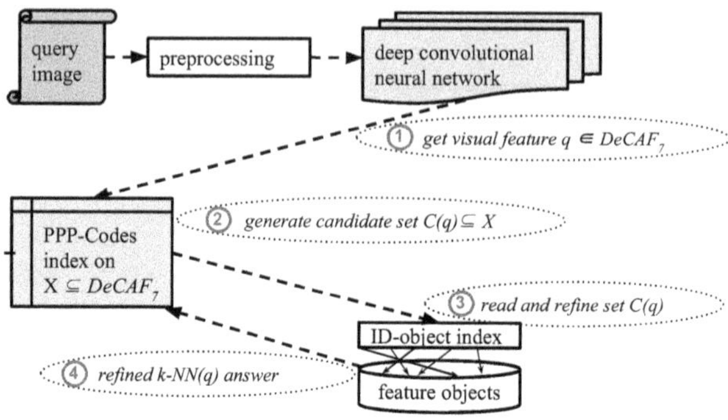

Figure 2: Schema of the demonstration system.

memory, 8 CPU cores and an SSD disk with the ID-object store maintaining the set of the $DeCAF_7$ features. The actual images to be displayed are stored separately.

The application provides several actions. The default one displays a random selection of images, which demonstrates the diversity of the collection. Each of the images can serve as a query image for the k-NN visual search as described above; in order to initiate such query, the $DeCAF_7$ feature is retrieved from the ID-object store. Also, an external image can be uploaded and serve as the query; in this case, the $DeCAF_7$ feature is first extracted by the neural network. The Profiset collection contains also keywords for each image and our application provides also text search realized via Lucene index. These keywords are not combined anyhow with the DeCAF features in order to demonstrate the pure strength of the deep convolutional neural networks.

Acknowledgments

This work was supported by the Czech Research Foundation project P103/12/G084.

3. REFERENCES

[1] P. Budikova, M. Batko, and P. Zezula. Evaluation Platform for Content-based Image Retrieval Systems. In *International Conference on Theory and Practice of Digital Libraries*, LNCS, pages 130–142. Springer, 2011.

[2] J. Donahue, Y. Jia, O. Vinyals, J. Hoffman, N. Zhang, E. Tzeng, and T. Darrell. DeCAF: A Deep Convolutional Activation Feature for Generic Visual Recognition. In *Proceedings of the International Conference on Machine Learning*, pages 647–655, 2014.

[3] Y. Jia, E. Shelhamer, J. Donahue, S. Karayev, J. Long, R. Girshick, S. Guadarrama, and T. Darrell. Caffe: Convolutional Architecture for Fast Feature Embedding. *arXiv preprint arXiv:1408.5093*, 2014.

[4] A. Krizhevsky, I. Sutskever, and G. E. Hinton. ImageNet Classification with Deep Convolutional Neural Networks. *Advances In Neural Information Processing Systems*, pages 1106–1114, 2012.

[5] D. Novak and P. Zezula. Rank Aggregation of Candidate Sets for Efficient Similarity Search. In *Database and Expert Systems Applications: 25th International Conference, DEXA 2014. Proceedings, Part II*, vol. 8645 of *LNCS*, pages 42–58. Springer, 2014.

[6] P. Zezula, G. Amato, V. Dohnal, and M. Batko. *Similarity Search: The Metric Space Approach.* Springer, 2006.

[2]`http://caffe.berkeleyvision.org`
[3]`http://disa.fi.muni.cz/profiset/`

Galean: Visualization of Geolocated News Events from Social Media

Vanessa Peña-Araya, Mauricio Quezada, and Barbara Poblete
PRISMA Research Group
Department of Computer Science
University of Chile, Santiago, Chile
{vpena, mquezada, bpoblete}@dcc.uchile.cl

ABSTRACT

Online Social Networks (OSN) have changed the way information is produced and consumed. Organizing and retrieving unstructured data extracted from these platforms is not an easy task. Galean is a visual and interactive tool that aims to help journalists and historians, among others, analyze news events discussed on Twitter. In this tool, news events are visually represented by the very countries from where the news originated, the date when they happened and their impact in the OSN. Galean considers countries as entities, as opposed to mere geographical locations as most of the tools in the state of the art. As a consequence, it allows users to explore and retrieve news not only by their geographical and temporal context, but also by the relationship among countries. With this tool users can search for behavioral patterns of news events and observe how countries are associated in specific events. We expect our work to become a public tool that helps conduct historical analyses of social media news coverage over time.

Categories and Subject Descriptors

H.3.3 [**Information Storage and Retrieval**]: Information Search and Retrieval—*Information filtering*; H.5.2 [**Information Interfaces and Representation**]: User Interfaces—*Graphical user interfaces*

Keywords

Social media analysis; spatio-temporal analysis; geovisualization; text analysis; historical analysis

1. MOTIVATION AND CONTRIBUTION

An event is usually understood as *something* that happened in a particular *place* and *time*. When a news event happens, users from OSN react to them by sharing the information or opinions they have about them. However, it is not an easy task to extract valuable knowledge from this huge volume of information. Even if news events are detected and stored in local databases it is hard to retrieve them later. This is mainly because the user does not always know what he or she is looking for and, if so, might not know the exact words to describe it.

In this paper we present Galean, an interactive visualization tool that represents events extracted from Twitter by their geographical and temporal context. It aims to help users explore and retrieve news events from OSN by the political geographical entities that participate in it. In addition, it aims to reveal links between countries based on their participation in particular news events, and behavioral patterns of the news. With this representation of news events, we work to deliver an interactive tool that can answer questions such as *what are the events related to this country on this date?* Or, *in which news events do these two countries participate together and how do they evolve?*

Most state of the art tools that work with geographical features of events extracted from OSN, aim to position them over where they happened or aim to detect events happening in a particular place. For example, Sakaki et al. [3] use the geographical metadata in tweets [1] to detect where the epicentre of an earthquake is and Watanabe et al. [5] to identify small localized events. SensePlace2 [1] gives a broader view by also considering the locations that tweets are about. However, this tool emphasizes dimensions of the events more than the events themselves. As a result, these tools ignore the relationships among countries that occur as a consequence of real world events, and therefore do not allow users to explore and query events by these relationships as our tool does.

We hope Galean will help journalists and ordinary OSN users explore and analyze news events from a historical point of view.

2. SYSTEM ARCHITECTURE

The system architecture of Galean is designed in a three-step process:

I.- Event identification: We detect news events that had high media coverage by gathering messages from verified news accounts from Twitter. The data set currently in use contains news events starting from August 2013. The detection and storage processes of news events are conducted every hour. Although Galean could use any news source, it is defined currently to use a set of tweets as input.

II.- Geo-temporal contextualization: besides the date in which

[1] Tweets: messages posted in the Twitter OSN

SIGIR '15, August 09-13, 2015, Santiago, Chile
ACM 978-1-4503-3621-5/15/08
http://dx.doi.org/10.1145/2766462.2767862.

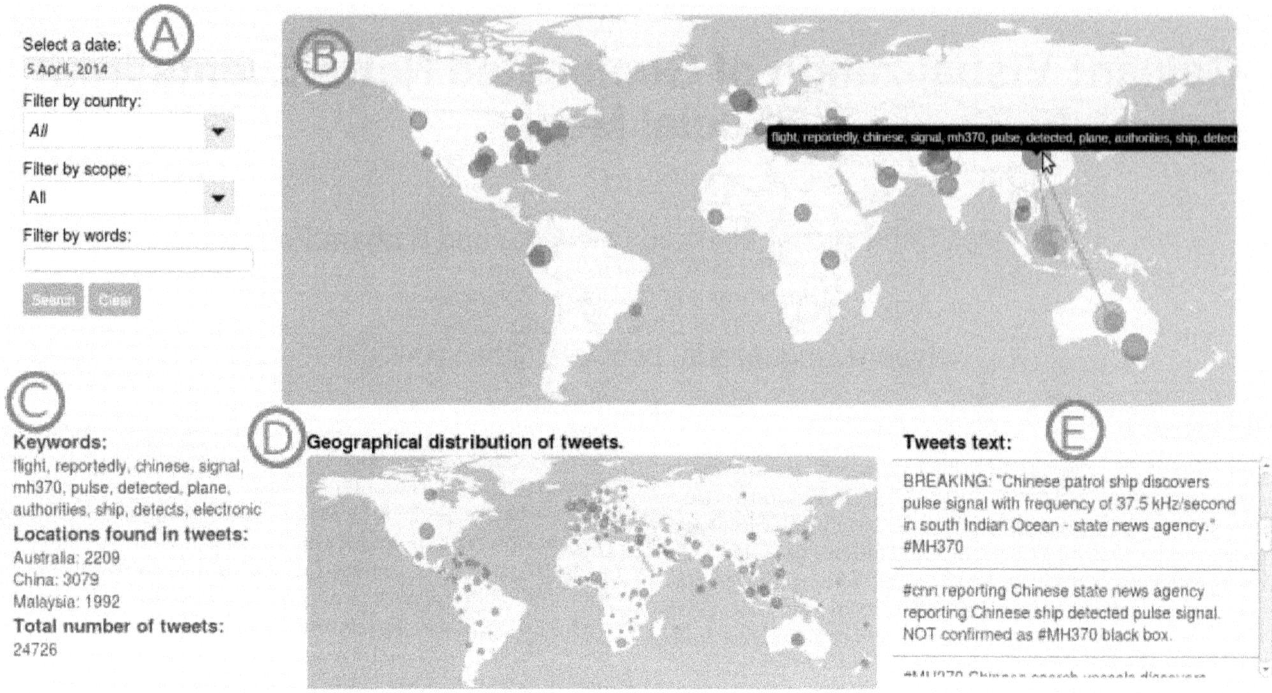

Figure 1: Screenshot of Galean's interface.

a news event was detected, we also extract the countries from where the news originated, and the countries from where Twitter users talk about the news. Both processes use CLAVIN [4], an open source geoparser. A more detailed description of the location-aware model of news events used by Galean can be found in [2]. *III.- Visualization:* The complete view of Galean is in Figure 1. To start using it, the user must select a particular date of interest in the filter area (section `A`, Figure 1). After this, all the news events detected on that date will be displayed as a bubble on the main map, as depicted in section `B` of Figure 1. Each of them are positioned over the country that was involved in the event with their size represent their impact in OSN, measured by volume of messages. When passing the cursor over international events (orange bubbles), the links between all the countries involved in the news event are revealed. By clicking a bubble, additional information about the news it represents appears in the view: miscellaneous data, propagation of the news over the world and tweets discussing the event, in sections `C`, `D` and `E` respectively in Figure 1.

3. DEMONSTRATION

Galean is an exploratory tool. By selecting a date to start with, the user has an idea of the news events that happened that day by country and impact. With this basic information the user navigates and finds news events according to what he or she is looking for. Figure 1 shows the overview of news events for April 5th, 2014. The selected event in that picture refers to the search of the Malaysian flight MH370 which disappeared March 4th of the same year. As can be observed, that event relates Malaysia, China and Australia. This is because a Chinese news agency declared at that time that a signal, that may have come from the black box of the missing flight, was received from a location near Australia. It is possible to see that the event has a lot of impact on Twitter, as shown in the map below. This map also highlighted in red that Malaysia, China and Australia were the protagonists of that event. The filters available in the left part of the view allow users to focus on news associated with one or more countries. With these features, Galean allows users to follow the evolution of a news event.

4. ACKNOWLEDGEMENTS

The authors were partially supported by a FONDECYT Grant 11121511 and the Millennium Nucleus Center for Semantic Web Research Grant NC120004. We also thank Alexandre Bergel and Omar Miranda for their help in early stages of this work.

References

[1] Alan M. MacEachren, Anuj Jaiswal, Anthony C. Robinson, Scott Pezanowski, Alexander Savelyev, Prasenjit Mitra, Xiao Zhang, and Justine Blanford. Senseplace2: Geotwitter analytics support for situational awareness. In *IEEE (VAST)*, 2011.

[2] Mauricio Quezada, Vanessa Peña-Araya, and Barbara Poblete. Location-aware model for news events in social media. In *SIGIR*, 2015.

[3] Takeshi Sakaki, Makoto Okazaki, and Yutaka Matsuo. Earthquake shakes Twitter users: real-time event detection by social sensors. In *WWW*, 2010.

[4] Berico Technologies. CLAVIN: Cartographic Location And Vicinity INdexer. `http://clavin.bericotechnologies.com/`, 2012–2013.

[5] Kazufumi Watanabe, Masanao Ochi, Makoto Okabe, and Rikio Onai. Jasmine: a real-time local-event detection system based on geolocation information propagated to microblogs. In *CIKM*, 2011.

SciNet: Interactive Intent Modeling for Information Discovery

Tuukka Ruotsalo[1], Jaakko Peltonen[2,4], Manuel J.A. Eugster[2], Dorota Głowacka[3], Aki Reijonen[3], Giulio Jacucci[3], Petri Myllymäki[3], Samuel Kaski[2,3]
Helsinki Institute for Information Technology HIIT
[1]Helsinki Institute for Information Technology HIIT, Aalto University, Finland
[2]Aalto University, Department of Information and Computer Science, Finland
[3]University of Helsinki, Department of Computer Science, Finland
[4]University of Tampere, School of Information Sciences, Finland
first.last@hiit.fi

ABSTRACT

Current search engines offer limited assistance for exploration and information discovery in complex search tasks. Instead, users are distracted by the need to focus their cognitive efforts on finding navigation cues, rather than selecting relevant information. Interactive intent modeling enhances the human information exploration capacity through computational modeling, visualized for interaction. Interactive intent modeling has been shown to increase task-level information seeking performance by up to 100%. In this demonstration, we showcase *SciNet*, a system implementing interactive intent modeling on top of a scientific article database of over 60 million documents.

Keywords

Intent modeling; Interactive information retrieval; Personalization; Visual information seeking

Categories and Subject Descriptors

H.3.3 [**Information Search and Retrieval**]

1. INTRODUCTION

Recent behavioral studies show that a large portion of users' information-seeking activities are exploratory and characterized by the complex and evolving nature of users' information needs [4]. As a result, the users face the problem of entering correct terms that describe their evolving search intents, so that the desired information can be retrieved on subsequent iterations [2]. We propose *Interactive intent modeling* promoting resourceful interaction between humans and information retrieval systems to enable information discovery that goes beyond search [6]. It tackles the vocabulary mismatch problem [2] by providing the user with knowledge about potential intents to discover, visualizes the intents as directions in the information space around the user's present position, and transfers the exploratory search to a recognition task in which users can direct their search via an interactive visualization to interact with the system's intent model [7].

Interactive intent modeling is based on two principles [6]: 1) Visualizing the current search intents and directions in the information space, and 2) Interactive adaptation of the intent model balancing exploring the information space and exploiting the user feedback.

SIGIR'15, August 09-13, 2015, Santiago, Chile.
ACM 978-1-4503-3621-5/15/08.
DOI: http://dx.doi.org/10.1145/2766462.2767863.

2. THE SCINET SYSTEM

The *SciNet* system, shown in Figure 1, implements interactive intent modeling on top of over 60 million scientific documents. The search starts with the user typing in a query, which results in a set of keywords being displayed and laid out on a radial display called the Intent Radar [8], and a ranked list of articles. The estimated intents, for which the results on the right side list have been retrieved, are visualized for the user (inner circle). The angular distance corresponds to similarity of intents and the radial distance from the centre corresponds to relevance. Predicted future intents, which are estimated for users to find directions on the radar away from their present intent estimate, are visualized in the outer circle of the Intent Radar. The user can provide positive feedback by dragging keywords closer to the center of the radar, and negative feedback by dragging them further away. Multiple keywords can be dragged at each iteration.

Figure 1 shows two iterations of a search session: the Intent Radar visualization of the first iteration (left) and the second iteration with both the visualization and the final result list. The user first issues a query "information visualization" and the system visualizes the intent model (inner circle) and suggested potentially interesting intents (outer circle) as keywords, and a ranked document list. The user increases the relevance of "visual information retrieval" (red arrow) by dragging it to the center of the radar. The system then computes and visualizes new intent model represented as a set of keywords (inner circle), including "image representation and indexing," "perception," and "visual data exploration." The system also computes projections in the intent space via pseudo-feedback and suggests relevant search directions for the user (outer circle), including "www," "information fidelity," "information visualization techniques," "interaction." The user can continue the search by selecting to exploit to more specific topics or to explore to more general but yet relevant topics.

3. ALGORITHMIC BUILDING BLOCKS

Learning the intent model. Given the evolutionary nature of search, as also demonstrated in our example search scenario, it is important to not only exploit the feedback elicited from the user

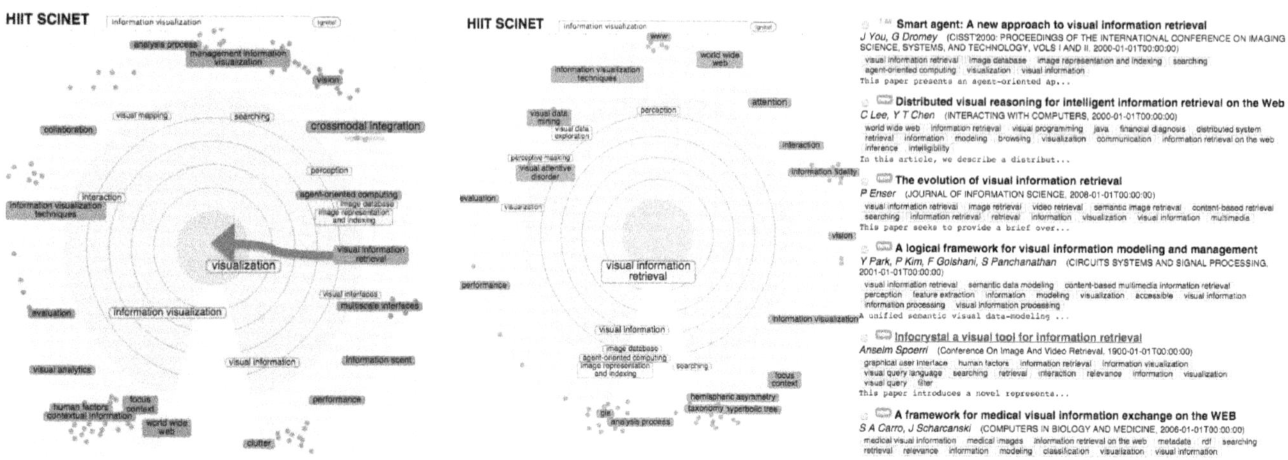

Figure 1: Two iterations of a search session with an initial query "information visualization". Left: The Intent Radar visualization of the first iteration. The user drags the keyword "visual information retrieval" to the center of the Intent Radar (red arrow). Right: The second iteration. Both the Intent Radar visualization and the final result list are shown.

but also balance it with exploration. To put it simply, users need to be able to focus on a specific location of the information space (exploit) and also be able to broaden their search through more general areas (explore). To learrn such models on-line, we use the *exploration–exploitation paradigm* of reinforcement learning [1, 3]. In this paradigm, the model (the search engine) and its environment (the user) form an online loop, and learning involves finding an optimal balance between exploration (selecting items from uncharted parts of the information space) and exploitation (selecting items most likely to be relevant given the current intent model) to acquire feedback on subsequent iterations. The learning mechanism predicts the model consisting of keyword relevances based on user interactions during the search session. The model is then used in combination with a statistical language model to rank the documents.

Interactive visualization. We optimize a data-driven layout for the search intents by probabilistic modeling-based nonlinear dimensionality reduction [9]. The task of the layout algorithm is to place keywords so that neighboring keywords on the display have neighboring characterizations. To highlight the structure in the outer circle layout, we apply a simple agglomerative clustering to angles of keywords in the outer circle and show for each cluster the label of the predicted most relevant keyword [7].

4. SUMMARY OF RESULTS

The *SciNet* system was studied in task-based experiments in which users were given 30 minutes to solve research tasks using information retrieval systems operating on a database of over 60 million scholarly articles. The system setup with interactive intent modeling was compared against conventional information retrieval system with a list-based visualization and interaction with typed queries. Interactive intent modeling was found to significantly improve users' task performance on complex tasks, helping users to move away from their initial query context, thus allowing them to increase recall by over 50% while preserving precision. Moreover, session-level recall for novel information that was assessed separately was found to improve by over 100% [7, 5]. The improvements can be attributed to interactive intent modeling. The interaction with intent visualization does not fully replace the query-typing interaction, but users still rely on typed keywords when initializing new search directions. However, interactive intent modeling offers an additional complementary way to express search intents to direct search towards novel, but still relevant information.

5. ACKNOWLEDGMENTS

Certain data included herein are derived from the Web of Science prepared by THOMSON REUTERS, Inc., Philadelphia, Pennsylvania, USA; the Digital Libraries of ACM, IEEE, and Springer. The search engine is commercialized by Etsimo Ltd. (www.etsimo.com).

6. REFERENCES

[1] P. Auer. Using confidence bounds for exploitation-exploration trade-offs. *J. Mach. Learn. Res.*, 3:397 – 422, 2002.

[2] G. W. Furnas, T. K. Landauer, L. M. Gomez, and S. T. Dumais. The vocabulary problem in human-system communication. *Commun. ACM*, 30(11):964–971, Nov. 1987.

[3] D. Glowacka, T. Ruotsalo, K. Konuyshkova, K. Athukorala, S. Kaski, and G. Jacucci. Directing exploratory search: Reinforcement learning from user interactions with keywords. In *Proc. IUI'13*, pages 117–128, New York, NY, USA, 2013. ACM.

[4] G. Marchionini. Exploratory search: from finding to understanding. *Commun. ACM*, 49(4):41–46, Apr. 2006.

[5] T. Ruotsalo, K. Athukorala, D. Głowacka, K. Konyushkova, A. Oulasvirta, S. Kaipiainen, S. Kaski, and G. Jacucci. Supporting exploratory search tasks with interactive user modeling. In *In Proc. ASIS&T*, pages 39:1–39:10, Silver Springs, MD, USA, 2013. American Society for Information Science.

[6] T. Ruotsalo, G. Jacucci, P. Myllymäki, and S. Kaski. Interactive intent modeling: Information discovery beyond search. *Commun. ACM*, 58(1):86–92, Dec. 2014.

[7] T. Ruotsalo, J. Peltonen, M. Eugster, D. Glowacka, K. Konyushkova, K. Athukorala, I. Kosunen, A. Reijonen, P. Myllymäki, G. Jacucci, and S. Kaski. Directing exploratory search with interactive intent modeling. In *Proc. CIKM '13*, pages 1759–1764. ACM, 2013.

[8] T. Ruotsalo, J. Peltonen, M. J. Eugster, D. Glowacka, A. Reijonen, G. Jacucci, P. Myllymäki, and S. Kaski. Intentradar: Search user interface that anticipates user's search intents. In *Proc. CHI EA '14*, pages 455–458. ACM, 2014.

[9] J. Venna, J. Peltonen, K. Nybo, H. Aidos, and S. Kaski. Information retrieval perspective to nonlinear dimensionality reduction for data visualization. *J. Mach. Learn. Res.*, 11:451–490, 2010.

Linse: A Distributional Semantics Entity Search Engine

Juliano Efson Sales[1], André Freitas[2], Siegfried Handschuh[2], Brian Davis[1]
[1]Insight Centre for Data Analytics
National University of Ireland, Galway
[2]Department of Computer Science and Mathematics
University of Passau

ABSTRACT

Entering *Football Players from United States* when searching for *American Footballers* is an example of *vocabulary mismatch*, which occurs when different words are used to express the same concepts. In order to address this phenomenon for entity search targeting descriptors for *complex categories*, we propose a *compositional-distributional semantics* entity search engine, which extracts semantic and commonsense knowledge from large-scale corpora to address the vocabulary gap between query and data.

Categories and Subject Descriptors

H.3.3 [**Information Storage and Retrieval**]: Information Search and Retrieval

Keywords

semantic search, entity search, distributional search.

1. INTRODUCTION

Entities naming *sets* and *categories* are fundamental for describing structured, semi-structured and unstructured data and are present from Wikis to databases. The natural language descriptors associated with these entities are fundamental to support users searching, querying or browsing structured or semi-structured data, which heavily depend on them to find the desired piece of information.

Users searching over a set of *natural language category descriptors* (NLCDs) demand principled mechanisms to support crossing the semantic gap between the user queries and the target NLCDs. The *vocabulary problem* occurs when different terms are used to express the same concepts. One of the first studies in this direction shows that 80% of people familiar with the same domain use different terms to name the same concept[4]. Search over collections which do not have high vocabulary redundancy is highly affected by the vocabulary problem, since users do not know which words were used to describe target entities, categories or documents.

Shifting from unique words to multi-word expressions enables differences not only in vocabulary, but also in ordering and *compositionality*, increasing the complexity in addressing the vocabulary mismatch. For example, *Football Players from United States* would be an acceptable paraphrase for *American Footballers*.

In order to address this problem, we have developed *Linse*, an entity search engine which implements a *compositional-distributional semantic model* to address the vocabulary problem for searching entities which describe complex categories (e.g. 'Buildings destroyed in the great fire of London and not rebuilt'). This paper demonstrates the basic mechanisms and principles behind the Linse entity search engine, showing how distributional semantics can support users in crossing the query-data semantic gap.

2. THE COMPOSITIONAL-DISTRIBUTIONAL SEMANTIC MODEL

Linse uses distributional semantic models [3] (semantic models which are automatically built from large-scale corpora) as a principled mechanism to address the vocabulary gap between users and data. On the top of the distributional model, a compositional model based on a *semantic pivoting mechanism* [5] is used to provide a semantic interpretation of the query under the Knowledge Base (KB) of category descriptors (NLCDs).

The Linse search engine decomposes every NLCD into a *semantic core* and three types of *specializations*: (i) specializations of the core defined by noun, adjective or adverb modifiers (e.g. 'Tall Athletes'); (ii) specializations defined by named entities ('Athletes from Russia') ; (iii) specializations defined by temporal references ('Athletes born in the 80s').

The Linse approach determines the *constituency structure* of every NLCD during indexing time, generating a graph containing a semantic core and its specializations, following the semantic representation model for categories described in [5]. Each core and specialization type is indexed in a different distributional vector space, which maps to different indexes.

The *query interpretation process* starts with the syntactic parsing of the query. The noun phrase head defines the query semantic core. For the example query 'ancestral wolves', the semantic core is 'wolves'. The semantic core is sent as a query to the *semantic core distributional vector space* which computes the distributional semantic re-

SIGIR '15, August 09-13, 2015, Santiago, Chile
ACM 978-1-4503-3621-5/15/08.
http://dx.doi.org/10.1145/2766462.2767871

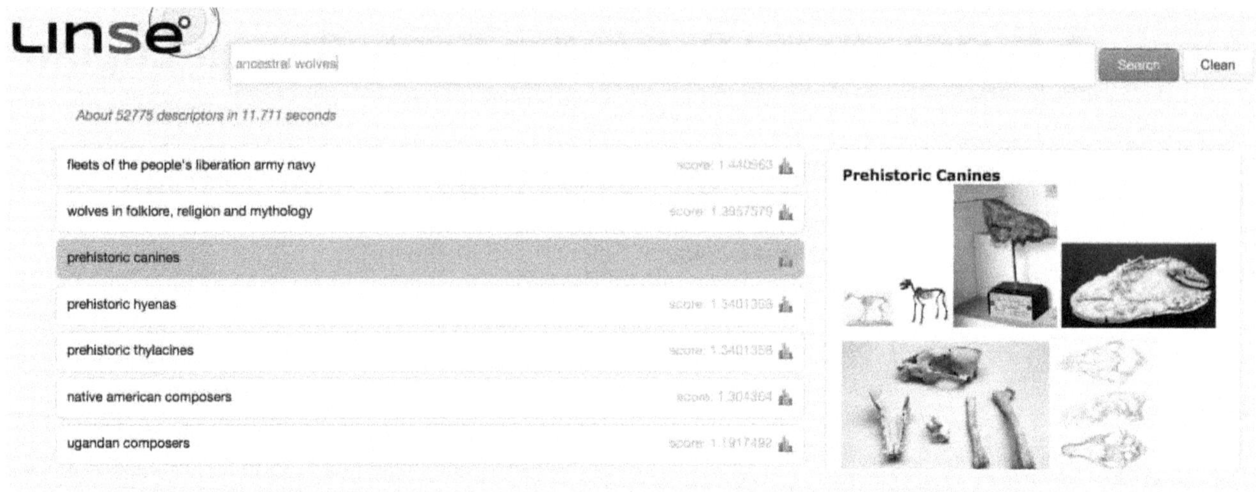

Figure 1: Screenshot of the Linse search result.

latedness between the query term and the indexed semantic cores, returning a set of most related semantic cores. For the example query, the corresponding 'canine' semantic core is returned.

The next step consists in selecting the next core modifier, the adjective 'ancestral', sending it as a query to the subspace of specializations of 'canine'. The use of 'canine' as a *semantic pivot* supports the reduction of the dimensionality of the distributional space, by only looking into specializations which are applied to 'canine'. Using the distributional semantic relatedness measure over the specializations subspace, it returns 'prehistoric canine' as an output. The ranking approach uses as a ranking score a weighted composition of the distributional relatedness measure between each query term and the matching NLCD terms. In the context of this work, Explicit Semantic Analysis [6] is used as a semantic relatedness measure.

Figure 1 shows an screenshot of the result set for the example query, which displays the search box, the ranked list of returned categories and their associated ranking scores. The use of the distributional semantic relatedness as a ranking function provides a comprehensive semantic matching mechanism [5] which is suitable for exploratory entity search scenarios.

For the demonstration, a knowledge base of more than 300,000 category descriptors corresponding to the Wikipedia category links were indexed. A set of natural language queries over the knowledge base are demonstrated in an online video[1]. Some of these queries with their corresponding NLCD mappings are listed on Table 1.

Linse was implemented using Java over Lucene and used the EasyESA framework [2] over the Wikipedia 2013 corpus.

3. SUMMARY

This paper demonstrated the Linse entity search engine. Linse uses a compositional-distributional model to provide a mechanism to search for complex category descriptors. The use of distributional semantic models provides a low-effort (automatically built from large-scale corpora) and comprehensive semantic matching strategy, which can be easily transported to other languages. The proposed model can be applied in different scenarios for entity search, varying from tag recommendation systems to Question Answering over Linked Data.

[1]http://treo.deri.org/linsedemo

Queries → NLCDs
literature journals from austria → austrian literary magazines
movie premieres in 2008 → 2008 film festivals
obsolete justice institutions of connecticut → defunct law enforcement agencies of connecticut
norwegian top singles → number-one singles in norway
italian social movements → political movements in italy
repeating events which were initiated in 1875 → recurring events established in 1875
horse enthusiasts from france → french racehorse owners and breeders

Table 1: Examples of query-NLCD mappings.

4. ACKNOWLEDGMENTS

This publication was supported by Science Foundation Ireland (SFI) under Grant Number SFI/12/RC/2289.

5. REFERENCES

[1] A. Freitas, et al., On the Semantic Representation and Extraction of Complex Category Descriptors, In Proc. of NLDB, 2014.

[2] D. Carvalho, et al., EasyESA: A Low-effort Infrastructure for Explicit Semantic Analysis, In Proc. of ISWC, 2014.

[3] P. D. Turney and P. Pantel., From frequency to meaning: Vector space models of semantics. J. Artif. Int. Res., 37(1) : pp. 141 - 188, January 2010.

[4] G. W. Furnas et al., The vocabulary problem in human-system communication. Commun. ACM, 30(11): pp. 964 - 971, November 1987.

[5] A. Freitas, E. Curry, Natural Language Queries over Heterogeneous Linked Data Graphs, In Proc. of IUI, 2014.

[6] E. Gabrilovich, S. Markovitch, Computing semantic relatedness using Wikipedia-based explicit semantic analysis. In Proc. of IJCAI, 2007.

Online News Tracking for Ad-Hoc Queries

Jeroen B. P. Vuurens
The Hague University of Applied Science
Delft University of Technology, The Netherlands
j.b.p.vuurens@tudelft.nl

Arjen P. de Vries
CWI
Delft University of Technology, The Netherlands
arjen@acm.org

Roi Blanco
Yahoo Research Barcelona, Spain
roi@yahoo-inc.com

Peter Mika
Yahoo Research Barcelona, Spain
pmika@yahoo-inc.com

ABSTRACT

Following news about a specific event can be a difficult task as new information is often scattered across web pages. An up-to-date summary of the event would help to inform users and allow them to navigate to articles that are likely to contain relevant and novel details. We demonstrate an approach that is feasible for online tracking of news that is relevant to a user's ad-hoc query.

Categories and Subject Descriptors

H.3.3 [**Information Search and Retrieval**]: Information Filtering

General Terms

Clustering, Multi-document summarization

1. TRACKING EVOLVING NEWS

Internet users are replacing traditional media sources such as newspapers or television shows more frequently by online news. Although the Web offers a seemingly large and diverse set of information sources ranging from highly curated professional content to social media, in practice most sources base their stories on previously published works and add a much more limited set of new information. Therefore, users that seek additional information on a topic, often end up spending significant amount of effort re-reading the same parts of a story before finding relevant and novel information. In such cases, an up-to-date summary of the event would help to inform users and allow them to navigate to articles that are likely to contain relevant and novel details. Online summarization is a crucial aspect of real-world products such as online live streams for natural disasters, product launches, financial or political events, breaking news notifications on mobile devices and topical daily news summaries like the Yahoo! news digest (`https://mobile.yahoo.com/newsdigest`).

In this demonstration, we suggest an alternative for tracking the news via Twitter hashtag subscriptions or Google Alerts. Compared to these existing approaches, the user is presented with a summary that contains the most important previously unseen facts along a timeline, topically related to a predefined ad-hoc query. The result is a timeline that is less redundant than Twitter and more insightful than the stream of headlines on Google Alerts. Instead of reporting social media utterances, we propose to give updates directly from the journalists' writings, by selecting relevant sentences with novel information from the news articles themselves.

The main contribution of this work is to demonstrate an approach that is feasible to tailor continuous news updates to ad-hoc queries. The technical contribution is to apply a multi-step three-nearest-neighbors clustering approach that can keep up with all the news arriving from hundreds of RSS feeds. For each of those feeds, we fetch the full articles from the source, and process their contents to identify the most novel and relevant sentences. The resulting system participates in the TREC temporal summarization task, but the demonstration gives more interpretable and comparable results than the TREC evaluation measures indicate. Also, users of the demo can track their own information needs.

SIGIR'15, August 09-13, 2015, Santiago, Chile.
ACM 978-1-4503-3621-5/15/08.
DOI: http://dx.doi.org/10.1145/2766462.2767872 .

2. EXISTING WORK

The system used can be viewed as a hybrid combination of techniques for query based online news tracking and summarization, adapted from [2, 1]. A side effect of broadcast news is that stories with near identical publication times are more likely to discuss related events [2], which is what we use in this study to cluster news. Our approach differs by a stronger emphasis on novelty of information emitted (like [3]). Hereto, we estimate the amount of previously unseen information to use only sentences that are likely to contain novel information.

3. TRACKING AD-HOC REQUESTS

For online news tracking, we propose to use articles that are published on online news sites. The title of news articles can be viewed as a short summarization of its content, and therefore used to determine if articles are likely to describe the same topic. Given the relative low-memory requirements of news headlines, this allows for fast in memory clustering without the need to partition the data. The publication of most news articles can be monitored using RSS feeds, which allows fast access to the articles' title and publication time.

In this demo, we summarize a stream of online news articles in a three-step process: *cluster titles*, *cluster sentences* and *qualify sentences*. In the first step, titles of newly published articles are continuously downloaded from RSS feeds. These titles are connected to their nearest neighbors based on similarity measure that considers their title and publication time. Salient sentences are found in sentence clusters of the nearest neighbor graph, when sentences from at least three different sources are most similar, indicating news facts that are more interesting rather than (opinion) information that is not supported. In step 2, per ad-hoc query a graph of sentences is created and maintained. The output of step 1 is monitored, and if a *query matching cluster of titles* is formed or modified, i.e. that contains a title that includes all query terms, then all sentences of the news articles in that cluster are added to the sentence graph of the ad-hoc query. Finally, in step 3, the *qualifying* sentences in the arriving news article are emitted to the user. For qualification, a sentence must (a) be among a cluster of at least three sentences from different news domains, (b) be ranked in the top-K of emitted sentences using a relevance model over the information seen in the last hour, and (c) add information previously not shown to the user.

4. FEASIBILITY

In this demo, we show that online news tracking can be done with reasonable latency in commodity machines. Typically, the monitoring of RSS feeds and maintaining a nearest neighbor graph over news headlines takes less than 10% of the capacity of a standard computer. The clustering and qualifying of sentences is processed independently for different ad-hoc queries and therefore can be processed in parallel and scaled up in production systems. Additionally, efficiency can be improved when the news timelines for known entities (e.g. Wikipedia) are cached in advance, allowing steps 2 and 3 for entity related queries to be simplified to a filtering task over a cached timeline.

5. DEMONSTRATION

We provide three ways to participate in the demo. At the stand, we will show a summary of topics that are trending at that time. For these summaries, the information is processed as if online and therefore represent what the user would have received when they subscribed to the query at the first update. Additionally, participants can experience receiving new updates on the topics they wish to track, by subscribing to a live generated RSS feed for current trends. Finally, we provide limited opportunity to enter ad-hoc queries, depending on the resources needed to downloading the articles for new topics.

Table 1: Timeline constructed for the query "Copenhagen" from Feb 14 2015 16:19.

Time	Sentence
2015-02-14 16:19:58	Copenhagen - Shots were fired on Saturday near a meeting in the Danish capital of Copenhagen attended by controversial Swedish artist Lars Vilks, Sweden's TT news agency reported.
2015-02-14 16:49:22	COPENHAGEN, Denmark - At least one gunman opened fire Saturday on a Copenhagen cafe, killing one man in what authorities called a likely terror attack during a free speech event organized by an artist who had caricatured the Prophet Muhammad.
2015-02-14 17:34:26	COPENHAGEN, Denmark (AP) – A gunman fired on a cafe in Copenhagen as it hosted a free speech event Saturday, killing one man, Danish police said.
2015-02-14 18:51:04	After searching for the gunman for hours, police reported another shooting near a synagogue in downtown Copenhagen after midnight.
2015-02-14 19:29:41	One person was shot in the head and two police were wounded in an attack on the synagogue in central Copenhagen, Danish police said, adding that it was too early to say whether the incident was connected to an earlier one at an arts cafe.
2015-02-15 01:56:20	French President Francois Hollande called the Copenhagen shooting "deplorable" and said Thorning-Schmidt would have the "full solidarity of France in this trial."
2015-02-15 03:52:40	Denmark was on high alert and a massive manhunt was under way on Sunday after a man sprayed bullets at a Copenhagen cafe hosting a debate on freedom of speech and blasphemy, killing one person and wounding three police officers.

In Table 1, we show an example of a time line constructed for the query "Copenhagen", after a terrorist attack on Februari 14th 2015. The first mention on Twitter of the hashtag #CopenhagenShooting was at 17:11 (`http://ctrlq.org/first/`), and the first information was added to Wikipedia at 17:06. A larger static example of the demo results can be viewed online, at `http://newstracker.github.io/`.

Acknowledgment

This demonstration has been developed with support of the Yahoo Faculty Research and Engagement Program and COMMIT/ project Infiniti, and was carried out on the Dutch national e-infrastructure with the support of SURF Foundation.

References

[1] J. Allan, R. Gupta, and V. Khandelwal. Temporal summaries of new topics. In *Proceedings of the 24th annual international ACM SIGIR conference on Research and development in information retrieval*, pages 10–18. ACM, 2001.

[2] J. Allan, R. Papka, and V. Lavrenko. On-line new event detection and tracking. In *Proceedings of the 21st annual international ACM SIGIR conference on Research and development in information retrieval*, pages 37–45. ACM, 1998.

[3] E. Gabrilovich, S. Dumais, and E. Horvitz. Newsjunkie: providing personalized newsfeeds via analysis of information novelty. In *Proceedings of the 13th international conference on World Wide Web*, pages 482–490. ACM, 2004.

DUMPLING: A Novel Dynamic Search Engine

Andrew Jie Zhou, Jiyun Luo, Hui Yang
Department of Computer Science, Georgetown University
{jz398,jl1749}@georgetown.edu, huiyang@cs.georgetown.edu

ABSTRACT

In this demo paper, we introduce a new search engine that supports Information Retrieval (IR) in a dynamic setting. A dynamic search engine distinguishes itself by handling rich interactions and temporal dependency among the queries in a session or for a task. The proposed search engine is called Dumpling, named after the development team's favorite food. It implements state-of-the-art dynamic search algorithms and provides: (i) a dynamic search toolkit by integrating the Query Change Retrieval Model (QCM) and the Win-win search algorithm; (ii) a user-friendly interface supporting side-by-side comparison of search results given by a state-of-the-art static search algorithm and the proposed dynamic search algorithms; (iii) and APIs for developers to apply the dynamic search algorithms to index and search over custom datasets. Dumpling is developed under the umbrella of a bigger project in the DARPA Memex program to crawl and search the dark web to support law enforcement and national security.

1. INTRODUCTION

Dynamic search is an emerging topic in Information Retrieval (IR) research [4]. In dynamic search, we model dynamic systems which change or adapt over time or a sequence of events using a range of techniques from artificial intelligence and reinforcement learning. Many of the open problems in current IR research can be described as dynamic systems, for instance, information retrieval in a session.

In a dynamic search setting, a user issues multiple queries during a session to accomplish a search task. The common process is that the user sends a query, gets the top ranked documents, changes her query and sends it again. As a result, a series of queries, a series of retrieved documents, and rich user interactions will be generated, until the session stops when the user finishes her search task. During a session, the temporal dependencies between queries are presented in that way that the previous queries and the previously obtained search results will influence how the user issues the current query and how the search result rankings could be optimized for the current query.

The dynamic search algorithms implemented in Dumpling include the Query Change Retrieval Model (QCM) [1] and the Win-win search algorithm [3]. Not only does it implement a dynamic search engine, Dumpling also provides a convenient user interface for a user to compare the results from the dynamic search engine and the static search engine. By comparing the retrieved documents, the user can easily evaluate the performance of different search engines. We have deployed Dumpling for DARPA's Memex program. The evaluations of the systems are done by obtaining real user feedback for the search results. They show that the dynamic search algorithms dramatically improve the search accuracy over the static search algorithms. To further test the performance of the dynamic search engine, Dumpling also provides simple APIs to update the dataset. Dumpling can automatically build an index and apply the dynamic search algorithm to a new dataset. Dumpling is not only a dynamic search system but also provides potential to further the research of dynamic search.

SIGIR'15, August 09-13, 2015, Santiago, Chile.
ACM 978-1-4503-3621-5/15/08.
DOI: http://dx.doi.org/10.1145/2766462.2767873 .

2. QUERY CHANGE RETRIEVAL MODEL

The Query Change Retrieval Model (QCM) analyzes the evolution of queries as well as previously retrieved documents to enhance the dynamic search. QCM's document ranking function is based on the previous query q_{i-1}, the current query q_i, the previously retrieved documents D_{i-1}, and the discount factor $\gamma \in (0,1)$: $Score(q_i, d) = P(q_i|d) + \gamma \sum_a P(q_i|q_{i-1}, D_{i-1}, a) \max_{D_{i-1}} P(q_{i-1}|D_{i-1})$. It measures the document relevance to the ith query based on the current reward (current document relevance) and the discounted sum of past accumulated rewards/relevance in a session. The most important feature of this formula is that the past queries and retrieved documents have less influence on the user's current search. The QCM model is highly effective and consistently won the top positions in the recent TREC Session Track evaluations [2].

3. WIN-WIN SEARCH

A user tends to query several times in a row during one search session. She changes keywords in the queries hoping to find more information. The intension of a user differs from one session to another. Sometimes, the user finds some relevant information by the first query, and then wants to find more detailed information about subtopics by the next query (We term this behavior as exploitation.) Other times, the user gets what they need by the first query, and then

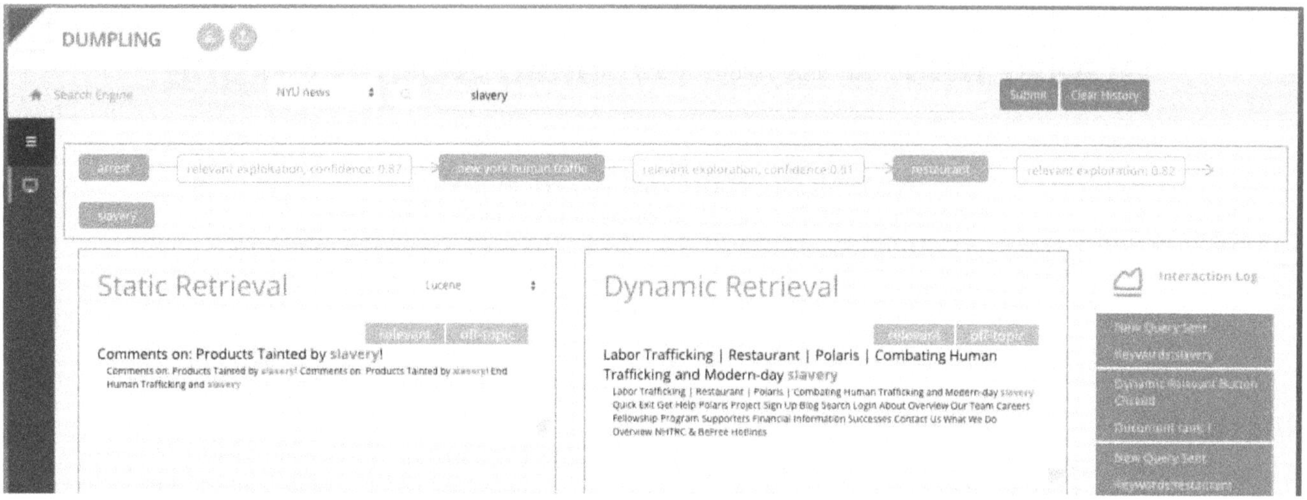

Figure 1: Dumpling User Interface

wants to change to a brand-new topic by the next (We term this behavior as exploration). In the model of the Win-win search algorithm, we categorize the user into 1 of 4 states: {*RT*: find something relevant and explore a new topic; *RR*: find something relevant and exploit the same topic; *NRT*: find nothing relevant and explore a new topic; *NRR*: find nothing relevant and exploit the same topic.} The user's state moves from one state to the next along with the evolution of queries. The belief of the user's state can be presented as $b_t = S_m$ $(t = 1, 2, ..., n)$ (n stands for the total number of iterations) and m= {RT, RR, NRT, NRR} [3]. Dumpling infers the user's current state by analyzing previous returned documents, the user's queries and the user's interactions during the session. Every time the user sends a new query, Dumpling updates the user's state using $b_{t+1}(s_j) = Pr(s_j|o_t, a_t, b_t) = \frac{O(s_j,a_t,o_t)\sum_{s_i \in S} T(s_i,a_t,s_j)b_t(s_i)}{P(o_t|a_t,b_t)}$. where t indicates the search iteration; s_i and s_j are any two states; $b_{t+1}(s_j)$ is the probability of the user being believed at state j in iteration $t+1$; o_t is the observation of the user's behavior; a_t is the search engine's action. Dumpling thus infers the user's state, and chooses appropriate retrieving algorithm and arguments.

4. USER INTERFACE & EVALUATION

Dumpling supports dynamic search to different datasets which can be chosen by a user. Currently we use datasets provided by the DARPA Memex program. The documents are crawled from the dark web including forum posts, online sex ads, child labor ads, etc. The search engine is located at `dumplingproject.org`. Due to the sensitivity of the data, our search results are password protected and not open to the public. Figure 1 shows the interface of Dumpling. It supports the following functionalities. Dumpling provides very convenient APIs to maintain the dataset. With Dumpling's API, the user can add, update and delete index based on new crawling results. The extensibility of Dumpling is enhanced by the easy-to-change dataset. The search engine provides side-by-side comparison between the dynamic search algorithm and static search algorithm (elastic search in our case). We also have a decision state pane to show our estimated decision making states of the user during a search.

algorithm	dynamic search	static search
Precision@10	0.52	0.32
# of Queries	362	
# of Sessions	178	

Table 1: Search Accuracy in Precision at 10.

Dumpling provides a convenient user interface for a user to compare the dynamic search results and the static search results. Dumpling gathers explicit feedback from real users in US agencies working on national security. The user can provide both positive and negative feedback of the search results and the feedback is used in the dynamic search algorithms. In Figure 1, in the first query, a user uses "arrest"; in the second query, the user uses "new york human traffic". From the user's perspective, she initially wants to know who was arrested recently. Then she wants to further exploit who is recently arrested by New York police because of human trafficking. For the static search algorithm, the retrieved documents only include New York human trafficking news, the keyword "arrest" seldom appears in the documents. For the dynamic search algorithm, the retrieved documents contain much more information about arresting, which better suits the user's needs.

5. ACKNOWLEDGEMENT

The research is supported by DARPA FA8750-14-2-0226, NSF IIS-1453721, and NSF CNS-1223825. Any opinions, findings, conclusions, or recommendations expressed in this paper are of the authors, and do not necessarily reflect those of the sponsor.

References

[1] D. Guan, S. Zhang, and H. Yang. Utilizing query change for session search. In *SIGIR'13*.

[2] E. Kanoulas, M. M. Hall, P. Clough, B. Carterette, and M. Sanderson. Overview of the trec 2011 session track. In *TREC'11*.

[3] J. Luo, S. Zhang, and H. Yang. Win-win search: Dual-agent stochastic game in session search. In *SIGIR'14*.

[4] H. Yang, M. Sloan, and J. Wang. Dynamic information retrieval modeling. SIGIR '14.

Promoting User Engagement and Learning in Amorphous Search Tasks

Piyush Arora
ADAPT Research Centre, School of Computing
Dublin City University, Dublin 9, Ireland
parora@computing.dcu.ie

ABSTRACT

Much research in information retrieval (IR) focuses on optimization of the rank of relevant retrieval results for single shot ad hoc IR tasks. Relatively little research has been carried out on user engagement to support more complex search tasks. We seek to improve user engagement for IR tasks by providing richer representation of retrieved information. It is our expectation that this strategy will promote implicit learning within search activities. Specifically, we plan to explore methods of finding semantic concepts within retrieved documents, with the objective of creating improved document surrogates. Further, we would like to study search effectiveness in terms of different facets such as the user's search experience, satisfaction, engagement and learning. We intend to investigate this in an experimental study, where our richer document representations are compared with the traditional document surrogates for the same user queries.

Categories and Subject Descriptors:H.3.3[Information Search and Retrieval]: search process, H.5.2[Information Interfaces and Presentation]: Interaction styles
Keywords: interactive IR; learning; engagement.

1. RESEARCH PROPOSAL

Searching information on the web has become an indispensable part of our daily activities. From finding answers to our daily questions to satisfying our curiosity, and increasingly, for educational purposes. We look towards the web to learn about different topics through MOOCs, wikipedia, and general web content. At present, search engines are optimized for look-up tasks and not for activities that require more sustained interactions with information. Current IR systems are not generally configured to support long search sessions [2]. We would anticipate that, in a longer session, a user might benefit from having the results change dynamically based on their engagement and interactions.

In our work we plan to explore the relationship between complex search tasks and the manner in which information is presented to the user to enable more active engagement and improve learning. As noted in [1], there are several factors which play an important role in learning such as a) *prior knowledge*, b) *coherence*, c) *motivation* and d) *knowledge actualization*. We want to focus on the coherence aspect in our research. The main question we will investigate in our work is: *How can search results be presented with respect to document content to improve user engagement?*

Our ultimate goal is to improve user engagement with retrieved information. It is our expectation that understanding document similarities and differences at a semantic level can help us to create better document surrogates (e.g. in terms of document summaries, topics, visualisations) which may in turn improve user engagement.

Li and Belkin [3] propose a faceted approach for conceptualizing search tasks. Following this categorisation, Jian et al. [2] investigate two facets of search tasks: product and goal. The product of a search task can be factual or intellectual and the goal of a search task can be either specific or amorphous. Thus they study four different types of task: known item (factual + specific), known subject (factual + amorphous), interpretive (intellectual + specific), and exploratory (intellectual + amorphous). We plan to adopt their categorization in our study of supporting and enhancing user engagement, focusing on known subject, interpretive and exploratory tasks. It is our hope that the content representations proposed in our research will form the basis of mechanisms to support more engaging search experiences in future search engines.

Acknowledgments: This work is supervised by Jennifer Foster and Gareth J.F.Jones. This research is supported by Science Foundation Ireland (SFI) as a part of the CNGL Centre for Global Intelligent Content at DCU (Grant No: 12/CE/I2267).

2. REFERENCES

[1] L. Freund, H. O'Brien, and R. Kopak. Getting the big picture: supporting comprehension and learning in search. 2014.

[2] J. Jiang, D. He, and J. Allan. Searching, browsing, and clicking in a search session: changes in user behavior by task and over time. In *Proc. of SIGIR*, pages 607–616, 2014.

[3] Y. Li and N. J. Belkin. A faceted approach to conceptualizing tasks in information seeking. *Information Processing & Management*, 44(6):1822–1837, 2008.

SIGIR'15, August 09-13, 2015, Santiago, Chile.
ACM 978-1-4503-3621-5/15/08.
DOI: http://dx.doi.org/10.1145/2766462.2767848.

Cross-Platform Question Routing for Better Question Answering

Mossaab Bagdouri
Department of Computer Science
University of Maryland
College Park, MD, USA
mossaab@umd.edu

ABSTRACT

The last two decades have made the Internet a major source for knowledge seekers to fulfill their needs. Several tools and platforms were developed to find answers to one's questions such as search engines and online encyclopedias. The wide adoption of social media pushed the possibilities even further by giving people the opportunity to stimulate the generation of answers that are not already present on the Internet. Some of these are primarily community question answering (CQA) services, while the others have a more general audience but can also be used to ask and answer questions.

Assessing which platform is best suitable for certain information need of a particular user, and subject to some specific constraints, is a problem that has seen little attention (e.g. [3]). Hence, we consider *cross-platform question routing* to automatically suggest where an input question should be asked or redirected to. Several stages are required to address this problem. First, we need to analyze the differences between the questions asked on different platforms. In fact, on a search engine, a user would provide the least context to the query. On a CQA website, she would summarize the question in a title and provide more context in a description. On the other hand, the (online) identity of the asker in a microblogging service is revealed to her friends, leading to a higher exposure of context. For this stage, we gather questions from different platforms to train a classifier on the distribution of question types [4] over these platforms. Services that are not restricted to questions and answers (e.g., Twitter) need special mining to find content that contains questions. We will extend the work of [2] to find out which posts are answer seeking questions.

Second, we need to characterize the users, as not all demographics have the same needs. For instance, the types of information seeked by a journalist are arguably different from those of a teenager. Thus, we build some classifiers that differentiate users based on the questions they might ask. We apply some algorithms that we developed to retrieve the Twitter accounts of Arab journalists, and adapt the taxonomy of the more general question types to this group of professionals.

Routing questions needs new evaluation measures that take in consideration various aspects beyond the traditional dimension of relevance. For instance, for a user who is seeking opinions of "ordinary" people about non-factoid questions, informality of the answers is a constraint that might be added to the evaluation [1]. The cost of wrong answers is an additional dimension to the evaluation that is often traded-off with response time. For example, a journalist cannot accept an unverified report and might spend a long time verifying it. On another hand, someone who is trying to get recommendations for a nearby restaurant might trade the correctness for a timely answer. Thus, we need to model the likelihood of whether and when a question will get a response, if a response contains an answer to that question and to which extent that answer is correct and satisfies the expectations of the asker.

Categories and Subject Descriptors

H.3.3 [**Information Storage and Retrieval**]: Information Search and Retrieval

Keywords

Question Answering; Question Routing; Social Media

ACKNOWLEDGMENT

This work was made possible by NPRP grant# NPRP 6-1377-1-25 from the Qatar National Research Fund (a member of Qatar Foundation). The statements made herein are solely the responsibility of the author.

REFERENCES

[1] M. Bagdouri, D. W. Oard, and V. Castelli. CLIR for informal content in Arabic forum posts. CIKM, 2014.

[2] M. Hasanain, T. Elsayed, and W. Magdy. Identification of answer-seeking questions in Arabic microblogs. CIKM, 2014.

[3] A. Oeldorf-Hirsch, B. Hecht, M. R. Morris, J. Teevan, and D. Gergle. To search or to ask: The routing of information needs between traditional search engines and social networks. CSCW, 2014.

[4] Z. Zhao and Q. Mei. Questions about questions: An empirical analysis of information needs on Twitter. WWW, 2013.

SIGIR'15, August 09-13, 2015, Santiago, Chile.
ACM 978-1-4503-3621-5/15/08.
DOI: http://dx.doi.org/10.1145/2766462.2767849 .

Time Pressure in Information Search

Anita Crescenzi
School of Information and Library Science, University of North Carolina
Chapel Hill, NC, USA
amcc@email.unc.edu

Categories and Subject Descriptors

H.3.3 [**Information Storage and Retrieval**]: Information Search and Retrieval—*Search Process*

Keywords

Search behavior; Time pressure

1. ABSTRACT

The primary purpose of this research is to explore the impact of perceived time pressure on search behaviors, searcher perceptions of the search system and the search experience. Are there observable behavioral changes when a searcher is time-pressured? To what extent are search behavior differences attributable to objective experimental manipulation versus to the subjective experience of time pressure? An important secondary purpose of this work is to identify appropriate outcome measures that allow for the comparison of session-level search behaviors when time is manipulated. This proposal builds on Crescenzi, Kelly and Azzopardi [3] and is intended to be part of a multi-method line of inquiry examining time-pressured information-seeking.

Why is it important to study time? Research has shown that time is an important element of information retrieval [4] and information-seeking [6]. Recent work has examined several temporal factors in interactive information retrieval (IIR) research including system response time [1], time limits [9], and the urgency of the information need [8]. While impact of perceived time pressure on search behavior is not well understood, there has been a great deal of research on how time pressure impacts decision-making. This research has shown that when making a decision under time pressure, people often reduce the amount of time to process pieces of information, work faster, focus on more general information or even satisfice [5]. As information search involves numerous decisions, examining similar adaptations may be present in time-pressured information search.

Time is also an important factor to consider in search and system evaluation. Comparison of interaction measures is complicated when the amount of time that a participant can interact with a system is constrained (e.g., time limits or system delays). Further, differences in search outcome measures (e.g., quality or number of documents found) may reflect the time spent searching as much as other experimental manipulations and time-normalization may be required [7]. Finally, time spent searching as an outcome measure is difficult to interpret [2].

The findings from this research are expected provide insight into time-pressured information search. A better understanding of time-pressured information search may ultimately influence search system design and better support time-pressured searchers.

SIGIR'15, August 09-13, 2015, Santiago, Chile.
ACM 978-1-4503-3621-5/15/08.
DOI: http://dx.doi.org/10.1145/2766462.2767851.

2. REFERENCES

[1] I. Arapakis, X. Bai, and B. B. Cambazoglu. Impact of response latency on user behavior in web search. In *Proc. of the 37th ACM SIGIR conference*, pages 103–112, 2014.

[2] P. Borlund, S. Dreier, and K. Byström. What does time spent on searching indicate? In *Proc. of the 4th IIiX Symposium*, pages 184–193, 2012.

[3] A. Crescenzi, D. Kelly, and L. Azzopardi. Time pressure and system delays in information search. In *Proc. of the 38th ACM SIGIR conference*, 2015.

[4] P. Ingwersen and K. Järvelin. Information retrieval in context. *ACM SIGIR Forum*, 39(2):31, Dec. 2005.

[5] J. W. Payne, J. R. Bettman, and E. J. Johnson. *The Adaptive Decision Maker*. Cambridge University Press, Cambridge, 1993.

[6] R. Savolainen. Time as a context of information seeking. *Library & Info. Sci. Research*, 28(1):110–127, Mar. 2006.

[7] N. J. Taylor, A. R. Dennis, and J. W. Cummings. Situation normality and the shape of search: The effects of time delays and information presentation on search behavior. *J. of the A. Soc. for Info. Sci. and Tech.*, 64(5):909–928, 2013.

[8] J. Teevan, K. Collins-Thompson, R. W. White, S. T. Dumais, and Y. Kim. Slow search: Information retrieval without time constraints. In *Proc. of the 7th HCIR Symposium*, pages 1–10, New York, New York, USA, 2013. ACM Press.

[9] A. Tombros, I. Ruthven, and J. M. Jose. How users assess web pages for information seeking. *J. of the American Society for Info. Sci. and Tech.*, 56(4):327–344, 2005.

Controversy Detection and Stance Analysis

Shiri Dori-Hacohen
Center for Intelligent Information Retrieval
School of Computer Science
University of Massachusetts Amherst
Amherst, Massachusetts
shiri@cs.umass.edu

ABSTRACT

Alerting users about controversial search results can encourage critical literacy, promote healthy civic discourse and counteract the "filter bubble" effect. Additionally, presenting information to the user about the different stances or sides of the debate can help her navigate the landscape of search results. Our existing work made strides in the emerging niche of controversy detection and analysis; we propose further work on automatic stance detection.

Categories and Subject Descriptors: H.3.3 [Information Storage and Retrieval]: Information Storage and Retrieval —*Information filtering, Clustering*

Keywords: controversy detection, stance detection, critical literacy

1. MOTIVATION

The challenge of navigating different sides of a debate on a controversial topic is a cognitive burden to the user, an increasingly challenging task with social and ethical implications [6]. We present existing work in the field and propose a further contribution that will facilitate healthy debates and serve users' information needs with regards to controversial topics: automated stance extraction for controversial topics, which will detect the various sides of the debate.

Related Work. The problem of controversy detection has been receiving increased attention (see [6] for a survey). In addition to detecting the controversial topic, another challenge is understanding what is controversial about it [1, 2]; a comprehensive approach for detecting stances of a debate has not yet been proposed. Recent work has used manually extracted stances which were used as classifiers to investigate users' opinions [7]. Further advances are needed in order to present users with explicit stances on controversial topics.

Our Contributions. We introduced the problem of detecting controversial topics on the web [3], and suggested a weakly-supervised algorithm to solve it [4]; we examined a hypothesis that controversies occur in neighborhoods of related topics, demonstrating that controversy exhibits homophily and improving the current state of the art [5].

SIGIR'15, August 09-13, 2015, Santiago, Chile.
ACM 978-1-4503-3621-5/15/08.
DOI: http://dx.doi.org/10.1145/2766462.2767844 .

2. PROPOSED RESEARCH

We propose an additional contribution: automatic stance extraction. We hypothesize that the stances of controversial topics can be automatically extracted from Wikipedia; we further posit that such extracted stances can be used to classify web pages and queries, determining whether their author or issuer holds these stances.

Methodology. We intend to extract stances (sides of the debate) for controversial topics using Wikipedia: for example, using the words inserted and deleted from the article, or looking at the editors graph. Finding ground truth for this problem is challenging; however, we have found a dataset that can be used to generate evaluations.

Issues for Discussion. Given the above, we'd like to discuss the definition of controversy, and challenges in evaluation of the stance extraction problem.

3. CONCLUSION

There are multiple subtleties involved with information seeking on controversial topics [6]. We describe some work already completed as well as additional proposed work, which can inform users of the controversy level of their search terms and assist their understanding of different stances or opinions on such topics.

Acknowledgments. This work was supported in part by the Center for Intelligent Information Retrieval and in part by NSF grant number IIS-1217281. Any opinions, findings and conclusions or recommendations expressed in this material are the author's and do not necessarily reflect those of the sponsor.

4. REFERENCES

[1] R. Awadallah, M. Ramanath, and G. Weikum. Harmony and Dissonance: Organizing the People's Voices on Political Controversies. *Proc. WSDM*, 2012.

[2] S. Das and A. Lavoie. Automated inference of point of view from user interactions in collective intelligence venues. In *Workshop on Social Computing and User Generated Content*, EC 2013.

[3] S. Dori-Hacohen and J. Allan. Detecting controversy on the web. In *Proc. CIKM*, 2013.

[4] S. Dori-Hacohen and J. Allan. Automated Controversy Detection on the Web. In *Proc. ECIR*, 2015.

[5] S. Dori-Hacohen, D. Jensen, and J. Allan. Stacked Models for Controversy Detection in Wikipedia. *Under review*, 2015.

[6] S. Dori-Hacohen, E. Yom-Tov, and J. Allan. Navigating Controversy as a Complex Search Task. *Proc. Workshop on Supporting Complex Search Tasks*, ECIR 2015.

[7] E. Yom-Tov, S. T. Dumais, and Q. Guo. Promoting civil discourse through search engine diversity. *Social Science Computer Review*, 2013.

Using Contextual Information to Understand Searching and Browsing Behavior

Julia Kiseleva
Department of Mathematics and Computer Science
Eindhoven University of Technology, Eindhoven, The Netherlands
j.kiseleva@tue.nl

ABSTRACT

There is great imbalance in the richness of information on the web and the succinctness and poverty of search requests of web users, making their queries only a partial description of the underlying complex information needs. Finding ways to better leverage contextual information and make search context-aware holds the promise to dramatically improve the search experience of users. We conducted a series of studies to discover, model and utilize contextual information in order to understand and improve users' searching and browsing behavior on the web. Our results capture important aspects of context under the realistic conditions of different online search services, aiming to ensure that our scientific insights and solutions transfer to the operational settings of real world applications.

Categories and Subject Descriptors: H.3.3 [**Information Storage and Retrieval**]: Information Search and Retrieval—*Search process*

General Terms: Algorithms, Performance, Experimentation

1. CONTEXTUALIZING SEARCH

Modern search still relies on the query-response paradigm, which is characterized by a sharp contrast between the richness of data in the index, and the relative poverty of information in the query, usually expressed in a few keywords to capture a complex need. This is particularly true in online search services, where the same query may be observed from many users, with considerable variations in their search intents. Contextual information is the obvious route to try to restore the balance, and behavioral data related to user's searching and browsing activities provides new opportunities to model contextual aspects of user needs.

The importance of contextual information in search applications has been recognised by researchers and practitioners in many disciplines, including recommendation systems, information retrieval, ubiquitous and mobile computing, and marketing. Context-aware systems [1] adapt to users' operations and thus aim at improving the usability and effectiveness by taking context into account. In this thesis we consider two types of behavior: **(1)** 'searching'—when users are issuing queries and we are trying to improve search results (SERP) taking context of sessions into account; and **(2)** 'browsing'—when users are surfing a website and we are predicting their movements utilizing context.

SIGIR'15, August 09–13, 2015, Santiago, Chile.
ACM 978-1-4503-3621-5/15/08.
DOI: http://dx.doi.org/10.1145/2766462.2767852.

The main research problem of this thesis is to investigate the value of context in searching and browsing user behaviour on web: *How to discover, model and utilize contextual information in order to understand and improve users' searching and browsing behaviour on web?* The general research problem is broken down to four specific research questions. We start by developing a general analytic framework that views context-aware search from the system's perspective: ***RQ1****: How to define a general analytical framework for context-aware systems?* This analytic part defines a general framework for modeling context, and introduces the notions of optimal contextual models and useful contextual models. Next, we look at the impact of specific contextual aspects: ***RQ2****: What is the impact of geographical location as a contextual information?* [2] ***RQ3****: How to discover users behavioral aspects as contextual information?* [3] We look at behavioral dynamics—changes in aggregated user behavioral features over time to detect changes in user satisfaction and drifts in query intent: ***RQ4****: How to define and to detect changes in user satisfaction with retrieved search results?* [4]. Our general research methodology is to conduct research on realistic data from various on-line search services, ensuring our results transfer to operational cases. This has a number of important consequences. Evaluation is key in operational environments, and we follow the current state of the art approach to evaluation, consisting of: **(1)** *offline stage*—where the progressive evaluation (time-wise), cross validation (object-wise) and human judgments procedures are employed; and **(2)** *online stage*—where the developed techniques are integrated into web systems. We employ traditional A/B and multivariate testing procedures providing reliable estimates of the performance of the alternative approaches.

Acknowledgments This research is supported by STW (CAPA project). Thanks to the ACM SIGIR for a Student Travel Grant.

References

[1] J. Kiseleva. Context mining and integration into predictive web analytics. In *WWW (Companion Volume)*, pages 383–388, 2013.

[2] J. Kiseleva, H. T. Lam, M. Pechenizkiy, and T. Calders. Predicting current user intent with contextual markov models. In *ICDM Workshops*, 2013.

[3] J. Kiseleva, H. T. Lam, M. Pechenizkiy, and T. Calders. Discovering temporal hidden contexts in web sessions for user trail prediction. In *Proceedings of WWW (Companion Volume)*, pages 1067–1074. ACM, 2013.

[4] J. Kiseleva, E. Crestan, R. Brigo, and R. Dittel. Modelling and detecting changes in user satisfaction. In *Proceeding of CIKM*, pages 1449–1458, 2014.

Transfer Learning for Information Retrieval

Pengfei Li
RMIT University
Melbourne, Australia
li.pengfei@rmit.edu.au

Categories and Subject Descriptors

H.3.3 [**Information Storage and Retrieval**]: Information Search and Retrieval

Keywords

Information retrieval, Learning to rank, Transfer learning

ABSTRACT

Learning to rank algorithms (LTR) are techniques that utilize machine learning to learn ranking functions for particular document and topic sets. LTR models are designed and trained to optimize the effectiveness of the ranking function on the assessed topics of a document set. One challenge of applying LTR on information retrieval systems is obtaining the relevance judgments. Transfer learning is a technique that can be used to train models for new datasets (*target domain*) using related datasets (*source domain*), under the circumstances where limited training data is accessible, and thus can help training LTR models in similar situations. The aim of this research is to study the issues of transfer learning techniques for information retrieval (TLTR) and develop new TLTR algorithms to help improve the effectiveness of information retrieval systems.

The idea of applying transfer learning to LTR is not new but requires deeper exploring. Transfer learning techniques have been extensively studied in machine learning community [2]. However, the study of applying transfer learning to LTR had not drawn too much attention until recent years. A few attempts have been tried. However, better understanding of the issues is needed for future research.

To better understand TLTR and develop new TLTR algorithms, several research questions are to be answered. Here we list the research questions we want to address in this study. ***Q1.*** *What are the factors that can affect the effectiveness of LTR algorithms on a dataset?* ***Q2.*** *Is it necessary to apply TLTR? Moreover, under what circumstances TLTR is needed?* ***Q3.*** *How should the relatedness of LTR tasks be measured?* ***Q4.*** *What is the difference between conventional transfer learning and TLTR?* ***Q5.*** *How to tackle so-called heterogeneous TLTR problems, where the feature spaces of datasets are different?* ***Q6.*** *How to measure the effectiveness of TLTR models?*

We tested the generalization of LTR models by training and testing in different datasets. We validated that the performances of LTR models will be leveraged when applying to a different dataset. Study of the stability of LTR models with respect to training data will also provide evidence that standard LTR is not sufficient to improve ranking effectiveness under certain circumstances. Our study showed that training LTR models do not require too many queries, but these queries should better represent the queries in the entire collection. The finding also suggests that identifying similar queries or query groups in the source domain might be a clue to solving TLTR problems. We proposed a TLTR algorithm that trains LTR models with queries that are the most similar to source domain queries, from the source domain. These queries are weighted with importance, calculated by query similarities. This approach is similar to most instance-weighting based TLTR algorithms [1, 3], but the algorithm we proposed requires no relevance judgment from the target domain.

Our study showed that transferring LTR models between different document sets might have a more terrible effect. However, our experiments are limited by lacking a pair of test collections with the same query set but different document sets. A further step of the research is to construct two test collections with different document sets, yet keep all other factors the same. The influences of the divergence between document sets on LTR algorithms will be studied based on the datasets. As mentioned before, heterogeneous TLTR is an area yet to be well explored. The study of how to tackle heterogenous TLTR is also under the scope of this study.

SIGIR'15, August 09-13, 2015, Santiago, Chile.
ACM 978-1-4503-3621-5/15/08.
DOI: http://dx.doi.org/10.1145/2766462.2767845.

References

[1] Peng Cai, Wei Gao, K.F. Wong, and Aoying Zhou. Weight-based boosting model for cross-domain relevance ranking adaptation. *Adv. Inf. Retr.*, pages 562–567, 2011.

[2] Sinno Jialin Pan and Qiang Yang. A Survey on Transfer Learning. *IEEE Trans. Knowl. Data Eng.*, 22(10):1345–1359, October 2010.

[3] Shangkun Ren, Yuexian Hou, Peng Zhang, and Xueru Liang. Importance Weighted AdaRank. *Adv. Intell. Comput.*, pages 448–455, 2012.

Enhancing Mathematics Information Retrieval

Martin Líška
Faculty of Informatics, Masaryk University, Botanická 68a, 602 00 Brno, Czech Republic
255768@mail.muni.cz

Categories and Subject Descriptors

H.3.3 [**Information Systems**]: Information storage and Retrieval—*Information Search and Retrieval*; I.7 [**Computing Methodologies**]: Document and text Processing—*Index Generation*

Keywords

query expansion, digital mathematical libraries, indexing mathematics, MIaS, MathML, formula, subformula unification, evaluation

Motivation

Mathematics Information Retrieval (MIR) is a domain specific branch of Information Retrieval. MIR is a broad term for all the activities related to obtaining information from a collection of resources and answering an information need that involves mathematics in the form of math expressions and formulae. MIR is very important for Digital Mathematics Libraries (DMLs) which gather mathematically oriented documents in which users need to search and navigate effectively. A concrete implementation usually means a search engine that is able to answer a query composed of mathematical expressions as well as standard textual keywords searching through a collection with a substantial amount of mathematics.

There are several research groups that aim at creating well performing and usable math search engine. Our group located at the Faculty of Informatics, Masaryk University, develops Math Indexer and Searcher (MIaS) [2] a math-aware search engine, currently deployed in EuDML (European Digital Mathematics Library). To the best of my knowledge, it is the only deployment of a MIR system in such a scale. Other deployments, e.g. DML-CZ, are planned.

The Goal

The goal is to design the ultimate math information retrieval system. The ultimateness can be understood as a combination of specific features that all together will support high precision as well as recall in searching documents with mathematical content.

Research Topics and Methods

The main research aspects of MIR are the following: *preprocessing* – unifying the input math notation; *indexing* – preparation of the internal structures and representation for similarity search; *searching* – interpretation of user query and expansion; *evaluation* – continuous evaluation of retrieval quality; *performance* – the internal representations must support a good overall performance.

Based on the NTCIR-11 Math-2 Task evaluation, MIaS approach is currently one of the best ranked in terms of the system's effectiveness [1]. In my work, I want to build upon the current performance of MIaS and research further methods and topics that could possibly make the system perform even better. The topics are the following:

Semantically Enhanced Search – integration of Computer algebra systems in the indexing as well as the searching phase as a computational power to reduce math expressions to a normalized form. Disambiguation of math structures from document and queries into known concepts in order to introduce semantics into the matching.

Subformula Unification – the ability to unify whole expression subtrees in order to allow the users to create queries containing wildcards in math expressions. In more complex query expressions wildcards can be critical in suppressing uninteresting parts of math expressions. The complexity of this aspect is heavily dependent on the representation of the data.

Query Expansion/Relaxation – mathematical queries can be relaxed by dividing it to smaller parts. This is can be a fallback method in case of unsuccessful complex query expressions. On the keyword level, mixed mathematical-textual queries can be relaxed by removing keywords from the individual parts of the query.

Combined Text-Mathematical Search – math expressions and text keywords need to be effectively combined for the system query in terms of logical operators as well as their mutual weighting.

Evaluation Framework – preparation of an automated evaluation framework for rigorously evaluating changes proposed to the retrieval process as listed above. This is possible with the presence of a test collection for MIR, such as NTCIR-11 Math-2 collection.

References

[1] M. Líška, M. Růžička, and P. Sojka. Math Indexer and Searcher under the Hood: History and Development of a Winning Strategy. In N. Kando, K. Kishida (Eds.), *Proceedings of the 11th NTCIR Conference*, pp. 127–134. NII, Tokyo, 2014.

[2] P. Sojka and M. Líška. Indexing and Searching Mathematics in Digital Libraries – Architecture, Design and Scalability Issues. In J. H. Davenport et al. (Eds.) *Proceedings of CICM 2011, LNAI 6824*, pp. 228–243, Berlin, Germany, 2011. Springer. `http://dx.doi.org/10.1007/978-3-642-22673-1_16`.

SIGIR'15, August 09-13, 2015, Santiago, Chile.
ACM 978-1-4503-3621-5/15/08.
DOI: http://dx.doi.org/10.1145/2766462.2767843.

Improving Search using Proximity-Based Statistics

Xiaolu Lu
RMIT University
Melbourne, Australia
xiaolu.lu@rmit.edu.au

Categories and Subject Descriptors

H.3.1 [**Information Storage and Retrieval**]: Content Analysis and Indexing—*Indexing methods*; H.3.4 [**Information Storage and Retrieval**]: Systems and Software—*Performance evaluation*

Keywords

k-term Proximity, Indexing, Efficiency

ABSTRACT

Modern retrieval systems often use more sophisticated ranking models. Although more new features are added in, term proximity has been studied for a long time, and still plays an important role. A recent study by Huston and Croft [2] shows that many-term dependency is a better choice for a large corpus and long queries. However, utilizing proximity-based features often leads to computational overhead, and most of the existing solutions are tailored to term pairs. Fewer studies have focused on many-term proximity computation, and the plane-sweep approach proposed by Sadakane and Imai [6] is still state-of-the-art. Consider a multi-pass retrieval process where the proximity features could be an effective first pass ranker if we can reduce the cost of the proximity calculation.

In this PhD project, we consider the following questions: (i) How important are the proximity statistics in the term dependency models and what is the cost of extracting the proximity features? (ii) Although all term dependencies are considered in ranking models, can we design an early termination strategy considering only partial proximity? Moreover, instead of viewing the term from the same level, can we utilizing its locality for obtaining more efficiency? (iii) How do we best organize the term proximity statistics to be more indexable, facilitating the extraction process? (iv) How do we best define the approximation form of term proximity in order to find the best trade-off between effectiveness and efficiency?

In a preliminary experimental study, Lu et al. [3] compare how different term dependency components affect the entire ranking models show that although the phrase component helps to improve the effectiveness in an overall sense, it degrades dramatically on some queries. Although the proximity part doesn't always improve the effectiveness, it is more stable.

From the computational perspective, we have found that extracting single term dependency proximity using the plane-sweep algorithm is not a bottleneck. But it is a computational intensive job when processing each dependency feature separately. However, the extra cost of considering proximity independently can be reduced by extracting all dependencies together [4]. Further, since most of retrieval systems keep both a direct file and an inverted file, it is possible to exploit both representation to maximize the efficiency.

Although the cost of extracting proximity features can be reduced compared to separate calculations, it is still less efficient when processing frequent query terms with long documents. Considering the characteristics of all term dependency features, there is some redundant information. Thus, it may be possible for us to design a rank-safe early termination strategy by only computing partial proximity features instead of extracting them all. Heuristically, to achieve this, we could map the proximity extraction problem into weighted interval ranking by taking TF and IDF values into account. Besides the early termination method, it is also worth seeking an indexable organization of proximity statistics. The plane-sweep method in the extraction process reveals possibilities for building auxiliary structures to augment existing index structures.

Usually, accurate distances between terms will be captured in ranking models, but the definition varies. Clarke et al. [1] consider the *cover* and scores over sets of the covers, whereas Metzler and Croft [5] utilize an unordered window. But capturing actual distance sets a higher requirement on both space and query time. Instead of calculating the distance between terms, an approximation of proximity can also be considered. Especially when using the proximity feature as an effective first pass ranker, efficiency will be considered as a higher priority, without sacrificing too much effectiveness. With suitable approximations, it may be possible to optimize the efficiency within a given threshold of effectiveness.

SIGIR'15, August 09 - 13, 2015, Santiago, Chile.

ACM 978-1-4503-3621-5/15/08.
DOI:http://dx.doi.org/10.1145/2766462.2767847.

References

[1] C. L. Clarke, G. V. Cormack, and E. A. Tudhope. Relevance ranking for one to three term queries. *Inf. Proc. & Man.*, 36(2):291–311, 2000.

[2] S. Huston and W. B. Croft. A comparison of retrieval models using term dependencies. In *Proc. CIKM*, pages 111–120, 2014.

[3] X. Lu, A. Moffat, and J. S. Culpepper. How effective are proximity scores in term dependency models? In *Proc. ADCS*, page 89, 2014.

[4] X. Lu, A. Moffat, and J. S. Culpepper. On the cost of extracting proximity features for term-dependency models. Submitted.

[5] D. Metzler and W. B. Croft. A Markov random field model for term dependencies. In *Proc. SIGIR*, pages 472–479, 2005.

[6] K. Sadakane and H. Imai. Text retrieval by using k-word proximity search. In *Proc. Symp. Database Appl. Non-Trad. Envs.*, pages 183–188, 1999.

Spoken Conversational Search: Information Retrieval over a Speech-only Communication Channel

Johanne R. Trippas
School of Computer Science and Information Technology
RMIT University, Melbourne
Johanne.trippas@rmit.edu.au

ABSTRACT

This research is investigating a new interaction paradigm for Interactive Information Retrieval (IIR), where all input and output is mediated via speech. While such information systems have been important for the visually impaired for many years, a renewed focus on speech is driven by the growing sales of internet enabled mobile devices. Presenting search results over a speech-only communication channel involves a number of challenges for users due to cognitive limitations and the serial nature of the audio channel [2]. Other research has shown that one cannot just 'bolt on' speech recognizers and screen readers to an existing system [5]. Therefore the aim of this research is to develop a new framework for effective and efficient IIR over a speech-only channel: a *Spoken Conversational Search System* (SCSS) which provides a conversational approach to determining user information needs, presenting results and enabling search reformulations. This research will go beyond current Voice Search approaches by aiming for a greater integration between document search and conversational dialogue processes in order to provide a more efficient and effective search experience when using a SCSS. We will also investigate an information seeking model for audio and language models.

Presenting a Search Engine Result Page (SERP) over a speech-only communication channel presents a number of challenges, e.g., the textual component of a standard search results list has been shown to be ineffectual [4]. The transient nature of speech poses problems due to memory constraints, and makes the possibility of "skimming" back and forth over a list of results (a standard process in browsing a visual list) difficult. These issues are greatly exacerbated when the result being sought is further down the list.

This research will advance the knowledge base by:

- Providing an understanding of which strategies and IIR techniques for SCSS are best for users.
- Defining novel technologies for contextual conversational interaction with a large collection of unstructured documents that supports effective search over a speech-only communication channel (audio).
- Determining new methods for providing summary-based result-presentation for unstructured documents.

Thus this research will transform search over a speech-only communication channel by using an inherently interactive and conversational experience.

Developing a suitable SCSS requires an iterative user-centered approach, allowing us to design with the user in mind while matching the user's mental model [3]. Within a mixed-methods methodology several techniques will be used to form design decisions, i.e., role plays, Wizard of Oz methodologies and crowdsourcing. These techniques will allow us to gather data about user interaction patters and understand their linguistic behaviour [1, 2], and form an information seeking model for audio.

Our preliminary study measured the impact of the length of web search summaries in audio communication channels. The analysis showed that users preferred shortened summaries for queries with a clear query intent [6]. These findings emphasized the importance of developing techniques that can both predict when a query needs to be refined and provide suggestions for refinement to a conversational interface.

Thus the overall findings will advance the development of spoken search user interfaces since we address established challenges of Voice Search, but also seek to integrate these challenges within a framework for a SCSS.

Categories and Subject Descriptors

H.5.1 [**Multimedia Information Systems**]; H.3.3 [**Information Search and Retrieval**]; H.5.2 [**User Interfaces**]

Keywords

Conversational Search; Interactive Information Retrieval; Search Result Summarisation; Spoken Retrieval

References

[1] L. Dybkjaer, N. O. Bernsen, and W. Minker. Evaluation and usability of multimodal spoken language dialogue systems. *Speech Communication*, 43(1):33–54, 2004.

[2] J. Lai and N. Yankelovich. Speech interface design. In *Encyclopedia of Language & Linguistics (Second Edition)*, pages 764–770. Elsevier, 2006.

[3] J. Rubin and D. Chisnell. *Handbook of Usability Testing: Howto Plan, Design, and Conduct Effective Tests*. Wiley, 2008.

[4] N. G. Sahib, D. Al Thani, A. Tombros, and T. Stockman. Accessible information seeking. *ACM*, 2012.

[5] N. G. Sahib, A. Tombros, and T. Stockman. A comparative analysis of the information-seeking behavior of visually impaired and sighted searchers. *Journal of the American Society for Information Science and Technology*, 63(2):377–391, 2012.

[6] J. R. Trippas, D. Spina, M. Sanderson, and L. Cavedon. Towards understanding the impact of length in web search result summaries over a speech-only communication channel. In *Proc. of SIGIR'15*, 2015.

SIGIR'15, August 09-13, 2015, Santiago, Chile.
ACM 978-1-4503-3621-5/15/08.
http://dx.doi.org/10.1145/2766462.2767850.

Finding Answers in Web Search

Evi Yulianti
School of Computer Science & Information Technology
RMIT University
Melbourne, Australia
evi.yulianti@rmit.edu.au

ABSTRACT

There are many informational queries that could be answered with a text passage, thereby not requiring the searcher to access the full web document. When building manual annotations of answer passages for TREC queries, Keikha et al. [6] confirmed that many such queries can be answered with just passages. By presenting the answers directly in the search result page, user information needs will be addressed more rapidly so that reduces user interaction (click) with the search result page [3] and gives a significant positive effect on user satisfaction [2, 7].

In the context of general web search, the problem of finding answer passages has not been explored extensively. Retrieving relevant passages has been studied in TREC HARD track [1] and in INEX [5], but relevant passages are not required to contain answers. One of the tasks in the TREC genomics track [4] was to find answer passages on biomedical literature. Previous work has shown that current passage retrieval methods that focus on topical relevance are not effective at finding answers [6]. Therefore, more knowledge is required to identify answers in a document. Bernstein et al. [2] has studied an approach to extract inline direct answers for search result using paid crowdsourcing service. Such an approach, however, is expensive and not practical to be applied for all possible information needs. A fully automatic process in finding answers remains a research challenge.

The aim of this thesis is to find passages in the documents that contain answers to a user's query. In this research, we proposed to use a summarization technique through taking advantage of Community Question Answering (CQA) content. In our previous work, we have shown the benefit of using social media to generate more accurate summaries of web documents [8], but this was not designed to present answer in the summary. With the high volume of questions and answers posted in CQA, we believe that there are many questions that have been previously asked in CQA that are the same as or related to actual web queries, for which their best answers can guide us to extract answers in the document. As an initial work, we proposed using term distributions extracted from best answers for top matching questions in one of leading CQA sites, Yahoo! Answers (Y!A), for answer summaries generation. An experiment was done by comparing our summaries with reference answers built in previous work [6], finding some level of success. A manuscript is prepared for this result.

Next, as an extension of our work above, we were interested to see whether the documents that have better quality answer summaries should be ranked higher in the result list. A set of features are derived from answer summaries to re-rank documents in the result list. Our experiment shows that answer summaries can be used to improve state-of-the-art document ranking. The method is also shown to outperform a current re-ranking approach using comprehensive document quality features. A manuscript was submitted for this result.

For future work, we plan to conduct deeper analysis on top matching questions and their corresponding best answers from Y!A to better understand their benefit to the generated summaries and re-ranking results. For example, how do the results differ on different relevance level of top best answers from Y!A that were used to generate summaries. There are also opportunities to improve the use of Y!A in generating answer summaries, such as by predicting the quality of best answers from Y!A corresponding to the query. We also aim to combine the related Y!A pages into our initial result list when there is a question from Y!A, which is well matched with the query. Next, it is important to think about an approach to generate answer summaries for the queries that do not have related result from CQA.

SIGIR '15, August 09-13, 2015, Santiago, Chile
ACM 978-1-4503-3621-5/15/08.
http://dx.doi.org/10.1145/2766462.2767846

Categories and Subject Descriptors

H.3.3 [**Information Storage and Retrieval**]: Information Search and Retrieval.

Keywords

Web Search, Answer, Summarization, CQA

REFERENCES

[1] Allan, J. 2004. HARD Track Overview in TREC 2004 - high accuracy retrieval from documents. *Proc of TREC*.

[2] Bernstein, M.S., Teevan, J., Dumais, S., Liebling, D. and Horvitz, E. 2012. Direct Answers for Search Queries in the Long Tail. *Proc of SIGCHI*, 237–246.

[3] Chilton, L.B. and Teevan, J. 2011. Addressing People's Information Needs Directly in a Web Search Result Page. *Proc of WWW*, 27–36.

[4] Hersh, W.R., Cohen, A.M., Roberts, P.M. and Rekapalli, H.K. 2006. TREC 2006 genomics track overview. *Proc of TREC*.

[5] Kamps, J., Pehcevski, J., Kazai, G., Lalmas, M. and Robertson, S. 2008. INEX 2007 Evaluation Measures. *Focused Access to XML Documents*, 24–33.

[6] Keikha, M., Park, J.H., Croft, W.B. and Sanderson, M. 2014. Retrieving Passages and Finding Answers. *Prof of ADCS*, 81-84.

[7] Lagun, D., Hsieh, C.-H., Webster, D. and Navalpakkam, V. 2014. Towards Better Measurement of Attention and Satisfaction in Mobile Search. *Proc of SIGIR*, 113–122.

[8] Yulianti, E., Huspi, S. and Sanderson, M. 2015. Tweet-biased summarization. *JASIST*. (2015).

SIRIP 2015 Chairs' Welcome

It is our great pleasure to welcome you to the *SIGIR Symposium on Information Retrieval in Practice (SIRIP 2015)*. The goal of SIRIP is to bring together information retrieval researchers, practitioners, analysts, and consumers, and to achieve knowledge transfer across these boundaries. It is our hope that everyone who attends SIRIP walks away with new understanding and at least one new idea to think about or explore. SIRIP 2015 is held on the third day of the main SIGIR conference, on Wednesday, August 12, 2015, in Santiago, Chile. SIRIP is attended by people registered for the main conference as well as other interested practitioners who chose register for it alone. The SIRIP program consists of three hour and half long sessions that include a mix of invited presentations, refereed papers, and a panel presentation.

Invited Talks

As has been traditional for the SIGIR Industry Track in past years, this year we invited preeminent industry practitioners to talk about interesting real world problems and emerging new technologies or approaches. Invited speakers were selected to represent a diverse set of companies and topics, including institutions that are already well represented within the IR community (such as Microsoft, Yahoo, Baidu, and Yandex) and those that represent new or emerging areas of interest (including LinkedIn, Bloomberg, and Sogou).

- *From Web Search Relevance to Vertical Search Relevance,* Yi Chang (Yahoo)
- *Finding Money in the Haystack: Information Retrieval at Bloomberg,* Jonathan Dorando (Bloomberg)
- *If SIGIR Had an Academic Track, What Would Be in It?* David Hawking (Microsoft)
- *WeChat Search and Headline: Tencent and Sogou Join Forces on Mobile Search and the Challenges We Face,* Chao Liu (Sogou)
- *Structure, Personalization, Scale: A Deep Dive into LinkedIn Search,* Asif Makhani (LinkedIn)
- *Location in Commercial Search Engines*, Vanessa Murdock (Microsoft)
- *Challenges and Opportunities in Online Evaluation of Search Engines,* Pavel Serdyukov (Yandex)
- *Lower Search Cost,* Dou Shen (Baidu)

Refereed Papers

In addition to invited talks, we also solicited the submission of short (4-page) research papers contributing original results obtained in an industry setting or with obvious industry impact. These were curated by the SIRIP chairs and are published as part of the SIGIR proceedings. The number of accepted refereed papers was, of necessity, small. We received eight high quality submissions from practitioners at institutions around the world, and were able to accept half of them for presentation at SIRIP. Acceptance criteria included an assessment of likely impact and interest to an industry audience, as well as originality, technical quality and expression.

- *Practical Lessons for Gathering Quality Labels at Scale*, Omar Alonso (Microsoft)
- *Incremental Sampling in Query Logs*, Ricardo Baeza-Yates (Yahoo)

- *Where to Go on Your Next Trip? Optimizing Travel Destinations Based on User Preferences*, Julia Kiseleva (Eindhoven University of Technology), Melanie Mueller (Booking.com), Lucas Bernardi (Booking.com), Chad Davis (Booking.com), Ivan Kovacek (Booking.com), Mats Stafseng Einarsen (Booking.com), Jaap Kamps (University of Amsterdam), Alexander Tuzhilin (New York University), and Djoerd Hiemstra (University of Twente)
- *Bringing Order to the Job Market: Efficient Job Offer Categorization in E-Recruitment*, Emmanuel Malherbe (Multiposting), Mario Cataldi (Université Paris 8), and Andrea Ballatore (University of California, Santa Barbara)

Panel Presentation

In addition to presentations, this year's SIRIP schedule includes a panel presentation designed to foster discussion and encourage all attendees to think about the avenues that they might use to influence the real-world search tools that people currently use. The panel features prominent academics with rich and varied experiences that have led to significant industrial impact.

- *Having Industrial Impact from Academia*. Moderator: Jimmy Lin (University of Maryland)

We hope that you find the SIRIP program interesting and thought-provoking, and that the symposium provides you with a valuable opportunity to share ideas with other researchers and practitioners from institutions around the world.

Hang Li
SIGIR '15 Industry Track Chair
Huawei, China

Jaime Teevan
SIGIR '15 Industry Track Chair
Microsoft Research, USA

From Web Search Relevance to Vertical Search Relevance

Yi Chang
Yahoo Labs, Sunnyvale, CA 94089
yichang@yahoo-inc.com

1. ABSTRACT

Web search relevance is a billion dollar challenge, while there is a disadvantage of backwardness in web search competition. Vertical search result can be incorporated to enrich web search content, therefore vertical search relevance is critical to provide differentiated search results. Machine learning based ranking algorithms have shown their effectiveness for both web search and vertical search tasks. In this talk, the speaker will not only introduce state-of-the-art ranking algorithms for web search, but also cover the challenges to improve relevance of various vertical search engines: local search, shopping search, news search, etc.

SIGIR'15, August 09-13, 2015, Santiago, Chile.
ACM 978-1-4503-3621-5/15/08.
DOI: http://dx.doi.org/10.1145/2766462.2776787.

2. BIO

Yi Chang is a director of sciences in Yahoo Labs, working on web search, vertical search and mobile search challenges. His research interests include information retrieval, applied machine learning, natural language processing and social media mining. Yi Chang has co-authored more than 80 referred journal and conference papers, and he has published the first book in this area of vertical search relevance. He has served as track chair, area chair, poster chair, and sponsorship chair for SIGIR, WWW and CIKM in the past a couple of years.

Finding Money in the Haystack: Information Retrieval at Bloomberg

Jonathan J. Dorando
Bloomberg L.P.
New York, NY, USA
jdorando@bloomberg.net

Konstantine Arkoudas
Bloomberg L.P.
New York, NY, USA
karkoudas@bloomberg.net

Parth Vasa
Bloomberg L.P.
New York, NY, USA
pvasa@bloomberg.net

Gary Kazantsev
Bloomberg L.P.
New York, NY, USA
gkazantsev@bloomberg.net

Gideon Mann
Bloomberg L.P.
New York, NY, USA
gmann16@bloomberg.net

ABSTRACT

The financial markets are a rich domain for search, and it is not simple to serving the entire scope of financial professionals, who make their living on accurate, timely, and deep information. The data sources are many and disparate. This includes domains with rich structured data such as company and security attributes, textual data like research reports, and time sensitive news stories. Not only is the domain complicated, but some of the techniques that work for web search have to be adapted and reconsidered in an enterprise context with fewer eyeballs but just as complicated questions.

At Bloomberg, we have been addressing these problems over the past four years in the search and discoverability group, heavily leveraging the insights from the academic and open-source communities to apply to our problems. We'll discuss about our efforts in Natural Language Question & Answer (NLQA), learning to rank, federated search, crowd sourcing, and how this all comes together to make search effective for our users.

SIGIR'15, August 09 - 13, 2015, Santiago, Chile.
 ISBN 978-1-4503-3621-5/15/08
DOI: http://dx.doi.org/10.1145/2766462.2776782.

If SIGIR had an Academic Track, what would be in it?

David Hawking
Microsoft (Bing)
Canberra, Australia
david.hawking@acm.org

ABSTRACT

It used to be the case that very little industry research was presented at SIGIR. Now the balance has radically changed – many accepted papers have industry authors and many rely on industry data sets – To the extent that a leading academic member of the SIGIR community has light-heartedly proposed the creation of an Academic Track.

Behind the levity lies the important question of how a researcher can make a meaningful contribution to the field, in the absence of petabyte-scale sets of documents and massive user-interaction logs. Theoretical contributions can revolutionize thinking, but have greatest impact when applicable in practice, and when empirically validated.

In my years at Funnelback and more recently at Microsoft I have been very aware of high-impact but not-well-solved IR problems involving relatively tiny datasets. Many of them are characterized by sparsity of user interaction data and are hence not well-suited to simple machine learning approaches or to large scale A/B testing. My talk will illustrate and attempt to characterize these problems and to suggest fruitful areas for academic research.

If time permits, I will mention some areas in which academic research has contributed to current large-scale industry practice.

Categories and Subject Descriptors

H.3.3 [**Information Storage and Retrieval**]: Information Search and Retrieval—*relevance feedback*

Keywords

Open IR problems for academics.

BIO

David Hawking is an applied scientist in the Relevance & Intent group of Microsoft. He is based in Canberra and works on Bing.

David has been an IR researcher since 1991 and, among other things, has worked on parallel IR, distributed IR, term proximity models, efficiency, automatic assessment of health webpage quality, evaluation, test collection development, web IR and enterprise search. In 1998 he left the Australian National University to continue his research at Australia's largest research organization CSIRO. CSIRO's industrial focus led to the commercialisation of the team's research and eventually to the spinning off of the Funnelback internet and enterprise search company in late 2005. David joined the spinoff as Chief Scientist in 2008 and worked in that role until joining Microsoft in 2013.

David continues as an adjunct professor at the Australian National University and has graduated nine PhDs. He has authored around a hundred publications in the IR area (see `david-hawking.net/publications.shtml`) and twice served as program chair for SIGIR. He chaired the Industry Track at SIGIR 2014 and was Web Track coordinator at the international Text Retrieval Conference (TREC) from 1997-2004. In this role he was responsible for the creation and distribution of widely used text retrieval test collections. He holds an honorary doctorate from the University of Neuchâtel (Switzerland), the 2005 Chris Wallace award (Australasia) for computer science research and the 2012 Tony Kent Strix award (jointly with Doug Cutting).

SIGIR'15, August 09 - 13, 2015, Santiago, Chile.
ACM 978-1-4503-3621-5/15/08
http://dx.doi.org/10.1145/2766462.2776784.

WeChat Search & Headline: Sogou Joins Force with Tencent on Mobile Search

Chao Liu
Sogou Inc.
liuchao@sogou-inc.com

ABSTRACT

Tencent Inc. is the biggest social network company in China. Its WeChat and QQ boast of 700 million and 800 million monthly active users (MAU), respectively. Sogou Inc., on the other hand, is a search leader in China, being the No. 2 and No. 3 on mobile/PC search market, respectively. This talk introduces how Tencent and Sogou join force on the battele of mobile search. Specifically, we discuss two products, namely WeChat Search and WeChat Headline, and illustrate how they leverage the strength of both companies to take the market. We further dive under the hood, and examine technical problems and solutions. In particular, we focus on unique aspects due to the particularities of WeChat, e.g., millions of articles generated from about 1 million official accounts, which are forwarded and broadcasted by hundreds of millions of users across the world. Some problems, e.g., de-duplication and ranking, might be similar to traditional IR, but some other aspects are not. In the end, we put forward some challenges for open discussion, and solicit comments from academia and fellow practitioners.

Categories and Subject Descriptors

J.4 SOCIAL AND BEHAVIORAL SCIENCES

General Terms

Algorithms, Design, Human Factors

Keywords

Social Search, Mobile Search.

SIGIR '15, August 09-13, 2015, Santiago, Chile.
ACM 978-1-4503-3621-5/15/08.
DOI: http://dx.doi.org/10.1145/2766462.2776781

BIO

Chao Liu is the Chief Scientist, and the General Manager of the Data Science Department in Sogou Inc. Dr. Liu is elected to China "Top 1000 Young Talents", the highest honor for oversea researchers returning to China. Before coming back to China, he was a researcher and the manager of the Data Intelligence Group in Microsoft Research at Redmond (MSR-Redmond). His research has been focused on Web search/ads and data mining, with about 40 conference/journal publications and many research results transferred to Microsoft Bing, Tencent SoSo, and Sogou Search engines. Dr. Liu has been on the program and organizing committees of many conferences, including SIGIR, SIGKDD, WWW, etc., and actively campaigns for the mutualism between academia and industry. Dr. Liu earned his PhD in Computer Science from the University of Illinois at Urbana-Champaign in 2007, and B.S. in Computer Science from Peking University (China) in 2003.

Structure, Personalization, Scale: A Deep Dive into LinkedIn Search

Asif Makhani
LinkedIn Corporation
Mountain View, CA USA
amakhani@linkedin.com

ABSTRACT

All of us are familiar with search as users. And as software engineers, many of us have worked on search problems in the context of web search, site search, or enterprise search. But search at LinkedIn is different. Our corpus is a richly structured professional graph comprised of 364M+ people, 3M+ companies, 2M+ groups, and 1.5M+ publishers. Our members perform billions of searches (over 5.7B in 2012), and each of those searches is highly personalized based on the searcher's identity and relationships with other professional entities in LinkedIn's economic graph. And all this data is in constant flux as LinkedIn adds more than 2 members every second in over 200 countries (2/3 of our members are outside the United States). As a result, we've built a system quite different from those used for other search applications. In this talk, we will discuss some of the unique challenges we've faced as we deliver highly personalized search over semi-structured data at massive scale.

SIGIR '15, August 09-13, 2015, Santiago, Chile.
ACM 978-1-4503-3621-5/15/08.
DOI: http://dx.doi.org/10.1145/2766462.2776785

Location in Search

Vanessa Murdock
Microsoft
1 Microsoft Way
Redmond WA
vanmur@microsoft.com

ABSTRACT

As users turn increasingly to handheld devices to find information, the research community has focused on real-time location signals (GPS signals) to improve search engine effectiveness. Location signals have been investigated for predicting businesses the user will frequent[3], assigning geographic coordinates to media files[1], and to improve mobile search ranking[2].

While the increased focus on real-time user location has produced excellent research, there remains a gap between the capabilities being developed in the research community, and the capabilities being developed by commercial search engines. The core of this discrepancy between the advances in research and advances in industry is understanding the user's location.

The vast majority of research on user location assumes that the user's location is known, because the user has provided a GPS signal. For many systems, there is no GPS signal available. The user may choose not enable it, or the system chooses not to prompt the user for the location because doing so degrades the user experience. For these interactions, the system relies on the user's IP address for location information.

Further, much of the current research uses public geocoded data such as Foursquare (http://www.foursquare.com visited June 2015), and Twitter (http://www.twitter.com visited June 2015). These data are an incomplete picture of places a user may visit, and are potentially biased in their representation of actual users. The information contained in these data is not the same type of information typically available to a commercial search engine.

In this talk we discuss gaps between current research on location, and industry advances in using location signals to improve search results. We focus on user location as one example of a gap between research and development.

Categories and Subject Descriptors

H.3.3 [**Information Storage and Retrieval**]: Information Search and Retrieval *–retrieval models.*

SIGIR '15, August 09-13, 2015, Santiago, Chile
ACM 978-1-4503-3621-5/15/08.
http://dx.doi.org/10.1145/2766462.2776783

General Terms

Algorithms, Experimentation.

Keywords

User location, local search, contextual ranking.

BIO

Vanessa Murdock is a Principal Applied Researcher at Microsoft for the past three years. Her research focuses on leveraging social media to improve local search.

Previously Dr. Murdock worked at Yahoo! Research in Barcelona, Spain, as a Senior Research Scientist. At Yahoo! Research she led the Geographic Context and Experience Group, doing research on topics related to geographic information retrieval and user-generated content. She has been awarded 8 patents, and has more than 30 patent applications pending, resulting in a Master Inventor Award from Yahoo! (2012). She received the OAA Award for Outstanding Achievement by a Young Alum from the University of Massachusetts in 2014.

Dr. Murdock publishes regularly in the field of information retrieval, and is active in the scientific community, reviewing for conferences and journals, organizing workshops and tutorials, and serving on the organizing committees for international conferences.

Dr. Murdock received a B.S. in Computer Science from Colorado State University in 2001 and an M.S. and Ph.D. in Computer Science from the University of Massachusetts Amherst in 2005 and 2006, respectively. Dr. Murdock also holds a Bachelor of Music, and worked as a professional musician for 10 years prior to her career in computer science.

REFERENCES

[1] Larson, M., Soleymani, M., Serdyukov, P., Rudinac, S., Wartena, C., Murdock, V., Friedland, G., Ordelman, R., and Jones, G. Automatic tagging and geotagging in video collections and communities. In *Proceedings of the 1st ACM International Conference on Multimedia Retrieval (ICMR)*. 2011.

[2] Lv, Y., Lymberopoulos, D., and Wu, Q. An exploration of ranking heuristics in mobile local search. In *Proceedings of SIGIR*. Portland, 2012.

[3] Shaw, B., Shea, J., Sinha, S., and Hogue, A. Learning to rank for spatiotemporal search. In *Proceedings of WSDM.* Rome, 2013.

Challenges and Opportunities in Online Evaluation of Search Engines

Pavel Serdyukov
Yandex
Leo Tolstoy 16
Moscow, Russia
pavser@yandex-team.ru

ABSTRACT

Yandex is one of the largest Internet companies in Europe, operating Russia's most popular search engine, generating 58.6% of all search traffic in Russia (as of April 2015). As all modern search engines, Yandex increasingly relies on online evaluation methods such as A/B tests and interleaving. These online evaluation methods test various changes in the search engine by analyzing the changes in the character of its interactions with its users. There are several grand challenges in online evaluation, including the choice of an appropriate online metric and the need to deal with the limited number of user interactions available for a search engine for experimentation. In my talk, I will overview our latest research on improving the sensitivity of well-known online metrics, on the discovery of more sensitive and robust online metrics, on scheduling and early stopping of online experiments.

SIGIR'15, August 09 - 13, 2015, Santiago, Chile.
ACM. ISBN 978-1-4503-3621-5/15/08
DOI: http://dx.doi.org/10.1145/2766462.2776786.

Short Bio Pavel Serdyukov is the Head of Research Projects at Yandex, where he manages a team of researchers working in the field of web search, data mining, computer vision and others. He has published extensively in top-tier conferences on the topics related to web search, personalization, enterprise/entity search, query log analysis, location-specific retrieval and recommendation. He co-organized a number of workshops at SIGIR, was a co-organizer of the Entity track at TREC 2009-2011, and co-organized a series of workshops/data mining challenges at WSDM in 2012 – 2014. He has served as a senior PC member at most recent WWW, WSDM and CIKM conferences and was also the General Chair of ECIR 2013 in Moscow. Before joining Yandex in 2011, he was a postdoc at Delft University, got his PhD from Twente University (2009) and his MSc from Max-Planck Institute for Computer Science (2005).

Lower Search Cost

Dou Shen
Baidu Inc.
Baidu Campus, No. 10 Shangdi 10th St
Beijing, China, 100085
shendou@baidu.com

ABSTRACT
Web search has been an effective approach for people to find the desired information or service. However, Web search is a pretty heavy task for most users since people need to launch a search engine's portal, phrase the right query and then go through search results to find the right information or service. To lower the search cost, commercial search engines have been improved in many ways, including query suggestion, relevant search, knowledge graph, ranking algorithm, user interface, and so on. I will briefly explain the progress along these features, especially for the largest Chinese search engine - Baidu. In addition to these approaches, another important way to lower search cost is to make Web search available and ready whenever a user intends to start a search, which becomes more important with the popularity of mobile devices. I will talk about the progress along this direction and the technologies behind it as well.

Categories and Subject Descriptors
H.4.0 [**Information Systems**]: Information Systems Applications – *General.*

General Terms
Algorithms, Experimentation

Keywords
Web Search; Search Cost; Keyword Recommendation.

SIGIR'15, August 09-13, 2015, Santiago, Chile.
ACM 978-1-4503-3621-5/15/08.
http://dx.doi.org/10.1145/2766462.2776788

Practical Lessons for Gathering Quality Labels at Scale

Omar Alonso
Microsoft Corporation
omalonso@microsoft.com

ABSTRACT

Information retrieval researchers and engineers use human computation as a mechanism to produce labeled data sets for product development, research and experimentation. To gather useful results, a successful labeling task relies on many different elements: clear instructions, user interface design, representative high-quality datasets, appropriate inter-rater agreement metrics, work quality checks, and channels for worker feedback. Furthermore, designing and implementing tasks that produce and use several thousands or millions of labels is different than conducting small scale research investigations. In this paper we present a perspective for collecting high quality labels with an emphasis on practical problems and scalability. We focus on three main topics: programming crowds, debugging tasks with low agreement, and algorithms for quality control. We show examples from an industrial setting.

Categories and Subject Descriptors

H.0 [Information Systems]: General

General Terms

Design, Experimentation, Human Factors

Keywords

Labeling; crowdsourcing; inter-rater agreement; debugging; Captchas; worker reliability; experimental design

1. INTRODUCTION

Researchers and engineers use human computation via platforms like CrowdFlower or Amazon Mechanical Turk as a mechanism to produce labeled data sets. Several areas of information management such as information retrieval, machine learning, recommender systems, and natural language processing rely heavily on such labels for product research and development.

Crowdsourcing has become increasingly important for curating, labeling, and processing Web-scale datasets. Many members of the information retrieval community have interest in crowdsourcing and would like to incorporate it into their research and practice. We share practical recommendations for practitioners who are already working with crowdsourcing platforms, and would like to step up their game.

SIGIR '15, August 9-13, 2015, Santiago, Chile.

ACM 978-1-4503-3621-5/15/08...$15.00
DOI: http://dx.doi.org/10.1145/2766462.2776778

Labeled corpora may be used to train and evaluate ranking algorithms or may be used as reference datasets for implementing and evaluating information retrieval techniques. Assigning a label is usually considered a judgment task, performed by a human (e.g., worker, expert, judge, annotator, rater, etc.), where the judgments may be more or less subjective. A judgment on the objective end of the spectrum may suggest a single right answer, so we can rely on a single worker or a small number of workers to accurately label an item. If the judgment is more subjective, we probably need to ask more workers the question, and use an aggregation method to determine the best candidate label.

In general, our approach for collecting labels not only looks at designing work from the standpoint of results, but also explicitly acknowledges the human aspects of human computation, and identifies other issues that include worker motivation, fatigue, subjective judgment, and making the most of worker characteristics and diversity.

In this paper, we assume a supervised or semi-supervised learning setting. That is, there is a human involved in the production of labels to bootstrap a learning mechanism or for evaluation purposes. We also add two constraints from real-world systems: scalability and continuity. By scalability, we mean gathering several thousands or millions of labels depending on the application. Rather than a one-off process for acquiring labels in a single step, we see this as a continuous process that runs at specific intervals (e.g., daily, weekly, etc.) as part of a bigger workflow for training, modeling, or evaluation.

We argue that gathering high quality labels at scale is not a straightforward activity. While it is desirable to use crowdsourcing techniques, the process should not be outsourced. Quite the contrary, teams that depend on these data need to have tight control on the many factors that can influence the outcome including specific crowdsourced data management techniques [6].

We now describe three areas that impact the overall quality of labels: wetware programing (or how to ask humans to perform a task), debugging human computation tasks, and algorithms for assessing work quality and worker performance.

2. WETWARE PROGRAMMING

We use the phrase "wetware programming" to describe a computation that is designed by a human and performed by another human in a crowdsourcing-like platform. The idea behind human computation is to use humans as processors in a distributed system for performing tasks that machines cannot do well yet. Human computation is usually performed via form-based tasks or games (e.g., GWAP). When comparing to a machine, the instruction set for humans is somewhat unknown, making it more difficult for an engineer to design and implement solutions based on human computation.

2.1 Design considerations

We outline a number of issues that engineers and developers face when writing software that uses human computation.

- Asking questions. All tasks require at some point a question. Is the document relevant for the query? Does the image contain adult content? Are both articles the same? Is the following entity the same as this Facebook page? Asking questions is part art and part science. Instructions are very important but, at the same time, workers will not read nor remember several pages of details. What we recommended is to be precise and to the point on the question that is asked and what is expected as a valid answer. Showing examples of what is acceptable and not is always desirable. If possible involve a technical writer or someone with an English major to write the instructions.
- User interface and content presentation. All the necessary information to perform the task should be self-contained: what is the task, what needs to be done, examples, tips, links, etc. A worker who is engaged with a task and content would produce better labels. The goal is to help the worker perform the task the best way possible. Having the ability for workers to leave feedback is also a good strategy for collection suggestions and improvements for the task.
- Processing speed. As expected, in general, humans are much slower than machines for computing. There is also variation among humans. Tasks that are not completed in time or with a high abandonment rate can be an indication of assignment difficulty or poor incentives.
- Cost and incentives. Regardless if the humans are experts or part of a crowdsourced pool, the right cost and incentive structure can help retain and attract good workers.
- Task difficulty. All human tasks involve a degree of difficulty. Even if we think that the request is very simple, it may have an important cognitive load so it is always desirable to create, if possible, the simplest unit of work that can be performed.
- Errors. Labeling tasks are very repetitive and we all humans are error prone. Collecting multiple answers does help to eliminate those errors due to poor attention by workers using consensus strategies.

2.2 Agreement and consensus

We need to be able to trust the data collected so far. If two or more workers agree on a judgment, the higher the chances that the label is correct. A good practice is to use inter-rater agreement statistics for measuring the agreement among workers. An inter-rater statistic produces a value between -1 and 1, where 1 is perfect agreement, 0 is due to chance, and -1 means total lack of agreement. The most common statistics used in practice are Cohen's kappa (2 raters), Fleiss' kappa (n raters), and Krippendorff's alpha (n raters with missing values). It is strongly recommended to always use a good inter-rater static and avoid things like percentage agreement.

2.3 Microtasks and workflows

Finally, it is very likely that each task or microtask will be part of a larger workflow so, overall, there is an upfront cost when instrumenting human computation as part of large systems. This step may look overwhelming at first but there is great benefit if implemented correctly. Data quality and experimental designs are preconditions to make sure we get the right kind of labels before we move further down the modeling pipeline. These labels will be used for rankers, machine learning models, evaluations, etc.

3. REAL-WORLD PROBRLEMS

Survey designers and researchers that produce annotated corpora have a good process in place to achieve good results. Engineers use a development process (e.g., agile, waterfall, etc.) to produce software. However, when dealing with a human instruction set, the process is a bit unclear. A number of issues with the adoption of human computation and crowdsourcing in organizations are due to a lack of development process and unrealistic expectations. Crowdsourcing works but requires attention and care. In other words, the work is outsourced to the crowd but not the process.

3.1 Development process

It is good practice to have a development process in place that allows fast iteration and experimentation. We do not claim that ours is unique but it has been tested in production with good results. It consists on the following three phases.

1. Prototype development. We start with a small data set and use it with our very own development team for testing the designs and gathering labels. If the team members do not understand the design or if the inter-rater agreement is low, we need to go back to the drawing board and re-design the task.
2. Early stage production. This step uses the same design and same data set as in the previous step but this time using a different crowd: hired editors (if they are available) or crowdsourced workers. The goal is to see if other workers can perform the same task and produce similar results. In other words, do workers agree with our own internal team? If the task design is still unclear and the agreement is low, we probably need to debug the task using the framework presented in subsection 3.4.
3. Continuous production. Now that we tested the design a number of times and the results are good, the next step is to enforce quality control, increase the size of the data set, and perform this step continuously.

3.2 Labels for evaluation

Relevance evaluation is one of the most widely used applications of crowdsourcing. The task is very simple: given a query and a web page, assess its relevance in a binary or graded relevance scale. The labels collected are used to measure the performance of a particular algorithm and for building test collections.

In practice, however, not all evaluation tasks are so simple. A common mistake is trying to do too much on a single task. That is, asking several questions while minimizing payment instead of a more practical alternative of decomposing a task into smaller ones. At the end, we want a single label but it does not mean that such label needs to be produced in a single task in one pass. In the context of machine translation, a very nice overview of task design and data acquisition is presented in [4]. In a different example, for evaluating the performance of a near-duplicate algorithm, the task was partitioned in two: one for detecting if a document is a news article and a second one to compare if two news documents are duplicates or near-duplicates. Each phase was conducted in two different platforms (MTurk and Microsoft's UHRS) with different payment schemes [3]. Figure 1 summarizes the workflow.

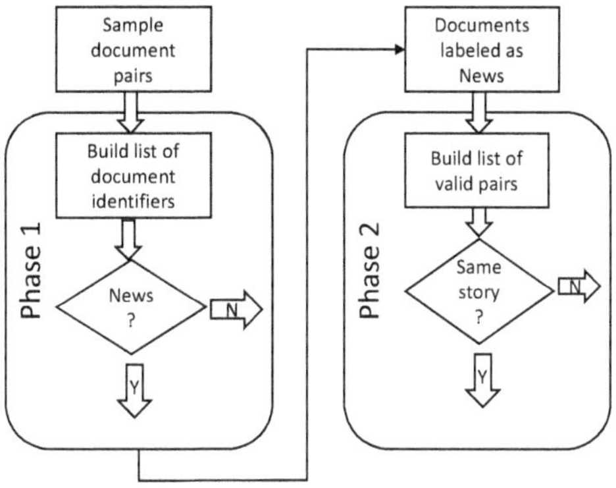

Figure 1. Two-phase evaluation for near-duplicate detection. Phase 1 uses Mechanical Turk while phase 2 uses UHRS. Both phases use different payment schemes and expertise.

3.3 Labeling and low agreement

In practice, a common approach is to start from the feature engineering or modeling phase and reverse the type of labels that are needed. For example, say that a given classifier model needs three types of labels ("yes", "no", "not sure"). One solution is to create a task so humans can provide those exact three labels for a class. A problem with this strategy is that the kind of labels that are needed for the machine (the model) do not necessary represent the same labels for humans. In other words, we should use labels that humans can perform best at and then map them into what input is required for the machine. This may include, for example, using a binary scale for a machine but a 5-point grade for humans.

There are cases where a task will produce results with low inter-rater agreement in many runs. The typical reaction by the engineer or developer is usually adversarial: identify the workers that are spammers or low performers and replace them. While this may be the case, the first thing that is needed is to debug the task. How do we know if the task is working? Debugging a task that uses a human instruction set has a number of problems and it is usually a difficult thing in practice.

3.4 Debugging framework

We now describe a framework for debugging subjective judgment tasks and for improving label quality before the crowdsourcing task is run at scale. The framework alternately varies characteristics of the work, assesses the reliability of the workers, and aims to improve task design by disaggregating the labels into components that may be less subjective to the workers, thereby potentially improving inter-rater agreement [2].

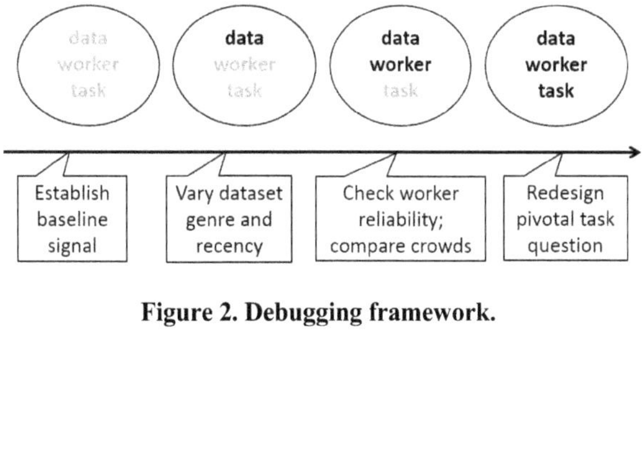

Figure 2. Debugging framework.

The framework presented in Figure 2 consists of a "data-worker-task" pattern where the aim is to dive into each of the three contingent factors with the end goal of debugging (and fixing) each potential problem.

1. Data. We first start with the data (the work to be done) with the aim of reducing the subjectivity of the data and narrowing the data genre. Many factors can cause conscious or unconsciously bias on the workers. Reducing the range on these factors can make the final results more accurate.
2. Workers. We then look at the performance of the workers. How can we detect poor quality work in the absence of a gold set to check workers' performance or high inter-rater agreement to identify normative answers? A Captchas-like technique called HIDDEN (Human Intelligence Data-Driven Enquiries) is useful for solving this problem. Instead of asking a completely orthogonal question like the traditional Captchas, the questions were designed to focus the workers' attentions on the aspects that they are about to judge. Figure 3 shows an example of HIDDENs. In order to complete the task, workers were asked to read the content three different times, attending to different aspects of the post. In other words, workers had to reflect on the tweet in multiple ways.
3. Task. Many subjective concepts are controversial because there are many different interpretations. By segmenting the factors that lead to the subjective decision, it is possible to narrow down the decision space. In our experience, we found that most of the problems occur on ill-defined questions that produce inconsistent answers.

Figure 3 shows an example of a production task using HIDDENs to label tweets in a classification task. We can think of Q1 as the algorithmic HIDDEN whereas Q2 is more semantic. Q3 is the question that we use to collect labels. By maintaining high inter-rater agreement on the HIDDENs we can iterate and debug a potentially problematic question, in our case Q3.

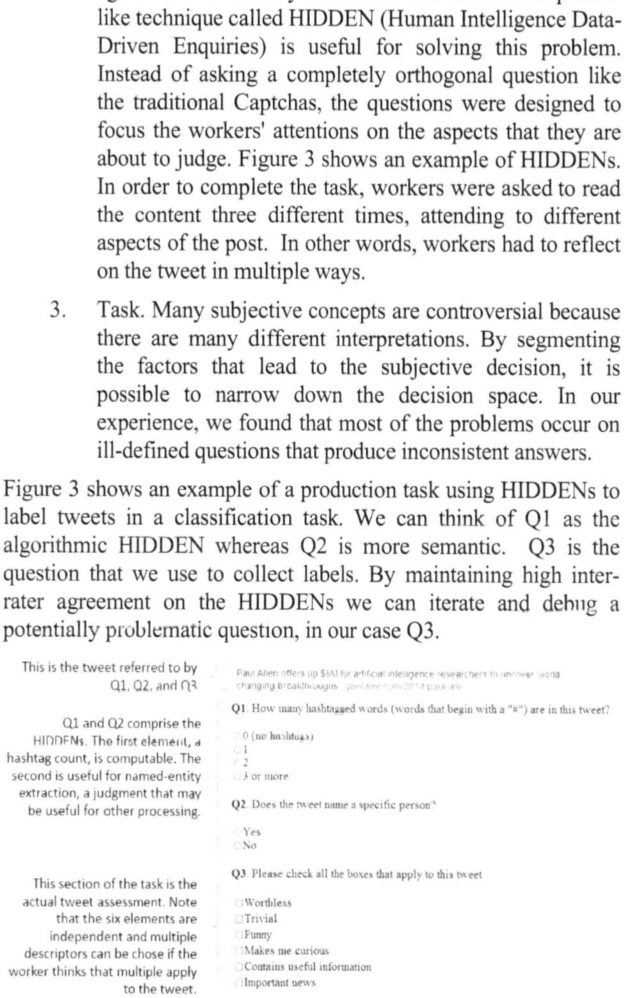

Figure 3. HIDDEN structure. The first question is completely objective and computable; the second is partially objective; and the third could be much more subjective.

4. ALGORITHMS AND QUALITY CONTROL

While there is quite of bit of research on quality control from an adversarial perspective (i.e., workers are spammers), in practice quality has to be applied to both requesters and workers. Workers may be spamming or not performing, but, at the same time, our own design may be so bad that is impossible for honest and experience workers to produce anything useful.

How do we measure work quality? If we can produce honey pots (known answers for questions), we can remove workers who are not passing them. Other options are to compare the performance of a worker to other workers in the same task or to use a tiered approach, where certain workers are more experts. An example of a tiered approach is the "find-fix-verify" pattern: one set of workers find and fix a problem and a separate set of workers verify that the correction is good. But more importantly, when and how should we enforce the quality control?

4.1 Quality checks

Quality control is an on-going activity, in particular in industrial environments that require tasks to run continuously. Quality control check points should be introduced as follows:

1. Before the task is on production. This can be done by using a qualification test or similar mechanism to filter, screen, select, train, and recruit workers.
2. During task execution time. We assess answers as worker produces them. This can be implemented by introducing honey pots as random checks.
3. After task has completed. Once the experiment is done, we compute the usual accuracy metrics and remove bad performers.

A new proposed approach for enhancing worker performance is by providing micro breaks [5]. As a lot of tasks are repetitive and, in certain cases, probably boring, providing workers with a break can potentially improve overall work quality.

4.2 Algorithmic solutions

As noted before, a good technique is to compare a label to a predefined answer. This is very cheap to implement but assumes that such gold set or ground truth exists or that is somewhat affordable to produce down the road. A second problem is to produce good honey pots that are not so easy to identify by workers. Qualification tests have also some disadvantages. There is an extra cost involved for designing and maintaining such tests. This may also turn off workers and hurt completion time.

Most of the algorithms for managing work quality are based on majority vote, EM-based and maximum likelihood. Majority vote is straightforward to implement and tends to produce good results. However, there are cases when it is not possible to get majority so easily. The algorithm "get another label" decides how many labels to use on a given task based on the distribution of all previously encountered tasks [7]. Vox Populi uses the aggregate label as an approximate ground truth and eliminates the workers that provide incorrect answers [8].

4.3 Explore-exploit and adaptive strategies

Very recently there are new directions that use adaptive approaches for managing crowds [1]. In explore-exploit techniques there is a quality-cost tradeoff. That is, maximizing the quality of the labels gathered while minimizing the overall cost per task. The idea of exploration is to try out alternatives to gather information. Exploitation is about choosing alternatives that perform well based on information already collected.

How many workers to ask in a given task is also a fair question to pose. For example, for the query {facebook} and the web page {www.facebook.com}, one worker should be enough to produce a good judgment. However for the query {mars expedition} and the web page {www.mars-one.com} is not clear how many workers are needed. Developing and implementing stopping rules that know when to stop asking a worker for a new label is very important.

5. CONCLUSION

Often perceived as boring and time consuming process, gathering high quality labels requires full attention so it is key to own the entire process end-to-end. These labels will be used for training set creation, modeling, and evaluation. There is no need to rush things. Repeatable label quality at scale works but requires a solid framework. The end goal is to get the labels right first and then move to modeling.

In this paper we presented the areas that need attention that should be useful for practitioners who are considering crowdsourcing at scale but are a bit unsure about how to implement and focus resources. We described a development process that is currently used in-house to test human computation tasks. We also introduced a reliability framework that shows the three aspects that need attention: workers, data and task design. We also outline a number of algorithmic solutions that can be used for managing quality.

Finally, lots of different skills and expertise are required for implementing successful tasks that can produce high quality labels. For example, social and behavioral science, human factors, algorithms, economics, distributed systems, and statistics. It is important to know our own limitations and be ready to collaborate with other teams.

6. REFERENCES

[1] I. Abraham, O. Alonso, V. Kandylas, R. Patel, S. Shelford, and A. Slivkins. "How Many Workers to Ask? Adaptive Exploration for Collecting High Quality Labels". http://arxiv.org/abs/1411.0149

[2] O. Alonso, C., Marshall, and M. Najork. "Debugging a Crowdsourced Task with Low Inter-rater Agreement". *Proceedings of JCDL*, 2015.

[3] O. Alonso, D. Fetterly, and M. Manasse. "Duplicate News Story Detection Revisited". *Proceedings of AIRS*, 2013.

[4] C. Callison-Burch. "Fast, Cheap, and Creative: Evaluating Translation Quality using Amazon's Mechanical Turk". *Proceedings of EMNLP*, 2009.

[5] P. Dai, J. Rzeszotarski, P. Paritosh, and E. Chi. "And Now for Something Completely Different: Improving Crowdsourcing Workflows with Micro-Diversions". *Proceedings of CSCW*, 2015.

[6] A. Marcus and A. Parameswaran. *Crowdsourced Data Management.* Foundations and Trends in Databases, 2015.

[7] V. Sheng, F. Provost, P. Ipeirotis. "Get Another Label? Improving Data Quality Using Multiple, Noisy Labelers". *Proceeding of KDD*, 2008.

[8] O. Dekel and O. Shamir. "Vox Populi: Collecting High-Quality Labels from a Crowd". *Proceedings of COLT*, 2009.

Incremental Sampling in Query Logs

Ricardo Baeza-Yates
Yahoo Labs
Sunnyvale, USA
rbaeza@acm.org

ABSTRACT

We introduce a simple technique to generate incremental query log samples that mimics well the original query distribution. In this way, editorial judgments for new queries can be consistently added to previous judgments. We also review the problem of how to choose the sample size depending on the types of queries that need to be detected as well as the conditions needed to get a good sample.

Categories and Subject Descriptors

H.3.3 [**Information Systems**]: Information Search and Retrieval

1. INTRODUCTION

In evaluating search engine quality, we are typically interested in the average performance over a large set of queries. Unfortunately, estimating this performance based on individual queries is not trivial because query frequencies follow a very biased distribution that can be modeled with a power law [2]. Hence, choosing the right sample size as well as the right sample is crucial and can have a dramatic impact on performance estimations as well as in any other measure inferred from the query sample.

Many times sample queries are often selected in an arbitrary fashion, due to many different reasons. For example, the queries are those where we have judgement evaluations and hence we can measure quality performance. However, most of the time those queries do not represent well the original query stream (*e.g.* biased towards popular queries, filtered for adult queries and/or identity information, etc.). Even when the sampling is done correctly, the resultant distribution may not have the same characteristics of the original query stream.

To measure search engine quality, many times editorial quality judgments are used. However, as the editorial judgment of large samples is expensive, we have a trade-off between cost and the error in the performance estimation. For this reason, the editorial work is spread over time and instead of generating a large sample to be used for several months, it is much better to generate incremental samples that reflect the changes in the query distribution but at the same time are consistent with each other. Therefore, we design a new sampling algorithm that addresses these requirements. To the best of our knowledge, we are the first to tackle this case.

The rest of the paper is organized as follows. In the following section we characterize query logs while in Sections 3 and 4 we address the issues of sample size and sample generation, discussing how to measure the goodness of a sample with respect to the original distribution. In Section 5 we present the new sampling algorithm that is able to generate a series of incremental samples, followed by some concluding remarks in Section 6.

SIGIR '15, August 09 - 13, 2015, Santiago, Chile.

ACM 978-1-4503-3621-5/15/08 ...$15.00.
DOI: http://dx.doi.org/10.1145/2766462.2776780.

2. MODELING QUERY FREQUENCIES

A query log is a time-ordered sequence of queries submitted to a search engine. Each query can have one or more attributes associated to the query, such as time, location, etc. The query frequency is usually modeled by a power law (there are other distributions that can be used but they are more complex, see [10]). That is, the query frequencies follow a distribution proportional to $f_1\ r^{-\alpha}$ where f_1 is the frequency of the most popular query, r is the rank of the query when frequencies are sorted from largest to smallest, and α is the exponent of the power law.

The exponent α depends on the specific search engine, how many languages are used in it, etc. For example, in [11], for the case of a Brazilian search engine, α was 0.59, while for another one that uses Spanish was 1.42 [7]. In [3, 8], for the case of a generic search engine, α was 1.84 and 2.38, respectively, more similar to the case of words in text documents. In this paper we use for our examples mobile query logs from 8 different countries obtained in the same period of time from a large web search engine. In our case α is below but close to 1. An example is given in Figure 1 where α is 0.88 if we force f_1 to be the actual value.

An important characteristic of query logs is that the long tail does not match well the power law model, because the tail is much longer than the one that corresponds to the power law fitting the head distribution. Indeed, singleton queries are a large percentage of the query vocabulary (number of different queries), typically 50% in a generic web search query log and in our mobile query logs they are in the range of 61% to 69% (in the case of Figure 1 is 68.8%). In the later case this implies more than 26% of the query

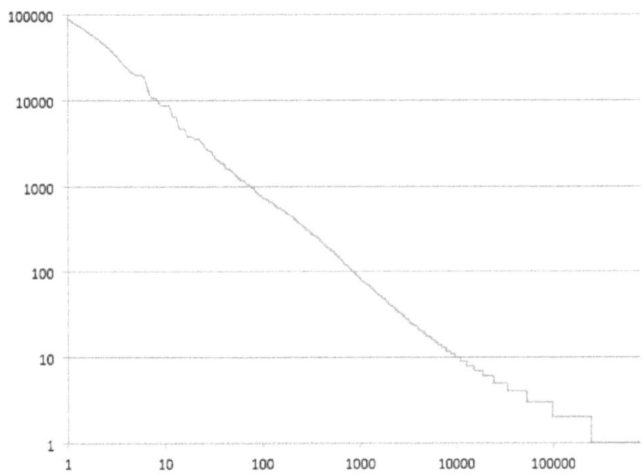

Figure 1: Mobile query log example.

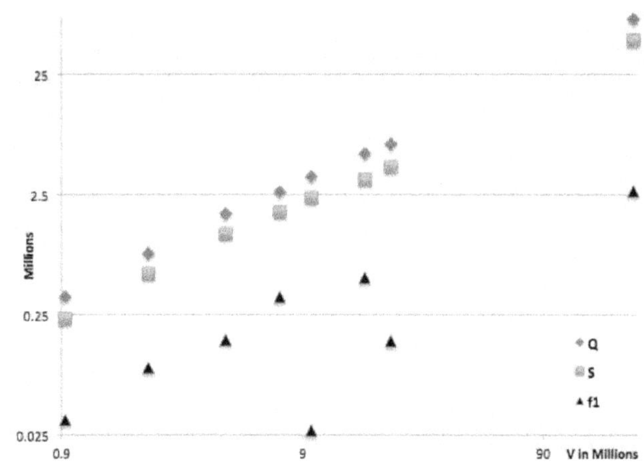

Figure 2: Characteristics of mobile query logs for 8 different countries.

volume (in our mobile samples this percentage ranges from 20% to 27%).

Let Q be the total number of unique queries in the query log and S the number of singleton queries. Hence, a better model for the query frequency is:

$$f_r = \begin{cases} \lceil f_1/r^\alpha \rceil & 1 \le r \le Q-S \\ 1 & Q-S < r \le Q \\ 0 & r > Q \end{cases}$$

Using this model we obtain the following formulas for the total volume of queries V:

$$V = \begin{cases} f_1(Q-S)^{1-\alpha}/(1-\alpha) + S + O(1) & 0<\alpha<1 \\ f_1 \ln(Q-S) + S + O(1) & \alpha = 1 \\ f_1/(\alpha-1) + S + O(f_1 Q^{-(\alpha-1)}) & \alpha > 1 \end{cases}$$

As in practice $S = O(Q)$, we have the following order of magnitude relations with respect to the volume of queries:

$$\begin{array}{lll} Q = O(V) & f_1 = O(V^\alpha) & 0<\alpha<1 \\ Q = O(V) & f_1 = O(V/\log V) & \alpha = 1 \\ Q = O(V^{1/\alpha}) & f_1 = O(V) & \alpha > 1 \end{array}$$

In our mobile query logs we have the first case that works well even across countries as shown in Figure 2. Notice how f_1 grows a bit more slowly as α is below 1. The two outliers are countries that use Kanji, so as expected, language also plays a role.

3. SAMPLE SIZE

Most research works use very small query sets, partly due to lack of data, or as we mentioned before, for lack of judged queries. On the other hand, in [9] it is shown that a random query sample of 650 queries is sufficient to reliably estimate if a search engine is better than another search engine. However, this work does not say anything regarding the right sample size if we want to estimate a measure in the query log itself, for example, the fraction of queries that mention a location or a given topic.

Let us assume that we want to be able to detect in the query log sample a certain class of queries that appears with probability p in the query stream. To estimate the sample size we could use the standard error formula for a binomial distribution of parameter p. However the standard error is not good for small values of p. In [4] and the associated comments, several techniques to estimate the error in a Binomial distribution are studied. For large samples, they recommend the Agresti-Coull [1] technique that also works well for values of p closer to 0, which is the case for many applications (it is certainly the case for click through rates in ads or results below the top ranked ones). Although not recommended, for small p also the Clopper-Pearson technique works well, but is a bit conservative. At the end we settled for the recommended technique because it also allows to find a formula for the sample size n. Indeed, we obtain

$$n \ge Z^2_{1-\alpha/2}\left(\frac{p'(1-p')}{\epsilon^2} - 1\right)$$

where ϵ is the maximum relative error that we want to have, $1-\alpha$ is the confidence interval, Z is the inverse of the standard normal distribution, and $p' = p + Z^2/2$. For example, if we want to estimate a class of queries that appears 10% of the time with a confidence interval of 90% and a relative error of at most 10%, we need a sample size of at least 2432 queries. With 650 queries the relative error would be almost 20% or then we can only measure with a 10% error a class of queries that appears 29% of the time or more. In practice, if we want to measure rare queries, such as using the search engine as a calculator, we will need much larger sample sizes.

4. SAMPLING TECHNIQUES

Query samples are weighted sets, in the sense that the same query can be sampled multiple times. Let $\mathcal{S}$ be a sample query set. For every $q \in \mathcal{S}$, we have a sample frequency $f_q(\mathcal{S})$, *i.e.*, the frequency of q in $\mathcal{S}$. From here we can estimate the prior probability p_q of q in the entire query log, if $\mathcal{S}$ is an i.i.d. sample of the distribution of queries:

$$p_q \approx \widehat{p}_q(\mathcal{S}) = \frac{f_q(\mathcal{S})}{\sum_{q' \in \mathcal{S}} f_{q'}(\mathcal{S})}\,.$$

As query frequencies are discrete and very biased, standard sampling techniques do not work well.[1] Indeed, the two

[1]The alias method of Walker or efficient techniques tailored to discrete distributions do not work well with large and biased data sets.

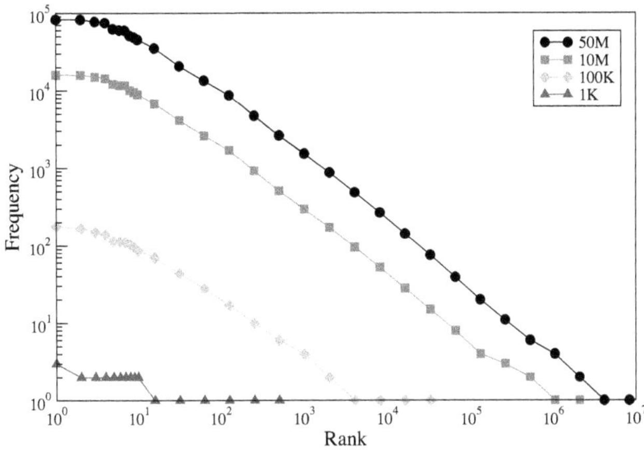

Figure 3: Query frequency distributions with varying sample sizes in a logarithmic scale.

main problems related to our query frequency characterization are:

(1) the frequencies do not mimic well the original distribution, specially for frequent queries, and

(2) the relative size of the set of singletons is quite different.

A good query sampling algorithm should solve the two problems above.

In [12] they analyze the two most used sampling techniques, which suffer of the two drawbacks just mentioned. The simplest one is obtained by removing repeated queries from the sample (but then there are no frequencies and any performance measure will be wrongly estimated). The second and most used one uses $\widehat{p}_q(\mathcal{S})$ above to estimate the real frequencies. However, in power law distributions, the $\widehat{p}_q(\mathcal{S})$ estimator is not accurate unless the sample is very large, or the α coefficient is close to zero (making the distribution close to uniform). We show this problem in Figure 3 by using a query log of 50M queries and construct samples (i.i.d. with replacement) of sizes 1K, 100K, and 10M. Observe that as the sample becomes smaller, the sample distribution approaches the uniform distribution, and then any performance measure underestimates the effect of frequent queries. They propose to partially solve issue (1) by using a much larger sample to estimate the query frequencies, for example, by using the frequencies of the 10M sample to better estimate the frequencies of the 1K sample in Figure 3. This technique allows to alleviate the underestimation of frequent queries. Nevertheless, issue (1) is not completely solved as the most frequent queries are not necessarily the same and (2) still remains. Indeed, the singletons set size for the query log of Figure 1 using the original frequencies to correct the sample frequencies is about half the original (34%).

5. A NEW SAMPLING TECHNIQUE

A solution to issue (1) is sampling via binning in a query log sorted by query frequency. That is, we first put all the most frequent queries, second the second most frequent queries, and so on. As a result, all identical queries will be contiguous as shown in Figure 4. To sample, we divide this frequency sorted query sequence in (almost) equal bins and

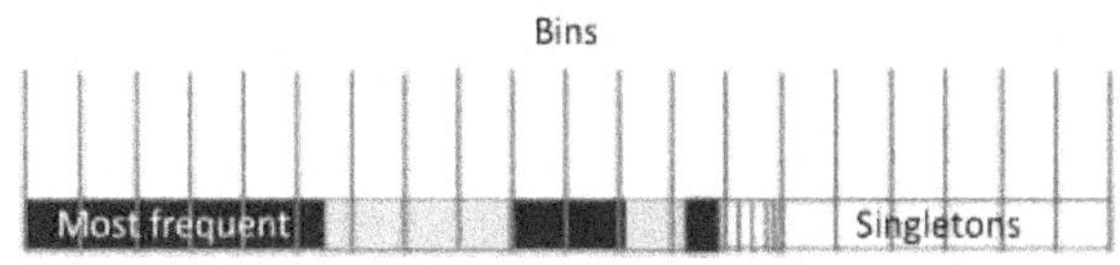

Figure 4: Sampling by binning.

we choose randomly one query of each bin as shown in Figure 4. For this, we just choose at random a number from 0 to the bin size minus 1, selecting the query in that position. Then we jump to the next bin adding the bin size, iterating until we reach the end of the distribution. If there are more than one bin for the same query, we will have repetitions that will give us the frequency of that query in the sample. In practice this algorithm can be simulated by only using the queries and their frequencies.

What is the right binning size? If we want to obtain M queries in the sample, the bin size will be $b = V/M$ for a query log with a volume of V queries. However, as many samples will be repeated the number of unique queries is less than the target sample size M. If we want to obtain M distinct queries in the sample, we need to adjust the bin size to get the closest possible to M.[2] For this we can use binary search to find the right sample size (we need to decrease the bin size to obtain more unique queries). This implies in the worst case $O(\log M)$ iterations.

Notice that all the queries that have original frequency larger or equal than the bin size will be represented in the sample. Hence, the order the queries in the head of the distribution is equal to the original distribution up to that point. In addition, the frequency in the sample will be scaled by the bin size (up to the value of 1). In fact, in the head of the distribution this is similar to stratified sampling, as we are sampling from groups that in most cases have the same query (that is, they are different strata as shown in the left of Figure 4). Hence, we do not need to correct the sample frequency as this frequency is just a scaling of the original frequency (modulo bin size).

The procedure above does not solve issue (2) as now the sample is heavily biased towards the head. To fix this we change the bin size when we reach the singletons in the sample. That is, when the query frequency in the original distribution is less than $b/2$, we stop and we recompute the bin size to match the singletons size ratio. If we want a ratio of $\beta = S/V$ of singletons volume, we now use $b' = (1-\beta)(Q-Q')/(\beta V')$ to achieve the desired ratio, where V is the total query log volume, Q is the number of distinct queries in the query log, and V' and Q' are the current values for the same variables in the partial sample already generated. Notice that in the set of original singletons we are actually doing a uniform sampling and that $b' > b$.

In Figure 5 we show the frequencies of a sample of 750 queries for the query log of Figure 1 using the new technique. In this case the volume ratio of the singletons is the same as in the original query log (26.6%) and as the sample is small, all non singletons queries are identical to the head of the original query log. As we are matching the ratio of sin-

[2]Depending on M, the final number might be not equal to M due to rounding.

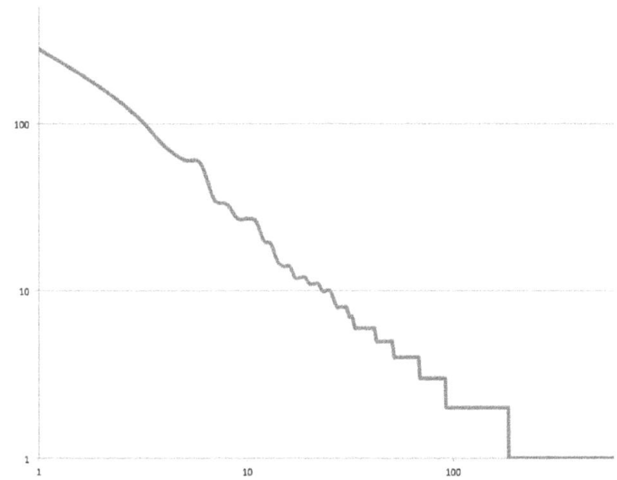

Figure 5: Sample example in logarithmic scale.

gletons, the percentage of singletons with respect to unique queries is a bit higher (75% instead of 69%), so this sample has a slight bias to the tail. Notice that the resemblance of both curves is very good, with a similar α.

A simplified deterministic variant of the previous algorithm is to use the queries at the right end of each bin. In the head of the distribution there are no changes as the queries are the same in most bins. In the tail, any query is as good as any query as the order is arbitrary, so in practice it is random. The same argument partially holds in the middle of the distribution and as we are using the right side query, getting again a sample biased towards the tail, being a bit harder than a completely random sample (which implies that we will not overestimate any measure that is biased to the head, *e.g.* commercial queries).

Now we show how we can do incremental samples with this algorithm. First, we select the largest b that is a power of 2 and that satisfies $b = V/M$. This will give us a sample of size M or larger. Now, if we double the sample size b and we use the same algorithm to generate the new sample, most of the queries will be the same (in the head this is trivially true), providing that we use the same initial random value (we can store this parameter as part of the sample). Hence, if we are enlarging a set of judged queries, about half of them will be already judged, so in practice the technique is almost incremental. This is even true if we use a different query log, as the correlation in time of query logs is very high. In [3] they show that the correlation of windows of a few weeks along a whole year was all the time larger than 0.99.

6. CONCLUDING REMARKS

We have presented a new sampling algorithm in query logs that mimics well the long tail of the distribution as well as the most frequent queries. An issue that we do not address, is that sometimes we want to make sure that additional attributes are well represented in the query sample (*e.g.* locations from where a given query is issued). However, the attributes of queries in a sample, in general, will not follow the distribution of a given attribute as the attribute distribution might not be uniform nor necessarily correlated with the query distribution. So, if a sample for a given attribute is needed, we can apply the binning technique on that attribute, independently of the queries. Otherwise, if we need all attributes associated to a query, we should apply the binning technique for each attribute separately, according to the different strata groups that can be defined in the query (e.g. top queries, singletons, etc.). This will give a more truthful random sample (notice that in general mimicking two or more non-correlated distributions is not possible). Another possibility is to apply the same algorithm to an expanded query log where the frequencies are taken over unique tuples that contain queries and the values of attributes of interest (continuous attributes such as time must be binned, *e.g.* by hours).

Another conclusion of our study, is that we may need different query frequency models for different alphabets and/or languages. Also, if the query distribution has a longer tail, we may need to take in account duplets (queries that appear twice), triplets, etc.

7. REFERENCES

[1] A. Agresti and B.A. Coull. Approximate is better than "exact" for interval estimation of binomial proportions. *The American Statistician* 52(2):119–126, 1998.

[2] R. Baeza-Yates and B. Ribeiro-Neto. Modern Information Retrieval: the concepts and technology behind search (2nd ed.). *Pearson Education*, 2011.

[3] R. Baeza-Yates, A. Gionis, F. Junqueira, V. Murdock, V. Plachouras and F. Silvestri. Design Trade-Offs for Search Engine Caching. *ACM Transactions on the Web*, 2(4), Article 4, 2008.

[4] L.D. Brown, T.T. Cai, and A. DasGupta. Interval estimation for a binomial proportion. *Statistical Science*, 16(2):101–133, 2001.

[5] C. Clopper and E.S. Pearson. The use of confidence or fiducial limits illustrated in the case of the binomial. *Biometrika* 26: 404–413, 1934.

[6] W. G. Cochran. Sampling Techniques (third ed.) Wiley & Sons, 2007.

[7] . R. Baeza-Yates and F. Saint-Jean. A Three Level Search Engine Index based in Query Log Distribution. In *SPIRE 2003*, Springer LNCS, Manaus, Brazil, October 2003.

[8] R. Baeza-Yates, A. Tiberi. Extracting Semantic Relations from Query Logs. In *ACM KDD 2007*, San Jose, California, USA, August 2007, 76–85.

[9] E. C. Jensen, S. M. Beitzel, O. Frieder, and A. Chowdhury. A framework for determining necessary query set sizes to evaluate web search effectiveness. In *Special Interest Tracks and Posters of the 14th Int'l Conf. on World Wide Web*, pages 1176–1177, 2005.

[10] M.E.J. Newman. Power laws, Pareto distributions and Zipf's law. *Contemporary Physics* 46 (5): 323–351, 2005.

[11] C. Saraiva, E. de Moura, N. Ziviani, W. Meira, R. Fonseca, and B. Ribeiro-Neto. Rank-preserving two-level caching for scalable search engines. In *Proc. 24th Annual Int'l ACM SIGIR Conf. on Research and Development in Information Retrieval*, pages 51–58, 2001.

[12] H. Zaragoza, B.B. Cambazoglu, R. Baeza-Yates. Web search solved? All result rankings the same?. In *Proc. CIKM 2010*: pages 529–538, 2010.

Where to Go on Your Next Trip? Optimizing Travel Destinations Based on User Preferences

Julia Kiseleva[1] Melanie J.I. Mueller[2] Lucas Bernardi[2]
Chad Davis[2] Ivan Kovacek[2] Mats Stafseng Einarsen[2]
Jaap Kamps[3] Alexander Tuzhilin[4] Djoerd Hiemstra[5]

[1]Eindhoven University of Technology, Eindhoven, The Netherlands
[2]Booking.com, Amsterdam, The Netherlands
[3]University of Amsterdam, Amsterdam, The Netherlands
[4]Stern School of Business, New York University, New York, USA
[5]University of Twente, Enschede, The Netherlands

[1]j.kiseleva@tue.nl [3]kamps@uva.nl [4]atuzhili@stern.nyu.edu [5]d.hiemstra@utwente.nl
[2]{melanie.mueller, lucas.bernardi, chad.davis, ivan.kovacek, mats.einarsen}@booking.com

ABSTRACT

Recommendation based on user preferences is a common task for e-commerce websites. New recommendation algorithms are often evaluated by offline comparison to baseline algorithms such as recommending random or the most popular items. Here, we investigate how these algorithms themselves perform and compare to the operational production system in large scale online experiments in a real-world application. Specifically, we focus on recommending travel destinations at `Booking.com`, a major online travel site, to users searching for their preferred vacation activities. To build ranking models we use multi-criteria rating data provided by previous users after their stay at a destination. We implement three methods and compare them to the current baseline in `Booking.com`: random, most popular, and Naive Bayes. Our general conclusion is that, in an online A/B test with live users, our Naive-Bayes based ranker increased user engagement significantly over the current online system.

H.3.3 [**Information Storage and Retrieval**]: Information Search and Retrieval—*Information filtering, Selection process*

General Terms: Design, Performance, Experimentation, Human Factors

Keywords: Industrial case studies, multi-criteria ranking, travel applications, travel recommendations

1. INTRODUCTION

This paper investigates strategies to recommended travel destinations for users who provided a list of preferred activities at `Booking.com`, a major online travel agent. This is a complex exploratory recommendation task characterized by predicting user preferences with a limited amount of noisy information. In addition, the industrial application setting comes with specific challenges for search and recommendation systems [11].

To motivate our problem set-up, we introduce a service which allows to find travel destinations based on users' preferred activities, called destination finder[1]. Consider a user who knows what activities she wants to do during her holidays, and is looking for travel destinations matching these activities. This process is a complex exploratory recommendation task in which users start by entering activities in the search box as shown in Figure 1. The destination finder service returns a ranked list of recommended destinations.

The underlying data is based on reviews from users who have booked and stayed at a hotel at some destination in the past. After their stay, users are asked to endorse the destination with activities from a set of 'endorsements'. Initially, the set of endorsements was extracted from users' free-text reviews using a topic-modeling technique such as LDA [5, 14]. Nowadays, the set of endorsements consists of 256 activities such as 'Beach,' 'Nightlife,' 'Shopping,' etc. These endorsements imply that a user liked a destination for particular characteristics. Two examples of the collected endorsements for two destinations, 'Bangkok' and 'London', are shown in Figure 2.

As an example of the multi-criteria endorsement data, consider three endorsements: e_1 = *'Beach'*, e_2 = *'Shopping'*, and e_3 = *'Family Friendly'* and assume that a user u_j, after visiting a destination d_k (e.g. 'London'), provides the review $r_i(u_j, d_k)$ as:

$$r_i(u_j, d_k) = (0, 1, 0). \quad (1)$$

This means our user endorses London for 'Shopping' only. However, we cannot conclude that London is not 'Family Friendly'. Thus, in contrast to the ratings data in a traditional recommender systems setup, negative user opinions are hidden. In addition, we are dealing with multi-criteria ranking data.

In contrast, in classical formulations of Recommender Systems (RS), the recommendation problem relies on single *ratings* (R) as a mechanism of capturing user (U) preferences for different items (I). The problem of estimating unknown ratings is formalized as follows: $F : U \times I \to R$. RS based on latent factor models have been effectively used to under-

SIGIR'15, August 09 - 13, 2015, Santiago, Chile.
© 2015 ACM. ISBN 978-1-4503-3621-5/15/08 ...$15.00.
DOI: `http://dx.doi.org/10.1145/2766462.2776777`.

[1]`http://www.booking.com/destinationfinder.html`

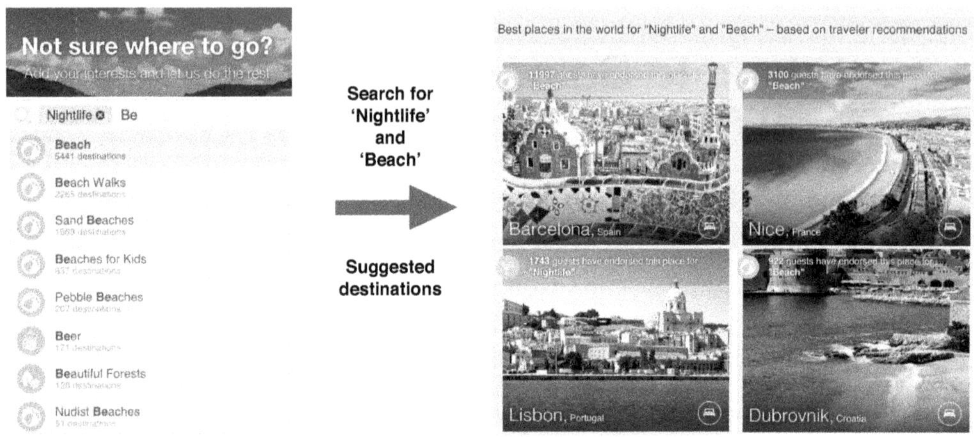

Figure 1: Example of destination finder use: a user searching for 'Nightlife' and 'Beach' obtains a ranked list of recommended destinations (top 4 are shown).

stand user interests and predict future actions [3, 4]. Such models work by projecting users and items into a lower-dimensional space, thereby grouping similar users and items together, and subsequently computing similarities between them. This approach can run into data sparsity problems, and into a continuous cold start problem when new items continuously appear.

In multi-criteria RS [1, 2, 12] the rating function has the following form:

$$F : U \times I \rightarrow (r_0 \times r_1 \cdots \times r_n) \tag{2}$$

The *overall rating* r_0 for an item shows how well the user likes this item, while criteria ratings $r_1, \ldots, r_n$ provide more insight and explain which aspects of the item she likes. MCRS predict the overall rating for an item based on past ratings, using both overall and individual criteria ratings, and recommends to users the item with the best overall score. According to [1], there are two basic approaches to compute the final rating prediction in the case when the overall rating is known. In our work we consider a new type of input for RS which is multi-criteria ranking data without an overall rating.

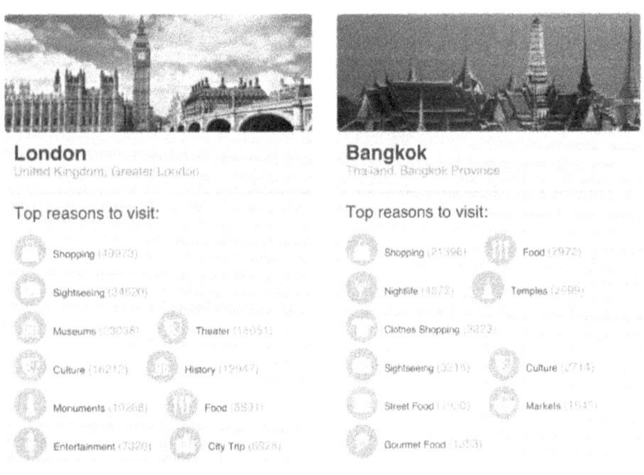

Figure 2: The destination finder endorsement pages of London and Bangkok.

There are a number of important challenges in working on the real world application of travel recommendations.

First, it is not easy to apply RS methods in large scale industrial applications. A large scale application of an unsupervised RS is presented in [9], where the authors apply topic modeling techniques to discover user preferences for items in an online store. They apply Locality Sensitive Hashing techniques to overcome performance issues when computing recommendations. We should take into account the fact that if it's not fast it isn't working. Due to the volume of traffic, offline processing—done once for all users—comes at marginal costs, but online processing—done separately for each user—can be excessively expensive. Clearly, response times have to be sub-second, but even doubling the CPU or memory footprint comes at massive costs.

Second, there is a continuous cold start problem. A large fraction of users has no prior interactions, making it impossible to use collaborative recommendation, or rely on history for recommendations. Moreover, for travel sites, even the more active users visit only a few times a year and have volatile needs or different personas (e.g., business and leisure trips), making their personal history a noisy signal at best.

To summarize, our problem setup is the following: **(1)** we have a set geographical destinations such as 'Paris', 'London', 'Amsterdam' etc.; and **(2)** each destination was reviewed by users who visited the destination using a set of endorsements. Our main goal is to increase user engagement with the travel recommendations as indicator of their interest in the suggested destinations.

Our main research question is: *How to exploit multi-criteria rating data to rank travel destination recommendations?* Our main contributions are:

- we use multi-criteria rating data to rank a list of travel destinations;
- we set up a large-scale online A/B testing evaluation with live traffic to test our methods;
- we compared three different rankings against the industrial baseline and obtained a significant gain in user engagement in terms of conversion rates.

The remainder of the paper is organized as follows. In Section 2, we introduce our strategies to rank destinations recommendations. We present the results of our large-scale online A/B testing in Section 3. Finally, Section 4 concludes our work in this paper and highlights a few future directions.

2. RANKING DESTINATION RECOMMENDATIONS

In this section, we present our ranking approaches for recommendations of travel destinations. We first discuss our baseline, which is the current production system of the destination finder at `Booking.com`. Then, we discuss our first two approaches, which are relatively straightforward and mainly used for comparison: the random ranking of destinations (Section 2.2), and the list of the most popular destinations (Section 2.3). Finally, we will discuss a Naive Bayes ranking approach to exploit the multi-criteria ranking data.

2.1 Booking.com Baseline

We use the currently live ranking method at `Booking.com`'s destination finder as a main baseline. We are not able to disclose the details, but the baseline is an optimized machine learning approach, using the same endorsement data plus some extra features not available to our other approaches.

We refer further to this method as 'Baseline'.

Next, we present two widely eployed baselines, which we use to give an impression how the baseline performs. Then we introduce an application of the Naive Bayes ranking approach to multi-criteria ranking.

2.2 Random Destination ranking

We retrieve all destinations that are endorsed at least for one of the activities that the user is searching for. The retrieved list of destinations is randomly permuted and is shown to users.

We refer further to this method as 'Random'.

2.3 Most Popular Destinations

A very straightforward and at the same time very strong baseline would be the method that shows to users the most popular destinations based on their preferences [6]. For example, if the user searches for the activity 'Beach', we calculate the popularity rank score for a destination d_i as the conditional probability: $P(\text{Beach}|d_i)$. If the user searches for a second endorsement, e.g. 'Food', the ranking score for d_i is calculated using a Naive Bayes assumption as: $P(\text{Beach}|d_i)\times P(\text{food}|d_i)$. In general, if the users provides n endorsements, $e_1, \ldots, e_n$, the ranking score for d_i is $P(e_1|d_i)\times\ldots\times P(e_n|d_i)$.

We refer further to this method as 'Popularity'.

2.4 Naive Bayes Ranking Approach

As a primary ranking technique we use a Naive Bayes approach. We will describe its application to the multi-criteria ranking data (presented in Equation 1) with an example. Let us again consider a user searching for 'Beach'. We need to return a ranked list of destinations. For instance, the ranking score for the destination 'Miami' is calculated as

$$P(\text{Miami}, \text{Beach}) = P(\text{Miami}) \times P(\text{Beach}|\text{Miami}), \quad (3)$$

where $P(\text{Beach}|\text{Miami})$ is the probability that the destination Miami gets the endorsement 'Beach'. $P(\text{Miami})$ describes our prior knowledge about Miami. In the simplest case this prior is the ratio of the number of endorsements for Miami to the total number of endorsements in our database.

If a user uses searches for a second activity, e.g. 'Food', the ranking score is calculated in the following way:

$$\begin{aligned} P(\text{Miami}, \text{Beach}, \text{Food}) = P(\text{Miami}) \times P(\text{Beach}|\text{Miami}) \\ \times P(\text{Food}|\text{Miami}) \end{aligned} \quad (4)$$

If our user provides n endorsements, Equation 4 becomes a standard Naive Bayes formula.

We refer further to this method as 'Naive Bayes'.

To summarize, we described three strategies to rank travel destination recommendations: the random ranking, the popularity based ranking, and the Naive Bayes approach. These three approaches will be compared to each other and against the industrial baseline. Next, we will present our experimental pipeline which involves online A/B testing at the destination finder service of `Booking.com`.

3. EXPERIMENTS AND RESULTS

In this section we will describe our experimental setup and evaluation approach, and the results of the experiments. We perform experiments on users of `Booking.com` where an instance of the destination finder is running in order to conduct an online evaluation. First, we will detail our online evaluation approach and used evaluation measures. Second, we will detail the experimental results.

3.1 Research Methodology

We take advantage of a production A/B testing environment at `Booking.com`, which performs randomized controlled trials for the purpose of inferring causality. A/B testing randomly splits users to see either the baseline or the new variant version of the website, which allows to measure the impact of the new version directly on real users [10, 11, 15].

As our primary *evaluation metric* in the A/B test, we use conversion rate, which is the fraction of sessions which end with at least one clicked result [13]. As explained in the motivation, we are dealing with an exploratory task and therefore aim to increase customer engagement. An increase in conversion rate is a signal that users click on the suggested destinations and thus interact with the system.

In order to determine whether a change in conversion rate is a random statistical fluctuation or a statistically significant change, we use the G-test statistic (G-tests of goodness-of-fit). We consider the difference between the baseline and the newly proposed method significant when the G-test p-value is larger than90%.

3.2 Results

Conversion rate is the probability for a user to click at least once, which is a common metric for user engagement. We used it as a primary evaluation metric in our experimentation. Table 1 shows the results of our A/B test. The production 'Baseline' substantially outperforms the 'Random' ranking with respect to conversion rate, and performs slightly (but not significantly) better than the 'Popularity' approach. The 'Naive Bayes' ranker significantly increases the conversion rate by 4.4% compared to the production baseline.

We achieved this substantial increase in conversion rate with a straightforward Naive Bayes ranker. Moreover, most computations can be done offline. Thus, our model could be

Table 1: **Results of the destination finder online A/B testing based on the number of unique users and clickers.**

Ranker type	Number of users	Conversion rate	G-test
Baseline	9.928	25.61% ± 0.72%	
Random	10.079	24.46% ± 0.71%	94%
Popularity	9.838	25.50% ± 0.73%	41%
Naive Bayes	9.895	**26.73% ± 0.73%**	93%

trained on large data within reasonable time, and did not negatively impact wallclock and CPU time for the destination finder web pages in the online A/B test. This is crucial for a webscale production environment [11].

To summarize, we used three approaches to rank travel recommendations. We saw that the random and popularity based ranking of destinations lead to a decrease in user engagement, while the Naive Bayes approach leads to a significant engagement increase.

4. CONCLUSION AND DISCUSSION

This paper reports on large-scale experiments with four different approaches to rank travel destination recommendations at `Booking.com`, a major online travel agent. We focused on a service called destination finder where users can search for suitable destination based on preferred activities. In order to build ranking models we used multi-criteria rating data in the form of endorsements provided by past users after visiting a booked place.

We implemented three methods to rank travel destinations: Random, Most Popular, and Naive Bayes, and compared them to the current production baseline in `Booking.com`. We observed a significant increase in user engagement for the Naive Bayes ranking approach, as measured by the conversion rate. The simplicity of our recommendation models enables us to achieve this engagement without significantly increasing online CPU and memory usage. The experiments clearly demonstrate the value of multi-criteria ranking data in a real world application. They also shows that simple algorithmic approaches trained on large data sets can have very good real-life performance [8].

We are working on a number of extension of the current work, in particular on contextual recommendation approaches that take into account the context of the user and the endorser, and on ways to detect user profiles from implicit contextual information. Initial experiments with contextualized recommendations show that this can lead to significant further improvements of user engagement.

Some of the authors are involved in the organization of the TREC Contextual Suggestion Track [6, 7, 16], and the use case of the destination finder is part of TREC in 2015, where similar endorsements are collected. The resulting test collection can be used to evaluate destination and venue recommendation approaches.

Acknowledgments

This work was done while the main author was an intern at `Booking.com`. We thank Lukas Vermeer and Athanasios Noulas for fruitful discussions at the early stage of this work. This research has been partly supported by STW and is part of the CAPA project.[2]

References

[1] G. Adomavicius and Y. Kwon. New recommendation techniques for multicriteria rating systems. *IEEE Intelligent Systems (EXPERT)*, 22(3):48–55, 2007.

[2] G. Adomavicius, N. Manouselis, and Y. Kwon. *Multi-Criteria Recommender Systems*, volume 768-803. Recommender Systems Handbook, Springer, 2011.

[3] D. Agarwal and B.-C. Chen. Regression-based latent factor models. In *Proceeding of KDD*, pages 19–28, 2009.

[4] D. Agarwal and B.-C. Chen. flda: matrix factorization through latent dirichlet allocation. In *Proceeding of WSDM*, pages 91–100, 2010.

[5] D. M. Blei, A. Y. Ng, and M. I. Jordan. Latent dirichlet allocation. *Journal of Machine Learning Research*, 3: 993–1022, 2003.

[6] A. Dean-Hall, C. L. Clarke, J. Kamps, P. Thomas, N. Simone, and E. Voorhees. Overview of the trec 2013 contextual suggestion track. In *Proceeding of TREC*, 2013.

[7] A. Dean-Hall, C. L. Clarke, J. Kamps, P. Thomas, and E. M. Voorhees. Overview of the TREC 2014 contextual suggestion track. In *Proceeding of Text REtrieval Conference (TREC)*, 2014.

[8] A. Halevy, P. Norvig, and F. Pereira. The unreasonable effectiveness of data. *Intelligent Systems, IEEE*, 24(2): 8–12, 2009.

[9] D. J. Hu, R. Hall, and J. Attenberg. Style in the long tail: Discovering unique interests with latent variable models in large scale social e-commerce. In *KDD*, pages 1640–1649, 2014.

[10] R. Kohavi, A. Deng, B. Frasca, T. Walker, Y. Xu, and N. Pohlmann. Online controlled experiments at large scale. In *Proceedings of KDD*, pages 1168–1176, 2013.

[11] R. Kohavi, A. Deng, R. Longbotham, and Y. Xu. Seven rules of thumb for web site experimenters. In *Proceeding of KDD*, pages 1857–1866, 2014.

[12] K. Lakiotaki, N. F. Matsatsinis, and A. Tsoukias. Multicriteria user modeling in recommender systems. *IEEE Intelligent System*, 26(2):64–76, 2011.

[13] M. Lalmas, H. O'Brien, and E. Yom-Tov. Measuring user engagement. *Synthesis Lectures on Information Concepts, Retrieval, and Services*, 6(4):1–132, 2014.

[14] A. Noulas and M. S. Einarsen. User engagement through topic modelling in travel. In *Proceeding of the Second Workshop on User Engagement Optimization*, 2014.

[15] D. Tang, A. Agarwal, D. O'Brien, and M. Meyer. Overlapping experiment infrastructure: More, better, faster experimentation. In *Proceedings of KDD*, pages 17–26, Washington, DC, 2010.

[16] TREC. Contextual suggestion track. Text REtrieval Conference, 2015. URL `https://sites.google.com/site/treccontext/`.

[2] `http://www.win.tue.nl/~mpechen/projects/capa/`

Bringing Order to the Job Market: Efficient Job Offer Categorization in E-Recruitment

Emmanuel Malherbe
Multiposting
Paris, France
emalherbe@multiposting.fr

Mario Cataldi
LIASD
Université Paris 8
Paris, France
m.cataldi@univ-paris8.fr

Andrea Ballatore
Center for Spatial Studies
University of California, Santa Barbara
Santa Barbara, CA, USA
aballatore@spatial.ucsb.edu

ABSTRACT

E-recruitment uses a range of web-based technologies to find, evaluate, and hire new personnel for organizations. A crucial challenge in this arena lies in the categorization of job offers: candidates and operators often explore and analyze large numbers of offers and profiles through a set of job categories. To date, recruitment organizations define job categories top-down, relying on standardized vocabularies that often fail to capture new skills and requirements that emerge from dynamic labor markets. In order to support e-recruitment, this paper presents a dynamic, bottom-up method to automatically enrich and revise job categories. The method detects novel, highly characterizing terms in a corpus of job offers, leading to a more effective categorization, and is evaluated on real-world data by Multiposting (http://www.multiposting.fr/en), a large French e-recruitment firm.

Keywords

E-Recruitment, Job Categorization, Classification

1. INTRODUCTION AND MOTIVATION

E-recruitment can be defined as the process of matching people to appropriate jobs using different on- and off-line strategies and technologies. As the number of candidates and jobs varies by expanding, shifting, and contracting, the recruitment process presents remarkable challenges in information management, indexing, and matching. The usage of the web helps employers reach larger population of candidates, lowering geographic barriers [10]. Several companies currently handle large volumes of job offers and applications across the globe, including Multiposting (multiposting.fr), LinkedIn (linkedin.com), and Monster (monster.com).

Conventional recruitment methods deployed in Human Resource Management (HRM) are notorious for being costly and time-consuming, particularly when applied to large pools of offers and candidates. Since the 1970s, job categorization has been used in human resources departments for personnel selection and promotion, as well as for salary administration [2], and is currently recognized as a major issue in recruitment [1, 4]. To tackle the complexity of the matching process, a common approach relies on the categorization of job offers, identifying and grouping salient characteristics, tasks, and skills. Top-down categorizations encode domain knowledge, and are commonly used to explore, search, and analyze data. While fully bottom-up, keyword-based techniques can be applied to e-recruitment, curated and human-readable categorizations are necessary to obtain high-quality results, reducing the noise in the matching.

Existing categorization strategies fail to identify the terms that capture salient aspects in the descriptions of potential candidates. Similarly, job descriptions contain vague and overly generic information, which is hard to exploit in the matching process. Moreover, the vocabulary used by employers and recruiters change over time, reflecting the evolution of the labor market. For this reason, the detection of these variations is key to design an effective job categorization strategy that reflects the underlying data more closely.

Let us consider for example a category descriptor related to computer programming. The 'programming languages' field might present a fixed list of keywords including popular languages (e.g., Java, C++, Python), without including recent languages such as Clojure or Swift that are likely to be in high demand in the immediate future. In this context, it is considerably hard, even for a domain expert, to update the descriptors, anticipating the rapid changes in the industry. To tackle the challenges of e-recruitment, top-down and bottom-up approaches need to be leveraged, updating expert-defined resources with dynamic knowledge extraction from the data.

In this paper, we propose a data-driven, bottom-up approach to enrich the textual descriptions of job categories. Given a domain categorization, the approach automatically updates the terms from the corpus of job offers. The enriched descriptions are then used to support a field-to-field similarity computation in the matching between jobs and candidate categories. The matching focuses on the differences between structured textual fields and the extracted terms, maximizing the probability of a correct classification. The proposed approach is evaluated in different application contexts on real-world data collected by Multiposting, one of the largest companies in the e-recruitment sector. The French company provides a web platform for e-recruitment, and processes more than 3M job offers per year and 100M applications in 50 countries.

SIGIR'15, August 09 - 13, 2015, Santiago, Chile.
 ISBN 978-1-4503-3621-5/15/08 ...$15.00.
DOI: http://dx.doi.org/10.1145/2766462.2776779.

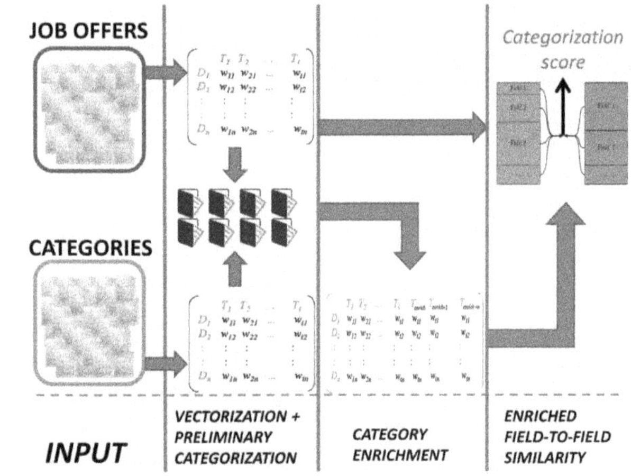

Figure 1: Flow diagram of the proposed hybrid job offer categorization method.

2. CONTEXT-BASED CATEGORY ENRICHMENT

The objective of this work is to support the categorization of a corpus of job offers by semantically enriching the job categories with recent and contextually relevant terms. The flowchart of the method is showed in Figure 1. In this study, we define two entities: job offers and job categories.

A *job offer* can be defined as a structured text document that formalizes an offer of employment, authored by an employer. A job offer contains textual fields, such as 'company description,' 'required skills,' 'education level,' depending on the specific conceptualization. Formally, a job offer o as a set of keyword vectors, each one representing a textual field $o = \{\vec{o_1}, ..., \vec{o_k}\}$ where k is the total number of textual fields in job offer o, and $\vec{o_i}$ (with $i < k$) is a vector of weighted keywords, which represents the frequency of terms of its i-th field. Each component $w_{k,i}$ of $\vec{o_i}$ is the term weight of the i-th vocabulary term in the k-th field of the considered job offer. This weight is calculated as:

$$w_{k,i} = \sqrt{tf_{k,i}} \left(1 + log\frac{|M|}{m_i}\right) \quad (1)$$

where $tf_{k,i}$ is the term frequency value of the i-th vocabulary term in k-th field. M is the entire set of job categories and m_i the number of job categories containing the i-th term in at least one field.

A *job category* is a description of a type of jobs provided by a domain expert, and has a structure analogous to that of job offers. We formalize a job category c as a set of vectors $c = \{\vec{c_1}, ..., \vec{c_l}\}$ where l is the number of textual fields in the job category description, and c_j a vector of weighted keywords that represent the frequency of terms of the j-th field of the job category (with $j < l$).

2.1 Enrichment of Job Categories

Given a corpus of job offers and job categories, we want to enrich a category c to a c' that includes new keywords to better reflect the job offers. As a first step, we retrieve the set of most representative categories for each job offer, quantifying the representativeness of categories through the cosine similarity of vector sums. Formally, for each offer $o \in O$, we compute the cosine similarity cos with category c as:

$$sim(o, c) = cos\left(\sum_{i=1}^{k} \vec{o_i}, \sum_{j=1}^{l} \vec{c_j}\right) \quad (2)$$

For each offer, we sort all categories in C in decreasing order in terms of similarity to $\vec{o}$. As the similarity values in this context follow a power law, we select a subset of categories so that the sum of their similarities sim reach 90% of the sum of all similarities $\sum_{j=1}^{l} sim(o, c_j)$, excluding the tail of categories with low similarities [8]. At the end of step, each job offer in O has a non-empty set of categories associated to it.

Using these sets, we search for the most contextually informative keywords for each category. The relevance weight $rw_{c,x}$ of a candidate keyword x for category c is computed as:

$$rw_{c,x} = log\left(\frac{\frac{r_x}{R_c - r_{c,x}}}{\frac{n_x - r_{c,x}}{N - n_x - R_c + r_{c,x}}}\right) \left|\frac{r_{c,x}}{R_c} - \frac{n_x - r_{c,x}}{N - R_c}\right| \quad (3)$$

where $r_{c,x}$ is the number of job offers associated to the category c containing the keyword x, and n_x is the total number of job offers containing x. R_c is the number of job offers associated to the category c, and N is the total number of job offers in the corpus. Intuitively, the keywords that appear frequently only in specific associations and rarely in others will tend to have higher weights.

Subsequently, for each category, we select the terms having a positive enrichment value as as a set of enriching keywords $K_{x \to c}$. This set is used to compute the enrichment vector to be added to the original job category vector c. The enrichment weight $e_{c,x}$ of the term x for category c is calculated as:

$$e_{c,x} = \sqrt{r_{c,x}} \left(1 + log\left(\frac{M}{m_x}\right) + rw_{c,x}\right) \quad (4)$$

where $rw_{c,x}$ is the relevance weight, $r_{c,x}$ is the number of job offers associated to the category. M the total number of job categories, and $m_x$is the number of job categories c containing the term x in its keywords set $K_{x \to c}$. The homogeneity of the function is assured by expressing $rw_{c,x}$ as a sum of probabilities while $log(\frac{M}{m_x})$ is assimilated to the probability of observing term x in a category [9].

Finally, we define the enriched job category as an extended set of vectors $c' = \{\vec{c_1}, \vec{c_2}, ..., \vec{c_l}, \vec{ev_c}\}$ where $\vec{ev_c}$ encodes the knowledge extracted from the corpus. The other vectors of the category remain unchanged.

2.2 Matching Job Offers and Job Categories

A job offer o can now be matched against the enriched job categories. For this purpose, we define a field-to-field similarity (FtFs) matching approach, taking into account both the information extracted from the corpus and the structure of the original data. First, we define a FtFs matrix as:

$$S(o, c') = \left\{\begin{matrix} s(o,c')_{1,1} & s(o,c')_{1,2} & ... & s(o,c')_{1,l} \\ s(o,c')_{2,1} & s(o,c')_{2,2} & ... & s(o,c')_{2,l} \\ ... & ... & ... & .... \\ s(o,c')_{k-1,1} & s(o,c')_{k-1,2} & ... & s(o,c')_{k-1,l} \\ s(o,c')_{k,1} & s(o,c')_{k,2} & ... & s(o,c')_{k,l} \end{matrix}\right\} \quad (5)$$

	Initial categories	Enriched categories	Offers
Documents	531	531	215,375
Terms	9,286	13,761	55,209
Fields	8	8	4

Table 1: The corpus of job offers and categories provided by Multiposting and Pôle Emploi.

Each element $s(o,c')_{i,j}$ represents the normalized similarity between the i-th field of the offer o (with $i < k$) and the j-th textual field of the enriched category c' (with $j < l$), that is:

$$s(o,c')_{i,j} = \frac{cos(\vec{o}_i, \vec{c}_j)}{\sum_{p=1}^{m} \sum_{q=1}^{l} cos(\vec{o}_p, \vec{c}_q)} \quad (6)$$

where cos denotes the cosine vector similarity. This similarity calculation leverages the differences between the fields. For instance, the offer of a programming job can have highly discriminant terms in the 'skills' field, but not in the 'employer description' field, which contains a set of general terms occurring in all offers by the same employer. Following this intuition, the similarity s between the offer o and the enriched category c' is therefore calculated as:

$$sim(o,c') = \sum_{i=1}^{k} \sum_{j=1}^{l} \lambda_{i,j}\ s(o,c')_{i,j} \quad (7)$$

where $\lambda_{i,j}$ is a similarity probability between textual field calculated based on a training data-set (see [5] for details). The higher $s(o,c)$, the more similar the offer o to the considered category c. The function has no upper bound, while the lower bound is 0.

At the end of this matching step, we have a matching score $s(o,c')$ for each enriched category c'. The last step consists of the selection of the most similar categories, obtaining the strength of association between job offer o and a set of enriched categories c'. This data-driven categorization embeds knowledge from the corpus of job offers, overcoming the limitations of the initial static categorization.

3. EVALUATION

The proposed categorization approach was evaluated through several experiments, using real job offers and job categories. For the evaluation, company Multiposting provided a corpus of 215,375 job offers, advertised on its online platform from 2009 to 2014. A set of 531 static job categories was obtained from Pôle Emploi, the French governmental agency that supports job seekers (www.pole-emploi.fr). The categories are part of the Répertoire Opérationnel des Métiers et des Emplois (ROME) nomenclature, which can be seen as the French equivalent of O*NET, a job categorization widely used in the US (www.onetcenter.org) [3].

A job category by Pôle Emploi is structured into 8 textual fields ('title,' 'definition, 'admission,' 'conditions,' 'environment' 'competences,' 'activities,' and 'labor mobility'), and is linked to manually defined similar categories. By contrast, the Multiposting job offers have only 4 textual fields: 'title,' 'job description,' 'candidate profile,' and 'company description.' Both offers and categories are in French. Table 1 summarizes the characteristics of these data-sets.

As ground truth to evaluate our approach, we produced an annotated set of 1,339 job offers, randomly selected from the corpus. Two teams of 3 domain experts performed a manual categorization, manually selecting the most fitting category for each job. When the experts disagreed about the categorization of a job, the conflict was discussed and resolved. In the instances where the conflicts were not easily settled, the job offers were discarded as too ambiguous.

To obtain a realistic picture, we applied four methods to the manually-generated data-set, comparing the performance of our approach with three alternative methods:

- Cosine Measure (*CM*): In this method, the corpus was categorized only with the cosine similarity measure in Equation 2. This approach does not enrich the categories and does not consider the field-to-field similarity of Section 2.2.
- Enriched Cosine Measure (*e-CM*): The categorization was performed by applying the standard cosine similarity measure (Equation2) to the enriched categories, but without using the field-to-field similarity.
- Field-to-Field Similarity (*FtFs*): This method categorizes the job offers only with the structural information (Section 2.2), without enriching the categories.
- Enriched Field-to-Field Similarity (*e-FtFs*): This is the proposed approach, which combines the previous methods.

Error rate (*E*). First, we observed the categorization errors with respect to the ground truth. The error rate E_1 is calculated as $1 - p$, where p is the categorization precision with respect to the top category selected by each of the four approaches. E_1 ranges from 0 to 1, where 0 means a perfect categorization, and 1 is an entirely wrong categorization.

Receiver Operating Characteristic (*AAC-ROC*). This measure evaluates binary classifiers by plotting two parameters: TP rate (fraction of True Positives) and FP rate (fraction of False Positives) [7]. To compare the methods, it is possible to reduce the ROC to a single scalar value by measuring the area above the curve (AAC), which quantifies the overall error.

Hinge-Loss (*HL*). The Hinge-Loss function computes the average distance between the proposed model and the valid data for multi-class categorizations[6]. For each job offer, HL considers the vector of similarity values of all categories generated by a method. This vector is then compared to the ground truth vector, in which the correct category is marked as 1, while the others are set to 0. The distance between a vector and the ground truth is inversely proportional to the quality of the categorization method.

As the top category is particularly important, we first observed the results for the top ranked category $argmax_c\ s(o,c)$ with indicators HL_1 and $AAC\text{-}ROC_1$. Subsequently, considering that the each category in the ROME nomenclature also points to similar categories, we tested if the candidate category proposed by each approach falls in this extended set of valid categories, with indicators E_{sim} and HL_{sim}.

As the results in Table 2 show, our Enriched Field-to-Field Similarity method (*e-FtFs*) outperforms the alternative methods with respect to all of the evaluation metrics. More specifically, *e-FtFs* obtained 0.25 for E_1, and 0.21 for E_{sim}. Considering the fact that job offers and categories were generated by different communities using different vocabularies, in different time ranges, we consider this error

	E_1	E_{sim}	HL_1	HL_{sim}	*AAC-ROC*
CM	0.38	0.33	0.797	0.722	0.234
e-CM	0.28	0.22	0.729	0.629	0.187
FtFs	0.28	0.24	0.673	0.484	0.168
e-FtFs	**0.25**	**0.21**	**0.645**	**0.472**	**0.152**

Table 2: Performance of the proposed approach (*e-FtFs*) compared with three alternatives, on a set of 1,339 job offers and 531 job categories.

rate promising. The HL indicators follow a similar trend, showing that the *e-FtFs* performs better than the other methods even when adopting a fuzzy categorization.

With respect the other indicators, HL shows higher error values. This is due to the fact that we compare the performance of a fuzzy classifier (the automatic method) with a binary one (the manual classification). As a result, the evaluation is very pessimistic: to obtain an error value equals to 0, the method should return a null vector with only the correct category set to 1. While both *e-CM* and *FtFs* outperform the simple cosine measure *CM*, the best performance is obtained only when combining the two methods into *e-Ftfs*, confirming the benefits of both the bottom-up category enrichment and the field-to-field similarity.

4. CONCLUSION

In this paper, we presented a novel categorization method targeted at industrial applications in e-recruitment. Our method semantically enriches the job categories, and then leverages the structure of textual documents using a field-to-field similarity comparison. The approach was evaluated on real-world data by the French corporation Multiposting. The experiments showed several improvements in the task of job categorization, providing a novel solution for weaving dynamic, bottom-up knowledge into static job categories.

The classification problem of job offers we tackled in this paper deserves further investigation. We plan to explore alternative families of categorization approaches, drawing on supervised and unsupervised machine learning techniques. While our current approach relies on a bag of words model, performance might be improved with more semantic knowledge, for example clustering synonyms, hypernyms, and hyponyms. To better support the exploration and search of job offers, we will integrate named entity recognition and classification (NERC) into the method, identifying companies, universities, and government agencies. The usability of the job categories might also be improved by grouping them into meaningful hierarchies, helping e-recruitment operators face rapidly changing labor markets.

References

[1] R. Boselli, M. Cesarini, F. Mercorio, and M. Mezzanzanica. How the Social Media Contributes to the Recruitment Process? In A. Rospigliosi and S. Greener, editors, *Proceedings of European Conference on Social Media (ECSM)*, pages 10–11, Brighton, UK, 2014.

[2] E. T. Cornelius, T. J. Carron, and M. N. Collins. Job analysis models and job classification. *Personnel Psychology*, 32(4):693–708, 1979.

[3] E. C. Dierdorff, J. J. Norton, C. M. Gregory, D. Rivkin, and P. M. Lewis. O*NET's National Perspective on the Greening of the World of Work. In A. H. Huffman and S. R. Klein, editors, *Driving Change with I-O Psychology*, pages 348–378. Routledge, New York, 2013.

[4] T. Gonzalez, P. Santos, F. Orozco, M. Alcaraz, V. Zaldivar, A. D. Obeso, and A. Garcia. Adaptive employee profile classification for resource planning tool. In *SRII Global Conference*, pages 544–553. IEEE, 2012.

[5] E. Malherbe, M. Diaby, M. Cataldi, E. Viennet, and M.-A. Aufaure. Field Selection for Job Categorization and Recommendation to Social Network Users. In *Proceedings of the IEEE/ACM International Conference on Advances in Social Network Analysis and Mining (ASONAM)*, pages 588–595. IEEE, 2014.

[6] R. Moore and J. DeNero. L1 and L2 Regularization for Multiclass Hinge Loss Models. In *Symposium on Machine Learning in Speech and Natural Language Processing (MLSLP)*, pages 1–5, Bellevue, WA, 2011.

[7] Z. Omary and F. Mtenzi. Machine learning approach to identifying the dataset threshold for the performance estimators in supervised learning. *International Journal for Infonomics (IJI)*, 3:314–325, 2010.

[8] Y.-J. Park and A. Tuzhilin. The Long Tail of Recommender Systems and How to Leverage It. In *Proceedings of the 2008 ACM Conference on Recommender Systems (RecSys'08)*, pages 11–18. ACM, 2008.

[9] I. Ruthven and M. Lalmas. A survey on the use of relevance feedback for information access systems. *The Knowledge Engineering Review*, 18:95–145, 2003.

[10] S. Snell, S. Morris, and G. Bohlander. *Managing Human Resources (17e)*. Cengage Learning, Boston, MA, 2013.

SIGIR 2015 Tutorials Chair's Welcome

This year's conference received twelve submissions, of which eight were accepted, and one was extended to an additional half-day. The decision was based on criteria of relevance to the SIGIR community, core quality and experience of presenters. The accepted tutorials include three full-day tutorials, and two morning-afternoon sequences. It was important for us to build a diverse yet comprehensive program that would address the needs of all attendees from newcomers, eager to acquire critical knowledge, to experts curious about side or emerging areas of research in Information Retrieval.

To this effect we made sure to cover a wide range of topics from fundamental ones ("Revisiting the Foundations of IR") to timely ones such as formal models ("Building and Using Models for Information Seeking, Search and Retrieval"), the handling of verbose queries ("Information Retrieval with Verbose Queries"), or related to leveraging Wikipedia ("Exploiting Wikipedia for Information Retrieval Tasks".) We also decided to allow for non-mainstream topics in order to expand the horizons of Information Retrieval practitioners and researchers with a full-day tutorial on "Music Retrieval and Recommendation".

In addition, we wanted to offer more flexibility to attendees in building their own personalized program as well as learning about timely topics. We thus included this year two morning-afternoon sequence of half-day tutorials. One such sequence deals with click models, starting in the morning with "An Introduction to Click Models for Web Search", while the afternoon session dives deep into "Advanced Click Models and their Applications to IR". The other sequence covers the always-critical topic of IR evaluation, with a morning session dealing with "Designing an End-to-End Evaluation Pipeline", and an afternoon session tackling user behavior in "Modeling User Behavior for Measuring Effectiveness". Note that in order to offer more flexibility to attendees, the morning and afternoon sessions of these two tutorials are each considered as stand-alone tutorials and can be taken independently.

We would like to thank the seventeen presenters, from Academia and Industry, who will travel to Chile from various parts of the world in order to give their tutorials, namely from Australia (Guido Zuccon), Austria (Peter Knees and Markus Schedl), Canada (Charles Clarke and Mark Smucker), India (Manish Gupta), Israel (Nir Ofek, Victor Makarenkov, and Bracha Shapira), United Kingdom (Leif Azzopardi, Emine Yilmaz), The Netherlands (Ilya Markov and Maarten de Rijke), Switzerland (Aleksandr Chuklin) and the United States (Michael Bendersky, Paul Kantor and Jin Young Kim).

We hope that you will find this program interesting and educational and that it will provide you with a valuable opportunity to learn from some of the most famous and experienced researchers in the ever-evolving field of information retrieval.

Yoelle Maarek
SIGIR 2015 Tutorials Chair
Vice-Chair SIGIR EC
VP Research EMEA, Yahoo Labs, Israel

Building and Using Models of Information Seeking, Search and Retrieval

Full Day Tutorial

Leif Azzopardi
University of Glasgow
Glasgow, United Kingdom
Leif.Azzopardi@glasgow.ac.uk

Guido Zuccon
Queensland University of Technology
Queensland, Australia
g.zuccon@qut.edu.au

ABSTRACT

Understanding how people interact with information systems when searching is central to the study of Interactive Information Retrieval (IIR). While much of the prior work in this area has either been conceptual, observational or empirical, recently there has been renewed interest in developing mathematical models of information seeking and search. This is because such models can provide a concise and compact representation of search behaviours and naturally generate testable hypotheses about search behaviour.

This full day tutorial focuses on explaining and building formal models of Information Seeking and Retrieval. The tutorial is structured into four sessions. In the first session we will discuss the rationale of modelling and examine a number of early formal models of search (including early cost models and the Probability Ranking Principle). Then we will examine more contemporary formal models (including Information Foraging Theory, the Interactive Probability Ranking Principle, and Search Economic Theory). The focus will be on the insights and intuitions that we can glean from the math behind these models. The latter sessions will be dedicated to building models that optimise particular objectives which drive how users make decisions, along with a how-to guide on model building, where we will describe different techniques (including analytical, graphical and computational) that can be used to generate hypotheses from such models. In the final session, participants will be challenged to develop a simple model of interaction applying the techniques learnt during the day, before concluding with an overview of challenges and future directions.

This tutorial is aimed at participants wanting to know more about the various formal models of information seeking, search and retrieval, that have been proposed in the literature. The tutorial will be presented at an introductory level, and is designed to support participants who want to be able to understand and apply such models, as well as to build their own models.

SIGIR'15, August 09-13, 2015, Santiago, Chile.
ACM 978-1-4503-3621-5/15/08.
DOI: http://dx.doi.org/10.1145/2766462.2767874.

Categories and Subject Descriptors

H.3.3 [**Information Storage and Retrieval**]: Information Search and Retrieval:Search Process; H.5.m [**Information Interfaces and Presentation**]:Miscellaneous

General Terms

Theory, Experimentation, Economics, Human Factors

Keywords

Search Behaviour; User Models; Retrieval Strategies; Evaluation

1. INTRODUCTION

The tutorial will be structured in four main parts: (1) Why Model and Early Models (1960-1980) (2) Contemporary Models (1980+), (3) Model building, and, (4) Making a model (as an hands-on activity for the participants). The day will conclude with a discussion of challenges and future directions. It should be noted that in the field of Information Retrieval we have developed lots of models - mainly retrieval models. However, this tutorial will focus on building models for interactive information seeking and retrieval, and so focus on modelling the user's interactions with the interface/system in order to characterise search behaviours. Such models are rarer, as they tend to be more complicated, and require a greater appreciation of how people interact with systems. Indeed, developing such models has been hailed as a (somewhat) grand challenge for Interactive Information Retrieval [15]. Furthermore, such models are becoming increasingly important as they form the basis of many performance measures, provide a better understanding of how people interact with such systems, and a way to evaluate the utility of various features/interactions.

1.1 Why Model and Early Models

In this part of the tutorial, we will develop the motivation and rationale for developing formal (by which we mean mathematical) models of Information Seeking and Retrieval (ISR). To begin, we will discuss and describe various conceptual and descriptive models of ISR, including Bates' Berry Picking Model [13] and the ISR framework proposed by Ingwersen and Järvelin [27], along with other such models (e.g. [14, 16, 17, 29, 28, 30, 23, 46]). This will provide the background for the tutorial where we point out the limitations of such models and motivate the need to develop models that are not only descriptive in nature, but predictive and crucially explanatory. To set the context, we will discuss the qualities of information, the poverty of attention, information as a good, and how information can be valued. This is important because information seeking is intrinsically embedded within a task. Once motivations and context are provided, we will then examine a number of early formal models (1960-1980s) that have been developed using Decision Theory, Economics and Cost-Benefit frameworks [1, 36, 22, 35]; the most notable being the Probability Ranking Principle (PRP) [35]. The following topics will be covered:

1. Types of Models (Conceptual, Descriptive, Formal)
2. An overview of Conceptual models
3. What is a model? Why formal, why mathematical?
4. Why formally model ISR? Why we need theory? At least, in theory!
5. The benefits and costs of formally modelling ISR
6. Why don't we have lots of formal models for ISR?
7. A discussion on the lack, and lack of usage, of formal models for ISR
8. The Information Age, Poverty of Attention, Mathlus' Law [21, 33]
9. Information as Good and the Value of Information [44]
10. Decision Making and Optimization Models [26, 31]
11. Optimality and Rationality [40, 39, 42]
12. Cooper's Model of Searching [22]
13. Probability Ranking Principle [35]

1.2 Contemporary Models

The second part of the tutorial will focus on three contemporary formal models. First we shall show how the PRP can be extended to consider interaction by presenting the Interactive Probability Ranking Principle [25]. Next, we shall delve into Information Foraging Theory (IFT), which has become very popular and is often used to motivate experiments, but yet infrequently used in terms of modelling and prediction. Here, we will focus on the patch model, and explain the different implications of the model/theory, and how user behaviour is expected to change under varying circumstances. We will explain how these implications can be generated through a graphical analysis (and for the more math savvy, how they can be analytically derived). Then, we will turn our attention to the initial model of Search Economic Theory (SET) [3] and explain how the model was developed, and how it is possible to graphically and computationally explore how these models can be used to make hypotheses about search behaviour. We will then show how the model was refined to include more variables (and thus become more realistic) [7].

A summary of the topics we shall cover in this section are:

1. Interactive Probability Ranking Principle [25]
2. Sensemaking and Cost Structures [37]
3. Optimal Foraging Theory [41]
4. Information Foraging Theory [32, 20, 34, 37, 38]:
    - Information Scent Model
    - Information Diet Model
    - Information Patch Model
    - Charnov's Marginal Value Theorem [19]
5. Economic Theories:
    - Optimal Search Behavior and the Pandora's Box Problem [42, 45, 44]
    - Optimal Amount of Information (when to stop and deciding at the margin) [18]
    - Search Economic Theory [3, 5, 6, 7]

During this session activity sheets will be given to participants to draw hypotheses from various models.

1.3 A Guide to Modelling

Part three will focus on optimisation models, in general, how to build such models, and how to use them to generate hypotheses using various methods (analytical, graphical and computational) [43, 31]. The essence of such models is to develop a cost function and a gain function given the different interactions that users can perform. Given these functions, it is then possible to establish under what conditions cost is minimized and/or gain is maximized. This section will explore the following topics:

- What choices are available? What are the limitations?
- What are the interactions, costs and benefits?
- What will vary? Parameters?
- Define the problem and the goal
- Construct a cost and gain function
- Solve, plot, compute
- Draw inferences

To help illustrate how to undertake the model building process, we will use an example based on the simple scenario of finding the first highly relevant document in a result list. We will describe how we can characterize the problem, enumerate the different variables, and show how the different variables impact the overall cost and the design of the interface. If time permits, then we will also include some notes on developing simulations to explore such models (i.e., computational approaches).

1.4 Practical Session

The final part of the tutorial will be dedicated to building a model. Participants will consider the problem of a user trying to find an app on a mobile phone or tablet. The goal here is to find the app that the user wants to use. So the focus will be on building a cost function to model the different ways in which the user can find the app, e.g. search or browse. To add realism to the scenario, we will consider different types of users, ones that can remember where the app is, and those who cannot (i.e., best and average/worse cases) as well as consider how screen size and app icon size can be modelled to arrive at an optimal size and layout for such interaction. During the practical session, participants will be encouraged to abstract away the details to form a representation of the problem, and identify the main variables that are likely to influence the interaction (i.e., number of apps on the phone, the number apps per page, the cost of moving between screens, etc). These will be used to formulate the costs, then we will be able to reason about when it is better to search for an app and when it is better to browse. We will also consider alternative designs, such as presenting the most used apps first, or a hierarchical browsing structure, and whether they are likely to be more efficient or not, or under what circumstances.

2. INTENDED LEARNING OUTCOMES

By the end of the tutorial, participants should be able to:

- Define and describe the different types of models
- Explain the rationale for formal models of ISR
- Describe and define the components and optimisation model
- Describe and explain the main contemporary models
- Explain and infer the predicted user behaviour given these contemporary models
- Design a formal model and generate hypotheses regarding user behavior

3. BIOGRAPHY

Leif Azzopardi is a Senior Lecturer within the School of Computing Science at the University of Glasgow. His research focuses on building formal models for Information Retrieval - usually drawing upon different disciplines for inspiration, such as Quantum Mechanics, Operations Research, Microeconomics, Transportation Planning and Gamification. Central to his research is the theoretical development of formal models for Information Retrieval, where his research interests include:

- Statistical Language Models for the retrieval of documents, sentences, experts and other information objects [12, 24];
- Probabilistic models of user interaction and the simulation of users for evaluation [2, 8, 9];
- Microeconomic models of information interaction, specifically how cost and effort affect interaction and performance with search systems [3];
- Methods which assess the impact of search technology on society in application areas such as search engine bias and the accessibility of e-Government information [11], and;
- Search for fun (i.e. the SINS of users) [4].

He received his Ph.D. in Computing Science from the University of Paisley in 2006, and he received a First Class Honours Degree in Information Science from the University of Newcastle, Australia, 2001. In 2010, he received a Post-Graduate Certificate in Academic Practice and has been lecturing at the University of Glasgow since then. He has given numerous invited talks on Formal Models of Information Seeking and Retrieval throughout the world and lectured at the Information Foraging Summer School (2011, 2012 and 2013) and Symposium of Future Directions in Information Access (2007-2013). His work on economic models [7] for search received a best paper honourable mention at SIGIR 2014. He recently released a free online book called, *How to Tango with Django* which is a noob's guide to web development in Python's Django (available free at: `www.tangowithdjango.com` [10]).

Guido Zuccon is a Lecturer within the School of Information Systems at the Queensland University of Technology. His research interests include formal models of search, ranking principles for information retrieval, and retrieval models for health search. Guido has actively contributed to the area of document ranking and search result diversification. During his PhD he performed an extensive analysis of document ranking principles [49] and introduced the quantum probability ranking principle [51, 47] and was the first to empirically evaluate the interactive PRP [48]. His work on formal models of search result diversification based on facility location analysis [50] received the best paper award at ECIR 2013 and then in 2014 he received a best reviewer award at ECIR.

He received a Ph.D. in Computing Science from the University of Glasgow in 2012, and he received a Master in Computer Engineering with summa cum laude from the University of Padua, Italy, in 2007. Before joining the Queensland University of Technology as a lecturer in 2014, he was a postdoctoral research fellow at the CSIRO, Australia.

4. REFERENCES

[1] C. W. Axelrod. The economic evaluation of information storage and retrieval systems. *Information Processing & Management*, 13(2):117–124, 1977.

[2] L. Azzopardi. Query side evaluation: an empirical analysis of effectiveness and effort. In *Proc. of SIGIR*, pages 556–563. ACM, 2009.

[3] L. Azzopardi. The economics in interactive information retrieval. In *Proc. of SIGIR*, pages 15–24. ACM, 2011.

[4] L. Azzopardi. Searching for unlawful carnal knowledge. In *Proc. of SIGIR Workshop: Search for Fun*, volume 11, pages 17–18, 2011.

[5] L. Azzopardi. Economic models of search. In *Proceedings of the 18th Australasian Document Computing Symposium*, ADCS '13, pages 1–1, 2013.

[6] L. Azzopardi. Economic models of search. In *Proceedings of the 18th Australasian Document Computing Symposium*, ADCS '13, pages 1–1, 2013.

[7] L. Azzopardi. Modelling interaction with economic models of search. In *Proc. of SIGIR*, pages 3–12, 2014.

[8] L. Azzopardi and M. de Rijke. Automatic construction of known-item finding test beds. In *Proc. of SIGIR*, pages 603–604, 2006.

[9] L. Azzopardi, M. de Rijke, and K. Balog. Building simulated queries for known-item topics: an analysis using six european languages. In *Proc. of SIGIR*, pages 455–462. ACM, 2007.

[10] L. Azzopardi and D. Maxwell. Tango with django: a begginners guide to web development in python / django, 2013.

[11] L. Azzopardi and V. Vinay. Retrievability: An evaluation measure for higher order information access tasks. In *Proc. of CIKM*, pages 561–570, 2008.

[12] K. Balog, L. Azzopardi, and M. de Rijke. Formal models for expert finding in enterprise corpora. In *Proc. of SIGIR*, pages 43–50, 2006.

[13] M. J. Bates. The design of browsing and berrypicking techniques for the online search interface. *Online Information Review*, 13(5):407–424, 1989.

[14] M. J. Bates. Training and education for online. chapter Information search tactics, pages 96–105. Taylor Graham Publishing, London, UK, 1989.

[15] N. J. Belkin. Some(what) grand challenges for information retrieval. *SIGIR Forum*, 42:47–54, 2008.

[16] N. J. Belkin. Some(what) grand challenges for information retrieval. *SIGIR Forum*, 42(1):47–54, 2008.

[17] N. J. Belkin, R. N. Oddy, and H. M. Brooks. Ask for information retrieval: part i: background and theory; part ii: results of a design study. *Journal of Documentation*, 38(2) 61-71 and 38(3) 145-164, 1982.

[18] U. Birchler and M. Butler. *Information economics.* Routledge, 2007.

[19] E. L. Charnov. Optimal foraging: attack strategy of a mantid. *The American Naturalist*, 110(971):141–151, 1976.

[20] E. H. Chi, P. Pirolli, and J. Pitkow. The scent of a site: A system for analyzing and predicting information scent, usage, and usability of a web site. In *Proc. of SIGCHI*, pages 161–168. ACM, 2000.

[21] E. Coiera. Information economics and the internet. *Journal of the American Medical Informatics Association*, 7:215–221, 2000.

[22] M. D. Cooper. A cost model for evaluating information retrieval systems. *Journal of the American Society for Information Science*, pages 306–312, 1972.

[23] S. Erdelez. Information encountering: a conceptual framework for accidental information discovery. In *Proc. of ISIC*, pages 412–421, 1997.

[24] R. T. Fernández, D. E. Losada, and L. A. Azzopardi. Extending the language modeling framework for sentence retrieval to include local context. *Information Retrieval*, 14(4):355–389, 2011.

[25] N. Fuhr. A probability ranking principle for interactive information retrieval. *Information Retrieval*, 11(3):251–265, 2008.

[26] F. S. Hillier and G. J. Lieberman. Introduction to operations research. *NY, US*, 2001.

[27] P. Ingwersen and K. Järvelin. *The Turn: Integration of Information Seeking and Retrieval in Context.* Springer-Verlag New York, Inc., 2005.

[28] K. Järvelin. IR research: systems, interaction, evaluation and theories. *SIGIR Forum*, 45(2):17–31, 2012.

[29] K. Järvelin and T. D. Wilson. On conceptual models for information seeking and retrieval research. *Information Research*, 9(1):9–1, 2003.

[30] C. C. Kuhlthau. Developing a model of the library search process: Cognitive and affective aspects. *RQ*, pages 232–242, 1988.

[31] K. G. Murty. Optimization models for decision making: Volume. *University of Michigan, Ann Arbor*, 2003.

[32] P. Pirolli and S. Card. Information foraging. *Psychological Review*, 106:643–675, 1999.

[33] A. J. Repo. The value of information: Approaches in economics, accounting, and management science. *Journal of the American Society for Information Science*, 40(2):68–85, 1989.

[34] H. L. Resnikoff, H. Resenikoff, and H. Resnikoff. *The illusion of reality.* Springer-Verlag New York, 1989.

[35] S. E. Robertson. The probability ranking principle in ir. *Journal of Documentation*, 33(4):294–304, 1977.

[36] D. H. Rothenberg. An efficiency model and a performance function for an IR system. *Information Storage and Retrieval*, 5(3):109 – 122, 1969.

[37] D. M. Russell, M. J. Stefik, P. Pirolli, and S. K. Card. The cost structure of sensemaking. In *Proc. of INTERACT/SIGCHI*, pages 269–276, 1993.

[38] P. E. Sandstrom. An optimal foraging approach to information seeking and use. *The library quarterly*, pages 414–449, 1994.

[39] H. A. Simon. A behavioral model of rational choice. *The quarterly journal of economics*, 69(1):99–118, 1955.

[40] H. A. Simon. Theories of bounded rationality. *Decision and organization*, 1:161–176, 1972.

[41] D. Stephens and J. Krebs. Foraging theory. *Princeton: Princeton University Press*, 1(10):100, 1986.

[42] G. J. Stigler. The economics of information. *The journal of political economy*, 69(3):213–225, 1961.

[43] H. R. Varian. How to build an economic model in your spare time. *American Economist*, 41:3–10, 1997.

[44] H. R. Varian. Economics and search. *SIGIR Forum*, 33(1):1–5, 1999.

[45] M. L. Weitzman. Optimal search for the best alternative. *Econometrica: Journal of the Econometric Society*, pages 641–654, 1979.

[46] T. D. Wilson. Human information behavior. *Informing science*, 3(2):49–56, 2000.

[47] G. Zuccon and L. Azzopardi. Using the quantum probability ranking principle to rank interdependent documents. In *Proc. of ECIR*, pages 357–369. Springer, 2010.

[48] G. Zuccon, L. Azzopardi, and C. van Rijsbergen. The interactive prp for diversifying document rankings. In *Proc. of SIGIR*, pages 1227–1228. ACM, 2011.

[49] G. Zuccon, L. Azzopardi, and C. K. Van Rijsbergen. An analysis of ranking principles and retrieval strategies. In *Proc. of ICTIR*, pages 151–163. Springer, 2011.

[50] G. Zuccon, L. Azzopardi, D. Zhang, and J. Wang. Top-k retrieval using facility location analysis. In *Proc. of ECIR*, pages 305–316. 2012.

[51] G. Zuccon, L. A. Azzopardi, and K. Rijsbergen. The quantum probability ranking principle for information retrieval. In *Proc. of ICTIR*, pages 232–240, 2009.

Advanced Click Models and their Applications to IR

SIGIR 2015 Tutorial

Aleksandr Chuklin
Google Switzerland &
University of Amsterdam
Zürich, Switzerland
a.chuklin@uva.nl

Ilya Markov
ISLA, University of Amsterdam
Amsterdam, The Netherlands
i.markov@uva.nl

Maarten de Rijke
ISLA, University of Amsterdam
Amsterdam, The Netherlands
derijke@uva.nl

ABSTRACT

This tutorial concerns with more advanced and more recent topics in the area of click models. Here, we discuss recent developments in the area with a particular focus on applications of click models. The tutorial features a guest talk and a live demo where participants have a chance to build their own advanced click model.

While this is the second part of the two half-day tutorials, it is not required for participants to attend the first one. In the beginning of this part, a short introduction to basic click models will be given so that all participants share a common vocabulary. Then, recent advances in click models will be discussed.

Categories and Subject Descriptors

H.3 [**Information Storage and Retrieval**]: H.3.3 Information Search and Retrieval

Keywords

Click models; web search

1. INTRODUCTION

Click models, probabilistic models of the behavior of search engine users, have been studied extensively by the information retrieval community during the last five years.

A good body of work has been published on click models over the past 5 to 10 years. Importantly, the area continues to be an active one, with new models aimed at describing and/or predicting behavioral data being proposed at each of the main information retrieval conferences (SIGIR, WSDM, WWW, CIKM) over the past few years. There is also a fair number of publications that use click models presented in the main information retrieval conferences as well as ACM journals such as TOIS. All this indicates that there is a substantial and continued level of interest in the topic.

Indeed, we now have a handful of basic click models, inference methods, evaluation principles and applications for click models, that form the building blocks of ongoing research efforts in the area. The time is right to organize and present this material to a broad audience of interested information retrieval researchers, whether junior or senior. Many of the click models available today have been proposed by different industrial and academic research groups—one of the key aims of our proposed tutorial is to bring these together and offer a unified perspective. To achieve this, we describe the basic click models, inference methods and evaluation principles. We supplement this with an account of available datasets and packages plus a live demo based on these. We also present click model applications accompanied by examples.

We expect the tutorial to be useful for both researchers and practitioners that either want to develop new click models, use them in their own research in other areas or apply the models described here to improve actual search systems.

SIGIR'15, August 09-13, 2015, Santiago, Chile.
ACM 978-1-4503-3621-5/15/08.
DOI: http://dx.doi.org/10.1145/2766462.2767882.

2. OBJECTIVES

A large body of research on click models has been developed. This research has improved our understanding of user behavior in web search and facilitated the usage of click models in various search-related tasks. Current studies use a broad range of notations and terminology, perform experiments using different and mostly proprietary datasets, do not detail the model inference procedures used and, thus, do not provide a general systematic view on the research area. This, in turn, slows down the development and hinders the application of click models. The goal of this tutorial is to bring together current efforts in the area, summarize the research performed so far and give a holistic view on existing click models for web search. More specifically, the aims of this tutorial are the following:

1. Describe existing click models in a unified way, i.e., using common notation and terminology, so that different models can easily be related to each other.
2. Compare commonly used click models, discuss their advantages and limitations and provide a set of recommendations on their usage.
3. Provide ready-to-use formulas and implementations of existing click models and detail general inference procedures to facilitate the development of new ones.
4. Give an overview of existing datasets and tools for working with click models and develop new ones.
5. Provide an overview of click model applications and directions for future development of click models.

Our target audience consists of researchers and developers in information retrieval who are interested in formally capturing user interactions with search engine result pages, whether for ranking purposes, to simulate user behavior in a lab setting, or simply to gain deeper insights in user behavior and interaction data. The tutorial will be useful as an overview for anyone starting research work in the area as well as for practitioners seeking concrete recipes.

The tutorial aims to provide a map of an increasingly rich landscape of click models. By the end of the half-day tutorial, attendees should be familiar with the basic definitions and intuitions of what we consider to be the core models, with inference tasks for these models, and with uses of these models. While our presentation is necessarily formal in places, we make a serious effort to relate the models, the inference procedures and the applications back to the core information retrieval task and to web search data by including a fair number of examples. We hope that this supplies attendees who are new to the area with effective means to start using click models in their own research.

3. DETAILED SCHEDULE

The advanced tutorial consists of two blocks of 1.5 hours. Each block will incorporate three types of activity: (1) presentation of the material, (2) live coding sessions, and (3) discussions at the end of each 1.5 hours. Additionally we plan to bring an author of a recent click model paper to give a short presentation and participate in the discussion. For the coding sessions, we will provide code examples and data samples. The participants will be able to either follow the examples on the slides or perform them live along with the presentation. During the discussion sessions at the end of each 1.5 hour block, we will offer the participants a number of quizzes aimed to (self-)assess the comprehension of the presented material. The schedule of the advanced tutorial is as follows.

Block 1 (1.5 hours)

1. Overview of Advanced Click Models

   Here we present main development directions of click models and discuss most prominent members of each class. We discuss models' assumptions, observed and hidden random variables, models' parameters and relations between parameters and random variables. This discussion is concluded with a summary of differences and similarities between the presented models. The following types of click models will be covered in this part:

   (a) Click models for aggregated search
   (b) Beyond a single query session
   (c) User diversity
   (d) Eye tracking and mouse movements
   (e) Nonlinear search engine result page examination
   (f) Using editorial judgements

2. Live Demo: Building an Advanced Click Model

   In this part, we use samples of publicly available datasets and open-source software packages to guide the participants through a process of extending a basic click model to incorporate some new ideas. In particular, we will use an open source package maintained by Markov[1] as well as samples from interaction data shared by Yandex.[2]

3. Recap and Discussion

[1]https://github.com/markovi/PyClick
[2]http://imat-relpred.yandex.ru/en/datasets

Coffee Break (30 minutes)

Block 2 (1.5 hours)

4. Live Demo: Building an Advanced Click Model (continued)

5. Guest talk: "Building a Click Model: From Idea to Implementation"

6. Click Model Applications and Future Directions In this part we discuss different applications for modern click models in different areas such as ranking, evaluation or user simulation. We also discuss future directions for click models, the area we believe to stay active in the coming years with more ideas coming in and being integrated and re-integrated.

   (a) Applications
      i. Inference of Document Relevance
      ii. Click Model-based Metrics
      iii. Simulating Users
   (b) Future Directions
      i. Rich User Feedback
      ii. Heterogeneous Search
      iii. Cross-Device and Cross-Session Search Tasks

7. Recap and Discussion

4. TYPE OF SUPPORT MATERIALS TO BE SUPPLIED TO ATTENDEES

- Complete draft of the book [1]
- Copy of the slides
- Code and data samples to follow live demos

Acknowledgements

This work was partially supported by the grant P2T1P2_152269 of the Swiss National Science Foundation, the European Community's Seventh Framework Programme (FP7/2007-2013) under grant agreement nr 312827 (VOX-Pol), the Netherlands Organisation for Scientific Research (NWO) under project nrs 727.011.005, 612.001.116, HOR-11-10, 640.006.013, 612.066.930, CI-14-25, SH-322-15, Amsterdam Data Science, the Dutch national program COMMIT, the ESF Research Network Program ELIAS, the Elite Network Shifts project funded by the Royal Dutch Academy of Sciences (KNAW), the Netherlands eScience Center under project number 027.012.105, the Yahoo! Faculty Research and Engagement Program, the Microsoft Research PhD program, and the HPC Fund.

All content represents the opinion of the authors which is not necessarily shared or endorsed by their respective employers and/or sponsors.

REFERENCES

[1] A. Chuklin, I. Markov, and M. de Rijke. *Click Models for Web Search*. Morgan & Claypool, 2015. To appear.

An Introduction to Click Models for Web Search

SIGIR 2015 Tutorial

Aleksandr Chuklin
Google Switzerland &
University of Amsterdam
Zürich, Switzerland
a.chuklin@uva.nl

Ilya Markov
University of Amsterdam
Amsterdam, The Netherlands
i.markov@uva.nl

Maarten de Rijke
University of Amsterdam
Amsterdam, The Netherlands
derijke@uva.nl

ABSTRACT

In this introductory tutorial we give an overview of click models for web search. We show how the framework of probabilistic graphical models help to explain user behavior, build new evaluation metrics and perform simulations. The tutorial is augmented with a live demo where participants have a chance to implement a click model and to test it on a publicly available dataset.

Categories and Subject Descriptors

H.3 [**Information Storage and Retrieval**]: H.3.3 Information Search and Retrieval

Keywords

Click models; web search

1. INTRODUCTION

Click models, probabilistic models of the behavior of search engine users, have been studied extensively by the information retrieval community during the last five years.

A good body of work has been published on click models over the past 5 to 10 years. Importantly, the area continues to be an active one, with new models aimed at describing and/or predicting behavioral data being proposed at each of the main information retrieval conferences (SIGIR, WSDM, WWW, CIKM) over the past few years. There is also a fair number of publications that use click models presented in the main information retrieval conferences as well as ACM journals such as TOIS. All this indicates that there is a substantial and continued level of interest in the topic.

Indeed, we now have a handful of basic click models, inference methods, evaluation principles and applications for click models, that form the building blocks of ongoing research efforts in the area. The time is right to organize and present this material to a broad audience of interested information retrieval researchers, whether junior or senior. Many of the click models available today have been proposed by different industrial and academic research groups—one of the key aims of our proposed tutorial is to bring these together and offer a unified perspective. To achieve this, we describe the basic click models, inference methods and evaluation principles. We supplement this with an account of available datasets and packages plus a live demo based on these. We also present click model applications accompanied by examples.

We expect the tutorial to be useful for both researchers and practitioners that either want to develop new click models, use them in their own research in other areas or apply the models described here to improve actual search systems.

SIGIR'15, August 09-13, 2015, Santiago, Chile.
ACM 978-1-4503-3621-5/15/08.
DOI: http://dx.doi.org/10.1145/2766462.2767881.

2. OBJECTIVES

A large body of research on click models has been developed. This research has improved our understanding of user behavior in web search and facilitated the usage of click models in various search-related tasks. Current studies use a broad range of notations and terminology, perform experiments using different and mostly proprietary datasets, do not detail the model inference procedures used and, thus, do not provide a general systematic view on the research area. This, in turn, slows down the development and hinders the application of click models. The goal of this tutorial is to bring together current efforts in the area, summarize the research performed so far and give a holistic view on existing click models for web search. More specifically, the aims of this tutorial are the following:

1. Describe existing click models in a unified way, i.e., using common notation and terminology, so that different models can easily be related to each other.
2. Compare commonly used click models, discuss their advantages and limitations and provide a set of recommendations on their usage.
3. Provide ready-to-use formulas and implementations of existing click models and detail general inference procedures to facilitate the development of new ones.
4. Give an overview of existing datasets and tools for working with click models and develop new ones.
5. Provide an overview of click model applications and directions for future development of click models.

Our target audience consists of researchers and developers in information retrieval who are interested in formally capturing user interactions with search engine result pages, whether for ranking purposes, to simulate user behavior in a lab setting, or simply to gain deeper insights in user behavior and interaction data. The tutorial will be useful as an overview for anyone starting research work in the area as well as for practitioners seeking concrete recipes.

The tutorial aims to provide a map of an increasingly rich landscape of click models. By the end of the half-day tutorial, attendees should be familiar with the basic definitions and intuitions of what we consider to be the core models, with inference tasks for these models, and with uses of these models. While our presentation is necessarily formal in places, we make a serious effort to relate the models, the inference procedures and the applications back to the core information retrieval task and to web search data by including a fair number of examples. We hope that this supplies attendees who are new to the area with effective means to start using click models in their own research.

3. DETAILED SCHEDULE

This introductory tutorial consists of two blocks of 1.5 hours. Each block will incorporate three types of activity: (1) presentation of the material, (2) live coding sessions, and (3) discussions at the end of the block. For the coding sessions, we will provide code examples and data samples. The participants will be able to either follow the examples on the slides or perform them live along with the presentation. During the discussion sessions at the end of each the 1.5 hour blocks, we will offer the participants a number of quizzes aimed to (self-)assess the comprehension of the presented material. The schedule of the introductory tutorial is as follows.

Block 1 (1.5 hours)

1. Introduction and Historical Notes

2. Aims of this Tutorial

3. Basic Click Models

   Here, we describe basic click models for web search, starting with the simplest random click model and arriving to the more sophisticated DCM, DBN and UBM models. We discuss models' assumptions, observed and hidden random variables, models' parameters and relations between parameters and random variables. This discussion is concluded with a summary of differences and similarities between the presented models. The following click models will be covered in this part:

   (a) Random Click Model
   (b) Position-Based Model
   (c) Cascade Model [3]
   (d) User Browsing Model [4]
   (e) Dependent Click Model [6]
   (f) Click Chain Model [5]
   (g) Dynamic Bayesian Network Model [1]

4. Click Model Inference

   In this part, we describe the process of training click model parameters from past click observations. We review two main inference techniques, namely maximum likelihood estimation (MLE) and the expectation-maximization algorithm (EM). We then give several examples of MLE and EM inference for existing click models to support the theory. Finally, we present the ready-to-use MLE estimates and EM update rules for the parameters of previously discussed click models. The detailed plan of this part is as follows:

   (a) Maximum Likelihood Estimation
      i. MLE Inference for RCM
      ii. MLE Inference for simplified DCM
      iii. MLE Inference for simplified DBN
   (b) EM Inference
      i. Expectation (E-step)
      ii. Maximization (M-step)
      iii. EM Inference for UBM
   (c) Alternative Inference Methods
      i. Bayesian Inference [7]
      ii. Probit Inference [9]
      iii. Matrix Factorization [8]

5. Recap and Discussion

Break (30 minutes)

Block 2 (1.5 hours)

6. Live Demo: Click Model Inference

   In this part, we use samples of publicly available datasets and open-source software packages to guide the participants through click model inference in practice. In particular, we will use an open source package maintained by Markov[1] as well as samples from interaction data shared by Yandex.[2]

7. Click Model Evaluation

   Here, we discuss different ways to evaluate click models and to compare them to each other. We start with traditional approaches, such as log-likelihood/perplexity evaluation and click-through rate prediction, and then discuss more application-oriented evaluation methods like NDCG evaluation. The outline of this part is as follows:

   (a) Log-Likelihood and Perplexity Evaluation
   (b) Click-Through Rate Prediction Evaluation
   (c) Relevance Prediction Evaluation

8. Data and Tools

   Here, we discuss publicly available datasets for experimenting with click models. We also describe open-source software packages and libraries that facilitate working with click models. The outline of this part is as follows:

   (a) Public Datasets
   (b) Software Libraries and Open-Source Projects

9. Recap and Discussion

4. TYPE OF SUPPORT MATERIALS TO BE SUPPLIED TO ATTENDEES

- Complete draft of the book [2]
- Copy of the slides
- Code and data samples to follow live demos

[1] https://github.com/markovi/PyClick
[2] http://imat-relpred.yandex.ru/en/datasets

Acknowledgements

This work was partially supported by the grant P2T1P2_152269 of the Swiss National Science Foundation, the European Community's Seventh Framework Programme (FP7/2007-2013) under grant agreement nr 312827 (VOX-Pol), the Netherlands Organisation for Scientific Research (NWO) under project nrs 727.011.005, 612.001.116, HOR-11-10, 640.006.013, 612.066.930, CI-14-25, SH-322-15, Amsterdam Data Science, the Dutch national program COMMIT, the ESF Research Network Program ELIAS, the Elite Network Shifts project funded by the Royal Dutch Academy of Sciences (KNAW), the Netherlands eScience Center under project number 027.012.105, the Yahoo! Faculty Research and Engagement Program, the Microsoft Research PhD program, and the HPC Fund.

All content represents the opinion of the authors which is not necessarily shared or endorsed by their respective employers and/or sponsors.

REFERENCES

[1] O. Chapelle and Y. Zhang. A dynamic bayesian network click model for web search ranking. In *WWW*, pages 1–10, 2009. doi: 10.1145/1526709.1526711.

[2] A. Chuklin, I. Markov, and M. de Rijke. *Click Models for Web Search*. Morgan & Claypool, 2015. To appear.

[3] N. Craswell, O. Zoeter, M. Taylor, and B. Ramsey. An experimental comparison of click position-bias models. In *WSDM*, pages 87–94, 2008. doi: 10.1145/1341531.1341545.

[4] G. E. Dupret and B. Piwowarski. A user browsing model to predict search engine click data from past observations. In *SIGIR*, pages 331–338, 2008. doi: 10.1145/1390334.1390392.

[5] F. Guo, C. Liu, A. Kannan, T. Minka, M. Taylor, Y.-M. Wang, and C. Faloutsos. Click chain model in web search. In *WWW*, pages 11–20. ACM, 2009. ISBN 9781605584874. doi: 10.1145/1526709.1526712.

[6] F. Guo, C. Liu, and Y. M. Wang. Efficient multiple-click models in web search. In *WSDM*, pages 124–131, 2009. doi: 10.1145/1498759.1498818.

[7] C. Liu, F. Guo, and C. Faloutsos. BBM: Bayesian browsing model from petabyte-scale data. In *KDD*, New York, NY, USA, 2009. ACM Press. ISBN 9781605584959. doi: 10.1145/1557019.1557081.

[8] S. Shen, B. Hu, W. Chen, and Q. Yang. Personalized click model through collaborative filtering. In *WSDM*, New York, NY, USA, 2012. ACM Press. ISBN 9781450307475. doi: 10.1145/2124295.2124336.

[9] Y. Zhang, D. Wang, G. Wang, W. Chen, Z. Zhang, B. Hu, and L. Zhang. Learning click models via probit bayesian inference. In *CIKM*, New York, NY, USA, 2010. ACM Press. ISBN 9781450300995. doi: 10.1145/1871437.1871496.

IR Evaluation: Modeling User Behavior for Measuring Effectiveness

Charles L. A. Clarke
Computer Science
University of Waterloo

Mark D. Smucker
Management Sciences
University of Waterloo

Emine Yilmaz
Computer Science
University College London

ABSTRACT

This half-day tutorial on IR evaluation combines an introduction to classical IR evaluation methods with material on more recent user-oriented approaches. We primarily focus on off-line evaluation, but some material on on-line evaluation is also covered. The broad goal of the tutorial is to equip researchers with an understanding of modern approaches to IR evaluation, facilitating new research on this topic and improving evaluation methodology for emerging areas.

Categories and Subject Descriptors

H.3.4 [**Information Storage and Retrieval**]: Systems and Software—*Performance evaluation (efficiency and effectiveness)*

General Terms

Experimentation, Measurement, Performance

Keywords

user models; effectiveness; efficiency; tutorial

1. OVERVIEW

An IR effectiveness measure makes a prediction about the benefits of an IR system to its users. For example, we might evaluate a search engine result page using the NDCG measure [18], or another traditional measure. In applying this measure, we assume that a larger NDCG value corresponds to a better result, providing more benefit to its user. Recent research extends traditional IR evaluation methodology to directly model user behavior while interacting with an IR system, with the goal of improving the quality of the prediction [8, 9, 11, 27, 39–41, 51–53].

In this tutorial, we cover IR evaluation methodologies and measures from a user modeling perspective. We start with a review of standard approaches to evaluation, building on the Cranfield paradigm [14], including a review of traditional measures from a user perspective. These measures include precision, recall, MAP [30–32,49,50], NDCG [18], ERR [10], and RBP [27]. We discuss efforts to extend these measures to address novelty and diversity [10,12,13], and to incorporate observed user behavior.

We then discuss sources of user behavior that can be used to develop and calibrate user models for IR evaluation [23]. These sources can be divided into two broad classes: lab studies and implicit feedback. Such lab studies include direct relevance assessments, think aloud protocols, eye tracking, as well as the observation of searchers completing search tasks. Implicit feedback requires the observation of users "in the wild", including clickthroughs, dwell times, and mouse movements [29].

Finally, we introduce techniques for developing evaluation methodologies that directly model key aspects of the user's interaction with the system. For example, for a standard web search result page, we might model the searcher's interaction with the summaries, their probability of clicking on a result, their time to read a page, and other factors. Both benefits and costs must be expressed in meaningful units. For example, benefits might be measured by the number of unique relevant documents seen, while costs might be measure by the time spent interacting with the system. Alternatively, benefits might be measured in time well spent, i.e., the time spent viewing relevant material [11].

By careful modeling of user behavior, we can evaluate systems not only in terms of their average behavior, but also in terms of variance across a population of users. In developing these measures, we must strike a balance between fidelity and complexity. We cannot model all aspects of user behavior, and simplification is required. Moreover, to make accurate predictions these models must be calibrated against actual user behavior; we provide detailed examples of how to achieve this aim.

2. OBJECTIVES

We assume an audience of early doctoral students and established researchers from outside IR. These individuals may have seen basic IR measures, e.g., NDCG from work on web search, but require a broader understanding of the important role that evaluation plays with respect to IR research. As new IR tasks emerge, we hope to equip researchers working on these tasks with the tools to appropriately and meaningfully evaluate their efforts. A full bibliography, partialy reproduced below, allows participants to extend their understanding of each topic after the tutorial.

SIGIR'15, August 09–13, 2015, Santiago, Chile.
Copyright 2015 ACM 978-1-4503-3621-5/15/08
http://dx.doi.org/10.1145/2766462.2767876 .

3. FORMAT

An outline of topics appears below, organized into four broad categories. The depth varies from topic to topic, with a emphasis on examples and insights. After a basic overview of evaluation methodologies, we discuss evaluation from a user viewpoint, examing how user models may be translated into evaluation measures. We then discuss approaches to studying user behavior to inform these models, both through laboratory studies and through inplicit feedback from live systems. Finally, we discuss how the results of these user studies may be applied to validate effectiveness measures. In addition, we provide exercises allowing attendees to compute measures, make relevance judgments, and otherwise actively engage in the process of IR evaluation. After the tutorial, the slides and exercises from the tutorial will be made openly available through the authors' personal websites.

4. TOPICS

1. Basic evaluation methodology
   (a) Cranfield paradigm
   (b) Test collections
   (c) Queries and topics
   (d) Relevance assessment; the pooling method
   (e) Precision; recall; mean average precision
   (f) *Exercise: computing MAP*
   (g) Significance testing; confidence intervals
   (h) Limitations on recall estimates
   (i) TREC and other evaluation experiments
2. A user oriented view
   (a) User models behind traditional metrics
   (b) Graded relevance and NDCG
   (c) The cascade model
   (d) Rank biased precision; expected reciprocal rank
   (e) *Exercise: computing ERR*
   (f) Expected browsing utility
   (g) Novelty and diversity; intent aware measures
   (h) Session based evaluation
   (i) Passage oriented evaluation; U-measure
   (j) Incorporating variability in user behavior
3. The role of user studies
   (a) Lab studies
   (b) Relevance assessment
   (c) Relevance, effort, and user satisfaction
   (d) *Exercise: relevance judgments*
   (e) Side-by-side and whole page judgments
   (f) Observational studies; eye tracking
   (g) Think aloud protocols
   (h) On-line evaluation; A/B testing
   (i) Clicks, skips and other implicit signals
   (j) Result interleaving
4. Calibration and validation
   (a) Costs and benefits; simulation
   (b) Time based calibration
   (c) Time well spent
   (d) *Exercise: simulating a search task*
   (e) Economic models of search
   (f) Foraging theory
   (g) Applications of reinforcement learning

5. FULL BIOGRAPHIES

5.1 Charles L. A. Clarke

Charles Clarke is a Professor in the School of Computer Science at the University of Waterloo, Canada. His research interests include information retrieval, web search, and text data mining. He has published on a wide range of topics — including papers related to question answering, XML, filesystem search, user interfaces, and statistical natural language processing — as well as the evaluation of information retrieval systems. He was a Program Co-Chair for SIGIR 2007 and SIGIR 2014. He is currently Chair of the SIGIR Executive Committee, and Co-Editor-in-Chief of the *Information Retrieval Journal*. He is a co-author of the graduate textbook *Information Retrieval: Implementing and Evaluating Search Engines*, MIT Press, 2010.

5.2 Mark D. Smucker

Mark Smucker is an Associate Professor in the Department of Management Sciences at the University of Waterloo. Mark's recent work has focused on making information retrieval evaluation more predictive of actual human search performance. Mark has been a co-organizer of two TREC tracks, a co-organizer of the SIGIR 2013 workshop on modeling user behavior for information retrieval evaluation (MUBE) and the SIGIR 2010 workshop on the simulation of interaction. He is a recipient of the SIGIR best paper award (2012) for his work with Clarke on the time-based calibration of effectiveness measures. He is also a recipient of the University of Waterloo, Faculty of Engineering's Teaching Excellence Award.

5.3 Emine Yilmaz

Emine Yilmaz is an Assistant Professor in the Department of Computer Science University College London and a research consultant for Microsoft Research Cambridge. She is the recipient of the Google Faculty Award in 2014/15. Her main interests are evaluating quality of retrieval systems, modeling user behavior, learning to rank, and inferring user needs while using search engines. She has published research papers extensively at major information retrieval venues such as SIGIR, CIKM and WSDM. She has previously given several tutorials on evaluation at the SIGIR 2012 and SIGIR 2010 Conferences and at the RuSSIR/EDBT Summer School in 2011. She has also organized several workshops on Crowdsourcing (WSDM2011, SIGIR 2011 and SIGIR 2010) and User Modeling for Retrieval Evaluation (SIGIR 2013). She has served as one of the organizers of the ICTIR Conference in 2009, as the demo chair for the ECIR Conference in 2013, and as the PC chair for the SPIRE 2015 conference. She is also a co-coordinator of the Tasks Track in TREC 2015.

6. REFERENCES

[1] Azzah Al-Maskari, Mark Sanderson, and Paul Clough. The relationship between IR effectiveness measures and user satisfaction. In *30th Annual International ACM SIGIR Conference on Research and Development in Information Retrieval*, pages 773–774, 2007.

[2] Javed A. Aslam, Virgil Pavlu, and Emine Yilmaz. A statistical method for system evaluation using incomplete judgments. In *29th Annual International ACM SIGIR Conference on Research and Development in Information Retrieval*, pages 541–548, 2006.

[3] Javed A. Aslam, Emine Yilmaz, and Virgiliu Pavlu. The maximum entropy method for analyzing retrieval measures. In *28th Annual International ACM SIGIR Conference on Research and Development in Information Retrieval*, pages 27–34, 2005.

[4] Stefan Büttcher, Charles L. A. Clarke, Peter C. K. Yeung, and Ian Soboroff. Reliable information retrieval evaluation with incomplete and biased judgements. In *30th Annual International ACM SIGIR Conference on Research and Development in Information Retrieval*, pages 63–70, 2007.

[5] Ben Carterette. Robust test collections for retrieval evaluation. In *30th Annual International ACM SIGIR Conference on Research and Development in Information Retrieval*, pages 55–62, 2007.

[6] Ben Carterette. System effectiveness, user models, and user utility: A conceptual framework for investigation. In *34th International ACM SIGIR Conference on Research and Development in Information Retrieval*, pages 903–912, 2011.

[7] Ben Carterette, James Allan, and Ramesh Sitaraman. Minimal test collections for retrieval evaluation. In *29th Annual International ACM SIGIR Conference on Research and Development in Information Retrieval*, pages 268–275, 2006.

[8] Ben Carterette, Evangelos Kanoulas, and Emine Yilmaz. Simulating simple user behavior for system effectiveness evaluation. In *20th ACM International Conference on Information and Knowledge Management*, pages 611–620, 2011.

[9] Ben Carterette, Evangelos Kanoulas, and Emine Yilmaz. Incorporating variability in user behavior into systems based evaluation. In *21st ACM International Conference on Information and Knowledge Management*, pages 135–144, 2012.

[10] Olivier Chapelle, Donald Metlzer, Ya Zhang, and Pierre Grinspan. Expected reciprocal rank for graded relevance. In *18th ACM Conference on Information and Knowledge Management*, pages 621–630, 2009.

[11] Charles L. A. Clarke and Mark D. Smucker. Time well spent. In *5th Information Interaction in Context Symposium*, pages 205–214, 2014.

[12] Charles L.A. Clarke, Nick Craswell, Ian Soboroff, and Azin Ashkan. A comparative analysis of cascade measures for novelty and diversity. In *4th ACM International Conference on Web Search and Data Mining*, pages 75–84, 2011.

[13] Charles L.A. Clarke, Maheedhar Kolla, Gordon V. Cormack, Olga Vechtomova, Azin Ashkann, Stefan Büttcher, and Ian MacKinnon. Novelty and diversity in information retrieval evaluation. In *31st Annual International ACM SIGIR Conference on Research and Development in Information Retrieval*, pages 659–666, 2008.

[14] Cyril W. Cleverdon. The Cranfield tests on index language devices. *AsLib proceedings*, 19:173–192, 1967.

[15] Gordon V. Cormack, Christopher R. Palmer, and Charles L. A. Clarke. Efficient construction of large test collections. In *21st Annual International ACM SIGIR Conference on Research and Development in Information Retrieval*, pages 282–289, 1998.

[16] Georges Dupret and Mounia Lalmas. Absence time and user engagement: Evaluating ranking functions. In *6th ACM International Conference on Web Search and Data Mining*, pages 173–182, 2013.

[17] Georges Dupret, Vanessa Murdock, and Benjamin Piwowarski. Web search engine evaluation using clickthrough data and a user model. In *16th International WWW Conference Workshop on Query Log Analysis: Social and Technological Challenges*, May 2007.

[18] Kalervo Järvelin and Jaana Kekäläinen. Cumulated gain-based evaluation of IR techniques. *ACM Transactions on Information Systems*, 20(4):422–446, 2002.

[19] Thorsten Joachims, Laura Granka, Bing Pan, Helene Hembrooke, and Geri Gay. Accurately interpreting clickthrough data as implicit feedback. In *28th Annual International ACM SIGIR Conference on Research and Development in Information Retrieval*, pages 154–161, 2005.

[20] Evangelos Kanoulas, Ben Carterette, Paul D. Clough, and Mark Sanderson. Evaluating multi-query sessions. In *34th International ACM SIGIR Conference on Research and Development in Information Retrieval*, pages 1053–1062, 2011.

[21] Gabriella Kazai and Mounia Lalmas. eXtended cumulated gain measures for the evaluation of content-oriented XML retrieval. *ACM Transactions on Information Systems*, 24(4):503–542, 2006.

[22] Gabriella Kazai, Emine Yilmaz, Nick Craswell, and Seyed M. M. Tahaghoghi. User intent and assessor disagreement in web search evaluation. In *22nd ACM International Conference on Information and Knowledge Management*, pages 699–708, 2013.

[23] Diane Kelly and Cassidy R. Sugimoto. A systematic review of interactive information retrieval evaluation studies, 1967–2006. *Journal of the American Society for Information Science and Technology*, 64(4):745–770, 2013.

[24] Jinyoung Kim, Gabriella Kazai, and Imed Zitouni. Relevance dimensions in preference-based IR evaluation. In *36th International ACM SIGIR Conference on Research and Development in Information Retrieval*, pages 913–916, 2013.

[25] Yiqun Liu, Yupeng Fu, Min Zhang, Shaoping Ma, and Liyun Ru. Automatic search engine performance evaluation with click-through data analysis. In *16th International WWW Conference Workshop on Query Log Analysis: Social and Technological Challenges*, May 2007.

[26] Alistair Moffat, William Webber, and Justin Zobel. Strategic system comparisons via targeted relevance judgments. In *30th Annual International ACM SIGIR Conference on Research and Development in Information Retrieval*, pages 375–382, 2007.

[27] Alistair Moffat and Justin Zobel. Rank-biased precision for measurement of retrieval effectiveness. *ACM Transactions on Information Systems*, 27(1):1–27, 2008.

[28] Benjamin Piwowarski, Andrew Trotman, and Mounia Lalmas. Sound and complete relevance assessment for XML retrieval. *ACM Transactions on Information Systems*, 27(1):1–37, 2008.

[29] Filip Radlinski and Nick Craswell. Optimized interleaving for online retrieval evaluation. In *6th ACM International Conference on Web Search and Data Mining*, pages 245–254, 2013.

[30] Stephen Robertson. On GMAP: and other transformations. In *15th ACM International Conference on Information and Knowledge management*, pages 78–83, 2006.

[31] Stephen Robertson. A new interpretation of average precision. In *31st Annual International ACM SIGIR Conference on Research and Development in Information Retrieval*, pages 689–690, 2008.

[32] Stephen E. Robertson, Evangelos Kanoulas, and Emine Yilmaz. Extending average precision to graded relevance judgments. In *33rd International ACM SIGIR Conference on Research and Development in Information Retrieval*, pages 603–610, 2010.

[33] Tetsuya Sakai. Evaluating evaluation metrics based on the bootstrap. In *29th Annual International ACM SIGIR Conference*, pages 525–532, 2006.

[34] Tetsuya Sakai and Zhicheng Dou. Summaries, ranked retrieval and sessions: A unified framework for information access evaluation. In *36th International ACM SIGIR Conference on Research and Development in Information Retrieval*, pages 473–482, 2013.

[35] Mark Sanderson and Hideo Joho. Forming test collections with no system pooling. In *27th Annual International ACM SIGIR Conference on Research and Development in Information Retrieval*, pages 33–40, 2004.

[36] Mark Sanderson, Monica Lestari Paramita, Paul D. Clough, and Evangelos Kanoulas. Do user preferences and evaluation measures line up? In *33rd International ACM SIGIR Conference on Research and Development in Information Retrieval*, pages 555–562, 2010.

[37] Mark Sanderson and Justin Zobel. Information retrieval system evaluation: effort, sensitivity, and reliability. In *28th Annual International ACM SIGIR Conference on Research and Development in Information Retrieval*, pages 162–169, 2005.

[38] Mark D. Smucker, James Allan, and Ben Carterette. A comparison of statistical significance tests for information retrieval evaluation. In *16th ACM Conference on Conference on Information and Knowledge Management*, pages 623–632, 2007.

[39] Mark D. Smucker and Charles L. A. Clarke. Modeling user variance in time-biased gain. In *6th Internation Symposium on Human-Computer Interaction and Information Retrieval*, pages 3:1–3:10, 2012.

[40] Mark D. Smucker and Charles L. A. Clarke. Stochastic simulation of time-biased gain. In *21st ACM International Conference on Information and Knowledge Management*, pages 2040–2044, 2012.

[41] Mark D. Smucker and Charles L.A. Clarke. Time-based calibration of effectiveness measures. In *35th International ACM SIGIR Conference on Research and Development in Information Retrieval*, pages 95–104, 2012.

[42] Ian Soboroff, Charles Nicholas, and Patrick Cahan. Ranking retrieval systems without relevance judgments. In *24th Annual International ACM SIGIR Conference on Research and Development in Information Retrieval*, pages 66–73, 2001.

[43] Karen Sparck Jones and C. J. van Rijsbergen. Information retrieval test collections. *Journal of Documentation*, 32(1):59–75, 1976.

[44] Jean Tague-Sutcliffe. The pragmatics of information retrieval evaluation. In *Information Retrieval Experiment: Experiment*, pages 59–102. Butterworth-Heinemann, 1981.

[45] Jean Tague-Sutcliffe. The pragmatics of information retrieval experimentation, revisited. *Readings in Information Retrieval*, pages 205–216, 1997.

[46] Ellen M. Voorhees. Variations in relevance judgments and the measurement of retrieval effectiveness. *Information Processing & Management*, 36(5):697–716, 2000.

[47] Ellen M. Voorhees and Donna K. Harman. *TREC: Experiment and Evaluation in Information Retrieval.* MIT Press, 2005.

[48] William Webber, Alistair Moffat, and Justin Zobel. Statistical power in retrieval experimentation. In *17th ACM Conference on Information and Knowledge Management*, pages 571–580, 2008.

[49] Emine Yilmaz and Javed A. Aslam. Estimating average precision when judgments are incomplete. *International Journal of Knowledge and Information Systems*, 16(2):173–211, August 2008.

[50] Emine Yilmaz, Evangelos Kanoulas, and Javed A. Aslam. A simple and efficient sampling method for estimating AP and NDCG. In *31st Annual International ACM SIGIR Conference on Research and Development in Information Retrieval*, pages 603–610, 2008.

[51] Emine Yilmaz, Milad Shokouhi, Nick Craswell, and Stephen Robertson. Expected browsing utility for web search evaluation. In *19th ACM International Conference on Information and Knowledge Management*, pages 1561–1564, 2010.

[52] Emine Yilmaz, Manisha Verma, Nick Craswell, Filip Radlinski, and Peter Bailey. Relevance and effort: An analysis of document utility. In *23rd ACM International Conference on Conference on Information and Knowledge Management*, pages 91–100, 2014.

[53] Yuye Zhang, Laurence A. Park, and Alistair Moffat. Click-based evidence for decaying weight distributions in search effectiveness metrics. *Information Retrieval*, 13:46–69, February 2010.

Information Retrieval with Verbose Queries

Manish Gupta
Microsoft
gmanish@microsoft.com

Michael Bendersky
Google, Inc.
bemike@google.com

1. COVER SHEET

Proposed duration is a full-day tutorial. The current plan is to divide the tutorial into two main parts, each focusing on applications of the discussed techniques to verbose natural language queries.
1. Query reduction, reformulation and segmentation techniques.
2. Query concept weighting, expansion and learning-to-rank.

Contact Information

Manish Gupta (main contact):
Email: gmanish@microsoft.com
Address: 3B6014, Microsoft Building 3, Microsoft Campus, Gachibowli, Hyderabad-500032, India.

Michael Bendersky
Email: bemike@google.com
Address: Google, 1600 Amphitheatre Parkway, Mountain View, CA 94043.

Intended Audience

Information retrieval with verbose natural language queries has gained a lot of interest in recent years both from the research community and the industry. Search with verbose queries is one of the key challenges for many of the current most advanced search platforms, including question answering systems (Watson or Wolfram Alpha), mobile personal assistants (Siri, Cortana and Google Now), and entity-based search engines (Facebook Graph Search or Knowledge Graph). Therefore, we believe that a tutorial on this topic at SIGIR is very timely and will attract a lot of interest from all conference participants.

Researchers in the field of analysis of search queries will benefit the most, as this tutorial will give them an exhaustive overview of the research in the direction of handling verbose web queries. We believe that the tutorial will give the newcomers a complete picture of the current work, introduce important research topics in this field, and inspire them to learn more. Practitioners and people from the industry will clearly benefit from the discussions both from the methods perspective, as well from the point of view of applications where such mechanisms are starting to be applied.

After the tutorial, the audience will be able to appreciate and understand the following: (1) What are the interesting properties of complex natural language verbose queries; (2) Challenges in effective information retrieval with verbose queries; (3) State-of-the-art techniques for verbose query transformations that yield better expected search performance; (4) State-of-the-art ranking methods for verbose queries, including supervised learning-to-rank methods (5) What user/industry segments can be affected by better retrieval with verbose queries and what are the possible applications.

Pre-requisites: Introductory-level knowledge in information retrieval, query log mining, web mining, algorithms, natural language processing and machine learning.

Brief Biography

Manish Gupta (*Homepage Link*) is a Senior Applied Scientist at the Bing team in Microsoft India R&D Private Limited at Hyderabad, India. He is also an Adjunct Faculty at International Institute of Information Technology, Hyderabad. He received his Masters in Computer Science from IIT Bombay in 2007 and his Ph.D. from the University of Illinois at Urbana-Champaign in 2013. Before this, he worked for Yahoo! Bangalore for two years. His research interests are in the areas of web mining, data mining and information retrieval. He has published more than 30 research papers in referred journals and conferences, including WWW, SIGIR, ICDE, KDD, PKDD, SDM conferences. He has also co-authored a book on Outlier Detection for Temporal Data.

Manish has an extensive experience in offering tutorials at top conferences. Following is a list of recent tutorials he has offered.

- **Manish Gupta**, Rui Li, Kevin C. Chang. Towards a Social Media Analytics Platform: Event and Location Detection for Microblogs. *WWW 2014*.
- **Manish Gupta**, Jing Gao, Charu Aggarwal, Jiawei Han. Outlier Detection for Temporal Data. *CIKM 2013*.
- **Manish Gupta**, Jing Gao, Charu Aggarwal, Jiawei Han. Outlier Detection for Graph Data. *ASONAM 2013*.
- **Manish Gupta**, Jing Gao, Charu Aggarwal, Jiawei Han. Outlier Detection for Temporal Data. *SDM 2013*.

He also taught a full credit course on "Web Mining" at IIIT-Hyderabad, India in 2013 and in 2014. He also participated in the organization of CMU Winter School in 2014.

Michael Bendersky (*Homepage Link*) is a Senior Software Engineer at Google, where he works on organizing the world's information and making it universally accessible and useful. He received his Ph.D. from the University of Massachusetts Amherst in 2012. Michael published more than 20 research papers on information retrieval with verbose natural language queries. His paper "Discovering Key Concepts in Verbose Queries", published at SIGIR 2008, has been widely cited as one of the seminal works in this research area. Since then, his papers on query segmentation, query

SIGIR'15, August 09-13, 2015, Santiago, Chile.
ACM 978-1-4503-3621-5/15/08.
DOI: http://dx.doi.org/10.1145/2766462.2767877.

expansion and query representations for information retrieval appeared at top-tier academic conferences, including SIGIR, CIKM, WSDM, WWW, ACL and SIGKDD.

Michael co-organized a successful series of workshops on "Query Representation and Understanding" held at SIGIR 2010 and 2011. He also served as a publicity chair for the WSDM 2014 conference.

2. MOTIVATION

Recently, the focus of many novel search applications shifted from short keyword queries to verbose natural language queries. Examples include question answering systems and dialogue systems, voice search on mobile devices and entity search engines like Facebook's Graph Search or Google's Knowledge Graph. However the performance of textbook information retrieval techniques for such verbose queries is not as good as that for their shorter counterparts. Thus, effective handling of verbose queries has become a critical factor for adoption of information retrieval techniques in this new breed of search applications.

Over the past decade, the information retrieval community has deeply explored the problem of transforming natural language verbose queries using operations like reduction, weighting, expansion, reformulation and segmentation into more effective structural representations. However, thus far, there was not a coherent and organized tutorial on this topic. In this tutorial, we aim to put together various research pieces of the puzzle, provide a comprehensive and structured overview of various proposed methods, and also list various application scenarios where effective verbose query processing can make a significant difference.

3. OBJECTIVES

After the tutorial, the audience will be able to appreciate and understand the following: (1) What are the interesting properties of complex natural language verbose queries; (2) Challenges in effective information retrieval with verbose queries; (3) State-of-the-art techniques for verbose query transformations that yield better expected search performance; (4) State-of-the-art ranking methods for verbose queries, including supervised learning-to-rank methods (5) What user/industry segments can be affected by better retrieval with verbose queries and what are the possible applications.

4. RELEVANCE TO INFORMATION RETRIEVAL COMMUNITY

As can be seen from the long list of referenced papers, in this tutorial, we will organize related work done by the information retrieval community in the past decade, present it as a coherent story, and summarize the research advances in the field of information retrieval with verbose queries. Thus, it is clearly relevant to the IR community. The theme of the proposed tutorial is most related to the "Queries and Query Analysis" area of SIGIR 2015. It is also related to a successful series of workshops on "Query Representation and Understanding" held at SIGIR 2010 and 2011.

To the best of our knowledge, no previous tutorials have been offered on this research topic.

5. TOPICS OUTLINE

Here is a brief outline of the topics covered by the tutorial with relevant references.

- Properties of Verbose Queries: Length distribution of queries [2, 45], query types, distribution of mean reciprocal rank wrt query length, part-of-speech distribution, information need specificity [35], repetition factor [37], percentage of searches covered by top-K% queries [37], smoothing mechanisms [46].
- Query Reduction to a Single Sub-Query
  - Types of Sub-Query Candidates: Noun phrases [4], named entities [21], individual words [33, 34], two-term combinations [26], all word subsets [16, 21, 22, 23], word subsets with one word deleted [3, 20], matching queries from personal query log, POS blocks, one to three word queries without stopwords [29], right part of the query [19].
  - Feature Sets
    - Post-Retrieval Features: LambdaRank and BM25 scores of top-K documents [3], query quality, query scope [23], query clarity, standard deviation at 100 documents, a normalised version of standard deviation at 100 documents, the maximum standard deviation in the ranked-list, standard deviation using a variable cut-off point, query length normalized standard deviation using a variable cut-off point.
    - Word Dependency Features: Mutual information between words [21, 22], word co-occurrence in pseudo-relevant documents [29], binary dependencies [33], quasi-synchronous dependencies [34].
    - Query Log based Features: Query log frequency [4], similarity with old queries [20], deletion history, rareness.
    - Statistical Features: TF, IDF [4, 19, 23, 34], simplified clarity score [23], term-term co-occurence, term-topic co-occurence, term-term context, term-topic context [26].
    - Linguistic Features: POS [26, 34], named entities [21, 26], acronyms [26], isBrandName.
    - Query Features: Query length [3, 34], presence of stop words [3, 34], presence of URL [3], similarity with original query [23], isRightMost.
  - Ask for User Input: [21, 22].
  - Methods to Combine the Signals: Word graph construction [21, 22], clustering and rules based approach, classifier [4, 23], LambdaRank [3], stop structure identification [19], rules based approach [20], regression [26], random walk [29], RankSVM [33], quasi-synchronous dependency language model [34].
  - Efficiency Aspect: One word deletion [3, 20], randomly pick up a few sub-queries, overlapping search results and snippets [22].
- Query Reduction by Choosing Multiple Sub-Queries
  - Subset Distributions using CRF-perf [40, 42].
  - Reformulation Trees with Subset Selection and Query Substitution Operations [41].
- Weighting Query Concepts
  - Regression [25, 47].
  - Sequential Dependence Model using Markov Random Fields [30].
  - Integrating Regression Rank with Markov Random Fields (MRFs) [24].
  - Weighted Sequential Dependence Model [7].

- A Fixed-Point Method [31].
- Parameterized Query Expansion Model [8].
- Query Hypergraphs [5].
- Multiple Source Formulation [9].

- Query Expansion by Including Related Concepts
  - Adding ODP category label to queries.
  - Latent Concept Expansion using Pseudo-Relevance Feedback [8].
  - Selective Interactive Query Expansion [22].
  - Supervised models for pseudo-relevance term selection [12].
- Query Reformulation
  - Translation-based Language Model [43].
  - Random Walks: Query Log-based Term-Query Graph [11], Click Graph [36].
  - Using Anchor Text [15].
  - Question Reformulation Patterns from Query Logs [44].
  - Unified framework for query refinement [18].
- Query Segmentation
  - Statistical Segmentation using Category-wise N-Gram Frequencies [32].
  - Performing Segmentation jointly with Parts-of-speech Tagging and Capitalization [6].
  - Supervised Segmentation using Decision-boundary, Context and Dependency Features [10].
  - Unsupervised Segmentation using Generative Language Models and Wikipedia [38].
- Query-Dependent Learning-to-Rank
  - Query-Dependent Ranking Models [17].
  - Two Stage Learning-to-Rank Models [14].
  - Learning from Click Data [39, 13].
- Applications of Verbose Query Processing: Finding images for books [1], question answering [19, 43], searching for cancer information, patent searches, fact verification [27], natural language interface for databases [28], e-commerce [32], search queries from children, music search, queries from user selected text.
- Summary and Future Research Directions

Following is a list of related topics that we do *not* cover as part of this tutorial: (1) Automatic Speech Recognition (ASR), (2) Processing null queries other than verbose queries, (3) Query by Document, (4) Query processing tasks for short queries.

6. FORMAT AND DETAILED SCHEDULE

A tentative schedule based on a full-day tutorial is as follows.

- 9:00 – 10:30 Properties of Verbose Queries / Query Reduction
- 10:30 – 11:00 Coffee Break
- 11:00 – 12:30 Query Expansion, Reformulation and Segmentation Techniques
- 12:30 – 14:00 Lunch Break
- 14:00 – 15:30 Weighting Query Concepts
- 15:30 – 16:00 Coffee Break
- 16:00 – 17:30 Query-Dependent Learning-to-Rank, Applications, Summary, and Future Directions

7. TYPE OF SUPPORT MATERIALS

The attendees can download slides from `http://goo.gl/64wY0w` [Draft Version]

No additional equipment is needed.

8. RELEVANT REFERENCES

The following is a list of references which will be used in the preparation of the tutorial material. Many other papers will also be referred.

9. REFERENCES

[1] R. Agrawal, S. Gollapudi, A. Kannan, and K. Kenthapadi. Enriching Textbooks with Images. In *Proc. of the* 20th *ACM Intl. Conf. on Information and Knowledge Management (CIKM)*, pages 1847–1856, 2011.

[2] A. Arampatzis and J. Kamps. A Study of Query Length. In *Proc. of the* 31st *Annual Intl. ACM SIGIR Conf. on Research and Development in Information Retrieval (SIGIR)*, pages 811–812, 2008.

[3] N. Balasubramanian, G. Kumaran, and V. R. Carvalho. Exploring Reductions for Long Web Queries. In *Proc. of the* 33rd *Intl. ACM SIGIR Conf. on Research and Development in Information Retrieval (SIGIR)*, pages 571–578, 2010.

[4] M. Bendersky and W. B. Croft. Discovering Key Concepts in Verbose Queries. In *Proc. of the* 31st *Annual Intl. ACM SIGIR Conf. on Research and Development in Information Retrieval (SIGIR)*, pages 491–498, 2008.

[5] M. Bendersky and W. B. Croft. Modeling Higher-Order Term Dependencies in Information Retrieval using Query Hypergraphs. In *Proc. of the* 35th *Intl. ACM SIGIR Conf. on Research and Development in Information Retrieval (SIGIR)*, pages 941–950, 2012.

[6] M. Bendersky, W. B. Croft, and D. A. Smith. Joint Annotation of Search Queries. In *Proc. of the* 49th *Annual Meeting of the Association for Computational Linguistics: Human Language Technologies (HLT)*, pages 102–111, 2011.

[7] M. Bendersky, D. Metzler, and W. B. Croft. Learning Concept Importance using a Weighted Dependence Model. In *Proc. of the* 3rd *ACM Intl. Conf. on Web Search and Data Mining (WSDM)*, pages 31–40, 2010.

[8] M. Bendersky, D. Metzler, and W. B. Croft. Parameterized Concept Weighting in Verbose Queries. In *Proc. of the* 34th *Intl. ACM SIGIR Conf. on Research and Development in Information Retrieval (SIGIR)*, pages 605–614, 2011.

[9] M. Bendersky, D. Metzler, and W. B. Croft. Effective Query Formulation with Multiple Information Sources. In *Proc. of the* 5th *ACM Intl. Conf. on Web Search and Data Mining (WSDM)*, pages 443–452, 2012.

[10] S. Bergsma and Q. I. Wang. Learning Noun Phrase Query Segmentation. In *Proc. of the 2007 Joint Conf. on Empirical Methods in Natural Language Processing and Computational Natural Language Learning (EMNLP-CoNLL)*, volume 7, pages 819–826, 2007.

[11] F. Bonchi, R. Perego, F. Silvestri, H. Vahabi, and R. Venturini. Recommendations for the Long Tail by Term-Query Graph. In *Proc. of the* 20th *Intl. Conf. Companion on World Wide Web (WWW)*, pages 15–16, 2011.

[12] G. Cao, J.-Y. Nie, J. Gao, and S. Robertson. Selecting Good Expansion Terms for Pseudo-Relevance Feedback. In *Proc. of the 31st Annual Intl. ACM SIGIR Conf. on Research and Development in Information Retrieval (SIGIR)*, pages 243–250, 2008.
[13] V. Dang, M. Bendersky, and W. B. Croft. Learning to Rank Query Reformulations. In *Proc. of the 33rd Intl. ACM SIGIR Conf. on Research and Development in Information Retrieval (SIGIR)*, pages 807–808, 2010.
[14] V. Dang, M. Bendersky, and W. B. Croft. Two-Stage Learning to Rank for Information Retrieval. In *Proc. of the 35th European Conf. on IR Research on Advances in Information Retrieval (ECIR)*, pages 423–434. 2013.
[15] V. Dang and B. W. Croft. Query Reformulation using Anchor Text. In *Proc. of the 3rd ACM Intl. Conf. on Web Search and Data Mining (WSDM)*, pages 41–50, 2010.
[16] S. Datta and V. Varma. Tossing Coins to Trim Long Queries. In *Proc. of the 34th Intl. ACM SIGIR Conf. on Research and Development in Information Retrieval (SIGIR)*, pages 1255–1256, 2011.
[17] X. Geng, T.-Y. Liu, T. Qin, A. Arnold, H. Li, and H.-Y. Shum. Query Dependent Ranking using K-Nearest Neighbor. In *Proc. of the 31st Annual Intl. ACM SIGIR Conf. on Research and Development in Information Retrieval (SIGIR)*, pages 115–122, 2008.
[18] J. Guo, G. Xu, H. Li, and X. Cheng. A Unified and Discriminative Model for Query Refinement. In *Proc. of the 31st Annual Intl. ACM SIGIR Conf. on Research and Development in Information Retrieval (SIGIR)*, pages 379–386, 2008.
[19] S. Huston and W. B. Croft. Evaluating Verbose Query Processing Techniques. In *Proc. of the 33rd Intl. ACM SIGIR Conf. on Research and Development in Information Retrieval (SIGIR)*, pages 291–298, 2010.
[20] R. Jones and D. C. Fain. Query Word Deletion Prediction. In *Proc. of the 26th Annual Intl. ACM SIGIR Conf. on Research and Development in Informaion Retrieval (SIGIR)*, pages 435–436, 2003.
[21] G. Kumaran and J. Allan. A Case For Shorter Queries, and Helping Users Create Them. In *Proc. of the Human Language Technologies: The Annual Conference of the North American Chapter of the Association for Computational Linguistics (HLT-NAACL)*, pages 220–227, 2007.
[22] G. Kumaran and J. Allan. Effective and Efficient User Interaction for Long Queries. In *Proc. of the 31st Annual Intl. ACM SIGIR Conf. on Research and Development in Information Retrieval (SIGIR)*, pages 11–18, 2008.
[23] G. Kumaran and V. R. Carvalho. Reducing Long Queries using Query Quality Predictors. In *Proc. of the 32nd Intl. ACM SIGIR Conf. on Research and Development in Information Retrieval (SIGIR)*, pages 564–571, 2009.
[24] M. Lease. An Improved Markov Random Field Model for Supporting Verbose Queries. In *Proc. of the 32nd Intl. ACM SIGIR Conf. on Research and Development in Information Retrieval (SIGIR)*, pages 476–483, 2009.
[25] M. Lease, J. Allan, and W. B. Croft. Regression Rank: Learning to Meet the Opportunity of Descriptive Queries. In *Proc. of the 31th European Conf. on IR Research on Advances in Information Retrieval (ECIR)*, pages 90–101, 2009.
[26] C.-J. Lee, R.-C. Chen, S.-H. Kao, and P.-J. Cheng. A Term Dependency-based Approach for Query Terms Ranking. In *Proc. of the 18th ACM Conf. on Information and Knowledge Management (CIKM)*, pages 1267–1276, 2009.
[27] C. W. Leong and S. Cucerzan. Supporting Factual Statements with Evidence from the Web. In *Proc. of the 21st ACM Intl. Conf. on Information and Knowledge Management (CIKM)*, pages 1153–1162, 2012.
[28] Y. Li, H. Yang, and H. Jagadish. Constructing a Generic Natural Language Interface for an XML Database. In *Proc. of the 2006 Conf. on Advances in Database Technology (EDBT)*, pages 737–754, 2006.
[29] K. T. Maxwell and W. B. Croft. Compact Query Term Selection using Topically Related Text. In *Proc. of the 36th Intl. ACM SIGIR Conf. on Research and Development in Information Retrieval (SIGIR)*, pages 583–592, 2013.
[30] D. Metzler and W. B. Croft. A Markov Random Field Model for Term Dependencies. In *Proc. of the 28th Annual Intl. ACM SIGIR Conf. on Research and Development in Information Retrieval (SIGIR)*, pages 472–479, 2005.
[31] J. H. Paik and D. W. Oard. A Fixed-Point Method for Weighting Terms in Verbose Informational Queries. In *Proc. of the 23rd ACM Conf. on Information and Knowledge Management (CIKM)*, pages 131–140, 2014.
[32] N. Parikh, P. Sriram, and M. Al Hasan. On Segmentation of E-Commerce Queries. In *Proc. of the 22nd ACM Intl. Conf. on Information and Knowledge Management (CIKM)*, pages 1137–1146, 2013.
[33] J. H. Park and W. B. Croft. Query Term Ranking based on Dependency Parsing of Verbose Queries. In *Proc. of the 33rd Intl. ACM SIGIR Conf. on Research and Development in Information Retrieval (SIGIR)*, pages 829–830, 2010.
[34] J. H. Park, W. B. Croft, and D. A. Smith. A Quasi-Synchronous Dependence Model for Information Retrieval. In *Proc. of the 20th ACM Intl. Conf. on Information and Knowledge Management (CIKM)*, pages 17–26, 2011.
[35] N. Phan, P. Bailey, and R. Wilkinson. Understanding the Relationship of Information Need Specificity to Search Query Length. In *Proc. of the 30th Annual Intl. ACM SIGIR Conf. on Research and Development in Information Retrieval (SIGIR)*, pages 709–710, 2007.
[36] D. Sheldon, M. Shokouhi, M. Szummer, and N. Craswell. LambdaMerge: Merging the Results of Query Reformulations. In *Proc. of the 4th ACM Intl. Conf. on Web Search and Data Mining (WSDM)*, pages 795–804, 2011.
[37] G. Singh, N. Parikh, and N. Sundaresan. Rewriting Null E-Commerce Queries to Recommend Products. In *Proc. of the 21st Intl. Conf. Companion on World Wide Web (WWW)*, pages 73–82, 2012.
[38] B. Tan and F. Peng. Unsupervised Query Segmentation using Generative Language Models and Wikipedia. In *Proc. of the 17th Intl. Conf. on World Wide Web (WWW)*, pages 347–356, 2008.
[39] W. Wu, H. Li, and J. Xu. Learning Query and Document Similarities from Click-through Bipartite Graph with Metadata. In *Proc. of the 6th ACM Intl. Conf. on Web Search and Data Mining (WSDM)*, pages 687–696, 2013.
[40] X. Xue and W. B. Croft. Modeling Subset Distributions for Verbose Queries. In *Proc. of the 34th Intl. ACM SIGIR Conf. on Research and Development in Information Retrieval (SIGIR)*, pages 1133–1134, 2011.
[41] X. Xue and W. B. Croft. Generating Reformulation Trees for Complex Queries. In *Proc. of the 35th Intl. ACM SIGIR Conf. on Research and Development in Information Retrieval (SIGIR)*, pages 525–534, 2012.
[42] X. Xue, S. Huston, and W. B. Croft. Improving Verbose Queries using Subset Distribution. In *Proc. of the 19th ACM Intl. Conf. on Information and Knowledge Management (CIKM)*, pages 1059–1068, 2010.
[43] X. Xue, J. Jeon, and W. B. Croft. Retrieval Models for Question and Answer Archives. In *Proc. of the 31st Annual Intl. ACM SIGIR Conf. on Research and Development in Information Retrieval (SIGIR)*, pages 475–482, 2008.
[44] X. Xue, Y. Tao, D. Jiang, and H. Li. Automatically Mining Question Reformulation Patterns from Search Log Data. In *Proc. of the 50th Annual Meeting of the Association for Computational Linguistics (ACL)*, pages 187–192, 2012.
[45] J. Yi and F. Maghoul. Mobile Search Pattern Evolution: The Trend and the Impact of Voice Queries. In *Proc. of the 20th Intl. Conf. Companion on World Wide Web (WWW)*, pages 165–166, 2011.
[46] C. Zhai and J. Lafferty. A Study of Smoothing Methods for Language Models applied to Ad hoc Information Retrieval. In *Proc. of the 24th Annual Intl. ACM SIGIR Conf. on Research and Development in Information Retrieval (SIGIR)*, pages 334–342, 2001.
[47] L. Zhao and J. Callan. Term Necessity Prediction. In *Proc. of the 19th ACM Intl. Conf. on Information and Knowledge Management (CIKM)*, pages 259–268, 2010.

Revisiting the Foundations of IR: Timeless, Yet Timely

Paul B. Kantor
Rutgers University and CCICADA
96 Frelinghuysen Dr., Piscataway NJ 08854-8018 USA
732-322-8412 paul.kantor@rutgers.edu

ABSTRACT

As we face an explosion of potential new applications for the fundamental concepts and technologies of information retrieval, ranging from ad ranking to social media, from collaborative recommending to question answering systems, many researchers are spending unnecessary time reinventing ideas and relationships that are buried in the prehistory of information retrieval (which, for many researchers, means anything published before they entered graduate school).

Much of today's received wisdom may be nothing more than the fossilized residue of lively debates concerning such things as . estimation of value and evaluation of systems. Returning to those discussions may open the door to genuinely new insights.

On the other hand, of the ideas that surface as "new" in today's super-heated research environment have very firm roots in earlier developments in fields as diverse as citation analysis, statistics, and pattern recognition. The purpose of this tutorial is to survey those roots, and their relation to the contemporary fruits on the tree of information retrieval, and to separate, as much as is possible in an era of increasing commercial secrecy about methods, the problems to be solved, the algorithms for solving them, and the heuristics that are the bread and butter of a working operation.

Among the important new topics whose foundations will be explored are the use of social media in search and advertising, and the growing management of personal image collections for search and for commercial purposes.

While some might think that an examination of the roots is of merely historical interest, it has practical value as well. When you know which earlier research has provided the origins for the things that you are interested in, you can use that fact to trace its other descendents, and often find rich and rewarding ideas in a literature that you would not normally reach, because it was not considered important by your instructors when you were learning about the problems. In addition to pattern recognition and citation analysis, the tutorial will also expose and review some of the relations to the fields of statistics and operations research.

Participants will become familiar with roots in Pattern Analysis, Statistics, Information Science and other sources of key ideas that reappear in the current development of Information Retrieval as it applies to Search Engines, Social Media, and Collaborative Systems. They will be able to separate problems from algorithms, and algorithms from heuristics, in the application of these ideas to their own research and/or development activities. Course materials will be made available on a Web site two weeks prior to the tutorial. They will include links to relevant software; links to publications that will be discussed; and mechanisms for chat among the tutorial participants, before, during and after the tutorial.

Specific Topics will include:

1. The earliest "automated retrieval;
2. Vectors and Logarithms: their pragmatic origins;
3. Probabilistic approaches. A frequentist foundation;
4. The quest for a theoretical foundation;
5. Generative approaches;
6. Network approaches;
7. Binding approaches together.

Certain materials that are very hard to find, including foundational IBM technical reports by H.P. Luhn and I.J. Good will be scanned and placed on a web site for the tutorial. Since this will not be a public site, we will need some information on advance registration to add participants to the site.

SIGIR '15, August 09-13, 2015, Santiago, Chile
ACM 978-1-4503-3621-5/15/08. http://dx.doi.org/10.1145/2766462.2767878

Categories and Subject Descriptors
H.3.0 General; H.3.3 Information Search and Retrieval

General Terms: Algorithms, Measurement, Performance, Theory

Keywords: Foundations of Information Retrieval

1 Overview and Rationale

The purpose of this tutorial is to survey those roots, and their relation to the contemporary fruits on the tree of information retrieval, and to separate, as much as is possible in an era of increasing secrecy about methods, the problems to be solved, the algorithms for solving them, and the heuristics that are the bread and butter of a working operation.

2 Relevance to the Information Retrieval Community

While some might think that an examination of the roots is of merely historical interest, it has practical value as well. When you know which earlier research has provided the origins for the things that you are interested in, you can use that fact to trace its other descendants, and often find rich and rewarding ideas in a literature that you would not normally reach, because it was not considered important by your instructors when you were learning about the problems. In addition to pattern recognition and citation analysis, the tutorial will also expose and review some of the relations to the fields of statistics and operations research.

3 Course Objectives

Participants will become familiar with roots in Pattern Analysis, Statistics, Information Science and other sources of key ideas that reappear in the current development of Information Retrieval as it applies to Search Engines, Social Media, and Collaborative Systems. They will be able to separate problems from algorithms, and algorithms from heuristics, in the application of these ideas to their own research and/or development activities.

4 Outline of the Tutorial

1. The earliest "automated retrieval:
    - A. Origins in the American Chemical Society research
    - B. Kent experiments;
    - C. Sets and modifications
        - (i) Boole combinations
        - (ii) Quorum type rules rules;
    - D. Key word selection
    - E. *Luhn; ranking texts*
        - (i) the origins of *tf*
        - (ii) the origins of *idf*
    - F. Ranking and retrieval
2. Vectors and Logarithms: their pragmatic origins
    - A. Weighting the Importance of Features
    - B. Controlling for document size
        - (i) Salton and the ray space approach
        - (ii) Fox's metrics
        - (iii) "Pivoting and Singhal
    - C. The unreasonable introduction of logarithms
    - D. Is there a "vector space of documents and queries"
        - (i) Queries as dual spaces
        - (ii) Non Euclidean metrics
    - E. Patterns in spaces
        - (i) Linear subspaces
        - (ii) Manifolds
        - (iii) Relative densities – relation to sensor problems
3. Probabilistic approaches. A frequentist foundation
    - A. Maron and Kuhns
    - B. One user among many – the "system orientation?"
    - C. One document and one users – subjective probability
    - D. One user and a feature-based class of documents
        - (i) The "cluster hypothesis"
        - (ii) The "smoothness of relevance"
    - E. Research in Pattern Recognition
        - (i) Estimating densities empirically
4. The quest for a theoretical foundation:
    - A. I.J. Good and the weight of evidence. The *"bin"*
        - (i) odds of relevance
        - (ii) the relevance of log-odds
    - B. Robertson and Sparck-Jones
        - (i) explaining" term weighting
        - (ii) estimating parameters from data
    - C. Naïve but successful
        - (i) Is there a "deep reason"?
        - (ii) Robertson and "BM25".
        - (iii) Hierarchical models
5. Generative approaches: Language models and topic modeling
    - A. A new layer of formalism
    - B. hidden relations to the older views
    - C. characterizing a literature, a topic or an interest
    - D. Conjugate distributions and hyperparameters
    - E. Mixtures of distributions
    - F. Random numbers of random variables.
6. Network approaches:
    - A. Graph theory and IR
    - A. Origins in citation studies
        - (i) Impact Factor
        - (ii) Network instabilities
        - (iii) Co-citation analysis
    - B. Warren; Garfield; Small; Narin;
    - C. Kleinberg. Directed graphs. Hubs and authorities
    - D. Brin & Page: Page Rank
    - E. Ask.com and the "media war"
    - *F.* Networks social and other for information finding
        - (i) Folksonomies and Tagging
        - (ii) Association of persons
        - (iii) Privacy and social stability.
7. Binding approaches together:
    - A. No one method works
    - B. The kinds of synthesis
        - (i) Feature expansion
        - (ii) Rule combination
    - C. The scope of synthesis
        - (i) Global
        - (ii) User-dependent
        - (iii) Task-dependent
    - D. Usage as a meta-feature
        - (i) Covert collection
        - (ii) Overt cooperation
8. Wild Speculations Can there be a theory of how information and users interact? Brains without brain models?
    - A. Quantum formulations: information collapses the users' wave function
    - B. HOTT (HOmotopy Type Theory): user experience as a path in info. space
    - C. An Appreciation of IJ Good.

5 Course Materials

Course materials will be made available on a Web site two weeks prior to the tutorial. They will include links to **relevant software**; links to **publications** that will be discussed; and mechanisms for **chat** among the tutorial participants, before, during and after the tutorial.

6 Some Relevant Monographs and Papers

[1] R.O. Duda, P.E. Hart, and D.G. Stork. Pattern classification. 2001.

[2] Geman, S. & Geman, D., 1984. Stochastic relaxation, Gibbs distributions, and the Bayesian restoration of images. Pattern Analysis and Machine Intelligence, IEEE Transactions on, (6), pp.721–741.

[3] I.J. Good. Probability and the Weighing of Evidence. Griffin, 1950.

[4] I.J. Good. Rational decisions. Journal of the Royal Statistical Society. Series B (Methodological), 14(1):107{114, 1952.

[5] I.J. Good. Maximum entropy for hypothesis formulation, especially for multidimensional contingency tables. The Annals of Mathematical Statistics, 34(3):911{934, 1963.

[6] IJ Good and RA Gaskins. Nonparametric roughness penalties for probability densities. Biometrika, 58(2):255{277, 1971.

[7] T. Hastie, R. Tibshirani, and J.H. Friedman. The elements of statistical learning: data mining, inference, and prediction. Springer Verlag, 2009.

[8] H.P. Luhn. A statistical approach to mechanized encoding and searching of literary information. IBM Journal of research and development, 1(4):309{317, 1957.

[9] H.P. Luhn. A business intelligence system. IBM Journal of Research and Development, 2(4):314{319, 1958.

[10] H.P. Luhn. The automatic creation of literature abstracts. IBM Journal of research and development, 2(2):159{165, 1958.

[11] P. Massart. The Tight Constant in the Dvoretzky-Kiefer-Wolfowitz Inequality. Ann. Probab. Volume 18, Number 3 (1990), 1269-1283

[12] Bishop, Christopher M. Pattern Recognition and Machine Learning. 1st ed. 2006. Corr. 2nd printing, 2006, XX, 740 p. 304 illus. in color. Springer

7 Selected Readings

Certain materials that are very hard to find, such as some papers by H.P. Luhn and I.J. Good will be scanned and placed on a web site for the tutorial. Since this will not be a public site, we will need some information on advance registration to add participants to the site.

ACKNOWLEDGMENTS

Thanks to John Prager and the Library at IBM for providing the classic papers.

IR Evaluation: Designing an End-to-End Offline Evaluation Pipeline

Jin Young Kim
Microsoft
jink@microsoft.com

Emine Yilmaz
University College London
emine.yilmaz@ucl.ac.uk

ABSTRACT

This tutorial aims to provide attendees with a detailed understanding of end-to-end evaluation pipeline based on human judgments (offline measurement).

The tutorial will give an overview of the state of the art methods, techniques, and metrics necessary for each stage of evaluation process. We will mostly focus on evaluating an information retrieval (search) system, but the other tasks such as recommendation and classification will also be discussed. Practical examples will be drawn both from the literature and from real world usage scenarios in industry.

Keywords

evaluation; measures; crowdsourcing; human judges; experiment design

1. TUTORIAL OBJECTIVES

The primary learning objectives of the tutorial are:

- Provide participants a thorough understanding of the full workflow and the methodological decisions involved in a human judge based (offline) measurement process.
- Provide a review of the state of the art relating to each step of the evaluation process, covering topics such as sampling methods, experiment and metric design, human (judge) resource management, judging interface design, and methods for the evaluation of judgments and metrics.
- Provide participants with further insights on offline measurement by means of real world examples and practical considerations both from the literature and from industry.
- Enable participants to make informed decisions on experiment design choices, metric selections, sampling methods and judging system designs based on their own needs.

ACM 978-1-4503-3621-5/15/08.
DOI: http://dx.doi.org/10.1145/2766462.2767875 .

2. BACKGROUND

Evaluation methodologies have played a significant role in the development of information retrieval and knowledge management systems. Human judgments, and evaluation metrics based on human judgments are critical to the advancement of a wide range of applications that rely on labelled data, such as those that make use of machine learning techniques, e.g., search, recommendation, etc. The labels and evaluation metrics guide the design of a technique, or directly become an objective function on which algorithms are trained.

However, designing suitable metrics, labelling systems and designing complete evaluation workflows and experiments from which reasonable and reliable conclusions can be drawn is no trivial matter. There are many decisions that need to be made when the quality of a system is evaluated, such as which metrics to use, how to obtain a representative sample of tasks, how to collect high-quality human judgments, etc. Erroneous or biased labels or unsuitable metrics can not only invalidate the evaluation of a system, but they can also cause serious issues when used in the training of machine learning components of the system.

In this tutorial, we aim to cover the theory and practice of human judgment based evaluation, including topics such as experiment and task design, human label collection, metric selection and evaluation. We review the end-to-end process of judgment-based evaluation and detail each step of the workflow. We first illustrate the basic principles in designing an offline evaluation experiment. We then describe the key stages, such as metric selection, query (or task) sampling, judging interface design, judge training, evaluation of the adopted metrics and the experiments.

3. SCOPE

This tutorial should be of interest to a wide range of SIGIR attendees. Many (if not most) SIGIR participants work on areas where the use of human judgments is indispensable for evaluation, including information retrieval (IR), information extraction, recommender systems, and so on. IR in particular has a long and rich tradition of label-based evaluation, and many of the techniques for IR evaluation are applicable to other fields.

This tutorial will provide a broad overview of the state-of-the-art, both in the theory and practice of human label based evaluation of search and other types of intelligent algorithms. Through this tutorial, those new to the concept of evaluation will come away with a solid understanding of how to design human judgment based evaluation experiments, while those with intermediate knowledge will gain deeper insights and further understanding of the mechanisms used in different stages of the evaluation process.

4. OUTLINE

- Designing Offline Measurements (20 mins) [23, 24, 25, 26, 27, 33, 34]
  - Introduction to measurement
  - Evaluation process overview
  - Major components: task, judgment, metric and experiment
  - When to use users (online) vs. judges (offline) for measurement
- Metrics for Offline Measurement (50 mins)
  - Experiment design
    * Understanding goals, criteria and requirements
    * Workflow design
  - Task sampling [27, 28, 29, 30, 31, 32, 35, 36, 37, 38]
    * Sampling criteria
    * Recent advances in task sampling (e.g., Priority queue)
  - Metric selection
    * Metric choices by model [6, 27, 39, 46, 47]
      · User model based metrics [11, 13, 20]
      · System based metrics [14, 15, 16]
    * Metric choices based on label type (absolute vs preference rating) [7, 22, 40]
    * Metrics choices based on metric properties [41, 42, 43, 44, 45]
      · Fidelity
      · Sensitivity
      · Reliability
      · Cross-metric agreement [1, 2]
    * Metrics for other tasks
  - Hypothesis testing for evaluation [48, 49]
- Break (20 minutes)
- Human Judgments for Offline Measurement (60 minutes)
  - Judging system design [3, 7, 8, 9, 10, 19, 22]
    * Lab versus online
    * UI design
    * Guidelines
  - Judge hiring & training [56, 57, 58, 59]
    * In-house vs crowdsourcing
    * Recruitment and incentives
    * Training
  - Online or adaptive judging workflows
    * Early stopping
    * Task and judge selection algorithms
  - Analysis & evaluation [21, 54, 55]
    * Judging noise and bias
    * Judging quality vs metrics and evaluation outcome
    * Statistical tools
- Practical Guide (30 minutes)
  - Examples from TREC [12, 27]
    * Evolution of the TREC Web Track judging process
  - Examples from Industry
    * Lessons from Bing offline measurement

5. TARGET AUDIENCE

The target audience includes any researchers and practitioners who have a need for human judge based evaluation, for example, to train or evaluate an IR system. Since we also cover many of recent papers in IR evaluation, this tutorial will be also helpful for those who wants to follow up on state-of-the-art research in this area. A college-level background in statistics is required and a basic domain knowledge in IR is helpful but not mandatory.

After attending the tutorial, we expect the audience to design, execute and evaluate human judge-based measurement for their need in an effective and efficient manner. They would be understand basic procedure, key decisions and trade-offs to make, and know where to look for when they need more guidance. Also, they will have some code to start with if they want to use some of the metrics explained.

6. PRESENTER BIOGRAPHIES

6.1 Jin Young Kim

Jin Young Kim graduated from UMass Amherst with Ph.D in Computer Science at 2012. His thesis focused on the retrieval and evaluation techniques for personal information. He is currently an Applied Researcher at Relevance Measurement team in Microsoft Bing, where he spends most of his time in improving the measurement of search quality, consulting on challenging measurement issues, establishing best practice on measurement across the company. He published dozens of papers in the area of ranking model, user modelling, and evaluation for IR. He was a lecturer for offline measurement in recent Microsoft internal course for new employees, and gave numerous talks in conferences including SIGIR, ECIR, CIKM, WSDM and WWW.

6.2 Emine Yilmaz

Emine Yilmaz is a lecturer (assistant professor) at the Computer Science Department of University College London. She is also working as a research consultant for Microsoft Research Cambridge. She obtained her Ph.D. from Northeastern University in 2008. Her main interests are information retrieval and applications of information theory, statistics and machine learning. She has published research papers extensively at major information retrieval venues such as SIGIR, CIKM and WSDM. She has previously given several tutorials on evaluation at the SIGIR 2012 and SIGIR 2010 Conferences and at the RuSSIR/EDBT Summer School in 2011. She has also organized several workshops on Crowdsourcing (WSDM2011, SIGIR 2011 and SIGIR 2010) and User Modeling for Retrieval Evaluation (SIGIR 2013). She has served as one of the organizers of the ICTIR Conference in 2009 and as the demo chair for the ECIR Conference in 2013.

7. REFERENCES

[1] Azzah Al-Maskari, Mark Sanderson, and Paul Clough, The relationship between IR effectiveness measures and user satisfaction. SIGIR '07.

[2] Al-Maskari, A., Sanderson, M., Clough, P., and Airio, E. The good and the bad system: does the test collection predict users' effectiveness? SIGIR '08.

[3] Peter Bailey et al., "Evaluating search systems using result page context," in IIiX, 2010.

[4] Ben Carterette. System effectiveness, user models, and user utility: a conceptual framework for investigation. SIGIR '11.

[5] Ben Carterette, Paul N. Bennett, David Maxwell Chickering, and Susan T. Dumais, "Here or There," in ECIR, 2008.

[6] Ben Carterette and Ian Soboroff. 2010. The effect of assessor error on IR system evaluation. SIGIR '10.

[7] Praveen Chandar and Ben Carterette. Using preference judgments for novel document retrieval. SIGIR '12.

[8] Chandar, P. and Carterette, B. Preference Based Evaluation Measures for Novelty and Diversity. SIGIR'13.

[9] Olivier Chapelle, Donald Metzler, Ya Zhang, and Pierre Grinspan. Expected reciprocal rank for graded relevance. CIKM '09.

[10] Charles L.A. Clarke, Maheedhar Kolla, Gordon V. Cormack, Olga Vechtomova, Azin Ashkan, Stefan Büttcher, Ian Mackinnon. Novelty and Diversity in Information Retrieval Evaluation. SIGIR '08.

[11] Nick Craswell, Onno Zoeter, Michael Taylor and Bill Ramsey. An experimental comparison of click position-bias models. WSDM '08.

[12] Steve Fox, Kuldeep Karnawat, Mark Mydland, Susan Dumais, and Thomas White. 2005. Evaluating implicit measures to improve web search. ACM Trans. Inf. Syst. 23, 2 (April 2005), 147-168.

[13] Peter B. Golbus , Javed A. Aslam , Charles L. Clarke, Increasing evaluation sensitivity to diversity, Information Retrieval, v.16 n.4, p.530-555, August 2013.

[14] Kalervo Järvelin and Jaana Kekäläinen. Cumulated gain-based evaluation of IR techniques. ACM TOIS, 20(4):422-446, October 2002.

[15] Katz, S. M. (1987). Estimation of probabilities from sparse data for the language model component of a speech recogniser. IEEE Transactions on Acoustics, Speech, and Signal Processing, 35(3), 400–401.

[16] Jinyoung Kim, Gabriella Kazai, and Imed Zitouni, Relevance Dimensions in Preference-based IR Evaluation. SIGIR '13.

[17] Alistair Moffat and Justin Zobel. Rank-biased precision for measurement of retrieval effectiveness. ACM Transactions on Information Systems, 27(1):2:1-2:27, December 2008.

[18] E. Pronin, "Perception and misperception of bias in human judgment," Trends in cognitive sciences, vol. 11, no. 1, pp. 37-43, 2007.

[19] Tetsuya Sakai and Ruihua Song. Evaluating diversified search results using per-intent graded relevance. SIGIR '11.

[20] Mark Sanderson, Monica Lestari Paramita, Paul Clough, and Evangelos Kanoulas, Do user preferences and evaluation measures line up? SIGIR '10.

[21] Falk Scholer, Diane Kelly, Wan-Ching Wu, Hanseul S. Lee, and William Webber. 2013. The effect of threshold priming and need for cognition on relevance calibration and assessment. SIGIR '13.

[22] Paul Thomas and David Hawking, Evaluation by comparing result sets in context, CIKM' 06.

[23] Jean Tague-Sutcliffe. The pragmatics of information retrieval evaluation. In Information Retrieval Experiment: Experiment, pages 59–102. Butterworth-Heinemann, 1981.

[24] Jean Tague-Sutcliffe. The pragmatics of information retrieval experimentation, revisited. Inf. Process. Management., 28(4):467–490, 1992.

[25] Jean Tague-Sutcliffe. The pragmatics of information retrieval experimentation, revisited. Readings in Information Retrieval. lnformation retrieval, pages 205–216, 1997.

[26] Ellen M. Voorhees. The philosophy of information retrieval evaluation. In CLEF '01: Revised Papes from the Second Workshop of the Cross-Language Evaluation Forum on Evaluation of Cross-Language Information Retrieval Systems, pages 355–370, London, UK, 2002. Springer-Verlag.

[27] Ellen M. Voorhees and Donna K. Harman. TREC: Experiment and Evaluation in Information Retrieval. MIT Press, 2005.

[28] Javed A. Aslam, Virgil Pavlu, and Emine Yilmaz. A statistical method for system evaluation using incomplete judgments. In SIGIR '06: Proceedings of the 29th annual international ACM SIGIR conference on Research and development in information retrieval, pages 541–548. ACM Press, August 2006.

[29] Ben Carterette, James Allan, and Ramesh Sitaraman. Minimal test collections for retrieval evaluation. In SIGIR '06: Proceedings of the 29th annual international ACM SIGIR conference on Research and development in information retrieval, pages 268–275, 2006.

[30] Ben Carterette and Rosie Jones. Evaluating search engines by modeling the relationship between relevance and clicks. In NIPS '07 : Proceedings of Advances in Neural Information Processing Systems, 2007.

[31] Ben Carterette, Virgil Pavlu, Evangelos Kanoulas, Javed A. Aslam, and James Allan. If i had a million queries. In Advances in Information Retrieval: 31st European Conference on IR Research, Lecture Notes in Computer Science. Springer-Verlag, April 2009.

[32] Matteo Cattelan and Stefano Mizzaro. IR evaluation without a common set of topics. In ICTIR '09: Proceedings of the 2nd International Conference on Theory of Information Retrieval, pages 342–345. Springer-Verlag, 2009.

[33] Filip Radlinski, Madhu Kurup, and Thorsten Joachims. How does clickthrough data reflect retrieval quality? In CIKM '08: Proceeding of the 17th ACM conference on Information and knowledge management, pages 43–52, New York, NY, USA, 2008. ACM.

[34] Kuansan Wang, Toby Walker, and Zijian Zheng. Pskip: estimating relevance ranking quality from web search clickthrough data. In KDD '09: Proceedings of the 15th ACM SIGKDD international conference on Knowledge discovery and data mining, pages 1355–1364, New York, NY, USA, 2009. ACM.

[35] Emine Yilmaz and Javed A. Aslam. Estimating average precision with incomplete and imperfect judgments. In Philip S. Yu, Vassilis Tsotras, Edward Fox, and Bing Liu, editors, Proceedings of the Fifteenth ACM International Conference on Information and Knowledge Management, pages 102–111. ACM Press, November 2006.

[36] Emine Yilmaz, Evangelos Kanoulas, and Javed A. Aslam. A simple and efficient sampling method for estimating AP and NDCG. In Sung-Hyon Myaeng, Douglas W. Oard, Fabrizio Sebastiani, Tat-Seng Chua, and Mun-Kew Leong, editors, SIGIR '08: Proceedings of the 31st Annual International ACM SIGIR Conference on Research and Development in Information Retrieval, pages 603–610. ACM Press, July 2008.

[37] Jianhan Zhu, JunWang, Vishwa Vinay, and Ingemar J. Cox. Topic (query) selection for IR evaluation. In SIGIR '09: Proceedings of the 32nd international ACM SIGIR conference on Research and development in information retrieval, pages 802–803, New York, NY, USA, 2009. ACM.

[38] Mehdi Hosseini, Ingemar J. Cox, Natasa Milic-Frayling, Milad Shokouhi, Emine Yilmaz: An uncertainty-aware query selection model for evaluation of IR systems. SIGIR 2012: 901-910

[39] Ben Carterette, Evangelos Kanoulas and Emine Yilmaz. Evaluating Web Retrieval Effectiveness". In Web Search Engine Research, chapter Evaluating Web Retrieval Effectiveness, Emerald Library and Information Science Book Series, 2011

[40] Paul N. Bennett, Ben Carterette, Olivier Chapelle, Thorsten Joachims: Beyond binary relevance: preferences, diversity, and set-level judgments. SIGIR Forum 42(2): 53-58 (2008)

[41] Javed A. Aslam, Emine Yilmaz, Virgiliu Pavlu: The maximum entropy method for analyzing retrieval measures. SIGIR 2005: 27-34

[42] Tetsuya Sakai: Evaluating evaluation metrics based on the bootstrap. SIGIR 2006: 525-532

[43] Voorhees, E. M. and Buckley, C.: The Effect of Topic Set Size on Retrieval Experiment Error, ACM SIGIR 2002 Proceedings, pp. 316-323, 2002.

[44] Sanderson, M. and Zobel, J.: Information Retrieval System Evaluation: Effort, Sensitivity, and Reliability, ACM SIGIR 2005 Proceedings, pp. 162-169, 2005.

[45] Chris Buckley and Ellen M. Voorhees. Evaluating evaluation measure stability. In SIGIR '00: Proceedings of the 23rd annual international ACM SIGIR conference on Research and development in information retrieval, pages 33–40, 2000.

[46] Olivier Chapelle, Donald Metlzer, Ya Zhang, Pierre Grinspan: Expected reciprocal rank for graded relevance. CIKM 2009: 621-630

[47] Emine Yilmaz, Milad Shokouhi, Nick Craswell, Stephen Robertson: Expected browsing utility for web search evaluation. CIKM 2010: 1561-1564

[48] Mark D. Smucker, James Allan, and Ben Carterette. A comparison of statistical significance tests for information retrieval evaluation. In CIKM '07: Proceedings of the sixteenth ACM conference on Conference on information and knowledge management, pages 623–632, New York, NY, USA, 2007. ACM.

[49] David Banks, Paul Over, and Nien-Fan Zhang. Blind men and elephants: Six approaches to TREC data. Information Retrieval Journal, 1(1-2):7–34, 1999.

[50] Mihai Georgescu and Xiaofei Zhu. 2014. Aggregation of Crowdsourced Labels Based on Worker History. In Proceedings of the 4th International Conference on Web Intelligence, Mining and Semantics (WIMS14).

[51] Matteo Venanzi, John Guiver, Gabriella Kazai, Pushmeet Kohli, and Milad Shokouhi. 2014. Community-based bayesian aggregation models for crowdsourcing. In Proceedings of the 23rd international conference on World wide web (WWW '14).

[52] Falk Scholer, Alistair Moffat, and Paul Thomas. 2013. Choices in batch information retrieval evaluation. In Proceedings of the 18th Australasian Document Computing Symposium (ADCS '13).

[53] Gabriella Kazai, Emine Yilmaz, Nick Craswell, and S.M.M. Tahaghoghi. 2013. User intent and assessor disagreement in web search evaluation. In Proceedings of the 22nd ACM international conference on Conference on information & knowledge management (CIKM '13).

[54] Luca Busin and Stefano Mizzaro. 2013. Axiometrics: An Axiomatic Approach to Information Retrieval Effectiveness Metrics. In Proceedings of the 2013 Conference on the Theory of Information Retrieval (ICTIR '13).

[55] Jinyang Gao, Xuan Liu, Beng Chin Ooi, Haixun Wang, and Gang Chen. 2013. An online cost sensitive decision-making method in crowdsourcing systems. In Proceedings of the 2013 ACM SIGMOD International Conference on Management of Data (SIGMOD '13).

[56] Djellel Eddine Difallah, Gianluca Demartini, and Philippe Cudré-Mauroux. 2013. Pick-a-crowd: tell me what you like, and i'll tell you what to do. In Proceedings of the 22nd international conference on World Wide Web (WWW '13).

[57] Omar Alonso. 2013. Implementing crowdsourcing-based relevance experimentation: an industrial perspective. Inf. Retr. 16, 2 (April 2013), 101-120.

[58] Gabriella Kazai, Jaap Kamps, and Natasa Milic-Frayling. 2013. An analysis of human factors and label accuracy in crowdsourcing relevance judgments. Inf. Retr. 16, 2 (April 2013), 138-178.

[59] Carsten Eickhoff and Arjen P. Vries. 2013. Increasing cheat robustness of crowdsourcing tasks. Inf. Retr. 16, 2 (April 2013), 121-137.

Music Retrieval and Recommendation

A Tutorial Overview

Peter Knees and Markus Schedl
Department of Computational Perception
Johannes Kepler University Linz
Altenberger Str. 69, 4040 Linz, Austria
peter.knees@jku.at, markus.schedl@jku.at

ABSTRACT

In this tutorial, we give an introduction to the field of and state of the art in music information retrieval (MIR). The tutorial particularly spotlights the question of music similarity, which is an essential aspect in music retrieval and recommendation. Three factors play a central role in MIR research: (1) the music content, i.e., the audio signal itself, (2) the music context, i.e., metadata in the widest sense, and (3) the listeners and their contexts, manifested in user-music interaction traces. We review approaches that extract features from all three data sources and combinations thereof and show how these features can be used for (large-scale) music indexing, music description, music similarity measurement, and recommendation. These methods are further showcased in a number of popular music applications, such as automatic playlist generation and personalized radio stationing, location-aware music recommendation, music search engines, and intelligent browsing interfaces. Additionally, related topics such as music identification, automatic music accompaniment and score following, and search and retrieval in the music production domain are discussed.

Categories and Subject Descriptors

H.5.5 [**Information Interfaces and Presentation**]: Sound and Music Computing—*Methodologies and techniques*; H.3.3 [**Information Storage and Retrieval**]: Information Search and Retrieval

Keywords

Music Information Retrieval; Music Recommendation; Content; Context; Listener

1. INTRODUCTION

As the amount of music available via streaming services, online stores, platforms like YouTube, and other web sources has skyrocketed over the last couple of years. Retrieving relevant music that matches the user's taste is a challenging, albeit important task to make accessible the ever-growing digital music repositories in an intelligent manner. Given the current rise of social media and user-generated contents, retrieving information about music as well as retrieving music itself heavily relies on text-based IR techniques, as text is still the widest used means of communication on the web. On the other hand, multimodal retrieval schemes for multimedia content demand for acoustic features and make hybrid (signal- and text-based) approaches attractive.

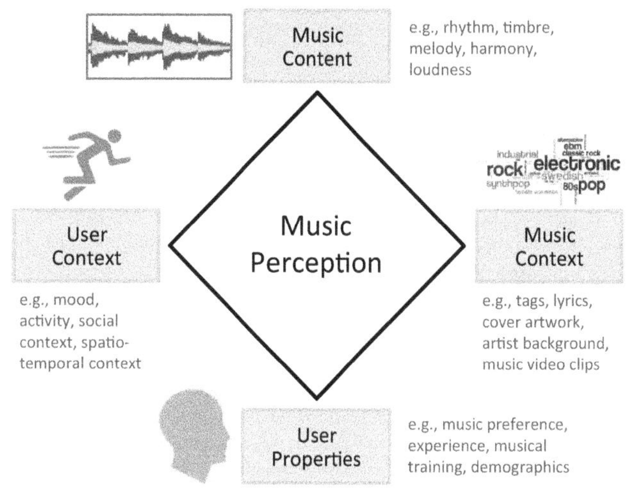

Figure 1: Four different categories of factors that influence music perception.

Music information retrieval (MIR) is a research field that aims – among other things – at automatically extracting semantically meaningful information from various representations of music entities, such as a digital audio file, a band's web page, a song's lyrics, or a tweet about a microblogger's current listening activity.

A key approach in MIR is to describe music via computational features, which can be broadly categorized into *music content*, *music context*, *user properties*, and *user context*, cf. Figure 1. While music content-based features are derived directly from the audio signal of the music file, music context refers to pieces of information that are not encoded in the actual audio file, nevertheless play an important role in human perception of music. Such aspects include the meaning of song lyrics, the background of an artist, the cover of an album, the sequence of songs selected by a DJ to constitute a playlist, or collaborative tags describing a release. Extract-

SIGIR'15, August 09-13, 2015, Santiago, Chile.
ACM 978-1-4503-3621-5/15/08.
DOI: http://dx.doi.org/10.1145/2766462.2767880.

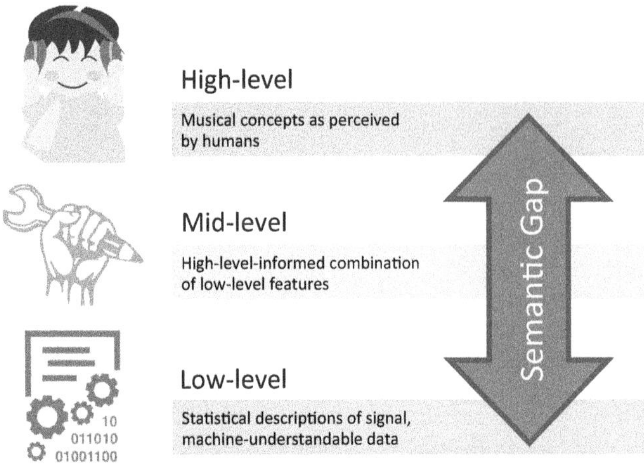

Figure 2: The different levels of feature abstraction and the "semantic gap" between them.

ing music content features requires access to the actual audio file; in contrast, contextual feature extractors require as input only editorial metadata (e.g., name of artist and song) to harvest music-related information from the web and consequently approximate similarities between music items. On the other hand, music content features are in general more objective than music context features as the underlying data source, i.e., the audio itself, does not change dynamically, in contrast to user-generated content or other kinds of contextual data sources. Both types of features (content and context), however, share a susceptibility to noise of different kinds. User properties refer to the listener's demographic information, musical education and experience, preferences and taste, as well as personality traits. The user context includes environmental aspects as well as physical and mental activities of the music listener. Particularly aspects of the latter two categories are often difficult to derive. Methods aiming at modeling these dimensions thus typically exploit traces of user-music interaction, such as listening histories or geo-location data, in order to learn a representation of (possibly latent) user state and context.

Depending on the chosen source, features might be closer to a concept as humans understand it (*high-level*) or closer to a strictly machine-interpretable representation (*low-level*). For instance, features derived from the music content or the sensor data captured with a user's personal device will be mostly statistical descriptions of signals that are difficult to interpret, i.e., low-level features, whereas information extracted from web sources, such as occurrences of words in web page texts, is typically easier to interpret. For all types of features in order to be processable, we need a numeric abstraction. Between these low-level numeric representations and the factors of musical perception that we want to model there is a discrepancy – commonly known as "semantic gap," cf. Figure 2. Particularly, the hybrid and user-centric techniques discussed strive to narrow this gap.

2. CONTENTS

MIR research has been seeing a paradigm shift over the last couple of years, as an increasing number of recently published approaches focus on the contextual feature categories, or at least combine audio-based techniques with data mined from web sources or the user's signals. This is reflected in the structure of the tutorial.

First, we introduce selected existing applications that rely on MIR technology to motivate the presented contents and relate them to real-world scenarios and applications, such as automated music playlist generation, personalized web radio, music recommendation systems, and intelligent user interfaces to music. Then, we summarize the ideas behind and discuss advantages and disadvantages of computational features extracted from music content and music context, as well as user-centric information. Each of these discussions is substantiated in a dedicated segment.

Regarding **music content** analysis, we give a brief introduction to signal processing methods (PCM, A/D Conversion, FFT, DCT, etc.) to lay the foundation for elaborated methods of music processing (e.g., [9]). We review some standard approaches to audio feature extraction on frame and block level as well as state-of-the-art similarity measures using features such as MFCCs [17], block-level features[29], and pitch class profiles [20]. We also briefly address features for related MIR tasks such as beat detection [4], melody extraction [21], or score following [1]. In addition, aspects of large-scale indexing [27] and the problem of hubness for retrieval in high-dimensional feature spaces are addressed [28]. Further attention is given to evaluating MIR systems beyond the traditional IR-related measures and the difficulties entailed by the need for objective quantification, e.g., [5, 31].

As for aspects of the **music context**, we focus on data accessible through web technology. To this end, we introduce the field of web-based MIR and give a detailed description and comparison of contextual data sources on music (e.g., web pages and blogs [10], micro-blogs [23], user tags [16, 14], and lyrics [18]) and discuss related methods to obtain this data (web mining, games with a purpose [15], etc.). These sources can be exploited in order to

- *mine descriptive and relational metadata* (e.g., band members and instrumentation, country, album covers, genres, related artists, e.g., [22, 12]), to
- *construct similarity measures* for music artists and songs based on collaborative and cultural knowledge (e.g., [10, 32], and to
- *automatically index and retrieve* music [11, 2].

Regarding the **user-centric aspects** (user properties and context) and their applications in music recommendation and other personalized systems, we discuss sources of music interaction traces (e.g., playlists [19], ratings [6], postings and micro-blogs [24], peer-to-peer networks [13, 30], and social networks [7]) and possibilities to mine the context directly from sensor data using smart devices [8]. Methods that use this data can then be applied for tasks such as playlist generation, tag prediction, and location-aware music recommendation. We further address methods that include information from both context data and content information, either by learning hybrid similarity measures or by optimizing audio-based or hybrid similarity functions in order to reflect preference of users [26]. Additionally, user requirements such as need for novelty, diversity, or serendipity are addressed [3, 33]. This last segment concludes with an outlook to the next years of MIR and the biggest challenges the field is facing.

The following outlines the structure of the tutorial:

1. **Introduction to Music Similarity and Retrieval**
   (a) The Information Retrieval Perspective
   (b) Factors of Music Similarity
   (c) Applications: Playlist Generation, User Interfaces, etc.
2. **Content-Based MIR**
   (a) Basic Methods of Audio Signal Processing
   (b) Audio Feature Extraction for Similarity Measurement
   (c) Music Understanding and Semantic Description
   (d) Evaluation of Music Similarity Algorithms
3. **Contextual Music Similarity, Indexing, and Retrieval**
   (a) Contextual Music Meta-Data: Comparison and Sources
   (b) Text-Based Features and Similarity Measures
   (c) Text-Based Indexing and Retrieval
4. **Collaborative Music Similarity and Recommendation**
   (a) Listener-centered Data Sources: Traces of Music Interaction
   (b) Collaborative Music Similarity and Recommendation
   (c) User-Awareness
   (d) Multi-Modal Combination
5. **Grand Challenges and Outlook**

3. BIOGRAPHIES OF THE PRESENTERS

Dr. Peter Knees is an assistant professor at the *Department of Computational Perception* at the *Johannes Kepler University Linz.* He holds a Master's degree in Computer Science from the *Vienna University of Technology* and a Ph.D. degree from the *Johannes Kepler University Linz.*

Since 2004, he co-authored over 60 peer-reviewed conference and journal publications, served as program committee member for several conferences relevant to the fields of music, multimedia, and text IR, including ISMIR, ACM Multimedia, ECIR Tutorials, and the Adaptive Multimedia Retrieval workshop and was an organizer of the *International Workshop on Advances in Music Information Research* series and the SIGIR 2014 *Workshop on Social Media Retrieval and Analysis.* He is teaching grad-level courses on *Multimedia Search and Retrieval, Learning from User-generated Data, Multimedia Data Mining,* and *Intelligent Information Systems* and has given tutorials and lectures on music IR at ECIR, SIGIR, and RuSSIR. In addition to music and web information retrieval, his research interests include multimedia systems, user interfaces, and recommender systems.

Dr. Markus Schedl is an associate professor at the *Johannes Kepler University Linz / Department of Computational Perception.* He graduated in Computer Science from the *Vienna University of Technology* and earned his Ph.D. in Computer Science from the *Johannes Kepler University Linz.* Markus further holds a Master's degree in International Business Administration from the *Vienna University of Economics and Business.* He (co-)authored more than 100 refereed conference/workshop papers and journal articles (published, among others, in SIGIR, ECIR, ACM Multimedia; Journal of Machine Learning Research, ACM Transactions on Information Systems, Springer Information Retrieval, IEEE Multimedia). He is an associate editor of the Springer International Journal of Multimedia Information Retrieval, serves on various program committees, and as reviewer (among others, for ACM Multimedia, ECIR, IJCAI, ICASSP, IEEE Visualization; Transactions of Multimedia, Transactions on Intelligent Systems and Technology, Information Sciences, Pattern Recognition Letters). He is co-founder of the *International Workshop on Advances in Music Information Research* (AdMIRe) and the *International Workshop on Social Media Retrieval and Analysis* (SoMeRA), the latter held in conjunction with SIGIR 2014. He recently co-authored an article titled "Music Information Retrieval: Recent Developments and Applications" in *Foundations and Trends in Information Retrieval* [25].

4. ACKNOWLEDGMENTS

This tutorial is supported by the European Union Seventh Framework Programme FP7/2007-2013 through grant agreements no. 601166 (PHENICX) and no. 610591 (GiantSteps), as well as by the Austrian Science Funds (FWF): P25655.

5. REFERENCES

[1] A. Arzt and G. Widmer. Towards effective 'any-time' music tracking. In *Proceedings of the Starting AI Researchers' Symposium (STAIRS)*, Lisbon, Portugal, 2010.

[2] L. Barrington, D. Turnbull, M. Yazdani, and G. Lanckriet. Combining audio content and social context for semantic music discovery. In *Proceedings of the ACM SIGIR*, Boston, MA, USA, 2009.

[3] O. Celma and P. Herrera. A new approach to evaluating novel recommendations. In *Proceedings of the ACM Conference on Recommender Systems (RecSys)*, New York, NY, USA, 2008.

[4] S. Dixon, F. Gouyon, and G. Widmer. Towards Characterisation of Music via Rhythmic Patterns. In *Proceedings of the International Symposium on Music Information Retrieval (ISMIR)*, Barcelona, Spain, 2004.

[5] J. S. Downie, J. Futrelle, and D. Tcheng. The international music information retrieval systems evaluation laboratory: Governance, access and security. In *Proceedings of the International Symposium on Music Information Retrieval (ISMIR)*, Barcelona, Spain, 2004.

[6] G. Dror, N. Koenigstein, and Y. Koren. Yahoo! music recommendations: Modeling music ratings with temporal dynamics and item taxonomy. In *Proceedings*

of the *ACM Conference on Recommender Systems (RecSys)*, Chicago, IL, USA, 2011.

[7] B. Fields, M. Casey, K. Jacobson, and M. Sandler. Do You Sound Like Your Friends? Exploring Artist Similarity via Artist Social Network Relationships and Audio Signal Processing. In *Proceedings of the International Computer Music Conference (ICMC)*, Belfast, UK, 2008.

[8] M. Gillhofer and M. Schedl. Iron Maiden while jogging, Debussy for dinner? - An analysis of music listening behavior in context. In *Proceedings of the International Conference on MultiMedia Modeling (MMM)*, Sydney, Australia, 2015.

[9] B. Gold and N. Morgan. *Speech and Audio Signal Processing: Processing and Perception of Speech and Music*. Wiley, 1999.

[10] P. Knees, E. Pampalk, and G. Widmer. Artist Classification with Web-based Data. In *Proceedings of the International Symposium on Music Information Retrieval (ISMIR)*, Barcelona, Spain, 2004.

[11] P. Knees, T. Pohle, M. Schedl, and G. Widmer. A Music Search Engine Built upon Audio-based and Web-based Similarity Measures. In *Proceedings of the ACM SIGIR*, Amsterdam, Netherlands, 2007.

[12] P. Knees and M. Schedl. Towards Semantic Music Information Extraction from the Web Using Rule Patterns and Supervised Learning. In *Proceedings of the Workshop on Music Recommendation and Discovery (WOMRAD)*, Chicago, IL, USA, 2011.

[13] N. Koenigstein, Y. Shavitt, and T. Tankel. Spotting Out Emerging Artists Using Geo-Aware Analysis of P2P Query Strings. In *Proceedings of the ACM SIGKDD International Conference on Knowledge Discovery and Data Mining (KDD)*, Las Vegas, NV, USA, 2008.

[14] P. Lamere. Social Tagging and Music Information Retrieval. *Journal of New Music Research: Special Issue: From Genres to Tags – Music Information Retrieval in the Age of Social Tagging*, 37(2):101–114, 2008.

[15] E. Law, L. von Ahn, R. Dannenberg, and M. Crawford. Tagatune: A Game for Music and Sound Annotation. In *Proceedings of the International Conference on Music Information Retrieval (ISMIR)*, Vienna, Austria, 2007.

[16] M. Levy and M. Sandler. A semantic space for music derived from social tags. In *Proceedings of the International Conference on Music Information Retrieval (ISMIR)*, Vienna, Austria, 2007.

[17] B. Logan. Mel Frequency Cepstral Coefficients for Music Modeling. In *Proceedings of the International Symposium on Music Information Retrieval (ISMIR)*, Plymouth, MA, USA, 2000.

[18] R. Mayer, R. Neumayer, and A. Rauber. Rhyme and Style Features for Musical Genre Classification by Song Lyrics. In *Proceedings of the International Conference on Music Information Retrieval (ISMIR)*, Philadelphia, PA, USA, 2008.

[19] B. McFee and G. Lanckriet. Hypergraph Models of Playlist Dialects. In *Proceedings of the International Society for Music Information Retrieval Conference (ISMIR)*, Porto, Portugal, 2012.

[20] H. Purwins. *Profiles of Pitch Classes: Circularity of Relative Pitch and Key—Experiments, Models, Computational Music Analysis, and Perspectives*. PhD thesis, Technische Universität Berlin, Germany, 2005.

[21] J. Salamon and E. Gómez. Melody extraction from polyphonic music signals using pitch contour characteristics. *IEEE Transactions on Audio, Speech and Language Processing*, 20:1759–1770, 08/2012.

[22] M. Schedl. *Automatically Extracting, Analyzing, and Visualizing Information on Music Artists from the World Wide Web*. PhD thesis, Johannes Kepler University Linz, Austria, 2008.

[23] M. Schedl. #nowplaying Madonna: A Large-Scale Evaluation on Estimating Similarities Between Music Artists and Between Movies from Microblogs. *Information Retrieval*, 15:183–217, June 2012.

[24] M. Schedl. Leveraging Microblogs for Spatiotemporal Music Information Retrieval. In *Proceedings of the European Conference on Information Retrieval (ECIR)*, Moscow, Russia, 2013.

[25] M. Schedl, E. Gómez, and J. Urbano. Evaluation in music information retrieval. *Foundations and Trends in Information Retrieval*, 8(2–3):127–261, 2014.

[26] M. Schedl, S. Stober, E. Gómez, N. Orio, and C. C. Liem. User-Aware Music Retrieval. In M. Müller, M. Goto, and M. Schedl, editors, *Multimodal Music Processing*, volume 3 of *Dagstuhl Follow-Ups*, pages 135–156. Schloss Dagstuhl–Leibniz-Zentrum für Informatik, Dagstuhl, Germany, 2012.

[27] D. Schnitzer. *Indexing Content-Based Music Similarity Models for Fast Retrieval in Massive Databases*. PhD thesis, Johannes Kepler University Linz, Austria, 2011.

[28] D. Schnitzer, A. Flexer, M. Schedl, and G. Widmer. Local and global scaling reduce hubs in space. *Journal of Machine Learning Research*, 13:2871–2902, October 2012.

[29] K. Seyerlehner, G. Widmer, M. Schedl, and P. Knees. Automatic Music Tag Classification based on Block-Level Features. In *Proceedings of the Sound and Music Computing Conference (SMC)*, Barcelona, Spain, 2010.

[30] Y. Shavitt, E. Weinsberg, and U. Weinsberg. Mining Music from Large-Scale, Peer-to-Peer Networks. *IEEE Multimedia*, 18(1):14–23, January 2011.

[31] J. Urbano and M. Schedl. Minimal test collections for low-cost evaluation of audio music similarity and retrieval systems. *International Journal of Multimedia Information Retrieval: Special Issue on Hybrid Music Information Retrieval*, 2(1):59–70, January 2013.

[32] B. Whitman and S. Lawrence. Inferring Descriptions and Similarity for Music from Community Metadata. In *Proceedings of the International Computer Music Conference (ICMC)*, Göteborg, Sweden, 2002.

[33] Yuan Cao Zhang, Diarmuid O Seaghdha, Daniele Quercia, Tamas Jambor. Auralist: Introducing Serendipity into Music Recommendation. In *Proceedings of the ACM International Conference on Web Search and Data Mining (WSDM)*, Seattle, WA, USA, 2012.

Exploiting Wikipedia for Information Retrieval Tasks

Bracha Shapira
bracha.shapira@gmail.com

Nir Ofek
nirofek@bgu.ac.il

Victor Makarenkov
vitiokm@gmail.com

Department of Information Systems Engineering
Ben-Gurion University of the Negev
Beer-Sheva, Israel

ABSTRACT

Wikipedia - the online encyclopedia - has long been used as a source of information for researchers, as well as being a subject of research itself [11, 12, 23, 5, 6] . Wikipedia has been shown to be effective in recommender systems, sentiment analysis, validation and multiple domains in information retrieval. One of the reasons for Wikipedia's popularity among researchers and practitioners is the multiple types of information it contains, which enables practitioners to select the right "tool" for their respective tasks. In addition to its great potential, this multitude of information sources also poses a challenge: which sources of information are best suited for a specific problem and how can different types of data be combined?
This tutorial aims to provide a holistic view of Wikipedia's different features - text, links, categories, page views, editing history etc. - and explore the different ways they can be utilized in a machine learning framework. By presenting and contrasting the latest works that utilize Wikipedia in multiple domains, this tutorial aims to increase the awareness among researchers and practitioners in these fields to the benefits of utilizing Wikipedia in their respective domains, in particular to the use of multiple sources of information simultaneously.

Categories and Subject Descriptors

H.3.3 [**Information Search and Retrieval**]: Miscellaneous

Keywords

Wikipedia, Information Retrieval, Machine Learning

1. BRIEF DESCRIPTION

We propose tutorial on Wikipedia[1] as a knowledge source that leverages various Information Retrieval and Machine learning tasks.

[1] www.wikipedia.org

SIGIR '15, August 09-13, 2015, Santiago, Chile
ACM 978-1-4503-3621-5/15/08
http://dx.doi.org/10.1145/2766462.2767879

- Length: half-day (3 hours plus breaks).
- Intended audience: intermediate and advanced audience, researchers and practitioners in (one or more of) the following fields: machine learning, information retrieval, recommender systems and natural language processing.

2. OBJECTIVES

Our aim for this tutorial is to provide our participants with a working knowledge in the following areas:

- Become familiar with the different sources of information available in Wikipedia and the various features that can be derived from them.
- Possess the understanding which of the Wikipedia features can be successfully applied in various domains.
- Become acquainted with the various ways in which machine learning can be used to leverage the knowledge stored in Wikipedia.
- How Wikipedia's structure of semi-structured textual entities can be used to leverage the search and retrieval missions.

3. RELEVANCE

We partition the applications utilizing Wikipedia in learning-based tasks into four application domains: recommender systems, ranking, information retrieval and knowledge acquisition and validation. Each of these domains can also be divided into tasks, which are reviewed in depth throught the tutorial. The full taxonomy of Wikipedia applications is presented in Figure 1. We now briefly review each of these domains.

1. **Information retrieval** - the goal of this application domain is to provide information which is best-suited for the information needs of the user. In this application domain Wikipedia is used for multiple purposes, including the enrichment of the original query (query expansion) and the identification of relevant entities (entity-based information retrieval).
2. **Recommender systems** - the goal of this application domain is to identify items that are best suited for a given user and to infer the similarity of various items. Because of its hyper connected structure and the massive amounts of information it contains, Wikipedia is highly useful in this domain.

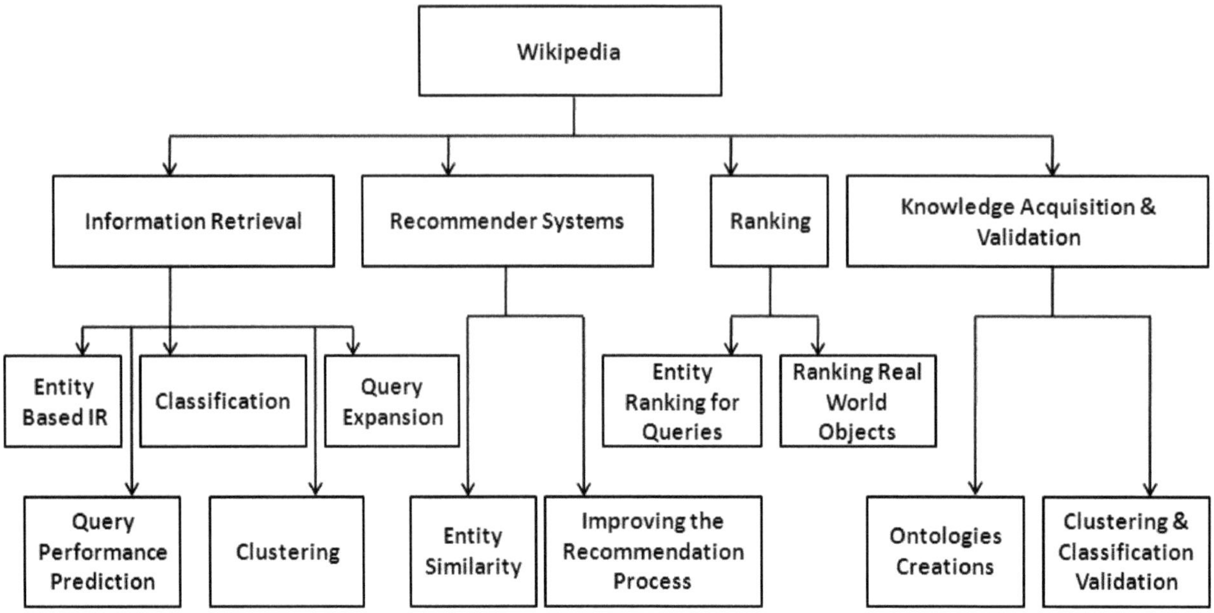

Figure 1: A taxonomy describing the application domains of machine learning in which Wikipedia can be utilized

3. **Ranking** - the goal of this domain is to determine the relative standing of items. Being a collaborative database, Wikipedia can be used to harness the "wisdom of the crowd" for this task.

4. **Knowledge acquisition and validation** - this application domain includes two tasks: a) the extraction of structured knowledge (ontologies) from Wikipedia and; b) the utilization of Wikipedia for the validation of hypothesis and conclusions.

In addition to a comprehensive review of the various domains in which Wikipedia can be utilized, we will also provide the participants with detailed references to the various studies which utilize Wikipedia's multiple features. Some of the information that will be provided to the participants is presented in Table 1.

4. FORMAT AND SCHEDULE

We suggest the following outline of the tutorial:

1. Introduction to Wikipedia - a short review of its size, scope, growth rate and additional statistics. We will then describe the different application domains presented in Figure 1, thus enabling the audience to identify the domains that are relevant and related to its fields of interest.

2. Wikipedia as a knowledge base - we provide an overview of the various ways by which Wikipedia's text, links, categories, page views etc. can be utilized in a machine learning context.

3. For each of the following domains, we provide a review of the domain, and the leading works in the field. Then, we focus on a single project which requires significant use of machine learning. Projects from the following fields will be reviewed:

   (a) Information retrieval - query performance prediction.

   (b) Sentiment analysis - measuring word relatedness.

   (c) Recommender systems and items similarity - we will review the different methods by which Wikipedia similarity could be utilized to improve ratings prediction

   (d) Ranking - we will describe methods that utilize different features of Wikipedia for the purpose of ranking real-world entities.

   (e) Knowledge acquisition and validation - we will demonstrate how knowledge acquired from Wikipedia could be used to validate solutions to "soft" problems (problems that do not have one "right" solution) such as clustering.

We suggest to provide hands-on faculty sessions, based on the outcomes and experience gained through leading projects and authoring papers [11, 12, 23, 13, 17, 2, 19, 18, 29] related to the abovementioned topics.

Table 1: **The domains in which each of the features reviewed in this section is applied and references to relevant studies**

	Recommender Systems	Ranking	Information Retrieval	Knowledge Acquisition and Validation
`Page text`	[24, 39, 16, 37]	[38, 4]	[38, 12, 32, 6]	[34, 35, 7]
`Categories`	[36, 30]	[25, 10]	[15, 1, 27, 28, 12]	[3, 33]
`Links`	[36, 40]	[26, 31]	[20, 9, 14, 12]	[22]
`Redirect pages`	[11]		[12]	
`Disambiguation pages`			[8]	
`Infoboxes`		[21], Wikiometrics (Section 4.2)		[34, 35]
`Page views`		Wikiometrics (Section 4.2)		
`Editing history`				

5. REFERENCES

[1] B. Al-Shboul and S.-H. Myaeng. Query phrase expansion using wikipedia in patent class search. In *Information Retrieval Technology*, pages 115–126. Springer, 2011.

[2] O. Arazy, N. Kumar, and B. Shapira. A theory-driven design framework for social recommender systems. journal of the association for information research articl, 2010.

[3] D. Buscaldi and P. Rosso. Mining knowledge from wikipedia for the question answering task. In *Proceedings of the International Conference on Language Resources and Evaluation*, pages 727–730, 2006.

[4] G. Demartini, C. S. Firan, T. Iofciu, and W. Nejdl. Semantically enhanced entity ranking. In J. Bailey, D. Maier, K.-D. Schewe, B. Thalheim, and X. S. Wang, editors, *WISE*, volume 5175 of *Lecture Notes in Computer Science*, pages 176–188. Springer, 2008.

[5] E. Gabrilovich and S. Markovitch. Overcoming the brittleness bottleneck using Wikipedia: Enhancing text categorization with encyclopedic knowledge. In *Proceedings of the 21st National Conference on Artificial Intelligence*, pages 1301–1306, July 2006.

[6] E. Gabrilovich and S. Markovitch. Wikipedia-based semantic interpretation for natural language processing. *Journal of Artificial Intelligence Research*, 34:443–498, 2009.

[7] A. Grappy and B. Grau. Answer type validation in question answering systems. In *Adaptivity, Personalization and Fusion of Heterogeneous Information*, pages 9–15. LE CENTRE DE HAUTES ETUDES INTERNATIONALES D'INFORMATIQUE DOCUMENTAIRE, 2010.

[8] B. Hachey, W. Radford, J. Nothman, M. Honnibal, and J. R. Curran. Evaluating entity linking with wikipedia. *Artificial intelligence*, 194:130–150, 2013.

[9] C.-C. Hsu, Y.-T. Li, Y.-W. Chen, and S.-H. Wu. Query expansion via link analysis of wikipedia for clir. *Proceedings of NTCIR-7*, pages 125–131, 2008.

[10] R. Kaptein, P. Serdyukov, A. P. de Vries, and J. Kamps. Entity ranking using wikipedia as a pivot. In J. Huang, N. Koudas, G. J. F. Jones, X. Wu, K. Collins-Thompson, and A. An, editors, *CIKM*, pages 69–78. ACM, 2010.

[11] G. Katz, N. Ofek, B. Shapira, L. Rokach, and G. Shani. Using wikipedia to boost collaborative filtering techniques. In *Proceedings of the Fifth ACM Conference on Recommender Systems*, RecSys '11, pages 285–288, New York, NY, USA, 2011. ACM.

[12] G. Katz, A. Shtok, O. Kurland, B. Shapira, and L. Rokach. Wikipedia-based query performance prediction. In *ACM SIGIR , SIGIR '14*, pages 1235–1238, 2014.

[13] L. R. N. O. Y. W. P. B. M. Y. S. B. K. Z. P. M. Kenneth Portier, Greta E. Greer and J. Yen. Understanding topics and sentiment in an online cancer survivor community. *JNCI Monographs*, 2013.

[14] M. Koolen, G. Kazai, and N. Craswell. Wikipedia pages as entry points for book search. In *Proceedings of the Second ACM International Conference on Web Search and Data Mining*, pages 44–53. ACM, 2009.

[15] Y. Li, W. P. R. Luk, K. S. E. Ho, and F. L. K. Chung. Improving weak ad-hoc queries using wikipedia asexternal corpus. In *ACM SIGIR*, pages 797–798. ACM, 2007.

[16] C. Lu, W. Lam, and Y. Zhang. Twitter user modeling and tweets recommendation based on wikipedia concept graph, 2012.

[17] V. Maidel, P. Shoval, B. Shapira, and M. Taieb-Maimon. Ontological content-based filtering for personalised newspapers. *Online Information Review*, 34(5):729–756, 2010.

[18] O. Maimon and L. Rokach. *Data mining and knowledge discovery handbook (2nd Edition)*. Springer-Verlag New York, Inc., New York, NY, USA, 2nd edition, 2010.

[19] E. Menahem, L. Rokach, and Y. Elovici. Combining one-class classifiers via meta learning. In *ACM CIKM*, CIKM '13, pages 2435–2440, New York, NY, USA, 2013. ACM.

[20] D. Milne, O. Medelyan, and I. H. Witten. Mining domain-specific thesauri from wikipedia: A case study. In *Proceedings of the 2006 IEEE/WIC/ACM international conference on web intelligence*, pages 442–448. IEEE Computer Society, 2006.

[21] R. Mirizzi, A. Ragone, T. D. Noia, and E. D. Sciascio. Ranking the linked data: The case of dbpedia. In B. Benatallah, F. Casati, G. Kappel, and G. Rossi, editors, *ICWE*, volume 6189 of *Lecture Notes in*

Computer Science, pages 337–354. Springer, 2010.

[22] R. Navigli and S. P. Ponzetto. Babelnet: Building a very large multilingual semantic network. In *Proceedings of the 48th annual meeting of the association for computational linguistics*, pages 216–225. Association for Computational Linguistics, 2010.

[23] N. Ofek and L. Rokach. A classifier to determine which wikipedia biographies will be accepted. *Journal of the Association for Information Science and Technology*, 66(1):213–218, 2015.

[24] A. Pak. Using wikipedia to improve precision of contextual advertising. In *Proceedings of the 4th Conference on Human Language Technology: Challenges for Computer Science and Linguistics*, LTC'09, pages 533–543, Berlin, Heidelberg, 2011. Springer-Verlag.

[25] J. Pehcevski, J. A. Thom, A.-M. Vercoustre, and V. Naumovski. Entity ranking in wikipedia: utilising categories, links and topic difficulty prediction. *Inf. Retr.*, 13(5):568–600, 2010.

[26] J. Pehcevski, A.-M. Vercoustre, and J. A. Thom. Exploiting locality of wikipedia links in entity ranking. In C. Macdonald, I. Ounis, V. Plachouras, I. Ruthven, and R. W. White, editors, *ECIR*, volume 4956 of *Lecture Notes in Computer Science*, pages 258–269. Springer, 2008.

[27] H. Raviv, D. Carmel, and O. Kurland. A ranking framework for entity oriented search using markov random fields. In *Proceedings of the 1st Joint International Workshop on Entity-Oriented and Semantic Search*, page 1. ACM, 2012.

[28] H. Raviv, O. Kurland, and D. Carmel. The cluster hypothesis for entity oriented search. In *ACM SIGIR*, pages 841–844. ACM, 2013.

[29] F. Ricci, L. Rokach, B. Shapira, and P. B. Kantor. *Recommender Systems Handbook*. Springer-Verlag New York, Inc., New York, NY, USA, 1st edition, 2010.

[30] V. Subramaniyaswamy and S. C. Pandian. Effective tag recommendation system based on topic ontology using wikipedia and wordnet. *Int. J. Intell. Syst.*, 27(12):1034–1048, 2012.

[31] A.-M. Vercoustre, J. Pehcevski, and J. A. Thom. Using wikipedia categories and links in entity ranking. In *Pre-proceedings of the sixth International Workshop of the Initiative for the Evaluation of XML Retrieval (INEX 2007)*, 2007.

[32] M. Vidal, G. V. Menezes, K. Berlt, E. S. de Moura, K. Okada, N. Ziviani, D. Fernandes, and M. Cristo. Selecting keywords to represent web pages using wikipedia information. In *Proceedings of the 18th Brazilian Symposium on Multimedia and the Web*, pages 375–382. ACM, 2012.

[33] J. Vivaldi, L. A. Cabrera-Diego, G. Sierra, and M. Pozzi. Using wikipedia to validate the terminology found in a corpus of basic textbooks. In *LREC*, pages 3820–3827, 2012.

[34] F. Wu and D. S. Weld. Autonomously semantifying wikipedia. In *ACM CIKM*, pages 41–50. ACM, 2007.

[35] F. Wu and D. S. Weld. Automatically refining the wikipedia infobox ontology. In *Proceedings of the 17th international conference on World Wide Web*, pages 635–644. ACM, 2008.

[36] Z. Wu, G. Xu, R. Pan, Y. Zhang, Z. Hu, and J. Lu. Leveraging wikipedia concept and category information to enhance contextual advertising. In *ACM CIKM*, CIKM '11, pages 2105–2108, New York, NY, USA, 2011. ACM.

[37] Z. Wu, G. Xu, Y. Zhang, P. Dolog, and C. Lu. An improved contextual advertising matching approach based on wikipedia knowledge. *Comput. J.*, 55(3):277–292, Mar. 2012.

[38] H. Zaragoza, H. Rode, P. Mika, J. Atserias, M. Ciaramita, and G. Attardi. Ranking very many typed entities on wikipedia. In *ACM CIKM*, CIKM '07, pages 1015–1018, New York, NY, USA, 2007. ACM.

[39] L. Zhang, C. Li, J. Liu, and H. Wang. Graph-based text similarity measurement by exploiting wikipedia as background knowledge, 2011.

[40] W. Zhang, D. Wang, G.-R. Xue, and H. Zha. Advertising keywords recommendation for short-text web pages using wikipedia. *ACM Trans. Intell. Syst. Technol.*, 3(2):36:1–36:25, Feb. 2012.

Workshop Chairs' Welcome

We are pleased to introduce the Workshop Program for the 38th Annual SIGIR Conference. We received 14 workshop proposals, each of which was peer-reviewed by three members of the Workshops PC. After discussion of all submissions in the Workshops PC, as well as with the PC Chairs of the technical program, 7 workshops were accepted (50% acceptance rate). We sought to include topics that covered the breadth of expertise in the SIGIR community, would appeal to a diverse range of SIGIR attendees, and would push the state-of-the-art in IR research. We greatly appreciate all authors who submitted a proposal for consideration and all reviewers for their help in selecting which proposals to include in the program. Finally, we are grateful to Microsoft Research for providing workshop fee waivers for thirty-five students.

This year's workshops include new explorations of established topics such as temporal information retrieval, personalization, and question answering. The Workshop on Temporal, Social and Spatially-aware Information Access (#TAIA2015), now in its fourth year at SIGIR, explores the relationship between temporal information access and other data sources. Similarly, the Workshop on Social Personalization & Search (SPS2015) studies the opportunities for improved personalization provided by social data. The Web Question Answering Workshop studies next generation QA systems that go beyond simple factoid questions.

In addition to these familiar topics, you will find workshops investigating entirely new subareas of information retrieval. The Workshop on Reproducibility, Inexplicability, and Generalizability of Results (RIGOR) focuses on testing the robustness of existing results in information retrieval. The Workshop on Privacy-Preserving Information Retrieval, which is in its second year, draws together researchers from the privacy and retrieval communities to improve the sensitivity of information retrieval research to user privacy concerns. The Graph Search Workshop studies information retrieval in highly structured information spaces, bringing some of the research topics from industry into a public academic venue. Last but not least, the Workshop on Neuro-Physiological Methods in Information Retrieval Research covers topics on the novel use of physiological data for information retrieval.

We believe this year's workshop program reflects the diversity of information retrieval research and are excited for the new directions it will enable and inspire. We hope you find this program interesting and thought-provoking.

Fernando Diaz
Microsoft Research
New York, NY, USA

Diane Kelly
University of North Carolina at Chapel Hill
Chapel Hill, NC, USA

Web Question Answering: Beyond Factoids

SIGIR 2015 Workshop

Eugene Agichtein
Emory University & Yahoo Labs, Haifa, Israel
eugene@mathcs.emory.edu

David Carmel
Yahoo labs, Haifa, Israel
david.carmel@ymail.com

Charles L. A. Clarke
University of Waterloo, Canada
claclark@uwaterloo.ca

Praveen Paritosh
Google inc. Mountain View, CA
pkp@google.com

Dan Pelleg,
Yahoo labs, Haifa, Israel
pellegd@acm.org

Idan Szpektor
Yahoo labs, Haifa, Israel
idan@yahoo-inc.com

Categories and Subject Descriptors: H.3.3 [Information Search and Retrieval]: Retrieval models

General Terms: Algorithms

Keywords: Web Question Answering

1. OVERVIEW

Automatic question answering is a central topic in information retrieval. Web search engines have made great progress at answering factoid queries, such as "how many people live in Australia?". These can provide a succinct answer, up to a few words in length, and sometimes offer additional information such as related facts or entities. However, for deeper questions which could benefit from a longer response (e.g., "history of Australia"), current search engine resort to returning a link to a detailed web document. Alternatively, such a question might be posted on a Community Question Answering (CQA) site ("Visiting Australia in May, what should I see?"), hoping to get a human authored and detailed response.

In this workshop we aim to explore the boundaries of Web question answering to better understand the spectrum of approaches and possible responses that are more detailed than a short fact, yet are more useful than a full document result. Is it possible to automatically answer diverse questions ranging from advice on fixing a broken sink to requests for opinions on the best basketball player of all time. In addition, questions submitted on the Web can be either short and ambiguous (such as Web queries to a search engine), or long and detailed (such as CQA questions). This workshop is particularly timely for two additional reasons: (1) there still exist many disagreements regarding the goals and nature of Web question answering services, mostly relating to the questions of "question intent" (what kind of queries benefit from question answering compared to other methods); and (2) leading search engines are eager to provide question answering services, especially for mobile devices. These issues make the WebQA task more challenging than traditional QA, and the most effective approaches remain an open question.

We plan to bring together researchers from diverse areas working on this problem, including those from NLP, IR, social media and recommender systems communities. As compared to the main SIGIR conference, out goal is to conduct a more focused and open discussion, encouraging the presentation of work in progress and late breaking initial results in Web Question Answering. Both academic and industrial participation will be solicited, including keynotes and invited speakers.

We encourage submissions describing ongoing research, late breaking, preliminary results, and position papers on the following topics:

- Social and User generated question analysis
- Identifying Question intent in Web queries
- Answer aggregation from various resources
- Answer summarization from various resources Using Collaboratively Generated Content for QA
- Inferring answers for Web questions using knowledge bases or graphs
- Answering opinion questions, including sentiment analysis
- Answering complex, multi-sentence questions
- Evaluation of question answering systems (e.g., via crowd sourcing)

This workshop coincides with and complements the LiveQA track at TREC 2015 (www.trecliveqa.org). LiveQA is a revival of the TREC Question Answering track, organized by some of the workshop chairs. The track provides a challenge and data for answering "real user questions", posted to the Yahoo Answers site. The LiveQA challenge evaluation is to be held shortly after the workshop, which would provide both the active and potential participants a way to discuss ideas and approaches.

SIGIR'15, August 09-13, 2015, Santiago, Chile.
ACM 978-1-4503-3621-5/15/08.
DOI: http://dx.doi.org/10.1145/2766462.2767861 .

Graph Search and Beyond

SIGIR 2015 Workshop Summary

Omar Alonso
Microsoft
Mountain View, CA
USA

Marti A. Hearst
UC Berkeley
Berkeley, CA
USA

Jaap Kamps
University of Amsterdam
Amsterdam
The Netherlands

ABSTRACT

Modern Web data is highly structured in terms of entities and relations from large knowledge resources, geo-temporal references and social network structure, resulting in a massive multidimensional graph. This graph essentially unifies both the searcher and the information resources that played a fundamentally different role in traditional IR, and "Graph Search" offers major new ways to access relevant information. Graph search affects both query formulation (complex queries about entities and relations building on the searcher's context) as well as result exploration and discovery (slicing and dicing the information using the graph structure) in a completely personalized way. This new graph based approach introduces great opportunities, but also great challenges, in terms of data quality and data integration, user interface design, and privacy.

We view the notion of "graph search" as searching information from your personal point of view (you are the query) over a highly structured and curated information space. This goes beyond the traditional two-term queries and ten blue links results that users are familiar with, requiring a highly interactive session covering both query formulation and result exploration. The workshop attracted a range of researchers working on this and related topics, and made concrete progress working together on one of the greatest challenges in the years to come.

Categories and Subject Descriptors: H.3.3 [**Information Storage and Retrieval**]: Information Search and Retrieval—*Query formulation, Search process, Selection process*

Keywords: Graph search; Semantic search; Personalization; Exploration; Query suggest

1. INTRODUCTION

Information on the Web is increasingly structured in terms of entities and relations from large knowledge resources, geo-temporal references and social network structure, resulting in a massive multidimensional graph. This graph essentially unifies both the searcher and the information resources that played a fundamentally different role in traditional IR, and offers major new ways to access relevant information. In services that rely on personalized information like social networks, the graph plays an even more important role, in other words: *you are the query*.

Graph search affects both query formulation as well as result exploration and discovery. On the one hand, it allows for incrementally expressing complex information needs that triangulate information about multiple entities or entity types, relations between those entities, with various filters on geo-temporal constraints or the sources of information used (or ignored), and taking into account the rich profile and context information of the searcher (and his/her peers, and peers of peers, etc). On the other hand, it allows for more powerful ways to explore the results from various aspects and viewpoints, by slicing and dicing the information using the graph structure, and using the same structure for explaining why results are retrieved or recommended, and by whom.

This new graph based information seeking approach introduces great opportunities, but also great challenges, both technical ranging from data quality and data integration to user interface design, as well as ethical challenges in terms of privacy; transparency, bias and control; and avoiding the so-called filter bubbles. Graph search is already available today in many flavors with different levels of interactivity. Social network-based services like Facebook and LinkedIn provide flexibility to search their personal network form many diverse angles. Web search engines like Google and Bing rely more on using graphs to show related content as a mechanism to include other possible contexts for a given query. Clearly, it is not limited to web, and can be applied to other highly structured data. Just to give an example, the hansards or parliamentary proceedings are fully public data with a clear graph structure linking every speech to the respective speaker, their role in parliament and their political party. Graph search allows to explore politics from the viewpoint of individual members of parliament or government.

At a high level, graph search seems limited to familiar entity types (e.g., Facebook entities) and templates. How far can this scale? Will this work on truly open domains? There is a huge potential to use the graph to go beyond recommendations for new friends and contacts or semantically related content. Unlocking the potential of richer knowledge sources for new search strategies requires us to think outside

SIGIR'15, August 09–13, 2015, Santiago, Chile.
ACM 978-1-4503-3621-5/15/08.
DOI: http://dx.doi.org/10.1145/2766462.2767855.

the box, by combining different insights from IR, semantic search, data integration, query expansion and user interfaces to name a few.

2. MANY OPEN RESEARCH QUESTIONS

We view the notion of "graph search" as searching information from your personal point of view (you are the query) over a highly structured and curated information space. This goes beyond the traditional two-term queries and ten blue links results that users are familiar with, requiring a highly interactive session covering both query formulation and result exploration.

This raises many open questions:

IR Theory What happens if search gets personal? Does this break the classic dichotomy between users and documents, as users are nodes in the social network data themselves? What is the consequence of ultimate personalization, as the local graph differs for all users? As the local graph structure is key, does this obviate the need for large central indexes? Do these types of requests fit in the classic paradigm (e.g., Broder's taxonomy)? How does this shift the balance between the control of the searcher and the ranker over the result set?

Data Integration Building a knowledge graph requires massive data integration at many levels: are there trade-offs in simplicity and level of detail (such as the classic knowledge representation trade-off)? What levels of granularity and comprehensiveness are needed for effective deployment? What quality is needed: is any noise acceptable? How to deal with near duplicate detection, conflation, or entity disambiguation?

Use Cases and Applications Rather than a universal solution, graph search is particularly useful for specific types of information needs and queries. What are the data and tasks that make graph search works? What kind of scenarios that would benefit from a graph model? In what context can switching perspectives by showing results from the vista of other persons useful?

Query formulation How to move from singular queries to highly interactive sessions with multiple variant queries? What new tools are needed to help a searcher construct the appropriate graph search query using refinements or filters to better articulate their needs, or explore further aspects? How can we augment query autocompletion to actively prompt user to interactively construct longer queries exploring different aspects?

Result Exploration There is a radical shift towards the control of the searcher—small changes in the query can lead to radically different result sets—how can we support active exploration of slices of the data to explore further aspects? Unlike traditional facetted search options, the result space is highly dynamic, how can we provide adaptive exploration options tailored to the context and searcher, at every stage of the process?

Evaluation How do we know the system is any good? How to evaluate the overall process, given its personalized and interactive nature? Can we rely on the direct evaluation of query suggestions and query recommendations? Are there suitable behavioral criteria for in the wild testing, such as longer queries, multiple filters, longer dwell-time, more active engagement, more structured-query templates? Can we use are standard experimental evaluation methods from HCI and UI/UX design?

Privacy Access to personal data is fraught ethical and privacy concerns, is there is similarly structured public data for scientific research? As an extreme form of personalization, how to avoid the uncanny cave, filter bubbles and echo chambers? How ethical is it to privilege a particular query refinement suggestion over the many other possible candidates?

3. CONCLUSIONS

The workshop brought together researchers from a range of areas in information access, who worked together on searching information from your personal point of view over a highly structured and curated information space. One of the main lines of discussion was the considerable industrial activity around social graphs. The most famous example is Facebook Graph Search, a feature that allows users to perform more sophisticated searches on their social network [1]. Bing has been integrating Facebook into their web search results for the last couple of years. Similarly, Google has been annotating search results with Google+ profiles. And all the rest of the search industry is moving in the same direction.

There are also crucial links with work on searching structured data, and work on the appropriate query languages, in particular as part of semantic search. These branches of research in particular focus on complex querying of structured text or data, whereas the graph search addresses also, and perhaps primarily, the process of constructing series of complex queries interactively. This is directly related to exploratory search and sense making. The graph structure provides natural facets for exploring the data, from a local point of view, allowing for a more dynamic structure than traditional faceted search using rigid, global, hierarchical structure. This challenges our understanding of search user interfaces design and evaluation, with search results moving from the found links, to the HIT page as snippets, and now to query suggestion as previews of possible query extensions.

Graph Search has fundamental consequences for information access and offers tremendous opportunities for building new systems and tools that allow users to explore information from many different angles, shifting control back to the user. This is a radical departure from current systems where the machine learning dominate the interaction: the entire information space is determined by the user, and the user is in the driver's seat when expressing her needs and exploring the space of options interactive.

Acknowledgments This research is funded in part by the Netherlands Organization for Scientific Research (ExPoSe project, NWO CI # 314.99.108; DiLiPaD project, NWO Digging into Data # 600.006.014).

References

[1] N. V. Spirin, J. He, M. Develin, K. G. Karahalios, and M. Boucher. People search within an online social network: Large scale analysis of facebook graph search query logs. In *CIKM'14*, pages 1009–1018. ACM, 2014. URL `http://doi.acm.org/10.1145/2661829.2661967`.

SIGIR 2015 Workshop on Reproducibility, Inexplicability, and Generalizability of Results (RIGOR)

Jaime Arguello[1], Fernando Diaz[2], Jimmy Lin[3], and Andrew Trotman[4]

[1] University of North Carolina at Chapel Hill [2] Microsoft Research
[3] University of Maryland, College Park [4] eBay Inc.

jarguello@unc.edu, fdiaz@microsoft.com, jimmylin@umd.edu

Categories and Subject Descriptors: H.3.4 [Information Storage and Retrieval]: Systems and Software—Performance evaluation

Keywords: evaluation; negative results

1. MOTIVATION

Many, if not most, published research papers in Information Retrieval (IR) describe the following process: the authors identify an opportunity to improve on a particular IR task, implement an experimental system, and compare its performance against one or more baselines (or a control condition, in the case of a user study). The quality of the research is judged based on the magnitude of the improvement and whether the methodological choices suggest external validity and generalizability, for example, whether the experimental setup is "realistic" or whether the baseline methods reflect the state of the art.

Unfortunately, research demonstrating the *failure* to reproduce or generalize previous results does not have a similar publication venue. This sort of result—often referred to as a 'negative result'—serves to control the quality of published research in a scientific discipline and to better understand the limits of previously published methods. Publication venues for such research exist in fields such as ecology,[1] biomedicine,[2] pharmacy,[3], and social science.[4]

The SIGIR 2015 Workshop on Reproducibility, Inexplicability, and Generalizability of Results (RIGOR) aims to provide a venue for publication and discussion of IR research that fails to reproduce a previously published result under the same or similar experimental conditions (e.g., same test collection and system configuration) and research that demonstrates the failure to generalize an existing approach to a new domain. To this end, we have developed a set of categories covering different ways in which a result may fail to reproduce or generalize as well as a set of reviewing principles unique to this style of research. We believe the RIGOR Workshop provides a forum in which to present and discuss an under-represented aspect of IR research.

[1]http://jnr-eeb.org/index.php/jnr
[2]http://www.jnrbm.com/
[3]http://www.pnrjournal.com/
[4]http://jspurc.org/intro2.htm

SIGIR'15, August 09-13, 2015, Santiago, Chile.
ACM 978-1-4503-3621-5/15/08.
DOI: http://dx.doi.org/10.1145/2766462.2767858.

2. SCOPE

We see papers in this workshop focusing on different scenarios in which previous results might fail to reproduce. Specifically, we invite submissions from the following four categories: repeatability of published experiments, reproducibility of published experiments on comparable data, generalizability of published results to comparable tasks, and inexplicability of unpublished experiments. We provide more details about these categories below.

2.1 Repeatability

Although IR experiments vary in subtle ways that may influence the precise values of, for example, evaluation numbers, we expect hypothesis tests to be robust to these subtle variations. A submission in this category demonstrates a failure to repeat a published result under approximately the same conditions in which the previously published experiments occurred. Examples include papers making claims such as:

(a) "published mean average precision (MAP) improvements on TREC8 for BM25 with Rocchio pseudo-relevance feedback are not reproducible."

Papers in this area serve to control the quality of results in IR research.

2.2 Reproducibility

IR experiments are often conducted on specific corpora, sets of queries, and relevance judgments. In many cases, these experiments can be conducted on other comparable corpora, queries, or relevance judgments. A submission in this category fails to reproduce a published result on a comparable dataset. Examples include papers making claims such as:

(a) "published MAP improvements on TREC8 for BM25 with Rocchio pseudo-relevance feedback are not reproducible on Reuters, a comparable news corpus and queries."

(b) "published production interleaving improvements on Bingle, a portal web search engine, for ranking with LTRx are not reproducible on Yandu, a comparable production environment."

Papers in this area serve to test the sensitivity of results in IR research to experimental conditions.

2.3 Generalizability

Many IR strategies have demonstrated effectiveness across different comparable task definitions (e.g., 'BM25 is an effective term weighting scheme for different text ranking tasks'). A submission in this category fails to reproduce a published result on a comparable task. Examples include papers making claims such as:

(a) "published MAP improvements on TREC8 for BM25 with Rocchio pseudo-relevance feedback do not generalize to the TREC Entity Track."

(b) "published production interleaving improvements on Bingle, a portal web search engine, for ranking with LTRx do not generalize to Twitbook post search, a comparable production search task."

Papers in this area serve to test the sensitivity of results in IR research to task definitions.

2.4 Inexplicability

Finally, in some cases, IR research involves testing hypotheses that we expect to be positive, based on prior work in IR or related disciplines. We would also like to test the the ability to generalize to tasks that are either vaguely comparable to or completely different from previously-studied tasks. A submission in this category fails to obtain improvements using well-established principles/methods or well-motivated approaches. Examples include papers making claims such as:

(a) "pseudo-relevance does not improve performance on image retrieval."

(b) "incorporating social signals does not improve production portal web search."

Papers in this area serve to test the sensitivity of results in IR research to task definitions and help understand the limits in applying straightforward techniques in novel domains.

SIGIR 2015 Workshop on Temporal, Social and Spatially-aware Information Access (#TAIA2015)

Klaus Berberich
Max Planck Institute for Informatics
Saarbruecken, Germany
kberberi@mpi-inf.mpg.de

James Caverlee
Department of Computer Science and Engineering
Texas A&M University
College Station, USA
caverlee@cse.tamu.edu

Miles Efron
Graduate School of Library and Information Science
University of Illinois
Champaign, USA
mefron@illinois.edu

Claudia Hauff
Web Information Systems
Delft University of Technology
Delft, the Netherlands
c.hauff@tudelft.nl

Vanessa Murdock
Microsoft Corporation
Redmond, USA
vanmur@microsoft.com

Milad Shokouhi
Microsoft Research
Cambridge, UK
milads@microsoft.com

Bart Thomee
Yahoo! Labs
San Francisco, USA
bthomee@yahoo-inc.com

1. OVERVIEW

Spatial and temporal context are tightly coupled. For example, users may visit a place during specific times of the day or on certain days of the week. Some places have special relevance during a specific time of the year, or only exist for a limited window of time. Understanding the spatial and temporal context of a user is often necessary to understand their information need. Understanding the user's spatial and temporal context is especially important on a mobile device where the space is limited, and the user expectation far exceeds the ability of the technology to satisfy him.

Users provide an unprecedented volume of detailed and continuously updated information about where they are, what they are doing, who they are with, and what they are thinking and feeling about their current activities. The provision of this stream creates an informal contract between the user and the information access application that is expected to provide results that are contextually relevant.

In this workshop, we build on the previous three successful editions [1, 2, 3], and explore spatial and temporal context in dynamic geotagged collections such as Wikipedia, traditional news sources, as well as social media sites such as Twitter, Foursquare, Facebook and Flickr. We also investigate the geo-temporal dynamics of user engagements with apps and search engines on mobile devices and cross-device.

SIGIR'15, August 09 - 13, 2015, Santiago, Chile.
© 2015 ACM. ISBN 978-1-4503-3621-5/15/08 ...$15.00.
DOI: http://dx.doi.org/10.1145/2766462.2767860.

We aim to bring together practitioners and researchers to discuss their recent breakthroughs and the challenges with addressing spatial and temporal information access, both from the algorithmic and the architectural perspectives.

Website:
`http://research.microsoft.com/en-us/people/milads/taia2015.aspx`

2. SCOPE

The workshop relates to all aspects of geographical and time-sensitive information access. TAIA2015 has a special focus on events, to include event detection, recommendation, and characterization. Research questions include:

- How can we detect and profile past & future events across social media channels and traditional media?
- How can we best leverage our understanding of a user's location and time context to improve the ranking of places and content?
- How can we detect event-centric queries and leverage temporal and spatial annotations in document to better serve them?
- How can we employ user generated content to describe places or paths according to their beauty, engagement, etc.
- Can we construct a profile of places of interest of users based on their social media streams?
- How can we profile small-scale events which are sparsely covered in social media?

- How can we model the footprint of a business from users' social tagging behavior?
- How can we model the impact on a business based on users' online behavior?
- How to mine geo-temporal patterns of app usage on mobile devices?
- How to perform geo-temporal analyses of cross-device search?

In addition, TAIA2015 welcomes contributions on the following issues that complement current technologies in spatial and temporal information:

- Publicly available dynamic collections (e.g., Wikipedia edits, Wikipedia page requests, Twitter, and news streams).
- Evaluation methodologies for geo-constrained and time-sensitive tasks.
- Timeline creation and summarization.
- Spatial modeling of social media and Web content.
- Spatial and temporal intent classification of queries.
- Spatial and temporal natural language processing tasks and techniques.
- Spatial and time-sensitive ranking including effective ranking for spatiotemporal context-sensitive queries, optimizing for both freshness and relevance, evaluating the results for context sensitive queries, etc.
- Temporal changes in document contents.
- Understanding Web dynamics, including trends and other temporal analysis on web and social graphs.
- Local search and recommendation.

3. FORMAT

The workshop will include two keynotes, a series of talks (20-30 minutes each) from accepted papers as well as a breakout session and discussions to identify research challenges and to foster understanding between the different communities. The two keynotes, given by Barbara Poblete (University of Chile) and Omar Alonso (Microsoft) provide a mix of academic and industrial perspectives on the workshop theme.

4. REFERENCES

[1] F. Diaz, S. Dumais, M. Efron, K. Radinsky, M. de Rijke, and M. Shokouhi. SIGIR 2013 Workshop on Time Aware Information Access (# TAIA2013). In *Proceedings of the 36th international ACM SIGIR conference on Research & Development in Information Retrieval*, SIGIR '13, pages 1137–1137, 2013.

[2] F. Diaz, S. Dumais, K. Radinsky, M. de Rijke, and M. Shokouhi. #TAIA2012. *SIGIR Forum*, 46(2):102–106, 2012.

[3] F. Diaz, C. Hauff, V. Murdock, M. de Rijke, and M. Shokouhi. SIGIR 2014 Workshop on Temporal, Social and Spatially-Aware Information Access (#TAIA2014). In *Proceedings of the 37th international ACM SIGIR conference on Research & Development in Information Retrieval*, SIGIR '14, pages 1298–1298, 2014.

NeuroIR 2015 – Neuro-Physiological Methods in IR Research

Jacek Gwizdka
School of Information
University of Texas at Austin
TX, USA
sigir2015@gwizdka.com

Joemon Jose
Dept. of Computer Science
University of Glasgow
UK
Joemon.Jose@glasgow.ac.uk

Javed Mostafa
Info. Science & BRIC
UNC at Chapel Hill
NC, USA
jm@unc.edu

Max L. Wilson
School of Computer Science
University of Nottingham
UK
max.wilson@nottingham.ac.uk

ABSTRACT
This Tutorial+Workshop will discuss opportunities and challenges involved in using neuro-physiological tools/techniques (such as fMRI, fNIRS, EEG, eye-tracking, GSR, HR, and facial expressions) and theories in information retrieval. The hybrid format will engage researchers and students at different levels of expertise, from those who are active in this area to those who are interested and want to learn more. The workshop will combine presentations, discussions and tutorial elements and consist of four segments (tutorial, completed research, work-in-progress, closing panel).

General Terms
Neuroscience, Experimentation, Measurement.

Keywords
H. Information Systems. H.3 INFORMATION STORAGE AND RETRIEVAL. H.3.3 Information Search and Retrieval. Subjects: Query formulation; Search process; Retrieval models

Author Keywords
fMRI, fNIRS, eye-tracking, EEG, GSR, HR.

1. MOTIVATION
The progress made in neuroscience in the last two decades allows one to expect that neuroscience (and related fields) will contribute to other disciplines. It has already happened in several social science disciplines, such as economics and marketing – neuroeconomics and neuromarketing have been established over a decade ago. The results from collaboration between behavioral economists and neuroscientists have supported advances in understanding of decision-making and human behavior [1]. More recently, information systems researchers started a new sub-field NeuroIS (Neuro Information Systems – [3]; NeuroIS.org, 2009). Information systems research studies the development and use of information and communication technologies in organizations and society. NeuroIS is "a subfield of information systems literature that relies on neuroscience and neurophysiological theories and tools to better understand the development, use, and impact of information technologies (IT)" [10].

Application of neuro-physiological methods for studying browsing tasks, information selection, and relevance judgment have emerged as critical areas of active research. The broad intersecting theme, among IR researchers and those with strong applied neuroscience background, is development of more robust models for information search – models which go beyond behavioral data and account for physiological and neurological responses to information as stimuli. This early work by information retrieval researchers resulted in a number of recent publications that appeared at SIGIR, ECIR, and related conferences. Selected recent publications include: [2,4,5,6,7,8,9,11,12,13,14,15].

However, the IR community is still widely unaware of these new methods. We propose the workshop to discuss and exchange experiences among researchers; build a community; plan future work; make others aware of potential usefulness of neuro-physiological methods and their applicability to their research; enable others to read and assess papers that employ such methods.

2. THEME AND PURPOSE
The workshop will have three main themes: 1) cases and problems in information retrieval that are particularly amenable to analysis based on neuro-physiological methods (e.g., relevance judgment studies), 2) comparative analysis of neuro-physiological tools and techniques and their applications in information retrieval research (e.g., fMRI versus EEG), and finally, 3) evaluation and statistical analysis methods for incorporating neuro-physiological methods in an IR research study.

For the theme 1 above, we will invite presentations and posters on current IR projects that are utilizing neuro-physiological methods. For theme 2, we will incorporate presentations and demonstrations of neuro-physiological techniques in the workshop. We will invite researchers with strong experience in utilizing portable tools such as eye-trackers and EEGs, encouraging them to bring with them some of these tools. We will also encourage researchers with recent experiences in applying fMRI and fNIRS and other methods based on large imaging instruments to participate. Finally, for theme 3, a certain number of presentations and posters will be sought that place emphasis on metrics, evaluation methods, and statistical techniques associated with neuro-physiological information retrieval data.

3. FORMAT AND PLANNED ACTIVITIES
The workshop schedule will combine presentations, discussions and tutorial elements and consist of four segments.

1) Tutorial - will offer guidance on how to start working with neuro-physiological tools in the context of IR. We will introduce and compare several tools, such as EEG, eye-tracking and fMRI, and will discuss best practices and useful tips, which will be helpful to all, not just those new to the area.

2) Completed research - experienced participants will present findings and lessons learned from their own work and will consider how neuro-cognitive and physiological tools, such as fMRI, fNIRS, eye-tracking, EEG, GSR, and analysis of facial expressions could further contribute to IR research questions.

SIGIR '15, August 09-13, 2015, Santiago, Chile
ACM 978-1-4503-3621-5/15/08.
http://dx.doi.org/10.1145/2766462.2767856

3) Work-in-progress - participants, and particularly those who are starting out in this area, will present their planned/current work in lightning talks; group discussions will provide feedback and guidance.

4) Closing panel - will discuss future directions and collaborations between workshop participants.

A workshop webpage https://sites.google.com/site/neuroir2015 will be maintained and added to http://www.neuroinfoscience.org website maintained by Jacek Gwizdka.

4. PARTICIPANTS' SELECTION

Selection of papers and posters will be conducted at two levels. Members of the program committee will be assigned responsibilities to conduct the first level review. At least two reviewers will be assigned per paper and at least one member will review each poster. A final review of all papers and posters will be conducted by the four members of the organizing committee. About 15 papers and 12 posters will be selected, and the associated researchers will be invited to attend the workshop. We anticipate a maximum of about 35 participants in this event, but we do not intend to limit participation.

5. ORGANIZERS

Jacek Gwizdka is an Assistant Professor and Information eXperience Lab co-director at School of Information at University of Texas, Austin. He studies cognitive aspects of human-information interaction; his research is situated at the intersection of interactive-information retrieval (IIR) and human-computer interaction (HCI). His current projects include application of cognitive psychology to the study of how people evaluate information relevance and neuro-physiological methods to implicit assessment of cognitive load. He also investigates effects of search results presentation and cognitive abilities on information search task performance. Dr. Gwizdka has been affiliated with University of Toronto, Rutgers University and University of Texas at Austin. He conducted research at industrial labs (Xerox PARC, FXPAL, HP Labs). He serves in various roles at international conference committees (e.g., CHIIR, IIiX, ASIS&T, ACM SIGCHI and SIGIR) and has co-organized successful workshops at several international conferences, including: IIiX (SaL2014), SIGIR (UIIR2009), CSCW (Email'2002). He is as an Associate Editor of Interacting with Computers and serves on editorial board of Information Processing & Management. More on Dr. Gwizdka's research can be found at: http://gwizdka.com

Joemon M. Jose is a Professor at the School of Computing Science, University of Glasgow. He is a fellow of the BCS, IET and a chartered information technology professional (CITP), member of the ACM and IEEE. He has a well-established reputation in research on multimedia information retrieval, developing advanced retrieval models, studying the role of emotion in search, personalization and adaptive retrieval. His current research interests include: neurophysiological feedback based systems for IR. He has published over 110 journal and conference articles and leads a team of 6 PhD students and 3 post-doctoral researchers. He was a co-chair of the ICMR 2014, and ECDL 2010 conferences, and had organized numerous conferences and events including AIR 2008, SSMS 2007, AIR 2006, AMR 2005, IRiX 2005 & IRFEST 2005. He was a guest editor for the Information Processing and Management on Adaptive Retrieval and a keynote speaker for the RIAO 2010 conference.

Javed Mostafa. Javed is the Director of the Carolina Health Informatics Program (chip.unc.edu) and the Director of the Laboratory of Applied Informatics Research (lair.unc.edu). His research concentrates on information retrieval problems, particularly related to search and user-system interactions in large-scale document/data repositories. He also serves as the Deputy Director of the Biomedical Informatics Core at the NC Translational & Clinical Sciences Institute (tracs.unc.edu) and has current research engagements in biomedical data mining, analysis, visualization, user interface design, and multi-modal human-computer interaction. Javed served as an associate editor for the ACM Transactions on Information Systems for eight years. He currently serves on the editorial board of the Journal of the Association for Information Science & Technology (http://www.asis.org/jasist.html) and he also serves as an associate editor of the ACM Transactions on Internet Technology (http://toit.acm.org/). Javed is interested in investigating the possible relationship between locations in the brain that specialize in certain activities and information seeking tasks. A related interest is information seeking evaluation methodologies that employ a broad spectrum of biological / physiological methods. Dr. Mostafa has significant experience in organizing research workshops, sponsored by several organizations, including the NSF (2 as PI), ACM DL (2005, 2006, and 2007), and SIGIR (2004).

Max L. Wilson is an Assistant Professor in Human-Computer Interaction and Information Retrieval (HCIR) at the University of Nottingham. Max holds a PhD in Human-Computer Interaction from the University of Southampton, and publishes widely in the space between HCI and Information Retrieval, including a book on Search User Interface Design with Morgan Claypool, and a chapter for Ruthven and Kelly's Interactive IR textbook. As well as being on conference committees (e.g. CHI 2010-2016, IIiX2010-14) and being on the editorial boards for IP&M and IJHCS, Max has organised several workshops, including the prior EuroHCIR and Searching4Fun workshops. Max's recent work published at ACM CHI2014 and CHI2015 have been on the use of fNIRS brain sensing for measuring mental workload in the pre-frontal cortex.

6. PROGRAM COMMITTEE

- Ioannis Arapakis, Yahoo Research, Spain
- Vincent N. Carrasco, Laboratory of Applied Informatics Research, SILS, University of North Carolina at Chapel Hill, USA
- Ashlee Edwards, SILS, University of North Carolina at Chapel Hill, USA
- Manuel Eugster, HIIT, Aalto University, Finland
- Roberto González-Ibáñez, Informatics Engineering, Universidad de Santiago, Chile
- O'Brien Heather, UBC, Canada
- Hideo Joho, Faculty of Library, Information and Media Science, University of Tsukuba, Japan
- Yvonne Kammerer, Leibniz-Institut für Wissensmedien - Knowledge Media Research Center, Germany
- Irene Lopatovska, Pratt Institute, USA
- Randall Minas, Information Technology Management Dept, Shidler College of Business, University of Hawaii at Manoa, USA
- Yashar Moshfeghi, Computer Science, University of Glasgow, UK
- Heather O'Brien, iSchool, University of British Columbia, Canada

- Luisa Pinto, Computer Science, University of Glasgow, UK
- Frank Pollick, Psychology, University of Glasgow, UK
- University of Glasgow, UK
- Erin Solovey, College of Computing and Informatics, Drexel, USA

7. RELATED WORKSHOPS AND PANEL

Two of the workshop organizers (Gwizdka & Mostafa) co-organized a very successful panel session at ASIST 2013 in Montreal entitled "Panel Title: Applications of Neuroimaging in Information Science: Challenges and Opportunities".

8. REFERENCES

1. Camerer, C.F., Loewenstein, G., and Prelec, D. Neuroeconomics: Why Economics Needs Brains. *Scandinavian Journal of Economics 106*, 3 (2004), 555–579.
2. Cole, M.J., Gwizdka, J., Liu, C., Belkin, N.J., and Zhang, X. Inferring user knowledge level from eye movement patterns. *Information Processing & Management 49*, 5 (2013), 1075–1091.
3. Dimoka, A., Pavlou, P.A., and Davis, F. NeuroIS: The Potential of Cognitive Neuroscience for Information Systems Research. *INFORMATION SYSTEMS RESEARCH*, (2010), isre.1100.0284.
4. Eugster, M.J.A., Ruotsalo, T., Spapé, M.M., et al. Predicting Term-relevance from Brain Signals. *Proceedings of the 37th International ACM SIGIR Conference on Research & Development in Information Retrieval*, ACM (2014), 425–434.
5. Gwizdka, J. Looking for Information Relevance In the Brain. *Gmunden Retreat on NeuroIS 2013*, (2013), 14. **BEST PAPER**
6. Gwizdka, J. Characterizing Relevance with Eye-tracking Measures. *Proceedings of the 5th Information Interaction in Context Symposium*, ACM (2014), 58–67.
7. Gwizdka, J. News Stories Relevance Effects on Eye-movements. *Proceedings of the Symposium on Eye Tracking Research and Applications*, ACM (2014), 283–286.
8. Moshfeghi, Y. and Jose, J.M. An effective implicit relevance feedback technique using affective, physiological and behavioural features. *Proceedings of the 36th international ACM SIGIR conference on Research and development in information retrieval*, ACM (2013), 133–142.
9. Moshfeghi, Y., Pinto, L.R., Pollick, F.E., and Jose, J.M. Understanding Relevance: An fMRI Study. In P. Serdyukov, P. Braslavski, S.O. Kuznetsov, et al., eds., *Advances in Information Retrieval*. Springer Berlin Heidelberg, 2013, 14–25. **BEST PAPER.**
10. Riedl, R., Randolph, A., Brocke, J. vom, Léger, P.-M., and Dimoka, A. The Potential of Neuroscience for Human-Computer Interaction Research. *SIGHCI 2010 Proceedings*, (2010).
11. Arapakis, I., Athanasakos, K., and Jose, J.M. A comparison of general vs personalised affective models for the prediction of topical relevance. SIGIR'2010, ACM (2010), 371–378.
12. Arapakis, I., Moshfeghi, Y., Joho, H., Ren, R., Hannah, D., and Jose, J.M. Enriching User Profiling with Affective Features for the Improvement of a Multimodal Recommender System. CIVR'2009, 29:1–29:8. **BEST STUDENT PAPER.**
13. Lopatovska, I. and Arapakis, I. Theories, methods and current research on emotions in library and information science, information retrieval and human-computer interaction. IP&M 47, 4 (2011), 575–592.
14. Maior, H., Pike, M., Sharples, S. and Wilson, M.L. (2015) Examining the Reliability of Using fNIRS in Realistic HCI Settings for Spatial and Verbal Tasks. In: Proc. CHI'15 (accepted).
15. Pike, M. F., Maior, H. A., Porcheron, M., Sharples, S. C., & Wilson, M. L. (2014, April). Measuring the effect of think aloud protocols on workload using fNIRS. In Proc. CHI'14 (pp. 3807-3816). ACM.

SPS'15 – 2015 International Workshop on Social Personalization & Search

Christoph Trattner
NTNU, Norway
chritrat@idi.ntnu.no

Denis Parra
PUC, Chile
dparra@ing.puc.cl

Peter Brusilovsky
University of Pittsburgh, USA
peterb@pitt.edu

Leandro Marinho
UFCG, Brasil
lbmarinho@dsc.ufcg.edu.br

Categories and Subject Descriptors

H.3.3 [**Information Storage and Retrieval**]: Information Search and Retrieval—*Information filtering*

Keywords

social personalization; social search & navigation; recommender systems; user modeling

1. OVERVIEW

For the Social Personalization & Search workshop[1], we invite researchers working in the fields of Information Retrieval, Personalization, User Modeling, and Recommender Systems where the social dimension plays a fundamental role. The workshop is examining several approaches that leverage the social side of the search process on two main contexts: (a) using social data for improving search and recommendations, and (b) search as a social process, collaborative IR (e.g., [1, 4, 3, 2]).

On the first context, we expect to attract contributions that use the social dimension in different methods for personalization and search, such as data from online social networks, social tagging systems, online forums and community-based Q&A. This topic is important because it involves leveraging new sources of information that are specific to social systems such as shared items and tags, user public profiles, online and offline social connections, and logs of user social activities in order to improve people's information access in a wide variety of tasks and devices.

On the second context, the social dimension is emphasized as collaboration, so we aim to discuss works that consider information seeking as a collaborative activity. Here, researches can potentially use explicit social communication information (such as online, offline chat) to boost the personalized search experience for each user, or in a community-wise sense, support the common goal of users working on the same search tasks, such as people planning a group trip.

We invite submissions that may include the following topics, but are not limited to:

- search and recommendations based on social links
- search and recommendations in collaborative tagging systems
- group-level search personalization
- search and recommendations in blogs and microblogs
- approaches for social personalization in recommender systems
- approaches on personalized social collaboration
- approaches on social linking
- methods for social search and navigation
- methods for social predictive models
- social methods for information visualization
- applications of the aforementioned topics to diverse domains (education, smart cities, music, etc.)
- any other methods that exploit new forms of social data for search and personalization
- applications of any of the above methods

The goal of this workshop is to share and discuss research that goes hopefully beyond classic personalization techniques, trying to capitalize potentially useful information available in social data for paving the way to more efficient personalized information access technologies. In addition to personalization, we also consider social search and navigation as topics that involve the importance of the social dimension on filtering and information access.

Acknowledgments: The authors would like to thank Alejandro Bellogín for his help with the organization of this workshop.

[1] http://socialcomputing.ing.puc.cl/sps2015/

SIGIR '15, August 09–13, 2015, Santiago, Chile.
ACM 978-1-4503-3621-5/15/08.
http://dx.doi.org/10.1145/2766462.2767859 .

2. REFERENCES

[1] A. Bellogín, I. Cantador, and P. Castells. A comparative study of heterogeneous item recommendations in social systems. *Inf. Sci.*, 221:142–169, 2013.

[2] E. Lacic, D. Kowald, L. Eberhard, C. Trattner, D. Parra, and L. B. Marinho. Utilizing online social network and location-based data to recommend products and categories in online marketplaces. In *Mining, Modeling, and Recommending'Things' in Social Media*, pages 96–115. 2015.

[3] D. Lee and P. Brusilovsky. Recommending talks at research conferences using users' social networks. *IJCIS*, 23(02), 2014.

[4] C. Trattner, D. Parra, L. Eberhard, and X. Wen. Who will trade with whom?: Predicting buyer-seller interactions in online trading platforms through social networks. In *Proc. of WWW'14*, pages 387–388.

Privacy-Preserving IR 2015: When Information Retrieval Meets Privacy and Security

Hui Yang
Georgetown University, USA
huiyang@cs.georgetown.edu

Ian Soboroff
NIST, USA
ian.soboroff@nist.gov

ABSTRACT

Information retrieval (IR) and information privacy/security are two fast-growing computer science disciplines. There are many synergies and connections between these two disciplines. However, there have been very limited efforts to connect the two important disciplines. On the other hand, due to lack of mature techniques in privacy-preserving IR, concerns about information privacy and security have become serious obstacles that prevent valuable user data to be used in IR research such as studies on query logs, social media, tweets, and medical record retrieval. We propose this privacy-preserving IR workshop to connect the two disciplines of information retrieval and information privacy and security. We look forward to spurring research that aims to bring together the research fields of IR and privacy/security. Last year, the first privacy-preserving IR workshop focused on mitigating privacy threats in information retrieval by novel algorithms and tools that enable web users to better understand associated privacy risks.

Categories and Subject Descriptors

H.3 [**Information Systems**]: Information Storage and Retrieval

Keywords

Privacy-Preserving Information Retrieval

1. MOTIVATION

With the emergence of online social networks and the growing popularity of digital communication, more and more information about individuals is becoming available on the Internet. While much of this information is not sensitive, it is not uncommon for users to publish sensitive information online, especially on social networking sites. The availability of this publicly accessible and potentially sensitive data can lead to abuse and expose users to stalking and identity theft. An adversary can digitally "stalk" a victim (a Web user) and discover as much information as possible about the victim, either through direct observation of posted information or by inferring knowledge using simple inference logic.

Information retrieval and information privacy/security are two fast-growing computer science disciplines. Information retrieval provides a set of information seeking, organization, analysis, and decision-making techniques. Information privacy/security defends information from unauthorized or malicious use, disclosure, modification, attack, and destruction. The two disciplines often appear as two areas with opposite goals: one is to seek information from large amounts of materials, the other is to protect (sensitive) information from being found out. On the other hand, there are many synergies and connections between these two disciplines. For example, information retrieval researchers or practitioners often need to consider privacy or security issues in designing solutions of information processing and management, while researchers in information privacy and security often utilize information retrieval techniques when they build the adversary models to simulate how the adversary can actively seek sensitive information. However, there have been very limited efforts to connect the two important disciplines.

In addition, due to lack of mature techniques in privacy-preserving information retrieval, concerns about information privacy and security have become serious obstacles that prevent valuable user data to be used in IR research such as studies about query logs, social media, tweets, session analysis, and medical record retrieval. For example, the recent TREC Medical Record Track halted over concerns about privacy in nominally de-identified data, and the TREC Microblog Track does not directly distribute tweets in order to support the right of Twitter users to make private or delete their tweets and accounts. The situation needs to be improved in a timely manner. All these motive us to propose this "privacy-preserving IR" workshop in SIGIR.

Co-located with SIGIR 2014, the first privacy-preserving IR workshop (PIR 2014) [3] received active participation. Most workshop attendees agreed that we need to continue to collaborate on this topic, and to seek both general and specific solutions to the privacy and security issues in various IR tasks. This year, we continue the efforts with a set of new focuses.

SIGIR'15, August 09-13, 2015, Santiago, Chile.
ACM 978-1-4503-3621-5/15/08.
DOI: http://dx.doi.org/10.1145/2766462.2767857.

2. THEME AND PURPOSE

User privacy is at risk whenever owners of publicly available network resources can be traced and recorded, and their user activities can be mined and inferred. The digital ecosystem involves not only such threats to personal privacy but also promising cures. For example, information-theoretic protocols may decompose each user's query into several sub-queries, ensuring they include no information about the user's intent.

Privacy and security has been discussed in a few recent IR conferences and workshops. The SIGIR 2012 "Community IR Evaluation using Private Data Collections" workshop discussed issues how private data such as medical records can be shared for open IR evaluations. The CIKM 2013 "Channeling the Deluge: Research Challenges for Big Data and Information Systems" Panel Session also briefly addresses the privacy issue in information systems. There are also privacy- and security-related workshops that less related to IR but more related to data mining, artificial intelligent, and machine learning. For instance, Computer and Communication Security (CCS) 2013 workshop on "Artificial Intelligence and Security". However, their focus is not mainly for IR and is very different from the proposed workshop. As far as we know, there have been very limited efforts to connect the two important disciplines of information retrieval and information privacy and security.

This workshop aims to spurring research that aims to bring together the research fields of IR and privacy/security, and mitigate privacy threats in information retrieval by constructing novel algorithms and tools that enable web users to better understand associated privacy risks. We believe this workshop in SIGIR can provide valuable opportunities to explore the connection between information retrieval and information privacy and security.

2.1 List of Questions

The workshop addresses several important topics that connect information retrieval, information privacy and security:

- Protecting User Privacy in Search, Recommendation and Beyond [1]: much damage can be caused as users can be identified in AOL query log data and Neflix log data, it is important to develop effective and efficient solutions to protect users' privacy in information retrieval applications.
- Dataset Distribution and Evaluation: How does privacy affect IR test dataset distribution and evaluation? For instance, web query logs and medical records could not be shared without privacy concerns to the public or the researchers. How to anonymize the datasets and make sure that they can be shared with a certain degree of privacy guarantee while at the same time preserves the utility of the data?
- Information Exposure Detection : new information retrieval and natural language processing technologies are needed to quickly identify components and/or attributes of a user's online public profile that may reduce the user's privacy, and warn one's vulnerability on the Web.
- Novel Information Retrieval Techniques for Information Privacy/Security Application: new information retrieval, evaluation, or machine learning techniques need to be designed that fit the practice of applications in information privacy and security.
- Private Information Retrieval Techniques for Enabling Location Privacy in Location-Based Services [2]: data about a user's location and historical movements can potentially be gathered by a third party who takes away the information without the awareness of the service providers and the users, how location-based services and recommender systems interact with Location Obfuscation techniques and other Privacy-Enhancing Technologies.

3. KEYNOTES

Speaker: Dr. Li Xiong, Emory University.

Title: Making Private User Data Accessible for Information Retrieval Research: Data Sharing with Differential Privacy

Abstract: Almost a decade has passed since the infamous AOL data leak. Up till today, data privacy concerns continue to prohibit valuable user data such as query logs and web browsing sessions to be shared and used for Information Retrieval (IR) research. As a result, lack of large scale datasets is still one of the major barriers facing academic IR researchers. This talk will give an overview of the recent developments in building and sharing statistical and synthetic datasets based on private data with the rigorous differential privacy guarantee. Then we will focus on techniques we have developed for sharing sequential data under differential privacy, addressing challenges such as high dimensionality and high correlations, which are also common characteristics in user behavior data. Empirical studies using real-world web browsing data will demonstrate the feasibility as well as challenges of applying differential privacy on user behavior data for IR research.

4. ACTIVITIES AND SCHEDULE

9:00–9:15am Welcome A brief welcome which illustrates the goal of this workshop and the schedule for the day. All participants introduce themselves, their research focus, and the specific interest in the topic of the workshop.

9:15–10:30am Keynote Talks

10:30–12:30pm Morning Presentations We have a morning presentation session for high quality papers that are accepted by the workshop.

12:30–1:30pm Lunch Break Participates have their lunch, can discuss about the morning talks on their own.

1:30–4:00pm Group Discussion There will be breakout groups on different themes to have further discussion in this section.

4:00–5:00pm Bring it All Together At the end of the day, we will get everyone together to discuss about the invited talks and posters.

5:00–5:15pm Conclusion The organizers will summarize the discussions and conclude the day.

5. WEBSITE

Our website is located at `privacypreservingir.org`.

References

[1] W. Jiang, L. Si, and J. Li. Protecting source privacy in federated search. In W. Kraaij, A. P. de Vries, C. L. A. Clarke, N. Fuhr, and N. Kando, editors, *SIGIR*, pages 761–762. ACM, 2007.

[2] A. Khoshgozaran and C. Shahabi. Privacy in location-based applications. chapter Private Information Retrieval Techniques for Enabling Location Privacy in Location-Based Services, pages 59–83. Springer-Verlag, Berlin, Heidelberg, 2009.

[3] L. Si and H. Yang. Pir 2014 the first international workshop on privacy-preserving ir: When information retrieval meets privacy and security. *SIGIR Forum*, 48(2):83–88, Dec. 2014.

Author Index

www.ingramcontent.com/pod-product-compliance
Ingram Content Group UK Ltd.
Pitfield, Milton Keynes, MK11 3LW, UK
UKHW051414290926
15471UKWH00009B/1594

9 781450 338899